THE TAXATION OF CAPITAL GAINS

Tony Appleby & Frank Carr

Finance Act 2000

Published by The Institute of Taxation in Ireland,
19 Sandymount Avenue, Dublin 4.

Telephone: (01) 668 8222
Fax: (01) 668 8387
E Mail: info@TaxIreland.ie
Website: www.taxireland.ie

First Published 1980.
Second Edition 1983.
Third Edition 1984.
Fourth Edition 1986.
Fifth Edition 1989.
Sixth Edition 1994.
Seventh Edition 1995.
Eighth Edition 1996.
Ninth Edition 1997.
Tenth edition 1998.
Eleventh edition 1999.
Twelfth edition 2000.

The authors of the first five editions were:
Tony Appleby and John Roche.

THE INSTITUTE OF
TAXATION
IN IRELAND

ISBN 0902565 84 2

The object of this book is to explain in broad detail the principles and practice of the Taxation of Capital Gains in the Republic of Ireland. The book is not intended as a detailed exposition of the extensive volume of statute and case law relating to that tax.

Neither the Institute nor the authors accept any responsibility for loss or damage occasioned by any person acting or refraining from acting as a result of the material in this book.

Any views or opinions expressed are not necessarily subscribed to by the Institute.

Professional advice should always be sought before acting on any issue covered in this book.

THE INSTITUTE OF TAXATION IN IRELAND

The Institute of Taxation in Ireland was founded in 1967. It has been admitted by the Confederation Fiscale Europeenne (CFE) as a member representing the Republic of Ireland. Under the provisions of the Finance Act 1990, any person who has been admitted as a member of the Institute of Taxation in Ireland has the right to be heard by the Appeal Commissioners and at a rehearing before a Circuit Court Judge (Finance Act 1995). The Institute and its AITI qualification are officially recognised in the State for purposes of the EC Directive of 21 December 1988 regarding Standards for Higher Education Qualifications Awarded on Completion of Professional Education and Training of at least Three Year's Duration.

The objects of the Institute include the promotion of the study of tax law and practice, the making of regular submissions on fiscal matters to the Government and through CFE, to the EU Commission, and the establishment of a high standard of professional ethics for persons engaged in the practice of tax consultancy.

To become an Associate, it is necessary to pass examinations set by the Institute. Designatory letters are AITI and FITI. Fellows, Associates, Members, Student and Subscriber Members of the Institute now number over 5,000, and are drawn mainly from the legal, accounting and banking professions and from the revenue service.

It is possible, outside of the examination system, to participate in many of the benefits of Institute membership by becoming a Subscriber. Full details are available from the Chief Executive, Institute of Taxation in Ireland, 19 Sandymount Ave, Dublin 4. Telephone (01) 66 88 222, Fax (01) 66 88 088 /66 88 387 E Mail: info@taxireland.ie Website: www.taxireland.ie

This book is based on legislation in force as at June 2000 which is:

- The Taxes Consolidation Act 1997,

- The Finance Acts 1998 to 2000 (inclusive),

- Case Law reported to March 2000.

References to legislation are contained in the margin alongside the appropriate text. A table of legislation referred to is included before the index. Throughout the text 'Ireland' and 'Irish' should be read as referring solely to the Republic of Ireland.

All legislative references in the text are to the "TCA97" (Taxes Consolidation Act, 1997) unless otherwise stated.

ABBREVIATIONS USED:

1975 Act..........	Capital Gains Act 1975
1978 Act.........	Capital Gains Tax (Amendment) Act 1978
AMA85...........	Age of Majority Act, 1985.
CA...................	Companies Act
CGT	Capital Gains Tax
CSA68.............	Continental Shelf Act, 1968
DRIA67	Diplomatic Relations & Immunities Act, 1967.
DDDAA97	Dublin Docklands Development Authority Act, 1997.
FA	Finance Act
FLA95.............	Family Law Act, 1995.
FL(D)A96	Family Law (Divorce) Act, 1996.
GIA58	Greyhound Industry Act, 1958
HA96	Harbours Act, 1996.
IA37	Interpretation Act, 1937.
IHIA94............	Irish Horseracing Industry Act, 1994.
IRLM	Irish Law Reports Monthly
ITA 1967.........	Income Tax Act 1967
LG(P&D)A63.	Local Government (Planning & Development) Act 1963
PA90	Partnership Act, 1890.
Para.................	Paragraph
S......................	Section
SA63	Succession Act, 1963.
Sch	Schedule
SLA82.............	Settled Land Act, 1882.
SI	Statutory Instrument
STC	Simon's Tax Cases
SPA54.............	State Property Act 1954
TC	Tax Cases
TCA97	Taxes Consolidation Act, 1997

FOREWORD

With each year that passes, the scope of capital gains tax becomes more far reaching. The Finance Act 2000 changes alone affected issues ranging from the taxation of collective investment undertakings, to disposals of non residential land and retirement relief for individuals.

The authors have in this edition further improved upon an outstanding work. The size of the publication is a reflection of their continuing commitment. They have made widespread use of examples which make it much easier to understand many of the complex concepts involved. They have also worked tirelessly to incorporate relevant materials published by Revenue and other sources.

The authors, Tony Appleby and Frank Carr, are to be complimented on producing a work of the highest quality.

MICHAEL MULLINS
President
Institute of Taxation in Ireland

INDEXATION FACTORS FOR CAPITAL GAINS TAX

Year Expenditure Incurred	Multiple for disposals in Year to 5 April:																	
	1984	1985	1986	1987	1988	1989	1990	1991	1992	1993	1994	1995	1996	1997	1998	1999	2000	2001
1974/75	3.759	4.140	4.397	4.598	4.756	4.848	5.009	5.221	5.355	5.552	5.656	5.754	5.899	6.017	6.112	6.215	6.313	6.582
1975/76	3.035	3.344	3.551	3.714	3.842	3.916	4.046	4.217	4.326	4.484	4.568	4.647	4.764	4.860	4.936	5.020	5.099	5.316
1976/77	2.615	2.881	3.059	3.200	3.309	3.373	3.485	3.633	3.726	3.863	3.935	4.003	4.104	4.187	4.253	4.325	4.393	4.580
1977/78	2.242	2.470	2.623	2.743	2.837	2.892	2.988	3.114	3.194	3.312	3.373	3.432	3.518	3.589	3.646	3.707	3.766	3.926
1978/79	2.071	2.282	2.423	2.534	2.621	2.672	2.760	2.877	2.951	3.059	3.117	3.171	3.250	3.316	3.368	3.425	3.479	3.627
1979/80	1.869	2.059	2.186	2.286	2.365	2.410	2.490	2.596	2.663	2.760	2.812	2.861	2.933	2.992	3.039	3.090	3.139	3.272
1980/81	1.618	1.782	1.893	1.979	2.047	2.087	2.156	2.247	2.305	2.390	2.434	2.477	2.539	2.590	2.631	2.675	2.718	2.833
1981/82	1.337	1.473	1.564	1.636	1.692	1.725	1.782	1.857	1.905	1.975	2.012	2.047	2.099	2.141	2.174	2.211	2.246	2.342
1982/83	1.125	1.239	1.316	1.376	1.424	1.451	1.499	1.563	1.603	1.662	1.693	1.722	1.765	1.801	1.829	1.860	1.890	1.970
1983/84	-	1.102	1.170	1.224	1.266	1.290	1.333	1.390	1.425	1.478	1.505	1.531	1.570	1.601	1.627	1.654	1.680	1.752
1984/85	-	-	1.062	1.111	1.149	1.171	1.210	1.261	1.294	1.341	1.366	1.390	1.425	1.454	1.477	1.502	1.525	1.590
1985/86	-	-	-	1.046	1.082	1.103	1.140	1.188	1.218	1.263	1.287	1.309	1.342	1.369	1.390	1.414	1.436	1.497
1986/87	-	-	-	-	1.035	1.055	1.090	1.136	1.165	1.208	1.230	1.252	1.283	1.309	1.330	1.352	1.373	1.432
1987/88	-	-	-	-	-	1.020	1.054	1.098	1.126	1.168	1.190	1.210	1.241	1.266	1.285	1.307	1.328	1.384
1988/89	-	-	-	-	-	-	1.034	1.077	1.105	1.146	1.167	1.187	1.217	1.242	1.261	1.282	1.303	1.358
1989/90	-	-	-	-	-	-	-	1.043	1.070	1.109	1.130	1.149	1.178	1.202	1.221	1.241	1.261	1.314
1990/91	-	-	-	-	-	-	-	-	1.026	1.064	1.084	1.102	1.130	1.153	1.171	1.191	1.210	1.261
1991/92	-	-	-	-	-	-	-	-	-	1.037	1.056	1.075	1.102	1.124	1.142	1.161	1.179	1.229
1992/93	-	-	-	-	-	-	-	-	-	-	1.019	1.037	1.063	1.084	1.101	1.120	1.138	1.186
1993/94	-	-	-	-	-	-	-	-	-	-	-	1.018	1.043	1.064	1.081	1.099	1.117	1.164
1994/95	-	-	-	-	-	-	-	-	-	-	-	-	1.026	1.046	1.063	1.081	1.098	1.144
1995/96	-	-	-	-	-	-	-	-	-	-	-	-	-	1.021	1.037	1.054	1.071	1.116
1996/97	-	-	-	-	-	-	-	-	-	-	-	-	-	-	1.016	1.033	1.050	1.094
1997/98	-	-	-	-	-	-	-	-	-	-	-	-	-	-	-	1.017	1.033	1.077
1998/99	-	-	-	-	-	-	-	-	-	-	-	-	-	-	-	-	1.016	1.059
1999/00	-	-	-	-	-	-	-	-	-	-	-	-	-	-	-	-	-	1.043

NOTE: No indexation is available for expenditure made within 12 months prior to the date of disposal.

The following table sets out the countries participating in the European Monetary Union and the fixed exchange rates for conversion of the existing currency of those countries to the euro.

EURO - FIXED CONVERSION RATES		
applying on introduction of euro on 1 January 1999		
Country	**1 EURO =**	**Existing Currency**
Austria	13.7603	Austrian schilling
Belgium	40.3399	Belgian franc
Finland	5.94573	Finnish markka
France	6.55957	French franc
Germany	1.95583	Deutschmark
Holland	2.20371	Dutch guilder
Ireland	0.787564	Irish pound
Italy	1936.27	Italian lira
Luxembourg	40.3399	Luxembourg franc
Portugal	200.482	Portuguese escudo
Spain	166.386	Spanish peseta

The CGT issues arising out of the introduction of the euro are discussed in various paragraphs:

- Overall Summary of position - paragraphs 4.2.1
- Consideration for disposal in foreign currency - paragraph 8.10
- Acquisition of asset in foreign currency - paragraph 9.1.2.2.
- Debt on a security - paragraph 38.2.

TABLE OF CONTENTS

CHAPTER 1   GENERAL PRINCIPLES 1

1   INTRODUCTION
        1.1   Legislation...1
        1.2   Case Law 3
2   CHARGE TO TAX
        2.1   Broad Outline 6
3   TERRITORIAL SCOPE OF THE CHARGE TO CGT
        3.1   Broad Outline - scope of the charge 9
        3.1.1   Irish resident and domiciled person 9
        3.1.2   Irish resident and non domiciled individual..........10
        3.1.3   Non resident persons 10
        3.2   Irish resident and domiciled persons.....................11
        3.3   Irish resident - non Irish domiciled individual
        3.3.1   Broad outline - Irish resident - non domiciled
                  individual...11
        3.3.2   What is a "remittance" question.............................18
        3.3.3   Notional sale proceeds 23
        3.3.4   Alienation of capital 27
        3.3.5   Remittance anti-avoidance 27
        3.4   Non-resident persons 29
        3.4.1   Broad Outline - Non-Residents.............................29
        3.4.2   Specified Assets - Gains 29
        3.4.3   Specified Assets - Losses......................................32
        3.5   Shares deriving value..32
        3.5.1   Broad outline - shares deriving value....................32
        3.5.2   Deriving value - when must the test be applied 33
        3.5.3   Deriving value - how is the test to be applied34
        3.5.4   Share valuations..35
        3.6   Branch assets...40
        3.6.1   What is a "branch or agency" 40
        3.6.2   Location of branch assets......................................42
        3.6.3   Use of branch assets/purpose for which held........42
        3.7   Location of Assets...44
        3.7.1   Location of Assets -statutory rules........................44
        3.7.2   Location of Assets - case law.................................48
        3.7.2.1   Letters of Allotment..48
        3.7.2.2   Goodwill attached to Buildings 49

4   DISPOSAL OF ASSETS
       4.1   Broad Outline - disposals of assets......................50
       4.2   What are Assets..51
       4.2.1   What are assets - Legislation.........................51
       4.2.2   What are assets - Case Law 51
       4.2.3   "Assets" means "property"..............................52
       4.2.4   "Assets" must be owned prior to disposal 53
       4.2.5   "Assets" - limitations on transfer 54
       4.2.6   Statutory compensation may be an asset 55
       4.2.7   The right to receive a sum may be an asset............58
       4.2.8   The right to sue may be an asset.......................59
       4.2.9   Letters of allotment..60
       4.2.10   "Assets" - broad summary of case law...............61
       4.2.11   Land and buildings as an asset..........................61
       4.3   Euro & Irish Currency not an "asset" 62
       4.4   What is a disposal? 63
       4.4.1   Broad Outline - what is a disposal?.......................63
       4.4.2   The meaning of disposal...................................64
       4.4.3   Part disposals...66
       4.4.4   Capital sums derived from assets 67
       4.4.5   Capital sum NOT derived from an asset................69
       4.4.6   Capital Sum - derived from which asset? 72
       4.4.7   Meaning of "capital sum"..................................75
       4.5   Compensation - as an asset 79
       4.5.1   Compensation - income or capital receipt?.............79
       4.5.2   Exempt compensation.......................................82
       4.5.3   Insurance policies 82
       4.5.4   Compensation and Roll-Over relief 84
       4.6   Effect of taxation on amount of compensation -
                "Gourley's Case"...84
5   RATES OF TAX
       5.1   Standard Rate 89
       5.2   Reduced Rate (Disposal - 6/4/94 to 2/12/97 only)
               90
       5.2.1   Broad outline - reduced rate - 6/4/94 to 2/12/97 .90
       5.2.2   Disposal 6th April 1994 to 3rd December 1997: 91
       5.2.3   Qualifying shares 91
       5.2.4   Qualifying company..93
       5.2.5   Qualifying trade condition 94
       5.2.6   Holding company 95
       5.2.7   Individuals only 96
       5.2.8   3 year ownership...96
       5.2.9   Miscellaneous matters.....................................97
       5.2.10   Application of rules – reorganisations, mergers, etc.....97
       5.2.11   Disposal of shares 101

	5.2.12	1995/1996 disposals only	102
6	DEVELOPMENT LAND		
	6.1	Broad Outline	105
	6.1.1	Overview - computational restrictions	105
	6.1.2	Tax Rates - development land : 20% - 40% - 60%	106
	6.1.2.1	Disposals on or after 1 December 1999	106
	6.1.2.2	Disposals pre 1 December 1999	107
	6.1.3	Land sold for residential development - after 5 April 2002.	111
	6.2	Meaning of Development Land	111
	6.3	Restriction on Indexation	120
	6.4	Restriction on certain reliefs	122
	6.5	Development Land - use of losses.	124
	6.6	Development - Small Gains	125
	6.7	Gains Arising to Companies	125
	6.8	Principal Private Residence	125
	6.9	Income Tax Provisions	125

CHAPTER 2   COMPUTATION RULES 129

7	COMPUTATION OF GAIN OR LOSS		
	7.1	Computation rules	129
8	CONSIDERATION FOR DISPOSAL		
	8.1	Broad Outline - Consideration	130
	8.2	Amount of Consideration	132
	8.3	Meaning of consideration	137
	8.4	Receipts taxed as income	139
	8.5	Capital Allowances	141
	8.6	Capitalised Value of Rent or Right to Income	141
	8.7	Asset used as Security	141
	8.8	Deferred or Contingent Proceeds	142
	8.8.1	General Rule	142
	8.8.2	Earnouts	145
	8.9	Apportionment of consideration	150
	8.10	Foreign currency	154
9	EXPENDITURE DEDUCTIBLE		
	9.1	Expenditure - main rules	155
	9.1.1	Broad Outline	155
	9.1.2	Value of consideration given	156
	9.1.2.1	Substitution of market value for consideration	159
	9.1.2.2	Foreign Currency	159
	9.1.3	Expenditure on provision of asset	161
	9.1.3.1	Own Labour	161
	9.1.4	Expenditure on asset	161

9.1.5	Cost of defending title	163
9.2	Incidental Costs	165
9.2.1	Cost of variation of marriage settlement	168
9.3	Foreign Tax	168
9.4	Asset used as security	169
9.5	Interest	172
9.6	Grants	174
9.7	Insurance	175
9.8	Expenditure : Capital Allowances	175
9.9	Contingent Liabilities	177
9.10	Assets Derived from Assets	178
9.11	Assets Acquired from Trust	181
9.12	Value Added Tax	182
9.13	Income Tax Relief	183
9.13.1	General Note - Share schemes	183
9.13.2	Business Expansion Scheme	184
9.13.2.1	Broad Outline - B.E.S. (CGT aspects)	184
9.13.2.2	Change in or withdrawal of relief	185
9.13.2.3	Multiple holdings, etc.	185
9.13.2.4	Main rule - deemed disposal of BES shares first	186
9.13.2.5	F.I.F.O.	187
9.13.2.6	Reorganisation of share capital	187
9.13.3	Research and Development	187
9.13.4	Relief for investment in films	187
9.13.4.1	Broad Outline - investment in films	187
9.13.4.2	Film relief 1987 - 1996	188
9.13.4.3	Film relief post FA96	189
9.14	Investment in renewable energy projects	193
9.15	Relief for employee share purchases	196
10	WASTING ASSETS	
10.1	Broad Outline	197
10.2	Restriction of Deductible Expenditure	198
10.3	Assets Qualifying for Capital Allowances	199
10.4	Method of Restricting Expenditure	200
10.5	Effect on Indexation	201
10.6	Merged Assets	201
11	PART DISPOSALS	
11.1	Part disposals - broad outline	203
11.2	Part disposals - detailed application	203
11.3	"No gain / no loss" disposals	208
12	EVENTS PRIOR TO 6/4/74	
12.1	Events prior to 6/4/74	209
13	ASSETS OWNED AT 6 APRIL 1974	

14   INDEXATION
       14.1   Indexation : broad outline 210
       14.2   Assets Acquired After 5/4/74 - Indexation..........211
       14.3   Indexation : Exceptions..211
       14.4   Indexation : Grant-Aided Expenditure.................214
15   TIME OF DISPOSAL
       15.1   Broad Outline 215
       15.2   Conditional Contract..220
16   ARM'S LENGTH RULES
       16.1   Broad Outline 223
       16.2   Acquisition...223
       16.2.1   Special rules for shares..224
       16.2.2   Antiavoidance - all assets 224
       16.3   Disposal - TCA97 s547(4)...226
       16.4   Connected Persons 227
       16.4.1   Acquisitions & disposals - general rule.................227
       16.4.2   Restriction of Relief for Losses...............................227
       16.4.3   Assets subject to right or restriction.....................228
       16.4.4   What is a Connected Person?..................................229
       16.4.5   Meaning of Control 231
       16.4.6   Disposal in a series of transactions.......................232
17   OPEN MARKET VALUE
       17.1   Broad Outline 234
       17.2   Unquoted Shares..235
       17.3   Exchange Control 235
       17.4   Quoted Shares 235
       17.5   Unit Trusts 236
       17.6   Appeals..236
18   DISPOSALS TO OR FROM TRADING STOCK
       18.1   Appropriation to trading stock...............................237
       18.2   Appropriation from Trading Stock 238
       18.3   Application to Members of a Group 239
       18.4   Meaning of trading stock..239

CHAPTER 3   RELIEFS, ALLOWANCES, AND
                 EXEMPTIONS 241

19   ANNUAL £1,000 ALLOWANCE TO INDIVIDUALS
       19.1   Broad Outline 241
       19.2   Married Persons 241
       19.3   Death..242
       19.4   Claim for Retirement Relief.....................................242
       19.5   Different Rates of Tax...242

20   LOSSES
      20.1   Broad Outline 102
      20.2   Non Allowable Losses...............................243
      20.3   Use of Losses 244
      20.4   Loss or Destruction of Asset 245
      20.5   Asset with Negligible Value.....................245
      20.6   Capital Allowance and Losses 250
      20.7   Connected Persons 250
      20.8   Development Land 250
      20.9   Groups of companies and shares.............250
      20.10   Corporation tax losses..............................250

21   GAINS AND LOSSES ON DISPOSAL OF CHATTELS
      21.1   Broad Outline 252
      21.2   "Wasting Chattels" 252
      21.3   "Non-Wasting Chattels" 252

22   EXEMPTION - WASTING CHATTELS
      22.1   Wasting chattels - broad outline 253
      22.2   No exemption for "wasting" business chattels 253
      22.3   Wasting chattels - part business use 254

23   £2.000 EXEMPTION - NON-WASTING CHATTELS
      23.1   Broad Outline 257
      23.2   Marginal Relief...257
      23.3   Sets of Chattels 258
      23.4   Losses...259
      23.5   Part Disposal of Qualifying Chattel 259
      23.6   Exceptions 261

24   PRINCIPAL PRIVATE RESIDENCE
      24.1   Broad Outline 261
      24.2   What is a "principal private residence".................262
      24.3   Separate Buildings (outhouses, gate lodge, etc.)..264
      24.4   Period of ownership....................................266
      24.4.1 Broad Outline 266
      24.4.2 Periods of absence.......................................269
      24.5   Part Used for Trade Purposes 271
      24.6   Change in Use or Structure of House 272
      24.7   More Than One Main Residence 275
      24.8   Married Persons 276
      24.9   Settled Property...276
      24.10   Profit Motive..277
      24.11   Dependent Relative 278
      24.12   Residence - Development Land 279
      24.13   Foreign dwelling...281

25   RELIEFS - REINVESTMENT OF DISPOSAL PROCEEDS
      25.1   Broad summary...281

26   ROLL-OVER RELIEF
      26.1.1   Broad Outline 283
      26.1.2   Claiming relief.......................................289
      26.2   Full Proceeds Re-Invested 290
      26.3   Partial re-Investment of Sale Proceeds 292
      26.4   Use Partly for Non-Trade Purposes.....................293
      26.5   Time Limit for Replacement of Asset 294
      26.6   Reinvestment in different trade.............................296
      26.6.1   Broad Outline 296
      26.6.2   Two or More Trades.....................................296
      26.6.3   Group Roll Over relief.................................298
      26.6.4   Cessation of Trade – Commencement of New Trade
               298
      26.7   Application to Non-Trading Activities.................300
      26.8   Farming activities.....................................301
      26.9   Sporting Bodies 301
      26.10   Anti-Avoidance..304
      26.11   Development Land Gains................................304
      26.12   Rollover relief on shares 307
      26.12.1   Broad Outline 307
      26.12.2   Conditions relating to shares disposed of:............308
      26.12.3   Conditions relating to new investment 309
      26.13   Revenue procedures. 315
      26.14   Company going non-resident 26.14
27   COMPULSORY PURCHASE ORDERS-RELIEF
      27.1   CPO Relief - Broad Outline 317
      27.2   Full proceeds not re-invested.........................318
      27.2.1   Less Than Full Proceeds Re-Invested 318
      27.2.2   More Than Full Proceeds Re-invested..................319
      27.3   Qualifying Assets.....................................319
      27.4   Time Limit for Re-Investment..........................322
      27.5   Development Land Gains323
28   RE-INVESTMENT OF COMPENSATION PROCEEDS
      28.1   Broad Outline 324
      28.2   Wasting Assets 324
      28.3   Circumstances of Relief...............................324
      28.4   Assets Not Wholly Lost or Destroyed 325
      28.5   Asset totally lost or destroyed: full reinvestment 327
      28.6   Compensation Partly Re-Invested......................328
      28.7   Time limit for reinvestment...........................329
      28.8   Tenants 329
29   DISPOSAL OF BUSINESS TO A COMPANY
      29.1   Broad Outline 330
      29.2   Conditions for Relief 330

	29.3	Going Concern	331
	29.4	Calculation of Relief	332
	29.5	Offshore Assets	335
30	**RETIREMENT RELIEF**		
	30.1	Broad Outline	336
	30.2	Conditions for relief	338
	30.3	Amount of relief	338
	30.4	Qualifying Assets	340
	30.5	Family Company	348
	30.6	Liquidation of Family Company	350
	30.7	Period of ownership/deemed ownership	352
	30.8	Calculation of £375,000 proceeds limit.	354
	30.9	Disposal of shares in family company:	358
	30.10	Marginal Relief	364
	30.11	Disposal to Child of owner	368
	30.12	Trusts	30.12
	30.13	Interaction with other reliefs:	376
	30.13.1	Transfer of business to a company	376
	30.13.2	Roll-over relief	376
	30.13.3	Relief for a company acquiring its own shares	376
	30.14	Offset of CGT against CAT	376
31	**DISPOSALS TO CHARITIES AND PUBLIC BODIES**		
	31.1	Broad Outline	377
	31.2	Subsequent Disposal by Charity, Etc.	377
	31.3	Charities - Settled Property	378
	31.4	Charities	378
32	**EXEMPT BODIES AND ASSETS**		
	32.1	Government and Other Securities	381
	32.1.1	General exemption on disposal	381
	32.1.2	Exchanges of government stocks	382
	32.2	Futures Contracts	383
	32.3	Strips of securities	383
	32.4.1	Superannuation Schemes	386
	32.4.2	Approved retirement Funds	386
	32.5	Scheme for Retirement of Farmers	388
	32.6	Employment grants and recruitment subsidies	388
	32.7	Exempt Bodies	389
	32.8	Exemption for certain gains	390
	32.9	Life Assurance Policies and Deferred Life Annuities	391
	32.10	Woodlands	392
	32.11	Annuities, Covenants, Etc.	392
	32.12	Diplomatic and Consular Officials	394
	32.13	Disposal of Interest in Settled Property	394

32.14	Relief for disposals of works of art	395
32.14.1	Broad Outline	395
32.14.2	Public Display - relief	395
32.14.3	Donations to National Collections - relief.	395
32.15	Chart of reliefs, exemptions, etc	396

CHAPTER 4   SPECIAL CLASSES OF PERSONS 401

33	MARRIED PERSONS	
33.1	Broad Outline	401
33.2	Married Woman Living With Her Husband	401
33.3	Assessment on Married Persons	403
33.4	Separate Assessment	404
33.5	Losses	405
33.6	Annual Exemption	405
33.6.1	Broad outline	405
33.6.2	Transfer of exemption to other spouse (pre 1998/99)	405
33.7	Disposal to Spouse	407
33.7.1	Disposal inter vivos between spouses	407
33.7.1.1	Treatment of spouse making disposal	407
33.7.2	Treatment of spouse acquiring asset from spouse	408
33.7.3	Disposals from estate of deceased spouse to surviving spouse	408
33.7.4	Spouses and Trusts	409
33.8	Marriage breakdown	409
33.8.1	Broad overview	409
33.8.2	Decree of Divorce	412
33.8.2.1	Broad Outline	412
33.8.2.2	Relief under TCA97 s1031	412
33.8.2.3	Transfers to which s1031 relief applies	413
33.8.3	Separation by Court Order or Formal deed	418
33.8.3.1	Broad outline	418
33.8.3.2	Relief under s1030	418
33.8.3.3	Scope of the relief	419
33.8.4	Informally separated spouses	420
33.8.5	Foreign divorce	421
33.8.6	Annullment of marriage	422
33.9	Meaning of "child"	423
33.10	Divorce and "connected persons"	424
33.11	Divorce and trusts	425
34	PARTNERSHIPS AND ASSOCIATIONS	
34.1	Broad Outline	426

	34.2	Partnerships assets	427
	34.3	The UK Statement of Practice	429
	34.4	Creation of the Partnership	429
	34.5	Admission of a New Partner	431
	34.6	Adjustment of Partnership Sharing Ratios	433
	34.7	Departure of partner	434
	34.8	Disposal of partnership assets	435
	34.9	Rate of CGT	436
	34.10	Irish practice	437
	34.11	Residence of Partners	438
	34.12	Unincorporated Associations	439
	34.13	European Economic Interest Grouping	440
35		CIUS; UCITS; UNIT TRUSTS.	
	35.1	Broad Overview	441
	35.2	Historical Overview	443
	35.3	Charge to CGT pre-FA89	446
	35.4	Reduced rate of CGT for trustees - pre FA89	447
	35.5	Reduced rate of CGT for Unit Holders - pre FA89	447
	35.6	CGT and CIUs — FA89 to FA93	448
	35.7	CGT & CIUs - FA 99 to FA 2000	449
	35.8	FA 2000 CIU tax regime	453
	35.8.1	Broad Outline	453
	35.8.2	Taxation treatment of a CIU under FA 2000	454
	35.8.3.1	Taxation of unitholder - non corporate	455
	35.8.3.2	Taxation of unitholder - corporate	457
	35.8.4	Taxation of the fund	458
	35.8.4.1	Returns & payment of tax by a CIU	461
	35.8.5	IFSC Funds	461
	35.9	Residence of trustees	462
	35.10	CIUs and Life Assurance	462
	35.11	Special Investment Schemes	462
	35.12	Offshore funds	464
	35.12.1	Broad outline	464
	35.12.2	Charge To Income Tax	466
	35.12.3	Material Interest	466
	35.12.4	Qualifying Fund	468
	35.12.5	Tax on Gain	468
	35.12.6	Shares held by non-resident entities	469
	35.13	Unit trusts and CIU's in the IFSC	469
	35.14	CIUs and double tax agreements	472
	35.15	Reorganisations and a CIU	472
	35.16	Unauthorised unit trusts	473

36   LIFE ASSURANCE
    36.1   Overview...477
    36.2   Life Assurance and Deferred Annuities - "old basis policies"...478
    36.3   Life Assurance - Finance Act 2000 regime 481
    36.3.1   Foreign life assurance...485
    36.4   Life assurance in the IFSC...................................486
    36.5.1   Life assurance companies 487
    36.5.2   Life Assurance - new business...........................490
    36.6   Special investment policies.................................490

37   SPECIAL PORTFOLIO INVESTMENT ACCOUNTS
    37.1   Broad Outline 491
    37.2   Special Portfolio Investment Accounts and CGT.491

CHAPTER 5   DEBTS AND OPTIONS.................495

38   DEBTS
    38.1   Broad Outline 495
    38.2   Debt on a security 495
    38.3   Property in Satisfaction of Debt...........................502
    38.4   Loss on Debt Acquired from "Connected" Person 502
    38.5   Trustees 503
    38.6   Bank Balances 503
    38.7   Bank Balances in Foreign Currency 505
    38.8   Foreign currency loans...505
    38.9   Exchange gains and losses of trading company...506
    38.10   Debentures - "paper for paper" 507

39   OPTIONS AND FORFEITED DEPOSITS
    39.1   Broad outline 508
    39.2   General rules..510
    39.3   Abandonment of an option 514
    39.3.1   Present position..514
    39.3.2   Historical position...517
    39.4   Option for trade assets 522
    39.5   Quoted options and traded options......................523
    39.6   Transfer of an option 523
    39.7   Option to buy and sell..523
    39.8   Forfeited deposits of purchase money...................524
    39.9   Leases and 'non-sale' transactions 524
    39.10   Assessment and return...525
    39.11.1 Employee share options..527
    39.11.2 Deferred payment in relation to share options 530

CHAPTER 6   SHARES AND SECURITIES..........533

40   SHARE TRANSACTIONS
40.1   Broad Outline - share transactions 533
40.2   Meaning of Shares 535
40.3.1 Receipt of Capital Distribution: 536
40.3.2 Shares and Liquidation 537
40.4   Sale of Rights 541

41   ISSUE OF SHARES - COST OF ACQUISITION
41.1   Basic Rule 542
41.2   Connected Person 543
41.3   Reverse Nairn Williamson scheme 544
41.4   Share Transactions - tax avoidance 546
41.5   Calls on shares...549
41.6   Extraction of Corporate Profits 549

42   REORGANISATIONS/REDUCTION OF SHARE CAPITAL
42.1   Overview...551
42.2   Definitions..553
42.2.1 "Reduction of share capital" is not defined. 553
42.2.2 "Reorganisation of share capital" is not defined .555
42.2.3 Bonus Issues...555
42.3   Rights Issues 556
42.4   Exchange of Shares in same company ('Paper for Paper') 560
42.5   Introduction of Further Consideration.................561
42.6   Shares Plus Other Consideration 563
42.7   Apportionment 564

43   COMPANY AMALGAMATIONS (by exchange of shares)
43.1   Overview..565

44   RECONSTRUCTIONS AND AMALGAMATIONS
44.1   Overview...569
44.2   Amalgamations 571
44.3   Reconstructions 571
44.4   Undertaking 572
44.5   Reorganisation : T. S. B.s and Building Societies..572
44.5.1 Conversion of building society: 573
44.5.2 Conversion of a trustee savings bank: 574
44.6   Reorganisation of co-operative society.................574
44.7   Demutualisation of assurance company 576
44.8   De-Mergers and Partitions of Family Companies577

45   REORGANISATIONS, ETC - ANTI-AVOIDANCE
45.1   Reorganisation of Share Capital 579
45.2   Debenture not a debt on a security 580

46		DISPOSAL AFTER RECONSTRUCTION, ETC.	
	46.1	Broad Outline	581
	46.2	Application of Provisions	581
	46.3	Time Limits	583
	46.4	Liquidation	584
	46.5	Charge on Principal Company	584
	46.6	Tax Unpaid	585
	46.7	Overall Time Limit for Assessment	586
	46.8	Disposal in the Course of Reconstruction or Amalgamation	586
47		CONVERSION OF SECURITIES	
	47.1	Outline - conversion of securities	586
48		SHARES-IDENTIFICATION	
	48.1	Outline	587
	48.2	General Rule	587
	48.3	Disposal within 4 Weeks of Acquisition	589
	48.3.1	General Outline – "Bed and Breakfast"	589
	48.3.2	Share identification rule	590
	48.3.3	Losses restriction rule	591
	48.3.4	Married couples	591
	48.4	Shares Acquired - 6/4/'74 to 5/4/'78	592
	48.5	Shares Held at 6 April 1974	595
	48.6	Shares obtained in a reorganisation (or amalgamation)	595
	48.7	BES shares	598
49		ACQUISITION BY A COMPANY OF ITS OWN SHARES	
	49.1	Background	598
	49.2	Overview	599
	49.2.1	Quoted buybacks	600
	49.2.2	Unquoted buybacks	601
	49.3	Unquoted shares	602
	49.3.1	Broad Outline	602
	49.3.2	Treasury shares : unquoted (s184)	605
	49.3.3	Main Conditions for relief : Unquoted	605
	49.3.3.1	Purpose of the transaction	605
	49.3.3.2	Trade Benefit (unquoted)	606
	49.3.3.3	Proceeds used to pay Inheritance Tax (unquoted)	608
	49.3.4	Residence of Shareholder (unquoted)	608
	49.3.5	Period of ownership of shares (unquoted)	609
	49.3.6	Reduction of vendor's interest in the company (unquoted)	610
	49.3.7	Connected persons	613
	49.3.8	Scheme or arrangement	613

49.3.9	Company acquiring shares from a dealer in shares	614
49.3.10	Returns	614
49.3.11	Information	614
49.4	Definitions - Share Buyback.	614
49.4.1	Overview	614
49.4.2	Quoted s173	615
49.4.3	Trading - s173	615
49.4.4	Group - s173	615
49.4.5	Trading group - s173	615
49.4.6	Shares - s173	615
49.4.7	Treasury shares - s184	615
49.4.8	Material interest - s185(3)	616
49.4.9	Associated persons - s185	616
49.4.10	Control - s173	617
49.4.11	Connected persons - s186	617
49.4.12	30% of shares or votes :	617
49.4.13	30% assets on winding up	618
49.4.14	Control of company:	618
49.4.15	Loan Capital:	618
50	EMPLOYEE SHARES	
50.1	Broad Outline	618
50.1.1	Finance Act 1998 - antiavoidance	619
50.2	Approved profit sharing scheme (CGT aspects)	621
50.3	Employee share ownership trusts	624
50.4	Save As You Earn	626
51	STRIPPING VALUE FROM ASSETS	
51.1	Outline Summary of provisions	627
51.2	Transfer of Value Derived from Assets	627
51.2.1	Shares in Companies	627
51.2.2	Interaction with other provisions	6321
51.2.2.1	Reorganisations, etc	632
51.2.2.2	Transfers between husband & wife	633
51.2.2.3	Transfers between members of a group of companies	633
51.2.2.4	The notional interest in the asset	634
51.2.2.5	Land	636
51.2.2.6	Other Assets	636
51.2.2.7	Persons acquiring the benefit	636
51.3	Transfer of assets at undervalue	636
51.3.1	Broad Outline - s589	636
51.3.2	Apportionment	639
51.3.3	Exception	639
51.4	Depreciatory Transactions in a Group	639
51.4.1	Broad Outline	639

	51.4.2	Scope of anti-avoidance Provisions......640
	51.4.3	Meaning of "Depreciatory Transactions" 640
	51.4.4	Effect of Provisions......641
	51.5	Dividend Stripping......642
	51.5.1	Broad Outline......642
	51.5.2	Scope of the Provisions......642
	51.6	Pre-disposal dividends......644
52	SHARE RELIEFS - SUMMARY CHART	
	52.1	Summary chart......648

CHAPTER 7   LEASEHOLD INTERESTS 651

53	LEASES - GENERAL INTRODUCTION	
54	GRANT OF LEASE......651	
	54.1	General outline - grant of lease......651
55	SALE OR ASSIGNMENT OF LEASEHOLD INTEREST	
	55.1	Sale of leasehold interest is a disposal......654
	55.2	Cost of acquisition......655
56	CHARGE TO CGT......657	
57	LEASE AS A WASTING ASSET	
	57.1	Wasted Expenditure - calculation......658
	57.2	Expenditure : Capital Allowances......661
	57.3	Leases owned at 6 April 1974......662
58	INTERACTION OF CGT WITH INCOME TAX	
	58.1	Income Tax - Sch D, Case V rules......663
59	TRANSACTIONS FOR CONSIDERATION	
	59.1	General......664
	59.2	Sale of a Long Lease......664
	59.3	Sale or assignment of a Short Lease......665
	59.4	Grant of a Long Lease (out of a Freehold or Long Lease)......665
	59.5	Grant of a Short Lease (out of a Freehold or Long Lease)......666
	59.6	Grant of a Short Lease Out of a Short Lease......667
	59.7	Expenditure Attributable to Part Disposal......667
	59.8	Consideration Chargeable......667
	59.9	Restriction of Loss......670
60	DEEMED PREMIUMS	
	60.1	Income Tax rules applied......670
61	DURATION OF A LEASE	
	61.1	Duration of lease - special rules......671
62	LEASES OF PROPERTY OTHER THAN LAND	
	62.1	Broad Outline - other leases......674

CHAPTER 8 ASSETS HELD IN A FIDUCIARY OR REPRESENTATIVE CAPACITY ...675

63	NOMINEES/TRUSTEES/EXECUTORS	
	63.1	Broad Outline 675
	63.2	Nominees and Bare Trustees...............................675
	63.3	Settled Property/Trustees. 676
	63.4	Personal Representatives.................................676
	63.5	Special trusts..677
	63.6	Joint Tenants 677
64	NOMINEES AND BARE TRUSTEES	
	64.1	Nominees 678
	64.2	Absolutely entitled against the trustees 679
	64.3	Assets of Insolvent Persons 684
	64.4	Companies in Liquidation.................................685
	64.5	Funds in Court 685
	64.6	Assets Transferred As Security.........................686
65	SETTLED PROPERTY	
	65.1	Broad Outline 689
	65.2	Trustees-Single Continuing Body..........................694
	65.3	Residence of a settlement.................................695
	65.3.1	Main rule 695
	65.3.2	Effect of "Professional Trustees" 697
	65.4	What is a Settlement? 698
	65.5	Property Settled on Trustees 702
	65.6	Dealings in Assets by Trustees—Actual Disposals 706
	65.7	Deemed Disposal by Trustees...............................706
	65.7.1	General Outline...706
	65.7.2	Death of Life Tenant...709
	65.7.3	Trustee relief - absolute interest passes on death of Life Tenant 711
	65.8	Meaning of Life Interest....................................714
	65.9	Deemed Separate Settlements...............................715
	65.10	Separate Settlements...716
	65.11	Losses Accruing to Beneficiary 725
	65.12	Disposal of Interest Under a Settlement................726
	65.12.1	Deemed disposal by beneficiary..........................726
	65.12.2	Exemption for beneficiary on disposal of interest 727
	65.12.3	Disposal of interest - non resident trustees...........730
	65.12.3.1	Broad Outline 730
	65.12.3.2	Limitation on use of exemption..........................731
	65.12.3.3	Exit disposal by beneficiary................................733
	65.12.3.4	Exit charge on trustees under s579B 733

65.13		Exit charge on trust going non resident	736
65.13.1		General rule	736
65.13.2		Defined Assets	739
65.13.2.1		General rule	739
65.13.2.2		Irish branch trade assets	739
65.13.2.3		Tax Treaty protected assets	739
65.13.2.4		Temporary change of residence due to death of trustee	740
65.13.2.5		Modification of Roll-over relief rules:	741
65.13.2.6		Collection of tax from former trustee	742
65.14		Trust becoming treaty protected	742
65.15		Return by trustees	744
65.16		Charitable Trusts	745
65.17		Foreign Trusts	745
66	PERSONAL REPRESENTATIVES		
66.1		Broad Outline	746
66.2		Personal Representatives	747
66.3		Gains Arising to Deceased Person up to Date of Death	747
66.4		Terminal Loss Relief	748
66.5		Assets Passing on Death	749
66.5.1		Assets to which the special "death" rules apply	749
66.5.2		Assets passing on or after 6 April 1978	750
66.5.3		Assets passing before 6 April 1978	752
66.6		Personal Representatives Becoming Trustees	755
66.7		Family Arrangements	755
66.8		Acquisition on Death of Spouse	758
66.9		Termination of Life Interest in settled property	758

CHAPTER 9   ANTI-AVOIDANCE 759

67	NON-RESIDENT ENTITIES		
67.1		Offshore aspects	759
67.1.1		Broad outline	759
67.1.2		History of Provisions	760
67.2		Non-Resident companies	765
67.2.1		Which non resident companies?	765
67.2.1.1		Resident	771
67.2.2		To whom may gains be attributed?	772
67.2.3.1		What can be attributed?	774
67.2.3.2		Excluded assets	779
67.2.4		Offshore losses	780
67.2.5		Interaction with DTR	781
67.3		Non resident companies - position pre 11/2/99	782

	67.3.1	Broad Outline - pre 11/2/99 only	782
	67.3.2	Scope of Provisions - pre 11/2/99 only	783
	67.3.3	Affect of Provisions - pre 11/2/99 only	783
	67.3.4	Exceptions - pre 11/2/99 only	787
	67.3.5	Deduction for Tax paid	789
	67.3.6	Losses - pre 11/2/99 only	790
	67.3.7	Double Tax Relief	792
	67.3.8	Tax Paid by Company	793
	67.3.9	Self Assessment	793
	67.3.10	Offshore funds	794
	67.3.10	Non-Resident "Groups" - limited relief for s590	794
68		NON-RESIDENT TRUSTS	
	68.1	Broad outline	800
	68.2	Section 579A - non resident trustees	801
	68.3	What settlements are affected question	801
	68.4	Beneficiary	802
	68.5	Capital Payments	803
	68.6	Gains to be attributed	805
	68.7	Attribution of gains	807
	68.8	Interaction with DTR	810
	68.9	Interaction with CAT	811
	68.10	Migrant Settlements	811
	68.11	S579 Rules	813
	68.11.1	Broad Outline - s579	813
	68.11.2	Scope of provisions - s579	814
	68.11.3	Effect of provisions - s579(2)	815
	68.11.4	Apportionment Between Beneficiaries - s579 rules	816
	68.11.5	Discretionary trusts - s579 rules	818
	68.11.5.1	Broad Outline	818
	68.11.5.2	Interest of discretionary beneficiary - case law	819
	68.11.5.3	Interest of discretionary beneficiary - Statutory Rules	820
	68.11.5.4	Statutory rules not a separate taxing code for discretionary trusts	822
	68.11.6	Pre 28 February 1974 settlements (s579)	822
	68.11.7	Payment of Tax by Trustees	829
	68.11.8	Losses	829
	68.11.9	Gains on Specified Assets	830
	68.11.10	Offshore Funds	831
	68.11.11	Self Assessment	831
69		FORM -V- SUBSTANCE	
	69.1	Historical Position	831
	69.2	The McGrath Case	833
	69.3	General Anti-Avoidance Law (s811)	837

70   ANTI-AVOIDANCE - GUIDE TO LOCATION
      70.1   Share transactions 839
      70.2   Anti-avoidance : Summary Chart.........................839

CHAPTER 10   COMPANY CHARGEABLE
**   GAINS...843**

71   INTRODUCTION
      71.1   Company chargeable gains 843
      71.2   Scope of the charge - Broad Outline.......................844
      71.3   Meaning of "company"..847
      71.4   Overseas branches - "participation exemption" ..848
72   AMOUNT CHARGEABLE TO C.T.
      72.1   Main rule - amount chargeable to CT 851
      72.2   Rate of C.T. on Gains – prior to FA 1982 856
73   RELIEF FOR LOSSES
      73.1   Broad Outline 856
      73.2   Capital losses of the company...............................857
      73.3   Buying losses: Anti Avoidance 859
      73.3.1 Broad Outline 859
      73.3.2 What is a "pre-entry" loss?...................................860
      73.3.3 What relief is available for a pre-entry loss?.........861
      73.3.3.1 Introduction 861
      73.3.3.2 Entry period gain 861
      73.3.3.3 Pre Entry Asset 863
      73.3.3.4 Trading Assets...865
      73.3.3.5 Wide Scope of Restrictions on Loss Relief 865
      73.3.3.6 Special rules - identification of assets 866
      73.3.3.7 Group Reorganisations 868
      73.3.3.8 Change in Identity of Group 868
      73.4   Trading losses and other deductions of the
              company 870
      73.5   Group losses872
74   "EXIT CHARGE" ON GOING NON-RESIDENT
      74.1   Overview...874
      74.2   Postponement of charge 876
      74.3   Exclusion for treaty States 881
      74.4   Collection of tax 883
75   RELIEFS - TRANSFERS BETWEEN COMPANIES
      75.1   Summary of reliefs...889
      75.2   Transfer of Business on Reconstruction, etc. 891
      75.2.1 Broad Outline 891
      75.2.2 Conditions - s615 relief....................................891

75.2.3	Operation of Relief	894
75.2.4	Disposal of Business	895
75.2.5	Returns	896
75.3	EU Mergers Directive - Transfer of Trade	896
75.3.1	EU Mergers Directive - outline of relief	896
75.3.2	EU mergers directive - relief	897
75.3.3	EU Mergers Directive - method of granting relief	900
75.3.4	EU Mergers Directive - Clawback of relief	900
75.3.5	EU Mergers Directive - Exclusions from relief	903
75.3.6	EU Mergers Directive - Anti-avoidance	903
75.3.7	EU Mergers Directive - Returns	903
75.4	Group Relief - post FA 99	904
75.4.1	Overview of Group Relief - post FA 99	904
75.4.2	Greoup relief - Companies resident in other EU Member States	905
75.4.3	Group relief - What constitutes a Group - post FA99	908
75.4.3.1	What constitutes a group - overview	908
75.4.3.2	Group relief - 75% Subsidiary - post FA 99	911
75.4.3.3	Group relief - Profits Test - post FA 99	912
75.4.3.4	Group relief - "Equity holders" - post FA 99	915
75.4.3.5	Group relief - assets on a winding-up test - post FA 99	917
75.4.4	Group relief - Anti-avoidance	918
75.4.4.1	Antiavoidance - Broad Outline	918
75.4.4.2	Antiavoidance - limited rights to profits or assets	918
75.4.4.3	Antiavoidance - variable rights, over a period of time	919
75.4.4.4	Residence and Groups	922
75.4.4.5	Special Transitional Arrangements - post FA 99	922
75.4.5	What Constitutes a Group? (Pre FA99)	923
75.4.5.1	Definitions (pre FA99)	924
75.4.5.2	Principal Company	924
75.4.5.3	75% Subsidiary (pre FA 99)	924
75.4.5.4	Non-resident structures (pre FA 99)	925
75.4.5.5	Ordinary Share Capital	928
75.4.5.6	Company Incorporated Outside Ireland	928
75.5	Transfers Between Group Member Companies	928
75.5.1	Transfers between group companies - outline	928
75.5.2	Indexation : Group transfers	929
75.6	State Bodies	930
75.7	Offshore Group Relief	931

76   GROUPS, TAKEOVERS, & REORGANISATIONS
        76.1   Group Effects of Takeover 931
        76.2   Winding up of Group Company 932
        76.3   Group relief and Reorganisations 933
        76.4   Part disposals within a group 936
        76.5   Exceptions to General Rule 937
        76.6   Extension of relief 940
77   TRANSACTIONS OUTSIDE A GROUP
        77.1   Transactions with non-group persons..................942
78   GROUPS AND DEVELOPMENT LAND
        78.1   Broad Outline — pre-24th April 1992...................944
        78.2   Disposal of Development Land 944
        78.3   Position — on or after 24 th April 1992 945
79   GROUP ROLL OVER RELIEF
        79.1   Broad Outline - Group roll-over 946
80   APPLICATION OF GROUP RELIEF TO TRADING STOCK
        80.1   Acquisition as Trading Stock 949
        80.2   Meaning of trading stock.....................................950
        80.3   Trading stock : Optional treatment 951
        80.4   Disposal of Trading Stock...................................955
81   COMPANY LEAVING GROUP—GENERAL RULE
        81.1   Company leaving group - outline 956
        81.2   Company leaving group - main rule.....................956
        81.3   Company leaving group - exceptions to main rule
               959
        81.4   Burman v Hedges & Butler (UK case) - pre FA 99
               963
        81.5   Roll-over relief : Co. leaving group. 966
        81.6   Assets Derived from Other Assets 966
        81.7   Company going non-resident 966
        81.8   Pre-disposal dividends 966
82   COMPANY LEAVING GROUP in course of MERGER
        82.1   Outline : leaving group in merger.........................967
        82.2   Merger 967
        82.3   Conditions..967
        82.4   Non-Resident Companies....................................967

CHAPTER 11   DOUBLE TAXATION RELIEF

83   DTR - BROAD OUTLINE OF RELIEF
        83.1   Outline - DTR 969
        83.2   TCA97 s826972
        83.3   Schedule 24 972
        83.3.1 Manner of granting Credit 972

	83.3.2	Requirement as to residence	973
	83.3.3	Limit on credit to be allowed	973
	83.3.4	Calculation of Irish Tax where credit is allowed for foreign tax	973
	83.3.5	Claim for credit relief	973
	83.3.6	Net basis of calculation	973
	83.3.7	Credit under mergers directive	973
	83.3.8	Unilateral Tax Credit	975
84	IRELAND / UK TAX TREATY		
	84.1	Broad Outline	976
	84.2	Terminology	976
	84.2.1	'Resident Of'	976
	84.2.2	Enterprise of a Contracting State	978
	84.2.3	Permanent Establishment	978
	84.3	Scheme of Relief — General	979
	84.4	Assets Generally	979
	84.5	Ships and Aircraft	980
	84.6	Shares	980
	84.7	Property of Permanent Establishment	981
	84.8	Immovable Property	982
	84.9	Credit Relief	983
85	OTHER TAX TREATIES		
	85.1	Ireland/Australia	984
	85.2	Ireland/Austria	984
	85.3	Ireland/Czech Republic	985
	85.4	Ireland/Denmark	985
	85.5	Ireland/Estonia	987
	85.6	Ireland/Finland	988
	85.7	Ireland/Hungary	989
	85.8	Ireland/Israel	989
	85.9	Ireland/Italy	990
	85.10	Ireland/Korea	990
	85.11	Ireland/Latvia	991
	85.12	Ireland/Lithuania	9921
	85.13	Ireland/Malaysia	992
	85.14	Ireland/Mexico	993
	85.15	Ireland/New Zealand	993
	85.16	Ireland/Poland	994
	85.17	Ireland/Portugal	995
	85.18	Ireland/Russia	995
	85.19	Ireland/Slovakia	996
	85.20	Ireland/South Africa	997
	85.21	Ireland/Spain	997
	85.22	Ireland/Sweden	998

85.23   Ireland/Switzerland 999
85.24   Ireland/USA 999
85..25   Ireland D. T. R. Agreements - list 1001

CHAPTER 12   ADMINISTRATION

86   CARE & MANAGEMENT OF CGT
      86.1   Responsibility for administration of CGT 1003
87   RETURNS, INFORMATION AND PAYMENT
      87.1   Application of Income Tax Provisions 1004
      87.2   Obligation to Make A Return 1005
      87.3   Time Limit for Submission of Return 1005
      87.4   Fraudulent or Negligent Return 1006
      87.5   Surcharge for Late Return 1006
      87.6   Returns of a partnership 10078
      87.7   Reorganisations etc 1007
      87.8   Penalties 1007
      87.9   Returns by Issuing Houses, Stockbrokers, etc....1008
      87.10   Returns by Auctioneers, etc 1008
      87.11   Returns by Nominee Shareholders 1008
      87.12   Returns by Party to a Settlement 1009
      87.13   Returns Relating to Non-Resident Companies &
                Trusts 1009
88   PRELIMINARY TAX
      88.1   Payments on account of CGT...............................1010
      88.2   Due date for payment of tax................................1011
89   INTEREST ON OVERDUE TAX
      89.1   General 1014
      89.2   Penalty Interest...1014
90   ASSESSMENT OF CGT
      90.1   Assessments...1015
      90.2   Other Special Assessment Rules..........................1017
      90.3   Statement of Affairs..1017
91   COLLECTION OF TAX FROM OTHERS
      91.1   Broad overview 1018
      91.2.1   Collection of Tax from beneficiary of trust 1018
      91.2.2   Collection of Tax from Former Trustees..............1020
      91.3   Gifts-recovery of tax from donee.........................1020
      91.4   Recovery of Tax from Shareholders.....................1020
      91.4.1   Broad Outline 1020
      91.4.2   Circumstances of Charge on Shareholders 1021
      91.4.3   Limit on Amount Recoverable.............................1021
      91.5   Recovery of Tax from Group Members...............1022

	91.5.1	Broad Outline	1022
	91.5.2	Time Limit	1023
	91.5.3	Recovery from Others	1023
	91.5.4	Company ceasing to be resident	1023
	91.6	Reconstructions	1023
	91.6.1	Agents, etc. of non-resident	1023
	91.7	Liquidators	1023
92	APPEALS		
	92.1	Appeal - Time Limit	1023
	92.2	Appeals – Manner of Making	1025
	92.3	Application of Income Tax Provisions	1026
	92.4	Regulations Relating to Appeals	1027
93	MARRIED PERSONS		
	93.1	Income Tax rules applied	1028
94	WITHHOLDING TAX		
	94.1	General Rules : withholding tax	1028
	94.2	Assets subject to withholding tax	1030
	94.3	Disposal of asset in parts	1032
	94.4	Capital Sum derived from asset	1032
	94.5	Rate of Withholding Tax	1034
	94.6	Amount on which withholding Tax is chargeable	1034
	94.6.1	Broad Outline	1034
	94.6.2	VAT on sale proceeds	1034
	94.7	Notional sale proceeds	1035
	94.8	Non-money Consideration	1035
	94.8.1	Broad Outline	1035
	94.8.2	Return of information	1036
	94.8.3	Payment of withholding tax	1036
	94.9	Exemption from withholding tax	1037
	94.10	Returns and Assessment	1040
	94.11	Adjustment of Liability	1040
	94.12	Irish Agent of non-resident	1040
95	LIABILITY OF TRUSTEES, ETC.		
	95.1	Trustees of settlement	1041
96	VALUATION OF ASSETS : POWER TO INSPECT		
	96.1	Power to inspect assets	1041
97	PAYMENT OF CAPITAL GAINS TAX		
	98.1	Broad Outline - payment of CGT	1041
	98.2	Unremittable Gains	1041
	98.3	Payment by Installments	1043
	98.4	Preferential Payment	1043
	98.5	Liquidators and Mortgagors, etc.	1043
	98.6	Credit against CAT	1043

98.7   Repayments of CGT 1045

CHAPTER 13   RESIDENCE AND DOMICILE

98   BROAD OUTLINE
        99.1   Broad Outline 1047
99   RESIDENT INDIVIDUAL (POST F. A.1994)
        99.1   Residence - broad Outline 1047
        99.2   Residence - statutory rules 1048
100   ORDINARILY RESIDENT (POST FINANCE ACT 1994)
        100.1   Ordinary Residence - statutory rules...................1048
101   RESIDENT — COMPANY
        101.1   Broad Outline - Company residence....................1049
        101.2   Central Management and control.........................1049
        101.3   Irish registered company 1050
102   RESIDENT : INDIVIDUAL (PRE F. A. 1994)
        102.1   Broad Outline - Old Residence rules....................1051
        102.2   Tests - pre 6 April 1994..1052
        102.3   Physical Presence in Ireland (not habitual and no
                  place of abode)..1054
        102.4   Maintenance of a Place of Abode (in Ireland
                  Available for Use) 1055
        102.5   Habitual Visits to Ireland (for Substantial Periods)
                 1055
        102.6   Coming for Permanent Residence........................1056
        102.7   Irish resident - leaving 1056
103   ORDINARILY RESIDENT (PRE F. A. 1994)
        103   Ordinary residence 1056
104   DOMICILE
        104.1   Broad Outline 1057
        104.2   Domicile of Origin 1057
        104.3   Domicile of Choice...1058
        104.4   Domicile of Dependence.......................................1058
        104.5   Claims procedures regarding domicile 1059

TABLE OF CASES ....

TABLE OF STATUTES ....

INDEX

1   INTRODUCTION

1.1   Legislation

On 28 February 1974, the then Minister for Finance, Mr. Richie Ryan laid a **white paper on capital taxes** before both houses of the Oireachtas. The white paper outlined the Coalition Government's proposals for a comprehensive system of capital taxation, including **capital gains tax (CGT), wealth tax and capital acquisitions tax.** All of these taxes were brought into effect within the following three years, although on a subsequent change of Government, wealth tax was abolished with effect from 5 April 1978.

The proposals on CAPITAL GAINS TAX, outlined in the white paper (with some amendments) were introduced into the legislation in the **CAPITAL GAINS TAX ACT 1975** (the "1975 Act"). The 1975 Act brought all legal entities, including both individuals and companies within the scope of the charge to CGT.

The **CORPORATION TAX ACT 1976** (CTA 1976) introduced major changes in the way in which companies were charged to tax, and made specific provision for the charging of companies capital gains. Prior to the CTA 1976 companies paid income tax and corporation profits tax on their income, and CGT on their gains. The CTA 1976 changed all that and introduced a single tax on company profits, which included both the company's income and chargeable gains. The corresponding adjustment was made to the CGT legislation to exclude gains chargeable to corporation tax (CT) from the scope of the charge to CGT. For corporation tax purposes (in broad terms) income was measured under the separate income tax rules, and gains were measured under the separate CGT rules. The resulting income and gains were charged to CT as the company's profit for the relevant accounting period.

Other reliefs (group relief, etc.) were introduced in the CTA 1976 which applied solely to companies. Adjustments were also introduced to deal with the arithmetic problems caused by the difference between the CT rate of tax (50% in 1976) and the 26% CGT rate of tax which applied in 1976.

The Finance Act 1982 excluded company gains on development land from the charge to CT, and such gains reverted once again to being solely within the scope of the charge to CGT.

The 1975 Act taxed capital gains arising on disposals of assets on or after 6 April 1974. Part of the gain on a disposal might have accrued in a period prior to 6 April 1974, and special rules were included in an attempt to eliminate that part of the gain.

Subject to the special rules for eliminating the pre 6 April 1974 part of the gain, the "taxable" gain was normally calculated by deducting the cost of the asset from the sale proceeds. No distinction was made between short term speculative gains, and gains on assets held for a long period of time. In addition, no recognition was given to the fact that the greatest part of most gains was attributable to inflation, rather than to any increase in the value of the asset in real terms.

Proposals to deal with the inflation and long term ownership issues were tabled by (the late) Mr. George Colley (in his capacity as opposition spokesman on Finance) as amendments to the Capital Gains Tax Bill 1975 during the Committee stage of its passage through the Dail. The proposed amendments were, however defeated by the Government of the time. In 1978 in his capacity as Minister for Finance (following a change of Government) he introduced new provisions to deal with these important issues. Provisions to deal with these issues were enacted in the Capital Gains Tax (Amendment) Act 1978.

The **CAPITAL GAINS TAX (AMENDMENT) ACT 1978** (the "1978 Act") recognised the inflation problem and provided in effect, that only a "real" gain (as distinct from a mere increase in value caused by inflation) would be taxed. Broadly speaking, it allows the taxpayer to increase his deductible expenditure in line with the increase in the CONSUMER PRICE INDEX since the expenditure was incurred. The indexed expenditure is deducted from the sale price to give the gain chargeable to CGT. This adjustment eliminating the part of the gain attributable to inflation ("INDEXATION") applies to all taxpayers (both corporate and individual) and to all assets, although its application to development land was restricted by the Finance Act 1982.

Over the years various attempts were made to recognise the distinction between long term gains, and short term 'speculative' gains - depending on the political party in power at the time, and the overall political climate.

Many different variations of a sliding scale of tax rates were used to recognise the distinction between a gain arising out of long term ownership of an asset, and a short term speculative gain. From 6th April 1978 a standard rate of 30% applied with a scale of rates tapering down to 'nil' in the case of assets owned for more than 21 years. In later years the standard rate of CGT varied from year to year (from 30% to 40%) with rates increasing for ownership of less than 6 years.

Later Finance Acts have continued the ongoing process of change in the CGT legislation, particularly in the area of anti-avoidance legislation, and legislation dealing with the attempts of the European Union, through its directives, to harmonise tax legislation throughout Europe.

Prior to 1997 the legislation relating to Income Tax, Capital Gains Tax and Corporation Tax was contained in different Acts:

- the Income Tax Act, 1967 (itself a consolidation of earlier legislation),

- the Capital Gains Tax Acts of 1975 and 1978,

- the Corporation Tax Act 1976

and each of those Acts was itself amended by the annual Finance Act since the main legislation was enacted.

All the legislation has now been consolidated into a single Act - the Taxes Consolidation Act, 1997, and all references to legislation in this book are to that Act (unless otherwise indicated).

The FA98 reduced the standard rate of CGT to 20%. It retained a 40% rate in respect of disposals of

- development land;

- overseas life assurance policies; and

- material interests in distributing offshore funds.

The F(No2) A98 extended the 20% rate of capital gains tax to disposals on or after 23 April 1998 and before 6 April 2002 of development land with planning permission (including outline permission) for residential development. The rate is to apply for a period of four years. It is proposed that a CGT rate of 60% should apply thereafter to certain development land disposed of for residential development. The FA 2000 extended the 20% rate to all development land disposals from 1 December 1999 to 1 April 2000.

The FA99 made major changes to the anti-avoidance legislation dealing with off-shore companies and trusts, and with trusts becoming non-resident. It also brought the definition of a "group" into line with that applying for corporation tax losses purposes.

s1(2)   Throughout the TCA97, the phrase *"the Capital Gains Tax Acts"* is used to mean all the legislation relating to CGT in the TCA97 itself, and in any other enactment.

1.2   Case Law

The Irish 1975 Act is taken almost word for word (in all but a few areas) from the UK legislation which existed at that time, apart from the obvious changes - i.e. instead of referring to the "United Kingdom" the Irish version refers to "the State", etc. In the UK, the tax (CGT) was first introduced in the FA.65. The Irish 1975 Act which followed 10 years later consisted in the main of a consolidation of the CGT sections of the UK FA 65, and the later UK amendments to that legislation. Many of the concepts introduced were new to Irish law and there were no Irish court decisions readily available to help in the interpretation of that new law.

As the UK had a 10 year start on Ireland with this tax, a considerable number of UK cases were available to help in the interpretation of the new Irish legislation, together with a substantial body of practice which had grown up there over the period. For this reason, the greater number of the judicial decisions referred to in this text are decisions of the UK courts, as in most instances, where the point had already been the subject of judicial consideration in the UK, it was not challenged again in the Irish courts. There are, of course, exceptions to this general rule, most notably in the area of tax avoidance.

Although UK decisions are influential in Irish courts, they are not binding precedents which the Irish courts must follow, and indeed in some instances the Irish courts cannot follow them. This distinction between the status of a judgement of an Irish court and that of a UK court must be very clearly understood in considering any UK cases. Any conclusions arrived at or any quotes from decisions of the UK courts must be viewed with a certain degree of caution.

In recent years, and particularly since the early 1980's many decisions of the UK courts have encroached into an area which could be more properly termed "law making" rather than the interpretation of law. This is particularly noticeable in the cases dealing with anti-avoidance schemes (see Chapter 9). The case law involving such schemes served to highlight the fundamental difference between Irish and UK judicial authority and practice.

This type of "law by the Judiciary" is a familiar feature of UK law. It has been applied in many areas, and is not confined to tax law.

For many years the principles to be applied in interpreting fiscal statutes as set out in Duke of Westminister v CIR were followed closely by the Courts in both Ireland and the UK. The principles set out in that case have been summarised by many judges - the following summary is taken from Lord Cairns (in Partington v Attorney General):

"As I understand the principle of all fiscal legislation, it is this; if the person sought to be taxed comes within the letter of the law he must be taxed however great the hardship may appear to the judicial mind to be. On the other hand, if the Crown, seeking to recover the tax, cannot bring the subject within the letter of the law, the subject is free, however apparently within the spirit of the law the case might otherwise appear to be"

The principles established in the Westminister case have been approved on many occasions in the Irish courts. This area is dealt with in more detail in paragraph 69.

There has never been any restriction on the ability of the UK Judiciary to make new law, other than the acceptability of such new law to Parliament. If Parliament did not like it, it could, and did in many instances (in effect) repeal it by subsequent legislation. There is no constitutional principle in England other than the paramouncy of Parliament. That paramouncy is absolute. However, subject to the right of Parliament to subsequently reject such law, there is no fetter on the right of the English judiciary to make new law on any matter before them, and this is frequently done where they see a remedy for an abuse or an injustice. For example, this principle was most notably followed by Lord Denning, beginning with his decision in the High Trees House case in 1947, and the National Provincial Bank case (neither of which had any direct bearing on tax matters) which ultimately led to the enactment of the UK Family Home Protection Act of 1986.

For many years it was obvious that a substantial industry was growing in the UK in the area of tax avoidance schemes, which were based mainly on the principles laid down in the Westminister case. The UK did not have any general anti avoidance legislation against the tax avoidance resulting from such schemes, and the UK Revenue were having a very difficult time in the courts. From the early 1980's the UK courts started to change their mind gradually about the application of the Westminister principles, and in effect, did a U-turn. By the end of the 1980's the UK courts had made a substantial body of "new law" to be applied in certain tax avoidance areas, by giving preference to the economic substance of what actually happened over the legal format of the transactions.

The Irish Revenue invited the Irish courts to take a similar view (P.W. McGrath v J.E.McDermott - Supreme Court, July 1988) but the Irish courts declined, and the Westminister principle remains the yardstick by which such matters are dealt with in Ireland. Following the decision in the McGrath case, general antiavoidance legislation dealing with tax avoidance schemes was introduced in the Finance Act 1989 (see paragraph 69).

The principles governing the separation of powers between the Judiciary and the Oireachtas in Ireland are totally different to those applying in the UK. The Irish position on this matter is set out in the 1937 Constitution. The Oireachtas is not paramount, it is the people of Ireland who are paramount and in whom the ultimate power resides. This power has been exercised, in that under the 1937 Constitution, the people have delegated the sole and exclusive power of making laws for the State to the Oireachtas.

Article 15.2.1 of the 1937 Constitution sets out in clear unambiguous terms :

"the sole and exclusive power of making laws for the State is hereby vested in the Oireachtas: no other legislative authority has power to make laws for the State".

This is one area of major difference between the Irish and UK courts.

In addition to other differences, UK courts have in some instances been known to refer to the Hansard record of the debates in Parliament as an aid to the construction of the legislation. Comments made in the UK Parliament on the intended meaning of UK legislation, even where it is identical to the Irish legislation, can be of little relevance to its interpretation by an Irish court.

The Irish courts have shown a willingness on many occasions to consider the interpretation of matters afresh, and arrive at a different conclusion from the UK courts on similar legislation. This is particularly so where they feel that the UK decision is not well founded in the context of Irish law. This differing approach has lead to a position where the UK court decisions can be totally at variance with those of the Irish courts. This variance is very noticeable in the area of *"form v substance"* which is dealt with in detail in paragraph 69.

It must also be borne in mind that although the Irish and UK legislation were practically identical in most areas in 1975, later Finance Acts have brought many changes both in Ireland and in the UK (and not necessarily the same changes in both countries) which have resulted in the Irish CGT law growing further apart from the UK law as the years passed.

Today there are many areas where the current Irish CGT law is totally different from that applying in the UK.

In the many "quotes" from UK decided cases referred to throughout the book, the references to UK Law have been replaced insofar as possible and meaningful with the equivalent Irish legislative references (where the wording of the Irish law is the same).

2   CHARGE TO TAX

2.1   Broad Outline

The basic charge to CGT is expressed in what appears on the surface to be very simple terms - in TCA97 s28:

s28   *"Tax shall be charged in accordance with this Act in respect of capital gains, that is,*

- *in respect of **chargeable gains** computed in accordance with this Act and*

- *accruing to a **person***

- *on the **disposal***

- *of **assets**."*

With the exception of some rare instances , a charge to CGT can arise only in respect of a transaction which meets ***all*** of the requirements stated above even where in fact they do not do so.

In addition, the CGT legislation in certain circumstances deems a transaction or a person to meet one or more of these requirements even where they do not do so in fact.

The ***persons*** and the ***assets*** which are within the charge to CGT are described in paragraph 3. This is generally known as the "territorial scope" of the tax.

Paragraph 4 deals with the ***disposal*** of ***assets***.

The general basic rules for the computation of a ***chargeable gain*** are set out in paragraphs 7, 8 and 9.

The CGT legislation does not state anywhere that a gain is to be computed by taking the sale proceeds and reducing it by the relevant costs.

Equally the Income Tax legislation charges income tax on the "full amount of the profits or gains" of a trade or profession, but nowhere in the Income Tax legislation is the term "profits or gains" defined. The TCA97 does not specify that receipts are to be reduced by the relevant costs to arrive at the "profits or gains" to be charged to tax.

The equivalent income tax issue was dealt with in a common sense manner by Lord President Clyde in Whimster & Co v IRC in the following words:

"The profits of any particular year or accounting period must be taken to consist of the difference between the receipts from the trade during the period and the expenditure laid out to earn those receipts"

Although it is not stated anywhere in the legislation, it is assumed that a **"gain" or "loss"** for CGT purposes must consist of the difference between

— the consideration for the disposal, and

— the deductible costs

of the relevant asset, subject to the specific rules set out in the legislation governing the amount of the consideration for the disposal to be taken into account, and what costs are deductible in the computation of any resulting gain or loss.

The legislation appears to proceed on that assumption.

Example 1

Joe Brown sold 1,000 shares in CRH PLC in February 2000, for a total consideration of £6,250. Joe is an Irish resident and domiciled individual. The indexed base cost of the shares (see paragraphs 9 and 14) was £1,000.

The transaction described above, the sale of shares by Joe, is a transaction which is within the charge to capital gains tax. That is because:

- *a chargeable **gain** has arisen on it i.e. the consideration (£6,250) exceeds the indexed base cost (£1,000) and therefore a gain, computed in accordance with the Act arises.*

- *The gain has accrued to a **person** i.e. Joe Brown, an individual.*

- *A transaction on which the gain arose to Joe was a **disposal**. Joe's sale of the shares is a disposal by him of those shares in the ordinary sense of "disposal".*

- *The gain arose to Joe on the disposal of something which constituted an **asset** in the ordinary meaning of that word i.e. shares in CRH PLC.*

- *The transaction is within the **territorial scope** (see paragraph 3.1) of the tax since Joe is Irish resident and domiciled.*

All of the requirements for a charge to tax existed.

Example 2

The facts are as in example 1 except that the base cost in the shares was £7,000.

*Although there has been a **disposal** of an **asset** by a **person**, the transaction did not give rise to a chargeable gain and accordingly a charge to capital gains tax cannot arise. The transaction is nonetheless within the ambit of the tax and the loss which has arisen may be taken into account in the computation of Joe's gains for the year of assessment, or later years.*

Example 3

Joe (the same individual as in example 1) financed his purchase of CRH PLC shares by borrowing $1,500 from his uncle in America. At the date he borrowed the dollars, he was able to convert them into IR£1,000. Having sold the CRH PLC shares for IR£1,000, Joe purchases $1,500 and repays the loan from his uncle. The purchase of the $1,500 on this occasion cost Joe IR£700.

A charge to capital gains tax does not arise on the transaction relating to the dollars because although:

- *a gain has arisen as computed in accordance with the Act and*

- *it has accrued to a person i.e. Joe,*

*it has not accrued on the **disposal** of an **asset** but rather on the discharge of a **liability**. The repayment of the debt did involve a disposal of an asset i.e. the dollars which Joe had purchased for the purpose, but the chargeable gain did not arise on the disposal of the dollars, since the value received by Joe for their disposal was identical to the cost of acquiring them on the same day. Instead the gain arose on repaying the loan.*

The basic concepts illustrated in the examples above are discussed in greater detail in the remainder of the book.

3   TERRITORIAL SCOPE OF THE CHARGE TO CGT

3.1   Broad Outline - scope of the charge

CGT is charged for a year of assessment which is the year ending on 5 April in each year.

A charge to tax cannot arise unless there is an actual or statutarily deemed disposal of an asset. The words *'disposal'* and *'asset'* are dealt with in paragraph 4.

s28(1)   The charge to CGT is made in respect of gains which *accrue* to a person on the disposal of assets.

The legislation does not define the term *accrue* nor does it provide general rules for determining the time when a gain *accrues* on the disposal of an asset. It does, however, set out rules for determining the *"time of disposal"* of an asset (see paragraph 15), but does not explicitly state that the gain *accrues* at the time of disposal of the asset. However, the legislation appears to proceed on the basis of that assumption.

A specific rule is given for determining the time when a gain accrues in the case of assets chargeable on a remittance basis (see paragraph 3.3).

A charge to CGT can arise in three different circumstances set out in the following three sub-paragraphs.

3.1.1   Irish resident and domiciled person

s29(2)   If the person making the disposal is

• either resident **or** ordinarily resident

• **and** domiciled

in Ireland for the year of assessment in which the gain accrues, he is within the charge to CGT on gains on the disposal of all chargeable assets.

The charge under this heading is not limited in any respect by the location of the asset, or the remittance of the proceeds of disposal. The charge applies on the full amount of the gain - irrespective of the location of the asset, or what happens to the proceeds.

The charge to CGT in the case of an Irish resident and domiciled individual is considered in detail in paragraph 3.2

3.1.2   **Irish resident & non Irish domiciled individual**

s29(2), (4)   If the person making the disposal is an individual, and is:

either resident **or** ordinarily resident

and NOT domiciled

in Ireland for the year of assessment in which the gain accrues, he is within the charge to CGT on :

gains arising on the disposal of Irish and UK assets (whether any part of the proceeds is remitted into Ireland or not),

and

amounts received in the State in respect of chargeable gains accruing on the disposal of assets located outside Ireland and outside the U.K.

A detailed consideration of the charge to CGT in the case of an individual who is resident or ordinarily resident in Ireland, but not domiciled in Ireland is set out in paragraph 3.3.

3.1.3   **Non resident person**

s29(3)   If the disposal is made by a person who is neither resident nor ordinarily resident in Ireland, no charge to tax can arise unless the asset is one of the *specified Irish assets* (see paragraph 3.4). Gains on the disposal of such assets are chargeable irrespective of the residence, ordinary residence or domicile of the person making the disposal.

A detailed consideration of the charge to CGT in the case of a person who is not resident or ordinarily resident in Ireland, is set out in paragraph 3.4.

Gains accruing to a non-resident company or non-resident trust may in certain circumstances be attributed to and taxed on Irish resident shareholders/beneficiaries.   Details are set out in paragraphs 67 (non-resident companies) and 68 (non-resident trusts).

The meaning of the terms 'resident','ordinarily resident' and 'domicile', is dealt with in Chapter 13.

The assessment period, and the charging rules vary slightly in the case of a company which is within the charge to corporation tax on capital gains. The relevant provisions are dealt with in Chapter 10.

s648   However, it is important to note that under s648 (s36 FA 1982), gains arising to companies on disposals of development land (after 27 January 1982) are chargeable to CGT and not corporation tax. The meaning of "Development Land" is set out in paragraph 6

3.2   **Irish resident & domiciled persons**

As a general rule, any person who is either resident or ordinarily resident (and domiciled) in Ireland in a year of assessment, is chargeable to CGT on all gains arising on assets disposed of by him during that year of assessment.

s29(2)   TCA97 s29(2) provides that:-

".......a person shall be chargeable to Capital Gains Tax in respect of chargeable gains accruing to him in a year of assessment for which he is resident or ordinarily resident in the State".

In the case of an Irish resident (or ordinarily resident) and domiciled person, it is immaterial whether the gain arises on an Irish or a foreign asset - he is chargeable to CGT on the full amount of all gains (as computed under the CGT Acts) whether all or any part of the proceeds are remitted into Ireland or not.

Example 4

Individual - Irish domiciled and Irish resident

> *Sean is domiciled in Ireland, and for 1999/00 he is also resident in Ireland. During 1999/00 gains accrue to him on the disposal of assets in Ireland, Germany and Canada.*

> *Sean is chargeable to CGT in Ireland for 1999/00 on all the above gains, whether they are remitted into Ireland or not, simply because he is Irish resident and domiciled.*

An exclusion from the charge to tax under this rule is provided in the case of a non-domiciled individual, but only for gains accruing on the disposal of assets located outside Ireland and outside the UK.

3.3   **Irish resident - non Irish domiciled individuals**

3.3.1   **Broad outline - Irish resident - non domiciled individual**

If an individual is resident (or ordinarily resident) but not domiciled in Ireland, the general charge to CGT which applies to a resident and domiciled person (as set out in paragraph 3.2) is modified by s29(4).

s29(4)   S29(4) states that the general charge to CGT based on residence or ordinary residence as set out in s29(2) .. *"shall not apply in respect of gains accruing from the disposal of assets situated outside the State and the United Kingdom.....to an individual..."*..who is not domiciled in Ireland.

Instead of the general charge to CGT under s29(2) on all worldwide assets, there is substituted by s29(4) a charge to CGT on non-domiciled individuals for Irish and UK situated assets, and also for certain foreign assets. The basis of charge in respect of those non-UK foreign assets is:

s29(4)

- *"on the amounts **received in the State in respect of** .. chargeable gains accruing from the disposal of assets situated outside the State and the United Kingdom .."*.

- it also deems such gains to accrue when the amounts are received in the State, and

- disallows relief for any losses accruing on the disposal of such assets - whether or not the proceeds of disposal are remitted into Ireland.

This basis of charge in respect of non-UK foreign assets is popularly known as "the *remittance basis*".

s29(2)

The general charge to tax under s29(2) remains in the case of gains accruing on the disposal of Irish and UK assets. The remittance basis only applies to gains arising on assets located outside Ireland, and outside the UK.

A "remittance basis" is also available in relation to income tax. The rules which identifies the persons entitled to the "remittance basis" for income tax purposes differ from the rules applying to identify the persons entitled to the remittance basis for capital gains tax purposes. A resident and domiciled Irish citizen who is not ordinarily resident in Ireland is entitled to the remittance basis for income tax. There is no provision extending the remittance basis for capital gains tax to such a person.

Example 5

Individual - Irish resident - domicile?

> Sean is resident in Ireland for 1999/00. In that year he sold assets located in Ireland, in the UK, and in Israel. Gains were computed in all cases under the CGT computation rules.
>
> **Domiciled :** If he is also domiciled in Ireland, he is chargeable on all gains on his world-wide disposals of assets (including all three above mentioned assets). The question of whether all or any part of the sale proceeds is remitted is not relevant in computing to his CGT liability.
>
> **Non Domiciled :** If he is not domiciled in Ireland, he is chargeable on:
>
> - gains accruing on the disposal of all assets located in Ireland and
> - gains accruing on the disposal of all assets located in the UK (whether remitted into Ireland or not) and
> - all other foreign gains (i.e. in this example - gains arising on the disposal of assets located in Israel) but only to the extent of amounts received in Ireland in respect of those gains.

Example 6

Individual - Irish resident/ordinarily resident with foreign domicile:

Alain is domiciled in France and is resident and ordinarily resident in Ireland. In 1999/00 he had gains arising on the disposal of Irish land and buildings, UK shares, and on farmland in Latvia. He also disposed of land in Romania, but incurred a CGT loss on the disposal of that land.

Irish Assets and UK Assets:
As Alain is resident in Ireland he is chargeable to Irish CGT for 1999/00 on the gains accruing on the sale of the Irish and UK assets, computed under the normal CGT rules.

Foreign Farms:
Alain is chargeable on the gain arising on the disposal of the farm in Latvia to the extent that amounts representing the gain are received in Ireland.

No relief is available for the loss on Romanian property.

s29(7)   **A gain which is taxed on the remittance basis is deemed to be a gain accruing when it is received in the State.**

This may not be in the same year of assessment as that in which the disposal was made.

The amount of the gain accruing on disposal of the asset is computed by reference to the actual date of disposal. This gain is not in itself chargeable. What is chargeable, is the amount received in the State in respect of that gain, and that amount is deemed to be a gain accruing in the year of assessment in which it is actually received in Ireland. The actual computed gain may in fact fall into charge in parts over a number of years, with the amount remitted in each year treated as accruing in that year.

Example 7

Individual - Irish resident - foreign domicile:

Jean Mark is domiciled in France, but is resident in Ireland for 1998/99 During the year 1998/99 gains arose on the disposal by him of some of his French assets. The proceeds of disposal amounted to (the Irish currency equivalent of) IR£10,000, and the full gain measured under Irish CGT rules amounted to IR£2,000.

During 1998/99 he remitted the full IR£10,000 sale proceeds to his bank account in Dublin.

The question of foreign tax, and relief in Ireland for it has been ignored, to simplify the illustration of the basic principles involved.

As he is resident in Ireland for 1998/99, the gain may be chargeable to CGT. The full gain (i.e. IR£2,000) is measured under Irish CGT rules by reference to the actual date of disposal of the asset.

Whether he is chargeable to CGT in respect of the gain will normally depend on whether he is resident (or ordinarily resident) in Ireland when the gain is remitted. In this case as the full gain has been remitted into Ireland in a year in

13

which he is resident, the full gain is chargeable as a gain of 1998/99. There are other circumstances which may affect the matter, and these are discussed following **example 8** *below.*

If part of the gain was remitted in 1998/99 and the balance in 1999/00, the gain would be charged to CGT partly in 1998/99 and partly in 1999/00 **to the extent the gain was remitted in each of those years,** *assuming he is resident in both years.*

If part of the gain was remitted into Ireland in a year when he was not resident or ordinarily resident in Ireland, no charge to CGT could arise in respect of that part of the gain.

The question of the *"extent to which a gain is remitted"* into Ireland in each of the years mentioned above is not just a simple arithmetic proportion of the gain, but can be difficult to measure. What is remitted after a disposal is (all or part of) the ***sale proceeds,*** and not the ***gain*** as measured under the CGT rules. This issue is discussed in more detail later in paragraph 3.3.2.

Example 8

Individual - Irish resident with foreign domicile when disposal occurred - change of domicile - part of gain remitted to Ireland when the individual is Irish resident and Irish domiciled.

Assume the facts are the same as in Example 7 above but that in the year 1999/00 Jean Mark became domiciled in Ireland, and was resident there that year.

In 1998/99, when he was French domiciled but Irish resident, Jean Mark remitted £1,000 of the proceeds to Dublin. On the assumption that the Revenue would treat the entire of that £1,000 as representing part of the gain, Jean Mark would be liable to tax in 1998/99 on that part of the gain ie £1,000.

In 1999/00 Jean Mark remitted to Ireland the balance of the proceeds of sale (£9,000). Jean Mark is not liable to capital gains tax in 1999/00 in respect of any part of the sum remitted in that year. This is because the basis of liability to capital gains tax in 1999/00 is that applicable to a domiciled and resident person (all gains accruing world-wide in that year) and not that applicable to a non domiciled but resident person (ie remittance basis for non UK foreign assets). Since the remittance basis rules have no application to him in 1999/00 the fact that he has remitted part of the gain to Ireland in that year is not relevant. The gain accrued to Jean Mark in 1998/99 and accordingly cannot give rise to a liability in the year 1999/00 when the rules applicable will attach a liability to Jean Mark only in respect of gains arising in that year.

The remittance from the proceeds of disposal of a non UK foreign asset can not give rise to a liability to capital gains tax when it is made in a year in which the taxpayer is either:

• not resident nor ordinarily resident in Ireland or

• domiciled in Ireland

In summary, the CGT Acts provide three separate bases for liability to CGT and in the opinion of the authors those three are mutually exclusive. One only of those bases can apply to any taxpayer for any given tax year. A taxpayer may be liable to a different basis in each successive tax year depending on his circumstances. The three bases are:

- *domiciled and resident/ordinarily resident* - Gains on disposals in the year world-wide.

- *not domiciled but resident/ordinarily resident* - Gains on disposals on Irish and UK assets in the year, and remittances in the year from disposals of other foreign assets made in years in which the taxpayer was similarly not domiciled but resident/ordinarily resident.

- *non resident/nor ordinarily resident* - Gains arising in the year on Irish specified assets only.

To round off the discussion of the treatment of non-donmiciled individuals, it is necessary to consider the position of an individual who reasised a gain on the disposal of a foreign (non-UK) asset at a time when he was neither resident, ordinarily resident nor domiciled in Ireland.

Example 9

Individual - not Irish resident/ordinarily resident and not domiciled in Ireland when disposal occurred - gain remitted to Ireland in later year when individual becomes Irish resident but still not Irish domiciled:

> *Alain is domiciled in France. He is not Irish resident (nor ordinarily resident) in the tax year 1998/99. He sold French assets in that year, realising a gain (measured under the Irish CGT rules). He becomes resident in Ireland for 1999/00, and remits the proceeds of those disposals into Ireland in 1999/00.*

> *Are the gains chargeable to CGT in Ireland in 1999/00, being gains remitted into Ireland in a year in which he is resident here ?*

s29(2)

> *S29(2), which is the basic charging section, does not charge the 1998/99 gains to CGT, as Jean Mark is neither resident nor ordinarily resident in Ireland for 1998/99, and the assets concerned are located abroad. Where Jean Mark "satisfies the Revenue Commissioners that he is not domiciled in the State" s29(2) does not apply for the period for which he is non-domiciled. Instead, s29(4) deems the gain to accrue when the amounts in respect of the gain are remitted into Ireland. If s29(4) is read in isolation, it may appear to impose a charge to CGT on Jean Mark in respect of the remittance of the 1998/99 gains, as it deems the gains to accrue when they are remitted - i.e. in 1999/00 and he is Irish resident in that year.*

s29(4)

The position is not entirely clear, but for the following reasons, the authors are of the opinion that such gains are not chargeable:

- s29(4) is a *relieving section*. It would be paradoxical if it had the affect of making a non-domiciled individual chargeable to CGT in Ireland on gains which were not chargeable under the normal charging rules if he were in Ireland in the year of disposal (when he was actually non-resident).

- s29(4) applies where the taxpayer *satisfies the Revenue Commissioners* that he is non-domiciled. The wording suggests that it is a relief to be claimed by the taxpayer, and not a charging provision to be imposed on him against his will. The initiative seems to lie with the taxpayer to assert his non-domicile.

- It may be beyond the Constitutional limits of the taxing powers of the State to tax a transaction entered into abroad, concerning foreign assets disposed of by an individual who at the time of the transaction was neither resident nor domiciled in Ireland.

- the wording of s29(4) *suggests* it applies only where s29(2) would otherwise have applied. It firstly states that s29(2) *shall not have application,* "but" a charge on the remittance basis shall apply instead. In Jean Mark's case, s29(2) had no application to the 1998/99 disposal, so s29(4) is not necessary to "un-apply" s29(2), nor indeed is it capable of un-applying it to a situation to which it never applied in the first instance.

In certain circumstances (e.g. where losses arising on foreign assets exceed gains on foreign assets) the normal charge under s29(2) may give a more favourable result to a non-domiciled individual than the remittance basis, since the latter denies any relief for foreign losses. In such a case it may be worth considering the position where the individual chooses not to assert his foreign domicile at that time (although in fact he was actually domiciled abroad). The position is not clear.

Normally, as part of the ordinary self-assessment Form 11 (Return of Income and Gains) an individual is asked to "tick" the box in which he claims to be non-domiciled. On the 1998/99 Form 11 it appears as question 52 on page 8. The remittance basis for a non-domiciled individual applies for the purposes of both income tax and CGT. Even if an individual wanted to try and avail of loss relief for foreign losses, any claim by him regarding his non-domicile position may not apply for just the particular year in which the claim is made, and the question of its affect on his income tax position also needs close attention.

Where only part of the sale proceeds is remitted into Ireland, there is always some difficulty in identifying whether or not the amount remitted contains any part of the gain. What is remitted into Ireland can only represent all or part of the actual *proceeds* of disposal. There is normally no specific remittance in respect of a gain as calculated under the CGT Acts. The legislation does not give any guidance as to how a remittance of part of the sale proceeds can be apportioned between the amount of any gain arising on the disposal, and the non-gain part of the proceeds. This matter is discussed further in paragraph 3.3.2.

The changes which have occurred in the rates of CGT have all taken effect by reference to the *time of disposal* of an asset. Because of the remittance basis rules, an individual can find himself in the position where, although the gain is deemed to accrue in the current year, the rate of tax which applies is that which refers to the actual time of disposal. The date on which the gain accrues is not necessarily the same as the time of disposal of the asset (see paragraph 15).

Example 10

> Helga, who is a long term resident of Ireland but domiciled in Germany, sold a valuable original painting by a well known German artist which she had kept in her holiday home in Germany. The gain on disposal measured under Irish CGT rules amounted to IR£ 10,000. The full proceeds were used by her as part of the purchase price of a new house in Ireland 6 years after the actual year of disposal of the painting.

> The gain is deemed to accrue when it is remitted into Ireland - ie. 6 years after the disposal, and is chargeable to CGT at the rate of tax applying 6 years previously.

In no circumstances does the 'remittance basis' apply to gains arising on the disposal of assets located in the UK. Gains arising on the disposal of U.K. assets are either

- **chargeable to Irish CGT on the full amount of the gain** (irrespective of whether the gain is remitted to Ireland or not) or

- *not chargeable at all*

    depending solely on the residence or ordinary residence of the individual making the disposal.

The remittance basis does not apply to:

- a company,

- trustees and other persons acting in a representative capacity.

The remittance basis applies ONLY to an individual.

s568(2)   Trustees and personal representatives of a deceased person (for the purposes of CGT) are deemed not to be individuals in their representative capacity.

There is an anomaly in the CGT Act's definition of the territorial scope of capital gains tax. It relates to unquoted shares deriving their value from land or mineral rights in the State. Such shares are specified assets. A person who is not resident or ordinarily resident is within the charge to Irish capital gains tax in respect of such shares, on the full gain arising. However if the shares in question are shares in a foreign incorporated company (so that they do not represent an asset located in Ireland, nor located in the UK - e.g. a Channel Island company, or a French company) a person who is resident in Ireland, but not domiciled here would be liable to capital gains tax on a disposal of such shares deriving their value from Irish land on a remittance basis. Paradoxically, a resident person has a more favourable treatment than a non-resident person. If the proceeds of disposal of the foreign shares (deriving value from Irish land) are not remitted into the State by the resident but non-domiciled person, they may entirely escape capital gains tax. But if the same person had been non-resident at the time of the disposal, they would be liable fully to capital gains tax. This normally does not arise in relation to shares which are Irish shares, or which are UK shares since the remittance basis does not apply to gains on the disposal of Irish or UK assets.

The location of an asset is central to the remittance basis. In order that the remittance basis should apply, the asset on which a gain arises must be located outside Ireland, and outside of the U.K. The rules in relation to the location of assets, for the purposes of capital gains tax, are explained in paragraph 3.7. For the most part these follow normal international rules (and common sense) but particular regard needs to be had to the special rule that applies regarding the location of a debt. The rule in that case is the opposite of the rule which applies in international law and has the effect of depriving an Irish resident of the remittance basis in relation to gains arising on movements on a foreign currency bank account held outside of Ireland.

3.3.2   What is a "remittance" ?

s29(4)(a)   The charge to CGT on remittance basis gains is made *on the amounts received in the State in respect of those chargeable gains.*

s29(5)   The only guidance in the legislation as to the amount to be treated as *received in the State in respect of those chargeable gains* is set out in s29(5), which states:

"....there shall be treated as received in the State in respect of any gain all amounts paid, used, or enjoyed in or in any manner or form transmitted or brought to the State...."

s72   S29(5) includes the income tax anti-avoidance provisions against what at the time was known as the "export overdraft" avoidance scheme, and variations on that theme. Those anti-avoidance provisions are to apply equally to CGT as they apply to income tax (see paragraph 3.3.5).

This sole CGT provision on remittances seems almost over-simplistic in its approach when compared to what appears to be a far more wide ranging income tax provisions.

The importance of the income tax wording is that it is generally accepted that the broad principles established in the many cases involving remittances from an income tax point of view, may also apply to CGT. However, in looking at this area it is vital to note the differences in wording between the Income Tax and CGT legislation on remittances, and also to note the wording on which the principles were established by the Courts in this area.

At least at first glance, the income tax wording appears to be far wider in scope than the equivalent CGT legislation. S71 provides that in the case of a non-domiciled person :

s71(3)   *"(Income) tax shall....be computed on the full amount of the actual sums received in the State from remittances payable in the State, or from property imported, or from money or value arising from property not imported, or from money or value so received on credit or on account in respect of such remittances, property, money or value brought into the State in the year of assessment without any deduction or abatement".*

FA65 Sch 2   The CGT wording is different from that used in the Irish Income Tax
Para 8 (UK)   Acts. It is clear that the relevant part of the (UK) FA.65 which first introduced CGT in the UK was taken from the UK legislation on remittances current in the UK at that time, contained in the (UK) FA65. The Irish CGT law in this area is mainly a copy of the equivalent UK CGT legislation. The overall result of this, is that Ireland ended up with remittance basis wording, which although different to the current Irish income tax wording, is the same as the UK wording for both income tax and CGT.

On closer study, it appears that the more modern CGT wording which treats an amount as being received if it is "paid, used or enjoyed ...or transmitted" could be regarded as being far more wide ranging than the older income tax wording.

In looking at the overall affect of the remittance basis on any taxpayer, it is vital to keep clearly in mind, that the only taxpayer concerned with a remittance basis is:

• an *individual,*

• who *is resident* or ordinarily resident in Ireland,

• who *is not domiciled* in Ireland.

• who has gains (or income) arising outside Ireland and outside the UK.

Such an individual will probably be equally concerned about having amounts treated as a remittance in respect of income as a remittance in respect of gains.

In terms of the overall principles established, the income tax cases can be catagorised into a number of broad areas as follows:

- *Receipts by the taxpayer can be traced to a foreign income source:*

In most circumstances, where foreign income arises to a person, it is reasonably clear whether it has been remitted into Ireland or not. However, difficult problems can arise where money representing the income has been invested in another asset, and it is the proceeds of sale of that other asset which is remitted into Ireland.

This point was dealt with in the UK case of Patuck v Lloyd. In that case, foreign income was invested abroad, and the sale proceeds of that investment were remitted. It was held to be a remittance of income. In the UK case of Harmel v Wright, a taxpayer invested foreign income in the share capital of a company. That company loaned the money to another company, which in turn loaned the money to the taxpayer. In the course of his judgement, Templeman J. said:

"...one does not need to strip aside the corporate veil if you find that emoluments, which mean money, come in at one end of a conduit pipe and pass through several traceable pipes until they come out at the other end to the taxpayer".

Harmel v Wright was decided under (U.K.) FA56 remittance legislation, and confirmed the concept established under previous legislation that if the receipt can be clearly traced to the foreign income, and is coupled with *"a corresponding diminution of the amount of the taxpayer's accrued income abroad"* then it will be treated as a remittance of the foreign income (per Lord Reid in Thomson v Moyse).

- *The receipt by the taxpayer must be from an income source:*

It is not sufficient that the taxpayer has income, and in addition, that money is remitted. The remittance must be traceable (however indirectly) to the foreign income. In Kneen v Martin, the taxpayer had both income and capital abroad in separate bank accounts. A remittance from the separate capital bank account was held **not** to be a remittance of income.

- *Receipts by the taxpayer from a mixed fund of income and capital:*

Serious problems can arise for a taxpayer if he keeps both income and capital in the same bank account and remits amounts into Ireland from that account. The UK court decisions in this area (to date) all relate to income tax, and the decisions were all given at a time when CGT did not exist in UK law.

Where funds are remitted from a foreign bank account containing both income and capital, it can be extremely difficult, if not impossible, to show whether any amount remitted to Ireland from that bank account has been made out of the income or out of the capital contained in that account.

It is normally presumed by the Revenue Authorities that remittances from a mixed bank account (of income and capital) are to be treated as first coming out of income, until the income content of the account is exhausted.

In the UK case of Scottish Provident Institution v Allan it was held that remittances to the UK (i.e. remittances not clearly made out of a specific income or capital source) must be presumed to consist of interest, not of capital, as long as the amount of capital transferred to Australia for investment still remained invested there.

In that case, the company had sent funds to Australia for investment there. In the UK Chancery Division, it was held that *"where a capitalist company.....has invested large sums for a period of 15 years in a colony, and has an agent employed not only to receive interest but also to receive the capital of the investment when paid up, and to reinvest it, even if unappropriated remittances are made to this country, I think everyone would agree that they must be dealt with according to the ordinary course of business and these remittances must be presumed to be paid in the first place out of interest insofar as they are income, and in the second place out of principal or capital. I think that the rule results from the fact that no prudent man of business would encroach upon his capital for investment when he has uninvested income lying at his disposal"*. The decision of the Chancery division was upheld in the House of Lords.

In the later UK case of Kneen v Martin, Slesser L.J. said *"the learned Attorney General argues that there is no such presumption. He points out that it is not a presumption merely of business practice, such as was mentioned in case to which I have referred (Scottish Provident Institution v Allan) but that it is a matter of presumption, as the language there used by the Commissioners, if there be any presumption at all it is in favour of the subject, and that the Crown have to prove that they are entitled to extract the tax. He goes on to argue that insofar as there is no presumption, unless the construction for which he contends is right, it would put an impossible obligation on the Crown and make a very complicated investigation before the Commissioners in any particular case to ascertain whether this could be capital or not. I am inclined to agree with him that there is no such presumption arising one way or the other, but I disagree entirely with the conclusion that, because there is no presumption - or at any rate no presumption that this is income - therefore it follows that his construction is the right one. It seems to me that this matter is just such a matter of fact as the Commissioners are eminently suited to enquire into.....I express no final opinion, but I will guard against it being thought that there is, as I see it, in their view such a presumption in favour of this being income rather than capital. The only ordinary obligation of the Crown is to show that the subject is liable to tax, for the moment I cannot see that any presumption of law arises one way or the other".*

It can be easily seen how such a rule could be applied for income tax purposes in the absence of CGT. Most informed individuals avoided this "mixed fund" problem in the past by keeping separate accounts for income and for capital. However, it is difficult to see the position as clearly today, with the added complication of CGT.

There is one point which is absolutely clear, and that is the remittance from a mixed fund account cannot in its entirety be both income and capital.

- *Compulsory Remittances:*

The question of a remittance made by a taxpayer because of the compulsory requirements of other laws was considered in the Irish case of J.M. O'Sullivan v Julia O'Connor (executrix of Evelyn O'Brien decd.).

Miss Evelyn O'Brien (decd.) was a US citizen, who retained her foreign domicile, but died resident in Ireland. The issue concerned balances held by her in US bank accounts. Under the Emergency Powers Finance No. 5 Order 1940, Miss O'Brien was required to offer the US dollar balances in those accounts (for sale) to the Irish Minister for Finance. The overall result of this, was that foreign income represented by the US dollar account balances was brought into Ireland.

It was held by Maguire J in the High Court (1947) having considered the decisions in many other relevant cases, that *"these cases appear to establish the proposition that the fact that there is compulsion does not alter the essential character of the transaction."*

- *Receipts by persons other than the taxpayer:*

In the UK case of Thompson v Moyse it was held that the use of foreign income to pay off debts within the UK due by the taxpayer fell to be treated as an income receipt by that taxpayer.

However, the issues arising out of funds being gifted to another person, and subsequently brought into the country by that other person, is a more difficult issue. This involves the alienation of income, and is dealt with separately in paragraph 3.3.4

The overall issue from the taxpayer's point of view, probably is whether there has been an amount paid, enjoyed or used in Ireland in respect of funds held abroad. It probably will be of lesser concern to him whether it is in respect of income or gains, as in most circumstances, both will be taxable - and the only difference will be the availability of personal allowances, and rates of tax applying to the separate taxes.

The "mixed fund" problem is a serious one for CGT. Apart from the situation of where money is remitted from a mixed fund of income and capital, there is a totally separate problem even where funds are remitted from an account containing only capital. That capital in itself, is a mixed fund for CGT purposes, as only part of it will represent the gain.

- In the case of income, what is remitted clearly must represent all or part of the income itself. This is clear from the decided cases on the subject. In the case of CGT all that can be remitted is the proceeds of sale. Where only part of the sale proceeds is remitted, how is the gain taxed? The gain is deemed to accrue to the individual to the extent of amounts received in Ireland representing the gain.

- Is the first part of the proceeds remitted the gain, or is the taxpayer to be treated as returning his original capital first, with the gain being the last to be remitted? Is the remittance to be apportioned to determine the amount of the gain included?

The legislation gives no indication or guidance as to how to deal with this problem. In practice, in dealing with CGT the Revenue maintain that the first amount received in Ireland is in respect of the gain. It appears at first glance that the reasoning set out by the judge in Scottish Provident Institution v Allen (mentioned earlier in this paragraph) could be thought to favour the Revenue Commissioners approach to the problems involved. It would be interesting to see if the approach of the Revenue would be the same if the amount was remitted out of a mixed fund containing both taxable income and capital gains.

Until the matter is clarified in the context of the current legislation by the Irish Courts a doubt must remain over the validity of such an arbitrary apportionment of sale proceeds. However, that still leaves the taxpayer in a difficult position. The onus is on him to make a self-assessment return, and severe interest and other penalties apply where the gain is not returned properly, or where payment of the tax is late.

3.3.3   Notional sale proceeds

A problem arises where the gain is measured by reference to notional proceeds (see paragraph 16). For CGT purposes there are two different matters to consider :

- the actual consideration for the disposal (if any), and

- the notional (deemed) consideration for the disposal.

As already mentioned, the identification of a part of the actual consideration remitted into Ireland as representing the gain is not entirely free of doubt.

The position is much more difficult where the gain is computed by reference to deemed notional consideration for the sale.

Only real consideration can actually be remitted. Notional consideration does not actually exist, and could not in any circumstances be remitted into Ireland. The legislation does not deem a notional remittance. What can be remitted to Ireland is all or part of any actual consideration held by the taxpayer. This can give rise to many difficulties.

A clear distinction must be made between the situations where the CGT rules

- deem a consideration where in fact there was no consideration at all, and

- deem a consideration which is different to the actual consideration.

Where the CGT rules deem a consideration, and there was in fact no actual consideration, there is no real problem. For example, no difficulty arises in the case of a gift for no consideration. Where there is no actual consideration for the disposal, it is absolutely clear that there is nothing which can be remitted to Ireland.

Example 11

Jean Mark is resident in Ireland, but is domiciled in France. In 1999/00 he made a gift of French land to his girlfriend Corinne. Under the CGT rules dealing with a disposal which is not a bargain made at arms length, he is deemed to dispose of the asset at market value. (see paragraph 16)

As there are no actual sale proceeds, there is nothing to actually remit to Ireland. There can be no remittance, and no gain to charge.

The real problems are confined to the area of where the CGT rules deem the sale proceeds to be more (or less) than the actual sale proceeds.

This could happen where an asset is disposed of at a substantial undervalue to a connected person. The disposal will be treated (for CGT) as being made at market value, and the gain calculated on that basis. Any part of the actual proceeds remitted will bear little relationship to the gain calculated by reference to the full market value of the asset. (see paragraph 16)

The following simple example illustrates the issues involved in deciding what a remittance is "in respect of".

Example 12

Where a non-domiciled individual

- *buys a foreign asset for £100, and*

- *sells it a number of years later for £150, and*

- *remits £20 of the proceeds into Ireland in 1999/00.*

- *assuming the full gain calculated under CGT rules is £40*

– *how much of the gain is chargeable in 1999/00 ?.*

To the extent the £20 is remitted in respect of the gain, the gain is chargeable to tax. However, there is no rule or guidance set out in the CGT legislation indicating the extent that a remittance out of the sale proceeds represents the gain.

What is remitted is certainly part of the consideration for disposal of the asset. The consideration certainly represents (in part) a recovery of his original capital. It also includes (in part) his profit on the sale. However, it would be difficult for any reasonable person to regard the part of the consideration remitted as being in respect of his profit alone.

Example 13

*In certain circumstances, the law disregards the actual consideration for disposal, and deems a different consideration. If (in **example 12** above) the law deemed his sale price to be £250, it would appear reasonable to assume that the only sum available to the individual out of which to remit any amount into Ireland, is the actual proceeds of £150. It is difficult to visualise any circumstances in which any part of the additional £100 deemed consideration could be regarded as being remitted into Ireland.*

It would appear that the only sum available to the individual out of which he can remit anything into Ireland is the actual consideration for the disposal (i.e. £150). The actual sale proceeds of £150 could hardly be regarded as representing any part of the deemed additional £100 sale proceeds. Any deeming provision cannot change what in fact the actual consideration is in respect of.

It would seem logical to assume that there cannot be a remittance of the part of the gain represented by the deemed excess over the actual sale proceeds (and which does not in fact exist).

The CGT position is further complicated by a number of artificial factors, such as indexation of costs for inflation, and deemed acquisition of assets at 6th April 1974, etc. but the broad principles remain unchanged.

Example 14

William is resident in Ireland, and domiciled in France. He sold a house in France to his brother in 1999/00 for IR£30,000 at a time when the house was valued at IR£55,000. The house base cost (including indexation) amounted to IR£10,000. He lodged the sale proceeds of IR£30,000 into his bank account in Dublin.

His chargeable gain for CGT purposes is IR£45,000 as he is deemed to sell the house to his brother for its market value of IR£55,000 (see paragraph 16). His gain based on the actual sale price of the house is IR£20,000.

*The charge to CGT is on the **amounts received in the State in respect of the chargeable gain.** The only amount received in the State is IR£30,000, which clearly represents the total actual sale proceeds of the house. It is clear that the IR£30,000 is the maximum amount which could be charged to CGT as being*

> *received in the State. However, it is also quite clear that the total IR£30,000 is not received in respect of the gain alone.*

If the principles discussed in *examples 11 to 13* above were applied to *example 134 - where the total actual proceeds are remitted to Ireland, the amount remitted to Ireland clearly represents a return of his capital (in part) and his profit (in part). No part of the additional IR£25,000 deemed sale proceeds could be contained in the amount remitted, as in fact that additional IR£25,000 was never received by William. It would appear to strain the use of the English language a little too far to suggest that any part of the deemed additional consideration was included in the remittance of the actual consideration.*

Example 15

> *Elizabeth is resident in Ireland, but domiciled in Germany. During 1999/00 she sold a property located in Latvia to her sister Bertha for IR£100,000. At the time of sale, the full market value of the Latvian property was IR£160,000. Let us assume that the total deductions allowed to Elizabeth in computing her gain (or loss) on the disposal amounts to IR£110,000. The gain computed for CGT purposes would amount to IR£40,000 taking the deemed sale proceeds as the market value of the property into account in computing the gain. During 1999/00 Elizabeth remitted IR£20,000 into Ireland.*

> *The issue for determination now, is how much (if any) of the gain is chargeable to CGT. Based on the deemed sale price of IR£160,000, she has a chargeable gain of IR£50,000. However, taking the actual sale proceeds into account, she has a loss of IR£10,000.*

> *The only amount which Elizabeth can remit to Ireland is all or part of the actual consideration. She cannot remit what she does not have. The actual consideration of IR£100,000 does not represent or contain any part of the notional IR£50,000 increase in the consideration over the actual figure of IR£100,000. The deemed additional £50,000 consideration was never received by her, and cannot be remitted. Based on the actual sale proceeds, there is a CGT loss. It is the additional deemed proceeds which give the artificial gain which she never actually received. It is difficult to see a justification for treating any part of the actual consideration as being in respect of a gain.*

It is understood that this reasoning is not accepted by the Revenue, who would seek to tax the £20,000 remitted into Ireland.

Our conclusion set out above, follows the reasoning set out in the UK case of Scottish Provident Institution v Allan. In that case, it was held that remittances from Australia must be of an income nature, as the sums retained in Australia equalled or exceeded the original capital invested. In this case, none of the capital is retained abroad, and it must follow that the remittance must include a return of Elizabeth's capital.

3.3.4 Alienation of capital

Following the decision in the UK case of Carter v Sharon, where income is alienated abroad, any remittance of that amount in the future by the current owner is not a remittance by the original owner. A similar principle would probably apply in the case of a gain, although if the full proceeds are not alienated, care would have to be taken to ensure that the part alienated represented the gain. In practice this may be an extremely difficult matter to prove.

Example 16

Jean Mark is resident in Ireland, but is domiciled in France. In 1999/00 he made a gift of French land to his girlfriend Corinne. Under the CGT rules dealing with a disposal which is not a bargain made at arms length, he is deemed to dispose of the asset at market value. (see paragraph 16). Some months later Corinne sold the land and brought the sale proceeds with her into Ireland.

*The treatment of Jean Mark on giving the gift to Corinne has already been dealt with in paragraph 3.3.3 (in **example 101**).*

The fact that Corinne has sold the land, and brought the sale proceeds into Ireland raises the question of Corinne's residence and domicile to establish whether she in chargeable to CGT in her own right.

The bringing into Ireland by Corinne of her sale proceeds is certainly (in the absence of other factors) not a remittance by Jean Mark.

3.3.5 Remittance anti-avoidance

s72

The FA91 introduced anti-avoidance provisions to counter income tax "remittance basis" avoidance schemes. The provisions are now TCA97 s72. The basic scheme took the form of a non domiciled taxpayer living on an overdraft while in Ireland, and paying it off abroad after he left Ireland. Many variations of that concept were used. S72 introduced provisions which deem a remittance to be made in certain circumstances.

s29(5)

S29(5) applies the provisions to CGT in the same manner as if the gain were foreign income by providing that:

"....s72 shall apply as it would apply if the gain were income arising from possessions outside the State".

The following is a broad outline of the relevant provisions relating to *"income arising from possessions outside the State"* :

s72

- Where a person who is resident or ordinarily resident in Ireland uses foreign income to pay off

  - a loan made to him in Ireland, or

  - a loan made abroad, but brought into Ireland, or

  - a debt incurred in paying off all or part of the above loans the amount of the foreign income used for that purpose is treated as a remittance of income into Ireland.

- The same rule applies where a loan is paid off out of foreign income before the non domiciled taxpayer remits the loan proceeds to Ireland.

s72
Prior to the FA97 the provisions only applied to a person who was ordinarily resident in Ireland. The FA97 extended the scope of the provisions to include an individual who is merely resident in Ireland. The scope of the provisions apply *"in relation to income applied in or towards satisfaction of a debt for money lent on or after 20th February 1997, or a debt incurred in satisfying in whole or in part any such debt......".* As stated above, this applies to capital gains as it applies to income.

Where income (or assets representing income) owned by the borrower is held by the lender (as security or otherwise), and is available to that lender to reduce or pay off a loan to the borrower, the borrowings may be treated as a remittance of income to Ireland. There must be an "arrangement" between the borrower and the lender, whereby the amount of the loan to be repaid depends in any way (directly or indirectly), on the value of the assets held by the lender.

Example 17

> Jan Brun is a Netherlands domiciled person living in retirement in Ireland. His living expenses in Ireland are financed from the proceeds of borrowings from a bank in Amsterdam. Periodically Jan disposes of shares held in companies outside of Ireland (and outside the UK) and uses the proceeds to repay the Amsterdam bank.

> Although Jan has not remitted into Ireland any part of the proceeds of his disposal of foreign shares, s72 will treat him as remitting those proceeds, to the extent that they are applied in discharging a foreign loan, and to the extent that the proceeds of the foreign loan were themselves remitted to Ireland.

s72
S72 does not provide rules for dealing with a mixed loan obtained abroad by the non-domiciled person. In *example 17* above, the loan which Jan had from his Amsterdam bank might have been partly used to fund living expenses in Ireland (and thus remitted into Ireland) and may have been partly used to purchase shares abroad. When the loan is discharged by the sales proceeds of the foreign shares, how does one determine whether what is being discharged is the part of the loan whose proceeds are remitted into Ireland, or the part of the loan which was used to finance the share purchases?

It is arguable that banking law should be applied to determine the order of offset of the repayment against moneys borrowed. That is a subject outside the scope of this book. The situation is not entirely clear.

3.4   Non-resident persons

3.4.1   Broad Outline - Non-Residents

It is important to note that normally (other than in respect of specified assets described in paragraph 3.4.2) a person is only chargeable to CGT on gains *accruing to him in a year of assessment for which he is resident or ordinarily resident in the State*. It follows, that if the individual is not resident (or ordinarily resident) in Ireland for the tax year in which the gain accrues, no liability to CGT can arise (other than in respect of specified assets). However, it should be noted that there is no absolute clarity of the position where certain "remittance basis"gains are involved - as set out in *example 8* and the discussion following that example. In such circumstances it may be advisable to try and obtain advance clearance from the Revenue before remitting such funds into Ireland.

Example 9 discusses the position of gains made by a non-domiciled individual while he was non-resident, which are remitted into Ireland by him after he becomes resident.

Paragraph 67 describes anti avoidance legislation that may attribute disposals by non residents to resident persons for CGT purposes.

3.4.2   Specified Assets - Gains

A person who is neither resident nor ordinarily resident in Ireland may still be within the charge to CGT. Gains arising on the disposal of certain Irish assets (specified in the Capital Gains Tax Acts) are chargeable to CGT irrespective of the residence or ordinary residence of the person making the disposal. The specified assets are:

s29(3)(a)
IA37 sch p14

(a)   *"Land in the State"*: The word land includes *"messuages, tenements, and hereditaments, houses and buildings of any tenure"*(paragraph 14 of the schedule to the Interpretation Act, 1937).

s29(3((b)
s29(6)

(b)   *"Minerals in the State or any rights, interests or other assets in relation to mining or minerals or the searching for minerals"*: This includes exploration or exploitation rights in a designated area [s29(6)] i.e. within the limits of the Irish 'Continental Shelf'.

CSA68 s1

S29(6) refers to a "designated area" as defined in s1 Continental Shelf Act 1968.

s13

"Exploration or exploitation rights" takes the meaning given to them in TCA97 s13.

s29(3)(c)

(c)   *"Assets situated in the State which, at or before the time when the chargeable gains accrued, were used in or for the purposes of a trade carried on by him in the State through a branch or agency, or which at or before that time were used or held or*

acquired for use by or for the purposes of the branch or agency"
(see paragraph 3.6)

Gains accruing to a person who is neither resident nor
ordinarily resident on the disposal of assets listed in paragraph
(b) above are deemed to be gains arising from a trade carried on
through an Irish branch trade of that person.

s29(1)   (d)   *"..Shares deriving their value or the greater part of their value
                     directly or indirectly .."* from such assets mentioned at (a) or (b)
                     but not (c) above *"other than shares quoted on a stock
                     exchange"*(see paragraph 3.5).

In paragraph (d) above, the legislation deems certain shares to be
"specified" assets for the purpose of bringing them within the scope
of the charge to CGT, where those shares derive the greater part of
their value from (a) or (b) above - i.e. from Irish land (the definition
of which extends to include buildings) and mineral, exploration or
other rights related to Irish land.

It should be noted that although "trade assets" are listed in (c) above
as a specified asset in the case of a direct ownership of such assets,
the legislation does not deem shares deriving value from underlying
trade assets of a company to be 'specified' assets by virtue of that fact
alone.

The practical difficulties involved in determining whether shares in a
company derive their value from "specified assets" of the company
(bringing any gain on the disposal of the shares within the scope of
the charge to CGT) or from other (non-specified) assets are dealt
with in the following sub-paragraphs.

FA95 s70   Since the introduction of CGT, a withholding tax has been applied to
              the assets specified above (in the absence of a Revenue clearance
s562   certificate). The FA95 extended the scope of the withholding tax to
              certain shares, securities and capital sums, which may not
              themselves be specified above, and in the ownership of a
              non-resident may not be within the territorial scope of the charge to
              CGT. Details are set out in paragraph 94.

Notwithstanding the extension of the withholding tax (FA95) to
certain shares, securities and capital sums which are not among the
specified assets, the charge to CGT on persons who are neither
resident nor ordinarily resident is not extended to these assets. If tax
is withheld (due to the absence of a clearance certificate as explained
in paragraph 94) the non-resident person who suffers the
withholding tax on such assets is entitled to a repayment of the tax
under Irish domestic law, even without regard to double tax
agreements.

s29(7) S29(7) states that gains arising to a non resident on the disposal of exploration or exploitation rights in a designated area (as referred to in sub-section 6) and minerals in the State and rights in relation to mining or minerals or the searching for minerals, are to be regarded as gains accruing on the disposal of assets used for the purposes of a trade carried on by that person in the State through a branch or agency. The significance of that provision would seem to be that where a non resident company makes a disposal of the assets mentioned, it would be chargeable to corporation tax on companies capital gains, rather than to capital gains tax. The treatment of the capital gains of companies is discussed in paragraph 71.

The provision might appear to create some anomaly in relation to the liability of a non resident to Irish CGT on the disposal of unquoted shares deriving their value from certain assets in Ireland. Unquoted shares deriving their value from land, or from minerals in the State, or mining rights etc are within the CGT net regardless of the resident status of the taxpayer. Shares deriving their value from the assets of a branch or agency in the State (the third category of specified Irish assets) are not within the charge to CGT in the same fashion but would be within the charge to CGT only if the person disposing of the shares was resident or ordinarily resident in the State in the year in which they did so. S29(7) in providing that minerals, and mineral rights should be regarded for capital gains tax purposes as branch assets, might appear to create some confusion as respects shares deriving their value from them. In the view of the authors, s29(7) does not affect the position relating to shares. If shares derive their value from minerals in the State, or mineral rights etc, and are unquoted, they are specified Irish assets notwithstanding that the minerals, and mineral rights etc themselves may fall to be treated for CGT purposes as if they were branch assets.

s29(3) S29(3), in referring to minerals and mining rights as being specified Irish assets, has a curious anomaly. It specifically provides that the reference is only to minerals in the State. It is therefore clear that the ownership of a mine in Northern Ireland is not a specified Irish asset and, in the hands of somebody neither resident nor ordinarily resident in the State, not within the scope of CGT for most purposes. However the definition continues by making a reference to "rights, interests, or other assets in relation to mining or minerals or the searching for minerals". Alone among the references to assets which are specified Irish assets, this reference is not qualified by the words "in the State". Having regard to the inherent limitations on the taxing power of the Irish State, and given that the definition of specified assets is for the purpose of defining the liability of persons neither resident nor ordinarily resident in Ireland, it would seem clear that the omission is unintentional and that the references to mining rights are to mining rights in the State. This is reinforced by s29(7) which would treat such assets as the assets of a branch in the State.

3.4.3   Specified Assets - Losses

s546(4)

A loss accruing to a person in a year of assessment for which the person is neither

- resident, nor

- ordinarily resident

in Ireland *"shall **not** be an allowable loss {for the purposes of the CGT Acts} **unless** under s29(3) the person would be chargeable to [CGT} in respect of a chargeable gain if there had been a gain instead of a loss on that occasion."*

s29(3)

As such a person is only chargeable to CGT in Ireland on the assets specified in s29(3), it follows that :

- only a loss on the specified Irish assets can be allowable, and

- any such loss can only be set off against a chargeable gain on another specified asset in that year. Of course if the person was resident or ordinarily resident in a later year loss relief would be available on a carry forward basis against any chargeable gain.

Details of the specified assets are set out above. The CGT rules for allowing relief for losses are set out in paragraph 20.

3.5   Shares deriving value

3.5.1   Broad outline - shares deriving value

There are a number of separate provisions, dealing with shares in a company, where the treatment depends on the assets from which the shares derive their value - for example:

- A **non-resident person** is within the scope of the charge to CGT on specified Irish assets. In the case of unquoted shares in a company, this depends on whether the shares *derive the greater part of their value* from **Irish land**, etc.

s29(3)

- A **withholding tax** at 15% applies to the sale proceeds of certain assets (in the absence of a specific exemption). Included amongst those assets, are unquoted shares *deriving the greater part of their value* from **Irish land**, etc..

s562

- A **reduced rate of 26% tax** applied (up to 3rd December 1997) to the disposal of certain shares in an Irish resident company which (inter alia) *derive the greater part of their value* from a **trade**.

s592

In dealing with the question of shares deriving value from the underlying assets of a company, there are two main issues which must be considered:

When must the test be applied : The date on which the test is to be applied is important, as the underlying assets of any company will normally change over a period of time. What the shares in a company may derive value from today may be quite different from what the same shares derived value from yesterday. This is considered in paragraph 3.5.2.

How is the test to be applied : Most companies own more than one single asset and will normally also have liabilities - some of which are directly related to specific assets. In such circumstances, do the shares in the company derive value from a combination of many different items? The way in which the law is to be applied in this area is not free of doubt, and many problems can arise. This is considered in paragraph 3.5.3.

3.5.2   **Deriving value - when must the test be applied?**

The position here is best illustrated by a brief example:

Example 18

> *Sunshine Ltd is a private Irish registered company. Although its shareholders are not resident in Ireland, the company itself is resident here. For many years its sole asset was a large office block in Dublin, which it rented to its tenants over the years. It sold the office block in December 1999, and taking indexation into account, the company had no chargeable gain. As a result, at 30 April 2000 (the company's financial year end) the company has nothing but cash on deposit. The cash was, of course, derived entirely from the sale of the property.*
>
> *The shareholders then decided to liquidate the company, and take the proceeds abroad to their home country.*
>
> *The main issue to be decided is whether the shares in the company are 'specified assets' for CGT purposes. If they are, a CGT charge would arise on any gain resulting from the disposal of the shares by the shareholders, and also the amounts paid to the shareholders by the liquidator may come within the "withholding tax" rules (see paragraph 94).*
>
> *For such an interpretation to prevail, it would mean that any company which at any time since its incorporation was within the definition (i.e. derived the greater part of its value from Irish land) is forever within the scope of the charge. This argument could be taken to ridiculous extremes - for example where an individual sold property and invested the proceeds in shares in a company. Are the shares then to be regarded as deriving their value from "Irish land" ?*
>
> *Although no interpretation of a point of law is entirely without doubt (in the absence of a clear decision on the matter by the Irish courts) it seems reasonable to assume that :*
>
> * *the company's assets must be looked at as they actually stand at the time of disposal of the shares, and*

> • *the historical source of the company's assets at the time of disposal of the shares is not itself relevant.*
>
> *On this basis, in the above example the share value is not derived from property - it is (at the time of disposal of the shares) derived from cash.*
>
> **It is understood that this interpretation is not (in practice) disputed by the Revenue Authorities.**

3.5.3   Deriving value - how is the test to be applied?

s29(1)

In the context of shares in a company, the phrase *"deriving their value or the greater part of their value directly or indirectly from"* can be interpreted in many different ways depending on your overall view of what shares 'derive value' from. It is understood that in practice this is an area which is causing problems for taxpayers in dealing with the Revenue Authorities.

There is no definition, or guidelines given in the Taxes Acts to identify the underlying assets of a company (if any) from which the shares are to be treated as deriving their value, although for CGT alone the concept occurs in many different places.

Some examples of where the phrase occurs are given above. The authors are not aware of any relevant decided cases in those areas which can give any guidance in the matter.

s535

There are however, many decided cases dealing with the area of **"capital sums derived from assets"**. Those cases give some indication as to the interpretation of the phrase "derived from". Many difficult and varied cases have been decided in that area by the UK Courts, and the decisions in those cases are helpful in determining the assets from which **"value"** is derived in any particular case. The cases dealing with "compensation" are particularly helpful (see paragraph 4.5).

In the UK case of Davenport v Chilver, Nourse J. said (referring to the derivation of the compensation received by the taxpayer under a UK Government Order appropriating assets of the USSR located within the UK to compensate certain UK residents for the loss of estates taken over from them by the Soviet Union after the revolution there - in this case an estate in Latvia)... *"I do not think that one can be said to derive from another unless it is in some sense the fruit of the tree. In Latvia the tree is dead. The fruit has dropped from one rooted in a loftier soil to which the blight cannot attain".*

Further cases are set out in paragraph 4.5

In the case of shares in a company, it seems logical that the commercial *basis of valuation* of those shares must be analysed in detail - before any conclusion can be reached as to which of the company's assets the shares derive value from.

If the company has no assets or rights, or anything of value, the shares in that company also have no value. In broad terms, the value of the shares in any company is linked directly to the value of the company itself. The overall company value is normally based on its assets and liabilities in a very broad sense (taking its earning potential as an asset). The value of a trading company would be geared mainly to the earning potential of its trade or business.

If an individual acquires an asset through his wholly owned company, in effect he owns the value of the underlying assets (through the value of his shares) although he may not directly own any asset itself other than the shares. Many individuals use companies to acquire, hold and/or deal in assets, mainly for family, commercial, or taxation purposes. This can lead us to conclude that ownership through a company is in fact an indirect ownership of the asset itself. Such a conclusion is a totally wrong. All a shareholder in a company owns is shares in that company.

3.5.4 Share valuations

In broad terms, a share in a company is merely a mixed bundle of rights and obligations. It does not confer ownership of any asset other than of the share itself. It is the company itself which owns the assets. The shareholder does however, normally have the ability to participate in the income generated by the use of the company's assets (i.e. through dividends) or to participate in the proceeds of disposal of the underlying assets on liquidation of the company. All a shareholder owns through his shareholding in a company is part of the overall *value* of the company itself.

The value of the company itself is derived from a number of different factors, depending on the activities, assets and liabilities of the company. That overall value of the company is then apportioned over all the issued share capital of the company. The value of non-controlling shareholdings is then normally further reduced, as forming part of a minority interest, etc.

- **General rules for valuations** : The valuation of any asset whether it be land, patent rights, or shares in a company can be very much a mixture of specialised knowledge, and common sense. This text does not deal with all the rules and conventions of such valuations. In the case of share valuations, the reader is referred to *"The valuation of shares in private companies" by B.H. Giblin*, also published by the Institute of Taxation in Ireland.

s547 The general commercial rules which are normally applied in valuing shares in private companies may be altered or amended by statutory rules which are applied in certain circumstances. The main statutory rules to be applied in arriving at the open market value of an asset for CGT purposes are dealt with in s547 (see paragraph 17). For the most part the statutory rules merely confirm that the normal rules applied in commercial practice apply to the valuation of unquoted shares for CGT purposes.

- **CAT Rules:** It is important to note that the specific mandatory rules which apply to the valuation of unquoted shares for the purposes of capital acquisitions tax do not apply for CGT purposes. This is particularly important in determining whether the shares are to be valued mainly on the basis of the underlying assets of the company, or on the company's profit earning potential. There are also major differences in deciding whether a holding is to be valued as forming part of a controlling interest. These factors can make a substantial difference to the value of unquoted shares. For CGT purposes, the normal rules and conventions of valuing company shares in practice apply.

- **Share Valuation : Trading Company :** In broad terms, it is normal practice in valuing an unquoted **trading** company to value that company on the basis of the value of its trade. That trade would be valued on the basis of its past earning record and estimated future earning potential. The value of the company's tangible assets (Land & Buildings, Plant & Machinery, Debtors, Stocks etc.) and its liabilities, although taken into account, would not be the main factor on which the company value would be determined. This makes a good deal of sense, when we consider that as long as the trade continues, there is little prospect of the underlying value of its main fixed tangible assets (i.e. land and buildings) actually being realised. Those assets - in the context of a trading company - are used mainly to support the income earning potential of the business, and are not held as investment assets to be sold whenever it appears that a financial gain could be realised.

This, of course, is only a broad outline, and there are many exceptions. Take the case of a company owning a valuable property which it uses solely as a business premises (for family reasons). Assume the business is only generating a small annual profit of (say) £10,000 - and the property itself could be sold for (say) £10m. In such a case, the value of the property would have to be regarded as more than merely incidental to the trade. This does not necessarily mean that the shares would take the value of the property. The property is not really worth anything like its true value for as long as the company decides to hold it and use it solely as a business premises for its existing business.

- **Share valuation : non-trading companies :** The normal commercial practice for valuing the shares of an unquoted **non-trading company** (for example - an investment company) is to value the underlying assets of the company.

The legislation does not provide rules or guidelines for determining from what specific assets (if any) shares derive their value, and in particular, whether they derive value from land, or from a trade or from a mixture of assets and liabilities. Where there is a mixture of assets in a company, the answer is often not entirely clear and may involve disputes with the Revenue . The matter is best illustrated by an example.

Example 19

Balance Sheet - TRADERS LTD		*per accounts (cost)*	*market value*
		IR£	IR£
ASSETS	Land & Buildings	200,000	300,000
	Goodwill	–	150,000
	Stock	290,000	290,000
	Debtors	210,000	210,000
		700,000	950,000
LIABILITIES	Trade Creditors	(300,000)	(300,000)
	Bank Overdraft	(250,000)	(250,000)
VALUE OF NET ASSETS		150,000	400,000
FINANCED BY :	Share Capital	1,000	
	Revenue Reserves	149,000	

The Balance Sheet of any business will normally show trade assets at their **"book written down value"** - which normally means the historic cost of the asset written down (depreciated) since it was acquired in accordance with the company's accounting policies. The assets are not necessarily shown on the Balance Sheet at their full market value.

The above example shows a typical trading company, with its premises, substantial creditors and borrowings, and a reasonable profit record (indicated by the extent of the accumulated revenue reserves). Its share value, in practice, would be determined mainly by its past profit/earning record and future profit expectations.

It is understood that the Revenue take the view in such a case that :

• all liabilities should be offset firstly against assets other than land

• the balance of the assets are then taken as those from which the shares derive their value.

In the above example, the following would be the result of applying that view:

	IR£
Market value of non-land assets	650,000
Less total liabilities	550,000
Balance = net non-land assets	100,000
Market value of Land	300,000
VALUE OF NET ASSETS	400,000

The overall value of the company's net tangible assets is £400,000. This would normally be attributed by the Revenue as to

- *£300,000 land and*

- *£100,000 other assets.*

The result of this artificial valuation and attribution is that the shares would be regarded as deriving the greater part of their value from land.

It should be clear to any reasonable person that the real value of the shares is derived from the successful conduct of a trade by the company and not from any single asset. The land is but one of many assets used by the company in the course of its trade - and does not even account for 50% of the total assets.

There is no basis, either in legislation, case law, or the practice of share valuations for the practice described above.

In this case the company carries on a trade. All of its assets are employed in the conduct of the trade. All of its income arises from the trade. Any purchaser of a controlling interest would normally value such an interest by reference to the value of the trade - i.e. of its maintainable earnings. In such a case it seems fair to say, that the shares derive their value from the conduct of the trade, and not from land in the State.

This practice (outlined in the above example) is even more untenable if in the example above, instead of a £250,000 bank overdraft (incurred for general trading purposes) £200,000 of the borrowings were represented by a mortgage loan taken out for the sole purpose of purchasing the land - and secured by a charge on that land.

The unreasonableness of that approach is further illustrated if we compare a company which owns its premises (Traders Ltd) with another similar company (Makers Ltd) which rents its premises.

Example 20

		Traders Ltd IR£	Makers Ltd IR£
ASSETS	Land & Buildings	200,000	–
	Goodwill	150,000	150,000
	Stock	290,000	290,000
	Debtors	210,000	210,000
Market value of total assets		850,000	650,000
LIABILITIES	Trade Creditors	(300,000)	(300,000)
	Loan to purchase land	(200,000)	–
	Bank overdraft	(50,000)	(250,000)
MARKET VALUE OF NET ASSETS		150,000	150,000

NOTES:

Both companies would be valued in practice on the basis of their earning potential, and let us assume that their profit records are very similar.

Both companies have the same overall value attributed to the shares, based on their (assumed) earning potential (i.e. £300,000). Traders Ltd has recently

> *bought its premises for £200,000 using a loan secured on the premises, and Makers Ltd rents its premises at a rent equal to the interest cost incurred by Traders Ltd on its property loan.*
>
> *Both companies derive their value from the trading activities. The only real difference between the companies, is that Traders Ltd has an additional 'asset' matched by a corresponding liability - i.e. the property, and the mortgage loan. The value of the shares in Traders Ltd can no more be said to derive from the land than the shares of Makers Ltd. The value of the shares in both companies are clearly derived from the value of their respective trades.*

The basis of valuing of shares in companies may vary so much from case to case, that it is doubtful whether there is any single correct rule which can be applied in all circumstances for determining the source of value of shares. It seems clear however, that in the case of a trading company the Revenue practice is not sustainable, and major doubts must be raised in the case of its application to a non-trading company.

The question of whether or not shares derive their value from land will arise in relation to a specific lot of shares. Where that lot of shares consists of 100% ownership, or a substantial controlling interest in a company, it would be reasonable to consider that the value of the shares derives from the activities and assets of the company, whether that be a trade, land or whatever. This is discussed above. However if the block of shares in relation to which the question is being asked is a minority interest, different considerations may arise. Whereas in general the value of controlling interests is often determined by a variety of factors such as the assets of the company, and its earnings record and future prospects for earnings, the valuation of a minority interest in many instances is determined by the future dividend prospects. If the value is largely determined by dividend prospects, the value is probably not influenced to any great extent by the composition of the assets of the company, whether they be land or anything else.

You could thus have a situation in which a block of 100% of the shares in a company may derive its value from land owned by the company, but where the focus is instead on a block of shares constituting (say) 3% of the share capital of the company, the value could be determined by dividend prospects unrelated to the value or composition of the assets of the company, and accordingly the shares might not derive their value from land. Thus some shares in a company might derive their value from land, and other shares may not, even where the shares are all of one class.

The distinction between a controlling holding, and a minority holding is well recognised in terms of the value which a block of shares have in the open market. Not only is the value of a minority holding usually significantly smaller than that of a majority stake, the factors which determine that value (ie that from which the value is derived) may be different in the case of the minority stake as compared to the majority stake in the same company,

Until the matter has been ruled on by the Courts, practitioners should be aware of the practice which the Revenue may seek to adopt in this area.

3.6   Branch assets

As noted at 3.4.2 above, a non-resident may be chargeable to CGT in respect of assets of an Irish branch or agency.

This raises a number of issues for consideration:

- what is a "branch or agency"

- the rules regarding the location of the assets,

- the conditions regarding the use to which the assets are put, or the purpose for which the assets are held.

The relief available in respect of certain overseas branches of an Irish resident company is described in paragraph 71.4.

s579(B)(6) Irish branch assets are excluded from the "exit charge" on trustees going non-resident (see paragraph 65.13.2.2). A similar exclusion in relation to a company going non-resident is described in paragraph 74.2.

3.6.1   What is a "branch or agency"

s5 The term "branch or agency" is defined in very broad general terms for CGT purposes as meaning:

"any factorship, agency, receivership, branch, or management but does not include the brokerage or agency of a broker or agent referred to in s1039"

s1039 S1039 deals with special provisions as to non-residents, and temporary residents. Although that part of the TCA97 is not applied generally to CGT, the specific provisions of s1039 are applied in determining whether or not an agent is regarded as a branch of a non-resident for the purposes of the charge to CGT.

This is part of the legislation was taken directly from the UK 1965 Act. It appears to be a complex and mainly incomprehensible attempt at defining the distinction between an agent and a principal (in terms of general commission agents).

s1039 S1039 states *"a broker or general commission agent, or.....an agent not being an authorised person carrying on the regular agency of the non-resident person......etc"*.

It is interesting to note that the UK equivalent of s1039 was omitted from the later UK consolidated CGT Act 1979.

The concept of "branch or agency" is also used in the Corporation Tax Acts. Possibly as a result, the terms are usually thought of as relating to companies. The expression is not restricted to companies in the Capital Gains Tax Acts. It can as easily refer to an individual, or partnership, or a trustee.

The branch or agency referred to is only one through which a *trade* is carried on.

In the UK case of IRC v Brakett, it was held that the taxpayer, who had been the settlor of an offshore settlement which owned an offshore company, and who was an employee (and the only employee) of that company constituted a branch or agency of that company in the UK where he resided. The judge said *"I do not think that it is necessary that an agent should be a person who is empowered to enter into contracturl relations on behalf of the non-resident company. Wherever the contracts are made, I find it difficult to imagine how a non-resident company which carries on a trade with any degree of continuity in the United Kingdom can do so otherwise than through a "branch or agency" as defined in the Taxes Management Act 1979 (UK)."* This decision would seem to give a very wide meaning to "branch or agency". It remains to be seen whether an Irish court would give a similarly wide meaning in particular to the word "agency". Normally the power to bind the principal to a contract is an inherent part of the nature of an agency.

The term "trade" does not include a "profession".

Example 21

> Greene and Orange Chartered Accountants, provide accountancy services principally in Dungannon in Northern Ireland, but also have an office in Letterkenny. Neither of the partners are resident or ordinarily resident in the State. The Letterkenny office is managed by an employee and it is visited only once a month by the partners. The partnership sold the goodwill, leasehold premises, and fixtures and fittings of the Letterkenny Office to its manager in December 1999.
>
> Notwithstanding that the fixtures and fittings referred to are situated in the State and notwithstanding that they are the assets of a branch in the State, the partners are not liable to Irish capital gains tax on the disposal since the assets in question were not in use for the purpose of a trade, but rather were used for the purpose of a profession. They are of course liable in respect of the land and buildings since these are separately specified assets in their own right.
>
> The partnership would be liable to capital gains tax in the State (subject to the double taxation agreement with the UK) in relation to the leasehold premises since it is an asset of a type separately specified without reference to the question of a branch. The goodwill and fixtures however are not of a separately specified category and would be within the charge only if they were used for the purpose of a trade carried on through a branch etc.

The word "branch" would not seem to necessarily refer to a subsidiary part of an organisation, notwithstanding that the branch of a tree is normally considered a subordinate part of the overall tree, in contrast to its trunk. It might be possible for a person who is resident in Northern Ireland to carry on a trade in the Republic (without becoming resident in the State) and for the location where that trade is carried on to be a branch, notwithstanding that he has no other trading location, whether in the State or in Northern Ireland. That point is not beyond dispute but it would seem anomalous if an individual's liability to capital gains tax in the Republic in such circumstances were determined by the question of whether he did or did not have another trading establishment outside the State, and on the relative size of the establishment in the State, compared to that outside the State.

There is a small anomaly in regard to the treatment of a company which is not resident in the State. A non-resident company is liable to corporation tax on *"any income from property or rights used by, or held by, or for, the branch or agencies."* This is not limited by reference to the location of the assets at the time that the income arises from them, in contrast to the position relating to the charge to tax on gains on the disposal of such assets. Thus a non-resident company would be liable to corporation tax on income arising from assets held outside the State for its Irish branch, but would not be liable to corporation tax on gains arising on the disposal of such assets.

3.6.2   Location of branch assets

s29(3)(c)
The assets must be situated in Ireland in order that a chargeable gain can arise on their disposal by a non-resident. The CGT law (s533) sets out specific rules for determining the location of assets for CGT purposes. Those rules are explained in paragraph 3.7.

The legislation does not state when this test (regarding the location of the assets) is to be applied. It would appear reasonable to apply the test only at the date of disposal of any particular branch asset coming within the possible charge under this heading.

3.6.3   Use of branch assets/purpose for which held

s29(3)(c)
It is clearly stated in s29 that the assets must (at or before the time when the chargeable gains accrued) be or have been:

• used in, or for the purposes of a trade carried on in Ireland by the non-resident (through a branch or agency), or

• assets which were used or held or acquired for use by or for the purposes of the branch or agency.

It would appear that an asset which was originally acquired for use in a trade carried on in Ireland by a branch of a non-resident will remain within the charge to CGT even after it has ceased to be used for the purposes of that branch trade. Once assets have been acquired for or used by an Irish branch of a non-resident it appears that they can only be removed from the scope of the charge to CGT if the actual assets are removed from Ireland prior to the disposal.

Example 22

French Fashions SA are a French incorporated and resident company. It has a branch in Ireland, consisting of a shop in Grafton Street where it has traded for a number of years. French Fashions SA decides to close its Grafton Street branch. It sells off the lease, and also sells off the shop fittings. However it transfers certain valuable art works, used to create a luxurious ambiance in the shop, to a London auction room and disposes of them there.

French Fashions SA is liable to Irish capital gains tax in accordance with s29(3)(c) on the disposal of the leasehold property, and on the fixtures and fittings which it disposed of in Ireland. All of these are assets used by French Fashions SA for the purpose of a branch in Ireland. The art works which were transferred to the London auction room are not within the charge to Irish capital gains tax, because, although used for the purposes of the branch trade in Ireland, they were not located in Ireland at the date of their disposal by auction in London.

Example 23

If French Fashions SA had, instead of disposing of the leasehold interest and the fittings, granted a sub-lease of the shop, together with the fittings to a new tenant at a rack rent, there would be no immediate capital gains tax liability because no capital sum would have been received on the granting of the new lease. If some years later French Fashions SA sell their lease, and the fittings in the shop, to their immediate landlord, French Fashions are within the charge to Irish capital gains tax on the disposals.

The lease, being interest in land in Ireland would be within the charge to Irish capital gains tax whether or not it had been in use previously for the purpose of a trade carried on through a branch. The fittings, although not in use for the purpose of a branch trade at the date of their disposal, nor for several years previously, are still within the charge to Irish capital gains tax because they are located in Ireland, and had been previously used by French Fashions SA for the purpose of a trade carried on through a branch.

If French Fashions had, after sub-letting the premises, purchased any additional fittings and leased them to its new tenant, a disposal of those new fittings would not be within the charge to Irish capital gains tax notwithstanding that they are located in Ireland, since they would not have been used by French Fashions SA for the purpose of a trade carried on in Ireland through a branch. This is on the assumption that the letting of such items would not constitute the carrying on of a trade, which is something that depends on all of the facts of a particular situation.

The case of S. Murphy (Inspector of Taxes) v Dataproducts (Dublin) Ltd [High Court, 29/1/88] concerned the question of whether interest on a bank account was "branch" income or "head office" income. Although not concerned with capital gains, the case had to consider whether or not the bank account was a branch asset. The bank account represented monies remitted from the branch to head office and which were held for the general purposes of the company, including (if the directors so decided) for the requirements of the branch. It was held, on the facts of the case, that the bank account was not a branch asset.

3.7   Location of Assets

3.7.1   Location of assets - statutory rules

s533

In the case of a non-resident person or non-domiciled individual the question of whether the gain arises on the disposal of an Irish asset or a foreign asset is important.

S533 sets out a number of 'situs rules' which determine whether an asset is an Irish asset or a foreign asset for CGT purposes. The place where an asset is located by general law, or where it is physically located is not the test to be applied in the case of assets within the scope of these rules, which fix the location of the asset for the purposes of capital gains tax. Indeed, there is a substantial body of case law dealing with other taxes which have no situs rules, the principles established in which would locate many of the assets listed below differently to the CGT rules for the purposes of other laws.

The rules are as follows:

- *Land & Buildings*

s533(a)

The situation of rights or interests (otherwise than as security) in or over immovable property (land and buildings etc.) is that of the immovable property.

- *Chattels*

s533(b)

Subject to the following rules, the situation of rights or interests (otherwise than as security) in or over tangible movable property is that of the tangible movable property.

- *Debts*

s533(c)

Subject to the following rules a debt (whether secured or unsecured) is situated in Ireland only if the creditor is resident in Ireland.

This is a reversal of the normal international rule which would locate the debt by reference to the residence of the debtor. As a result of this specific rule, what would in general law be regarded as a "foreign debt" is treated for Irish CGT purposes as an Irish asset when owned by an Irish resident, and vice versa.

There is an exception to the general rules outlined above. That is, a judgement debt is situated where the judgement is recorded.

Example 24

John has £Stg 10,000 on deposit with Midland Bank in London. John is also owed £Stg 2,000 by his brother-in-law, Edgar who lives in London. John has secured a judgement against Edgar in relation to the debt, Edgar having failed to repay it on the due date.

Under normal international rules governing the location of assets, the bank account and the debt would both be regarded as located in the U.K. However, under the rules which are peculiar to Irish CGT the bank account is regarded as located in Ireland, but the judgement debt against Edgar is regarded as located in the UK, where the judgement was obtained and registered.

In *example 23,* the fact that the bank account is deemed located in Ireland rather than the UK would not matter greatly since John would be liable in respect of any gains arising from the bank account no matter which country it is regarded as located in. If however the bank account had been with Deutsche Bank in Frankfurt, and if John was not domiciled in Ireland, the rule would have very real consequences. John would not be entitled to the remittance basis on gains arising in relation to the bank account as it would not be an asset located outside Ireland and outside of the UK. In principle, every time a cheque is written on that bank account there is a disposal of part of the debt owed by the bank to John. As explained in paragraph 38.7 a bank account in foreign currency represents a form of debt (a debt owing by the bank to its customer) which is a chargeable asset notwithstanding that it is not a debt on a security. There is a minor exception to that explained in paragraph 38.7.

Where a bank account is owned by more than one person, jointly, it may be difficult to apply the statutory rule as to the location of the bank account. The statutory rule states that the bank account is situated in the State "only if the creditor is resident in the State". Where there is more than one creditor, the only plausible reading of this rule is that the bank account would be located in the State only if both creditors are resident in the State. Where both account holders (i.e. creditors in the statutory language) are not resident in the State, it would seem that the bank account cannot be regarded as being located in the State even if it were an account held at an Irish branch of a bank. Nothing, however, is likely to turn on that.

The legislation does not provide any rule as to the location of a bank account whose creditor is not resident in the State. That is a curious omission which could be relevant to a non-domiciled person who is ordinarily resident (but not resident) in the State. Such a person would be liable to Irish capital gains tax, potentially on the remittance basis in relation to assets located outside of Ireland and outside of the U.K. In such a case the bank account would not be regarded as located in Ireland. If the ordinarily resident accountholder drew a cheque on it and received cash from, for example, the Paris branch of the same bank, if would seem that he would regarded as disposing of an asset located outside of Ireland and would not necessarily have remitted the proceeds into Ireland.

- *Shares And Securities*

s533(d)   Shares or securities issued by any municipal or governmental authority, or by any body created by such an authority, are situated in the country of that authority - see also note below in paragraph 3.7.2.1 regarding letters of allotment.

- *Registered Shares And Securities*

s533(e)   Subject to the previous rule, registered shares or securities are situated where they are registered and, if registered in more than one register, where the principal register is situated.

The legislation does not provide rules for determining the location of shares and securities which are not registered.   A typical example of shares and securities which are not registered are those held in bearer form.   A "bearer share" is the name given to a share the ownership of which depends on the possession of the share certificate, rather than on the owners name being registered in a register.   When s533 does not provide a rule relating to bearer shares, the normal rule of international law would apply which would regard such shares as being located where the share certificate is physically to be found.

- *Ships And Aircraft*

s533(f)   A ship or aircraft is situated in Ireland only if the owner is resident in Ireland. An interest or right in or over a ship or aircraft is situated in Ireland only if the person entitled to the interest or right is resident in Ireland.

This rule could be significant in the case of a company not resident in Ireland, but trading there through a branch or agency. As explained in paragraph 72.1, such a company is within the charge to Irish tax on capital gains in relation to assets located in the State, and used in or for the purposes of the trade, or used or held or acquired for such purposes.   If the Irish branch owned a ship or an aircraft, the company would not be liable to Irish capital gains tax on a disposal of those assets even if they were physically in Ireland at the date of disposal, and notwithstanding that they were held for the purpose of the trade of the branch.   TCA97 s533 deems a ship or aircraft to be located, not where they physically are, nor indeed where they are registered, but rather where the company which owns them is resident.

- *Goodwill*

s533(g)

The situation of goodwill of a trade, business or profession is at the place where the trade, business or profession is carried on - see also note in paragraph 3.7.2.2 below regarding the position of goodwill in relation to the premises in which the business is carried out.

The statutory rule is difficult to apply where a trade is carried on in more than one place.

Example 25

Pierre is domiciled in France but resident in Ireland. He is an interior decorator with consulting rooms in Paris, Dublin and Los Angles. Pierre trades under his own name, which is well known among rich potential customers throughout the world. His customers at each of his three consulting rooms are drawn from many countries. Pierre has received an offer from a multi-national company for his business, including the use of his name. Where is Pierre's goodwill located for capital gains tax purposes?

Since Pierre carries on his business at least in part in Dublin, it would seem undeniable that under the artificial statutory rules that determine the location of assets, part at least of his goodwill is located in Ireland. The commercial reality of course is that his goodwill is located in every country in which his name is known but that is not relevant to the statutory rule set out in s533.

The legislation is not of much assistance in determining whether it is all, or part, or what part, of Pierre's goodwill that is located in Ireland. The issue is very relevant from the view point of the remittance basis of taxation, to which Pierre is entitled, and which is explained in paragraph 3.3. Is this liable on "an arising" basis only in relation to the gain on that part of the goodwill which is located in Ireland, and on a remittance basis in relation to the Paris and Los Angles goodwill, or because the trade is carried on at least in part in Ireland is all of the goodwill to be regarded as located in Ireland and therefore is the entire gain in relation to the goodwill taxable on an arising basis rather than on a remittance basis?

The question could be conveniently answered if Pierre had a separate goodwill in relation to each of his three establishments, because then there would of course be three separate assets and the problem would not arise. But if the goodwill of Pierre essentially attaches to his name and is an indivisible single asset, then it would seem to follow that it is either entirely located in Ireland, or not located in Ireland at all. Unfortunately, neither the legislation or case law offers any guide as to how the question should be answered.

s29(4)

S29(4) which deals with the remittance basis states that it applies to assets situated outside the State and outside the United Kingdom. In the example above the goodwill is situated outside the State and outside the United Kingdom by reason of the fact that the trade is carried on (at least in part) in places outside the State etc. But it is also located in the State by reason of the trade being carried in the State also. The solution may well be, if the statutory language is not clear, that there is no basis for taxing Pierre at all.

• *Patents, Trade Marks, Etc.*

s533(h)

Patents, trade marks and designs are situated where they are registered. If they are registered in more than one register, you must look to where each register is situated. Copyright, franchises, rights and licences to use any copyright material, patent, trade mark or design are situated in Ireland if they, or any rights derived from them are exercisable in Ireland.

• *Exploration And Exploitation Rights*

s29(6)
CSA68 s1

Any gains accruing on the disposal of exploration or exploitation rights in a designated area, (basically the Irish Continental Shelf) are treated as gains on the disposal of assets situated in the State. The term *"designated area"* takes its meaning from s.1, Continental Shelf Act, 1968.

The statutory rules of s533 determines the location only of those assets which are referred to in s533. The Section does not purport to be comprehensive. The location of assets not referred in s533 would be determined according to the rules of international law. Thus, for example, in the case of a debt where the creditor is not resident in Ireland, the debt will be regarded as located (in accordance with international law) where the debtor is located provided however that the debtor is not located in Ireland. S533 will permit a debt to be located in Ireland only if the creditor is resident in Ireland. Another example is that of a bearer share, which, as explained above, will be regarded as located wherever it is to be found.

3.7.2   **Location of assets - case Law**

3.7.2.1   **Letters of Allotment**

The UK case of Young v Phillips had to consider the location for CGT purposes of letters of allotment in respect of shares of a company registered in England.

s5

TCA97 s5 states that *""shares" includes stock, and shares or debentures comprised in any letter of allotment or similar instrument shall be treated as issued unless the right to the shares or debentures thereby conferred remains provisional until accepted and there has been no acceptance."*

The letters of allotment with which Young v Phillips was concerned were not provisional. The judge none the less rejected the argument that the letters of allotment were to be treated as shares already issued, and to have a location as if they were shares. The judge pointed out that the rule relating to the location of shares was provided only in respect of *"registered shares"* and he was not prepared to treat the deeming provision in the UK equivalent of s5 as equating a letter of allotment with a registered share.

In dealing with the location of a letter of allotment, the judge noted that instruments which were capable of being disposed of where they physically were, without the requirement to do anything, or involve any person, at any other place, were treated in law as being located in the place where they physically were. He referred to the case of Stern v The Queen, in which it was held that blank forms of transfer and powers of attorney endorsed on share certificates in United States railway companies were located where the forms and certificates were to be found, because there was evidence of an active market in that place in which the forms and certificates could be disposed of, without reference to the United States.

However the Letters of Allotment in the Young v Phillips case related to a private company, and not to a publicly quoted company and there was not evidence before the court as to the existence of a market in letters of allotment in English private companies on the Island of Sark (in the Channel Islands) which is where the Letters of Allotment were physically to be found on the date of their disposal. In the absence of evidence that the letters of allotment could have been disposed of in a market in Sark, the judge held that they must be located in England where the shares to which they related would be registered.

The judge explained his apparent disregard of the fact that the letters of allotment were in fact disposed of in Sark (which might be some evidence of an ability to dispose of them there!) by pointing out that the disposal in question was between connected parties. It is to be noted that the decision in Young v Phillips does not amount to a rule of law that letters of allotment relating to shares in private companies are to be treated as located where the shares to which they refer would be registered. The judgement rather turned on a finding of fact that a market in such letters of allotment did not exist on the Island of Sark, and the judgement would need to be applied with care to any different set of circumstances.

3.7.2.2   Goodwill attached to Buildings

It can sometimes be difficult to determine whether goodwill exists as an asset in its own right, distinct from land and buildings in which a trade is carried on. In the UK case of Butler v Evans it was held that the question of whether goodwill existed as a separate asset distinct from premises was essentially a matter of fact and not of law. On the facts of that particular case, it was held that goodwill was a distinct asset from the premises in which a retail shop was located.

4   DISPOSAL OF ASSETS

4.1   Broad outline - disposals of assets

s28(1)   One of the most important areas of the CGT legislation is the meaning of the phrase *disposal of assets*. It is crucial to the charge to tax which only applies to a gain accruing on the *disposal of assets*.

Notwithstanding the importance of this phrase, neither the term *disposal* nor the term *asset* are comprehensively defined for CGT purposes. It is now more than 30 years since the legislation was first introduced in the UK Finance Act 1965, and over 20 years since its enactment in Ireland, and throughout the intervening years the CGT law has had many subsequent amendments, and much judicial attention. After all that time and attention to the law by Revenue authorities and judiciary, it is still not possible to extract an accurate and complete definition either of

- what the term *asset* means in the context of the CGT legislation, or

- of the meaning of the term *disposal.*

This general area (of *disposals* and *assets*) has resulted in more cases being brought before the courts than any other area of CGT, which in itself testifies to the complexity of the subject.

A general guideline can be obtained from the legislation, and specific guidance taken in certain areas which have been the subject of consideration by the courts. This leaves a large area at the core of the CGT law, where the legislation is unclear, and there are no guidelines laid down by the courts.

To complicate matters further, the CGT legislation sets out many circumstances where it

- *deems a disposal of an asset* where there has in fact been no real disposal, and

- *deems that there has been no disposal of an asset* where in reality there has been an actual disposal.

Not everything from which a capital sum is derived, or in respect of which a capital gain may be made, is necessarily an asset. An obvious example of something other than an asset in respect of which a capital gain may be made or from which a capital sum may be derived, is a **liability**. A gain arising on the disposal of a liability is not within the charge to capital gains tax.

4.2   What are Assets

4.2.1   What are assets - legislation.

s28(1)
A charge to tax can only arise where there is a disposal of an asset. The term 'asset' is not exhaustively defined in the legislation, and generally takes its normal meaning. The word "asset" in its ordinary sense has a very wide meaning. In one context it can mean investments, land and buildings, and property of all types, while in another context it can mean the possession of good health, good looks or good education.

The only general guidance to be obtained from the CGT Acts, is contained in TCA97 s532 which states that:

s532
"All forms of property shall be assets for the purposes of this Act whether situated in the State or not, including:-

• *options, debts, and incorporeal property generally,*

• *any currency, other than Irish currency* (the UK £Stg. was also excluded from the meaning of "asset" prior to 1980/81) *and*

• *any form of property created by the person disposing of it, or otherwise becoming owned without being acquired".*

This would not normally be looked upon as a "definition" but merely as a statement of particular items to be included within the meaning of the term "assets". Nonetheless, the UK courts have treated this reference to property as providing a *limitation* on what otherwise would be the very wide ordinary meaning of the word "assets".

4.2.2   What are assets - case law

The decisions of the UK Courts have established three broad principles:

— the word "asset" for CGT purposes is synonymous with "property".

— an asset (property) must be owned by the disponer prior to the disposal.

— the position is not affected by limitations on the transferability of the property.

Apart from these broad principles, the decisions of the Courts have served only to identify specific items which are or are not to be regarded as assets for CGT purposes.

4.2.3   **"Assets" means "property".**

One of the clearest statements given by the UK courts as to the meaning of the word "assets" was given by Nicholls LJ in the case of Kirby v Thorn EMI . Thorn EMI had sold a number of subsidiaries, and in addition to the consideration received for the disposal of the subsidiaries had been paid a sum in return for an undertaking *not to compete* with those subsidiaries in the future. Thorn EMI argued that the sum of money in question was derived from the curtailment of their "liberty to compete", but that it was not liable to capital gains tax because the liberty to compete, or to trade, was not "property" and hence was not an asset. Nicholls J. dealt with that argument as follows:

"I agree that the liberty or freedom to trade, enjoyed by everyone, is not a form of "property" within the meaning of (the CGT legislation). This liberty, or freedom, is a "right" if that word is given a very wide meaning, as when we speak of a person's "rights" in a free society. But in (the CGT legislation) the words used are "assets" and "property". "Property" is not a term of art, but takes its meaning from its context....the context in the instant case is a taxing act which is concerned with assets and disposals and acquisitions, gains and losses. I can see no reason to doubt that in (the CGT legislation) "property" bears the meaning of that which is capable of being owned, in the normal legal sense, and that it does not bear the extended meaning that would be needed if it were to include a person's freedom to trade."

In the passage quoted above the Court of Appeal made three points:

- "Assets" are synonymous with "property". This is not explicitly stated in the legislation, but the view of the UK Court of Appeal would no doubt have influence in an Irish court.

- Property means "that which is capable of being owned, in the normal legal sense".

- The right or freedom to trade, or to compete is not "property" and therefore is not an asset for CGT purposes.

However, it is important to note, that although the "freedom to trade" was held not to be an asset for CGT purposes, the Court also held that the parent company (Thorn EMI) did have a goodwill in its subsidiaries, and that goodwill was an asset from which a chargeable gain could arise.

In the UK case of National Provincial Bank Ltd. vs Hastings Car Mart Ltd., Lord Wilberforce said in a House of Lords judgement at [1965] AC 1247:

"Before a right or interest can be admitted into the category of property or of a right affecting property it must be definable, identifiable by third parties, capable in its nature of assumption by third parties, and have some degree of permanence or stability".

The case was concerned with the rights of a married woman in the family home owned by her husband and not with taxation.

4.2.4   **"Assets" - must be owned prior to disposal**

The UK case of Kirby v Thorn EMI also held that there was a disposal of an asset within the meaning of the CGT legislation only where the asset existed immediately prior to the disposal in the ownership of the person making the disposal. If an asset came into existence only through the act of disposal itself, then it was not, in relation to that disposal, an asset within the meaning of the CGT legislation.

s532(c)   In Kirby v Thorn EMI the Crown argued that [the UK equivalent of s532] which provides that property includes *any form of property created by the person disposing of it* indicates that the Act contemplates a disposal by the creation of an asset. This was rejected by Nicholls LJ..."[*Under s532(c)]...... property is an asset for the purposes of the Act even where it is created by the disponer. It was submitted that it would be anomalous to recognise the disposal of an asset created immediately before the disposition, but to exclude the case where an asset is created by the disposition. But from the second limb of [s532(c)] ... "or otherwise coming to be owned without being acquired"..... it is clear that in the first limb of [s532(c)] it is assumed that the person making the disposition was the owner of the property created by him. Whether the result is to be regarded as an anomaly or not, this is consistent with the Act applying to dispositions of assets by disponers, regardless of the length of time for which they may have owned the assets prior to the disposals, but not applying (subject to express provision) in circumstances where, prior to the disposition, the disponer had no asset".*

s534   He also dealt with the further contention by the Crown, that it was clear that the draftsman had in mind that a disposal could be an act of creation, as [s534(b)] provides for a part disposal where an interest or a right in or over the asset is created by the disposal, as well as where it subsists before the disposal. Dealing with this contention, Nicholls LJ said:...*"I do not feel able to draw from this, the conclusion that the Crown submitted followed, namely that an asset created by a disposition must be assumed to have been intended to fall within the ambit of the tax unless expressly excluded".*

s532(c)   The meaning of the part of s532(c) referring to an asset *"otherwise becoming owned without being acquired"* was also dealt with by Nourse J in Davenport v Chilver. *"It is a matter of everyday legal parlance to talk of someone acquiring a right under a statute. In my view the second part of [s532(c)] is not directed to this kind of right at all. Counsel for the Crown argued that if it was not it would be difficult to know to what it was directed. That may be so, although it would seem to me that it might apply, for example, to the goodwill of a business which had been built up by the person whom it was sought to tax. In any event, the difficulty of not knowing to what a very general provision of this nature may be directed is not justification for seeking to apply it to something to which it is clearly not directed".*

There are of course certain statutory exceptions to the general rule that the asset must be owned by the person making the disposal prior to the actual disposal, e.g. the grant of an option can be regarded as the disposal of an asset in certain circumstances. The option has no existence prior to the moment of its grant (i.e. of its disposal). The very act of granting it creates it. Were it not for the statutory exception, the grant of an option would not be regarded as the disposal of an asset, nor would any amount received for such a grant be regarded as derived from an asset within the meaning of the legislation.

4.2.5   **"Assets" - limitations on transfer**

Although Nicholls J. held that asset/property means "that which is capable of being owned", its meaning is not confined to that which the owner may transfer to others. This matter was dealt with in the UK case of O'Brien v Bensons Hosiery (Holdings) Ltd. There the House of Lords held that a sum of money paid to a company by a director in consideration of the company's releasing him from his obligations under a service agreement was a capital sum derived from that service agreement; and that the service agreement in question was an asset of the company. It was agreed that the service agreement was not capable of being transferred by the company to any other party (at least not without the consent of the employee). It was argued that for that reason it was not an asset of the company. The point was dealt with by Lord Russell as follows:

"It was contended for the taxpayer that the rights of an employer under a contract of service were not "property" or an "asset" of the employer, because they cannot be turned to account by transfer or assignment to another. But in my opinion this contention supposes a restricted view of the scheme of the imposition of capital gains tax which the statutory language does not permit. If, as here, the employer is able to extract from the employee a substantial sum as a term of releasing him from his obligations to serve, the rights of the employer appear to me to bear quite sufficiently the mark of an asset of the employer as something which you can turn to account, notwithstanding that its ability to turn it to account is by a type of disposal limited by the nature of the asset."

Lord Russell also rejected the argument that because the Capital Gains Tax legislation requires in certain circumstances that the consideration for the disposal of an asset (or its acquisition) should be treated as being the *open market value* of the asset, that only property which has a market value is an *"asset"* for the purposes of the Capital Gains Tax legislation. He said *"in my opinion it is erroneous to deduce from s.22(4)* [UK equivalent of TCA97 s547]....*a*

s547

principle of general application for the purposes of capital gains tax that an asset must have a market value."

4.2.6   **Statutory compensation as "an asset"**

Among the issues arising in a number of UK cases dealing with compensation, were :

• whether compensation, per se, was within the scope of CGT, and

• whether statutory rights were an asset for CGT purposes.

Apparently conflicting decisions arose in a number of those cases dealing with compensation derived from statutes. The key to understanding the apparent conflict, is understanding the fundamental distinction made in those cases between

• a capital sum derived from an asset, and

• an amount paid in the nature of reimbursement of expenses or costs, which is not a capital sum derived from an asset.

The cases involved were (in chronological order):

—Davis v Powell (compensation held not to be derived from an asset)

—Davenport v Chilver (compensation held to be derived from an asset), and

—Drummond v Austin Brown (compensation held not to be derived from an asset).

The basic principles were set out first in Davis v Powell. In that case a tenant farmer was paid compensation under the (UK) Agricultural Holdings Act 1948. The compensation provisions of the Act applied where the tenancy of an agricultural holding terminated by reason of notice to quit, and in consequence, the tenant quit the holding. In broad terms, the compensation was quantified in the Act as *"the loss or expense directly attributable to the quitting of the holding which is unavoidably incurred by the tenant upon or in connection with the sale or removal of his household goods, implements of husbandry, fixtures, farm produce or farm stock on or used in connection with the holding, and shall include any expenses reasonably incurred in the preparation of his claim for compensation".*

The statute also set out a minimum and a maximum amount of compensation.

In the course of his judgement, Templeman J. said:

"The plain object of this section is to provide by statute that a landlord shall make good to a tenant the loss or expense which he unavoidably incurs in connection with the matters mentioned in the section; and to avoid any quibbling and quarrels about matters it is said that he is not to get less than

one year's rent or more than two, and if he wants more than one year, he must prove his loss. That is a very sensible provision for giving a tenant compensation for loss or expense unavoidably incurred. Looking at section 34 (of that UK 1948 Act) by the light of nature and asking 'Can that amount be liable to CGT', the answer is 'Nonsense', you cannot make a gain out of a sum of money which is given to compensate for loss or expense unavoidably incurred".

Towards the conclusion of his judgement, he gave a summary of the basic principles which he applied in this case:

"It seems to me that it would be onerous in the extreme if a gain was held to be made out of a sum of money given to compensate for loss or expense without proper provision being made for deduction of such loss or expense actually suffered, and no such provision being made in the statute, I am not prepared to assume that the legislature has enacted anything so monstrously unjust or perverse".

The principles applied by Templeman J. in Davis v Powell were followed with approval in Drummond v Austin Brown. In that case it was held that compensation obtained by a tenant on determination of his tenancy by the landlord was not derived from an asset. The obligation to pay compensation to the tenant arose under the (UK) Landlord and Tenant Act 1954. It did not arise out of any of the terms of the lease which was terminated, nor did it arise as a result of private contract between the landlord and tenant. In the course of his judgement in the Court of Appeal Fox LJ. said:

"In our opinion the £31,384 was not derived from the lease. The word "derived" suggests a source. The right to the payment was, in our view, from one source only, namely the statute of 1954. The lease itself gives no right to such a payment. It was the statute, and the statute alone, which created the right to the payment. The statute simply created an entitlement where none would otherwise have existed. And in creating that entitlement it did not require that any provision be written into the lease. Thus, there is no deeming provision which would in any way require one to treat the lease as being the source of the entitlement. We do not think that the sum can be said to be derived from any asset."

The case of Davenport v Chilver considered what appeared on the face of it, to be a similar case to Davis v Powell and Drummond v Austin Brown. In the Chilver case the daughter of a deceased Mrs. Chilver became entitled to **compensation** relating to certain properties in Latvia which had been nationalised by the government of that country, and which prior to nationalisation, had been owned in part by Mrs. Chilver and in part by her two daughters. Under an agreement between the United Kingdom and the USSR, a fund was established to which persons whose property had been nationalised could apply for compensation. The entitlement to compensation was regulated by means of a government order made under the (UK) Foreign Compensation Acts 1950 and 1969. At the time when the compensation fell to be claimed, Mrs. Chilver was dead and the right under the statutes to compensation in respect of her assets was held by her two daughters. It was argued by the daughters that the compensation which they received was derived from a statute, and on the basis of the decision in the Powell, and Austin Brown cases, was not derived from an asset. In the Chancery division, Nourse J rejected this claim, saying:

*"It seems to me that Miss Chilver's right (to compensation) is one of very different order from Mr. Powells. Once the intended payment had been made to the (Compensation) Commission the affect of the 1969 order was to confer on Miss Chilver a right to share in a designated fund, subject to proof of title and value. That is a right which can, I think, fairly be described as an independent proprietary right, whereas the right to compensation under (the Landlord and Tenant Act) is a claim against the pocket of the landlord for expenses which the tenant's pocket is deemed already to have met. **It is a mere right of reimbursement**....There is no difficulty in saying that the 1969 order conferred on Miss Chilver, who had owned nothing beforehand, a form of property, and therefore an asset within (the CGT legislation)."*

Nourse J. here was making two separate points:

* The payments in the Powell case were merely reimbursing the tenant for the costs he would incur in giving up his tenancy. He described it as "a mere right to reimbursement".

* Reimbursement by its very nature excludes the possibility of gain, since it merely puts one back in the position that one was in before incurring expense.

He identified the asset from which Miss Chilver's compensation was derived, not as the statute, but as the right conferred by the statute on Miss Chilver, to the compensation. The statute might not be "property" owned by Miss Chilver, but the right to compensation which it conferred on her was such property. If that right to compensation was itself the source of the compensation, then the compensation was derived from an asset within the meaning of the CGT legislation.

Nourse J. also distinguished the case of Davis v Powell decision when he said:

"The learned judge (in the Davis v Powell case) did not have to consider whether the statutory right to compensation might itself have been a form of property and therefore an asset within (the CGT legislation). It was not necessary for him to look beyond the lease, that being the asset in respect of which the claim....was made (by the Inland Revenue)."

In the Powell case, Templeman J. did not have to rule on the point.

The Powell and Austin Brown cases were also discussed in the judgement in Zim Properties v Proctor (described below) as follows:

"(The Powell and Austin Brown cases) do not evince any principle beyond the general principle....that not every right to a payment is an "asset" for capital gains tax purposes."

4.2.7   "Asset" may include a "right to receive" a sum

The Davenport v Chilver case applies an argument that has arisen on several occasions in CGT cases in the UK. That is that a particular sum

— is derived from the right to receive that particular sum,

— rather than from whatever circumstance conferred the right to receive it on a person.

The logical consequence of applying such a principle is that every sum which a person receives, which is not a pure gift, is derived from a right to receive the sum, and accordingly is derived from an asset. That approach could be taken to extremes which are nonsensical.

This was recognised in Zim Properties Ltd. v Proctor where Warner J. said:

"I have no difficulty in accepting that not every right to a payment is an "asset" within the meaning of that term in the capital gains tax legislation. Perhaps the most obvious example of one that is not is the right of a seller of property to payment of its price. The relevant asset, then, is the property itself. But what that shows, however, to my mind, is no more than that the interpretation of the capital gains tax legislation requires, as does the interpretation of any legislation, the exercise of common sense, rather than just the brute application of verbal formulae."

This quotation should not be taken literally. In fact, probably "every right to a payment" may be an asset notwithstanding the comments of Warner J above. The important point is that the right to receive the sum is not necessarily the asset from which the particular capital sum was derived for CGT purposes. That topic is explored in greater detail in paragraph 4.4.

The identification of "**the right to receive a sum**" as an asset had already arisen earlier in the important case of Marren v Ingles where it found approval in the House of Lords. The facts in Marren v Ingles were described by Templeman L.J. (as he then was) as follows:

"On 15 September 1970 the taxpayers sold shares for £750 per share plus the right, to which I shall refer as the right to a future sum, to receive in certain unpredictable events an unquantifiable sum on an unascertainable date.....On 15 September 1970 the taxpayers received an asset. That asset was the right to a future sum and the nature of that asset was that it was incorporeal property."

Such was Lord Justice Templeman's characterisation of a transaction described by the Appeal Commissioners as "the vendors agreed to sell a total of 60 A ordinary shares....at a price per share of £750 plus "half of the profit"". The expression "half of the profit" was defined in the sale agreement in respect of the shares as half of the difference between the middle market price of the shares immediately after they were quoted, should they ever be quoted, to the extent that it exceeded the amount of £750 per share. In other words, the shares were originally sold for a consideration of £750 per share, which amount might fall to be increased (to an unspecified extent) if at any time in the future the shares should fall to be quoted on the stock exchange (which event was not certain). In the event the shares were quoted and the vendors of the shares received a further £2,055 per share under the contract which they had entered into in 1970 for the sale of the shares.

The implications of Marren v Ingles are discussed later in connection with the meaning of the word "disposal". All that need be noted at this point is that the decision which was approved in the House of Lords supported the view that **"the right to receive"** is an asset. There could be no doubt that it is an asset, and it did not require a judgement of the House of Lords to convince anyone of that.

The real issue is whether the sums received by the vendors of the shares on the occasion of the shares being quoted, were derived from

— the shares which they sold, or

— from the right to receive the additional consideration.

That issue is considered in more detail later (see paragraph 4.4.6).

4.2.8 "Right to sue" as an asset

Zim Properties Ltd. v Proctor is another UK case which identified an asset where one was not immediately apparent. Zim Properties Ltd. had entered into a contract to sell certain properties. The contract stated that time was of the essence i.e. that failure to complete various stages of the contract within the date stipulated on the contract would be a fatal breach of the contract. In the event Zim Properties were unable within the time limits stipulated to produce satisfactory proof of title to the properties to the purchaser who was able to repudiate the contract on those grounds. Zim Properties sued their lawyers on the grounds that the lawyers should have been aware of the difficulties which they faced in proving title to the properties, and therefore should not have permitted the contract to state that time was of the essence, without making particular provision relating to the difficulty of proving title. Zim Properties claimed that the properties were worth in the open market at the date the contract was repudiated less than their value when the contract was entered into and that they should be compensated by their solicitors for the loss occasioned by the repudiation of the contract.

They claimed that this compensation was derived from the properties which were the subject matter of the contract for sale (and in respect of which they had deductible base cost). The Revenue argued that the compensation was not derived from the properties (which had suffered no physical damage) but rather were derived from Zim Properties right of action against their solicitors arising out of the alleged negligence of the solicitors.

Warner J. summed up his conclusion in the case as follows:

"It seems to me that in the present case, if one looks at the taxpayer companies claim against the firm as it was pleaded, it would be true to say that the essence of it was that the taxpayer company had, in reliance on the negligent advice of the firm, acted to its detriment in entering into a contract in inappropriate terms and that the taxpayer company was thereby subjected to the risk of financial loss according to matters completely outside its control."

Warner J. accepted in those circumstances that **"the right to sue"** was the asset from which the compensation was derived. In arriving at this conclusion, he based his decision on the judgement given in the House of Lords in O'Brien v Bensons Hosiery (Holdings) Ltd, and said:

"It would in my view be inconsistent with the decision in O'Brien v Bensons Hosiery (Holdings) Ltd. to hold that a right to bring an action to seek to enforce a claim that was not frivolous or vexatious, which right could be turned to account by negotiating a compromise yielding a substantial capital sum, could not be an "asset" within the meaning of that term in the capital gains tax legislation. I propose, for the sake of convenience, to refer to the right that the taxpayer had, in that sense, to bring an action against the firm as its "right to sue" the firm."

Since the decision in the Zim Properties case the law has been amended by FA82. That amendment does not in any way affect the treatment of the consideration received, but merely ensures that the taxpayer cannot have a deductible base cost in respect of an asset which consists of the right to sue (see paragraph 16.2). It leaves the taxpayer in the position where the full consideration received is treated as the gain for CGT purposes.

4.2.9   **Letters of allotment**

In the case of Young v Phillips, Letters of Allotment in respect of shares were recognised as being assets (chooses in action) distinct from shares. That case was concerned not so much with the character of the letters of allotment as assets, but with the situs of the asset in question (the place where they were located).

4.2.10   **"Assets" - broad summary of case law**

The broad conclusions which may be drawn from the UK cases described above may be summarised as follows:

- In the CGT legislation, "assets" mean that which may be owned privately i.e. property.

- Something may be property notwithstanding that it is not transferable, provided it can be turned to account.

- Basic human rights (e.g. the right to compete) are not assets for the purposes of the CGT legislation.

- Statutes are not assets for the purposes of the CGT legislation **but** rights conferred by statutes may be assets for the purposes of the CGT legislation.

- The "right to receive" a sum is an asset.

- The "right to sue" is an asset.

4.2.11   **Land and buildings as an asset**

If a person who owns a site of land builds a building upon it, most non-technical laymen would, in common parlance, consider that he has acquired a new asset (i.e. the building which he has built upon the land). It would be common to view the building as a distinct asset from the land. In law, this is an incorrect view of the matter. The owner of land is, in broad terms, the owner of all buildings upon the land. When a person builds a building upon land, he changes the value of the land, the uses to which the land can be put, and the physical nature of the land. However, he does not change the nature of the asset which he owns. The nature of that asset was and remains, an interest in land.

Example 26

> *John bought a two acre site from his father in 1998. Two years later he had saved sufficient money to arrange for a contractor to build a house upon the site.*
>
> *John has not acquired a new asset in 2000, when the house is complete. All he owned before the contractor commenced work was the two acre site. In law, all he owns after the house is complete is the two acre site. At all times he is the owner of the land, and of all permanent fixtures upon it by reason of being the owner of the land. He does not separately own the land, and a house.*

s538

TCA97 s538 deems that strict legal position not to apply in certain circumstances. The section states that for the purpose of a disposal occasioned by the entire loss, destruction, dissipation, or extinction

s538(3)

of an asset (as provided for in s538(1)) or for the purposes of a disposal arising by reason of a "negligible value claim" under s538(2), **"a building and any permanent or semi-permanent structure in the nature of a building, may be regarded as an asset separate from the land on which it is situated".**

s538(3) goes on to state that in the event of a building being deemed to be disposed of by reason of s538(1) or s538(2) [see paragraph 4.4.2] the owner of the land shall be deemed to have sold, and immediately reacquired, the site of the building and any land occupied along with it for ancillary purposes. The deemed disposal and reacquisition of the site is for a consideration equal to its market value at the time.

S538 is discussed further in paragraph 20.5.

The UK case of Watton v Tippett, which is discussed in paragraph 26.1.1, considered whether a factory building subsequently sub-divided into two units constituted a single asset or two separate assets.

4.3	**Euro & Irish Currency - not an "asset"**
s532	As noted in paragraph 4.2.1, the legislation states that the term *asset* includes *"any currency other than Irish currency"*
s541A	As and from 1 January 1999 the euro is the currency of Ireland, and the Irish pound is a denomination of that currency.

The legal position has been well summarised in the Forfás EMU Business Awareness Campaign documentation issued in 1998.

Document 16 (*"The Legal Framework for the euro"*) states:

— *From 1 January 1999, the euro will be the currency of participating Member States.*

— *There will be a transitional period from 1 January 1999 until 31 December 2001 during which the principle of "no compulsion/no prohibition" will apply whereby economic agents will be free to use the euro, but will not be compelled to do so. Euro notes and coins will not be availanble until 1 January 2002.*

— *National currencies will continue to exist as denominations of the euro (during the transitional period).*

— *Euro notes and coins will be put into circulation on 1 January 2002: from that date they will be legal tender in all the participating Member States.*

— *From 1 January 2002, all contracts and legal instruments will be deemed to be in euro, at the fixed conversion rate, and the legal changeover will be complete - except that national currency notes and coins may remain legal tender for at most 6 months (this period may be shortened by national law).*

The countries participating in the EMU and the fixed conversion rates of exchange applying between those currencies and the euro are set out in the *TABLE on page vii* in the preliminary pages at the beginning of this book.

The national currencies of each of the participating States which joined the EMU on 1 January 1999 continue to exist for a 3 year period to 31 December 2001 as denominations of the euro. The Irish pound is also a denomination of the euro during that period.

It could be argued that as the Irish pound and the other national currencies which participate in the euro are all merely denominations of the euro, that they are all "Irish currency" (albeit not legal tender in Ireland) within the meaning of the CGT Acts.

An alternative view is that notwithstanding that the other national currencies are now also denominations of the euro, those national currencies will not be Irish currency, and after 1 January 1999, the Deutschemark, the French Franc etc., will remain currency other than Irish currency for CGT purposes (until 1 January 2002 when the euro becomes the common national currency of all participating Member States).

The matter is not beyond doubt, but s541A seems to favour the former view.

Other aspects of currency transactions are discussed in paragraphs 8.10 and 9.1.6 and 38.2.

4.4 What is a disposal?

4.4.1 Broad outline - what is a disposal?

s534

Although TCA97 s534 and s535 deal with the subject of *"disposal of assets"* they do not attempt to provide a comprehensive definition of what constitutes the disposal of an asset. What they do is to give an extended meaning to the ordinary meaning of that phrase. In particular it is provided that:

s534(a)

• a *disposal* of an asset normally *includes a part disposal* of an asset (unless the context otherwise requires),

s534(b)

• there is a *part disposal* of an asset where:

 −an interest or right in or over the asset is created by the disposal (as well as where it subsists before the disposal), and

 −on a person making a disposal, any description of property derived from the asset remains undisposed of.

s535(1)

• there is a disposal of an asset by its owner where a capital sum is derived from that asset (even if no asset is acquired by the person paying the capital sum) - see also paragraph 4.4.4,

Certain transactions are deemed not to constitute the disposal of an asset for the purposes of the CGT legislation. Examples of such transactions are:

s567(2)   — The transfer of an asset by a nominee or trustee to the person for whom he is the nominee, or to the person who is absolutely entitled against him as trustee to the asset.

s537(1)   — The transfer of an asset to another person by way of security for a liability or obligation. An example would be where a borrower transfers shares which he owns into the name of the lender where the shares are held by the lender solely as security for the borrowing. In such a case any transactions in respect of the asset by the person holding them as security shall be treated as transactions of the person entitled to the asset i.e. the person who transferred it to him as security,

s569   — The transfer of assets of an insolvent person to the trustee or assignee in bankruptcy,

s573   — Assets acquired on death by the personal representatives of the deceased person.

           — A list of specific items, transactions and events which are deemed not to be disposals for CGT purposes or which are otherwise exempt from a charge to CGT are set out in paragraph 32.

In the following text, the meaning of the term *disposal* is considered (in the context of CGT). The extension of that meaning to part disposals, and capital sums derived from assets is then considered.

4.4.2   The meaning of disposal

It is helpful to remember, in considering what the ordinary meaning of "disposal" may be, that we are discussing the disposal of "assets" in the context of the CGT legislation. As we have seen, in that context, "assets" mean property. In its ordinary meaning, a disposal of property occurs when a person gives up the rights which he has in an item of property.

It was stated by Nicholls LJ in the Court of Appeal (in Kirby v Thorn) *"there is no statutory definition of disposal but, having regard to the context, what is envisaged by that expression is a transfer of an asset (i.e. of ownership of an asset), as widely defined, by one person to another. The Act presupposes that, immediately prior to the disposal, there was an asset and that the disposer owned it."*

In the context of CGT, the term "disposal" does not necessarily imply any positive action on the part of the owner of the property. It is clearly contemplated in the legislation that the compulsory acquisition of land by a local authority having powers to compulsorily acquire property, constitutes the disposal of an asset by the person from whom the local authority compulsorily acquires it.

TCA97 s538 provides:

s538
"Subject to the Capital Gains Tax Acts and in particular to s540 , the occasion of the entire loss, destruction, dissipation or extinction of an asset shall for the purposes of those Acts, constitute a disposal of the asset whether or not any capital sum by way of compensation or otherwise is received in respect of the destruction, dissipation or extinction of the asset".

The affect of this sub-section is to treat any transaction or event upon, or as a result of which an asset *entirely* ceases to exist, as a disposal of that asset. An asset may cease entirely to exist without any positive action by its owner being taken to bring that about.

FA98 s67
However, it should be noted that special rules apply in computing the CGT consequences of such a deemed disposal arising from the "striking off" of a company where its assets pass to the State, and are subsequently passed back by the State to the shareholders - see paragraph 20.5.

Example 27

John owns a valuable painting by Jack B. Yeats. It is entirely destroyed during an accidental fire at his house, where the picture was kept.

John is treated as disposing of the picture on the occasion on which it is destroyed by fire, even though that resulted from no action of his.

The following are some everyday examples of transactions which would be regarded as the disposal of assets in the ordinary sense of the word:

- A sale of land

- A gift (as decided in the UK case of Turner v Follet)

- The determination of a lease of land, on the expiry of the period of the lease.

- The death of an animal

- The repayment of a debts

- The forgiveness of a debt

- The redemption of shares

- Shares ceasing to exist on a company being struck off the Companies Office register

- The destruction of an item of furniture in a fire

- An option ceasing to exist on the expiry of the period during which it could be exercised;

- An option ceasing to exist upon the exercise of the option.

s540   It should be noted that there are special rules dealing with options which modify the operation of the general rule regarding disposals. Those special rules are set out in paragraph 39.

4.4.3   Part disposals

s534(1)   TCA97 s534 provides that references in the CGT Acts to a "disposal" include a references to a "**part disposal**." It goes on to state that generally there is a part disposal of an asset where, on a person making a disposal, any description of property derived from the asset remains undisposed of. Further details of the wording of s534 on part disposals is set out in paragraph 4.4.3, and the main consideration of the area (part disposals) is set out in paragraph 11.

As already noted, a disposal includes a part disposal. From the point of view of determining whether a particular transaction or event results in a disposal of an asset, it is not important whether it is a disposal, or a part disposal of that asset. It is only when we come to the actual computation of the gain or loss that it is relevant. In very broad terms, if only part of the asset is disposed of, then only part of the cost is allowed in computing the gain or loss on disposal. This is the only importance of the distinction between a disposal and a part disposal of an asset.

Example 28

John owns his own house. On marrying Mary, he transfers a half share in the house to Mary. The house is thereafter owned by them to the extent of 50% each as tenants in common.

John has disposed of a half share in the house, but he retains a half share. He has made a part disposal of the property.

There are many special rules which apply between married persons (see paragraph 33) and also a special relief which applies on the disposal of an individual's principal private residence (see paragraph 24). However, none of those special rules change the fact that he has made a part disposal of the house. Those rules only affect the calculation of the amount the gain or of the tax (if any) payable as a result of the transaction.

S534 also states that there is a part disposal of an asset where an interest or right in or over the asset is created by the disposal.

Example 29

John and Mary have just married. John doesn't own a house. Mary's father grants John a two year lease of a house which Mary's father owns.

The granting of the lease creates a right over the house, which did not exist prior to it being granted. The granting of the lease represents a part disposal by Mary's father of his interest in the house (the land) - see Chapter 7 (leases).

It can on occasions be difficult to determine whether a particular disposal represents the disposal of an asset, or whether it represents the disposal of a section of a larger asset (of which the item disposed of forms only part). This distinction can be important in determining the amount of a gain or loss arising on that disposal. The question of part disposals is dealt with in paragraph 11.

The UK case of Strange v Openshaw confirmed that the grant of an option was to be treated as the disposal of an asset consisting of the option; and not as a part disposal of the asset over which the option was granted.

4.4.4 Capital sums derived from assets.

In the ordinary sense of the word "disposal" the receipt of a capital sum from an asset may not, in itself, be regarded as a disposal of the asset. It would not necessarily involve the cessation of (or transfer of) ownership rights in the asset, or the entire extinction of the asset.

s535(2)

TCA97 s535 provides that, subject to exceptions in the Act, there is *"a disposal of assets by their owner where any capital sum is derived from assets notwithstanding that no asset is acquired by the person paying the capital sum...."*

For a disposal to occur under this rule, a taxpayer should receive:

• a **capital sum** which is

• **derived from**

• an **asset**

The meaning of "asset" has been examined in paragraph 4.2 above. In the following paragraphs, the meaning of **"capital sum"** is examined, and in particular, the difficulties of determining which asset (if any) a capital sum is **derived** from.

However these are not necessarily the only circumstances in which a disposal of an asset will be deemed to occur by reason of s535(2). After the words quoted above, s535(2) goes on to state:

"and this paragraph applies in particular to:

(i) *Capital sums received by way of* **compensation** *for any kind of damage or injury to assets or for the loss, destruction or dissipation of assets or for any depreciation or risk of depreciation of an asset,*

(ii) *Capital sums received under a policy of* **insurance** *of the risk of any kind of damage or injury to, or the loss or destruction of, assets,*

(iii) *Capital sums received from the* **forfeiture** *or surrender of rights, or from refraining from exercising rights, and*

(iv) *Capital sums received as* **consideration for use** *or exploitation of assets."*

Great difficulty has been experienced in the interpretation of s535(2), as evidenced by a difference of opinion between members of the UK Judiciary on the interpretation of that sub-section. The sub-section (as set out above) consists of :

- a general introduction, deeming a disposal where a capital sum is derived from an asset, followed by

- four "lettered" paragraphs, dealing specifically with receipts derived from compensation, insurance, forfeiture of rights, and consideration for the use of an asset. The four lettered paragraphs are introduced by the words *'and this paragraph applies in particular to -'*

The problem was well summarised by Ralph Gibson LJ in giving his judgement in the UK Court of Appeal (in Pennine Raceways v Kirklees MC) when he said:

"A question was raised in argument as to whether Warner J was right in holding that a case could not fall within the particular provisions of any of the lettered paragraphs of [s535(2)] unless the case was shown to be covered by the introductory words of the section, namely a 'capital sum ....derived from assets'. Nourse J (as he was then) in Davenport v Chilver held that as a matter of construction, the particular examples contained in the lettered paragraphs stand on their own feet and, if necessary, prevail over the general words. Warner J (in Zim Properties v Proctor) took the view and the contrary view was not argued before him, that the opinion of Nourse J must be regarded as mistaken in the light of speeches of Lord Wilberforce and Lord Frazer in Marren v Ingles". He then proceeded to mention a book in which it was suggested that the view of Warner J was based on a misreading of passages in Marren v Ingles. Having noted that he had not heard full argument on the point, and that it was not necessary for him to decide the issue, he proceeded .. *"but my inclination is to agree with the conclusion of Nourse J".*

The interpretation of Nourse J was commented on favourably in the same case by Ralph Gibson LJ where he said at page 134:

"In my judgement, the cases covered by the words [in s535(2) quoted above] are intended to be within the deemed disposal provision without proof of further requirement."

On the same issue, Stuart Smith LJ (Pennine Raceways v Kirklees MC) in dealing with the difference of opinion in interpretation, stated *"I am content to assume that the narrower construction favoured by Warner J is correct".*

Until the matter is ruled on by an Irish court, it would be unwise to base any material matter on an unnecessary interim personal interpretation.

In the case of Chaloner v Pellipar Investments the UK High Court rejected the submission that Marren v Ingles was authority for the proposition that the reference in s535(2) "did not apply to any case where the payer of the capital sum received an asset "in exchange" for the capital sum." Rattee J said "*Lord Fraser (in Marren v Ingles) – clearly expressed the view that "not withstanding" in [s535(2)] meant "whether or not", with the result that the subsection applied whether or not an asset was acquired by the payer of the relevant capital sum in exchange for the capital sum.*"

s535(2)

He went on to express his view that the consideration received for the disposal of an asset (which is what was involved in the Pellipar Investments case) could not be "capital sums received as consideration for use or exploitation of assets" as referred to in s535(2)(IV). That is one of the specific instances described in the legislation of a capital sum derived from an asset. Rattee J said "*those words are apt to include capital sums received as consideration for the use or exploitation of assets, title to which remains unaffected in their owner – but are not apt to include capital sums received as consideration for a grant of the owner's title to the assets, whether absolutely or for a term of years.*"

4.4.5   Capital sum NOT derived from an asset

An obvious example of a capital sum which is not derived from an asset is a capital sum received by way of *gift*. In such a case the capital sum is derived (in all probability) from the benevolence of the disponer who makes the gift. The gratitude or goodwill or sense of obligation of another person is not an asset in the sense in which the word is used in the Capital Gains Tax Acts. It was noted in paragraph 4.2.3 that the UK courts have equated the word "asset" in the context of the Capital Gains Tax Acts with property, i.e. with something which may be owned.

A second example of a capital sum which might be derived from something other than an asset is a capital sum which is derived from a **liability**. Such an event would be rare and it is difficult to think of a practical instance of such an event. An example might be a sum received by a debtor from his creditor in return for his agreement to repay a debt earlier than its due date. The creditor might make such a payment if he was under financial pressure and required early repayment. More usually however, he would agree to accept a lesser sum than the nominal amount owing, in return for early discharge of the debt. In the latter instance there would certainly be a capital profit arising from the liability, but no capital sum would have been received by the debtor.

The UK cases of Davis v Powell and Drummond v Austin Brown provide a third example of a capital sum not derived from an asset.

Those cases were concerned with **statutory compensation**. In the Drummond v Austin Brown case, Fox LJ in the Court of Appeal said *"the word "derived" suggests a source. The right to the payment (of the compensation) was, in our view, from one source only, namely the statute of 1954....It was the statute, and the statute alone, which created the right to the payment....We do not think that the sum can be said to be derived from any asset."*

In Davis v Powell, Templeman J (as he then was) dealt with the case of Mr. Powell, a taxpayer who was paid £591 by way of compensation for disturbance under the Agricultural Holdings Act of 1948. Templeman J said:

".... it does not seem to me that the compensation paid under (the Agricultural Holdings Act 1948) is derived from the asset, namely the lease. It is not derived from an asset at all; it is simply a sum which Parliament says should be paid for expense and loss which are unavoidably incurred after the lease has gone"

While those two cases concerned with statutory compensation are interesting instances where the courts held that capital sums received by a taxpayer were not derived from assets, they do not establish any general principle that sums derived either directly or more remotely from a statute are not derived from an asset. It was stated in the judgement in Zim Properties v Proctor:

"(The Powell and Austin Brown cases) do not evince any principle beyond the general principle.... that not every right to a payment is an "asset" for capital gains tax purposes".

Neither should the decisions in the Powell and Austin Brown cases be taken to imply that all capital sums received by way of compensation are inherently outside the scope of capital gains tax. In the case of Davenport v Chilver the compensation received by a taxpayer by virtue of the UK statutory order was held to be derived from an asset for the purposes of capital gains tax.

The UK case of Pennine Raceways v Kirklees MC is another instance in which statutory compensation was held to derive from an asset, for the purposes of capital gains tax. Pennine Raceways Ltd. received compensation under the Town and Country Planning Act 1971 (UK) for loss of income and other costs incurred as a result of the revocation of the planning permission which they held and which permitted them to conduct drag racing on a disused airfield. The taxpayer argued that the compensation received was derived from the statute and that on the basis of the decisions in the Powell and Austin Brown cases, the compensation was not derived from an asset and accordingly did not give rise to a disposal for the purposes of capital gains tax. The Court of Appeal firmly rejected the suggestion that the Powell or Austin Brown case had established any principle that all statutory compensation lay outside the ambit of capital gains tax. In the course of his judgement, Croom-Johnson LJ said:

"The authorities cited by counsel....do not support the general proposition that compensation awarded by statute is outside .... the [UK] Capital Gains Tax Act 1979. One must look in each case to see whether the capital sum is "derived" from the asset or from something else, and in this connection one should properly approach the question in the way adopted by Warner J. in Zim Properties v Proctor (1985) STC 90 at page 107 where, after saying that it would be a mistake to say that the asset from which a capital sum is derived must always be the asset that constitutes its immediate source", he went on to say: "The true view is hinted at by Fox J. in O'Brien v Benson's Hosiery (Holdings) Ltd. (1979) STC 735 when he referred to the reality of the matter. One has to look in each case for the real (rather than the immediate) source of the capital sum. In the present case the company had an asset, which was the licence, and that licence depreciated in value when the planning permission was revoked. For that depreciation they are entitled to a capital sum by way of compensation, and their right to the compensation is given by - the Town and Country Planning Act 1971 - because their asset has sustained loss or damage which is directly attributable to the revocation of permission. It is clear that the capital sum is "derived" from the asset".

Stewart-Smith LJ in the same case expressed much the same point in the following manner:

"....The mere fact that the right to compensation is statutory as opposed to one arising as common law does not of itself prevent the capital sum being derived from the asset."

In the 1995 case of Davis v Henderson the UK Special Commissioners held that sums paid to a tenant on giving up his tenancy under the Landlord and Tenant Acts were covered by the principle in Davis v Powell notwithstanding that the issue of a notice to quit by the landlord to the tenant occurred after negotiations between them, and after the tenant had requested that such a notice be served on him as a pre-condition to quitting the tenancy. An additional sum paid to get early possession of the property was agreed to be taxable.

- **Published Revenue Commissioners precedent:**

- In a published precedent the Revenue Commissioners have accepted that the premium paid under the EU scheme of **Installation Aid for Young Farmers** is a capital sum not derived from an asset. Their thinking is not further elaborated but presumably the sum is regarded as being derived from a statute, and any question of a "right to receive" is (correctly in the authors' view) disregarded as being the source (see further details in paragraph 4.4.6).

4.4.6   **Capital sum - derived from which asset?**

In Drummond v Austin Brown in the Court of Appeal, Fox LJ said *"The word "derived" suggests a source"*.

In order to determine whether a particular capital sum is derived from an asset, one must consider the source of that capital sum. Although this task may seem straight forward, a difficulty arises in that you may have to chose between an immediate source, and a less immediate or more indirect source.

The difficulties which have tended to arise in cases which have appeared before the UK courts in relation to capital sums received by taxpayers have been not so much to determine whether the capital sums are derived from an asset, from a liability, or from neither (a matter which is rarely in doubt) but rather to identify the precise asset from which the capital sum is derived.

The UK case of Marren v Ingles concerned the identification of which of a number of assets a capital sum was derived from. That case, and the related case of Marson v Marraige are discussed in detail in paragraph 8.8 (dealing with contingent proceeds). The taxpayer had disposed of shares in return for:

"£750 per share plus the right,.....to receive in certain unpredictable events an unquantifiable sum on an unascertainable future date."

Subsequently the taxpayers did receive a sum of money in respect of a contingent future right to additional consideration. Templeman LJ held that the capital sum ultimately received was derived, not from the original sale of shares, but from the right to receive a future sum (the unquantifiable sum due on the happening of certain contingent events, at a future unascertainable date). The shares, whose sale gave rise to the right to receive the sum, might have been seen as a more remote source from which the sum was derived.

The decision had to be made between these two sources. The decision of the court was in favour of the **"right to receive"** that contingent future sum, as being the relevant source .

The case of Davenport v Chilver was concerned with compensation paid to the Chilver sisters in respect of land expropriated in Latvia by the USSR.

In addition to seeking compensation for the land which they themselves had held in Latvia, the Chilver sisters also received compensation in respect of land which had been held in Latvia by their mother, and which also had suffered nationalisation. The nationalisation had occurred before the death of Mrs. Chilver and therefore the Chilver sisters had not been able to inherit the land in Latvia from their mother. Mrs. Chilver had died before the compensation scheme was put in effect so she did not, in her own right, ever acquire rights to compensation before her death, and therefore her daughters did not inherit such rights from her as an asset. In that case, Nourse J said

"Miss Chilver acquired (from her mother) no more than a hope that she would one day receive her share of compensation. It was no different from the hope of succeeding under the will of a living person - a mere spes successionis. That is something which has never been treated as property in England law. In my judgement it is not a form of property and therefore not an asset for the purpose of (the CGT legislation)."

At this point it might seem that the Chilver sisters could not have been said to have derived a capital sum from an asset. They had not owned the land in Latvia in respect of which they were being compensated (in right of their mother). The compensation was coming to them under a statute and was in the nature of compensation. Although in the Austin Brown and Powell case the statutory compensation with which those cases were concerned was held not to be derived from an asset, Nourse J did not feel that they established any principle which bound him in the context of the Chilver case. He held that the compensation was derived from the "right to receive" conferred by the statute and hence from an asset. He justified his disregarding of the two earlier decisions on compensation on the grounds that the Judges in those cases had not been asked to consider whether the compensation was a capital sum derived from **"the right to receive"** conferred by the Statute. He did not explicitly state that those cases were wrongly decided, nor was it within his power to override those decisions. Nonetheless, it is difficult to totally reconcile the decision in Davenport v Chilver with the decisions in the Powell and Austin Brown cases.

The decision in Davenport v Chilver, and the earlier decision in Marren v Ingles, create a difficulty in that, except in the case of gifts, any capital sum received is usually received because the recipient has a right to receive it. In many instances there may therefore be more than one asset from which it may be argued that a capital sum is derived. It may be derived most immediately from the right to receive the capital sum, but derived less immediately from some other asset, in relation to which the right to receive the sum arose. In the Marren v Ingles case the "right to receive" the future contingent consideration arose from the sale of shares. That future contingent consideration, when it was received, was no doubt viewed by the recipients as merely being the final part of the consideration for the shares they had sold. But so far as the Courts were concerned, it was derived, not from the shares, but from "the right to receive".

Some of these difficulties were recognised in Zim Properties Limited v Proctor by Warner J when he said:

"I have no difficulty in accepting that not every right to a payment is an "asset" within the meaning of that term in the capital gains tax legislation. Perhaps the most obvious example of one that is not is the right of a seller of

property to payment of its price. The relevant asset, then, is the property itself. What that shows, however, to my mind, is no more than that the interpretation of the capital gains tax legislation requires, as does the interpretation of any legislation, the exercise of common sense, rather than just the brute application of verbal formulae".

One of the arguments used to justify the conclusion in Marren v Ingles that the final traunch of consideration was derived from the right to receive it, rather than from the earlier sale of shares, was that subsequent to the sale of shares, and before the receipt of the final traunch, there existed an undoubted asset - "the right to receive". That asset could have been sold at any time prior to the final traunch being received. Had it been sold, the moneys received from its sale would quite clearly have been derived from the sale of that right to receive, and not from the earlier sale of shares.

That is certainly true, and there is no doubt that, following on the original sale of the shares, and before the receipt of the final traunch of consideration in the Marren v Ingles case, the vendor of the shares did hold an asset (his right to receive the future contingent traunch of consideration). But the fact that he held such an asset, and the fact that if he had sold such an asset, his gain on the sale of that asset would not be derived from the earlier sale of shares, does not necessarily mean that it was the asset from which the subsequent final traunch of consideration was derived.

Undoubtedly it was most convenient in the Marren v Ingles case that the judges were able to reach the conclusion which they did reach, as it saved considerable computational problems which do not arise in a straight forward case of a sale of property. But the function of judges (in the Irish courts, as opposed to the UK courts) is to interpret the law as they find it, and not particularly to solve problems. Until the Irish courts have had occasion to consider the matter, some doubt must exist as to whether they will adopt the approach of attributing capital sums to "the right to receive" those sums rather than to some less immediate asset.

The issue was referred to in the case of Pinewood Developments Ltd., Healy Homes Ltd. and Daniel Healy v the Minister for the Environment and Ireland. That High Court case concerned an award of damages by the European Court of Human Rights. The issue was whether the damages were derived from land owned by the plaintiffs, or from more basic rights which are not assets within the meaning of the Capital Gains Tax Acts. The issue was not considered by the Courts as it was possible for them to deal with the case before them by reference to other matters.

Unfortunately none of the cases to date indicate clear rules by which one may determine when a "right to receive" is the relevant asset from which the subsequent capital sum is derived, and when it is not.

4.4.7   **Meaning of "capital sum"**

s535(1)
The extensive guidance from income tax cases, both in Ireland and in the UK, as to the distinction between sums of money which are capital, and those which are revenue are not as relevant to the consideration of the meaning of the phrase "capital sum" in the context of CGT. TCA97 s535(1) gives a detailed definition of the phrase for the purposes of the CGT legislation, and that meaning is not necessarily the same as the ordinary meaning of the phrase. The definition given in s535 is:

"Capital sum" means any money or moneys worth which is not excluded from the consideration taken into account in the computation under Chapter 2 (of Part 19)".

This definition does not necessarily exclude receipts of an income nature from the meaning of *capital sum,* but merely excludes items specifically excluded by Chapter 2 of Part 19. That Chapter sets out the rules for computing a gain or loss on disposal of an asset. The rules contained in that Chapter are wide and complex. As a very broad rule, amounts taxed as income are not taken into account in the computation of a gain or loss for CGT purposes. However, this is only a broad general rule, and not every receipt of an income nature is necessarily excluded under this broad rule.

s551(2)
The exclusions referred to above (in the definition of capital sum) are set out in s551(2) in the following terms:

"Any money or moneys worth charged to income tax as income of, or taken into account as a receipt in computing income, profits, gains or losses for the purposes of the Income Tax Acts of the person making the disposal"

s544(2)
This provision is further expanded by s544(2), in that it provides that any references in s551 to sums taken into account as receipts (or as expenditure) in computing profits, gains or losses for the purposes of the Income Tax Acts shall include references to *"sums which would be so taken into account but for the fact that any profits or gains of a trade, profession or employment are not chargeable to income tax or that losses are not allowable for those purposes"*:

s551
S551 then goes on to provide an exception to this general rule, in that certain sums are not to be excluded from consideration in a CGT computation even though they may be taken into account in the computation of income. The exceptions are:

s707
s551(2)
• certain sums taken into account in accordance with s707 in computing the expenses of management of life assurance companies.

s551(3)
• sums taken into account in computing a balancing charge on the disposal of plant and machinery, or an industrial building.

s551(4)

- the capitalised value of the right to a rent (as in a case where rent is exchanged for some other asset) or of a right of any other description to income or to payments in the nature of income over a period, or to a series of payments in the nature of income.

These specific exceptions are not excluded from the meaning of *capital sum*, and may be taken into account as proceeds of disposal (or part thereof) for CGT purposes.

The definition of "Capital Sum" is very wide. It is so wide that it is impossible to discuss comprehensively the range of receipts which might fall within it.

- **Revenue Commissioners published precedent:**

— In a published precedent the Revenue Commissioners have indicated that the premium payable by the European Union in respect of the *grubbing up of orchards* is regarded as a capital receipt rather than an income receipt. The precedent does not identify the asset from which the capital receipt is deemed to be derived ie whether it is the farmland or whether it is from a separate right existing under EU legislation. The topic of the identification of the asset from which the capital sum is derived has been considered in paragraph 4.4.6.

— In a further published precedent the Revenue Commissioners have stated *"The EEC Scheme of Installation Aid for Young Farmers,* which was introduced by EEC Council Regulation No. 797/85 provides for the payment to farmers of a single premium. Such a payment may be treated as a capital sum which will not give rise to a charge to capital gains tax as there is no disposal of an asset."

s544(2)

An obvious difficulty could arise in relation to income which is in one form or another exempted from income tax. In the case of tax exempt receipts of a trade, profession or employment, the position is clear. Such receipts are deemed to be taken into account for income tax purposes by s544(2) - see above. The other main income tax exemptions are normally given in terms of the income being *"disregarded for all purposes of the Income Tax Acts"*, which may not necessarily extend to CGT.

Such items would include stallion fees, and income from woodlands. It seems unlikely that a court would accept the argument that when the Oireachtas confers an exemption from income tax on what is clearly "income", it is to be taken as automatically imposing a charge to CGT, although making no specific mention of this CGT charge. However, it must be accepted that the position is not entirely clear. It is difficult to accept that an exemption from income tax merely creates an exposure to liability to capital gains tax.

Other areas where no income tax is payable may arise out of reliefs, but this is an easier problem to deal with. Where relief is involved, the receipt is taken into account in computing income, and it is the tax payable which is relieved.

A person neither resident nor ordinarily resident in Ireland may be within the charge to Irish capital gains tax if they hold shares in a company deriving its value from land in Ireland. This is discussed in paragraph 3.4. If such an non resident person received a dividend from such a non resident company, that dividend would have no connection with the Irish tax system in any income tax context. It would not be taken into account in computing any Irish income tax and the fact that it is not taken into account would not be because any trade, profession or employment (see s544(2) is not within the charge to Irish income tax. Rather it arises because dividends from that non resident company are not within the charge to Irish income tax. Although the conclusion might seem very strange indeed, that opens up the risk that such a dividend is a capital sum derived from an asset which is within the charge to Irish capital gains tax. That in turn would raise withholding tax issues - see paragraph 94. This issue is a distinct matter from that of pre-disposal dividends which are discussed in paragraph 51.6.

Compensation paid by one member of a group of companies to another group member is discussed in paragraph 76.12.

s20
s129

A distribution from an Irish resident company (no matter what the form of the distribution) is chargeable to income tax under sch F. (TCA97 s20). Irish resident companies are chargeable to corporation tax rather than to income tax. TCA97 s129 provides that corporation tax shall not be charged on the distributions of a company resident in the State nor shall such distributions be taken into account in computing income for corporation tax. This rule is subject to a number of exceptions, in particular relating to dividends on certain preference shares, which are subject to corporation tax even when paid between resident companies.

s129

It is to be noted that s129, which forbids the taking into account of dividends of a resident company in computing income for corporation tax purposes, does not prohibit them being taken into account for the purpose of computing chargeable gains for corporation tax purposes.

s583

TCA97 s583 provides that a person, on becoming entitled to receive in respect of shares in a company any capital distribution from the company, should be treated for capital gains tax purposes as if he had made a part disposal of his shares in return for the capital distribution. Specifically for the purpose of that section only, "capital distribution" is defined as any distribution from a company other than one which in the hands of the recipient constitutes income for the purposes of income tax.

s78 TCA97 s78(6) substitutes corporation tax for references to income tax, insofar as the CGT Acts are applied to a companies capital gains.

The combination of provisions outlined above have given rise to some controversy in the UK. The Inland Revenue, in a statement of practice SP4/89 "company purchase of own shares" have taken the view that where a company buys back its own shares any distribution from the company in relation to that transaction may be taken into account in the capital gains tax computation on the disposal of the shares by another resident company. On the other hand, they are of the view that any dividend paid by a company does not represent a capital distribution from the company and does not give rise to a disposal or part disposal of shares.

The view expressed by the Revenue is strongly dissented from by Bramwell in paragraph 13-22 of the 1994 edition of Capital Gains Tax by Bramwell, published by Sweet & Maxwell.

It is not intended to go over the arguments here, as in the opinion of the authors, the arguments do not point decisively to any one conclusion. Any arguments based on a reading of the words of the relevant sections leave the matter open to further argument.

One argument which might recommend itself to a Court would be:

s129 • the proceeds of a buyback of shares (insofar as they exceed the sum originally subscribed) are not inherently income. They are income for the purposes of income tax solely because the income tax acts impose a charge to tax upon the excess under schedule F. In truth however, it is a capital sum which is specifically brought within the charge to income tax subject to the provisions of s129.

s76 • S76 provides that "except where otherwise provided by the tax acts, the amount of any income shown for the purposes of corporation tax be computed in accordance with income tax principles, all questions as to the amounts which are or are not to be taken into account as income, or in computing income - - being determined in accordance with income tax law".

s129 • S129 provides that distributions shall not be taken into account in computing income for corporation tax purposes which is certainly an exception to one element of s76. However s129 does not state that a distribution is not to "be taken into account as income". It merely says it is not to be taken into account in computing income. The two matters are separately dealt with in s76, and s129 would seem to be an exception to one only of the two matters.

s76 • The fact that a distribution may be required "to be taken into account as income" by s76 does not result in any charge on a company in receipt of a distribution because s129 provides that corporation tax is not chargeable on distributions of a company resident in the state.

s583

- On the argument above, it would follow that because under income tax principles (to be followed for corporation tax purposes in determining what is income) distributions by resident companies are treated as income, it follows that they are indeed income for the purposes of the corporation tax acts although not chargeable to corporation tax on income. It follows therefore that they are not a "capital distribution" as referred to in section 583, because in the hands of a resident company, they do constitute income for the purposes of corporation tax, albeit corporation tax is not charged upon them by reason of a specific exemption.

The authors are not aware of the attitude of the Revenue Commissioner to the approach of the UK Inland Revenue as set out in Statement of Practice SP4/89.

A "close company" may also be able to argue that a distribution from an Irish resident company is taken into account in the computation of income for corporation tax purposes, in the particular context of surcharge on undistributed investment income

- **Revenue/Chief Inspector's CGT Manual:**

—On a reorganisation of share capital, a shareholder may sometimes receive a small cash sum in lieu of an entitlement of a fraction of a share in the course of the reorganisation. If that sum is small, the Revenue Commissioners at paragraph 19.4.6.16 of their CGT manual indicate that it should not be treated as a capital sum derived from the shares, but may, with the consent of the shareholder, be treated as a reduction of his base cost.

This treatment may not suit a taxpayer who has not otherwise used his annual CGT exempt amount.

4.5 Compensation as an asset

4.5.1 Compensation - income or capital receipt?

Where compensation is received and the receipt is related to a business activity, the question of whether the receipt is chargeable as income, or as the proceeds of disposal of an asset may be a difficult one to resolve.

In Lang v Rice the taxpayer received compensation from the Northern Ireland Office, following the bombing of his Belfast business premises. The premises were rented, and not owned by the taxpayer. The compensation was in four separate parts, i.e.

—Loss of Trade Stock

—Damage to and loss of contents of the buildings,

—Consequential Loss (Loss of profits) and

— Tenant's Improvements.

He was assessed to CGT on the consequential loss compensation. The Revenue contended that it was a once and for all capital payment which was made when it was known that the business had ceased permanently, to compensate for the loss of the business. It was held that the compensation was nothing more than compensation for the loss of profits which could have been earned during the period which it would have taken to reinstate the premises following the damage. Accordingly it was an income receipt.

In Glenboig Union Fireclay Company Ltd v IRC a company whose business was mining for fireclay received compensation from a railway company for the fireclay in an area of its land reserved by the railway company under statutory powers. It was held in the House of Lords that the compensation was not income, but consideration for a capital asset which had been rendered unavailable for the purpose of the fireclay company's business. As Wrenbury LJ said, *"the compensation was the price paid for sterilising the asset from which otherwise a profit might have been obtained"*.

In London and Thames Haven Oil Wharves v Attwooll the taxpayers jetty was damaged by the negligent handling of an oil tanker. They received compensation which was divided between the physical damage to the jetty, and consequential loss (loss of profits) due to the jetty being out of use for the 380 days which it took until the repairs were completed.

The question for consideration by the court was whether the receipt for the consequential loss was income in the hands of the taxpayer. It was held in the Court of Appeal that the compensation was income, because it was not received in respect of the sterilisation of a capital asset : it fell to be treated as a trading receipt of the taxpayer.

The position of such receipts was summarised by Diplock LJ in that case in the following words:

"An alternative way in which Mr Monroe puts it is that the £21,000 compensation was paid to the taxpayers for not using their capital asset, the jetty. But I think that this is no more than ingenious semantics designed to bring the case within some of the words used in the Glenboig case. It was paid for the loss which they suffered because owing to the wrongful act of the tanker owners they were unable to use the jetty just as the taxpayer in the Ensign case was unable to use his ship by reason of a paramount power of the Crown, in the Burmah case by the ship repairers breach of contract and in the British Colombia Fir and Cedar Lumber Company case because the taxpayer was unable to use his premises because of the occurence of the risk insured against.

These cases are to be contrasted with cases where compensation is paid for the destruction or permanent deprivation of the capital asset used by a trader for the purposes of his trade. There the asset thereafter ceased to be one by the use or exploitation of which the trader carries on his trade. As a result of such destruction or deprivation the trader ipso facto abandons that part of his trade which involves the use of the capital asset of which he has been deprived..... Even if the compensation payable for the loss of the capital asset has been calculated in whole or in part by taking into consideration what profits he would have made had he continued to carry on a trade involving the use or exploitation of the asset, this does not alter the identity of what the compensation is paid for, to wit, the permanent removal from his business of a capital asset which would otherwise have continued to be exploited in the business".

The principle set out above were approved in Raja's Commercial College v Gian Singh & Co Ltd.

The judgement in the Attwooll case referred to above was critically considered in the Court of Appeal in the UK in the case of Deeny v Gooda Walker. In the Gooda Walker case the so called "replacement principle" set-out in the Attwooll case was challenged. That principle was stated in the Attwooll case by Diplock LJ as follows:

"Where, pursuant to a legal right, a trader receives from another person compensation for the traders failure to receive a sum of money which, if it had been received, would have been credited to the amount of profits (if any) arising in any year from the trade carried on by him at the time when the compensation was so received, the compensation is to be treated for income tax purposes in the same way as that sum of money would have been treated if it had been received instead of the compensation. The rule is applicable whatever the source of the legal right of the trader to recover the compensation."

Interestingly, the Court of Appeal was divided on the question of whether such a rule was valid. Two of the judges held that it was, and one judge had reservations. Simon Brown LJ who held at it was a valid rule, said:

" – for the various payments to be held to be taxable receipts, the taxpayers in obtaining them must properly be regarded as having acted in the ordinary course of their business enterprise. In that sense the receipt can properly be said to arise from the taxpayers business. – The plain fact is that the proper conduct of business from time to time requires resort to that law to recover sums of money which would otherwise be lost to the business' profitability."

The dissenting judge, Saville LJ, said: *" – I cannot accept the "replacement principle" but instead apply the test propounded in the cases I have cited, namely whether the receipt in question arises from, in this case, the underwriting business of the member. This, after all, is what the statute itself provides."*

In effect, Saville LJ was saying that not every compensation received for the loss of a business receipt, or the incurring of a business expense necessarily in every circumstances arises from the trade in question. One had to independently ask whether it did so arise. The majority of the Court of Appeal felt that the principle in the Attwooll case was satisfactory. The matter has not had to be decided in Ireland to-date.

In the case of Beveridge v Ellam the UK Special Commissioners ruled that not all payments received for the sterilisation of an asset were necessarily capital in nature. The case concerned periodic payments made by the French Government to an employee made compulsorily redundant by an industrial firm, in line with a government programme to create new job opportunities for younger people. The Special Commissioner noted that the payments were not instalments of a predetermined capital sum. He accepted that they were made in compensation for the sterilisation of the taxpayer's right to pursue his profession and exercise his skills (something which the Commissioners held that the taxpayer would be unlikely to do in all the circumstances, following his redundancy). Nonetheless it was held that a series of payments which were not instalments of a capital sum were income in nature notwithstanding that they were to compensate for the sterilisation of a capital asset.

The Beveridge v Ellam case was concerned with an assessment to income tax, and not with an assessment to capital gains tax. It did not consider whether the taxpayer had derived a capital sum, consisting of the right to receive the subsequent payments (as opposed to the payments themselves) which right was derived from an asset i.e. the ability to carry on a profession. While the goodwill of a profession is a chargeable asset, and the receipt of a capital sum derived from it could give rise to a chargeable gain, the freedom or ability to practice a profession is unlikely to be a chargeable asset so the point as to whether the taxpayer did or did not derive a capital sum, in the form of the right to the subsequent income stream, may be academic.

4.5.2   Exempt compensation

Many forms of compensation are specifically exempt from tax. Further details are set out in paragraph 32.8 in the reference there to compensation received for personal or professional wrongs or injuries suffered by an individual, and to compensation to hepatitis sufferers.

4.5.3   Insurance policies

The owner of a property which has suffered damage may receive compensation for that damage from an insurance company, if the risk of damage had been covered by a policy of insurance.

s535(2)(a)(i)   S535(2) provides that there is a disposal of assets by their owner where a capital sum is received under a policy of insurance in respect of damage or injury to him or in respect of loss or depreciation of assets.

s535(2)(b)   s535(2) then goes on to state that notwithstanding the provision quoted above, which ensures that the receipt of insurance compensation in respect of the loss of an asset, or damage to an asset will always be treated as the occasion of the disposal of an asset, neither the rights of the insured under a policy of insurance (other than a life policy), nor the rights of the insurance company are to be regarded as an asset on the disposal of which a gain can arise. s535(2)(c) makes it clear that this deeming provision does not apply where the right to receive compensation under a policy is assigned *after the event* giving rise to the damage or injury or loss in respect of which the compensation would be received.

The affect of the various provisions described above could be summarised as follows:

- The receipt of insurance compensation for the loss or destruction of an asset will always be the occasion of a deemed disposal of that asset.

- The assignment of the right to receive compensation, after the event giving rise to the compensation has occurred, is the disposal of an asset. That asset is not the rights of the insured person under the policy, but rather is the property which was damaged or lost.

- The assignment of rights under an insurance policy, at a time then the event which might give rise to compensation had not occured is the disposal of an asset on which disposal no gain can accrue. It is an exempt disposal.

Example 30

Coffinships Ltd. have a policy of insurance over their vessel, MV Rustbucket. On hearing that MV Rustbucket is in the path of a typhoon in mid Pacific, Coffinships Ltd. takes a gamble and sells its rights under the insurance policy over the vessel to the highest bidder. MV Rustbucket is lost in the storm and the purchaser of the rights under the policy receives a substantial sum from the insurance company.

The loss of MV Rustbucket is the occasion of a disposal of that asset, being the entire destruction of the asset. However as no compensation is receivable by Coffinships Ltd. in respect of the destruction, the computation would reveal only a loss. The sale of its rights under the insurance policy (prior to the sinking) by Coffinships Ltd. was the disposal of an asset, but it was a disposal which cannot give rise to a chargeable gain since it occurred prior to any event giving rise to compensation.

s535(2)(b)   The position of the speculator who purchased the insurance rights is more ambiguous. He receives a substantial sum which is derived from the insurance rights which he purchased. s535(2)(b) provides

that the rights of the insured under a policy of insurance are exempt
assets. Are the rights under which the speculator receives the sum of
money the rights of the insured under the policy of insurance? On
the face of it, it would seem to be so, and accordingly it would seem
that the gain arising to the speculator would not give rise to a
chargeable gain. It could of course give rise to an income tax charge
as an adventure in the nature of a trade, or as one of the activities of
a trade, but that is a separate matter.

Example 31

Let us consider the situation in **example 30** *if Coffinships Ltd. had delayed
selling its rights under the insurance policy until after MV Rustbucket
had been hit by the storm, and had sunk.*

*In that case, whether or not Coffinships Ltd. had received confirmation of the
sinking at the time of the sale, its rights under the insurance policy would no
longer be exempt. Any sum received by it from the sale would be taken in as
consideration in respect of a disposal or part disposal of MV Rustbucket.*

4.5.4   **Compensation and Roll-Over relief**

Where a capital sum is received as compensation for the damage,
loss or destruction of an asset, relief may be available if the money is
used to replace or restore the asset. This relief is discussed in
paragraphs 26 and 28.

4.6   **Effect of taxation on amount of compensation - "Gourley's Case"**

The UK case of British Transport Commission v Gourley involved an
action for personal injuries. A large part of the damages related to
the plaintiff's loss of earnings. The damages would be free of tax in
the hands of the plaintiff. It was held in the House of Lords that as
the liability to pay income tax on his earnings was a liability
established by law, the plaintiff could only claim as his loss the
amount he would actually have received - i.e. the amount he would
have received after deduction of income tax. To allow a claim for the
total gross earnings would result in the plaintiff receiving a windfall.

Gourley's case merely established what appears to be a common
sense rule for determining the amount of damages. There is no
reason for the plaintiff to receive more than the loss he actually
incurred, solely because of the affect of taxation on income.
Gourley's case concerned a situation where the damages were (in
effect) replacing lost income which would have been chargeable to
income tax if the claimant had not been deprived of it, and had
received it as income in the ordinary course of his life.

Gourley's case was followed in the UK by West Suffolk County
Council v W Rought Ltd a case which involved compensation for the
compulsory acquisition of a leasehold factory occupied by the
company for the purposes of its business. At that time, corporation

tax had not been introduced, and a company was also chargeable to income tax on its income. The company's claim against the council was for loss of profits. An important factor in this case, was that the Revenue had made it clear that in their view (and the reasoning for Revenue view is not clear) no income tax was chargeable on the compensation claimed. The House of Lords proceeded on that basis, and in order to ensure that the company did not recover any more compensation than represented their real financial loss, the Lords applied the general principle established in Gourley's case, and held that the Lands Tribunal, in assessing compensation, should have estimated to the best of their ability the amount of additional taxation which W. Rought Ltd would have had to bear if it had actually earned the amount which it had been prevented from earning.

Both of these cases arose before the advent of CGT, and the only issue was whether the compensation was chargeable to tax as income of the recipient. If it was, then the affect of taxation was taken into the calculation of the net compensation payable, to ensure that the claimant did not receive more than his actual loss.

CGT was first introduced in the UK in 1965, and in Ireland, in 1975. With the advent of CGT, the question of applying the principle established in Gourley's case was made far more difficult and complex. The principle remained the same, in that the claimant should receive no more than his actual loss, taking the affect of taxation into account in appropriate circumstances. The difficulty is in establishing the appropriate circumstances.

In the Rought case, the UK Revenue indicated clearly that they would not be seeking to tax the compensation as income, which left the way clear for the court to apply the Gourley case without any difficulty. It is difficult to see the Revenue being as helpful today, and the real question of applying Gourley's case to compensation rests with the issue of whether the compensation is subject to taxation.

In Stoke-on-Trent City Council v Wood Mitchell & Co Ltd, part of the company's land was taken over by the Council under their compulsory purchase powers. The problem concerned part of the compensation referable to disturbance. The question was whether the £12,228 in respect of temporary losses suffered should be adjusted to take account of corporation tax. The Lands Tribunal held that it was income, and as such chargeable to corporation tax in the hands of the company. As such, no deduction should be made from the compensation for taxation, and the amount should be paid in full. The company would suffer taxation on that amount under the normal corporation tax rules in due course. The Court of Appeal upheld the decision of the Lands Tribunal. Gourley's case and the Rought case were distinguished.

The significant difference between Stoke-on-Trent and the Rought case, was that the Revenue had made their view known in the Rought case, indicating clearly that they would not be seeking to tax the compensation. No such assurance had been forthcoming in the Stoke-on-Trent case. The Revenue declined the invitation of the Court of Appeal to give their view on the matter, and it was left to the court to consider whether the changes in statute law (introducing CGT and corporation tax) resulted in Wood Mitchell & Co becoming liable to pay CGT (corporation tax on gains) on the gain arising out of the compulsory acquisition of the property by the Council. The position of the Revenue Authorities is important. If they later levied tax - after it had been deducted in arriving at the amount of compensation payable, it would, in effect, amount to double taxation of the same receipt. The principle established in Gourley's case and the Rought case was intended solely to secure that a successful claimant did not recover more than his real loss.

The position was well summarised by Roskill LJ (in delivering the judgement of the Court of Appeal) when he said "...*the company, in the absence of any assurance from the Inland Revenue that no attempt would be made to levy tax on this sum, stood in peril of receiving considerably less than that which they would have received had their capacity to earn continued unaffected by compulsory acquisition.*

In such circumstances, the more natural course, which would avoid any risk of injustice, would be for the company to receive the full sum, leaving the question of liability to tax (if any) to be adjusted thereafter between the company and the Inland Revenue. We take the view that the principles laid down in Rought's case can only be applied if after examination of the relevant statutory provisions it is clear beyond peradventure that the sum in question would not be taxable in the hands of the company. If that is clear, then it would be wrong to require the Council to compensate the company beyond the amount of the loss which the company would in truth suffer. But if it is not, then it seems to us unjust that in a doubtful situation the council can get the benefit of a reduced payment while leaving the company exposed to the risks we have mentioned. Considerations of abstract justice might be thought to suggest that the claimants should receive the full sum, and then in due course account to the Inland Revenue for any tax properly chargeable on that amount".

This issue frequently arises in dealing with compensation for loss of income, and not so often in a CGT situation.

In most cases, the compensation is merely replacing income which would otherwise have been earned by the claimant had his capacity to earn been unaffected by the event which gave rise to the claim. The application of the rule in Gourley's case is necessary where the compensation is exempt from tax, and the earnings which it replaces would have been charged to tax, to ensure that the claimant only recovers his real loss.

The first issue to decide, is whether the compensation is replacing something which would otherwise have been chargeable to tax. If it would not in any event have been chargeable to tax, then Gourley's case has no relevance, and there is no question of deducting any tax on payment of the compensation.

If what has been lost (the subject matter of the compensation) would in the ordinary course of events have been chargeable to tax, the question now is whether the compensation itself is chargeable to tax. It is possible that the compensation is chargeable to a different tax to that which what has been lost would have been subject to. For example, the income would have been charged to income tax (or corporation tax on income in the case of a company) and the compensation could be chargeable to CGT.

There are many cases where compensation measured in terms of the loss of income has been held to be a capital receipt, which is not chargeable as income. This is particularly so where the compensation results from the destruction of the profit making apparatus of the recipient of the compensation. Some of these cases are mentioned in paragraph 4.4. There are also many other cases involving the loss of an agency, where the status of the compensation may depend on the extent to which the disposal of the agency affects the overall profit making apparatus of the taxpayer. This is a more complex matter, where what would have been received would have been chargeable to income tax, but that is now replaced by a charge to CGT on the gain arising from the compensation proceeds. In the Pennine Raceway case (see below) the member of the Lands Tribunal dealing with it stated.. *"I have received no argument on the question whether the profits after deduction for corporate income tax, ought to be grossed up for corporate capital gains tax"* and asked the question of the Court of Appeal as to whether his construction of the matter was correct. However, the matter was not argued before the Court of Appeal, and they answered that question with a plain - NO.

In Pennine Raceway v Kirklees Metropolitan Council the company had planning permission to conduct drag races under licence on a disused airfield. The planning permission was revoked by the Council, and the company claimed compensation. The compensation was assessed by the Lands Tribunal at £202,744, measured by reference to the estimated loss of profits to the company. The tribunal took the view that the compensation was not profits chargeable to corporation tax in the hands of the company, and deducted £100,337 representing "corporation income tax" which would have been paid by the company if those profits had been earned in the relevant years. Later, the Revenue indicated that they would assess the company to CGT. The company appealed to the Court of Appeal on a number of matters, including whether the compensation should have been subjected to a deduction of tax on payment. In this case, no clear guidance was available from the Revenue Authorities as to how they would view the matter.

After much deliberation regarding the taxation aspects of the matter, Croom-Johnson LJ came to the conclusion that if there was any possibility of the company becoming chargeable to tax, or if the position was uncertain, that the principles of the Stoke-on Trent case should be followed, and accordingly, the compensation should be paid gross, without any deduction for tax.

This leaves any such tribunal trying to determine the compensation due in an extremely difficult position, as the whole question of what asset (if an asset at all) compensation is derived from is a very difficult area to be in any way certain about.

The question of from what a capital sum is derived is considered in more detail in paragraph 4.4.6.

The other side to this is to consider what should happen if the subject matter of the compensation (which was lost) would not have been chargeable to tax in the normal course of events, but the compensation is now to be taken into account as the proceeds of disposal of an asset for CGT purposes. Is Gourley's case to be applied as increasing the compensation to balance out matters for the affect of taxation ?

In the case of Deeny v Gooda Walker Ltd (in vol liq.), the UK high court held that where both the lost profits and the compensation were chargeable to tax, it was not appropriate to engage in an enquiry into the respective amounts of tax, and the exposure to tax on each account should be deemed to cancel each other.

Further discussion of the Gooda Walker case, and in particular of certain aspects of the judgement of the UK Court of Appeal can be found in paragraph 4.5.1.

The interaction between compensation and CGT has been considered by the Irish High Court in the case of Peter C. Herron and Others v The Minister for Communications. The case concerned compulsory acquisition of land by the Minister for Communications. An arbitrator assessed compensation at the amount of £428,000 but added a rider to the affect that if that sum were found to be liable to capital gains tax, he would make a further award to take account of the CGT liability. The High Court held that an award of compensation on the compulsory acquisition of property should represent the whole value of the entire interest which the claimant had in the property in question. The compensation awarded should represent the value to the claimant of the land as it stood on the date and time when it was compulsorily acquired. Capital gains tax was a personal obligation which arose subsequent and separately from the compulsory acquisition. Accordingly, the compensation awarded should fully reflect the value of the land, and it was not be appropriate to adjust it to have regard to the capital gains tax situation.

5   RATES OF TAX

5.1   Standard Rate

s28(3)
The standard rate of CGT for 1999/00 is 20%. Different rates have applied in past years.

FA98 s65
The 20% standard rate applied to disposals on or after 3 December 1997.

A rate of 40% applies in relation to disposals of

F(No2)A98 s3
- development land (but note the exception for certain development land disposals between 23 April 1998 and 30 November 1999 and all disposals of development land between 1 December 1999 and 5 April 2000 where the 20% rate will apply), or

- shares deriving their value from development land and

- a material interest in an offshore fund, and

- certain offshore life assurance policies.

The 40% rate applies only to the last two mentioned offshore assets where the disposal is on or after 1 December 1989.

The treatment of development land, and the rates of CGT applying to such disposals are set out in paragraph 6.

The changes which have taken place in CGT rates have all taken effect by reference to the date of disposal of an asset. Gains are charged to CGT by reference to the year in which the gain accrues. In most circumstances the two dates are the same, but there are a number of instances where they are different.

As explained in paragraph 3.3.1 dealing with remittances , the rate applying to gains taxed on the remittance basis is the rate appropriate to the year in which the asset was disposed of, and not the rate appropriate to the date on which the proceeds are remitted into Ireland.

Where roll-over relief is claimed on disposal of an asset, the gain is deemed not to arise until the replacement asset ceases to be used for trade purposes (see paragraph 26). When the gain is eventually deemed to arise, the rate of CGT is the rate applying at the date of disposal of the old asset which gave rise to the gain in the first instance.

s590
s579A
S579A and s590 can attribute the gains of an offshore trust and an offshore close company to Irish resident persons. Where they do, the gain is deemed to accrue in the year in which they received a capital

payment from the trust or company as the case may be. That may be in a different year to that in which the date of disposal (by the offshore trust or company) occurred.

Where s590 applies on its own (ie without s579A also applying) the CGT rate would be determined by the date of disposal of an asset by the non resident company. This is because what is attributed to the onshore shareholder is the actual gain accruing to the company on an actual disposal of an asset. However where s579A applies to attribute the gains either of a trust, or of a company owned by a trust, the attribution is not of an actual gain but rather of a notional gain. Accordingly there is no actual underlying disposal of an asset in relation to the notional gain being attributed. Therefore in such a case the CGT rate would be determined by the date of the capital payment and would be the CGT rate appropriate to the year in which the capital payment occurs.

In chapter 10 there is an explanation of the application of the corporation tax rates in taxing the capital gains of most companies operating in Ireland . Special rules , which are explained in chapter 10 , have the affect of ensuring that the effective rate of tax on such gains is 20%(or 40% in respect of offshore funds, etc.) and not the nominal corporation tax rates of 25% or 24%.

| 5.2 | **Reduced Rate (Disposal - 6/4/94 to 2/12/97 only)** |

| 5.2.1 | **Broad outline - reduced rate - 6/4/94 to 2/12/97** |

| s592 | A reduced CGT rate of **27%** was introduced in the Finance Act 1994. |

The rate was reduced further by FA97 to **26%** in respect of disposals made on or after 6th April 1997. In respect of disposals on or after 3rd December 1997, the reduced rate no longer applies. From that date the *standard rate is* **20%**.

In broad terms, the reduced rate of CGT applies to gains arising on the disposal :

- on or after **6th April 1994 and before 3rd December 1997** (see paragraph 5.2.2)

- by an **individual** (see paragraph 5.2.7)

- of **certain qualifying shares** (see paragraph 5.2.3)

- in an **Irish resident trading company** (in certain circumstances this can include a holding company of a trading group) - see paragraph 5.2.4.

- provided the shares had been *owned* by that individual for a period of not less than **3 years** prior to the disposal (see paragraph 5.2.8). In the case of a disposal prior to 6th April 1996, the shares had to be held for a period of 5 years.

The relief applies where the value of all the shares in the company is derived to the extent of not less than 75% from the underlying trade of the company itself and/or the trade of a connected company (see paragraph 5.2.5).

It is important to note that the reduced rate does **not** apply to:

— a disposal by a *company*,

— a disposal of an *unincorporated business*.

— a disposal of shares, which derive their value (or the greater part of their value) from '**development land**' [s.66(1)] - see paragraph 6 for a discussion of development land, and paragraph 3.5.3 for determining whether shares derive value from land.

5.2.2   Disposal 6th April 1994 to 3rd December 1997:

FA94 s66(9)   The reduced rate only applies where the disposal was made *after 5th April 1994 and before 3rd December 1997.* See paragraph 15 for details of the rules regarding the time of disposal of an asset.

5.2.3   Qualifying shares:

s592(1)   The term "qualifying shares" is defined in TCA97 s592(1) to mean:

• ordinary shares

— defined to mean - all issued share capital of the company - by whatever name called - other than share capital the holders whereof have the right to a dividend at a fixed rate, but have no other right to share in the profits of the company

If a class of shares is entitled to a dividend at a fixed rate, and also is entitled to a share in profits over and above that of the fixed rate dividend, they would not be excluded by this requirement. They would however seem to fall within the category (referred to below) of shares having a preferential right to dividends i.e. the right to a dividend at a fixed rate. The explanation for this apparent duplication of requirements may be that you could have a situation where all of the several classes of shares in a company are entitled to a fixed rate of dividend; but some classes only, and not others, are entitled to share in the profits beyond that fixed rate of dividend. In such a situation none of the shares could be said to have a preferential right to a dividend, by reason of the fixed rate referred to, since all classes of shares are entitled to that fixed rate pari passu. The rate may be fixed, but it is not preferential since all share equally. In that example however those classes of shares entitled only to the fixed rate, but not to participate further, are excluded by reason of the requirement described, notwithstanding that the right is not preferential. The other classes of shares, entitled

to participate further, are not excluded by either this
requirement, or by the reference below to a preferential right to
dividends.

—which are fully paid up,

—having no present or future **preferential** right :-

  —to dividends,

  —to the assets of the company on a winding up, or

  —to be redeemed.

The question of preferential rights can only arise where the company
has more than one class of shares in issue. If all issued shares are of
the same class they will all have the same rights, and none will have
preference over others.

"Preferential right" is not defined and therefore has its ordinary
meaning in the context of company law. Where there is more than
one class of shares, and one class has a right not possessed by
another class, it may be argued that the class having the right is
preferred over the other class, and that its right is a "preferential
right". An example of such a situation might be where the A shares
have voting rights, but the B shares do not. It is sometimes argued
that the A shares in such a situation have a preferential right. If that
argument were correct, it would exclude from this relief, and many
other reliefs in several taxes which are dependent on the rights of
shares not being preferential, any class of shares in a company which
has rights which are not held by every other class in the company.
That is not likely to be the intention of the Oireachtas, which must be
presumed to be aware of the normal practice of business persons in
arranging share rights. If it were their intention to exclude so wide a
body of shares from relief, one would have expected it to be stated in
more explicit terms.

An alternative interpretation of "preferential right" is that it is a right
shared by several classes of shares, but which one class is entitled to
in priority to other classes. In other words, "preferential right" refers
to a right for which there is a queue of persons entitled to the right,
and the right of those at the top of the queue may be regarded as
preferential to the right of those further down the queue. On that
interpretation, a right which is held by one class of shares to the
entire exclusion of other classes is not a preferential right since it is
held to the exclusion of other classes, rather than in priority to them.
That interpretation more closely accords with the normal use of the
expression "preference shares". In ordinary parlance, such shares are
shares with a prior right to receive dividends, but not with the
exclusive right to receive dividends. Their right to dividends is
preferential, but not exclusive. Until such time as the matter has been
clarified by the courts, the phrase remains ambiguous.

5.2.4   **Qualifying company:**

In simple broad terms, a qualifying company is an *unquoted Irish resident trading company.* In certain circumstances a holding company can also be a qualifying company as explained in paragraph 5.2.6.

FA97 s76(b)   The meaning of "unquoted" for this purpose was changed by the FA 1997, and the current definition is as follows:

s592(1)   *..'unquoted company' means a company none of whose shares, stocks, or debentures are listed in the official list of a stock exchange or quoted on an unlisted securities market.*

There is no requirement that the company be incorporated in Ireland.

However, the legislation does not leave matters as simple as that. In relation to a disposal of qualifying shares, a company will be a qualifying company if all of the following conditions are met:

s592(2)(a)   **At the date of acquisition of those shares**, the company must have :-

- been an unquoted company (even if it is quoted at the date of disposal),

- been resident in Ireland (and not resident elsewhere), and

- had an issued share capital the total market value of which did not exceed £25m (irrespective of the total value of those shares at the date of disposal)

s592(2)(b)   **For a period of 3 years immediately preceding the date of disposal** of the shares, the company must have been resident in Ireland (and not resident elsewhere), **and either**

- *must have existed* wholly or mainly to carry on one or more qualifying trades **or**

- *its "business"* must have consisted wholly or mainly of

  - the holding of shares in one or more connected companies, **or**

  - both the holding of such shares and the carrying on of one or more qualifying trades.

In the three years between 6th April 1994 and 5th April 1997 the requirements relating to the business of the company and the period for its existence described above had to be met for a period of *five years* immediately preceeding the date of disposal of the shares. This was so notwithstanding that from 6th April 1996 onwards the
FA97 s76(a)   required period of ownership of the shares was reduced to *three years*. The FA97 which removed this anomaly did not do so retrospectively. It is not known if the Revenue Commisioners operate a concession in this area.

The company is regarded as meeting these conditions at any point in time, where its shares derive not less than 75% of their value from its own trade or the trade of connected companies, or from both.

The meaning of a 'connected company' is dealt with in detail in paragraph 5.2.6 In very broad terms it means an Irish resident trading company in which the qualifying company owns not less than 20% of the voting rights.

5.2.5   Qualifying trade condition:

s592(1)   All trades with a number of specific exceptions are qualifying trades. The specific *exceptions* are trades of *dealing in* all or any of the following items:

- —shares,

- —securities,

- —land,

- —currencies,

- —futures, or

- —traded options.

s592(3)(a)   A company is regarded as meeting the qualifying trade test if not less than 75% of the market value of ALL the issued share capital of the company is *derived from* the carrying on of a qualifying trade (either carried on by the company itself, or by the connected companies in which it holds shares) throughout the *3 year* period immediately preceeding the date of disposal of the shares.

s592(4)   Where the activities carried on by a company partly consist of a qualifying trade, and partly of a non-qualifying trade, they are treated as two separate trades for the purpose of determining whether the shares derive not less than 75% of their value from qualifying trading operations.

The question of whether the shares in a company derive value from the trade, or any other specific asset or assets of the company has caused difficulties in dealing with the Revenue Authorities. This matter is dealt with in detail in paragraph 3.5.

s592   • **Revenue Commissioners published precedent:**

- *"Where 75% of the market value of a company is not derived from qualifying trades solely by reason of retained cash surplus, and where the cash surplus derives from trading activities within the meaning of s592 and the profits are used for the purposes of the trade, the reduced rate will be allowed."*

- This precedent as published is fairly meaningless. If indeed the cash is used for the purposes of the trade, no question would seem to arise but that the shares derive their value as to 75% at least from the qualifing trade. It is a fact that some trades (particularly seasonal trades or deposit taking trades), require higher levels of cash to be held than may be required in other trades. Whether or not a cash balance is in use in the trade or represents a separate investment asset is a question of fact which can only be answered in each separate case.

5.2.6   Holding company

s592(5) In certain circumstances, shares in a holding company can qualify for the reduced rate of CGT.

FA97 s76(a) In order to qualify a holding company (throughout the period of *three years* (5 years pre 6 April 1997) immediately preceding the date of disposal of its shares) must be a company

- whose business consists wholly or mainly of the holding of shares in one or more "connected companies ("connected companies" are explained below).

  or

- whose business consists wholly or mainly of

  − holding shares in one or more connected companies

      and

  − the carrying on of one or more qualifying trades.

Both a holding company and a mixed "holding *and* trading" company may be a qualifying company.

Connected Company :

Where the qualifying company holds shares in another company (or companies) the other company is regarded as connected with the qualifying company if:

- **at the date of acquisition** of its shares by the qualifying company, that other company was an unquoted company,

- it is resident in Ireland (and not resident elsewhere), and

- the qualifying company can exercise not less than 20% of the total voting rights in that other company.

s592(3)(c) Where the business of a 'connected company' consists of the holding of shares in other companies, those other companies which are 'connected' with the 'connected company' are also treated as connected with the 'qualifying company' even though the qualifying company would not necessarily have a direct or indirect 20% holding in those companies.

Example 32 (6/4/94 to 2/12/97 only)

> A Ltd owns 25% of the voting shares in B Ltd. B Ltd has a business of holding shares in other companies. B Ltd owns 30% of the voting shares in C Ltd and also owns 30% of the voting shares of D Ltd.
>
> All companies are Irish resident, and unquoted.
>
> For the purpose of determining whether the market value of the shares in A Ltd is derived to the extent of not less than 75% from qualifying trades, B Ltd, C Ltd and D Ltd are all connected with A Ltd, even though A Ltd has only a 25% share of B Ltd. and its indirect holding in C Ltd and D Ltd is less than 20%.

5.2.7   Individuals only:

s592(6)

The reduced rate can only be claimed by individuals. It should be noted that trustees and personal representatives of a deceased person (in their representative capacity) are deemed not to be individuals for the purposes of CGT .

There is no requirement as to the residence of the individual. A non-resident individual is only within the charge to CGT in the case of unquoted shares, where the shares derive their value from Irish land, minerals, etc. (see paragraph 3.4.2). Obviously the reduced rate would be of little significance to a non-resident individual who is not within the charge to CGT on the gain in the first instance. The question of what assets the shares in a company derive their value from has caused difficulty. The matter is dealt with in paragraph 3.5.

5.2.8   3 year ownership:

s592(6)

The individual must have owned the shares in the same capacity for a **continuous period** of not less than *3 years* ending with the date of disposal.

In relation to disposals made prior made to 6 April 1996, the minimum required period of holding was *5 years.*

s592(1)

Where shares are acquired by an individual **on the death** of another individual, he is deemed to acquire the shares at market value at the date of death of that deceased person. Where the shares are acquired **on the death of his spouse**, he is also deemed for the purpose of the reduced rate of tax, to acquire the period of ownership of his deceased spouse.

s1028

Such a provision (passing on the deceased spouse's period of ownership) is not necessary where the asset passes from one spouse to another during their lifetime. In such circumstances, the asset is deemed to have been acquired by the spouse now owning the asset, at the same time as it was acquired by the other spouse, and at the same cost. The combined period of ownership by both spouses, and the original acquisition cost are preserved by the existing provisions of s1028 (married persons - see paragraph 33).

• **Revenue Commissioners published precedent :**

— In their published precedents the Revenue Commissioners would
seem to disagree with the comments above in that they state, *"in
relation to shares transferred from one spouse to another, that the periods
of ownership cannot be aggregated "in strictness". However, in practice
the periods or ownership may be aggregated".* The basis for the
Revenue Commissioners' differing view is not known, and in the
light of the abolition of the relief, may no longer be of much
interest.

5.2.9   Miscellaneous matters:

s592(1)

For the purposes of the reduced rate :

— the term **'trade'** includes 'a profession'.

— the term **'unquoted'** refers to a company, none of whose shares,
stocks, or debentures, are listed in the official list of a stock
exchange, or dealt in on an unlisted securities market.

5.2.10   Application of rules – reorganisations, mergers, etc.

s592(7)
s592(8)

In certain circumstances, the CGT legislation deems a person

• to own shares which have long ceased to exist,

• not to own shares which he in fact actually owns.

Such circumstances usually arise following a reorganisation,
reconstruction, amalgamation, or merger - where the person has
disposed of his existing shares in exchange for other shares in the
company, or perhaps for shares in another company. What gives
rise to this, is the effect of the 'relief' set out in TCA97 s584.

s584

The following is a brief summary of that relief for the sole purpose of
setting the broad scene necessary to explain the further provisions of
s592(7)(8). In broad terms, s584 gives relief for a wide variety of
possible transactions involving company reconstructions,
amalgamation, mergers, etc. The basic principles of the relief fall
into three broad areas (see paragraph 42 et seq.):-

• A straightforward **share for share swop** - where existing ('old')
shares are surrendered, or transferred to a company issuing shares
in exchange for them.

In such circumstances (subject to the overall rules of TCA97 s584)
that relief would apply to *deem* that for CGT purposes:

— there is no disposal of the old shares, and

— there is no acquisition of any new shares.

For CGT purposes, as you are deemed not to have acquired any new shares, you cannot own any new shares - they do not exist for CGT purposes. Equally, you have not made any disposal of the old shares, and accordingly, you still own them.

Instead, the legislation treats the new shares now held as if they were in every respect the old shares, acquired at the same cost and time as the old shares were acquired.

You can end up with what on the surface appears to be a ridiculous result, of owning shares for (say) 20 years (the period of ownership of the old shares) in a company which was only incorporated in the current year - see paragraph 42 et seq.

s584(4)

- **A share for share swop involving the giving of further consideration** in addition to transferring the existing shares. In these circumstances, the relief (TCA97 s584) would *deem* the new holding (as a total unit) to be the old shares in every way, but with the addition of further enhancement expenditure equal to the further consideration given in the reorganisation (see paragraph 42.5).

s584(5)

- **A share for share swop also involving the withdrawal of part of the share value** from the company. In such circumstances, the relief (TCA97 s584) *deems* that no shares have been either acquired or disposed of, but treats the new holding (in total) as being in every respect what remains of the old shares after the part disposal represented by the consideration received (see paragraphs 42 to 44).

s592

The main problem here, is that the new shares could be shares in a different company to that in which the old shares were issued, with a different share valuation (looking at the £25m value limit on acquisition), and a different trade pattern at times relevant to determining the position for the reduced rate of tax. These provisions could cause problems in applying the normal rules of s592. The further rules needed in such circumstances are set out in TCA97 s592(7),(8).

s592(7)

Where :

- no further consideration was introduced at the time of the disposal (other than the original shares themselves - i.e. excluding (b) above), and

- both the new holding *and* the original (old) shares are qualifying shares for the purposes of the reduced rate of CGT,

the new holding of shares (in total) is deemed to have been acquired at the acquisition date of the shares comprised in the original (old) holding for the purposes of determining the rate of CGT.

FA97 s76(a)   Further rules also apply which vary according to whether the new shares are held for

s592(8)   — less than *3 years* (5 years pre FA97) or,

— not less than *3 years* (5 years pre FA97).

The entire area of reconstructions, amalgamations is full of deeming provisions, and it is unfortunate that this legislation dealing with the reduced rate of CGT is not more clear in its references to the *3 year* period of ownership prior to disposal of the shares. It is not totally clear whether the reference is to the actual period of ownership, or the period of ownership deemed as a result of applying the rules of the s584.

s584   A detailed examination of the provisions would lead one to consider that the more meaningful interpretation is for the references to the period of ownership in this provision is to be taken as a reference to the actual period of ownership - ignoring the "deeming" provisions of s584 - which apply for all other purposes of the CGT legislation. However, as many have found to their cost, the interpretation of law does not necessarily produce the most meaningful result.

The position is discussed in detail below.

References to an ownership period of not less than 3 years should - in respect of disposals prior to 6th April 1996, be read as a period of not less than 5 years.

NEW SHARES - OWNERSHIP NOT LESS THAN 3 YEARS :

s592(8)(a)   Where s592(7) *"applies, and has effect, and the new holding is held for a period which is* **not less than 3 years***"*, a number of further provisions also apply:

Market value requirement:

The requirement that the company must have a market value not exceeding £25m at the date of acquisition of the shares, is to apply to the original (*old*) shares at the date of acquisition of those original shares and not to the actual date of acquisition of the current holding.

This provision is the same as where the new holding is held for a period of less than 3 years.

Shares issued in different company:

Where the shares now held are issued by a company which is not the company which issued the original shares, the requirements that the company be

— unquoted and

— Irish resident

at the date of acquisition of those shares is to be applied to the original company, and not to the company in which the current shareholding subsists.

The requirement that the company be Irish resident throughout the specified *3 year* period, and the requirement regarding its activities and the deriving of not less than 75% of its share value from trading activities throughout that period are to be applied to the new company, ignoring the original 'old' company.

This provision is different to where the new holding is held for a period of less than 3 years.

s592(8)(b)   This point is important, as different provisions apply in some areas where s592(7) *"applies, and has effect, and the new holding is held for a period which is **less than 3 years**".*

NEW SHARES - OWNERSHIP LESS THAN 3 YEARS :

The provisions which apply in such circumstances are:

Market value requirement:

The requirement that the company must have a market value not exceeding £25m at the date of acquisition of the shares, is to apply to the original (*old*) shares at the date of acquisition of those original shares and not to the actual date of acquisition of the current holding.

*This provision is also the same as where the new shares have been held for a period of **not less than 3 years.***

Shares issued in different company:

Where the shares now held are issued by a company which is not the company which issued the original shares, the requirements that the company be

• unquoted and

• Irish resident

at the date of acquisition of those shares is to be applied to the original company, and not to the company in which the current shareholding subsists.

*This provision is also the same as where the new shares have been held for a period of **not less than 3 years.***

The requirement that the company be Irish resident throughout the specified *3 year* period, and the requirement regarding its activities and the deriving of not less than 75% of its share value from trading activities throughout that period is to be applied *partly to the new company, and partly to the old company* - i.e. to the new company from the date of acquisition of the new holding, and to the old company for the part of the total specified **3 *year*** period before the date of acquisition of the new holding.

Looking at sections 67 and 68 in total, it appears that the most logical interpretation, is that the reference to the new shares being held 'for a period' must be a reference to the period for which they were actually held, ignoring the deeming provisions of Schedule 2, paragraph 2.

Example 33 (6/4/94 to 2/12/97 only)

> *Joe Smith inherited 500 shares in Smith Factories Ltd from his father in June 1994. The shares had been held by the father for 10 years prior to death. Joe inherited 200 shares in Smith Factories Ltd. from his wife, who died in the same traffic accident as his father, in June 1994. His wife had owned the shares since her marriage in May 1991. Joe had acquired 200 shares in the same company on his marriage in May 1991. Smith Factories Ltd. was an unquoted trading company worth £5,000,000 in 1991 and in 1993. On 1 January 1995 Smith Factories Ltd. was taken over by Combine PLC, a quoted company, in a share for share swap to which the provisions of TCA97 s584 applied. Joe sold his shares in Combine PLC on 31 December 1996.*

> *Combine PLC had an OMV of £100,000,000 in 1995 and 1996, derived from trades, and was Irish resident.*

> *The tests regarding being unquoted and relating to overall value are applied to Smith Factories Ltd. and not to Combine PLC.   Only the shares acquired in May 1991 by Joe, and those inherited from his wife qualify for the reduced rate of CGT.   Joe is treated as having acquired his wife's shares when she actually acquired them, i.e. May 1991 and it is at that date that Smith Factories Ltd. must meet those tests; which it does. The shares inherited from his father do not qualify for relief, being held by Joe for less than 3 years. His father's period of ownership is not taken into account.*

> *The company test regarding deriving value from trades is applied to Combine PLC from 1 January 1995 to 31 December 1996, and to Smith Factories Ltd. for the period 1 January 1992 to 31 December 1994 (being the balance of the 5 year period).*

5.2.11   Disposal of shares

A taxpayer contemplating a disposal of shares should ensure that the relief is not lost by reason of the form in which the disposal is made.

The sale of a trade by a company, followed by liquidation of the company to extract the cash proceeds, could result in the individual shareholder being taxed at the 40% CGT rate (pre 3rd December 1997) on disposal of his shares. At the date of disposal of his shares, the only asset of the company is cash, and it is no longer a trading company. This appears to be the strict interpretation of the law, but only time will tell if the Revenue authorities will apply it strictly, or allow relief in such circumstances.

Where a shareholder receives an offer for his shares from another company, the offer may take the form of shares in the acquiring company in exchange for his existing shares. As explained in Chapter 8 in certain circumstances, he may be treated as not making any disposal of his shares if he accepts that offer. Instead, the new shares acquired will take the same cost and acquisition date as his existing shares. On the ultimate disposal of those new shares, the tax rate may not be 26%. The detailed rules which determine whether the reduced rate is available are described above.

- **Revenue Commissioners published precedent :**

− The lower rate applied only in relation to a disposal of qualifying shares. In some cases shares may be disposed of in return (partly at least) for a deferred contingent consideration. This is typically described as an *"earn out"* and arises where the additional consideration is contingent on the achievement by the company of certain targets. In the UK case of Marren v Ingles (see paragraph 4.4.6) certain such earn outs were treated as not being derived from the shares disposed of, but rather from a separate asset consisting of the right to receive such deferred contingent consideration. The receipt of such deferred contingent consideration, were Marren v Ingles correctly decided (which the authors believe was not) and were it to be followed in Ireland (which has not been decided by the Courts) would call in question the availability of the lower rate of tax. In their published concessions the Revenue Commissioners have stated *"As the amounts received in an earn out are in respect of a right separate to shares which were disposed of, they will not qualify for the relief. However, in practice, cash earn outs may be treated as qualifying for the relief."* From this it would seem that the Revenue Commissioners accept that Marren v Ingles would be followed in Ireland, a matter about which the authors have considerable doubt. The reference in the published precedent to consideration consisting of cash should be read in the context of share for share relief. The Revenue Commissioners have a separate published precedent in relation to relief under s586 in the context of an earn out - see paragraph 8.8.2.

5.2.12   **1995/1996 disposals only**

s584   Where a taxpayer, prior to 6 April 1994, as part of a reorganisation, reconstruction, or amalgamation to which s584 applied, obtained shares which either are:

- not qualifying shares or

- are in a company which is not a qualifying company,

and obtained those shares in exchange for qualifying shares in a qualifying company, the rules relating to qualifying shares, and relating to qualifying companies, are relaxed, **for 1995/96 disposals only**, where certain conditions are met. These conditions are:

- The new holding of shares obtained in the reorganisation etc. must have been *acquired on or before the 5th day of April 1994*. Although it is not explicitly clear from the legislation, the reference here to the date of acquisition of the new holding appears to be a reference to the actual date of acquisition, and not a reference to the date of acquisition as deemed by s584, which would normally be the date of acquisition of the old holding.

- The old holding (the original shares) must have been held by the individual throughout the *period of 5 years before the date of acquisition of the new holding.* This requirement should be contrasted with the provisions of s592(7),(8), described above where the date of acquisition of a new holding was deemed to be the date of the original old holding, thus enabling the period of ownership of both the old shares and the new shares to be combined, for the purpose of meeting the requirement that shares should have been held for 5 years prior to disposal. No similar relaxation of the rules is available in the present case. The old shares must have been held for 5 years, in their own right, and without regard to the period for which the new shares have been held. It is therefore not possible to combine the relaxation of rules provided for in the 1994 legislation relating to reorganisations, and that provided in the 1995 legislation.

Example 34

John acquired shares on 1 January 1990 (the original shares). On 1 January 1994 he exchanged those shares for shares in Newco, in a transaction to which TCA97 s584 applied. John disposed of the new holding on 6 April 1995.

For the purposes of the reduced tax rate John will be deemed to have held the new holding of shares for a period in excess of 5 years. This is because s592(7) will deem the new holding to have been acquired at the same date as the old holding for these purposes i.e. at 1 January 1990. If however Newco is not a qualifying company, whereas the original company in which John acquired shares was a qualifying company, John will be disappointed to hear that he cannot avail of the relief provided by the 1995 legislation because the original holding was not held by him for 5 years or more prior to the share swap.

- There is one further requirement which must be met in order that the relaxation of rules in the 1995 legislation should apply to the transaction. That requirement is that the company in which the new holding of shares is held must be a company which would *not be a qualifying company* for the purposes of the legislation, *but for* the provisions of the 1995 legislation. It would seem that the 1995 legislation does not apply to relax the rules in favour of the taxpayer where the company in which the new holding is held (Newco in the example above) is, in its own right, a qualifying company. This is a most peculiar restriction of the relief provided by the 1995 legislation.

Example 35

John acquired shares in Company A, and shares in Company B, on 1 January 1985. On 1 April 1994 he entered into two transactions as a result of which he exchanged his shares in Company A for shares in Company C, and in which he exchanged his shares in Company B for shares in Company D. The provisions of TCA97 s584 applied to both transactions. Company A and Company B were qualifying companies, and the shares in those companies were qualifying shares. The shares which John obtained in Company C and the shares which he obtained in Company D are not qualifying shares. Company C would be a qualifying company but Company D is not a qualifying company.

*The provisions of the 1995 legislation may apply to the shares held in Company D so as to apply the reduced rate of CGT to a disposal of those shares in 1995/96. However the 1995 legislation cannot apply to extend the reduced rate of CGT to a disposal of the shares in Company C, **because that company is a qualifying company!** This does not seem a very sensible position, as regards the shares in Company C. It remains to be seen how the Revenue will apply the legislation in practice.*

*Where the conditions outlined above are met the requirements of the 1994 legislation relating to the reduced rate of CGT are applied in a modified manner to a disposal of the new holding of shares **in 1995/1996 only.***

Whether or not the new holding of shares which is being disposed would otherwise be qualifying shares, they will be regarded as being qualifying shares.

Whether or not the new holding of shares has been held for a period of not less than 5 years, they will be regarded as having been so held.

Requirements relating to a qualifying company are applied in the following modified manner:

- The requirement that the company be an **unquoted** company resident in the State and not resident elsewhere, the market value of whose share capital should not exceed £25m, is applied at the date of the acquisition of the original shares, and not at the date of the acquisition of the new holding and;

- The requirement is applied to the **original company** in which the taxpayer held the shares, and not to the new company in which he now holds shares as a result of the reorganisation etc. Obviously this latter modification applies only where the new shares are held in a different company to that in which the original shares were held. Where the reorganisation consisted only of a change in the rights of shares, for example, but the new shares and the original holding might be held in the same company, this particular modification is neither relevant nor has application.

- The requirement relating to the **residence of the company**, and the purpose for which it exists, are applied to the original company (where that is different from the company in which the shares being disposed of are now held) and are applied throughout a period of 5 years immediately preceding the date of the acquisition of the new holding rather than to the period of 5 years immediately preceding the date of the disposal of the shares, which would otherwise be the case.

Example 36

> John held all of the ordinary shares of John Trading Ltd., and had held those shares since 1 January 1985. The shares would be qualifying shares for the purpose of s592, and John Trading Ltd. was a qualifying company for the purpose of that legislation. On 1 April 1994 John accepted an offer for his shares from Mega Company PLC. Mega Company PLC is a quoted company, which acts as a holding company for a property investment group (principally). Mega Company PLC issued John with preference shares in exchange for his ordinary shares in John Trading Ltd. On 1 June 1994 John disposed of 50% of his holding in Mega Company Ltd. and he disposed of the balance on 1 June 1995.

> The rate of CGT applying to any gain on John's disposal on 1 June 1994 will be 40%. The lower rate of CGT would not apply because the shares were not qualifying shares, nor was the company in which the shares were held a qualifying company. The 1995 provisions relaxing these requirements for the lower rate of CGT do not have application for disposals prior to 6 April 1995.

> The reduced rate of CGT will apply to the disposal on 1 June 1995. John meets all of the conditions. The company whose shares he was now disposing of would not be a qualifying company but for the 1995 legislation. The shares are not qualifying shares, but for the 1995 legislation. However he had held his original shares for more than 5 years, and in the 5 years prior to the share swap, John Trading Ltd. had met all the requirements for being a qualifying company. Therefore John will be treated as having made a disposal on 1 June 1995 of qualifying shares, which he had held for more than 5 years, in a qualifying company.

> If John had delayed making his disposal of the second lot of shares until 1 June 1996, he would not be able to avail of the reduced rate of CGT. The relaxation of the requirements relating to qualifying shares, and in relation to a qualifying company, which are outlined above, **apply only to disposals in 1995/1996.**

6   DEVELOPMENT LAND

6.1   Broad Outline

6.1.1   Overview - computational restrictions

Since the passing of FA82 a distinction has been made between "development land", and other assets. Special computational rules, and rates of tax have applied over the years to gains arising on the disposal of development land.

In computing a gain or loss on the disposal of development land, the following points should be noted:

- indexation may be restricted,

- roll-over relief is not generally available (subject to exceptions),

- relief for reinvestment of the proceeds of a CPO is not available,

- there is a restriction on the relief available for the set off of losses,

- relief for the disposal of a principal private residence may be restricted.

- development land gains arising to a company which is within the charge to CT are chargeable to CGT and not to CT. Nonetheless a form of group relief is available for transfers of assets between members of a group.

6.1.2   Tax Rates - development land : 20% - 40% - 60%

F(no.2)A98 s3   The tax rate applicable to disposals of development land has been
FA2000 s86   the subject of frequent modification in recent years. The FA 2000
FA2000 s52   introduced parallel changes to the rates of tax applying where
income tax or corporation tax on income is the appropriate tax arising on the disposal of development land. The discussion below separately deals with the position prior to FA2000 (paragraph 6.1.2.2) and then with the regime introduced by the FA 2000 paragraph 6.1.3)..

6.1.2.1   Disposals on or after 1 December 1999

FA2000 s86   S86 FA 2000 introduced new rules relating to the rate of capital gains tax applying to disposals of development land. The new rules apply to disposals on or after 1 December 1999. As noted in paragraph 6.1.3, the rules will change on 6 April 2002 in relation to some disposals only of development land, as described in that paragraph.

Where a disposal is made of development land (which as noted, includes shares deriving their value from development land) on or after 1 December 1999, the rate of capital gains tax applicable is 20%.

The following table gives a very brief overview of the various tax rates (income tax and capital gains tax) applying to development land, following FA 2000. It is highl6y summarised insofar as land dealing and development is concerned.

Tax Rates on profits and gains from land disposals pre 6/4/2002	company		individual	
	Pre 1/12/99	Post 1/12/99	Pre 1/12/99	Post 1/12/99
RESIDENTIAL DEVELOPMENT LAND				
Dealing	28%	20%	46%	20%

Tax Rates on profits and gains from land disposals pre 6/4/2002	company		individual	
	Pre 1/12/99	Post 1/12/99	Pre 1/12/99	Post 1/12/99
Other	20%	20%	20%	20%
NON-RESIDENTIAL DEVELOPMENT LAND				
Dealing	28%	25%	46%	46%/44%
Other	40%	20%	40%	20%
NON-DEVELOPMENT LAND				
Dealing	28%	25%	46%	46%/44%
Other	20%	20%	20%	20%

6.1.2.2.　　　Disposals pre 1 December 1999

F(No 2)A98 s3　Notwithstanding the reduction in the standard rate of CGT to 20%, *the normal rate of CGT chargeable on a gain arising on the disposal of development land prior to 1st December 1999 is 40%.* This rate also applies to gains on shares deriving their value from development land.

s649A　The F(No2)A98 adopted a "carrot and stick" approach in an attempt to encourage people to make more land available in the short-term future for residential development (and that approach was further extended by FA99). It provided that the standard 20% CGT rate would apply to qualifying land disposals over a specified period, and at the same time introduced a penal 60% CGT rate for such disposals after the end of that specified period.

- It allowed the *20% rate of CGT* to apply to qualifying disposals of land in the period beginning 23 April 1998 and ending on 5 April 2002. This end date was brought forward to 30 November 1999 by
FA2000, s86　FA 2000, s86. The disposals qualifying for the standard rate are:

　　　—a disposal to *a housing authority* [within the meaning of s23 of the Housing(Miscellaneous Provisions) Act 1992] which land is specified in a certificate in writing given by the housing authority as land being required by it for the purposes of the Housing Acts 1966 to 1998,

FA99 s91　　　—a disposal to the *National Building Agency Ltd,* and a *body standing approved for the purposes of s6 of the Housing (Miscellaneous Provisions) Act 1992* subject to similar conditions as apply to a housing authority - see above (added by FA99 in respect of disposals from 10 March 1999).

— a disposal of *land with residential planning permission* - ie. a disposal in respect of the whole of which, at the time at which the disposal is made permission for residential development had been granted under LGP&DA63 s26 and such permission has not ceased to exist,

FA99 s91

— a disposal of *land zoned for residential use* - ie. a disposal in respect of the whole of which, at the time at which the disposal is made, is, in accordance with a development objective (as indicated in the development plan of the planning authority concerned), for use solely or primarily for residential purposes (added by FA99 in respect of disposals from 10 March 1999).

F(No2)A98 s3

• It provided for a *CGT rate of 60%* to apply to disposals after 5 April 2002 where the land is zoned on the development plan of the planning authority concerned for use solely or primarily for residential purposes.

Notwithstanding the above general rules, the 20% rate was *NOT* available in the case of disposals pre 1 December 1999 :

• of development land with residential planning permission, (or where it is zoned for residential use) where the disposal is under a conditional contract and the condition related to the obtaining of permission for development other than residential development, or

• to a disposal to a "connected person" - for example it does not apply to a gift between father and son, or a sale between an individual and his brother. The meaning of "connected person" for CGT purposes is discussed in paragraph 16.4.4

Example 37

John Brown enters into a contract for the sale of 100 acres of his farm to Developers Limited. The 100 acres presently has planning permission for residential development. The contract is conditional on John Brown seeking and successfully obtaining, within 18 months of the date of the contract (28 May 1998) planning permission for a hotel, golf course and conference centre on the land.

*Notwithstanding that the land is presently the subject of residential planning permission, the 20% CGT rate will **not** apply because the contract is conditional on an alternative non-residential planning permission being obtained. Under the terms of the contract, the purchaser is not obliged to go ahead unless John Brown successfully obtains the non-residential planning permission. If he did successfully obtain that planning permission, then the date of the contract would be the date upon which he obtains the permission and at that date he would presumably, have both residential planning permission (which already exists)* *and alternative non-residential planning permission on the land. It is not the presence of two planning permissions which appears to be the problem, but rather the fact that the contract under which the disposal was made was conditional on obtaining the second planning permission.*

The legislation does not explicitly address the situation which would exist if John Brown, before entering into any contract for the sale of the land, obtained the second planning permission relating to hotel etc. and if both that and the residential planning permission existed on the land at the date of sale under an unconditional contract.

FA99 s91

FA99 further amended rules relating to the rate of CGT which has application to a disposal of development land. The amendment applied to disposals on or after the 10 March 1999. The FA99 rules are broadly the same as those introduced by the F (No 2)A 98. The principal changes are

- a disposal to the National Building Agency Limited or to a body approved for the purposes of Section 6 of the Housing (Miscellaneous)Provisions Act 1992, and certified as being required for the purposes of the Housing Acts, 1966 to 1998, will attract a 20% rate.

- a disposal of development land which is zoned for use solely or primarily for residential purposes, and which is to an unconnected party and is not conditional on obtaining non residential planning permission will attract a 20% rate.

Following the FA99 changes (noted above) it is no longer necessary for the land to actually have planning permission at the time of disposal. It is sufficient that it is be zoned on the county development plan primarily for residential use. However, if it is zoned otherwise than primarily for residential use, but actually has planning permission for residential development, it will still qualify for the 20% rate,

It is understood that it is the view of the Revenue Commissioners that it is only where the zoning in the county plan is expressly stated to be "For use solely or primarily for residential purposes" that the 20% rate will apply where its application is based on zoning as described above. It is understood that it is their view that other forms of zoning which provide for residential use (eg agricultural with option for residential use) do not meet the requirement for the 20% rate. The precise wording of zoning may therefore be of critical importance and not all zoning that permits or provides for residential use will be accepted by the Revenue as meeting the requirements for the 20% rate.

The Revenue interpretation of the requirement relating to residential zoning might appear more strict than their published ruling in relation to residential planning permission, described below.

The 20% rate should apply in a case where the land has planning permission for residential purposes, or is zoned primarily for residential purposes. It is necessary that that condition be met by *"whole of the land* (which is the subject of the disposal) *at the time at which the disposal is made"* . That phrase might contain some implication that if a single block of land were being sold, and only part of that land met the requirements described above relating to zoning or planning permission, that none of the land would attract the 20% rate. Although that interpretation could be put on the words used, it would seem perverse. If that were correct, the absence of planning permission on a very small corner of a large piece of land might result in the application of the 40% rate to the entire area. That would scarcely be sensible. It is more likely that the alternate interpretation, that so far as a gain arises on that part of the land meeting the conditions for the 20% rate, the 20% rate will apply to a gain on that part, is the correct interpretation. That would then leave the question of the apportionment of base cost, and of consideration, between the area of land qualifying for the 20% rate, and the balance of the land.

However, many areas of tax law are not necessarily based on what a reasonable person would regard as common sense, and where the position is not absolutely clear, consideration should be given to trying to clear the tax position with the Revenue Commissioners in advance of the transaction.

In some cases it may be more convenient for the parties to specify in the contract for sale, how they apportion the consideration. The topic of apportionment of consideration is discussed in paragraph 8.9, and a method of avoiding any doubt in the interpretation of the above provisions may well lie in that area.

A number of provisions in the Taxes Acts deem a taxpayer to dispose of an asset, usually at open market value. In many instances the taxpayer is deemed to then reacquire it at the same value. In the case of an asset appropriated to trading stock, the legislation merely deems a disposal. The Revenue Commissioners have confirmed that such a deemed disposal is not to be treated as a disposal to a connected person, on the basis that a person cannot be connected with themselves. Such disposals therefore could potentially attract the 20% rate of capital gains tax.

The 20% rate of CGT relates to disposals pre 1 December 1999 of

- certain *development land* **ONLY,**

  − and *NOT* to

- *shares deriving value from development land.*

Such shares remain chargeable at the 40% rate of CGT in respect of a pre 1 December 1999 disposal.

As noted in paragraph 5.2.1, the reduced 26% rate of CGT which applied from 6th April 1974 to 3rd December 1997 does not apply to gains arising on shares which derive their value from development land.

• **Revenue Commissioners - tax briefing:**

—The Revenue Commissioners, in Issue 33 of Tax Briefing, September 1998, stated that *"Planning permission granted for a holiday cottage could be regarded as planning permission granted for residential development."*

6.1.3   Land sold for residential development - after 5 April 2002.

A CGT rate of 60% rate will apply to disposals after 5 April 2002 where the land is zoned on the development plan of the planning authority concerned, as for use solely or primarily for residential purposes.

The 60% rate referred to relates to disposals of land, but does not relate to disposals of shares deriving their value from the land in question. Such disposals would seem to fall within the 20% rate.

The test of whether the land is zoned for residential use must be applied at the date of disposal (after 5 April 2002).

This could result in harsh treatment of the owner of land held at 5 April 2002 where the zoning is changed (say) from industrial to residential after 5 April 2002.

The complex rules relating to the CGT rate applicable on the disposal of development land seem all the more odd when it is considered that the rate of corporation tax applicable to the profits of a corporate dealer in land (after 1/1/2000) is 25% and can be as low as 20% in some cases. The major difference between the CGT rate (potentially 60%) and the CT rate (of 25%) on dealing in land may prove to be unsustainable. As long as the major difference in tax rates exists, it will create pressure on corporate land owners to view their land acquisitions and subsequent disposals as being a trading matter outside the scope of the charge to CGT. It may also create more corporate land owners, with companies being formed for the sole purpose of trying to avail of the lower corporate "land dealer" CT rate.

6.2   Meaning of Development Land

FA82 s36

The FA82 introduced a new concept of development land, which applied to disposals on or after 28 January 1982.

In broad terms, where there is a disposal of land and

• the consideration for disposal of the land

— exceeds

the current use value of the land,

it is development land.

The meaning of development land is not related in any way to the use to which the land is put. It is defined only in terms of the price received on disposal.

The concept of "development land" extends to include a disposal of unquoted shares which derive the greater part of their value from such land.

s648

"Development land" means land in the State the consideration for the disposal of which, or the market value of which at the time at which the disposal is made, exceeds the current use value of that land at the time at which the disposal is made, and includes shares deriving their value or the greater part of their value directly or indirectly from such land, other than shares quoted on a Stock Exchange.

s648

The most important aspect of the definition is the meaning given to the phrase *current use value.* This phrase is defined separately in relation to land, and shares deriving value from land.

Current Use Value -

(a) *Land* :

"in relation to land at any particular time means the amount which would be the market value of the land at that time if the market value were calculated on the assumption that it was at that time and would remain unlawful to carry out any development (within the meaning of secton 3 of the Act of 1963) in relation to the land other than development of a minor nature".

The Act of 1963 referred to is the Local Government (Planning and Development) Act 1963.

(b) *shares deriving their value from land.*

"in relation to shares in a company (being shares deriving their value.. ......from land, other than shares quoted on a stock exchange) at any particular time, means the amount which would be the market value of the shares at that time if the market value were calculated on the same assumption, in relation to the land from which the shares so derive value, as is mentioned in paragraph (a)".

There is a reference in the definition of "development land" above to shares *"deriving their value.......from such land".*

"Such land" refers to land *"the consideration for the disposal of which, or the market value of which at the time at which the disposal is made, exceeds the current use value of that land at the time at which the disposal is made".* Where the disposal in question is a disposal of shares, there will be no consideration for the disposal of the land because there is no disposal of the land per se. In such a case there is only the market value of the land which can be compared with the current use value of the land. Although at first reading, it might seem that the phrase "at the time at which the disposal is made" refers to a disposal of land, it is equally capable of referring to a disposal of shares, and the definition as phrased in relation to shares, is not logical.

Some of the ambiguity in the definition of development land can be demonstrated in the following examples.

Example 38

John is a farmer and has run into some financial difficulty. To raise cash to meet bank demands, he sold 50 acres of land for £¼ million to his father. The open value market value of the 50 acres is approximately £200,000 as is its current use value. John's father paid over the odds for the land in order to assist his son, without appearing make a gift to him at the expense of his other sons.

In the computation on Johns disposal of land, open market value of £200,000 would be substituted for the actual consideration passing, of £250,000.

Is the land development land? The open market value does not exceed current use value and on that basis it is not development land. However the actual consideration for the disposal did exceed the current use value. If the tax payer is obliged to regard land as being development land if either or both of the consideration or the market value exceeds current use value, then this is development land. That conclusion would seem a bit bizarre and may be avoided if the test is applied not to the actual consideration but the deemed consideration - i.e. open market value, since this is a transaction between connected parties (see paragraph 16).

Example 39

John is still under pressure from the bank and decides to sell another 50 acres, this time with some long term if uncertain development potential. The current use value is £200,000 and the market value £225,000. John receives a number of offers for the land, including offers at £225,000 but decides to accept an offer of £200,000 in the hope that it will preserve his indexation and give him a 20% capital gains tax rate rather than a 40% rate that would apply to non residential development land.

If it is only the consideration passing that has to be compared with current use value, this is not development land. But the market value does exceed current use value. If that test also must be applied (despite the fact that the Capital Gains Tax Act does not substitute open market value for actual consideration in the circumstances described above) then this is development land (as ones instinct would say it is).

The two examples above indicate the potential significance of the ambiguity, and the real difficulty of determining the correct meaning of some ambiguous drafting.

The definition of development land requires

   – the *current use value* of the land to be compared with

                    – the *consideration for the disposal* or the *market value* of the
land at the time of disposal

It is not immediately clear whether the current use value

- must be compared to both the market value and the consideration for the disposal, or

- whether a choice is allowed depending on the circumstances of the disposal.

This question pre-supposes that the consideration for the disposal and the market value could be different amounts.

s547 In certain circumstances, the actual consideration for the disposal is itself replaced by the market value of the asset. This would occur, for example, with a transaction between connected persons, or where the transaction is not a bargain at arm's length. In such a case, the consideration for the disposal is deemed to be the market value of the asset.

On the other hand, where an asset is disposed of between unconnected third parties at a price other than what some expert may consider to be its full potential value (for example because of a foolish buyer or a foolish seller) the agreed price must be taken as being the open market value as between those parties. To have to take account of the fact that some other unconnected person at some time in the future may agree to a higher (or lower figure) would mean that the CGT consequences of any transfer of an asset could never be finally concluded.

There is one circumstance in which the dual test of consideration and open market value as compared to current use value is particularly significant. That is in the case of a part disposal of land or of shares deriving their value from land. The topic of part disposals is discussed in paragraph 11. The critical point to bear in mind is that the Acts state that a part disposal is to be treated as a disposal of the asset. In other words, a part disposal is treated as a total disposal of the asset save in one respect, ie that the base cost is restricted. If therefore there is a part disposal of land, it is quite possible that the consideration passing on the part disposal might be less than the current use value of the land. However, if the test to be applied is not only the consideration passing, but also a comparison of open market value of the land with current use value, then the land may yet be development land.

Example 40

John (in Example 38 and 39 above) is getting used to being under pressure from his bank and finds it necessary to dispose of another 50 acres of land. He is unwilling to see it pass out of the family forever and therefore grants a long lease of the land, rather than entering into an outright sale. He leases the land for a rent of £10,000 per annum, and a premium of £100,000. The lease is for a *period of 60 years. The current use value of the land at the date of disposal is £200,000, and its open market value at that date is £250,000.*

The premium of £100,000 (no part of which is chargeable to income tax since it is a long lease) is the consideration to be taken into account in a part disposal computation on the land. That sum however is less than the current use value of the land. If that were the only test to be applied, the land would not be development land. However the open market value of the land (which in this case is its value if the land were disposed of entirely on the open market by way of outright sale and not by way of the granting of a long lease) is £250,000, and that exceeds the current use value. Therefore the land is development land.

The fact that the premium charged is an open market premium, having regard to the period of the lease and the rent set) is not relevant. The alternative test to a comparison of consideration passing with current use value is to compare the open market value of the land with the current use value. That is not the consideration that would pass in an identical transaction to that giving rise to the part disposal, if it were in the open market to an unconnected party, but rather is the market value of the land if the land were absolutely disposed of by way of outright sale in the open market.

LG(P&D)A63
s2, 3, 4

In the context of the meaning of "current use value" the term ***"development of a minor nature"*** is itself defined as meaning development (not being development by a Local Authority or statutory undertaker) which under or by virtue of s4 Local Government (Planning and Development) Act 1963 is exempted development for the purposes of the Local Government (Planning and Development) Acts 1963 and 1976.

The term 'statutory undertaker' takes the meaning assigned to it by s2 Local Government (Planning and Development) Act 1963, which is as follows:

"statutory undertaker" means a person authorised by a British or Saorstat Eireann statute or an Act of the Oireachtas or an order having statutory force to construct, work, or carry on a railway, canal, inland navigation, dock harbour, gas, electricity, or other public undertaking".

This part of the meaning of development land, has eliminated a doubt which existed under the previous definition in relation to whether or not land sold to a Local Authority for certain development was excluded.

The term 'development' is defined in s3 Local Government (Planning and Development) Act 1963 as follows:-

3.(1) "Development" in this Act means, save where the context otherwise requires, the carrying out of any works on, in, or under land or the making of any material change in the use of any structures or other land.

(2) For the purposes of subsection (1) of this section and without prejudice to the generality thereof -

(a) where any structure or other land or any tree or other object on land becomes used for the exhibition of advertisements, or

(b) where land becomes used for any of the following purposes:

(i) the placing or keeping of any vans, tents or other objects, whether or not movable and whether or not collapsible, for the purpose of caravanning or camping or the sale of goods,

(ii) the storage of caravans or tents,

(iii) the deposit of bodies or other parts of vehicles, old metal, mining or industrial waste, builders' waste, rubble or debris,

the use of the land shall be taken as having materially changed.

(3) For the avoidance of doubt it is hereby declared that for the purposes of this section the use as two or more dwellings of any structure previously used as a single dwelling involves a material change in the use of the structure and of each part thereof which is so used.

The exempted development within the meaning of section 4 of that Act is:-

(1) (a) development consisting of the use of any land for the purposes of agriculture or forestry (including afforrestation), and development consisting of the use for any of those purposes of any building occupied together with land so used;

(b) development by the council of a county in the county health district;

(c) development by the corporation of a county or other borough in such borough;

(d) development by the council of an urban district in such district;

(e) development consisting of the carrying out by the corporation of a county of other borough or the council of a county or an urban district of any works required for the construction of a new road or the maintenance or improvement of a road;

(f) development consisting of the carrying out by any local authority or statutory undertaker of any works for the purpose of inspecting, repairing, renewing, altering or removing any sewers, mains, pipes, cables, overhead wires, or other apparatus, including the breaking open of any street or other land for that purpose;

(g) development consisting of the carrying out of works for the maintenance, improvement or other alteration of any structure, being works which affect only the interior of the structure or which do not materially affect the external appearance of the

> *structure so as to render such appearance inconsistent with the character of the structure or of neighbouring structures;*
>
> (h) *development consisting of the use of any structure or other land within the curtilage of a dwellinghouse for any purpose incidental to the enjoyment of the dwellinghouse as such;*
>
> (i) *development consisting of the carrying out of any of the works referred to in the Land Reclamation Act, 1949.*
>
> (2) (a) *The Minister may by regulations provide for any class of development being exempted development for the purposes of this Act and such provision may be either without conditions or subject to conditions and either general or confined to a particular area or place.*
>
> (b) *Regulations under this subsection may, in particular and without prejudice to the generality of the foregoing paragraph, provide, in the case of structures or other land used for a purpose of any specified class, for the use thereof for any other purpose being exempted development for the purposes of this Act.*
>
> (3) *References in this Act to exempted development shall be construed a references to development which is:-*
>
> (a) *any of the developments specified in subsection (1) of this section, or*
>
> (b) *development which, having regard to any regulations under subsection (2) of this section, is exempted development for the purposes of this Act.*

Further exemptions are to be found in the Local Government (Planning and Development) Regulations 1994, made under the authority refered to in 2(a) above.

The UK case of Morgan v Gibson considered the meaning of "development land". The dicta in Lord Scarman's judgement in Watkins v Kidson from which it appeared that development value was to be equated with "hope value" was approved.

There is a popular misconception that development land refers only to "a green field" and cannot refer to land already built on. This is incorrect. The test as to whether land is or is not development land is based solely on a question of value. Would the market value of the land be lower if the land could never obtain planning permission? If so it is development land, and if not, it is not development land. The physical condition of the land is irrelevant to the question, save insofar as it impacts on its value.

A city site already built on would be development land if its market value reflected the hope that the site could be cleared and redeveloped, or the hope of securing an alteration in its use. On the other hand, a "green field" suited for housing development might not be development land if its value in its current use (e.g. as the grounds of a large country house) exceeds its value for housing development; or if neighbouring householders would pay a higher amount to secure it as an addition to their gardens, than a builder would as a building site.

In determining whether or not land is development land it does not matter whether or not the land presently has planning permission for a change of use, or for any particular form of development. If it has such planning permission, then its current use value must be determined by making the assumption that it does not have that planning permission, and further assuming that it never would obtain that planning permission, or any other planning permission.

The definition of development land suggests that if the assumption that no planning permission would ever be available would reduce the market value of a piece of land, that the land is then development land. But almost any land, no matter what its present use or location, would suffer some reduction in value, no matter how small, on the basis of such an assumption being made regarding it. It cannot have been the intention of the Oireachtas that all land in the State, with some minor exceptions such as the summit of Carrantuohill, should be treated as development land. Were there such an intention, it would surely have been more clearly expressed.

The test as to whether land is or is not development land involves, in every case, the valuation of the land. Such a process cannot lead to a precise and certain result (since it is no more than an opinion as to the outcome of a hypothetical event) but usually results in a range of values being identified within which market value is likely to fall. As a matter of common sense (endorsed for use in capital gains tax cases by the UK case of Zim Properties Ltd. v Proctor) only a difference in value in excess of the normal "range of error" inherent in the valuation process relating to land, should be regarded as being significant in determining whether land is or is not development land. This proposition, that minor variations in valuation should not determine the question, received some support from the Supreme Court decision in the Daly case, where the constitutional requirement of proportionality was stated to apply to tax laws. The tax penalties which apply if land is development land are severe. It would seem unjust that a minor difference in the value of land (or more precisely, in an experts opinion as to the value of land) should attract such severe consequences.

• **Revenue/Chief Inspector's CGT manual :**

— In part 19 paragraph 8.2, it is acknowledges that *"the valuation of property is not an exact science. Nevertheless it is normally possible to determine from all the relevant facts that the market value of a particular asset lies within a particular price range."*

Unfortunately the courts have not had an opportunity to consider the matter so there can be no certainty regarding it.

The case of J. McMahon (Inspector of Taxes) v Albert Noel Murphy, heard before Justice Lynch in the High Court on 25 November 1988 *gave a good example of development land.* Certain land, which lay close to a town in which little or no development had taken place, was solely in agricultural use on 5 April 1974. The case concerned the valuation of the land at that date. The Revenue Valuation Office had valued it solely on its value as agricultural land (the use to which it was being put) and refused to place any higher value on it to represent the hope value of development, on the grounds that they were not aware of any developer being in the market for land in that area on that date. The taxpayer had always had it in mind that the land might one day be developed and would not have sold the land for agricultural value. The judge ruled that all reasonable potential uses of the land should be taken into account in arriving at its value and that that included (in the particular instance in question) its potential use for development. Accordingly a valuation that reflected potential development value, and which was significantly higher than agricultural value was adopted. Agricultural value was £800 per acre, whereas the market value was held (reflecting hope value) to be £4,000 per acre. Since the development value was based on the assumption or hope that planning permission could be obtained in relation to the land so that it might be developed and put to alternate uses, it is clear that the land was development land as, in the absence of planning permission, its value would not be much greater than £800 per acre, and that is very significantly less than its true open market value.

- **Revenue Commissioners - Tax Briefing :**

- The Revenue Commissioners, in Issue 35 of Tax Briefing, March 1999 have stated *"Where a chargeable gain accrues on the grant of a right of way over development land which has planning permission for residential development, the right of way itself does not have planning permission for residential development. Accordingly the gain accruing on the grant of the right of way is chargeable to capital gains tax at 40%"*. The authors have reservations regarding this view. The grant of a right of way is not the total disposal of the land which is covered by the right of way and therefore is only a part disposal of that land or a larger block of land of which it is part.   A part disposal is a disposal of the land. Accordingly, the issue is whether the land (and not the right of way per se) has planning permission for residential development. Furthermore, a right of way is likely (of its nature) to relate to part only of a holding of land and will rarely (save in exceptional circumstances) extend to the total holding. For that reason also what is involved is likely to be part disposal and regard should be had to the planning status of all of the land which is held as a single asset for CGT purposes, and not merely that part of the land which is the subject matter of the right of way. The determination of what constitutes a single asset in terms of land is itself a complex matter and is discussed in paragraphs 4.4, and 11.

It should be noted that the Revenue statement pre-dates FA99 which would apply a 20% rate of corporation tax where land is zoned solely or primarily for residential purposes, regardless of the actual planning permission upon a portion of land.

Only land in the State can be development land. This is specifically stated in the definition, and in any event is implicit in the references to the Planning Acts in the definition of development land.

Example 41

John owns a farm which straddles the border with Northern Ireland, being partly in Fermanagh and partly in Cavan. Although the land is currently in agricultural use, its value is derived principally from extensive deposits of gravel on the land. Planning permission would be required to develop these gravel deposits.

John sells his farm to a quarrying company for £1m. £600,000 of this relates to the land in Northern Ireland and £400,000 relates to the land in the Republic. The current use value of the land in Northern Ireland is £150,000, and the current use value of the land in the Republic is £100,000.

The land in the Republic, being land in the State whose open market value, and the consideration for whose disposal, exceeds current use value, is development land and will suffer the higher rate of capital gains tax, restriction of indexation etc. The land in Northern Ireland, although its economic circumstances are identical to that of the land on the other side of the border, is not development land because it is not land in the State (whatever John's political views on that may be!). Accordingly the 20% rate of capital gains tax will apply to that disposal and full indexation will be available.

The question of when land constitutes a single asset, and when different blocks of land constitute separate assets, is discussed in paragraph 11. In the example above, difficulties of interpretation would arise if John's farm constituted a single asset. Since the land taken as a whole (the single asset) is not land in the State, can it be treated as development land? If, as we have done in the example above, the land on each side of the border is conveniently treated as a separate asset, the problem disappears. But it is not clear that a block of land inherited by John from his father as a unit on a single occasion and farmed by him as a single farm, and in every way commercially and physically inter-linked, does constitute more than a single asset.

6.3 Restriction on Indexation

In computing a gain or loss on the disposal of development land, on or after 28 January 1982, the relief due in respect of indexation is restricted. (See paragraph 14 for general rules on indexation).

s651 The effect of the restriction is to allow indexation only in respect of the part of the cost (or MV 6 April 1974) attributable to the current use value at the date of acquisition or 6 April 1974 (if later). No indexation is allowed in respect of enhancement expenditure.

Example 42

Land was acquired in 1972 at a cost of £10,000: planning permission was obtained in 1973. Market value at 6 April 1974 was £100,000. Enhancement expenditure incurred in 1976 was £30,000. Current use value at 6 April 1974 was £15,000: the land was sold in March 1998 for £300,000.

The gain is calculated as follows:	£	£
Sale proceeds March 1998		300,000
MV 1974		100,000
Enhancement Expenditure 1976		30,000
C.U.V. at 6/4/74	15,000	
Indexed @ 6.112	91,680	
Uplift in indexed CUV		76,680
CGT deductions		206,680
GAIN		93,320

The restriction of indexation can apply to **shares in an unquoted company** which derives its value from development land. The current use value in such a case is taken to be the value which the shares would have if development of its land were to be permanently impossible.

A difficulty may arise in the application of the legislation if the company did not own the development land in question at the date when the shareholder acquired his shares. The value of shares at a particular date cannot be affected by any assumption made regarding land which it did not own on that date, but only acquired at a later date. In such a case it would seem that the open market value and current use value of the shares would be the same, and no restriction of indexation would arise.

Example 43

Joe subscribed £100,000 for shares in Properties Limited, a newly created company on 30 June 1997. On 31 July 1997 Properties Limited applied the £100,000 in acquiring land as an investment. On 1 July 1998 Joe, having received an offer, sold his shares for £400,000, reflecting an increase in the value of the land due to having obtained planning permission during the period of his ownership of the shares.

Joe's shares derive their value from development land on the date at which he disposed of the shares i.e. 1 July 1998. In principle therefore indexation is available only in respect of the current use value of the shares at the date on which he acquired the shares i.e. 30 June 1997. At 30 June 1997 the shares were worth £100,000. No assumption made relating to the land which the company acquired a month later could affect the value of the shares at 30 June 1997.

Accordingly the current use value of the shares at 30 June 1997 is the same as their cost price i.e. £100,000, and no restriction of indexation arises.

6.4   **Restriction on certain reliefs**

s652   As a general rule,

- *roll-over relief* - TCA97 s652(1) (see paragraph 26.11) and

- *relief available for the reinvestment of the proceeds of a compulsory purchase of certain assets* - s652(2) (see paragraph 27)

do not apply to a gain arising on the disposal of development land on or after 28 January 1982.

There are a number of exceptions to this general rule, where the reliefs will apply, even though the disposal is regarded as being of development land. The exceptions are:

s652(6)   • **Disposal by sporting bodies:**

An exception to the restriction on the use of *roll-over relief and CPO relief* is made where the disposal is by a *"body of persons established for the sole purpose of promoting athletic or amateur games or sports, being a disposal which is made in relation to such of the activities of that body as are directed to that purpose"*. Such a gain will still qualify for relief under the normal rules.

The phrase "athletic or amateur games or sports" would seem to mean that games or sports which are athletic may be a qualifying purpose even if such games or sports are not exclusively amateur. "Athletic" has no defined meaning in the legislation and would seem to refer to any game or sport requiring muscular strength, skill and co-ordination. It is arguable that the reference to "amateur games" could include even the activities of a body promoting amateur chess.

Sports bodies which employ some professional players, while their membership is principally comprised of amateur players, may still exist solely to promote amateur sport, the use of professionals being an end to that means. The position of such sports bodies is not clear and the issue is open to debate.

s235   The definition quoted above is similar to that which appears in TCA97 s235. That definition was the subject matter of a case which reached the Irish Supreme Court - Revenue v ORMG. There the Supreme Court (in a majority decision) held that two persons cannot constitute a "body of persons". They did not indicate what was the minimum number of persons which could constitute a "body of persons". In his judgement, the late McCarthy, J, reviewed the background to the legislation, as far back as the Finance Act 1927. That Finance Act confined the relief to the games of Gaelic football, hurling and handball. This history of the legislation might open up some argument as to whether the word "or" in the expression "athletic or amateur sports" may not be intended to mean "and". The word "or", rather confusingly, can sometimes mean "and" depending on context, although that is not the usual meaning of the word.

s652(2)
- **Disposal of land - for local amenity or environmental reasons.**

The restriction on *roll-over relief* will not apply to a disposal of development land (on or after 6th April 1995) where *"the relevant local authority gives a certificate in writing to the person making the disposal stating that the land being disposed of is subject to a use which, on the basis of guidelines issued by the Minister for the Environment, is inconsistent with the protection and improvement of the amenities of the general area within which that land is situated or is otherwise damaging to the local environment"*.

For this purpose, the *relevant local authority* means *"the council of a county, or the corporation of a county or other borough or, where appropriate, the urban district council, in whose functional area the land being disposed of is situated"*.

It is anomalous that this relief is applied only to "roll-over relief" under s611 and not to "CPO relief" under s612.

This is discussed further in paragraph 26.11.

s73(1)
- **Compulsory purchase of farm land for road building or road widening**

A further exception is made, in that the restriction on the use of *CPO relief* (see paragraph 27) does not apply to a disposal of *farm land* (on or after 6th April 1995) where that land is disposed of to an authority possessing compulsory purchase powers

— *"for the purpose of enabling that authority to construct, widen, or extend a road or part of a road, or*

— *for a purpose connected with, or ancilliary to the construction, widening or extension of a road or part of a road by the authority"*.

Farm land for this purpose means *"land occupied and used only for the purposes of farming"*.

LG(P&D)A63
s29
A *compulsory disposal* in this context means a disposal to an authority possessing compulsory purchase powers. It must be made pursuant to the exercise of those powers, or the giving of formal notice of intention to exercise those powers. The term 'compulsory disposal' would not include a disposal to which the provisions of s29 Local Government (Planning and Development) Act 1963 apply. That section is the one under which a person can require the planning authority to purchase the land in certain circumstances where planning permission has been refused.

This is also dealt with in paragraph 27.5.

- **Disposal of racecourse land**

s597

With effect from 21st April 1997, the disposal of land by an authorised racecourse is not excluded from roll-over relief under s597. However, the exclusion of such land from CPO relief remains.

To avoid the exclusion from relief under s597 (roll-over relief) it is necessary that the land in question:

IHIA94 s2

— should be an asset of an authorised racecourse within the meaning of s.2, Irish Horseracing Industry Act 1994 and must be used for the provision of appropriate facilities or services to carry on horseracing at racemeetings, or to accommodate persons associated with horseracing, including the public.

There is some ambiguity in this requirement, in that the part of the requirement regarding the land being used for the provision of facilities, etc. makes it clear that it is appropriate facilities at a racemeeting, whereas land held for the purpose of accommodating persons associated with horseracing would not appear to be confined to land used to accommodate them at racemeetings. For that reason, the land may not even be located directly at the racecourse.

— must have been owned by the authorised racecourse for at least 5 years ending with the time of disposal.

— the new replacement land must be in the ownership of the authorised racecourse.

These provisions apply notwithstanding that the authorised racecourse may not be carrying on a trade in the conduct of racemeetings.

6.5   Development Land - use of losses.

s653

The FA82 (now TCA97 s653) restricts the use of losses against development land gains, where the gain arises on or after 28 January 1982. The only losses which can be deducted from such gains, are post 27 January 1982 losses on disposals of development land. Other losses cannot be set against such gains.

Subject to that restriction, the normal loss rules apply (see paragraph 20). Losses (including losses on the disposal of development land) may be set first against any gains chargeable at the highest rate of CGT. There is no rule requiring losses on development land to be set against development land gains in priority to other gains.

6.6   Development - Small Gains

s650   The above rules relating to development land (including the tax rates) do not apply to an individual in a year of assessment if the total consideration from disposals of development land in that year do not exceed £15,000. In applying this rule, husband and wife are treated separately.

It should be noted that this exception to the normal rules is given by reference to the amount of the consideration for the disposal. The amount of the actual gain or loss is not relevant.

s649A(2)(b)   The standard 20% rate of CGT applies to a sale of development land where the total consideration from such disposals in the year of assessment does not exceed £15,000 (irrespective of whether the land is sold for residential development or not).

6.7   Gains Arising to Companies

s649   As a general rule, gains arising to an Irish resident company are chargeable to corporation tax as part of the profits of the company for the accounting period in which the gain arises. Development land gains arising to a company on disposals made on or after 28 January 1982 are chargeable to CGT, and not to corporation tax. The effect of this provision is to exclude such gains from the profits of the company for corporation tax purposes. Accordingly, relief for trade losses, group relief, and other deductions from profits cannot be set against such development land gains. The special rules governing the transfer of development land between companies in a group, are set out in paragraph 78.

6.8   Principal Private Residence

The treatment of development land which also qualifies for relief as a principal private residence of an individual, is set out in paragraph 24.12.

6.9   Income Tax Provisions

As already mentioned, if the consideration for the disposal of an asset is chargeable as income, it is not chargeable to CGT. In view of the income tax anti-avoidance provisions in the case of land transactions, this rule is particularly important in relation to such disposals.

The income tax anti-avoidance provisions are wide and complex. The following outline of the income tax position is only intended as a general guide. The practitioner is referred to the appropriate legislation should the need arise.

6.9.1   S.17 F(MP)A 1968 - TCA97 s640

s640   This deals with the circumstances in which a transaction in land (not otherwise caught as trade) is deemed to be a trade, and the profits are chargeable under Case 1.

The provisions apply where an interest in land is disposed of in the course of a "business" of dealing in or developing land. The terms "dealing" and "developing" are given extremely wide meanings. The provisions are mainly intended to close specific loopholes in the general law as to whether or not a particular transaction constitutes a trade.

In the past, income tax was avoided on profits arising out of land transactions in many and varying ways. The following are some of the successful methods used in the past by taxpayers to avoid income tax on the profits arising from transactions in land, which for the main part depended on the taxpayer being able to show that the transaction did not constitute a trade for the purposes of Schedule D, Case I:

- *A developer granted a long lease at a premium - as nothing was sold, no trade existed.*

Example 44

> *A developer bought a site, and built an office block on that site. Let us assume that the developed property is valued at £5m. It is clear that if he had sold the office block, the profit would have been charged to income tax under Schedule D, Case I as the profits of his property developing trade. Instead of selling the property, he granted (say) a 500 year lease for an annual rent of £1 and a premium of £5m.*
>
> *At the time of this type of arrangement, there was no CGT, nothing was sold so there was no trade, and as the lease was for a period exceeding 50 years, the premium could not be treated as rent income.*

- *A disposal of land not acquired as trading stock e.g. farmer turns developer. The farmer was merely realising the fixed assets of his farming trade. What he sold was not stock in trade, and accordingly a Schedule D, Case I profit did not result from the sale.*

- *A disposal of land owned by company in the course of liquidating the company.*

Example 45

> *A builder formed a company, and the company was used to build a shopping centre. On completion of the building, the company was placed in voluntary liquidation. The liquidator sold the buildings to the purchaser, and the proceeds were received by the builder as the proceeds of liquidation of the company (for the disposal of his shares).*

> *This type of scheme was used prior to 1974 (Pre CGT). The liquidator was not carrying on a trade when he sold the property - he was merely realising the assets of the company in the course of liquidating that company. The actual builder had disposed of nothing but his shares in the company.*

- **The sale of shares in property owning company (the company developed the land - the shareholder is merely realising his investment).**

Example 46

> Let us assume, in **example 45**, that instead of liquidating the company, the builder sold the shares in the company to the person who wished to buy the property.
>
> All the builder had sold was the shares in his company. This was the disposal of an investment - not a trade. The company had sold nothing - it still owned the developed property.
>
> The purchaser now owned the company which in turn owned the property, and to add insult to injury, instead of paying 6% stamp duty on the purchase of the property, he paid only 1% stamp duty on the transfer of shares.

Two cases decided by the Irish Courts highlight the main areas attacked by s640:

s640

BIRCH v DELANEY (Supreme Court - July 1936)
Denis Delaney was a builder, who disposed of his houses, not by an outright sale of his full interest in the houses, but by granting a long lease at a premium to the "purchaser". In practical terms, the purchaser bought the house subject to a ground rent. It was held that Denis Delaney was merely granting leases, and the profits could not be charged under Case 1. S640 deals with this situation by deeming the transaction to be a trade. It provides that where the profits would be chargeable under Case 1 if the full interest in the property were sold, that the disposal of anything less than the full interest (ie a lease) is deemed to be a trade in certain circumstances.

s640

SWAINE v VE (Supreme Court - March 1964)

A builder acquired land for the purpose of farming it. He subsequently changed his mind and developed it. It was held that the subsequent sale of the developed property was not a disposal of trading stock, and accordingly, not chargeable under Case 1. S640 provides that if the profit would be chargeable if the land was trading stock, that it is deemed to be chargeable under Case 1 notwithstanding that it was not acquired as trading stock.

The section also deals with a disposal by a liquidator, by deeming him to continue the trade of the company.

s640

In a later case (J Mara v Hummingbird Ltd) the taxpayer developed a property with the intention of letting it, and holding it as an investment. He was, however, subsequently persuaded to sell it. The transaction was attacked by the Revenue under s640. The case was decided against the Revenue, as that section only applied where the full interest was not sold, or where it was not acquired in the course of a business of dealing in or developing land. S640 includes an amendment introduced by FA81 s28 to include a situation where the full interest in the property is sold.

6.9.2   **FA81 s29 - TCA97 s641**

s641

This section, deems certain capital profits on the disposal of land, (directly or indirectly) to be income chargeable under Case IV. It is extremely wide in its potential application.

It charges any gain of a capital nature (not otherwise charged as income) arising on the disposal of:

- land acquired with the main object of realising a profit on its disposal (including property deriving value from land).

- land held as trade stock

- land developed by a company with the main object of making a gain on its disposal.

The legislation effectively looks through any schemes or arrangements, whether concerning the land or value derived from it whereby the land or control over it is effectively disposed of.

7   COMPUTATION OF GAIN OR LOSS

7.1   Computation rules

The CGT legislation sets out a series of rules for determining

* the amount of the *consideration for the disposal* and,

* the amount of the *deductible expenditure*.

Those rules are not contained in any one place, but are spread out through different sections of the legislation. The overall approach taken by the legislation is to set out the overall general rules which apply to all disposals. The legislation also sets out special rules which apply only in specific circumstances.

s28   TCA97 s28 states that a capital gain is......." *a chargeable gain computed in accordance with this Act..*"

The CGT Acts merely sets out rules for calculating

— the proceeds of disposal, and

— the deductible expenditure.

It does not explicitly state (nor is it stated anywhere else) that a gain is to be computed by deducting the cost of the asset from the proceeds of its disposal. The legislation however, proceeds on that assumption which can be logically inferred.

The approach taken in this text is similar, in that it attempts

* to explain the broad rules which apply to all disposals, and

* then deals with the special rules which apply only in specific circumstances.

The failure of the capital gains tax legislation to explicitly state how a gain or a loss is to be computed was recognised in the UK case of Garner v Pounds Ship Owners and Ship Brokers where it was stated: *"The implication of (the capital gains tax provisions dealing with the computation of a gain on disposal) though nowhere stated expressly, is that in the case of an arm's length disposal for a monetary consideration such consideration is the starting point for the computation of the gain. There is no basic rule indicating how that consideration is to be identified, but there are various provisions indicating the matters to be taken into account. There is also a detailed provision indicating the deductions which may be made".*

The topic of "disposal of assets" was dealt with in paragraph 4.

The rules for calculating the amount of the proceeds of disposal to be taken into the computation of a chargeable gain or allowable loss for CGT purposes are dealt with in paragraph 8.

The computation of the amount of deductible expenditure is dealt with in paragraph 9.

The following comments made by Lord Wilberforce in the Aberdeen Construction case, have often been quoted, especially in other UK cases, and are worthy of consideration, before reading the detailed rules relating to computation of gain or loss:

"The legislation imposing (capital gains tax)....is necessarily complicated, and the detailed provisions, as they affect this or that other case, must of course be looked at with care. But a guiding principle must underlie any interpretation of the Act, namely, that its purpose is to tax capital gains and to make allowance for capital losses, each of which ought to be arrived at on normal business principles. No doubt anomalies may occur, but in straight forward situations,....the court should hesitate before accepting results which are paradoxical and contrary to business sense. To paraphrase a famous cliché, the capital gains tax is a tax on gains; it is not a tax on arithmetical differences".

Reasonable though these words of Lord Wilberforce may be, the fact remains that capital gains tax is a tax on gains computed in accordance with the capital gains tax legislation. That legislation and "business sense" are not closely related.

8 CONSIDERATION FOR DISPOSAL

8.1 Broad Outline - Consideration

The CGT legislation sets out a series of rules for calculating the amount of the consideration for the disposal to be taken into the computation of the CGT gain or loss. There are in broad terms, two separate issues to be considered:

• what is the amount of the consideration for the disposal, and

• how much (if any) of that consideration is to be taken into the CGT computation of the chargeable gain or allowable loss ?

There are many instances where the CGT law:

• deems a disposal of an asset to have taken place, where in fact there has been no real disposal, and

• deems that no disposal of an asset has taken place, where in reality there has actually been a disposal.

There are also many instances where the legislation *deems* notional consideration for a disposal for CGT purposes, and that consideration replaces the actual consideration in the computation of the gain or loss, irrespective of the amount (if any) of the actual consideration, and irrespective of whether any consideration has actually been received by the person making the disposal.

s547

Example 47 (no actual consideration)

Mary gifted a holiday cottage valued at £30,000 (which she had owned for many years) to her daughter Susan on the occasion of Susan's 18th birthday.

In this case, there is no actual consideration at all, but the legislation deems the asset to be disposed of for a price equal to its open market value

s547
s10.

Example 48 (transfer at undervalue)

James transferred a painting valued at £40,000 to his grandson for a consideration of £5,000.

Where a person transfers an asset at an undervalue to a person connected with him the legislation deems the asset to be disposed of at a price equal to its open market value .

s1028

Example 49 (transfer between husband and wife)

Tim transferred an investment property valued today at £100,000 to his wife, Helen for full consideration. It had been bought on the open market by Tim in 1980 for £30,000 (including incidental costs of acquisition). Helen transferred £100,000 cash from her personal bank deposits as consideration for the property.

On a transfer between husband and wife (living together as such) the legislation deems the transfer to be at the transferor's base cost. This cost (£30,000) is substantially less than the actual price paid by Helen of £100,000.

s573

Example 50 (asset passing on death)

John died on 1st January 2000. Under his will a valuable painting passed to his niece, Anne.

In such circumstances, the law deems that John has not made any disposal, even though Anne has actually acquired an asset .

These are but a few examples of occasions where the CGT law *deems* the position to be what could be totally different to what actually happened.

In some circumstances the legislation may deem the disposal to be made for a price equal to the market value of the asset, or in some circumstances deems a sale price equal to the cost of that asset (which itself could be a deemed figure). In other circumstances the law may deem a disposal where none actually exist. The circumstances in which the legislation substitutes an *artificial deemed sale price* in place of the actual sale price (if any) are dealt with mainly in:

• paragraph 13 (assets held at 6th April 1974),

• paragraph 16 (connected persons/bargains not at arms length)

• paragraph 33 (married persons)

- paragraph 75 (transfers between members of a group of companies).

- paragraph 51.6 (pre-disposal dividends on disposal of subsidiary by group).

Once the consideration has been determined, it is then necessary to establish the extent to which that consideration is to be taken into account in computing any gain or loss on the disposal.

8.2   Amount of Consideration

s547   In certain circumstances TCA97 s547 can substitute open market value as being the consideration to be taken into account for CGT purposes, in place of the actual consideration arising in a transaction. Other provisions, e.g. disposal between spouses (see paragraph 33.1) or group relief provisions (see paragraph 75) substitute base cost for capital gains tax purposes for the actual consideration, in the CGT computation. But where specific provisions substituting a deemed or notional consideration for actual consideration do not have application then the consideration to be taken into account in a capital gains tax computation is the actual consideration received by the person making the disposal.

In the UK case of Aberdeen Construction v IRC the House of Lords had to consider a case in which £250,000 was offered for shares in a company, on condition that a loan of £0.5 million owing from that company to the vendor be waived. It was accepted by all of the judges in the House of Lords that the shares were virtually worthless were such a loan not waived. The issue which the House of Lords had to consider (among others) was whether the £250,000 in question was

– solely consideration for the shares which were the subject matter of the contract, or

– whether it represented consideration for both the acquisition of the shares, and for the agreement to waive the loan, and whether accordingly it had to be apportioned between these two purposes.

All of the judges were agreed that the answer depended on a proper construction, not of the CGT legislation, but rather of the sale contract in respect of the shares. Three of the judges held that the figure of £250,000 was consideration both for the shares, and for the waiver of the loan, and accordingly had to be apportioned. Two of the judges held that the terms of the contract relating to the shares were such that the £250,000 was expressed to be consideration for the shares only.

Lord Russell of Killowen (one of two dissenting Law Lords) said:

"It is I believe agreed on all hands that if Westminster had said to the taxpayer company "I am not interested in the Rock Fall shares while your debt remains outstanding. Go away and extinguish it and I will then bid you a quarter million pounds for the shares, the taxpayer company's first point could not have succeeded. The distinction between that situation and a contract such as was made, viz. to buy the shares for £250,000 on condition the debt be extinguished, is too fine for me to appreciate. Recognition of the distinction I think, with respect, stems from an understandable reluctance to hold that the ambush of this legislation should catch the taxpayer company with a taxable capital gain when it has lost a substantial sum in its unhappy venture in Rock Fall".

Viscount Dilhorn said:

"The offer was expressed to be one to buy the whole issued share capital of Rock Fall for £250,000 and it would in my view be wrong to interpret it as including an offer to pay a part of that sum for the waiver of the loan. Just as a man may offer to buy a secondhand car for £x on condition that it passes its MOT test or offer to buy a house for a certain sum if certain repairs or alterations are made without agreeing to pay a sum towards the expense of the test or for the repairs or alterations, so here, in my opinion , it is not right having regard to the terms of the letter to conclude that Westminster had agreed to pay for the waiver and so to attribute any part of the price to the obtaining of the waiver. If apportionment of the price at £250,000 between the issued share capital and for the waiver was justifiable in this case, why should the apportionment be limited to these items? Taxation losses were to remain (as a condition of the contract) for the benefit of Westminster. Presumably they were of value to Westminster for otherwise that would not have been made a condition of the contract. If they were of value and any apportionment was justified, I can see no reason for limiting it to the waiver. Some of it surely would be attributable to the acquisition by Westminster of the taxation losses.

It is not open to us to rewrite the bargain made between the parties, and I do not think it is right to hold that part of the £250,000 was paid for the waiver. The letter states that the price was to be paid for the issued share capital and does not state that it was to be paid for anything else."

The quotations given above were from the judgements of the two law lords who dissented from the majority opinion of the House of Lords, which was that the contract had provided for the payment of £250,000 both for the acquisition of shares, and for the waiving of the loan.

The important principle upon which all the judges in the Aberdeen Construction case were agreed was that the consideration for the disposal of the shares was the consideration provided for in the contract for the disposal. While there was disagreement as to the meaning of the contract, there was no disagreement on that principle. The interpretation placed on the contract by the majority of the House of Lords does not lay down any rule of law which could or should influence an Irish court. With all respect, the authors consider that the opinion of the majority of the House of Lords as to the construction of the contract was, as suggested by Lord Russell, influenced by a wish to avoid harshness to the taxpayer, and may not be followed by Irish courts.

A broadly similar transaction to that which occurred in the Aberdeen case was the subject of a subsequent case, Booth v Buckwell. In that case however the contract for the disposal of share had specified one sum of money to be consideration for the shares, and a second sum to be consideration for the discharge or partial waiver of a loan. Browne - Wilkinson J. held that the decision in the Aberdeen case did not bind him, as in the Aberdeen case only a single sum was specified as consideration, and accordingly, once it was held that it was consideration for both the shares and the waiver of a loan, apportionment was inevitable. That was not the case where separate sums were specified for each item viz. the shares, and the waiver of the loan. He said *"where parties to a composite transaction have, as a result of negotiations between themselves, provided that part of the consideration is to be paid for one part of the transaction and part for another, they cannot subsequently seek to reallocate the consideration for tax purposes. They have chosen to carry through the transaction in a particular manner, and the taxation consequences flow from the manner adopted. The Crown's position may well be different in certain cases. After all the Crown was not a party to the transaction."*

s547

It does not appear to the authors that the question of whether or not the Crown (or the Irish State as the case may be) was a party to the transaction is relevant. In the absence of specific statutory provisions such as TCA97 s547, there is no authority to go behind the consideration specified by parties (acting in good faith in this regard).

The UK case of Marren v Ingles concerned a contract for the sale of shares for an immediate (or almost immediate) and certain sum of money, together with a further sum of money to be paid at an unspecified future date in the event of the company whose shares were sold being floated on the Stock Exchange. The amount of the second payment was dependent on the price at which the shares would be floated on the Stock Exchange, were they so floated. In fact they were floated two years after the date of the contract for the original disposal. In that case, the Revenue and the taxpayer agreed that the original disposal of the shares was for an immediate sum of money, together with a chose in action consisting of the contingent future right to receive a further payment. The case was concerned with the taxation consequences which flowed from the receipt of that further payment two years later. The case was not concerned with the determination of the consideration which should have been taken into account on the original disposal of shares in 1970.

That question was considered only by one judge, Lord Fraser of Tullybelton in the House of Lords. He stated at page 505 *"the first question is whether the right to half of the profit (the second sum which was paid in 1972) is properly to be regarded as a separate asset, or simply as a deferred part of the price of the shareholdings (disposed of in 1970). In my opinion the former view is correct."* Lord Fraser advanced no reasons for this latter statement. All of the judgements in the case of Marren v Ingles proceeded on the basis that the agreement between the Revenue and the taxpayer regarding the 1970 disposal was correct. They did so notwithstanding that the contract for the sale of the shares in 1970 clearly stated the consideration to consist of two sums of money, and not one sum of money together with a chose in action. As an inevitable consequence of the second sum of money being delayed in its payment, a chose in action necessarily arose in the hands of the vendor, but it was not a consideration for which he had stipulated in the contract. The short quotation from Lord Fraser's judgement given above is the sole instance in the case, in any of the courts in which it was heard, in which the correct determination of the consideration for the disposal of shares in 1970 was considered.

In the authors' opinion this case ought not to be regarded as authority, influential or otherwise, for the proposition that the actual consideration negotiated by parties acting in good faith can be disregarded, and that there can be substituted for it short lived legal rights which come into existence in consequence of the agreement between the parties (such as *"the right to receive"* a deferred and/or contingent further amount of consideration). Such a proposition would in any event run counter to the decision of the House of Lords in the case of Stanton v Drayton. In that case, Lord Fraser said at page 590 *"the cases of Osborne v Steel Barrel Company Ltd. and Craddock v Zevo Finance Company Ltd. are ample authority for saying in the words of Lord Wright in the latter case, that the Crown is not entitled to go behind the agreed consideration in a case where, as in the present case the transaction is not alleged to be dishonest or otherwise not straightforward".* In the same case Lord Roskill said *"What the consideration is in any particular case must be determined by reference to the contract which the parties concerned have concluded".*

The UK case of Stanton v Drayton was concerned with the capital gains tax consequences of a contract under which a company acquired from Eagle Star Insurance Company Ltd. a portfolio of investments at the price of £3,900,000 odd. The price was satisfied, in accordance with the agreement between the companies by the allotment by the taxpayer company to Eagle Star of 2.4 million (odd) ordinary shares of 25p each in the taxpayer company, the issue price of each share being 160p. Although the case arose in relation to a subsequent disposal of part of the portfolio of shares, and was primarily concerned with the consideration given for those shares by the taxpayer company, that determination of the consideration given for the shares was clearly relevant to the question of the consideration received by Eagle Star for the shares.

Although the contract for the acquisition of the portfolio of shares had placed a price on the shares of £3.9 million odd, and had agreed that that price was to be satisfied by the issue of 2.4 million shares odd fully paid up as 160p, the Revenue argued that the value of the consideration given for the portfolio was a lesser figure. It based this argument on the fact that the Stock market value of the shares, immediately after they were issued, was only 125p per share. The House of Lords unanimously ruled against the Revenue. Lord Fraser of Tullybelton having reviewed the judgements in Osborne v Steel Barrel Company Ltd.and Craddock v Zevo Finance Company Ltd, said:

"From these judgements I extract the following propositions relevant to the present appeal. (1) A company can issue its own shares "as consideration for the acquisition of property"....(2) The value of consideration given in the form of fully paid shares allotted by a company is not the value of the shares allotted but, in the case of an honest and straightforward transaction, is the price on which the parties agreed....

The latter point was expressed even more forcibly in the House of Lords by Lord Wright where he said:

"No authority was cited for the claim of the Revenue in a case like this to go behind the agreed consideration and substitute a different figure.....One consequence of taking the agreed value of the shares as conclusive is that cases may occur in which that value may seem surprising, because the market value of the newly allotted shares on the day when they are first quoted proves to be much higher or much lower than their value agreed between the parties. That might happen, for example, because of some unexpected political event occurring between the date of the agreement and the date of the first quotation. But, provided the agreed value has been honestly reached by a bargain at arm's length, it must, in my opinion, be final and it is not open to attack by the Crown."

s552   The case of Stanton v Drayton was concerned with the deduction available to a taxpayer in respect of *"the amount or value of the consideration, in money or money's worth, given by him or on his behalf wholly and exclusively for the acquisition of the asset"* as stated in TCA97 s552. In the opinions of the authors, the comments above relating to the value of the consideration given by the person acquiring an asset are equally applicable and relevant for capital gains tax purposes to the value of the consideration received by the person disposing of the same asset.

The UK Spectros case (discussed in paragraph 8.9) highlights the principle that the consideration which parties to a contract have agreed in clear terms should be respected for tax purposes.

Where two unconnected persons dealing at arm's length exchange objects or assets, each will have a disposal of an asset (ie the object or other asset which he gave in exchange for that which he received). The consideration which each receives for their disposal is the value of that which they receive. Usually where two parties acting at arm's length exchange assets, the assets will be of identical open market value. That is not necessarily the case. One party may simply have made a bad bargain.

- **Revenue/Chief Inspector's CGT manual:**

—Paragraph 19.2.6.2 of the Revenue Commissioners manual on capital gains tax notes that in such a situation the fact that the two taxpayers place values on the assets which each received, which are not identical *"is not itself sufficient to challenge the arm's length nature of the transactions, although in practice, unless the difference is clearly substantial, all parties may well agree on a common value".*

The case of Garner v Pounds Shipowners and Shipbrokers concerned a case where an option was granted over certain land for an amount of £399,750. Under the terms of the contract the sum was not to be released unless and until certain covenants relating to the land were released, and the vendor undertook to use his best endeavours to secure such release. The vendor expended £90,000 in a successful effort to secure the release of the covenants. The Court of Appeal held that, on a consideration of the terms of the option agreement, the entire consideration of £399,750 was expressed to be consideration for the grant of the option, and no part of it was expressed to be consideration for securing the release of the covenants. Accordingly, the entire consideration fell to be taxed on a disposal of the option and no deduction was available for the expenditure incurred in securing the release of the covenants.

8.3   Meaning of consideration

The capital gains tax legislation does not provide a definition for *"consideration"*. The meaning of *"consideration"* was considered in the UK case of Fielder v Vedlynn. There it was stated:

"It was common ground before the Special Commissioner and before me that the definition in law of "consideration" was as set out in the speech of Lord Lindley giving the advice of the Privy Counsel in Flemming v Bank of New Zealand , quoting from Lush J. in 1875 [who himself was citing Comyns' Digest (at B.1-15) going back to the 17th century]: "a valuable consideration in the sense of the law, may consist either in some right, interest, profit, or benefit accruing to the one party, or some forbearance, detriment, loss, or responsibility, given, suffered, or undertaken by the

other...." As Lord Lindley observed, that definition had for hundreds of years been accepted as correct."

Ancient though the definition may be, and although approved by many judges, it is not a definition likely to be a great deal of help in many cases.

The case of Fielder v Vedlynn concerned shares which were disposed of for an agreed sum of money, which was to be left outstanding for a period; together with guarantees given by persons other than the purchaser, that the purchaser would meet the obligation to pay the sum of money in question. It was agreed by all concerned that the sum of money represented the full open market value of the shares which were disposed of. Nonetheless the Revenue sought to have a value placed upon the guarantees which were given, and to have those guarantees treated as additional consideration, over and above the cash sum. The judge accepted that the guarantees did represent part of the consideration given for the shares which were disposed of. However he went on to say *"but in my judgement it does not mean that in this case and on this transaction the value to the taxpayer company of the consideration that it received, which consideration included the guarantees, was more than the price paid to it."*

The case does highlight one important point. If the consideration for a disposal is specified to be a sum of money, then the value of the consideration must be taken to be that sum of money. There appears to be no precedent for the view that consideration specified as a sum of money may be valued at a lesser figure, taking into account such factors as the credit worthiness of the person who has undertaken to pay it. That follows, on the basis that it is the money which has been specified as the consideration, and not a debt (notwithstanding that a debt may come into existence in any case where the payment of the money is deferred).

s563   TCA97 s563 provides that *"consideration for the disposal shall be brought into account without any discount for postponement of the right to receive any part of it and without regard to the risk of any part of the consideration being irrecoverable or to the right to receive any part of the consideration being contingent: provided that if any part of the consideration so brought into account is shown to the satisfaction of the inspector to be irrecoverable, such adjustment, whether by way of discharge or repayment of tax or otherwise, shall be made as the case may require."*

These words may justify the decision arrived at in Fielder v Vedlynn, in that if no regard is to be had to the risk of part of the consideration in that case (the money) being irrecoverable, then it would follow that no value could be placed on the guarantees, since the guarantees had value only to the extent that doubt as to the recoverability of the balance of the consideration existed. You can place value on the guarantees, only by having regard to the risk that the sum of money would not be recoverable, but a CGT deduction deduction for any such item is expressly forbidden by s563.

8.4 Receipts taxed as income

s551   The broad rule, is that receipts which are taxed as *income* (or taken into account in computing income) are not taken into account as consideration for CGT purposes. Only receipts which are not taxed as income are taken into account. This matter is considered also in paragraph 4.4.7

For income tax purposes, it is necessary to distinguish between "income' receipts and 'capital' receipts. In principle, only receipts of an income nature are chargeable to income tax, although there are certain statutory exceptions.

The CGT legislation does not use the word *capital* receipts to describe the consideration to be taken into account in the computation of a gain or loss for CGT purposes. Instead it deals with the issue by taking into account all receipts other than those which are

- taxed as income,
- taken into account in computing income, gains, or losses for income tax, or corporation tax purposes, including any sums which would be taken into account but for the fact that:

  - any profits or gains of the trade, profession, or employment are not chargeable to income tax or corporation tax, or

  - any losses are not allowable for income tax or corporation tax purposes.

Similar provisions apply in the case of expenditure (and are dealt with in paragraph 9 below).

Any reference to receipts chargeable to tax includes income or profits taxable by deduction at source.

What remains , in effect, are capital receipts - i.e. the consideration for the disposal for CGT purposes. Some receipts which would normally be regarded as being of a capital nature are deemed by statute to be income. Such items would include capital sums received for the:

s757   — sale of patent rights,

s643   — certain land sales,

s100   — sale of land with right of reconveyance,

s99   — assignment of certain leases created at an undervalue.

There is also the question of receipts which in effect are taxed as income by being taken into account in computing a balancing charge for capital allowances purposes. Special rules are provided for dealing with assets attracting **capital allowances**. Those rules are set out in paragraph 9.8.

s551(2)   The amount of any receipt which is taken into account as income (or in computing income) for income tax or corporation tax purposes is not taken in as part of the disposal proceeds for CGT purposes. This, however, does not mean that the asset (or part of it) has not been disposed of. It merely means that in the computation of the gain (or loss) you exclude that part of the sale proceeds taken into account in arriving at income for income tax or corporation tax purposes. In certain cases, the entire proceeds are taken into account as income (for example - the sale of patent rights) and in other cases only part of the proceeds is taken into account for income tax purposes (for example - the grant of a short lease of land at a premium - part of the premium is chargeable as income)

Example 51

Bill owns a freehold property and grants a 26 year lease to John at a premium of £10,000 and an annual rent of £2,000.

He has disposed of an interest in the property (part disposal) by granting a lease. Part of the premium is chargeable to income tax, together with the rent. The consideration taken in for CGT is:

Premium	*£10,000*
Less - chargeable to income tax	**£5,000*
Proceeds of disposal for CGT (balance)	*£5,000*

* £10,000 - (£10,000 x [(26-1)/50] = £5,000.

In the case of Inspector of Taxes v Thomas Keleghan, the Revenue sought to raise an income tax assessment under Schedule E on what the taxpayer argued was the proceeds of disposal of a loan note obtained by him in return for the sale of shares in a company. The basis for the Revenue claim was a side letter between the purchaser and vendor of the original shares whereby it was stated that the loan notes were granted in part as an inducement for the vendor to become an employee of the purchaser. This particular aspect of the case failed as the Appeal Commissioners found that no contract of employment came into existence, and accordingly there was no source in relation to which an income tax assessment could be raised. Accordingly no part of the consideration fell to be disregarded for capital gains tax purposes as having been charged to income tax.

The case highlights the dangers that can be involved in a share disposal where it is important to the purchaser that the vendors of the shares should continue to work for the company being purchased or for other parts of their own group.

8.5 Capital Allowances

s551(3)

Capital receipts taxed by way of 'balancing charge' are not excluded from the sale proceeds under the above rule. The legislation does however, set out special rules for dealing with the overall position of assets attracting capital allowances, and those rules are set out in paragraph 9.8.

8.6 Capitalised Value of Rent or Right to Income

s551(4)

The general rule regarding income/capital receipts does not preclude the taking into account of the capitalised value of a rent (as in a case where the rent is exchanged for some other asset) or of a right to income (or to payments in the nature of income over a period, or to a series of payments in the nature of income).

8.7 Asset used as Security

s537

All assets are deemed to be disposed of free of any right or restriction by way of security. Where any such right or restriction attaches to the asset on its disposal, the full amount of that right or interest is taken into account as being part of the consideration for the disposal of the asset.

Example 52

John owns a commercial property which is let to a tenant. He has financed its purchase by a mortgage loan (secured on the property) which stands at the amount of £100,000.

John is anxious to sell the property. A purchaser offers him a cash sum of £250,000 for the property, and offers additionally to take on liability for the mortgage. John estimates the value of the offer therefore to be £350,000, which is, he reckons, a good price. He accepts the offer.

Although the only cash passing to John is £250,000, the purchaser has assumed the liability to repay the mortgage and therefore the amount of the mortgage at the date of the disposal must be treated as additional consideration received by John, and given by the purchaser. Accordingly the consideration for the purposes of computing the gain on the disposal of the property, and for computing the acquisition cost of the purchaser, is £350,000.

If the transaction above were with a brother of John, so that s547 and s549 together would treat the acquisition and disposal to be for a consideration equal to the market value of the asset, s537(3) would have application in regarding the asset as being disposed of and as being acquired free of any charges or security that in fact attached to it. Therefore in computing open market value under s547 regard will be had to the open market value of the premises entirely free of the mortgage.

S547 is stated to be "subject to the capital gains tax acts" where s537 is not stated to be subject to other sections. Nonetheless, if the interaction of the two sections in the case of a transaction between connected parties results in the consideration being treated as being open market value, there would seem to be no further scope for adding to that consideration the amount of the security or

charge. In other words s547 would seem to over-ride the provisions of s537
relating to including the security or charge in the amount of the consideration.
This is the only logical conclusion that can be drawn from the fact that s537 also
states that the asset is to be regarded as acquired and disposed of free of that
security or charge.

8.8   Deferred or Contingent Proceeds

8.8.1   General Rule

s563(1)   In computing a gain or loss, the full amount of the consideration (not
taxed as income etc as referred to in paragraph 8.4) for the disposal
must be taken into account,

- ignoring any discount for postponing the receipt of the proceeds,
  and

- without regard for any part of the consideration being
  irrecoverable or contingent on the happening of some future
  event.

If any part of the proceeds are subsequently proven to be
irrecoverable, any necessary adjustments are made by way of
discharge or repayment of tax at that time.

UK case law would suggest that these provisions apply only where
the consideration is 'contingent', and not to a situation where the
consideration itself also is wholly uncertain in amount. Where an
asset is sold and part of the proceeds is not only contingent on the
happening of a future event which may or may not occur, but cannot
be quantified unless and until the contingency actually happens, the
right to the future contingent proceeds is treated as a separate asset.

- An example of this would be a sale of land for an immediate sum
  with a further amount payable based on the extent of the actual
  development of the property if it ever happens.

- Another example would be the sale of shares in a private company
  for an immediate sum and a contingent further payment related to
  the quoted price if the company goes public.

If such a contingency actually happens, the proceeds are treated as a
capital sum derived from the separate asset, and taxed as such by
reference to the time of payment of the proceeds (see paragraph
4.4.6).

The date of the original disposal of the asset which gave rise to those
rights would not be relevant. That would be a separate disposal.

The UK cases on which these observations are based are Marren v
Ingles and Marson v Marriage. The issue has not come before an
Irish court to date. In the opinion of the authors the UK decisions in
those cases are open to criticism and may not deserve to be regarded

as influential by an Irish court. For a more detailed criticism of the judgement in those cases, see "Marren v Ingles revisited" by Frank Carr, Irish Journal of Taxation (1995 issue).

The UK case of Randall v Plumb is described in greater detail in paragraph 9.10. In that case a taxpayer had received a sum of money from a company in consideration of the grant to the company of an option to acquire land. The money fell to be repaid to the company should the option not be exercised, and fell to be treated as part of the consideration for the land should the option be exercised. The option had a period of up to 20 years. It does not appear to have been in dispute in the case that the sum in question fell to be taken into account in the computation of a gain arising on the grant of the option (or alternatively by reason of the receipt of the sum). The case turned on what allowance should be made for the contingency in respect of its repayment.

s563 None of the prohibitions on taking certain factors into account in valuing consideration, which are set out in s563 and referred to in the opening paragraph above, would have been relevant to the case. If the sum were indeed consideration, or a capital sum derived from an asset, it was already received and accordingly no contingencies relating to its recoverability were in question. What was in question was contingencies relating to its refundability. The UK legislation was not on all fours with the Irish legislation and accordingly the grounds on which the judge held a contingency to repay might be taken into account in the valuation of consideration, were not very relevant in Ireland. A proposition accepted by the court, i.e. that the sum was consideration for the grant of the option, would seem open to dispute notwithstanding that it was not objected to by the taxpayer (or so it would seem). On the facts disclosed in the case, the most that could be said was that the right to hold the money without accounting for interest, until it fell to be repayable, was the only consideration given for the grant of the option in that case. The moneys themselves were not consideration for the grant of the option. The taxpayer gave, in return for the moneys not only the option, but also the undertaking to repay the moneys, so that the moneys were consideration for both matters and not just for the grant of the option. The case of Randall v Plumb should be treated with caution, in applying it in the context of Irish legislation.

s981 Where the proceeds of sale are payable in installments, the Revenue Commissioners **may** in certain circumstances grant relief by deferring the payment of part of the tax due (see paragraph 97.3).

In the UK case of Coran v Keighley it was held on the facts of that particular case that the sale of land coupled with the granting of a mortgage loan by the vendor to the purchaser for part of the proceeds, did not constitute a payment of the outstanding part of the proceeds by installments. It was held that there were two separate transactions - the sale of the property for the full consideration, and the loan to the purchaser.

The UK case of Garner v Pounds Shipowners/Shipbrokers concerned the payment for the grant of an option which was to be released to the grantor only if and when certain covenants relating to the land over which the option was granted were released by a third party. The grantor incurred significant expenditure securing the release of the covenants. The consideration amounted to £399,750, and the expenditure to secure the release of covenants amounted to £90,000.

The Court of Appeal said *"The first step is to decide whether the taxpayer company's right to receive the £399,750 was subject to a contingency - - for that purpose it is necessary to return to the option agreement, which, unlike that in Randall v Plumb, did not provide for the £399,750 to be paid immediately to the taxpayer company. It was to be held by stakeholders until such time as the covenants were released and the lease granted, at which time it might be paid to the taxpayer company. If, on the other hand, its best endeavours to procure the releases on the grant were unsuccessful, then, if the option was not exercised, the £399,750 was to be refunded to (the purchaser). If the option was exercised, the £399,750 would be payable to the taxpayer company as part of the purchase price. In this state of affairs, it can fairly be said - - both that there was a postponement of the taxpayer company's right to receive the £399,750 and that the right was contingent. The right was postponed while the £399,750 was held by the stakeholders and contingent on the successful outcome of the taxpayer company's best endeavours or the exercise of the option. It follows that the £399,750 is to be brought into account at its full value and that Randall v Plumb is distinguishable."*

The Judge then went on to consider a separate matter, which was whether there was a basis for a deduction of the £90,000 spent in obtaining the release of covenants, as was required by the contract in order that the option moneys should become payable.

He said, *"In the present case the £399,750 was expressed by the option agreement to be paid only for the grant of the option. It was not expressed to be paid both for the grant of the option and for the taxpayer's company's obligations to use its best endeavours to procure the releases of the covenants."*

Accordingly it was held that the entire of the £399,750 fell to be regarded as consideration for the option. The deduction for the £90,000 was then denied on the grounds that securing the releases of the covenants (which the vendor had undertaken to use its best endeavours to do, and which was a precondition to securing the release of the option moneys) was not expenditure on granting the option itself. Since the £399,750 was being taxed as proceeds for granting an option, no deduction fell to be made from it for expenditure, incurred not in granting the option, but in fulfilling a condition relating to the release of the option moneys.

8.8.2   **Earnouts**

One of the most frequent transactions which give rise to deferred or contingent consideration is the so called "earn out". This is a reference to a transaction where shares or a business are sold for a consideration, that either in whole or in part is payable in the future (after the disposal) and whose amount is dependent on the prosperity of the business sold, or the prosperity of the business carried on by the company whose shares are sold. In principle the comments in paragraph 8.8.1 above apply in this situation. To date such a transaction has not been ruled on by the Irish courts. In practice the Revenue Commissioners apply the approach set out in the UK case of Marren v Ingles, where part or all of the consideration is deferred, and where the amount of the deferred contingent consideration is wholly unascertainable.

The example given below illustrates the approach which it is understood would be followed by the Revenue Commissioners in such a case.

Example 53

Joe Brown is founder, managing director and sole beneficial shareholder in Brown Software Ltd. The company was formed when Joe subscribed £1,000 capital in May 1990. In August 1997 Joe signed a contract for the sale of all of the shares to Multinational Computing PLC. The consideration was the sum of £5 million payable immediately; together with a further sum to be paid (provided he was then employed by the company) in August 1999 equal to 50% of the amount by which the turnover in the year ended 31 July 1999 of the company exceeded its turnover in the year ended 31 July 1997.

Joe has made a disposal in the tax year 1997/98 and must make a return in respect of the disposal not later than 31 January 1999. Applying the principles laid down in Marren v Ingles in the UK, the Revenue Commissioners would require Joe to estimate the market value on 31 August 1997 of the contingent right to receive, in August 1999 a further traunch of consideration in respect of the shares. Such a right is not an easy thing to value, as there is no active market in such rights. The fact that it is deferred would be relevant and would require discounting; the fact that the recovery of any sum whatever is dependent on a wholly uncertain event - the amount of the turnover of Brown Software Ltd. in the year ended 31 July 1999 and on Joe remaining as a manager until then - would require a further discounting for uncertainty. Any person paying out immediately good money to acquire such an uncertain future right would certainly require a good margin of profit to compensate them for the risks which they are taking. This book does not propose to consider how such a right ought to be valued. That is a matter for an expert valuer. It is assumed that Joe agrees with the Revenue that the value of the contingent future amount, in August 1997, is £0.5 million. In August 1999, Joe having worked hard in the interval to ensure that Brown Software prospered, it was found that its turnover had increased in the two years by £4 million with the result that Joe received a further payment of £2 million in August 1999.

Joe's computations for CGT will be prepared as follows on the basis of the judgement in Marren v Ingles, and on what is understood to be Revenue Commissioner practice in Ireland at present:

1. ***1997/98 computation*** £

   Consideration for disposal of shares 5,500,000

   Consisting of £5 million cash and "moneys worth" of £0.5 million, being the value of the right to receive further sums

   Less base cost (Indexed) (1,153)

   Taxable gain 5,498,847

   Less personal allowance (self & wife) 2,000

   Chargeable to CGT @ 26% 5,496,847

   Tax payable 1,429,180

2. ***Computation for 1999/2000***

   Consideration for disposal (right to receive future sum) 2,000,000

   Less base cost indexed from 1997/98 to 1999/00 516,500

   Taxable gain 1,483,500

   Less personal allowance 1,000

   Gain chargeable to CGT 1,482,500

   Tax @ 20% 296,500

   The total tax payable on the combined disposals = 1,725,680

It should be noted that the 26% rate of tax appropriate to a disposal of the shares in Brown Software Ltd. is not available in relation to the disposal two years later of the "right to receive further moneys". That right, although an asset, is not a qualifying share for the purpose of the 26% rate. It is not a share at all, although it arose out of a transaction concerning shares. Furthermore, the rate was abolished with effect from 3rd December 1997.

The justification which might be offered for the deduction of £500,000 as base cost of the "right to receive further moneys" would be that the right was acquired in consideration of part of the shares. Parting with the shares represented expenditure on acquiring the right. The value of the shares so given would equal the value of the right and that was determined as £500,000 at the date of the transaction in August 1997.

Reference has been made above in paragraph 8.8.1 to reservations as to whether the case of Marren v Ingles was correctly decided, and as to whether it would be followed by the Irish courts. This should be borne in mind in considering the example above.

The treatment of "an earnout" above may be contrasted with the treatment of an earnout which is expressed in slightly different fashion;

Example 54

The background to the formation of Brown Software Ltd. is the same as in **example 53** above. In August 1997 Joe Brown accepted an offer from Mega Computers PLC for all of the shares in Brown Software Ltd. The consideration consisted of £5 million payable immediately; and a further £2 million payable in August 1999 provided the turnover of Brown Software Ltd. in the year ended 31 July 1999 amounted to not less than £15 million. This turnover target was comfortably achieved and Joe received his additional £2 million in August 1999. Joe's computations, in accordance with the Capital Gains Tax Acts, and on a basis which it is believed would be acceptable to the Revenue Commissioners would be as follows:

3.　Computation 1997/1998

	£
Consideration for disposal of shares	7,000,000
(Consisting of the immediate payment of £5 million and a contingent future payment of £2 million)	
Less base cost indexed for inflation	1,153
Gain	6,998,847
Less annual exemption	2,000
Chargeable gain	6,996,847
Tax @ 26% on the chargeable gain	1,819,180

No further computation is required to be submitted by Joe in 1999/2000, when the final payment is made to him. That has been fully accounted for in his 1997/98 computation. The 1997/98 computation included the second payment of £2 million, notwithstanding that at the time that computation was prepared and submitted there was no certainty that the amount would be received. s563 requires that any such uncertainty be disregarded in the preparation of a computation, and that no discounting for the fact that there is a delay in payment should be made.

Example 55

Assume the facts to be the same as in **example 53** above except that Joe's contract provided that in addition to the immediate payment of £5 million, and a contingent payment of £2 million in 1999, Joe was entitled to a further payment of £1 million in the year 2000, if the turnover of Brown Software Ltd. in the year ended 31 July 2000 was at least £20 million. In the event, although Joe qualified for the additional payment in 1999, the company did not reach the turnover target in the year 2000, and the third payment never fell to be paid to Joe.

Joe's computation would be as follows:

4.　Computation 1997/98:

	£
Consideration for disposal of shares	8,000,000
(Consisting of the immediate payment of £5 million and contingent future payments of £3 million)	
Less base cost indexed for inflation	1,153
Gain	7,998,847
Less annual exemption	2,000
Taxable gain	7,996,847
Tax @ 26%	2,079,180

In August 2000 it became apparent that Joe would not receive the full £8 million. The last £1 million would not become payable to him. Joe is entitled, under s563 to require the inspector to adjust his tax returns and assessments for the year ended 1997/98 so that his liability is computed by reference to a sales consideration of £7 million (which he actually received) and not the £8 million by reference to which it was originally prepared. The difference in tax must be repaid to him in accordance with s563.

The entitlement to interest on such a repayment would depend on the repayment consisting of preliminary tax; or of the repayment being made on the determination on appeal. It is unlikely to be in the latter circumstance as there is no right of appeal against an assessment raised in accordance with the taxpayer's return. Where tax has been paid both by a payment of preliminary tax, and by a final payment of capital gains tax after an assessment has been raised, it may be difficult to demonstrate that all of the repayment relates to preliminary tax, as opposed to being a repayment of all or part of the second and final payment of capital gains tax which was made following the raising of the assessment. That final payment did not carry interest on a repayment save on the settlement of an appeal.

As can be seen above, from the viewpoint of a taxpayer the UK Marren v Ingles principle (where it is applicable, and it is limited to where consideration is contingent, future, and wholly unascertainable) does defer payment of part of the tax to a future date, and softens the blow on the taxpayer in having to make a payment of tax before he has actually received all of the consideration. It could however serve to increase the capital gains tax rate applicable to part of the consideration for the disposal of shares, from the 26% rate applicable to the disposal of shares per se, to the 40% rate that would have applied to the disposal of the "right to receive" the final traunch of the consideration had the FA98 not reduced the rate to 20%.

The application of the principles set out in the UK case of Marren v Ingles (were it to be followed in Ireland by the courts) could disadvantage a taxpayer making a disposal to which the principles apply in a number of ways. There are a number of reliefs which might not be available in relation to the second disposal of the "right to receive the contingent future payments".

These include:

- The reduced rate of tax (for disposals up to 3rd December 1997)

- Rollover relief (where the assets disposed of would have qualified)

- Retirement relief (if the original disposal would have qualified)

- Exemption for government stocks and unit trusts/UCITS

- Principal private residence

- Rollover relief on shares

It is understood that where consideration which includes an earnout is entirely shares or debentures, and where no other form of consideration is involved, the Revenue Commissioners will permit the application of the "paper for paper" rules of s584 to apply even to the shares or debentures received subsequent to the disposal and which at the date of the disposal represented future contingent and unascertainable consideration. A strict application of the Marren v Ingles principle would deny "paper for paper" treatment to the deferred contingent right to receive future shares, since that right is not in itself shares or debentures. This treatment, if it is considered to be applicable, *should be confirmed with the Revenue Commissioners in every instance* and should not otherwise be relied on.

• **Revenue Commissioners published precedent:**

— In a published precedent, the Revenue Commissioners have stated *"Where part of a consideration for a take over consists of shares or securities to be issued at a future date if a contingency is satisfied, the earn out element will be treated as a security and relief under Section 586 may be due. This will apply only in so far as the earn-out element does not or could not take the form of cash."*

• **Revenue Commissioners published precedent:**

— In a further published precedent they state *"As the amounts received in an earn out are in respect of a right separate to shares which were disposed of, they will not qualify for the reduced rate of capital gains tax. However, in practice cash earn outs may be treated as qualifying for the reduced rate."* The reduced rate has since been abolished.

Paradoxically, in the case of a non-resident non-ordinarily resident person (i.e. one who is liable to Irish tax on capital gains only in respect of the disposal of specified assets in the State) the "Marren v Ingles" principle might operate so as to exempt him from tax on any gain arising on the second disposal of the deferred contingent unascertainable right, although he might be within the charge in relation to the first disposal of the specified asset.

The question of whether a payment is consideration for the disposal of land, or of goodwill, or is rather consideration for the disposal of "the right to receive a future unascertainable contingent amount" is also relevant to the obligation of the person making the payment to withhold the 15% withholding tax (where applicable).

It is unfortunate that the Revenue Commissioners have not to date clarified whether they consider that the judgement in Marren v Ingles would be followed in Ireland. A statement by the Revenue Commissioners cannot determine that matter but it could reduce some of the uncertainty for taxpayers.

The implications of Marren v Ingles for the purchase of an asset are considered in paragraph 9.1.2.

s563 As noted previously s563 does include a relief for part of the consideration for the disposal of an asset proving to be uncollectible or irrecoverable. In other words it provides a bad debt relief, insofar as the consideration for the disposal of an asset is represented by a debt. s563(1)(b) refers to "any part of the consideration so brought into account" being irrecoverable, but it would be absurd if the same provision did not apply also where the entire of the consideration proved irrecoverable.

The UK case of Loffland Bros. North Sea Inc. v Goodbrand was concerned with a claim for relief under this proviso. In that case an asset had been disposed of for a consideration expressed in US dollars, which was payable by instalments over a nine year period. All of the dollars were duly paid over. However due to fluctuations in the exchange rate as between the dollar and the pound sterling over the nine year period, the pound sterling equivalent of the dollars which were received ultimately proved to be substantially less than the pound sterling equivalent of the total dollar consideration which was taken into account in the computation of the gain. The Special Commissioners had held that since the sterling equivalent "taken into account" had not been fully realised subsequently, bad debt relief should be available in respect of it. This conclusion was rejected by the High Court which said that the reference to consideration being irrecoverable was, in the circumstances, a reference to the dollars proving irrecoverable. All of the dollars were recovered.

8.9   Apportionment of consideration

The disposal of an asset may be part of a larger transaction involving the disposal of other assets, or other matters. Such composite or related transactions can give rise to difficulties in apportioning the consideration payable as between the different assets being disposed of, or the different matters which are the subject of the agreement.

s547   Where the parties to the disposal/acquisition are connected, or the transaction is not one at arm's length, or in a variety of other circumstances to which TCA97 s547 has application (see paragraph 16) open market value may be substituted for the consideration actually arising in the transaction on the disposal of the assets. However where s547 does not cause open market value to be substituted for the actual consideration to which the transaction gives rise, the computation is determined by reference to the actual consideration. The case of Aberdeen Construction Group Ltd. v IRC was concerned with a contract under which shares were sold, and a loan account was waived, for a single composite consideration. The case of Booth v Buckwell dealt with a situation where shares were disposed of for a consideration which was specified in the contract, and a loan account was compromised, or partly waived, for a separate consideration, also specified in the contract.

The transaction with which the Aberdeen Construction Group Ltd. case was concerned is described in paragraph 9.10. The case was discussed in the subsequent Booth v Buckwell case and the critical issue in it was described as follows:

"All their lordships agreed that the decisive question in that case was the true construction of the bargain which the parties had made between themselves. The only difference between the majority and the dissenting minority was not as to the construction of any taxing provision but as to the true construction of the contract in that case. On its true construction, did it provide that the £250,000 was paid for the shares alone, as the minority held, or was it paid for the shares and for the waiver of the debt? The majority having held that the £250,000 was payable as consideration for both these purposes, it followed that the £250,000 had to be apportioned between the two."

The method of apportionment was left to the Special Commissioners.

The subsequent UK case of Booth v Buckwell was concerned with a contract under which a company agreed to sell the shares in its subsidiary for a specified price, and to accept a further specified sum of money in full discharge of a loan owing to it by the subsidiary, which was substantially higher than the sum of money which it agreed to receive in discharge of the loan. Browne-Wilkinson J. held that the nature of the contract was similar to that in the Aberdeen case i.e. it was a composite contract involving interrelated obligations to sell the shares and to waive (or partly waive) a debt. However he rejected the suggestion that he should follow the Aberdeen case in apportioning the total consideration passing as between the two subject matters of the contract. He distinguished the case from the Aberdeen case on the grounds that the Aberdeen case had involved a single specified consideration in respect of the two subject matters of the contract (sale of shares, and the waiver of a debt); whereas in the Booth v Buckwell case the parties to the contract had themselves stipulated separate consideration for the sale of the shares, and for the waiver of the debt (in part). He said:

"In my judgement, where parties to a composite transaction have, as a result of negotiations between themselves, provided that part of the consideration is to be paid for one part of the transaction and part for another, they cannot subsequently seek to reallocate the consideration for tax purposes. They have chosen to carry through the transaction in a particular manner, and the taxation consequences flow from the manner adopted. The Crown's position may well be different in certain cases. After all, the Crown was not a party to the transaction.

So, in this case, the transaction could have been carried through by the new company repaying the debt in full, the price being paid for the shares being reduced accordingly. Alternatively, the Aberdeen method could have been adopted; that is one lump sum could have been paid, both for the purchase of the shares and for the total extinguishment of the loan account. The taxation consequences of the method adopted would vary in each case. Once the parties have chosen to adopt one method, in my judgement the taxation consequences must follow and it is not open to them subsequently to argue that for tax purposes the transaction ought to be treated as if a different method had been adopted."

Brown Wilkinson J. recognised that the consequence of his decision in the Booth v Buckwell case was harsh for the taxpayer. They made a substantial loss on their loan to the subsidiary, and received no relief for that loss because the loan was not a debt on a security, and hence was outside the charge to capital gains tax. In contrast, they appeared to make a substantial gain on the shares and were subject to tax on that. Yet overall they had made almost no gain at all.

The Booth v Buckwell judgement might appear to be unsatisfactory in that, according to the facts recited in the case stated, one might be led to believe that the parties to the transaction were connected with one another, and that open market value rules should have replaced the consideration stipulated in the contract. The point does not appear to have been raised in the case. The judge also appears to have taken a very literal reading of the contract in question, particularly as regards the references in it to the allocation of consideration between the two matters with which it was concerned. Notwithstanding these criticisms however the case serves as a warning on the importance of considering the tax consequences when allocating consideration in a contract.

s547

The principle that the consideration to be taken into account in the computation of a gain is the actual consideration which the parties have agreed to between themselves (in the absence of the substitution of open market value by s547, or some other value by provisions such as the group relief provisions) was confirmed in the UK High Court decision in the case of Spectros International v Madden. In that case Spectros International entered into a contract to sell a subsidiary. Prior to entering into the contract it had taken a dividend of $20 million from the subsidiary, which the subsidiary had financed by means of a bank loan guaranteed and secured by Spectros. Following on the extraction of that dividend from the subsidiary, the subsidiary was worth only $1,000. The contract between Spectros and the purchaser (ABI) however provided for the payment of $1,000 to Spectros, and the payment by ABI of $20 million to the subsidiary's bank in discharge of its borrowing, and provided that the entire sum of $20,001,000 was consideration for the sale of the shares in the subsidiary. The court concluded that the form of the contract which the parties had chosen to enter into was not one for the sale of a company worth $1,000, for the sum of $1,000, together with an undertaking by the purchaser to secure the discharge of the subsidiary's borrowings, but rather a contract under which the vendor sold the shares for $20,001,000 and undertook to secure that the bank borrowings of $20,000,000 were discharged, by directing part of the sale's proceeds to that end.

The judge, Lightman J, said, *"in the ordinary case, where a holding company sells a subsidiary, and the subsidiary is indebted to the holding company or some other person, and the purchaser under the sale agreement agrees to discharge the subsidiary's debt, the payment of the debt will not necessarily or indeed (perhaps) ordinarily constitute additional consideration of monetary value for the shares. The obligation of the purchaser may constitute added value, e.g. if the subsidiary is insolvent and the debt is due to or guaranteed or secured by the vendor. When however the subsidiary is solvent and the shares are sold for full value, no question of added value, let alone added value in monetary terms, will arise. What distinguishes this case is the unusual fact that the parties have here agreed to allocate to the purchase money the sum required to be expended by the vendor in the discharge of the debt and provided for application of that part of the purchase money in its discharge. The parties have chosen this result, and the court must respect their choice......I conclude, therefore, like the Special Commissioners, that upon the true construction of the three agreements the consideration for the disposal of the shares was $20,001,000. I see nothing unreal or unbusinesslike in this view: There may well have been good reason for structuring the transaction this way. I fully accept that it results in a hefty bill for corporation tax which any of a number of alternative structures suggested by (counsel for the taxpayer) would have avoided. But that is a matter which should have been (if it was not) taken into account when the form of the agreements was negotiated and agreed"*.

The UK case of Garner v Pounds Ship Owners and Ship Breakers in many ways resembled the Aberdeen Construction case. It resembled it not only in that similar issues arose, where it had to be considered whether the consideration was both for an asset which was the subject matter of the contract, and also for the vendor undertaking certain other steps, but also resembled it in that arguably the High Court was influenced heavily by the hardship to the taxpayer and may have done less than full justice to the law as a result.

The taxpayer owned land. He granted a third party an option to acquire that land at a particular price. The land was subject to disadvantageous covenants at the time. The agreement relating to the grant of the option stipulated that the consideration for the option was to be £400,000 but that the £400,000 would not be payable unless and until the vendor secured the release of the covenants over the land. The vendor undertook to use his best endeavours to do that.

In the event it cost him £90,000 to secure the release of the covenants. That sum was not deductible in a computation relating to the disposal of an asset consisting of the option (which was never exercised). The judge held, relying on the Aberdeen case, that the contract was one under which the consideration of £400,000 was in part for the grant of the option, and in part for the vendor undertaking to secure the release of the covenants; and further held that it was reasonable to apportion the consideration by reference to hindsight, and to assign £90,000 as being the amount of the consideration referable to the obligation to attempt to secure the release of the covenants.

The Court of Appeal reversed the High Court decision and held that no part of the consideration was attributable to the undertaking to secure the release of the covenants, and that the entire consideration was expressed, by the agreements entered into, to be for the grant of the option. Furthermore, no deduction was available in relation to the expenditure of £90,000, since it was not expenditure on granting the option (which was the asset disposed of) but rather was expenditure incurred under a separate contractual obligation ie to use best endeavours to secure the release of covenants.

- **Revenue/Chief Inspector's CGT manual :**

— The Revenue capital gains tax manual, at paragraph 19.2.14.14. has a reference to apportionment. The reference is not to apportionment of consideration, but rather to apportionment of acquisition costs. It states *"Any apportionment should be made by reference to the values at the time of acquisition. In practice, however, where, for example, a block of flats or tenements or terraced houses is involved, the initial "cost" may be ascertained on the basis of current valuations for rating purposes".*

8.10   **Foreign currency**

The consideration for the disposal of an asset may consist of an amount of foreign currency. In order to bring such consideration into the computation of a gain it is necessary that the consideration (since it is not an amount of Irish currency) be valued (see paragraph 8.3). That value must be ascertained as at the date of the contract. The value must be expressed in Irish pounds (or alternatively, the *euro* from 1 January 1999) and not in any other currency, regardless of the circumstances. It is therefore necessary in an instance where the consideration consists of foreign currency, to value the amount of that foreign currency in Irish pounds at the date of the contract. This would usually be done by reference to the market exchange rate between the two currencies on the relevant date.

The CGT issues arising out of the introduction of the euro as the common national currency of most EU Member States from 1 January 1999 is discussed in paragraphs 4.3 and 9.1.6. Broad details of the countries participating in the European Monetary Union and adopting the euro as their currency, and the fixed exchange rates applying between the existing currencies and the euro are shown in the **TABLE** on page vii (in the preliminary pages at the beginning of this book).

s563 The UK case of Loffland Bros. North Sea Inc. v Goodbrand involved the disposal of oil rigs in the North Sea for the sum of US $38,610,000. This sum was payable in instalments over a nine year period. The £stg./US$ exchange rate varied over that nine year period with the result that the £Stg. value of the dollars received, as and when they were received, amounted to £Stg.23,853,508. However the value of the US$38,610,000 on the date of the contract had amounted to £Stg.33,313,201. The figure which had to be taken into the computation of the gain on the disposal of the oil rigs was the figure of £Stg.33,313,201, since it was the sterling value of the total dollar consideration at the date of the contract, notwithstanding that the total dollar consideration was not payable on that date. As explained in paragraph 8.8, a claim for "bad debt relief" on the shortfall in the sterling value of the consideration for the disposal of the oil rigs, between the value of the dollars at the date of the contract, and the value ultimately realised from the dollars, was refused.

9   EXPENDITURE DEDUCTIBLE

9.1   Expenditure - main rules

9.1.1   Broad Outline

To compute the chargeable gain, the amount of the sale proceeds is reduced by the expenditure deductible under the CGT Acts. Broadly speaking, s556 provides for this expenditure to be indexed by reference to the increase in the consumer price index since the expenditure was incurred.

The approach adopted in the following paragraphs is to deal initially with the basic rules governing the allowability of expenditure. After that, the special rules applicable to expenditure incurred on wasting assets and part disposals are dealt with. When the rules governing the allowability of expenditure have been dealt with, the s556 provisions on indexing that expenditure are explained.

s554 The general rule is that any expenditure allowable for income tax purposes is not allowable for CGT. This prohibition is extended to include expenditure which *would be* allowed for income tax purposes *on the assumption* that the asset was used as a fixed asset for trade purposes (even if the asset in fact was never used for the purposes of a trade and no income tax allowance was ever received for the expenditure).

s552   Subject to this basic rule, the allowable deductions are as follows:

- the amount or value of consideration in money or money's worth given by the taxpayer wholly and exclusively for the acquisition of the asset together with the incidental costs of acquisition (see paragraph 9.2).

  If the asset was not acquired (e.g. if it was created by its owner) the amount to be taken into account is the expenditure wholly and exclusively incurred in providing the asset (see paragraph 9.1.3).

- expenditure wholly and exclusively incurred on the asset for the purpose of enhancing the value of the asset. Such expenditure is only allowable if it is reflected in the state or nature of the asset at the time of disposal (see paragraph 9.1.4).

- expenditure wholly and exclusively incurred in establishing, preserving or defending title to, or right over, the asset (see paragraph 9.1.5).

- the incidental costs of making the disposal (see paragraph 9.2)

- foreign tax not creditable (see paragraph 9.3).

No deduction is allowed for qualifying expenditure in a computation under the CGT Acts, more than once from any sum, or from more than one sum.

s544(7)   Any assessment to income tax, or decision on a claim under the Income Tax Acts, and any decision on appeal under the Income Tax Acts, against any such assessment or claim *is conclusive* so far as any provision of the CGT legislation depends on the provisions of the Income Tax Acts.

Special rules govern expenditure qualifying for capital allowances (paragraph 9.8) and expenditure on wasting assets (paragraph 10).

9.1.2   Value of Consideration given

The UK case of Stanton v Drayton considers the meaning of the words used in s552 *"The amount or value of the consideration, in money or money's worth, given by the person or on the person's behalf wholly and exclusively for the acquisition of the asset...."*.

s552   Lord Fraser of Tullybelton said at page 588 *"(that) means that the allowable deduction is to be restricted to "the amount of the consideration, if it is in money, or the value in money's worth if it is not in money". He went on to say at page 590 "I see no indication that "value" is used as meaning market value....s.22(4) (the UK equivalent of s547) provides that the acquisition of such an asset shall be deemed to be for a consideration equal to the "market value" of the asset, and the obvious reason is that no agreed value, arrived at by an arm's length transaction, is available but in the ordinary case under paragraph 4(1)(a)* [the UK equivalent of s552] *such a value is available - namely the price agreed between the parties. Consequently there is no need to look to the market value, and no need to read in the word "market" before "value" where Parliament has not seen fit to use it."*

The case of Stanton v Drayton was concerned with the value of the consideration given by a company when it issued its own shares in exchange for a portfolio of shares and securities acquired by it. It is discussed in greater detail in paragraph 8.2.

In the UK case of Whittles v Uniholdings it was stated *"it must be wrong in principle to value the acquisition cost of an asset on any date other than that on which it is acquired"*. Uniholdings had borrowed in dollars, and thus acquired dollars as an asset. The consideration given was the promise to repay an equivalent amount of dollars at a later date. At issue was the question of whether the value of that promise was to be determined by reference to the dollar/sterling exchange rate on the date on which the dollars were borrowed, and the promise was given, or by reference to the exchange rate when Uniholdings had to acquire dollars in the market in order to repay the borrowing. As indicated in the quote above, it was determined that the value of the promise was to be determined by reference to the exchange rate when the promise was given i.e. on the acquisition date of the assets acquired in return for the promise.

The UK case of Marren v Ingles is discussed in paragraph 8.8.2. In that paragraph the discussion concentrates on what was the subject matter of the case ie the computation of the amount of the consideration, where part of the consideration was deferred, contingent, and uncertain in amount. The case was not concerned with the base cost of the purchaser of the shares with whose disposal the case was concerned.

The conclusion in the case was that where shares were disposed of for an immediate cash sum, and the possibility of an additional unquantified cash sum becoming payable if uncertain future events occurred, the consideration given for the shares was to be treated as being the cash sum immediately paid, and the market value at the date of disposal of the right to receive the contingent future sums. The contingent future sums themselves were not treated as consideration for the shares, but rather were treated as consideration for the disposal of the right to receive those sums.

The "Marren v Ingles principle" has not been approved by the Irish courts as the matter has not yet come before them. It has been criticised. The case itself did not consider the base cost to the purchaser of the shares.

In the House of Lords, Lord Fraser stated in his judgment in the Marren v Ingles case in relation to the final sums paid and the contingency upon which additional consideration became due "the sum was paid to satisfy or extinguish the right (to receive the sum) and not as any part of the consideration for the shareholdings; full consideration for them had already been given" - -

If that comment were a correct interpretation of the transaction (the authors have strong reservations as to whether the case was correctly decided) it would seem to have the unavoidable implication that the consideration given by the purchaser for the shares consisted of:

(a) The up front sum payable under the contract and

(b) The value of the contingent obligation to pay an unquantified sum on an uncertain future date.

It equally follows that the final tranche of payments made by the purchasers of the shares in the Marren v Ingles case, in 1972, did not constitute consideration for their acquisition of the shares. They were described above as the discharge of a liability and not as acquisition consideration. That final tranche of consideration would not seem to be capable of being taken into account as enhancement expenditure as it was not reflected in the state or nature of the shares in the hands of the purchaser.

Although published Revenue precedents (see paragraph 8.8.2) suggests that the Revenue Commissioners would intend to apply Marren v Ingles as if it had been correctly decided, none of the published Revenue material appears to address the issue of the base cost of the purchaser. It is not clear whether the Revenue intend that the treatment of the vendor would be mirrored by the treatment of the purchaser. The disadvantages of Marren v Ingles being applied to the purchaser far outweigh the disadvantages of it being applied to the vendor. In most instances, in a buoyant economy, the final payout will exceed the value of the contingent right to receive it, at an earlier date when the asset was disposed of. Accordingly the purchaser's base cost, on Marren v Ingles principles, will usually be less than the sums which he will ultimately pay out by reason of his acquisition of the asset. The excess of the payments is "dead money" on that basis and qualifies for no tax relief.

In the author's opinion, in the circumstances outlined in the Marren v Ingles case, the consideration given by the purchaser for shares consists of all of the moneys paid by the purchaser to the vendor, whether immediately, or at some date in the future on the crystallisation of a contingency. In the opinion of the authors, the comment of Lord Fraser quoted above is simply wrong. Until the Revenue Commissioners indicate their views on the matter, purchasers should be aware of the potential difficulties they face.

In some circumstances of course, a purchase may, on the foot of the Marren v Ingles principle, obtain a higher base cost than he would otherwise be entitled to. This will arise where the ultimate pay-out either never occurs (due to the failure of the contingency to crystallise) or is paid out in a sum much smaller than anticipated, so that the value of the contingent future right at the date of the disposal of the asset actually exceeds the sum ultimately paid out.

9.1.2.1.   Substitution of market value for actual consideration

As explained in paragraphs 13, 16, 33, and 75 primarily, in certain cases the actual consideration for the acquisition of an asset (if any) may be ignored for CGT purposes, and a different consideration is substituted.

9.1.2.2   Foreign Currency

Where an asset is acquired in **foreign currency**, and subsequently sold, the cost deductible from the Irish currency value of the sale proceeds is the Irish currency value of the acquisition cost at the date of acquisition. This was the decision in the UK case of Bentley v Pike. The gain cannot be computed by reference to the Irish currency value of the difference between the cost of the asset and the sale proceeds measured in the foreign currency (if both acquisition and disposal were in the same currency).

Example 56 (Pre euro)

In the UK case of Bentley v Pike a German asset was acquired at a cost DM 132,780 (£Stg equivalent was £Stg.11,446). The asset was sold for DM 152,241 (£Stg equivalent was £Stg.23,175 - owing to a change in the exchange rate).

It was held in Bentley v Pike that the gain was not to be measured by the £Stg. difference between the DM cost and the DM selling price of the asset which would have yielded a gain of approx. £Stg.3,000, but that

- *the purchase must be separately converted into local currency (£Stg.) at the date of acquisition (£Stg.11,446), and*

- *the sale price must be separately converted into local currency (£Stg.) at the date of sale (£Stg.23,175).*

The chargeable gain for CGT is the difference between the £Stg. cost at the date of acquisition, and the £ Stg. sale price. The gain is therefore £Stg.23,175.

It should be noted that the rule in Bentley v. Pike was not based on any specific provision of the UK Capital Gains Tax Acts that explicitly dealt with the treatment of amounts arising in foreign currency. Rather it was a rule deduced from the fact that Capital Gains Tax must be computed in the currency of the State.

FA98 Sch 2   The FA98 has made explicit provision for the problem of conversion of foreign currency expenditure. It has done so in the context of the introduction of the euro as the currency of the State. That occurred on the 1 January 1999, at which date the Irish pound became a denomination of the euro.

Further discussion regarding the CGT aspects of the introduction of the euro on 1 January 1999, and the transitional period to 1 January 2002 are set out in paragraph 4.3. Details of the countries participating in the EMU and the fixed exchange rates between their existing currencies and the euro are listed in the **TABLE** on page vii (in the preliminary pages at the beginning of this book).

s552(1A)

The new CGT rule is to be found in s552(1A). It provides that a sum allowable as a deduction, incurred in the currency other than the currency of the State must be expressed in terms of the currency of the State by reference to the rate of exchange applying at the time that the liability to pay the sum was incurred.

This appears to be a legislative expression of the rule expressed in the UK case of Bentley v. Pike. However, s552(1A) does not go on to explicitly state that (in terms of the Bentley v. Pike example above) the Deutschmark amount, having been expressed as an amount of Irish pounds by reference to the Irish pound/Deutschmark exchange rate applying at the date the liability or cost was incurred, should be further converted into euro at the rate of 1 euro = IR£0.7875644 (at which the euro is introduced as Irish currency on 1 January 1999) as it is not necessary to do so - the Irish pound converted into euro at the fixed exchange rate between the IR£ and the euro yields the same value (although expressed in euro rather than Irish pounds).

Example 57 (Post euro)

Taking the facts in Bentley v. Pike above, but assuming that the person acquiring and disposing of the asset was resident in Ireland (instead of in the UK) and that the disposal transaction took place after 1 January 2002, at which time the disposal must be in euro. Let us also assume that the disposal proceeds amounts to 20,000 euro. How will the liability to tax on the disposal be determined?

By that date the euro will be the currency of Germany, and the Deutschmark will no longer exist. The euro will also be the currency of Ireland. No problem arises in relation to the sales proceeds, from the view point of currency rates. Notwithstanding that the sale may have occurred in Germany, the sales proceeds will arise in the common currency of Ireland and Germany.

*Assuming for the purposes of simplicity that the punt equivalent of the Deutchmark acquisition costs set out in **example 55** are the same as the £Stg. equivalent figures given there, the acquisition costs for Irish CGT purposes in relation to a disposal after 1 January 2002 would involve converting the acquisition cost of DM132,780 into Irish pounds at the rate ruling at the date the liability was incurred. It is assumed that the amount paid would convert to IR£11,446 at that date. The amount of Irish pounds must now be converted into euro at the conversion rate applying between the Irish pound and the euro on 1 January 1999. That rate is IR£0.787564 = 1 euro. The IR£11,446 therefore converts into 16,351 euro.*

The computation therefore is as follows:

Consideration for disposal	20,000	euro
Acquisition cost	16,351	euro
Chargeable Gain	3,649	euro

Indexation has been ignored for the purposes of simplicity. In practice it would not matter whether it was applied to the Irish pound equivalent of the acquisition expenditure, or the euro equivalent. Equally it would not matter if it was applied to the original Deutschmark cost, since all the subsequent exchange conversion factors are fixed.

s79

Most foreign exchange gains arising to a trading company are now chargeable to corporation tax as income of the company, and accordingly would be excluded from the consideration taken into account in computing chargeable gains.

It was decided in the UK case of Loffland Bros. North Sea Inc v Goodbrand that CGT relief is not available for currency fluctuations between the amount of the consideration converted to local currency at the date of disposal, and the amount actually received - see paragraphs 8.8, and 8.10.

9.1.3 Expenditure on provision of asset

In the UK case of Garner v Pounds Shipowners and Shipbrokers, an option was granted for a consideration of £399,750. The option agreement required the vendors to use their best endeavours to secure the release of certain covenants over land, which was the subject matter of the option. The proceeds of the sale of the option would not be released unless and until those covenants were released. The vendor incurred £90,000 of expenditure in securing the release of the covenants. In the Court of Appeal a deduction for the £90,000 expenditure was rejected. The Appeal Court quoted with approval the High Court comment *"The asset was provided long before the expenditure was incurred. The expenditure may have been incurred pursuant to the option, but not in providing it."*

9.1.3.1 Own Labour

It was held in the case of Oram v Johnson that expenditure on the cost or enhancement of an asset does not include the notional cost of the taxpayer's own labour.

9.1.4 Expenditure on asset

s552(1)(b)

In Aberdeen Construction Group Ltd. v IRC the High Court in the UK held that a company, which under a contract for the disposal of shares in a second company, had bound itself to waive a loan owing to it from that second company, had not by reason of waiving the loan, incurred enhancement expenditure on the shares. Lord Emslie said *"by no reasonable stretch of the imagination is it possible to classify the making of the loans or their waiver as expenditure wholly and exclusively incurred "on" the shares and I find it impossible to say that either were reflected in the state or nature of the shares which were sold. The waiver of the loans may well have enhanced their value but what paragraph 4(1)(b) (UK equivalent of s552(1)(b)) is looking for is, as a result of relevant expenditure, an identifiable change for the better in the state or nature of the asset, and this must be a change distinct from the enhancement of value".*

The Aberdeen Construction case is described in greater detail in paragraph 9.10.

s552(1)(b)

The UK case of Chaney v Watkis is also concerned with the UK equivalent of s552(1)(b), dealing with enhancement expenditure. Mr. Chaney owned the freehold of a cottage in which his mother-in-law was a protected tenant. His mother-in-law agreed to give up her tenancy and provide him with vacant possession in return for the sum of £9,400. It was accepted by the Revenue that if that payment had been made, it would have represented deductible enhancement expenditure. But the payment was not made because by a further agreement the mother-in-law agreed to accept in its place a life tenancy in part of another property owned by Mr. Chaney. The Revenue sought to deny Mr. Chaney a deduction in respect of the sum of £9,400 on the grounds that he had not incurred the expenditure. They also denied him a deduction for the expenditure he incurred in providing his mother-in-law with alternative accommodation (by way of a life interest in part of a second property owned by him) on the grounds that that expenditure was expenditure on a second property owned by Mr. Chaney, and not on the cottage which he sold. The judge ruled that the fact that expenditure incurred by Mr. Chaney in providing his mother -in-law with alternative accommodation was on the second property which he retained was not *"inconsistent with expenditure also being incurred by the taxpayer in enhancing the value of his interest in the property (the cottage which he sold) by obtaining vacant possession".*

Although the point was not actually at issue in the case, the judge expressed the view that changes which occurred between the date of a contract for the sale of an asset, and the completion of that sale (usually the conveyance) could be taken into account in judging whether or not expenditure was reflected in the state or nature of an asset at the date of its disposal. This was relevant because the vacant possession obtained by Mr. Chaney was obtained subsequent to the contract which he entered into for the sale of the cottage, but before the completion of the sale. *"The date of disposal"* in relation to a disposal on foot of a contract is stated by s542 to be *"the time the contract is made, and is not, if different, the time at which the asset is conveyed or transferred."*

The judge concluded that Mr. Chaney's obligation to provide his mother-in-law with alternative accommodation did represent expenditure incurred by him in order to obtain vacant possession of the property which he was selling, and he remitted the matter to the Appeal Commissioners to place a value on that obligation. He indicated that the necessity to place a value on the obligation, rather than accepting that the figure of £9,400 should be taken to be that value, arose because the parties were not dealing with each other at arm's length.

• **Revenue/Chief Inspector's CGT manual :**

— In the Revenue Commissioners capital gains tax manual it is noted that *"Expenditure incurred in repairing and putting into a fit state for letting a property acquired in a dilapidated condition is normally inadmissible as a deduction under Case V of Schedule D. For capital gains tax purposes, however, such expenditure (including expenditure on decorations) may in general be regarded as allowable expenditure under Section 552 (1)".*

9.1.5   **Cost of defending title**

It was held in the UK case of Emmerson v Computer Time International that the payment of arrears of rent by a liquidator as a condition imposed by the landlord on the assignment of the company's leasehold interest by the liquidator, was an expense incurred for the purposes of establishing, preserving or defending the company's title to the lease.

In order that expenditure incurred in establishing, preserving or defending title to, or right over, the asset should be deductible expenditure, it is necessary that it should have been wholly and exclusively incurred for those purposes. In the ordinary way the payment of rent by a lessee in respect of a premises (although it does serve the purpose of preserving his title to his leasehold interest which would be forfeited if he did not pay the rent) is not exclusively incurred to preserve his title. In part it is incurred simply to have possession of the premises, and because there is a legal obligation on him in any event to pay it. The position of the liquidator was different in that in the ordinary way the landlord would have been entitled only to such repayment as any creditor of the company would have received, usually a percentage only of the full debt. The liquidator's decision to pay the full arrears, in the Emerson case, was not for the purpose of securing occupation of the premises, nor was it meeting a legal obligation by reason of past occupation but was solely to ensure his ability to sell the lease, which could not be done without the landlord's consent.

Whereas the cost of establishing one's title to property may well be a capital expense in the ordinary way, and therefore even in the case of

a person carrying on a trade or profession, it is not a deductible
expense for income tax purposes by reason of being capital, the cost
of defending title is usually regarded as being an expense of a
revenue nature. It would therefore normally be a deductible expense
of a trade for income tax purposes. For that reason, the costs of
defending title, or preserving title (as opposed to establishing title)
are rarely likely to be deductible in respect of an asset used for trade
or professional purposes, notwithstanding that they are listed
amongst the deductible classes of expenditure. All of the listed
classes of deductible expenditure are subject to the overriding rule
that no sum which is deductible for income tax purposes may be
deducted for the purposes of capital gains tax.

Example 57

> *John Bloggs carries on an undertaking business on a premises in Clonmel. The
> neighbouring premises, a yard, was owned by a family who had long left the
> area. John Bloggs had been accustomed for many years to using the yard
> (without the owner's permission, their whereabouts not being known) for the
> purpose of parking his hearses at night, and for storing coffins etc in a lean-to
> shed which he erected there.*
>
> *After approximately 15 years of occupying the neighbouring yard in this fashion
> John Bloggs made application to the courts for a squatters title to the yard. He
> incurred £3,000 of legal expenses on this in 1995.*
>
> *In 1997 the long lost family reappeared, and sought administration of the estate
> of the last registered owner of the yard. The administrator took an action
> against John Bloggs seeking arrears of rent for his many years of occupation, and
> title to the yard. John Bloggs successfully defended this action at a cost of
> £8,000. However he was obliged to bear his own costs in the matter.*
>
> *Both the £3,000 incurred in 1995 and the £8,000 incurred in 1997 fall within
> the description of expenditure incurred wholly and exclusively to establish and
> defend title to an asset. The £3,000 in 1995 was capital in nature, in creating
> for Joe Bloggs a new asset to wit his legal title to the yard. As such it would not
> be deductible for the purpose of computing profits of his undertaking business.
> It is therefore part of the base cost of the yard for the future.*
>
> *The £8,000 incurred in 1997 was incurred in defending a title he already
> possessed to the yard and in defending a claim for rent. This expenditure is
> revenue in nature and would be a deductible expense of his undertaking trade.
> As it was deductible for income tax purposes, it did not fall to be included in his
> base cost of the asset for capital gains tax purposes, notwithstanding that it falls
> within the category of expenditure ordinarily deductible.*

- **Appeal Commissioners Ruling:**

— The Appeal Commissioners have ruled that probate tax is
   allowable as an acquisition cost of an asset, under s552(1) TCA 97.

9.2   **Incidental Costs**

s552(2)   The incidental costs of acquisition (or disposal) must be incurred wholly and exclusively for the purpose of the acquisition (or disposal) of the asset, and must fall into one or other of the following categories:

- fees, commission, or remuneration for the professional services of any
  - surveyor
  - valuer
  - auctioneer
  - accountant
  - agent
  - legal advisor
- costs of transfer or conveyance (including stamp duty),
- cost of advertising to acquire the asset.
- cost of advertising to find a buyer in the case of a disposal, and reasonable valuation costs necessary to compute any gain or loss on that disposal.

Although s552(2) provides for a deduction in terms of "professional services", it would not seem to be a requirement that the services provided should be provided by somebody actually carrying on a profession. An auctioneer is not normally regarded as carrying on a profession and the inclusion of an auctioneer (and a valuer) in the list of persons providing eligible services would suggest that no particular meaning should be given to "professional" in this context. However it may have the meaning that only a payment for services rendered by one of the listed categories of persons would be deductible if that person is actually carrying on a business in an organised manner of providing such services. The point does not appear to have been litigated and must therefore remain ambiguous.

Example 58

John Bloggs, in order to meet bank debts, has decided to dispose of a farm in Tipperary and a rental property which he owns in Dublin. The farm is put up for sale by private treaty through a local auctioneer and a fee of £5,000 becomes duly payable to the auctioneer on the sale of the farm.

The house in Dublin is sold by private treaty also. However it was not put up for sale in the normal way through an auctioneer by reason of the need for rapid disposal. Instead, a friend who owned a number of property companies undertook to find a buyer for a minimum price of £400,000 within seven days, with closing of the sale within 21 days, in return for a fee of £4,000.

Notwithstanding that both fees described above were incurred by John Bloggs for the same purpose, ie to secure the services of a third party in finding a buyer for his properties, only the first fee would appear to be allowable as deductible expenditure. The first fee was paid to an auctioneer for his services (notwithstanding that these services did not consist of the conduct of an auction but rather the conduct of a private sale). The payment in relation to the Dublin apartment was not paid to a person who carried on the business of finding buyers for properties. It was paid to somebody who took a casual opportunity of profit by reason of his connections and knowledge of the market-place. He performed the same function as the Tipperary auctioneer in the transaction but he could not have been said to have rendered the professional services of an auctioneer. That is both because he was not an auctioneer, and the services rendered by him, although akin to the services of an auctioneer, were not rendered in the carrying on of a business of auctioneering. Neither would the payment to the friend in relation to the Dublin property seem to fall under the heading "Costs of advertising to find a buyer". There was no question of advertising involved even though the purpose was to find a buyer.

It might be argued that the friend was alternatively "an agent". As described above, he would not in fact be an agent since he had no power to bind John Bloggs to any contract. He was merely a person providing a service and no more an agent than John's barber would be an agent. Even if he were an agent, it was not an agency carried out by him in an organised business and therefore would probably fall foul of the requirement that his services be "professional services."

No allowance is available for the cost of agreeing the tax position with the Inspector, nor is any allowance given for interest (with the limited exception set out in paragraph 9.5), although the cost of both of these items can be quite substantial.

s552(2) The UK case of Couch v Caton's Administrators was concerned with a deduction in respect of fees paid to a valuer. The fees paid arose in connection with the submission of a tax return to the Inspector of Taxes, and in respect of subsequent negotiation with the Inspector of Taxes and the conduct of a case before the Appeal Commissioners. The Revenue accepted that the costs which related to the initial valuation which was the basis of the tax return made to the Inspector of Taxes were deductible costs under s552(2) in its UK equivalent. This is the paragraph which provides that the cost of a valuation for the purpose of a computation is part of the incidental costs. The Revenue disputed that part of the valuation fee which related to negotiations with them, and the conduct of an appeal before the Appeal Commissioners. In the High Court, the judge upheld the Revenue interpretation. He said:

"If the solicitors, counsel and expert witnesses retained by the taxpayer for the purposes of an appeal against the assessment were to be asked what they were being paid to do it is my view most unlikely that they would answer that they were making a valuation of the shares or ascertaining their value. They would not so answer because that is not what they were doing. It is more likely that they would answer that they were together playing their respective roles in presenting to the special commissioner the taxpayer's

*case on the question of value. They would so answer because that is what
they were doing. — By the appeal stage the only person who can with any
accuracy be described as making the relevant valuation — is the special
commissioner. — The cost incurred by the taxpayers for the purpose of the
appeal are correctly characterised as costs incurred for the purpose of
conducting a tax controversy with the Revenue. I consider that the same
can be said of any costs incurred in the course of any negotiation with the
Revenue over the question of value, and regardless of whether it is
successful or not."*

In the authors opinion, the decision in the Catons Administrators
Case is a bit surprising, especially in the context of self assessment,
where a taxpayer has an obligation to consider any views expressed
by the Revenue Commissioners which might suggest that his
valuation of the shares in his return of income was incorrect.
Arguably, correspondence and negotiations with the Revenue
Commissioners on this point occur *"in ascertaining market value where
required by this Act"* as referred to in s552.

Valuation fees are referred to twice in s552(2).

—The fees, commission or remuneration paid for the professional
   services of any valuer are part of the incidental costs where they
   are incurred *"for the purposes of the acquisition or as the case may be
   the disposal"* of the assets. An example might be where a valuer is
   employed to advice the taxpayer on the price which he should
   seek for the asset, or in actually conducting negotiations for the
   sale of the asset.

—Expenses reasonably incurred in ascertaining market value as
   required by the CGT Acts. It is this latter provision which was the
   subject matter of the Catons Administrators Case described above.
   The expenses here referred to arise subsequent to the disposal, or
   acquisition.

An example of the circumstances in which they might arise is any
case where either the acquisition or the disposal of the asset was a
transaction with a connected party, so that s547 substitutes open
market value for the actual consideration passing. In such a case it
will usually be necessary, in order to prepare a computation, to
obtain the advice of a valuer as to the open market value of the asset.

This reference to the costs of a valuation for the purpose of the
computation is the only reference in s552 to the deductibility of the
costs of preparing the tax computation and agreeing the gain with
the inspector. It seems rather anomalous that the costs of making a
valuation should be singled out in this manner for a deduction,
while all of the other costs involved in employing a tax agent for the
purpose are not referred to.

It should be noted that what is referred to in the second instance
above is the costs incurred in making a valuation. Such costs need

CHAPTER 2

EXPENDITURE DEDUCTIBLE

not necessarily be incurred in relation to somebody who would be conventionally described as a "valuer". In contrast, the other type of costs referred to immediately above are specifically those paid "for the professional services of a valuer".

- *Revenue/Chief Inspector's CGT Manual:*

— Paragraph 10.5, part 19, Chief Inspector of Taxes notes on the Consolidated Taxes Act 1997 states that part of a liquidator's fees may be apportioned as a cost of the disposal of the company's assets.

Special rules apply to incidental costs of disposal incurred on the occasion of a beneficiary becoming absolutely entitled to settled property as against the trustees. These rules are described in paragraph 65.7.

9.2.1 Cost of variation of marriage settlement

The cost incurred by the trustees, arising out of the variation of a marriage contract settlement, to enable the assets to be paid out to the beneficiaries earlier than was otherwise possible, was held in the UK case of CIR v Chubbs Trustees to be an incidental cost of the disposal of the assets by the trustees.

9.3 Foreign Tax

s828(4) Any foreign tax payable on the disposal of an asset is allowable as a deduction in computing the gain, but only to the extent that relief is not already provided for it by some other method, e.g.-

- under the terms of a double taxation relief agreement between Ireland and the other country involved, or

- by the unilateral double taxation relief introduced in Sch24 Part 2.

Normally under a DTR agreement, the foreign tax would be deducted from the Irish tax payable on the gain rather than in arriving at the gain.

Example 59 (ignoring indexation)

Sale of land in a country with no DTR agreement with Ireland - assume £20,000 sale proceeds, Allowable Cost is £10,000, and foreign tax paid of £2,000.

	£	£
Selling Price		20,000
Cost	10,000	
Foreign tax	2,000	12,000
GAIN		8,000
	£8,000 @ 20% =	£1,600

Example 60

Sale of land in a country with a DTR agreement with Ireland (dealing with CGT) - assume £20,000 sale proceeds, Allowable Cost is £10,000, and foreign tax paid of £1,000.

		£
Selling Price		20,000
Cost		10,000
GAIN		10,000
	£10,000 @ 20% =	£2,000
Less credit for foreign tax		£1,000
CGT Payable		£1,000

Double Tax Relief is dealt with further in Chapter 11.

Sch24, Part 2

The FA98 introduced a unilateral tax credit, which can apply even where a double tax agreement does not exist with the state which levied the foreign tax. However the unilateral tax credit is confined to the situation where an Irish resident company is in receipt of a dividend paid by a company resident outside of Ireland. It has no direct relevance to Capital Gains Tax. There is an indirect relevance insofar as the credit for foreign taxes in relation to a dividend, where the Irish resident company has a 25% holding in the share capital of the overseas company paying the dividend, can extend to taxes paid by the overseas company on the profits for which the dividend is paid, and those taxes for which credit is available in relation to the dividend, can include taxes akin to Capital Gains Tax in Ireland.

9.4   Asset used as security

s537

All assets are deemed to be acquired free of any right or restriction by way of security. Where any such right or restriction attaches to the asset on its acquisition, the full amount of that right or interest is taken into account as being part of the acquisition cost of the asset.

Example 61

John owns a property. He acquired the property with the aid of a £50,000 loan from his cousin in the United States of America. The loan was interest free and not repayable until a fixed date in 10 years time. It is secured on the property. John wishes to sell the property but it does not seem to him to be sensible to repay an interest free loan when he does not have to. The property is worth £100,000 on the open market, unencumbered by a mortgage, but John is able to get a purchaser willing to pay him £60,000 for the property subject to the mortgage.

John is treated as selling the property for £110,000 - £60,000 paid to him by the purchaser and the £50,000 liability effectively assumed by the purchaser.

s537(3)

S537(3) requires that the full amount of the liability assumed by the purchaser be added to any other consideration given. In the example above, the current value of an interest free loan not repayable for a further 10 years is very much less than its face value. Notwithstanding this, no discounting is provided for, and it is the amount of the liability, and not the value of the liability in the market place, which is taken into account as consideration. If the liability in question had been a loan carrying interest at the rate of (say) 20% per annum, the amount taken into account as additional consideration on the disposal would still be the capital sum outstanding ie £50,000, even though the open market value of having such a liability taken over by another person is several times greater than the open market value of having an interest free long term liability taken over by another person.

The wording of the legislation does not give rise to any great injustice or difficulty where a person who acquires an asset which remains subject to a right of security in respect of a debt of the person making the disposal, assumes the liability to pay that debt without further claim upon the person making the disposal. In such a case the person making the disposal is effectively relieved of his debt and the person making the acquisition is obliged to incur the expenditure to repay the debt, without right of recompense against the person making the disposal.

However the words of the legislation are not clearly limited to such a situation. It is possible that an asset might be disposed of by one person, and acquired by another, while remaining subject to a security in respect of the liabilities of the person making the disposal, but without the person making the acquisition agreeing to take on the sole obligation to discharge that liability. In other words, the obligation to pay off the debt might remain with the person making the disposal. Indeed it might very well be an express condition of the sale that they should do so within a fixed period, or should apply part of the sales proceeds to do so. In such a case the price agreed between the two parties for the asset might well not be a discount from the true market value of the asset so as to reflect the debt. In such a case the operation of s537(3) would nonetheless seem to include the full amount of the liability as additional consideration for the disposal and the acquisition.

What s537(3) requires is firstly that the disposal be treated as free of the rights of security. That in itself does not imply anything in the current situation since the consideration passing remains the consideration passing, and the assumption to be made does not oblige us to substitute any different value to that agreed. Secondly the section requires that the consideration be increased by "the full amount of the liability thereby assumed by the person acquiring the asset". In the circumstances outlined the person acquiring the asset has assumed the liability in the sense that he accepts the right of the creditor to dispose of the asset in order to discharge the debt to the creditor. But in such an instance the person acquiring the asset would usually stand in the shoes of the creditor and be entitled to claim recompense from the person making the disposal, where they have not agreed to the contrary. In such a case the person making the disposal would have to reimburse the person making the acquisition, and the inclusion of the amount of the liability as additional consideration produces an unrealistic result.

It may be that the answer to the conundrum is that where an asset is disposed of subject to a right of security, but the person acquiring it has not taken on the obligation to discharge the debt in place of the person making the disposal of the asset, that he is not regarded as taking on any part of the liability at that time and that therefore no adjustment falls to be made. This could be rationalised on the basis that no part of the liability would be undertaken by him unless and until they exercised their rights and disposed of the asset and pocketed the proceeds.

Example 62

> Bloggs Limited sold a property in Dublin and one in Cork to Property Limited. Both properties were pledged as security for the debts of Bloggs Limited to various banks.
>
> The Dublin property was sold for £500,000. It was subject to a mortgage by a bank in the amount of £1m. Property Limited undertook to discharge that mortgage and to indemnify Bloggs Limited against it. The property was to be sold with the security remaining in place. The bank were not a party to the transaction. Bloggs duly paid £1m discharging the bank's claims and secured a lifting of the charge on the property. The section would require that the consideration passing between Bloggs Limited and Property Limited of £500,000 should be increased by the £1m bank liability discharged on the property.
>
> The property in Cork was sold for £800,000. It was sold subject to a mortgage to a bank in the amount of £400,000. The contract for sale provided for an undertaking by Bloggs Limited's solicitors that the bank debt would be discharged by it on behalf of Bloggs Limited out of the sales proceeds of the property within five working days of the closing of the sale. The consideration of £800,000 was duly paid over and title was taken to the property while still subject to the bank mortgage. The solicitor duly honoured his undertaking by using £400,000 of the sales proceeds to pay off the bank and secure a release of the mortgage on the property. In the view of the authors the section should not apply so as to increase the consideration of £800,000 by the sum of £400,000, being the amount of the liability to the bank which was charged on the property when the property was transferred. This is because Property Limited had not undertaken to discharge the bank debt on behalf of Bloggs Limited and therefore did not assume it, notwithstanding that had Bloggs Limited's solicitor for any reason failed to discharge his undertaking to pay off the bank out of the sales proceeds, the bank could have seized the property to discharge their debt.

Where an asset is disposed of and acquired subject to a security, but without the liability which is secured being undertaken by the transferee, the security probably represents contingent liability,(ie a liability which would crystallise only if the security is realised or exercised). Contingent liabilities are discussed in paragraph 9.9.

s547

S537 (3) does not explicitly describe its interaction with S547, which can substitute open market value for actual consideration in certain circumstances. It is however reasonable to assume that where S547 substitutes open market value for actual consideration passing, it also substitutes it for the deemed additional consideration which S537(3) would give rise to. In the example above, if John sold the property to a connected party on the terms described, he would be deemed to have disposed of the property for £100,000, its open market value and not the £110,000 which is the total of the sum received by him, and the amount of the liability taken over.

The UK case of Thompson v Salah concerned artificial arrangements which unsuccessfully attempted to avoid tax on the sale of a property subject to a mortgage.

9.5   Interest

s552

Interest paid by an individual or any non-corporate body is not allowable as a deduction for CGT purposes. There are no exceptions to this rule.

s553

Generally, for CGT purposes, interest, even if charged to capital, is not allowed as a deduction in calculating chargeable gains. The only exception is made in the case of a company. In relation to a company there is an exception so that interest is deductible if:

- the company incurs expenditure on the *construction* of any :

  − building,

  − structure

  − or works

- that expenditure was allowable as a deduction in computing a gain arising on the disposal of the asset,

- that expenditure was defrayed out of borrowed money, and

- the company charged to capital all or any part of the interest on that borrowed money referable to a period or part of a period ending on or before the disposal.

The amount of the capitalised interest is deductible in such circumstances.

It should be noted that

− the legislation refers to the "construction" cost of a building and not to the cost of buying a building already constructed, or of buying the site for a building to be constructed.

− this provision permitting the deduction of capitalised interest is available only to a company, and not to an individual or any other non-corporate entity.

The provision is to be found, in almost identical terms, in both s552(3) and in s553.

There is an important difference between the manner in which the relief for interest is expressed in s552, compared with s553. In s552 relief is provided for interest only in so far as such interest has not been taken into account for the purposes of relief under the Income Tax Acts, or could have been so taken into account but for an insufficiency of income or profits or gains. In contrast, s553 grants the relief without any such restriction. Apart from this point, the terms for the relief under the two sections are identical.

Example 63

Bloggs Limited have borrowed money to build a new factory building. The building was complete on 1 January 1999, at which time borrowings in relation to the construction work amounted to £1m. In the year ended 31 December 1998 the interest on the borrowings amounted to £80,000. That was capitalised as part of the cost of the building in the accounts of Bloggs Limited for that year end. However Bloggs Limited, which is a trading company, claimed a deduction for the interest in computing its trading profits. A further sum of £100,000 arose in the year ended 31 December 1999, in respect of interest on the original loan. This interest was charged to the profit and loss account, and a deduction was claimed for it in the Case I computation for trading income.

Under s552(3) Bloggs Limited would not be entitled to relief in respect of the interest of the year 31 December 1998. That is because relief was claimed for the interest in computing trading income. The same situation would apply in the year ended 31 December 1999, with the additional reason that the interest was not capitalised by the company. However s553 does grant relief for the interest in the year ended 31 December 1998, since relief under that section is available without reference to a claim for relief in computing trading income. However relief for the year ended 31 December 1999 would be denied under s553 also as the interest was not capitalised by the company.

The comments on s552 and s553 above must be qualified by reference to s554. Section 554(1) denies a deduction under s552 to any expenditure allowable as a deduction in computing the profits or gains or losses of a trade. That raises the question of whether s554 denies a deduction for interest which might be deductible by reason of s553, as opposed to interest deductible by reference to s552(3). Section 554 is concerned solely with denying a deduction under s552. Although the point is not beyond debate, it appears to the authors that s553 is not itself the basis for a claim for a deduction in respect of the interest but rather that it includes in the construction cost of a building the amount of that interest, for the purpose of computing relief for that expenditure under s552. Therefore s553 does not directly give relief but merely enables s552 to give relief for the interest as if it were construction expenditure. That being so, s554 operates to exclude the deduction under s552 in so far as the interest was included in trade expenses. The point is not beyond dispute. It is very difficult to understand why s552(3) and s553 exist in almost identical terms side by side, dealing with the identical subject matter, and differing only by reference to whether or not interest has been claimed as a deduction in computing the profits of a trade. This is made all the more surprising since that point, the deductibility in computing profits of a trade, is in any event dealt with in s554.

In order that interest should be deductible it is necessary under both s552 and s553 that "the company charge to capital all or any part of the interest". "Charge to capital" here would seem to be a reference to the capitalisation of the interest in the accounts of the company and not to be a reference to whether or not the interest is, in taxation terms, capital rather than revenue in nature. The fact that interest is charged to capital in the accounts of a company would not in itself prevent the company from obtaining a deduction for such interest in computing the income of a trade.

The interest which is deductible under s553 and s552 is interest referable to a period prior to the disposal, and not merely interest up to the point at which the construction of the building is complete. In *example 63* above, Bloggs Limited would have been entitled to claim a deduction for CGT purposes for interest on the borrowings up to the date of disposal in 2002, had the interest been capitalised by them throughout the period, and had it not been allowable as a deduction in computing the profits or gains or losses of a trade or profession.

S554 not only excludes the deduction under s552 for interest deductible in computing the profits of losses of a trade or profession, but further requires that if the expenditure would have been deductible had the asset which is being disposed of been held as a fixed asset of a trade, that a deduction be denied to that expenditure. Thus for example a deduction would be denied even if the premises being disposed of was a rental premises rather than a premises held for the purposes of a trade, in so far as the interest on the construction costs of the premises would have been deductible had they been held as the fixed asset of a trade.

Interest which is a distribution is not deductible in computing the income of a company in accordance with s129. However there appears to be no prohibition on claiming a deduction for interest incurred by a company, meeting the conditions outlined above, whether or not that interest is treated as a distribution by s130 or any other section.

9.6 Grants

Any expenditure which has been or is to be met directly or indirectly by any grant, either in Ireland or elsewhere is not allowable as a deduction (to the extent that it is met by the grant).

s565 *"There shall be excluded from the computation under this Chapter of a gain accruing on a disposal any expenditure which has been or is to be met directly or indirectly by any government, by any board established by statute, or by any public or local authority whether in the State or elsewhere".*

Some tax practitioners have a doubt as to whether grants paid by the European Union (or by any of the EU funds) come within this rule. The issue is whether the Commission of the European Union could properly be regarded as a government or board established by statute, or a public or local authority. Although its funds are partly derived from the governments of the member states (mainly through a levy based on the domestic value added tax of each member State) the connection between the provision of funds to the EU by the member State, and the source of grants paid out by the EU is remote. There must remain a doubt as to whether such grants are to be regarded as being provided directly or indirectly by a government.

9.7 Insurance

s552
No allowance can be claimed for insurance premiums, under a policy insuring a risk of any kind of damage, injury, loss or depreciation of asset. Insurance is further discussed in paragraph 4.5.3.

9.8 Expenditure : Capital Allowances

Special provisions for dealing with expenditure qualifying for Capital Allowances are included in the CGT Acts.

s555
Expenditure qualifying for capital allowances (or a renewals allowance) is allowable in full in computing a gain on the disposal of an asset. Similarly, receipts which are effectively taxed by way of a balancing charge are not excluded from the proceeds taken into account in computing the gain for CGT purposes. Capital allowances are, however, taken into account in computing an allowable loss. TCA97 s555 provides that:

s555(1)
"...in the computation of the amount of a loss accruing to the person making the disposal, there shall be excluded from the sums allowable as a deduction any expenditure to the extent to which any capital allowance or renewals allowance has been or may be made in respect of that expenditure".

In effect, capital allowances are not taken into account in arriving at a gain for CGT purposes. However, in deciding whether a loss is to be allowable, capital allowances obtained on expenditure incurred must be taken into account.

If a gain results, that gain is charged to CGT in the normal manner ignoring the effect of any capital allowances or renewals allowance granted in respect of the asset.

If a loss results, that loss is restricted - it must be computed by deducting the allowances (net of any balancing charge) effectively granted in respect of the asset from the deductible expenditure (before indexation). A renewals allowance is a deduction allowable in computing profits or losses for income tax or corporation tax purposes by reference to the cost of acquiring an asset in replacement of another asset. A renewals allowance is treated as a deduction in respect of the asset being replaced and not of the new asset acquired.

Example 64

Peter acquired an "Industrial Building" for £100,000. Over the years he received capital allowances of £60,000 in respect of it. He sold the building for £220,000

Computation:	£
Sale Proceeds:	£220,000
Cost (ignoring indexation)	£100,000
GAIN	£120,000

As a gain arises, capital allowances granted have no relevance to the computation.

Example 65

Jim acquired an industrial building on 1 March 1997 for £300,000. He sold it on 8 March 2000 for £250,000. He has made a commercial loss of £50,000 on the transaction.

Computation:	£	£
Sale Proceeds		250,000
Cost	300,000	
IBAA(assumed)	(5,600)	
Balancing Allowance	(44,400)	
		250,000
Chargeable gain/allowable loss		£NIL

* Indexation does not apply in this case as it would produce a loss which would not otherwise result (see paragraph 14.3).

The rule operates to restrict a loss - it does not affect the computation of a gain.

Where the operation of the rule would have the effect of transforming an allowable loss into a chargeable gain, it would be applied only to bring about a break-even situation ie a no gain/no loss situation. In the example above, had the balancing allowance been (say) £60,000 the computation would nonetheless be as set out above.

s289(6),
s295,
s312(5),
s280

Where the person disposing of the asset was treated for tax purposes as having acquired it at the tax WDV of the person from whom he acquired it, any allowances granted to the person from whom he acquired it (insofar as they have not been used to reduce a CGT loss) are treated as having been granted to the person making the disposal.

The special treatment of wasting assets where expenditure on them attracts capital allowances is described in paragraphs 10.3 and 57.2.

9.9 Contingent Liabilities

s562

There are only three cases specified in the legislation where the value of a contingent liability attaching to a person on the disposal of an asset is not deductible. These are:

- The contingent liability of a person who assigns a lease of land (or other property) and retains a liability to the person from whom he acquired the lease, in the event of the default of the person to whom he assigned the lease.

- The contingent liability of a person who disposes of land or an interest in land by way of sale, lease or option, where he assumes a responsibility for 'quiet enjoyment' or other obligations in connection with the disposal.

- Where an asset (other than land) is disposed of, a contingent liability (actual or implied) may remain with the person making the disposal in respect of warranty or other representations made in connection with that disposal (e.g. under the Sale of Goods Act).

Such contingent liabilities are not deductible in arriving at the gain or loss on the disposal of the asset. If, however, the liability is actually enforced at a subsequent stage, whatever adjustments as are necessary will be made to effectively allow the expenditure incurred.

The value of all contingent liabilities other than those specifically excluded (above) must be taken into account in the computation of a gain or a loss on the disposal of an asset.

The UK case of Randall v Plumb was concerned with the treatment in a CGT computation of a contingency. The taxpayer had granted an option to a company to acquire certain lands from him at any time during an approximately 20 year period, for a fixed price of £100,000. In consideration of the grant of the option, the taxpayer received the sum of £25,000. The option agreement provided that this sum would be repayable to the company in certain circumstances (broadly if planning permission for a certain development was not obtained by various dates), and would form part payment of the consideration for the property should the option be exercised. The sum of money would thus either be repayable by the taxpayer to the company should the option not be exercised by reason of planning permission not been obtained, or would be applied in part payment of the consideration for the disposal of the land if the option were exercised or would be retained by him if planning permission were granted but the option was not exercised.

The case turned on how this contingency to repay should be reflected in the computation which fell to be prepared by reason of either the grant of an option by the taxpayer, or the receipt by him of a capital sum derived from the land (depending on which view the court might take of the matter).

s562

The Court had to consider the UK equivalent legislation to s562. However the UK equivalent differed in one important respect from the Irish legislation. The UK equivalent legislation provided that *"no allowance shall be made in the computation under this schedule...."* for the contingencies which the paragraph then went on to specify and which are expressed in similar words to those employed in s562 (with the exception of subsecton 1(b)(iii) which did not appear in the UK legislation). The UK legislation therefore appeared to forbid the taking into account of the contingency either in computing the consideration to be taken into account, or in computing the deductible expenditure. In contrast the Irish legislation provides that *"no allowance shall be made under s552...."* for the contingencies which the paragraph then lists. s552 is the section which sets out the rules for computing deductible expenditure. It is not concerned with the computation of the amount of consideration to be taken into account. This is important because it is clear from the judgement in the UK case that it turned on the computation of the consideration, and not on the question of deductible expenditure. In the event the judge held that because the obligation to repay moneys was not the type of contingency specifically excluded in the UK equivalent to s562, it was permissible to take it into account in valuing the consideration.

s562

s552

Had the case been decided under Irish law, s562 would not be relevant at all since it does not apply to the calculation of the consideration. However s562, in the subsection referred to above which does not appear in the UK legislation, is sufficiently widely expressed to prevent any deduction (as expenditure) for the contingency to repay the capital sum received, or consideration received. This is not relevant however since the rules of s552 dealing with deductible expenditure would never have permitted such a deduction in the first place.

9.10   Assets Derived from Assets

s559

On the disposal of an asset, which has derived its value from another asset in the same ownership, it is necessary to arrive at the allowable cost to be deducted in calculating the gain on the disposal. Part of the cost of the original asset from which it derived its value is attributed to it. The apportionment is made on the basis of the respective market values of the original asset and the 'derived' asset at the date of disposal of the 'derived' asset.

s559 provides:

"(1) *If and so far as, in a case where assets have been merged or divided or have changed their nature or rights or interests in or over assets have been created or extinguished, the value of an asset is derived from any other asset in the same ownership, an appropriate proportion of the sums allowable as a deduction in respect of the other asset under paragraphs (a) and (b) of s552(1) shall, both for the purpose of the computation of a gain accruing on the disposal of the first-mentioned asset and, if the other asset remains in existence, on a disposal of that other asset, be attributed to the first-mentioned asset.*

(2) *The appropriate proportion shall be computed by reference to the market value at the time of disposal, of the assets (including rights or interests in or over the assets) which have not been disposed of and the consideration received in respect of the assets (including rights or interests in or over the assets) disposed of".*

If, for example, a lessee of property subsequently acquired the landlords superior interest in the property during the currency of the lease, the two interests would normally be treated as merging, and the new asset would have derived its value partly from the leasehold interest. In such circumstances, on a disposal of the new merged asset, account would be taken of both the qualifying expenditure on the leasehold interest, and the cost of acquiring the landlords superior interest.

On a disposal of the freehold, the leasehold which had merged with it would no longer exist as a separate asset. Accordingly the appropriate proportion (see sub-section 2 quoted above) would be 100% of the deductible cost of the leasehold.

In any circumstances in which the original asset from which the new asset's value is derived continues in existence, the apportionment of the base cost of the original asset between the two assets will occur on the date of the disposal of whichever of the two assets, the original or the new asset, is first disposed of. Thus if the old asset is the first disposed of, the attribution will occur on the date of that disposal and similarly, if it had been the new asset which was first disposed of. It should be borne in mind that a disposal includes a part disposal (see paragraph 4.4.3). It would seem therefore that even a minor part disposal of either the new asset or the old asset could trigger the apportionment of the base cost of the original asset by reference to relative values on the date of what might be a very minor part disposal.

Many instances of assets merging, dividing, or changing rights etc, in so far as they apply to shares in a company, would be covered by the share reorganisation provisions of the capital gains tax acts and not by the provisions relating to "assets derived from assets". The topic of reorganisations of share capital is discussed in paragraph 42.

The UK equivalent of this provision was considered in Aberdeen Construction Group Limited v IRC. In that case Aberdeen Construction Group had acquired, over a period of time, all the shares in Rock Fall Limited. In addition, over the period of time it had made loans to Rock Fall Limited totaling £500,000. Subsequently, the shares in Rock Fall Limited were sold to an unconnected company for £250,000. The sale of the shares was conditional upon Aberdeen Construction Group Ltd waiving the £500,000 loan due from Rock Fall Limited.

On behalf of the taxpayer it was argued:

- That the £250,000 proceeds was in respect of both the shares and the loan and should be apportioned to both, or

- That the loan was a debt on a security which would give rise to an allowable loss (see paragraph 38), or

s559

- That the shares derived value from the waiver of the loan and accordingly part of the 'cost' of the loan should be attributed to the shares (under the UK equivalent of TCA97 s559).

It was held by a majority in the House of Lords that (based on the terms of the contract) the £250,000 proceeds should properly be attributed to both the shares and the loan, and accordingly should be apportioned to both the for the purposes of CGT.

Although not all the Lords agreed with the decision in favour of the taxpayer, they were unanimous in their rejection of the alternative argument that the shares derived value from the loan within the meaning of s559.

In the course of his judgement Lord Russell of Killowen said, "*the second contention of the taxpayer is based on (TCA97 s559) which contention, if correct, would lead to some apportionment as under the first contention. That paragraph is cross-headed "assets derived from other assets". If broad terms were legitimate in connection with any part of this complicated legislation one would say that the paragraph is designed to provide for computation of capital gains where one asset has gained in value at the expense of another asset in the same ownership. Had it been expressed in such broad terms, it would be clear that in the circumstances the Rock Fall shares asset had gained in value by the extinction of the taxpayer company's other asset, the debt. But the paragraph has limiting factors or qualifying conditions for its operation. So far as presently relevant, it was necessary for the taxpayer company to contend that the debt and the shares had been "merged", or (perhaps) that the shares had "changed their nature". I find these contentions wholly unacceptable. Release of a company from its debt does not achieve anything that can be described as merger of the debt with the shares in the company; nor does it change the nature of those shares. If the contrary were true it would equally be appropriate to say that (within the paragraph) the debt was a right or interest over the shares, which had been extinguished; but of course it was not such. At one time I speculated whether it could be said that the waiver of the debt was a case of extinction of "rights or interests in or over" the asset consisting of the debt, a suggestion quite rightly not advanced by counsel for the taxpayer company. The speculation was soon terminated by counsel for the Crown who pointed out that total extinction of the asset cannot come within the language: the part is not the whole. Accordingly, I would reject the second contention".*

Merged assets are considered further in paragraph 10.6, and in particular the issues arising when a "wasting" asset is merged into a non-wasting asset.

Further consideration is given to the question of the question of *"derived from"* in paragraph 4.

s559

In the UK case of Bayley v Rogers dealing with a case where a tenant received a new lease by court order under landlord and tenant legislation, on the expiry of an old lease, the court rejected the notion that the new lease was derived from the old lease so as to cause the application of the UK equivalent of s559. The case is considered further at paragraph 55.2 and at paragraph 61.

The "assets derived from another asset" concept also arises in the anti-avoidance legislation relating to "pre-entry losses" (i.e.- arising to a company before it becomes a member of a group). This is discussed in paragraph 73.2.

9.11 Assets Acquired from Trust

s552

Where a person becomes absolutely entitled to property as legatee, or as against the trustees of settled property, the cost of transferring the assets to him are allowable as incidental costs of any subsequent disposal of the assets by him.

This deduction covers both his own costs relating to the transfer, and those of the trustees, (or personal representatives if he acquired the asset as legatee).

• **Revenue/Chief Inspector's CGT Manual :**

— In the Revenue Commissioners capital gains tax manual at Paragraph 19.3.5.14 it is stated that a deduction in relation to costs borne by the trustees should be allowed to the beneficiary only "if no claim has been made by the trustees". No such limitation appears in s552 but it would seem that any "double claim" in relation to the same expenses (once by the trustees and once by the beneficiary) would be resisted by the Revenue. Whether they would do so successfully or not is another matter.

The general treatment of trustees and settlements is dealt with in Chapter 8.

9.12   **Value Added Tax**

Where expenditure incurred on the

- acquisition

- enhancement, or

- incidental costs of acquisition or disposal

of an asset includes VAT, the amount of the expenditure taken into account for CGT purposes must be reduced by the amount of VAT recoverable in relation to the expenditure. To the extent it is recoverable, no cost has in fact been incurred.

Example 66

		£
Cost of asset...£1,000 + £210 VAT	=	1,210
enhancement expenditure ...£500 + £105 VAT	=	605
solicitors' fees on sale...£100 + £21 VAT	=	121

If the person is registered for VAT, and the asset is a business asset, the VAT would usually be deductible from VAT due to the Revenue on the VAT return for the period(s) in which the expenditure was incurred. If no VAT was due to the Revenue in those periods, the VAT incurred on the expenditure would be repaid by the Revenue. The cost for CGT purposes is the amount excluding VAT, i.e. £1,600 (£1,000 + £500 + £100).

Where the VAT is not recoverable, it would, of course form part of the cost of the asset for CGT purposes.

It should be noted, that in certain circumstances VAT is recoverable, even though the person who incurred the expenditure is not registered for VAT in Ireland, e.g.

- An unregistered farmer is entitled to a repayment of VAT on certain grant aided work on the land.

- Certain non-residents, who are not registered for VAT in Ireland, are entitled to a repayment of VAT incurred in Ireland on goods and services acquired by them for business purposes.

Also, as a general rule, persons registered for VAT in Ireland, are entitled to a refund of VAT incurred in other E.U. countries in respect of goods and services acquired for the purposes of their business.

- **Revenue/Chief Inspector's CGT Manual :**

- The treatment outlined above is confirmed in the Revenue Commissioners capital gains tax manual at paragraph 19.2.2.1.

Although it is the treatment conventionally applied, the statutory basis for the treatment outlined above is not obvious. It appears to turn on the notion that the operation of input credit in some sense represents a reimbursement to a person who has incurred VAT inclusive expenditure. While that may be so in an economic sense, it is a reading of VAT legislation which is open to challenge. In principle the entitlement to input credit is not related to the payment of any particular sum.

This becomes particularly clear where an input credit serves to reduce a liability for VAT in respect of supplies but does not result in any repayment of VAT.

9.13　　　Income Tax Relief

9.13.1　　General Note - Share schemes

An individual may qualify for an income tax deduction for all or part of the capital cost of certain qualifying shares, under the various income tax relief schemes.

These deductions are available under:

s488 - s509
- the Business Expansion Scheme (relief for investment in corporate trades) - see paragraph 9.13.2.

- relief for investment in companies involved in research and development- see paragraph 9.13.3.

s481
- relief for investment in film companies - see paragraph 9.13.4.

- Relief for investment in renewal energy projects - see paragraph 9.14

s479
- relief for employee share purchases- see paragraph 9.15.

All of these reliefs are subject to many conditions, but where the investment in the shares qualifies for relief under these provisions, the individual investor will get a deduction for income tax purposes for the cost of the shares (subject to the limitations of the relief). When the shares are disposed of, the allowable cost for CGT must be ascertained, to establish whether a gain or a loss arises on that disposal for CGT purposes.

In all cases, special rules are set out in the legislation for dealing with the CGT position on the ultimate disposal of those shares.

Other CGT aspects of Employee Share Schemes are discussed in paragraph 50.

9.13.2   Business Expansion Scheme

9.13.2.1   Broad Outline - B.E.S. (CGT aspects)

s506

The relief for investment in corporate trades (business expansion scheme) was introduced in the FA84. In broad terms it applies to qualifying shares issued on or after 6 April 1984. Over the years, the conditions for the relief have been substantially amended, but the CGT treatment of the shares on disposal, is the same today as it was in 1984.

An income tax deduction may be received on all or part of the amount invested in the shares. On disposal of the shares, all or part, or none of that relief may be clawed back, depending on the circumstances.

The consideration for the disposal (for CGT purposes) is normally clear, and the special rules deal mainly with the calculation of the part of the 'cost' of the shares to be taken into the computation of the gain or loss on disposal for CGT purposes.

In broad terms, the legislation provides for the income tax relief to be ignored, and the gain computed for CGT purposes as if no income tax relief had been granted. If a CGT loss would result, the cost of the shares for CGT purposes is reduced, to exclude relief for any resulting loss.

The special rules for calculating the CGT gain or loss on disposal are set out in s506.

Where relief for income tax has been given, and not withdrawn, the full cost is allowable as a deduction in calculating the gain or loss for CGT purposes. However, this rule is restricted where it would result in a CGT loss on the disposal.

Where a CGT loss would result from ignoring the income tax allowance, the sums allowed as a deduction for CGT purposes (ignoring the income tax relief) are reduced by the lower of:

• the full amount of the income tax deduction, or

• the excess of the amount qualifying for an income tax deduction over the sale proceeds.

This rule does not apply to a disposal from one spouse to another (under the CGT provisions dealing with married persons living together) - see paragraph 33.

Example 67

NOTE - The following example is not intended as an example of the operation of the BES rules - it is intended merely as an example to clarify the above CGT computation rules.

William purchased qualifying BES shares in 1992 for £30,000. In 1998 he sold the shares for a total consideration of £20,000.

The consideration for the sale of the shares is clear - it is £20,000.

The CGT cost of the shares (ignoring income tax relief) is £30,000. This will clearly result in a CGT loss, so the £30,000 cost must be reduced by the lower of:

- *the amount of the income tax deduction - £30,000 or*

- *the excess of the income tax deduction (£30,000) over the amount of the sale proceeds (£30,000 - £20,000), i.e. £10,000.*

In these circumstances, the cost for CGT purposes is:

Total cost	*£30,000*
reduction (excess)	*£10,000*
qualifying cost for CGT	*£20,000*

This will, in effect, leave a no gain, and no loss position for CGT.

9.13.2.2   Change in or withdrawal of relief

The above rule applies where income tax relief has been given, and has not been withdrawn.

s506   s506(4) provides that... *"there shall be made all such adjustments of capital gains tax, whether by way of assessment or by discharge or repayment of tax, as may be required in consequence of the relief being given or withdrawn."*

9.13.2.3   Multiple holdings, etc.

An individual holding shares in any company, may hold some which qualify for BES relief, and some which do not qualify. Shares may have been acquired at different times. The company may have been involved in a reconstruction or reorganisation, resulting in the shares now held being different from those originally issued. Additional rules are set out for dealing with many such potential difficulties.

Although there are specific CGT rules, which would deal with such problems, s506 applies the specific (income tax - B.E.S.) rules of TCA97 s498 in certain circumstances.

In relation to shares in respect of which relief has been given and not withdrawn, any question

- as to which of any such shares issued to a person at different times a disposal relates, or

- whether a disposal relates to such shares or to other shares,

is to be determined as for income tax purposes, under the BES rules set out in s498.

s498   In other words, if a taxpayer disposes of shares of a class in which he holds shares that attracted BES relief, the normal CGT rules for identifying which shares are deemed to be disposed of do not apply. Instead, special rules set out in s498 are used to identify the shares which are deemed to be sold. This special rule makes sense, as it ensures that the same shares are treated as being disposed of for both income tax (BES Clawback) purposes and for CGT purposes. The s498 rules may be broadly summarised as follows:

- shares which attracted BES relief are treated as being disposed of before shares in the same class which did not attract BES relief. This rule applies regardless of when the shares were actually acquired.

- As between shares of the same class which attracted BES relief, the shares are to be treated as being sold are to be selected on a F.I.F.O. basis.

9.13.2.4   Main rule - deemed disposal of BES shares first.

s498   Where an individual holds ordinary shares of the same class in the same company, some of which qualify for B.E.S. relief, and some of which do not, any disposal of ordinary shares of that class in the company is treated as being made out of the shares qualifying for B.E.S. relief - to the extent of the B.E.S. qualifying shares of that class held. s498(4) which determines the income tax position, is applied in the same manner for CGT purposes.

Where shares are issued to shareholders, in proportion to their existing holding of shares in the company, the new holding (i.e. the existing holding of shares plus the new shares issued, in total) is treated as being the same asset as the original holding of shares (before the new issue). Such an issue of shares could be for consideration (e.g. a rights issue) or could be free (e.g. a bonus issue). The CGT rules on 'reorganisations' are set out in detail in Chapter 6.

Where any part of the original holding of shares qualified for BES relief, a further rule applies in determining which shares have been disposed of under the s498(4) rule set out above. This further rule only applies where the new shares are not issued for payment.

- the new holding (in total) is treated as shares in respect of which BES relief has been granted, and

- a disposal of the whole or part of the new holding, is treated as a disposal of the whole or a corresponding part of those shares.

9.13.2.5   **F.I.F.O.**

s498(4)   Where shares of any class in a company have been issued to him at
different times, the normal CGT rule of 'first in - first out' is applied
in determining which shares have been disposed of by a shareholder.

9.13.2.6   **Reorganisation of share capital**

s506   Where an individual holds ordinary shares in a company, and B.E.S.
relief has been given in relation to some of his shares, but not to
others, if there is a reorganisation of the shares the normal CGT rules
for a reorganisation are modified.

The rule deeming the new holding (in total) to be the same as the
existing holding (before the new share issue) is modified to, in effect,
split the old and new holdings, into those qualifying for BES relief,
and those not qualifying.

The rules apply separately to the B.E.S. qualifying shares and to
other shares, so that the shares of each kind are treated as a separate
holding of original shares, and identified with the new separate
(total) holdings.

9.13.3   **Research and Development**

FA86 s30   Relief was introduced for qualifying investments in shares in a
research and development company in FA86 and has since been
repealed.

Similar problems may arise with this relief as with the B.E.S. relief.

The specific rules applying to the computation of the gain or loss on
disposal for CGT purposes are set out in FA86 s30.

The CGT rules are similar to those applying to B.E.S. relief shares - as
set out above.

Prior to FA93 relief for research and development projects was
separate to relief for BES investment. The FA93 has brought certain
research and development projects within the scope of B.E.S. Relief.

9.13.4   **Relief for investment in films**

9.13.4.1   **Broad Outline - investment in films**

s481   This relief was introduced in FA87 s35. In broad terms, it allows a tax
deduction from the profits of the investor company (for corporation
tax purposes) for amounts invested in certain Irish film-making
companies. The FA93 extended the relief to certain qualifying
individuals.

The 1987 relief was due to expire on 5 April 1996 (generally). The
FA96 confirmed the budget announcement in January 1996 of the

introduction of a new "Section 35 film relief" to replace the 1987 relief. The new relief (now s481) was introduced with affect from budget day in 1996 and the old relief was prematurely terminated at that date, but subject to complex transitional provisions that enabled the 1987 relief to continue in a modified form, and subject to various conditions, up to 5 April 1996, side by side with the new "Section 35" film relief (now more properly refered to as s481 relief). The CGT rules relating to the 1987 relief, and to the 1996 relief, are separately described below. Film relief primarily concerns income tax or corporation tax on income, and it is not proposed to describe its operation in terms of those taxes. For a more complete description, reference should be made to the companion volumes, Income Tax (McAteer & Reddin) and Corporation Tax (Carr, Brennan & Moore) published by the Institute of Taxation in Ireland.

9.13.4.2   **Film relief 1987 - 1996**

As with other reliefs, there are numerous conditions and anti-avoidance provisions related to the relief.

s481

Once again, there are special rules for dealing with the CGT issues which arise because all or part of the cost has been allowed as a deduction from income. The rules set out in s35, FA87 are different in some respects, but are similar in others to the BES rules.

FA87 s35

S35(20) sets the overall scene, by restating the general CGT rule - if a deduction is available from income for the expenditure, then no deduction is available for the same expenditure for CGT purposes.

This general rule is then modified in later subsections of s35(20) - which give relief, but only in the case of a subscription for qualifying new ordinary shares which have been held for a period of three years prior to the disposal. In such a case, the relief available is the same as for B.E.S. shares (set out above) - the full expenditure is allowable, but is restricted to deny relief for a loss.

Where the shares have not been held for the three year period, relief may still be available where the full proceeds have been reinvested in further qualifying shares - provided the shares being disposed of have been held for at least 12 months prior to the disposal.

s35(20)(d) applies the treatment described above in relation to shares held for three years, to shares held by a company for more than one year where the investment is in a "small film" project. The treatment also applies to an investment of £1,050,000 or more, held for at least one year, with a form of marginal relief for an investment of between £350,000 and £1,050,000, given proportionately. This extension of the relief to shares held for one year or more applies only to an investment held by a company.

9.13.4.3   **Film relief post FA96**

s481   As stated at the outset, the relief introduced for investment in films
by the FA96 is a separate, new and distinct relief from that
introduced by the FA87, notwithstanding that many of the
conditions relating to the relief, and its manner of operation, are
similar. One major difference between the FA96 relief, and the FA87
relief (as amended subsequently) is that the FA96 provides for an
income tax/corporation tax deduction of only 80% of the amount of
the investment which qualifies for relief, whereas the FA87 provided
for a 100% relief.

Where an individual has obtained relief in respect of an investment,
so much of the amount of the investment in respect of which he
obtains an income tax deduction (i.e. 80% of the part of his
investment which qualified for relief) is excluded from the
taxpayer's cost of acquisition of the shares in the film company.

This treatment (which is in line with the general rule in relation to
cost of acquisition expenditure and its interaction with income tax
reliefs) is modified where the investment in the film company was
an investment by way of subscription for new ordinary shares and
those shares are retained by the individual for at least one year after
their acquisition. In such a case the full amount of the cost of the
investment in the film company qualifies (in the normal way and
subject to the normal rules) as part of the cost of acquisition of the
shares. However insofar as this would give rise to a loss on a
disposal of the shares, the sums subscribed for the shares are
reduced. The reduction is of an amount sufficient to eliminate the
loss, or, where it is a lesser amount, is an amount equal to that part
of the subscription which qualified for income tax relief i.e. generally
80%. In other words, a loss can arise on the disposal of such ordinary
shares in a film company, held for a full year, to the extent that it
arises on taking into account, in respect of the sum subscribed for the
shares, only that part which did not qualify for an income tax
deduction. In most instances that will be 20% on the sum subscribed,
up to the limit which qualifies for relief.

A s481 investment raises two CGT issues:

—In some cases - preference shares or ordinary shares held for less
   than a year - part of the cost of the shares is not deductible in a
   CGT computation.

—Even where a full deduction is permitted for the cost of the shares,
   the amount of any loss arising may be restricted.

Example 68

> *Joe subscribes £10,000 for 10,000 £1 preference shares in Mega Productions
> Ltd., and also £10,000 for 10,000 £1 ordinary shares in Mega Productions Ltd.
> The investment is made in December 1996 and is the only qualifying investment*

made by Joe in a Section 481 film company in the year ended 5 April 1997. Mega Productions Ltd. is a qualifying company for the purposes of film relief. In January 1998 Mega Productions Ltd. is liquidated (having completed the making of its film and selling on the rights to the film) and Joe receives £100 in respect of his preference shares, and nothing in respect of his ordinary shares, from the liquidator.

Disposal of preference shares	£	£
Consideration for disposal		100
Deductible expenditure:		
Sum subscribed	10,000	
Less amount in respect of which income tax deduction obtained under section 481 (80%)	8,000	
Deductible cost of acquisition		2,000
Allowable loss		1,900

Computation in respect of disposal of ordinary shares	£
Consideration for the disposal	Nil
Deductible expenditure:	
Sum subscribed for shares	10,000
Preliminary calculation of allowable loss	10,000
Less restriction by lesser of amount of loss (£10,000) or income tax deduction received (£8,000)	8,000
Final allowable loss	2,000

Had Joe received the sum of £3,000 (say) from the liquidator in respect of the ordinary shares the computation would be as follows:

	£
Consideration received for disposal	3,000
Less sums subscribed for shares	10,000
Preliminary calculation of allowable loss	7,000
Less restriction by lesser of loss (£7,000) or the s481 deduction obtained for income tax (£8,000)	7,000
Final allowable loss	Nil

s481 The treatment of a company which has made an investment in a film company and obtained relief under s481, is different from that described above in relation to an individual investor.

The basic rule is that a company may not obtain a deduction in a capital gains tax computation for that part of an investment in a film production company which qualifies for relief under s481. Whereas an individual is denied a deduction only in respect of the 80% of the sum subscribed for shares, in respect of which he gets an actual deduction of an equal amount, a company is denied a deduction for capital gains purposes in respect of the entire of the investment in relation to which 80% is deductible for the purposes of s481 film relief.

It is understood that this distinction in the legislation between the base cost of shares for an individual as compared to a company was unintentional. The Revenue may apply a concession in this area so as to reduce the base cost of a company by 80% of the sum subscribed only, but no announcement to that effect had been made at the date of writing. In all examples below the strict statutory position is illustrated. However, as in the case of an individual, this rule is relaxed where the investment is in ordinary shares of the film company, and those shares are held for a period of at least one year after subscription. In such a case the restriction on sums deductible for capital gains purposes is removed. If however the computation throws up a loss, then a restriction is imposed, in the same fashion as in relation to an individual, in either the amount of the loss, or the amount of the actual deduction obtained under s481 in respect of the subscription, whichever is the lesser.

Example 69

Mercury Ltd. invested £1 million in the preference shares of Mega Productions Ltd. and £1 million in the ordinary shares of Mega Productions Ltd. The sums invested qualified for relief under s481. The investment is made in December 1996. On the liquidation of Mega Productions Ltd. in January of 1998 Mercury Ltd. received from the liquidator £10,000 in respect of the preference shares, and nil in respect of the ordinary shares. A computation in relation to the disposal would be as follows:

	£
Computation on disposal of Preference shares:	
Consideration received	*10,000*
Deductible expenditure:	
Sum subscribed (£1 million),	
***less** amount qualifying for s481 relief (£1 million)*	*Nil*
Chargeable gain	*10,000*

It should be noted that the entire sum subscribed, insofar as it would have qualified the company for an 80% deduction, is disallowed in the case of a company, whereas it is only the amount equal to the 80% deduction which was disallowed in the case of an individual investor.

	£
Computation on disposal of ordinary shares:	
Consideration received	*Nil*
Deductible cost:	
Sum subscribed	*1,000,000*
Preliminary calculation of loss	*1,000,000*
Reduced by the lesser of the loss or the actual deduction obtained (80%)	*800,000*
Final allowable loss	*200,000*

The treatment of these shares being ordinary shares held for longer than a year, differs from the treatment of the preference shares as illustrated above.

For the purposes outlined above new ordinary shares are defined as meaning new ordinary shares forming part of the ordinary share capital of a qualifying company (in s481 film relief terms) which, throughout the period of one year commencing on the date such shares are issued, carry no present or future preferential right to dividends, or to a company's assets on its winding up, and no present or future preferential right to be redeemed.

For the purpose of simplicity indexation has been ignored in the examples above. Insofar as the subscription for shares or any part of it is allowable as a deductible cost, it attracts indexation. As noted elsewhere, indexation cannot be used to create, or to increase, an allowable loss.

Where the disposal is of new ordinary shares which have been held for a period of one year, the restriction on the capital gains deduction for the sum subscribed applies only where an allowable loss would arise from the deduction. Where the computation discloses a chargeable gain, or a break even position, the sum subscribed is deductible in full, without any restriction being imposed for the fact that an income tax deduction has been obtained by reference to part or all of the sums subscribed.

Example 70

*Assume that Joe in **example 68** above received £13,000 from the liquidator in respect of the ordinary shares, and £13,000 in respect of the preference shares.*

Once again indexation is being ignored for the sake of simplicity.

Preference share computation:	£
Consideration received	13,000
Deductions for sum subscribed:	
Sum subscribed £10,000, less amount of income tax deduction, £8,000	2,000
Chargeable gain	11,000
Ordinary share computation	
Consideration received	13,000
Deduction for acquisition cost:	
Sum subscribed for shares	10,000
Chargeable gain	3,000

There is no restriction in this example on the deductibility of the sums subscribed for the new ordinary shares held for at least one year. This is because the subscription is for "new ordinary shares" rather than preference shares and because the computation disclosed a gain, and not a loss.

Similar treatment arises in the case of a corporate investor where the computation discloses a gain rather than a loss, and where the investment is in new ordinary shares held for at least one year.

s481

TCA97 s481 does not provide any *rules to identify shares* disposed of by an investor with sums subscribed by him for shares which

s580

have qualified for income tax relief under s481. Although unlikely, it

s581

is possible that an investor might invest sums in excess of those qualifying for relief, or have subscribed for shares in the company in a manner which did not qualify for relief (e.g. before the necessary approvals and certifications have been obtained) as well as subscribing for shares which did qualify for relief. It would seem therefore that the provisions of TCA97 s580 (the FIFO rules) would have application, subject to the "4 weeks rule" of TCA97 s581(see paragraph 48.3) for this purpose.

9.14   **Investment in renewable energy projects**

s486B

TCA97 s486B provides a company chargeable to corporation tax with a deduction from its profits (i.e. both from income and from chargeable gains) of an amount equal to the sum of money paid by it for new ordinary shares in a qualifying company which exists solely for the purpose of undertaking a qualifying energy project. A qualifying energy project is a project approved by the Minister for Public Enterprise which generates electricity from solar power, wind power, hydro power, and/or biomass.

There is a limit of £10m on the deduction which a company may obtain in this fashion in any one accounting period of 12 months, with a pro-rata reduced limit in accounting periods of lesser length.

As with all reliefs for investments, there are numerous conditions. Since the relief is primarily a corporation tax relief these are not described here. Further details may be obtained from the companion volume, Corporation Tax, published by the Institute of Taxation in Ireland.

S486B(14)(a) provides that a company which obtains relief for expenditure on shares under the section may not also obtain a deduction for the same expenditure in computing chargeable gains in relation to the shares, or otherwise. The result of this rule would be that where a company obtains relief for the full amount which it invests in shares in a qualifying energy company, it would have no base cost in those shares for capital gains tax purposes. This rule is relieved by s486(B)(14)(b) which provides that provided the shares are retained by the investing company for a period of five years from their acquisition, no part of their expenditure on the shares shall be disallowed by reason of their having obtained relief under s486B in respect of that expenditure.

S486B(6)(b) also has a five year retention period - if the shares are not retained by the investing company for five years, the relief under s486B is withdrawn. It is clear from the wording of sub-section 6(b) that a relief which is withdrawn is to be regarded as a relief which was never granted, for the purpose of determining whether or not the base cost for CGT purposes has been effected by the initial granting of relief. Sub-section 6(b) provides that in the event of a disposal within five years "a claim to relief under this section shall not be allowed in respect of the amounts subscribed for those shares, and if any such relief has been given, it should be withdrawn." The primary effect of disposal within five years therefore is to deny an entitlement to relief, and the withdrawal of relief already granted is clearly intended to be equivalent to the denial of relief.

Example 71

Trading Group PLC invest £8m in ordinary shares in Wind Energy Ltd, a company which is a qualifying company for the purpose of relief under Section 486B. Payment is made for the shares on 1 October 1998 and the shares are issued by Wind Energy Ltd on 31 October 1998. Trading Group PLC ends a 12 month accounting period on 31 December 1998. On 30 June 2002, Trading Group PLC dispose of half of their shares in Wind Energy Ltd for the sum of £6m. On 1 November 2003 it disposes of the balance of its shares for the sum of £7m.

In the accounting period ended 31 December 1998 Trading Group PLC initially receive a deduction in the amount of £8m, in computing their profits. However, this must be reopened when they subsequently dispose of half of the shares within the five year retention period (on 30 June 2002). Trading Group PLC must therefore be treated as not having been entitled to a deduction in respect of that part of the expenditure that related to the shares disposed of. In this case that is clearly half of the original expenditure i.e. £4m. Trading Group Plc's taxable profits for the accounting period ended 31 December 1998 will therefore be increased by the amount of £4m, over and above the sum as originally computed.

The capital gains tax computation in relation to the disposal of the shares in the year 2002 (ignoring indexation for simplicity purposes) would be as follows:

Base Cost	£4,000,000
Consideration for disposal	£6,000,000
Chargeable Gain	£2,000,000
CGT @ 20%	£ 400,000

The rate of corporation tax for 1998 is 32% and accordingly the gain must be adjusted to the sum of £1,250,000. That adjusted gain at a rate of 32% yields corporation tax of £400,000. The base cost is unaffected by the fact that relief was initially granted, since the relief was withdrawn on the disposal of the shares.

The disposal in the year 2003 occurred one day after the completion of five years from the date of acquisition of the shares. That date would appear to be 31 October 1998, the date the shares were issued, and not 1 October 1998, the date payment was made for them. The computation for the accounting period ended 31 December 2002 would be as follows:

Base Cost of shares	£4,000,000
Consideration for disposal	£7,000,000
Chargeable Gain	£3,000,000
CGT @ 20%	£ 600,000

Assuming a corporation tax rate of 32%, it is necessary to adjust the chargeable gain up to an amount of £1,875,000. That, at a corporation tax rate of 32%, yields a corporation tax charge of £600,000.

Because the shares had been retained for a full five year period the base cost of the shares is not diluted by reason of corporation tax relief having been obtained on the original subscription.

From the example above it will be seen that the base cost of the shares is identical, whether or not they are retained for a five year period!

s486B There is an ambiguity in s486(B)(14)(b). It provides that there is to be no reduction in base cost of shares held for a five year period after acquisition, where "none of those shares is disposed of by the company". In the example above, Trading Group PLC paid a sum of £8m for ordinary shares in Wind Energy Ltd. That constituted a single payment. Part of those shares were disposed of within the five year period. A very literal reading of subsection 14(b) might suggest that all of the shares acquired by means of the single payment of £8m, had to be retained for five years in order that the base cost of any of them should be unaffected by the relief granted under s486B. This conclusion would be absurd, and it would seem more correct to regard the payment for each share as being a separate investment, even if all were paid for by a single cheque.

s580 S486B does not provide share identification rules for determining which shares are first disposed of, where shares were acquired at a number of different times in an energy company. TCA97 s580 provides share identification rules for all CGT purposes. This is discussed in paragraph 48. The general rule is "first in first out" but this is subject to a number of exceptions and qualifications. It would seem logical that the same rule should be used for the purpose of determining whether or not relief was actually granted. However, the "first in first out" rule is an artificial rule and it is not clear that it can be applied to any situation for which there is not statutory authority to apply it. In the absence of an artificial rule such as that provided by the "first in first out" rule, the normal method of identifying shares would be by reference to the share number i.e. one would look to the actual shares disposed of. Since the base cost of shares is identical, whether they are held for less than five years, or for more than five years (as demonstrated above) the absence of a comprehensive share identification rule in s486B may be of no practical assistance.

9.15   **Relief for employee share purchases.**

This income tax relief was introduced in the FA86 and is now s479.

s479   In broad terms the relief permitted an eligible employee in relation to a qualifying company a deduction equal to the amount of a subscription by him for eligible shares in the qualifying company. The amount of the deduction was limited to £750 in aggregate (a lifetime aggregate) for the years 1986/87 to 1993/94. This lifetime limit was raised to £3000 from the 6 April 1994, and was further raised to £5,000 by FA96 (with effect from 6th April 1996).

The relief can be withdrawn where the shares are disposed of within a period of three years from their acquisition. This period was one of five years in relation to disposals up to 12 February 1998. Where the disposal occurs after the fourth anniversary of their acquisition, only 75% of the relief will be withdrawn. The rules in s498 (business expansion scheme) are applied to identify disposals in relation to

s506   which relief was claimed, where a person holds both shares in relation to which he obtained relief, and other shares of the same class. However, the rules of s498 are applied only for the purposes of a clawback of the s479 relief (they are expressly applied in relation to BES relief shares by s506). They are not applied to identify the shares disposed of for CGT purposes. Accordingly, an anomaly can arise with a single disposal being treated as being in respect of different shares for CGT purposes and for income tax purposes. This is assumed to be a flaw in the drafting of the legislation rather than an intentional anomaly. The law as it is enacted is reflected in the examples set out below.

Where there has been a reorganisation for the purposes of capital gains tax, resulting in a person who obtained relief for shares acquiring a new holding in respect of those shares, the new holding is treated as being shares in respect of which he obtained relief.

Where shares in respect of which the relief has been obtained and has not been withdrawn, are disposed of, the expenditure which attracted the relief is excluded from the base cost of the shares for capital gains tax purposes.

Example 72

Joe Brown subscribed for one thousand £1 ordinary shares in Wonder Products Limited on the 30 June 1984. On the 30 June 1986 he subscribed for a further one thousand £1 ordinary shares at £1.50 per share. £750 of this expenditure attracted relief under s.12. On the 30 June 1989 Joe disposed of one thousand shares at a price of £2 each.

For CGT purposes Joe is treated as disposing of the shares which he acquired in 1984. For the purposes of s479 however the rules of s498 will treat him as disposing of the shares acquired in 1986 and will result in a withdrawal of his relief under s479.

CGT Computation	£
Consideration	*2,000*
1984 Base Cost (ignoring indexation)	*1,000*
Taxable gain	*1,000*

Indexation has been ignored for the sake of simplicity.

Example 73

Mary Brown obtained relief under s479 on a subscription of £1,000 for one thousand £1 shares in Megastores PLC. These are the only shares which she acquired in the company. After five years she disposed of the shares for £2,000.

	£
Consideration	*2,000*
Base cost (expenditure of £1,000, less £750 relief for a pre-1994/95 acquisition)	*250*
Taxable Gain	*1,750*

Indexation has been ignored for the sake of simplicity. It would apply only to the figure of £250 above, and not to the £1,000 of expenditure actually incurred.

See paragraph 50.2 for a discussion of the CGT aspects of approved profit sharing schemes and Employee Share Ownership Trusts, and paragraph 39.11 for a discussion of share option schemes for employees.

10   WASTING ASSETS

10.1   Broad Outline

s560

In normal circumstances, the full amount of the expenditure incurred in acquiring and enhancing an asset is allowable in arriving at the chargeable gain. The 1975 Act, however, restricts the allowable expenditure in the case of the disposal of a wasting asset.

The term 'wasting asset' is defined in s560(1) as follows:

"...wasting asset means an asset with a predictable life not exceeding 50 years but so that-

(a)   *freehold land shall not be a wasting asset whatever its nature and whatever the nature of the buildings or works on it,*

(b)   *"life" in relation to any tangible movable property, means useful life, having regard to the purpose for which the tangible assets were acquired or provided by the person making the disposal,*

(c)   *plant and machinery shall, in every case, be regarded as having a predictable life of less than fifty years, and in estimating that life it shall be assumed that its life will end when it is finally put out of use as being unfit for further use, and that it is going to be used in the*

normal manner and to the normal extent and is going to be used
throughout its life as so estimated, and

(d) *a life interest in settled property shall not be a wasting asset until the*
predictable expectation of life of the life tenant is fifty years or less,
and the predictable life of life interests in settled property and of
annuities shall be ascertained from actuarial tables approved by the
Revenue Commissioners".

Sch14 Para2   In addition to these rules, TCA97 Sch14 which deals with leases,
provides that a lease of land shall not be a wasting asset until the
time when its duration does not exceed fifty years. Under this rule, a
lease may initially not be a wasting asset, but will become so at the
time when it has fifty years or less to run. (Chapter 7 deals with the
computation of gains on the disposals of leasehold interests).

An exemption from CGT in respect of tangible movable wasting
assets is described in paragraph 22.

The Inland Revenue in the UK, in a press release on 10 February 2000
said the following on the topic of whether a shotgun constituted
machinery in this context.

"In our view there has to be a subtle difference between clocks and shotguns.
Once you have wound up a clock, it continues to tick more than once,
whereas with a shotgun once you have pulled the trigger, you only get one
discharge out of the barrel. That said, we accept that you have to go on and
consider what happens if you have an automatic weapon or machine gun
which effectively fires continuously. While we take the view that the matter
is not free from doubt, we would generally accept the argument that all
types of gun should be treated together under the general description of
'machinery' so that they would have a predictable life of less than 50 years."

10.2   Restriction of Deductible Expenditure

s560(3)   The general rule in the case of a disposal of a wasting asset is that the
cost of the asset and subsequent enhancement expenditure (as
reduced by any predictable residual or scrap value at the end of its
useful life) are treated as wasting away during the life of the asset.
The owner is treated as having used (or enjoyed) the part of the cost
attributable to his ownership during that period of ownership, and
only the unused part of the cost is available as a deduction for CGT
purposes.

The cost and enhancement expenditure, in arriving at the allowable
deduction in computing the gain or loss on disposal, are wasted in
direct proportion to the expiration of the expected life of the asset
(i.e. on a 'straight line' basis).

For this purpose, an estimate of the residual or scrap value at the end
of the useful life of the asset must be made at the date of acquisition
of the asset.

Example 74

If you pay £1,000 for an option to buy shares at a certain price within (say) six months, the option is an asset with an expected life of 6 months and the cost is £1,000. If after three months have elapsed you sell the option to someone else, giving them the right to avail of the option, what they have bought is an option to buy the shares at the stated price within the three months remaining. The first three months have wasted during your ownership and when you are arriving at the cost to be allowed against the sale price of the option you will only take into account (in this case) half of the cost.

10.3   Assets Qualifying for Capital Allowances

s561

The restriction on the amount of expenditure which is allowable, applies to all wasting assets with the exception of business assets used solely for trade purposes and qualifying for capital allowances. In the case of an asset which is used solely for the purposes of a business and qualifies for capital allowances, although it is a wasting asset, the expenditure is not wasted. The full cost of such an asset qualifies as a deduction subject to the normal restriction in the computation of a loss in the case of assets qualifying for capital allowances.

Where the asset is used partly for non-trade purposes or otherwise qualifies in part only for capital allowances, the expenditure is apportioned by reference to the extent to which the expenditure qualified for capital allowances. The part apportioned to trade purposes will not be restricted.

As outlined in paragraph 10.1, plant and machinery is in all cases and at all times treated as a wasting asset. At first sight this might be thought to refer solely to such matters as factory machinery, in which case the treatment as a wasting asset would in most cases correspond with economic reality. However the word "plant" can encompass a wide range of items, as remote from factory machinery as the books used by a barrister. A barrister's books are an example of an asset which might very well have a useful life in excess of 50 years. The fact that an item of plant might not have a useful life as short as 50 years should not result in any difficulty since plant will almost invariably attract capital allowances in the hands of its owner. A rare example of plant which would not attract capital allowances for its owner would be leased plant where the lessee bears the burden of wear and tear. In such an instance the plant would suffer a restriction of its base cost expenditure in the hands of the lessor regardless of its true economic life, merely because it is plant.

The position is a bit more complex in the case of machinery. Whereas plant can be plant only if it is used for the purpose of a trade or profession by some person, there is no necessity for an item of machinery to be used for the purpose of anybody's trade. An antique clock is an example of an item of machinery which typically would not be in use for anybody's trade. An antique duelling pistol also would constitute an item of machinery as would an antique camera. Such items might well be expected to have a useful life in excess of 50 years, even disregarding the fact that they are collectors items. Nonetheless, they are wasting assets regardless of their useful life and in many cases will not be exempt from the consequences in terms of restriction on base cost etc by reason of attracting capital allowances.

The exclusion from "wasting assets" treatment also applies to any asset in respect of which the taxpayer has incurred any expenditure which has qualified in full for any capital allowance. This alternate basis for exclusion from wasting asset treatment is not dependent on the person having used the asset solely for the purpose of a trade or profession throughout the period of ownership. Neither is the expenditure qualifying for capital allowance restricted to acquisition cost and enhancement cost, as is the case in the alternate basis for exclusion noted above. Given the apparently very wide ambit of the second basis for exclusion from wasting asset treatment, it is not clear what significance the first basis has at all! The expenditure attracting the capital allowance has no de minimis amount and could be very small relative to the value of the asset.

10.4 Method of Restricting Expenditure

s560(3)

A wasting asset is normally deemed to be 'used up' on a straight line apportionment basis. If, for example, an asset, at the date of acquisition, had an expected useful life of twenty years, and was sold after fifteen years, three-quarters of the expenditure would be disallowed.

s560(3) provides that, in computing a gain on the disposal of a wasting asset, the cost of the asset,
"...after deducting the residual or scrap value, if any, of the asset, is written off at a uniform rate from its full amount at the time when the asset is acquired or provided, to nothing at the end of its life".

It further provides in the case of enhancement expenditure, that it is to be:-

"written off at a uniform rate from the full amount of that expenditure at the time when that expenditure is first reflected in the state or nature of the asset to nothing at the end of its life".

An exception to this straight line write off is made in the case of expenditure incurred in the acquisition of a lease of land. The normal wasting asset rules do not apply to such a lease. The expenditure attributed to the wasted part of the expenditure incurred on the acquisition of a lease of land is calculated from tables set out in TCA97 Sch14. The effect of these tables is to weight the expenditure towards the later years of the lease. The entire area of leasehold interests in land is complex and is dealt with in Chapter 7.

Where the expenditure concerned has been incurred on the enhancement of an asset, it is only wasted from the time it was first reflected in the state or nature of the asset, and not from the date of acquisition of the asset, nor from the date of payment for that expenditure.

10.5   Effect on Indexation

Indexation is applied to expenditure which is allowed as a deduction. The effect of the wasting provisions is to disallow a proportion of expenditure. Accordingly, the indexation provisions apply to the amount of expenditure remaining after the wasting provisions have been applied.

10.6   Merged Assets

s559   Another circumstance where the expenditure attributable to a wasting asset must be taken into account, is on the disposal of an asset following the merger of a wasting asset with that asset (see paragraph 9.10).

s560   A typical example of assets merging, is where a leaseholder buys out the freehold of the property. In such a case, usually the leasehold will merge with the freehold and be extinguished entirely. What remains is a freehold interest. It is interesting to note that the Revenue have sought to apply the wasting asset rules of paragraph 10 in determining the expenditure to be allowed in calculating a gain on disposal of the asset (the freehold). The wasting asset (the leasehold) has disappeared, and all that remains is the freehold interest, and it is that (non-wasting asset) which is being disposed of. There is no wasting asset being disposed of.

It is difficult to see how s560 (wasting assets) can have application on the disposal of a freehold interest in land. That paragraph only has application on the disposal of a wasting asset.

Example 75

On 30 June 1993 Joe Brown paid £20,000 for the transfer to him of a lease on a premises. At the date of the transfer to him the lease had ten years to run. On the 31 July 1993 Joe succeeded in buying out the freehold interest immediately superior to his leasehold interest, for the sum of £50,000. The freehold interest and the leasehold interest now merged, leaving Joe only with a freehold interest. On the 30 June 1998 Joe disposed of the freehold interest for £75,000.

s559   *Since the freehold derives its value in part from the leasehold interest having merged with it and extinguished, thus providing vacant possession of the premises, the provisions of s559 apply so as to attribute to the freehold an appropriate proportion of the base cost of the leasehold. In accordance with s559(2) that appropriate proportion is 100%, since the leasehold no longer exists and no part of it remains undisposed of when the freehold has been disposed of. The question now arises as to whether all of the £20,000 paid for the leasehold interest is to be attributed to the freehold, or only half of that sum, since at the date of the disposal of the freehold the lease, had it still existed, would have been half way through the remaining period of its life since acquisition by Joe.*

The restriction of the base cost of a wasting asset provided for by s560 applies only on the computation of a gain on the disposal of a wasting asset. No such computation is involved here and for that reason, in the authors' opinion, the entire £20,000 is to be attributed to the freehold, so that the total base cost of the freehold (ignoring indexation) is £70,000 made up as follows:

- *£20,000 in relation to the lease, and*

- *£50,000 in relation to the purchase of the freehold itself*

This view may be disputed by the Revenue.

The UK case of Lewis v Walters dealt with facts superficially similar to those set out in *example 75* above. The freehold of a property was owned by a lady, and a leasehold interest granted out of that freehold was held by her husband. On the death of the lady, the freehold was inherited by her two children. They were also the executors of their father's will, and his heirs, when he died some years later. At that point the two children jointly owned the freehold, and held the leasehold interest of the same property as executors of their father's will (of which they were the beneficiaries). They sold the property by entering into a contract for the sale of the freehold (as its owners) and for the sale of the leasehold interest (as executors of their father's estate). They were duly assessed to tax on the disposals which were treated as the disposal of two separate assets, the freehold, and the leasehold interest in the same house. The leasehold interest (which at the time has approximately 16 years left to run) was treated by the courts as a wasting asset.

The judgement in the case of Lewis v Walters was not in conflict with the discussion of *example 75* above because in Lewis v Walters, the freehold interest and the leasehold interest never merged while in the possession and ownership of the two children who ultimately sold the two interests. The two interests did not merge because, although held by the same two individuals, they were not held by them in the same capacity. The freehold interest was held by them as beneficial owners, and the leasehold interest was held only as the executors of an estate. It is noted in the judgement that in the hands of the purchaser of the two interests, the interests merged. Had the two children completed the administration of their deceased father's estate prior to selling the property, and appointed the leasehold interest to themselves beneficially, it would have been possible for the leasehold interest to merge with the freehold interest, and for a sale to take place of the freehold interest only (the leasehold interest no longer existing). But that was not what occurred.

11   PART DISPOSALS

11.1   Part disposals - broad outline

s557   Special rules are provided for calculating the part of the cost which is allowable as a deduction in arriving at a gain (or loss) on the disposal of part of the asset.

If (for example) a person buys ten acres of land, some of which is good agricultural land, some of which is woodland and some of which is bog and marsh land, it would be unrealistic to assume that on the sale of five acres of good land, only half of the original cost would be allowable as a deduction. In such a case it is obvious that a greater part of the cost price is referable to the good land than (say) the marsh or bog land. How do you calculate the part of the cost to be allowed in computing the gain? TCA97 s557 sets down rules for calculating the allowable part of the cost in the case of the disposal of part of an asset. s557 provides that:

"Such portion of the expenditure shall be allowable as a deduction in computing under this schedule the amount of the gain accruing on the disposal as bears the same proportion to the total of the said sums as the value of the consideration for the disposal bears to the aggregate of the said value and the market value of the property which remains and the balance of the expenditure shall be attributed to the property which remains undisposed of".

The rules are normally illustrated in practice by the formula:-

$$\text{Base cost of asset} \quad \times \quad \frac{A}{A + B} \quad \text{where}$$

A = Proceeds of part disposal

B = Value of the remaining property at the date of sale.

Paragraph 77.4 discusses part disposals which are *intra group* transactions.

11.2   Part disposals - detailed application

The effect of this formula is to apportion the allowable cost (including any relevant enhancement expenditure) between the part of the asset being sold and the part remaining, on the basis of the market value of the respective parts of the property at the date of sale. In the case of an asset owned at 6 April 1974 the 'cost' is deemed to be the market value at that date. The formula would be applied to this 'deemed cost' on a subsequent part disposal of that asset.

The formula only applies to the expenditure that it is necessary to apportion.

Example 76

Bill inherited a 200 acre farm on the death of his father in June 1985. The market value at that date was £140,000. In the summer of 1986 he modernised the farm, during the course of which he constructed farm buildings at a cost (net of grant) of £80,000. In May 1990, he bought the adjoining farm (80 acres) for £70,000. Some of the original farm land was useless for farming. In February 1998 he sold 40 acres (of those inherited) for £190,000. What is his chargeable gain (assuming it is not development land)?

Having acquired the farm on the death of his father, he is deemed to have acquired it at that date at 'market value' (see paragraph 66.5).

Let us assume that the market value of the 160 acres remaining out of the original farm, at the date of disposal of the 40 acres was £500,000.

	£
The sale proceeds amount to-	190,000

The cost is arrived at by applying the 'part disposal' formula

$$\text{Total Cost of Asset} \quad x \quad \frac{A}{A+B}$$

$$£140,000 \quad x \quad \frac{£190,000}{£190,000 + £500,000}$$

	£
= *£38,550 indexed @ 1.390*	53,584
GAIN	136,416

*This allowable cost of £38,550 is indexed up in the normal manner: (see paragraph 14).

s557(4) *There is no need to apportion any part of the cost of the buildings since they enhanced the part of the land remaining undisposed of, nor the additional farm as it is separate asset, and not part of the asset which was sold.*

It is not always clear when the part disposal rules apply. The problem arises most frequently in relation to land. It may be best illustrated with an example.

Example 77

John inherits an estate of 2,000 acres of land of varying quality and value. Some time later he disposes of a half acre site close to a main road (which formed part of the estate), on which there is outline planning permission to build a house.

Has John made a part disposal of his estate of 2,000 acres, or has he disposed of a single asset consisting of a half acre site?

Before considering the answer, it might be useful to indicate the relevance of the question.

If John has merely disposed of an entire asset consisting of a half acre site, there could be little doubt but that the asset disposed of is development land.

Accordingly his entitlement to indexation, losses, and other matters may be restricted and the applicable CGT rate may be affected. Development land is discussed in greater detail in paragraph 6. There can be little doubt that the small site would be regarded as development land as the consideration for its disposal is clearly greater than the current use value of that site (without the planning permission).

However if the disposal is regarded as a part disposal of the 2,000 acre estate, it is arguable that what is being sold is part of the entire estate, the value of which is not quantifiably affected by the planning permission on a small section of the land. That position is not entirely clear, but it is arguable.

The question of whether the item disposed of is part of a larger asset, will also affect the cost to be allocated against the disposal proceeds. In broad terms, if it is a part disposal, a proportion of the overall cost of the inherited land will be apportioned to the sale. If it is not regarded as a part disposal, the market value (at the date of the inheritance) of the 1/2 acre itself will be apportioned to the sale. These two separate figures could be totally different.

It is important to realise that the CGT legislation does not give any indication as to how you determine whether a disposal of land is a part disposal of a large holding, or the disposal of an asset in its own right.

The UK case of Watton v Tippet, which is discussed at paragraph 26.1, turned on the question of whether the disposal of part of a sub-divided factory building was a part disposal of the entire building, or a disposal of a separate asset consisting of the sub-divided portion of the building. In that case the Judge observed that *"if - - two properties were acquired under the same contract and at the same time when they were not physically separated, provided they could be treated as separate assets and that the consideration was apportioned between them at the time of sale - -"* the disposal of one of them would not be a part disposal of an asset consisting of them both, but would be the entire disposal of a separate asset. The comment is not as helpful as it might seem, since the judge specified that for that to apply the asset disposed of and the asset retained should be capable of being treated as separate assets. That after all is what the question is all about, so it hardly provides an answer.

The primary function served by the "part disposal rules" in the overall scheme of the acts appears to be confined to providing a method of apportioning the allowable cost between that which is disposed of, and that which (acquired on the same occasion and by the same transaction) is retained. On that basis it might seem sensible to treat land which is acquired in a single transaction on a single occasion as constituting a single asset. However, this principle clearly is not sufficient in itself. If John inherits a farm of land in Kerry, and a farm of land in Donegal, on the death of his uncle, they would both represent land acquired by the same transaction on the same occasion. But it would defy common sense to suggest that they are together a single asset. Common sense (which it should be mentioned has little to do with tax law) would suggest that to be a single asset land should not only be acquired on a single occasion in a single transaction, but each part of it should be in physical proximity to every other part, and it all should form a single natural economic asset. To some extent the matter is bound to be a grey area and will depend on the facts of each situation.

- **Revenue/Chief Inspector's CGT Manual :**

– In paragraph 19.2.8.3 of the Revenue Commissioners capital gains tax manual, Inspectors are advised that where the portion of an asset which is disposed of is small relative to the whole, and where it is in any event necessary to obtain a valuation at the acquisition date (or 6 April 1974 where relevant), part disposal treatment should not be insisted on in order to save the taxpayer the expense of producing a second valuation in relation to the one computation, ie a valuation at the date of the part disposal, of the portion of the asset which was retained at that date. The instruction is illustrated by a number of examples including the disposal of 10 acres of agricultural land out of a 100 acre farm; and the disposal of two half acre sites from a 30 acre farm. These are given as indications of disposals that would be regarded as small relative to the total.

Apart from giving guidance to both the Inspector and the taxpayer as to when there is scope for avoiding part disposal treatment where that simplifies matters, the extract from the manual would indicate that in the circumstances outlined, the Revenue consider that what is involved is a part disposal rather than a disposal of the entire of the smaller asset. However, the example given by the Revenue does not go into such details as whether the land all forms one natural economic block of land, whether they were acquired on the same date and in the same transaction etc. Such circumstances may determine whether or not a disposal is a part disposal or not, as a matter of strict law.

Similar problems do not tend to arise in relation to shares, even though shares may be acquired as a block on a single occasion. It is clear from the structure of the CGT Acts (e.g. the share identification rules described in paragraph 48) that each share constitutes a separate asset for the purposes of capital gains tax.

- **Revenue/Chief Inspector's CGT Manual :**

– At Paragraph 19.2.14.3 of the Revenue Commissioners capital gains tax manual it is stated *""asset" is not defined in the Act and is therefore to be given its natural meaning subject, however, to the inference from Sections 552 and 557 that the "asset" is whatever is covered by a specific item of expenditure on an acquisition, whether made by purchase or otherwise"*.

The authors would agree that "asset" should be given its natural meaning. However they believe that the identification of expenditure follows from an identification of the asset in question, rather than vice versa as suggested in the quote above.

- **Revenue/Chief Inspector's CGT Manual :**

— The Revenue manual in sub-paragraph 14.5 goes on to state that any acquisition of land by contract or inheritance or gift, should be regarded as a single asset no matter what it may comprise of. However it appears to relax this instruction by saying that the treatment of individual dwelling-houses (where several were bought as a lot) each as a separate asset should not be objected to; and where it is the normal practice to sell flats in a building as separate assets, each flat may be treated as a separate asset even though the building as a whole is owned by one person.

- **Revenue Commissioners CGT Manual :**

— Sub-paragraph 14.11 of the Revenue manual states *"where a physical part (or an interest in or right over a part) of an area of land comprising a number of acquisitions is disposed of, the rules for part disposals should be applied to the smallest separate acquisition or a number of acquisitions out of which the part disposal is made".*

The following example would illustrate the intention behind the Revenue instruction.

Example 78

John Maguire inherited his father's farm in 1996. In 1997 he purchased an adjoining farm and now farms the two areas of land which are side by side, as a single farm. In 1998 he disposed of a half acre site which formed part of the land inherited from his father.

The Revenue instruction would imply that the disposal of the half acre site is to be treated as a part disposal of the land acquired from his father, and that the land purchased in 1997 does not enter into the calculation in any fashion. The Revenue instruction also implies that it is their belief that strictly speaking the sale of the half acre site is a part disposal of the land inherited from the father, and not an entire disposal of an asset consisting of half an acre. However, as noted previously in the Revenue Commissioners capital gains tax manual, the Inspector is instructed to accept "entire disposal" treatment of the half acre as an asset in itself, in the interests of avoiding unnecessary expenditure on valuations, where a valuation was required in relation to the acquisition cost. That instruction in the present case would imply that if the taxpayer wished to submit a computation based on the open market value of the half acre site at the date he inherited it, and treat its disposal as the entire disposal of a single asset, and not a part disposal of the farm inherited, that the Revenue should accept that treatment. In contrast, had the half acre site been located on the farm purchased in 1997, the Revenue instruction would not require the Inspector to accept "total disposal" of a half acre asset, since no valuation was required in relation to the acquisition. Had the acquisition of the 1997 farm been from a connected party of course, a valuation would be required and therefore the taxpayer would in those circumstances again be entitled to treat the half acre site as an asset in itself.

It has to be emphasised the comments above are based on extracts from the Revenue Commissioners' manual, and not from legislation. They therefore describe either Revenue practice, or Revenue interpretation of the law, and not necessarily the authors' view of the law.

— **Revenue/Chief Inspector's CGT Manual :**

— In Paragraph 19.2.14.13 it is stated that the "total disposal" of a single asset treatment should be given to a taxpayer, where it might alternatively be argued that part disposal of a larger asset is involved, if the taxpayer gives an undertaking to adopt the same procedure on all subsequent disposals out of the larger asset. However the Revenue instructions permit the taxpayer to adopt that approach only in limited circumstances (where the disposal is small relative to the total valuation on the acquisition). It is not clear what significance should be attached to the undertaking.

— Where a "total disposal of a single asset" approach is taken where a small part of land is sold out of a larger area of land, Paragraph 19.2.14.15 advises the Inspector that in the event of an irreconcilable dispute with the taxpayer on any apportionment of deductible costs, the Inspector should take the matter to appeal and insist on the strict statutory "part disposal" approach.

11.3   **"No gain / no loss" disposals**

In some circumstances, typically intra group transfers, a transaction is deemed to take place for a consideration that produces a "no gain/no loss" situation. In such a case there are two consideration figures available - the actual consideration, and the deemed consideration for the purpose of the "no gain/no loss" rule. The part disposal calculation is always carried out by reference to the actual consideration, rather than to the deemed "no gain/no loss" computation.

Example 79

*Assume the facts are the same as in **example 76** except that the 40 acres sold in February 1994 were sold to Bill's wife. As explained in paragraph 33.7 disposals between husband and wife who are "living together" at the date of the disposal are on a "no gain/no loss" basis. In other words, they are for a deemed consideration which secures that on the disposal there is neither a gain nor a loss. In order to determine the deemed consideration it is therefore necessary to compute the base cost, since the deemed consideration will necessarily equal the base cost in order to secure that there is neither a gain nor a loss on the disposal. A problem presents itself in that under the formula described in Paragraph 11.1, it is necessary to know the consideration for a disposal, in order to compute the base cost in relation to the disposal. This Gordonian knot is cut by a rule which disregards the "no gain/no loss" treatment solely for the purpose of computing* *the base cost. Since husband and wife are connected persons, in the absence of the "no gain/no loss" rule, open market value would be substituted for the consideration passing. In the present instance that can be taken to be the sum actually paid by Bill's wife, £190,000. The cost figure (before indexation) of £38,550 is therefore arrived at in the same manner as at **example 69** That in turn determines the deemed consideration on the disposal.*

Similar treatment will apply in any situation where there is simultaneously a part disposal, and the legislation deems the transaction to be on a "no gain/no loss" basis.

s547

The situation may be further complicated in that the transaction involving a "no gain / no loss" treatment may be with a connected party. In such a case, if the "no gain / no loss" rule is disregarded, s547 may impose open market value in place of the actual consideration. In such a case it is the open market value which would be adopted as the consideration for the purpose of part disposal computations.

12 EVENTS PRIOR TO 6/4/74

12.1 Events prior to 6/4/74

s544(8)

s544(8) sets out a rule to be applied in the computation of a gain or loss for CGT purposes, by reference to events occurring prior to 6 April 1974.

"Insofar as the provisions of the Capital Gains Tax Acts require the computation of a gain by reference to events before the 6th day of April 1974, all those provisions, including the provisions fixing the amount of the consideration deemed to be given on a disposal or an acquisition, shall apply except so far as expressly excluded".

This subsection was previously s51(2) CGTA 1975. Prior to consolidation that subsection contained the words "Part 1 of Schedule 1 and Schedule 2 and 3 and" after the word "including".

Schedule 1 contained the computation rules (consideration chargeable, expenditure deductible, wasting asset rules, part disposal rules, etc.). Schedules 2 and 3 dealt with reorganisation and reduction of share capital, and leases of land and other assets.

Example 80

William sold an asset in January 1998 for £300,000. The market value of the asset at 6 April 1974 was £30,000. Ignoring other factors, the gain would be computed as follows:-

	£
Sale Proceeds	*300,000*
Cost (MV 1974) 30,000 indexed @ 6.112	*183,360*
GAIN	*116,640*

209

If we now look back to the actual cost of the asset, we may find that in fact a loss arose, or perhaps a real gain of less than £116,640, either of which would affect the outcome for CGT purposes. In arriving at the original 'cost' for this purpose, if a part disposal had been made out of the asset prior to 6 April 1974, an amount of the pre 6 April 1974 expenditure would be excluded using the normal part disposal rules which apply to a post 5 April 1974 part disposal. Only the balance of the pre 6 April 1974 expenditure would be taken into account in the computation of the gain or loss on the 1994 disposal.

13   ASSETS OWNED AT 6 APRIL 1974

s556

The old time apportionment rules which applied to gains arising on the disposal of assets owned at 6 April 1974 were repealed with effect from 6 April 1978. All assets held at 6 April 1974 are now ***deemed to be sold and reacquired at market value on that date***. This rule applies, with a few minor adjustments (of a computational nature) where the disposal of the asset takes place on or after 6 April 1978. The computational adjustments arising in certain circumstances are set out in paragraph 13.

14   INDEXATION

14.1   Indexation : broad outline

s556

This relief has the effect of eliminating the part of the gain attributable to inflation. It is available to all taxpayers and applies to practically all expenditure. It is not necessary to be resident in Ireland to obtain this relief.

There is only one item of expenditure which cannot be indexed - that is expenditure incurred within one year of the date of disposal of the asset. Indexation only applies to expenditure where the disposal of the asset concerned takes place on or after 6 April, 1978.

There is a restriction in the amount of indexation available on a disposal of development land (see paragraph 6.3).

To arrive at expenditure deductible in the case of an asset owned at 6 April 1974 (in calculating a gain or loss) it is necessary to 'index' the cost (market value at 6 April 1974) by reference to the 'multipliers' set out in the 1978 Act. The 1978 Act contains a table, showing the multipliers to be applied to expenditure in the case of disposals of assets in 1978/79. Regulations are issued for each subsequent year of assessment setting out the multipliers for disposals in those later years. The multipliers for 1978/79, and those introduced by regulation for 1979/80 and later years are set out in table form at the front of the book.

An asset owned at 6 April 1974 (regardless of when it was actually acquired) is deemed to be acquired at 6 April 1974 at a cost equal to its market value at that date. That 'cost' is deemed to be incurred in

1974/75, and accordingly the multiplier relating to 1974/75 applies (see paragraph 13).

Example 81

An asset costing £1,000 was acquired in 1964. The value at 6/4/74 was £10,000. The asset was sold in February 1998 for £100,000.

	£	£
Sale proceeds		*100,000*
Value 6/4/74	*10,000*	
Indexed x 6.112 =		*61,120*
Gain		*38,880*

14.2   **Assets Acquired After 5/4/74 - Indexation**

The same principles apply. The cost is 'indexed' using the multiplier referable to the year in which the cost was incurred. The same rule applies to enhancement expenditure incurred after 5 April 1974. Enhancement expenditure incurred prior to 6 April 1974 would be reflected in a market value (deemed cost) at that date.

Example 82

An asset was acquired in 1963 for £1,000 (Value 6/4/74 £10,000). Further (allowable) enhancement expenditure was incurred in :-

June 1975 -	*£5,000*
Aug. 1976 -	*£2,000*
Jan 1994 -	*£3,000*

The asset was sold in March 1999 for £150,000.

		£
Sale proceeds		*150,000*
Cost		
Market value 6/4/74	*£10,000 x 6.215 =*	*62,150*
Expenditure		
- Jun 1975	*£5,000 x 5.020 =*	*25,100*
- Aug 1976	*£2,000 x 4.325 =*	*8,650*
- Jan 1994	*£3,000 x*1.... =*	*3,000*
		98,900
Gain		*51,500*

*No indexation for expenditure incurred within 12 months of disposal.

14.3   **Indexation : Exceptions**

s556(4)   There are exceptions to the general rules on the application of indexation and the use of market value at 6 April 1974. Where these rules would have the effect of:-

- increasing an actual loss (giving relief for more than the real loss incurred)

or

- increasing an actual gain (charging more than the real gain realised)

or

- turning an actual gain into a loss (giving relief for a loss, where in fact a real gain arose)

or

- turning an actual loss into a gain (charging a gain, where an actual loss arose

certain subsidiary rules come into effect. TCA97 s556(4) provides that

s556(2)

- s556(2) - indexation of expenditure, and

s556(3)

- s556(3) - provision deeming asset to be sold and reacquired at market value on 6 April 1974.

will not apply -

(a) *If as a consequence of the application of those subsections a gain would accrue on that disposal to the person making the disposal and either a smaller gain or a loss would so accrue if these subsections did not apply, or*

(b) *if as a consequence of the application of those subsections a loss would so accrue and either a smaller loss or a gain would accrue if those subsections did not apply,*

and, accordingly, in a case to which paragraph (a) or (b) applies, the amount of the gain or loss accruing on the disposal shall be computed without regard to the provisions of subsections 2 and 3 but, in a case where this subsection would otherwise substitute a loss for a gain or a gain for a loss, it shall be assumed, in relation to the disposal, that the relevant asset was acquired by the owner for a consideration such that neither a gain nor a loss accrued to him on making the disposal".

A literal reading of s556(4) as quoted above would limit its application (inter alia) in denying relief for a loss created by indexation to a situation where both

— indexation was available, *and*

— the asset was deemed to be acquired at market value at 5th April 1974.

On such a reading the sub-section would have no application on the disposal of an asset acquired after 5th April 1974. Such an interpretation is not normally followed in practice, not least by the Revenue authorities.

The following examples illustrate the effect of the above rules, as they are usually applied in practice:

Example 83 *(where CGT rules result in greater loss than that actually realised).*

			£
Asset purchased in 1970 for			*4,000*
Market value 6/4/74	=		*800*
Sale price December 1998	=		*3,000*
Computation			
Sale proceeds	=		*3,000*
MV 6/4/74	=	*800 @ 6.215*	*4,972*
Loss using indexing rules	=		*1,972*
Actual loss	=	*(4,000-3,000)*	*1,000*

The rules cannot have effect to increase an actual loss and therefore the allowable loss is reduced to £1,000 - the actual loss suffered.

Example 84 *(where CGT rules result in greater gain than that actually realised).*

			£
Asset purchased in 1970 for			*4,000*
Market value 6/4/74	=		*600*
Sold June 1998 for	=		*5,100*
Computation			
Sale proceeds	=		*5,100*
MV 6/4/74	=	*£600 @ 6.215*	*3,729*
Gain using indexation	=		*1,371*
Actual gain	=	*(5,100-4,000)*	*1,100*

These rules cannot increase the actual gain so the chargeable gain is reduced to £1,100 - the gain actually realised.

Example 85 *(where CGT rules result in a loss, but an actual gain arose on the disposal).*

			£
Cost 1970			*4,000*
Market Value 6/4/74	=		*950*
Sale proceeds September 1998	=		*4,500*
Computation			
Sale Proceeds	=		*4,500*
MV 6/4/74	=	*indexed @ 6.215*	*5,904*

Loss using indexation		1,404
Actual gain	= (4,500 - 4,000)	500

The rules cannot be used to turn an actual gain into a loss so where this happens the disposal is treated as giving 'NO GAIN-NO LOSS'

Example 86 (where CGT rules result in gain, but loss actually suffered on the disposal).

		£
Cost 1970		4,000
Market Value 6/4/74	=	200
Sale Price August 1998	=	3,000

Computation		
Sale proceeds	=	3,000
MV 6/4/74 x 6.215	=	1,243
Gain using indexation		1,757
Actual Loss	= (4,000-3000)	1,000

These rules cannot be used to change actual loss into a gain. Where this happens, the transaction is treated as giving: 'NO GAIN-NO LOSS'

14.4   **Indexation : Grant-Aided Expenditure**

As discussed in paragraph 9.6 in arriving at allowable expenditure it is necessary to deduct certain grants or subsidies received in respect of it.

Example 87

	£
Cost	10,000
Grant	3,000
Allowable Cost	7,000

It is this £7,000 net expenditure that is 'indexed' in calculating the gain.

s556(8),(9)   *Assets acquired prior to 6 April 1974, must be valued at 6 April 1974. The market value at that date is the deemed cost. Where the cost of any such asset was met partly by way of grant, the market value at 6 April 1974 must be reduced by the amount of the grant.*

Example 88

	£
Asset Cost (say 1960)	*10,000*
Grant(in 1960)	*3,000*
MV 6/4/74	*40,000*

In the case of a disposal of the asset on or after 6 April 1978, the deemed cost is

	£
MV 6/4/74	*40,000*
Less Grant	*3,000*
	37,000

It is this £37,000 deemed net cost that is to be indexed.

Indexation is applied in relation to expenditure in a tax year, regardless of when within the tax year that expenditure is incurred. In other words, £100 spent on 6 April 2000 attracts the identical uplift by way of indexation as does £100 spent on 5 April in 2001, notwithstanding that it is incurred almost a year later. In every case of course the asset has to be held for a year before indexation is available, but subject to that indexation applies to expenditure in a year without distinguishing when within the year the expenditure was incurred. Thus expenditure of £100 on 5 April 2000 will in due course attract a year's more indexation than would the same amount spent on 6 April 2000.

The same rule applies equally in relation to a disposal. A disposal on 6 April 2000 will attract a full year's indexation for the year 2000/2001 notwithstanding that the asset was held for only one day in that tax year. It receives the same indexation as would an asset which was not disposed of until 5 April 2001, 364 days later.

The maximum indexation is obtained where the investment is made on 5 April in a tax year, and the relevant disposal is not made until 6 April in a tax year more than one year away. In that case an investment held for 367 days attracts three years indexation. In contrast an asset acquired on 6 April in a tax year and disposed of on the following 4 April (ie held for 364 days) attracts no indexation.

15   TIME OF DISPOSAL

15.1   Broad Outline

s542

The time at which a disposal is made may be of vital importance. For example, if an asset was disposed of before 6 April, 1974, no CGT liability could arise. Similarly, indexation applies only to disposals on or after 6 April, 1978, and the special rules for dealing with transactions involving development land introduced in FA 1982 in all cases, apply only to disposals on or after 28 January 1982 and before 6th April 1992, to some extent.

In most cases, the time of disposal is clear and no legislation is required to clarify the position. In certain cases, however, specific rules apply; these are as follows:

s542(1)(a)

• Disposal by CONTRACT

If an asset is disposed of and acquired under a contract the time of disposal and acquisition is the time the contract is made and not the date the property is actually conveyed or transferred. If however, the contract is conditional, the disposal is treated as being made at the time the condition is satisfied. (see paragraph 15.2).

Example 89

John Black decided in June 1999 to sell a rental property which he owned as an investment in Dublin. The property was advertised for sale and on 28 June 1999 a written offer "subject to contract" was received. John decided to accept the offer and the solicitor issued a contract to the purchaser's solicitor. This was returned signed by the purchaser on 5 July 1999. John signed it on the same day. The contract called for the payment of an immediate deposit of 10% of the purchase price, with the balance being paid on the closing of the sale, which date was set for 28 August 1999. A cheque for the deposit had accompanied the contract when returned signed from the purchaser. On 28 August 1999 John attended at a solicitor's office where the purchaser paid over the balance of the sales proceeds, and John signed the Deed of Transfer of the property to the purchaser and delivered it to the purchaser's solicitor.

The disposal of the investment property took place on foot of a contract. Therefore the date of disposal of the property was the date the contract was entered into. That date was 5 July, being the date when John signed the contract which had already been signed by the purchaser. At that point and only at that point both parties became bound by a contract. The prior offer did not constitute a contract because it was expressly stated to be "subject to contract". The date of disposal is not 28 August, the date upon which the title was actually transferred to the purchaser. That might seem to be the date of disposal to the man in the street, but the CGT legislation has laid down an artificial rule that the date of disposal is the date the contract is entered into, and not the date upon which the property is transferred in fulfilment of the contract.

In the example above the delay between the entering into a contract on 5 July, and the actual implementation of the contract by the transfer of the property on 28 August was relatively short and of no great significance. If however a contract was signed on (say) 5 March 1999, with completion of the contract by transfer of the property and payment occurring on 20 April 2000, the disposal would occur not in the year 2000/2001 (which is when the property was actually handed over to the purchaser and was finally paid for) but in the year 1999/2000, which would be the year in which the disposal occurred.

Example 90

John Brown has decided to mark his daughter's 21st birthday by gifting to her an apartment which he owns as an investment. John announced this to his daughter and her friends during her 21st birthday party on 31 January 2000, to loud applause. After several reminders by his daughter, he instructed his solicitor to draw up legal documents to transfer the title of the property to her, and this was done on 31 July 2000.

The disposal is not under a contract. One of the necessary conditions for the existence of a contract, the giving of valuable consideration by the daughter, was missing. Therefore the date of disposal is not determined by the date of any contract, and could not be since there was no contract. The date of disposal in this case falls to be determined not by any rule provided in the CGT Acts, but in accordance with Land Law. Under Irish Land Law a disposal would not have occurred until the Deed of Transfer was executed on 28 July 2000. The promise at the birthday party did not affect John Brown's ownership of the property, or transfer any ownership to his daughter. The promise was unenforceable by the daughter against him. There was no disposal of the property in law until the Deed of Transfer was executed. That therefore fixes the point at which the date of disposal occurs in that instance.

Had John Brown approached matters differently, and instead of verbally announcing his intention of gifting the property at the birthday party, presented his daughter with a contract under which she purchased the property for the sum of £1, and had they both signed the contract before the admiring guests, the subsequent disposal on the completion of the contract would be on foot of a contract. It would of course still in effect be a gift, but it would be a gift carried through by way of a contract. In such a case the date would be determined by the statutory rule relating to disposals under contract ie the date of disposal would be 28 January 2000, the date of the birthday party and of the signing of the contract, and not the subsequent date of transfer of legal title of 28 July 2000.

In the UK case of Johnson v Edwards an asset was to be sold under a contract effected prior to the operative date of CGT. The asset was actually sold after the commencement of CGT. The question for decision by the Court was whether the rule deeming the disposal to take place at the date of contract would apply in the case of a "pre-CGT" contract. The Court decided that the rule did not apply in such a case and consequently the disposal was liable to CGT notwithstanding the fact that the disposal was under a contract dated prior to the operative date of CGT. It was held that the provision could be fairly construed in a way which did not have retrospective consequences. However, that case was concerned with the introduction of the rule into the pre-existing UK CGT code by the UK Finance Act of 1971. It may not be authority for the same proposition in the context of the Irish CGT legislation where the rule was in place from the commencement of the Irish 1975 Act.

In the UK case of Aspden v Hindersley assets to be transferred under a Consent Order in divorce proceedings made before the decree absolute were regarded as being disposed of under a contract. Depending on the facts of the case, it may be a conditional contract.

- **Disposal under CPO:**

s542(1)(c)

Where there is a compulsory acquisition, the time of disposal and acquisition is the earlier of:

    (i)   The time when compensation is agreed, ignoring variations on appeal, and

    (ii) the time when the acquiring authority enters on the land.

The rule described above applies only where the authority having powers of compulsory purchase acquires the property by exercising those powers. The rule described above would not apply if the taxpayer, aware that the authority had the power to compulsorily acquire, voluntarily entered into a contract with them for the sale rather than have the authority exercise their compulsory powers. Even if a contract is negotiated under threat of the exercise of compulsory powers, the time of disposal is that set down for a disposal under a contract in that instance, and not a disposal under a CPO.

- **Disposal under HIRE PURCHASE arrangement:**

In the case of a hire purchase transaction the time of disposal is the time when the person hiring first obtains the use of the asset. If at the end of the hire period, ownership of the asset does not in fact pass, then all necessary tax adjustments will be made (on the basis that there was in fact no disposal in the first instance).

s539

This rule also applies to other transactions by virtue of which *"the use and enjoyment of an asset is obtained by a person for a period at the end of which the property in the asset will or may pass to that person."*

The issue of whether to apply this rule to a contract for the sale of Cabs - where ownership of the cab licence did not pass until after all payments had been made by the purchaser - was considered in the UK case of Lyon v Pettigrew (see below in paragraph 15.2).

The practical application of the treatment laid down by s539 for a hire purchase transaction is not as clear cut as might be expected. This is best illustrated by an example.

Example 91

HP Limited agrees to provide Johns Sawmills Limited with a new piece of plant. The item of plant could be purchased directly from the suppliers by Johns Sawmills Limited for £10,000, if they had wished to do that. By reason of HP Limited's superior purchasing power it is able to acquire the item for £9,500. It provides it to Johns Sawmills Limited on a typical hire purchase agreement providing for 3 payments of £4,500 each over a 3 year period, and providing Johns Sawmills Limited with an option to acquire the item at the end of the 3 year period for £500.

S539 requires that HP Limited be treated as disposing of the item of plant on the day the hire purchase agreement is entered into, and that Johns Sawmills Limited be treated as acquiring the item of plant by way of sale on that date. That rule will be of no consequence to HP Limited since it is probably not within the charge to capital gains tax on any dealings in plant, since it is within the charge to tax on income on such transactions. Nonetheless, the deeming provisions apply to Johns Sawmills Limited.

What is the deemed acquisition price of the item of plant by Johns Sawmills Limited? S539 does not offer any guidance on this matter. It is not clear that there are any grounds for resorting to open market value since the parties are not connected, and there is no indication that the deemed transaction is deemed to be otherwise than at arm's length. One answer is that it may be that it is the actual cost price of the equipment - but is that the £9,500 actually paid by HP Limited, or is it the £10,000 which it would have cost Johns Sawmills Limited to acquire it directly? Economic analysis may be resorted to to separate out the hire purchase payments to a notional capital element, and a notional interest element.

Old UK tax case law in an income tax context would support the view that in some hire purchase contracts part of the hire payment is capital in nature. However that analysis is usually dependent on the option purchase price at the end of the agreement being significantly lower than the expected market value at that date. If in fact, the option purchase price of £500 was the parties best estimate of the likely market value of the asset at the end of 3 years, there would be no grounds for saying that any part of the hire payments are capital in nature.

There is a further difficulty in treating the hire payments as representing the acquisition cost, in the whole or in part. S552 defines what is deductible as acquisition cost. That includes expenditure wholly and exclusively to acquire the asset. Hire payments are not payments to acquire an asset but are payments for its use at a time when it is not owned by the lessee.

s539 The authors presume that the Revenue will accept the actual cost to HP Limited as the basis for the computation. However the matter is not referred to in the Revenue's capital gains tax manual. The manual does state that in any case in which the hiree (ie the person who has rented the equipment from the hire purchase company) claims a capital gains tax loss in respect of the repossession of the asset by the vendor, the claim should be submitted to head office. Such advice is not surprising in view of the lack of guidance which s539 provides in the treatment of this area.

There is one other ambiguity in the treatment set out in s539 in relation to hire purchase. At the commencement of the hire purchase contract, the person who owns the asset and has provided it for the purpose of the contract is deemed to have disposed of the asset. If that person is not providing the asset in the course of a trade of which that asset would be treated as trading stock (and that is quite possible) what is the position of that person thereafter? Factually they own the asset. But s539 has deemed them to already have disposed of it. What happens if they now actually dispose of it ie sell it subject to the benefit of the hire purchase contract? S539 does not provide a clear answer.

A disposal under a hire purchase contract is a disposal on foot of an option agreement. The lessee usually has an option to acquire the asset, but is not obliged to acquire the asset. The special treatment provided for options is discussed in paragraph 39. The normal treatment applied to a disposal as a result of the exercise of an option to purchase is that the date of the exercise of the option determines the date of disposal. This rule is not applied to a hire purchase contract on the exercise of an option to purchase. Instead, as outlined above, the date of disposal is the date when the asset is first provided to the lessee.

- **CAPITAL SUM DERIVED FROM ASSETS:**

In the case of disposals mentioned in paragraph 4.4.4 (capital sums derived from assets) the time of disposal is the time the capital sum is received.

s542(2)   Strictly speaking the CGT Acts specifies the time of disposal to be the time of receipt of the capital sum only in the four specific examples of a capital sum derived from an asset which are given in the legislation, and which are listed in paragraph 4.4.4.

s535(2)(a)   *"For the purposes of subparagraphs (i) to (iv) of section 535(2)(a), the time of disposal shall be the time when any capital sum is received".*

The legislation refers to these four specific examples but not to capital sums derived from assets in general. Since however s542 does not lay down any other rule as to the time of disposal in relation to other transactions constituting capital sums derived from an asset, it may appear reasonable to suppose that in other instances, the time of disposal is also the time when the capital sum is received. However, the fact that it may be reasonable, is not necessarily the correct basis of interpretation, and other interpretations of this issue are possible.

- **Disposal of LIFE ASSURANCE POLICY**

The special rules for determining the date of disposal of certain life assurance policies and contracts for deferred annuities are set out in paragraph 32.9.

15.2   **Conditional Contract**

TCA97 s542(1)(b) provides:

"If the contract is conditional (and, in particular, if it is conditional on the exercise of an option), the time at which the disposal and acquisition is made
s542(1)(b)   *is the time the condition is satisfied".*

The meaning of 'conditional' in this context was considered in the UK case of Lyon v Pettigrew. The taxpayer was the proprietor of 11 taxis, and their licences to ply for hire. He signed contracts for the sale of six of them, together with their licences. The contracts provided for a sale price of £6,000 for each taxi and licence, to be paid over 150 weeks in equal installments. Under the contract, the ownership of the taxi passed immediately, but ownership of the licence was to pass only on payment of the last installment in each case. It was contended for the taxpayer that the final passing of ownership of the licence subject to payment of the full proceeds was a condition which deferred the time of disposal until the final payment was made.

It was held by Walton J in the Chancery Division (based on the English law concerned) that the licence could not be divorced from the vehicle . The only question remaining to be decided following the decision on that point, was whether both the licence and the car passed under the original agreement (at the date of that agreement), or whether the agreement was 'conditional' thereby deferring the time of disposal until the final payment was made.

In dealing with the meaning of 'conditional' in this context Walton J said:

"The words 'contract is conditional' have traditionally, I think, been used to cover really only two types of cases. One is a 'subject to contract' contract, where there is clearly no contract at all anyway, and the other is where all the liabilities under the contract are conditional on a certain event. It would for example, be possible for a hotelier to make a booking with a tour operator conditionally on the next Olympic Games being held in London. Then, until it had been decided that the next Olympic Games were going to be held in London, there would be no effective contract: the whole contract would be conditional, the whole liabilities and the duties between the parties would only arise when the condition was fulfilled".

Walton J was referred to the judgement of Russell LJ in Eastham v Leigh London and Provincial Properties Ltd. Although not dealing with CGT, that case was concerned with another tax, the effect of the provisions of which was dependent on whether a contract was conditional.

In that case Russell LJ said:

"The answer, to my mind is a short and simple one: I cannot accept that it is correct to say that because the grant of the lease was dependent upon the fulfillment by the tenant of those obligations which constituted the consideration for the grant of the lease, the contract to acquire can properly be described as a conditional contract at all. It is a contract for sale and purchase, or, rather, grant and acceptance of a lease; what is provided for in the contract is not a condition of the contract at all, it is simply a provision that the one party shall carry out certain works in consideration of a

promise thereafter to grant a lease. Indeed it appears to me that once it is accepted that it is one contract of acquisition and not two contracts the matter is completely answered. If there be one contract I cannot see, with respect, how the postponement of the carrying out of one part of the contract until the fulfillment of the consideration by the other party can in any way be properly described as a 'condition' of the contract as distinct from a perfectly ordinary part of, or term of, the contract".

A conditional contract is a contract which is subject to a condition precedent. The conditions to which a contract may be subject can be analysed as between conditions precedent, and conditions subsequent. A condition precedent is a condition which must be fulfilled before there is a binding arrangement between the parties. The most common example of a condition precedent is an option. An option consists of an offer (usually to sell or possibly also to buy) which is irrevocable for a specified period. No contract to buy or to sell, as the case may be, comes into existence until the option is exercised i.e. until such time as a person to whom the option has been granted accepts the offer of the other party to buy or to sell as the case may be. The exercise of the option is a condition precedent.

A condition subsequent is a condition which one of the parties has bound themselves to comply with, but which does not have to be fulfilled before both parties are contractually bound by the agreement entered into. An example might be where the vendor of a house agrees in a contract not to make any alterations to the house prior to the date of closing of the sale. Both parties to the contract are bound by the contract whether or not that condition is fulfilled. A failure to fulfill the condition would give rise to a right on the part of the purchaser to secure damages, or possibly to secure specific enforcement of the contract in the courts. But he would be bound by the contract whether or not the condition is fulfilled.

- **Revenue Commissioners - Tax Briefing**

- In Tax Briefing Issue 36 - June 1999 the Revenue Commissioners confirmed that in their view a contract which is conditional on the obtaining of planning permission is a conditional contract. They state "Obtaining planning permission is a condition precedent to the performance of the contract. The time of disposal is the time at which planning permission is obtained." The Revenue go on to confirm that a contract which provides that disposal and acquisition is subject to a loan approval being obtained is a conditional contract in this context and "the time of disposal is the time at which loan approval is obtained."

- **Appeal Commissioners Ruling**

- The Appeal Commissioners have ruled that a requirement in a contract for the sale of land or for "the production of the vendors of a map suitable for registration in the Land Registry showing the property coloured in red" was not a condition precedent and did not render the contract a conditional contract.

16   ARM'S LENGTH RULES

16.1   Broad Outline

s547
In certain circumstances, the CGT legislation requires you to ignore the actual price at which an asset passes from one person to another, and instead it substitutes a deemed price - usually market value of the asset at the date of the transaction. The meaning of "**market value**" is described in paragraph 17.

The main rule on this is TCA97 s547, which sets out the rules for determining the circumstances in which the market value of the asset must be substituted for the actual transfer price (if any).

s549
S549 of the same Act brings transactions between 'connected persons' within the same rules.

The rules have been substantially amended since the law was first enacted in the 1975 Act.

The most important point to note, is that the Irish law in this area deals separately with 'acquisitions' and 'disposals', which means that the same rules will not necessarily apply to the person making the disposal, and the person acquiring the asset.

The rules dealing with the acquisition of an asset are dealt with in s547(1), and those dealing with disposals are set out in s547(4).

16.2   Acquisition

In certain cases, a person is deemed to acquire an asset for its market value, irrespective of the actual price (if any) he paid for it. This applies to:

• *Not Bargain At Arm's Length*

s547(1)(a)
Where he acquires the asset otherwise than by way of bargain made at arm's length (this particularly includes a gift).

• *Distribution*

s547(1)(b)
Where he acquires the asset by way of a distribution from a company in respect of shares in the company (e.g. by way of a distribution in a winding up).

• *Consideration Cannot Be Valued*

s547(1)(c)
Where the asset is acquired wholly or partly for a consideration that cannot be valued.

• *Employment, Etc.*

s547(1)(c)   Where the asset is acquired wholly or partly in connection with his own (or another's) loss of office or employment or diminution of emoluments or otherwise in consideration for or in recognition of his (or another's) services or past services in any office or employment or of any other service rendered or to be rendered by him (or by another).

• *Connected Person*

s549(2)   Where the asset is acquired from a 'connected person' (see 16.4 below).

16.2.1   Special Rules for shares

The rules outlined above were modified with effect to acquisitions on or after 24 June 1982, in relation to share issues by a company to a person connected with it. This topic is discussed in detail in paragraph 41.5.

In brief, under the rules outlined above, but for the 1982 modification, any share issue (which was not a reorganisation of share capital) made by a company to a person connected with it, would have a base cost for that connected person of *open market value* regardless of his actual expenditure on the shares. Since the issue of shares is not the disposal of an asset, what could be a very high base cost for a share could be created without any corresponding CGT charge on the company. This point was brought out in the UK case of Harrison v Nairn Williamson described in detail in paragraph 41. Where a company, on or after 24 June 1982 issues shares otherwise than by way of bargain made at arms length to a person connected with the company, the base cost to that person in the shares will be the lower of the consideration he actually gave for them, or the amount of the increase in the value of his overall shareholding in the company as a result of the new issue of shares. The open market value rule described above will not apply.

16.2.2   Antiavoidance - all assets

s547(3)   A further restriction of the application of s547 was introduced in FA92 s62, which added a further subsection, now s547(3).

s547(3) provides that s547 - otherwise deeming a person's acquisition of an asset to be at market value (where it is acquired in the circumstances outlined above) is not to apply where:

— *there is no corresponding disposal of the asset,*

   and

— there is no consideration in money or money's worth given for the asset,

or

— the consideration for the asset is of an amount or value which is lower than the market value of the asset.

This new rule applies in the case of assets acquired on or after 7th May 1992. It should be noted that 547(3) only applies in the case of the acquisition of an asset since it applies only where there is no corresponding disposal.

Example 92

Examples of assets being acquired without a corresponding disposal, would include:

- *shares acquired on the issue of those shares by a company.*

- *the right to sue, arising from negligence (see case of Zim Properties, paragraph 4.4.6)*

- *statutory rights to compensation (see paragraph 4.4.5)*

- *non purchased goodwill of a business*

- *a non purchased patent*

In the absence of a specific rule deeming an asset to be acquired at market value, the normal rules apply - the asset is acquired at its actual cost - if any !

SPA54 s31   The FA98 introduced a further circumstance in which the acquisition of assets, otherwise than by way of a bargain made at arms length, will not involve their being acquired for a deemed consideration equal to their open market value at the time. That is where assets accrued to persons by reason of the Minister for Finance waiving his entitlements to those assets under s31 of the State Property Act 1954. In certain circumstances property, in the absence of any other lawful owner, passes to the state. The most relevant of circumstances is where a company is struck off the register of companies and thereby dissolved, while still having assets. It is the normal practice of the Minister for Finance to identify the persons who are "morally entitled" to such assets (usually the shareholders and creditors in the case of a company as mentioned) and to pass the assets to them, usually retaining a sum to cover the costs incurred by the state, or requiring payment to be made to the state by those receiving the assets. With effect from any assets transferred in this fashion by the Minister on or after 12 February 1998, the base cost of those acquiring the assets will be confined to the amount (if any) which they are obliged to pay in return for having the assets transferred to them by the Minister. This restriction was introduced in conjunction with anti avoidance legislation designed to defer negligible value loss relief on shares in a company whose assets pass to the state on the company being dissolved. The matter is referred to further in paragraph 20.5.

Example 93

Shops Ltd. had neglected to make returns to the companies office for decades. In March 1998 the Registrar of Companies struck the company off the register. At that date the company was the owner of a shop in Cork. The consequence of the company being struck of the register was that the ownership of the shop passed to the state. The shop was then worth £500,000.

The Minister exercised his rights under s31 of the State Property Act 1954 to transfer the shop in equal shares to John and Mary, who each had held 50% of the shares in Shops Ltd. at the date it was struck of the register. The transfers were made in return for payment by each of them of £60,000, which is applied by the Minister in payment of the companies liabilities.

Notwithstanding that the bargain between John and Mary, and the Minister could hardly be said to be a bargain made at arms length, the base cost of John and Mary in the Cork shop is limited to £60,000 each, and not the £250,000 which would be the base cost if the same transaction had occurred prior to 12 February 1998. The new subsection 1A of s547 does not concern itself with the Capital Gains position of the company which was dissolved, and whose assets passed to the state otherwise than by way of a bargain made at arms length, and for zero consideration.

16.3   Disposal - TCA97 s547(4)

s547(4)

s547(4) sets out the specific arm's length provisions which are to apply to the disposal of an asset. In certain circumstances an asset will be deemed (for CGT purposes) to be sold for its market value, irrespective of the actual sale price. These provisions apply :

- where the asset is disposed of otherwise than by way of a bargain made at arm's length (this particularly includes a gift) or

- where the disposal of the asset is wholly or partly for a consideration that cannot be valued or

s549

- where the asset is disposed of to a connected person.

s547(4)(b)

Although the provisions relating to a disposal substitute market value in the case of a gift, the rule does not apply to a *gift* made prior to 20 December 1974. As a gift prior to 20 December 1974 cannot therefore give rise to a chargeable gain, any loss made on such a disposal is not an allowable loss (see paragraph 20 for the general rules on losses)

- **Revenue/Chief Inspector's CGT Manual:**

- The Revenue Commissioners capital gains tax manual at paragraph 19.1.16.4 indicates what appears to be a concessional treatment, where an employer transfers an asset at under value to an employee or director. Where the employee or director is charged to tax under Schedule E on the amount of the under value, and the transfer is not in satisfaction of a pre existing debt for unpaid remuneration, provided the employer is chargeable to tax under Case I or Case II Schedule D, the consideration for his disposal is to be treated as the cash consideration, if any, received by him from the director or employee. However, where that is less than the cost of the asset, no allowable loss would be allowed to the employer. The employee's cost of acquisition is unaffected by this concession and would be the market value of the asset.

16.4 Connected Persons

16.4.1 Acquisitions & Disposals - General Rule

s549   Acquisitions and disposals between *connected persons* are treated as if they were not "bargains at arms length", bringing the transaction within the scope of s547.

16.4.2 Restriction of Relief for Losses

s549(3)   A loss arising on the disposal of an asset to a *connected person* is not allowable except insofar as it can be set against a chargeable gain arising on the disposal of some other asset to the same person.

Example 94

> John sold quoted shares on the stock exchange on 31 March 1998. He realised a chargeable gain of £10,000 on that disposal. On 4 April 1998 he sold shares in the family company to his brother. The transaction gave rise to a loss (disregarding indexation which cannot increase a loss) of £5,000. The price at which he sold the shares to his brother reflected open market value, which would otherwise have been substituted for the consideration, by reason of their being connected persons.

> John is liable to capital gains tax on the chargeable gain of £10,000, without relief for the loss which arose on the transaction with his brother. Had John disposed of the quoted shares to his brother on the same terms as on which he disposed of them on the stock exchange to a third party, the chargeable gain would have arisen on a transaction with the same connected person as that which whom he had the transaction on which the loss of £5,000 arose. In such circumstances the loss on the sale of the family company shares would have been allowable against the gain on the disposal of the quoted shares. John's brother could have disposed of the quoted shares on the stock exchange immediately without any further capital gains tax implications.

> It should be noted that the restriction on the relief for a loss is that it is confined to gains arising on the disposal to the **same connected person** as was involved in the transaction giving rise to the loss.

Example 95

> John disposed of quoted shares at open market value to his brother, and realised a chargeable gain of £10,000. On the same day he disposed of other quoted shares at open market value, to his sister and realised an allowable loss of £5,000.

John may not obtain relief for the loss arising on the transaction with his sister (a connected person) against the gain arising on the transaction with his brother (also a connected person) because the gain and the loss did not arise on a transaction with the same connected person.

There is an exception to the restriction on relief for loss arising on a transaction with a connected person. That is where the loss arises on a gift in settlement, where the gift is in trust to be applied for educational, cultural or recreational purposes for the benefit of members of an association, the majority of whom are not connected persons.

16.4.3   Assets subject to right or restriction

s549(6)   Where an asset acquired from a *connected person* is subject to any right or restriction enforceable by that person, or by some other person connected with him, then the market value of the asset is to be taken as:

— The market value of the asset ignoring the right or restriction

reduced by

— The market value of the right or restriction **OR** the amount by which the value of the asset would be increased if the right or restriction did not exist, **whichever is the less.**

Example 96

A farmer owning land close to Dublin, wishes to gift some of the land to his son, to enable that son to start his own farming business; the land has development potential. He also wishes to ensure that the son does not immediately develop the land. He therefore imposes a restrictive covenant whereby the erection of any buildings or other structures on that land is prohibited.

The agricultural value of the land is £50,000. The land has for some time been zoned by the County Council for industrial development, and outline planning permission was granted to the farmer for the building of industrial units. The full market value of the land is £500,000. If we assume the market value of the restriction is £300,000, the deemed consideration for the disposal by the farmer, and the acquisition cost of his son is as follows:

Market Value of land (ignoring the restriction)	£500,000
Less smaller of Market value of restriction: i.e. £300,000 or	
increase in value of land without the restriction: i.e. (500,000-50,000) = £450,000	
DEDUCT	£300,000
Deemed consideration for acquisition	£200,000

s549(7)   In certain cases, however, the right or restriction is ignored and the full market value of the property is taken. This rule is applied in the following circumstances:

228

- Where the right or restriction is of such a nature that if it was enforced it would effectively destroy or substantially impair the value of the asset, without bringing any corresponding advantage either to the person making the disposal or to a person connected with him

  or

- Where the right or restriction is an option or other right to acquire the asset

  or

- In the case of incorporeal property, where the right or restriction is a right to extinguish the asset in the hands of the persons paying for it by forfeiture or merger or otherwise. This condition, however, does not apply to a right of forfeiture or other right exercisable on a breach of a covenant contained in a lease of land or other property. In addition, it does not apply to any right or restriction under a mortgage or other charge on property.

Arising out of the McGrath case (see paragraph 69) the FA89 amended the application of the rule in certain circumstances. The right or restriction is not ignored in determining open market value where the person who makes the disposal is not within the charge to CGT in respect of the disposal. This amendment applies to disposals made on or after 25 January 1989. It also applies to disposals prior to that date, where they gave rise to an allowable loss for which relief is due on or after that date.

16.4.4   What is a Connected Person?

s10

S10 defines "connected".

- *Spouse And Blood Relatives*

s10(3)

Husband, wife or relative. Relative includes brother, sister, uncle, aunt, niece, nephew, ancestor, lineal descendant or a person adopted under the Adoption Acts 1952 to 1974 or under the law of any place outside the State.

- *Child - connected person:*

In setting out details of the individuals with which another individual is to be regarded as connected, s10(3) includes a relative of that individual. s10(1) then defines relative, as including a *lineal descendant,* and persons *adopted under the Adoption Acts 1952 to 1974, or the law of any place outside the State.*

It is interesting to note that the word "*child*" is not used for the purposes of s10. However, the meaning of the word *child* is

important for other purposes of the CGT Acts, and its meaning is
dealt with in paragraph 33.9.

The use of the term *lineal descendant* would include most
children. It clearly includes a child born naturally to a married
couple. The question of a legally adopted child (under the specific
Acts mentioned) is also clear.

Lineal descendant also includes grandchildren, great
grandchildren, and so on to any degree.

- *"In Laws"*

s10(3)   Husband or wife of a relative. The husband or wife of a relative of
the individual's husband or wife.

- *Trustees*

s10(4)   A Trustee of a trust is connected with the settlor if the settlor is an
individual, but not if it is not an individual, e.g. a company. The
trustee is also connected with any person connected with that
settlor.

A trustee of a settlement is connected with a body corporate which
is connected with the settlement. A body corporate is connected
with the settlement in any year if it is a *close* company (or would
be so if Irish resident) and the shareholders include either the
trustees or a beneficiary of the settlement.

- *Partners*

s10(5)   A person is connected with any partners of his and with the
husband or wife or relatives of any of his partners.

There is however one important exception to this rule. A person is
not connected with another person solely by reason of their being
partners, where the transaction in question is the acquisition or
disposal of partnership assets pursuant to bona fide commercial
arrangements. The significance of this exception is discussed in
further detail in paragraph 34.

- *Companies*

s10(6)   A company is connected with another company:-

(i) If the same person has control of both or a person has control
     of one and persons connected with him or he and persons
     connected with him have control of the other or

(ii) If a group of two or more persons has control of each
     company and the groups consist either of the same persons or
     could be regarded as consisting of the same persons by
     treating (in one or more cases) a member of either group as
     replaced by one or more persons with whom he is connected.

s10(7)   A company is connected with another person if that other person has control of it, or if he and persons connected with him together have control of it. (see paragraph 16.4.5 - re. "control").

s10(8)   Any two or more persons acting together to secure or exercise control of, or to acquire a holding in a company are treated in relation to that company as connected with one another. They are also treated as connected with any person acting on the direction of any of them to secure or exercise control of a company or to acquire a holding in the company.

The question of when persons act together to control a company was considered in the UK case of Steele v European Vinyls Holdings BV. In that case it was held that the fact that shareholders vote together in support of a proposal does not mean that they are acting together to control the company if their actions were not predetermined by an agreement - eg. a shareholders agreement. Thus, the fact that a company owned 50/50 by two shareholders can do little of importance without their joint consent (in practice) does not mean that the two shareholders act together to control to control the company where each of them is free decide his approach to issues as they arise.

16.4.5   Meaning of Control

Control, for the purposes of the CGT Acts, takes the meaning assigned to it by s432 (previously s.102 CTA 1976), the relevant part of which is reproduced below:

(2)   *"For the purposes of this Part a person shall be taken to have control of a company if such a person exercises, or is able to exercise or is entitled to acquire, control, whether direct or indirect, over the company's affairs, and in particular, but without prejudice to the generality of the preceding words, if such a person possesses or is entitled to acquire*

s432   (a)   *the greater part of the share capital or issued share capital of the company or of the voting power in the company; or*

(b)   *such part of the issued share capital of the company as would, if the whole of the income of the company were in fact distributed among the participators (without regard to any rights which he or any other person has as a loan creditor), entitle such a person to receive the greater part of the amount so distributed; or*

(c)   *such rights as would, in the event of the winding up of the company or in any circumstances, entitle such a person to receive the greater part of the assets of the company which would then be available for distribution among the participators.*

(3)   *Where two or more persons together satisfy any of the conditions of subsection (2), they shall be taken to have control of the company.*

(4)   For the purposes of subsection (2) a person shall be treated as entitled to acquire anything which such a person is entitled to acquire at a future date, or will at a future date be entitled to acquire.

(5)   For the purposes of subsections (2) and (3), there shall be attributed to any person any rights or powers of a nominee for such a person, that is to say, any rights or powers which another person possesses on such a person's behalf or may be required to exercise on such person's direction or behalf.

(6)   For the purposes of subsections (2) and (3), there may also be attributed to any person all the rights and powers of any company of which such person has, or such person and associates of such person have, control or any two or more such companies, or of any associate of such person or of any two or more associates of such person, including those attributed to a company or associate under subsection (5), but not those attributed to an associate under this subsection; and such attributions shall be made under this subsection as will result in the company being treated as under the control of five or fewer participators if it can be so treated.

The definition in s432 of "control" is discussed in paragraph 67.2.1 in the context of non-resident companies.

16.4.6   Disposals in a series of transaction

s550   In certain circumstances a number of individual assets, when valued together as a unit, would have a greater value than the total of the values attributable to the individual assets. In such a case, s550 provides that the greater value will apply to transfers of such assets between *connected persons*. The meaning of "connected persons" is dealt with in paragraph 16.4.4.

Example 97

Jim owns four derelict houses which provide a suitable site for development. The site covered by the four houses is valued at £160,000 whereas the value of each house taken separately would be only £10,000, total £40,000. Jim gifts the houses to his son in four separate transactions.

As market value is to be applied to transactions between connected persons, the market value of £10,000 would under the normal provisions be applied to each transaction. Under the special provisions, mentioned above, the market value relating to each transaction would be

$$160{,}000 \ x \ \frac{10{,}000}{40{,}000} \ = \ £40{,}000$$

The value of the consideration deemed to be received (under the general arm's length rules) will therefore be £40,000 in respect of each disposal and not £10,000.

Had Jim gifted one house each to four sons, notwithstanding that the transactions would be with related parties, s550 would not have application in determining the open market value of each transaction. That is because s550 has application only where one person acquires assets by means of two or more transactions with a connected party. In this instance each of the sons would have acquired only one asset by means of one transaction. The same conclusion would apply if Jim had transferred two of the houses to John, and two of the houses to John's wife. These two transactions would not fall to be aggregated for the purpose of determining the open market value of the houses in respect of each transaction.

S550 applies only to a transaction between connected parties. A transaction between connected parties always has the actual consideration in the transaction disregarded for the purposes of capital gains tax, and open market value (as defined in the Capital Gains Tax Acts) substituted. Therefore s550 always has potential application to a transaction between connected parties.

The provisions as set out in s550 are as follows:

"Where a person is given or acquires from one or more persons with whom he is connected, by way of two or more transactions, assets of which the aggregate market value, when considered separately in relation to the separate other transactions, is less than the aggregate market value of those assets when considered together, then for the purposes of the Capital Gains Tax Acts the market value of the assets where relevant, shall be taken to be the larger market value and that value shall be apportioned rateably to the respective disposals".

s550   S550 appears to be deficient in that it does not specify which market value is to be used in calculating tax on the respective disposals.

Example 98

George owned a pair of antique pistols. On 30 June 1989, he gave one of the guns valued at £5,000 to his son; the market value of the pair on that date was £15,000. On 31 March 1999 he gave his son the remaining gun, then valued at £7,500. The pair had a value of £25,000 at that time.

In calculating the chargeable gain, the question arises as to which market value would be apportioned to the respective disposals. If the March 1999 market value of £25,000 was apportioned between the disposals, the 1989 disposal will be deemed to have been for a consideration of £15,000. This would be a most unfair result as the figure of £15,000 is far in excess of the highest possible value attributable to the asset at that time. Similarly, it would not seem correct to apportion the 1989 Market Value to the disposals.

It is suggested that the best way of dealing with the matter would be to regard the 1989 disposal as being half the Market Value of the pair at that time i.e. £7,500, similar treatment applied to the 1999 disposal giving rise to a deemed consideration of £12,500.

However, the position is not entirely clear.

It might further be argued from the wording of s550 that the market value, computed on this peculiar basis, can be attributed to an asset only on the occasion of the second or later acquisition or disposal with a connected person. The particular definition of market value applies where a person is given or acquires from one or more persons with whom he is connected, by way of two or more transactions, certain assets. On the occasion of the receipt of the first asset in such series, he would not be a person who has acquired (or disposed of if that is relevant) assets by way of two or more transactions. It may be argued therefore that the section can have no application to the first transaction and that the words used are not sufficiently clear and mandatory to require that the computation in relation to that first transaction should be reopened, possibly in a subsequent tax year, when a second or later transaction occurs. As the matter has not been considered by the Irish courts, such an argument can only be speculative.

Anti avoidance legislation relating to the splitting of sets of items is also to be found in s602. This is discussed in paragraph 23.3.

17   OPEN MARKET VALUE

17.1   Broad Outline

s548(1)   In broad terms, open market value means *"the price which those assets might reasonably be expected to fetch on a sale in the open market"*.

s548(2)   In arriving at the open market value, it is not permitted to take into account any reduction in value which would result from the placing of all the assets on the market at the same time.

References in the legislation to market value are references to ***"open market value"*** However, a reference to "value" in an unqualified manner is not necessarily a reference to open market value.

In the case of J. McMahon (Inspector of Taxes) v Albert Noel Murphy, Justice Lynch in the High Court on 25 November 1988 held that in arriving at the market value of land regard should be had to all reasonable potential uses to which the land could be put. Attention should not be confined, in the valuation exercise, to one use only, such as the use in which it was then employed. The case concerned land which at 5 April 1974 was in agricultural use, and was close to a town in which little development had taken place. The Revenue Valuation Office were of the opinion that no developer was in the market at that date for land in the area. The taxpayer would not have sold the land at that date for agricultural value and had in mind the possibility that it would one day be developed. The judge ruled that agricultural value was not the appropriate value and that regard should be had to other potential uses of the land, in arriving at a decision as to its value.

17.2 Unquoted Shares

s548(4)

In the case of unquoted shares, the open market price is to be estimated on the basis that there is available to any prospective purchaser, all the information which a prudent prospective purchaser of the asset might reasonably require if he was buying the shares from a willing seller by private treaty at arm's length.

17.3 Exchange Control

CGTA 1975 s49(7) provided that where an asset was subject to exchange control restrictions (under the Exchange Control Act 1954) to such an extent that part of the price paid by the purchaser cannot be retained by the seller, the market value was to be adjusted having regard to the difference between the amount payable by the purchaser and the amount receivable by the seller.

This provision was no longer relevant due to the abolition of Irish Exchange Control and was repealed by FA 1997 prior to the 1997 consolidation of the CGT legislation.

17.4 Quoted Shares

The rules for ascertaining the market value of quoted shares are quite detailed. They are as follows:-

s548(3)(a)

Shares listed in the stock exchange official list - Irish

(i) The last price at which bargains were recorded

or

(ii) Where normal (not special) bargains were recorded at the relevant date, the price at which those bargains were recorded. If more than one price was recorded take the price halfway between the highest and lowest of the two prices.

The lowest price under (i) or (ii) is taken as the open market value of the shares.

s548(3)(b)

Shares listed in the stock exchange daily official list:

(i) Take the lower of the two prices shown for the relevant date plus one-quarter of the difference between the two figures.

or

(ii) Where normal (not special) bargains were recorded in that list for the relevant date you use the price at which the bargains were actually recorded. If more than one such price was recorded you take a price halfway between the highest and lowest.

The open market price used for CGT purposes is the lower of the prices resulting either (i) or (ii) above. Where share are listed on both the Stock Exchange Official List - Irish; and the Stock Exchange Daily Official List, the lower of the two valuation figures is to be taken.

These rules do not apply to shares where some other Stock Exchange affords a more active market.

If the Stock Exchange concerned, or one of the Stock Exchanges concerned is closed on the relevant date, you ascertain the market value by reference to either the "latest previous date", or "earliest subsequent date" on which it is open, whichever gives the lowest value.

None of these rules relating to quoted shares apply where as a result of special circumstances, the prices quoted are, by themselves, not a proper measure of the market value. It was established in the UK case of Hinchcliffe v Crabtree, that the fact that the directors of a company had information which would affect the quoted prices of the shares if that information was also available to the Stock Exchange, is not a "special circumstance".

- **Revenue/Chief Inspector's CGT Manual :**

— The CGT manual at 19.2.8.5 states that the Valuation Office gives priority to valuation cases where there is a non-resident vendor and instructs Inspectors to mark such referrals as "Urgent - non-resident case".

— The manual states that Inspectors have authority to settle land valuation cases on their own authority, but requires unquoted share valuation cases to be referred to head office. Inspectors are also instructed to always retain the 1973/74 accounts, which should never be destroyed.

17.5   Unit Trusts

s548(5)   In the case of a unit trust the value taken is the lower of the buying and selling prices published on the relevant date, or on the latest date prior to that date if no prices are published on the relevant date.

17.6   Appeals

s548(6)   An appeal against the value of shares or securities, other than quoted shares or securities, is to be determined in the same manner as an appeal against an assessment (see paragraph 92).

18   DISPOSALS TO OR FROM TRADING STOCK

18.1   Appropriation to trading stock

s596   A chargeable gain or allowable loss may arise if a person appropriates a capital asset to be trading stock of a trade carried on by him. The asset "appropriated" is deemed for CGT purposes to be disposed of at its market value at the time of appropriation.

Example 99 – *Appropriation to Trading Stock*

> *Maeve runs an antique and fine art shop. In June 1993 she bought a painting for her personal collection; it cost £3,500. In March 1998 she decided to put it into her shop stock for sale; at that date its market value was £4,250.*
>
> *Maeve is deemed to have sold the painting at its market value in March 1998. The gain is as follows:*

	£
MV March 1998	*4,250*
Cost £3,500 indexed @ 1.081	*3,783*
Gain	*467*

> *If the market value of the painting in March 1998 was £3,250, Maeve would have an allowable loss of £250.*
>
> *The painting would be brought into trading stock for income tax purposes at its market value at the date of appropriation as stock in trade.*
>
> *Instead of paying tax on the gain the taxpayer may elect to deduct the gain from the market value in arriving at the value of the stock to be brought in for income tax purposes. In the above example, Maeve could elect to have the gain of £467 deducted from the market value of £4,250. In this case the amount brought into stock for income tax purposes is £3,783 (£4,250-£467). If there had been an allowable loss of £250 she could have brought the painting into stock for income tax at a value of £4,500 (£4,250+£250) up to 29 May 1990. An election is not permitted where an appropriation after that date would give rise to an allowable loss.*
>
> *Had the painting being retained in the private collection for more than a year, indexation would have been available on the occasion of the deemed disposal on appropriation to trading stock. The chargeable gain would have been correspondingly reduced by the amount of the indexation. If the amount of the indexation were (say) £200, the chargeable gain on the tax above would have been £550. The "cost price" of the picture for the purpose of computing income tax on a subsequent disposal, where Maeve elects to have the gain deducted from the income tax cost, would be £3,700. In effect, the amount of the indexation was not subjected to income tax, just as it would not have been subjected to capital gains tax.*

The UK Special Commissioners, in the case of N Ltd. v Inspector of Taxes considered a case in which a taxpayer group transferred shares in a subsidiary to a newly incorporated subsidiary. The newly incorporated subsidiary was alleged to have commenced a trade in securities, and claimed to appropriate its newly acquired shares in the fellow subsidiary, to trading stock. The case largely turned on findings of fact that the newly created subsidiary was not carrying on a trade and that accordingly the alleged appropriation to trading stock did not occur. The case considered whether the existence of tax avoidance motives indicated that a trade did not exist.

It should be noted that the treatment outlined in s596 on the appropriation of an asset to trading stock applies only where the taxpayer carried on a trade. In some instances it may be relevant to consider whether a trade has commenced at the time of the alleged appropriation. The rules determining when a trade commences are discussed in the companion volume "Income Tax" by McAteer & Reddin, published by the Institute of Taxation in Ireland. Having regard to the definition of "trading stock" (see paragraph 80.2) which refers to "property such as is sold in the ordinary course of the trade" would seem that "trading stock" can only exist for capital gains tax purposes in the context of a trade which has already commenced. If that is so, then the appropriation of an asset to trading stock cannot occur prior to the commencement of the trade.

As is indicated in paragraph 80.2, even if a company is carrying on a trade and determines to appropriate an asset to be trading stock of that trade, such a formal decision by the company may be insufficient to constitute appropriation to trading stock if, having regard to all of the circumstances, the asset thereafter does not constitute trading stock of the trade. The UK Nova Securities case discussed in paragraph 80.2 further illustrates this point.

From the 1 January 2000 a corporation tax rate of 25% will apply to income arising from a trade of dealing in land. In many cases land which is dealt in is development land. The contrast between the 40% Capital Gains Tax rate which may apply to some development land currently (and the 60% rate which may apply from 2002 onwards) is likely to focus attention on the issue of whether or not a company holding development land does so as a trading asset, or as a capital asset. Where a company is able to successfully demonstrate that it held the land as a trading asset at the date on which it disposed of it, it may thereby qualify for the 25% rate of corporation tax. However, in order to ensure that the entire gain is subject to that rate, and no part of it is subject to the 40% rate which might otherwise apply, it would be necessary also to demonstrate that the land had been trading stock when originally acquired by the company. If that were not the case, and the land were appropriated to trading stock at a date after its acquisition, the deemed disposal at the date as outlined above would occur.

18.2   Appropriation from Trading Stock

If a person appropriates an asset from his trade (or retains it on cessation of the trade for non trade purposes) he is deemed to have acquired it at the amount brought into the accounts of the trade for income tax (or corporation tax) purposes in respect of the asset.

The value at which items are to be taken into the accounts (computation of profits for income tax purposes) was considered by the UK Courts in the case of Sharkey v Werner. The decision in that case is not normally followed in practice by the Irish Revenue, who will normally treat the asset as being appropriated from stock at cost for income tax purposes. Similar treatment should follow for CGT purposes. The Irish High Court decision in the Belville Holdings Ltd case may cast some doubt on this position.

18.3 Application to Members of a Group

The application of these rules to the transfer of assets between companies which are members of a group for CGT purposes, is set out in paragraph 80.

18.4 Meaning of trading stock

The meaning of trading stock for the purposes of CGT is considered in paragraphs 80.2 and 80.3.

19   ANNUAL £1,000 ALLOWANCE TO INDIVIDUALS

19.1   Broad Outline

s601(1),(2)   Individuals only are entitled to an annual exemption of £1,000. If the chargeable gains do not exceed £1,000 in a year of assessment no tax is chargeable. If the gains of the year exceed £1,000, only the excess is chargeable.

The exemption relates to the amount of the gain, and not the amount of the consideration for the disposal.

If an individual has no gains in a year of assessment, he cannot carry the benefit of the exemption forward. Effectively, it is lost.

s568   The exemption is confined to individuals. Companies, trustees, etc. cannot claim this allowance. Although trustees, personal representatives, etc. may be individuals, they are deemed not be individuals in their representative capacity.

For 1981/82 and previous years the exemption was £500, and for 1982/83 to 1991/92 (incl.) the annual exemption was £2,000 for each individual.

19.2   Married Persons

s1028   Only one £500 exemption was available to a married couple up to and including the year 1979/80. In a case where 'separate assessment' was claimed for CGT the £500 exemption for the year of assessment (up to and including 1979/80) had to be apportioned to each spouse in proportion to the 'chargeable gains' of each spouse in that year.

For 1980/81 and subsequent years each spouse has a separate entitlement to the annual exemption (1993/94 and later years £1,000 each).

Prior to 1998/99, in certain circumstances any unused part of the annual exemption of one spouse could be used in that year by the other spouse, in addition to that person's own annual exemption. The circumstances in which the surplus exemption of one spouse could be used by the other are set out in paragraph 33.6.2.

This facility to transfer all or part of the allowance between spouses *does not apply* for 1998/99 or later years of assessment.

19.3   **Death**

s601(4)   Where an individual dies during a year of assessment, the annual exemption can be claimed by his personal representatives against gains arising to the deceased person in that year of assessment, up to the date of death.

19.4   **Claim for Retirement Relief**

s601(5)   The annual exemption cannot be claimed for any year of assessment in which relief is also claimed by that individual in respect of the "sale of a business on retirement". (See paragraph 30).

Denial of relief in this case is only in relation to the individual who claims retirement relief. Where that individual is a married person, this claim for retirement relief does not debar his spouse from claiming the annual exemption in relation to any disposals by the spouse (assuming the spouse also did not claim retirement relief in that year).

Example 100

Mike disposes of property in relation to which he is entitled to claim (and does claim) retirement relief in the year ended 5 April 1999. In the same year, Mike and his spouse, Mary, dispose of quoted shares held jointly by them, in relation to which a chargeable gain of £3,000 arises to each of them. Mike is not able to claim his annual exemption of £1,000 in relation to the disposal of his interest in the quoted shares. This is by reason of his having claimed retirement relief in the same year. However Mary is entitled to claim the annual exemption in relation to the chargeable gain accruing to her.

If, in the example above, the shares had belonged entirely to Mike at the time when he was contemplating disposal, it would seem that he might have been able to firstly dispose of them to his wife (whether by gift or sale), thus permitting his wife to dispose of them on the open market and avail of the annual exemption.

19.5   **Different Rates of Tax**

s601(3)   As in the case of losses, the annual exemption applies first to gains chargeable at the highest rate of CGT for the year, any unused balance being set against gains chargeable at the next lower rate, and so on.

Example 101

Bill has chargeable gains in 1998/99 (before set off of his £1,000 annual allowance :

£800 gain	*liable*	*@ 40%*
£1,400 gain	*liable*	*@ 20%*

His £1,000 allowance is set first against the £800 gain, and the unused balance of £200 is set against the £1,400 gain. If Bill was married, his wife's separate £1,000 allowance could only be set against her own gains - if she had any in that tax year. If she had none, her separate £1,000 allowance is lost.

20   LOSSES

20.1   Broad Outline

s546(2)

A loss is calculated in the same manner as a gain. The same rules apply as to the consideration chargeable and the expenditure allowable. However, Indexation cannot either create or increase a loss.

Example 102

John acquired quoted shares for a cost of £5,000. He disposed of them for a consideration of £6,000. Indexation of the cost of acquisition between the date of acquisition and the date of disposal amounted to £2,000. The computation is as follows:

Acquisition cost	£5,000
Indexation	£2,000
Deductible cost	£7,000
Consideration for sale	£6,000
Loss	£1,000

This is not an allowable loss because it arises entirely due to indexation. The sales proceeds of £6,000 exceeded the acquisition cost of £5,000, so there was in fact a gain but for indexation. The indexation is allowed to eliminate the gain but it cannot create a loss. Accordingly the disposal gives rise to neither a chargeable gain nor an allowable loss.

20.2   Non Allowable Losses

s546(3)

If a gain on the disposal of an asset would not be chargeable, then a loss arising on the disposal of that asset is not allowable.

Example 103

Pierre disposed of quoted shares on the Paris Bourse in 1996, at a time when he was not resident or ordinarily resident in Ireland. In 1998/99 he became resident and domiciled in Ireland and realised a chargeable gain on the disposal of further shares on the Paris Bourse.

Pierre is not entitled to relief against his 1998/99 chargeable gains for the losses incurred in 1996. The transaction in 1996, had it yielded a gain rather than a loss, would not have given rise to a chargeable gain since Pierre was not at the time within the Irish capital gains tax territorial scope. The same principle would apply to losses arising to a non-resident company in relation to assets which are not specified Irish assets (see paragraph 3.4.2), should the company subsequently have chargeable gains after it becomes resident in Ireland (see paragraph 20.10).

s546(4);
s29(4)(c)

In addition, where the person making the disposal is an individual, and is not domiciled in Ireland, any losses accruing to him on the disposal of assets situated outside Ireland and outside the UK are not allowable losses for CGT purposes whether the proceeds of sale are remitted into Ireland or not (see paragraph 3.3).

Example 104

John is resident and ordinarily resident but not domiciled in Ireland. He has a loss on the disposal of property in France.

No relief can be claimed in Ireland, as a gain (if one arose) would have been chargeable on a remittance basis.

Example 105

Bill is resident but not domiciled in Ireland. He has a loss on the disposal of Irish land.

The loss is allowable, as a gain (if one arose) would have been chargeable in Ireland.

A special treatment applies to losses arising on the disposal of non wasting tangible moveable property. This is described in paragraph 23.4.

The exemption in respect of wasting chattels is described in paragraph 22. To the extent that such chattels are exempt, losses arising on them are not allowable losses.

20.3   Use of Losses

s31

As a general rule, tax is chargeable on the total gains of the year, after deducting allowable current year's losses, and losses forward from earlier years. Unused losses are carried forward to be set off in the next earliest possible year against net gains of that year. In any year, losses may be set against gains liable at the highest rate of tax.

s546(6)

TCA97 s546(6) provides that -

"For the purposes of section 31, where, on the assumption that there were no allowable losses to be deducted under that subsection, a person would be chargeable under the CGT Acts at more than one rate of tax for a year of assessment, any allowable losses falling to be deducted under that subsection shall be deducted:-

(a)   if the person should be so chargeable at two different rates, from the chargeable gains which would be so chargeable at the highest of those rates and, so far as they cannot be so deducted, from the chargeable

gains which would be so chargeable at the next highest of those rates, and so on.

(b) if the person would be so chargeable at three or more rates, from the chargeable gains which would be so chargeable at the highest of those rates and, so far as they cannot be so deducted, from the chargeable gains which would be so chargeable at the next highest of those rates, and so on".

s546(5)   Except in the case of a CGT loss arising to an individual in the year of his death (see paragraph 66) relief by way of set off of a loss against chargeable gains cannot be given for a year of assessment earlier that the year of assessment in which the loss actually arose.

Relief cannot be given more than once for any loss (or part of a loss).

There are a number of restrictions on the set off of losses, and those restrictions are referred to later in this paragraph.

20.4   Loss or Destruction of Asset

s538   The entire loss, destruction, dissipation, or extinction of an asset is a disposal of that asset - which may give rise to a loss claim. Similarly, however, a gain may arise if compensation is received (see paragraph 4.5).

20.5   Asset with Negligible Value

s538   Normally only a realised loss is allowable. However, if the inspector is satisfied that the value of an asset has become negligible, he may allow loss relief as if the asset had been sold and reacquired at market value, and the loss in fact realised.

Where an inspector allows the loss relief claim, the loss arises not at the date at which the asset lost its value, but rather at the date on which the claim for the loss relief is made.

This is discussed also in paragraph 4.4.

Example 106

John has disposed of quoted shares in 1997/98, realising a gain of £5000. When he comes to calculate what his preliminary tax payment in respect of Capital Gains Tax will be, which he does in October 1998, he looks about for means of reducing the chargeable gain. John owns shares in a private investment company which was very unsuccessful, and had lost all of its assets in the early 1980's. The company had been kept in existence since then in a dormant way, because it was not worth anybody's bother to wind it up. John requests his inspector of taxes to allow a claim for loss in relation to the shares in the investment company having become of negligible value (he had the base cost in them of £2000) and the inspector agreed, in October 1998.

Notwithstanding that the loss in respect of which the Inspector agreed to permit loss relief had existed in an economic sense since the early 1980s, and therefore existed throughout 1997/98, the strict statutory position is that relief cannot be claimed against the gain which was to be realised in 1997/98, as the loss is deemed to arise for capital gains tax purposes at the date the claim for relief is made ie October 1998. However the published Revenue precedent indicates that the Revenue would in this instance permit the relief to be granted for 1997/98 since the loss had existed in that year and the claim for the loss was made within 12 months from 5 April 1998.

Alternatively, John could have obtained relief by winding-up the private investment company prior to 5 April 1998. Although the Revenue precedent makes no reference to the circumstances, it is likely that the fact that John might subsequently (eg in October 1998) put the company into liquidation would not preclude him from making a negligible value claim and seeking relief in relation to that claim for the year 1997/98. A liquidation in October 1998 would ordinarily crystallise the loss in 1998/99 with no possibility of it being carried backwards. But it would seem that it is open to John to additionally make a negligible value claim and to seek relief on the basis of that negligible value claim in 1997/98, rather than on the basis of the liquidation in 1998/99. The claim on the basis of the negligible value claim is permitted by the Revenue to be carried backwards to a taxable period ending within 12 months from the date of claim.

- **Revenue Commissioners published precedent:**

— In their published precedents the Revenue Commissioners have stated that a claim made within 12 months of the end of a year of assessment or accounting period for which relief is sought will be admitted provided that the asset was of negligible value in the period concerned.

s538(2) — A strict reading of s538(2) would suggest that the date upon which relief is to be given is the date upon which the Inspector agrees to grant the relief. However it appears to be the view of the Revenue Commissioners that the correct statutory position is that the relief is available in the year of claim rather than in the year in which the Inspector arrives at his decision (where it is different). As indicated above, the Revenue Commissioners will permit some degree of retrospection.

FA98 s67 The FA98 introduced some anti avoidance legislation in this area which appeared to be aimed at a situation where a company having assets with uncrystalised capital gains, is struck from the companies register - typically for failure to make returns. In such a case the assets pass to the State. Usually the State does not retain assets in such a case but it seeks to identify the persons who would have been entitled to them on the liquidation of the company, and transfers the assets to them, usually retaining a small part to cover the costs incurred by the State. The State is not obliged to act in that fashion and can in fact retain the assets for the benefit of the State if it so chooses. It is therefore a very dangerous matter for a company to be struck of the share register, while holding assets.

In a situation as outlined above, where the assets pass to the State and are subsequently transferred by the State (at its discretion) to the beneficial owners of the shares in the company, the shareholders would ordinarily have incurred a loss on the disposal of the shares in the company (having received no consideration for the disposal) : and would have an open market value base cost in relation to the assets transferred to it by the State, since it had obtained them otherwise than by way of a bargain made at arms length.

SPA54 s31   The FA98 inserted s538(2A). This subsection defers relief for a loss claimed by virtue of s538 (in respect of the shares in the "struck-off" company) until the assets obtained from the State under the State Property Act 1954 have in turn been disposed of. It also provides that where the assets acquired from the State in this fashion are disposed of piece meal, in a number of tax years, a claim for loss is rateably allowed only as the assets are disposed of in each year.

s538(2A)   Where s538(2A) applies, it is not possible to accelerate the allowance for loss on a negligible value claim by the share holders who receive assets from the state transferring those assets to their spouse, so as to trigger the relief, without also triggering a gain on the disposal of the assets. The assets in such a case are treated as disposed of only when the spouse in turn disposes of them.

s538(2A)
s547   The new anti avoidance legislation is a little anomalous. The purpose of a negligible value claim is to crystallise a loss at a time when an asset has not been disposed of. The new s538(2A) applies only where a body corporate has been dissolved and as a result the company's property passes to the State under the State Property Act, 1954. The dissolution of a company is the occasion of a disposal of the shares in that company. In the ordinary way therefore, there will be no scope to crystallise a gain by way of a negligible value claim in relation to the shares, where the fall in value is in fact caused by the company being deprived of its assets by their passing to the State. The passing of the assets to the State, and the disposal of the shares on the dissolution of the company, would be simultaneous. S538(2A) will therefore seem to apply only to a situation where a negligible value claim has been made by reference to a fall in value which occurred prior to the dissolution of the company, and the companies assets transferred to the State. It seems extraordinary that such an unlikely sequence of events should be the subject matter of special legislation. The new subsection 2A applies only on a waiver by the State of its right to property under the State Properties Act 1954, on or after 12 February 1998. The trigger date is the date on which the State returns the property to the beneficial owner of shares in the company - and not the date of the negligible value claim. The subsection could have application to re-open a loss claim made prior to 12 February 1998. S547 has also been amended in relation to the waiver of the right of the State to the property on or after 12 February 1998 by denying the shareholders an open market value base cost for the assets transferred to them by the State.

The operation of subsection 2A is not illustrated by way of example as there are doubts as to how the subsection can have application in the context of the dissolution of a company, as opposed to in the context of a company with a continuing existence.

s538

Where there is a claim for relief for loss on an asset where the value has become negligible (which in effect gives relief for unrealised losses) *'any permanent or semi-permanent structure in the nature of a building'* may be treated as an asset separate from the land on which it is situated. Where the taxpayer claims relief for the unrealised loss in such circumstances, he is also deemed to have sold any land occupied with the buildings for purposes ancillary to the use of the buildings, at its current market value. This may have the effect of reducing (or eliminating) the loss relief on the 'deemed' disposal of the buildings. In effect, relief is available for the unrealised loss on the buildings to the extent that it exceeds the unrealised profits on the land comprised in the remainder of the asset.

This special treatment in relation to structures is necessary because a structure does not constitute an asset in itself. Rather the only asset is the interest in the land on which the structure is built. It is possible therefore that a building which may have cost a large sum may have become (as a building viewed in isolation) of little or no value. It may have become obsolete or dilapidated. However the building is not an asset, and but for the provision described here which enables it to be treated as if it were an asset in itself, a negligible value claim would not be possible. It is the land on which the structure or building is built that constitutes the asset and it is possible that the land may have retained considerable value notwithstanding that the structure built upon it has become of little or no value. Were it not for the provision described above a negligible value claim would not be possible in such circumstances since the asset, the land, would not have become of negligible value despite the deterioration in value of the building per se.

Example 107

> In 1989 John bought a 100 acre farm for £300,000. In 1990 he obtained planning permission to build a workshop on half an acre of the farm from which he intended to carry on some carpentry business. The building cost £25,000 to build. At the time the half acre site (which would have had an average cost of £1,500), was worth £5,000 by reason of the planning permission. The carpentry business was not successful and ceased after a year. The building was not otherwise used or maintained and by 1999 the roof, doors and windows were substantially rotted and the building was dangerous.
>
> John was advised by a local auctioneer that the site was now worth at least £30,000 as planning permission could be obtained for housing on it. However the structure on the site was in itself worthless and contributed nothing to the value of the site. If anything it was a liability reducing the value of the site. Any purchaser of the site would certainly knock it.

But for subsection 3 of section 538 enabling John to treat the dilapidated building as an asset separate from the half acre site, he would not be able to make a negligible value claim in these circumstances. A half acre site was (presumably) worth £30,000 immediately after the workshop had been completed on it. It was still worth £30,000. However the building, which had cost £25,000 and presumably had a value of approximately £25,000 once built, was now worthless, but was not an asset in itself.

If John makes a claim for negligible value relief in relation to the building, he would receive relief of £25,000, being the difference between the current market value and the base cost (ignoring indexation which cannot create or augment a loss). However he will also have to treat himself as having disposed of the site at its open market value and therefore would recognise a gain on the difference between its current market value of £30,000 and its base cost of £1,500 (together with indexation on that amount). The result of such an election would be that John's base cost in the half acre site would be increased to £30,000 but he might have incurred a small amount of capital gains tax by reason of the difference between the negligible value relief on the building, and the deemed disposal of the underlying site. Why therefore should John have done it? If John is going to dispose of the site anyway, it would be a senseless move. If however John had intended to knock the building before sale, or before redeveloping the site himself, the construction cost, which represents enhancement expenditure on the site, would cease to be available to him in relation to the site since it would no longer be reflected in the state or nature of the site once the building was demolished. A negligible value election and deemed disposal of the underlying site as outlined above would be a means whereby he would be able to "lock in" that original construction cost notwithstanding the intended demolition of the building prior to a disposal to a third party of the site, or an appropriation by him of the site to trading stock of a trade of dealing in and developing land.

- **Revenue/Chief Inspector's CGT Manual :**

— In the Revenue Commissioner's capital gains tax manual they emphasise that not all structures attract the "deemed separate asset" treatment described above. Whereas any building attracts that treatment potentially, a structure attracts it only if it is in the nature of a building. The manual gives the example of a tennis court which is demolished to make way for a swimming pool. Although the tennis court was a structure, it was not a structure in the nature of a building.

- **Revenue/Chief Inspector's CGT Manual:**

— In paragraph 9.1. part 19, Instructions on Taxes Consolidation Act issued to Inspector of Taxes, it is stated that a precise computation of the increase in value of the land will not be required where it is clear that it is not more than 5% of the loss sustained.

A claim to have the land and the building treated as separate assets lies at the taxpayer's discretion. He is not obliged to make such a claim and if he does not, the treatment cannot be imposed by the Revenue.

In the UK case of Williams v Bullivant, it was held that the notional sale and reacquisition could not be regarded as taking place earlier than the date of the relevant claim for negligible value relief. The taxpayer had realised chargeable gains in 1973/74; on 28 February 1974 the value of certain shares held by him became negligible. He lodged the claim on 28 February 1978 seeking to have the notional loss treated as arising in l973/74 and allowable against the gains arising in that year. Vinelott J., reversing the decision of the Commissioners, held that the loss was deemed to arise in 1977/78, the year in which the claim was lodged.

The UK case of Larner v Warrington was decided on a similar point.

20.6   Capital Allowance and Losses

s555   The effect of capital allowances in restricting the allowable expenditure in computing amount of a loss for CGT purposes is set out in paragraph 9.8.

20.7   Connected Persons

s549   Certain restrictions apply in the case of a loss arising on the disposal of an asset to a connected person. The details are set out in paragraph 16.4.

20.8   Development Land

s649   Substantial restrictions were imposed by the FA 1982, on the set-off of losses against post 27 January 1982 development land gains. Details of the restrictions are set out in paragraph 6.5.

20.9   Groups of companies and shares

s621
s622   Anti-avoidance legislation relating to depreciatory transactions and dividend stripping discussed in paragraph 70 may affect the computation of a loss arising on the disposal of shares.

20.10   Corporation tax losses

As explained in paragraph 73.4 the trading losses of a company, or in certain circumstances of other companies in a loss group with that company, may be relieved against a company's capital gains chargeable to corporation tax.

s78   Where capital losses arise on the disposal of assets by a company while it is within the charge to corporation tax, they are taken into account as a deduction in the accounting period in which they arose, or by way of relief against the capital gains of certain later accounting periods.

Example 108

> *Belle Profits SA is a French Yoghurt distributor. In its accounts year ended 30 June 1996 it disposed of its subsidiary, Belle Profits (Germany) GmbH, at a loss of £1 million. In the year ended 30 June 1997, Belle Profits SA was taken over by an Irish food company and thereafter was managed and controlled from Ireland. Its head office in Paris was disposed of at a gain of £5 million, shortly after the transfer of management and control to Ireland.*

> *An accounting period of Belle Profits SA ended on the occasion of it coming within the charge to Irish corporation tax. When the head office was disposed of, it was within the charge to Irish corporation tax. However its previous loss on the disposal of Belle Profits GmbH arose at a time then it was not within the charge to corporation tax, and accordingly cannot be deducted from the gain on the disposal of the head office, for the purpose of computing the corporation tax liability on that gain. Any trading loss arising in the accounting period which commenced on the transfer of management and control to Ireland may be offset against the gain on the disposal of the Paris head office, as may a trading loss in the following accounting period (generally speaking).*

> *This topic is covered in greater detail in paragraph 73.2.*

Capital losses cannot be "group relieved" by being surrendered between group companies in the manner in which trading losses may. Within a group, advantage is taken of capital losses by transferring property pregnant with gains to a group company entitled to losses, prior to the disposal of the property to outside the group. As explained in paragraph 75.5 such an intra group transfer of assets does not trigger a chargeable gain or allowable loss. A company entitled to loss relief may sometimes be acquired by a group in order that it may avail of its tax relief entitlement as explained. The UK case of Bromarin AB and Another vs. IMD Investments Ltd concerned the interpretation of a contract for the sale of such a "loss" company. It would be of interest to anyone negotiating or drafting such a contract, but as it does not concern tax directly, it is not described here.

The FA99 enacted provisions designed to counter the purchase by a group of a company having existing capital losses, or owning an asset on whose disposal capital losses would arise. The mischief that the anti-avoidance legislation is aimed at would be that, following the purchase of such a company, the purchasing group would transfer to the purchased company an asset on whose disposal a gain would crystallise. The purchased company would then dispose of the asset and realise a gain against which it would be entitled to off-set any capital losses it had previously crystallised but for which it had not previously obtained relief. Alternatively, it might, in the same accounting period as that on which it disposed of the asset (which it obtained intra group) at a gain, dispose of assets it had already held at a loss, and avail of relief for that loss. The topic is discussed in greater detail in paragraph 73.3.

21 GAINS AND LOSSES ON DISPOSAL OF CHATTELS

21.1 Chattels - broad outline

Two separate and mutually exclusive reliefs are given in taxing gains arising on the disposal of tangible movable property (chattels).

There is a total exemption for tangible moveable property which is a wasting asset.

There is an exemption for tangible moveable assets which are not wasting, provided the consideration does not exceed £2000. These two exemptions are described in greater detail in paragraphs 22 (wasting chattels) and paragraph 23 (non wasting chattels).

Tangible movable property refers to an asset

— which can be touched (i.e. is tangible) and

— is capable of being moved.

Example 109

John disposes of a painting; quoted shares; and a building.

The painting is capable of being touched i.e. it is tangible. It is also capable of being moved from place to place. It is therefore tangible movable property i.e. a chattel.

The shares represent a bundle of rights. Notwithstanding that ownership of the shares may be indicated by possession of a share certificate (which is tangible and movable) the shares themselves are distinct from the share certificates, and are mere rights. They are not capable of being touched. Equally, they are not capable of being moved as they have no physical existence. They are not tangible movable property.

A building (which in law is represented by ownership of the land on which the building stands) is tangible. You can touch the building, and you can touch the land. But neither the land nor the building is movable. Therefore it is not tangible movable property i.e. it is not a chattel.

21.2 "Wasting Chattels"

s603

Broadly speaking, most wasting chattels are exempt from CGT. This exemption is dealt with in paragraph 22. The relief applies to all tax payers. The meaning of "wasting asset" is described in paragraph 10.

21.3 "Non-Wasting Chattels"

s602

This category would comprise most chattels not classified as "wasting" chattels. In the case of durable (or non-wasting) chattels, the exemption only applies if the sale proceeds do not exceed £2,000, with marginal relief applying to sale proceeds marginally exceeding the £2,000 limit. In addition, this relief only applies to individuals.

Details of this exemption are set out in paragraph 23. The exemption limit relates to the consideration for the disposal, and not to the amount of the chargeable gain.

22 EXEMPTION - WASTING CHATTELS

22.1 Wasting chattels - broad outline

s603

Tangible movable property which is a wasting asset (a wasting chattel) is completely exempt from CGT irrespective of the sale price. The relief applies to all taxpayers, but is subject to special rules for business chattels (see paragraph 22.2 and 23.3).

In any case where a gain is not assessable to CGT a loss is not allowable, and so a loss on the disposal of exempt wasting chattels is not allowable for CGT purposes.

s560

As outlined in paragraph 10, a 'wasting' asset is one which has a predictable useful life of 50 years or less. Plant and Machinery is always a wasting asset (see Paragraph 10.1) regardless of its usefull life.

Examples of wasting chattels would be livestock, bloodstock, yachts, etc. Jewellery and antique furniture, for example, would not normally be wasting chattels, but an antique clock, being machinery, would be a wasting asset. An example of a wasting asset that does not qualify for relief is an option. While it is a wasting asset, it is not tangible movable property (i.e. not a chattel).

The restriction of deductible expenditure in respect of those wasting assets which do not come within the exemption is described in paragraph 10.

22.2 No exemption for "wasting" business chattels

s603(2)

The exemption does not apply to wasting chattels used for the purpose of a trade or profession to the extent that the expenditure qualifies for capital allowances. Neither does the exemption apply to commodity futures.

Although such business chattels are not given the exempt status of other wasting chattels, they are nevertheless wasting chattels. This is important as the relief applicable to non-wasting chattels will not apply to them either (see paragraph 23).

The exclusion from exemption is stated by s603 to apply in two circumstances.

- If throughout the period of ownership of the person making the disposal the asset had been used solely for a trade or profession and the taxpayer could have claimed capital allowances either in

respect of the acquisition cost (s552(1)(a) expenditure) or
enhancement expenditure (s552(1)(b) expenditure). Whether or
not such allowances were claimed does not matter, provided the
person would have been entitled to claim them. The trade or
profession need not be one carried on by the person making the
disposal eg he could have leased it to someone carrying on a trade.

The requirement that the asset had been used solely for the
purpose of a trade or profession throughout the period of
ownership is not strictly applied. Where trade/professional use
has applied for part only of the period of ownership, or where the
trade/professional use was not the sole use, the exclusion of the
exemption is applied in an amended form as explained in
paragraph 22.3.

• The second basis for exclusion is where the person making the
disposal has incurred expenditure on the asset which has qualified
in full for any capital allowance. An example of expenditure on an
asset which will qualify for capital allowance, but which asset may
not have been used by the taxpayer for the purpose of a trade or
for a profession, would be expenditure on the acquisition of an
item of plant or machinery which is let by a non trading lessor to a
trading lessee. In such a case the lessor, (provided he bears the
burden of wear and tear) would be entitled to capital allowances
in respect of the expenditure notwithstanding that the leasing
transaction did not occur in the course of any trade carried on by
him.

The UK case of Burman (Inspector of Taxes) -v- Westminster Press
Limited concerned the entitlement of the taxpayer to the exemption
in relation to an item of plant on which capital allowances were
granted for expenditure incurred on provision of the plant.
However, a number of years later, the plant was sold at a gain
without having been brought into use by the taxpayer company. On
the sale of the plant, the relevant allowances were withdrawn. It was
held that, in fact, the exemption was available. However, the
decision seemed to turn on the fact that, under the U.K. legislation in
force at the material time, the recapture of the particular allowances
granted was achieved by the withdrawal of the allowances as if no
entitlement existed in the first place and not by a compensatory
balancing charge. Thus, at the time of the disposal, the plant did not
qualify for capital allowances. The decision may not have application
in Ireland where recapture of allowances is by way of balancing
charge.

22.3   **Wasting chattels - part business use**

s603(3)   If a wasting chattel is used partly for a trade or profession, and
partly for other purposes, (or has otherwise qualified only in part for

capital allowances) the gain is apportioned and the 'qualifying part' is chargeable while the 'non-qualifying part' is treated as an exempt wasting chattel.

This apportionment treatment can apply either because the wasting chattel was partly used for private purposes (see example 97 below) or because it was not used for trade/professional purposes throughout the period of ownership. An example of the latter circumstance would be where a car was in business use by a doctor for some years up to the point at which he retired from the profession, after which it was in use solely for private purposes for another period of time and was then disposed of. In this circumstance the apportionment carried out is not a time apportionment (as might be expected) but rather is on the same basis as where there is mixed private and business use ie an apportionment in the ratio to extent to which expenditure attracted capital allowances, and to which it did not.

Example 110

If a car cost £3,000 and was used 50% for business and 50% for private purposes, capital allowances would effectively have been allowed on 50% of the cost.

The part qualifying for capital allowances is not exempt. The other 50% qualifies for the exemption and, therefore half of any gain arising on the disposal would be exempt from CGT.

Example 111

On 30 June, 1997, Paddy paid £1,000 for a new machine to be used in his manufacturing business. In calculating his income tax liability based on the year ended 31 December 1997 he claimed capital allowances of £150 on the machine. On 1 May 1998, he sold the machine for £1,250. The machine has a predictable life of ten years.

As the asset is used wholly for business purposes and attracts capital allowances, the wasting chattel exemption does not apply, and the allowable cost will not be 'wasted' in calculating a gain (see paragraph 10.3). As the asset is a 'wasting' chattel, the £2,000 exemption for durable chattels does not apply (see paragraph 23). The gain is calculated as follows:

Sale proceeds		*£1,250*
Cost	*£1,000*	
Less Allowed for Income Tax	*£ Nil (see note)*	*£1,000*
Chargeable Gain		*£250*

Note: The £150 capital allowances are ignored in calculating the gain. If a loss arose, it would be deducted in calculating that loss (see paragraph 9.8).

Example 112

Jack paid £800 for a second-hand lathe on 30 June 1996 for use in his furniture manufacturing business. In his tax computations based on the year ended 31 December 1997 he claimed capital allowances at 15%. On 1 January 1998 he sold the lathe for £750. The machine had a predictable life of ten years.

Sale proceeds			£750
Cost-£800 less allowances (net) £50			£750
Loss			£NIL
Note (1)	Capital Allowances claimed	800@ 15% =	£120
	WDV of asset	680	
	Sale proceeds	750	
	B/C		£(70)
	Net allowance		£50

Note (2)   As set out in paragraph 9.8, capital allowances are taken into account only to reduce a loss.

Example 113 (Asset Partly Qualifying for Relief)

Dr. Bill purchased a new Rolls Royce car for use in his practice at a cost of £70,000 on 1 January 1996

His accounts are made up to 31 December each year. For 1996/97 and 1997/98 he claimed wear and tear at 20% on the motor car. The Inspector agreed that the car is used one half for private purposes. At the date of purchase (1/1/96) the maximum qualifying cost for capital allowances purposes was £14,000

On 1 December 1998 he sold the car for £84,000. The car had a predictable useful life of 40 years.

What (if any) is his chargeable gain?

To the extent that the asset qualifies for capital allowances, it does not qualify for the wasting assets exemption. In normal circumstances the allowances will only be granted on £14,000 expenditure (under income tax rules then applying). Because of the 50% private use, the capital allowances are only effectively granted on £7,000. The balance of £63,000 is treated for Capital Gains Tax purposes as if it represented expenditure on a separate asset. The gain referable to that amount of expenditure qualifies for the relief.

The gain referable to the expenditure attracting capital allowances is not exempt from Capital Gains Tax.

The sale price of £84,000 must be apportioned between the expenditure qualifying for capital allowances and the expenditure not qualifying. To the extent it qualifies for capital allowances, it is treated in effect as a separate asset, to which the wasting chattel rules do not apply - i.e.

$$\frac{7,000}{70,000} \quad x \quad £84,000 \quad = £8,400$$

The balance, i.e.. £69,300 (77,000-7,700) is the proportion of the sale proceeds relating to the sale of the wasting chattel qualifying for relief in full.

The related expenditure (i.e. £7,700) qualified for capital allowances. The full cost of £7,700 is therefore allowable and must be indexed up.

	£
i.e. £7,700 x 1.054	8,116
Sale proceeds	8,400
GAIN	284

23   £2,000 EXEMPTION - NON-WASTING CHATTELS

23.1   Broad Outline

s602

A gain arising to an individual on the disposal of non-wasting tangible movable property (chattels) is exempt from CGT provided the sale proceeds do not exceed £2,000. The amount of the GAIN is not relevant in deciding whether the exemption applies. This exemption does not apply to a wasting asset - such an asset is either exempt under the wasting chattel provisions, or is chargeable under the normal rules. Examples of durable chattels would be jewellery, silverware, antique furniture, paintings, etc.

The relief is not limited by the number of durable chattels sold in each year. The exemption is given for each separate asset provided the sale price of that particular asset does not exceed £2,000.

If, for example, an individual sells 25 separate non-wasting chattels in the same year of assessment, any sold for £2,000 or less are exempt from CGT. Special rules apply in the case of a part disposal of such chattels, and the sale of parts of a 'set' (see paragraph 23.3).

This relief should not be confused with the annual allowance (currently £1,000 for an individual). That allowance is dealt with in paragraph 19.2.

23.2   Marginal Relief

s602(3)

Marginal relief is available if the sale price exceeds £2,000. The CGT payable cannot exceed half of the excess of the sale price over £2,000. In arriving at the CGT payable on the disposal, the annual allowance is set against any other gains first and only any unused balance of it is set against the gain on the chattel for the purpose of determining whether or not marginal relief applies.

Example 114

John is married. He purchased an antique silver tray for £600 in August 1996 and sold it in July 1997 for £2,200. He had other gains in 1997/98 of £1,500. His wife had no gains chargeable for this year.

	£
Sale proceeds (silver tray)	2,200
Cost	600
Gain	1,600
Annual Exemption (2,000-1,500)*	500
Chargeable gain	1,100

Tax 40% = £440 (before marginal relief).

* In 1998/99 and later years the annual exemption will be limited to a total of £1,000 for any individual - any unused balance of the annual allowance of the spouse of an individual can no longer be set against gains of the other spouse.

Calculation of Marginal Relief:

The amount of CGT payable on the disposal of the silver tray, setting off allowances and losses forward, etc. (insofar as possible against other gains of the year) is £440.

CGT payable on the disposal of this asset is reduced to 1/2 of the excess of the sale proceeds over £2,000, i.e. CGT payable is reduced to (£2,200-£2,000) x ½ = £100. The overall affect of the relief is to leave Bill with a CGT bill amounting in total to £100 for the year.

As in the case of the wasting chattel exemption, special rules apply in calculating the marginal relief in the case of a part disposal (see paragraph 23.5)

23.3   **Sets of Chattels**

s602(5)   Where several assets have formed part of a set, and were all owned at one time by one person and are disposed of by that person (whether or not at different times) the individual disposals will in certain circumstances all be grouped together as one single transaction for the purpose of applying the exemption applicable to non wasting chattels.

This provision only applies where the assets (or some of them) comprised in the set are disposed of by the owner of the set:

• to the same person

   or

• to persons acting in concert

   or

• to persons who are 'connected' (see paragraph 16.4).

In any other circumstances, each part of the set disposed of is treated as a separate asset for the purposes of this exemption. The Act does not define the term 'set', and so it must be given its ordinary meaning. In general it would comprise more than two items. Two similar items would more properly be described as a "pair".

- **Revenue/ Chief Inspector's CGT Manual**

  — In the Revenue Commissioners capital gains tax manual at Paragraph 19.7.2.7 it is stated: *"A practical approach is to say that broadly, a group of articles form a "set" if they are (a) essentially similar and complementary, and (b) their value as a whole is greater than the sum of the values of the parts."*

  The manual goes on to give as examples of items which do not constitute "sets":

  A collection of coins is not normally a set but all values minted in one year will usually form a set. Presumably the thinking is that a collection of coins will usually not have a value greater than the sum of the value of the individual coins whereas a collection of coins on a "theme" will be worth more as a group, than the sum of their separate values.

  A collection of stamps is not normally a set even if all on one theme but all the values of a commemorative issue or a definitive issue of one country will normally constitute a set.

  Provisions also exist treating certain disposals of assets to connected persons as if the separate sales were all parts of a set for the purposes of determining open market value- see paragraph 16.4.6.

23.4   Losses

s602(4)   As gains on such durable chattels are exempt from CGT where the sale price does not exceed £2,000, it is only reasonable to assume that some restriction will be made on relief for losses incurred on the sale of such assets. The Act provides that in calculating the allowable loss, the sale proceeds, if less than £2,000, are to be taken as £2,000 for the purposes of computing the loss. In consequence, a durable chattel with a base cost of less than £2,000 cannot generate an allowable loss.

Example 115

> *Fred owns a silver tray which he purchased for £2,100 in June 1997. He sold it for £1,600 in March 1998.*

The allowable loss is calculated as follows:	*IR£*
Cost	2,100
Deemed Sale Price	2,000
Allowable Loss	100

23.5   Part Disposal of Qualifying Chattel

Special provisions apply where the disposal is of a right or interest in or over the chattel.

s602(6)   In applying the exemption, marginal relief, and the rules for restricting losses, the consideration is to be taken as including both the actual consideration for the part disposal and the value of the interest retained.

Where the total of the actual consideration plus the value of the interest retained does not exceed £2,000 the relief applies in full to the part disposal (i.e. it is exempt). Where the aggregate of the consideration and the value retained exceeds £2,000, the maximum tax payable (marginal relief) is calculated as follows:-

[(Consideration for Disposal + Value Retained) - £2,000] x

$$\frac{1}{2} \times \frac{\text{Consideration}}{\text{Consideration + Value Retained}}$$

Example 116

	£
Assumed - Proceeds of Part Disposal	*800*
Assumed - Value of Interest Retained	*1,400*
Aggregate	*2,200*

Taking the above figures as the relevant figures in the case of a part disposal of a non-wasting chattel, the marginal relief is calculated as follows:

$$(£2,200 - £2,000) \quad x \quad \tfrac{1}{2} \ x \quad \frac{£800}{£2,200} \quad = £36$$

The Tax payable on the part disposal cannot exceed £36.

Where the aggregate of the consideration and the value retained is less than £2,000 and a loss results from the transaction, the loss is restricted. The consideration is deemed to be the actual consideration plus a fraction of the difference between the aggregate of the actual consideration plus the value retained and £2,000. The fraction to be taken into account is the actual consideration divided by the aggregate of the consideration plus the value retained.

Example 117

	£
Proceeds of Part Disposal	*800*
Value of Interest Retained	*1,000*
Aggregate	*1,800*

The consideration for the purposes of calculating the CGT loss is deemed to be:

$$£800 + (\ £200 \ x \ \frac{£800}{£1,800} \ ) \quad = £889$$

23.6   **Exceptions**

s602(7)   This £2,000 exemption and the related marginal relief *do not apply* to gains arising on the disposal of:

- wasting assets
- currency of any description
- commodity futures

24   **PRINCIPAL PRIVATE RESIDENCE**

24.1   **Broad Outline**

CGT exemption exists in relation to a gain arising on the disposal of a principal private residence.

In paragraph 24.2 the question of what constitutes a residence is discussed.

In paragraph 24.3, the question of whether a residence can extend to more than one building is considered.

The extent of the exemption depends on the period for which the building has been occupied as a principal private residence, during the period of ownership. In paragraph 24.4 "period of ownership" and "period of occupation" are considered.

The exemption may be lost in whole or in part where a building is used exclusively for trade or professional purposes. This is considered in paragraph 24.5.

A person may not have more than one principal private residence at any one time. This is discussed in paragraph 24.7, and its application to a married couple is discussed in paragraph 24.8.

The relief is available in relation to property held in trust, where it is occupied as a principal private residence by a life tenant. This is described in paragraph 24.9.

The relief is not available in respect of a house purchased wholly or mainly for the purpose of making a gain on its disposal. This is described in paragraph 24.10.

Relief can extend to a property occupied by the taxpayer's dependent relative. This is described in paragraph 24.11.

The relief is restricted if the house constitutes development land. The restriction is described in paragraph 24.12.

The application of the relief to a foreign building is discussed in paragraph 24.13.

The interaction of the relief with CPO relief is discussed in paragraph 27.3.

24.2   **What is a "principal private residence"**

s604   An individual's principal private residence, together with land occupied as its garden or grounds up to a maximum of one acre *(exclusive of the site of the house)* is exempt from CGT if disposed of by the individual who has used it as his principal private residence throughout his period of ownership.

A principal private residence does not necessarily consist of 'bricks and mortar'. In the UK case of Makins v Elson it was decided that a caravan, which was jacked up on bricks, and complete with all the normal services including water, electricity, telephone, etc. (together with the appropriate land not exceeding 1 acre) was a principal private residence for the purposes of the relief.

Another UK case involving a *caravan* was Moore v Thompsom. In that case it was held by the Commissioners on the facts, that the caravan was not a dwelling house capable of being regarded as the main or only residence of the taxpayer. The decision of the Commissioners was upheld in the Chancery Division. The case was distinguished from Makins v Elson, in that the wheels were still on the caravan, and no water and electricity services were laid on. In addition, whereas Mr. Makins lived continuously on the site in the caravan with his family, in this case it was only used periodically for brief visits.

In order to avail of the relief relating to the disposal of a principal private residence it is necessary that it be a dwelling house which has been occupied by the taxpayer (or in certain circumstances by the beneficiary of a trust) *"as his only or main residence"*. The UK case of Goodwin v Curtis concerned a UK taxpayer who acquired a dwelling house and occupied it for only a very brief period. The taxpayer had acquired a house with the intention of occupying it as a permanent residence, but due to changes in his circumstances, he almost immediately entered into arrangements to resell it and in consequence occupied the house for only a few weeks. During the time while he occupied the house it was the only accommodation owned by him which was available to him as a dwelling. The judge, Sir John Vinelott, quoted Lord Denning in the Court of Appeal decision in the case of Fox v Stirk and Bristol Electrical Registration Officer where he said inter-alia *"temporary residence at an address does not make a man resident there. A guest who comes for the weekend is not resident. A short stay visitor is not resident."* Sir John Vinelott said *"in my judgement (the Commissioners) were fully entitled to take the view that the farmhouse was used not as a residence but as mere temporary accommodation for a period that the taxpayer hoped would be brief and which in fact lasted some 32 days between completion of the sale to him and completion of the sale by him."*

The judge concluded that the brevity of stay in the house was such that during the time he lived there the taxpayer did not reside there, and it was not his residence. The case gave no indication as to the minimum period of occupation of a house which in the view of the English Courts would constitute "*residence*". The Fox case from which Lord Denning's quote was taken was not concerned with taxation, nor with whether or not a dwelling house was a person's residence but rather with whether certain persons were resident in a particular constituency for electoral purposes. The decision in the Goodwin v Curtis case is open to criticism but should nonetheless be noted.

If the land used as garden or grounds is to be exempted, it must be sold not later than the date of disposal of the residence. In the case of Varty v Lynes a taxpayer had a residence with less than one acre of land. He sold the house and some of the land, but retained the balance of the land and some time later sold it, (with planning permission). It was held that the subsequent sale of the land (which would have qualified for relief if sold with the dwelling house) did not qualify for relief. The status of the land as part of the residence must be decided not later than the time of disposal of the house. If it is sold after the disposal of the residence, it will not qualify for relief.

The relief applies to a gain accruing to an individual on the disposal of (or of an interest in) -

"*(a) a dwelling house or part of a dwelling house which is, or has been occupied by the individual as his or her only or main residence, or*

land which the individual has for his or her own occupation and enjoyment with that residence as its garden or grounds, up to an area (exclusive of the site of the dwelling house) not exceeding one acre".

- **Revenue/Chief Inspector's CGT Manual :**

  — In paragraph 19.7.3.2 of the Revenue Commissioners manual on Capital Gains Tax it is stated "*The word 'residence' has its normal meaning and for an individual this is a dwelling in which he habitually lives. In other words it is his home. It follows that actual physical occupation of the dwelling house by the individual is necessary before a claim can be accepted that it is or was his residence. Whilst each case must depend on its own facts, a dwelling house should not be regarded as an individual's residence where the occupation is on a purely temporary basis. For example, an individual may acquire a house and then decide not to make it his residence and before disposing of it he may arrange to make his home in a second house so that the first house clearly never was his residence. Nevertheless he may stay in the first house for a very short period in an attempt to show it was his main residence. The exemption should not be granted in respect of such a period of nominal occupation.*

Similarly a few nights spent in a house whilst repairs and redecoration are carried out prior to its disposal would not be sufficient to establish a claim for an exemption."

24.3   **Separate Buildings (outhouses, gate lodge, etc.)**

The question has arisen on many occasions, as to whether a separate building can be regarded as part of the main residence, for the purposes of this relief.

A number of UK cases have resulted from that issue, and are set out below.

Markey -v- Sanders and Williams -v- Merrylees are two cases dealing with whether a dwelling-house constituting the taxpayer's only or main residence can consist of two or more buildings which are not physically joined together. In Markey -v- Sanders, it was held that a bungalow built on an estate did not fall to be treated as part of the dwelling-house on the grounds that, inter-alia, it was situated a considerable distance from the main house and was deliberately sited for privacy away from the main house. On the other hand, in Williams -v- Merrylees, Vinelott J in the Chancery division declined to overturn a decision of the Commissioners that a modest lodge serving a substantial residence and used by a caretaker could properly be regarded as part of the taxpayers dwelling house for the purposes of the relief.

In Batey -v- Wakefield a taxpayer built a dwellinghouse for himself and his family on 1.1 acres of land. In 1966, he built a chalet bungalow on the land for a caretaker and his wife who acted as housekeeper. The bungalow had its own access to a different road from that of the main house and two buildings were separated by a hedge and the width of a tennis court. The buildings were separately rated.

It was held in the Court of Appeal that the bungalow formed part of the main residence. The word "dwelling-house" or "residence" could comprise several buildings not physically joined together and a staff flat with its own access could accurately be described as part of the larger house. The fact that the bungalow was physically separate from the main house was irrelevant in ascertaining the entity which constituted the residence of the taxpayer and the fact that it comprised separate accommodation did not conclusively determine that separate accommodation was not part of the dwellinghouse.

In the UK case of Lewis v Lady Rood it was held that a cottage occupied by a gardener did not form part of the main residence. The Court of Appeal accepted the Revenue contention that no building can form part of a dwelling house which includes a main house unless that building is appurtenant to and within the curtillage of the

main house. In explanation of of this concept, Balcolm LJ quoted
from the dictum of Buckley LJ in the case of Mentheun-Campbell v
Walters :

*"In my judgement, for one corporeal hereditament to fall within the
curtillage of another, the former must be so intimately associated with the
latter as to lead to the conclusion that the former in truth forms part and
parcel of the latter. There can be very few houses indeed which do not have
associated with them, at least some few square yards of land, constituting a
yard or a basement area or a passageway or something of the kind, owned
and enjoyed with the house, which on a reasonable view could only be
regarded as part of the messuage and such small pieces of land would be
held to fall within the curtillage of the messuage. This may extend to
ancillary buildings, structures or areas such as outhouses, a garage, a
driveway, a garden and so forth. How far it is appropriate to regard this
identity as parts of one messuage or parcel of land as extending must
depend on the character and the circumstances of the items under
consideration."*

On the basis of this test, it was decided that the cottage was not part
of the main house. It was 175 meters from the house and they were
separated by a large garden with no intervening buildings other than
green houses and tool shed.

In the UK case of Honour -v- Norris the taxpayer and his wife
acquired several self contained flats in Ovington Square, London in
order to provide sufficient accommodation for himself and his
family.

Flat 10 provided accommodation for the taxpayer's elder children
and guests, accommodation for the taxpayer and his family whilst
construction work was being carried out on other flats and on rare
occasions, sleeping accommodation for the taxpayer and his wife.

On the sale of flat 10, the taxpayer claimed relief on the basis that it
constituted (together with another flat in which he normally lived)
part of one dwellinghouse which was his only or main residence.

In the High Court, Vinelott J. found against the taxpayer.

*"It is sufficient for the purposes of this case to say that in my judgement of
the proposition that flat number 10 together with (other flats) form part of a
single entity which could sensibly be described as a dwellinghouse split into
different buildings and performing different but related functions is an
affront to common sense. Flat 10 was acquired because it was a separate
dwellinghouse conveniently close to the taxpayer and his wife's main
dwellinghouse and with a view to it being used .... to provide occasional
bedroom accommodation for the taxpayer's two children and his guests and,
on rare occasions, sleeping accommodation for the taxpayer and his wife. It
was no more part of a dwelling-house than, for example, a guest house
bought in a neighbouring village by the owner of a country house who*

found that his house was not always adequate to accommodate his children and guests."

- **Revenue/Chief Inspector's CGT Manual :**

—In paragraph 19.7.3.2 of the Revenue manual on Capital Gains Tax it is stated *"The term 'dwelling house' is not defined for the purposes of the section. It should however, be interpreted as including any premises at which the taxpayer normally resides even though he may also carry on his business on the same premises. Outbuildings which are 'attached' to the house in the general sense should be regarded as part of the dwelling house, but a building or part of a building which is a separate dwelling house should be excluded from the exemption."*

24.4   Period of ownership

24.4.1   Broad Outline

Where an individual has not occupied the property as his principal private residence during his entire period of ownership, part of the gain may be chargeable. In such a case the exempt part of the gain is the proportion which the period of such occupation (during the period of ownership) bears to the period of ownership. In making the calculations any period of occupation or ownership before 6 April 1974 is ignored.

s604 Since the extent of the relief depends in part on the use to which the property was put during the period of ownership, it is important to be able to determine what constitutes the period of ownership. s604 does not provide an exhaustive definition of "the period of ownership". Accordingly, unless one of the special circumstances described below applies, the expression has its normal meaning i.e. the period of time for which the taxpayer has owned the property.

s604(1) One special circumstance dealt with by s604(1) is where the taxpayer has had different interests in the property at different times. The rule provided by the Act is that in such a circumstance his ownership is deemed to commence from the date of his acquisition of an interest, which acquisition gives rise to expenditure which it deductible in a CGT computation. That expenditure includes expenditure on the acquisition of an interest in the property. Where the interest was acquired otherwise than by way of a bargain made at arm's length (e.g. by way of gift or by way of inheritance) the individual is deemed to have incurred such acquisition expenditure, in an amount equal to open market value. In most instances therefore there should be some expenditure related to an acquisition of an interest in a private residence, and it is a matter of determining the earliest such expenditure.

Example 118

Joe signed a lease of a house in 1980. He did not pay any premium and the landlord was not a connected party and it was in all respects an arm's length lease. In 1996 Joe got tired of paying rent and bought out the freehold of the property from the landlord. In 1998 Joe sold the property (in which his interest now consisted solely of the freehold interest).

Joe first acquired an interest in the property in 1980 (a leasehold interest). However no deductible expenditure arose in relation to that interest, on the facts stated above. Accordingly that interest is disregarded for the purpose of determining when his ownership of the property commenced. The first interest in the property whose acquisition gave rise to deductible expenditure was the purchase of the freehold in 1996. Accordingly it is from the date of acquisition of that interest that Joe's ownership is deemed to commence. Joe's activities in the house prior to acquiring the freehold (whether in terms of using it as a principal private residence, or using it for other purposes) are not relevant to the relief under s604.

Example 119

Joe's father in his will leaves a house in trust jointly to John and Jim (his sons) for their joint lives, and with the remainder interest to pass to the survivor of the two. His death occurs in 1980. In 1996 John bought out Jim's half share in the life interest and also his contingent rights in the remainder interest, thus becoming the absolute owner of the property. In 1998 he sold the property outright.

s604(5)

John's period of ownership would appear to have commenced in 1996, and not in 1980, in so far as concerns the 1998 disposal. This would seem to follow from the fact that what John received in 1980 was an interest under a settlement and he would be exempt on any disposal of that interest, in accordance with s604(5) - see paragraph 65.12. Accordingly the consideration which he is deemed to have given for that interest (open market value since he took it otherwise than by way of a transaction at arm's length) would not seem to be expenditure allowable as a deduction in the computation of a gain to which s604 relates. There would be no occasion to prepare any computation or to compute any gain. The first occasion upon which John incurred expenditure in acquiring an interest, in circumstances where the expenditure would be deductible, was in 1996.

s604(9)

There is a further exception to the ordinary meaning of "period of ownership". Where one spouse transfers an interest in the principal private residence to the other (whether by sale, or by gift, or by inheritance) the transferee's period of ownership begins at the beginning of the period of ownership of the transferor spouse. Any period during which the house was the only or main residence of the transferor spouse will also be treated as a period during which it was the only or main residence of the transferee spouse, in relation to a disposal of that property. That deeming provision (in s604(9)(c)) would not seem to affect identification of the principal private residence of the transferee spouse, at a time prior to the interest being transferred to the surviving spouse, where what is involved is a disposal of property other than the principal private residence transferred between the spouses.

Example 120

Mary occupied No.1 Main Street as her principal private residence from 1985 until her marriage to John in 1995. She then went to live with her husband John in No.2 Main Street, which John had acquired as his principal private residence in 1990. 12 months after the marriage in 1995, John transferred a half interest in No.2 Main Street to Mary.

In relation to any disposal of No.2 Main Street, Mary's period of ownership is deemed to begin in 1990, when her husband John's period of ownership commenced. Because it was John's principal private residence from that date up to 1995, it is deemed to also be the private residence of Mary during that period, in relation to a disposal of No.2 Main Street.

s604(8)   *Notwithstanding the rule that a person may not have more than one principal private residence at any one time [s604(8)], the fact that Mary is deemed to have occupied No.2 Main Street as her principal private residence from 1990 onwards, insofar as concerns any disposal of No.2 Main Street by her, would not seem to affect the fact that her principal private residence from 1985 to 1995 was in fact No.1 Main Street. This is not made explicit in the legislation but it might be deduced from the words used in subsection 9(1) "account shall be taken of any part of that period during which it was his only or main residence as if it was also that of the other". This falls short of stating that it shall be deemed to be the principal private residence of the transferee ("the other"). It merely required one to take account of the period **as if** it were the principal private residence of the transferee, but it does not say that it was the principal private residence of the transferee.*

Subsection 8 states for the purposes of this section an individual shall not be treated as having more than one main residence at any one time. In the example above, Mary would not be treated as having more than one main residence, strictly speaking, but rather she is treated in the period 1990 to 1995 as having one main residence (or actual residence at No.1 Main Street) and the period 1990 to 1995 is taken account of as if it had been a period during which No.2 Main Street was the principal private residence. But that seems to fall a hairs breath short of actually treating Mary as having a main residence at No.2 Main Street. There is some ambiguity in the point. The contrary interpretation, which would treat Mary as having owned No.2 Main Street from 1990, but deny her the status of having had it as her main residence from that date by reason of her occupation of No.1 Main Street as a main residence from that date up to 1995, would probably be unconstitutional, as penalising the married state.

s604(9)   *The second restriction proposed by s604 on the number of properties which a person may occupy simultaneously as a principal private residence, which is the restriction in s604(9)(a) that a husband and wife, while living together, may be treated as having only one principal private residence, would not be relevant in the example above to the period 1990 to 1995 since in that period John and Mary were not living together (or at any rate were not married).*

S604(9), which can treat a transferee spouse as having a period of ownership which predates their actual period of ownership, applies only where one spouse disposes of his interest in the dwelling house or part of the dwelling house which is their only or main residence, to the other. In the example above, John disposed of only half of his interest which is not the same thing as disposing of part of the house.

He did not therefore dispose of his entire interest. However TCA97 s534(a) provides that references to a disposal of an asset include references to a part disposal of an asset, and that would seem to treat John's disposal of half of his interest, as being a disposal of his interest for these purposes.

24.4.2 Periods of absence

In arriving at the period (post 5/4/74) throughout which the property is occupied as a principal private residence, the 1975 Act sets out certain circumstances in which the property is *deemed* to be so occupied.

• Foreign employment

s604(5)

Any period of absence (after 5/4/74) throughout which the individual worked in an employment or an office all the duties of which were performed outside the State, may be *deemed* to be a period of occupation for principal private residence relief purposes.

• Revenue/Chief Inspector's CGT Manual:

— The Revenue Commissioners, in their capital gains tax manual at Paragraph 19.7.3.8 indicate a concessional treatment in the case of a husband and wife living together, where one spouse is the owner of the principal private residence, but a period of absence is caused by the foreign employment, or conditions of employment of the other spouse. In such a case, provided that throughout the period neither spouse had a residence or main residence eligible for relief, the provisions indicated above in relation to foreign employment and condition of employment are deemed to apply. It also notes that absence by the taxpayer (who would normally live alone) who was in a hospital etc while the residence remained unoccupied it is to be regarded as a period of occupation. Occupation rent free of the residence during such a period in hospital etc. by a relative of the claimant for the purposes of security etc. would not invalidate the concessional treatment.

• Condition of employment

Any period (after 5/4/74) of absence, not exceeding four years (or periods of absence which together do not exceed four years), throughout which the individual was prevented from residing in his house because of any condition imposed on him by his employer requiring him to reside elsewhere may be deemed to be a period of occupation of the property as a principal private residence provided the condition was reasonably imposed to secure the effective performance of his duties.

- **Last 12 Months**

  The last 12 months of ownership are deemed to be a period of residential occupation for the purpose of calculating the relief, provided the house was (at some time) his principal residence.

- **Residence In House Before and After Absence**

  The house is treated as occupied as a residence by the individual during the permitted periods of absence by reason of his employment if it is actually his only or main residence both before and after the period concerned and provided during that period he had no other residence or main residence which would have been eligible for relief as his principal private residence.

  Reference has been made in paragraph 24.2 to the view taken by UK courts that use as a residence implies use with a degree of permanence. There has been experience of Revenue challenge to the relief where, on a person returning after a period of absence arising from an employment, their occupation of the residence was for a very brief period only (weeks). The matter has not been tested before the courts in Ireland. Given that the legislation has not chosen to make reference to any required minimum period of use, it is doubtful if the Irish courts would feel able to fill that gap. For that reason the authors do not believe that the Revenue challenge is well based. However the matter is uncertain.

  'Period of ownership' and consequently 'period of occupation' cannot include any period prior to 6 April 1974.

  The 'last 12 months' deemed residence applies without any of these conditions, (provided it is - or was - his main residence). However, to avail of the deemed period of residence during the absence caused by his employment, it is necessary for him to actually reside in the premises after the absence. The 'deemed' period of residence in the last 12 months of ownership is not sufficient in itself to satisfy this condition.

Example 121

John is unmarried. He bought a house in Dublin for £10,000 on 1 January, 1970. It was his home until 30 September 1975 when he was required to move to Cork to set up a new branch of his employer's business. He stayed in a rented house in Cork until 31 December 1977 and during that period, let his Dublin home. On his return he reoccupied his Dublin home. On 31 March 1988 he moved to Limerick permanently and let the house in Dublin. On 31 March 1994 he sold the house for £160,000. He has no other chargeable gains for 1993/94.

The market value of the property at 6 April 1974 was £25,000.

The chargeable gain is calculated as follows:

Period of Ownership

6/4/1974 to 31/3/1994	=	20 years

Period of Occupation

Actual - 6/4/1974 to 30/9/1975	=	$1^1/_2$ years
Deemed - 30/9/1975 to 31/12/1977	=	$2^1/_4$ years
Actual - 1/1/1978 to 31/3/1988	=	$10^1/_4$ years
Deemed - 1/4/1993 to 31/3/1994 (last year)	=	1 year
Total	=	15 years

Chargeable Gain

Sale Price	£160,000
Market value 6 April 1974 (as indexed) £25,000 indexed @ 5.656	£141,400
Total Gain	£18,600
Chargeable Gain = 18,600 x $^5/_{20}$	£4,650

The chargeable gain is reduced by the annual exemption, and CGT is chargeable on the balance of £3,650.

Note: *In calculating the fraction to be applied to the total gain, all periods of both occupation and ownership prior to 6 April 1974 are ignored. Fifteen years out of the twenty years ownership are exempt. One quarter of the gain only is chargeable.*

24.5   Part Used for Trade Purposes

s604(6)   Where part of the house is used *exclusively* for the purposes of a trade or profession, it is necessary to apportion the gain to the respective parts of the house, and the exemption can only apply to the non-business part.

It should be noted that the apportionment of the gain is required only where part of the house is being used *exclusively* for trade or professional purposes. If part of the house has been used for trade or professional purposes, but not exclusively so, apportionment of the gain on the disposal of the house in order to restrict the principal private residence exemption, is not required.

Example 122

John is a solicitor working from home. One room in his house is equipped as an office and is used by his secretary and also by clients as a waiting room. It is not used in anyway as part of the dwelling house. A second room is used by John as his private office. It is also used in the evenings by Johns' children as a room in which to study. John also uses it during the weekends as a room in which to listen to music or read books while other family members watch television in the family room.

On the disposal of the property John would have to apportion the gain between the room used exclusively for business purposes (the secretaries' office) and the rest of the house. However no apportionment is required in relation to the room used as Johns' office, as the business use is only partial.

Paragraph 30.4 deals with the interaction with retirement relief.

- **Revenue/Chief Inspector's CGT Manual :**

s604(7)
— Paragraph 19.7.3.10 of the Revenue Commissioners capital gains tax manual it is stated *"Where a room is used almost entirely for business purposes, with only occasional private use, it should be contended that Section 604(6) applies to restrict relief, the small residential use falling to be disregarded on de minimis grounds; alternatively it should be argued that the occasions of private use are changes of use within Section 604(7) giving rise to a "just and reasonable" adjustment".* The authors would not agree with the view expressed - see paragraph 24.6.

24.6   Change in Use or Structure of House

s604(7)
Section 604(7) provides that principal private residence relief may be given, instead of on the basis described above, on a different basis.

That different basis is such basis as the inspector and the individual may agree. Where they do not agree, the basis would be what the Appeal Commissioners on appeal consider to be "just and reasonable".

The circumstances in which the normal method of computing the relief is set aside, and is replaced by an unspecified method which meets the requirements of being "just and reasonable" are where (at any time in the period of ownership):

- *"there is a change in the dwelling house or the part of it which is occupied as the individual's residence, whether on account of a reconstruction or conversion of a building or for any other reason, or"*

- *"there have been changes as regards the use of part of the dwelling house for the purpose of a trade, business or profession, or for any other purpose".*

The two circumstances outlined above are distinct from each other. The first circumstance relates to "a change in the dwelling house". That expression is vague. It is so vague that, taken out of context, it could relate to a change in the value of the house, or a change in the street number of the house. However, in the context of the particular example given in the section - reconstruction or conversion - it appears to be the case that the change in question must be a physical change in the building. It is true that the section goes on to say that the change can be "for any other reason", an expression which is very wide indeed. Nonetheless the ejusdem generis rule would apply to limit the interpretation of general rule to matters similar to the specific examples given. An example of physical change to a house which is a principal private residence would be the adding on of a "back kitchen". That is something which occurs frequently. That is a physical change to the building that is used as a principal private residence. But surely it is not intended that on every occasion that a physical change takes place to a building, that the normal method of computing principal private residence relief is to be set aside, and an unspecified method is to be negotiated between the tax payer and the Inspector. Presumably the only occasion upon which a physical change to the building used as a principal private residence would give rise to the application of s604(7) is where it would be "unjust and unreasonable" to apply the normal method of granting principal private residence relief, subsequent to the change in the building.

Example 123

Joe Smith occupies a very small property on a large site in a swanky residential neighbourhood. His house much smaller than his neighbours houses, all of which are very expensive houses. Joe secured planning permission to significantly extend his house, making it more in keeping with the houses of his neighbours, and more appropriate to the neighbourhood. In consequence of the work carried out by Joe, the market value of his house increased very significantly, and by an amount much higher than the cost to Joe of carrying out the construction work.

The house had been owned by Joe for ten years prior to Joe carrying out the construction work, and for five of those ten years it had been rented out, and not been used by Joe as his principal private residence.

If Joe were to dispose of the property shortly after carrying out the construction work, a large part of the gain would be taxable, by reason of principal private residence relief having regard to the period when it was not used as his principal private residence. But the growth in value did not occur while the house was rented out. The growth in value occurred during the period when it was a principal private residence.

In the circumstances outlined, the usual time basis of apportionment would not seem to be just and reasonable, and hopefully the inspector would react favourably to a request to treat the gain which accrued by reason of the construction work as entirely within the relief without any apportionment to the period when the house was not his principal private residence.

However, the strict interpretation of the legislation is not free of doubt.

The second basis for seeking a "just and reasonable" treatment relates to a change in the use of the dwelling house for business purposes .

In the other instance given above of a physical change in the building the reference was to *"a change in the dwelling house or the part of it which is occupied as the individual's residence"* This difference in wording might suggest that where the basis for invoking s604(7) is change in the use of the property, that can be a change in the use of the property only at a time when some part of it is in use as a principal private residence. A change from business use of the entire property over to residential use would not seem to clearly fall within the words.

It is difficult to imagine circumstances where "just and reasonable" can be invoked by reason of a change in the part of the house in use for business purposes, other than where the gain on the disposal of the property did not arise evenly over the period of ownership, but instead arises disproportionately either before or after a change occurred in the percentage of the building in use as a private residence.

Example 124

*The circumstances in which the second basis for invoking subsection 7 might apply could be very similar to those outlined in **example 122** above. If, the increase in the value of John's house occurred entirely in a period after he had discontinued the use of part of it for professional use (e.g.- as a solicitor) and indeed may have been caused precisely by such a change, it would seem unjust that the benefit of the relief should be diluted in relation to that increase in value, when it had nothing to do with the period when part of the house was in use as a business.*

As noted in paragraph 24.5, the Revenue Commissioners appear to consider that they are entitled to invoke s604(7). It seems rather extraordinary that the Revenue Commissioners should consider that they are entitled to describe the manner in which legislation (which in practice they drafted) operates is other than just and reasonable. One's instinct would suggest that subsection 7 was provided for the benefit of the taxpayer solely, and not for use by the Revenue Commissioners as a means of reducing the relief available to the taxpayer. It is easy enough to see how the operation of s604 could in certain circumstances be other than just and reasonable where it restricts the relief available to the taxpayer. But would it ever be unjust or unreasonable, for a taxpayer to get more relief under s604 than he might otherwise obtain if the section had been differently worded? The authors are not convinced that the Revenue Commissioners are entitled to invoke s604(7) but the legislation does not explicitly deal with this point, and the Revenue Commissioners obviously do not agree with the authors.

There may be circumstances in which it is unjust to deny a relief, or dilute a relief, to a taxpayer and thereby take more or his money for the State than would otherwise be the case. But how can it ever be "unjust" to apply to a taxpayer a relief in accordance with the law in circumstances which leaves him with more money than would otherwise be the case? We must bear in mind that the money in question belongs to the taxpayer in the first place. It may be unjust to take it from him, but can it ever be unjust to leave it with him? For that reason the authors are of the view that s604(7) can be invoked only by the taxpayer, and not by the Revenue. However the contrary view of the Revenue should be noted.

- **Revenue/Chief Inspector's CGT Manual :**

— At paragraph 19.7.3.9 of the Revenue Commissioners capital gains tax manual, a concessional treatment is indicated to cope with a situation where a person has a house constructed on land they already own, and they subsequently occupy the house as their principal private residence. The matter dealt with in the concession is the question of the period of ownership. The concession indicates that where the house *"is completed within a year of the date of occupation and occupied as his only or main residence on completion, the period from the date of acquisition of the land to physical occupation of the house may be regarded as part of the period of occupation as main residence for exemption purposes."*

Where the interval between the acquisition of the land and the completion of construction exceeds one year a different treatment is indicated as set out in the following example which is to be found in paragraph 19.7.3.25 of the capital gains tax manual:

Example 125

In June 1985, an individual bought a piece of freehold land of less than one acre for £20,000. In June 1988, construction begins thereon of a house for the landowner's occupation. This is completed at a cost of £40,000 and occupied in June 1989. The house and the land are sold in June 1993, for £120,000 and as the house is the owner's main residence from June 1989, the whole of the gain on the house itself is exempt. The chargeable gain on the land is calculated as follows:

Sale proceeds	120,000
Cost of land 20,000 x 1.287 = 25,740	
Cost of house 40,000 x 1.167 = 46,680	72,420
Overall gain	47,580
	=====
Gain apportioned to land £25,740 x £47,580 =	16,911
£72,420	
Exempt fraction (June, 1988 - June, 1993) = 5	
(June, 1985 - June, 1993) 8 x £16,911	10,.570
Chargeable gain	6,341
	=====

24.7   More Than One Main Residence

s604(8)   The only house which can qualify for relief, is one occupied by the owner as a residence at some time after 5 April 1974. An individual cannot have more than one 'principal private residence' qualifying for relief at any one time.

The problem of deciding which house qualifies as the 'principal private residence' during any period is to be dealt with in the following manner:

- The taxpayer notifies the inspector of his choice (in writing within 2 years of the beginning of the period for which he is electing to treat the house as qualifying) and if the inspector agrees, the question is settled as regards that particular period.

  or

- In the absence of any such agreement the inspector decides which house qualifies, and notifies the taxpayer (who has a right of appeal against any such determination by the inspector).

In the UK case of Griffin -v- Craig-Harvey it was held that the election of the taxpayer as to which of a number of residences shall be treated as his principal private residence had to be made within two years of the beginning of the period in which he had most recently acquired a residence. That an election could be made by him at anytime, and be valid for a preceding period of two years prior to the election, was rejected. On each occasion that an additional residence was acquired a new right to make an election arose, and a new two year period during which such an election could be made commenced.

In Ireland, such an agreement is valid only with the agreement of the Inspector.

24.8   Married Persons

s604(9)   A married couple can have (at any one time) only one principal private residence for the purposes of this relief, so long as they are living together. Where more than one residence is involved (at any time) an election as to which property is the 'principal private residence' (see paragraph 24.6) must be made by both. A determination from the inspector on the question of which house qualifies, also must be sent to both. Either of them may appeal.

Where one spouse transfers a 'principal private residence' (or part of it) to the other spouse (including a transfer on death) the acquiring spouse is deemed also to acquire the transferring spouse's period of ownership, and period of occupation for the purposes of this relief - see *Example 120* which deals with married persons.

24.9   Settled Property

s604(10)   Where property is the subject of a settlement and under the terms of the settlement, a beneficiary is entitled to occupy the property and in fact occupies it as his principal private residence, the same relief will be given to the trustees on the disposal of the property as would apply to the occupying beneficiary if that person owned the property himself. (The general treatment of settlements is dealt with in paragraph 65).

In the UK case of Sansom v Peay the question arose as to whether a beneficiary under a discretionary trust who was occupying a house as a residence at the discretion of the trustees was 'entitled to occupy' the property, and so bring the property within the scope of the relief. Mr. Justice Brightman held in the Chancery Division, that a beneficiary occupying a property as a result of the exercise of the discretion of trustees, was 'entitled to occupy' that property, and as such, the property qualified for relief on sale by the trustees.

24.10   Profit Motive

s604(11)   Principal Private Residence relief is not given in the case of any house purchased wholly or mainly for the purpose of making a gain on the disposal. In addition, relief is not given for the part of the gain attributable to enhancement expenditure incurred wholly or mainly for the purpose of realising a gain on the disposal of the house.

The UK case of Jones v Wilcock heard before the UK Special Commissioners dealt with a case where the Revenue alleged that a private residence was purchased for the purpose of realising a gain from its disposal. The case had concerned the not uncommon situation of a taxpayer purchasing a residence in need of renovation, at a time of rising house prices. The taxpayer expected to have to sell the house within a few years as their family circumstances changed. Although they hoped to realise a gain on resale, the Special Commissioner held that that hope did not constitute a purpose in purchasing the property and that the purpose in purchasing the property was solely to provide themselves with a suitable residence.

He distinguished between their hope that they would realise a gain when it was necessary to resell the house, and their purpose in acquiring the house. He was also influenced by the lack of any evidence of commerciality in the manner in which the house was acquired or renovated - the lack of detailed costings, or other indication of a concern for profit. He said *"I find that the taxpayer....did not buy (the house) or make the improvements even in part for the purpose of turning the house to account as if the purchase, improvements and sale were something like an adventure in the nature of trade; using counsel's phrase, "as a speculator". There is before me no evidence of commerciality such as low costings carefully calculated to produce the maximum return. The taxpayer kept no accounts. He does not know exactly how much the improvements cost. The object of making the improvements, I find, is to provide an agreeable home. A gain at the end of the day was a hope and even, still, an expectation, but it was not a purpose within [the UK equivalent of section 25(10)]."*

In the UK case of Goodwin v Curtis a taxpayer bought and sold a number of dwellings in rapid succession, and occupied one dwelling for a period of 32 days only. On a question of fact, it was held that his transactions had not been trading transactions. As is noted in paragraph 24.2, relief was denied on the grounds that the short period of occupation of the property deprived it of the quality of being a residence.

24.11   Dependent Relative

s604(11)

In addition to the relief available to an individual on the disposal of his own residence, further relief may be available in respect of a gain arising to him on the disposal of a house which was used by a dependent relative as that relative's sole residence.

The relief applies to an individual where he disposes on or after 6 April 1979 of a dwelling - house which at any time in his period of ownership has been the sole residence of a dependent relative of that individual. The house must have been provided by the individual to that dependent relative free of rent or any other consideration, (i.e. it must have been provided gratuitously).

The relief also applies to the disposal of an interest in the house, and also in a case where only part of the house is occupied by the dependent relative, in the same manner that it would apply if it was the individual's only or main residence qualifying for relief as such.

In the case of any individual, only one house can qualify for this additional relief at any one time. In the case of a married man whose wife is living with him, only one of them can claim the relief for 1979/80. Where either the wife or the husband claim relief in respect of such a house for 1979/80, the Inspector must be satisfied that the other spouse has relinquished any claim which that spouse may have during the same period in respect of a different property and another dependent relative. For 1980/81 and subsequent years relief can be claimed separately by each spouse in respect of a dwelling house owned by that individual spouse, and occupied by a dependent relative of that spouse.

Dependent relative means in relation to an individual,

- *a relative* of the individual (or of the wife or husband of the individual)

    – who is incapacitated by old age or infirmity from maintaining himself/herself, or

- the *widowed mother* or

FA97 s146(1)   • the *widowed father*

— whether or not so incapacitated - of the individual or of the wife or husband of the individual.

There is no income test applied to the definition of "dependant relative" in s604 (11). This is in contrast to s466, which deals with dependant relative allowance (income tax), and where a very strict income test is applied.

In the UK case of Eglen v Butcher a taxpayer claimed that his children were dependent relatives, on the grounds that their youth was an infirmity preventing them from maintaining themselves. This was rejected by the judge who said *"To my mind both the state of being incapacitated and infirmity connote some departure from normal physical and mental ability, whether due to congenital defect or due to illness, accident or disease. - - Whilst the section recognises incapacity from old age, it does not in terms recognise incapacity from youth. Can youth as such be described as and included in infirmity? In my judgment it cannot."*

24.12   Residence - Development Land

s604(12)

The relief given to an individual on the sale of his residence, does not apply to the part of the gain reflecting "development value". The relief is calculated only by reference to the gain which would have arisen if the property was both bought and sold for it's value solely as a residence.

This restriction on the relief is contained in s604(12) and applies where the disposal takes place on or after 25th January 1984.

The gain on the disposal of the property is calculated in the normal way (as development land), and the resulting gain is reduced by the restricted residence relief. The balance of the gain is chargeable in full as a development land gain.

Example 126

Claire bought a property on 31 January 1987 for its residence value of £20,000. Incidental costs of acquisition amounted to £5,250. The asset was sold to a developer on 28 February 1994 for £300,000. Its value as a residence at that time was £70,000. The incidental costs of disposal were £5,000. Throughout her period of ownership of the property, it was her principal private residence.

The gain chargeable is calculated as follows:-

	£	£
Sale proceeds (Development Lands)		300,000
Cost (current use value)	20,000	
Indexed @ 1.190	23,800	
Incidental costs : acquisition 5,250		
: indexed @ 1.190	6,223	
: disposal	5,000	35,023
GAIN		264,977
Less residence relief		38,810
Gain taxable @ 40%		226,167

Residence Relief:

	£	£
sale price as residence		70,000
"residence" cost (indexed)	23,800	
incidental cost of acquisition (as indexed)	6,223	
incidental cost of disposal		
£5,000 x $\dfrac{70,000}{300,000}$ =	1,167	
		31,190
"residence" gain (qualifying for full relief)		38,810

In calculating the gain which would arise on the sale solely as a residence, the incidental costs of a disposal are apportioned proportionately.

This restriction in relief does not apply where the disposal is by an individual whose total consideration for disposal of such properties in the year of assessment does not exceed £15,000. In arriving at the total of £15,000, only disposals of properties which would normally have qualified for residence relief are included.

Example 127

*If, in **example 126**, the facts were as stated save that the cost price of the residence in January 1987 was £50,000, the computation would be as follows:*

Development land computation:	£	£
Sales proceeds (development lands)		300,000
Cost	50,000	
Indexation based on current use value at date of acquisition, £20,000 x 1.190	3,800	
Incidental costs: acquisition	5,250	
Indexation on incidental acquisition costs, £5,250 (20,000 / 50,000) x 1.190	399	
Incidental costs of disposal	5,000	64,449
Gain		235,551
Less residence relief (see below)		43,711
Gain taxable		191,840

Residence relief:		
Sale price as residence		70,000
"Residence" cost (indexed)	23,800	
Incidental cost of acquisition proportionate to residence cost (indexed)	1,322	
Incidental cost of disposal £5,000/ (70,000 x 300,000)	1,167	
Total		26,289
(Residence) gain (qualifying for full relief)		43,711

The treatment generally of development land is described in greater detail in paragraph 6.1.

24.13 **Foreign dwelling**

There is no explicit requirement in s604 that a dwelling should be located in the State, in order that principal private residence relief should apply to it. In the absence of such an explicit requirement, a property overseas (e.g. in the UK) could constitute such a residence. This could be particularly relevant to an individual who is ordinarily resident, but no longer resident, in the State. Such an individual is within the charge to capital gains tax in respect of his world wide assets, if he is domiciled in Ireland. A person may be ordinarily resident in the State for up to 3 years after ceasing to be resident there.

Some of the provisions of s604 would have little relevance to a foreign property e.g. those relating to development land, and also to absences due to employment abroad, causing a person not to occupy a dwelling as a residence. While such provisions appear to have been written without regard to the possibility that the principal private residence might not be located in the State, they would not seem in themselves sufficient to impose a requirement that a principal private residence be located in the State.

25 **RELIEFS - REINVESTMENT OF DISPOSAL PROCEEDS**

25.1 **Broad summary**

In certain circumstances the CGT Acts give relief from an immediate charge to tax which would otherwise occur on the disposal of an asset where the consideration for the disposal of the asset is reinvested.

Where a person disposes of certain specified assets so as to give rise to a potential charge to tax on a capital gain, there are be three reliefs which may be available to him which avoid, or defer, the charge to tax. Those reliefs are:

- **Rollover relief :** the relief is discussed in paragraph 26. It mainly relates to situation where there is a disposal of certain trade asset (specified in the legislation) and the disposal proceeds are reinvested in further specified trade assets within the time allowed. The relief can also extend to include certain shares. The reason for the disposal is not relevant.

  The relief is given (in broad terms) by deeming that gain not to arise until the replacement asset ceases to be used for the purposes of the business. In effect it defers the charge to tax.

- **Compulsory purchase orders relief :** This relief is described in paragraph 27. Unlike rollover relief, relief under this provision is limited to where the disposal takes place as a result or in consequence of a CPO. The assets to which the relief can apply are broadly similar to those specified for roll over relief, but also extends to include certain non-business assets. There is a time limit within which a qualifying reinvestment must be made.

  The relief is given by deferring the immediate charge to tax. The way in which the tax is deferred depends on the amount of the disposal proceeds reinvested in the replacement asset.

- **Reinvestment of compensation proceeds :** This relief is discussed in paragraph 28.

The rollover relief and compulsory purchase order relief are very similar but, confusingly, differ in a number of points of detail. In some circumstances a disposal might be eligible for both reliefs. Whichever relief is claimed is the relief which would apply. Where no claim is made, neither relief need apply and the ordinary rules relating to a disposal would apply. At a time of rising capital gains tax rates, or where capital losses are available, or where other loss relief is available in the case of a company, a taxpayer might find it to his advantage not to claim either relief.

The principal features of the rollover and CPO reliefs are contrasted below in a table. Of necessity, this table can be no more than a very general guide to the reliefs and should not be relied on without reference to the discussion in paragraph 26.1 et seq. and paragraph 27.

	Roll over relief	CPO relief
• Must relief be claimed	yes	yes
• Relief for Plant & Machinery	yes	yes
• Relief for Land & Buildings	yes	yes
• Relief for Goodwill	yes	yes

	Roll over relief	CPO relief
• Irish assets only	no	yes
• Trade assets only	yes	no in case of land, but yes for plant & Machinery /goodwill
• Time limit for reinvestment - 1 year before & 3 years after	yes	yes
• Extends to shares	yes	no
• relief excluded if replacement asset acquired with view to gain on its disposal	yes	no
• Extent of relief dependent on whether asset used solely for specified purposes during ownership	yes	no
• Relief where reinvestment in different trade	yes	no
• Form of relief	gain deferred	no disposal - old base cost attaches to new asset
• Exclusion from relief for development land	yes	yes
• Exceptions to development land exclusion - "dirty industries"	yes	no
• Exception to development land exclusion for farm land disposed of to local authority	no	yes
• Exception to development land exclusion for certain sporting bodies	yes	yes

26 ROLL-OVER RELIEF

26.1.1 Broad Outline

s597 In general terms, this relief consists of a deferral of the payment of capital gains tax (or part of that tax) arising on the disposal of certain business assets, where the proceeds (or part of the proceeds) are re-invested in business assets. For the relief to apply both the asset sold and the asset acquired must fall within one (but not necessarily the same one) of the following categories:) *as set out in s597(3):*

(a) **Plant and Machinery** used solely for trade purposes.

(b) *Except where the trade is a trade of dealing in or developing land,* (where any profit on disposal would form part of the trading profits of that trade) *or of providing services for the occupier of land in which the person carrying on the trade has an estate or interest -*

(i) **any building or part of a building** *and any permanent or semi-permanent structure in the nature of a building occupied (as well as used) only for the purpose of the trade,*

(ii) *Any* **land** *occupied (as well as used) only for the purposes of the trade.*

(c) **Goodwill. Of a trade.**

FA98 s71(1) This list is extended by FA98 in the case of disposals made by a *sporting body* on or after 27 March 1998 to include certain financial assets of that sporting body -

(d) **Any financial assets** *owned owned by a body of persons referred to in paragraph (f) of subsection(2) ; for the purposes of this paragraph* **"financial assets"** *means shares of any company and stocks, bonds, and obligations of any government, municipal corporation, company or other body corporate."* - see paragraph 26.9.

In the case of land and buildings, mere visits to a site, coupled with the intention to build, and the application for planning permission do not satisfy the 'used' and 'occupied' test for the purpose of the relief. This was decided in the UK case of Temperley v Visabell.

The UK case of Anderton v Lambe was concerned with two farmhouses on a farm farmed in partnership by Mr. and Mrs. Lambe and their two sons. The houses had qualified for farm capital allowances for income tax purposes. Each of the houses was occupied by one of the sons as a residence i.e. as a farm house. Its basis of occupation was a licence from the partnership, rather than a tenancy. The Court held that the occupation of the houses was by the sons in their individual capacity, and not by the partnership per se, notwithstanding that the houses were owned by the partnership and were used as farmhouses. Accordingly they did not meet the test in relation to land and buildings of being *"occupied and used solely for the purpose of the trade"*.

The UK case of Dodd v Mudd was concerned with a claim for rollover relief on the gain arising on the disposal of the goodwill of an accountancy practice. The taxpayer claimed rollover relief against expenditure on acquiring a 75% interest in a large house, to be used as a private hotel. The other 25% interest in the house was acquired by his wife, and the house was held by them as tenants in common.

Part of the house, amounting to 25%, was used by them as a private residence, and the balance was used for trade purposes. Vinelott J. ruled that the gain on the sale of the goodwill could be rolled over only against 75%, of 75%, of the total expenditure on the acquisition of the house. That proportion represented the expenditure by the taxpayer on his interest in the portion of the house used for trade purposes. Because the house was held in its entirety as tenants in common, Vinelott J. rejected the argument that the husband should be regarded as having acquired the entire of the portion of the building used for trade purposes, with the private portion being regarded as having been acquired by the wife.

In passing, Vinelott J. expressed a reservation as to whether, where what is acquired is only an interest in an asset, that interest could itself be said to be an asset used for the purposes of a trade (as distinct from the asset in which the interest existed). In other words whereas he was happy that the house itself was in use for the purpose of the trade, it was not clear to him that the joint tenancy of the 75%, which the husband had in the property, was an asset in use for the purpose of the trade. However he did not rule on this point as it was not in dispute in the case. The authors are not aware of this point being raised as a difficulty by the Revenue in practice.

- **Revenue Commissioners published precedent:**

- In their published precedents the Revenue Commissioners have stated that a *"taxi plate"* does not come within the qualifying assets set out in Section 597 (3). It has been claimed that a "taxi plate" is "goodwill" or alternatively that it is "plant". The Revenue do not accept this. The attitude of the Revenue Commissioners to a *taxi plate* appears more severe than that which they adopt to a *milk quota,* which they regard as forming part of land. A taxi plate is a positive permission to use a motor vehicle for the purpose of the trade of taxi operations. A *milk quota* is an entitlement to produce a particular level of milk before the imposition of certain financial penalties. It is not in itself a permission to produce milk (no permission is required for that purpose) but rather it is an exclusion from penalties. The two would seem fairly similar in nature.

There is provision for partial relief where the assets disposed of were used partly for non-trade purposes.

The investment in the replacement assets must take place within the 4 year period, commencing 1 year before and ending 3 years after the date of the disposal.

The deferral is granted by treating the gain as not arising until the "new asset" ceases to be used for the purpose of the trade. It does not reduce the cost of the "new" asset. The gain merely remains in abeyance until the new asset is sold. However, in calculating the tax applicable to the deferred gain, (on the disposal of the new asset) the date of disposal of the "old asset" is the relevant date for the purposes of indexation and rates of tax.

In order to obtain a full deferral of the gain, the entire consideration for the disposal must be re-invested. If only part is re-invested, a deferral is allowed up to the amount by which the gain exceeds the amount not re-invested. If the amount not re-invested exceeds the gain no deferral is allowed. It should be noted that the relief refers to re-investment of sale proceeds - not of the gain. In practice, the revenue may be willing to regard the re-investment of the proceeds net of any incidental costs of disposal as qualifying for full relief.

Example 128

Fred sold his factory in 1998 - the details are as follows:-

Sale proceeds	*£50,000*
Cost (indexed)	*£40,000*
Gain	*£10,000*

In 1998 he bought a new factory for £84,000.

The entire sale proceeds of £50,000 are re-invested so the £10,000 gain is held in abeyance until the new factory is sold or it otherwise ceases to be used for the purposes of the trade. The position at that stage depends on the extent to which the proceeds of the sale of the new factory are re-invested (see paragraph 26.2 below).

Example 129

John sold his factory in June 1998 - the details are as follows:

Sale proceeds	*£50,000*
Cost (indexed)	*£40,000*
Gain	*£10,000*

In 1998 he bought a new factory for £48,000.

As only part of the sale proceeds was re-invested, the gain on the 1998 disposal will be taxed up to the amount not re-invested.

The balance of the gain is treated as not arising until the replacement asset ceases to be used for the purpose of the trade.

i.e. Gain	*£10,000*
Amount re-invested	*£2,000*
@ 20% = £400 (Payable)	
Deferred gain	*£8,000*

Although roll-over relief arises mainly in trading situations, it is also available to professions and other activities - see paragraph 26.7.

The UK case of Watton v Tippett had to consider whether a taxpayer who disposed of a part of an asset soon after acquisition could claim rollover relief on the resulting gain by reference to the expenditure on the acquisition of the remaining part of the asset, which had been acquired within the required time period. The asset in question had been a factory premises which the taxpayer converted for use for indoor sports. He divided the premises into two separate parts by means of a partition, and disposed of one part. The judge rejected this claim and said:

"It is important to observe that a part disposal of an asset is to be treated as a disposal of the asset, not as a disposal of part of the asset. A part disposal of an asset may or may not involve a disposal of a severable part. – The consideration for unit 1 cannot be severed and treated as paid in part for unit 1A and in part for the retained part of unit 1. So – if a taxpayer were to buy from the same vendor two adjacent properties under two separate but contemporaneous contracts, there would be no reason in principle why the sale of one should not be treated as the sale of old assets and the retained part as new assets for the purpose of (rollover relief). The description of assets as "old" and "new" is functional and not temporal. It may be that the result would be the same as if the two properties were acquired under the same contract and at a time when they were not physically separated, provided they could be treated as separate assets and that the consideration was apportioned between them at the time of sale. That case can be considered when it arises. The insuperable difficulty in the instant case is that unit 1 was acquired as a single asset and for an unapportioned consideration. – The difficulty which confronts the taxpayer is that the sale of unit 1A was strictly a part disposal of unit 1 and not a disposal of part of unit 1. The disposal of unit 1A having been a part disposal of unit 1, it cannot be said that the consideration arising from the sale of unit 1A was applied in the acquisition of "other assets". "

In other words, the taxpayer acquired a single asset and his disposal of part of it was a part disposal of the entire of that single asset, and accordingly there was no "other asset" against which he could rollover the gain. Had he bought two separate assets at the same time, it would have been possible to rollover the gain on the disposal of one against the acquisition of "the other asset".

In the Court of Appeal the High Court judgement in the case of Watton v Tippet was confirmed. The Appeal Court judges criticised the drafting of the rollover relief, and in particular references to the proceeds of disposal of the "old" asset being applied in the acquisition of "new" assets. The judge said that the word *applied* prima facie indicated some direct relationship between the proceeds of the first disposal and the expenditure on the new assets. It was accepted by them that the structure of the relief clearly did not envisage any such direct tracing between the receipt of the consideration, and the expenditure on the new asset. All that was involved appeared to be a coincidence of amounts within a fixed time frame. They were unhappy with this situation, but did not go so far as to rule that this conventional Revenue treatment is incorrect.

In the opinion of the authors, it seems clear that the legislation does not envisage any direct tracing between the proceeds of disposal of the old asset and the actual moneys used to pay for the new asset. This is particularly clear where the qualifying expenditure on the acquisition of the new asset is allowed within the time frame commencing 12 months prior to the date of disposal of the old asset, even where the money was borrowed and replaced by the sale proceeds of the old assets.

- **Revenue/Chief Inspector's Manual:**

  - In the Chief Inspector of Taxes' manual it is stated in relation to s597 "The relief may be allowed where the investment of the whole (or part) of the disposal proceeds does not technically involve an acquisition, eg where on property already owned a replacement building is erected and is occupied and used for the trade, or where additions are made to buildings already owned and occupied and used for the purposes of the trade."

The Revenue statement above does not in explicit terms refer to enhancement expenditure. The types of expenditure they give in their example are technically enhancement expenditure. It is not clear that the Revenue concession necessarily extends to all forms of enhancement expenditure. The equivalent UK statement of practice is more explicit in extending to all enhancement expenditure. Any person in doubt on the point should clarify it with the Revenue on a case by case basis.

HA96 s96, s97   TCA97 Sch26 provides that a new port company formed under the Harbours Act 1996 may be treated as the same person as that from
Sch26   whom an asset was acquired in the course of a transfer on the vesting of port assets in accordance with s. 96 or 97 of the Harbours Act 1996. This applies for the purpose of roll over relief under s597.

- **Revenue Commissioners - Tax Briefing:**

  - In the article in *"Tax Briefing"* issue 12 (October 1993) the Revenue Commissioners stated that where a trader applies the proceeds of disposal on capital expenditure to enhance the value of existing assets (of a qualifying catagory) such expenditure is treated for the purpose of rollover relief as if it was incurred in acquiring other assets, provided:

    - the enhanced assets are used only for the purposes of the trade, and

    - on completion of the enhancement work, the assets are immediately taken into use and used only for the purposes of the trade.

- **Revenue/Chief Inspector's CGT Manual :**

— At Paragraph 19.6.2.9 of their capital gains tax manual, the Revenue Commissioners point out that *"in the case of a married couple where the old assets were solely owned by one spouse but the new assets are acquired jointly by both spouses, full roll-over relief would not be clearly due. However, if both spouses had been actively engaged in the trade and so continue after the acquisition of the new assets, roll-over relief may be allowed provided the other requirements are satisfied."*

It may well be that the practice indicated in this statement is not concessional but is properly based on the statute. There does not appear to be any requirement that the new assets acquired by the reinvestment proceeds should be owned by the person who made the disposal of the prior assets. The requirement is that *"the new assets on their acquisition are taken into use and used only for the purposes of the trade."* Since the "claw-back" provisions of Section 597(4)(b) apply by treating the original disposal as occurring at a later date when the "new assets" cease to be used for the purpose of the trade, there is nothing in the structure of the section which would require the taxpayer claiming the relief should be the sole owner of the asset. The requirement rather is that he should be the person who incurs the expenditure on its acquisition. Normally that will result in his being the owner. Where he acquires the new asset on his own behalf, and on behalf of another person (who does not bear any cost of the acquisition) the requirements would seem to be met.

- **Revenue Commissioners - Tax Briefing:**

— The Revenue Commissioners, in Issue 35 of Tax Briefing, March 1999 stated that where an individual disposed of an asset which was used for the purposes of a trade carried on by a company in which the individual is a major shareholder, roll over relief would not be available. This is because the trade for which the asset was used was not carried on by the individual who owned the asset. This should be contrasted with the relief available for companies in a group situation. (See paragraph 79).

26.1.2   **Claiming relief**

It is understood to be the view of the Revenue Commissioners that relief should be claimed when the necessary expenditure on new assets has ben incurred, and not in submitting the return for the period in which the old assets were disposed of where the expenditure had not then been incurred. The legislation does not explicitly deal with the point.

The matter can be one of some importance. The acquisition of a "new asset" can take place as long as three years after the disposal of the "old asset". If the Revenue interpretation is correct, a claim for roll-over relief cannot be made in making a return in relation to the disposal of the old asset even if expenditure on the new asset is planned and almost certain to occur within the three year period. Thus capital gains tax would have to be accounted for and paid on the disposal of the old assets, and relief by way of repayment obtained when the new investment is made. This imposes a cash flow disadvantage which, in theory at least, could deprive the taxpayer of the necessary funds to make the acquisition of the new asset!

The interpretation placed on the legislation by the Revenue Commissioners would seem to be correct, notwithstanding the disadvantages it involves.

26.2   Full Proceeds Re-Invested

s597(4)

If the consideration for the disposal of the old assets (i.e. the full sale proceeds) is re-invested, the full gain (on the disposal of the old assets) is treated as not arising until the new qualifying assets cease to be used for the purposes of the trade. When the new assets cease to be used for trade purposes the gain deferred on the disposal of the old assets may be deferred further. This further deferral is available provided the full sale proceeds arising on the disposal of the new assets are re-invested in further new qualifying assets.

Example 130

Peter carries on a manufacturing trade. In March 1972 he acquired his factory premises for £60,000 (mv 6/4/74 was £80,000). In June 1997 he sold the premises for £680,000 and purchased another for £750,000. In March 1998 he decided to change the location of his operation. He sold the new premises for £800,000 and used the proceeds towards the cost of new plant (cost £180,000) and a unit in a new industrial estate (cost £620,000).

In 1998 his health deteriorated and in September of that year he retired, selling the plant for £210,000 and the building for £675,000. He did not qualify for "retirement" relief.

Peter's liability to tax on these transactions is calculated as follows:

Disposal 1997:

Sale proceeds	£680,000
MV 6/4/74 (indexed) £80,000 x 6.112	£488,960
Gain	£191,040

The full proceeds of £680,000 were invested in new qualifying assets so that gain is deemed not to arise until the new assets cease to be used for the purposes of the trade. When the gain eventually becomes taxable, the rate of CGT is whichever rate would have been payable at the actual date of disposal, if the gain had not been deferred.

Disposal March 1998:

Sale proceeds (building)	£800,000
Cost (no indexation-12 month rule)	£750,000
Gain	£ 50,000

Again, however, the full proceeds were invested in new qualifying assets so the gain and that arising in 1997 are deferred.

Disposals September 1998

Sale Proceeds	Plant	£210,000
	Buildings	£675,000
		£885,000
Cost (no indexation - as assets held for less than 1 year)	Plant	£180,000
	Buildings	£620,000
		£800,000
Gain		£85,000

As the sale proceeds are not re-invested all deferred gains (i.e. £191,400 from 1997 and £50,000 from March 1998) are now deemed to arise in addition to the £85,000 gain in September 1998. The rate of CGT is the rate which would have been payable on the individual disposals if the gains had not been deferred.

Although the "plant" is a chattel, and would normally have a life not exceeding 50 years, it is not treated as an exempt wasting chattel because it qualifies for capital allowances - see paragraph 22.

In some cases the disposal which will crystallise charges deferred by rollover relief may be entitled to retirement relief. Retirement relief is described in paragraph 30. As explained in paragraph 30.13.2, in such circumstances retirement relief cannot directly relieve the crystallisation of the rolled-over gains. However, it may be worth while seeking concessional treatment on the matter from the Revenue Commissioners. This should be confirmed directly with the Revenue Commissioners in each separate case.

The form of the relief is that of a deferral. The chargeable gain which arises on the disposal of the old assets is not regarded as crystallising at the time of that disposal, but rather it is treated as crystallising when the "new assets" cease to be used for the purpose of the trade, without further roll-over relief being available on that occasion. This is a different form of relief to the one where the gain is treated as reducing the base cost of the new assets.

The crystallisation of the chargeable gain (ie the clawback of the relief) occurs on the assets ceasing to be used for the purpose of the trade. That is not necessarily the same thing as the disposal of the new asset by the taxpayer. The new asset might cease to be used for the purpose of the trade while still remaining in the taxpayer's ownership eg because he appropriates it to private use. It is also possible that an asset could continue to be used in a trade notwithstanding that the taxpayer has ceased to own it eg where he sells it and leases it back. In the latter instance it is not so clear that the claw-back of relief is not triggered by the disposal by the taxpayer of the new assets, notwithstanding their lease back and notwithstanding the fact that they may never have physically ceased to be used for the purposes of the trade. The ambiguity arises as it is not clear whether the Courts would regard the reference to the "new asset" as being a reference to the ownership rights of the taxpayer in that asset, or a reference to the physical asset itself. On a sale and lease back, the taxpayer would have ceased to be the absolute owner of the asset and thereafter be entitled to the use of the asset not as an absolute owner but as a lessee. Was the "new asset" his absolute ownership title or was it the physical asset? Since ownership titles cannot be brought into use in a trade in any sensible way, and since it is physical assets (in the case of plant and machinery etc) which are used in a trade, a better interpretation would seem to be that a sale and lease back does not trigger a claw-back of the relief. However, the matter is uncertain.

26.3   **Partial re-Investment of Sale Proceeds**

s597(5)   Paragraph 26.2 deals with the situation where the full proceeds are re-invested. Where only part of the proceeds are re-invested, partial relief will be available if the part not re-invested is less than the gain arising.

It could be argued that "gain" in this context is to be calculated without indexation. However, if this is correct it would make a nonsense of several other reliefs.

Where partial relief applies the gain arising is deferred to the extent that it exceeds the amount not re-invested.

Example 131

> *Alan disposed of his factory premises for £120,000 on 15th December 1997 giving rise to a chargeable gain of £15,000. He spent £110,000 on new premises.*
>
> *He had acquired the original premises in December 1984.*
>
> *Alan's liability is calculated as follows:*

	£
Chargeable gain arising	*15,000*
Proceeds not re-invested	*10,000*
Deferred gain-chargeable eventually at 20%	*5,000*
Taxable gain (1997/98)	*10,000*
Taxed at 20%	*2,000*

> *The deferred gain of £5,000 will be chargeable when the new premises ceases to be used for the purposes of the trade. If the sale proceeds of the new premises were invested in further new qualifying assets the gain of £5,000 may be further deferred, and so on. (See paragraph 26.2). If losses arose in the year in which the deferred gain came into charge they may be set off against it.*

> *It is understood that in practice the Revenue are willing to treat the continuing deferral (in the case of a partial re-investment) in this manner, although the strict legal position is not entirely free from doubt.*

26.4 Use Partly for Non-Trade Purposes

s597(9)

Where qualifying assets have not been used for trade purposes throughout the entire period of ownership, the cost and sale proceeds are apportioned as if there were two separate assets. Any apportionment has to be made "having regard to the time and extent to which it was and was not used for those (trade) purposes". The gain attributable to the "asset" used for trade purposes qualifies for relief.

Example 132

> *On 6th April 1970, X Limited purchased a warehouse for £60,000. The warehouse was used for the purposes of the company's trade up to 5 April 1978. From 6 April 1978 to 5 April 1997 it was let . The building was sold on 5 April 1997 for £550,000 (net of expenses). The market value of the warehouse at 6 April 1974 was £80,000. X Limited used the entire proceeds of sale to re-invest in qualifying assets.*

	£	£
Sale Proceeds		*550,000*
Market Value - 6 April 1974	*80,000*	
Indexation @ 6.112		*488,960*
Chargeable Gain		*61,040*

> *Gain attributable to Qualifying Asset:*
> $4/23$ *years x £61,040 =*　　　　　　　　　　　　　　*26,539*

> *Only £26,539 of the gain is eligible for roll - over relief. The balance of the total chargeable gain is liable to tax in the normal way.*

The UK case of Richart v J. Lyons & Co. Limited is authority for the rule that in calculating the periods of trade use and non-trade use, no account is to be taken of any period of time when a chargeable gain was not accruing, i.e. , in *example 132*, ignore the period from 6th April 1970 to 5th April 1974.

The Lyons case is also authority for the proposition that a deemed disposal and reacquisiton at 6 April 1974 of an asset that in fact was held prior to that date, does not interrupt the "period of ownership" of the asset. This particular ruling can have significance in other contexts in which period of ownership may arise e.g. period of ownership of shares for the reduced rate of CGT (abolished from 3 December 1997) or retirement relief.

In the case of E.P. O'Coindealbhain (Inspector of Taxes) v K.N. Price, Justice Carroll in the High Court on 29 January 1988 held that a farm of land, which throughout the period of ownership had been let on conacre to a third party and had not otherwise been used by the taxpayer, had not been occupied by the taxpayer for the purpose of a trade, or for farming and that accordingly an entitlement to rollover relief did not arise on its disposal, notwithstanding that the proceeds of disposal were invested in the purchase of a new farm.

Justice Carroll held that the taxpayer had neither occupied the old farm nor had he carried on a trade of farming on it. The occupation, and the trade of farming were by the conacre tenant.

26.5   **Time Limit for Replacement of Asset**

s597(7)   An amount equal to the sale proceeds (or part thereof) must be expended within the period of 1 year before and three years after the disposal. The Revenue Commissioners have power to allow an extension of this time limit.

It is sufficient that an unconditional contract for the acquisition of the replacement assets is entered into within the time limit mentioned. Provisional relief will be given where such an unconditional contract is entered into, and any necessary adjustments can be made as and when (and if) the assets are actually acquired.

It is necessary that the replacement assets should "on the acquisition" be "taken into use, and used only, for the purposes of the trade". In the UK case of Campbell Connelly and Company Limited-v- Barnett, roll-over relief was denied in part because of a delay in employing the assets acquired in the trade. A company disposed of a premises and shortly afterwards acquired the freehold of another premises. The newly acquired premises had a sitting tenant and it was not until almost nine months later that vacant possession was obtained and the premises occupied for the purpose of the trade. The case was complicated by the fact that the freehold was acquired by the taxpayer company, whereas the sitting tenant was bought out by the parent company of the taxpayer so that the new asset was acquired only in part by the taxpayer. But the fact that the delay of the order mentioned occurred before putting the premises into use for the purpose of the trade was in any event fatal to the claim for relief.

The decision in this case should be contrasted with the decision in the case of Clarke-v-Mayo, a UK case concerned with retirement relief. It had to consider the meaning of the phrase "immediately before the material disposal — the asset was in use for the purposes of that business". The judge held that the words "immediately before—" *should not be construed in isolation but in the context of retirement relief as a whole. In that context the words "immediately before" might be construed as meaning "sufficiently proximate in time to the material disposal or cessation so as to justify the conclusion that the transaction in question formed part of it".* In the Campbell Connelly case however the judge gave no similar broad purposive interpretation to the expression "on the acquisition thereof". It is difficult to argue that the decision in Campbell Connelly is correct and that the decision of Clarke -v- Mayo is also correct. If a purposive interpretation is appropriate in one case, surely it was equally appropriate in the other. It is open to argument that where an asset is put into use in a business within a reasonably short time after being acquired, but in particular in circumstances which make it clear that its acquisition, and its use in the business, are closely related, that the words "on the acquisition there of" cover the situation, and relief ought to be available. The matter is not free from doubt.

The UK case of Steibelt v Paling considered the requirement that the new assets must, on acquisition, be taken into use and be used only for the purpose of a new trade (s597(4)(a)(II). The court concluded that the UK Inland Revenue statement of practice on rollover relief correctly interpreted the law in this particular respect and did not represent a concession. That statement of practice provided *"where a 'new asset' is not, on acquisition, immediately taken into use for the purposes of a trade, it will nevertheless qualify for relief under (TCA 97 s597) provided (a) the owner proposes to incur capital expenditure for the purposes of enhancing its value; (b) any work arising from such capital expenditure begins as soon as possible after acquisition, and is completed within a reasonable time; (c) on completion of the work the asset is taken into use for the purpose of the trade and for no other purpose; and (d) the asset is not let or used for any non trading purpose in the periods between acquisition and the time it is taken into use for the purpose of the trade."*

In the January 1997 issue of Irish Tax Review (Institute Matters, item 16) it is reported that "the Irish Revenue view was that they would continue to apply the law as it was understood prior to this case (Campbell Connolly & Co. Ltd. v Barnett) in Ireland".

In the case of Milton v Chilvers the UK Special Commissioners held that the meaning of **"on the acquisition"** in its context was **"following on the acquisition".** That did not imply immediacy, but it did exclude dilatoriness. The taking into use and the acquisition had to be reasonably proximate to one another.

• **Revenue/Chief Inspector's CGT Manual :**

— In their capital gains tax manual the Revenue Commissioners at Paragraph 19.6.2.10 refer to the Revenue Commissioners' power to extend the period in which reinvestment must occur in order to avail of the relief. They give as an example of circumstances where the period should be extended, where a Local Authority uses its compulsory purchase powers to acquire a property in advance of their need to use the property, and allow the former owner to remain in possession for a period of time which may exceed 3 years. The manual says, *"In such a case a claim for an extension of the time limit may be allowed by the District Inspector for a period of 12 months after the property ceases to be used by the trader for the trade, if the disposal proceeds are reinvested in qualifying assets within this extended period. Any other claim for extension of the time limit should be submitted to head office."*

26.6   **Reinvestment in different trade**

26.6.1   **Broad Outline**

The general rule in relation to rollover relief is that the proceeds of a disposal must be reinvested in specified assets (of a type specified in paragraph 26.1) which must be in use for the purpose of the same trade as were the assets which were disposed of. There are three exceptions to the requirement that the reinvestment be in assets for the same trade.

These are:

• where two or more trades are carried on simultaneously by the same taxpayer;

• where the taxpayer ceases a trade, and commences a new trade within a specified time period;

• where the relief is claimed by a company, and the company is in a group.

These three exceptions to the normal rule are described in greater detail below.

26.6.2   **Two or More Trades**

s597(11)(a)   Normally the relief applies where the disposal and re-investment relate to the same trade. However, the relief also applies (in the same manner) to a person who carries on two or more trades, provided:

• the trades are in different localities

and

• the trades deal wholly or mainly with goods or services of the same kind.

As noted in paragraph 26.6.4 the Revenue Commissioners consider that the reference to carrying on two or more trades can extend to the carrying on simultaneously of two or more trades, or where one trade ceases and another commences. That interpretation may be concessional in that the wording of the legislation would suggest that subsection 11(a) applies only to two trades carried on simultaneously. The equivalent UK legislation specifically provides that the two trades may be carried on either successively or at the same time. However the Irish legislation is structured differently and provides in two separate paragraphs for two trades being carried on, and trades being carried on successively. The latter is subject to time constraints.

In such a case the relief is calculated as if all the separate trades were one single trade; the disposal may be in one trade and the re-investment in the other.

Example 133

> *Joe Brown Ltd. runs a supermarket in Dun Laoghaire, and has a cash and carry outlet in Tallaght where he wholesales much the same line of goods which are sold in his supermarket. The company also operates a hairdressing salon in a shopping centre in Bray.*

> *The company has taken advantage of increasing property values in Tallaght to sell off part of the warehouse there out of which the cash and carry business operates. The proceeds of the sale amounted to £250,000. £100,000 was then applied to acquiring a neighbouring unit in Bray, in order to expand the hairdressing salon. The balance of £150,000 was applied in acquiring new racking and storage systems for the supermarket.*

> *The three operations carried on by Joe Brown Ltd. are self-evidently separate trades. They are in different locations, providing different services and products, to a different range of customers. They do not trade under a single corporate image. There is little exchange of staff between them.*

> *Although all of the proceeds of sale have been reinvested in assets of the type which qualify for the relief i.e. plant, or buildings, and although all of the new assets are used for the purposes of trades carried on by Joe Brown Ltd. the £100,000 invested in the extended premises at Bray does not qualify for rollover relief. The hairdressing trade carried on in Bray is in a different locality to the cash and carry trade in which the disposal was made (thus satisfying one condition for the relief) but the trades do not deal wholly or mainly with goods or services of the same kind. Accordingly it is not possible to rollover from the cash and carry trade into the hairdressing trade. On the other hand, although the cash and carry trade and the supermarket are very different in their nature, they do deal mainly with goods of the same kind, and they are carried on in different localities. Accordingly the £150,000 expenditure does qualify for rollover relief.*

There is no guidance available as to what "different localities" means. In the example above, all three trades were carried on in the greater Dublin area. However each location is several miles away from the other so that they would not in any normal way be said to be in the same locality. "Locality" is not the same word as "location", nor is it a reference to "premises". If in the example above the supermarket and the hairdressing salon were in separate units in the

same shopping centre in Dun Laoghaire (rather than one being in
Dun Laoghaire and the other being in Bray) it is likely that they
would be regarded as being in the same locality (albeit in different
premises, and perhaps not in the same location). The requirement
that the trades be in different localities, in order that reinvestment
can be rolled over from one trade to the other, introduces an
ambiguity into the legislation which is undesirable. It is also unclear
why such a requirement should be introduced since there would not
seem to be any reasons of policy for it.

A published Revenue Commissioners precedent in this area is noted
in paragraph 26.6.4

26.6.3   **Group Roll Over relief**

Group rollover relief is discussed in paragraph 79.

26.6.4   **Cessation of Trade – Commencement of New Trade**

s597(11)(b)   Roll-over relief also applies to a person who ceases to carry on a
trade, and subsequently commences a new trade, provided:

- he carried on the old trade for at least 10 years prior to its cessation

  and

- he commences a new trade within two years of the date of
  cessation of the old trade.

The relief is calculated as if the two trades were the same trade.
There is no requirement in this case, that the two trades should be
similar.

The reference to "within a period of two years from the date on
which he ceased to carry on the trade or trades" would seem capable
of extending to a period of two years before he ceased to carry on the
trade or trades, as well as to a period of two years after he ceased to
carry on the trade or trades. The point is not beyond doubt however.

Where a person ceases to carry on more than one trade, it is not clear
how the two year period should be calculated, if the two trades did
not cease on the same date. The legislation makes specific provision
for the possibility that the taxpayer carried on, and ceased, more
than one trade but the period of two years is to be calculated "from
the date on which he ceased to carry on the trade or trades". If a
person carried on two trades, and ceased the two trades with an
interval of a year between ceasing each one, it would seem a
reasonable interpretation to say that the date on which he ceased to
carry on the two trades was the date on which he ceased to carry on
the last of the two trades to cease.

The case of Steibelt v Paling in the UK concerned a claim for
roll-over relief in the context of a person who had ceased the trade of

carrying on a public house, and subsequently commenced the trade of carrying on a licensed restaurant. The licensed restaurant was located on a barge. It took a considerable period of time to renovate the barge and acquire the necessary licences and finance in order to commence the trade. The original trade was sold in October 1986 but the new trade did not commence until August 1995. The Court held that the gap between the carrying on of the two trades was such that the two trades could not be regarded as being carried on successively. This particular interpretation is not of relevance in Ireland where the word "successively" is not used.

The case also considered the refusal by the Inland Revenue to exercise the discretion granted to them by the UK equivalent of s597(7) to extend the three year period after the disposal of the old assets in which the expenditure on the new asset must occur. The court held that the Appeal Commissioners, in attempting to overrule the Inland Revenue's decision not to extend the period, acted outside their powers. Only the superior courts, on the foot of a judicial review could overrule the exercise of a discretion statutorily granted to the Revenue.

If a person ceases a trade which he has carried on for less than 10 years, he cannot avail of rollover relief by the reinvestment that takes place in a trade which he then commences. In such a situation a taxpayer would be able to achieve rollover relief only on the basis of carrying on two or more trades in different localities (see paragraph 26.6.1 above) or by reference to group relief (if he can organise matters so that group relief would apply) as described in paragraph 26.6.3. In order to get within the relief described in paragraph 26.6.1, he would have to commence the new trade prior to ceasing the old trade; and they would have to be carried on in different localities; and they would have to be concerned with goods or services of the same kind.

Example 134

> Joe Brown Ltd. (see **example 133** *above) closed its cash and carry in Tallaght and sold off the forklift trucks, and palleting and racking. It reinvested the proceeds in equipment and fixtures required to convert the premises into an amusement arcade.*

> *Joe Brown Ltd. will get rollover relief even though the trade that ceased, and the new trade which had commenced are in the same locality, and even though they were concerned with goods and services of a very different nature. This is because the rollover relief being claimed is not in respect of a disposal in a continuing trade, into a second continuing trade (see 26.6.1 above) but is from a trade which had ceased, into a new trade which has commenced. Accordingly the type of restrictions described in 26.6.1 above do not apply.*

- **Revenue Commissioners - published precedent :**

– In their published precedents the Revenue Commissioners have stated *"Where a trade carried on for less than 10 years ceases and a*

*similar trade commences, strictly, relief is not due as Section 597(11)(b)
requires that the old trade be carried on for at least 10 years. However,
Section 597(11)(a) allows relief for two trades, wholly or mainly
concerned with goods of services of the same kind are carried on. This is
read as applying where the trades are carried on simultaneously or
successively, thus covering a cessation of one trade and the
commencement of a similar trade."*

26.7   **Application to Non-Trading Activities**

s597(2)   Roll-over relief is also given to certain persons who are not carrying
on a trade, subject to the same rules that would apply if they were
trading.

The relief applies (with the necessary modifications) to all the
following:

(a)   The discharge of the functions of a public authority.

(b)   The occupation of woodlands managed (by the occupier) on a
commercial basis and with a view to the realisation of profits.

(C)   A profession, office or employment.

• **Revenue/Chief Inspector's CGT Manual :**

– In Paragraph 19.6.2.3 of their capital gains tax manual, the
Revenue Commissioners give as examples of the application
of the relief to an office or employment, the sale by an
insurance agent of his "insurance book" or the sale by an
employee of a luxury hotel, of his right to tips. They describe
these "rights" as "essentially goodwill".

(d)   Such of the activities of a non-profit making body of persons,
whose activities are wholly or mainly directed to the protection
or promotion of the interests of its members in the carrying on
of their trade or profession, as are so directed.

(e)   The activities of a non-profit making body of persons whose
activities are wholly or mainly carried on otherwise than for
profit. The relief applies in the case of land and building only if
they are both occupied and used by the body and the case of
other qualifying assets, only if they are used by the body.

(f)   Such of the activities of a body of persons established for the
sole purpose of promoting athletic or amateur games or sports
as are directed to that purpose (see paragraph 26.9).

(g)   Farming (see paragraph 26.8).

26.8   **Farming activities**

s597(2)(g)   It was necessary to add farming to the list of activities to which
rollover relief would apply because farming is not a trade. For the

purposes of the Income Tax Act it is deemed to be a trade, but it is not in fact or in law a trade for any other purpose.

The way in which the relief is applied to farming is a little ambiguous. The section did not state that farming was to be deemed to be a trade for the purpose of the section. It just states that the section applies, with any necessary modification, to farming as it applies in relation to a trade. That wording leaves some scope for objecting that it is not possible to rollover disposal proceeds arising in a trade, into expenditure in farming, in the manner in which it is possible to rollover from one trade to another, as described in the paragraphs above. Similar comments apply to each of the other categories of activities to which the relief is applied, but which do not constitute trades.

- **Revenue/Chief Inspector's CGT Manual :**

s567(2)(g)

—In paragraph 2.5 of Chapter 19, point 6.2 *"The relief afforded by s597 applies to farming as it applies in relation to a trade. All farming carried on by a person should be treated as one trade irrespective of the size of the holding or holdings and so long as there is continuation. Thus the benefits of the relief will be available to a farmer who disposes of his holding and invests in another holding or in a business (say a retail shop)."*

26.9   Sporting Bodies

s597(2)(f)

As noted in paragraphs 26.1, and 26.7 above, rollover relief can apply to *"such of the activities of a body of persons established for the sole purpose of promoting athletic or amateur games or sports that are directed to that purpose"*.

It seems peculiar that the relief should be specifically confined to such of the activities of the body of persons as are directed to the purpose of promoting athletic games etc., if it is also a requirement that that be the sole purpose of the body of persons. If indeed the body of persons were established for the sole purpose of promoting athletic games etc., any activities not directed to that purpose would be ultra vires the body of persons.

The meaning of the phrase quoted above describing the body of persons is discussed in paragraph 6.4, in relation to the application of rollover relief to development land, where a more favourable treatment is available to the sporting bodies described, than is available to the general body of taxpayers.

In addition to the comments made in paragraph 6.4, it is worth noting that in order that rollover relief should be available, the body claiming the relief must be "established for the sole purpose of promoting athletic or amateur games or sports". It is not clear that a body which is established both to promote sports of the type described, and to promote culture, and/or to pursue political objectives would constitute a body entitled to the relief. The rather peculiar wording referring to "such as the activities - - as are directed to that purpose" might suggest that there was some intention that the relief should be available to a body which pursues a number of objectives other than the promotion of athletic games etc., but that would seem to fly in the face of the clear words used "body of persons established for the sole purpose of promoting athletic or amateur game" etc. Persons relying on the relief should carefully examine the instruments creating the body of persons, in order to see how the objectives of the body are defined.

Although a body of persons established solely for the promotion of athletic games etc. would probably be established for charitable purposes (whether it be in the category of the promotion of education, or of other purposes beneficial to the community), there is no requirement in the legislation that the body claiming rollover relief in relation to its activities should be a charitable body. However a body established for the purpose of making profits from their activities are almost certainly not established *solely* for the purpose of promoting athletic games etc. A body which earns profits in the course of the activities that are directed towards promoting athletic games (e.g. admission to games etc.) and which devotes those profits to the further promotion of those athletic games etc. would probably not be debarred from falling into the category of sporting bodies described above, by reason of their trading activities.

Where a body of persons established solely for the promotion of athletic games etc., as described above, is entitled to relief, the relief applies not only to the 3 categories described in paragraph 26.1 (land and buildings, plant and machinery, and goodwill) but, in relation to disposals on or after the date of passing of the Finance Act 1998, applies also to disposals of shares of any company, and the stocks and bonds of any corporate body, or government or municipal corporation.

Example 135

The Amateur Mud Wrestling Association, a body established solely for the purpose of promoting the amateur sport of mud wrestling, have been raising funds for the purpose of erecting an indoor arena in which to conduct the sport, outdoor venues in winter having proved unattractive to competitors. The money raised has been invested in quoted stocks and shares, pending the accumulation of a sufficiently large sum, to go ahead with the construction. The trustees of the Amateur Mud Wrestling Association, having entered into contracts for the building of the arena, disposed of the stocks and shares thereby realising a substantial gain. The proceeds of the disposal were applied in payments to the contractors who are building the arena.

Since the building of an arena for the conduct of the sport is an activity for the purpose of promoting the sport, rollover relief should be available on any gains arising on the sale of the quoted shares, since they have been applied towards the *construction activity. The position is perhaps less certain if the trustees, on disposing of the quoted shares, had acquired UK government stocks as a short term investment, pending payments to the contractor. UK government stocks would be financial assets of a type which qualify for rollover relief for the sporting body, but the question arises as to whether the proceeds of the sale of quoted shares, when invested in UK government stocks, are being "directed" to the sole purpose for which the body has been established i.e. promoting athletic or amateur games or sports.*

The answer probably is that provided the investment in the government stocks is with a view to ensuring that the trustees are able to meet their obligation to the contractor who is building the stadium, the investment is for the purpose of promoting an amateur sport. In other words, provided the investment in the government stocks isn't ultra vires the trustees (who are established for the sole purpose promoting amateur mud wrestling) it must be an action which is directed towards the sole purpose for which the association has been founded.

If however the trustees of the association abandoned the notion of building a stadium, and left the accumulated funds invested in a portfolio of shares as a form of long term nest egg for the association, it might be more difficult to establish that the proceeds of any disposal of shares (as would occur from time to time in the management of the portfolio) had been directed towards the sole purpose for which the association was established.

As stated in paragraph 26.1, and as illustrated in *example 135* above, the range of assets which qualify for roll-over relief is extended in the case of an amateur sporting body than it is in the case of any other body. It extends to *"any financial assets owned by"* an amateur sporting body. The wide definition of financial assets is set out in paragraph 26.1. Part of the definition requires they must be *owned* by that sporting body.

It seems clear enough that roll-over relief would apply on a disposal of such financial assets by an amateur sporting body.

It is a little less clear that the roll-over relief would apply where an amateur sporting body disposes of (for example) land, in return for financial assets, such as stock issued by a company. In order that the roll-over relief in relation to the land should apply it is necessary that the financial assets into which the land proceeds have been "rolled" should be owned by an amateur sporting organisation. It is certainly the case that once such assets have been acquired by an amateur sporting organisation, they would then be owned by it. But if the organisation "rolls-over" from a land disposal into stock obtained in exchange, would the stock be regarded as being owned by the organisation at the moment or roll-over? In s593 7(3) where the assets which are assets for the purpose of roll-over relief are defined, only financial assets are defined in terms of their ownership. This may be intended to do no more than limit the availability of the relief in relation to financial assets to amateur sporting bodies, but it could also have the intent of limiting the relief to a situation where the financial assets are, immediately prior to and at the moment of the application of the relief, owned by the amateur sporting body. If that were the case, it would not be possible to roll-over from another asset into financial assets. On balance the authors favour the view that the reference to "owned" was intended to do no more than confine the relief to sporting bodies, and does not confine the relief to disposals of financial assets to the exclusion of the possibility of "rolling over" into such assets. The position is unclear.

26.10   Anti-Avoidance

s597(8)   Roll-over relief does not apply unless the replacement asset is acquired for trade purposes, and not wholly or partly for the purpose of making a gain on the disposal of it.

Special provisions apply to the application of roll-over relief where

- a company or,

- trustees of a settlement,

become non-resident or treaty protected. These provisions are discussed in paragraphs 26.14, 65.13.2.5, and 74.1..

26.11   Development Land Gains

s652   Roll-over relief is not available in the case of gains arising on the disposal of development land on or after 28 January 1982.

There are SIX *exceptions to this exclusion* of development land from roll-over relief :

(1)   *Sporting bodies* : certain sporting bodies may claim the benefit of the relief (see paragraph 6.4).

(2)   *Authorised racecourses :* authorised racecourses are entitled to roll over relief if they meet certain conditions (principally the land having been owned by the racecourse for at least five years prior to the disposal and used for the purposes of race meetings, or providing facilities for persons associated with horseracing) - see paragraph 6.4.

(3)   *Dirty industries:* in the case of disposals on or after 6th April 1995, roll-over relief is available on a disposal of development land provided the authority in whose area the land is situated gives a certificate that the land being disposed of is subject to a use that is inconsistent with the protection and improvement of the amenities of the general area, or otherwise damages the local environment. This certification process must be in accordance with guidelines issued by the Minister for the Environment. These add nothing to the statutory requirements.

Example 136

An example might be a company carrying on a scrap metal recovery business on a a derelict site in a residential area. Such a derelict site is likely to be development land (since it would probably command a higher price as housing land than it would for use as a scrap metal business).

The conduct of a scrap metal business in a residential area is likely to be injurious to the local amenities and would probably damage the environment in itself. Were the owner of that site to decide to sell his existing site and relocate onto an industrial estate, he would be making a disposal of development land.

Any gain on the disposal of his site would, if not certified by the local authority as described, be denied rollover relief. CGT could be payable notwithstanding that he may need the entire proceeds of sale to acquire the new premises on the industrial estate. However if certification is granted, rollover relief will be available to him in the normal manner.

The example given above is perhaps a rather extreme example. A scrap metal recovery business would be a most unpleasant neighbour in a residential area. It would be possible for an industry which is much less noisy, and less noxious, to be inconsistent with the protection and improvement of the amenities of a residential area. Even a small light industrial unit, causing no particular noise or effluent pollution, may be an undesirable neighbour in a residential area. It is understood that the attitude of local authorities to the certification process seems to vary from authority to authority. Some authorities appear to take the view that if a particular activity would not receive planning permission were it now to apply for planning permission, by reason of the zoning of the area and its predominant usage, then it is appropriate to give the necessary certificate in order to persuade the enterprise to move elsewhere. Other local authorities appear to require a high degree of pollution of one type or another, before they are willing to certify.

The local authority have little discretion in the matter of giving the certificate. Where an application meets the requirements of the guidelines issued, then the local authority must issue the certificate and has no discretion in the matter. The requirements laid down in the guidelines relate to the use being inconsistent with existing zoning (an objective matter - it either is or is not inconsistent) and with damage to amenities. The latter is a subjective matter where the local authority do have a degree of discretion in arriving at their judgment. But if it can be objectively demonstrated that there is damage to amenities, then the local authority have no discretion in the matter and must grant the certificate.

S652(2) does not state at what point in time the certificate must have issued, in order that roll-over relief should be available on a disposal. Must it be in place-

- prior to the disposal?

- at the date of the disposal?

- before the closing of the sale?

- before a return of capital gains falls to be made?

- before an assessment is raised?

The matter may not be of great significance in that, as noted above, the issue of a certificate is not a discretionary matter. Where the conditions for its issue as set out in the guidelines exist, then the local authority must issue the certificate. The doctrine that "that which must be done is to be treated as done" may have application in a situation where a local authority issues the certificate subsequent to the date of disposal, or subsequent to the closing of the sale etc. If the taxpayer was entitled to have such a certificate from the local authority at an earlier date, it is doubtful if the legislation is intended to have effect so as to deny the taxpayer the relief solely by reference to the date upon which the certificate issued. However there must be some cut-off date which can hardly be later than the date upon which an assessment in respect of gains for the year in question becomes final and conclusive. The law in this area is uncertain. The taxpayer is at risk where he does not have the local authority certificate in place at the date of the contract.

(4) *Farm land:* Farm land disposed of to an authority possessing compulsory purchase powers (which generally speaking will be a local authority) where the land is used solely for the purpose of farming and the disposal is made to enable the road authority to construct, widen or extend a road or part of a road, or for ancillary purposes. It is to be noted that the disposal need not be made on foot of a compulsory purchase order provided the authority to which the land is transferred possesses compulsory purchase powers. Thus a negotiated sale by contract to a local authority for the purposes specified would be within the relief even if no question arose of the exercise of compulsory purchase powers.

(5) Assets used by an *authorised greyhound track* in the provision of appropriate facilities or services for greyhound racing may be entitled to rollover relief notwithstanding that they are development land, in relation to disposals made on or after 6 April 1998. An authorised greyhound race track means a greyhound track having a licence under section 2 of the Greyhound Industry Act 1958. In order that the development land should be entitled to rollover relief, it is necessary that the land should have been owned by the authorised greyhound track for a period of 5 years ending with the date of disposal

and should during that period have been used by them to provide facilities for greyhound racing, and that the new assets should likewise by used by them and owned by them, for the purpose of providing facilities for greyhound racing. However s597 (11) (b), dealing with a person who ceases to carry on a trade, and commences to carry on a new trade within a period of 2 years, does not apply to a disposal of development land by an authorised greyhound race track.

(6)   *Dublin Docklands:* the exclusion of development land from rollover relief does not apply to a disposal by reason of a compulsory purchase by the Dublin Docklands Development Authority under s28 (1) of the Dublin Docklands Development Authority Act, 1997.

It should be noted that the exclusion does not apply to a straight forward sale of land to the Dublin Dockland Development Authority, but only to a disposal by reason of an order made under s28 (1) as referred to above.

26.12   Rollover relief on shares

26.12.1   Broad Outline

s591   Where the proceeds of certain share disposals made after 5 April 1993 are reinvested in the acquisition of certain other shares within 3 years from the disposal, any gain which would have arisen on the disposal is deemed not to arise until the new shares (or shares which in turn replace them) are disposed of.

Both the original shares disposed of, and the new shares acquired must meet certain conditions.

The relief is available only to individuals. It is not available to a company, or to a trustee.

Example 137

John Brown acquired 10% of the shares in Cloth Manufacturers Ltd. on 30 June 1993. From that date he was a part time director of the company. In January 1997, because of conflicts of interest with another clothing company of which he was an employee, John Brown sold his shares to the other shareholders in Cloth Manufacturers Ltd. The shares had cost him £10,000. The sales proceeds amounted to £50,000. In June 1997 Joe invested £75,000 in a new company, Brown Cloths Ltd. in which he commenced to trade as an importer and distributor of Clothing Materials. From that date he was a full-time working director of Brown Cloths Ltd.

In May 2015, Joe, having then reached his 65th birthday sold his shares in Brown Cloths Ltd. to his children for their estimated open market value, of £1 million.

Although Joe has made a disposal in the year 1996/97, the gain arising on that disposal (sales proceeds of £75,000, from which is deducted the indexed acquisition cost amount to £10,640) is deemed by section 27 not to accrue in 1996/97. Joe has met the requirements for the rollover relief on shares and accordingly the crystallisation of the gain is deferred until he disposes of the new shares in Brown Cloths Ltd. This disposal occurs in the year 2015.

Assuming that the law remains unchanged (in this area) up to the year 2015, on the disposal of the shares in Brown Cloths Ltd. two separate gains may arise:

— Any gain on the present disposal of shares in Brown Cloths Ltd, and

— The gain on the disposal of shares in Cloth Manufacturers Ltd which was deferred from 1996/97 when the actual disposal took place.

s599

If the current law remains unchanged, the disposal of shares in Brown Cloths Ltd would qualify for retirement relief (s599 - see paragraph 30) and Joe would be free of CGT in respect of the shares in Brown Cloths Ltd on transfer to his children.

The gain deferred on the disposal of shares in Cloth Manufacturers Ltd in 1996/97 is now deemed to arise in 2015, and (under current CGT law) is chargeable to CGT at the rate of tax which would have applied at the date of disposal - i.e.- January 1977 - a reduced rate of 27% (see paragraph 5 of 9th or 10th Edition for details of the rates of tax).

*Notwithstanding that the gain **"arises"** on the same occasion as the gain on disposal of shares in Brown Cloths Ltd, it does not qualify for retirement relief. The entitlement to any relief would have been determined by reference to the facts at the time of the actual disposal of those shares - and at that time there were no grounds for claiming such relief.*

The roll-over provisions merely defer the time when the gain is deeded to arise - they do not change the date of disposal of the asset.

26.12.2   **Conditions relating to shares disposed of:**

From 6 April 1995:

• The business of the company must consist wholly or mainly of the carrying on of a trade or of holding shares in 51% subsidiaries whose business consists wholly or mainly of the carrying on of a trade (or in relation to disposals after 5th April 1995, a profession).

"Wholly or mainly" has its ordinary meaning but no guidance is given as to how the business of a company is to be measured for this purpose.

s643

All trades qualify for this purpose, including dealing in shares and securities. So also would a trade of dealing in land, to the extent a gain on the disposal of shares is not charged to income tax under TCA97 s643.

• The investor must have been a full time or part time director (or employee) of the company and/or of its subsidiaries.

The above conditions must be met for the shorter of

—a period of 3 years ending with the disposal, or

—the period from the company's commencement to trade to the date of disposal.

There is no minimum holding period for *the shares* being disposed of.

Pre 6 April 1995:

The conditions outlined above apply in respect of disposals made on or after 6th April 1995.

The conditions applying to disposals made prior to 6 April 1995 were more stringent, and additionally included the following:

• The company must be unquoted. 'Unquoted' means not listed on a stock exchange list or dealt in on the USM.

• The investor disposing of the shares must hold at least 15% of the voting rights in the company. "Voting rights" are not defined and it is unclear if they mean only voting rights which extend to all matters arising at a meeting of the company, or those which apply to some such matters only.

• The investor must have been a full time working director of the company and/or of its subsidiaries. For this purpose, *full time* is defined as devoting substantially the whole of his time in a managerial or technical capacity to the business of the company or of its subsidiaries. The meaning of "full-time" and relevant case law is discussed further in paragraph 30.4.

The conditions above must be met for the shorter of a period of 3 years ending with the disposal or the period from the company's commencement to trade to the date of the disposal. There is no minimum holding period for the shares being disposed of.

26.12.3   **Conditions relating to new investment**

• The new investment must be acquired by a *subscription for ordinary share capital* of the new company. A purchase of existing shares from an existing shareholder will not qualify for the relief.

s591   S591, which grants the relief, as originally introduced in the FA93 did not appear to exclude relief where shares were purchased from an existing shareholder, rather than being acquired by way of subscription for a new issue. The section refers throughout (where relevant) to an individual "acquiring" a qualifying investment but does not qualify the manner in which the investment is to be acquired. An amendment to the FA95 introduced a new paragraph (bb) in FA93 s27(5), now s591(6)(c). S591(6)(c) provides that an individual will be regarded as acquiring eligible shares in a qualifying company only if the company uses the money raised through the issue of the relevant shares for the purpose of enabling it, or enlarging its capacity, to undertake qualifying trading operations. The implication of this amendment is that the relief is confined to an investment which results in the company raising money through the issue of eligible shares. By implication that excludes the relief where the shares are acquired by purchase from an existing investor. This amendment applies as regards disposals (in relation to which the relief is sought) made on or after 6 April 1995. The position as regards relief on shares disposed of prior to that date must be open to doubt, notwithstanding the apparently clear words of the legislation, which would, prior to the Finance Act 1995, not appear to have excluded relief where the new shares were purchased rather than subscribed for. There must also be some doubts as to whether it is possible to introduce such a fundamental restriction to the relief by implication, rather than by explicit requirement.

s591(6)
- The investor must acquire *at least 5% of the ordinary share capital* of the new company within 1 year of disposing of the original shares and 15% within 3 years of the disposal. This requirement regarding the acquisition of a 5% minimum holdings within a 1 year period is relaxed in one circumstance. That circumstance is where the taxpayer meets all of the other conditions for relief other than this condition or, other than the condition relating to the taking up of employment or a directorship within a particular period (see below).

s591(6)
Where the taxpayer holds the position of full-time director or full-time employee in the new company and retains that position for a two year period which commences at some time in the period between acquiring shares in the new company, and 3 years after the disposal of the shares in the old company, he may obtain the relief by way of a repayment of capital gains tax notwithstanding not having met the 5% shareholding within 1 year requirement. It is also necessary, for this relaxation of the conditions to apply, that the capital gains tax should already have been fully paid. It is for that reason that the relief is available in these circumstances by way of repayment. Any repayment arising for this reason does not carry interest.

S591, as originally introduced as FA93 s27, required, in order that the relief be available, that the investor "become at any time during the initial period" a *full-time employee or full-time director* of the company. A person who is already a full-time employee, or a full-time director of the company prior to the initial period could not meet this requirement since he could not "become" what he already was. This condition is referred to below. The alternate condition described above (which will satisfy the requirements for the relief where some of the other conditions are not met) requires that "the individual has, throughout a period of 2 years beginning within a specified period, been a full-time employee or full-time director of the qualifying company". Such a condition could be met by a person who is already a full-time employee or full-time director prior to the commencement of the specified period, or the initial period.

Where the original shares were disposed of during the year ended 5 April 1994, the new 5% holding may be acquired at any time up to 5 April 1995.

- The *new company* must not be that whose shares were disposed of, or a member of a group with that company. For this purpose a group is defined by reference to 51% minimum shareholdings.

- The investor must become a *full time director or employee* of the new company within a year of the disposal and retain that position until at least 3 years after the disposal or, if earlier, until a winding up of the company for commercial reasons.

In relation to disposals made prior to 6th April 1995, it was required that the investor become a full-time working director of the new company. It was not sufficient that he merely become a full-time employee.

FA96 s63   *In respect of disposals made on or after 6 April 1996* the requirement is relaxed provided the individual has met all of the other conditions for relief other than the requirement relating to becoming a full-time director or employee, and other than the requirement that he obtain 5% of the ordinary share capital within one year and 15% within 3 years. It is also, if the requirement is to be relaxed, necessary that he should have paid the capital gains tax on the original disposal in full. In such circumstances, provided the taxpayer becomes a full-time employee or a full-time director of the company and remains so for a two year period which begins some time between the date of his acquiring the eligible shares in the new company, and ending on a date 3 years after the disposal of the original holding the relief will apply notwithstanding that the two conditions referred to were not met. If this condition is met, relief is available by way of repayment of capital gains tax.

- The new company must be *incorporated in the State.*

- The company must be an *unquoted company,* i.e. a company none of whose shares , stocks or debentures are listed in the official list of any stock exchange or quoted on any unlisted securities market of a stock exchange. However, where a company was an unquoted company at the date the new investment was acquired, it will not be deemed to cease to be a qualifying company solely by reason of its shares (there is no reference to stock or debentures in this case) becoming quoted on the developing companies market of the Irish stock exchange, in the three years after the date of the disposal of the original investment. The exclusion relating to the developing companies market has effect from 6 April 1997.

- In the 3 year period following the disposal of the original shares, the new company must be *resident in the State* and exist wholly or mainly to carry on a *trade* there (includes a *profession* in relation to disposals made after 5th April 1995).

s591(5)

This is a more restrictive condition than applies to the company whose shares were disposed of. The latter could carry on a trade anywhere, or could be a holding company of trading companies. For this purpose (unlike in the case of the original shares) a trade is defined as one carried on with a view to profits whose revenue in the period of 3 years from the disposal of the original shares is not derived as to more than 25% from dealing in shares, securities, land, currencies, futures or traded options. This definition applies only to new shares acquired after 23 May 1994.

s9

- In the 3 year period following the disposal of the original shares the new company must *not be a 51% subsidiary* of another company; or under the control of another company; or under the control of another company and of persons connected with that other company. A company is treated for this purpose as connected with persons who control it, or with a company with which it is commonly controlled (TCA97 s10).

- The new company must *not be liquidated* in the 3 year period following the disposal of the original shares unless it is for commercial reasons and the liquidation is completed within a 3 year period.

- The company in which the investor has invested his money must use that money to *undertake qualifying trading operations* within a period of three years after the date of disposal (by the investor) of the original holding. This requirement was introduced by FA 1995, but it is interesting to note that the official "explanatory memorandum" published with the Act states that this provision was inserted "in order to put the matter beyond doubt" That statement would appear to imply that the authorities believed that such a requirement always existed. It is difficult to see what could have given rise to such a belief.

- The relief does not apply unless the new shares are acquired for *bona fide commercial reasons* and not wholly or partly for the purposes of realising a gain from the disposal of the new shares. This restriction is difficult to interpret. Few shares are acquired without the prospect of realising a gain on their disposal being in the mind of the investor, even if it is not immediately in prospect, or certain. Indeed in the real world such a prospect would seem inseparable from an acquisition being made for commercial reasons.

s591(9)

s591(11)

A breach of any of these conditions leads to a withdrawal of the relief, the deferred gain being deemed to arise in the tax year in which the breach of condition occurs and to be reportable for that year. On a withdrawal of relief within the 3 year period from the original disposal (but not on a disposal of the new shares outside that period) the amount of the gain arising is computed by adjusting the deferred gain as follows:

- by giving relief for any allowable losses arising in the tax year in which the original shares were disposed of or in previous tax years, to the extent not otherwise already relieved in or before that first mentioned tax year.

- by increasing the gain by an amount equal to a rate of interest calculated at the rate applying to overdue tax on the original gain reduced by the loss relieved as just described, and for the period from the due date for payment of CGT for the tax year in which the original disposal occurred to the due date for payment of CGT for the tax year in which the gain crystallises.

As described in paragraph 89.2, the due date for payment of CGT may vary depending on several circumstances. The date referred to above may be the Preliminary Tax due date for the relevant years. It appears that there is an ambiguity in the legislation in this matter.

Although the gain is treated as crystallising in the tax year in which the new shares are disposed of, or in which there is a breach of conditions relating to the new shares, indexation is calculated only to the date of actual disposal.

Example 138

Joe Brown has been the financial controller of Corrig Makers Ltd. for several years and holds 5% of the issued ordinary and preference share capital of the company. In June 1997 he sold all of his shares to the majority shareholder in the company, and gave up his employment in the company. The proceeds of sale of the shares amounted to £200,000 and Joe's base cost in the shares (indexed) amounted to only £1,000.

Joe applied the consideration in acquiring and investing in a company called Always Open Stores Ltd. He paid £50,000 to acquire all the existing share capital of the company, invested a further £50,000 in new ordinary share capital of the company, and lent the company £100,000. This transaction occurred in November 1997 and Joe immediately became a full-time director and employee of Always Open Stores Ltd. In November 2000 Joe converted his loan of £100,000 into ordinary share capital of the company, as a condition for a bank loan then being negotiated.

Joe's disposal of his shares in Corrig Makers Ltd. discloses a chargeable gain of £199,000. Insofar as part of the proceeds were applied by Joe in purchasing shares, rather than in subscribing for new shares, rollover relief is not available on that portion of the proceeds. Thus £50,000 used to acquire the existing share capital of Always Open Stores Ltd., in November 1997, is not eligible for relief.

The £50,000 which was applied in November 1997 in subscribing for new share capital is eligible for relief under s591, as all of the conditions have been met. The £100,000 converted into share capital in November 2000 does not qualify for relief, as it was a loan to a company , and the investment in the share capital occurred more than 3 years after the date of disposal, which was 30 June 1997.

Joe's computation for 1997/98 would be as follows:

	£
Consideration	200,000
Indexed base cost	1,000
Chargeable gain	199,000
Part of chargeable gain treated as not accruing until new investment in Always Open Stores Ltd. is disposed of	50,000
Chargeable gain arising in 1997/98	149,000

Had Joe converted the £100,000 loan into ordinary share capital of Always Open Stores on 31 May, 2000, the investment would have been made within 3 years of the date of the disposal of the original shares and would therefore qualify for relief. Had that occurred, Joe would make a claim for additional relief (in relation to the £100,000 investment) after 31 May 2000, and his tax liability for 1997/98 would be correspondingly adjusted, and a repayment of tax made to Joe. Joe cannot claim the relief in his return of income and gains for 1997/98 in respect of the £100,000 investment because the claim can only be made after the investment has been made. Joe must therefore make a return disclosing the gain in the computation outlined above, even if it is foreseen by him that he will convert the loan within the 3 year period permitted.

In the example above, Joe might have invested the entire £200,000 proceeds of sale of the original holding into ordinary shares in Always Open Stores Ltd. in November 1997, as an alternative to the steps outlined above. The company might then have used £50,000 of that sum to buy back the shares of the existing shareholder, leaving Joe as the sole shareholder in the company. It is not clear in such a case that the relief would be available in relation to £50,000 of the sum invested by Joe. It is a condition for relief that the company should, within the specified period, use the money for the purpose of enabling it, or enlarging its capacity, to undertake qualifying trading operations. There can be circumstances in which the buyback of shares from an existing shareholder may be for the benefit of the trade of a company (e.g. where that shareholder is elderly and wishes to retire out of the business and make way for new vigorous management). Whether or not the application of the moneys to a buyback of shares in such a situation would be their application *"for the purpose of enabling it, or enlarging its capacity, to undertake qualifying trading operations"* is an arguable matter, and not beyond doubt.

26.13   **Revenue procedures.**

The following comments by the Revenue Commissioners have been published in Irish Tax Review.

TALC minutes 14 December 1998

Question : D3. Reinvestment Relief

(a)   S.591(2)(c) - "consideration must be applied"

Is this to be given a literal meaning, ie must the consideration received be the same funds used to purchase shares. For example, if an individual borrows partly or wholly to invest will the requirement that the "consideration ... obtains for any material disposal ... is applied ..." be breached.

(b)   Full Time Director/Full Time Employee (definition of s250 used)

It is a requirement that the individual is a full time director or employee. This is defined in s250 as a person *"required to devote substantially the whole of his or her time to the service of the company"*. How is this to be applied in cases where an individual is a full time employee with the reinvestment company but has:

   - one or more non executive directorships

   - involvement (small time input) with other ventures or projects.

(c)   Qualifying Company - s591(7)(a)(i)(II)

The company in which the investment is made must be a company which *"exists wholly for the purposes of carrying on wholly or mainly in the State of one or more qualifying trades"*.

The words "exists wholly" could be interpreted to exclude a company which carries on a trade but who also has a trading subsidiary company. If this is correct, then a normal trading company which has a subsidiary company (eg manufacturing subsidiary, R&D subsidiary etc) would not be a qualifying company.

Is this intended to be the case?

Response

(a)   The Chief Inspector of Taxes advised that they will be interpreting this provision strictly.

(b)   The Chief Inspector of Taxes advised that practitioners refer to the Palmer Case in the UK which was held in January 1998, where it was decided that the meaning of the words were that the Director had to spend virtually all of his working time devoted to the company. However, the CIOT confirmed that Directors who were also involved in Trade Associations, Professional Bodies or Sporting Organisations should not be prejudiced under this requirement.

(c)   The Chief Inspector of Taxes advised that this was the case.

26.14   **Company going non-resident**

If an Irish company ceases to be Irish resident, the application of roll over relief both in relation to the company itself and in relation to other companies in a group relationship with it, may be affected.

s627   The restriction of rollover relief was introduced in FA 1997. It takes the form of an *"exit charge"* based on a deemed disposal of its assets by a company on the occasion of it becoming non-resident. This is discussed in paragraph 74.

Certain companies are excluded from the "exit charge" and from the restrictions on rollover relief. These companies which could be broadly described as companies controlled by a company based in a State with which Ireland has a tax treaty (either as to 90% in the case of a direct holding, or as to 50% + in the case of an indirect holding) are more particularly described in paragraph 74.

 Where a company has disposed of "old" assets and before investing in new assets (in relation to which it could claim rollover relief) it ceases to be Irish resident it may not claim rollover relief in respect of an investment in new assets made after it became non-resident. There is an exception to this rule where assets are located in Ireland and are acquired for the purposes of an Irish branch trade (or agency) of that company. The legislation dealing with this exception states that the restriction does not apply in two circumstances:

- where the new assets are , immediately after the company goes non-resident, situated in Ireland and in use for the purposes of a trade or agency of the company, and

- where the new assets are acquired at a date later than the date on which the company went non-resident situated in Ireland, and are in use for the purposes of an Irish trade carried on by the company through a branch or agency.

As the context in which these exceptions arise are the acquisition of new assets after the company has become non-resident it is difficult to understand the reference in the first circumstance (above) to assets in use for the purposes of a trade in the State immediately after the company became non-resident. One may speculate that it is intended to cover a situation where assets which were leased and in use for the purposes of a trade immediately before going non-resident, are subsequently purchased. The second catagory of assets referred to above - those which are situated in the State after the company has become non-resident , and are in use at a later date for the purpose of a trade, is more readily understandable.

References to assets situated in the State include, for this purpose, assets used or intended for use in connection with exploration or exploitation activities carried on in the State or within the limits of the Irish continental shelf.

Similar provisions exist where a trust becomes non-resident - see paragraph 65.13.2.5.

27 COMPULSORY PURCHASE ORDERS-RELIEF

27.1 CPO Relief - Broad Outline

s605

A measure of relief is given where certain specified assets are acquired by an Authority possessing compulsory purchasing powers, provided the proceeds are re-invested. Details of assets qualifying for the relief are set out in paragraph 27.3.

The relief applies to qualifying assets disposed of after 5 April 1978, provided the person making the disposal to such an Authority can prove:

- The disposal would not have been made but for the exercise of (or the giving of formal notice of intention to exercise) those powers by the Authority. Provided notice of intention is served, the powers need not be exercised.

and

- the entire sale proceeds (and no more) are re-invested in replacement assets of the same class as the assets disposed of (special provisions apply where more or less than the sale proceeds is re-invested-see paragraph 27.2).

Where the relief applies (subject to the detailed conditions set out below) the transaction is treated for CGT purposes as if there was no disposal of the old assets, and no acquisition of the new assets. The new replacement assets are treated as if they in fact were the old assets, with the same acquisition date, same cost, and same market value (where applicable) at 6 April 1974 as the old assets.

Example 139

John owns Irish land. The local council serves formal notice on him of its intention to acquire the land (if necessary by use of its compulsory purchasing powers).

John sells the land to the council for £100,000 and a few months later acquires other Irish land for £100,000.

For CGT purposes, he is treated as if he had not sold the original land and had not acquired the new land-the new land carries the same acquisition date, cost and 6/4/74 value (if held at 6/4/74) for CGT purposes as the old land, thus preserving the effect of indexation, and the period of ownership.

Relief is also given (subject to further rules) where more or less than the full sale proceeds is re-invested.

27.2

Full proceeds not re-invested

The general rule mentioned above gives relief where exactly the full sale proceeds are re-invested. In practice, it would be more normal to expect the person concerned to pay either more, or less, for the replacement asset. Relief is provided for this situation.

27.2.1

Less Than Full Proceeds Re-Invested

s605(3)

Where less than the full sale proceeds is re-invested, the taxpayer is treated as making a part disposal to the extent of the amount not re-invested. Relief then applies only to the part of proceeds actually re-invested.

Example 140

Bill bought a farm in June 1970 for £70,000. He has farmed the land since then. The market value at 6 April 1974 is agreed at £220,000.

In June 1997, a Local Authority acquired the land (under its compulsory purchase powers). The purchase price finally agreed was £850,000. It is not development land.

Bill re-invested in other farm land in June 1998, which cost him £700,000 and used the £150,000 balance to pay off a bank loan.

Bill is treated as making a part disposal of land for £150,000. In applying the part disposal 'formula', the part not re-invested is treated as consideration received, and the amount re-invested is treated as the amount value remaining after the part disposal.

i.e. Sale proceeds £150,000

Cost-(using part-disposal formula-see paragraph 11)

$$\text{MV } 6/4/74 \text{ } x \text{ } \frac{A}{A + B} = \text{Cost}$$

$$£220,000 \text{ } x \text{ } \frac{£150,000}{£150,000 + £700,000} = £38,823$$

The 'cost' of £38,823 must now be indexed

£38,823 x 6.112 = £237,826

NO GAIN : NO LOSS -

Note: *As Bill held the land at 6/4/74 he is deemed to have sold and reacquired it at market value on that date*

With regard to the balance of £700,000 which was re-invested, he is treated, in effect, as if he has no disposal and no acquisition. On any subsequent disposal (or part disposal) of the new £700,000 property, he is treated as owning that asset since June 1970, and it will have:

$$- \text{ a cost of } \quad \frac{£700,000}{£150,000 \ + \ £700,000} \text{ x } £70,000 \ = \ £57,647 \text{ at June 1970}$$

and

– a Market Value of (£220,000 - £38,823) = £181,177 at 6 April 1974

27.2.2   More Than Full Proceeds Re-invested

s605(2)   Where the person making the disposal invests more than the full sale proceeds of the old asset, he is treated for CGT purposes as if he has:-

- Acquired a new separate asset at the date of acquisition with a cost equal to the amount of the excess of the amount re-invested over the sale proceeds of the old asset, and

- Made no disposal of the old asset.

Example 141

*If we take the facts in **example 140** but assume that instead of re-investing £700,000 out of the £850,000 sale proceeds, that he invested £900,000 (i.e. more than the sale proceeds of the old assets).*

If it is assumed that he sold the new acquisition for £1,500,000 in August 1999, his liability would be calculated as follows:

	£	£
Sale proceeds		1,500,000
Cost		
MV 6/4/74 £220,000 x 6.313 (old asset)	1,388,860	
Deemed cost June 1988		
50,000 x 1.303 (deemed new asset)	65,150	1,454,010
GAIN		45,990

27.3   Qualifying Assets

s605(5)   The assets qualifying for this relief must be located in the State, and are divided into two separate 'classes':

Trade Assets ("Class I")

- Plant or Machinery used for trade purposes

- Buildings or part of building or similar permanent or semi-permanent structure - used and occupied only for trade purposes

- Land used and occupied only for trade purposes

- Goodwill of a trade.

Land and buildings which would otherwise be included within the scope of "Class I" above are excluded from that class where the trade concerned is a trade of dealing in or developing land and a profit on the disposal of such land would form part of the trading profits.

Also excluded from "Class I" are land and buildings where the trade concerned is one of providing services to the occupier of land and the person making the disposal has an interest in the land. An example of this would be where the owner of let property was carrying on a trade of providing maintenance and other services related to the property for the occupier.

Other Assets ("Class II")

- Any Land Or Buildings, provided

- they are not within Class 1 and do not consist of a dwelling house in respect of which the person making the disposal could claim relief as a principal private residence (see paragraph 24).

To qualify for the relief, you must dispose of a Class I asset and re-invest in Class I assets. Alternatively, you can dispose of Class II asset and re-invest in a Class II asset. You cannot get relief if you dispose of Class I asset and re-invest in a Class II asset (or vice versa).

As noted above, CPO relief extends to land or buildings which are not in use for the purpose of a trade. This may be contrasted with rollover relief (see paragraph 26) where the relief is restricted to assets used for the purpose of a trade (and certain other purposes). CPO relief can extend to any land or buildings in the State, regardless of the purpose to which they are used, other than a principal private residence.

s604

CPO relief does not extend to land in respect of which a claim could be made for principal private residence relief. It must be borne in mind that such a claim may be possible even if the building or land was not in use as a principal private residence at the date of its disposal. Where the person making the disposal used the land or building as his principal private residence for any period of time during his ownership of it, a disposal may give rise to a claim for relief under s604. The rule which denies CPO relief in such circumstances is harsh, since the amount of relief available under s604, by reason of principal private residence relief, may in some circumstances be quite small relative to the relief which might be available on a disposal if CPO relief applied. Whereas a taxpayer is entitled to choose between rollover relief, and CPO relief, where he is eligible for both, he cannot choose between principal private residence relief and CPO relief - the possibility of a claim under principal private residence relief entirely excludes CPO relief.

For the purposes of the relief, the two classes of assets (trade assets and other assets) are treated quite separately. It is not possible to "rollover" from a disposal of one class of assets, into an acquisition of another class.

Example 142

John Brown has carried on a trade in a "filling station" supplying petrol etc. to motorists, for many years. He disposes of the land, buildings, and plant and machinery on the site to a local authority, following the service on him of formal notice of intention to exercise compulsory powers for the purpose of road widening. John invests the proceeds in purchasing a large house in Dublin which is divided into flats occupied by tenants.

The CPO relief does not apply because the assets disposed of are all trade assets falling within Class 1, whereas the asset acquired is an asset within Class 2.

Similar consequences would have followed had the details of the disposal and acquisition been reversed i.e. if the property subject to the CPO had been the rental property, and if John had reinvested in a filling station. Relief would still not be available, for the same reason. This restriction seems rather odd. One could understand the reasons of policy which might restrict rollover relief on the disposal of trading assets, to reinvestment in other trading assets. It is difficult to understand why relief should be available on the disposal of non-trading land and buildings, only if reinvested in other non-trading land and buildings, but not if reinvested in trading assets.

In order that the relief should be available it is necessary not only that the disposal should be the result of the exercise of compulsory purchase powers, or the giving of formal notice of intention to exercise those powers, but that the taxpayer should satisfy the Revenue Commissioners that the disposal would not otherwise have taken place. This requirement might be a means of ensuring that all disposals to local authorities are not brought within the relief by the vendor and the local authority agreeing in negotiations to the local authority giving a formal notice of intention to exercise powers, notwithstanding that both parties are content that the transaction should go ahead without compulsion. If the availability or otherwise of the relief is likely to be a significant financial concern to the vendor, in any case in which the relief is claimed, it would seem likely that a disposal would not go ahead on any other basis, at any rate on the terms negotiated. The UK Special Commissioners decision in the case of Davis v Henderson (1995) raised somewhat similar issues. In that case, the Special Commissioners held that a tenant who negotiated with his landlord in relation to his quitting his tenancy, and who had requested the landlord to serve a notice to quit upon him so that the sums payable to him would in part at least arise under the Landlord and Tenant Acts, and be free of capital gains tax, was nonetheless entitled to be treated as receiving sums under those Acts.

"Class 1" assets are confined to those used for the purpose of a trade. "Trade" is not given any extended meaning and accordingly does not encompass a profession, or an employment.

s655

s3

"Trade" is given the same meaning as in the Income Tax Acts (TCA97 s3). In its original meaning in the Income Tax Acts, "trade" did not include farming, or the commercial management of woodlands. s655 states that "all farming in the State shall be treated as the carrying on of a trade". That falls short of extending "trade" to include farming. Nonetheless it would seem extraordinary if farming fell into Class 2, rather than Class 1. It seems likely that it is intended that farming should be regarded as the conduct of a trade for the purposes of CPO relief but the point is not beyond dispute and in certain circumstances it might benefit a taxpayer if farming were regarded as a Class 2 rather than a Class 1 activity e.g. where the assets which he wishes to rollover into are Class 2 rather than Class 1 assets. It is worth noting that s597, dealing with rollover relief, specifically applies the relief to farming, and to commercially managed woodlands, and does not proceed on the assumption that "trade" would encompass either of those activities.

Class 1 assets for CPO relief purposes do not extend to assets used for several purposes to which rollover is applied by s597. These include the discharge of the functions of a public authority; occupation of commercial woodlands; a profession, office or employment; non-profit making bodies and activities; sporting bodies. The peculiar position of farming has already been referred to. It would seem beyond argument that commercially managed woodlands fall into Class 2, and not into Class 1. Thus activities of commercial management of woodlands is not treated as a trade for income tax purposes, even by statutory extension of the ordinary meaning of "trade". It must of course be realised that CPO relief applies to all land in the State, other than that on which principal private residence relief can be claimed, and that accordingly the fact that these bodies and activities are excluded from being in Class 1 means only that the relief does not apply to plant and machinery, or to goodwill, disposed of by them; and that for the purposes of the relief, they cannot reinvest in trading assets.

27.4   **Time Limit for Re-Investment**

s605(4)

As with roll-over relief, the "replacement assets" must be acquired (or an unconditional contract entered into) within the period of-

- 1 year before the disposal

  and

- 3 years after the disposal.

The roll-over relief provisions regarding the application of relief where an asset is being acquired under contract, and the power of the Revenue to extend the time limit apply in the same manner to this relief (see paragraph 26.5).

27.5 Development Land Gains

s652

This relief is not available in the case of a gain arising on the disposal of Development Land on or after 28 January 1982 except in the case of

(a) *certain sporting bodies:* (see paragraphs 6.4 and 26.9)

(b) *farm land:* an exception is available where farm land is disposed of for the purpose of enabling a local authority to construct , widen, or extend a road or for purposes which are ancillary to such work. This exception extends only to land occupied and used only for the purposes of farming. FA95 s73 [now TCA97 s652(5)] which introduced this exception, does not explicitly state that the farming land must be occupied by the taxpayer who is disposing of it. Prima facie it could apply to the owner of land who has rented land to a tenant who uses it exclusively for farming purposes.

- **Revenue Commissioners published precedent :**

- This interpretation is confirmed in a published Revenue concession which states *"There is no requirement that the person making the disposal has to have farmed the land himself and thus, let land can qualify as long as it has been occupied and used by the lessor for the purposes of farming"*. It is assumed that the published concession contains a typographical error and that the reference to "lessor" should have been a reference to "lessee". Any other interpretation would render the comment meaningless.

s654

s232

"Farming" is defined as in s654. That definition excludes market garden land. S652(5) does not state that the question of whether or not land is occupied for the purpose of farming shall also be determined in accordance with s654, but it is interesting to note that "occupation" is defined in that section and includes having the right to use any land by virtue of any easement, or to graze livestock thereon. The word "occupation" is also defined in s232, in relation to land. There it is defined as "having the use thereof".

Occupation of woodlands is not likely to be regarded as the occupation of land for the purpose of farming. This is probably so arising from the ordinary meaning of "farming" but is reinforced in the definition of "farming" in s654 and of "woodlands" in s232.

• **Revenue Commissioners published precedent :**

— In their published precedent the Revenue Commissioners note a Circuit Court decision to the effect that *bee-keeping* is to be regarded as husbandry. It would seem to follow that land occupied for bee-keeping is occupied for the purpose of farming and is therefore farm land.

28   RE-INVESTMENT OF COMPENSATION PROCEEDS

28.1   Broad Outline

s536

As mentioned previously (in paragraph 4.4), capital sums derived from assets may be treated as giving rise to a disposal (or part disposal) of those assets. However, where the capital sum is received as compensation for the damage, loss or destruction of an asset, relief may be available if the money is used to replace or restore it. The relief does not apply automatically-it must be claimed by the taxpayer.

• **Revenue Commissioners CGT Manual :**

— In Paragraph 19.1.7.3 of the Revenue capital gains tax manual it is stated *"The word "replacement" should be interpreted reasonably. If the new asset is of a similar functional type to the old asset, a claim may be admitted."*

28.2   Wasting Assets

s536(4)

The relief does NOT apply to a capital sum derived from a wasting asset. Wasting assets are discussed in paragraph 10.

28.3   Circumstances of Relief

The relief may be claimed in three different circumstances:-

• *Asset Not Wholly Lost Or Destroyed.*

Where the asset is not wholly lost or destroyed and the entire capital sum (or all of it except for a small part which is not reasonably required for the purpose) is applied in restoring the asset (see paragraph 28.4).

• *Asset Lost Or Destroyed -all Proceeds Re-invested.*

Where the asset is lost or destroyed and the whole of the capital sum is applied in replacing the asset (see paragraph 28.5).

• *Asset Lost Or Destroyed-part Re-invested*

Where the asset is lost or destroyed and only part of the capital sum is applied in replacing the asset. (In this case relief will not be available if the part not applied in restoring the asset is greater than the gain (see paragraph 28.6)).

28.4   **Assets Not Wholly Lost or Destroyed**

s536(1)   In a case where the asset giving rise to the capital sum has not been wholly lost or destroyed, the capital sum will not be treated as a disposal (or part disposal) of the asset provided the entire capital sum is used to restore the asset (or the entire sum, with the exception of a part which is not reasonably needed for the restoration and which is "small" when compared to the entire sum).

The legislation does not lay down any guidelines as to what is considered 'small'.

• **Revenue/Chief Inspector's CGT Manual :**

—In paragraph 7.1 of Part 19 of the instructions on the Taxes Consolidation Act issued by the Chief Inspector of Taxes, it is stated that in practice "small" should be taken as meaning *"not exceeding 5% in comparison with the amount of the capital sum as a whole. Where the compensation is received in respect of damage to an asset which is part of a larger unit, the test of smallness in relation to the value of the asset should be applied to the smallest unit which could reasonably be sold as such. For example, if a cottage is damaged, the unit is the cottage and not the estate on which it stands."*

Where the receipt of the capital sum is not treated as a disposal (under these provisions) the cost of the asset (before indexation) which was restored is reduced by the amount of the capital sum for the purpose of computing any gain or loss on a subsequent disposal of the restored asset.

No relief is given under this rule, unless the entire proceeds (apart from the 'small' exception mentioned above) are used to restore the asset.

In addition, no relief is available where the aggregate total of the allowable cost and enhancement expenditure referable to the asset (before indexation) is less than the amount of the capital sum, or the part of it which would have been taken into the CGT computation as 'sale proceeds' if the relief did not apply in a case where the entire proceeds are not applied in restoration.

As mentioned previously, relief is ordinarily provided whether the entire sum is applied in restoring the asset, or the entire sum, except for a small part not reasonably required for the purpose, is applied in restoring the asset. Where the entire sum is applied in restoring the asset the treatment described above (the relief) is available whether the compensation exceeds the allowable cost and enhancement expenditure, or whether it does not. In contrast, where the entire sum, save for a small part not reasonably required for the purpose, is applied relief will be available only if the compensation proceeds do not exceed the base cost (before indexation) and before incurring the restoration expenditure.

Where the entire amount of the compensation (without any allowance for a small part etc.) is applied in restoring the asset, it would seem that the reduction of base cost, by deducting the compensation proceeds from the base cost, is to be carried out even where the compensation proceeds exceed the base cost. Logically, the base cost cannot be reduced below zero so that the maximum amount of reduction that can occur is in fact the amount of the base cost. This may provide an unexpected bonus to the taxpayer.

Example 143

Michael owns a holiday home in Galway. Vandals broke in and caused extensive damage. He received £5,000 compensation for the malicious damage caused.

In normal circumstances, the £5,000 compensation would be treated as the proceeds of a part disposal for CGT purposes.

If, however, he used the £5,000 to restore the asset, he can claim to be treated as NOT making any disposal. If he claims this relief, the cost and enhancement expenditure (before indexing) of the old asset is reduced by £5,000.

If Michael spent only £4,900 of the compensation (that being all that was required) in restoring the damage to the house, his entitlement to claim that there had been no disposal, and to reduce the base cost by the amount of the compensation, would depend on whether or not the amount of the compensation did or did not exceed his base cost in the asset. If Michael's base cost were £4,000 then he could not claim to have the receipt of compensation treated as not being a disposal. If on the other hand, his base cost were £5,000, or greater, he could claim to have the receipt of the compensation treated as not being a disposal, and to have the base cost reduced by the amount of the compensation.

Example 144

The following details relate to a building partly damaged by fire in December 1992

Cost 30/6/1992	£10,000
Fire Insurance proceeds, all of which was spent on restoring the building	£6,000
Sold 31/3/1993 for	£15,000

Calculation Of Gain

December 1992	*as the full proceeds are applied in restoring the asset - deemed no disposal (if relief claimed). for CGT purposes.*	
March 1993		
Sale Price		£15,000

Cost 30/6/92	10,000	
Less Capital sum received	6,000	
		£4,000
Chargeable Gain		£11,000

> **Note**: *If indexation applied, the net (£4,000) expenditure would be indexed from the date of acquisition.*

The treatment of the compensation proceeds in such a case is similar to the treatment of a grant received. It is assumed that the £6,000 expenditure represents repairs to the damaged property-not capital expenditure, and so the re-investment of the proceeds would not normally have qualified as a deduction in computing a gain or loss for CGT purposes (it must be assumed that the asset was used for trade purposes, and therefore the repair cost would have been allowed as an income tax deduction - and so is excluded for CGT purposes - see paragraph 9).

28.5   Asset totally lost or destroyed: full reinvestment

s536(2)

This relief applies where the asset is lost or destroyed and the compensation proceeds received for the loss of the asset are used in full to replace the asset. The taxpayer is allowed one year in which to buy the replacement asset. The inspector may extend this period. The relief must be claimed by the taxpayer.

Where the entire compensation proceeds are used to replace the asset he is treated as if:

- the destroyed asset was disposed of at such a price as gives no gain and no loss on the disposal

  and

- the consideration for the new replacement asset is reduced by the excess of:

the compensation proceeds and any residual or scrap value of the old asset

  over

the amount taken in above as disposal proceeds.

Example 145

Paddy bought an old painting by an internationally recognised artist in June 1985 for £30,000.

In January 1998 the painting was totally destroyed in a fire. The insurance proceeds amounted to £110,000.

In February 1998 Paddy replaced the painting with another painting by the same artist at a cost of £115,000.

As Paddy re-invested the entire proceeds, he is entitled to claim full relief:

	£
Cost of old asset	30,000
Compensation	110,000
Excess	80,000

Paddy is treated as if he had disposed of the asset at no gain, no loss, i.e. £30,000. This amount of the compensation received is used against the total cost of the old asset; the excess over that part of the proceeds, i.e. £80,000 is, in effect, treated in the same manner as a 'grant' received towards the cost of the new asset.

	£
Cost of new asset	115,000
Less excess	80,000
Allowable cost	35,000

In arriving at the gain chargeable on a subsequent disposal of the new asset, the net cost of £35,000 will be indexed.

28.6   **Compensation Partly Re-Invested**

If the amount not used to replace the asset exceeds the gain, no relief can be claimed.

s536(3)   Where only part of the compensation proceeds are used to replace the asset, and the amount not used for this purpose does not exceed the gain, relief may be claimed as follows:

• the taxpayer is treated as having made a disposal and the gain is reduced to the amount not used to replace the asset, *and*

• the cost of the 'new' asset is reduced by the balance of the gain (which is deferred).

Example 146

*If we take once again **example 145** (Paddy's painting) but assume that he only spent £105,000 in replacing the asset.*

The position would be as follows:

	£	£
Proceeds		110,000
Cost (incl. enhancement expenditure)	30,000	
Indexed...x 1.390		41,700
Gain		68,300

The gain is reduced to the amount not re-invested,

	£
i.e. Proceeds	110,000
re-invested	105,000

not re-invested   5,000

The gain is therefore reduced to £5,000. Tax is calculated on the £5,000 in the normal manner.

The cost of the new asset is reduced by the balance of the gain:

	£
Gain	68,300
Chargeable now	5,000
Balance deferred	63,300

On the disposal of the new asset, its cost is reduced, i.e.

	£
Expenditure	105,000
Less gain deferred	63,300
Cost	41,700

Note: *It is interesting to compare the result of applying the relief in this case, with the situation where the proceeds are fully re-invested (see paragraph 28.5). Partial re-investment can give higher relief in certain circumstances, because of the loss of indexation which occurs where relief is claimed on full re-investment of the proceeds.*

28.7 Time limit for reinvestment.

s536

In order that relief under s536 should be available, it is necessary that the expenditure on the replacement of the asset should take place within one year of receipt of the compensation. The Inspector may allow a longer period.

- **Revenue/Chief Inspector's CGT Manual :**

— Paragraph 7.2 of the instructions relating to the Taxes Consolidation Act issued by the Chief Inspector of Taxes (Part 19) permits an inspector to extend the replacement period up to 2 years where delay can reasonably be regarded as unavoidable. A delay beyond 2 years has to be referred to head office.

28.8 Tenants

- **Revenue/Chief Inspector's CGT Manual :**

— In the Revenue Commissioners manual on capital gains tax it is stated that the lessee of a property should not be treated as deriving a capital sum from an asset where he receives insurance proceeds in relation to damage to the asset, to the extent that he applies those proceeds in discharging an obligation to restore any damage to the property.

This is a distinct matter from roll-over relief in respect of insurance proceeds. Such roll-over relief would not apply in the circumstances described since a lease with less than 50 years to run is a wasting asset. The instruction in the Revenue manual is presumably concessional. It does not indicate how it would interact with any claim by the lessee that his expenditure constituted enhancement expenditure on his leasehold interest, assuming such a claim could be asserted.

29   DISPOSAL OF BUSINESS TO A COMPANY

29.1   Broad Outline

s600

Where a non-corporate person (i.e. individual, trust, partnership) transfers a business (as a going concern) to a company, a measure of relief is given to the extent that the sale proceeds are taken by way of shares in the company. The relief, in effect, consists of a deferral of the tax payable on the amount of the consideration taken in the form of shares in the company.

s600(6)

"The relief will not apply....... unless it is shown that the transfer is effected for a bona fide commercial reasons and does not form part of any arrangement or scheme of which the main purpose or one of the main purposes is avoidance of liability to tax".

In accordance with s61 FA 92, this restriction applies only to a transfer effective on or after 24 April 1992.

The interaction of this relief with "retirement relief" is described in paragraphs 30.7 and 30.13.1

29.2   Conditions for Relief

All of the following conditions must be complied with before the relief applies:

(a) There must be a transfer of a business to a company from a person who is not a company.

(b) The business must be transferred as a going concern.

(c) The whole of the assets of the business or all of those assets other than cash must be transferred.

(d) The transfer must be wholly or partly for shares in the company.

• **Revenue/Chief Inspector's CGT Manual :**

— The Revenue Commissioners, in their manual relating to capital gains tax state that if all of the assets of a business other than cash are not transferred to the company, the relief provided by Section 600 will not be available and a capital gains tax charge may arise on those assets which are transferred to the company. That emphasises the importance of carefully identifying what

constitutes the "assets of the business" when planning for
incorporation. It would seem obvious when determining what
constitutes the "assets of the business" for this purpose, regard
would be had only to the assets as they exist at the moment of
transfer.

Example 147

*Joe Adams has decided to incorporate his undertaking business. He has carried
it on in premises owned by his father, on a rent free basis for several years.
Immediately prior to the incorporation Joe obtains a 2 year 9 month lease from
his father for the premises in question.*

s600

*On the face of it, the asset of the business (in so far as concerns the premises) for
the purpose of s600 is the 2 year 9 month lease, and not whatever interest
(possibly none at all in the circumstance described) which Joe may previously
have had in the premises.*

There can be obvious difficulties in determining whether or not an
asset is a business asset eg a motor car used partly for private
purposes and partly in the business. Another example of potential
difficulty is where the business of a partnership is being
incorporated, and where the premises is owned solely by one of the
partners. Because of the importance of ensuring that all business
assets are transferred on the occasion of incorporation, it is probably
safe to proceed only on the basis of prior clarification of such issues
with the Revenue Commissioners (assuming such clarification is
provided).

Where a single building is in use partly as a private residence, and
partly for the purpose of the trade, there are obvious practical
difficulties in transferring the property as a whole to the company.
An example of such a building could be a public house, or shop,
where the family accommodation and the commercial premises are
all in one building. One apparently obvious solution would be to
separate out the commercial parts of the premises and make it
subject to a lease. There is a difficulty in doing that in that the courts
generally will not permit a person to grant a lease to themselves.
This is probably yet another situation requiring concessional
treatment from the Revenue (should such be available).

29.3 Going Concern

It was held in the UK case of Gordon -v- IRC that the question of
whether a business was transferred as a 'going concern' was to be
decided at the date of the transfer. In that case a farming partnership
of husband and wife transferred the farm business (and all the
assets, etc.) to a company, to avail of the CGT deferral. At the same
time negotiations were in progress for the sale of the farm, which
was actually sold by the company within a few months of the
transfer.

In the Court of Session (Scotland), the Lord President (Hope) in giving judgement stated... *"The business which he transfers to the company must be transferred to it 'as a going concern'. The word 'as' is linked to the word 'transfers', and this shows that it is the state of the business at the date of the transfer which must be considered. There is no requirement that the business shall answer to the description of being a going concern at any future date or that it shall continue to be a going concern for any period after the date of transfer, nor is the relief said to be affected by what the transferee may do with the business once it has been received by it .....The rollover relief does not depend on the date on which the disposal was made which in terms of (s.10 of the 1975 Act) was the time when the contract was made. Nor does it depend on the state of the business at the date fixed by the contract for the transfer if the transfer did not in fact take place on that date. What is in issue is whether the business was a going concern at the date when it was actually handed over from one party to the other."*

The judge in the Gordon case quoted an earlier Australian case (a reference under the Electricity Commission (Balmain Electric Light Company Purchase) on the meaning of "going concern" as follows:

"To describe an undertaking as a going concern imports no more than, at the point in time to which the description applies, its doors are open for business; that it is then active and operating, and perhaps also that it has all the plant etc.. which is necessary to keep it in operation, as distinct from its being only an inert aggregation of plant...."

29.4   **Calculation of Relief**

The gain is calculated on the normal basis, ignoring any relief which may be available under this provision.

* The gain is apportioned (on the basis of market value) between

  − the value of shares taken in consideration of the transfer, and

  − the value of other consideration (i.e. cash, assets, loan account, etc.).

* The part of the gain apportioned to the other consideration is assessed, and the tax is collected in the normal manner.

* The part of the gain apportioned to the value of the shares taken in the company is not assessed. Instead, relief is given by deducting that part of the gain from the allowable cost in calculating a gain or loss on the ultimate disposal of the shares received in consideration for the transfer. Unlike roll-over relief, the gain is not merely held in abeyance; the cost of the shares is reduced. On a subsequent sale of the shares, with a reduced cost, the gain (if any) on the disposal of those shares will be increased, and the tax may, in effect, be payable at that stage. If, however, the value of

the shares fell substantially before the disposal, the tax on the gain deferred on the transfer of the business may never be collected.

Example 148

William, who started in business on 30 June 1965, transferred his business (all of its assets) to "WILLIE Ltd" in exchange for 10,000 ordinary shares of £1 each in WILLIE Ltd and £30,000 cash on 31 March 1989. The value of the shares at 31 March 1989 is agreed at £95,000.

William's assets as shown by his balance at 31 March 1989 were:

		Cost £	MV 6/4/74 £
Premises (at cost 30/6/65)		7,000	20,000
Goodwill (*William's estimate in 1989)		12,000*	4,000
Debtors		4,000	N/A
Stock in Trade		10,000	N/A
Cash		3,000	N/A
		36,000	
Less creditors	6,000		N/A
Taxation due	2,000	8,000	N/A
		£28,000	

During the negotiation with WILLIE LTD, the following market values (at 31 March 1989) were agreed:

	£
Premises	100,000
Goodwill	20,000
Debtors	3,000
Stock in Trade	10,000
Agreed value of business and assets at 31/3/89	133,000

The following are to be paid by WILLIE LTD, on behalf of William:

	£	£
Creditors	6,000	
Taxation	2,000	8,000
Net consideration due to William		125,000

On 31 March 1993 William sold his £10,000 ordinary shares in WILLIE Ltd to TAKEOVER Ltd for £150,000

GAIN ON SALE OF SHARES

The first matter to be looked at is the 1989 transfer of the business to the company:

	£	£
The value of the assets is		133,000
Taken in cash	30,000	
Debts paid on behalf of William	8,000	38,000
Value of shares (balance)		95,000

	£	£
Premises:6/4/74 value = £20,000 x 4.848=	96,960	
proceeds	100,000	
		3,040
Goodwill:6/4/74 value = £4,000 x 4.848 =	19,392	
proceeds	20,000	
		608
Debtors - no chargeable gain		
Stock - no chargeable gain		
Cash - no chargeable gain		
TOTAL GAIN		3,648
DEFERRED GAIN = 95/133 x £3,648 =		£2,605

This part of the gain is not taxed; instead, the cost of the shares is reduced by the deferred gain.

	£	£
i.e.		95,000
Less deferred gain		2,605
"cost"		92,395

CHARGEABLE GAIN:

$^{38}/_{133}$ x £3,648.....   1,043

This part of the gain is taxed in the normal manner, at the appropriate rate.

The next step to complete the picture is the calculation of the gain on the subsequent sale of those shares in 1993.

	£	£
Sale proceeds		150,000
Cost	92,395	
92,395 indexed @ 1.146		105,884
GAIN		44,116

Tax is calculated in the normal way on this gain.

Where the acquiring company takes over the liabilities of the business (on transfer of the business to the company) the value of the liabilities taken over represents *consideration other than shares* for the transfer.

Concessionally, the Revenue Commissioners may treat the transfer of bona fide trade liabilities as not being consideration other than shares for the purpose of calculating the relief.

- **Revenue Commissioners published precedent:**

—In their published concessions the Revenue Commissioners have stated *"Liabilities of the business included in the transfer rank as consideration for the transfer because the discharge of liabilities of the transferor by the transferee is equivalent to the payment of cash by the transferee to the transferor. In practice, however, where an individual transfers a business to a company, in exchange for shares only, and assets exceed liabilities, bona fide trade creditors taken over will not be treated as consideration."*

29.5 Offshore Assets

Part27 Ch2

As outlined in paragraph 35.12, in certain circumstances part 27 chapter 2 of TCA97 can impose an income tax charge on the disposal of "a material interest in a non qualifying offshore fund". Such an offshore fund can include a non resident company as well as a collective investment undertaking.

Although the incorporation of a business does not give rise to an immediate charge to Capital Gains Tax, if a material interest in a non qualifying offshore fund is included among the assets of the business which is being incorporated, a charge to income tax may arise (on an amount which is computed largely as a capital gain on the same disposal would be calculated). That income tax charge is not relieved in the same fashion as the CGT charge arising on incorporation is relieved.

To avoid double taxation on the subsequent disposal of the shares received on the incorporation of the business, the sum which is charged to income tax is deducted from the gain referred to in paragraph 29.4, before the apportionment between shares and other consideration is made. Accordingly any charge to CGT that does arise on the incorporation (by reason of part of the consideration being other than shares) is proportionately reduced to take account of the amount also charged to income tax, and the extent to which the base cost of the shares would be reduced by the relieved gain is in turn reduced by the amount charged to income tax, thus effectively increasing the base cost of the shares by the proportionate amount charged to income tax.

30   RETIREMENT RELIEF

30.1   Broad Outline

s598
s599

In broad terms *retirement relief* is a relief given to an individual on the sale of all or part of the qualifying assets of his business, provided he is aged 55 years or more at the date of disposal. The relief applies automatically where the conditions are met. No formal claim is necessary. Where all conditions are met, the relief takes the form of a reduction in the tax (CGT) payable on gains accruing on the disposal of the qualifying assets. In most circumstances, the relief reduces the tax payable to nil. It is important to note, that the relief may only be temporary, and could, in effect, be withdrawn by reference to certain events happening subsequent to the relieved disposal.

There are two separate sections in the 1975 Act dealing with this relief:

- s599 deals with a *disposal to a child* of the individual owner, and

- s598 deals with a *disposal* which is not within the scope of s599.

s599(1)(a)

Where the disposal is to a *child of the individual owner*, there is no limit on the proceeds of disposal, or gain, which may qualify for relief. However, there is, in effect, a clawback of the relief from that child, if the child does not retain the assets for a period of 6 years.

Where the disposal does not fall within s599, there are two mutually exclusive separate reliefs :

s598(2)

- *Full relief* from CGT payable on the disposal of qualifying assets provided the aggregate sale proceeds of such assets does not exceed the specified limit (currently £375,000).

- *Marginal relief* may be available where the (aggregate) sale proceeds exceeds £375,000.

Both the full, and marginal reliefs are potentially subject to recomputation in the future if the taxpayer makes further disposals of qualifying assets, and increases the aggregate of such disposal proceeds. The revised sale proceeds aggregate applies to current and also to past years. Applying this revised aggregate to earlier years, may result in a full or partial clawback of relief already granted in those earlier years. The aggregate proceeds exemption limit has increased over the years and thedetails are set out in the table below:

RETIREMENT RELIEF - AGGREGATE EXEMPTION LIMIT	
Date of disposal	**aggregate**
Prior to 6/4/91	50000
6/4/91 to 5/4/95 [FA91 s42(a)]	200000
6/4/96 to 30/11/99	250000
On or after 1/12/99	375000

Retirement relief only applies to an individual. A company, or person holding the business in a fiduciary or representative capacity (who would be deemed not to be an individual in that capacity) does not qualify for this relief.

s577(A)

The FA98 inserted s577A which can provide retirement relief to the trustees of the settlement on the occasion of a person becoming absolutely entitled to the assets of a settlement on the giving up of a life interest by a life tenant. This is further described in paragraph 30.12.

The relief extends to an individual sole trader, an individual partner in a partnership, or an individual who holds his business interests through a company (on the disposal of all or part of the shares in his *family company*).

Like all reliefs, it is subject to many conditions. Although this relief is commonly referred to as *retirement relief*, it has nothing to do with retirement. The actual retirement of the individual owner is not a condition for obtaining the relief. The relief is available even though the owner who disposes of all or part of his business assets, remains actively engaged in the business after the disposal.

A number of important amendments were made to this relief in the FA95. The changes made are clearly indicated in the text, and take affect only in relation to disposals made on or after 6th April 1995. If a reader has difficulties relating to disposals prior to 6th April 1995, he is referred to the 6th edition of this book (FA94 edition) which dealt with the problems existing under the pre 1995 legislation.

The UK legislation relating to retirement relief differs from the Irish legislation. The UK legislation involves the concept of the disposal of a business or of part of a business which is not a concept which appears in the Irish legislation. Accordingly a number of UK cases relating to retirement relief, which were concerned with this particular aspect of the UK legislation, are not relevant in considering the Irish legislation. These include McGregor v Adcock, Atkinson v Dancer, and Jarmin v Rawlings , amongst others.

30.2   **Conditions for relief**

The relief applies where the disposal is made -

• by an individual

• who is aged 55 years or more at the time of the disposal,

In addition, the disposal must be :

• of qualifying assets (see paragraphs 30.4 and 30.5)

• which have been owned by that individual for the qualifying period (see paragraph 30.4 and paragraph 30.7).

There is also an aggregate *"lifetime"* limit applied to the disposal proceeds (other than to a child of the individual making the disposal). The current aggregate limit is £375,000. The measurement of the aggregate limit can be difficult, and is dealt with in paragraph 30.8. Marginal relief may apply where that limit is exceeded, and that is dealt with in paragraph 30.10.

30.3   **Amount of relief**

Where the relief applies,

s599   • On a disposal to which s599 applies (i.e. to a child of the individual making the disposal) the relief is the full amount of the CGT payable on the disposal of the qualifying assets.

s598   • On a disposal to which s599 does not apply,

−if the proceeds does not exceed the limit (currently an aggregate total of £375,000) the relief is the full amount of the CGT payable on the disposal of the qualifying assets.

−if the proceeds exceeds the limit, the normal relief does not apply. Instead a marginal relief may apply to limit the CGT payable to the one half of the excess of the sale proceeds over the allowable limit for the relief.

The rules for calculation of the limit (currently £375,000) are set out in paragraph 30.8, and details of the rules for calculating the marginal relief are set out in paragraph 30.10.

The relief consists of a reduction in the amount of tax (CGT) payable on the gain. To calculate the relief, it is necessary to first calculate the CGT which would have been payable on the disposal, ignoring any relief. The relief is then granted as a deduction of all (or part in the case of marginal relief) of the CGT which would otherwise have been payable on the disposal of the qualifying assets.

s598(2)(b)   In determining the amount of CGT payable on the disposal of qualifying assets (for the purposes of computing the amount of the relief) all allowances, losses etc. are set against other gains of the individual for that year insofar as that is possible.

The amount of CGT payable in respect of the gain on the disposal of the qualifying assets is calculated by measuring :

- the amount of CGT payable on all gains including the gain on disposal of the qualifying assets,

- the amount of CGT payable ignoring any gain on disposal of the qualifying assets.

The difference between the two amounts is the CGT payable on the disposal of the qualifying assets.

Example 149

John sold a building used by him for the purpose of his business at arms length to a total stranger. He had owned the building and used it for business purposes for the past 17 years. He also sold a painting, which was not a business asset. The relevant details are as follows:

	Sale Price	Gain
	IR£	IR£
Building	160,000	20,000
Painting	10,000	2,000

John is unmarried, and has no other gains or losses to be taken into account in calculating the tax payable for that year. He is 56 years of age, and has never sold any other qualifying assets. Both sales took place during 1999/2000.

His gains of the year amount in total, to £22,000, less the £1,000 personal exemption. This leaves a total of £21,000 chargeable to CGT @ 20% = £4,200.

The only remaining question is the amount of the retirement relief to be deducted from the CGT payable.

The CGT payable including the £20,000 gain on the qualifying asset is £4,200. The tax which would be payable ignoring that gain is £1,000 @ 20% = £200. The difference of £4,000 represents the CGT payable on the qualifying asset (i.e. setting the £1,000 personal exemption exclusively against the other gain of the year). The CGT as calculated of £4,200 is then reduced by the relief of £4,000 leaving the tax payable of £200 on the painting.

However, the annual exemption of £1000 provided for by s601 is not available in any year in which retirement relief is claimed under s598 or under s599. Accordingly it is necessary to recompute the CGT in this case without reference to the annual exemption. This has the effect of increasing the tax payable by £200 (the annual exemption amount of £1000 at 20% equals £200). This leaves a final CGT bill of £400.

30.4   **Qualifying Assets**

It is not necessary for the individual to dispose of his business - but merely to dispose of all or any part of his qualifying assets (subject to the age condition, and the sale proceeds limit - if any) to qualify for the relief.

In broad terms the relief applies to gains arising on the disposal of business assets, and where the business is carried on through a company, the relief can also extend to include shares in that company.

s598(1)   The term 'qualifying assets' is not defined as such, but is stated to include two specific items:

* **the chargeable business assets** of the individual which, apart from *tangible movable property* he has owned for a period of not less than 10 years ending with the date of the disposal,

   and

* **shares or securities of a company** which has been:

   — a trading or farming company and his family company,

      or

   — a member of a *trading group* of which the *holding company* is that individual's family company

   during a period of 10 years ending with the disposal, and of which he has been a working director for a period of not less than 10 years (during which 10 year period he has been a *full-time* working director for not less than 5 years).

The meaning of the phrase 'during a period' of not less than 10 years was considered in Davenport v Hasslacher. It was held that it could only mean 'throughout the entire period of 10 years', and not merely 'at any time during that 10 year period'.

The FA98 amended the definition of "qualifying assets" to add on the requirement that not only should the chargeable business asset have been owned by the person for a period of not less than 10 years ending with the disposal, but also that they should have been the chargeable business assets of the individual throughout that period of 10 years ending with the disposal. That amendment applies with effect to any disposal on or after 6 April 1998.

The amendment resolves a doubt which had existed as to whether, where a person had owned assets for a period of 10 years, and on the date of the disposal they were chargeable business assets (but perhaps had achieved that status only a short time before the disposal), they were or were not qualifying assets. The amendment resolves the matter for disposals on or after 6 April 1998, but does not resolve it for disposals prior to that date. The fact that the

340

amendment was considered necessary might be an indication that the pre-existing wording did not require that the assets should have been chargeable business assets throughout the minimum 10 year period of ownership, in order to be qualifying assets, but that is not certain. The amendment may be intended as no more than clarification. In any event the interpretation by the Oireachtas of existing legislation, in making an amendment, is not to be taken as a guide to the true meaning of the prior legislation. On balance, and on a reasonable reading of the plain words which existed in relation to disposals prior to 6 April 1998, there was not a requirement that the assets owned by the individual for the minimum 10 year period, should have been throughout the period capable of qualifying as chargeable business assets.

Example 150

John carries on a trade of manufacturing dog food. He also owned a lock up garage for over 20 years, and for most of that period had rented it out to various tenants. In 1996 John resumed occupation of the lock up garage, as he needed it to store raw material for the expanding dog food business. In 1998 John sold the dog food business, including the lock up garage.

The lock up garage was not in use for the purpose of Johns trade throughout the 10 years ending with the disposal. It had been in that use for approximately 2 years, notwithstanding that John had owned it for almost 20 years. Accordingly, if the disposal occurred after 6 April 1998, it is not a qualifying assets for the purpose of retirement relief.

If the disposal had occurred in March 1998 the position is not as clear. John would have at least an argument to put up that the correct construction of the legislation then applying did not require that the asset should have been in use for the purpose of the trade throughout the 10 year period ending with its disposal, provided it was in that use at the date of its disposal, and had been owned by him for 10 years ending on that date.

FA98 s72   The fact that the amendment was expressed to take affect only in relation to disposals on or after 6 April 1998, notwithstanding that it was published earlier in the Finance Bill, would lend some support to the view that it was not intended as a clarifying section, but rather was intended to affect change in the legislation. Had the purpose merely been clarification, presumably the section would have been expressed to have application from an earlier date.

The FA98 has also amended the definition of "qualifying assets" in relation to certain farm land where the disposal in respect of which relief is claimed occurs on or after 6 April 1998. Elderly farmers sometimes rented their land to tenants under a scheme known as the Scheme of Early Retirement from Farming. This is a scheme run by the Department of Agriculture and Food under EU regulation. It is designed to encourage the passing on of land to younger farmers. It was found that where a farmer had rented out his land under the scheme, he no longer qualified for retirement relief in relation to that land (notwithstanding that he was still the owner and may have been the owner for the past 10 years) as the land was no longer in use by him for farming. Rather it was used by a tenant for farming. The amended definition applying to the disposals of land on or after 6 April 1998, would treat as a qualifying asset *"land used for the purposes of farming carried on by the individual which he or she owned and used for that purpose for a period of not less than 10 years ending with the transfer of an interest in that land for the purposes of complying with the terms of the scheme"*.

The amended wording used, quoted above, is rather ambiguous, if its purpose is indeed to provide retirement relief to farmers who are no longer farming the land in question, but are renting it out to others who carry on the farming. It would seem to require that the land :

- be used for the purposes of farming by the individual making the disposal, at the date at which he makes the disposal, and, additionally,

- should have been used for the purpose of farming by that individual for a period of not less than 10 years ending with the grant of a lease or licence under the Scheme.

The wording used would not seem to extend to a situation where the land was rented out, and remained rented out under the scheme, at the date of its disposal.

Example 151

John had carried on farming on his 50 acre farm for 40 years, until 1996, when he granted a lease of the land to his son under the early retirement scheme run by the Department of Agriculture. In 1998 John transferred the freehold of the land to his son, John junior.

In 1998 the land was not in use by John for the purpose of farming, notwithstanding that it had been so used by him for a period of not less than 10 years ending at the date at which he granted the lease under the scheme. On the face of it, it would seem he was not entitled to retirement relief.

If alternatively, John had cancelled the lease to John junior and resumed occupation of the land, and resumed the carrying on of farming on the land for no matter how short a period it would seem he would meet the requirements of using the land for the purposes of farming at the date of the disposal, and of having done so for a period of not less than 10 years up to the time at which he granted the lease under the scheme.

Since there would seem to be no particular purpose in a father terminating the sons lease and briefly reoccupying the land prior to transferring it to the son, it remains to be seen how the Revenue will interpret the section, or how they would administer it in such circumstances.

It may be that the correct interpretation (and probably that which was "intended") is that the requirement that the land be used by the taxpayer for the purposes of farming is a requirement which fell to be met, not at the date of disposal of the assets in relation to which retirement relief is claimed, but rather at the date at which he granted a lease for the purposes of the Scheme of Early Retirement for Farming.

- **Revenue/Chief Inspector's CGT Manual :**

—The Revenue Commissioners, in their capital gains tax manual at Paragraph 19.6.3.12 provide a concessional relief in relation to a partnership situation. The situation dealt with is one in which an asset is owned privately by a partner, but is provided for the purpose of the partnership business. The difficulty which arises is that if rent is paid, the asset is, in the hands of the partner individually, an investment and not a trading asset. The instruction given is that where market value rent is paid, retirement relief should be available on the basis that *"a fraction of the asset (equal to the fraction represented by the partner's share of the partnership profits)"* should have been regarded as a chargeable business asset. Where the rent paid is less than market value the manual states that *"a larger fraction of the asset than that stated above"* may be regarded as a chargeable business asset. Such cases should be submitted to head office. If no rent is charged, the asset is regarded as a chargeable business asset in its entirety.

As stated above, in order that shares should be qualifying assets one condition is that the taxpayer should have been a "full time working director" for at least 5 of the 10 years ending with the disposal. These need not be the last 5 year of that period.

"Full time working director" does not have its ordinary meaning but is defined in s598 (1). It means "a director required to devote substantially the whole of his or her time to the service of the company in a managerial or technical capacity". The meaning of "substantially the whole of his time" was considered in the UK High Court case of Palmer v Maloney. In that case the taxpayer worked for a company for between 85% and 90% of his time but devoted between 10% and 15% of his time to a business carried on as a sole trader. That business was significant in scale and profitability.

Laddie J. said:

"The definition of full-time working officer in para 1 (2) is not couched in terms of main and subsidiary activities. It stipulates that the tax concessions are only available where the director or officer devotes in substance the whole of his time to the service of the company. It seems to me that the intention behind these provisions is to encourage the taxpayer to concentrate all his hours of work in supporting the company. To obtain the favourable tax treatment he must in substance have remained wedded to the

company or group of companies alone. He must have forsaken all others. It is only that loyalty which is rewarded under the 1992 Act. The use of the word 'substantially' therefore in my view means 'in substance'. As Mr Walters put it: the 1992 Act sets a high test; entitlement will not be excluded by de minimis considerations. But subject to that, the whole of a person's working time must be devoted to the company if the retirement relief is to be secured. Mr Walters was right in my view also to point out that the 1992 Act requires the taxpayer to devote substantially the whole of his time, not merely a substantial portion of his time, to the service of the company."

The Judge went on to say that the percentage of hours was not the sole criteria. He was influenced by the commercial significance of the sole trade also. He held that the taxpayer did not devote "substantially the whole of his time" to the service of the company.

CATA76 Sch2 Para9 A number of Irish cases concerned with Capital Acquisitions Tax, and with favourite nephew relief might encourage the hope that an Irish Court would take a different view of the matter. In CATA76 Sch2, Para 9, a very similar phrase is used "work substantially on a full time basis". In Sch 2 para 9 there is a statutory definition of the phrase that requires that 24 hours a week, or 15 hours a week, be worked depending on certain circumstances. It is not possible to read a definition from one tax code into another but the Irish Courts may be influenced by the CAT definition. The matter remains to be tested.

The reference to the taxpayer being "required" to work full time seems odd. A director of a family company can rarely be required to do anything. The word appears to be without significance in this context.

For some odd reason, a full time director who does manual work, and not technical or managerial work, would seem to be denied relief. That is a problem unlikely to arise in practice.

- **Revenue/Chief Inspector's CGT Manual :**

– In their capital gains tax manual the Revenue Commissioners, at Paragraph 19.6.3.3 state *"Where an individual is required to devote substantially the whole of his time to the service, in a managerial or technical capacity, of more than one company and the companies constitute a "trading group" of companies or carry on complementary businesses so as to form a composite unit of business, he may be regarded (on the disposal by way of sale or gift of the whole of his shares in all the companies) as a full time working director of any of the companies, which in relation to him, is a "family company". If the relief is claimed on the disposal of one, or some only, of the companies, the case should be referred to head office."*

The concessional treatment outlined above is likely to have frequent application since most corporate businesses are carried on through a group of companies rather than through a single company. Where the family group consists of a holding company and some subsidiaries, the controlling shareholder will usually be a director of all of the companies. Being a director of several companies will not in itself necessarily mean that the person will have failed the test that they should be *"a director required to devote substantially the whole of his or her time to the service of the company"*. If some of the companies are dormant, the amount of time devoted to the duties of director of those companies may be negligible, and the time devoted to the trading subsidiary may still represent substantially the whole of a person's time. However where there exists more than one trading company in a group, the difficulty addressed by the concession above arises.

Even in the absence of the concession above, it could be argued that where there is a holding company which owns a number of trading subsidiaries, the involvement of the controlling shareholder in the affairs of the subsidiaries is part and parcel of his duties as director of the holding company. It is in order to increase the value of the holding company that he engages in activities in the other companies. He is merely forwarding the interests of the holding company, and in so doing carrying out his duties as a director of the holding company. The truth is that where a person holds trading subsidiaries through a holding company, he has no direct interest in the value or trading activities of the subsidiaries in themselves. His interest rather is in the value of the holding company, and the activities of the trading companies only indirectly reflect themselves in those values. It is therefore very reasonable to say that anything he does for the subsidiaries is done merely to enhance the value of the holding company, and as the director of the holding company. This argument could not be advanced where there is more than one trading company and they are not related together in a group. In contrast, the Revenue concession does extend to cover a number of trading companies not formally related in a group.

s598(1)
A **trading company** means a company whose business consists wholly or mainly of the carrying on of one or more trades or professions.

A **trading group** means a group of companies consisting of the holding company and its 75% subsidiaries, the business of whose members taken together consists wholly or mainly of the carrying on of one or more trades or professions.

The term **75% subsidiary** has the meaning assigned to it in s9 - see paragraph 75.4.3.2.

The term **chargeable business asset** was redefined in FA95 s70. This new definition replaces an earlier definition, which (apart from the inclusion of certain group companies) has remained unchanged since the drafting of the 1975 Act. The original definition was unsatisfactory, and lead to a position where the relief was in effect being operated by what could only be called "Revenue concession". This was a very unsatisfactory way to "legislate" for a relief, and it is good to note that the position has been changed by the FA95, which enacted the necessary legislative changes to give effect to what was actually happening in practice (by concession). This new definition is now in s598(1).

s598(1)   s598(1) defines *chargeable business asset* as an asset which is, (or is an interest in) an asset used for the purposes of:

- a trade, or

- farming, or

- a profession, or

- an office or employment

carried on by the *individual* or the *individual's family company* (or a company which is a member of a trading group of which the holding company is the individual's family company) *other than an asset on the disposal of which no gain accruing would be a chargeable gain.*

The addition of the text highlighted at the end of the previous sentence is the main change between the old definition and the new FA95 definition of chargeable business asset. The additional words make it clear that such items as debtors, stocks, bank balances, etc. are not normally included in the term *chargeable business asset*, as no chargeable gain would result from their disposal. In arriving at the £375,000 limit on qualifying assets, it is clear that only assets which would yield a chargeable gain on disposal are included.

Goodwill is specifically included in the statutory definition as a chargeable business asset.

Excluded from the definition of *chargeable business asset* are

- shares and securities, and

- other assets

which are held as investments.

In the UK, the Special Commissioners have concluded that shares and securities are excluded whether or not they are held as investments.

The previous definition also excluded a principal private residence qualifying for residence relief (see paragraph 24). There is no such specific exclusion in the FA95 amended definition.

Where 100% principal private residence relief is available in relation to a dwelling, that dwelling could not be a chargeable business asset having regard to the FA95 amendment referred to above, since no chargeable gain would arise on its disposal. However many residences carry less than 100% principal private residence relief either by reason of having a development land aspect, or because they did not meet the conditions for relief throughout the period of ownership. Such dwellings, attracting less than 100% relief would seem to be capable of being chargeable business assets if they meet the requirement of being used for the purpose of a trade etc. A dwelling is capable of being in mixed use, and frequently is in the case of a profession such as doctor or solicitor, where the "office" may be in the home.

- **Revenue/Chief Inspector's CGT Manual :**

— A form of concessional treatment is indicated in paragraph 19.6.3.16 of the Revenue Commissioners capital gains tax manual where it states. *"Where instead of disposing of the whole or part of the business by sale or gift an individual (or partnership) closes the business down permanently and (as nearly as may be at the same time) disposes of the assets by sale or gift, the individual (or partnership) should, subject to the other conditions of Section 598 be treated as having disposed of qualifying assets."* The point being catered for here is that if the business is first shut down, and the assets are subsequently disposed of, at the date of the disposal they would no longer be chargeable business assets since they would not at that date any longer be in use for the purpose of a trade etc. Broadly analogous concessional treatment is available in the case of a liquidation. This is explained in Paragraph 30.6.

- **Revenue Commissioners - Tax Briefing:**

— In Tax Briefing Issue 36 - June 1999 the Revenue Commissioners expressed the view that a person who carried on a trade of taxi driver as well as allowing another person to operate as a "cosy" driver would be disposing of a qualifying asset for the purpose of retirement relief when they disposed of the taxi plate. It said *"Revenue take the view that the taxi plate is used for the purposes of a trade carried on by the taxi operator. The fact that the taxi plate is also used by a cosy driver does not alter this. Taxi plates are now generally operated on a 24 hour basis; the cosy driver is in operation only when the owner (ie the individual claiming retirement relief) is not carrying on his/her trade. Accordingly the whole of the asset is used for the purposes of the trade with the taxi operator for the hours during which he/she carries on the trade and the same asset is used by a cosy driver when the trade is not carried on."* The Revenue ruling has an apparent implication that the taxi plate which is in use solely by cosy drivers would not be in use for the purpose of a trade of a person owning the plate. Whether or not that is the case might depend on the facts of each situation. If the cosy driver is a mere employee then it is probable a trade is being carried on. If the cosy driver is simply renting the plate and bearing all of the costs of operating the taxi during the rental period, then it may be that a trade is not being carried on by the owner of the plate who may merely hold it as an investment. On the other hand, there may be a profit sharing arrangement or the owner may bear some of the expenses and in such a case it becomes more difficult to determine whether or not a trade exists.

In the same issue of Tax Briefing the Revenue state that farmland let in conacre for a number of years prior to retirement by a retiring farmer over the age of 55 years is not regarded as a chargeable business asset as it had not been used for the purposes of trade of farming throughout the period of ten years ending with the date of disposal.

The UK Special Commissioners in the case of Hatt v Newman held that the letting of furnished rooms was not a trade for the purpose of retirement relief (or any other purpose). They also confirmed that the requirement that the assets be chargeable business assets is a test to be applied at the date of the contract, where the disposal is under contract.

30.5 Family Company

s598(1)

A family company is one in which the individual concerned owns

- 25% or more of the voting rights,

or

- 10% or more of the voting rights, and his family (including the individual) own 75% or more of the voting rights.

In relation to an individual, family means:

- his spouse,

- a relative of his, and

- a relative of his spouse

Relative means brother, sister, ancestor, or lineal descendant.

It should be noted that the various percentage holdings described above must be held during a period of 10 years ending with the disposal, in order for the shares to be qualifying assets.

Example 152

Joe inherited 50% of the shares in a trading company at 30 June 1986 on the death of his father. The balance of 50% of the shares is held by an unconnected person. On 28 August 1996 Joe disposed of 30% of the shares in the company to a new investor. As the shares amounted to 25% or more of the voting rights and had been held for 10 years, they were shares in a family company, for the purpose of retirement relief. In April 1997 Joe disposed of his remaining 20% of the company to his brother. Although these shares had been held for more than 10 years, the company was not a family company for the 10 years ending on the date of the disposal in April 1997. It had ceased to be the family company in August 1996, on the occasion of the first disposal. Accordingly the second disposal could not qualify for retirement relief. Neither does the second disposal fall to be aggregated with the first for the purpose of the computation of the limit on proceeds (see paragraph 30.8).

Where an individual holds less than 10% of the voting rights of a company, it is not his family company even if all of the remaining shares in the company are held by his family. If a parent disposed of shares to his children by degrees, he could find himself in a position where he has passed over more than 90% of the shares to his children and therefore retains less than 10%. A transfer of that final retained percentage to his children would not qualify for retirement relief because the company would no longer be his family company, notwithstanding that it is controlled by the family. This particular difficulty was the subject matter of an amendment to s598 (then s26 CGTA 1975) by s.60 of the Finance Act 1996. The amendment had application from 23 April 1996. It provides that where a holding company would be a family company but for the fact that an individual had, in the three years following 6 April 1987, transferred shares in the company to a child, the company should nonetheless be deemed to be the individual's family company. This provision is now s598(1)(b).

FA96 s60

s598(1)(b)

Example 153

Holdings Ltd. was wholly owned by Joe until 1980, when he transferred 50% of the shares in it to his eldest son John. In 1985 he transferred 25% to a second son, Willie. In June 1988 he transferred 20% to Willie. He now wishes to transfer the remaining 5% to Willie.

Prior to 23 April 1996 Holdings Ltd. would not be Joe's family company, for the purposes of the transfer of the remaining 5% to Willie. That is because Joe held less than 10% of the voting rights in the company. After 23 April 1996 however the company is his family company once again because the sole reason it was not previously his family company was the transfer in June 1988 to Willie of the 20% holding. Had Joe retained that holding, he would now hold in excess of 10% of the shares. It was therefore the sole obstacle to the company being his family company.

The limited form of relief introduced by the Finance Act 1996 (S598(1)(b) TCA 97) refers only to a situation where a parent transferred shares to his child in the 3 years ended 5 April 1990, thereby causing the company to cease to be his family company. The significance of 5 April 1990 is that it was with affect from that date that s598 was amended so as to include within the relief, the transfer of shares in a family holding company. It therefore extends a limited form of relief for those who reduced their holding in the family holding company to below 10% at a time when their percentage holding in the company had no significance, as retirement relief did not apply to the company. It is nonetheless a niggardly relief, and it is difficult to see why the relief should not have been applied without restriction as to time. It does underline the importance of a parent ensuring that in making lifetime transfers of family company shares to his children, he does not permit his holding ever to drop below 10% of the voting rights, without entirely disposing of his holding.

It should be noted that no similar relaxation has been provided in relation to a family company which is not a holding company.

30.6 Liquidation of Family Company

In broad terms, where the family company is liquidated, the individual shareholder is treated for CGT purposes as disposing of his shares, and the consideration for the disposal is the amount (if any) received from the liquidator (the capital distribution).

The retirement relief applies in such a case, in the same manner as if the individual had merely disposed of the shares (or securities) in the company.

s598(7) However, an exception is made where the individual receives a distribution in specie of chargeable business assets. In such circumstances, the relief does not apply.

Example 154

Joe Brown owns all of the shares in Dynasty Limited, a trading company. Joe has got fed up of dealing with auditors and has decided to carry on the business as a sole trader. A liquidator is appointed to the company. The liquidator uses the cash balances of the company, and cash collected from debtors to clear the creditors, and distributes the balance of the assets to Joe in specie. These consist of a premises, plant and machinery and stock. The premises are worth £300,000. The plant and machinery £200,000, and the stock £250,000. The total value received by Joe therefore is £750,000. All of this represents a capital sum derived from the shares in Dynasty Ltd.

The shares qualify for retirement relief as being Joe's family company. The premises and the plant both represent the chargeable business assets. The stock however is not a chargeable business asset since no capital gain would arise on its disposal. Any gain on its disposal would have been chargeable to tax as income.

Retirement relief is not available on the disposal of the shares by Joe.

Had the liquidator instead sold the premises and plant (possibly to Joe) and distributed to Joe the proceeds of sale, retirement relief should have been available in line with the published Revenue concession (mentioned below). Reliance on the concession is necessary since in such a case the company would no longer be carrying on a trade at the date of the distribution of the proceeds of sale to Joe. Such an approach, of selling the plant and buildings, might have stamp duty costs especially in relation to the buildings, which would not have arisen on an appointment in specie by a liquidator.

Where chargeable business assets held by a company are disposed of, and the company is **subsequently liquidated,** the relief strictly would not apply - as at that stage the assets of the company would consist of the proceeds of disposal of the business, and not the business itself.

Where the company assets are disposed of not more than 6 months prior to the disposal of the shares or appointment of a liquidator, and with a view to the disposal of shares or the appointment of a liquidator of the family company, the Revenue may, by concession, permit the proceeds such a disposal to be treated as chargeable business assets for retirement relief purposes.

This extra statutory concession was published by the Revenue Commissioners in "Tax Briefing" issue 26, dated April 1997.

- **Revenue/Chief Inspector's CGT Manual :**

—The extra statutory concession referred to above is also published in the Revenue Commissioners capital gains tax manual at Paragraph 19.6.3.14. The paragraph also deals with the possibility that on a liquidation, the liquidator might make a number of distributions to the shareholders. Such multiple distributions during the course of a liquidation give rise to a part disposal of shares in the company on the part of the shareholders who receive the distributions. If that strict treatment were followed, it would be necessary to recompute the conditions for retirement relief on the occasion of each part disposal. In the manual, the Revenue Commissioners indicate that *"In practice the date of appointment of the liquidator may be treated as the date of the notional disposal, so that chargeable business assets in hand at that date will be included in the disposal as such, notwithstanding that the assets are subsequently sold by the liquidator. For the purposes of apportionment between chargeable business assets and other assets the values at the date of appointment of the liquidator may be taken as the values at the time of the notional disposal of the shares and where an asset is subsequently sold at arm's length by the liquidator, the sales proceeds may be taken as the value of that asset."*

- **Revenue/Chief Inspector's CGT Manual :**

—Further concessional treatment in relation to the liquidation of a family company is indicated at Paragraph 19.6.3.15 of the Revenue Commissioners capital gains tax manual indicates as follows:
  " Where the business of a family company is disposed of to one or more of its shareholders, including a disposal by way of capital distribution, and the business is continued by the acquiring shareholder (or shareholders in partnership), there is an occasion of charge on the company. If the individual (or partner) retires within ten years of acquiring the business (or a share in the business), the relief should be computed on the basis that -(a) the retiring individual (or partner) had owned the whole or a part of the business throughout the period during which he was a shareholder of the family company as well as when he was a sole trader

(or partner) of the business — taken over from the company, and (b) the part which qualifies for relief is the proportion represented by his share in the business held throughout the period of ten years (whether as shareholder in the company, sole trader or partner)."

30.7   **Period of ownership/deemed ownership**

s598(1)(d)   In determining the period of ownership and the period of a directorship for the purposes of this relief, the following additional rules apply:

- **Ownership by spouse:**
  The period of ownership of the taxpayer's spouse is taken into account as if it were a period of ownership of the taxpayer.

- **Replacement of assets (roll-over relief):**
  Where assets (which qualify for roll-over relief) are sold, and the proceeds are reinvested in further qualifying assets, the period of ownership of the assets which were sold is taken into account as if it were a period of ownership of the new assets.

- **Transfer of business to company:**
  Where the qualifying assets are shares or securities in a family company, and the individual concerned had previously transferred his business to the company wholly or partly for shares in such a manner as to comply with the conditions necessary to obtain relief on the transfer of his business to the company (see paragraph 29), the period of ownership of the business transferred is taken into account as part of the period of ownership of the shares in the company. Other aspects of the interaction of the two reliefs are described in paragraph 30.13.1

s600   In these circumstances, the period of ownership of the business transferred to the company is also regarded as a period during which he was a full-time working director of the company.

- **Transfer of business from company:**

  Where a business is transferred by a family company to one of more of its shareholders (whether on the liquidation of the company or otherwise) a concessional treatment is available as described in 30.6 above.

- **Death of spouse:**
  Where the taxpayer's spouse dies, the period during which the deceased spouse was a full-time working director, up to the date of death of that spouse, is taken into account as part of the taxpayer's own period of full-time directorship of the company.

- **Share swap:**
  Where a share for share swap occurs, to which the provisions of
s586   s586 applies, the holder of the shares is deemed not to have

disposed of his old shares, or acquired new shares. The new shares are considered to be the same asset as the old shares acquired when the old ones were acquired. Accordingly it seems that the period of ownership of the new shares should be the period of ownership of the old shares. However difficulties can arise as regards retirement relief since the shares are now shares in a company which is a holding company, whereas the original shares may have been shares in a trading company. Furthermore the period during which the shareholder worked for the original company is not a period for which he had worked for the new company. Notwithstanding these difficulties the Revenue may, by concession, "look through" the new company and permit retirement relief to apply, where it would have been available but for the share for share swap having occurred.

This concessional treatment should always be confirmed with the Revenue authorities in advance of making any disposal.

- **Revenue Commissioners published precedent :**

- In their published precedents the Revenue Commissioners have indicated a concession in relation to the 10 year ownership requirement. They state *"Where an individual is terminally ill and a sufficient percentage of the time limit has expired the Revenue accepts that the requirements of Section 598 are met."* The published precedent does not indicate what period of ownership is considered sufficient in the context of a terminally ill person. It would seem reasonable to speculate that the concession is granted in recognition of the fact that on the death of the terminally ill person there would be a tax free uplift in base cost, enabling the personal representative to dispose of the assets without a charge to capital gains tax. However a terminally ill person might require the proceeds of sale in his lifetime so the concession probably recognises that human situation.

- **Revenue Commissioners published precedent :**

- There is a further published precedent in relation to period of ownership which relates to a company transferring its trade to a subsidiary in the 10 years prior to the disposal of an asset. The circumstances appear to envisage that the company in question had not been a holding company throughout the 10 years ending with the disposal. It states *"In strictness, relief is not due, as the holding company has not been a holding company through the 10 years ending with the disposal. In practice, relief will be allowed where all other requirements of the section are met."*

- **Revenue Commissioners published precedent:**

  — In their published precedents the Revenue Commissioners have stated *"Where a holding company is interposed or removed during the 10 years prior to disposal the taxpayer will not satisfy the requirements that he has held the shares for 10 years and has been a working director for 5 years. A "look through" approach may be taken (by the Revenue Commissioners) and the taxpayer will be treated as satisfying both conditions."*

- **Revenue Commissioners published precedent:**

  — A concession is also available in relation to leasehold property and is stated as follows: *"Where a lease expires and a new lease is granted, the old lease and the new lease are separate assets. In practice the periods of ownership may be aggregated."*

30.8   **Calculation of £375,000 proceeds limit**

s598(2)   If the aggregate total proceeds of disposal of all *qualifying assets* does not exceed £375,000, full relief is available for the CGT payable on gains accruing on the disposal of those assets. Marginal relief may apply instead if the proceeds exceed the £375,000 figure. As already mentioned in paragraph 30.4, qualifying assets (in relation to a disposal) by an individual means

- his chargeable business assets and

- shares in his family company

Many problems existed prior to the change in the definition of *chargeable business assets* in the FA 1995. The matter has now been clarified by the inclusion of the words *"other than an asset on the disposal of which no gain accruing would be a chargeable gain"*. The previous definition merely referred to all assets, and without the additional qualification now added, many uncertainties arose. It is good to see that the position has now been clarified in terms of legislation, rather than as it was previously, by Revenue concession.

s599(5)   The proceeds of any disposals qualifying for relief under s599 - on *disposal to a child* of the individual making the disposal, are ignored in calculating the £375,000 limit.

s598(6)(c)   Any disposal of qualifying assets between *husband and wife* are normally regarded as being at such a figure as to give no gain/no loss on the disposal. For the purpose of this relief, such disposals are taken into account at market value in calculating the total aggregate disposal proceeds.

The figure of £375,000 is a lifetime limit for the individual taxpayer for all disposals of qualifying assets since 6th April 1974 made after he has reached the age of 55 years. If for example, a later disposal brings the aggregate disposal proceeds to date over the £375,000 aggregate limit, the earlier relief may be withdrawn. There is, of course, a 10 year time limit on assessments to withdraw any earlier relief.

S598(6)(a) states:

"The total of the amounts of relief given under this section for any year of assessment, and all years of assessment before such year, shall not exceed such amount as would reduce the total amount of capital gains tax chargeable for all those years of assessment below the amount which would be chargeable if the disposals of qualifying assets had all been made in the year of assessment".

The affect of this important sub-section of s598 is illustrated by a short example:

Example 155

John is now 56 years of age. During the current tax year he sold off part of his chargeable business assets for £100,000. Three years ago he had sold off part of the business assets for £160,000, and CGT of £10,000 was assessed and paid on the gains which accrued on that disposal. A previous sale of business land and buildings took place in 1973 for a consideration of £150,000. He still retains the balance of chargeable business assets valued today at £300,000.

Clearly, the sale in 1973 cannot give rise to chargeable gains, so the assets involved can not be regarded as qualifying assets, and are not aggregated. In any event, the disposal was prior to his 55th birthday and for that reason also is not aggregated.

Three years ago, a sale took place of business assets. Retirement relief cannot apply to that sale, as he was not 55 years of age at the time of sale. CGT has been assessed and paid on that disposal.

Disposals made at a time when the taxpayer was not yet 55 years of age do not fall to be taken into account for the purpose of clawback. This is because clawback operates by assuming the prior disposals to have occurred in the current year, and by limiting the aggregate relief to the amount that would be available on such a basis. Since relief is available only where the disposal is made by the taxpayer, being then 55 years or older, disposals prior to reaching his 55th birthday do not affect the calculation one way or the other. Nonetheless, the legislation is somewhat ambiguous in that it could be argued that the deeming of earlier disposals to occur in a current year has the effect of deeming them to be disposed of by a person who has now reached his 55th birthday. That interpretation would run counter to the general scheme of the section, which focuses on disposals on or after the taxpayer reaching his 55th birthday, and is not concerned with earlier disposals.

This would mean that the aggregate would be calculated solely by reference to the £100,000 disposal in the current tax year, and full relief would be granted.

If and when John finally disposes of the balance of his qualifying assets, the aggregate would then amount to a figure in excess of the allowable aggregate limit. The result of this, is that the relief already granted for the current year, by reference to a £100,000 disposal, will have to be recalculated by reference to a figure in excess of the pre 1/12/99 £250,000 limit, resulting in a clawback of the relief (subject to the 10 year time limit for assessment).

Depending on the actual sale proceeds, marginal relief may apply instead to both the £100,000 disposal and also the later disposal.

s598(6)(b)

Provisions are made for a ***clawback of relief*** where an individual who has claimed this relief (on disposal to persons other than his child) makes a further disposal of qualifying assets at a later stage which brings his overall aggregate total to a figure in excess of the overall limit.

s598(6)(b) provides that *"any necessary adjustment may be made by way of assessment or additional assessment and such assessment may be made at any time not more than 10 years after the end of the year of assessment in which the last of such disposals is made"*.

The normal assets of a business would include

- Cash at bank

- Trading stock

- Trade debtors

- Plant & Machinery

- Land & Buildings,

- Goodwill.

The question of liabilities is ignored, as they are clearly not assets to be taken into account in arriving at the £375,000 limit.

The disposal of cash, trading stock and debtors of a normal business will not give rise to a chargeable gain, and so are excluded from the clawback calculations.

The other items, Land & Buildings, plant & Machinery, and goodwill (to the extent they refer to disposals of those assets since the individual became 55 years of age) are not excluded, and so must be taken into account in arriving at the overall £375,000 limit.

Example 156

Joe is aged 60 years, and has decided to retire from business in March 1996. He has carried on the business as a sole trader for the past 40 years, and it may be assumed for the purposes of this illustration (where appropriate) that the qualifying assets have been owned by him for a period in excess of 10 years.

Immediately prior to the sale of the business, the assets of the business were as follows:

	IR£
Land & Buildings	100,000
Trade Debtors	30,000
Trade Stocks	40,000
Goodwill	60,000
Plant & Machinery	10,000
Cash at bank	8,000
TOTAL ASSETS	248,000

Joe intends retaining the cash for his own use, and selling off the other assets to an unconnected third party who has agreed to purchase the business. Joe has had no previous disposals of qualifying business assets.

The actual gains or losses (if any) are calculated on the disposal of the land & buildings, goodwill, and plant & machinery in the normal manner. For the purposes of the example, let us assume that the total gains on those qualifying assets amounts to £27,000 (before any relief). The tax payable is calculated on the resulting net chargeable gains (taking losses into account where they arise), and tax is calculated at the rate of 40% (then applying)

It is only then that the question of measuring the relief arises - i.e. the extent to which the actual tax itself is to be reduced by the retirement relief. In practice, this involves looking at the proceeds received for the sale of the qualifying assets. The assets which could have given rise to a chargeable gain yielded a total of £170,000 which is below the £250,000 limit (then applying).

This means that the total capital gains tax payable on all the disposals is relieved (i.e. reduced to nil), i.e.

	£
Gains	£27,000
Annual exemption not available	NIL
Chargeable	£27,000

The CGT payable @ 40% amounts to £10,800. The relief of £10,800 is deducted from the CGT payable, leaving no tax payable on the disposal of those qualifying assets.

Example 157

*If, in **Example 156** above, Joe made further disposals of his qualifying assets 2 years later (in 1997/98) for a sum of £100,000, realising chargeable gains of £5,000 (before relief) two separate problems would arise:*

- *the relief for that later year would be calculated on the basis of a total disposal of qualifying assets of £270,000. This exceeds the then aggregate limit of £250,000, and so full relief is not available. The figure of £270,000 may however be close enough to the limit to give Joe marginal relief.*

- *The relief for 1995/96 (above) would be revised on the basis that the total sales of qualifying assets was £270,000. This would have the affect of withdrawing the relief already obtained for that year. The question of marginal relief would be based on a whether the full CGT payable on the qualifying assets (without any relief) was less than one half of the excess the deemed disposal proceeds of £270,000 over the then £250,000 exemption limit (i.e. - £10,000).*

The relevant calculations are set out below.

1995/96 disposal:

CGT as originally computed (before relief)	*£10,400*
Maximum CGT under marginal relief -	
(£270,000 - £250,000) x 1/2	*£10,000*

The original relief will be withdrawn, and the Inspector will assess the tax due, limited by marginal relief, of £10,000.

1997/98 disposal

Cumulative gains on qualifying disposals:	
(£27,000 + £5,000) less annual allowance	*£31,000*
Tax @ 40% (pre 3rd December 1997)	*£12,400*

Maximum CGT payable limited by marginal relief, for all qualifying disposals to date is £10,000. This amount has already been assessed for 1995/96, so no further tax is payable (at this time) on the 1997/98 disposal.

30.9   Disposal of shares in family company:

s598(1)   Shares (or securities) in a 'family company' may be qualifying assets for the purpose of "retirement" relief. However, the legislation also recognises that a company, as in the case of any other person carrying on a business, may hold assets other than business assets. The company may hold investments, or even a substantial bank deposit account which would have nothing to do with the value of its trade, or business assets. The value of the shares would reflect all the underlying assets of the company, as well as the value of its trade, and trading assets.

As in the case of an individual, the retirement relief only applies to the individual's qualifying assets. So with a company, the legislation attempts to divide the consideration for the disposal of the shares in that company between the part reflected by the value of the chargeable business assets, and other assets which do not qualify for relief.

A statutory basis for apportioning the consideration (for the disposal of the shares) is set out in s598(4), as substituted by the FA95.

To understand the statutory basis of apportionment, it is important to understand the meaning of two terms used by the legislation to describe the apportionment:

• *chargeable assets,* and

• *chargeable business assets.*

The term *chargeable business assets* has been described in detail in paragraph 30.4.

s598(5)

The definition of chargeable asset is given in s598(5) ...."*every asset of the company is a **chargeable asset** except one on the disposal of which by the company or a member of the trading group, as the case may be, at the time the disposal of the shares or securities, no gain accruing to the company or a member of the trading group, as the case may be, would be a chargeable gain*".

In effect, the term *chargeable assets* means all assets which could give rise to a chargeable gain on disposal, and would include the *chargeable business assets.*

s598(4)

s598(4) set out two bases of apportionment. i.e. :

• where the individual's family company *is not a holding company* -the proportion of the consideration referable to the chargeable business assets is "*the proportion which the part of the company's chargeable assets at the time of the disposal which is attributable to the company's chargeable business assets bears to the whole of that value*".

In effect, the apportionment is made on the basis of:

$$\text{consideration} \times \frac{\text{chargeable business assets}}{\text{chargeable assets}}$$

• where the individual's family company *is a holding company,* the basis of apportionment takes account of the fact that one member of the group may hold shares in another group member, and such shares would normally be regarded as chargeable assets. It also takes account of the fact that the actual business assets may be held by a subsidiary (that more than one company is involved) - i.e. the part of the consideration deemed to refer to the chargeable business assets is ... "*the proportion which the part of the value of the chargeable assets of the trading group (**excluding shares or securities of one member of the group held by another member of the group**) at the time of disposal which is attributable to the value of the chargeable business assets of the trading group bears to the whole of that value*".

In effect, the basis is the same as that for a single company, but is taken by reference to the assets of the entire group, rather than the assets of a single company, and shares held in other group members are ignored in arriving at the part of the proceeds taken into account for retirement relief.

Example 158

Joe is aged 60 years, and has decided to sell the shares in his family trading company. He has owned the shares in the company for the past 20 years and worked as a full-time working director of the company for the first 15 years of that period. He has been a part time director for the last 5 years. Joe has had no previous disposals of qualifying business assets since his 55th birthday. Immediately prior to the disposal of the shares, the assets of the company were as follows:

	£
Land and Buildings	150,000
Plant & Machinery	20,000
Goodwill	250,000
Government stocks (investments)	50,000
Quoted shares (investments)	5,000
Trade stocks	30,000
Trade debtors	40,000
Cash at bank	60,000

The total liabilities of the company amount to £55,000.

The agreed sale price of the shares in the company is £550,000.

For the same reasons explained in paragraph 30.4 the trade debtors, trade stocks, and cash at bank are neither chargeable business assets nor chargeable assets.

The government stocks are not chargeable assets and neither are they chargeable business assets because they are exempt from CGT. The quoted shares are chargeable assets since they are assets upon whose disposal a chargeable gain can arise, but they are not chargeable business assets since they have not been used for the purpose of a trade but rather were held for investment purposes.

The land and buildings, plant and machinery, and goodwill are all chargeable assets and also chargeable business assets being both chargeable to CGT and used in the trade.

The value of the chargeable business assets therefore in total amounts to £420,000 (150,000 + 20,000+ 250,000).

The value of the chargeable assets amounts to £425,000 (the same as above, with the addition of the quoted shares of £5,000).

The amount of the sale proceeds of the shares to be treated as referring to the sale of chargeable business assets is:

$$£550,000 \ x \ \frac{420,000}{425,000} \ = \ £543,529$$

It should be noted that the amount taken in as referring to the chargeable business assets under the statutory formula can give a nonsensical result. The total chargeable business assets of the company is £420,000. The formula attributes a part of the consideration to chargeable business assets which is far in excess of the actual value of those assets. What has happened, is that the formula has taken a fraction based on assets chargeable to CGT of the total value of the shares which is only derived to the extent of approx. 2/3rds from those assets.

In some cases the statutory formula will give a reasonable result, in other cases, the result of applying it will be a total farce - or would be if the matter was not serious.

If, on the other hand, the individual had stripped the non-chargeable assets from the company before the sale (i.e.. the government stock, and cash) the result of applying the formula would be reasonable. However, to do so may only cause problems with other taxes, and not really solve the real problem.

Although, in *example 158* the statutory formula treats an unrealistically large part of the consideration as referring to the sale of chargeable business assets, it also treats the same figure as being the sale proceeds in arriving at the £375,000 limit (£250,000 pre 1/12/1999).

This would give a very favourable result on a disposal to a child of the owner, where the sale proceeds are not relevant. However, on disposal to a third party, it causes major problems.

The problem may be more clearly explained by a simple example.

Example 159

Assume the company assets are as follows:

Land & Buildings	£150,000
Stock	£250,000
Quoted shares	£5,000
Total	£405,000

There are no liabilities, and the shares are sold for £405,000.

Before looking at the application of the statutory formula, let us apply a little common sense to the position. It is assumed that the purpose of the formula, is to apportion the sale proceeds between the chargeable business assets, and the other assets. It is obvious that the chargeable business assets, if they were owned directly by the individual taxpayer, and not by the company, are limited to the land and buildings. The other assets are clearly not chargeable business assets.

The statutory formula apportions the consideration for the disposal of the shares in the following manner:

$$£405,000 \times \frac{150}{155} = £391,935$$

The sum of £391,935 is deemed to represent the consideration for the disposal of the land & buildings. This is clearly a nonsense, as the total market value of the land & buildings is actually £150,000.

The affect of this, is that the deemed proceeds of chargeable business assets of £391,935 exceeds the £375,000 exemption limit. Full retirement relief is not available, although it would have been available if the assets were held personally by the individual.

The fault lies in the statutory wording used to describe the mandatory statutory formula.

Because of the importance of retirement relief in its application to the disposal of shares in a family company it is necessary to look at the statutory wording in greater detail. Retirement relief on disposals to persons other than a child of the taxpayer are set out in s598(2). As explained above, there are two forms of relief set out in s598(2) -

- a complete exemption where the consideration for the disposal does not exceed £375,000, and

- a marginal relief where the consideration for the disposal does exceed £375,000.

s598(4)

S598(4) describes how these two reliefs are to be applied to a disposal of shares in a family company. It is easy to see why such specific provision is needed. Where an individual disposes of chargeable assets other than shares it is a simple matter to distinguish between chargeable business assets and other assets, and to apply the relief only to a consideration arising in respect of the chargeable business assets. However where the disposal is of shares, the assets from which the shares derive their value may include both chargeable business assets, and other assets. It is therefore necessary, in order to ensure that the relief is not made available to the part of the consideration for the shares which is derived from assets which are not chargeable business assets, to provide for some basis of apportionment, or of restriction of the relief. That may be presumed to be the purpose of s598(4).

S598(4) states that on a disposal of shares in a family company *"the amount of the consideration to be taken into account for the purposes of sub-section 2 in respect of those shares or securities"* is to be the proportion which the chargeable business assets bear to the whole of the chargeable assets of the company at the date of disposal.

s598(2)

S598(2) provides a complete exemption from CGT where the consideration does not exceed £375,000. s598(4) requires us to reduce the consideration received for shares in a family company below the actual figure, for the purpose of applying s598(2) relief. The lesser the proportion of chargeable business assets to the chargeable assets of the company the smaller the amount of consideration which will be taken into account for the purposes of s598(2) and therefore, paradoxically, the more likely it is that the consideration will not exceed £375,000! Where the consideration for shares exceeds £375,000, the greater the proportion of chargeable business assets to total chargeable assets in the company, the less likely it is that the consideration for the purposes of sub-section 2 will be brought below £375,000! A straightforward reading of s598 therefore gives rise to extraordinary results in the case of shares in a family company.

The results of applying a straightforward reading of s598(2) and s598(4) are so extraordinary as to compel one to consider an alternative interpretation. S598(4) determines the amount of the actual consideration for the disposal of shares that is to be taken into account for the purposes of s598(2). The purpose of s598(2) is to determine the amount of relief on the disposal. It may be argued therefore that any part of the consideration not taken into account for the purposes of s598(2) should be brought into an ordinary computation of capital gains tax, without reference to s598. Alternatively, it might be argued that the entire of the consideration for the disposal of the shares should be brought into an ordinary computation of capital gains tax without regard to s598, and that relief under s598 should then be deducted from the tax so ascertained. Either interpretation is attractive and would make a degree of sense if the legislation were indeed structured in that manner.

Unfortunately it is difficult to apply either alternative interpretation to the words that have been used in s598. s598(2) provides that if the amount of the consideration for the disposal does not exceed £375,000 relief is to be given in respect of the full amount of capital gains tax chargeable on any gain accruing on the disposal. Those words seem incapable of any interpretation other than that on a disposal of shares in a family company, if the amount of consideration taken into account for the purposes of s598(2) does not exceed £375,000, no capital gains tax may be charged in respect of any aspect of the disposal. The words used are clear and mandatory and do not admit any possibility of applying the alternative interpretations suggested above. "The disposal" referred to is clearly the disposal of the shares in the family company, and not some notional separate disposal of part only of those shares. The legislation makes no reference to any such notional part disposal.

No matter how extraordinary the results produced by s598, it would seem to be beyond the powers of an Irish court (which may not legislate even where it believes the Oireachtas has blundered in its drafting of legislation) to correct matters by placing a "reasonable" interpretation on the words used in s598. Readers should nonetheless be warned that the Revenue Commissioners may well take a different view of the legislation.

• **Revenue/Chief Inspector's CGT Manual :**

— Such a differing view is reflected in the capital gains tax manual published by the Revenue Commissioners, at paragraph 19.6.3.5. where the following example is given (see *Example 160* below).

Example 160 (taken from Revenue Commisssioners CGT Manual)

> *A company is incorporated in 1980 with an issued share capital of 100 ordinary shares. A, who has been a full time working director since 1980, decides to retire in 1995/96. He disposes of all 100 shares for a consideration of £300,000, resulting in a gain of £90,000. The aggregate limit for relief at that time was £250,000.*

The value of the assets of the company at the date of disposal are:-   £

Freehold premises	210,000
Shop equipment	8,000
Goodwill	20,000
Quoted stocks and shares	50,000
Stock in trade and cash	<u>17,000</u>
	305,000
Less bank overdraft	<u>5,000</u>
	300,000

The proportion of consideration on disposal attributable to chargeable business assets is:-

$$\frac{238,000 \text{(premises + equipment + goodwill)}}{288,000 \text{ (premises + equipment + goodwill + quoted stocks & shares)}}$$

The threshold has not been exceeded viz:-

$$300,000 \times \frac{238}{288} = £247,916$$

The gain which is relieved from tax is as follows:-

$$\frac{90,000 \times 247,916}{300,000} = £74,375$$

The balance of the gain is taxable (£90,000 - £74,375 = £15,625)

Notwithstanding the fact that, in the example above, the consideration attributable to chargeable business assets is less than £250,000 (the pre 1/12/99 limit) the Revenue Commissioners conclude that a tax liability arises on the disposal of the shares.

Until the matter has been clarified in the Courts, doubt must remain as to the correct interpretation of this obscurely drafted legislation.

30.10   **Marginal Relief**

Where the individual making the disposal exceeds the £375,000 limit for the proceeds of disposal of qualifying assets, the full relief is not available. However, he may still be entitled to claim the marginal relief.

The affect of marginal relief is to reduce the CGT payable on the gains on qualifying assets to an amount equal to one half of the excess of the disposal proceeds over the £375,000 limit.

Example 161

*If in **example 160** above, the sale proceeds of the business premises were £256,000, and the gain remained the same at £20,000, the tax payable on the disposal of the premises would be reduced from £8,000 to a maximum of one half of (£256,000 - £250,000) i.e. £3,000 (the pre 1/12/1999 limit was £250,000).*

To this would be added the tax payable on the disposal of the painting, making a total CGT payable by John for 1995/96 of £3,400.

*The tax payable on the gains on qualifying assets, which is to be reduced is calculated on the same basis as set out in **example 160 above - i.e. by setting losses and allowances as far as possible against other gains of the year first.***

The legislation does not specify a cut-off point for marginal relief, as it is self imposed. When a stage is reached where one half of the excess, exceeds the tax payable under normal rules - there is no relief, and marginal relief cannot apply, as it cannot increase the liability.

Example 162

Joe is aged 65 years, and has decided to retire from business in March 1995. He has carried on business as a sole trader for the past 40 years. His business consists of retail shops in several locations. His disposals of qualifying assets subsequent to his 55th birthday were as follows:

1. *1988: Sale of shop to unconnected party - £40,000*

2. *1989: Gift of shop at open market value of £50,000 to his son*

3. *1992: sale of shop to unconnected party for £170,000*

4. *1993: sale of shop to unconnected third party for £100,000*

5. *Sale of shop to son for £150,000*

In 1995, Joe still owns one shop valued at £100,000.

Retirement relief would apply to Joe in relation to the disposals described above in the following manner:

***Disposal 1 :** The 1988 consideration for the disposal of the shop does not exceed the aggregate limit (£50,000) then applying . Accordingly, full relief is available for any CGT payable on that disposal.*

***Disposal 2 :** There is no limit on the consideration for disposals to his child. In addition, the disposal to his child is not aggregated in arriving at the limit relating to other disposals.*

Separate relief, under s599 (described in paragraph 30.11) would apply to this disposal to his child.

***Disposal 3 :** On the occasion of the sale in 1992 for the sum of £170,000, two issues arise. Firstly it is necessary to consider whether the relief previously* granted in 1988 needs to be adjusted. The aggregate consideration (ignoring the transfer to the son) in 1992 amounts to £210,000. At that date (1992) the relevant limit to the aggregate of consideration for disposals which would be exempt was £200,000 (increased on 6 April 1991 from the previous limit of £50,000). The aggregate consideration exceeds that limit and therefore in 1988 the disposal could have the relief granted to it withdrawn by the Revenue, if it proves necessary to do so in order to ensure that the total relief granted in relation to all disposals up to 1992 does not exceed the relief that would be available had they all occurred in 1992.

The next point to consider is what relief would be available if all disposals (1, 2, and 3 above) had occurred in 1992. On the assumption that the 1988 disposal had an indexed base cost of £10,000, and the 1992 disposal had an indexed base cost of £100,000, the total gain will amount to £100,000. However under marginal relief the total tax payable cannot exceed half the difference between the aggregate consideration and the figure of (in 1992) £200,000. That amounts to a sum of £5,000. That is less than what the tax otherwise would be if the reliefs did not apply, and it therefore represents the maximum tax which is chargeable. Since it is also less than the tax which would be chargeable (but for the application of the marginal relief) on the most recent 1992 disposal, it is not necessary for the Revenue to reopen the 1988 disposal on which they had applied complete exemption. They are able to collect all the tax due to date by means of an assessment on the current 1992 disposal.

Disposal 4 : The 1993 disposal has the affect of bringing the aggregate consideration on qualifying disposals up to that date to the sum of £310,000. Once again the same questions have to be looked at i.e. what relief is available on the current disposal, and is there any necessity to reopen the previous disposals. It is assumed that the indexed based cost for the 1993 disposals was £90,000. The aggregate consideration to date clearly exceeds the £200,000 limit (then applying) for total relief, and accordingly only marginal relief can apply. Accordingly the maximum, CGT payable is limited to half of the difference between the aggregate of £310,000, and the limit of £200,000 i.e. £55,000. That is considerably in excess of the tax which would otherwise fall to be paid on the 1993 disposal, which would be £10,000 at 40% i.e. £4,000. Accordingly, marginal relief will not apply to the 1993 disposal in the sense of providing any relief.

The Revenue are also entitled to re-open the assessments on the two previous disposals, in 1992 and in 1988, with a view to seeing that the total s598 relief obtained on the three disposals to date does not bring the tax liability on those three disposals to below £55,000. The exemption in 1988 reduced the tax liability on that disposal by £9,000 (assuming the 30% CGT rate applicable in that year applied). The 1992 disposal should have attracted tax of £29,000 but in fact it attracted tax of only £5,000 due to marginal relief. The 1993 disposal has attracted its proper share of tax i.e. £4,000. Therefore the aggregate tax properly chargeable on the three disposals to date, but for the s598 relief would be as follows:

Disposal 1 :	1988	£9,000
Disposal 3 :	1992	£28,000
Disposal 4 :	1993	4,000
Total		£41,000

> *This total is less than the maximum amount of tax which marginal relief permits to be charged i.e. £55,000   so marginal relief provides no benefit. Accordingly the Revenue are entitled to reopen the 1992 and 1988 assessments and to withdraw the relief in total from those years.*
>
> **Disposal 5** : *The 1995 disposal to the son has no implications since it is not included in the aggregation for the purposes of s598.*
>
> **Disposal 6** : *The fact that Joe has retained a further property does not affect the calculations. If he subsequently disposes of it, he could then require a further aggregate of considerations on disposals of qualifying assets since his 55th birthday to be made with a view to determining what relief if any would be available on its disposal.*

In the examples above the annual CGT exemption available to individuals (but not in a year where retirement relief has been claimed) has been ignored for the sake of simplicity. So also has the increase in the indexed base cost of prior disposals, which would arise when the notional tax computation has to be made on the assumption that all disposals since the 55th birthday occurred in the most recent year of disposal.

The operation of the clawback can be affected by **changes in the rates** of CGT over a period of time. The clawback operates by requiring one to calculate the amount of tax which would be payable if all disposals within the ambit of s598 had all occurred in the most recent year in which a disposal occurred. The amount of tax payable on those disposals is then compared with the maximum amount of tax which can be chargeable, where marginal relief applies. Where the rate of tax applying in the most recent year of disposal differs from the rate which applied in the years in which previous disposals occurred, the aggregate of tax payments which is compared with the marginal relief limit will not be the actual tax payments made but will be the tax payments which would have been made had the current rates applied to all disposals. Accordingly this notional tax amount may be greater or less than the actual tax payments made to date, and the amount of marginal relief correspondingly available may be greater or less than would otherwise be the case.

Where a taxpayer who has reached his 55th birthday disposes of some only of his qualifying assets to his *spouse*, that transfer is treated as being at open market value for the purpose *(only)* of computing the aggregate of consideration on disposals of qualifying assets for the purpose of the exemption / marginal relief. The purpose of this provision may be to ensure that a taxpayer does not avoid the inclusion in his aggregate (for the purpose of the exemption or of marginal relief) of some of his qualifying assets, which he might transfer to his spouse who might then make the transfers to unconnected third parties.

Example 163

s598

Joe meets the requirements for relief on his total qualifying assets of £500,000, in relation to which his base cost is only £1,000. Joe wishes to sell all of his qualifying assets in order to retire from business. In June 1995 he sells half of the assets for a consideration of £250,000, to an unconnected third party. This disposal attracts the exemption under s598, since the aggregate consideration in respect of disposals of qualifying assets since his 55th birthday does not exceed £250,000 (the pre 1/12/1999 limit). In July 1995 Joe gifts the balance of his qualifying assets to his wife who shortly afterwards disposes of them to the same unconnected third party for £250,000.

Joe has not succeeded in protecting the exemption which he obtained on the first sale. Although for CGT purposes the transfer to his wife would be treated as being on a no gain / no loss basis i.e. for the sum of £500 (being his base cost in those assets), for the purpose of aggregation it is treated as being for the sum of £250,000. Accordingly marginal relief is computed on the occasion of the transfer to the spouse and shows that tax relief would only be available on any transfer since his 55th birthday, to the extent that the aggregate tax payable exceeded £125,000 (half the difference between £250,000 and the aggregate consideration of £500,000). Joe has paid no tax on the first transfer, and is not liable to tax on the second transfer since it is a transfer to his spouse. However the Revenue may now reopen the assessment on the first transfer and clawback the exemption granted to Joe. The tax payable would be £99,800, being 40% of the gain of £224,500 (the base cost being £500).

Notwithstanding the fact that the assets transferred to Joe's wife were included in the aggregation of consideration of £250,000, Joe's wife is treated as having acquired them only for a cost of £500. Accordingly, on her disposal of the assets to a third party for a consideration of £250,000, a gain arises of £224,500. Joe's wife is not entitled to retirement relief on her disposal. This is because, notwithstanding that the period of ownership of her spouse in the assets is treated for the purpose of the section as also being her period of ownership, the assets were not assets used for the purpose of a trade carried on by her and accordingly are not chargeable business assets and therefore not qualifying assets. As a result of Joe's ill advised transfer to his wife, the total tax liability considerably exceeds what it would have been if Joe disposed of all of the assets directly to the third party.

30.11   Disposal to Child of owner

Where the disposal of qualifying assets is to a child of the owner, there is no limit for the purpose of relief on the amount of proceeds of disposal involved. The £375,000 lifetime limit which would otherwise apply is ignored.

s599(5)

In addition, the proceeds of disposal to a child is ignored in calculating the limit for disposals to persons other than a child of the owner of the qualifying assets.

For this purpose :

s599(1)(a)

• the term *child* includes a nephew or niece who has worked substantially on a full-time basis for the period of 5 years ending with the disposal in carrying on, or assisting in the carrying on of, the trade, business or profession concerned, or the work of, or connected with the office or employment concerned [s599(1)(a)].

s56

- an illegitimate child who has not, on or before the date of disposal, been legitimated or adopted in the manner described in s.36(a)(ii) of the FA77, shall, if the disposal is made to him by his mother on or after the 6th day of April 1979, be the child of his mother [s.27((1)(d)], but this was changed by FA 1988.

s1084

The treatment of illegitimate children has been altered by the Status of Children Act 1987, in that they are treated in effect as the children of both parents for tax purposes. The changes brought into force by the Status of Children Act 1987, were applied for the purposes of certain taxes (including CGT) by s.16, FA 1988 now s1084 (see paragraph 33.9).

Example 164

*The same taxpayer as in **example 163** sells off his business, as described in the previous example. Shortly after his 55th birthday, he had transferred part of the land and buildings used in the trade to his son.*

The transfer of the land and buildings to the son are totally relieved under s599.

That transfer to the son does not affect the calculation of relief under s598 on the disposal of the remaining assets to the unconnected third party. The chargeable business assets taken into account in calculating Joe's aggregation of consideration for the purposes when s598 remains £170,000, as computed in the previous example.

An individual may avail of the exemption under s599 no matter how valuable the assets may be which he transfers to his children, and no matter how large the gain which would otherwise be chargeable in respect of the disposals. There is no limit on the aggregate consideration for qualifying disposals for relief under s599.

The definition of qualifying assets for the purpose of s599 relief is the same as that already described for s598 relief in relation to disposals to third parties.

S599 relief is subject to a *clawback*. If the assets which are the subject of the relief are disposed of by the child within 6 years of the relieved transfer, the original relief granted to the parent on that relieved transfer may, in effect, be withdrawn. The relief is withdrawn, not from the parent who had the benefit of the relief, but by way of an assessment on the child who received the assets. The clawback is measured by a charge to CGT on the child, of the amount of tax which would have been payable if s599 had not applied to the original transfer of assets to him from his parent.

The 6 year period during which a disposal of a transferred asset can lead to a clawback, was 10 years in the case of disposals by the child made prior to 6 April 1995.

Example 165

> William, who is entitled to retirement relief, transferred all his qualifying assets
> by way of gift to his son George in 1993. The assets were valued at that time at
> £300,000. William's base cost of those assets to be deducted in computing the
> gain on the disposal was £10,000 (including indexation). In July 1995 George
> sold the assets (which were transferred to him by his father) for a total
> consideration of £500,000.
>
> Because George disposed of the qualifying assets within 6 years of the transfer
> from his father, he is now liable to
>
> - pay any CGT arising on his own disposal of those assets, and
>
> - pay the CGT his father would have paid on the 1993 disposal, if relief under
>   s599 did not apply to the transfer.
>
> It is therefore necessary to calculate what the amount of tax which would have
> been paid by his father if no relief was available under s599 at the time of the
> transfer.

s599(4)(a) S599 provides that on a subsequent disposal by the child within 6
years, "*the capital gains tax which, if subsection (1) [of s599] had not
applied, would have been charged on the individual on his disposal of those
assets to the child shall be assessed and charged on the child, in addition to
any capital gains tax chargeable in respect of the gain accruing to the child
on his disposal of those assets*".

As already mentioned, there are two reliefs which can affect the tax
payable on gains accruing on qualifying disposals by individuals
who are over 55 years at the time of the disposal:

- relief on disposal to a child of the owner (s599), and

s598 • relief under s598 for disposals not coming within s599

The general rules of interpretation of law, would suggest that in
normal circumstances, the specific relief available on a qualifying
disposal between a father and his child, would apply to such
circumstances to the exclusion of the more general relief applying to
a disposal between unconnected persons. That specific relief is given
by s599(1).

In the event of a subsequent disposal of those assets by the child, the
amount of CGT to be charged on the child, is the amount which
would have been payable by his father on the original transfer to
him, if relief under s599(1) did not apply to that transfer.

The only reason for excluding relief under s598 on the original
transfer, was that s599 was more specific to the circumstances of the
actual transfer between father and child. If s599 did not exist, or for
any reason did not apply, there does not appear to be any reason
why the relief offered by s598 should not apply.

This also makes a good deal of sense, in that to interpret the
combined affect of the two sections in a different manner, would

suggest that the draftsman intended that the relief for a transfer from parent to child would carry a far greater potential penalty than a similar transfer between strangers.

Had s598 relief applied, the aggregate consideration (£300,000) would have exceeded the 1993 limit for an exemption (£200,000) and marginal relief would have ensured that the total CGT payable could not exceed half the difference between £200,000 (the 1993 limit) and the aggregate consideration of £300,000, i.e. £50,000.

Since the £50,000 is far lower than the tax which would ordinarily be payable, it is the tax which would have arisen on the transfer from the father to the son in 1993, had s598 relief not applied. Therefore £50,000 is the tax which now becomes payable by the son in respect of the 1993 transfer. Additionally, he has of course to compute his own CGT liability by reference to the base cost of £300,000 (suitably indexed) and any enhancement expenditure which may have arisen in the two year period, and the consideration of £500,000 on the disposal.

- **Revenue Commissioners published precedent:**

- In their published precedents the Revenue Commissioners have stated that *"If a "share for share" reorganisation comes within Section 584 it will not constitute a disposal for the purposes of Section 599 (4)."* In other words if the child has received shares from the father and he later participates in a share for share transaction in relation to those shares which qualifies for relief under s584, that share for share transaction will not trigger the claw-back.

Where an owner wishes to retire and pass on a family company to his children, it might seem a straightforward solution that he should sell the shares to his children. He might alternatively gift them, but where he is not sufficiently wealthy to afford to divest himself completely without some recompense, it may be necessary for him to sell the shares. An immediate difficulty arises in that the children may not be in a position to pay the consideration, or to meet repayments on any borrowings raised in order to pay for the shares. Considerable tax costs could arise in extracting money from the family company in order to repay borrowings used to pay for the shares, or to directly provide the consideration for the shares. This is so whether the moneys are taken out by way of distribution (e.g. dividend) or salary.

In contrast, the sale of the shares in the family company to a third party can raise cash but is subject to the limit of £375,000 consideration, and marginal relief thereafter.

In some family situations this may point towards a mixed transaction, in which shares worth £375,000 are sold to a specially formed company owned by the children, and the balance of the shares are otherwise transferred directly to the children. The transfers to the children are not aggregated for the purposes of computing retirement relief on the disposal to the company owned by the children. The disposal to the company owned by the children does not benefit from the relief available in relation to a disposal to the children i.e. it has a £375,000 limit applied to it as with any disposal to a person other than the children. It may then be possible to structure matters so as to pass cash from the family company to the new "children's company", in order to finance the payment to the parent who has disposed of the shares. *That structuring involves taxation issues outside the scope of this book as may the transaction referred to above.*

Where assets have been disposed to a child and retirement relief is applied, the death of a child within six years of the transfer does not trigger a clawback of the relief. This is because a taxpayer is not treated as disposing of assets on death, for the purposes of capital gains tax.

30.12   **Trusts**

s577A   As explained in paragraph 65.7, a trustee may be treated as
FA98 s69   disposing of the trust assets at open market value on the occasion when persons come absolutely entitled as against the trustee to those assets. Where that occasion is the death of a life tenant (see paragraph 65.7.2) no charge to tax arises on the trustees. However, if the life interest comes to an end for other reasons e.g. the life tenant renouncing the interest in the settlement, and if the settlement comes to an end on that renunciation by reason of the remainder man becoming absolutely entitled as against the trustees on that occasion, then a charge to tax could arise on the trustees. S577A may provide relief in such a situation. The section was inserted by the FA98 in relation to deemed disposals by trustees on or after 12 February 1998.

S577A provides that

- where the trustees of settled property are deemed to dispose of and immediately reacquire the assets by virtue of 576 (1) and

- there are so deemed on the occasion of a person becoming absolutely entitled to the assets as against the trustee and

- those persons become absolutely entitled on the occasion of the person then entitled to the life interest relinquishing that life interest,

then the trustees will receive the same relief as would have been available to the life tenant who relinquished the interest, if that life tenant had been the absolute owner of the assets in question throughout the period during which he was life tenant, and as if any expenditure by the trustee on the asset which would be deductible under s552(1) on a disposal by the trustee, had been incurred by the life tenant. The section does not state that such expenditure shall be deemed to be incurred at the times at which it was incurred by the trustee, but presumably the legislation would be interpreted as if there was such a deeming.

If the persons who become absolutely entitled to the assets on the life tenant relinquishing his interest, are the children of the life tenant, then s559 would apply (provided all the conditions for relief are met) so as to grant total relief to the trustee. If the persons who become entitled are not the children of the life tenant who relinquishes the interest, then s598 is capable of application both so as to exempt trustees from any gain on disposals not greater than £375,000 in value, or to apply marginal relief.

The relief which is to be available to the trustees is the relief which would have been available to the life tenant had he made the disposal. Accordingly, the provisions of s598 that require the aggregation of disposals of qualifying assets would apply. Where the life tenant had himself made previous disposals (after reaching the age of 55 years) of qualifying assets, those disposals would have to be aggregated with the amount which the trustees are now deemed to have disposed of, in order to determine whether complete relief under s598 (2) (a) (i) would apply, or whether marginal relief under (ii) would apply.

In contrast however, in applying s598 to actual disposals by the life tenant of assets which he himself absolutely owned, the deemed disposal arising to a trustee, to which s577A applies , is not aggregated with disposals by the life tenant of his own assets, for the purpose of determining what relief is to be available to the "life tenant" in relation to those actual disposals of his own qualifying assets. The aggregation rule applies in one direction only - for the purpose of computing relief for the trustees, actual disposals by the life tenant of his own qualifying assets are aggregated with the deemed disposal of the trustee, but the deemed disposal by the trustee is not aggregated with actual disposals by the life tenant of his own qualifying assets, for the purpose of computing relief for the life tenant on those actual disposals of his own assets.

It is not clear from s577A, or from s598, as to how an actual disposal of his own qualifying assets made by the former "life tenant" subsequent to the deemed disposal by the trustees on the occasion when he relinquished his life interest, would be taken into account, for the purpose of a clawback of the relief given to the trustees. Although retirement relief under s598 which was granted to a taxpayer in relation to disposal of qualifying assets owned absolutely by that taxpayer is subject to recomputation and clawback when the taxpayer makes subsequent disposals of qualifying assets in later tax years, it is not clear that such a clawback provisions can apply to the trustees, either by reference to the actions taken by the former life tenant in relation to his own qualifying assets, or in relation to subsequent deemed disposals by the trustees of other qualifying assets which they may hold. On balance, it would seem that the clawback could not operate where there are no subsequent deemed disposals by the trustees to which the section would have application. If the trustees became entitled to relief on a second occasion in relation to different assets, there would seem to be no possibility of clawback or aggregation operating unless the life tenant is the same life tenant as in the case of the previous life interest which was relinquished.

s577A S577A does not confer retirement relief on the trustees in all circumstances in which a life tenant relinquishes his interest, with the result that other persons become absolutely entitled against the trustees to the assets. All it does is to grant to the trustees the same relief that the life tenant would have been entitled to had he been the absolute owner of the assets throughout the period for which he was life tenant. If he had been life tenant for less than 10 years, or if the trade carried on by the trustees (where the asset is a trade asset as opposed to shares in a family company) had not been carried on by the life tenant, then the life tenant would not have been entitled in his own right to retirement relief had he owned the assets, and accordingly the trustees would not receive relief. Similarly, if the amount of shares held by the trust were not sufficient to meet the requirements for the company be a "family company", then once again relief might not be available. In this case however it would seem that shares owned absolutely by the life tenant could be aggregated with the shares held by the trust, and for the purposes of s577A treated as absolutely owned by the life tenant.

Example 166

John is the life tenant of the X trust which owns 20% of the shares in X Ltd., a trading company. John owns 10% of those shares absolutely. S577A deems John to be the absolute owner of the 20% held by the trust (for the purpose of computing any relief due to the trustee) and accordingly for those purposes Johns share holding would be 30%, sufficient to make it a family company.

It should be noted however that were John to disposes of his own 10% he cannot be regarded as being the owner of the 20% of which he is life tenant, for the purpose of determining whether or not the company is a family company in relation to Johns own disposal. In the situation above, where John holds absolutely only 10%, X company would be a family company only if 75% of the votes were exercisable by John and by members of his family. The 20% held by the trustees is of no benefit to him in qualifying for the relief.

Example 167

John settled the shares in X limited on trusts retaining a life interest to himself, in 1995. He had acquired the shares in 1986. John relinquished his life interest in March 1998 and the trust thereby came to an end, with his son John junior becoming absolutely entitled to the shares as against the trustee.

The trustees have owned the shares for only 7 years. The section deems John to have been the absolute owner for that period. It would seem that he is therefore entitled to aggregate that period of ownership with his actual prior period of ownership, so as to demonstrate that he was the owner for not less than 10 years in total.

Not every relinquishment of the life interest will attract the relief. Relief is specifically available only in relation to a charge arising under s576 (1) on the occasion when a person becomes absolutely entitled to it as against a trustee by reason of a life interest coming to an end on it being relinquished by the life tenant. No other charge to tax is subject to the relief.

Example 168

The trustees of the X trust, of which John is a life tenant, accept a take over offer for the shares in X company and disposes of them for £1m. X company, were it absolutely owned by John, would be a qualifying asset of his. Following on the take over John relinquishes his life interest and John's son, John Junior (who under the trust deed is the remainderman) automatically becomes absolutely entitled as against the trustees to the trust assets. No relief is available under s577A because the gain which arose to the trustees did so on the sale of shares, and not on a deemed disposal under s576 (1). That latter deemed disposal related to the proceeds of the sale, and not to the shares in X Co.

Example 169

John is the life tenant of the X trust, which owns X Company, a company which if John owned it absolutely, would be a qualifying asset of his. The trust deed provides a life interest to John, and grants discretion to the trustees to appoint a remainder interest among a class of beneficiaries which includes Johns children. John renounces his life interest and the trustees immediately afterwards appoint the shares in X Co. to John's son, John Junior.

No relief will be available. The charge to tax on the trustees arises under s577 (3) - the termination of a life interest in possession in settled property, the assets then not ceasing to be settled property - and not under s576 (1) - a person becoming absolutely entitled to any settled property against the trustee. Although John Junior does become absolutely entitled, and the trustees are deemed to dispose of the assets on that occasion under s576 (1) no gain arises to them on that disposal under s576 (1) because the gain has already been triggered by the immediately prior deemed disposal under s577 (3).

This problem would have been avoided had the trustees appointed the remainder interest to John Junior prior to John renouncing his life interest.

30.13   Interaction with other reliefs:

30.13.1   Transfer of business to a company

It should be noted that there is no relief from this clawback which may be triggered on a subsequent transfer by that child of his business to a company. The relief for such transfers (see paragraph 29) deals with the child's own gain on transfer of the assets. It does not prevent the clawback of his parent's gain which is chargeable on him because of the disposal of the assets to the company (see also paragraph 30.6).

30.13.2   Roll-over relief

A gain which was deferred by a taxpayer under the roll-over provisions, is deemed not to *"accrue until he ceases to use the new assets for the purposes of the trade"* (see paragraph 26).

On a disposal of qualifying assets, more than one gain may arise:

- the actual gain on disposal of the qualifying assets, and

- a gain arising on an earlier disposal which was deferred under the roll-over relief provisions against the purchase of the qualifying assets.

The deferred gain is deemed to accrue at the time of disposal of the qualifying (new) assets. However, it does not arise on the disposal on the qualifying assets, and so cannot avail of the retirement relief.

Notwithstanding the comments above on the strict interpretation of the legislation, it is possible that concessional treatment may be available from the Revenue Commissioners. This should be confirmed directly with the Revenue Commissioners in each separate case.

30.13.3   Relief for a company acquiring its own shares

There does not appear to be any specific prohibition on the application of the two reliefs to the same transaction, in certain circumstances (see paragraph 49) provided the conditions for both reliefs are met.

30.14   Offset of CGT against CAT

A gift of a qualifying asset may give rise to a charge to CAT as well as to CGT. Where CGT is relieved, there is no possibility of an offset of any CGT. If the CGT is later clawed back, it cannot be offset against CAT on the original gift as it does not arise on the same event- see paragraph 97.6.

31   DISPOSALS TO CHARITIES AND PUBLIC BODIES

31.1   Broad Outline

s611   Where a disposal of an asset is made (otherwise than under a bargain at arm's length):

- to the STATE

- to a CHARITY, or

FA31 s28(3)   • to certain NATIONAL INSTITUTIONS or other PUBLIC BODIES defined in FA31 s28(3)

normal provisions (see paragraph 16) substituting market value may not apply. In such a case, provided the disposal is a gift, or is made for a consideration not greater than cost, the disposal and acquisition will be deemed to be for a consideration which would ensure that neither a gain nor a loss accrues on the disposal.

Example 170

Pat bought a house of historical and national interest in June 1984 for £20,000. In June 1992 he made a gift of the house to a charitable trust. At that time the house was valued at £85,000. It was not his principal private residence.

As the making of a gift is a disposal for CGT purposes, Pat is treated as disposing of the house to the trust. However, under the provisions outlined above, he is deemed to have disposed of the property to the trust for £20,000 (giving no gain/loss).

31.2   Subsequent Disposal by Charity, Etc.

To complete the picture, it is necessary to consider what would happen if the trustees subsequently disposed of the property.

If the subsequent disposal by the trustees is exempt under the general relief for charities (see paragraph 31.4) no problem arises. However, if that disposal is not exempt a charge to CGT arises on:

- the gain arising to the trustees on the disposal

  and

- the gain which would have arisen if arm's length provisions had applied to the original disposal to the trustees.

Both gains are assessed on the trustees.

Example 171

Let us assume that the trust sold the property (as in Example 170) for £95,000 in March 1993 and the proceeds were not applied for charitable purposes.

The tax is calculated as follows

TAX ON FIRST DISPOSAL

Market Value at Date of Disposal	£85,000
Cost as indexed (20,000 x 1.341)	£26,820
Gain	£58,180
£58,180 @ 40% =	£23,272

i.e. the tax that would have been payable by Pat if the relief given on the disposal to the charity did not apply.

TAX ON SECOND DISPOSAL

Consideration Received	£95,000
Market Value on Date of Acquisition	£85,000
Gain	£10,000
£10,000 @ 40% =	£4,000

No indexation arises as the asset is held for less than 1 year. The tax due on both disposals is payable by the trustees.

If the proceeds of the disposal by the trustees were not applied for charitable purposes, any gain arising would be chargeable (see paragraph 31.4).

31.3   Charities - Settled Property

s611(2)

In certain circumstances, the assets of a settlement (or part of those assets) are deemed to be disposed of, and immediately reacquired by the trustees at market value. This would normally happen:

- On the death of a life tenant, where the property remained within the trust (see paragraph 65.7.2)

  or

- When a beneficiary becomes absolutely entitled as against the trustees to all or part of the trust assets (see paragraph 65.1).

Where on the death of a life tenant the property is held on trust for a charity or other body qualifying for relief under the provisions outlined in paragraph 31.1 above, the trustees are deemed to dispose of the assets (and reacquire them) at such a value as gives no gain and no loss on the disposal. The same provisions apply where the charity (or other qualifying body) becomes absolutely entitled as against the trustees to all or part of the trust assets.

This relief in the case of settled property is conditional on no consideration being received by any person, for, or in connection with any transaction by virtue of which the charity or other qualifying body became entitled to the assets.

31.4   Charities

s609(1)

A gain is not chargeable if it accrues to a charity provided it is applicable and applied for charitable purposes.

The exemption is dependent on the gain being both "applicable and applied for charitable purposes". Whether or not the gain is applicable for charitable purposes will depend on the trusts applying to the property which is being disposed of ie are they exclusively charitable trusts. A further requirement, that the gain be actually applied for charitable purposes, is potentially a source of difficulty. No time limit is set down for the test. It is inherently improbable that there is any expectation that the gain be applied to charitable purposes in the year in which it arises, and the legislation itself makes no such requirement. There being no time limit in the legislation, it is not clear how long can elapse with the gain retained by the charity unapplied, before the exemption can be challenged. The matter does not appear to have been litigated before the courts. It would seem reasonable to say that if the application of the gain has occurred prior to an assessment being raised, it is a complete answer to the assessment, no matter how long a period has elapsed since the gain originally arose.

No tracing mechanism is applied for determining how one would identify a gain with a subsequent application for charitable purposes of funds by the charity. Is it "first in first out", "last in first out" or some other method? The absence of any such mechanism for relating the accrual of a gain and subsequent application of funds would suggest that no close examination of the matter is intended by the legislation.

The entitlement to the exemption for capital gains tax purposes in s609 uses slightly different words to the corresponding exemption for income tax purposes in s207 where the expression is "income - - applicable to charitable purposes only, and insofar as the same are applied for charitable purposes only". The inclusion in the income tax phrase of "insofar" offers some support for the notion that income which is applicable for charitable purposes, but has not at a point in time been applied fully to those charitable purposes might be deprived of its exemption by reason of partial non application. In contrast, the capital gains tax exemption does not use the expression "insofar as" in referring to application of the gain and therefore does not clearly deal with a situation where part of a gain is applied to charitable purposes, and part is not.

A charity may obtain funds from gifts and donations, income earned, or gains realised. All three sources of funds are subject to separate taxation reliefs which are dependant in all three cases on the funds being applicable to charitable purposes. However the income tax and the CGT reliefs further require that they be applied to charitable purposes. The difficulty of relating the application of funds to the source of funds becomes greater when it is realised that not only is it necessary to determine which gains may have been applied, but it is necessary to determine whether any particular application of funds was from funds received from gifts, from income, or from gains in the first place. A similar problem arises in relation to the remittance basis of taxation (see paragraph 3.3). There is no clear answer as to how it can be determined whether a charity which expends money on charitable purposes has done so from income, or from realised gains. The case law referred to in paragraph 3.3 would suggest that there is a presumption likely to be adopted by the courts that any application of funds will be primarily from income or gains, as opposed to gifts but it does not assist in the distinguishing between the application of income or gains.

s609(2)

If, for any reason, property owned by a charity ceases to be subject to charitable trusts, it will be treated as if it was sold for its market value on that date, and any gain arising as a result of the deemed sale will be chargeable to CGT.

In the UK case of Prest v Bettinson a testatrix left the residue of her estate to executor trustees on trust for sale, directing them to distribute the proceeds of sale (after payment of certain annuities) to five institutions (four of which were charities). It was contended that the gain on the disposal of the properties accrued to the charitable institutions, and accordingly, four fifths of the gains were exempt. It was held by the Court that the gains could not accrue to the charities unless they were absolutely entitled as against the trustees. As they were not so entitled (because of the requirement to pay the annuities out of the residue) the gains accrued to the executors, and not the charities.

The question of whether a donation from one charity to another is sufficient to warrant the amount being regarded as applied to charitable purposes, was considered in IRC v Helen Slater Charitable Trust Ltd. Slade J in his judgement stated that *"any charitable corporation which, acting intra vires, makes an outright transfer of money applicable for charitable purposes to any other corporation established exclusively for charitable purposes, in such manner as to pass to the transferee full title to the money, must be taken, by the transfer itself, to have 'applied' such money for 'charitable' purposes within the meaning of [TCA97 s611] unless the transferor knows or ought to know that the money will be misapplied by the transferee. In such circumstances, ...the transferor corporation is in my judgement entitled to claim exemption...without having to show how the money has been dealt with by the transferee".*

32   EXEMPT BODIES AND ASSETS

32.1   Government and Other Securities

32.1.1   General exemption on disposal

s607   The following securities are not chargeable assets, and no chargeable gain or allowable loss can arise on their disposal :

- Securities (including savings certificates) issued under the authority of the Minister for Finance,

- Stock issued by any of the following authorities

  - a local authority

  - a harbour authority (mentioned in the First Schedule to the Harbours Act, 1946)

  - Land bonds issued under the Land Purchase Acts

- Debentures, debenture stock, certificates of charge or other forms of security issued by:

  - The Electricity Supply Board

  - Board Gais Eireann (FA92 s24)

  - Radio Telefis Eireann

  - The Industrial Credit Corporation plc (FA89 s95)

  - Bord Telecom Eireann (FA88 s70)

  - Irish Telecommunications Investments plc (FA88 s70)

  - Coras Iompair Eireann

  - The Agricultural Credit Corporation Ltd,

  - Bord na Mona

  - Aerlinte Eireann Teo

  - Aer Lingus Teo

  - Aer Rianta Teo

  - The Housing Finance Agency, under Section 10 of the Housing Finance Agency Act 1981 (FA82 s41)

  - An Post, which are guaranteed by the Minister for Finance (FA 1984, s.66)

  - A designated body within the meaning assigned by Section 1 of the Securitisation (Proceeds of Certain Mortgages) Act 1995 (FA96 s36)

- Stocks or securities issued in the State by certain European Bodies with the approval of the Minister for Finance, i.e. issued by the European Economic Community, the European Coal and Steel Community, the European Atomic Energy Community, and the European Investment Bank.

Although no chargeable gain or allowable loss can arise on the disposal of these securities, it should be noted that any 'accrued' interest reflected in the sale proceeds may be charged to tax as income.

As described in paragraph 32.3, strips of Government securities are generally within the income tax code rather than the capital gains tax code and accordingly the exemptions described above are not relevant to them in most instances.

s815   Where a security is sold before the date for payment of the interest attaching to it, the sale price will reflect the amount of interest accrued. In broad terms, where the disposal takes place after 25th January 1984, s815 provides for the accrued interest to be charged to income tax under Schedule D, Case IV.

There are a number of exceptions to this rule, the main ones being:

- where the security has been owned by the person making the disposal for a continuous period of 2 years prior to the disposal. Personal representatives of a deceased person are regarded as being the same person as the deceased person they are representing for this purpose

- where the security is held as trading stock

- transfers between spouses (married persons living together)

- where the interest is regarded as a distribution under the Corporation Tax Act (as amended).

32.1.2   Exchanges of government stocks

s751B; FA99 s59   S751B was inserted by FA99 s59. The subject matter is a transaction under which the owner of a government bond exchanges that bond for a new security issued by the government under the exchange programme on Irish government bonds run by the National Treasury Management Agency. The section applies to exchanges in the period 11 February 1999 to 1 January 2000.

The section provides for a deferral of any chargeable gain arising on the exchange, until the new bonds are disposed of. In view of the fact that no chargeable gains arise on the disposal of government stocks, this section should have limited application.

It is understood that the exchange programme extends to certain stocks not covered by the exemptions described in paragraph 32.1.1

and accordingly provision was made for deferral of the chargeable gains in respect of those stocks.

32.2   **Futures Contracts**

Certain Government and other securities (see paragraph 32.1 above) are treated as not being assets for CGT purposes, so no chargeable gain or allowable loss can arise on the disposal of such securities.

s607(2)   This treatment was extended, by s.32 FA 1989, to include futures contracts for such securities [now in s607(2)].

To qualify for this CGT exemption, the futures contract must be:

- an unconditional contract for the acquisition or disposal of any such exempt instrument (listed in paragraph 32.1 above)

- require delivery of the instrument in respect of which the contracts are made.

The requirement that the instrument be 'delivered' is deemed to be satisfied, where a person who has entered into a futures contract dealt in or quoted on a FUTURES EXCHANGE or STOCK EXCHANGE closes out the futures contract by entering into another futures contract, so dealt in or quoted, with obligations which are reciprocal to those of the contract so closed out, and thereafter settles in respect of both futures contracts by means (if any) of a single cash payment or receipt.

32.3   **Strips of securities**

A security (including a Government security) may be stripped, i.e. the obligation of the issuer to pay interest and to pay capital may be separated from each other into separate units. Thus a security which promises repayment of capital on a particular date, and payments of interest over a period of time, may be "stripped" into two securities, one consisting of the entitlement to receive the repayment of capital on redemption, and the other consisting of the entitlement to receive the interest income during the period in which the security is an issue. These separated rights are described as strips of securities.

s55   TCA97 s55 permits the Minister for Finance to designate certain Government securities as being ones which may be stripped. The Finance Act also provided for a separate tax code in relation to the holding of such strips of securities. The most important feature of this code is that a holder of a strip of securities is brought within the charge to income tax under Case III of Sch D in relation to gains arising on the disposal or redemption of that security, where he is not already within the charge under Case I as a dealer in securities.

The consequences of imposing an income tax charge on the gains arising from the disposal or redemption of strips is to render valueless the capital gains exemption in relation to Government securities, where the strips are strips of a Government security. The exemption remains, but as the charge to tax in relation to the strips is under income tax and not under capital gains tax, its existence is of theoretical interest only.

As the topic of strips is therefore primarily an income tax topic, only brief details of the treatment for tax purposes of strips is provided in this paragraph.

• On the occasion of creating a strip, the person creating the strips from a security held by him at that time is deemed to dispose of the security at open market value. If the person is already within the charge to tax as a dealer in securities, that may have income tax/corporation tax on income consequences. Where the person is entitled to an exemption from CGT as the holder of a Government stock, that deemed disposal will not give rise to a chargeable gain.

• The deemed acquisition cost for each strip, on the occasion of it being created, is a proportionate part of the "opening value" of the security at the date it was stripped. In the case of a dealer in securities, it would be a proportionate part of the market value of the security at the time it was stripped. In the case of a non dealer however the "opening value" which is apportioned over the strips is the lower of the open market value of the security , or its nominal value.

Where a non dealer strips a security, he is therefore deemed to have disposed of the security at open market value at that time; but the aggregate of the acquisition cost to him of the various strips which he creates may actually be lower than that open market value of the security. This will arise if the nominal value of the security is less than the open market value. By reason of the deemed disposal of the security on the occasion of stripping it, the original acquisition cost of the security has no relevance to the acquisition cost of the strips for tax purposes thereafter.

• A dealer in shares who acquires a strip, other than by stripping a security, has an acquisition cost equal to the amount he paid for it. A non dealer however who acquires a strip of an exempt Government security (not any other type of security) may have an acquisition cost for the strip less than the amount which he paid for it. His acquisition cost is deemed to be equal to the lower of the amount paid for its acquisition, and a proportion of the nominal value of the security on the occasion of it being stripped, apportioned to the various strips in proportion to their market value at that time.

- The holder of a strip of a security is deemed to dispose of the security at open market value either at the end of an accounting period (in the case of a company within the charge to corporation tax) or the end of the tax year in other instances. This deemed disposal may give rise to a gain or a loss (usually a gain except in exceptional market conditions); but the gain or loss is one within either Case I of Sch D (in the case of a dealer) or within Case III of Sch D (in the case of any other person). It is not a chargeable gain or allowable loss for capital gains tax purposes.

- The reconstitution of a security from the various strips into which it had been broken is treated as being the occasion of the disposal of the strips at market value at that time, and the acquisition of the security for the aggregate of the market value of the strips, at that time. Once again this deemed disposal and deemed acquisition is an event relevant to income tax, and not to capital gains tax.

- The disposal of a strip (whether by redemption, sale, gift, etc) is the occasion for a potential charge to income tax under Case I Sch D (dealers) or Case III of Sch D (non dealers). As the entire consideration for the disposal of the strip will be brought into an income tax computation, the disposal should have no consequences for the purposes of taxation on capital gains.

  The only occasions when a stripped security enters the capital gains tax net is on the occasion of its stripping (when the security is deemed to be disposed of) and on the occasion of its reconstitution from strips (when there is a deemed acquisition). All transactions in between are subject to income tax and should have no implications for capital gains tax.

The taxation treatment of strips described above applies to any form of security (eg. issued by a quoted company) which is subjected to strips, and not only to Government securities. It does not apply to shares. There is one particular treatment described above which is peculiar to a strip of a Government security, i.e. the acquisition cost of a Government security acquired otherwise than by stripping the security, in the hands of a non dealer. However a non dealer acquiring a strip of a security other than a Government security, and otherwise than by way of stripping a security would have an acquisition cost for that security equal to the amount paid for its acquisition.

The legislation relating to strips does not specifically address the treatment of strips held at death. Though death is the occasion of a deemed disposal of assets for capital gains tax purposes, it would not ordinarily be the occasion of a disposal of assets, and the strips legislation of s55 does not deem it to be so. If that interpretation is correct, it would follow that on the occasion of death, any strips of securities held at that date would fall within the capital gains tax regime rather than the income tax regime (but other than in the case of dealers). Assets passing on death generally are dealt with in paragraph 66.

s812   TCA97 s812 may also be relevant to the stripping of a security, and to the tax treatment of strips. It is an income tax section and its interaction with the strips legislation above (also primarily an income tax topic) is outside the scope of this book. Reference should be made to the companion volume published by the Institute of Taxation in Ireland, "Income Tax".

32.4.1   Superannuation Schemes

s608   A gain accruing on investments to an approved (for income tax purposes) Superannuation Fund is not chargeable to CGT.

If only part of the Superannuation Fund is approved, the gain is exempt to the same extent that the income derived from the asset would be exempt from income tax.

A contract entered into by an approved Superannuation Fund in the course of dealing in financial futures or traded options dealt in or quoted on a futures exchange in Ireland is to be regarded as an investment. Accordingly, any gain accruing to an approved superannuation fund on such a contract would not be a chargeable gain.

32.4.2   Approved retirement funds

S784A
FA 2000, s23   The FA 99 inserted a number of sections, commencing with s784A, into the Taxes Acts. They introduced the concept of an approved retirement fund, and of an approved minimum retirement fund. These concepts were, from a taxation viewpoint, radically amended by s23 of the FA2000 which inter alia amended s784A.

Very few such funds were created prior to FA 2000 and accordingly the commentary below is confined to the new tax regime applied to the funds by FA 2000. Suffice it to say that the FA99 tax regime treated funds as transparent for tax purposes so that the pensioner was liable to tax in respect of the income of the fund, and in respect of the capital gains of the fund. However such income and gains could be distributed to him without further tax consequences. Where the original capital was distributed, ie the capital of the pension fund, a charge to income tax arose.

The approved retirement fund (ARF) and the approved minimum retirement fund (AMRF) were introduced as an alternative to the traditional pension arrangements which centred on a compulsory purchase of a retirement annuity from the funds accumulated by the pensioner during his working years. Such a traditional approach typically deprived the pensioner of his capital, leaving him only with an income for his life (together with, in most cases, an income for the life of a surviving spouse or minor dependants). The approach taken by the ARF and AMRF is one in which the purchase of a retirement annuity is no longer compulsory. Rather the pensioner retains the capital of his accumulated pension fund, which is held by a trustee on his behalf. He may spend that capital in his lifetime, or he may bequeath it to whomsoever he pleases (subject to rights of children and spouses under the Succession Act). The capital of an ARF is the absolute property of the pensioner, and he may do with it as he pleases. There are tax consequences depending on what he does do with it, but there are no legal restrictions on his right to spend it as he pleases, or not to spend it if he so chooses.

The principal distinction between an ARF and an AMRF is that an AMRF cannot be accessed, as regards its capital, by a pensioner until he reaches the age of 75 years. At that mature age, he is free to spend it as he pleases. A pensioner is obliged to put a minimum part of his pension fund into the AMRF, on the occasion of the establishment of the ARF. That minimum amount is usually £50,000, where the pension fund is of at least of that value.

Not all pensioners are entitled to elect to have an ARF rather than a purchased annuity. That right was confined by the FA99 to self-employed persons, proprietary directors, and employees not in pensionable employments. FA2000 extended it to employee in pensionable employments to the extent of the fund created by their AVCs. Therefore an employee in pensionable employment is within two regimes, ie a compulsory annuity purchase in relation to that part of the pension fund provided by his employer, and the right to elect for an ARF in relation to the part of the fund provided by the employee.

The tax regime provided for by the FA2000 in relation to an ARF and an AMRF (the same regime applies to both - s784C(7)) is as follows:

- The fund is exempt from capital gains tax on chargeable gains arising. It is also exempt from income tax on its income.

- The pensioner is no longer treated as being liable to tax in respect of the capital gains or income of the fund ie the fund is no longer transparent for tax purposes.

- Tax arises on all payments from the fund to the pensioner or to others who become entitled to the fund. The nature of the tax, and the rate of tax, vary, especially following the death of the pensioner. In the pensioner's lifetime the rate of tax will be his marginal rate of income tax. All payments from the fund to him are treated as income, whether they are paid out of the income of the fund, the capital gains of the fund, or the original capital of the fund. PAYE is operated on the payments and in the absence of a TFA, would be operated at the higher rate of income tax.

Following the death of the pensioner, the transfer of the fund, or payments from the fund may be subject to either income tax or capital acquisitions tax. However as no capital gains tax would arise on a transfer on death of the assets of the ARF both because the ARF itself is exempt from capital gains tax, and (less likely to be relevant but a fall-back argument) as a matter of civil law the assets of the ARF are the absolute property of the pensioner and therefore, for CGT purposes in so far as CGT can apply, should be entitled to an uplift to open market value on his death. (See paragraph 66.5).

32.5   **Scheme for Retirement of Farmers**

Any sums paid to farmers under the European Communities (Retirement of Farmers) Regulations 1974 is not taken into account as part of the consideration for the disposal of any asset.

This applies whether the amount is taken as a lump sum or as an annuity.

32.6   **Employment grants and recruitment subsidies**

s226   With affect from 6 April 1996 several types of incentives provided by the Government, or by government boards, or by the European Union, which are aimed at the creation of employment, or assisting unemployed persons to re-enter the work force, are disregarded for all the purposes of the Tax Acts. Primarily such an exemption is of significance in the context of taxes on income, but it also extends to capital gains tax.

The schemes covered by the exemption include:

— Back to Work allowance scheme

— FAS schemes

— certain County Enterprise Board schemes

— European Union Leader Community initiative schemes

— European Union Operational Programme for Local, Urban and Rural Development

— Special European Union Programme for Peace and Reconciliation in Northern Ireland and the Border Counties

— joint Northern Ireland / Ireland INTERREG programme

— International Fund for Ireland initiatives

32.7　　　　　**Exempt Bodies**

s610
Sch15, Pt1

A gain is not chargeable to CGT if it arises to:

(a)　a *registered trade union,* to the extent that its income is exempt from income tax under s213

(b)　an *unregistered friendly society* whose income is exempt from income tax under s211(1)

(c)　a *registered friendly society* whose income is exempt from income tax under s211(1)

(d)　a *local authority* (within the meaning of S.2(2) of the Local Government Act, 1941, and includes a body established under the Local Government Services (Corporate Bodies) Act, 1971)

(e)　The *Central Bank of Ireland*

(f)　a *health board*

(g)　a *vocational education committee* established under the Vocational Education Act, 1930

(h)　a *committee of agriculture* established under the Agriculture Act, 1931

(i)　the *National Treasury Management Agency*

(ii)　A licenced body under the *National Lottery* Act, 1986.

(j)　*Bord Failte Eireann*

(jj)　*National Pensions Board*

(k)　The *Dublin Regional Tourism Organisation* Ltd

(l)　The *Dublin and County Regional Tourism Organisation* Ltd

(m)　The *South Eastern Regional Tourism Organisation* Ltd

(n)　The *South-West Regional Tourism Organisation* Ltd

(o)　The *Western Regional Tourism Organisation* Ltd

(p)　The *North-West Regional Tourism Organisation* Ltd

(q)　The *Midland East Regional Tourism Organisation* Ltd

(r)　*Tramore Failte* Ltd

(s)　the *Irish Horseracing Authority* (from 1/12/94)

(t)　*Irish Thoroughbred Marketing* Ltd (from 1/12/94)

(u)　*Tote Ireland* Ltd (from 1/12/94)

(v)　A designated body within the meaning assigned by S1 of the **Securitisation** (Proceeds of Certain Mortgages) Act 1995 (from 30 November 1995).

(w) The *Dublin District Milk Board*; the *Cork District Milk Board*; the interim board established under Statutory Instrument No.408 of 1994; and in respect of disposals to the two milk boards referred to, *Dailysan Ltd. and Glenlee (Cork) Ltd* (from 5 December 1994),

(x) *Dublin Docklands Development Authority* (from 30th April 1997).

(y) *National Rehabilitation Board*

(z) The *Investor Compensation Company* Ltd (from 10 September 1998)

(za) The Commission for *Electricity Regulation* (from 14 July 1999)

Although FA97 exempted harbour authorities and port companies from tax on profits and gains for a limited period, the exemption does not appear to extend to chargeable gains on a disposal of assets.

32.8   **Exemption for certain gains**

s613   The following are deemed not to be chargeable gains:

(a) a bonus payable under the *Government installment savings scheme* (within the meaning of S.53 FA 1970)

(b) Prizes on *prize bonds*, under S.22 F (MP) A 1956

(c) sums received by way of *compensation for or damages for any wrong or injury* suffered by an individual:

- in his person, or

- in his profession.

(d) Winnings from *betting*, including pool betting, or *lotteries or sweepstakes*, or games with prizes. In addition, rights to such winnings, prizes, etc. obtained by participating in any such activities are deemed not to be chargeable assets for CGT purposes.

s191   A Tribunal was established in 1995 to provide *compensation to persons who contracted Hepatitis C* from certain blood or blood products or allied products. Any compensation paid by the Tribunal, or following a civil action for damages in respect of personal injury is treated by s191 as a payment made for damages in respect of a personal injury. As such, the payments in question are exempt from capital gains tax.

Typical examples of payments which are exempt as being compensation for personal or professional wrongs or injuries of an individual would be the compensation received by the victim of a road accident; or the damages received by the victim of a libel or slander. Were it not for the specific exemption contained in s613, such receipts might well be regarded are capital sums derived from the right to sue (if the Zim Properties case were followed by the Irish courts) and as such might have been liable to capital gains tax.

No special meaning is given in the legislation to "profession". In its ordinary meaning the word encompasses a limited range of occupations. Provision is not made for an exemption in respect of compensation or damage for wrong or injury suffered by an individual in his trade, or indeed even in an activity which may constitute a mere hobby. Neither is provision made for an exemption for damages for an injury or wrong suffered by an individual in an employment. It is not clear why an exemption has been provided in relation to a profession, but not in relation to any of the other forms of activity in which an individual may occupy his life. One can only assume that it reflects a snobbish view that only a professional person has a reputation that has value.

"Profession" is defined for CGT purposes to include a vocation. It is probably that the practice of politics is a vocation, in which case the exemption would apply to the substantial sums collected with some frequency by politicians from newspapers on grounds of libel. It is not known whether the Revenue apply any more liberal interpretation of the provision than is suggested by the bare word "profession."

32.9   Life Assurance Policies and Deferred Life Annuities

s593
s594

No chargeable gain accrues on the disposal of an assurance policy or a contract for a deferred annuity on the life of any person issued by a life assurance company within the charge to Irish corporation tax. The exemption also extends to a disposal of interests in or rights over such an asset.

This exemption however, does not apply where the person making the disposal-

- is not the original beneficial owner

    and

- acquired the rights (or interests) for a consideration in money or money's worth.

The FA2000 introduced a new tax regime in relation to certain life assurance policies. This new regime (while preserving the capital gains tax exemption) imposes a withholding tax, to be operated by the life assurance company and recouped from the policy holder's fund, in relation to disposals of policies. This is not a direct charge to tax on the policy holder who continues to enjoy the exemption enjoyed above, but it is the policy holder who effectively bears the cost of the tax charge and it therefore makes the exemption described above rather notional.

The date of disposal of such assets is determined by the earliest of the following:

• payment of the sums assured under the policy

• payment of the first installment of the annuity

• surrender of the assurance policy

• surrender of the rights under the annuity contract.

The consideration for the disposal of a contract for a deferred annuity is deemed to be the market value of the right to receive the first and subsequent installments of the annuity.

As indicated, the above is merely a broad outline of the provisions.

The detailed provisions are set out in paragraph 36.

32.10   Woodlands

s564

In the case of an individual the proceeds of the sale of standing timber and saleable underwood are not taken into account for CGT purposes. The relief does not apply to companies, or other bodies of persons.

Where land is sold with standing timber on it, the proceeds must be apportioned, and the part of the proceeds referable to standing timber excluded from the computation in relation to the disposal of the land. The same principles apply to compensation or insurance proceeds received in respect of standing timber or saleable underwood.

Although the cost referable to the trees must be excluded, there is no explicit requirement that the incidental costs of disposal should be excluded, or be apportioned between the consideration in respect of the timber (which is being excluded from the computation) and the consideration in respect of the land. It would seem that the entire incidental costs of disposal remain deductible notwithstanding the fact that a major part of the disposal consideration may be excluded from the computation.

A disposal of woodland is a disposal of land. A disposal of woodland is not exempt and accordingly an allowable loss can arise on the transaction. The relief provided by s564 consists of disregarding a certain part of the consideration. It does not consist of exempting the asset from CGT and accordingly the consequences of causing expenditure to be ignored, or losses to be other than allowable losses, do not arise.

32.11   Annuities, Covenants, Etc.

s613(3)

No chargeable gain will accrue on the disposal of a right to (or to any part of):

- Any allowance, annuity, or capital sum payable out of a superannuation fund established mainly for employees and their dependents.

- An annuity, (other than under a contract for a deferred annuity) granted by a company as part of its business of granting annuities on human life, whether or not including installments of capital.

- Annual payments which are due under a covenant made by any person provided they are not secured on any property.

The interpretation of the words "annual payments which are due under a covenant" was considered in the UK case of Rank Xerox v Lane.   The taxpayer company held the exclusive right to exploit the Xerox reproduction process. By two agreements, dated 1964 and 1967, it assigned those rights in certain countries to another company in consideration of a royalty. Both agreements were executed under seal although the seal was not necessary. In 1969, the taxpayer company paid a dividend to its shareholders by distributing in specie the right to receive the royalties (valued at £8,400,000). The Revenue claimed that this was a disposal of an asset. The taxpayer contended that what was disposed of was a right to "annual payments...due under a covenant", and accordingly, no gain could accrue on the disposal.

Lord Salmon stated (at page 746) *"In my view, it (annual payments ... due under a covenant) refers only to a unilateral promise made by deed which is therefore enforceable in spite of the absence of consideration and the paragraph certainly has nothing whatsoever to do with business or any other bilateral agreements."*

At page 747, Lord Russell of Killowen said *"In my opinion 'due under a covenant' is fairly to be construed as something narrower in scope than 'due under an agreement' would have been. I construe the phrase as meaning due by reason of the fact that the promise is under seal, because of the existence of the seal. If the presence of the seal adds nothing to the obligation to make the annual payments, I do not consider that the payments were 'due under a covenant made by a person'."*

In the course of his judgement, Lord Wilberforce said..."...'covenant' *in this part of the Act has a clear and special meaning, corresponding to practice, of an unilateral and voluntary enforceable promise as distinguished from an 'agreement' supported by consideration".*

A promise by one person to pay money to another person is not legally enforceable unless it is made for valuable (but not necessarily equal) consideration; or if the promise is made in writing and the document is under seal. That is the background to the distinction made by Lord Wilberforce above.

32.12   **Diplomatic and Consular Officials**

DRIA67   Certain exemptions from Irish tax are provided for Diplomatic and
Consular Staff representing foreign countries. The exemptions are
given by virtue of the Diplomatic Relations and Immunities Act
1967.

Article 34.

A Diplomatic Agent (i.e. the head or member of the Diplomatic staff
of the mission) is exempt from all dues and taxes personal or real,
national, regional or municipal, except...'*dues and taxes on Private
Income having its source in the receiving State and Capital Taxes on
Investments made in Commercial Undertakings in the receiving State'*.

In the Diplomatic Relations and Immunities Act 1967, the phrases
'sending State', and 'receiving State', are used to denote the Country
being represented, and the Country in which the representation is
being carried on by the Diplomat.

Article 49.

Consular Officers and Consular Employees and members of their
families forming part of their households are exempt from all dues
and taxes, personal or real, national, regional or municipal, except :
*'dues and taxes on Private Income, including Capital Gains, having its
source in the receiving State and Capital Taxes relating to Investments
made in Commercial or Financial undertakings in the receiving State'*.

32.13   **Disposal of Interest in Settled Property**

s613(4)   If a person disposes of an interest under a settlement (e.g. an annuity
or life interest) the gain is not chargeable,

*"Unless (a) the person making the disposal is not the person for whose
benefit the interest was created by the terms of the settlement and (b) he
acquired the interest for a consideration in money or money's worth, or
derived the interest from somebody who so acquired it."*

Where a person with an interest under a settlement becomes (as the
holder of that interest) entitled as against the trustees to any settled
property, he is deemed to have disposed of his interest in return for
obtaining the property. This rule does not affect the exemption
outlined in the previous paragraph.

This exemption is considered in more detail in paragraph 65.12, as is
the exclusion from exemption where the settlement has been
non-resident.

32.14   **Relief for disposals of works of art.**

32.14.1   **Broad Outline**

Relief is provided in relation to certain works of art which

- have been on loan for public display or
- which are donated to National collections.

The separate relief for assets transferred to a charity may also be relevant in appropriate circumstances - see paragraphs 31.1, 31.3 and 31.4.

32.14.2   **Public Display - relief**

s606

The relief is provided by treating any disposal of the asset after the period of loan to be for such consideration as to secure that neither a gain nor a loss accrues on the disposal.

The conditions for relief are as follows:

- the asset must be a picture, print, book, manuscript, sculpture, piece of jewellery, or work of art
- the asset must be loaned to a gallery or museum in the State approved of for this purpose by the Revenue Commissioners
- the Revenue Commissioners must be of the opinion that the asset has a market value of not less than £25,000 at the date when it is loaned to the gallery or museum; in forming their opinion, the Commissioners may consult with experts
- the asset must be displayed in the gallery or museum for a period of not less than six years from the date it is loaned and the public must be afforded reasonable access.

The original 1991 legislation was effective from 18 April 1991.

32.14.3   **Donations to National Collections - relief.**

s1003

Taxpayers who donate certain works of art to certain national collections may obtain a credit for the value of the items donated against liabilities incurred by the taxpayer to income tax, corporation tax, capital gains tax, gift tax or inheritance tax. Where the value exceeds the taxes in question, the excess is not refundable or repayable to the taxpayer.

The significance of this relief is limited by the fact that the selection committee, whose approval is required to enable a donation to receive the tax relief, will not approve for the donation of items *whose value is less than £75,000.* The committee may approve the donation of items in any year whose *aggregate value does not exceed £3,000,000* (£750,000 pre 2000)

The items which may be gifted, and which may be approved for the relief, include any kind of "cultural item" including in particular any archaeological item, archive, book, estate record, manuscript and painting and any collection of cultural items. The item must be an outstanding example of the type involved, pre-eminent in its class, and its export from the State must constitute a diminution of the accumulated cultural heritage of Ireland. These daunting requirements are reinforced by the further condition that the item must have a value of not less than £75,000, although that value could extend to a collection of items being gifted as a collection. These requirements were deemed met in 1995 by 2 items :

— The sketch notebooks of the artist Jack B Yeats, and

— a painting of the GHQ staff of the IRA by Leo Whelan.

The bodies who are approved as recipients for a gift to which the relief could apply include the National Archives, the National Gallery of Ireland, the National Library of Ireland, the National Museum of Ireland, the Irish Museum of Modern Art, or any other body mainly funded by the State or by a public or local authority as may be approved by the Minister for Finance.

The expression, "cultural items" is very vague and correspondingly wide. However one of the tests to be applied before approval by the selection committee for the purpose of the relief is that its export from the State should constitute a diminution of Ireland's accumulated cultural heritage. Except in extreme cases (such as occurred to the old London Bridge) a building or similar structure (normally) cannot be exported and so is not likely to qualify.

Where a person obtains relief under s1003 in respect of a donation he may not receive relief under any other provision of the Tax Acts, the Capital Gains Tax Acts, or the Capital Acquisition Tax Acts, in respect of that gift. It would seem therefore that the relief in relation to items publicly displayed, described in paragraph 32.14.2, cannot be availed of in relation to the donation of an item which is subsequently donated to a public institution, and in relation to which donation relief under s1003 is obtained.

32.15   **Chart of reliefs, exemptions, etc.**

An overall broad summary of the main reliefs and exemptions for CGT is set out in chart form on the following pages.

MAIN CGT RELIEFS & EXEMPTIONS		
Relief, exemption, etc	**Statutory Reference**	**Book Reference**
• Foreign Trusts exemption	FA93 s49 repealed 1997	Para 65.14
• Non domiciled liable on remittance basis	s29	Para 3.3
• Non residents liable only on specified assets	s29	Para 3.4
• Purchase by a company of its own shares	s173 et seq.	Para 49
• Exemption for certain subsidies	s226	Para 32.6
• Group relief for trading losses, management expenses & charges.	s456	Para 73.4
• Assets becoming of negligible value - loss relief available.	s538	Para 20.5
• Abandonment of an option (not for consideration) may be exempt	s540	Para 39
• Disposal of a debt (not a debt on a security) may be exempt	s541	Para 38
• Indexation of expenditure (for inflation)	s556	Para 14
• Cost of asset may be attributed to another asset where assets have been divided, merged, etc.	s559	Paras 9.10, 10.6 & 39.3.1
• Exemption for woodlands	s564	Para 32.10
• Nominees/Bare trustees not liable	s567	Paras 64.1 & 65.1
• Losses in year of death carried back 3 years against gains	s573	Para 66.4
• Tax free uplift in base cost of assets on death of owner	s573	Para 66.5
• Deed of family arrangement effective from date of death	s573	Para 66.7
• Professional trustees may be treated as non-resident	s574	Para 65.3
• Trustee losses may be available to beneficiary	s576	Para 65.11

MAIN CGT RELIEFS & EXEMPTIONS		
Relief, exemption, etc	Statutory Reference	Book Reference
• Tax free uplift in base cost of assets when trust ends on death of life tenant	s577	Para 65.7.2
• No disposal on reconstructions or reorganisations of capital	s584	Paras 42 - 47
• No disposal on conversion of securities	s585	Para 47
• No disposal on certain share for shares swops	s586	Paras 42 - 47
• No disposal by shareholders on certain reconstructions or amalgamations of companies	s587	Paras 42 - 47
• Reduced 26% rate of CGT on disposal of certain shares (pre 3/12/97)	s592	Paras 5.2
• Life Assurance Policy (Irish) not normally a chargeable asset	s593	Paras 32.9 & 36
• Relief for disposal of business assets for individuals over age 55	s598; s599	Para 30
• Replacement of certain business assets - Deferral of gain.	s597; s536; s620	Paras 25 to 28
• Relief for transfer of business to company	s600	Para 29
• Small gains annual exemption	s601	Para 19
• Chattels (non-wasting) worth less than £2,000 not chargeable	s602	Para 23.1
• Wasting Chattels (non-business) are not chargeable assets	s603	Para 22
• Principal Private Residence - relief available	s604	Para 24
• Roll-over relief for compulsory acquisitions	s605	Para 27
• Works of Art - conditional exemption (public display)	s606	Para 32.14
• Exemption for securities of European Institutions & certain Semi-State Bodies.	s607	Para 32.1
• Government and Semi State stocks are not chargeable assets	s607	Para 32.1

MAIN CGT RELIEFS & EXEMPTIONS		
Relief, exemption, etc	**Statutory Reference**	**Book Reference**
• Approved Superannuation/pension schemes exempt	s608	Para 32.4
• Charities usually exempt	s609	Paras 31
• Exemption for Trade Unions, Friendly Societies, Local Authorities, Health Boards, VEC, and Committees of Agriculture.	s610	Paras 32.7
• Relief for disposals to State, Charities & Public Bodies	s611	Para 31
• Farm Retirement Scheme - EC payments exempt.	s612	Para 32.5
• Exemption for gambling winnings	s613	Para 32.8
• Exemption for Installment Savings Scheme bonus.	s613	Para 32.8
• Exemption for disposal of certain pension rights	s613	Paras 32.4 & 32.11
• Exemption for disposal of interest under a settlement.	s613	Paras 32.13 & 65.12
• Relief on reconstruction or amalgamation of companies	s615	Para 75.2
• Relief for intra group transfers of assets	s617	Para 75.4
• Transfer of trade between companies - relief	s631	Para 75.3
• Transfer of assets between companies - relief	s632	Para 75
• Transfer of development land between group companies - relief	s633	Para 78
• Unit Trusts - certain units exempt.	s731	Paras 35 & 63.5
• Special Investment Schemes (unit trusts) relief	s737	Para 35
• Double Taxation relief	s828	Chap 11
• Deduction for foreign tax	s828	Para 9.3

MAIN CGT RELIEFS & EXEMPTIONS		
Relief, exemption, etc	Statutory Reference	Book Reference
• Special portfolio investment accounts relief (brokers accounts)	s838	Para 37
• Tax payment by installments where payment of consideration is deferred	s981	Paras 8.3 & 97.3
• Payment of CGT by transfer of art object	s1003	Para 32.14
• Deferral of tax where gains cannot be remitted from abroad	s1005	Para 97.2
• Surrender of losses between spouses	s1028	Para 33.5
• No gain on transfer of assets between spouses	s1028	Para 33.7

33   MARRIED PERSONS

33.1   Broad Outline

s1028

Gains and losses of each spouse are calculated separately as if they were single persons.

Provided both agree, losses which would normally be available to one spouse, can be used by the other spouse against gains in a year of assessment.   This rule applies not only to losses of the current year, but also to losses coming forward from previous years.

Normally the tax due by both is assessed on and collected from the husband (although since 6 April 1974 the gains of both spouses can be assessed on and collected from the wife in certain circumstances).

Normally a disposal of an asset from one spouse to another does not give rise to either a gain or a loss for CGT purposes (see paragraph 33.7). This does not mean that disposals from one spouse to another can be totally ignored, as there are some circumstances where such disposals, although not in themselves giving rise to a gain or a loss, can affect the amount of tax payable on other disposals, eg. if retirement relief is claimed.

33.2   Married Woman Living With Her Husband

s1015

The special rules dealing with the assessment of gains on married persons, and the special reliefs available, apply only in the case of a married couple where the wife is a *"married woman...living with her husband"*. Whether the wife is such a married woman is to be determined in accordance with the rules set out in s1015. That sub-section provides that a *'wife shall be treated as living with her husband unless either -*

(a)   *they are separated under an Order of a Court of competent jurisdiction or by a Deed of Separation,*

         or

(b)   *they are in fact separated in such circumstances that the separation is likely to be permanent"'*

FA80 s18

This rule as to the circumstances in which a wife is to be regarded as a "married woman living with her husband" for tax purposes, was substituted by FA 80 s18. Prior to that change, the current rule also applied, but in addition, a wife was not regarded as "a married woman living with her husband" in any year of assessment where

— one spouse was Irish resident and

— the other was non-resident

for that year. The Irish pre-1980 Finance Act rule was the same as that now applying in the UK. Our existing rule is now different as it does not repeat the part of the previous rule related to the residence of the married persons.

The most celebrated UK cases on the meaning of the expression *"married woman living with her husband"* was Gubay v Kington. That case turned on the pre 1980 Irish Finance Act rule (and followed the legislation as it stood at that time in the UK) and in particular on the part of it relating to the residence of the married persons. Accordingly it has no present relevance in Ireland.

s1028   Capital gains tax differs from capital acquisitions tax and stamp duty in its treatment of married couples, in that the principal exemption for intra-spouse transactions requires more than that the couple should be parties to a lawful marriage. That condition alone is sufficient to attract the capital acquisitions tax and stamp duty exemptions for intra spouse transfers. For capital gains tax relief under s1028 in respect of disposals between parties to a marriage, it is necessary that they should not only be married, but that the wife should be *"a married woman......living with her husband"*. As indicated above, that expression does not have its ordinary or natural meaning. The only circumstance in which a married woman will not be treated as living with her husband is where she has been formally separated i.e. separated by a court order or a deed of separation, or there is a factual separation which is likely to be permanent.

Example 172

Joe Brown married Mary in 1990. In 1994 Joe left the rented accommodation where they lived, and went to live in England. He did not leave a forwarding address or tell his wife of his intention of leaving. In 1996 Mary formed a relationship with another man and they set up house together. In 1997 a child was born to them. Mary has not formalised her separation from her husband by means of a court order, or a deed of separation.

In the unlikely event that Joe should ever wish to transfer an asset within the charge to Irish capital gains tax to Mary, he would not be able to avail of relief under s1028 in respect of an intra spouse disposal. The circumstances of their separation (in particular the fact that Mary is living with another man and has had a family with that other man) would point to their separation being likely to be permanent.

Mary cannot avail of the intra spouse exemption in relation to transfers between her and her new companion (the father of her child). Although they are living together, they are not married.

The position is to be contrasted with capital acquisitions tax, and stamp duty, in relation to both of which Mary and Joe would be entitled to an exemption in respect of an intra spouse transfer.

Example 173

> Joe married Mary in 1990. In 1994 Joe was made redundant and could not get a new job in Ireland. He went to England and has found work there. Mary is unable to join him as she has to look after an invalid parent in Ireland. Joe and Mary see each other once a year for approximately one week, when Joe returns to Ireland on holiday.
>
> Although Joe and Mary can scarcely be said to be living together in any ordinary sense, they have not been formally separated by a deed of separation or order of a court, nor do the circumstances of their separation suggest that it is likely to be permanent. On the death of Mary's parent, or on Joe finding an Irish job, circumstances point to their being reunited. Accordingly s1028 will regard Mary as being a married woman living with her husband notwithstanding their physical separation. They are accordingly entitled to the intra spouse exemption in relation to disposal of assets between them. The fact that Joe may not be resident or ordinarily resident in Ireland, while Mary is so resident is not relevant.

s1028

TCA97 does not define what constitutes separation for the purpose of s1028. As noted in the above example, physical separation (living in different houses, or living in different countries) would constitute separation in the ordinary sense but not necessarily separation which is likely to be permanent. In the cases of some marriage breakdowns, the married couple may continue to each live within the same house, but while living completely separate lives. In extreme cases this can go so far as couples living in the same house without speaking to each other for decades. It is likely that in such a case, where the parties have arranged their domestic affairs so as to minimise contact within the house and give a physical expression to their desire to lead separate lives within the house, that the couple may be regarded as separated and the circumstances may well indicate that such separation would be permanent, after a period of time. It would however be rarely in the interests of such a couple to assert that they are in fact separated, at least from the viewpoint of capital gains tax and in practice it is unlikely that the point will be raised by the Revenue.

33.3   Assessment on Married Persons

s1028(1)

The CGT arising on gains accruing to a wife (being a married woman living with her husband) in any year of assessment is normally assessed and charged on her husband.

This general rule regarding the assessment of one spouse on the combined gains of both spouses is subject to the right of married persons to be assessed and charged individually on their own gains (provided they elect to be treated in such manner - see paragraph 33.4).

Even where the gains of a wife are assessed and charged on the husband, no additional CGT can be chargeable over and above the amount which would have been charged if they were separately assessed - *"this subsection shall not affect the amount of capital gains tax chargeable on the husband apart from this subsection nor result in the additional amount of capital gains tax charged on the husband by virtue of this subsection being different from the amount which would otherwise have remained chargeable on the married woman."*

For 1994/95 and subsequent years of assessment, the *income tax* law was amended to allow for the "wife" to be assessed on the joint incomes of herself and her husband in certain circumstances.

The circumstances in which this rule can apply depends on the year of assessment in which the marriage took place:

- *Married pre 1993/94* : only on joint election by husband and wife before 6th July in the year of assessment.

- *Married in 1993/94 or subsequent year* : either by election (as above) or where the Inspector considers that the total income of the wife exceeds the total income of the husband for that year, then he may assess the wife.

s931(2)

s931(2) provides that :
" The provisions of the Income Tax Acts relating to the care, management, assessment, collection, and recovery of income tax, shall subject to any necessary modifications apply in relation to capital gains tax as they apply to income tax chargeable under Schedule D."

Accordingly, the rules outlined above in relation to income tax apply also to CGT, so that a wife may be assessed in respect of her husband's gains in the circumstances outlined.

It is not clear whether the reference (in the post 1993/94 period) to an Inspector considering that the total income of the wife exceeds the total income of the husband for the year has to be restated for CGT purposes as being an Inspector's belief that the chargeable gains of the wife exceed the chargeable gains of the husband. That might seem a sensible adaptation. However the only adaptation provided for in the legislation is one which is necessary. It does not seem necessary (notwithstanding that it might seem sensible) to substitute a reference to capital gains tax for the reference to income tax in the expression referred to. On balance the authors believe that in the absence of a joint election by the married couple, the Inspector may assess the wife only where he believes her income (without regard to her capital gains) exceeds the income of the husband.

33.4   **Separate Assessment**

s1028(2)

An election for separate assessment can be made by either spouse by giving notice in writing to the Inspector before 6th July following the end of the year of assessment.

The election for separate assessment continues to take effect until it is withdrawn. Where such an election is made by either spouse, both are separately assessed to CGT. The rule on disposals from one spouse to another, however, still applies (see paragraph 33.7).

The notice of withdrawal of the claim for separate assessment has no effect unless given in writing to the Inspector before 6th July following the end of the year of assessment for which it is to take effect.

33.5 Losses

s1028(3) *Surplus* losses of one spouse (whether arising in the current year of assessment or carried forward from prior years - including years prior to the date of marriage) are set against gains of the other spouse in a year of assessment.

This provision does not apply if either spouse gives notice to that effect within 3 months after the year end to the Inspector. Where such notice is given, the losses are carried forward against subsequent gains of the spouse to whom the losses accrued.

33.6 Annual Exemption

33.6.1 Broad outline

s1028(4) Each spouse is entitled to a separate annual exemption.

33.6.2 Transfer of exemption to other spouse (pre 1998/99)

In addition, in certain circumstances (prior to 1998/99) the unused part of the annual exemption of one spouse could be transferred to the other spouse. Where both husband and wife were chargeable to CGT in any year of assessment (or would have been but for the annual exemption) and the gains of one spouse are less than the annual exemption of that spouse, the unused part of the annual exemption could be transferred to and used by the other spouse, in addition to that individual's own annual exemption. This facility of transferring the unused part of a spouse's exemption to the other spouse was withdrawn for 1998/99 and subsequent years.

s1028(4) The provision allowing the transfer of the unused part of the annual exemption from one spouse to another was contained in s1028(4). The relevant provision was as follows :-

"(4) Where, apart from subsection (1),[charge on husband for gains of wife] the amount on which an individual is chargeable to CGT under s31 for a year of assessment (hereafter in this subsection referred to as "the first-mentioned amount") is less than £1,000 and the spouse of the individual (being, at any time during that year of assessment, a married woman living with her husband, or that husband) is, apart from subsection

*(1), chargeable to capital gains tax on any amount for that year, s601(1)
[annual exemption] shall have effect in relation to the spouse as if the sum
of £1,000 mentioned therein were increased by an amount equal to the
difference between the first-mentioned amount and £1,000"*

Example 172 (pre 1998/99 only)

*Seamus and Ann are married, and living together (within the meaning of
s1015). In 1997/98 Seamus has gains of £800 and Ann has gains of £2,900.*

1997/98		£	£
Seamus	— Gains		800
	— Exemption (part)		(800)
	— Chargeable		£NIL
Ann	— Gains		2,900
	— Exemption-self	1,000	
	— Seamus £200 (balance)	200	1,200
	— Chargeable		1,700

s1028(4)

*It would appear from a strict interpretation of s1028(4), that if either the
husband or wife do not have chargeable gains in a year of assessment, the
unused annual exemption of the spouse who has no chargeable gains cannot be
used by the other spouse. The unused balance can only be transferred where
both have gains in the same year of assessment. If only one spouse has a gain,
and the other has disposed of no assets during that year, only one annual
exemption is available to the spouse who has the chargeable gain.*

*However, in practice it is understood that the Revenue Commissioners applied
exemption by allowing the unused balance of the annual exemption of one
spouse to be used by the other (in addition to his own) in a case where only one
spouse is chargeable to CGT in the year of assessment. If in the above example,
Ann had the total gains of £3,700, and Seamus had none, Ann would, in
practice, be allowed the full £2,000 exemption.*

FA98 s75

The FA98 s75 in a unique example of a reversal of the pro-married
couples stance adopted in all tax legislation following the Murphy
case, brought to an end the ability of spouses to transfer between
each other the unused portions of their annual allowance. That
facility no longer applies from 1998/99 onwards.

Example 175

*The facts are as in **example 174** above, say that the gains arose in 1998/99.*

Seamus - gains	£800.00
Exemption (part)	£800.00
Chargeable	Nil
Ann - Gains	£2,900.00

Exemption - self	£1,000.00
Balance of Seamus's exemption not available to her	Nil
Chargeable	£1,900.00

In practice, for 1998/99 and later years, Ann could obtain the benefit of Seamus's surplus exemption by the timely transfer to him of an asset pregnant with gain (on a no gain : no loss basis) and allow the gain on disposal to a third party to crystalise in the hands of Seamus.

33.7 Disposal to Spouse

33.7.1 Disposal inter vivos between spouses

33.7.1.1 Treatment of spouse making disposal

s1028(5) Disposals from one spouse to the other (where both are living, and "living together" at the date of disposal) are treated as made at such a price as gives no gain and no loss to the spouse making the disposal.

Where the asset was acquired by the transferring spouse prior to 6/4/74, the transfer is treated as being at market value at 6/4/74 plus subsequent enhancement expenditure. Where the asset was acquired by the transferring spouse after 5/4/74, the transfer is treated as being at cost plus enhancement expenditure. In both cases, the amount before indexation is taken.

s1028(5) proviso This relieving provision does not apply if

- until the disposal the asset disposed of was trading stock of a trade carried on by the spouse making the disposal, or

- if the asset is acquired as trading stock for the purposes of a trade carried on the spouse acquiring the asset.

Trading stock is dealt with in paragraph 18.

s1028(6) The rule for disposal at no gain-no loss, takes effect in priority to the normal 'arm's length' provisions that apply between connected persons. (paragraph 16).

As described in paragraph 37, the Revenue Commissioners were of the view that the transfer by a person to a special portfolio investment account (SPIA) belonging to that person's spouse, was not a transfer to which the intra spouse disposal relief applies. That view is probably incorrect prior to FA99. The FA99 has so legislated in relation to a SPIA that an intra spouse exemption cannot occur within a SPIA.

33.7.2 Treatment of spouse acquiring asset from spouse

s1028(5)

The spouse acquiring the asset is treated (in calculating a gain or loss on any subsequent disposal of the asset acquired) as if that spouse had acquired the asset at the same date as the disposing spouse originally acquired it.

This ensures that the acquiring spouse (on a subsequent disposal of the acquired asset) is deemed to have the same :

— cost,

— market value at 6th April 1974 (if relevant),

— indexation, and

— period of ownership

in relation to that transferred asset, as the spouse from whom the asset was acquired.

It is important to realise that there *is a disposal* on the transfer of an asset from one spouse to another under the intra spouse relief rules.

The only matters affected by the specific rules on such a disposal are:

• the amount of the deemed consideration for the disposal (i.e. the deemed transfer price), and

• the passing on of the disposing spouse's period of ownership of the asset transferred.

The point may be important in calculating the amount of *"retirement relief"* (see paragraph 30) on disposal of business assets where the amount of the relief may be dependent on the total disposal proceeds of all qualifying assets (which would include business assets transferred to his spouse by the individual who is claiming the retirement relief).

33.7.3 Disposals from estate of deceased spouse to surviving spouse.

s573

On death there is no disposal by the deceased of his assets, and the normal "death" provisions apply in priority to the normal "intra spouse" provisions. Following the death of either spouse, it would be difficult to establish that the wife is a *"married woman living with her husband"*. The general provisions dealing with assets passing on death are dealt with in Chapter 8.

s592

In a case where the asset is acquired by one spouse on the death of the other (from the estate of that other spouse) specific provision is made to ensure the continuity of the period of ownership to the surviving spouse for the purpose of determining the (now repealed) reduced rate of CGT (see paragraph 5.2.8).

No such provision is necessary for 'indexation', as the surviving spouse is deemed to acquire the asset at its market value at the date of death, thus eliminating any gain which accrued up to the date of death.

Where a *"trust"* is created by the will of a deceased spouse the intra spouse relief has no application to benefits taken by the surviving spouse from such a trust, whether on death or later. The surviving spouse in such a case is in no different a position than any other beneficiary. The question of trusts is dealt with in Chapter 8.

33.7.4   Spouses and Trusts

There is an anomaly in the tax treatment of spouses in relation to a trust which is best described by way of an example.

Example 176

> *John and Mary are married and living together as husband and wife. John has decided to make provision in his lifetime for Mary. At the same time he is anxious to ensure that the family business will be passed to his children when both he and Mary are dead. He therefore grants Mary a life interest in half of the shares in the company, and he also makes her an outright gift of a holiday home which he owns in Kerry.*

> *The gift of the holiday home in Kerry is treated as being made on no gain no loss basis. However, the gift of the life interest in the shares in the family company is treated differently. It is treated, not as a disposal to Mary, but rather as a disposal to notional trustees of a notional settlement created by giving Mary a life interest in the shares. It is therefore not a disposal to a spouse but rather a disposal to a trustee and as such does not attract the relief for disposals between spouses. This is so regardless of the identity of the trustee (i.e. the person in whose name the shares are registered after the creation of the life interest). A trustee is a person separate in identity from the individual or company who may hold the office. Therefore even if the shares were registered in Mary's name on the occasion of her being granted a life interest, so that she was also trustee of the shares, the transfer would still not attract the intra spouse exemption since Mary would not have taken an absolute interest in the shares beneficially.*

33.8   Marriage breakdown

33.8.1   Broad overview

Prior to 1997 there was no statutory provision for a married couple to obtain a divorce under the laws of the Republic of Ireland. There was in fact a total prohibition on any form of divorce under the Constitution of Ireland which provided in Article 41 (together with many other matters related to the "family" and "marriage") in very explicit terms:

> **"41.3.2   *No law shall be enacted providing for the grant of a dissolution of marriage".***

In 1995, the Irish People by referendum approved the removal of the total constitutional ban on divorce by replacing the relevant part of Article 41 with a different provision which allows for divorce in certain circumstances . In very broad terms

- it allows for **"no fault" divorce**
- after a *four year separation,*
- subject to *proper provision being made for a dependent spouse and children,*
- it also requires the legislation to ensure the applicant's and respondant's *awareness of alternatives to divorce proceedings,* and to assist in *attempts at reconciliation.*

The referendum showed a very small majority in favour of the proposed amendment allowing for divorce in the circumstances proposed. Owing to the narrowness of the margin in the voting, those opposed to the amendment challenged the result of the referendum in the Irish courts. The final result in favour of the amendment to Article 41 was confirmed by the Supreme Court in 1996.

FL(D)A96 The legislation was enacted in the Family Law (Divorce) Act, 1996, which was signed by the President on 27th November 1996. S.1 of that Act provides for it to come into operation 3 months after the date of its passing - i.e. on 27th February 1997.

Even though "divorce" is now available under Irish law, it is available subject to the Court satisfying itself regarding compliance with the conditions imposed by the Family Law (Divorce) Act, 1996 (which takes account of the requirements of the amended Article 41 of the Constitution of Ireland).

Legal costs are inevitable in most cases in an application for a decree of divorce, particularly in the area of satisfying the Court that the conditions for the granting of a decree of divorce have been met. Those costs could be substantial depending on the circumstances of the individual case. Because of this, many separated couples will not necessarily be rushing to the Courts with an application for a decree of divorce. For this reason alone it is expected that many of the existing "permanent" separations and subsequent new relationships, including marriages not recognised by State law may remain as part of the overall social situation in Ireland for the forseeable future.

The question of the CGT issues arising out of the breakdown of a marriage must be looked at in the context not only of the CGT legislation, but also (in a very broad terms) in the context of the relevant family law, and the operation of extra statutory concessions operated by the Rvenmue Commissioners in this area. This book does not in any way purport to deal with family law, and refers to it only in a broad sense for the sole purpose of putting the relevant taxation provisions into their proper context.

The affect of taxation on marriage breakdown is also dealt with in a companion volume published by the Institute of Taxation in Ireland - "Tax Implications of Marital Breakdown" by Hilary Walpole.

Where a valid marriage exists there are many different ways in which, following the breakdown of that marriage, one or both parties to the marriage can organise their personal and financial affairs for the future.

- after a period of 4 years separation, they can apply to the Court for a decree of divorce.

- they can separate under the terms of an order of the Court

- they can separate by voluntary deed of separation, the terms of which may or may not be made an order of Court.

- they can separate informally without any written agreement.

- they can separate following a "foreign" divorce which is not recognised by Irish State law.

- they can separate by a "Church" annullment of the marriage (which annullment is not recognised by State law). The "Church" annullment may or may not be followed by a Church marriage (which is also not recognised as a valid marriage by State law).

The position must also be considered, where on the application of either or both spouses, the "marriage" is annulled by a civil court (as distinct from the church court). This is different to a divorce, in that to issue a decree of nullity, the court must find that no valid marriage existed in the first instance.

The other issues which require consideration arise where one or other party to such a marriage enters into a further relationship in the future, and perhaps even a marriage which is not recognised by State law.

There are two separate relieving provisions dealing with marriage breakdown (where the spouses are still married in law, but not treated as a married couple for CGT purposes because they are permanently separated)

- s1030 which deals mainly with transfers of assets between separated spouses on or following a formal separation, and

- S1031 which deals with transfers of assets between separated spouses on or following the granting of a decree of divorce (see paragraph 33.8.2.2)

In the following paragraphs the CGT implications of these issues are examined.

33.8.2   **Decree of Divorce**

33.8.2.1   **Broad Outline**

FL(D)A96 s10   The Family Law (Divorce) Act, 1996 came into operation on 27th
February 1997.

S.10(1) of that Act provides:

*"Where the court grants a decree of divorce, the marriage, the subject of the
decree, is thereby dissolved and a party to that marriage may marry again".*

It follows that the parties to that marriage are no longer husband and
wife, and in the absence of specific provisions to the contrary, a
chargeable gain could arise on the disposal of assets from one of
them to the other. The intra spouse relief can no longer apply.

One of the conditions for the granting of a decree of divorce is that
proper provision (to the satisfaction of the Court) is made for a
dependent spouse and dependent children of that family. This may
involve the disposal of assets by one spouse to the other. Where such
a disposal takes place after the granting of a decree of divorce,
specific provisions are made to allow certain transactions to keep the
intra spouse relief.

It should be noted that it is only a disposal from one spouse to the
other which attracts the intra spouse relief. There is no CGT relief
involved where one spouse disposes of assets to anyone other than
his spouse (now former spouse) even though the proceeds may be
required for the sole purpose of meeting obligations under a Court
order to provide for the other (former) spouse and perhaps also for
the children of that marriage.

33.8.2.2   **Relief under TCA97 s1031**

s1031(2)   TCA97 s1031 provides:

"(2) Notwithstanding any other provision of the Capital Gains Tax
Acts, where **by virtue or in consequence of** *an order made under Part
III of the Family Law (Divorce) Act, 1996,* **on or following the granting
of a decree of divorce,** *either of the spouses concerned disposes of an asset
to the other spouse then, subject to subsection (3), both spouses shall be
treated for the purposes of these Acts as if the asset was acquired from the
spouse making the disposal for a consideration of such an amount as would
secure that on the disposal neither a gain nor a loss would accrue to the
spouse making the disposal".*

Subsection (3) referred to above secures that the relief will not apply
where the asset concerned:

— formed part of the trade stock of a trade carried on by the spouse
  making the disposal, or

— is acquired as trading stock for the purposes of a trade carried on by the spouse acquiring the asset.

This is merely continuing the normal restriction which applies to the ordinary intra spouse relief (see paragraph 33.7).

s1031(4)   s1031(4) provides for the passing on of the disposing spouse's acquisition cost and acquisition date to the acquiring spouse.

"Where subsection (2) applies in relation to the disposal of an asset by a spouse to the other spouse, then, in relation to a subsequent disposal of the asset .... the spouse making the disposal shall be treated for the purposes of capital gains tax as if the other spouse's acquisition or provision of the asset had been his or her acquisition or provision of the asset."

As with the normal intra spouse relief, the provisions are in two separate parts:

- ensuring that no gain or loss accrues to the spouse making the disposal, and

- treating the acquiring spouse as if that spouse were the one who originally acquired the asset (to preserve the period of ownership, indexation, etc.).

FL(D)A96 s35   Similar provisions were enacted in the Family Law (Divorce) Act, 1996. Those provisions are repealed by s.71(4) FA 1997, which in effect replaces them with effect from the passing of the FA 1997 (10th May 1997).

33.8.2.3   Transfers to which s1031 relief applies

s1031   The relief provided by s1031 only applies where:

- by *virtue or in consequence of an order* made under Part III of the Family Law (Divorce) Act, 1996,

- *on or following* the granting of a decree of divorce,

- assets are transferred **from one spouse to the other spouse**.

Foreign divorces are discussed in paragraph 33.8.5.

Part III of the Family Law (Divorce) Act, 1996, contains sections 11 to 30 inclusive, and makes provision for the Court to make orders relating to many different matters which may arise in divorce proceedings. Many of those provisions which have nothing to do with CGT.

The following is a very broad summary of some of the main provisions of the Family Law (Divorce) Act, 1996, insofar as those provisions relate to the financial affairs of the parties involved in the divorce proceedings.

- *Maintenance pending suit orders* (s12) : such an order would normally be made to provide for a dependent spouse pending the hearing of the divorce application by the Court.

- *Periodic lump sum payment orders* (s13) : a dependent spouse may apply for such an order at any time during the lifetime of the other spouse. Similar provisions apply in the case of a dependent child. The payment may be for the benefit of the dependent spouse or child or both. Security for the continuity of payment may be required, perhaps by way of an "attachment of earnings order". Such an order ceases on the remarriage of the recipient spouse (to the extent that the payments relate to that individual).

- *Property adjustment orders* (s14) : On granting a decree of divorce or at anytime thereafter (on application by a dependent spouse or child) the Court may during the lifetime of the other spouse make a property adjustment order, i.e..:

  — transfer property from one spouse to the other, or to a dependent child (property in possession or in reversion)

  — settle property for the benefit of such dependents,

  — vary the terms of any ante-nuptial or post nuptial settlement (including a settlement made by will or codicil),

  — extinguish the interest of either spouse under such a settlement,

  Such an order cannot be made

  — in favour of a spouse who following divorce has remarried, or

  — in respect of the family home in which either spouse who following divorce, and having remarried, ordinarily resides with his/her spouse.

  The Court has discretion to apportion costs of complying with such an order.

- *miscellaneous ancillary orders* (s15) : such orders may be made on the application of a dependent spouse at anytime during the lifetime of the other spouse (or on behalf of a dependent child). Orders under this section relate to the *family home*, and may confer rights of residence on one spouse to the exclusion of the other (for life, or for a certain or contingent period) or may direct that the property be sold and apportion the sale proceeds between the individuals concerned in an appropriate manner.

  This provision of granting a right of residence does not apply to a family home of spouse who has remarried and is living in that property with his/her current spouse.

- *Financial compensation orders* (s16) : orders under this section relate to the giving effect to, or assigning rights under, or continuing payments relating to *life assurance policies*. Such an order can be made on the application of either spouse or on behalf of a dependent child. The order ceases on remarriage of the spouse receiving the benefit of the order.

- *Pension adjustment orders* (s17) : under this section, the Court may make provision for a dependent spouse or child to take part of the pension benefits arising under the other spouse's pension scheme, including death in service benefits, and a share in contribution repayments on leaving the scheme.

- *Orders for provision for spouse by estate of deceased spouse* (s19) : under this section, the Court may make such provision as it considers appropriate for a dependent spouse or child out of the estate of a former spouse. An order under this section cannot be made more than 6 months after representation is first granted under the Succession Act, 1965, nor can an order be made in favour of a spouse who has remarried.

- *Orders for sale of property* (s.19) : where the Court has made:

  −a secured periodic payment order

  −a lump sum order, or

  −a property adjustment order,

  It may make an order directing that the sale of such property as is specified in the order (being property in which both spouses have a beneficial interest in possession or reversion). It may also direct that the property be offered for sale to persons or class of persons specified in the order. The order may also direct how the proceeds of disposal are to be dealt with.

The above is merely a broad summary of some of the possible orders which can be made by the Court in connection with the application for, or on or following the granting of a decree of divorce.

Although many of the orders may be made for the sole purpose of providing income, or securing living accommodation for a dependent spouse and/or children, such payments are not necessarily paid out of income. Assets may have to be sold to provide the cash source for the payments required to comply with the Court order. The CGT treatment of assets transferred as security is dealt with in Chapter 8.

Where security is required, it may involve the transfer of an asset (as security). Normally this matter is dealt with by assignment of a life assurance policy, but it could involve the transfer of other assets as security. Rights granted over assets may involve a (part) disposal, or perhaps a "value shift" where a right of residence is involved in a property (which may or may not be the principal private residence of the spouse making the disposal)

In broad terms, such orders as are appropriate (at the discretion of the Court) will normally be made at the time of the granting of a decree of divorce. However, it is important to realise that further orders may be made at anytime during the lifetime of either spouse on the application of a dependent spouse (or on behalf of a dependent child) if in the opinion of the Court circumstances warrant such new orders.

There are restrictions on the making of further orders by the Court. In most cases, an order cannot be made following divorce relating to family home in which a remarried spouse is living with his/her current spouse. A further restriction recognises that on remarriage following divorce, a remarried spouse may lose his/her rights to be financially supported by the former spouse.

It is probable that prior to a divorce, the spouses will have separated in circumstances which are likely to be permanent. This will not invariably be the case, but it is likely to be the case in many instances. As mentioned earlier, where the married couple are not living together as husband and wife, the various intra spouse reliefs do not apply to them. Strictly speaking, at such a time in relation to any informal transfer of assets between them (not made under a deed of separation or a court order) they are not entitled to the intra-spouse reliefs. However a court order made in consequence of the divorce decree restores the intra spouse exemption to the couple in relation to transfers made under that court order. It does not of course retrospectively extend any relief to transfers made by them at a time when they were not living together as man and wife, and which was not made under a court order or a formal deed of separation.

It is equally the case that any informal transfer of assets between spouses, subsequent to the divorce, does not benefit from an intra spouse relief. If for any reason the former spouses wish to transfer assets between each other during their lifetime, subsequent to the divorce, the intra spouse relief will be available to them only if they seek a further court order to sanction the transfer of the assets. It remains to be seen whether the courts would make an order where parties are not in dispute, and where the sole purpose of seeking such an order is to obtain a tax advantage. There is as yet little or no experience in this area.

The relevant legal and other costs should be carefully weighed against the taxation costs which would otherwise be involved.

Although no CGT may be payable by the disponer in respect of such a transfer on foot of a court order or under a deed of separation, it is important to also consider the CGT affect on the recipient of the property, and possible taxation consequences arising out of other taxes involved in such a course of action.

Example 177

Joe and Mary were married in 1960. In 1967 Joe left the family home and set up house with another woman, with whom he subsequently had children. In 1985 Joe realised that 50% of the shares in his trading company, Always Open Stores Ltd., remained registered in the name of his wife. He reached a deal with her to buy the shares from her for £500,000. In August 1997 Joe and Mary agreed to seek a divorce, so as to enable Joe to marry a companion with whom he was now living. The court order, made to give affect to the divorce, provided for the transfer to Mary of two rental properties in Dublin worth £400,000 in total, (Joe's base cost being £20,000 only) and the sum of £360,000. Joe raised this sum of money by selling quoted shares on the stock exchange.

The sale of shares in Always Open Stores Ltd. by Mary to Joe in 1985 was a disposal by Mary at a time when she was not a woman living with Joe as husband and wife. Accordingly the intra-spouse relief, strictly speaking, did not apply to it and Mary would be liable to capital gains tax in the normal manner. Since Joe and Mary were not living together as husband and wife in 1985/86, Joe cannot be assessed by the Revenue Commissioners in respect of Mary's gain on the transaction.

The transfer of the rental properties to Mary by Joe on foot of the court order giving affect to their divorce, benefits from the intra-spouse exemption and no capital gains tax arises on the transaction. Mary's base cost in the properties however is not their £400,000 open market value at the date in August 1997 when she obtained the properties, but rather Joe's historic base cost (£20,000 in this case). On any subsequent disposal of those properties, Mary will face significant capital gains tax by reason of the low base cost, relative to the value of the properties.

Notwithstanding that Joe disposed of the quoted shares in order to fund the payment to Mary under the divorce decree, the disposal of the shares on the stock exchange to a third party cannot avail of the intra spouse relief. It was not a disposal to Mary, but one made to raise cash to pay to her. Accordingly it is liable to capital gains tax in the normal manner.

The application of the intra-spouse relief on the occasion of divorce is a two edged sword. It benefits the spouse making the transfer of property, in that that spouse is treated as making the disposal on a no gain no loss basis, and cannot be exposed to capital gains tax on the transaction. The spouse to whom the property is transferred however takes the property at the historic base cost of the transferring spouse. In most instances that will be lower than the open market value of the property and accordingly an uncrystallised capital gains tax liability is effectively transferred along with the property. There is therefore a sense in which an invisible liability is passed over with the property thus reducing its true value.

Example 178

In December 1997, Mary, in the example above, decided to raise cash and to do so placed one of the rental properties up for sale. Joe decided to buy back the property from her, and a price of £200,000 was agreed for the property.

The transfer, not being made on foot of an order of the court giving affect to the divorce, does not carry the intra-spouse relief (Joe and Mary being no longer spouses, or living together as man and wife). Accordingly Mary is liable to capital gains tax on the transaction. Mary's base cost is the historic base cost which Joe had on the property i.e. £20,000. Mary is therefore liable to capital gains tax on the difference between the £200,000 open market value of the property, and the base cost of £20,000, suitably indexed, and adjusted for cost of disposal etc.

33.8.3   Separation by Court Order or Formal deed

33.8.3.1   Broad outline

From the point of view of CGT on the transfer of assets, the position remains the same whether the Court grants

—a decree of divorce or

—a decree of judicial separation.

The position is that the wife is no longer *a married woman living with her husband.* As such the original intra spouse relief cannot apply to transfers of assets between them. The overall position is the same where the couple separate by virtue of a deed of separation agreed between them, whether or not it is made an order of Court.

Provided they are separated in such circumstances that the separation is likely to be permanent, the broad overall CGT position of the couple remains the same. The fact that they may remain husband and wife in the eyes of State law, is not relevant to the CGT treatment of the transfer of assets between them. However, where they are not divorced, they remain "connected person" which may affect the transfer price, or deemed transfer price of any asset transferred between them.

As in the case of divorce, transfers of assets between such spouses will not (in the absence of specific provisions) qualify for the normal intra spouse relief.

33.8.3.2   Relief under s1030

s1030

The relief provided is very similar to that provided in the case of a grant of a decree of divorce.

s1030 provides that:

"*(2) Notwithstanding any other provision of the Capital Gains Tax Acts, where by virtue or in consequence of :*

  (a) an order made under Part II of the Family Law Act, 1995 on or following a decree of judicial separation within the meaning of that Act, or,

  (b)   an order made under Part II of the Judicial Separation and Family Law Reform Act, 1989, on or following the grant of a decree of Judicial Separation where such order is treated, by

> *virtue of s.3 of the Family Law Act, 1995 as if made under the*
> *corresponding provision of the Family Law Act, 1995, or,*
>
> (c)   *a deed of separation, or,*
>
> (d)   *a relief order (within the meaning of that Act) made following the*
> *dissolution of a marriage", or following the legal separation of*
> *spouses, or*
>
> (e)   *an order or determination to like effect which is analogous to the*
> *order referred to in paragraph (d), or a court under the law of a*
> *territory other than the State made under or in consequence of*
> *the dissolution of a marriage or the legal separation of spouses,*
> *being a dissolution or legal separation that has entitled it to be*
> *recognised as valid in the State".*

...either spouse disposes of an asset to the other spouse, both spouses shall be treated as if the asset was transferred for such a consideration as to ensure that neither a gain nor a loss accrues to the spouse making the disposal. The normal intra spouse provisions also apply to the acquisition of the asset by the acquiring spouse, and the exclusion of trading stock.

The provisions of s1030 apply and are deemed to take effect as and from 1st August 1996.

FLA95 s52   The Family Law Act, 1995, provided similar relief in s52 of that Act. The provisions of the Family Law Act, 1995 have now been repealed by FA97 s72.

FA2000 s88   The part of subsection 2(d) quoted above that refers to foreign divorce and separation orders was inserted by the FA2000. The effect of the amendment is to extend the tax provisions relating to divorce to such divorces and separations. However it is extended to them only to the extent that the divorce is recognised in Ireland. This is dealt with further in paragraph 33.8.5.

33.8.3.3   Scope of the relief

Unlike the conditions for relief for intra spouse asset transfers following a divorce, the relief under s1030 is available for transfers of assets between spouses following a "formal separation" whether or not a Court is involved. A simple legally binding deed of separation between the spouses is sufficient to bring any such transfers within the scope of the intra spouse relief, provided any such transfer occurs by virtue or in consequence of that deed.

The orders which can be made by the Court follow closely the broad categories already summarised in the case of divorce - in paragraph 33.8.2.3 above.

33.8.4   Informally separated spouses

The special rules applying to married persons, only apply where a wife is regarded as 'living with her husband' - see 33.2 above. If they are in fact separated, in such circumstances that they are no longer treated as married for CGT purposes, the reliefs which apply on transfers of assets between married persons, and the other provisions applying to married persons will no longer apply to them.

A *separation* frequently involves a transfer of assets from one spouse to another. In an informal separation such transfers are not carried out under the terms of a deed of separation or a Court order. This new tax status existing between the separated spouses needs careful consideration, particularly if gains are likely to arise on the disposal of assets from one spouse to another.

s549
s10

In the absence of relief, the question of the *'consideration'* for disposals between informally separated spouses needs to be considered. Are they connected persons ? Although they no longer come within the category of *'a married woman living with her husband'*, they are still 'husband and wife' in law. The definition of 'connected persons' in s10 does not exclude separated spouses from the meaning of the general legal terms 'husband' and 'wife' and so they must be regarded as 'connected' for CGT purposes. Market value applies to any assets transferred from one of them to the other (to the exclusion of any actual consideration passing).

The restriction on the use of losses resulting from the transfer of an asset between connected persons will also apply.

One asset which will always need careful consideration, is the family home. An individual can only have one principal private residence qualifying for relief (at any particular point in time). A married couple living together can only have one principal private residence qualifying for relief. When they cease to be living together (in a tax sense) they can each have a separate principal private residence.

It is important that serious consideration is given to any possible future transfers between them while they are still regarded as 'married and living together' for CGT purposes, particularly where substantial assets are held by the two spouses, or where substantial asset values are to pass between them (perhaps as part of an overall separation settlement).

s1026

s1023

The FA83 introduced measures (now s1026) to give relief in respect of maintenance payments. Part of those provisions allowed the two separated spouses to elect for income tax purposes to be charged to income tax as a married couple. s1026 has the affect of changing s1023 in a case where a qualifying maintenance payment was made by one spouse to the other, allowing them to elect for joint assessment as if they were not separated. This provision, however, seems to have little to do with CGT, which provides for specific rules to apply in the case of a married woman 'living with her husband'. That 'definition' has not changed.

The present treatment of separated spouses, is to a great extent dealt with by Revenue *"extra statutory concession"* - arising mainly out of the pre-1996 Irish constitutional ban on divorce which resulted in a large number of separations, and second church "marriages" by separated persons (which were not recognised by the State). Now that the constitutional ban on divorce has been removed, the issue of whether, and to what extent those Revenue "concessions" will remain after the introduction of divorce legislation needs to be closely monitored. It is expected that divorce proceedings (as presently available) may be costly, even where there is no dispute between the parties involved. For this reason alone, not everyone will be in a financial position to actually avail of the current arrangements (assuming they wish to do so).

Some individuals do, however, obtain a 'Catholic Church' annulment of the marriage (if it was originally a Catholic Church wedding). The number of individuals obtaining such church annulments is not great. If a church annulment is granted, the individuals can remarry in the Catholic Church. The State does not recognise the annulment, and does not recognise the 'second marriage'.

The Revenue Commissioners normally treat such 'remarried' couples (by concession) as if they were legally married for income tax and capital gains tax purposes, and treat them to all intents and purposes as if they were legally married. This applies to both foreign divorces not recognised in the State, and Church annulments, which are followed by a remarriage, whether abroad or by the Catholic Church. This concessional treatment is not extended to other taxes. The future position of such concessional treatment is not known at the date of writing.

The concession does not apply to capital acquisitions tax nor to stamp duty.

33.8.5   Foreign divorce

Where the parties to the original marriage have obtained a valid foreign divorce which is recognised by the State, they are both free to remarry at any time. After a valid divorce they are no longer "married" and the intra spouse relief cannot apply to transfers of assets between them.

The general rule was that a divorce granted in a jusisdiction where either spouse was domiciled was recognised in Ireland as a valid divorce. A 1999 High Court judgement extended this rule to recognise a divorce granted in a jurisdiction where either spouse was ordinarily resident.

No relief was provided under the FA 97 (now s1030 as originally enacted) for disposals from one spouse to another consequent on a foreign divorce.

FA2000 s88   Where a foreign divorce is recognised as valid in Ireland (likewise with a foreign legal separation) the like provisions from the viewpoint of capital gains tax are applied as apply to an Irish divorce or legal separation. However this is so only in relation to disposals made on or after 10 February 2000. In relation to disposals made prior to that date, the position is that no relief is available in relation to disposals between couples not living together as man and wife.

Not all foreign divorces are recognised by the State. Where the foreign divorce is not recognised as valid under Irish law, the position is that the couple involved are probably not living together, and will probably be treated as permanently separated. Where either party enters into a subsequent marriage, although that subsequent marriage is bigamous under Irish law, the couple involved will normally be treated as married to each other (by concession) if they so claim for the purposes of income tax and CGT. This concession should be confirmed in advance in all cases.

33.8.6   **Annullment of marriage**

The consequences of a Court annullment of a marriage are quite different to those following a separation or a divorce. The granting of an annullment by the Court requires the Court to find that no valid marriage existed in the first instance. It is not a question of dissolving a marriage - there never was any marriage from the start.

The Court annullment of a marriage raises many practical difficulties not only for the two individuals involved, but also the children (if any) of that marriage.

Very few individuals obtain a State/Court annullment, mainly on account of the cost of the Court proceedings involved, and the uncertainty of the final outcome of those proceedings.

In strict law "annullment" by a Court means that the two individuals were never married and the intra spouse relief should never have applied to them. Any transfer of assets between them following the annullment of the marriage are fully within the scope of the charge to CGT should any gains arise. As far as the authors are aware, in practice the Revenue have not tried to alter the position of transactions which have occurred prior to the date of the annullment. Such transactions have been left stand. Any relief claimed by the individuals on the grounds that they were validly married at the time is not normally withdrawn.

However, it should be borne in mind, that although no gain or loss arose to the "spouse" making the disposal at the time of the intra spouse disposal, the recipient "spouse" acquired the base cost and date of acquisition of the disposing spouse - in effect any resulting gain is deferred, and may crystalise on a subsequent disposal by the acquiring spouse.

An annulment by church authorities is without legal consequences in Ireland. Only an annulment granted by a court has legal consequences. The discussion above is solely in terms of an annulment by the court. However an annulment by church authorities may be a factor indicating that the separation of a couple is likely to prove permanent and that accordingly they can no longer be regarded as living together as man and wife. As previously explained, it is an essential condition for the intra-spouse exemption on the transfer of assets that the couple live together as man and wife, in the sense defined for CGT purposes.

33.9   Meaning of "child"

s6
s10

In some circumstances, reliefs are available in the case of a disposal to a *child* (e.g. - retirement relief - see paragraph 30). A disposal to a *lineal descendant* (e.g. a child) being a "connected" person, may also lead to the application of a number of anti-avoidance provisions. The restricted meaning of the term "lineal descendant" for the purposes of s10 (which replaced s.33, 1975 Act - connected persons) is dealt with in paragraph 16.4.

Although, in most situations, the question of whether an individual is the legally recognised child of another is quite clear, there are some situations where the position is not clear. The question of the legal relationship (if any) between an illegitimate child and his blood parents (who may or may not be legally recognised as his parents) may not be totally clear. Also the question of the legal relationship between an adopted child and his natural blood parents needs to be considered.

s6

TCA97 s6 defines the term *child (and adopted child)* for Income Tax and CGT purposes as (unless the contrary intention appears) including references to :

- a son or daughter

- a stepchild

- a child who is adopted under the Adoption Acts 1952 to 1991, or

- the subject of a foreign adoption (as defined - by s1 Adoption Act 1991)

s6

In the case of an adopted child, the relationship which previously existed with his natural parents, is deemed to cease.

Further amendments were made by FA92, which extended the reference to Adoption Acts to include the Adoption Act 1991.

s10

The interaction of this expanded definition of "child" in s6 with the definition of "relative" in s10 is unclear.

The FA88 introduced provisions (now s8) to deem that for the purposes of specific tax Acts (*"the Acts"*), i.e.:

- the Taxes Acts,

- the Capital Gains Tax Acts,

- the Capital Acquisitions Tax Act 1976 (and later amending Acts), and

- the statutes relating to Stamp Duty (and instruments made thereunder)

s8

"Notwithstanding any provision of the Acts or the dates on which they were passed, in deducing any relationship between persons for the purposes of the Acts, the Acts shall be construed in accordance with section 3 of the Status of Children Act, 1987".

In effect, this means, that an illegitimate child is treated as the *child of both parents*.

For CGT purposes this provision applies in relation to disposals made on or after 14th January 1988.

Minor child:

AMA85 s2

A minor child is one which is under the age of 18 years. This provision came into force on and from 6th April 1986.

s7

Prior to 6th April 1986, the age of majority was 21 years.

33.10   Divorce and "connected persons"

A husband and wife are treated as connected for the purposes of the Capital Gains Tax Acts whether or not they are living together as man and wife. They may therefore be treated as connected even at a time when the intra-spouse exemption is not available to them (see paragraph 33.8.3).

Following on a decree of divorce, the former spouses are no longer husband and wife and accordingly are no longer connected parties, unless they qualify as connected parties by some reason other than marriage.

Persons who are "cohabiting", on no matter how stable a basis, but who are not married under a marriage recognised in Ireland, are not connected persons on the basis of their being husband and wife, as they do not in law have that status. The principal significance in terms of the Capital Gains Tax Acts of the parties to a transaction being connected is that the transaction will always be regarded as being a bargain not at arm's length, and accordingly as one in which section 9 of the 1975 Act will substitute open market value for the consideration actually passing.

Example 179

*In **example 177** above Mary sold shares to her separated husband, Joe in 1985. She did so for the sum of £500,000. If Mary had not been properly advised on the transaction, and Joe had concealed information regarding the financial affairs of the company from her, it is possible that the open market value of the shares may have been greater than the price paid.*

In such a circumstance Joe and Mary are regarded as being connected, and notwithstanding that Mary may have done her (uninformed and ill-advised) best to get the maximum price from Joe, if the true open market value was greater than the £500,000 paid, that true open market value can be treated as being the consideration on the transaction. It would be on the higher open market value that Mary would have to compute her capital gain, and that higher open market value would represent Joe's base cost in the shares.

33.11   **Divorce and trusts**

As noted in paragraph 33.7.4, the creation of a trust by one spouse, under which the other spouse takes an interest, is not entitled to the relief for intra spouse transfers. It is instead treated as a disposal to a notional trustee at open market value. This treatment applies equally where the transfer is made on the occasion of a divorce settlement.

If the transfers described in *example 176* in paragraph 33.7.4 had been transfers carried out as part of a divorce settlement under order of a Court, the same results would apply as described in that example. The intra spouse exemption would not apply to the life interest in the shares in the family company granted by John to Mary. This seems a particularly unsatisfactory position since a life interest may, in the context of a divorce where there are children, be seen to be the most satisfactory form of settlement by the parties involved. The spouse providing shares in a family company to a divorcing spouse may well be concerned to ensure that they do not "pass out of the family" forever, and will be available to the children of the marriage after the death of the spouse to whom they are given. However, if this objective is met by way of one spouse taking a life interest, there may be a CGT cost.

34   PARTNERSHIPS AND ASSOCIATIONS

34.1   Broad Outline

A partnership is not a separate legal entity, distinct from the individual partners. Normally it is merely a contractual commercial relationship which exists between the partners making up the partnership. In this sense it is different from a company, which is a legal person in its own right totally separate from its shareholders.

IA37 s11(c)   A partnership is not in the ordinary sense "a person". However it is a body of persons and "*person*" is defined in the Interpretation Act 1937 as including an unincorporated body of persons. This definition applies for the purpose of the Capital Gains Tax Act. On that basis it might be thought that a partnership, which is an unincorporated body of persons, might be chargeable as a "*person*" to Capital Gains Tax.

This is not so.

s30   TCA97 s30 provides that:

- Tax in respect of chargeable gains accruing to partners on the disposal of any partnership asset are to be assessed and charged on the partners separately and

- Any partnership dealings in assets are to be treated as dealings by the partners and not by the firm as such.

The main effect of these provisions is that a partnership is not a body chargeable to capital gains tax, but rather that the individual partners are to be charged to capital gains tax in respect of capital gains arising on the disposal of partnership assets.

s10(5)   There is one further capital gains tax provision dealing with partnerships. It is contained in s10(5) and provides that a person is to be treated as connected with any person with whom he is in partnership, and with the husband or wife or relative of any individual with whom he is in partnership. It goes on to provide an exception to his deemed connection. That exception is in relation to the acquisition or disposal of partnership assets pursuant to bona fide commercial arrangements. In the case of such acquisitions or disposals, a person would not be treated as connected with another person by reason solely of their being partners. They may of course be treated as connected for other reasons e.g. because they are related.

Example 180

A and B are in partnership. They acquire a premises for £100,000 for use in their trade. Five years later they find that the premises is too small. They sell the premises and acquire a new premises. Sales proceeds are £150,000.

Ignoring, for the purposes of the example, roll over relief, indexation and incidental costs of acquisition and disposal, a chargeable gain of £50,000 might seem to arise to the partnership.

This gain is not assessed on the partnership but rather must be apportioned as between A and B, and assessed separately for each and be charged upon each of them.

The two statutory provisions described above are the sum total of the capital gains tax provisions relating to partnerships. They have a deceptive appearance of simplicity. They do not provide a very helpful guide to the Capital Gains Tax implications of the many complex transactions which can arise in a partnership.

In 1975 the Inland Revenue in the UK (where the legislation is similar) recognised the difficulties in applying capital gains tax legislation to partnerships. They issued a **Statement of Practice** which set out their practice in regard to the application of capital gains tax in many specific types of transactions which can arise in the normal course of a partnership. The Revenue Commissioners in Ireland have stated that they would not necessarily follow this statement of practice but deal with each case on its merits.

The UK statement of practice is useful in highlighting the many practical difficulties which arise in attempting to apply CGT legislation to partnerships. In some cases the practice which it outlines is consistent with capital gains tax legislation. In other cases, it is difficult to reconcile the Inland Revenue practice with the legislation and it may in those instances represent a pragmatic attempt to apply an extra statutory (concessional) coherent scheme to the taxation of partnerships.

In the remainder of this paragraph, the UK statement of practice, notwithstanding the reservations just stated, will be used as a framework to highlight the many practical difficulties which arise in practice in the application of capital gains tax legislation to partnerships.

34.2   **Partnerships assets**

Before beginning an examination of the UK statement of practice it is necessary to consider the legal position regarding the ownership of partnership assets. A partnership is not, in the ordinary legal sense, a person in itself. This is so notwithstanding the definition used in the Interpretation Act 1937. The partnership assets are not owned by a person consisting of a partnership, but rather are jointly owned by all of the partners. The partnership assets are thus assets which are in joint ownership. Joint ownership (whether it be joint tenancy or tenancy in common) is quite a common form of ownership of assets.

PA90 s20, s39   However the interest of a partner in the assets of a partnership is a very particular form of joint ownership. A partner is entitled to have each of the partnerships assets employed for the purposes of the partnership's business; and on a dissolution of the partnership to have the partnership assets sold, and the proceeds primarily applied in the discharge of the liabilities of the partnership; and to have any surplus remaining distributed in accordance with the partnership agreement.

In addition to involving joint ownership of partnership assets, a partnership may give rise to a partner having other assets arising from the partnership. The partnership agreement will usually create obligations by each of the partners towards his fellow partners. Those obligations of other partners may represent an asset of the partner to whom they are owed, which asset is a distinct matter from the partnership assets per se.

Although it is common to speak of a partner's *"share in the partnership"* that share is not in itself a single recognisable legal asset. It is a composite term applied to his interest (joint) in each of the partnership assets, and to the rights obtained by him by virtue of the partnership agreement, vis-à-vis his fellow partners. For capital gains tax purposes it is the individual partnership assets in which he has an interest, and his rights vis-à-vis his fellow partners, that are assets for capital gains tax purposes, and not the *"share in the partnership"*.

Not all assets owned by the partners in a partnership, nor all assets used by a partnership, are partnership assets. Only assets owned jointly by the partners *as such* are partnership assets.

The Partnership Act 1890 sets out some rules to help determine which assets are partnership assets.

Example 181

A and B are in partnership as solicitors. The building which the partnership occupies as tenant was put up for sale by the landlord. A and B agreed to purchase the property jointly, each acquiring a 50% interest in the property. It is not their intention that the property should be a partnership asset, notwithstanding that it will be used by the partnership.

The property is not a partnership asset notwithstanding that it is owned by the partners and is in use for the purpose of the partnership trade. The important point is that it is owned by the partners jointly as individual investors, and not as partners, and that that was their intention. If A and B had determined that they, as partners, would acquire the property as a partnership asset, then it would have been a partnership asset.

Given that partnership assets are owned jointly by the individual partners, it follows that events such as the creation of a partnership; the dissolution of a partnership; the admission of new partners; and changes in partnership interests may all be the occasion of the disposal of interests by the individual partners in partnership assets, and of the acquisition of such interests by individual partners in partnership assets.

Example 182

> *A and B go into partnership to farm land. A provides the farm land which is introduced to the partnership as a partnership asset. B provides farm machinery which he introduces to the partnership as a partnership asset. On the formation of the partnership, the land and machinery, which were previously separately wholly owned by A and by B respectively become partnership assets in which both A and B have an interest.*
>
> *It follows therefore that the creation of the partnership involves a part disposal of the land by A, and an acquisition of an interest in the land by B; and a part disposal of the machinery by B, and an acquisition of an interest in the machinery by A.*

Example 183

> *A and B (the partners in **example 182** above) admit a new partner, C. On his admission C becomes a part owner of each of the partnership assets i.e. of the land, and of the plant and machinery.*
>
> *It follows that both A and B have made a part disposal of their interest in the land, and in the machinery, and that C has acquired an interest in the land, and in the machinery.*

The capital gains tax consequences of the creation of a partnership, and of the admission of new partners, are considered in greater detail in the section which follows, in the light of comments by the Inland Revenue in their statement of practice on partnerships.

34.3   The UK Statement of Practice

The UK statement of practice is being considered because it provides a useful framework within which to analyse the application of CGT law to a partnership. Although it has not been adopted by the Revenue Commissioners in Ireland (who have said they will not necessarily follow it) it is contemporaneous with the Irish capital gains tax legislation and therefore the problems which it addresses ought to have been known to the draftsman of the Capital Gains Tax Act 1975 at the time the legislation was being drafted (which draft was an exact copy of the UK provisions which existed at that time).

34.4   Creation of the Partnership

The UK statement of practice does not deal explicitly with the creation of a partnership. This is perhaps understandable since the assets involved are not partnership assets until the partnership has been created and therefore, insofar as any disposals are concerned which arise by reason of the creation of the partnership, the disposals are not disposals of partnership assets (although they may well represent the acquisition of partnership assets).

As outlined in *example 182* above, on basic principles the contribution of assets by a partner on the creation of the partnership can amount to a part disposal by that partner of the assets in question, and a corresponding acquisition of an interest in the assets by the other partner.

Because the partner introducing the assets to the partnership continues to be a part owner of the asset, there can be no more involved than a part disposal. It is not an outright disposal of the asset by the partner to "the partnership".

In principle a partner contributing assets as partnership assets must receive consideration for those assets unless the transaction constituted a gift. If the transaction is not one at arms length, or is between persons who are connected (other than by reason of being partners where the creation of a partnership is a bone fide commercial transaction), or where a gift is involved, the Capital Gains Tax Act will deem consideration equal to the open market value of the interest disposed of, to be received by the partner. Open market value might also be substituted where the consideration received is of a type which cannot be valued e.g. an undertaking by the other partner to apply himself full time to the conduct of the partnership's affairs.

As will be seen below, it would be expected that similar consequences would follow on the admission of a new partner to an existing partnership but in that instance the Inland Revenue have provided that where no payment is made by the incoming partner (or anybody else on that occasion) and no revaluation of partnership assets occurs, they are content that the disposals by the existing partners and the acquisition by the incoming partner, should be treated as being at the base cost of the individual assets concerned. It seems anomalous that such a concessional treatment would be available (in the UK) on the admission of a new partner, but not available on the creation of a partnership. However the Inland Revenue's approach in relation to the admission of new partners is a concessional approach, and does not seem to be strictly based on the legislation, and accordingly too much cannot be made of this anomaly.

The UK statement of practice deals explicitly with the situation where the incoming partner is connected with one or more of the existing partners, or where his entry into the partnership is otherwise not a transaction at arm's length. As explained in paragraph 16, in such circumstances the open market value of what is acquired and disposed of should be substituted for the actual consideration (if any) passing in a transaction. The statement of practice however provides that *"market value will not be substituted if nothing would have been paid had the parties been at arm's length"*. At first sight, this might seem like the same thing as open market value.

However what is involved is not the open market value of a fractional share of the various partnership assets, but rather the sum which an incoming partner would pay to become such a partner, if the transaction were at arm's length. Bearing in mind that the incoming partner may be assuming many non-monetary obligations (attendance to the company's business etc.) and exposing himself to unlimited liability in a trading situation, it may be the case in many instances that a payment would not arise on the admission of a new partner in a transaction at arm's length, even where the partnership assets are substantial.

The occasion of the creation of a partnership is also the occasion upon which each partner enters into obligations (e.g. to apply himself to the partnership affairs) to his fellow partners, and receives the benefit of similar obligations undertaken by his fellow partners. Such obligations constitute an asset for each partner. Since such assets rarely if ever give rise to capital gains, their existence is normally overlooked for capital gains tax purposes. Since they do not preexist the creation of the partnership, entering into the obligations does not constitute the disposal of an asset, but the receipt of the benefit of the obligations will constitute the acquisition of an asset by each separate partner. Arguably a partner gives a consideration for the acquisition of that asset, usually his corresponding obligation under the partnership agreement. This would represent deductible expenditure in relation to the asset only if it were consideration in moneys worth. It is questionable if the obligations undertaken by a partner towards his fellow partners constitute moneys worth.

- **Revenue/Chief Inspector's CGT manual**

— Part 19 of the instructions on the Consolidated Taxes Act 1997 published by the Chief Inspector of Tax, at paragraph 5.3 states "The setting up of a partnership or changes in partnership which involves a change in the asset sharing ratios may involve a disposal".

34.5 **Admission of a New Partner**

The admission of a new partner is in many respects similar in its consequences as regards assets, as is the initial creation of the partnership. A new partner obtains an interest in each of the partnership assets. That amounts to a part disposal by each of the original partners of their interest in those assets. If the new partner introduces assets to the partnership, the original partners will acquire an interest in those assets and the incoming partner who contributes the new assets will have made a part disposal of those assets.

The UK Statement of Practice treats as a single topic, the admission of a new partner, the departure of a partner from the partnership, and adjustments in *"partnership sharing ratios"* as between partners. For the moment we are concerned only with the admission of a new partner. The statement of practice recognises the acquisitions and disposals outlined above and it goes on to state that *"the disposal consideration will be a fraction (equal to the fractional share changing hands) of the current balance sheet value of each chargeable asset provided there is no direct payment of consideration outside the partnership"*. It is to be noted that the reference is to the current balance sheet value, which is not necessarily the same thing as the open market value or the historic cost of the assets in question.

The statement of practice goes on to qualify this rule by stating that where no adjustment is made through the partnership accounts (for example, by revaluation of the assets coupled with a corresponding increase or decrease in the partner's current or capital account at some date between the partner's acquisition of the asset and a reduction in his share) the disposal is treated as made for a consideration equal to his capital gains tax base cost and thus there will be neither a chargeable gain nor an allowable loss at that point.

Example 184

> A and B are in partnership. The partnership assets consist of a building acquired by the partnership at a cost for £100,000. C is admitted to the partnership without making a payment. The partnership agreement provides for him having a $^1/_3$rd interest in the partnership assets.
>
> The UK statement of practice would treat each of A and B as disposing of $16^2/_3\%$ of the building for a consideration of £16,666 to each partner, and would treat C as acquiring $33^1/_3\%$ interest in the building for a consideration of £33,333, notwithstanding that he has not made any payment, or contributed any assets to the partnership assets. This treatment does not appear to be well based in legislation.
>
> This treatment would be applied even if the building had an open market value in excess of its £100,000 cost - say a value of £150,000 as in **example 185** below.The figures would nonetheless be based on the book value and not the market value.

Example 185

> The situation is the same as that described in **example 184** above but prior to the admission of C, the building was valued as being worth £150,000. This figure was included in the company's accounts, and the capital account of each of A and of B was credited with £25,000 in respect of the revaluation surplus.
>
> The UK statement of practice would result in A and B being each treated as disposing of 16.67% of the building for a consideration equal to £25,000 each, and C would be treated as giving full consideration for a 33.33% interest in the building of £50,000.
>
> The UK statement of practice specifically states that the part disposal rules (which take into account the open market value of the interest in the property

> *which is retained) will not be applied in relation to the part disposals involved in the introduction of a new partner. Instead the calculation is done on a simple proportional basis as outlined above.*

It is not easy to see the legal basis for the UK treatment of the consideration passing in respect of the part disposals, and of the acquisition involved when a new partner is admitted to a partnership. The approach does reduce the capital gains tax cost which might be involved in admitting new partners to a partnership and might be therefore seen as politically desirable, but it would seem to be a concessional treatment as opposed to one based on legislation. The concession will usually (but not always) be advantageous to the existing partners, but will sometimes be disadvantageous to the incoming partner. It is not clear why an incoming partner in such a situation should be obliged to accept a lower base cost for the assets which he has acquired than the base cost which might be determined in accordance with the legislation.

The analysis of the determination of the consideration which would be deemed to pass in the transactions described above, if approached on a strict legislative basis, are similar to the analyses set out above for the part disposals and acquisitions involved on the creation of a partnership.

34.6   Adjustment of Partnership Sharing Ratios

s549

In an existing partnership the partners will sometimes agree to vary for the future the ratio in which they share profits and losses. Such a variation inevitably involves a variation at least in the value of their interest in the partnership assets. An agreement might also deal with a variation in the interest which they have in the assets at that point in time.

The UK statement of practice applies the same treatment to such changes in partnership sharing ratios as it applies to the admission of a new partner. In other words where assets have not been revalued from the date a partner acquired his interest in them, the transaction will be treated as being on a no gain/ no loss basis. It would otherwise be treated as involving acquisitions and disposals for a consideration equal to the balance sheet value (at the date of the change) of the assets.

It is not entirely clear that in law an agreement to change the ratios in which future profits will be shared, at a time when assets are stated in the partnership accounts at their full market value, represents a disposal of an interest in those assets but whether or not there is a disposal and acquisition on such an occasion, there would certainly seem to be such a disposal and acquisition where the ratios are changed at a time at which the partnership assets do not stand at their full open market value in the partnership accounts. In such a case it is as difficult to see the legislative basis for the Inland

Revenue approach as it is in the case of the admission of a new partner. The strict legislative position would seem to be in accordance with that outlined above for the acquisitions and part disposals arising on the creation of a partnership.

The UK statement of practice goes on to say that where payments are made between partners outside of the partnership (i.e. not out of partnership assets) in connection with changes in partnership sharing ratios, such payments are to be regarded as additional consideration (over and above that which would arise from the treatment described above) for the part disposal of the assets. They would correspondingly represent additional consideration for the acquisition of an interest in assets on the part of the partner making the payment.

• **Revenue Commissioners published precedent :**

— The Revenue Commissioners, in their published precedents, have commented on changes in "asset sharing ratios" in a partnership. The precedent is discussed in paragraph 34.10. It is broadly in line with the (UK) Inland Revenue treatment, although not expressed in identical terms. It is open to the same objections on grounds of logic as those expressed above in relation to the UK practise.

34.7   **Departure of partner**

On the resignation of a partner, his interest in the partnership assets is reduced to zero, and the interest of the surviving partners in those assets is correspondingly increased. He will usually also take out of the partnership assets a sum (usually in cash) equal to the balance on his current account and his capital account.

The UK statement of practice treats the retirement of a partner in the same manner as it treats any other reduction in profit sharing ratio. In other words, where assets have not been revalued since the departing partner acquired his interest in them, his disposal of his interest in those assets is treated as being on a no gain/no loss basis (and the corresponding acquisitions treated on a similar basis). Where assets were revalued the consideration will be by reference to a fraction of the balance sheet value of the assets (rather than their open market value). Where payments are made to the partner (whether outside the partnership or from partnership assets in respect of his disposal of his interest in the assets) that payment is treated as additional consideration. Where the departing partner is connected with the surviving partners, open market value is not substituted where it would be greater than the amount which would be paid on such an occasion if the parties were at arm's length.

The UK statement of practice goes on to state that the purchase of an annuity for the departing partner by the partnership or the surviving partners is treated as the payment of a sum equal to the cost of the

annuity, to the departing partner. However the payment by the
partnership to the departing partner of an annuity which is not more
than can be regarded as a reasonable recognition of the past
contribution of work and effort by the partner to the partnership will
not be regarded as consideration for a disposal of his interest in the
partnership assets. The statement of practice goes on to provide the
formula for determining a level of annuity which would not be
regarded as more than reasonable recognition of past effort.

34.8   **Disposal of partnership assets**

s30   S30 provides that tax in respect of chargeable gains accruing to
partners on the disposal of a partnership asset is to be assessed and
charged on them separately, and partnership dealings in assets are to
be treated as dealings by the partners and not by the firm as such.

Where a partnership disposes of an asset, each partner disposes of
his interest in that asset. It is this latter disposal which is the real
disposal (the partnership not being a person in law). The explicit
terms of s30 also require them to treat that disposal by each partner
of his interest in the asset as being the relevant disposal for capital
gains tax purposes. The tax on the disposal must be assessed
separately in relation to each partner and each partner must then be
charged with the tax which results from the amount assessed on
him.

Example 186

> Top Accountants are a long established partnership. The existing 3 partners
> were not members of the partnership when it was originally formed nor at the
> time when the company acquired its premises in 1980, at a cost of £100,000. In
> 1995 the partnership disposes of the premises for £200,000.
>
> Ignoring indexation, and incidental expenses, for the sake of simplicity, it might
> seem that the capital gain resulting is £100,000. This is not correct. Were the
> partnership per se the chargeable person for capital gains tax purposes, that
> would be the correct answer. However the partnership is not the chargeable
> person for capital gains tax purposes nor is capital gains tax assessed at the
> partnership level. Instead it is assessed on each partner separately, and the
> acquisition of assets, and the disposal of assets, by the partnership is treated as
> an acquisition and a disposal by each partner. It is therefore necessary to allocate
> the consideration (£200,000) among the partners, and to determine the base cost
> to each partner in respect of his share in the asset. That base cost will have been
> built up from the deemed acquisitions (or disposals) in relation to that asset
> which will have occurred in respect of each partner, on the occasion of his
> joining the partnership, and on subsequent changes in the membership of the
> partnership, or subsequent changes in partnership sharing ratios, as described
> above.

The Capital Gains Tax Act does not describe how the consideration
received from the disposal of a partnership asset is to be apportioned
among the partners. The UK statement of practice states "*the proceeds
of disposal will be allocated between the partners in the ratio of their shares*

in asset surpluses at the time of the disposal. Where this is not specifically laid down the allocation will follow the actual destination of the surplus as shown in the partnership accounts; regard will of course have to be paid to any agreement outside the accounts."

This method seems as reasonable as any other is likely to be.

Example 187

A and B are in partnership. They acquire a premises for £100,000 in 1980. In 1990 they admit C to the partnership. On that occasion C does not make any payment or introduce any new assets. The partnership agreement provides that each of the partners is to have an equal share in the partnership. In 1990 the property was worth £200,000 but this valuation has not been incorporated in the partnership accounts. In 1996 the property is sold for £300,000.

In the interests of simplicity, incidental costs and indexation are ignored in this example. It is also assumed for the purpose of the example that the treatment outlined in the UK statement of practice would be followed by the Revenue Commissioners in relation to the transactions (although this cannot be assured).

In 1990 A & B would each be treated as disposing of $\frac{1}{6}$ interest in the property to C, and C would be treated acquiring a one-third interest in the property. The transaction would be treated as occurring at the base cost of A and B in the property i.e. A and B would be treated as disposing of their $\frac{1}{6}$ for £16,666 each, and C would be treated as having given consideration of £33,333 for his interest. Part disposal rules would not be applied in the normal fashion (involving taking into account current market value in allocating base cost). The transaction would be treated as being carried out on a no gain/no loss basis.

A & B would be treated as each having a base cost of £33,333 being £50,000 original cost at the time the property was acquired, less part of the cost allocated to the part disposal when C was admitted.

In the partnership accounts for 1996, a gain of £200,000 would have been recognised on the disposal of the property and each of A, B, and C, would be credited with £66,666, being their respective share in that surplus.

Although the UK statement of practice is not explicitly clear on the point, it seems likely that the sales consideration of £300,000 would be allocated as to $\frac{1}{3}$rd each to A, B, and C. Accordingly each would be treated as having a chargeable gain of £66,666. In the example, this figure is the same as the accounting surplus but that would not normally be the case, where indexation and incidental costs are taken into account.

34.9   **Rate of CGT**

The period of ownership of assets may be relevant in determining the capital gains tax rate applicable prior to 3rd December 1997 where the asset consists of shares in a trading company (see paragraph 5.2). The period of ownership would have to be determined separately in relation to each partner. The period of ownership may also be relevant in relation to retirement relief. It is not known what approach the Revenue would take where the interest of a partner in an asset has varied over his period in the partnership as new partners were admitted, and partners left, and as partnership sharing ratios were adjusted. In principle he might be seen to have different periods of ownership for different percentages of his interest in the asset but that would seem an impractical approach in practice.

34.10   **Irish practice**

The Revenue Commissioners are not bound by the UK statement of practice and have declined to endorse it. Nonetheless it highlights problems which would arise from a strict application of the legal position to the conduct of partnership affairs. Insofar as the UK statement departs from the strict legal position, it is an attempt to minimise CGT liabilities arising on routine partnership transactions. Tax advisors should be aware of the UK statement and bring it to the attention of the Revenue where strict application of CGT rules produce a less satisfactory result.

It is to be hoped that the Revenue Commissioners will assist taxpayers who have obligations under self assessment, by producing their own statement of practice in this area.

• **Revenue Commissioners published precedent:**

— The Revenue Commissioners in their published precedents, make two references to partnerships.

— They state that where a partnership has written off goodwill in its balance sheet and the partner makes a subsequent disposal of his share in partnership assets, including goodwill, that partner is treated as realising a loss on the goodwill if he has a cost greater than nil. The precedent does not discuss in what circumstances the partner would have a cost greater than nil, or how one would determine that cost. The precedent as published is ambiguous in that it would suggest that a loss arises on a subsequent disposal without regard to the proceeds of disposal! Presumably what is intended is that a disposal for zero consideration of goodwill which is worthless and for that reason was written off, will generate a loss.

— The Revenue Commissioners have stated that *"Occasions of charge arise on disposals between partners. A change in asset sharing ratios involves a disposal/acquisition, most commonly on retirement of a partner or admission of a new partner. Where (1) no consideration is involved, (2) there is no revaluation of assets, (3) other than as partners the individuals are not connected persons within the meaning of Section 10, (4) the transaction is a bona fide commercial arrangement not forming part of a tax avoidance scheme - no gain is triggered and a reallocation of balance sheet values is acceptable."*

The published precedent does not discuss what treatment would apply where a revaluation of assets had occurred prior to the change in the asset sharing ratios. Presumably (but it must be stressed that this is not stated in the precedent) the treatment proposed in the precedent would apply to any assets which had not been the subject of the revaluation. Neither does the precedent indicate what treatment would be given if consideration were involved albeit consideration of less than open market value. In such circumstances would open market value be substituted for the actual consideration? It would seem anomalous if £1 consideration were sufficient to bring about such a fundamental change from the situation where there is no consideration. The published Revenue precedent is broadly (but not identically) in line with the UK Statement of Practice as discussed in Paragraph 34.6.

- **Revenue/Chief Inspector's CGT Manual :**

— At Paragraph 19.2.9.5 of the capital gains tax manual of the Revenue Commissioners it is stated *"Where the respective interests of the partners in a partnership change without any monetary or other consideration passing (either as a result of the custom of a particular partnership or of partnerships generally in a particular profession or trade) there is a disposal on the transfer of a partnership interest, but no chargeable gain if, under bona fide commercial arrangements, no consideration in money or moneys worth passes. There may, however, be an allowable loss if, in other circumstances, the disponer of the interest acquired it earlier for consideration in money or moneys worth. In practice, Section 10(5) should be regarded as also applying to a person joining a partnership."*

To date the only public comment by the Revenue Commissioners, contained in their manual in relation to capital gains tax, is to the effect that the setting up of a partnership or changes in partnership which involve a change in the asset sharing ratios may involve a disposal.

34.11   Residence of Partners

Once the gain (or loss) is apportioned to the individual partners, the question of any CGT liability is determined by reference to the residence (or ordinary residence) of each individual partner separately. The residence of the partnership as such has no relevance for CGT. The only other matter affecting chargeability is the fact that each individual partner will be assessed on his apportioned part of any gains attributable to the "specified Irish assets", irrespective of his residence or domicile. (see paragraph 3.3).

34.12   **Unincorporated Associations**

Apart from statutory exceptions, an unincorporated association is
not a legal entity, however real its existence may seem to the
members of the club and to the man in the street. In Leahy v AG for
New South Wales Viscount Simonds refers to:

*"the artificial and anomalous conception of an unincorporated society
which, though it is not a separate entity in law, is yet for many purposes
regarded as a continuing entity and, however inaccurately, as something
other than an aggregate of its members".*

In general law, such an unincorporated society cannot own property.
It is usual for property to be vested in trustees for the members,
whose rights and obligations are governed by the contract into
which they enter when they become members - usually the rules of
the association.

In broad terms, both income tax and CGT are chargeable on
'persons' within the scope of the charge to those taxes.

In the UK case of Carlisle and Silloth Golf Club v Smith it was held
that the golf club (an unincorporated association) was assessable to
income tax on income received from nonmembers. In the UK case of
American Foreign Insurance Association v Davies it was also held
that an unincorporated association could be the subject of an
assessment to income tax. In Income Tax Commissioners for London
v Gibbs Lord Macmillan said:

*"The important thing to ascertain is the meaning of the word 'person' in the
vocabulary of the Income Tax Acts. The word constantly occurs
throughout the Acts, and I think that it is most generally used to denote
what may be termed an entity of assessment, i.e. the possessor or recipient of
an income which the Acts require to be separately assessed for tax
purposes".*

The Interpretation Act 1937 states in s11 that

IA37 s11   *'The word "person" shall unless the contrary intention appears, be
construed as importing a body corporate (whether a corporation aggregate
or a corporation sole) and an unincorporated body of persons as well as an
individual'.*

CGT is chargeable in respect of chargeable gains accruing to a
'person' on the disposal of assets.

In determining whether such associations are chargeable to CGT, it
is necessary to look for statutory rules to establish whether such an
association is itself a 'person'. It is also necessary to consider
whether a 'person' who cannot own property can have a disposal of
that property for CGT purposes.

The issue was considered in the UK case of Frampton v IRC. In that
case, the trustees of Worthing Rugby Football Club sold land (vested

in them under the rules of the club) which had been used as the club sports grounds and club house. In that case, Peter Gibson J held that the UK equivalent of s.11 of the Interpretation Act 1937 (which defines 'person' in similar terms)

"requires me to read 'person' as including an unincorporated association unless the contrary intention appears, (which it did not) and...that an unincorporated association is to be treated for the statutory purpose as a person to whom gains can accrue. That means that an unincorporated association is to be treated for those purposes as a person which can itself acquire, own, and dispose of assets, including land. That is entirely in accord with the treatment of an unincorporated association as an entity of assessment for income tax purposes in respect of income".

With regard to the issue of the club being unable to own land in general law, he said.

"For income tax...an unincorporated association can be treated as an entity of assessment if it takes part in an activity no more active than having income accrue to it, for example, from investments. For capital gains tax purposes, it must take part in an activity in the sense that chargeable gains arise only on disposals. Ownership is not sufficient".

s5
s2

In the case of Revenue -v- ORMG the Supreme Court in 1983 held that two persons could not constitute a body of persons. They did not suggest what was the minimum number of persons that could constitute a body of persons. The test which the Supreme Court appeared to apply was to consider whether the ordinary usage of the words could encompass only two persons. The appeal in question was concerned with an income tax matter. TCA97 s5 defines "body of persons" for the purposes of the Capital Gains Tax Acts as having the same meaning as it has in s2 for Income Tax. Therefore the decision of the Supreme Court is valid equally for capital gains tax.

34.13   European Economic Interest Grouping

s1014

A European Economic Interest Grouping (EEIG) is a form of legal entity created under the European Union legislation, as applied in Ireland. It is designed to provide a form of legal entity which would have the same legal form in civil and tax law throughout the European Union. It combines features of a partnership with those of a company.

For Irish tax purposes (including CGT), an EEIG is treated as if it were a partnership. Accordingly, acquisitions and disposals by the EEIG are treated as acquisitions and disposals by the members (partners). Any gains or losses are apportioned between the members (partners) as if it were a partnership, and a charge to CGT arises on any member who is either resident or ordinarily resident in Ireland. Gains on 'specified assets' are, of course, chargeable on all members irrespective of their residence or ordinary residence.

The obligation to make a tax return and pay preliminary tax in respect of gains, would rest primarily with each member of the EEIG, but the EEIG itself would also have a responsibility to make an overall tax return (similar to the overall partnership return required from a partnership).

s5 The definition of "company"for CGT purposes (TCA97 s5) specifically excludes an EEIG.

35 CIUS; UCITS; UNIT TRUSTS.

35.1 Broad Overview

Collective investment undertakings **(CIU's)** is the name given to a range of investment vehicles that enable investors with relatively limited sums available for investment, to spread their investment over a large number of companies. The hope is that by so doing they will spread their risks so as to minimise the risk of losing their money. There is also the hope that by spreading their investment, they are more likely to pick a few winners.

If an individual has only about £10,000 to invest in quoted shares, it is unlikely to be worth his while to invest in more than approximately 4 companies. Minimum brokerage commissions among other factors dictate this. The investor however might wish to have exposure to a larger number of companies. This can be achieved if he gets together with a large number of other investors and they pool their moneys. This basic idea is what has given rise to collective investment undertakings.

Traditionally in Ireland the form of collective investment undertaking which was best known was the unit trust. A second form, not well known in Ireland but available principally in the UK, is the investment trust.

A unit trust is, as its name suggests, a trust. It is not a company. The trustees have an obligation to redeem the units of a unit holder at his request in return for his proportionate share of the assets of the unit trust. Because of this, the value of a unit in a unit trust cannot differ to any significant extent from the value of the proportionate share of the underlying assets.

In contrast an investment trust (despite its name) is a company. It is not obliged to redeem shares. The shareholders in it may dispose of their investment only by finding a willing purchaser. Because there is no commitment to redeem shares for a proportionate share of the underlying assets at the request of the shareholder, the market price of shares in a unit trust can and does vary (sometimes significantly) from the value of the underlying assets of the investment trust.

A unit trust is known as an open-ended vehicle. It is open-ended in the sense that its capital can increase or decrease with ease. An investment trust is an example of a closed ended vehicle i.e. its capital is relatively fixed.

Investors in mainland European countries have similar needs to those in Ireland and in the UK. The concept of a trust is not well developed in law in mainland European countries and the vehicles that developed there take the form of companies. Company law in continental countries permits certain investment companies to operate in the manner described above in relation to a unit trust i.e. redeeming its share capital for a proportionate share of assets, at the request of the shareholder. This type of company is widely known as a SICAV. The initials are those of the name of the type of company in the French language. Vehicles similar to the investment trust also developed in mainland Europe and these are known as a SICAF. As the last letter of the name suggests, capital is fixed in such a body and it does not redeem its shares at the request of the shareholder.

SI 78 of 1989   In 1985 the European Union published a directive (85/611/EC) popularly known as the "UCITS Directive". "UCITS" stands for Undertakings for Collective Investment in Transferable Securities. The directive aimed to enable UCITS formed in any member state of the European Community to be marketed freely in any other state. This directive was implemented into Irish law in 1989 by Statutory Instrument No. 78 of 1989. It has also been implemented into the domestic law of the other member states of the European Union.

The Dublin International Financial Services Center sought to attract to it collective investment undertakings, principally those who would be marketing throughout the European Union under the authority of the 1985 UCITS directive. As a result it was necessary to make provision in Irish law for forms of collective investment undertakings hitherto unknown in Ireland i.e. the SICAV and the SICAF.

Ireland now possesses the following collective investment vehicles:

- **UCITS** i.e. unit trusts, variable capital companies and fixed capital public limited companies. The variable capital company is akin to a SICAV. It can redeem its capital at will. The fixed capital public limited company has a small core of non-redeemable shares and has the bulk of its capital in issue as redeemable preference shares.

- **Authorised unit trusts.**

- **Variable capital investment companies** formed under Part XIII of the Companies Act 1990. These companies are also the equivalent of a "SICAV". They are open-ended in that they can redeem their capital at will. A designated variable capital investment company is permitted to market its shares to the public, and exists only in the IFSC. There it is free of tax. A non-designated variable capital company is not permitted to market its shares to the public. If it operates outside the IFSC, it is taxed just like an ordinary company. If it is licensed to operate in the IFSC, it would enjoy a 10% tax rate. A non-designated company managed in Shannon or the IFSC may be free of tax if all its investors are themselves vehicles for collective investment by 50 or more persons.

In the description which follows a "collective investment undertaking" (CIU) means:

- An *authorised unit trust*

- A **unit trust, variable capital company** (SICAV) or *fixed capital public limited company* formed under the UCITS regulations

- A *designated variable capital investment company* formed under Part XIII of the Companies Act 1990, or such a non-designated company, all of whose investors are vehicles for collective investment by 50 or more persons.

It does not include an investment trust, which is treated like any other investment company.

Another popular form of investment in Ireland in the past has been the so called "unit linked fund". This is the name usually given to a life assurance policy the value of which is related to the value of units in a unit trust. The investment is strictly speaking a life assurance policy and not a unit trust directly, and is dealt with in paragraphs 32.9 and 36 dealing with "Life Assurance".

The tax treatment applying to different categories of collective investment undertakings and unit holders in the various periods is subject to detailed conditions, transitional provisions and exceptions.

35.2   Historical Overview

s731(2)

The 1975 Act imposed CGT on the trustees of a unit trust in respect of gains accruing to the trustees on the disposal of trust assets. It also imposed CGT on unit holders in respect of gains arising on the disposal of units. This is now s731(2)

FA77 s35

From 1976/77 to 1988/89 inclusive the charge to CGT on the trustees and on the unit holders of certain resident registered unit trusts was at half of the rate of CGT otherwise applying.

FA88 s36

s734

The FA88 applied a 10% rate for unit trusts operating in the International Financial Services Centre in Dublin. The 1989 Provisions (referred to in next paragraph) replaced the 10% tax rate with a tax exemption, but did not impose a withholding tax obligation as it did to other CIUs. The 1993 provisions (see below) do not apply to CIUs in the IFSC, which remained subject to the 1989 provisions up to 1 April 2000..

FA89 s18

s734

The FA89 (now TCA97 s734) introduced a new tax regime for Irish resident unit trusts. This extended also to other forms of resident collective investment undertakings including UCITS. From 6 April 1990 (generally) resident collective investment undertakings (CIUs) were not liable to tax on gains arising from disposal of the CIU's assets. They were liable to account for a withholding tax at the standard rate of income tax on distributions to members, whether of income or of capital gains, and in respect of undistributed income. The withholding tax did not extend to undistributed gains. A member of a resident CIU (including a unit holder) was liable to income tax in respect of distributions from the CIU out of income subject to a credit for the tax withheld by the CIU. A member was treated as making a part disposal of his units in the CIU to the extent he received a distribution out of the gains of the CIU, again with credit for the tax withheld by the CIU. A member of a CIU was liable to CGT on disposals of units in the CIU.

s738

From 6 April 1994 (generally and subject to transitional provisions) a resident CIU was liable to CGT at the standard rate of income tax on gains arising on the disposal by it of assets. Where the CIU takes a corporate form the charge arising on it was corporation tax on companies' capital gains rather than CGT. A member (other than a company) was exempt from CGT or income tax on distributions to him of gains of the CIU and on gains arising on the disposal of units in the CIU.

If a company was chargeable to corporation tax on chargeable gains on disposals by it of units in a CIU the proceeds of disposal were treated as being after deduction of tax at the standard rate of income tax, and a credit was given to the company against the corporation tax on chargeable gains, for the deemed withholding tax.

The FA2000 introduced a new tax regime which has application from 1 April 2000 to certain collective investment undertakings only. The new regime applies only to those CIUs which first issued units on or after 1 April 2000 and also to CIUs that on 31 March 2000 were specified collective investment undertakings (ie IFSC CIUs). The new regime does not apply to collective investment undertakings (other than those in the IFSC) already existing with units in issue on 31 March 2000. Those existing CIUs remain subject to the 1994 regime described above. They remain subject to that regime not merely in relation to units already in issue at 31 March 2000 but also in relation to any units that might issue after that date.

The new regime introduced by FA2000 is described in greater detail below in paragraph 35.8. However it may be summarised as being one in which no Irish taxation is levied on either the income or the capital gains of the CIU. Neither is there a charge to tax directly on a non corporate unitholder at any point. A corporate unitholder iis chargeable totax on a grossed up amount of payments from the CIU other than on a redemption or cancellation. There is what is effectively a withholding tax operated upon any occasion on which the unitholder receives a distribution from the CIU in respect of his units, or redeems his units, or otherwise disposes of his units. This tax is levied on the CIU itself. The amount of the tax charged on the CIU (known as "the appropriate tax") varies depending upon the occasion giving rise to the charge ie whether a distribution of income, a redemption of the unit, or a disposal to a third party of the unit by the unitholder. The charge to tax on the CIU on any various events which would give rise to such a charge, does not arise in the case of certain unitholders, including a non resident who has made a suitable declaration.

The new regime therefore is one which applies an effective withholding tax to Irish residents (with certain exceptions) but not to non residents; and provides "a gross fund". The new regime enables IFSC funds to continue in operation providing tax free products to non residents without any significant change. It also enables non IFSC Irish resident CIUs to similarly provide tax free products to non residents.

s737   The FA93 introduced a special investment scheme, which is an authorised unit trust meeting certain conditions. The rate of CGT applying to gains accruing to the trustees of such a unit trust is 10% rather than the 24% rate applying to other authorised unit trusts formed before 1 April 2000 & outside the IFSC. However such a unit trust is liable to CGT both on realised gains and on unrealised gains arising on a deemed disposal of its investments at open market value on 5 April in each year. Unit holders of a special investment scheme are not liable to CGT on disposal of units in the scheme. Depending on transitional provisions, the special investment scheme applied to a unit trust from either 1993/94 or 1994/95. The FA2000 confines this special tax regime to units issued before 1 January 2001.

s740 et seq.   The FA90 introduced a new tax regime in respect of Irish resident members of a non-resident offshore fund (including a unit trust). Since 6 April 1975 a member of such a fund was liable to CGT in respect of gains arising from capital distributions from such a fund, and on disposal of units/shares in such a fund in the same manner as applied to gains generally. From 6 April 1990 a gain arising in respect of a unit/share in a non-qualifying offshore fund (broadly one which did not satisfy the Revenue Commissioners that it distributed at least 85% of its income, or meet certain other conditions) is subject to taxes on income (income tax or corporation tax as appropriate). There are transitional provisions in respect of units/shares held at 6 April 1990 by the person making a disposal. The CGT treatment of resident unit/shareholders in other distributing offshore funds remains as provided for in the original Act i.e. the unit holder/shareholder is liable to CGT on disposals of units in the normal manner. However, the rate of CGT applying is 40% and not the standard rate of 20%.

CGT treatment of Unit Trusts and CIUs - summarised

	Unit holder i4n Resident UT/CIU	Resident unit trust/CIU	Non corporate Unit holder in offshore unit trust/CIU	IFSC unit trust/ciu
1975/76	liable	liable	liable	N/A
1976/77 to 1989/90	liable at 1/2 rate	liable at 1/2 rate	liable	N/a (76/77 to 87/88) : 10% rate 88/89
1990/91 to 1993/94	liable	exempt	Income tax if non-distributing - CGT if distributing	exempt
1994/95 to 1/4/2000	exempt	liable @ 26% or 10%	as above	exempt
New Funds & all IFSC funds from 1/4/2000	exempt but WHT	exempt	as above 40% CGT rate	exempt

This chart is highly summarisedoverview of a complex area. It should not be relied on without reference to the detailed text.

35.3   Charge to CGT pre-FA89

The trustees of a resident unit trust were liable to CGT in respect of gains realised on trust assets. Where a unit holder received a capital distribution from the trust he was treated as having disposed of an interest in his units. Capital distribution means any distribution from a unit trust, including a distribution in the course of terminating the unit trust, in money or money's worth except a distribution which in the hands of the recipient constitutes income for the purposes of income tax. Gains earned by a unit trust in any year of assessment were not chargeable gains if throughout that year all the trust units were held by persons who would be exempt from CGT on disposals of their units. This did not apply if the unit holder was exempt merely because of non-residence. The exemption had to be for some other reason, e.g. if the units were held by a charity.

CGTA75 s31(3)

Units of a trust were not chargeable assets if throughout a year of assessment the assets of the trust were not chargeable assets. Irish Government stocks are an example of assets which are not chargeable assets.

Gains arising on the disposal of units were not chargeable in certain cases where the trust was operated in conjunction with life insurance policies. In this case the trustees must have been resident in Ireland at all times since 5 April 1974.

35.4   **Reduced rate of CGT for trustees - pre FA89**

CGTA75 s32(1)   For 1976/77 to 1989/90, the rate of tax payable on gains arising to the trust was reduced by HALF in the case of a unit trust

- which was a registered unit trust scheme within the meaning of s.3 of the Unit Trusts Act 1972

  and

- the trustees of which were resident and ordinarily resident in Ireland

  and

- the prices of units which were published regularly by the managers

  and

- All the units in which were of equal value and carry the same rights.

The reduced rate applied only where the following conditions were satisfied at all times since the trust was registered under the 1972 Act:

CGTA75 s32(5)   • not less than 80% of the units were held by persons who acquired them pursuant to an offer made to the general public

  and

- the number of unit holders was not less than 50 and no one unit holder was the beneficial owner of more than 5% of the units in issue at any time

  and

- the value of quoted securities held by the trustees on behalf of the unit trust was not less than 80% by value of the total trust assets, and the value of the holding in any one company did not exceed 15% by value of the total of such securities held by the trustees.

CGTA75 s32(6)   The Revenue Commissioners could treat a unit trust as qualifying for the reduced rate even if one or more of the conditions above were not satisfied, before a certain date.

35.5   **Reduced rate of CGT for Unit Holders - pre FA89**

Non-corporate unit holders in a qualifying trust also received the 50% reduction in the rate when calculating the tax payable on the disposal of their units from 1975/76 to 1989/90. A corresponding reduction in the effective rate of corporation tax applied to corporate unit holders disposing of their units in a qualifying unit trust.

35.6   CGT and CIUs — FA89 to FA93

S31 of the 1975 Act had imposed a charge to CGT on the trustees of a unit trust and provides a rule for determining whether they are resident in the State. S32 of the Act provided that in respect of qualifying unit trusts i.e. registered unit trusts meeting certain conditions (see paragraph 35.4) the rate of CGT applying to the Trustees would be half of that otherwise applying. The trustees of non-qualifying unit trusts remained liable to CGT at the full appropriate rate.

SI No 78 of 1989 SI No.78 of 1989 implemented in Ireland the E.U. Directive on undertakings for collective investment in securities (UCITS) and widened the range of available forms of collective investment beyond the existing unit trust to include variable capital companies (SICAVs).

FA89 s18(1) FA89 s18 introduced a new CGT code for collective investment undertakings (CIUs) which comprised registered unit trusts (amended to authorised unit trust by FA91) and any other UCITs authorised under S.I. No.78 of 1989.

FA89 s18(3) S18 provided that a CIU would not be liable to CGT or C.T. on any
FA89 s18(4)(b) gains accruing to it but that any unit/shareholder to whom the gains were distributed would be liable to CGT as if the distribution were a capital distribution and to the extent he would have been liable if the gains had accrued to him directly. The receipt of a capital distribution is treated by the 1975 Act as a part disposal of the units in respect of which it is received.

FA89 s18(4)(b) CGT was charged at the rates appropriate to the period in which the distribution was made and not that appropriate to the period when the gains accrued to the unit trust.

FA89 s18(5) The CIU was obliged to deduct tax at the standard income tax rate
FA89 s18(6) from distributions of income or gains, and the unit holder was entitled to credit for the withheld tax. This withholding did not apply to the cancellation, redemption or repurchase of a unit. The unit holder was treated as having received the gross payment, for the purpose of the computation of tax.

FA89 s18(5) A specified CIU, i.e. one licensed to operate in the IFSC (see paragraph 34.13) did not operate withholding tax on payments.

FA89 s18(4) A unit holder was liable to CGT at the full rate on gains arising on
FA89 s18(7) the disposal or part disposal of units.

FA89 s18(9) A distribution from a corporate CIU (e.g. a SICAV) was not treated as a distribution within the meaning of TCA97 s130.

The exemption in 1975 Act s31 for units in a unit trust which held only exempt assets (e.g. gilts unit trusts) remained available under the 1989 regime.

FA89 s18(12)   The FA89 provisions had effect from 6 April 1990 but could enter into effect in the year prior to that date for any CIU which agreed an earlier date with the Revenue Commissioners. It had effect for specified CIUs in the IFSC from 24 May 1989.

Example 188

> Go for Bust Unit Trust (an authorised unit trust resident in the State) had gains of £1,000,000 accruing to it on disposal of trust assets in the accounts year ended 31 December 1992. It distributed £500,000 of these gains to its unit holders on 31 December 1992. Joe, a resident unit holder, received 1/1000th of the distribution.
>
> The trustees were not liable to CGT on the gains. They were obliged to withhold tax on the distribution at the then standard rate of 27% and account to the Revenue for it. The deduction amounted to £135,000.
>
> Joe received £365 from the unit trust. He was deemed to receive £500, and allowed a credit for £135 tax withheld. The £500 represented a capital sum derived from his units and was a part disposal of those units. The indexed base cost of the units amounted to £7,500 and the OMV at 31 December 1992 was £10,000.

Computation:	£
Capital sum received	500

$$\frac{£500}{£10,000 + £500} \times £7,500 \ (base\ cost) \quad = \quad 357$$

	£
Taxable Gain	143
Joe's annual exemption was otherwise fully used.	
Tax payable @ 40% (1992/93 rate)	57
Less credit for tax withheld	(135)
Tax refund due to Joe	78

35.7   **CGT & CIUs - FA 1993 to FA 2000**

s738   The FA93 (now TCA97 s738) introduced a new system of CGT for resident CIUs (other than those in the IFSC) and for unit holders. Separate systems were introduced for resident CIUs generally, and for special investment schemes (see 35.11). The definition of CIU was expanded to include an *Authorised Investment Company* within the meaning of Part XIII of the Companies Act 1990 (a SICAF). Such entities exist in Ireland only in the IFSC.

TheFA95 expanded the definition to include Shannon or IFSC managed non-designated investment companies under Part XIII of the Companies Act 1990, all of whose investors are vehicles for collective investment by 50 or more non-residents.

The new regime introduced by the FA 93 continues to apply to CIUs in existence on 31 March 2000 (outside the IFSC). The regime introduced by the FA 2000 has application only to CIUs which first issued units on or after 1 April 2000, or which are in the IFSC (ie specified collective investment undertakings).

FA93 s17(2);   *The 1993 regime* applied in respect of the chargeable period of a CIU
FA93 s17(1)(c)   ending after 5 April 1994 if the CIU was carrying on a collective investment business on 25 May 1993 and otherwise in respect of any chargeable period ending after 24 May 1993. For the purpose of the new regime, a corporate CIU (e.g. a SICAV) was deemed to have ended an accounting period on 5 April 1994.

s738   *The 1993 regime* outside the IFSC (see paragraph 35.13) insofar as capital gains are concerned has the following features:

- A resident CIU is liable to CGT (or CT on company gains if a corporate CIU) on gains arising from disposals of its assets.

- A CIU operating as such on 25 May 1993 is deemed to have acquired the assets held by it on 5 April 1994 (other than exempt Government Securities) at OMV on that date. There is no corresponding deemed disposal.

- A CIU is deemed to dispose of and reacquire all of its assets (other than exempt Government Securities and strips of securities of any kind) on the last day of each chargeable period (i.e. accounting period if corporate and otherwise period of account ending in the tax year). This deemed disposal/acquisition is ignored for the purposes of identification of assets actually disposed of.

- Any gain or loss arising on the deemed disposal of assets at the end of a chargeable period is recognised as to one seventh in that period and in each period over the next 6 years. If a succeeding period is of less than a year, the amount recognised is proportionately adjusted. Any gains or losses whose recognition has been deferred in this manner are recognised in the period in which the collective investment business ceases, if they are then still unrecognised.

FA99 s87   - FA99 s87 retrospectively provided that the normal treatment applying to certain foreign currency securities on the introduction of the Euro would not apply to a CIU within the meaning of s738. The normal regime would have required a dfisposal and re-acquisition of the security on the date of introduction of the Euro (where it was denominated in a non-irish currency which became a member of the Euro). Instead the deemed disposal wuill occur at the end of the accounting period in which the changeover occurred, and will be subject to the 7 year spreading which applies to all gain or losses.

- Gains or losses on actual disposals are recognised in the period in which they occur.

  As respects disposals occurring on or after 28 March 1996, where interest is received in respect of certain securities in the year following their disposal, a part of the acquisition cost of the security equal to the amount of the interest is not deductible in the computation in the year of disposal, but is carried forward to the subsequent year, and is treated as a loss arising on the disposal of securities in that year.

s607   The securities to which this treatment applies are the exempt government and semi state securities and also securities of any body corporate not including shares.

  However insofar as the loss computed on the actual disposal (having regard to the deemed disposal and reacquisition of OMV at the beginning of the period) exceeds the true loss arising on the disposal of the asset (disregarding the deemed disposal and reacquisition at the end of each period), the excess of that artificially computed loss over the true loss is recognised as to one-seventh only in that period, and as to one-seventh in each period over the succeeding 6 years. In other words it is treated in the same manner as is a loss arising on the deemed disposal and reacquisition at the end of each accounting period. Gains or losses on actual disposals made before 28 March 1996 however are recognised in full in the period in which they occur.

- Losses on disposals which are recognised in a period are firstly set against gains recognised in the same period. They may then be set against income of the same period, to the extent not relieved against gains. Any unrelieved amount of loss is then deemed to arise in the next chargeable period.

- Indexation is not available to the CIU in the computation of gains.

- The exemption in s607 in respect of government stocks and other stocks is not available to a CIU.(see paragráph 32.1)

- Distributions by a CIU do not entitle the recipient to a credit for tax paid by the CIU.

s739   - Unitholder other than a company : Distributions by a CIU constitute neither income nor a capital sum in respect of a unit for a non-corporate recipient. The non-corporate unit holder is exempt from CGT on gains arising on a disposal of a unit in a CIU acquired after 5 April 1994. Where the unit being disposed of was held by the unit holder (or by a prior holder whose acquisition of the unit is deemed to be his) on 5 April 1994, a disposal of the unit after 5 April 1994 is within the charge to CGT. However the chargeable gain cannot exceed that which would arise if the unit had been disposed of (at the date at which it was actually disposed of) at 5 April 1994 OMV and employing 1993/94 indexation factors. Equally an allowable loss cannot be less than would have arisen on that basis. Where the substitution of 5 April 1994 OMV for actual consideration turns a gain into a loss or vice versa, the disposal is deemed to be on a no gain, no loss basis.

- Units held by a company: A company remains chargeable to corporation tax on chargeable gains in respect of the disposal of units in a CIU. The actual proceeds or consideration are treated as being after deduction of capital gains tax at a rate equal to the standard rate of income tax, and are grossed up accordingly. Credit is then given against the resulting corporation tax liability, for the notional withholding. Where the credit exceeds the actual liability on that disposal, the excess can be repaid to the company.

Transitional provisions, similar to those for non-corporate unitholders, apply to units held on 6 April 1994.

- The rate of CGT or CT on companies' capital gains applying in the computation of tax on the gains of a CIU is the same as the standard rate of income tax. Where that rate changes during the accounting period of a corporate CIU, an average rate, proportionate to the length of the parts of the period to which each rate applied, is used. A 10% rate applies to Special Investment Schemes (see 35.11).

Example 189

Go for Bust Unit Trust in the year ended 30 June 1994 disposed of shares in Diamond Mines Ltd. for £50,000 consideration. The open market value at 30 June 1993 had been £35,000 and at 5 April 1994 £40,000. The Unit Trust acquired during the year shares in Iron Mines Ltd. for £30,000, and shares in Tin Mines Ltd. for £10,000. At 30 June 1994 Iron Mines Ltd. shares were worth £39,000 and Tin Mines Ltd. were worth £8,000. The CGT liability of the Unit Trust is computed as follows:

Gains realised (Diamond Mines Ltd.) (being gain over 5/4/94 OMV)	£10,000
$1/_7$th of net gains deemed realised:	
[$1/_7$th x (gain of £9,000 less a loss of £2,000)]	£1,000
Taxable gains	£11,000
CGT @ 27%	£2,970

The 1993 regime does not apply to certain CIUs until chargeable periods ending after 5 April 1998 or ending after 5 April next following their ceasing to meet certain conditions. The excepted CIUs are those operating at 25 May 1993:

- which had invested 80% of their resources in land, or shares in Irish resident companies not quoted on the Irish Stock Exchange or USM, or

- which were index linked CIUs which made no payment to unit holders until redemption of units.

s607 As noted above, the exemption in s607 relating to certain securities did not apply to a CIU. They continued to apply to any unit trust which was not a CIU. A corresponding exemption from CGT on disposal of units in a unit trust holding solely such securities existed until 5 April 1994. It was repealed by the Finance Act 1994 from that date, but gains accrued at that date to a unit holder remained exempt. This was achieved by a deemed disposal and reacquisition at OMV on that date by unit holders in such unit trusts. Where the deemed disposal and reacquisition would cause a greater gain or smaller loss to arise on a subsequent disposal, the deemed disposal does not apply.

The 1993 regime was superceded by the FA2000 regime in respect of many (but not all) CIUs. This replacement took place at various dates depending on the nature of the CIU.

35.8 Finance Act 2000 CIU tax regime.

35.8.1 Broad Outline

FA2000 s58 The FA2000 introduced a new tax regime which has application to CIUs which first issued units on or after 1 April 2000, and to specified collective investment undertakings (ie IFSC CIUs).

s739B The new regime may be summarised briefly as being one in which:

- no Irish taxation is levied on the income or capital gains of the fund;

- a form of withholding tax levied on the fund is charged on the occasion when a unitholder (with some exceptions, principally non resident unit holders) receives a distribution from the fund, or has his units redeemed, or otherwise disposes of his units.

- A non-corporate unitholder is not directly subject to any taxation in relation to distributions from the fund, or disposals of units in the fund. A corporate resident unit holder is liable to CT on the grossed up amount of annual distributions, but not on redemptions.

The following are collective investment undertakings (CIUs) for the purpose of the FA2000 taxation regime:

- An authorised unit trust other then a Special Investment Scheme (see paragraph 35.11) or an exempt unit trust.

- A unit trust, a variable capital company (SICAV) or a fixed capital public limited company formed under the UCITS regulations of 1989.

- An authorised investment company within the meaning of Part XIII of the Companies Act 1990 provided it is authorised to sell its shares to the public, or its shareholders are exclusively other collective investors. These other collective investors would typically be a life assurance company or pension fund but can be any form of vehicles which is a collective investment vehicle with 50 or more unitholders, none of whom have contributed more than 5% of the capital.

- An investment limited partnership within the meaning of the Investment Limited Partnerships Act 1994.

- Any limited company (whether limited by shares or guarantee) wholly owned by one of the entities described above and held solely to provide limited liability protection in dealings on future contracts, option contracts, or similar financial instruments.

In order that the FA2000 regime should apply to the entities above, they must not be an offshore fund (see paragraph 35.12). Broadly that would probably require that they should be Irish resident in order to avail of the benefits of the FA2000 tax regime.

In addition to meeting the requirements set out above, the FA 2000 regime will apply to a CIU which is not a specified collective undertaking (ie one in the IFSC) only provided it first issues units on or after 1 April 2000. Therefore the regime cannot apply to CIUs existing prior to that date outside the IFSC.

The operation of appropriate tax, and the tax treatment generally of a CIU and of a unit holder under the FA2000 regime is similar to that which the Finance Act 2000 applies to life assurance.

Example 194 in paragraph 36.3 should be referred to. The example is equally valid as an illustration of the operation of the taxation system in relation to a CIU and a unit holder, as it is in relation to a life assurance company, and a policy holder. Much the same events give rise to much the same tax.

35.8.2   Taxation treatment of CIU under FA 2000

s739C   S739C exempts a CIU under the FA2000 regime from tax on income and on capital gains. The exemption in relation to income is wide but conceivably not exhaustive. The exemption applies to income which in the hands of an individual resident in the State would constitute income for the purposes of income tax.

The exemption in relation to capital gains applies to those gains which would be chargeable gains in the hands of a resident person if it is assumed that the asset being disposed of was a chargeable asset, and if it is further assumed that no exemption from capital gains tax applied.

It is difficult to think of anything which would not be exempt under the exemptions described above, but they are not expressed as a carte blanche exemption from income tax, capital gains tax, and corporation tax, in every circumstance. In practice however that is what they probably amount to.

S739C also provides an exemption from DIRT to a CIU eligible for the Finance Act 2000 regime. The exemption from DIRT is not dependent on the making of any declaration to the deposit taking institution paying the interest.

35.8.3.1   Taxation of unitholder - non corporate

s739G   The taxation of a unitholder in respect of a unit which is within the FA 2000 tax regime depends on whether the unitholder is a company (see paragraph 35.8.3.2) or another form of person eg an individual or a trust.

An individual (regardless of residence status) is not liable to income tax on any payment he receives arising out of his rights as a unitholder. Such payments would typically include distributions, and redemption proceeds.

A unitholder is also exempt from capital gains tax on any gain arising on the disposal of the unit.

The exemptions from income tax and capital gains tax described above are dependent on a charge to "appropriate tax" having arisen on the CIU on the event on which an exemption is claimed ie on the payment of a distribution, or the redemption of the unit, or the disposal of the unit by the unitholder. "Appropriate tax" is a form of withholding tax which is described below. In consequence, although no charge to tax arises on the individual unitholder, there is nonetheless an effective charge to tax at the rate of "appropriate tax".

The rate of appropriate tax can be either the standard rate of income tax, or the standard rate of income tax plus 3%, depending on the nature of the payment made to the unitholder by the CIU.

Where the payment made to the unitholder by the CIU is on the redemption or repurchase or cancellation of the units, then the rate which will apply is the standard rate of income tax plus 3%. In the year 2000/2001 that rate would equate to 25%.

Where the payment is an annually recurring payment which is not on the redemption etc of the unit, the rate of appropriate tax is the standard rate of income tax.

What has been said above can be rather crudely summarised as saying that on the final disposal of the unit, the rate applying is the higher rate of the standard rate of income tax plus 3% but on "income type distributions" from the fund, the tax rate applying is the standard rate of income tax.

One consequence of the exemption from income tax and from capital gains tax for the unitholder is that he is unable to mitigate the impact on him of "appropriate tax" by use of losses, or allowances, or other reliefs.

The tax treatment outlined above, ie an exemption from income tax and from capital gains tax, will apply only where the fund has been liable to appropriate tax on the occurring of the event in relation to which the exemption is claimed. It follows therefore that where the fund is exempt from appropriate tax in relation to the event (eg in relation to the payment of a distribution to a particular unitholder), the exemption described would not apply.

In principle, where appropriate tax has not been deducted on an occasion (eg payment of a distribution, or redemption of units) by reason of the liability to appropriate tax being zero when computed, the exemptions would not seem to apply. However in such an instance it is unlikely that any income or chargeable gain would arise in any event. It is course possible that on a disposal of a unit no appropriate tax is levied by reason of a loss arising on the disposal. In such a case arguably it is an allowable loss since no exemption from capital gains tax applies to the disposal. It is possible that the courts would hold that an appropriate tax of zero has been deducted in such a case. The matter is unclear.

Where appropriate tax is not withheld on an event, then the non corporate unitholder does not receive the exemption from income tax or capital gains tax referred to above. Where the event is the payment of a distribution by the fund or the redemption of units by the fund, the unitholder is treated as being in receipt of income chargeable to tax under Case IV of Schedule D. Where the event is a disposal of units (other than by redemption) the unitholder would be within the capital gains tax regime in the normal way as for any other chargeable asset.

It must be borne in mind that many of the unitholders in respect of whom appropriate tax is not chargeable on the fund would be entitled to other exemptions from income tax or capital gains tax generally, under other provisions of the Taxes Acts.

A non resident unitholder is one instance of a unitholder in respect of whom appropriate tax will not be charged (assuming the necessary declarations have been lodged). A specific exemption from income tax is provided to such unitholders where they are a company not resident in the State, or a person other than a company who is neither resident nor ordinarily resident in the State. A specific exemption from capital gains tax is not provided to such unitholders but it is almost inconceivable that they would be within the charge to capital gains tax anyway, since a CIU is unlikely to derive its value from specified assets (see paragraph 3.4).

35.8.3.2   **Taxation of unitholder - corporate**

If the unitholder is a company, any payment from the fund to the unitholder (other than on a redemption or buyback of units) will be treated as a sum received under deduction of income tax at the standard rate and will be charged to tax under Case IV of Schedule D on the grossed up amount. If however the company is chargeable to tax under Case I in respect of the payment from the fund (eg if the company is a dealer in securities or a bank) then the charge to tax on the grossed up amount is under Case I. Where the payment from the fund is in respect of the cancellation or redemption or repurchase of the units by the fund, the amount treated as income under Case I is reduced by the consideration given by the company to acquire the units. Nonetheless, a grossing up of the sum paid by the fund takes place and it is from the grossed up sum that the acquisition cost of the units is deducted.

The company will receive a credit for the notional withholding tax in respect of which the payments were grossed up. Where this notional withholding tax exceeds the company's liability to corporation tax for the period, the excess is refundable.

Where a company disposes of a unit provided appropriate tax has been levied on the fund on the disposal there will be no further charge to tax on the company. However this treatment does not apply if the company is a Case I dealer in respect of the units. In such a case the treatment will be as described above for a Case I dealer ie the total payment is grossed up, a deduction is available for the acquisition cost, and the net amount is chargeable under Case I, with credit for withholding tax.

Where the unitholder is a company, but appropriate tax has not been levied on the event (whether it be payment of a distribution, redemption or disposal) the sum received by the unitholder is treated as income arising under Case IV of Schedule D. There is no grossing up here (there having been no appropriate tax levied). Neither is there any provision for the deduction of the acquisition cost, where the event is the disposal of a unit.

It should be noted that where grossing up occurs above, the sum added to that which is received by the unitholder, in order to achieve the grossing up, is not necessarily the amount of the appropriate tax levied on the fund. Rather it is computed by reference to the standard rate of income tax, and by reference to the sum received. As will be seen in the discussion below on "appropriate tax", that tax is leviable at the rate of 3% in excess of the standard rate of income tax, and it is not always levied on the sum received.

As a broad overview of what has been said above:

- a corporate unit holder is liable to corporation tax on the grossed up amount of "distributions of an income type". Credit is given for appropriate tax deducted.

- a corporate unit holder is not liable to corporation tax on companies capital gains and sums received on the redemption, repayment, or repurchase or other disposal of a unit provided appropriate tax has been applied.

- a company which is a Case I dealer in securities is liable to corporation tax on Case I income on the occasion of the disposal of a unit. The amount taken into account is the grossed up amount, and credit is given for the appropriate tax.

35.8.4   **Taxation of the fund**

s739C   A CIU to which the FA2000 applies is not liable to tax on either its income arising to it, or on capital gains arising to it. It is therefore what is normally known as a "gross fund".

s739D   The only charge to tax which arises on the CIU under FA2000 is what is called "appropriate tax". This in reality, if not in strict form, is a withholding tax. It applies to all payments made by the fund to the unitholder, whether distributions out of income and gains, or redemption or repurchase of units. It also applies on the occasion of the unitholder assigning his units to another person (other than a repurchase or redemption by the fund).

The rate of appropriate tax can be either the standard rate of income tax, or the standard rate of income tax plus 3%, depending on the nature of the payment made to the unitholder by the CIU.

Where the payment made to the unitholder by the CIU is on the redemption or repurchase or cancellation of the units, then the rate which will apply is the standard rate of income tax plus 3%. In the year 2000/2001 that rate would equate to 25%.

Where the payment is an annually recurring payment which is not on the redemption etc of the unit, the rate of appropriate tax is the standard rate of income tax.

What has been said above can be rather crudely summarised as saying that on the final disposal of the unit, the rate applying is the higher rate of the standard rate of income tax plus 3% but on "income type distributions" from the fund, the tax rate applying is the standard rate of income tax.

s739E   The amount upon which appropriate tax is levied can vary depending on the event which causes it to be levied. These are described below.

- **Payments by the CIU to the unitholder other than on redemption, repurchase etc.**

  The appropriate tax is charged on the amount of the payment.

- **Payments by the CIU on the occasion of repurchase or redemption of units.**

  In this instance the amount on which the appropriate tax is levied depends on whether or not the CIU has made an election on behalf of all of its unitholders that first in first out rules will apply to identify the units being disposed of by a unitholder. This election must be made at the time the CIU is set up, or, where it existed at 31 March 2000 and was a specified collective investment undertaking then (ie an IFSC CIU) the election must be made on 1 April 2000. The election is irrevocable. A CIU is not obliged to make the election.

  Where the election has been made, appropriate tax is levied on the amount of the payment by the CIU to the unitholder but after deducting from it either the sum subscribed by the unit holder to the CIU to obtain the unit or, where he otherwise obtained the unit, the market value at the date he acquired it. In effect, it is the gain over acquisition cost/acquisition value that is subject to the appropriate tax. No question of indexation arises in computing the amount subject to appropriate tax.

  If the election has not been made, the amount on which appropriate tax is calculated is the payment by the CIU to the unitholder reduced once again by his acquisition cost/market value. However in this case the acquisition cost/market value is not computed by reference to the historic facts of a specific unit, but rather is computed on the average of all of the units held by the person immediately prior to the repurchase, redemption etc. The deduction is a part of the total acquisition cost/market value at acquisition of all the units held by the unitholder at the date of the redemption, equal to the proportion of the number of units being redeemed etc, compared to the total number of units held prior to redemption.

  The formula described seems to proceed on the assumption that all units in a CIU are identical. If they are not, the formula would produce unexpected results.

- **Transfer by unitholder of his units to another person.**

  Once again the amount by reference to which appropriate tax is calculated depends on whether or not an election for the application of the FIFO rules to identify the units being disposed of, has been made. This election has been described above.

  Where the election has been made the redemption, repurchase etc can be identified as being in relation to specific units acquired at specific dates, in specific circumstances. Therefore the sum which is deductible from the payment by the CIU will be either the sum subscribed by the unitholder to obtain those units, or, where he acquired them otherwise than by subscription, the market value at the date of acquisition.

Where the election has not been made the deduction from the sum paid by the CIU is again computed as being the average of the cost/market value of the units acquired by him. The calculation proceeds as described above on the occasion of a redemption, where an election has not been made.

As can be seen from the description above, appropriate tax arises as a charge on a CIU on the occasion of distributions by it, redemptions by it, or assignments of units by unitholders. These events will not give rise to appropriate tax where they are in respect of certain classes of unitholders:

- A pension scheme which has made an appropriate declaration.

- A life assurance company which has made an appropriate declaration.

- Another CIU which has made an appropriate declaration.

- A special investment scheme (see paragraph 35.11) which has made an appropriate declaration.

- An exempt unit trust under s731(5)(a) which has made an appropriate declaration.

- A charity which is exempt from tax under s297(1)(b) which has made a suitable declaration.

- An IFSC licensed management company of a CIU in the IFSC or Shannon or an other licences IFSC or Shannon operator which has made a suitable declaration.

- An ARF or an AMRF (see paragraph 32.4) which has made a suitable declaration.

- A non resident person who has made a suitable declaration, where the CIU has no reason to believe it to be incorrect.

- A unitholder in a CIU which was a specified collective investment undertaking in the IFSC at 31 March 2000 and the unitholder was a unitholder at that date, and the unitholder has made a declaration to the effect that all of the unitholders at that date were non residents.

- An intermediary on behalf of a non resident who has made a declaration that the beneficial owner is a non resident, and where the CIU has no reason to believe it to be incorrect.

A CIU on whom appropriate tax has been levied is entitled to deduct it from the amount of a payment to the unitholder, where the chargeable event is such a payment. Where the chargeable event is an assignment of units by the unitholder the CIU is entitled to cancel part of his units equivalent in value to the appropriate tax. Therefore while appropriate tax is charged on the CIU, it is effectively borne by the unitholder.

35.8.4.1   **Returns and payment of tax by a CIU**

A CIU must make two returns in relation to appropriate tax each year. One return must be made on 30 July (covering the six months to 30 June) and the second must be made on 30 January covering the six months to 31 December. The return must be made whether or not appropriate tax has become payable. The appropriate tax itself is payable on the due date of the return, in respect of the six month period in which it arose. There is provision for the raising of assessments and for appeal in the normal fashion. Overdue appropriate tax carries interest at the rate of 1% per month.

The return of appropriate tax must be in a form prescribed by the Revenue Commissioners. The various declarations referred to above must all be in a form set out in Schedule 2B TCA 97.

There is provision that an exchange of units by a unitholder on the occasion of a reconstruction or amalgamation of CIUs will not be treated as the occasion of a disposal triggering appropriate tax, as described above.

35.8.5   **IFSC funds**

s739D   FA2000 makes provision for the possibility that an IFSC fund had resident unitholders. As this is a matter of very little interest in most cases, it will not be described in any detail here. An appropriate tax charge will arise at the rate of 40% to a CIU in respect of such resident unitholders, as at 31 December 2000. The charge is on the excess of the value of the units at that date over the sums subscribed to acquire them, or the market value at date of acquisition, where they were otherwise acquired. There are certain unitholders who are exempt in respect of this charge.

35.9   **Residence of trustees**

s731(3)   The trustees are regarded as a body of persons separate from the individuals who from time to time fill the position of trustees. That body will be deemed to be resident and ordinarily resident in Ireland unless:

- the general administration of the trust is carried on outside Ireland

  and

- the trustees or a majority of them for the time being are not resident or not ordinarily resident in Ireland.

The residence of trustees is dealt with in more detail in paragraph 65.3.

35.10   **CIUs and Life Assurance**

s731(6)   S. 31(5A), 1975 Act exempted gains on units in certain resident unit trusts owned by life assurance companies from the tax year 1976/77. The exemption was preserved by s.35, FA 1990 with effect from 6 April 1990 (which was the date from which the Finance Act 1989 provisions relating to CIUs had effect, generally) by excluding such a CIU from the 1989 regime. It is now in s731(6).

FA92 s36   Such a CIU was permitted to elect into the 1989 regime from 1 April 1992 on payment of the CGT (at half the appropriate rate) that would have arisen if they disposed of their assets at OMV at 31 March 1992. The election had to be made by 1 November 1992.

A CIU which was excluded from the 1989 regime in this manner remained under the 1975/76 regime which applied from 1975/76 i.e. the CIU was liable to CGT at half the appropriate rate.

A CIU owned by a life assurance company (whether or not it had elected into the 1989 regime) became liable to the 1993 regime in the same way as any other CIU.

35.11   **Special Investment Schemes**

s737   Special investment schemes (SIS) are a class of authorised unit trusts, and are one of four special savings products created by the Finance Act 1993. These four savings products were introduced on the final ending of exchange controls to persuade investors to retain funds within Ireland. Three of the four products now attract a 20% rate of tax (the special deposit account is now taxed at 15%) and all are related in that the limits to the amount which an individual may invest in them is related partly to his total investment in all of them.

Special investment schemes will effectively come to an end from 1 January 2001. This has been brought about by an amendment to s737 by the FA2000. The amendment changed the definition of the special investment unit and confined it to units issued between 1 February 1993 and 1 January 2001. It follows therefore that units issued from 1 January 2001 will no longer attract the tax treatment described below as applicable to special investment schemes. However the FA2000, which made major amendments to the treatment of collective investment undertakings generally, did not end the tax regime described below in so far as it applies to special investment schemes existing on 1 January 2001. They will continue to be subject to the tax regime described below, notwithstanding that they may issue no new units which are subject to this tax regime.

The CGT treatment described in paragraph 35.7 relating to CIUs generally does not apply to a *special investment scheme*. Its CGT treatment is however similar in many respects.

- The SIS is liable to CGT on gains arising on disposal of its assets, at a rate of 10%up to 6/4/1999 and at a rate of 20% thereafter.

- An SIS is deemed to dispose of and immediately reacquire all of its assets, on 5 April in each year, at OMV. This extends to Government securities. The deemed disposal is ignored for the purposes of identification of assets actually disposed of.

- Any gain or loss arising in a period on the annual deemed disposal of the assets of an SIS is recognised in that period (and not over seven years as in other CIUs)

- Gains and losses on actual disposal are recognised as they occur. However, as respects disposals occurring on or after 28 March 1996, where interest is received in respect of certain securities in the year following their disposal, a part of the acquisition cost of the security equal to the amount of the interest is not deductible in the computation in the year of disposal, but is carried forward to the subsequent year, and is treated as a loss arising on the disposal of securities in that year.

s607   The securities to which this treatment applies are the exempt government and semi state securities and also securities of any body corporate not including shares.

- Losses are relieved firstly against gains in the same period. They may then be relieved against income of the same period. Any unrelieved losses are deemed to accrue in the next period.

- Indexation is not available to an SIS.

- The government stocks exemption in s607 is not available to an SIS.(see paragraph 32.1)

- An SIS is not liable to CGT on gains arising from eligible shares in qualifying companies for the purposes of the BES scheme. However losses on such shares are allowable.

- A unit holder in an SIS is not liable to CGT on disposal of his units or receipt of capital distributions from it. Neither is he entitled to any credit for tax paid by the SIS.

The conditions which must be complied with by an SIS, and the limits on the amount which may be invested by an individual are not described in this book. These details are described in Income Tax, by McAteer & Reddin, published by the Institute of Taxation in Ireland, and a companion volume of this book.

Example 190

> Go for Bust Unit Trust is a Special Investment Scheme. The facts are as in **example 189** above. The computation for the year ended 30 June 1994 is as follows:
>
> | | |
> |---|---:|
> | Realised gains | £10,000 |
> | Unrealised gains less unrealised losses | £7,000 |
> | Taxable gains | £17,000 |
> | | |
> | Tax at 10% | £1,700 |

35.12   Offshore funds

35.12.1   Broad outline

The liability to Irish CGT of a unit trust or corporate collective investment undertaking which is not resident in the State is as described in relation to any non-resident person in paragraph 3.4.

In principle a resident or ordinarily resident unit holder or shareholder in such a non-resident entity is liable to CGT (or C.T. on companies' capital gains as the case may be) on gains arising on the disposal or part disposal of his units or shares as he is on assets generally. There are particular features relating to the computation of gains or interests in offshore funds which are described in paragraph 35.12 below.

The CGT treatment described in paragraphs 35.01 to 35.10 inclusive does not apply to a collective investment undertaking not resident in the State, or to a unit holder in such a body.

As a very broad overview, it may be said that the special rules introduced in 1990, and as amended in 1998, as they apply to offshore funds have the consequence that :

- the post 1990 gains arising in respect of some offshore funds are charged to income tax, and there are special measures to ensure that double taxation does not occur when a charge to CGT might arise in the normal way on the disposal of an interest in those funds and

- the rate of CGT applying on disposals after 12 February 1998 on the disposal of an interest in an offshore fund which is not such an interest as exposed the holder to an income tax charge on a disposal, is 40%. This applies in place of the standard rate of CGT (presently 20%).

FA98 s66 The 40% rate of CGT referred to above is introduced by FA 1998 on the occasion on which it reduced the standard rate of CGT to 20%. It may seem paradoxical that such a penal rate should be applied to the disposal of an interest in a fund which is exempt from the income tax charge on disposals e.g. because it distributes its income. Such "distributing funds" hitherto seem to be regarded by the Revenue authorities as "good funds" and were not penalised. The explanation as to why they should be singled out for the 40% rate of CGT (while in principle what the Revenue authorities might regard as a "bad fund" i.e. a non distributing fund, attracts only a 20% rate on disposal of an interest), may lie on the fact that it is most unlikely that a CGT charge would arise in relation to a post 1990 gain on the holding of an interest in a non distributing offshore fund - a "bad fund". Such a gain is likely to be liable to income tax, and the amount charged to income tax is not also chargeable to CGT. Accordingly, insofar as gains arise post 1990, they are likely to arise only in relation to distributing offshore funds i.e. the "good funds". They in turn are now penalised, as the non distributing funds were in 1990, but in a different fashion.

The 40% CGT applies to a disposal of a material interest in a distributing offshore fund where the disposal takes place on or after 12 February 1998, even if the gain had largely arisen (in an economic sense as oppose to a tax sense) prior to that date.

The 40% rate also applies to the disposal of an interest in a resident company, or in a resident unit trust, if at any time on or after the later of

- 1 January 1991, or

- the time when the interest was acquired,

the company, or the unit trust as the case may be, had been a distributing offshore fund at a time when the interest in it constituted a material interest in the fund.

This rule ensures that the 40% rate of CGT cannot be avoided by causing a non resident fund to become resident, prior to the disposal of interests in it. Any period of non residence after the 1 January 1991 (or the date in which the taxpayer required his interest if later) is sufficient to ensure that the 40% CGT rate will apply on the disposal of a material interest by the taxpayer. As explained below, in certain circumstance an offshore fund can include a non resident company.

35.12.2   Charge To Income Tax

s747

The FA90 imposed (in what is now s747) a charge to **income tax** on all or part of the gains arising on the disposal of a **material interest** in certain non-resident CIUs (offshore funds) and thus affected the computation of CGT on the same disposal.

s743(1)

An offshore fund is any of:

— a non-resident company

— a non-resident unit trust

— any other foreign co-ownership arrangement, or similar arrangement under foreign law.

35.12.3   Material Interest

s743

A material interest in such an offshore fund is one where the holder, at the date of acquisition could reasonably expect to realise within seven years from his holding an amount equal to his proportionate share of the fund's assets. In very broad terms, an interest consisting of a loan; a life assurance policy; a shareholding held for trade reasons and meeting other conditions; or a plus 50% shareholding is not a material interest.

In the case of a shareholding in a company the conditions to be a material interest (which is not directly related to the size of the holding) could be met where the shares are redeemable at the shareholders option; or are subject to a put option at an appropriate price; or where an agreement exists to liquidate the company within seven years. These circumstances are not exhaustive.

Example 191

John has decided to invest in central and eastern European "emerging markets". Because he does not have a large amount of capital with which to invest, and because his stock broker is reluctant to undertake direct investment in eastern European equities, John decides instead to invest in a unit trust which specialises in investment in those equities. It is the Magic Management Commissar Fund, which is structured as a unit trust, the trustees of which are resident in Luxembourg.

John invests only £5000 in the fund, the total assets of which amount to £75m. The rules of the fund which are set out in the trust deed of the unit fund provide that the trustees are obliged to repurchase a unit holders units, at the request of the unit holder at any time, for a consideration equal the unit holders proportionate entitlement in the total value of the fund at that time.

Notwithstanding that John's interest in the Luxembourg fund is infinitesimally small, his holding is a "material interest" because it is an interest which gives him the right to realise his proportionate share of the funds assets within seven years from the date of his acquiring his holding.

Generally speaking, most unit trusts and other collective investment undertaking are structured so as to grant to the unit holder the right to require the fund to buy out his interest at any time, for his proportionate share of the funds assets. Therefore all holdings in funds which are structured in that way, are material holdings for the purposes of the legislation. One exception to this is the closed ended type fund, of which the type most familiar to Irish investors is likely to be the UK investment trust vehicle. Although an investment trust is designed to enable "small investors" to spread their investment over a very large range of quoted securities, and although it therefore fulfills the same function as a unit trust, it is usually in a corporate form (notwithstanding the name "investment trust") and does not undertake to buy back or redeem its shares on demand. Usually it is quoted on the stock exchange and the share holder disposes of his interest by selling them at the going market price. For various reasons that market price traditionally is at a discount on the asset value of the investment trust at the time. Because the share/unit holder in an investment trust is dependent on there being another willing purchaser in the market place for his shares, in order that he may realise his investment, he does not have the assurance that he can realise his proportionate share of the assets within a seven year period from the date of acquisition. His holding therefore would not be a material interest.

In continental countries, there is a vehicle similar the to UK investment trust which is usually referred to as a SICAF. Such a vehicle is usually not obliged to buy back or redeem shares at the option of the unit holder. In contrast, continental SICAVs are akin to unit trusts and usually are obliged to buy back or redeem the unit holder's interest at his request. An interest in a SICAF will therefore usually not be a material interest, and a holding in a SICAV usually will be a material interest, but in order to determine the matter in any particular instance regard should be had to the rules governing the vehicle.

Example 192

John, Pat and Mike are business acquaintances who have substantial experience in the retail trade in Ireland. They have decided to go into a joint venture in order to develop an amusement arcade and casino in Douglas in the Isle of Man. It is their intention, once the venture is successfully established, to attempt to sell it, most likely to a major UK quoted company in the gambling/leisure sector. The parties have therefore agreed on setting up a company through which to carry out the investment, that at the end of a five year period the company will be liquidated and the proceeds of liquidation distributed equally between the members.

The company, Casino Ltd., has a board of directors consisting of John, Pat and Mike, and also an Isle of Man resident managing director, and a non executive director resident in the UK who has particular expertise in the gambling/leisure sector. For convenience the board meets only in the Isle of Man, and the company is therefore resident in the Isle of Man, and not resident in Ireland.

Because John, Patrick, and Mike, may reasonably expect (by reason of their agreement to liquidate after 5 years) to realise their proportionate share of the assets of Casino Ltd., a non resident company, within seven years of setting up the company, Casino Ltd. is an offshore fund. The share holding of each of the three share holders is a material interest.

As explained in paragraph 35.12 below, the consequences of a holding in an offshore entity being regarded as a material interest in an offshore fund are very significant from an overall tax view point (by reason of an income tax charge being imposed on gains) and by reason of the fact that the CGT computation is quite different to the computation you would normally expect on the disposal of the share.

35.12.4   Qualifying Fund:

The income tax charge is applied only to the disposal of a material interest in a fund which the Revenue Commissioners do not certify to be a non-qualifying fund. To be certified a fund must meet several conditions principally the distribution of at least 85% of its profits. The conditions for certification are considered in greater detail in the companion volume Income Tax by McAteer & Reddin.

s744

For convenience, an offshore fund which is not certified to be non-qualifying is referred to in this chapter (though not in the Capital Gains Tax Acts) as a qualifying fund.

- **Revenue Commissioners published precedent:**

— In a published Revenue precedent, the Revenue Commissioners state *"An offshore fund would qualify for certification as a distributing fund not withstanding the fact that no distribution is made and the fund has a nominal level of income, where the level of income does not exceed 1% of the average value of the fund's assets held during the accounting period."*

35.12.5   Tax on Gain:

s745
Sch20

Income tax is chargeable on any part of the gain arising on the disposal of a material interest in a qualifying fund which is an offshore income gain (a gain chargeable to income tax). An offshore income gain is computed in the same manner as a capital gain on the disposal of the material interest but without benefit of indexation. For this purpose interests held at 6 April 1990 are deemed to have been acquired on that date at OMV, thus excluding gains arising before that date from the income tax charge.

s747

The amount of the offshore income gain is deducted from the consideration for the disposal in the *CGT* computation. In the case of an interest acquired after 6 April 1990 this will in every case result in a no gain no loss result. In the case of an interest held at 6 April 1990, there may be a capital gain or allowable loss resulting. By reason of the offshore income gain being calculated on an unindexed basis it will exceed the true indexed gain arising after 6 April 1990. As a result part of the pre 6 April 1990 gain is subjected to income tax rather than CGT, and not only the post 6 April 1990 gain.

- **Revenue Commissioners published precedent :**

— A published Revenue precedent indicates that where a disposal of a material interest in an undistributing offshore fund is made by a trust, it is the trustees and not any beneficiary who is liable to tax under s745. This is on the basis that the gain arising from the disposal is capital in nature and is not available for distribution to a beneficiary whose interest is confined to the income of a fund (ie a life tenant or a tenant for a limited period is not assessable).

35.12.6   Shares held by non-resident entities

s590 | S590 (see paragraph 67) is unlikely to apply to a non-resident corporate collective investment undertaking (e.g. a Luxembourg resident SICAV) since it has application only to a company which would be a close company if resident in the State.

s746 | The application of s590 to a non-resident close company which holds units in a qualifying offshore fund is amended so that it may attribute an offshore income gain arising to the non-resident close company, to a resident shareholder, in the same manner that it may attribute a capital gain.

s579 | S579 (see paragraph 68) does not apply to a unit holder in a non-resident unit trust since, although a trust, it is not a settlement because it lacks an element of bounty (see paragraph 65.4).

s746 | S579 may apply to a non-resident settlement holding units in a qualifying offshore fund so as to attribute the offshore income gain to a beneficiary, in the same manner as it would apply in the case of a capital gain.

35.13   Unit Trusts an CIUs in the IFSC

As described in paragraph 35.8 above FA 2000 introduced a new regime for collective investment undertakings. That new regime extends to specified collective investment undertakings (defined below) within the IFSC existing on 31 March 2000, or created thereafter. Accordingly s451 and s734, which previously had application to the taxation of a specified collective investment undertaking, will not have effect in relation to them from 1 April 2000.

s739B Insofar as a CIU has solely non resident unitholders, the new F2000 regime does not provide any significantly different tax regime to that which previously applied. It provides a gross (ie exempt from Irish tax) fund, with complete exemptions from Irish tax for the unitholder in relation to his holding of units.

The regime applying up to 1 April 2000 is described below. The treatment from 1 April 2000 is described in paragraph 35.8.

s451 S451 made special provision for certain unit trusts and life assurance businesses operating in the IFSC. The subsection applies to a life assurance company based in the IFSC engaged in life assurance business with policy holders and annuitants who reside outside Ireland and to a unit trust

(i)   registered under the 1972 Act,

(ii)   the business of which is carried on in the Customs House Docks Area (CHDA) or is carried on in Ireland and would be carried on in the CHDA but for circumstances outside the control of the persons carrying on the business and

(iii) whose unit holders are persons resident outside the state.

(iv)   which is issued a certificate by the Minister for Finance.

Under s451, the rate of capital gains tax (before credit for foreign tax) on chargeable gains accruing from securities or possessions in any place outside Ireland which are investments of such a life assurance business or investments of such a unit trust was not to exceed 10%.

S734 *exempted* a Specified Collective Investment Undertaking *(an SCIU)* from Irish tax on income and on gains.

s734 A SCIU is a body meeting the following requirements:

1.   It is either an authorised unit trust; a UCITS; an authorised investment company designated to raise capital from the public; or an authorised investment company not designated to raise capital from the public but all of whose investors are themselves vehicles for collective investment by 50 or more persons, including a life assurance company or pension fund.

2.   Most of its business in the State is carried on in the IFSC or Shannon either by itself or a licensed management company.

3.   All of its unit holders are non-resident in the State, save for the undertaking itself if it holds its own units or its management company if it holds units.

FA98 s42 With affect from 28 March 1998 unitholders may also include an IFSC licenced company, or a Shannon licensed company carrying on operations which would qualify for an IFSC certificate and not more than 25% of whose share capital is owned directly or indirectly by persons resident in the State.

s738
FA93 s17 (now TCA97 s738) which introduced the tax regime which currently applies to collective investment undertakings generally does not apply to an SCIU.

s734(9)
Distributions by a corporate SCIU were not treated as distributions within the meaning of TCA97 s130.

A unit holder in an SCIU did not enjoy an exemption from CGT in respect of his units. However having regard to the requirement that he should be a non-resident, and having regard to the restricted investment policies of an SCIU, a liability to CGT is unlikely to arise, even in theory.

An *authorised investment company* formed under Part XIII of the Companies Act 1990 may be licensed to operate in the IFSC even if not designated. Such a company would be a private investment vehicle. Such a non-designated authorised company is liable to corporation tax at the 10% rate on its trading income. Insofar as it had any capital gains (e.g. from activities outside its IFSC licence) it would be liable to corporation tax on such gains at the normal rates, currently (effectively) 20% or 40%. In practice such a company is unlikely to have any gains of a capital nature.

s734(1)
The FA95 introduced an exception to this rule (now TCA97 s734(1)(a)(c)). A non-designated company managed in Shannon or the IFSC, all of whose investors are vehicles for collective investment by 50 or more non-residents, or are life assurance companies, or pension funds, were treated as if they were designated - i.e. tax free.

FA98 s42
FA98 s42 relaxed the requirement that investors should be non residents etc., and extended the class of persons who can hold units/shares to resident persons provided they do not hold more than 25% of the share capital, whether directly or indirectly or through an Irish resident company.

• **Revenue Commissioners published precedent:**

A number of published Revenue precedents refer to specified collective investment undertakings in the context of s734.

— A Lloyds syndicate with Irish resident members may invest in SCIU without damage to its exempt status.

— Where the units in the SCIU are held for non residents by an Irish resident nominee company, the exempt status will not be affected provided the nominee company is in the business of holding shares in a nominee capacity and advance approval is received from the Revenue Commissioners.

— Take-over of a foreign fund which has Irish resident investors would not prejudice the tax exempt status of an SCIU provided the Irish investors are removed from the fund within three months of the date of the take-over.

35.14   **CIUs and double tax agreements**

FA89 s18(10)
FA93 s20

The FA89, by deeming for the purpose of double tax agreements a CIU to be neither resident nor liable to tax in the State, deprived a CIU of the benefit of some, but not all, of the double tax agreements entered into by the State. The effect of the deeming provision depended on the wording of each treaty. This deeming provision was repealed by the FA93.

The entitlement of a CIU to claim the benefits of a double tax agreement now depends upon the wording of each separate double tax agreement, and also to the attitude of the Revenue Authorities in the other treaty State. Some States accept that a CIU is a person capable of obtaining treaty benefits, whereas others take the position that it is a transparent body whose members should claim treaty protection (if they are entitled). In practice, due to the multiplicity of members in most CIUs it is impractical for individual unit holders to claim the treaty benefits.

A corporate CIU is in principle entitled to the benefits of the unilateral tax credit introduced by the FA98 (TCA 97 Sch24, Para9A and Para9B). However it would be entitled to the unilateral tax credit only if it received a dividend from a company in which it had at least a 25% shareholding. That would be an unusual situation for most CIUs.

35.15   **Reorganisations and a CIU**

s584

A CIU may take the form of a unit trust or of a company. The reorganisation provisions of s584 were always capable of application to a corporate CIU e.g. on the occasion of a rights issue, bonus issue or change of rights.

s733

FA90 s87 (now s733) extended this treatment to authorised unit trusts and to unit trusts organised under the 1989 UCITS Regulations (SI No78 of 1989). This is likely to be relevant principally to umbrella funds, which encompass several sub-funds. The provisions of s584 relating to conversion of securities, company amalgamations, and company reconstructions are not similarly extended.

S739H (inserted by FA 2000) introduces a further capital gains tax relief for a reconstruction or amalgamation of:

- any authorised unit trust

- UCITS created under the UCITS regulations

- authorised investment company under Part XIII of the Companies Act

- or investment limited partnership within the meaning of the 1994 Act and

- any limited company owned by such used solely to transact futures contracts, options contracts, or other financial instruments with similar risk characteristics, and not being an offshore fund.

s739H

S739H provides relief in respect of a "share for undertaking three party swap". In other words it provides a deferral for the fund of capital gains tax where one of the funds described above issues units to the unitholders of another of the funds described above, in return for the fund transferring to it all of the undertaking of the second mentioned fund.

35.16   Unauthorised unit trusts

s731

The treatment of authorised or registered unit trusts is described above in paragraph 35.1, and following paragraphs. It is possible to have another category of unit trust, which is not an authorised or registered unit trust. The treatment of such a unit trust is governed by s731. That section sets out a code of treatment for unit trusts which are not authorised/registered unit trusts.

s5(1)

A unit trust, for the purposes of s731, is defined in s5(1). It will exist where there are the following features:

- There is a property held by a trustee in trust.

- The interests of the beneficiaries in the assets of the trusts are divided into units which are held by unitholders.

- The trust represents an arrangement made for the purpose, or having the affect, of enabling the unitholders to participate in the profits or income from the property held by the trust.

Despite the formal language of the definition, it is evident that the unit trust can come into existence relatively simply. It requires no more than that property be vested in a trustee on behalf of a number of people, and that the interests of those people in the property be divided into units. Such an arrangement can come about without any necessity of registration or approval under the Unit Trust Acts. It can come about as a result of private arrangements between companies or individuals.

s574; s567

Before considering the rules laid down by s731 for the treatment of unauthorised/unregistered unit trusts, it is as well to remember some other provisions of the Capital Gains Tax Acts relating to trusts.

1.   S574 through to s578 sets out a comprehensive code under which settlements (i.e. trusts with an element of bounty) are taxed. That code is relatively self-contained, and provides a different tax regime than would apply generally. In most cases, a unit trust would not constitute a settlement, and accordingly

would not be governed by those sections. Although a unit trust will always be a trust, it usually does not have an element of bounty, but is a purely commercial arrangement between the unitholders, and between the unitholders and the trustee. It is not usually intended to confer a benefit on anybody in a gratuitous manner.

2.   S567(2) provides that the actions of a nominee i.e. a bare trustee are to be treated as the actions of any person on whose behalf he acts. Generally, a nominee is not a taxable person in himself and it is the person on whose behalf he acts that is the taxable person in relation to the nominee's actions. Transfers from a person to a nominee on his behalf, or from a nominee to the person for whom he is acting, are not regarded as disposals, or acquisitions, for the purposes of the Acts. This treatment applies in any instance where a person is absolutely entitled as against the trustee. S567(1) defines the circumstances in which a person is to be regarded as absolutely entitled against a trustee. Those circumstances are that the person has the exclusive right to direct the trustee as to how the asset should be dealt with.

A unitholder in a unit trust will generally not be absolutely entitled as against the trustee of the unit trust, and accordingly the trustee of a unit trust is not a nominee for a unitholder. A unitholder is not absolutely entitled against a trustee because he would usually not have the exclusive right to direct the trustee as to how to deal with an asset. Generally, the assets of a unit trust are held by the trustee under trust to sell those assets and to distribute the proceeds amongst the unitholders in accordance with their entitlements. The unitholders would not have any particular rights to direct the trustee as to how to deal with any particular asset in the trust, notwithstanding that on a winding up of the trust they would be entitled to have a proportionate share of the proceeds of sale of the assets returned to them.

s731   S731 should be read against that background.

The trustees of an unauthorised unit trust are to be treated for capital gains tax purposes as a single and continuing body of persons. The consequence of this is that changes in the identity of the trustees are without capital gains tax implications. If a trustee resigns and is replaced by a new trustee, a transfer of asset from one to the other does not constitute a disposal of assets by the retiring trustee, or an acquisition of assets by the incoming trustee. For capital gains tax purposes the transaction has no significance.

As the trustees are treated as a body of persons, the rules relating to their residence do not follow directly from the residence of the trustees in their private capacity. The body of trustees is treated as being resident, and as being ordinarily resident in the State unless certain conditions are fulfilled. Those conditions are:

- that the general administration of the unit trust be ordinarily carried on outside the State and;

- the trustee or a majority of them for the time being are not resident, or ordinarily resident in the State.

As can be seen, the fact that some of the trustees are resident in the State will not make the trustees, as a body, resident in the state provided a majority of the trustees are not so resident, and provided the general administration of the trust is carried on outside the State. Both conditions must be met in order that the trustees should be neither resident nor ordinarily resident in the State. Even where the administration of an unauthorised unit trust is carried on outside the State, it can be become resident within the State on the occasion of the resignation of trustees or the appointment of new trustees, or the death of an individual trustee, if those events upset a balance of residence of the trustees.

An unauthorised unit trust is a taxable entity in itself for the purposes of capital gains tax. The trustees are liable to capital gains tax in respect of chargeable gains accruing to the unit trust in any year of assessment. Obviously their liability to capital gains tax is dependent on their being within the territorial scope of capital gains tax i.e. on their residence status as a body, or their ordinary residence status, and on the question (where they are not resident or ordinarily resident) of whether the assets being disposed are specified assets. The territorial scope of capital gains tax is discussed in paragraph 3.

Where chargeable gains arise on a disposal by the trustees of trust assets, it is the trustees, and not the unitholders, who are chargeable to capital gains tax.

The units in the unit trust held by unit holders represent assets of the unitholders for the purposes of capital gains tax. It is these units, and not the underlying assets of the unit trust, which are treated as being the assets of the unitholder. A sale of a unit, or a gift of a unit would represent a disposal of an asset, (i.e. of the unit) and the tax treatment of the unitholder would be no different to his treatment in relation to the disposal of assets generally.

S731 specifically provides where a unitholder becomes entitled to receive a capital distribution in respect of his unit, he is to be treated as disposing of an interest in the unit. Generally speaking, that disposal would be a part disposal since in most instances it would not entirely eliminate a unit. Part disposals are dealt with in paragraph 11. For this purpose, a capital distribution means any distribution from the unit trust (including that in the course of winding it up) other than one which constitutes income of the unitholder for the purpose of income tax.

s613
Because a unit trust generally does not contain an element of bounty, it will usually not constitute a settlement. Accordingly a unit in a unit trust will not constitute an interest arising under a settlement. The exemption provided in s613 in relation to the disposal of an interest arising under a settlement would accordingly not usually be available in relation to the disposal of a unit in an unauthorised unit trust. That exemption is discussed in paragraph 65.12.

The tax treatment of an unauthorised unit trust, as described above, followed quite closely the tax treatment applied to a settlement. The provisions relating to unauthorised unit trusts do not make any reference to the tax consequences of a unitholder becoming absolutely entitled as against the trustee to any of the assets of the trust.

S574 to s578 dealing with settlements make elaborate provision for such circumstances. The explanation probably is that in the nature of a unit trust, a unitholder will never become absolutely entitled as against the trustee to any assets, save on the occasion of the winding up of the unit trust. s731 does provide that a capital distribution on the occasion of a winding up is to be regarded as a disposal or part disposal of the unit in respect of which it is made.

s731(3)
Where a unit trust is wound up by distribution to the unitholders of the assets of the trust in specie, the transfer by the trustees of assets to the unitholders would constitute a disposal by the trustees of those assets. That is not specifically referred to in s731 but would follow as a matter of necessity from the fact that the trustees are not mere nominees for the unitholders and that accordingly, transactions between them are not disregarded for capital gains tax purposes.

s731(6)
There is an exemption available in relation to the disposal of units in certain unauthorised unit trusts, and to the disposal of assets by the trustees of certain unauthorised unit trusts. The exemption in question relates to a trust which has at all times since the 6th April 1974 (or since it was established if later) been resident and ordinarily resident in the State and which exists solely for the purpose of enabling the public to participate in investment in certain life assurance related products.

s731(7)
The FA 1994 repealed a previous exemption in relation to units in a unit trust all of whose assets consisted of exempt government or semi-state stocks. Unitholders holding the units on the 6th April 1994 were deemed to dispose of, and reacquire the units on that day at open market value, thus receiving a tax free uplift in open market value before becoming subsequently exposed to capital gains tax on later disposals. This provision is contained in s731(7).

An exemption also exists for the trustees of an unauthorised unit trust provided all of the issued units in the trust are assets such that any gain accruing if they were disposed of by the unit holder would be wholly exempt from capital gains tax. However where the units are exempt by reason of being held by a non-resident person, or by

s739 reason of the exemption available under s739 in relation to UCITS, the trustees are not exempt in relation to gains arising on trust assets.

An example of a situation where the exemption for the trustees might apply is where all of the units in the unit trust are held by charities.

- **Revenue/Chief Inspector's CGT manual :**

- In the Revenue Commissioners capital gains tax manual at paragraph 19.2.7.1 the following advice is given to Inspectors: *"Some unit trust units are quoted on the stock exchange. Such quotations should be disregarded"*. That advice is given in the context where it is necessary to value a unit eg where the consideration for the acquisition or for the disposal of a unit is deemed by the legislation to be open market value rather than the actual consideration (if any) passing on the transaction.

- The manual goes on to note that where a dividend equalisation payment is made by a unit trust to a unit holder at the end of the period in which he acquired the unit, the equalisation payment should be treated as reducing his allowable expenditure for the unit. The Inspector is instructed not to pursue this matter where the amount of tax arising would be trivial.

36   LIFE ASSURANCE

36.1   Overview

As was the case with collective investment undertakings, the tax treatment of life assurance was significantly changed by FA2000. And, as with collective investment undertakings, the changes result in the preservation of the old system of taxation summarised above, in relation to some policies, and the introduction of an entirely different regime in relation to other policies. Going into the future, there are therefore two tax regimes potentially applying to life assurance policies, largely depending on when the policies were issued.

The FA2000 regime (which as was mentioned does not replace the regime described above, but rather complements it in respect of new policies) can be summarised as follows:

- It is a single regime applying both to domestic life policies (ie those issued by life companies operating outside the IFSC to Irish resident persons or non resident persons) and also to companies operating in the IFSC, who are now free to issue policies to either resident or non resident persons.

- The fund representing the policyholders interests is a gross fund ie exempt from Irish taxation on both income and on capital gains.

- In principle the policy holder (whether resident or non resident) is exempt from Irish tax on a disposal of the policy.

- However what is effectively a withholding tax is operated by the life company on any occasion upon which the policy holder extracts cash from that policy in any fashion, or otherwise disposes of the policy. This tax is levied at the rate of 3% over the standard income tax rate and applies to any payments from the life assurance company to the policy holder, and applies on the occasion of any disposal of the policy to a third party by the policy holder. Subject to suitable declarations, policies held by non residents do not attract this effective withholding tax.

The CGT treatment of pre FA2000 life assurance reflects that of collective investment undertakings in many ways prior to FA2000. It had four principal features:

- A CGT charge at the standard rate of income tax on the capital gains accruing to a policyholder's fund of a life assurance company.

- A special class of life assurance policy where the capital gains of the policyholders fund are taxed at 10%.

- A CGT exemption for policyholders in relation to policies issued by companies within the charge to Irish CT (i.e. An Irish resident company or an Irish branch of a non-resident company).

- A charge to CGT on the gain arising on the disposal of a foreign policy. The gain is computed without indexation. The annual exemption in relation to CGT may not be offset against the charge.

36.2   **Life Assurance and Deferred Annuities - "Old Basis Policies"**

The tax treatment described below is that which applied to life assurance policies prior to the FA2000. In general, it has application in relation to all life policies issued up to 31 December 2000. There is provision in the FA2000 for life assurance companies commencing life business after 1 April 2000 and before 31 December 2000, to elect to apply the FA2000 regime from 1 April or commencement of business, but subject to that the old regime applies to all policies issued up to 31 December 2000. It continues to apply to those policies for so long as those policies exist. Its application to policies in existence at 31 December 2000 does not come to an end at that date - it will continue to apply to such policies indefinitely.

s593

No chargeable gain accrues on the disposal of an assurance policy or a contract for a deferred annuity on the life of any person. The exemption also extends to a disposal of interests in or rights over such an asset.

This exemption however, does not apply where the person making the disposal:-

- is not the original beneficial owner

  and

- acquired the rights (or interests) for a consideration in money or money's worth.

The exemption does not apply either to:

- certain foreign policies (paragraph 36.3)

- certain corporate policies (these are described below).

The date of disposal of such assets is determined by the earliest of the following:

- payment of the sums assured under the policy

- surrender of the assurance policy

- payment of the first installment of the annuity

- surrender of the rights under the annuity contract.

The consideration for the disposal of a contract for a deferred annuity is deemed to be the market value of the right to receive the first and subsequent installments of the annuity.

- **Revenue/Chief Inspector's CGT Manual**

- In paragraph 1.1 of Chapter 19.5.1 of the Revenue Commissioners manual on Capital Gains tax it is stated *"the payment of premiums under a policy by any person to whom the benefit of the policy is assigned (thereby relieving the original beneficiary of a liability) should not in itself be regarded as the giving of consideration in money or money's worth for the disposal of the rights under the policy."*

This treatment does not apply to a foreign policy issued on or after 20 May 1993 - see paragraph 36.3.

FA94 s58

s595

The treatment of gains arising on life assurance policies held by a company within the charge of corporation tax was changed by s.58, F A 1994. The section inserted a new s. 20B into the 1975 Act (now TCA97 s595) which has effect in relation to a policy of life assurance, or a contract for a deferred annuity on the life of any person, entered into or acquired by a company on or after 11 April 1994. The new section affects only policies held by a company chargeable to corporation tax and issued by life assurance companies within the charge to corporation tax. It does not affect the treatment of policies which are "foreign policies". The new treatment does not apply to a disposal by a company of a policy which arises from a claim arising due to the death, disablement etc. of the insured person.

The broad thrust of the new legislation is to treat the sum received by a company from the disposal of a relevant policy as being a sum received under deduction of income tax. The company in receipt of the sum is then charged to corporation tax at the standard rate on the grossed up amount (i.e. a notional withholding tax is added to the amount received) and credit is given against the tax liability for the notional withholding amount.

Example 193

ABC Limited insures the life of its managing director for £100,000, on 30 April 1994. It is entitled to the sum of £100,000 on 30th April 1995, or on the death of its managing director, if earlier. It pays a premium of £95,000. On 30 April 1995, the policy having been for a period of one year only, the company receives the sum of £100,000. The managing director survived for the year.

If the policy was taken out with a company within the charge to Irish corporation tax (i.e. is not a "foreign" policy - see paragraph 36.3) the company is treated as follows:

	£
Sum received	100,000
Consideration given	95,000
(no indexation is available)	
Gain arising	5,000
Notional tax withheld (27/73)	1,849
Deemed gross receipt	6,849
CGT @ standard rate (40%)	2,740
Less tax credit	1,849
Net tax due	891

Since the company is chargeable to Corporation Tax and not to CGT the amount of the claim would of course have been adjusted upwards so as to give the same tax charge of £2,740, when the then appropriate corporation tax rate of 38% was applied to it. It is interesting to see the same example if it is assumed that the disposal occurred in 1998/99, the figures otherwise remaining the same.

Sum received	£100,000
Consideration given	£95,000
Gain arising	£5,000
Notional tax withheld (24/76)	£1579
Deemed gross receipt	£6,579
CGT @ standard rate (20%)	£1,315
Tax Credit	£1,579
Tax refund due	£264

It would seem that the result of the application of s595, in a situation where the rate of capital gains tax is lower than the standard rate of income tax, is to provide a corporate investor with a tax refund, and lower the effective internal rate of tax (taking the taxpayer and the fund together as a unit) to 20%.

The treatment does not apply where the disposal of the policy arises due to the death, disability etc. of the person whose life is insured. Thus if the payout had occurred due to the death of the managing director, no part of the proceeds would be liable to corporation tax on capital gains. In certain circumstances part of the proceeds might be treated as an income receipt of the company but that is a separate topic.

The example above is intended solely to illustrate the operation of s595, in circumstances where it does have application. The treatment of the proceeds of insurance policies taken out by a company on a *"Keyman"* may involve the proceeds being treated as income, rather as capital gains, depending on the circumstances. The example above is not intended to deal with, or illustrate, the distinction between those circumstances, and should not be taken as an indication as to whether the proceeds would be treated as income, or as capital gains. The Revenue Commissioners have issued a detailed statement on the treatment of Keyman insurance, to which reference may be made.

Life assurance policies taken out by a company before 11 April can be treated as entered into on or after that date where their period is extended on or after that date or another policy is substituted for the original policy, under an option provided for in the original policy.

36.3   Life Assurance - Finance Act 2000 regime.

The FA2000 introduced a new tax regime for life assurance policies. It did not replace the old regime (described in paragraph 36.2) above but rather co exists with it. The FA2000 regime has application to life assurance policies issued on or after 1 January 2001 by any company within the charge to corporation tax in Ireland. Such a company can either be a resident life assurance company, or a non resident life assurance company trading here through a branch.

s730B   Additionally, the new regime is capable of application to policies written on or after 1 April 2000 by a life company commencing business here on or after that date, provided the company so elects. It is likely that any company commencing business in that period would make the necessary election. If they fail to do so, a special charge to tax will be levied on 31 December 2000 at the rate of 40% on the increase in value of the policy between the date of issue and 31 December 2000, after allowing a deduction for the premiums paid in the period. Since it is not likely that any life company would expose its policy holders to that tax charge, it will not be further referred to in this book. The charge in question is levied directly on the life company but is taken from the policy-holders fund.

The new regime also applies to certain policies issued prior to 1 January 2001, where they relate to pension business, general annuity business, and permanent health insurance business.

The new regime has the following features:

- It applies equally to life policies issued by IFSC licensed operators on or after 1 January 2001, as it does to those issued in the domestic market in Ireland. All are now placed on the same basis.

- No Irish tax is chargeable on the income or chargeable gains allocated to or expended on behalf of policy-holders. In other words the fund is a gross fund. Under the alternate pre Finance Act 2000 regime, a charge to tax at the standard rate of income tax is effectively levied on this income and gains.

- The exemption described above for the original holder of a life policy (s593) continues to apply.

s593
- The charge to tax on a corporate holder of a policy which applied in the pre-FA2000 regime (s595) does not apply to the corporate holder of a policy within the FA2000 regime. Such a corporate holder is entitled to the exemption from capital gains tax provided by s593.

s730E
- A form of withholding tax is imposed on any occasion after 1 January 2001 upon which the life company makes a payment to the policy holder, or the policy holder otherwise disposes of the life assurance policy. The rate of tax charged is 3% in excess of the standard rate of income tax. It will not be clear what rate that will be when the new regime commences for most life companies, on 1 January 2001, until the budget of December 2000. The amount upon which the tax is levied varies depending on the nature of the event upon which it is charged ie part encashment, total encashment or assignment of the policy.

s730E
- There is an exemption from the withholding tax described where the life company is in possession of a non residence declaration which it has no reason to believe is incorrect. In other words, there is no withholding tax applied on a non residents life policy, whether that be issued in the IFSC, or issued by any company outside the IFSC. For a non resident, a life assurance policy is totally tax free, both as regards direct Irish taxes on the life assurance fund, in relation to tax on the policy holder himself, or in relation to the withholding tax referred to.

The amount upon which the withholding tax (effectively borne by the policy holder but formally levied on and paid by the insurance company, albeit out of the policy holders fund) is as follows:

- *Maturity or surrender of policy:* Sums paid by the life policy, less premiums paid in respect of the policy (to the extent not already taken into account in any previous charge of the withholding tax).

- *Surrender of part of policy:* The sum received for the surrender, less a proportion of the premiums paid on the policy (to the extent not already taken into account in any previous charge of the withholding tax). That proportion is in the ratio of the sum paid to the value of the policy immediately prior to the part surrender.

- *Assignment of the policy:* The value of the policy immediately prior to the assignment, less premiums paid in respect of the policy (to the extent not already taken into account in a prior withholding tax charge).

- *Part assignment of the policy:* The sum received, less a proportion of the premiums paid (to the extent not already taken into account in any previous charge of the withholding tax). The proportion is determined in the fashion described above for a part surrender.

As indicated above, the amount of premiums that are deductible in computing the amount on which the withholding tax is charged is not necessarily the full amount of the premiums of the policy. In a case where a charge has previously arisen on the maturity or surrender of the policy. Premiums are not deductible to the extent they were deducted in the computation of a previous charge. Several occasions of charge could arise in relation to a single policy, in the normal course of events. There might be part surrenders (or encashments) of the policy by the original policy holder; he might assign that policy to a third party in whole or in part; the policy might then mature or be surrendered. Each occasion would be an occasion of charge but only the first occasion would have a deduction computed by reference to all premiums paid to that date. The subsequent occasions of charge would have a deduction computed by reference only to premiums paid to the extent not previously deducted.

The life assurance company is entitled to recover the withholding tax (referred to as "appropriate tax" the same term as is used in relation to the withholding tax on collective investment undertakings albeit it is not the same tax) in a manner that places the burden effectively on the policy holder. They may do so by way of a withholding from payments to the policy holder (where that is the occasion of charge) or they may compensate themselves by withdrawing the moneys from the policy fund, thus reducing the value of the policy.

The life assurance company must account for the appropriate tax (withholding tax) twice a year, on 30 January and on 30 July. A return must be made even if no appropriate tax was owing. There is power for an Inspector to raise an assessment, and normal appeal procedures.

The following example illustrates how these rules described above would apply during the typical events which arise in relation to a life assurance policy.

Example 194

On 31 January 2001 John Brown took out a life assurance policy with an Irish resident life company. He paid an initial premium of £5,000. On 31 January 2002 and on 31 January 2003 he paid further premiums of £5,000 on each date. On 30 June 2003 he encashed part of his policy for the sum of £2000. On 31 December 2003 he transferred the policy (then worth £25,000) to his son Michael. Michael paid the premium due on 31 January 2004, and on 31 January 2005 encashed the policy, then worth £40,000.

During the lifetime of the policy neither the income nor the gains accruing to the life assurance company in respect of the policy were subject to Irish tax.

On 30 June 2003 a chargeable event "to appropriate tax" occurred. This was the part encashment of the policy. The policy was then worth £20,000. £15,000 of premiums had been paid in respect of it. The sum received from the partial encashment was £2,000. The amount upon which appropriate tax fell to be charged was £2,000, reduced by the proportionate amount of the premiums. The proportion would be that of 2,000: 20,000 applied to premiums of £15,000, giving a sum of £1,500. Appropriate tax would therefore be levied on £500. The rate of tax would be the standard rate of income tax plus 3%. For these purposes it is assumed that the standard rate of income tax would be 20%, so a charge of 23% on £500 would arise ie a sum of £115. John Brown would therefore receive from the insurance company a cheque in the amount of £1,885 (£2,000 reduced by £115). The Insurance company would have to account to the Revenue for the £115 withheld not later than 30 July 2003.

The next chargeable event to occur is the transfer of the policy by John to his son Michael. No further premiums had been paid between the previous chargeable event on 30 June, and this chargeable event on 31 December. The policy was now worth £25,000. Once again appropriate tax falls to be charged, this time on the value of the policy less premiums paid to that point in so far as not previously allowed. The premiums paid to that point amounted to £15,000, but £1,500 had been previously deducted in a computation of appropriate tax. Therefore only £13,500 will be deducted from the value of the policy (£25,000) on the occasion of this second computation. A charge of 23% on the difference, £6,500, therefore falls to be levied. This amounts to £1,495. The occasion of charge is not one upon which any money is moving from the life company to the policy holder and therefore a direct withholding from such a payment cannot occur. Instead, the life company can reimburse itself for the charge to appropriate tax by withdrawing this sum of £1,495 from the investments representing the policy. Effectively therefore the policy is reduced in value by an equal sum. The value of the policy in the hands of Michael therefore becomes £23,505.

The next occasion for a charge to tax is when Michael encashes the policy. At this point in time one additional premium of £5,000 has been paid, and the policy is worth £40,000. Of the £20,000 of premiums paid to date, £15,000 have *been previously taken into account in appropriate tax computations. Therefore only £5,000 of premiums fall to be deducted from the value of £40,000, leaving a sum of £35,000 to be charged to tax at the standard rate of income tax plus 3% (assumed therefore to be 23% in total). A tax charge arises therefore of £7,105. The life assurance company pay to Michael a cheque for £32,895. They must account to the Revenue for the appropriate tax of £7,105 which arose on this event not later than 30 July 2005.*

Had Michael been both not resident, and not ordinarily resident in Ireland (let us assume he was resident in the UK since the year 2000) no appropriate tax will be chargeable on the making by him of a non residence declaration to the life company. Accordingly the last charge to appropriate tax above, that on encashment by Michael, would not have arisen, and Michael would have received a cheque for £40,000. His tax treatment in the UK is of course a separate matter with which we are not concerned. The transfer of the life policy from father to son in December 2003 may also have had gift tax implications, with which we are not concerned here. It should be noted however that where CGT is offsetable against gift tax arising on the same event, the tax charge on the transfer from father to son in this instance is not CGT, it is "appropriate tax" which is a separate and distinct type of tax which is neither income tax nor capital gains tax. It is not offsetable against gift tax arising on the same event.

It does not matter whether the encashment by Michael of the policy in 2005 was because the policy had reached its maturity date, or because he encashed it early, or due to the death of his father (the life assured). The tax arises whether the encashment occurs in life or on death. There is no "death exemption" involved in appropriate tax.

36.3.1   Foreign life assurance

s594

The CGT treatment described above on disposal of a policy does not apply to a policy of *life assurance* or contract for a *deferred annuity* issued on or after 20 May 1993 by a company not within the charge to corporation tax in respect of its life assurance fund (a foreign life policy). A policy in existence at 20 May 1993 whose term is extended, or which is varied subsequently may be treated as being issued on or after 20 May 1993.

s594(4)

The FA95 excluded from this treatment to certain foreign reinsurance contracts in respect of life assurance contracts. In broad terms, the extension applies to contracts from 1 January 1995.

s594(2)

The FA97 excluded from the treatment in respect of "foreign life assurance policies" a policy written by an IFSC life assurance company, where it is written on the basis that the policyholder has been residing outside the State continuously for at least a six month period. Life assurance companies in the International Financial Services Centre in Dublin were entitled to tax privileges principally on the basis that they deal only with non resident persons. This exclusion deals with the situation where a person takes out a policy with such an Irish company, but later becomes resident or ordinarily resident in Ireland, and is so resident on the occasion of a disposal of the policy. This extension takes effect from 6 April 1997 and would seem to have retrospective effect in relation to policies issued by an IFSC company on or after 20 May 1993, where the disposal occurs after 6 April 1997.

A capital gain on the disposal of a foreign life policy is computed without indexation. The charge to CGT in respect of a gain on the disposal of a foreign life policy is made without regard to the exemption for the first £1,000 p.a. of chargeable gains in s1028 (see paragraph 19). Losses, whether arising on the disposal of a foreign life policy or on any other disposal, may not be relieved against a gain on the disposal of a foreign life policy.

The treatment may be in breach of EU law as stated in the Safir case.

36.4   **Life assurance in the IFSC**

A special regime applies to life assurance companies licensed to operate in Dublin's *International Financial Services Centre*.

The special regime described below applies only to policies issued by IFSC life assurance companies prior to 1 January 2001. Policies issued after that date are subject to the FA2000 regime described in paragraph 36.3. The regime described below however will continue to have application into the future in relation to policies issued prior to 1 April 2000. The two regimes will coexist.

Broadly speaking, life assurance companies within the charge to Irish CT are exempt from Irish tax in respect of the income and the capital gains which accrue to policy holders' funds. Policy holders of such companies are not liable to Irish tax in relation to their policies. However companies licensed to operate in the IFSC enjoy these benefits only on the basis that they do not issue policies to persons who are resident in the State. It was generally considered that that requirement meant that should a policy holder who was non-resident at the time of taking out the policy become resident in the State at a later stage, it was necessary that the policy contain a condition requiring it to be brought to an end on his becoming resident in the state.

The FA97 introduced the relaxation of this rigid exclusion of Irish residents from the categories of persons who might hold "IFSC life assurance policies". The new regime permits the policy holder to retain his policy on becoming resident in the State, and permits the life assurance company to retain its taxation privileges in relation to that part of the fund which relates to the policy, now held by a newly resident person. However, on an encashment or maturity of the policy, the life assurance company must operate a withholding tax (for which it accounts to the Revenue Commissioners) which is calculated at the standard rate of income tax. It is calculated on the increase in the value of the policy from the date on which the person resumed residence in Ireland, or became resident in Ireland while holding the policy, to the date of encashment or maturity. The premiums paid during this period of residence are permitted to be deducted from the increase in value, before applying the taxation charge.

It must be borne in mind that an IFSC life assurance company is not a foreign life assurance company, in that it is within the charge to corporation tax in respect of its life fund, albeit it does not actually pay tax by reason of a specific exemption. Therefore the "foreign life assurance" regime does not apply to a person who holds a life policy issued by an IFSC licensed life assurance company. Instead the regime which applies to the holders of policies issued by life assurance companies within the charge to corporation tax applies i.e. a policy holder is exempt from tax on his disposal of the policy, or encashment etc. The affect of applying the withholding tax to the sum paid to him is very broadly to equate his position with that of a person who had taken out a life insurance policy with a non-IFSC licensed life assurance company within the charge to Irish corporation tax. The fund representing the policy held by such a person would have suffered tax on its income and gains over the period of the policy at the standard rate of income tax. Whereas that income tax is paid annually in the case of a non-IFSC Irish life assurance policy, in the case of a life assurance policy issued by an IFSC licensed company but held by a person who is now Irish resident, the tax is paid as a lump sum on encashment/maturity. The regime is therefore not identical and only broadly similar in that the IFSC policy holder has the advantage of a deferral of the tax charge.

As relatively few policies affected by the special arrangements for individuals who become resident in Ireland having previously taken out an IFSC policy, are likely to arise, the topic is not explored here in further detail. Readers are referred to an article on the topic in the July 1997 issue of Irish Tax Review, by John Caslin, where the 1997 legislation is explored in detail, with worked examples illustrating the several circumstances in which it can apply.

36.5.1 Life assurance companies

s711
s711(1)

The FA93 introduced a new tax treatment for chargeable gains accruing to a fund maintained in respect of life business by a life assurance company which is within the charge to corporation tax.

The FA93 regime has application only in relation to policies issued by life assurance companies prior to 1 January 2001. The FA2000 introduced a new regime which has application to the taxation of life assurance companies in relation to policies issued from 1 January 2001. From 1 April 2000, a life assurance company is treated as carrying on two trades - one (consisting of its old business written before 1 April 2000) taxed as described below, and the second (new business written on or after 1 January 2001) taxed under a different regime described in paragraph 36.5.1. *Both regimes co-exist.*

The 1993 regime has the following features:

- Indexation is not available in the computation of chargeable gains.

s711(1)
- The exemption for Government and other stocks in s607 does not apply.

- Allowable losses may be set against chargeable gains in the same period and any excess is treated as a management expense, other than an acquisition expense (which would not be fully recognised in that period). Loss relief under s31 does not apply.

- The rate of corporation tax applying to the company gains in respect of investments referable to life business is the standard rate of income tax.

s719
- Assets (other than s607 exempt securities) held for the life assurance fund (not including pension business or special investment business (see paragraph 36.5)) are deemed disposed of and reacquired at OMV at the end of each accounting period. Such deemed disposals are ignored for the purposes of rules relating to the identification of shares disposed of.

  The exception relating to the deemed disposal of s607 exempt securities does not apply as and from 26 March 1997 to such securities which are held under a swap arrangement for assets which are not themselves such s607 exempt securities. Neither does the exception apply to government/s607 securities which are held in the form of a strip of a security. Security strips are discussed in greater detail in paragraph 32.3 .

- Chargeable gains or allowable losses arising from the deemed annual disposal of assets are recognised in equal amounts over seven years, commencing with the period in which the deemed disposal from which they arose occurred.

  A proportionate amount is recognised in accounting periods of less than a year. Any amounts otherwise not recognised up to then at the cessation of a business are then recognised.

- With regard to disposals on or after 28 March 1996, where interest is received from a security in the period following that in which it is disposed of, a corresponding part of the acquisition base cost of the security is excluded from the computation on the disposal in that period, and that corresponding part of the acquisition cost is treated instead as a loss arising on the disposal of the security in the succeeding period in which the amount of interest is received.

  In respect of disposals occurring on or after 28 March 1996, so much of the loss which is computed on the disposal (having regard to the deemed reacquisition price at the beginning of the period at which the disposal takes place) as exceeds the true loss which arises on the disposal if the deemed disposals and reacquisitions at the end of each period were disregarded, is recognised as to one seventh in the period in which the disposal occurs and similarly in each of the succeeding 6 periods.

Sch32 Para24
- As a transitional measure a life company was deemed to dispose of and reacquire all assets (other than exempt securities) at OMV on 31 December 1992. An accounting date was deemed to end at that date for the purpose of computing CT on the life business. Any net gain or loss arising on the deemed disposal was recognised *over seven years.*

s720
The FA95 introduced special rules relating to the phasing in of the "seven year spread" in relation to unrealised gains and losses. The special rules relate to unrealised **reinsurance gains or losses** which are deemed to accrue. Instead of spreading the unrealised reinsurance gains or losses over seven years, only a portion of those unrealised gains or losses which are deemed to arise in the year ended 31 December 1995 are spread. That portion is 2/7ths of the gains or losses deemed to arise in 1995. The remaining 5/7ths are recognised in 1995. Similarly, gains or losses deemed to arise in the years ended 31 December 1996 through to 1999 are only partially spread over a seven year period. 3/7ths of those arising in 1996 will be spread, 4/7ths of those in 1997, 5/7ths of those in 1998, and 6/7ths of those in 1999. The portion not spread is recognised immediately in the year in which it is deemed to arise.

s722
S722 permits a life assurance company to reduce the payment on maturity or encashment of a unit linked policy issued before 6 April 1974 by the amount of corporation tax at full rate on the chargeable gain arising on disposing of assets to meet the payment. S722 does not seem to have been amended to take account of the reduced effective tax charge (effectively 24% and not 32%) which applies generally.

FA99 s87
FA99 s87 retrospectively amended s541A (which had been inserted by FA98). It did so to modify the manner in which a taxpayer is deemed to have disposed of certain foreign currency denominated loans on the occasion of the introduction of the Euro. It provided that, rather than a deemed disposal and reacquisition occurring on the date of the introduction of the Euro, it would occur at the end of the accounting period of the life company, in which the change over occurred. Any gain or loss arising is taken into account for the purpose of the "seven year spreading" of capital gains and losses. This treatment does not apply to assets held for a Special Investment Policy. (see paragraph 36.6).

36.5.2   **Life assurance - new business.**

FA 2000, s53   The FA 2000 regime applies not only to business written on or after 1
                January 2001. It also applies to certain other business written prior
s730A   to that date including policies relating to pension business, general
                annuity business, and permanent health insurance. It applies both to
                IFSC companies, and to companies operating outside the IFSC.

                The new regime is briefly stated in s53 of the FA 2000 which
                introduced a new s730A. Subsection 4 provides that the profits of a
                life assurance company are to be charged to corporation tax in
                respect of new basis business, under Case I of Schedule D. It is likely
                that gains on the disposal of investments held by a life assurance
                company as part of its trade of life assurance would be regarded as
                Case I profits and accordingly outside the capital gains tax regime. It
                is of course possible that a life assurance company would hold
                shares (typically in subsidiaries) otherwise than in the course of the
                trade. In relation to such shares it would be within the capital gains
                tax regime but no special provisions would apply.

36.6   **Special investment policies**

s723   A special investment policy is one of the savings products
                introduced by the FA93 (now TCA97 s723). It was taxed at a rate of
                10% on income and gains until 6 April 1999, when the rate applicable
                became 20%. It takes the form of a life assurance policy. It is related
                to the other special savings products in that the limit to the amount
                which an individual may invest in a policy is affected by the amount
                he has invested in other special savings products.

FA 2000, s62   A special investment policy cannot be issued after 31 December 2000.
                This restriction was introduced by s62 of the FA 2000.

                The tax treatment of a special investment policy, insofar as capital
                gains are concerned, has the following features:

                • The corporation tax rate applying to life assurance company gains
                  on the disposal of assets of a special investment fund is 10% to 6
                  April 1999, and 20% thereafter. A special investment fund is the
                  fund of assets held by the company for the purpose of its business
                  of the issue of special investment policies.

                • The life assurance company is deemed to dispose of and reacquire
                  all of the assets of its special investment fund at OMV at the end of
                  each accounting period. The gain or loss arising is recognised in
                  the period and is not spread over seven years as would be the case
                  for other life assurance fund gains.

                • Gains on the disposal of eligible shares for the purpose of BES
                  relief are exempt from CGT. Losses on such shares are allowable
                  losses (even though gains are exempt).

- The policy holder is exempt from CGT on disposal of a policy in the same manner and subject to the same conditions as applies to any policy issued by a company within the charge to corporation tax.

The conditions which must be met by a life assurance company in relation to Special Investment Policies, and those which must be met by a policy holder are not described here. They are described in the companion volume in this series, Income Tax by McAteer and Reddin.

37   SPECIAL PORTFOLIO INVESTMENT ACCOUNTS

37.1   Broad Outline

A special portfolio investment account (SPIA) is one of four related investment products introduced by the Finance Act 1993 and now in TCA97 s838. Three are taxed at a rate of 20% on both income and capital gains. A special deposit account now attracts income tax at 15%. They are all related in that the limits to the amount an individual may invest in one product is related to the amount he has invested in the other three products.

37.2   Special Portfolio Investment Accounts and CGT

s838

A special investment account (SPIA) takes the form of investments held as nominee by a stock broker designated for the purposes of the tax legislation by the Revenue Commissioners.

The designated broker acts solely as a bare trustee. The investments held by him in the SPIA are the absolute property of the taxpayer on whose behalf they were acquired by the broker. All payments, receipts, acquisitions and disposals in relation to investments in the SPIA made to or by the broker are made to or by him as agent for his client, the taxpayer.

The tax treatment of an SPIA, insofar as it concerns capital gains, has the following features:

- CGT is not chargeable on capital gains arising in relation to investments held in the SPIA.

- The designated broker must account to the Revenue for 10% (20% from 6/4/99) tax on gains arising in each tax year on disposals or deemed disposals of investments in the SPIA. For this purpose, the gains are treated as if they were relevant interest for the purpose of Deposit Interest Retention Tax, arising on a Special Savings Account.

491

- The individual owner of the SPIA has no liability to income tax or capital gains tax in relation to income or capital gains arising from SPIA investments.

- Because CGT is not chargeable on SPIA capital gains, any allowable losses accruing to the owner of the SPIA on other assets cannot be relieved against the gains.

- Capital losses arising on SPIA investments are not allowable losses for CGT purposes and cannot be relieved against chargeable gains arising to the SPIA owner on assets held outside the SPIA.

- Capital losses on investments held in the SPIA may be relieved against income or other capital gains in the SPIA in the same tax year in the computation of the tax payable by the broker. Any loss not relieved in this manner may be relieved similarly in subsequent tax years.

s601

- The annual exemption in relation to capital gains in s601 does not apply to capital gains arising on SPIA assets. This means that the exemption may be applied entirely to other gains; but does not affect the computation of the tax liability to tax on SPIA gains.

- Indexation is not available in the computation of SPIA capital gains for the purpose of the tax liability arising to the broker.

- The investments in the SPIA are deemed disposed of and re-acquired at OMV on 5 April in each tax year, for the purpose of the computation of the tax liability of the broker.

- Gains arising on the disposal of eligible shares for the purpose of BES relief are not taken into account in the computation of the tax liability of the broker. Losses on such shares are taken into account.

s607

However, as respects disposals occurring on or after 28 March 1996, where interest is received in respect of certain securities in the year following their disposal, a part of the acquisition cost of the security equal to the amount of the interest is not deductible in the computation in the year of disposal, but is carried forward to the subsequent year, and is treated as a loss arising on the disposal of securities in that year. The securities to which this treatment applies are the exempt government and semi state securities (s607) and also securities of any body corporate not including shares.

- BES relief is not available in respect of investments made by an individual through an SPIA.

s547
s549
s573
s1028

It would appear that s547 (Consideration); s549 (Connected Persons); s1028 (Married Persons) pre FA 99, s573 (Death), and any other provision of the Capital Gains Tax Acts relevant to the computation of a capital gain or loss which is not specifically excluded by the legislation relating to an SPIA, have application in relation to the computation of the amount of gains chargeable to the 10% tax payable by the broker on transactions involving the assets of an SPIA, notwithstanding the exclusion of a charge to CGT on the capital gains of an SPIA. It is understood that the Revenue have expressed the view that s1028 (spouse exemption) may not apply to a transaction between a person and his spouse's SPIA. The basis for this view prior to FA99 is not known.

FA99 s65

The possibility that s1028 (intra trust spouse transfers) would apply to a SPIA was countered by FA99 s65, with effect from 1 December 1998. It provided that an investment would be within the SPIA legislation only if it was acquired by the broker at open market value. If the broker acquired from a spouse of the owner of the account, he would be treated by s1028 as acquiring the investment at the disposing spouse's base cost. If that is not the same as open market value at the date of the transfer to the broker, then the investment acquired by the broker from the spouse will not be within the SPIA legislation.

The fact that the legislation was amended may indicate some lack of confidence by the Revenue in their view that the intra spouse exemption could not apply to a SPIA in the first place.

The effect of the amendment would seem to be that an investment acquired otherwise than at open market value is not, after the 1 December 1998, included in the exemption from CGT on its disposal, which is available to the holder of a SPIA in the normal way. In other words, a disposal of such an investment gives rise to a CGT charge on the holder of the SPIA, rather than on the broker. Although it is not entirely clear, on balance it seems likely that where a share had been acquired other than at market value prior to the 1 December 1998, but is disposed of only after that date, then notwithstanding that it was a "SPIA" investment when acquired, on disposal it would not be such an investment and the exemption from CGT for the SPIA holder would be lost.

A transfer of investments already owned by an individual to his SPIA would not be a disposal of those investments for the purposes of CGT (being only a transfer to a nominee) but the investments would not attract the tax treatment described above, since they would not meet the statutory requirement to be investments acquired by the designated broker by an expenditure of money. Any payment of money by the broker would be a transfer to the individual of money held by the agent as his nominee, and as such is unlikely to be regarded as expenditure by the broker in the context of the section. The matter is not free from doubt.

Following the reduction of the standard rate of CGT to 20% (FA98) it may make little sense for a taxpayer to invest in a SPIA. The restrictions on annual exemption, loss relief, and indexation, and in particular the deemed annual disposal at open market value, may outweigh the product's advantages in terms of a lower nominal rate of tax. Many taxpayers hold their quoted shares for long periods without disposing of them. Such taxpayers in particular may find the deemed annual disposal in a SPIA works to their disadvantage overall.

- **Revenue Commissioners published precedent:**

  – The commentary above is based on the belief that the broker who holds a SPIA is a mere nominee for the taxpayer who provided him with the funds. That interpretation is not accepted by the Revenue Commissioners. In a published Revenue precedent relating to the disposal of shares by one spouse to the designated broker for a SPIA held in the name of the other spouse, they state *"The disposal of shares by an individual to a designated broker acting as trustee for a SPIA which is beneficially owned by that individual's spouse would not be regarded as a disposal to that individual's spouse. The disposal would be an occasion of charge to CGT by reference to the market value of the assets in question."* The authors are not aware of any basis for the Revenue view. Taxpayers should however be aware of the Revenue view as quoted- see comments above regarding FA99 amendments to SPIA rules.

38   DEBTS

38.1   Broad Outline

s541
s532(1)

A debt is an asset for CGT purposes. However where a debt is disposed of by the original creditor, the gain arising will not be a chargeable gain. The exemption also applies where the disposal is by the personal representatives of the original creditor or by his legatee.

s585

This exemption does not apply to the disposal of a "debt on a security". This phrase is not defined but is stated to have the meaning given to it by s585. That section does not define "debt on a security" but states that the term 'security' includes:

"any loan stock or similar security whether of any government or of any public or local authority or of any company whether secured or unsecured...".

The definition of "security" goes on to exclude certain Government and other securities which are exempted from CGT (see paragraph 32). If the debt is not a debt on a security no chargeable gain arises on a disposal and correspondingly, no allowable loss can arise.

38.2   Debt on a security

The meaning given to the phrase "debt on a security" under similar UK legislation has been considered by the UK courts. Their views are summarised below. The views of the Irish courts are described further down. It is the views of the Irish courts which determine the law in Ireland. The views of the Irish courts do not correspond with those of the UK courts in all respects.

Brief overview of the views of UK Courts:

- "Whatever else it may mean, the phrase debt on a security, is not synonym for a secured debt" (Cleveleys Investment Trust v IRC).

s541
s585

- "If it defines anything, it defines security, not debt on a security, and in view of the words, whether secured or unsecured, the latter must include some unsecured debts." (Cleveleys Investment Trust v IRC)

- "The only basis on which a distinction can be drawn is between a pure unsecured debt as between the original borrower and lender on the one hand, and a debt (which may be unsecured) which has if, not a marketable character, at least such characteristics as enable it to be dealt in and if necessary converted into shares or other securities" (Aberdeen Construction Group v IRC).

- "It can be seen, however, in my opinion, that the legislature is endeavoring to distinguish between mere debts, which normally (though there are exceptions) do not increase but may decrease in value, and debts with added characteristics such as may enable them to be realised or dealt with at a profit" (WT Ramsay Ltd v IRC).

- The word "debt" does not include a contingent right to receive an unidentifiable sum at an unascertainable date. It must be at least a liability to pay a sum which is at the time it is to be treated as a debt, ascertainable or capable of ascertainment (Marren v Ingles).

- Certain debts may be deemed to be a debt on a security - see paragraph 38.10.

The meaning of debt on a security has been statutorily extended (see paragraph 38.10)

In the UK case of Whittles v Uniholdings it was held that where Uniholdings had entered into a forward contract to purchase dollars (in return for a sum of sterling to be paid by Uniholdings to a bank) the right it had under the contract to receive the dollars on the due date for closing the contract did not constitute a "debt", and accordingly it was a chargeable asset.

In the case of Tarmac Roadstone Holdings Ltd. v Williams, the UK Special Commissioners considered the fact that loan notes which required the issuer's consent for transfer (which consent could be withheld without reason); and which were redeemable at the option of the issuer ahead of their due date for redemption "were not in the nature of investments which could be dealt in as such" by reason of those features. Accordingly they held that they were not debts on a security. This was so notwithstanding that the loan notes had many of the formal features of a debt on a security, in that they carried interest, and were recorded on a register, and had a fixed redemption date (subject to the right of the issuer to redeem earlier).

The UK Special Commissioners also considered whether a debt was a debt on a security in the case of Taylor Clark International Ltd. v Lewis. The Commissioner said *"we regard as significant the absence of any term or period of the loan, and the possibility of its immediate repayment at any time, would seem to us to point to the absence therefore of the "structure of permanence" referred to by Lord Wilberforce in W.T. Ramsey Ltd. v IRC"*. In the particular circumstances of the company which issued the loan note, the Commissioners considered that the loan would not in reality be marketable without the benefit of security and it was not clear that the security available to the original holder of the note would be transferable with the note. This did not amount to a finding that a debt on a security necessarily had to be secured, but was merely an observation that in the particular circumstances of the issuer there would be little market for the note in the absence of security.

The question of what constitutes a "debt on a security" has been considered by the Irish High Court in the case of J.J. Mooney v Noel McSweeney (Irish Tax Review, July 1997). In that case, the court considered the judgement in the UK case of Taylor Clarke International Limited (referred to above) in the following terms:

"The four characteristics of a loan on a security as proposed in Taylor's case arise only because in separate loan transactions, the loans have been disallowed for those stated reasons but those reasons do not necessarily identify what is or what is not a debt on a security. The essence must be the additional "bundle of rights" acquired with the granting of the loan so as to make it marketable and potentially more valuable than the value of the loan upon repayment. The potential increase in value must not be illusory or theoretical. It must be realistic at the time when the loan and rights are acquired by the lender".

It seems clear from the comments made on the UK Taylor case that it carried little weight with the Irish court.

The McSweeney case concerned a loan made by the taxpayer to a company in which he was a major shareholder. The loan was as part of an overall package of refinancing of the company in which several financial institutions participated. The loan was a subordinated loan, not carrying interest. However it was convertible on a predetermined basis into shares in the company at the option of the loan note holder. Mr. Justice Morris said:

"It is clear from the earlier judgements that eminent members of the English and Scottish bench found difficulty in defining and identifying the nature of "a debt on a security". All have agreed that it does not mean simply "a debt which is secured" or put another way, it is not the opposite to an unsecured debt.....In W.T. Ramsay Ltd. v CIR Lord Wilberforce at page 329 refers to debts on a security as "debts with added characteristics such as may enable them to be realised or dealt with at a profit" or again that the debt has "such characteristics as enable it to be dealt in and if necessary converted into shares or other securities". These are the elements which identify a debt on a security and are no more than common sense. The pure loan is exempt from CGT because it can never exceed the value. With the additional rights to convert into stock a debt on a security may appreciate in value and can be marketed at a profit. This is the clear distinction between the two types of debts....It is not relevant that a purchaser may have had difficulty because of local or transient commercial considerations in finding another purchaser. Once the transactions contained the characteristics which would in the ordinary course of commerce render it marketable, then it meets the criteria."

This judgement of the Irish High Court makes it clear that a debt may be a debt on a security notwithstanding that it does not carry a rate of interest. In that respect, the judgement marks a distinct break from a number of UK judgements which appeared to proceed on that self-evidently mistaken basis.

A debt on a security could be expressed either in Irish currency or in a foreign currency. No matter what currency it is expressed in, a debt on a security is a chargeable asset.

The judgement in the McSweeney case is the decisive statement of the law on the meaning of "debt on a security" in Ireland. It is this judgement and not the UK judgements to which reference should be made in determining what constitutes a debt on a security.

In the case of Inspector of Taxes v Thomas Keleghan, the High Court had occasion to consider the meaning of "debt on a security". The case was concerned with a transaction which had its origins in 1990 when the taxpayer sold shares in Gladebrook Limited to Siucre Eireann CPT for the sum of £8.6m. The consideration was satisfied by the issue of loan notes (debentures). The loan notes in question were redeemed for cash in February 1993. The Inspector of Taxes sought to assess the gain on the disposal of the loan notes to capital gains tax. The taxpayer's principal defence against this was his argument that the loan notes did not constitute a debt on a security, and accordingly no charge to tax could arise on their disposal, he being the original holder of the notes.

It should be noted that the FA96, by inserting subsection 7 into s541, ensures that as respects disposals of a debenture on or after 28 March 1996, a debenture obtained on a share exchange will always be regarded as a debt on a security. However Mr Keeghan's disposal of his loan note had pre-dated that provision which accordingly was not relevant at the time.

The loan note in question was complex. It had the following features:

- It was expressed to be non transferable except in the case of death.

- It allowed for conversion into shares in the event of a public flotation of the issuing company prior to 1 October 1991. However the conversion would be at a discount calculated on a sliding scale.

- From the earliest date on which it could be redeemed, the notes commenced to carry a rate of interest. The rate of interest was the Dublin intra bank offered rate for six month funds. That would be a variable rate but quite a low rate.

- The notes were redeemable at 30 days notice any time up to 1997. It is not clear from the facts stated in the case whether the redemption was at the option solely of the company, or whether the note holder also could demand redemption.

The details given of the loan note in the case are unsatisfactory. It is not clear what was meant by the loan notes being convertible into shares at a discount. In fact the whole basis of conversion into shares was not clearly described. Neither is it clear if the interest rate was a fixed interest rate determined on a particular date by reference to the Dublin intra bank market at that date, or was it one which varied as the Dublin intra bank market rate varied.

The judge found that the debt was not a debt on a security on two grounds. The first of these grounds was a straightforward application of the decision in the McSweeney case. The judge held that the interest rate and conversion rights were not of such a nature as would give the note "the capability of having an enhanced value". That was of course simply a finding of fact in relation to that particular loan note.

However the primary grounds on which the judge held it was not a debt on a security was the simple fact that the loan note was stated on the face of it to be non transferable. He said "*Both on the face of the note itself and in the conditions of issue it is provided that neither the note or any part thereof shall be transferable or assignable and accordingly if marketability is an essential element of a debt on a security, then this loan note cannot come within the definition, and it is a simple promise to repay a debt, which cannot constitute a chargeable gain by virtue of the provisions of s541.*"

This aspect of the judgment may be considered something of a new development in the understanding of the meaning of "debt on a security". It would not previously have been widely considered that a formal prohibition on transfer of legal ownership of a loan note would in itself be a sufficient bar to the loan note being a debt on a security. It is always possible to turn such a loan note to account by selling the beneficial interest (and thereafter holding the legal title in trust for the purchaser); or by agreeing to exercise the conversion rights for the benefit of a third party, so that they become the owner of the shares into which the loan note is converted.

The judgment on this point should be seen as a finding of fact in relation to the particular loan note in respect of which it was given. It is not a statement of law that in all circumstances, any loan note containing a formal prohibition on transfer is necessarily for that reason only not a debt on a security. It cannot be excluded as possible that a particular loan note could exist which notwithstanding a prohibition on transferability, would nonetheless be marketable, and capable of increasing in value, and of being the subject of a capital gain. That however is merely the view of the authors on this particular aspect of the judgment. It may well be that the courts will decide that the judgment in the Keleghan case is of universal application and that a bar on assignment is a complete answer to a charge that a debt is a debt on a security (provided it was not obtained in a share for paper exchange).

In paragraph 38.1 it is stated that "debt on a security is not defined". S541 does contain the phrase "a debt on a security within the meaning of s585". As explained in paragraph 38.1, s585 does not at all refer to a debt on a security, or give any meaning to it. What s585 does is to give a meaning to "security". Accordingly, the authors believe that it may be validly argued that the reference to "within the meaning of s585" governs solely the word "security" in the expression "debt on a security". If that is so, then the expression could be taken to read (substituting the s585 definition of security into the phrase used in s541) *"debt on a loan stock or similar security, whether of any government or of any public or local authority or of any company whether secured or unsecured but excluding securities within s6 and s7"*. If that meaning were applied to the expression, it would follow that an enquiry as to whether a debt was a debt on a security would focus on whether it was as a loan stock or similar to loan stock, and constituting a debt. However, the judgements in the McSweeney case and the Keleghan case now decisively state the law in Ireland and did not take this approach, nor have the UK cases.

On 1 January 1999 the euro was introduced as the currency of Ireland. The euro was also introduced into most of the other Member States of the EU on the same date.

Details of the participating States, and the fixed exchange rate between each participating currency and the euro are set out in the Table in the preliminary pages at the beginning of this book.

Where a debt on a security is expressed in foreign currency e.g. as a Deutshemark debt, the introduction of the euro for the Deutschemark as the currency of Germany, and the fact that the euro is also the currency of Ireland, does not affect the status of the debt as a chargeable asset. It is a chargeable asset because it is a "debt on a security" and it remains such no matter what currency it is expressed in.

s541A However the question does arise as to whether the substitution of the euro for the Deutschemark, as the currency of Germany, involves any disposal of a Deutschemark "debt on a security" at the 1 January 1999.

FA98 Sch2 The FA98 sch 2 para 9 inserted s541A to deal with the specific
Para9 position of a *foreign currency bank debt*, where where an amount is owed to a person in a currency other than Irish currency. S541A deems the bank debt to be:

• disposed of on 31 December 1998, and

- Immediately reacquired by that person at its market value.

The disposal will crystalise any gain or loss accruing at that date, although it will be treated as not accruing until the debt is actually disposed of. The reacquisition, gives the person to whom the debt is owed a new starting point combining a new acquisition date and new value.

It must be remembered that a bank debt is merely a debt, and is no different from any other foreign debt, and it is not in itself itself currency.

If the debt is a "debt on a security" for CGT purposes, it is a chargeable asset. If it is not a chargeable asset, the currency in which it is to be repaid does not alter its status for CGT purposes. It is either a "debt on a security" or it is not.

The treatment of currency, and the specific *exemption for Irish currency* is dealt with in paragraph 4.3, 8.10, and 9.1.2.2.

For example, where a *debt on a security* is expressed in Deutschemark, the Deutschemark continues to exist after the 1 January 1999, and the debt can be repaid in Deutschemark after that date and up to the 1 January 2002. The fact that the Deutschemark is no longer a national currency, but merely a denomination of the euro, does not seem a fact which would cause the Deutschemark denominated debt, to be regarded as being disposed of merely because of the introduction of the euro. It remains the *same debt* albeit the status of the currency in which it is to be be repaid may have changed.

If a debt on a security, written in Deutschemark prior to the 1 January 1999, still exists on 1 January 2002, it would no longer thereafter be possible to repay it in Deutschemark.

The EU Council regulations provide that :

- Where a payment is to be made by crediting an account, a debtor may pay either in euro or in the national currency of the Member State where the creditor has his account. The payment must be credited by the Financial Institution to the account in the denomination of the account (ie. either national currency or euro).

- Contracts and other legal instruments denonimated in a national currency will continue to be performed in that currency during the transitional period to 31 December 2001 (similarily those denominated in euro will be performed in euro) unless both parties agree otherwise,

- Spefic exceptions to this rule are made in the case of the National Debt, and the Stock Exchange (which changed fully to euro contracts from 1 January 1999).

• From 1 January 2002, all contracts are *deemed* to be in euro at the fixed conversion rate.

It is unlikely that the provisions could give rise to a successful arguement that the debt has been disposed of on the introduction of the euro, or on 1 January 2002 when the changeover to the euro is complete.

It would be surprising if the Revenue Commissioners took a different view, since the philosophy lying behind s541(1A)in dealing with euro matters, is to try as far as possible not to accelerate the due date of CGT merely by reason by introduction of the euro.

38.3   Property in Satisfaction of Debt

s541(3)   Where property is acquired by a creditor in satisfaction of a debt, the disposal and acquisition of the property will not be treated as being for a consideration greater than the market value of the property, irrespective of the value of the debt. Where the person acquiring the property is the original creditor and he makes a gain on the disposal of that property, there is a limit to the amount of the gain which is chargeable. The limit is the gain which would have arisen if he had acquired the property for a price equal to the amount of the debt.

Example 195

Mike owes Peter £5,000. In satisfaction of the debt he gives Peter a painting. At the date Peter acquires the painting it is worth £4,500. He sells it two years later for £6,000.

Peter cannot claim an allowable loss of £500 on the satisfaction (i.e. disposal) of the debt, as any gain on the disposal would not have been chargeable.

On sale of the painting his gain (ignoring indexation) is limited to:

Sale Price	£6,000
Less deemed consideration (amount of the debt)	£5,000
GAIN	£1,000

38.4   Loss on Debt Acquired from "Connected" Person

s541(4)   If a person acquires a debt from the original creditor (i.e. - from the person to whom the debt was originally due) any gain arising on a subsequent disposal of that debt would not be exempt. Where, however, the person who acquired the debt from the original creditor was connected with that original creditor (or his personal representatives or legatee) no allowable loss can arise on the subsequent disposal of the debt by that person. This restriction also applies where the debt was acquired directly or indirectly by one or more purchases through persons all of whom are connected with the person making the disposal.

This restriction on allowable losses applies to a company as it would apply to any other person. The restriction would apply, for example, where a debt is transferred from one member of a group to another member of a group. The actual transfer between group members does not trigger any chargeable gain due to group relief, even if the debt were a chargeable asset due to being a debt on a security, and even if the transferor company was not the original creditor. Notwithstanding that group relief applies to a transfer within the group of the debt, the rule which will restrict loss relief on a subsequent disposal by the transferee group company, will apply.

A further example of an unexpected instance where the restriction on loss relief would apply is where a debt is transferred between spouses. Even if the transferor spouse were the original creditor, so that had he made a disposal to a third party, no chargeable gain would have arisen, the transferee spouse would hold the debt as a chargeable asset and is liable to capital gains tax on any disposal of it (eg by repayment). Notwithstanding that the transferee spouse is fully chargeable to tax on the debt, the entitlement to loss relief on the transferred debt is denied. This particular treatment seems unsatisfactory in the case of transfers between spouses, and transfers between group companies, since the general structure of the CGT Acts is to attempt to treat such transfers as being tax neutral.

38.5 Trustees

s541(5)

Where the original creditor is a trustee, and the debt when created is settled property, when any person becomes entitled as against the Trustees to the debt he is treated as if he was the personal representative or legatee of the original creditor for the purpose of the above provisions.

38.6 Bank Balances

As explained in Paragraph 3.7.1, a bank account, being a debt, is regarded as located where the account holder is resident. It is not necessarily located where the bank, or the bank branch in question, is located.

This is different from the rule with applies in the case of income tax (and which applies for most commercial law purposes). A bank account in a French bank owned by an Irish resident person is an Irish located asset for CGT purposes, but is a French source of income for income tax purposes. Remittance basis would be available to a non-domiciled Irish resident person in relation to the interest, but not in relation to the gains on such an account.

FA98
Sch 2

FA98, Sch2 included a number of provisions related to the proposed substitution of the Euro for the Irish pound as the currency of Ireland on 1 January 1999. At that date the Euro was also substituted as official currency in several other states in Europe, with the present currency of those states (Deutschemark, French Franc, Italian Lira etc.) ceasing to exist as currencies, and becoming denominations of the Euro.

s541A   TCA 97 s541A was inserted by FA98 Sch2 para9 to deal with bank accounts which, prior to 1 January 1999, were expressed in what was then a foreign currency. The section provides that:

- the taxpayer is deemed to have disposed of the entire of the bank account immediately prior to the substitution of the euro for the Irish currency, and for the foreign currency in which the bank account was expressed.

- any tax resulting from the deemed disposal referred to above will be chargeable and assessable only when an actual disposal of the bank account occurs. Such actual disposals would usually occur when amounts are withdrawn from the account.

Example 196

John has always been a strong admirer of the Deutschemark, and has kept a Deutschemark bank account. He is domiciled and resident in Ireland. At 31 December 1998 the balance on his Deutschemark bank account stood at 248,330 Deutschemark. At that date, the equivalent amount of Irish pounds would have been £100,000 (assumed). On 1 January 1999 the number of Euro to which John would be entitled in respect of the amount standing in his Deutschemark bank account would be 70,000 Euro (assumed). The relevant rates of exchange are assumed for these purposes, and do not represent actual rates of exchange.

On 1 January 1999 both the Irish pound and the Deutschemark are denominations of the Euro, which is the currency of Ireland, and the currency of Germany.

John is deemed to have disposed of his Deutschemark bank account on 31 December 1998 for its then Irish pound equivalent of £100,000. However no tax liability becomes immediately due as a result of that deemed disposal. A tax liability will not arise until such time as John disposes of all or part of his bank account. The normal manner of making a disposal of a bank account is to withdraw sums from the account, whether by writing cheques, or otherwise.

In May 1999 John decides to buy quoted securities, rather than keeping his money in a bank account. He draws all of the 70,000 Euro from the account. On that date John is disposing of a debt (sum of money owing to him from a bank) which is not a chargeable asset, being a debt not a debt on a security, and expressed in the currency of the state. That disposal does not give rise to a chargeable gain directly, but it does resurrect the gain on the deemed disposal of the bank account on 31 December 1998. The tax arising on that deemed disposal now becomes due and payable as if the deemed disposal had occurred in May 1999. John would be liable to Capital Gains Tax in 1999/2000 in respect of the deemed disposal, and will be liable to pay Capital Gains Tax by 1 November 2001.

s541A   S541A does not provide rules for determining the times the balance on an account at 31 December 1998 is disposed of, where that account is a running account, with lodgements and withdrawals occurring regularly.

Example 197

> *John, the same taxpayer, with the same facts as in **example 196** above, lodged 30,000 Euro to his bank account in February 1999. In May 1999 his withdrawal from the account was in the amount of 70,000 Euro, out of the then balance of 100,000 Euro (being the 70,000 Euro which he had in December 1998, and the lodgement of 30,000 Euro in February 1999). Is John to be treated as disposing of the entire of his December 1998 bank balance (being the equivalent of 70,000 Euro) or is he to be treated as disposing of only part of the December 1998 balance (in the amount of 40,000 Euro), with the balance of the withdrawal being treated as representing the February lodgement? Although the Capital Gains Tax Acts do not provide any special rule for answering this question, banking law would offset sums withdrawn from an account firstly against the earliest sums lodged to the account, leaving the balance on the account represented by the most recent lodgements. On that basis, John would be treated as disposing of the entire of his December 1998 balance when he withdrew 70,000 Euro in May 1999.*

S541A applies only to debts owing from a bank, in foreign currency. The section does not apply to other debts in foreign currency.

38.7   Bank Balances in Foreign Currency

s541(6)

The exemption from CGT on the disposal of a debt does not apply to a debt owed by a bank, where the funds standing to the credit of the person's account with the bank are not in Irish currency. This exception to the normal rule does not apply where the foreign currency was acquired by the person for the personal expenditure outside Ireland, of himself and his family or dependents. This includes the cost of maintaining a residence outside Ireland. The normal exemption would apply to the debt represented by the foreign currency held by the bank in such a case.

The relevance of the Euro is explained in paragraph 38.2.

38.8   Foreign currency loans

s80

The FA93 (with retrospective affect) treated as a trading receipt the gain or loss arising to a company in connection with the repayment of certain foreign currency loans, the interest on which would be treated under s130 as a distribution. These were usually so called high coupon "s84 loans". These gains and losses would in some instances otherwise be capital gains or losses of a company.

As the subject is more properly in the area of corporation tax, it is not described further here. Reference may be made to the companion volume in the series, Corporation Tax by Brennan, Moore, & Carr.

38.9   **Exchange gains and losses of trading company**

s79   Many exchange gains or losses of a trading company are now treated by s79 as being part of the income of the company, notwithstanding that on basic principles they might more properly be regarded as capital gains or capital losses. As the topic is more proper to corporation tax on income, it is not proposed to examine it further here. Reference may be made to the companion volume, Corporation Tax, published by the Institute of Taxation in Ireland.

This treatment as income extends in particular to gains and losses arising in relation to money held by the company, or liabilities incurred by the company for the purposes of its trade. Such liabilities extend not only to trade creditors, but could also extend to bank indebtedness and borrowing incurred for the purpose of the trade. Gains or losses arising on transactions entered into for the purpose of hedging the exchange exposure on the assets and liabilities just referred to, are also treated as income.

The FA96 further extended the classes of gains and losses in relation to foreign exchange which are not treated as capital gains or allowable losses by including gains or losses arising from the hedging of corporation tax liabilities by a company whose functional currency is not Irish currency. That extension of special treatment applies as respects accounting periods ending on or after 1 April 1996.

It is of particular relevance to companies operating in Shannon or in the IFSC and which may be subject to controlled foreign company (CFC), or other anti-avoidance legislation, in another tax jurisdiction.

Any exchange gains or losses arising on the taxation liability would of course be outside the scope of capital gains tax (or corporation tax on companies capital gains) since they would arise in relation to a liability. Capital gains tax arises only on gains arising from the disposal of an asset. However a hedging instrument designed to hedge against the exchange exposure on the corporation tax liability would be an asset, and the gain arising on such a hedging instrument was therefore potentially within the scope of tax on capital gains, notwithstanding that the matching gain/loss on the tax liability was not. The affect of the 1996 amendment therefore has been to give matching tax treatment to the exchange gain or loss on the tax liability, and the parallel exchange gain or loss on the hedging instrument.

Unlike gains or losses arising on the other assets and liabilities within the scope of s79, those arising on the corporation tax liability and its hedging instrument are not treated as income but are simply disregarded entirely for tax purposes.

38.10   Debentures - "paper for paper".

s584
s586
s587

Under s584, s586 and s587, provided certain conditions are met it is possible for a person to swap shares or debentures in a company for other shares or debentures, without being treated as disposing of the original assets. (see paragraph 42).

If a person swapped shares or debentures (which were in the form of debts on a security) for debentures which were in a form that did not constitute a debt on a security, and the reorganisation, reconstruction and amalgamation provisions referred to above applied to the swap, no chargeable gain would arise to the taxpayer on that occasion. Neither of course would a chargeable gain arise on a subsequent disposal of the new debentures, since they would not be chargeable assets, not being a debt on a security (see paragraph 38.1).

s541
s584(2)
s586(2)
s587(2)

FA96 s61 has amended s541 to provide that where a company issues a debenture in a reorganisation to which paragraph s584(2) applies (reorganisation of a company's share capital); or one to which s586(2) applies (company amalgamations by exchange of shares); or one to which s587(2) applies (company reconstructions and amalgamations), the debenture so issued shall be (regardless of what they may otherwise be) debts on a security for the purposes of the capital gains tax acts. Similarly, if a debenture is issued to a debenture holder who has obtained his original debenture under the sections referred to (as described above) in respect of such a debenture this additional debenture is also to be regarded as a debt on a security, no matter what its features may be.

This provision applies to the disposal of a debenture on or after the 28th day of March 1996. It therefore has application on the disposal of a debenture which was obtained in a "shares or debenture for debenture" swap or capital reorganisation completed prior to 28 March 1996.

Example 198

Joe swapped his 100 shares in Oldco Ltd. for £100,000 of debentures in Newco Ltd. on 30 June 1995 in a swap to which paragraph 4(2) applied. The debentures carried no interest, were repayable on demand, were unsecured and in Irish pounds. They were accordingly not debts on a security. On 31 January 1996 Joe obtained repayment of £50,000 of the debentures. On 30 May 1996 the balance of £50,000 was repaid.

The original swap was not treated as a disposal of the shares or as an acquisition of the debentures, by reason of s586(2).

The 30 January 1996 repayment was a disposal of part of the debentures. Because they were not a debt on a security, no chargeable gain arose on the transaction.

The 30 May 1996 repayment is treated as a disposal of a chargeable asset and a chargeable gain or allowable loss may arise on the disposal. This is because s.61

FA 1996 (as incorporated in s541(7)) deems the debentures to be a debt on a security, on a disposal after 28 March 1996.

The FA97 extended the 1996 provisions (see s541(7)) in a minor way to provide that any debenture obtained by reason of a transaction which falls within the merger directive provisions (s631, s632 and s637) would also be a debt on a security.

It further provided that any debenture obtained by reason of rights attaching to debentures obtained in a reorganisation or a merger directive transaction would also be a debt on a security. However, the 1997 provisions did not go further to provide that a debenture received by reason of rights attaching to a debenture obtained in a reorganisation or merger directive transaction would also be a debt on a security.

The FA97 extension of the provisions (incorporated in TCA97 s541(7)) applies to the disposal of a debenture on or after 26 March 1997. This could apply to a debenture acquired prior to that date, and in such a case would have retrospective effect.

39   OPTIONS AND FORFEITED DEPOSITS

39.1   Broad outline

An option is specifically included as an 'asset' for CGT purposes (see paragraph 4.2).

The first matter to deal with, is what is an option ? This is not defined in the Taxes Acts. It was described by Mr. Justice Goff at the UK Chancery Division stage of the hearing of Sainsbury v O'Connor in the following terms -

"An option is not a conditional contract but an irrevocable offer which is open to acceptance by the exercise of the option. In the meantime, the grantor is under a contractual obligation not to put it out of his power to do what he has offered to do; but subject thereto, he retains not only equitable ownership, but also the rights of beneficial enjoyment normally attaching to equitable ownership".

It is clear from this, that an option is not in itself a contract. It is an offer. The exercise of the option fulfills the 'acceptance' condition required for a contract, and it then becomes a contract.

The Irish case of Edward J. Kearns v T.A. Dilleen Inspector of Taxes, is considered in detail in paragraph 39.3.2. In the course of the judgement in the Supreme Court the following was stated by Mr Justice Barron:

"The reality of a transaction is not governed by the words used to describe it. The word "option" involves choice the purpose of which in the usual option purchase agreement is to enable the option holder to have further

time whether or not to purchase. When over 98% of the price is paid for the option to purchase the element of choice is removed from the transactions. The form of the transaction may be that of an option but in substance it is not an option. No one would pay 98% of the price of a property for the choice to pay less than a further 2% to acquire the property or give up the 98% already paid and be left with neither the money or the property. Even if the usual option price had been paid the scheme could not have succeeded on that ground alone."

This comment may cast some doubt on the definition of an option quoted above from the Sainsbury v O'Connor case. However, the comments, although those of Supreme Court Judge, are obiter dicta, in that the case had already been decided on another ground. They appear to come perilously close to substituting economic substance for legal form and legal substance, an approach rejected in the McGrath case. It also comes close to basing a decision on supposed facts (the likelihood of an option being exercised) upon which (in the case in question) there was no finding of fact by the Appeal Commissioners who are the sole fact-finding body. It would conflict with common sense to say that in a circumstance in which 98% of the ultimate total consideration for an asset has been paid on foot of an option, that a person will always wish to pay the remaining 2%. If a deal has gone sufficiently bad, 2% may be very little to rescue from it, but few people would neglect the opportunity to rescue it if the asset had become entirely worthless. Some assets may not only be entirely worthless, but can be onerous e.g. shares in an unlimited company. If such an unlimited company ran into financial difficulties, the person holding options over shares might be unwilling to accept those shares for any price whatever. Nonetheless, the comments of Mr Justice Barron cannot be safely ignored, until the Courts have had a further opportunity to deal with the matter.

There are many different types of options which could be entered into. For example, an option may bind the person who granted the option (the 'grantor') to buy an asset, or to sell an asset, or perhaps to both buy an asset and sell an asset. The option can either be exercised, sold on to someone else, or merely abandoned. The option may be quoted - see paragraph 39.5. All of these variations depend on the terms and conditions of the option.

If the option is for a period of less than 50 years, it may be a 'wasting asset' for CGT purposes (see paragraph 10). Options involve both the grantor and the grantee, and the implications for both must be considered.

A lessee under a hire purchase agreement usually has the option to acquire the asset in certain circumstances. Notwithstanding that such an acquisition is on foot of the exercise of an option to purchase, it is not treated in the same way as other options. There is a special treatment laid down in the legislation for disposals under hire purchase contracts. This is explained in Paragraph 15. It affects principally the date of disposal and of acquisition of an asset acquired on foot of a hire purchase agreement. Other provisions relating to an option (eg the consequences of the abandonment of an option) can apply equally to the option element of a hire purchase agreement as they do to any other option.

The date of disposal of an asset, and of acquisition of an asset where it occurs through the exercise of an option is described in Paragraph 15.2.

s540

In a straightforward situation where a person acquires an option to purchase an asset, and subsequently exercises the option and buys the asset, he would normally regard the cost of the asset as including both the cost of the option, and the purchase price of the asset under the option. This is only applying common sense to the reality of what is happening. The CGT legislation approaches the problem in the same way, by treating the cost of an asset acquired under an option as including, both the cost of the option and the cost of acquiring the asset under the option. Similarly, the vendor is regarded as selling the asset for the total of the amount received for the grant of the option itself, plus the consideration receivable under the option for the actual sale of the asset - the option being regarded a merely part of the overall transaction to acquire or dispose of the related asset.

The main tax problems arise where the option is not exercised (e.g. where it is abandoned) and there is no other asset actually sold or acquired to link with the option. In these circumstances, the option stands alone, and special rules are set out for dealing with this, and other situations which can arise with options.

s540

The legislation dealing with the CGT treatment of options was contained in s.47, 1975 Act, as amended by CGT(A)A 1978, s.17 and Sch 2, and F.A. 1992, s.63 and is now found in TCA97 s540.

39.2   **General rules**

s540(2)

The CGT rules initially treat the grant of an option as the disposal of a separate asset (i.e. the option itself) subject to changing that treatment if an asset is actually acquired or disposed of under the option. In that case the option and the asset merge into a single transaction - the acquisition and disposal of that asset (with both the option price plus the asset price being treated as the cost of acquisition and also as the disposal price for the vendor).

The general rule in the Capital Gains Tax Acts is that a person is to be treated as disposing of an asset in a transaction only if they had owned the asset prior to and at the time of entering into the transaction. The asset must exist and be owned by the vendor at the moment of disposal. An asset brought into existence by a transaction is not treated as being disposed of for capital gains tax purposes, by the transaction which creates it. That general rule is subject to exceptions, and the provisions of s540, in deeming the grant of an option to be the disposal of an asset consisting of the option, consists of one such specific exception. The general rule is discussed in paragraph 4.2.4.

s540(2) states that... *'Without prejudice to the provisions of s534 and s535* (capital sums derived from assets - see paragraph 4.4) *the grant of an option .... is the disposal of an asset (namely, of the option), but subject to the following provisions of this section as to treating the grant of an option as part of a larger transaction.'*

This general rule, regarding the option as standing alone where it is not exercised, extends to include:

"(a)   *the grant of an option in a case where the grantor binds himself to sell an asset he does not own, and because the option is abandoned, never has occasion to own, and*

(b)   *the grant of an option in a case where the grantor binds himself to buy an asset, which, because the option is abandoned, he does not acquire."* - s540(2).

s540(3)(4)   The second part of this concept, treating the option as part of the acquisition (or disposal) of the asset itself - where the option is exercised - is dealt with in s540(3),(4). The position of the grantor of the option, whether it binds him to buy or to sell, is dealt with in s540(3):

"(3)   *Where an option is exercised, the grant of the option and the transaction entered into by the grantor in fulfillment of his obligations under the option shall be treated as a single transaction, and accordingly for the purposes of the Capital Gains Tax Acts:-*

(a)   *if the option binds the grantor to sell, the consideration for the option shall be part of the consideration for the sale, and*

(b)   *if the option binds the grantor to buy, the consideration shall be deducted from the cost of acquisition incurred by the grantor in buying in pursuance of his obligations under the option."*

s540(4)   Where the option is exercised, the exercise of the option is not regarded as the disposal of an asset - i.e. the option is not treated as a separate asset. This applies whether the option is exercised by the original grantee of the option, or any subsequent holder of that option. In such a case, the acquisition of the option, and the transaction entered into under that option merge into a single transaction and following from that, s540(4) provides:

'(a)   *if the option binds the grantor to sell, the cost of acquiring the option shall be part of the cost of acquiring the asset which is sold, and*

(b)   if the option binds the grantor to buy, the cost of the option shall be treated as a cost incidental to the disposal of the asset which is bought by the grantor of the asset.'

Where an option is exercised, the grant of the option and the related transaction together form a single transaction. The treatment of the consideration received for the option itself, depends on whether the grantor bound himself to buy or sell the asset concerned.

If the option bound the grantor to sell an asset, the consideration for the option forms part of the disposal proceeds of the asset.

The UK case of Strange v Openshaw confirmed that the grant of an option was to be treated as the disposal of an asset consisting of the option; and not as a part disposal of the asset over which the option was granted.

The following examples illustrate the operation of these rules.

s540(3)(a)   *Example 199- Exercise of option to sell : treatment of grantor*

Peter grants an option to Philip for £1,000 binding Peter to sell certain investments to Philip for £50,000 if called upon to do so with 6 months of the date of the option. Philip exercises his rights under the option, and Peter sells to investments to him for the agreed price.

The total sale proceeds of the disposal of the investments is calculated (for CGT purposes) under s540(3)(a) as follows:

Sale price of investments	*£50,000*
Sale proceeds of grant of option	*£1,000*
Total sale proceeds	*£51,000*

If the option bound the grantor to sell an asset, the CGT cost of acquiring the property in the case of the grantee includes both the price paid for the option, and the cost of acquiring the asset under that option.

s540(4)(a)   *Example 200 - Exercise of option to sell : treatment of grantee*

Suzanne grants Helen an option for £5,000, which binds her to sell a certain property to Helen for £75,000 if called upon to do so within a specified period from the date of the option. Helen exercises her rights under the option and calls upon Suzanne to sell her the property.

Helen has paid £5,000 to Suzanne for the option, and has also paid £75,000 under the terms of the option for the purchase of the property. The CGT cost to Helen in acquiring the property is the option cost of £5,000 plus the actual price paid for the property - i.e. a total of £80,000.

If the option binds the grantor to buy an asset, the consideration he receives for the grant of the option is deducted from the cost of acquisition of the asset acquired under the option.

s540(3)(b)   *Example 201 - Exercise of option to purchase : treatment of grantor*

Peter grants an option to Philip for £1,000 binding him (Peter) to buy certain investments from Philip for £50,000 if called upon to do so with 6 months of the date of the option. Philip exercises his rights under the option, and Peter buys the investments from Philip for the agreed price.

The cost of the investments to Peter, calculated under the rule in s540(3) is as follows:

Purchase price	£50,000
Less - received for option	£1,000
Base cost for CGT	£49,000

Where the option binds the grantor to buy an asset, the position of the grantee, is that he has incurred expenditure in acquiring the option, and when the option is exercised, he has received the agreed price for the asset. Combining the two transactions, the grantee is treated as if he has sold the asset for the option price, and the cost of acquiring the option, is treated as an incidental cost of disposal of the asset.

s540(4)(b)   ***Example 202 - Exercise of option to purchase : treatment of grantee***

Suzanne grants Helen an option for £5,000, under which Suzanne binds herself to purchase a certain asset from Helen for £75,000 if called upon to do so within six months after the date of the option. Helen exercises the option within the period allowed.

Helen is treated as selling the property to Suzanne for £75,000. In determining her cost in calculating the gain or loss on disposal, Helen will take the normal cost of that property into account, and is also allowed to treat the £5,000 option cost as an incidental cost of the disposal of the property

There are many circumstances where the actual consideration for a disposal is ignored, and 'market value' is substituted for CGT purposes. The rules dealing with options do not in any way affect those 'consideration rules' (see paragraph 16). The sole purpose of the 'option rules' is to deal with the adjustment to the 'consideration' for the acquisition or disposal of the asset, arising out of the amount received or paid for the option itself. It should be noted, that the consideration for the option itself, is also subject to the 'consideration - arms length' rules.

The UK case of Garner v Pounds Ship Owners and Ship Breakers is an interesting example of capital gains tax applying to the grant of an option which was not subsequently exercised. In that case the option agreement bound the grantor to use his best endeavours to secure the release of certain covenants over land (the land being the subject matter of the option).

The release of the covenants was secured at a cost of £90,000. An issue in the case was whether the £90,000 was a deductible expense in the computation in relation to the gain on the disposal of the option (on the occasion of it being granted). The judge noted that as the grantor had never acquired the option (which only came into existence when he granted it) no deduction could be claimed for the £90,000 that was being the cost of acquisition. The judge also held that it was not a cost of "producing" the option as it was a cost incurred subsequent to the option being granted.

The rule that the grant of an option, and the transaction entered into on its exercise, are to be treated as a single transaction, applies only where the subsequent transaction on the exercise of the option is one involving the grantor of the option. This is explicitly stated in s540. No rule is provided for the situation where an option is granted, but the subsequent exercise of the option involves somebody other than the grantor.

Example 203

Joe Bloggs owned shares in Bloggs Trading Limited. On 1 January 2000 he granted an option to Martha Brown to acquire all of the shares for £1m. The consideration for the grant of the option was the sum of £100. The option was expressed to be for a period of one year and to be enforceable against Joe Bloggs, and against his successors in title to the shares.

On 30 January 2000 Joe Bloggs died unexpectedly. On 30 June 2000 his executors obtained probate of his estate. On 30 September 2000 Martha Brown exercised the option against the executors and called on them to sell the shares to her, which they did.

S540 does not appear to require that the grant of an option by Joe Bloggs be treated as part of the same transaction as the disposal of shares by his executors to Martha. In the absence of any express provision dealing with the new situation, Joe Bloggs must be treated as having granted an option and thereby disposed of an asset. The consideration,(assuming it is an arm's length transaction) would be £100. The executors would be treated as selling the shares for the sum of £1m. The consideration paid to Joe Bloggs prior to his death for the grant of the option would not be aggregated with it.

A similar situation could arise if, subsequent to the grant of the option by Joe Bloggs, he sold, gifted, or settled the shares subject to the option.

39.3   The abandonment of an option

39.3.1   Present position

s540(5)   Where the option is abandoned (e.g. where it is not exercised, and not passed on to someone else) the option stands alone as a separate asset for CGT purposes. It is necessary to look at the treatment of

• the grantor (who has received a sum for granting the option) and

• the grantee (who has paid a sum to acquire the option).

S540(5) provides that:

"(a)   The abandonment of an option by the person for the time being entitled to exercise it shall constitute the disposal of an asset (being the option) by that person."

S540(5)(b) then goes on to restrict relief for a loss arising on the abandonment of an option.

Prior to 7th May 1992, the abandonment of an option was not a disposal of the option. The Courts have clarified that an abandonment of an option for consideration has always been a disposal for CGT purposes.

Most options refer to a specific period of time within which they are effective. After that period has passed the option simply lapses and ceases to exist. It is also possible that the option is abandoned for value, e.g. a consideration is paid to the holder of the option not to exercise his rights under that option. This raises the question of whether the 'abandonment of an option' for consideration is in fact an 'abandonment' for this purpose. What does the term 'abandonment' mean in this context?

The point has been considered in a number of UK cases, and also in an Irish case. These cases all related to the position prior to 7 May 1992 at times when s540 had provided that the abandonment of an option was not a disposal of the option - and accordingly not capable of generating a taxable gain.

In the UK cases, a majority of the judges have held that an abandonment for consideration is within the meaning of "abandonment" in the UK equivalent of the Irish s540. The decision in the Irish case on this point has gone against the judgements in the UK cases, and held the contrary view. Mr. Justice Costello in his judgement in the High Court delivered on 26 November 1993 in the case of Dilleen v Kearns, ruled that an abandonment for full consideration in that case was not an 'abandonment' of an option within the meaning of s540.

Since the abandonment of an option is now treated as a disposal, a computation of gain or loss is required and accordingly, the consideration for the disposal and the base cost must be identified.

In the case of the grantor, the value of the sale proceeds received by him for granting the option is normally clear - but there may be circumstances where s547 or s549 may require the substitution of market value where the transaction is not a bargain at arms length, or where it was between connected persons (see paragraph 16).

In the case of the grantee, the main issue is that he has paid a sum in acquiring the option but he has not exercised any rights under that option, and they are now gone, perhaps expired with the time period of the option. He has nothing, but has paid out a capital sum. What relief (if any) is available for that capital sum ?

The grantee has clearly incurred a loss - and the question of whether any relief is available for that loss must be considered. The general rule, is that any loss arising on the abandonment of an option is not available for CGT loss relief. Relief is given only in the case of:

- an option to acquire trade assets,
- a quoted option for shares, and
- a traded option,

subject to the separate conditions (set out in s540) which apply in the case of each of these types of options. The treatment of losses arising on such options is dealt with in paragraphs 39.5 and 39.6 below.

The special treatment referred to above for an option to acquire trade assets does not appear to extend to an option to acquire assets for the purpose of a profession, office, or employment carried on by the person. "Trade" has the same meaning in the Capital Gains Tax Acts as it has in the Income Tax Acts [s.2(2)]. The option in question must be to acquire assets which the person having the option intends (on acquisition) to use for the purpose of a trade carried on by him, which he commences to carry on within two years of his acquisition of the option.

s559

The question of the 'cost' of the option is a more difficult matter, and in particular, what (if any) part of the cost of the related asset can be attributed to the option. s559 allows part of the cost of an asset to be attributed to another asset, where in certain circumstances the value of that other asset has been derived from the value of the main asset (see paragraph 9.10). There can be little doubt but that the value of the option has derived from the asset over which the option subsists. Many varying opinions have been expressed on this point, but there is no general agreement, and indeed the amount may well vary considerably from case to case, depending on the circumstances.

Example 204

In January 1994 Jim Farmer granted an option to Bill Neighbour to purchase 100 acres of agricultural land from him at any time in the next 3 years, for the sum of £200,000. The consideration paid by Bill for the option was £5,000. At the time the option was granted, they farmed adjacent farms, and Jim was of the opinion that the land had no value apart from its agricultural use.

The following year it became clear that the local Council was looking to purchase land in that area for use as a tiphead. Jim could not get Bill to abandon his option, and could not sell his land (which was subject to the option) to the County Council. In fact it became clear during discussions with the Council, that they would prefer the location of Jim's land. Instead, they purchased 100 acres from Bill for an agreed price of £2m. Bill retained the option over Jim's land. The following year, the option expired, and ceased to exist as the time period ran out.

It is clear that Jim has received the sum of £5,000. Has he any deductible 'cost' (apart from any legal fees) ? There is no doubt, but that he has lost considerably by the transaction, and the option has cost him dearly. That, however, does not

> *mean that he is entitled to a deduction for any part of that cost in calculating a gain or loss for CGT purposes.*

There are many circumstances where the value of the asset is reduced after the granting of the option, and perhaps directly because of the grant of the option. There are equally as many circumstances where the value of the option is substantially increased, in that it takes its value from the asset over which it subsists.

s559

The general rule where assets derive value from other assets (in the same ownership) is dealt with in s559. On the disposal of an asset which has derived value from another asset (i.e. the option), part of the cost of the asset may be attributed to the derived asset (i.e. the option).

It is understood that the Revenue Commissioners would resist any such claim. Until such time as an actual case is decided by the Courts, it is unlikely that there will be any general agreement on this point.

The following paragraphs dealing with options have been written on the assumption that, where the option stands alone (i.e. where it is abandoned) that no part of the cost of the related asset can be attributed to it.

39.3.2 Historical position

Prior to 7th May 1992 (s.63 F.A. 1992), s540(4) provided that *"the exercise or abandonment of an option ..... shall not constitute a disposal of an asset ...by the person entitled to exercise it"*. That section then went on the deal with the case of where the option was exercised, and the option merged with the actual transfer of the asset to form a single transaction for CGT purposes. No further mention was made of the 'abandonment' of an option. This lead to a number of tax avoidance schemes, based on the assumption that if the abandonment of an option was not a disposal, then no gain could arise on such a transaction.

That provision was used in the UK for tax avoidance purposes, and following what appeared to be the initial success of that scheme before the Appeal Commissioners, and Chancery division in the UK, it was tried in Ireland as well.

FA92 s63

In Ireland, the FA92 changed the law to clarify the position - that the abandonment of an option **is a disposal** for CGT purposes, subject to a restriction of loss relief. The original s.47(3) (now s540(4)) provided that 'the exercise or abandonment of an option' does not constitute a disposal for CGT purposes. The words 'or abandonment' were removed by FA92 s63.

Although the law has now changed, the previous legislation gave rise to a number of Court cases, in which the meaning of the term 'abandonment' was considered in the context of options.

In the UK case of Golding v Kaufman, the taxpayer had a right under an option agreement to call on an unconnected third party to purchase certain shares owned by the taxpayer at a price determined under the option agreement. The third party did not want to buy the shares, and he paid the taxpayer £5,000 to forgo his rights under the option agreement - i.e.. to abandon the option. The Revenue assessed the taxpayer on the entire option proceeds, as being a capital sum derived from an asset (see paragraph 4.4). The taxpayer appealed, contending that it was a payment in respect of the abandonment of an option, and consequently not chargeable to CGT.

The word 'abandonment' is not defined in the CGT legislation.

The Commissioners who heard the appeal, held in favour of the taxpayer. The Revenue appealed against the decision of the Commissioners, and the case came before Vinelott J., in the Chancery Division.

In the course of his judgement he said,

"If the words 'abandoned' and 'abandonment' are construed solely in the context of ..s.47 (now s540).. it is, I think, difficult to reach any confident conclusions to the precise meaning to be attributed to those words. The difficulty cannot be resolved by reference to dictionaries or even to other contexts in which these words are used. As with other words in common use, the words 'abandoned' and 'abandonment' are of infinite scope and may cover a range of related meanings. Their precise scope or connotation can only be ascertained by examination of the particular context in which they are used."

In considering the context in which the word 'abandonment' was used, Vinelott J considered the interrelationship between (*the equivalent Irish provisions are referred to below*):

s535(2)
- s535(2).....dealing with capital sums derived from assets (see paragraph 3.4),

s538
- s538...dealing with the loss, destruction or dissipation of an asset (see paragraphs 3.4 and 18.4) and

s540
- s540.......dealing with options.

Although he held that the word 'abandonment' is clearly used in its wider sense including an abandonment for value (a view since ruled against by Mr Justice Costello in the Irish High Court) he held that s540 was merely qualifying s538 which gives relief for a loss arising from the 'loss destruction, dissipation or extinction' of an asset. It did not mean that there was no disposal within the meaning of s535(2). In approving the contention of the Crown who argued for such a construction of the legislation, Vinelott J said:

"It explains why..s.12(3) (now s538)..applies whether or not a capital sum is received, and why..s.12(3) and s.8(2) (now s535(2)) is not expressly made subject to the provisions of..s.47 (now s540). S.47(3) (now s540(4)) before the F.A. 1992 amendment ... creates an exception to the general rule that the extinction of an asset is to be treated as a disposal for the purposes of creating an allowable loss."

The UK case of Welbeck Securities Limited v Powlson also dealt with the abandonment of an option. In that case, the taxpayer company received £2m in consideration of which it agreed to release and abandon an option to participate in a property development. The Court of Appeal decided that, on its true construction of the equivalent UK legislation, s540(4) - as it stood before the Irish FA92 amendment - did not confer an exemption from the chargeable disposal which arose under s535(2) when the sum of £2m was received by the taxpayer company for the surrender of the option.

A similar situation was considered by the Irish High Court in the case of T.A. Dilleen (Inspector of Taxes) v Edward J Kearns. judgement was delivered in that case by Mr Justice Costello on 26 November 1993.

s811

The case was frankly admitted to be a 'tax avoidance scheme', although that in itself was not relevant to the outcome of the case - in accordance with the decision of the Supreme Court in the McGrath case (see paragraph 69). The transactions were prior to the commencement of the general anti-avoidance provisions of TCA97 s811.

The following is a brief outline of the case insofar as they are relevant to the decision in the case regarding the treatment of the 'abandonment of an option':

Mr. and Mrs K owned all of the share capital of a company (Coldstream), Mr K owning 5,000 shares, and Mrs K owning 11,000 shares. The scheme involved each of them granting an option to the other to buy their shares in the company, i.e.

• Mr K granted his wife an option to purchase his shares, the sum of £841,666 being payable on the grant of the option, and £15,000 on its exercise.

• Mrs K granted her husband an option to purchase her shares, the sum of £1,686,834 being payable on the grant of the option, and £27,500 on its exercise.

A short time later, they both sold their own shares (subject in each case to the option in favour of the other spouse) to an unconnected company for the amount payable on exercise of the option (i.e. £15,000, and £27,500 respectively). The shares were now owned by that unconnected company, but were subject to the options held by Mr & Mrs K.

On the same day, the purchasing company entered into and concluded a contract with each of the two spouses, whereby it paid to each of them a sum of money to abandon the option. In each case the amount paid was equal to the amount already paid by those individuals to purchase the option in the first instance - i.e. £843,166 to Mrs K, and £1,689,344 to Mr K. The unconnected company had bought all the shares for a total of

	£
Purchase of shares (From Mr K)	27,500
Purchase of shares (from Mrs K)	15,000
Payment to abandon option (Mr K)	843,166
Payment to abandon option (Mrs K)	1,689,344
TOTAL	2,575,000

The unconnected company now owned all the shares, and the options were gone. It then sold on the shares to another body corporate owned by Mr & Mrs K for £2,577,200.

The Revenue assessed Mr & Mrs K on the basis that the combined sums received for the abandonment of the options (£2,532,500) represented the proceeds of the disposal of assets - i.e. the options.

The question for decision by the Court was whether the £2,532,500 (in total) received by Mr & Mrs K for abandoning their options:

s535(2)
- amounted to the proceeds of disposal of an asset (the options) by virtue of s535(2) *(capital sums received in return for forfeiture or surrender of rights, or for refraining from exercising rights)*,

or

- whether the transaction was excluded from the scope of s535, because the 'abandonment of an option' is not a disposal for CGT purposes - under s540(4).

The Appeal Commissioners held in favour of the Revenue, and the Circuit Court held in favour of the Taxpayer. The case than came before Mr Justice Costello in the High Court. In considering the case, he also considered the reported UK cases of Golding v Kaufman, and Welbeck Securities v Powlson (see above).

In those UK cases, two separate points were considered, and a similar approach was adopted by the taxpayer and the Revenue in the Irish case.

(1) **whether the term 'abandonment' in the context of s540(4) was broad enough to include an abandonment for full consideration.**

The majority of judgements in those UK cases held in favour of the term 'abandonment' being wide enough to include an abandonment for full consideration. However, in the Irish case, Mr Justice Costello preferred the view of the minority dissenting judgement of Bingham, LJ in the UK, which held that an abandonment for consideration was not a real abandonment of an option. In the course of his judgement, Mr Justice Costello said *"It seems to me that when the Oireachtas used the phrase 'abandonment of an option' in section 47(3) of our 1975 Act (now s540(4)) it was not using a term of art and so the Court must construe it in its ordinary meaning. The Court should look at the whole of the transaction which has given rise to the assessment and consider whether in the ordinary meaning of the term it can be said that the taxpayer has 'abandoned' an option. And in doing so the substance of the transaction is what should be considered and not merely the words used to give it effect.......if he institutes proceedings asserting his right to the option and settles his claim by accepting a substantial sum of money in return for not doing so, it seems to me that he cannot be said to have "abandoned" his option. He has put his option to good use and has obtained an advantage for himself by doing so. He has not discarded a right which is of no value to him - he has traded it for valuable consideration.......And the same considerations will apply if, as in this case, the option holder accepts from a third party a sum of money in consideration for an agreement not to exercise the option. The parties may use the term 'abandonment', to describe what the option holder will do but in reality it is no such thing."*

In the Supreme Court Mr Justice Barron said *"a true abandonment is a unilateral action; when you give up a right for a consideration the action is no longer unilateral. Consequently there was no abandonment of the option in this case."*

(2) **whether s540(4) [*abandonment of an option*] is an exception to the general charge under s535(2) [*capital sum derived from an asset*].**

s540(4)

On this point, Mr Justice Costello agreed with the conclusions of the UK Judges on the same point, ...*"All that s.47(3) (now s540(4)) of the 1975 Act does is to provide that the abandonment of an option is not to constitute the 'disposal of an asset' - it does not exempt from liability a transaction involving the receipt of a capital sum on the abandonment of an option. As there is no valid reason why the Oireachtas should have intended to exempt from capital gains tax a capital sum received on the release of an option, and as there are no other provisions of the 1975 Statute to displace the construction of*

S.47(3) (now s540(4)) to which I have referred, I must conclude that S.47(3) does not operate to exempt the capital sums received by the taxpayer and his wife from the liability clearly arising from s.8(2)(a) (now s535(2))".

Mr Justice Murphy, in the Supreme Court, said *"the legislature isolated the exercise of an option and its abandonment from the remainder of the transactions in which these events occur and left intact the charging provisions relating to or arising from any other events in such transactions. Although an abandonment of an option is not a disposal the receipt of a capital sum arising from a consideration for such an abandonment could be a disposal and liable under (TCA97 s535)."*

Where a person makes a payment to another in order that that other should abandon an option, the question arises as to whether the payment would form any part of the base cost of the person who makes the payment. The person making the payment acquires no asset as a result of the payment. It would seem therefore that the only basis upon which a claim might be made for a deduction is that the payment represented enhancement expenditure on an asset owned by the person making the payment. It is doubtful if a claim for enhancement expenditure would be successful. To be successful it is necessary that the payment be reflected in the state or nature of the asset. If the result of the payment is that a person having an option over the asset abandons that option, a restraint on the ownership rights of the owner of the asset is removed; the asset itself is unaffected. The matter is not beyond doubt, but in the authors opinion the state or nature of the asset has not been affected by the lifting of the option and no deduction is available for the payment made to secure its abandonment.

39.4   Option for trade assets

s540(7)   If a person acquires an option to purchase assets for use in his trade, the abandonment (or disposal) of that option (despite the general rule to the contrary) can give rise to an allowable CGT loss. In addition, the normal rule which would treat the option as a wasting asset, does not apply.

This relief applies where the grantee intends to use the assets, either for the purpose of a trade then carried on by him, or which he commences within 2 years of the option being granted.

This, in effect gives relief for the full sum expended on the option, as no part of the cost is 'wasted'.

39.5   Quoted options and traded options

s540(8)

The same rule as for the abandonment of an option to acquire trade assets applies in the case of a quoted option to subscribe for shares in a company, and a traded option.

This, in effect gives relief for the full sum expended on the option, as no part of the cost is 'wasted'. For this purpose,

- a 'quoted option' means:

  "an option which at the time of abandonment or other disposal, is quoted, and, dealt in on a stock exchange in the State or elsewhere, in the same manner as shares."

- a "traded option" means:

  'An option which, at the time of abandonment or other disposal, is quoted on a stock exchange or futures exchange in the State or elsewhere.'

39.6   Transfer of an option

The transfer of an option from the person who held it to another person, is the disposal of an asset (the option).

An option may be a 'wasting asset' so the cost for CGT purposes may have to be 'wasted' in arriving at the chargeable gain (see paragraph 10).

Example 205

Lucy grants Jennifer an option for £6,000, which binds Lucy to sell a certain property to Jennifer for a specific amount set out in the option agreement, if called upon to do so within six months. After two months, Jennifer sells the option to David for £4,500.

Jennifer's gain is calculated as follows:

	£	£
Consideration for disposal		4,500
Cost	6,000	
Wasted - £6,000 x $^2/_6$ =	2,000	
		4,000
GAIN		500

Where the transfer of the option is not at arms length, the normal CGT rules deeming a consideration of "market value" may apply.

39.7   Option to buy and sell

s540(9)

Where the option binds the grantor, both to buy an asset and to sell an asset, the transaction is treated as two separate options - with half of the option consideration applying to each separate option. This arbitrary apportionment applies even where (as is often the case) the two options differ substantially in value.

39.8   **Forfeited deposits of purchase money**

s540(10)   It may happen that a deposit of purchase money will be forfeited if the related transaction is abandoned. In such a case, the amount forfeited is treated as if it was consideration paid for an option binding the grantor to sell, which was not exercised.

It is in effect, treated as the abandonment of an option. The normal rules (dealt with above) will apply.

There is a disposal of an asset (i.e. of an option) by the person keeping the deposit, and there is a loss on the disposal by the person who paid the deposit. Loss relief is not available unless the transaction comes within one of the exceptions (see above).

Example 206

> *Properties Limited enters into a contract with John Smith, a farmer, to buy his land from him for a total consideration of £500,000. The contract is unconditional. On signing the contract, Properties Limited pay a deposit of £50,000. Under the terms of the contract this deposit will be forfeited should Properties Limited fail to perform their obligations under the contract i.e. to proceed with the purchase. Before the closing of the sale Properties Limited go into receivership and the receiver refuses to complete the contract. As a result John Smith becomes entitled to retain the £50,000 deposit, and may be able to sue Properties Limited for breach of contract.*

> *Had Properties Limited proceeded with the completion of the contract, and paid the balance of moneys and taken conveyance of the land, the £50,000 deposit paid on the signing of the contract would be treated as part of the sales consideration for the land, both for the tax purposes of Properties Limited, and of John Smith Limited and that indeed is what the £50,000 is. However no sale actually took place since the contract was not completed. s540(10) provides that the forfeited deposit is to be treated similarly to consideration for the grant of an option. Accordingly it is not to be treated as a capital sum derived from the land, nor as consideration for the disposal of the land. Instead the provisions of s540 that applied to the abandonment of an option all apply to the forfeited deposit. No part of the base cost of the land may be taken into account in a computation relating to the deposit moneys in the hands of John Smith (see comments at the end of paragraph 39.3.1 above). Properties Limited (unless they are a trading company, in which case the CGT treatment will be of no interest anyway) will be treated as having acquired a wasting asset, and will not be able to obtain an allowable loss by reason of the transaction. The denial to John Smith of any part of the base cost of the land in computing his gain in the transaction may appear harsh, and is probably a different treatment to that which most taxpayers would assume would apply to the transaction.*

39.9   **Leases and 'non-sale' transactions**

s540(1)   The rules regarding options also apply to a transaction which is not a sale, including an option to grant a lease at a premium.

s540(1) provides:

'In this section -

'references to an option include references to an option binding the grantor to grant a lease for a premium, or enter into any other transaction which is not a sale, and references to buying and selling in pursuance of an option shall be construed accordingly'.

The legislation makes specific reference only to an option relating to the grant of a lease at a premium. An option could be granted entitling a person to call for the grant of a lease without a premium, but at a specified rent. If the rent in question were below market value, the amount of the consideration for the grant of the option (which might commercially be a substitute for a premium) could be quite large. s540(1) goes on to refer to an option to "enter into any other transaction which is not a sale" and that would seem to encompass an option to enter into a lease which does not involve a premium. There must however be some doubt about the matter, since it is arguable that where the legislation specifically directed its attention to leases, and chose to refer only to leases at a premium, that that is the extent to which it intends the provision to apply to leases.

39.10   Assessment and return

At first glance, an option could be thought to come within the rules applying to a conditional contract, in which case there would be a specific rule to determine the time of disposal for CGT purposes - see paragraph 15.2.

However, it is clear that an option is not a conditional contract in itself. In the words of Mr Justice Goff in the UK case of Sainsbury v O'Conner *"an option is **not** a conditional contract but an irrevocable offer which is open to acceptance by the exercise of the option".* Mr Justice Goff was merely stating a clear concept in law - that for a contract to exist there must be both an offer and an acceptance of that offer. If either part is missing there is no contract.

An option is merely the granting of a right of choice, which is granted by the option agreement. The grantor has disposed of a separate asset - the option itself, as distinct from the asset to which the option refers. The right of choice acquired by the grantee of the option, is a separate asset. Any contract which may exist relating to the asset to which the right of choice refers, may be conditional on the exercise of the option. In that sense any eventual contract to acquire the asset (which may exist or come into existence) may be said to be conditional on the exercise of an option. However, the grant of the option itself cannot be regarded as the disposal of an asset under a conditional contract, as the option agreement does not amount to a contract.

This does not change the fact that the grant of an option is the disposal of an asset for CGT purposes.

The disposal of an asset has implications for payment, assessment, and returns. There was no real difficulty for the taxpayer, until the advent of a self assessment system for CGT. Now there are potential problems. A number of specific difficulties arise in dealing with options, in that the grant of an option may or may not be the disposal of an asset, depending on whether or not it is exercised.

The difficulties are best illustrated by an example:

Example 207

> On 31st March 1994, Joe grants an option to Bill to purchase a property for £100,000 at any time in the following 5 years. The consideration for the grant of the option was £5,000.
>
> If the option is not exercised by 31st March 1999, s540 will treat Joe as having made a disposal on 31st March 1994 (in the tax year 1993/94). The disposal is of the option itself, and Joe will not have any base cost (apart from legal fees - of say - £100) in relation to that option. Joe has a taxable gain of £4,900. Assuming he is single, with no other gains of 1993/94, the tax ultimately payable will be £1,560.
>
> The due date for payment of the preliminary tax is 1 November 1994. The disposal should be returned on the 1993/94 form 11, due to the Inspector on or before 31st January 1995.
>
> This position is absolutely clear - provided the option is not exercised. However, Joe cannot be certain of that until 31st March 1999.
>
> If, on the other hand, Joe takes the view that the option will eventually be exercised, and accordingly makes no return or payment in relation to the option, relying on the merging of the option with the subsequent sale to give a disposal in a later year, he is potentially exposed to interest and a surcharge for 1993/94 should the option not be exercised.
>
> If, on the other hand Joe makes a payment, and includes the 'disposal' on his return for 1993/94, the Inspector is entitled to raise an assessment for that year in accordance with the taxpayer's return and an appeal is not possible against such an assessment. The legislation does not appear to provide for the reopening of the year by reference to facts coming to light in subsequent years (i.e. the actual exercise of the option). How is Joe to get a refund of the tax paid ?

s956

The Inspector does have the right to amend an assessment 'to take account of any fact or matter arising by reason of an event occurring after the return is delivered'. That is provided by s956, and operates without time limit. The right of the taxpayer to compel the Inspector to exercise that power in favour of the taxpayer is not absolutely clear, and may require proceedings in the High Court in the event of a dispute.

- **Revenue/Chief Inspector's CGT Manual :**

- The Revenue Commissioners capital gains tax manual, at Paragraph 19.1.11.2 states that where the option period is relatively short, an assessment need not be raised until it is known that the option has not been exercised. "Relatively short" is not defined.

In the UK case of Strange v Oppenshaw it was held that the grant of an option was the disposal of an asset i.e. of the option and might be assessed as such at a time when the option was unexercised, and still had a period to run in which it might be exercised. The case did not consider how the matter fell to be treated if, subsequent to the raising of an assessment relating to the grant of the option, the option was exercised and the grant of the option fell to be treated as part of the larger transaction for the sale of the subject matter of the option.

The UK case of Randall v Plumb is an example of an instance in which the Inland Revenue in the UK raised an assessment on a taxpayer in respect of an option which he had granted to a company to acquire land. The assessment was raised while the option still had a period of time left to run during which it could have been exercised, and at a time when it was not known whether or not the option would be ultimately exercised. The option in question was for a period of approximately 20 years.

Where an option is granted, and is subsequently exercised, the grant of the option is not treated as the disposal of an asset. However the asset to which the option related is regarded as being disposed of once the option is exercised. The date of disposal in relation to that underlying asset disposed of on foot of the contract is the date upon which the option is exercised (assuming the contract not to be subject to any other conditions precedent). In effect, the contract relating to the sale of the underlying asset is treated as a conditional contract during the period in which the option is outstanding, and the exercise of the option will usually render the contract relating to the underlying asset unconditional. Strictly speaking however there is no contract relating to the underlying asset while the option is unexercised - there is simply an irrevocable offer to buy, or to sell (as the case may be) but pending exercise of the option (i.e. acceptance of the offer) the contract doesn't exist. Nonetheless, a contract which is subject to the exercise of an option is usually thought of as a classic example of a conditional contract. The requirements relating to reporting the disposal of the underlying asset, and payment of any tax arising, all are triggered by or related to the date of exercise of the option.

39.11.1   Employee share options

A share option is a common feature in the remuneration package of a company executive. It usually consists of the right to subscribe at a specified price for a specified number of shares in his employer company during a specified period of time. For income tax reasons, the option is usually granted allowing the employee to purchase the shares at a price not less than the open market value of the shares at the time the option is granted to him.

s547 S547 provides that where a taxpayer acquires an asset *'in consideration for or in recognition of the persons or another persons services or past services in any office or employment or of any other service rendered or to be rendered by the person or another person'* his acquisition is deemed to be for a consideration equal to the market value of the asset (see paragraph 16).

If the employee does not exercise the option, the matter is irrelevant for CGT purposes. The option will simply cease to exist after the period of time allowed for its exercise has elapsed.

If the option is exercised by the employee or is sold or gifted by him, the question arises of the base cost of the shares for CGT purposes to be used in calculating a gain or loss on a subsequent disposal of those shares. The base cost of the option itself, is clear. It is the market value of the option at the date of grant of the option.

The question then arises of the base cost of the shares themselves. They are issued at the 'option' price, which may be totally different to the market value at the date of issue of those shares, and in practice, is usually less.

s547(3) The position is complicated by the fact that s547 was amended by the FA92, which inserted a new sub-section which is now s547(3). That new sub-section applied to disposals made on or after 7 May 1992. It would therefore apply to the disposal of shares acquired after that date on foot of an option, whether the option was granted before or after that date.

The affect of sub-section 3 is that s547(1), which substitutes open market value for actual consideration in certain circumstances, does not have application to the acquisition of an asset where

— there is no corresponding disposal of the asset, and

— there is either no consideration in money or moneys worth for the asset or

— the consideration given is lower than the market value of the asset.

The grant of an option is of course the disposal of an asset, and where it is given by reason of an employment, the employee's services will usually be consideration for that disposal and acquisition. s547(3) should therefore not operate so as to exclude the application of open market value on the grant of an option by a company to an employee. However where the option is then exercised by the employee, the subscription for shares is not a disposal of an asset by a company. In most instances a share option will be exercised by an employee only if the consideration (if any) which he must give on the exercise of the option is less than the value of the shares at the time at which he exercises it. In most instances therefore the conditions for s547(3) having affect will be present, and accordingly the substitution by s547(1) of open market value in respect of the shares acquired, will not occur.

s547   S547 provides that the grant of the option is to be regarded as part of the transaction involving the subscription for the share, where the option to subscribe is exercised, and the consideration given for the option is to be regarded as consideration given for the share. Accordingly any actual consideration given by the employee either in consideration of the grant of the option, or in respect of the subscription for the share, will be regarded as consideration given for the share, as also should the value of the services given in respect of the grant of the option. In other words, the option will be treated as being granted at open market value at the date of grant, and this consideration is uplifted by any additional consideration given as a subscription for the share at the time of its issue.

s128(10)   TCA97 s128(10) treats any gain which is chargeable to income tax in accordance with s128 as being additional consideration given by the employee for the shares acquired on the exercise of the option.

It should be noted that in computing the gain realised by the exercise of the option (which gain is chargeable to income tax under s128) the value of the services of the employee, which were given in return for the option, are not taken into account as consideration. This exclusion of "the performance of any duties in or in connection with an office or employment" from the consideration given for the option is solely for the purposes of s128(4) and no similar exclusion is applied to the computation of a gain under the Capital Gains Tax Acts. This interpretation would seem to create an anomaly. This is best illustrated by an example.

Example 208

Tony is granted an option by his employer, Scrooge Plc, to subscribe for 1,000 £1 ordinary shares at a price of £1 each. He is granted this right by reason of his employment at a time when the shares are valued at £3 each. Some time later Tony exercises the option, at a time when each £1 ordinary share in Scrooge Plc is worth £10 and takes up 1,000 shares in Scrooge Plc.

Tony is liable to income tax on the sum of £9,000 in accordance with Section 128. That sum is computed as being the difference between the £1,000 which he subscribed for the shares, and the market value of those shares on the day he exercised his option (£10,000).

What is Tony's base cost for his shares should he now choose to dispose of them? It would seem to be as follows:

Actual sum subscribed -   *£1,000*

Gain chargeable to income tax under s128, to be treated as consideration in accordance with s128(10) -   *£9,000*

Value of services given in return for the grant of the option -   £2,000

Total -   **£12,000**

If Tony disposed of his shares immediately on exercising his option (which is a not infrequent occurrence in practice, since employees often cannot finance the holding of the shares they acquire under option schemes), he would be deemed on this basis to make an immediate loss of £2,000. This is the difference between the open market value of the shares of £10,000 and the base cost calculated as above. This might seem a rather surprising conclusion. It is not clear, however, on what basis Tony can be denied a deduction for the value of his services, being part of the consideration given for the grant of the option. It would appear to be available by reason of s540 (3) - options and s552 (1) - deductible amounts. Such a deduction is denied for the purposes of s128, but not for the purposes of capital gains tax. Had the value of Tony's services been taken into account in computing the income tax charge under s128, they could not of course be taken in again for CGT purposes since the same amount cannot be deducted for the purposes of both taxes without specific statutory approval.

In relation to disposals of shares prior to 7 May 1992, the base cost for shares subscribed for on foot of an option granted by reason of a person's employment, should be the open market value of the share at the time of the subscription.

All of the comments above regarding base cost of a share issued through a share option scheme are subject to the application of s547(3) which limits the consideration which a person may be treated as having been given for new shares, where he is connected with the company, and his shares are issued other than by way of a bargain made at arm's length. The provisions of this anti-avoidance legislation is explained in greater detail in paragraph 41.

39.11.2   Deferred payment in relation to share options

Prior to the FA 2000 share options had one major disadvantage, as a means of enabling employees to become long term shareholders in their employer company. Since a charge to tax might arise on the occasion of the exercise of an option, on that occasion the taxpayer would find that not only did he have to finance the purchase of the share (albeit on favourable terms) but he also had to pay tax in relation to the share. In many instances it was found by employees that they could meet the tax payment only by disposing of some of the shares in the market. This was seen as defeating the objective of promoting long term employee share ownership.

FA 2000, s27   The solution to this produced by FA 2000 s27 was to insert s128A into the TCA97. This section grants a deferral of the due date for the tax that arises on the exercise of the share option. Whereas the charge under s128 arises on the exercise of a right obtained by reason of an employment to obtain any form of asset, the deferral provisions of s128A relate solely to a right to acquire shares in a company.

s128A In order that the deferral of the due date of the tax can be availed of it is necessary that the shares should not be disposed of in the same tax year as that in which the option was exercised.

Example 209

Joe Bloggs received options over 1000 shares on 5 April 2000 from his employer. On 7 April 2000 he received options over a further 1000 shares, also from his employer.

On 8 April John exercised both sets of options and acquired 2000 shares. He sold 1000 of these share immediately, and retained the remainder indefinitely.

John is entitled to the tax deferral provided by s128A in relation to the 1000 shares he retained. However s128A has no application to the 1000 shares disposed of, because they were disposed of in the same tax year as that in which the share option was exercised.

The deferral of tax provides a deferred due date for the tax but that due date depends on when the shares acquired under the option are disposed of. As noted above, if they are disposed of in the tax year in which the option is exercised, no deferral arises. But where the deferral does apply the due date will be the earlier of the two following dates:

- 1 November in the *year of assessment following that in which the shares are disposed of*. This would be the normal CGT due date, so that the income tax charge under s 128 becomes payable on the same date as CGT on the disposal of the shares will be payable.

- 1 November in the *eight tax year following the year in which the option is exercised.*

It must be emphasised that the tax which is deferred is the income tax charge arising on the exercise of the option. It is not a capital gains tax charge. The disposal of the share may give rise to a capital gains tax charge but the due date of that capital gains tax is quite unaffected by s128A.

If a loss arises on disposing of the shares ultimately, that will be a capital gains tax loss. It will not in any way affect the fact that a due date for payment of an income tax charge under s128 may arise on the occasion of the disposal, under the terms of s128A. The tax deferral introduced by the FA2000 relates solely to the income tax charge on the exercise of the option and does not impact at all on the capital gains tax charge.

S128A has one peculiarity. It has no share identification rule provided. Where a person has shares in a company acquired at several different times, and perhaps some acquired in circumstances in which s128 imposes a charge to income tax, but others acquired without such an exposure, the application of s128A becomes difficult where shares are disposed of in the eight year period following the exercise of an option. In the absence of share identification rules, the only method of identification of the shares disposed of with shares acquired for the purpose of determining how s128A affects the due date for income tax, is to have regard to the actual shares sold ie share cert numbers. In contrast, the capital gains tax rules on the identical disposal will identify the shares disposed of with shares acquired under statutory rules. These are generally the first in/first out rules, as modified by the four week rule (see paragraph 48). It can therefore happen that an anomalous situation will arise in which a disposal of shares may for capital gains tax purposes be treated as a disposal of different shares to those being treated as disposed of for the purposes of s128A. This can result either in a very favourable tax position, or a very penal tax position, depending on how the taxpayer manages his affairs.

40   SHARE TRANSACTIONS

40.1   Broad Outline - share transactions

A share in a company is an intangible asset. It has been described as "a bundle of rights".

Each share is an asset separate from every other share. Where the holder of 100 shares sells 10 of those shares, it is a disposal of 10 separate assets, and it is not a part disposal of a single asset of 100 shares.

Special anti-avoidance rules apply to the base cost of shares acquired by subscription (see paragraph 41.4).

Development land rules can apply to shares deriving their value from development land (see paragraph 6).

Shares deriving value from certain specified Irish assets are chargeable assets even in the ownership of a non-resident (see paragraphs 3.4.2 and 3.5).

Special rules apply to the disposal of shares by exchange for other shares or debentures. In some cases the exchange is not treated as a disposal of the shares (see paragraph 42).

Special rules also apply to changes in share rights ; shares issued on the incorporation of a business, or in exchange for an undertaking. These are all dealt with in paragraphs 42 et seq. In some cases these events may be treated as not involving a disposal of shares.

A buyback of its own shares by a company may involve taxes on income, or it may involve capital gains tax, depending on the circumstances (see paragraph 49).

There are anti-avoidance rules that may treat shares as being disposed of where no real disposal has occurred e.g. where value is stripped out of shares or where a pre-disposal dividend from profits generated intra group is received (see paragraph 51).

Capital gains tax rules interact with income tax rules relating to several employee share schemes, and the business expansion scheme and film investment relief schemes (see paragraph 50).

A special low tax rate may apply to certain share disposals prior to 3rd December 1997 by individuals (see paragraph 5.2).

Special share identification rules determine the identity of shares disposed of, rather than share registration numbers or share certificates being referred to for this purposes (see paragraph 48).

When a person disposes of his share, a charge to CGT may arise. The treatment of the tax computation is broadly the same as for other assets in the many cases where the special features of the legislation (many of which are referred to above) do not apply.

Example 210

Joe formed a company on 1st June 1991 subscribing £100,000 for an issue of 100,000 Ordinary shares of £1 each. The company prospered and on 30 June 1992 he sold 25,000 shares for £50,000; on 31 December 1998 he sold the balance of the shares for £300,000. His capital gains are calculated as follows

1992 DISPOSAL (1992/93):	£
Consideration received	50,000
Cost as indexed: 25,000 x 1.037	25,925
GAIN (1992/93)	24,075

1998 DISPOSAL (1998/99):	
Consideration received	300,000
Cost as indexed: 75,000 x 1.161	87,075
GAIN (1993/94)	212,925

The normal part disposal rules are not applied as each share is a separate asset.

A charge to tax arises not only on a sale, but on any disposal of an asset. The word "***disposal***" has a wide meaning and includes transactions other than a straight sale. In respect of shares, such transactions would include:

• A disposal in a winding-up:

• An exchange of shares in a company reconstruction, or in the amalgamation of companies (but subject to a statutory exception - see paragraph 42 et seq.):

• A sale of "rights" - of a right to subscribe for shares at an agreed price.

• The acquisition by a company of its own shares.

The legislation includes a considerable number of provisions dealing with transactions such as these, which do not involve a straight sale of shares for a cash consideration. Taking the examples listed above:

• the position regarding the disposal of shares in a winding up is clarified by the special rules dealing with capital distributions received from companies in respect of shares - see paragraph 40.3.

• an exchange of shares is a straightforward disposal, the consideration being the value of the shares received: however, the legislation provides substantial relief in this area - see paragraph 42.

- a sale of "rights" generally would not be regarded as a disposal of the shares concerned; the legislation however effectively treats it as such and attributes to the disposal, part of the cost of the original shares held - see paragraph 42.3.

- special rules apply in certain circumstances to the acquisition by a company of its own shares - see paragraph 49.

40.2   Meaning of Shares

s5   TCA97 s5 gives to the word *"shares"* in the capital gains tax legislation, an extended meaning. It states that it includes *"stock"*.

In the UK case of Aberdeen Construction Group Ltd. v IRC Lord Russell of Killowen said in relation to stock."...*loan stock, ...suggests to my mind an obligation created by a company of an amount for issue to subscribers for the stock, having ordinary terms for repayment with or without premium and for interest"*.

In the Aberdeen Construction case, although the judges in the House of Lords differed as between each other on many issues, there was agreement that a loan from a parent company to a subsidiary in that particular case did not constitute loan stock.

- **Revenue/Chief Inspector's CGT Manual :**

- In Paragraph 19.1.13.3 of the Revenue Commissioners capital gains tax manual, the view is expressed that "loan stock", where the expression occurs in the definition of "security" in Section 585, *"should be regarded as meaning in general a class of debt the holdings in which are transferable by purchase and sale."*

- **Revenue/Chief Inspector's CGT Manual :**

- In their capital gains tax manual the Revenue Commissioners state that *"A stock unit (or simply "stock") is essentially similar to a share but it is measured by the nominal amount of the issued capital which it represents."* The Revenue Commissioners view of stock does not appear to acknowledge the normal understanding, that it is a liability, albeit a long term liability in a way which share capital is not. In contrast, the definition given in the Aberdeen Construction Group Limited case above makes reference to repayment terms.

s55   The FA97 introduced a special income tax regime in relation to strips of securities (now TCA97 s55). This is described in paragraph 32.3. "Securities" for the purposes of that income tax legislation cannot include shares of a company but may include stock insofar as the stock of a company has been "stripped". Transactions relating to such stripping, and to the strips, may fall within the regime described in paragraph 32.3, which is an income tax regime, rather than within the capital gains tax regime described in the remainder of this part of the book.

40.3   **Receipt of Capital Distribution:**

s583   s583 provides that a person will be deemed to dispose of an interest in his shares where he receives a "capital distribution" from the company in respect of those shares. Capital distribution means:

"any distribution from a company (including a distribution in the course of dissolving or winding-up a company), in money or moneys worth except a distribution which in the hands of the recipient constitutes income for the purposes of income tax".

s129; s130   Most distributions from Irish resident companies after 5 April 1976, including distributions out of capital profits, are subject to income tax under the provisions of Schedule F. This income tax charge does not apply to distributions in the winding-up of a company. It can be reasonably assumed therefore that capital distributions for CGT purposes will arise mainly in the dissolution or winding-up of a company or under the special rules dealing with the acquisition by a company of its own shares - see paragraph 49.

Example 211 -Redemption Of Shares

Joe subscribed for 1000 £1 redeemable preference shares in Cups Limited, an Irish resident company, on 1 July 1993. On 31 December 1996 the shares were redeemed by the company at a a premium of 25p each.

The position is as follows:

	£
Received on redemption	1,250
Initial sum subscribed for the shares	1,000
Distribution (excess over amount subscribed)	250
Add tax credit - @ 23/77 of £250	75
Chargeable to income tax under Schedule F	325

Although Joe has disposed of his shares for CGT purposes, and made a profit, there is no chargeable gain. The profit is chargeable to income tax and therefore is not chargeable to CGT. For the purposes of the example it is assumed that the redemption does not come within the special rules in s173 et seq. dealing with the purchase by a company of its own shares - see paragraph 49.

- see also paragraph 49 where the UK Inland Revenue's treatment of CGT on a share buyback by a company is discussed in the context of shares held by another resident company.

40.3.1   **Shares and Liquidation**

Example 212 - Capital Distribution on Winding-Up

Jack formed a company on 1 January 1987. He subscribed at par for the share capital of 100,000 £1 ordinary shares. With the cash received from the share issue, the company bought Government stocks for £100,000. On 1 January 1994 Jack decided to liquidate the company when the gilts were worth £300,000. At that time the company also had cash of £15,000. Payments by the Liquidator including the Company's tax liability, amounted to £6,000. The balance of the assets were distributed to Jack in respect of his shares in the company.

On receiving the distributions from the Liquidator, Jack is deemed to have made a disposal of an interest in his shares with the value of the distribution representing the consideration for the disposal.

Jack's tax liability is calculated as follows (see note below - part disposal):

	£
Market value quoted shares	
(disposed of by Liquidator in specie to Jack)	*300,000*
Cash (15,000-6,000)	*9,000*
Assets available to shareholder	*309,000*
Cost of shares in the company 100,000 x 1.230	*123,000*
Gain	*186,000*
Less annual exemption	*1,000*
Chargeable Gain	*185,000*
Tax payable £185,000 at 40%	*74,000*

For the sake of simplicity and merely to illustrate the point involved, the computation on *example 212* above has been worked on the assumption of a total disposal by Jack of the shares in the company. Strictly speaking, the receipt by Jack of the distribution of the company's remaining assets in specie and in cash, represented a part disposal of its shares. It had not represented a total disposal of the shares because, for as long as the shares remained legally in existence, he had some remaining rights of property in them. Since the shares however were entirely without value once all of the companies assets have been distributed either to the shareholders or to the creditors, a part disposal computation would have produced the same result as a computation on the total disposal of the shares. The computation above would therefore be identical to the computation as a part disposal computation.

This point can be of greater importance where the liquidation is a lengthy process. Some liquidations go on over long periods of years, and assets may be distributed to the shareholders in several separate tranches. In such a case, it may be necessary to prepare the computation in relation to the capital distributions received from the liquidator, on the basis that there has occurred a part disposal. In such circumstances, to enable the shareholder to apply the part disposal apportionment of the qualifying CGT cost, it is important to calculate the "remainder value" of the shares. In practice it may be necessary to estimate of balance of funds of the company remaining available to shareholders. This would normally require the assistance of the liquidator.

Example 213

*If the facts were the same as in **example** 212 except that the investments of the company were in quoted shares rather than government stocks; and the liquidator had been able to dispose of part of these only before the 5th of April 1994. After providing for the capital gains tax liability of the company on the disposal of the quoted shares, and making due provision against other expenses which might arise, the liquidator paid out £ 50,000 to Jack on the 5th of April 1994. On the 31st of May 1994, the balance of the shares having been disposed of, and all liabilities, including CGT arising on the disposal of quoted shares, having been discharged, the liquidator paid out the balance of the assets (a sum of £197,000) to Jack. The company was struck-off the register of companies on the 31st October 1994.*

Computation for 1993/94	*£*
Capital distribution by liquidator	*50,000*
CGT cost to Jack of shares in company	*100,000*
Estimated value of shares after receipt of distribution	*197,000*
Consideration for disposal	*50,000*
Base cost attributable to this disposal (indexed @ 1.230)	

$$£100,000 \ x \ \frac{50,000}{£50,000 + £197,000} \ @ \ 1.230 \qquad 24,899$$

Gain	*25,101*
Less annual exemption (assumed)	*1,000*
Chargeable gain	*24,101*
Tax payable @ 40% (assumed)	*9,640*

Computation for year ended 1994/95;	*£*
Capital distribution received from liquidator	*197,000*
Balance of cost of shares	
£ 100,000 less £20243 used in 1993/94 = £79757	
Indexed from January 1987 i.e. @ 1.252	
	99,856
Gain	*97,144*
Less annual exemption (assumed)	*1,000*
Chargeable gain	*96,144*
Tax payable @ 40%	*38,458*

In the example above the liquidation was sufficiently straight forward and close to completion, on the occasion of the first capital distribution, to enable the estimate of the value of the shares on that occasion to be made accurately for the purpose of a part disposal computation. In practice, where there are interim distributions by the liquidator in the course of a complex liquidation, that may not be possible and the market value remaining in the shares after each part disposal will usually represent no more than the best estimate possible in the circumstances. Subsequent events may show that the assumptions regarding the value of assets and extent of liabilities, which underlie the estimate, were not entirely correct. Provided however the estimate was not grossly incorrect in a manner which would not be reflected in a price for the shares in the event of a third party seeking to buy them at that point in time, there should be no need to re-open the computations.

s535(2)   S535(2) provides that the receipt of a capital sum derived from an asset is to be treated as a part disposal of that asset. On that basis alone, the distributions by the liquidator to a shareholder in the
s583   course of a liquidation would constitute a disposal or part disposal of its shares. It therefore seems a little unnecessary that s583 specifically provides that a capital distribution from a company must be treated as the disposal of an interest in shares. However, since it has so provided, it is probably on the basis of this specific provision that the disposal is to be deemed to take place, rather than the more general provision in s535(2).

As indicated in the example above, a liquidation of a company will usually involve at least two classes of disposals of assets.

On the one hand, there will be disposals of chargeable assets by the liquidator. This may be either where he sells assets in order to raise cash to pay creditors, or to make a distribution to shareholders; or where he distributes assets in specie to the shareholders. Both types of transactions (sale and distribution in specie) represent disposals by the liquidator and may give rise to chargeable gains chargeable to corporation tax.

The shareholder will make disposals or part disposals of his shares as he receives capital distributions from the liquidator. If the company is insolvent, no capital distribution is paid by the liquidator to the shareholders.

The occasion of the company being struck-off the share register is the occasion of the total extinguishment of the shares, and that is the occasion of final disposal by the shareholder of its shares. That occasion in such a situation (an insolvent company) will usually crystallise a loss. Of course a shareholder might also crystallise a loss when making a negligible value claim at a time before the final liquidation of the company (see paragraph 20.5)

- **Revenue/Chief Inspector's CGT Manual :**

  - The CGT manual at paragraph 19.3.8 deals with the possibility that a liquidation would involve more than one distribution of assets by the liquidator to shareholders. It instructs the Inspector in such circumstances not to raise the question of capital gains tax on an interim distribution until after two years from the commencement of the liquidation, unless the distribution, when aggregated with other previous distributions, exceeds the total cost of the shares. It also instructs him to accept reasonable calculations by the shareholder as to the remaining value of the shares, in relation to any part disposal calculations, provided the shares are unquoted; provided the liquidation is expected to be completed within two years of the first distribution and is in fact so completed. The time limits noted above may possibly have been expressed prior to the introduction of self-assessment. The question of a liability to capital gains tax on interim distributions from a liquidator is not a matter left to an Inspector to raise. A shareholder has an obligation to make a return of gains on an annual basis and to account for tax accordingly. For that reason reliance should not be placed on the statement in the capital gains tax manual without specific clearance from the Revenue Commissioners.

- **Revenue/Chief Inspector's CGT Manual :**

— At paragraph 19.3.8.6 of the CGT manual, it is stated that where a company being wound up voluntarily makes compensation payments for loss of office to employees or office-holders, such compensation payments should be treated as being additional distributions of assets by the liquidator to the shareholders. In other words, the payments should be apportioned over the shareholders, even though they may not have been the persons who received such compensation payments. The basis for this treatment is not stated in the manual. Although it is not explicitly stated, it would seem that the Revenue statement is not intended to refer to statutory redundancy payments, or to payments which represent legally enforceable claims for damages for wrongful dismissal.

The authors doubt whether the treatment described above has a sound basis in law where it is blindly applied irrespective of the circumstances.

Presumably the basis is a presumption that a liquidator would make a voluntary payment only with the consent of all of the shareholders who would otherwise be entitled to the assets.

In such circumstances the payment might be viewed as an application of the shareholders assets by the liquidator on behalf of the shareholders, no different than if the shareholders had received the assets from the liquidator and had themselves made the voluntary payment. However there could be circumstances in which a voluntary payment is made by a liquidator not by reason of the wishes or consent of the shareholders, but because it is in the best interest of the liquidation e.g where the payment was made to ensure that persons do not interfere with the liquidation or with the company assets.

40.4   **Sale of Rights**

The CGT treatment of a rights issue which is taken up (ie. the right is exercised by the shareholder to whom it is granted) is explained in paragraph 42.3.

s583   Where a person receives (or becomes entitled to receive) a provisional allotment of shares or debentures in a company (i.e. a rights issue) and he disposes of his rights, he is treated as if the consideration received for the disposal of the rights was a capital distribution received by him from the company in respect of his original shares.

Example 214

John acquired 1,000 £1 ordinary shares in WEEDS LTD in July 1984 for £1,000. WEEDS LTD decided to make a RIGHTS ISSUE to the existing shareholders in March 1994. The offer to the shareholders was one share for every two shares held, at £1.50 per share. The market value of all shares in the company after (and including) the rights issue, is £1.80 per share.

If John takes up the 500 shares, he will own 1,500 shares. On a subsequent disposal, he would be treated as acquiring 1,500 shares in July 1984 for £1,000 and incurring enhancement expenditure on those shares (now represented by 1,500 shares) in March 1994 of £750 (see paragraph 42.3).

If, however, he decides not to take up the shares, and to sell the right to take up the shares to someone else the position would be as follows:

Let us assume that John sold the rights to Bill for £150.

John has made a part disposal of his original shares.

TOTAL COST
Original shares July 1984... Cost... £1,000

COST ALLOWABLE AGAINST PROCEEDS OF PART DISPOSAL
The Normal Part Disposal Rules Apply:

Cost =   £1,000
Sale proceeds =   £150
Market Value of remaining shares after disposal =   1,000 @ £1.80=   £1,800
Allowable cost

$$£1,000 \; x \; \frac{\text{Sale proceeds (£150)}}{\text{Sale proceeds (£150) + Value of remainder (£1,800)}} \qquad £77$$

Calculation of GAIN :	£
Sale proceeds	150
Allowable cost £77 @ 1.366	105
Gain	45

41   ISSUE of SHARES - COST OF ACQUISITION

41.1   Basic Rule

The act of issuing shares does not give rise to a chargeable gain on the company making the issue. Before a charge to tax can arise there must be a disposal of an asset and, on issuing shares, a company is not disposing of any asset. This point was considered in detail in the UK case of Stanton v Drayton Commercial Investment Co Ltd. There is a disposal of an asset for CGT purposes only if the asset existed prior to the alleged disposal (see paragraph 4.2.4). A company does not own a share prior to creating it by the act of its issue, and so the issue of a share cannot be the disposal of an asset. An exception is where a company holds its own shares as *Treasury Shares* which it may sell.

s549

As a share issue does not involve any disposal by the company, the "connected person" rules of s549 and s10 cannot apply to a subscription for shares in a company.

s547

S547, which can substitute open market value in certain circumstances, could apply for other reasons (e.g. where a subscription is not by way of a bargain made at arm's length) but the application of s547 to a share subscription is severely restricted. These restrictions are described in detail in paragraph 41.4. They may be summarised as follows (but for a more complete statement see paragraph 41.4):

* *Where the shareholder subscribing for the shares is connected with the company and a subscription is otherwise than by way of a bargain made at arm's length, his base cost for the shares on the occasion of the subscription will be the lower of market value or cost. Market value in this context has a particular meaning.*

* *Where the taxpayer subscribing for the shares is not connected with the company, but where the subscription is for less than market value for any other reason, his base cost is the sum subscribed for the share.*

These particular restrictions on s547 (open market value) relate principally to a subscription for shares and would not relate to a purchase or sale of shares already issued.

41.2   **Connected Person**

Where a shareholder disposes of shares which he has received as a result of a new issue, the amount deductible in computing the chargeable gain will usually be the actual amount (indexed) paid to the company for the shares. However, problems can arise if the shares are not issued under a bargain made at arm's length and if the company and the shareholder are "connected" within the meaning of s10 (see paragraph 16). In these cases, the question arises as to whether the shares would be held to be acquired at their market value (which may not always be the amount actually paid for the shares).

s547

Under s547, an acquisition of any asset otherwise than by way of bargain at arm's length is deemed to be for a consideration equal to the market value of the asset. Accordingly, if a person acquires shares as a result of a new issue which is made otherwise than by way of bargain at arm's length, the amount deductible for the purposes of a future disposal (pre FA 1982) was the market value of the shares at the date of issue.

FA82 s62

In respect of an allotment of shares on or after 24 June 1982 to a person connected with the company, the consideration deemed to have been paid by that person for their new shares would be equal to the lesser of:

- the amount or value of the consideration given by him for the new shares, and,

- the amount by which the market value of the shares in the company which he held immediately after the allotment of the new shares exceeds the market value of the shares in the company which he held immediately before the allotment, or, if he held no such shares immediately before the allotment, the market value of the new shares immediately after the allotment.

It is important to note that this legislation applies only where the issue is to a connected person within the meaning of the 1975 Act. Further consideration of these provisions is set out in paragraph 16. The background to the 1982 legislation lay in a well known UK tax case - Harrison v Nairn Williamson which is described further below.

The general rule (pre FA82) that an issue of shares is acquired by the shareholder (if a connected person) at market value at the date of issue was confirmed in that case. It was decided on UK legislation similar to that contained in s.9 of the 1975 Act (now TCA97 s547), but with a significant difference.

The UK provisions relating to both acquisitions and disposals were combined in s.22(4), FA(UK) 1975 which read (in part) as follows:

".....a person's acquisition of an asset and the disposal of it to him shall....be deemed to be for a consideration equal to the market value of the asset-(a)where he acquires the asset otherwise than by way of a bargain made at arm's length.....".

In the Harrison v Nairn Williamson case, the taxpayer company had paid £210,000 for loan stock in such circumstances that immediately after the issue, the aggregate value of the loan stock and the share capital of the company was only £73,500. It was agreed that the loan stock was issued otherwise than by way of bargain at arm's length. The taxpayer company subsequently sold the loan stock (which by then had been converted into preferred stock) for £39,900. The taxpayer company contended that the consideration for the acquisition of the loan stock was £210,000, and that the market value at date of issue could not be substituted under the "bargain at arm's length rules". The taxpayer's contention was based on the proposition that the rule applied only when there were both an acquisition and a disposal, whereas on the issue of the stock there was an acquisition by the stockholder but no disposal by the company.

The Court of Appeal decided against the taxpayer company. While accepting that the issue of the loan stock by the company did not constitute a disposal it was considered that market value could be substituted (in respect of the person making the acquisition), if the circumstances of the transaction attracted the operation of the section. It was in effect decided that market value could be substituted if there was an acquisition without a corresponding disposal.

The Irish legislators largely avoided these difficulties by dividing the bargain at arm's length rule into s547(1) for acquisitions and s547(4) for disposals. Nevertheless, the Harrison v Nairn Williamson decision is an important factor in considering the Irish legislation.

41.3   **Reverse Nairn Williamson scheme**

S547   The legislation dealing with the consideration contained in s547and the decision in Harrison v Nairn Williamson led to arrangements operated both in Ireland and the UK for the mitigation of capital gains. These arrangements popularly known as *reverse Nairn Williamson schemes* (Harrison, the Inspector of Taxes did not get a mention) can be illustrated by the following example:

Example 215

> *Jim, Robert and Philip owned all the issued share capital of MV Limited - which consisted of 900 £1 ordinary shares (they owned 300 each). The shares had been acquired in June 1974 at par on the formation of the company. The shareholder received an offer in May 1982 of £240,000 for the 900 shares.*

Clearly a substantial gain would have arisen on a straight disposal of the shares. For example, Jim's gain would have been as follows:

	£
Consideration Received for his 300 shares	80,000
Cost - £300 indexed @ 3.342	1002
Gain	78,998

In an attempt to reduce the CGT payable, they arranged for the company to issue more shares. The company therefore issued a further 10,000 £1 ordinary shares at par, Jim receiving 3,250, Robert 3,300 and Philip 3,450.

Clearly, the shares were not issued under a bargain made at arm's length so that the shareholders acquired their shares at market value at date of issue.

Assuming the offer of £240,000 plus £10,000 cash introduced for the new shares represented the market value of the company and dividing that value pro rata, Jim's gain on the sale of his shares would now be calculated as follows:

	£
Sale Proceeds	*81,422
Cost-1974 (indexed) £300 x 3.342 =	1,003
Cost-1982 (market value at date of issue)	*74,541
	75,544
Gain	£5,878

*Note: Jim is now disposing of his original 300 shares plus the additional 3,250 shares acquired by him immediately before the sale. Also, the value of the company has increased by the additional £10,000 cash introduced for the new shares issued. The part of the total proceeds referable to Jim's shares is as follows:

$$- \text{ Sale proceeds £250,000} \times \frac{3,550}{10,900} = £81,422$$

The cost of the original shares remains unchanged. However the question arises of the deemed cost of the new 3250 shares acquired by Jim for cash (at par). The shares are obviously worth a considerable amount more than par - as there is an offer of £240,000 for the company. The issue of shares at par to Jim could not be considered a bargain at arms length. The 1975 Act deems Jim to acquire the shares at market value at the date of issue. The cost is therefore:

$$- \text{ Cost (MV) 1982 £250,000} \times \frac{3,250}{10,900} = £74,541$$

It can be seen, by the simple device of issuing further shares to existing shareholders, a substantial tax saving could be made. It was, of course, important that the shares issue did not attract the reliefs available under s583 to s586 (Reorganisations).

Relief would have applied to a "proportionate allotment" of shares to the existing shareholders. For that reason the issue of shares was not proportionate between the three shareholders.

Schemes of this nature lead to the introduction of anti-avoidance legislation in s.62 of the FA 1982, now s547(2).

41.4   Share Transactions - tax avoidance

The interacting anti-avoidance provisions that have accumulated over the years may be summarised as follows:

- Originally shares acquired by a subscription not at arm's length had an open market value base cost.

- Allotments on or after 24 June 1982 not at arm's length and to a connected person carry a base cost equal to the lesser of the consideration given, or the increase the acquisition leads to in the value of the overall shareholding by the taxpayer and the company.

- In relation to disposals of shares on or after 7 May 1992 the original open market value rule described in the first bullet point does not apply for an under market value acquisition of a share where there is no corresponding disposal of the share (ie typically a share subscription at under market value). However the rule in the second bullet point above may still apply.

- The rule in the second bullet point above applies to shares allotted on or after 24 June 1982, regardless of the date of disposal. The rule in the third bullet point applies to shares disposed of on or after 7 May 1992, regardless of when allotted or acquired.

Because of the complexity of these interacting rules it is as well to attempt a further summarisation before getting into the detail.

The rules described above in summary, and in detail below, <u>typically</u> apply to shares acquired for less than market value. That is a broad generalisation. If the shares were pre existing shares at the date of acquisition (ie were not acquired by being subscribed for) the open market value rule of the first bullet point above is likely to apply to determine the base cost in all circumstances.

If the shares were acquired at under value by subscription/allotment by a person connected with the company then for a current disposal (ie one on or after 7 May 1992) the base cost will not be open market value. Instead the base cost will be determined by the second bullet point above ie by the lower of the consideration given, or the overall increase in the value of the taxpayer's shareholding as a result of the subscription/allotment.

The relevant rules are described in greater detail below. The overview above should not be relied on in itself and is intended only to enable the reader to understand how the various provisions interact.

s547(2)
s586(3)
s587(4)

Sections 62 and 63 FA 1982 were aimed at two artificial avoidance devices which were used to reduce, or perhaps eliminate entirely, a charge to CGT. S.62 dealt with what was generally known at the time as the reverse Nairn Williamson scheme (described in paragraph 41.3). It is now s547(2).

S.63 dealt with a loophole in the 1975 legislation dealing with reorganisation and reduction of share capital. It was possible using that legislation to artificially increase the cost of the shares to market value at the date of disposal. It is now s586(3) and s587(4).

s547

The FA82 made the following amendment to s9 of the 1975 Act (now s547(2)) to ensure that such "unauthorised relief" could not be availed of in the future.

(2) (a) *In this subsection 'shares' includes stock, debentures and any interests to which s584(3) applies and includes any option in relation to such shares, and references therein to an allotment of shares shall be construed accordingly."*

(b) *Notwithstanding subsection (1) and s584(3) where, **on or after 24th day of June, 1982,** a company, otherwise than by way of a bargain made at arm's length, allots shares in the company (hereafter in this subsection referred to as 'the new shares') to a person connected with the company, the consideration which the person gives or becomes liable to give for the new shares shall, for the purposes of the CGT Acts, be deemed to be an amount (including a nil amount), equal to the lesser of-*

(i) *the amount or value of the consideration given by him for the new shares, and*

(ii) *the amount by which the market value of the shares in the company which he held immediately after the allotment of the new shares exceeds the market value of the shares in the company which he held immediately before the allotment or, if he held no such shares immediately before the allotment, the market value of the new shares immediately after the allotment.*

In the 1997 consolidation of the legislation the words *"on or after 24th June 1982"* were dropped. They remain relevant to base cost insofar as it was affected by pre 24 June 1982 transactions.

The effect of the amendment, is to ensure that where shares are issued by a company to a connected person otherwise than by way of a bargain made at arm's length (on or after 24 June 1982) the consideration which the person gives for the new shares is to be treated for CGT purposes as being the lesser of:

- The amount or value of the consideration given by him for the shares,

and

- The amount by which the market value of all the shares in the company which he held immediately after the allotment of the new shares exceeds the market value of all the shares in the company which he held immediately before the allotment (or, if he held no such shares immediately before the allotment, the market value of the new shares immediately after the allotment).

The amendment goes on to include in the meaning of the term *shares,* stock, debentures, and any interests to which paragraph 5 (2) of Schedule 2 applies, and also includes any option in relation to such shares.

s547(3)

FA92 s62

A further amendment of s.9, 1975 Act (now s547) was made by FA 1992 in respect of disposals on or after 7th May 1992. This added a new sub-section (now s547(3)) (which applies open market value to a transaction in certain circumstances). The new s547(3) provides that s547(1) is not to have application to the acquisition of an asset where:

- there is no corresponding disposal of the asset (and the issue of a share by a company is not the disposal of an asset) and either;

- there was no consideration in money or moneys worth given for the asset which was acquired or;

- the consideration for the asset was less than market value.

One of the most common examples of the acquisition of an asset in relation to which there is no corresponding disposal is the issue of a share by a company. Accordingly where a company issues a share for a consideration which is less than the market value of the share, s547(1) which substitutes open market value for actual consideration in certain circumstances does not have affect.

Despite the fact that s547(1) does not apply, s547(3) - the FA 1992 amendment - continues to apply provided its conditions are met. Accordingly the issue of a share for a consideration less than market value to a person connected with the company would result in a base cost for those shares as described above as a result of the application of s547(2) - i.e. an amount equal to the lower of the consideration given for the shares, or the increase in value of the shareholders overall shareholding in the company as a result of the issue.

It seems strange that s547(2), which was introduced to prevent the application of s547(1) resulting in tax avoidance opportunities, should apply even where s547(1) may no longer have application by reason of s547(3).

41.5   **Calls on shares**

s582   Where a person gives any consideration in respect of an issue of shares or debentures in a company at a time more than 12 months after the allotment of those shares or debentures, the expenditure is treated as enhancement expenditure incurred on the date of payment.

Example 216

> Sam applied for, and was allotted on 1 January 1995, 5,000 £1 ordinary shares in SAMUEL LTD. 60p per share was payable on application. A further call of the balance of 40p per share was paid by SAM in June 1996.
>
> In March 1998, Sam sold the shares at £4 each.

Calculation of Gain :	£	£
Sale proceeds		20,000
Allowable cost:		
Original cost (1995/96)	3,000	
Enhancement expenditure (1996/97)	2,000	
The original cost is indexed from 1995/96. The multiple is 1.037 The indexed cost is therefore...	3,111	
The "enhancement" expenditure is indexed from 1996/97. The multiple is 1.016. The indexed cost is therefore	2,032	
Total expenditure (indexed)		5,143
Gain		14,857

s122A   FA98 s15 inserted TCA97 s122A. That section has application to shares obtained by reason of an employment. Among the circumstances in which the section has application is where partly paid up shares are acquired by reason of an employment. The section can give rise to an income tax charge. The topic is not directly relevant to capital gains tax and is not considered further here. Reference should be made to the companion volume, Income Tax by McAteer and Redmond, published by the Institute of Taxation in Ireland.

41.6   **Extraction of Corporate Profits**

s817   TCA97 s817 is intended to counteract what are described as schemes to avoid liability to tax under Schedule F. Such schemes are any scheme or arrangement to which a close company is a party, or which it has arranged, one of the purposes of which is to avoid liability under Schedule F by converting into a capital receipt an amount which would otherwise be available for distribution as a dividend.

Where on or after 25 January 1989, a shareholder disposes of shares or loan stock in a close company without thereby significantly reducing his interest in any business carried on by the close company, the excess of the proceeds of disposal of the shares over the consideration given for their original issue may be treated as a distribution made by the close company. Such a distribution would be chargeable to income tax under Schedule F in the hands of an individual.

The shareholder's interest in the close company's business is measured by reference to:

- the percentage of ordinary share capital of the company held by him.

- the percentage of profits he would receive on their distribution.

- the percentage of assets he would receive on a winding up.

The section does not define what would constitute a significant reduction in the shareholders interest in the business, measured in this way.

s817 The section does not apply to a disposal made for bona fide commercial reasons and not as part of tax avoidance arrangements.

s431 The provisions of s817 apply in relation to a close company. That close company can include a quoted company (see paragraph 67.2.1 re. Meaning of *close company*).

The consequences in terms of CGT of the application of the section is that the proceeds of disposal of shares, to the extent charged to income tax, are disregarded in the CGT computation, which is otherwise made in the usual way. In some cases this would result in an allowable loss.

Example 217

Joe Smith inherited 200 £1 shares in Smith Factories Ltd. in 1980. In March 1999 he sold these shares to Smith Holdings Ltd. for £20,000. The revenue reserves were then £19,800. Joe Smith owned all the issued shares in Smith Holdings Ltd.

If the section applies to him, Joe Smith is chargeable to income tax under Schedule F as if he had received a dividend of £19,800, being the excess of the sales proceeds over the capital subscribed. The CGT computation is as follows:

Consideration received	£200
(Being £20,000 sales proceeds less £19,800 charged to income tax)	
Unindexed base cost (assumed)	(£5,000)
allowable loss	£4,800

This loss is on a transaction with a connected person and so is subject to restrictions on its use (see paragraph 16.4).

42   REORGANISATIONS/REDUCTION OF SHARE CAPITAL

42.1   Overview

Where a person sells his shares for cash or receives a capital distribution from a company in respect of his shares and that distribution is in cash or property, he has, in real commercial terms disposed of an interest in his shares.

In contrast there may be situations where, for example, a company which is insolvent is forced by its creditors to reconstruct and the shareholders receive different shares in exchange for their existing shares. It may be that the existing ordinary shareholders, for example, will be asked to surrender their ordinary shares in return for non-voting preference shares. In such a case, it is clear that the shareholders have got nothing tangible out of the company and should not therefore be regarded as being subject to CGT in relation to that transaction.

This type of situation and others of a similar nature are recognised in the legislation. Relief is provided under the provisions relating to reorganisation and reduction of share capital (but see anti-avoidance provisions in paragraph 45 below).

These basic rules are applied to a variety of transactions in the shares of a single company e.g. where a shareholder receives bonus shares from the company; or subscribes for a rights issue in the company; or swaps his shares in the company for other shares, stock or debentures in the same company; or where the rights attaching to his shares are changed. In broad terms, all such transactions are looked on as a reorganisation of the share capital of a single company as a result of which the shareholder ends up owning more or less what he had owned before the transaction or something closely traceable to it. The application of the rules to the reorganisation of the capital of single company is examined in greater detail below.

The transactions to which these rules are applied in the case of a single company involve;

- the reduction of share capital of a company (see paragraph 42.2) and
- the reorganisation of the share capital of a company (see paragraph 42.3.).

The CGT Acts also apply these same principles to transactions that involve more than one company e.g. where a shareholder in one company exchanges his shares in that company for shares in another company. That application of these principles to more complex transactions involving more than one company is examined in paragraph 43.

The three basic rules of the reorganisation and reduction of share capital provisions are:

- where the *original shares* are exchanged for *new shares in the same company* there is deemed to be no disposal of the old shares and the new shares are treated as being acquired at the original cost and acquisition date of the old shares for the purposes of any future disposal.

- where the *original shares* are exchanged for *new shares in the same company plus other consideration,* there is deemed to be a part disposal for a consideration equal to the cash or value of the other assets received; the new shares acquire the original cost (to the extent that it is not attributable to the part disposal) and acquisition date of the original shares.

- where the *original shares plus other consideration* are exchanged for *new shares in the same company,* the new shares acquire the original cost and acquisition date of the old shares; in addition, the other consideration paid is regarded as "enhancement expenditure" incurred on the date it is paid over.

The rules relating to reorganisations, reduction of share capital, and amalgamations which are considered in paragraphs 42 to 44 inclusive, largely focus on the position of shareholders in the companies which are parties to the transactions. The position of the companies involved in the transactions is considered in paragraph 76, which concerns the transfer of businesses, and of trades between companies.

The interaction of the reliefs discussed in this and the following sections (broadly the provisions of s584) with group relief (a form of relief available to companies in relation to the transfer between them of assets) is considered in paragraph 76.

s747(6) Notwithstanding the fact that an exchange of shares or debentures is generally treated as not giving rise to a disposal (subject to the conditions outlined in the paragraphs which follow) where a company acquires another company in this fashion, and the acquired company is or was on 6 April 1990 (or if later, the date on which the consideration is given for the acquisition by the person holding it at the date of the exchange) a non qualifying offshore fund, then, for the purposes of chapter 2 of part 27, TCA 97, the share exchange may be treated as giving rise to a disposal. Chapter 2 of part 27 is concerned with imposing an income tax charge on the occasion of the disposal of certain assets and is not directly concerned with CGT. Despite the fact that a share exchange may be treated as giving rise to a disposal for the purposes of chapter 2 of part 27, dealing with offshore funds and income tax, that does not mean that it is treated as giving rise to a disposal for the purposes of CGT.

The significance of chapter 2 of part 27 in relation to offshore funds is solely that it may give rise to an income tax charge on a share for share exchange, but it otherwise is of no direct relevance to CGT. Normally, where chapter 2 of part 27 gives rise to a deemed disposal for income tax purposes, the sum charged to income tax is disregarded in a CGT computation. This goes some way to avoiding double taxation. In the present case however, a disposal may be deemed to occur for income tax purposes, giving rise to an income tax charge, but there is no corresponding disposal for CGT purposes, and accordingly some other method of avoiding double taxation is necessary. That is provided by s747 (6) which treats the amount charged to income tax (as an offshore income gain) as additional consideration given by the taxpayer for the new holding of shares arising from the exchange.

FA99 s59: s751A
   S751A(FA99 s59) deals with the situation where shares are held as trading stock or where the profit on their sale would otherwise be an element in the computation of trading profits. In such circumstances capital gains tax would not apply to a disposal of the shares, whether on a reorganisation or otherwise. The matter would be entirely within the realms of taxes on income. Accordingly reliefs provided for capital gains tax purposes would have no application.

S751A provides that where, for capital gains tax purposes, a transaction to which it applies would not have been treated as a disposal, then it shall not be treated as a disposal either for the purposes of a computation under Case 1 of Schedule D. Rather, the deductible cost of the original holding will be attached to any new holding resulting from the reorganisation.

42.2   Definitions

42.2.1   "Reduction of share capital" is not defined.

s584

CA63 s72   No guidance is given as to what constitutes a reduction of share capital. It would include a reduction of share capital by a company limited by shares or guarantee subject to confirmation by the High Court under s.72 of the Companies Act 1963. The paying off of redeemable share capital would not constitute a reduction of capital for this purpose.

Example 218

> *Haywire PLC has gone through a period of years in which it had severe trading losses. In consequence its shareholders funds are represented by issued share capital of £20 million consisting of 15 million £1 ordinary shares, and 5 million £1 preference shares; and a profit and loss account deficit of £16 million. It has now returned to profitability but cannot pay a dividend in the foreseeable future by reason of the large profit and loss account deficit. It needs to raise new share capital but cannot do so due to its inability to pay dividends.*

Haywire PLC receives permission from the High Court to reduce its share capital by cancelling one preference share out of every two preference shares held by each shareholder; and by cancelling 13 ordinary shares out of each 15 ordinary shares held by each shareholder. At the conclusion of that exercise the company's balance sheets shows ordinary share capital of £2 million; preference share capital of £2 million; and a zero balance on the profit and loss account. The company will now be in a position pay dividends from future profits as they arise, and accordingly is now able to raise new share capital.

Cancellation of the shares which was sanctioned by the court would, in the normal sense of the words, be a disposal of those shares. However by reason of the provisions of s584 the reduction of a company's share capital is not treated as involving any disposal of shares, nor any acquisition of new shares. Instead, the shares held at the end of the process are regarded as being the same shares as all of the shares held at the beginning of the process.

Therefore in the example above, a shareholder who had held 300 ordinary shares before the reduction in capital would hold only 40 ordinary shares after the reduction in capital. However those 40 shares are treated as being a group of shares identical in terms of acquisition cost, and date of acquisition to the original 300 shares. All of the acquisition cost which had previously attached to the 300 shares now attaches to the smaller group of 40 shares, without any reduction.

Of course in an extreme case, a shareholder might be able to obtain a recognition that he has suffered loss by making a negligible value claim, where the shares had indeed become of negligible value. That however has nothing to do with the reduction in capital described above.

A reduction in capital can, paradoxically, sometimes involve the acquisition of new shares.

Example 219

*Haywire PLC, the company described in **example 218** above, decides to reduce its share capital. The scheme of reduction approved by the court is not that outlined above, but is one under which each holder of two preference shares will receive one ordinary share in return for the cancellation of the two preference shares. Each holder of 15 ordinary shares has 13 of those ordinary shares cancelled.*

A preference shareholder in such a case is not treated as disposing of his preference shares, or as acquiring new ordinary shares. Instead the new ordinary shares that he ends up with as a result are treated, from the view point of the computation of capital gains subsequently, as if they were the identical preference shares which he previously held, acquired at the same time and in the same manner, and for the same consideration, as he had given for the preference shares.

This latter aspect, that the shareholder receives new shares in exchange for the cancellation of old shares can also take place otherwise than in the context of a reduction of capital, and is further referred to in paragraph 42.2.2. in the context of a reorganisation of share capital. In practice it is of no importance as to whether such an exchange in the context of a reduction in share capital is regarded as being part of that reduction in share capital, or is regarded as being instead a reorganisation of share capital. The tax treatment which follows is identical in both instances.

42.2.2   "Reorganisation of share capital" is not defined

The CGT Acts do not define the phrase "reorganisation of share capital" but does state that it includes:

s584
- any case where the person is, whether for payment or not, allotted shares in or debentures of the company in respect of and in proportion to (or as nearly as may be in proportion to) his holding of shares in the company, or any class or shares in the company; and

- any case where there are more than one class of shares and the rights attached to shares of any class are altered.

It should be noted that for this purpose, shares will include stock (see paragraph 40.2).

For the purposes of the relief therefore, reorganisation would include such transactions as a bonus issue of shares, a rights issue, the issue of ordinary shares in exchange for a cancellation of preference shares, and a bonus issue of debentures to existing shareholders.

In the UK case of Dunstan v Young Austen Young Limited it was held that the provisions of s584(1)(a),(b) do not exhaustively define those increases in capital which fall within the meaning of reorganisation of a company's share capital. An increase in share capital could be a reorganisation, even if it did not come within the precise wording of s584(1), provided that the new shares are acquired by the existing shareholders because they are existing shareholders and in proportion to their existing beneficial holdings.

s816; s584(4)
A person who receives a bonus share from a company may, if he might have elected to instead receive cash, be taxed as if he had received a dividend in an amount equal to the cash. Such a person is treated as having given consideration for the bonus shares equal to the deemed cash dividend.

42.2.3   Bonus Issues

The treatment of a bonus issue of shares, or a bonus issue of debentures to existing shareholders is identical, both in company law terms and in terms of their taxation treatment. A bonus issue is an issue of shares or debentures to existing shareholders without those shareholders being obliged to provide any new consideration for what they receive. It involves the capitalisation of part of the reserves of the company, so that the reserves are reduced, and the share capital (or in the case of a bonus issue of debentures, loan stock) of the company has increased.

Example 220

John owns 60 £1 ordinary shares in Shops Ltd. The other 40 £1 ordinary shares in issue are held by Joe. The company, in addition to having a share capital of £100, has accumulated profits of £200,000. As a condition of receiving a bank loan, it is obliged to capitalise some of these profits. This insures that the amount of profits which are capitalised cannot be paid out subsequently by way of dividend thereby reducing the assets available to the bank as security for its loan. The bank has required that £100,000 of the accumulated profits be capitalised. Accordingly, 60,000 £1 ordinary shares are issued to John by way of bonus issue, 40,000 £1 ordinary shares are issued to Joe. Neither John nor Joe provide any consideration for these shares. After the bonus issue, the share capital of the company is of 100,000 £1 ordinary shares and accumulated profits of £100,000. The total value of the shareholders funds is unchanged, but the make up, as between share capital and reserves, has been changed.

In recognition of the fact that in substance neither John nor Joe is any better off as result of what has occurred, a bonus issue of shares is always treated for capital gains purposes as a reorganisation of share capital. Accordingly neither John nor Joe is treated for capital gains tax purposes as having acquired any new shares on the occasion of the bonus issue. The 60,060 shares now held by John are deemed to be the same 60 shares that John originally held, acquired on the same occasion, and for the same consideration as those original 60 shares. Joe is treated similarly. If John and Joe had acquired their shares by subscribing for the original share capital of the company at par, the base cost which John would have for a 60,060 shares would be £60 adjusted for inflation.

Example 221

John, whose situation is described in **example 220** *above, decides to sell half of his share holding to Joe. He sells 30,030 shares to Joe for £60,000. John and Joe are unconnected and the transaction is a bargain at arm's length.*

The 30,030 shares being disposed of by John have the same base cost, and the same acquisition date, as do 30 of the original shares which he subscribed for in the company. The computation (ignoring indexation for the sake of simplicity) would therefore be as follows;

	£
Consideration	60,000
Less base cost of shares	30
Gain	59,970

Scrip dividends (shares in lieu) are discussed in paragraph 42.5.

42.3 Rights Issues

s584

A rights issue would normally be regarded as a reorganisation of share capital. Such an issue normally involves a proportionate allotment of shares to existing shareholders.

Example 222

Joe acquired 1,000 ordinary shares in Beermats Ltd for £2,000 in January 1989. The company made a rights issue in February 1999 of 2 shares for each share held at £1.50 per share. Joe took up his full entitlement. In March 1999, he sold his total shareholding for £8,000.

	£
Sale proceeds	8,000
Cost - 1988/89: £2,000 indexed @ 1.282 =	2,564
Enhancement expenditure 1998/99 (not indexed) =	3,000
	5,564
GAIN - 1998/99	2,436

Joe is treated as not acquiring any new shares in 1999. The additional consideration paid for the rights issue is treated as enhancement expenditure incurred on the shares acquired in 1989.

The use of these provisions in mitigation of taxation is well illustrated in the UK case of IRC v Burmah Oil Co Ltd. In that case the taxpayer company (Burmah Oil Co Ltd) held shares in a subsidiary H Ltd. That subsidiary had incurred a substantial deficit represented by a loan from Burmah of approximately £159m. The taxpayer company took steps to create an allowable loss for CGT purposes, which were, broadly, as follows:

- The loan was repaid by H Ltd, out of funds loaned by another company, but in fact provided indirectly by Burmah.

- Burmah then gave approximately £159m to H Ltd in payment of a rights issue of shares made by that company, of 700,000 ordinary shares at a premium of £227 per share.

- On receipt of the funds for the rights issue, H Ltd repaid the loan from the other group company.

- H Ltd was then liquidated and Burmah Oil Co received approximately £296,000 in respect of its shareholding.

In calculating the loss arising on the disposal of the shares in H Ltd Burmah sought to deduct the cost of the shares acquired in the rights issue in addition to the cost of its original shareholding.

The Revenue contended:

- that the new shares should be regarded as having been acquired at market value at the date of issue, and

- that having regard to the scheme as a whole the amount paid for the new shares was not true consideration given for those shares.

The first contention of the Revenue was rejected particularly on the grounds that, under the reorganisation provisions there was deemed to be no acquisition of new shares; the amount actually paid for the new shares fell to be treated as further consideration for the old shares.

However, it was held that the transactions entered into by the taxpayer company when considered as a whole, involved no real loss so that there should be no allowable loss for CGT purposes. This aspect of the case would be unlikely to be followed by Irish Courts following the decision in the "McGrath" case - see paragraph 69.2.

Such a scheme would now be defeated under anti-avoidance legislation since introduced both in Ireland and the UK - see paragraph 41.4.

s547

As explained in paragraph 41.4 the effect of s. 62 Finance Act 1982, which amended s. 9 of the 1975 Act (now s547), is to restrict the consideration which a connected person is treated as giving for shares to the lesser of the actual consideration, or the amount by which the market value of all of the shares in the company which he holds immediately after the subscription exceeds the market value of his shareholding in the company immediately prior to it. That provision applies only in relation to a subscription for shares which is otherwise than by a bargain at arm's length.

The application of s547(2) to the Burmah Oil case described above would be to have treated Burmah Oil as having given consideration on the rights issue, not of the actual £150 million which it paid but probably of approximately zero, being the impact which the subscription had on the value of its shareholding in that insolvent company.

s584

Because a Rights issue normally involves the allotment of shares in a company to the existing shareholders in the proportion of their holdings of shares, it usually falls within the definition given in s584 of a reorganisation of share capital. A rights issue of shares must be distinguished from a bonus issue of shares. A bonus issue of shares consists of the capitalisation of part of the reserves of the company and a distribution to the members (for no consideration) of the shares so created by capitalising reserves. By definition, such a bonus issue is always made

- in proportion to the existing shareholdings, and

- in the respect of existing shareholdings.

A rights issue on the other hand involves an offer to the members of the right to subscribe for new shares, usually at what is considered to be a favourable price. Since a rights issue will involve existing shareholders giving additional consideration in order to receive the new shares, it will sometimes be the case that not all shareholders will take up their rights to shares.

Where some shares are not taken up by the shareholder to whom they are offered (or indeed in some cases by anybody) but remain unissued, the shares as finally issued may not be issued to the members in proportion to their holdings prior to the issue. In such a circumstance is there a reorganisation in the meaning of the specific statutory example referred to in the first bullet point in paragraph 42.2.2 ? It must be borne in mind that that definition of a reorganisation refers to shares being allotted in respect of and in proportion to the shareholders holding of shares in the company. It refers to allotment and not to issue of shares. An allotment of shares occurs when a shareholder is given the right to have his name placed on the register of members in respect of one or more shares. The shares in respect of which is he is entitled to have his name registered on the register as the holder of them, are regarded as having been allotted to him. A rights issue in its ordinary sense would therefore involve each shareholder receiving the right to be entered on the register as the holder of certain shares, should they choose to exercise that right, and to pay the subscription monies in respect of the shares.

More usually however the rights to subscribe for new shares, which are not taken up by existing members are either offered to those members who do take up rights, or are sold to third parties. In such a situation all of the shares on offer would have been taken up. Where that is the case, those members who do take up the rights allotted to them receive shares proportionate to their old shareholding in the company. They will therefore be involved in a reorganisation of share capital. To the extent that they additionally take up rights which other members refused to take up they will receive an allotment of shares which is not in proportion to their previous shareholding in the company. That additional allotment would not seem to fall within the reorganisation provisions, not being in proportion to the original shareholding.

Third parties who purchase or otherwise acquire the rights which existing members do not take up, and who as a result are issued shares in the company are not receiving those shares either in respect of an existing shareholding of theirs in the company, or in proportion to it, and likewise are not treated as being involved in a reorganisation of share capital. Thus a single rights issue may involve some members receiving shares which involve a reorganisation; and some third parties receiving shares which are not treated as part of a reorganisation; and some existing members receiving some shares which are part of a reorganisation, and some which are not.

- **Revenue/Chief Inspector's CGT Manual :**
- The Revenue Commissioners, in their capital gains tax manual at Paragraph 19.4.6.16(2) state *"Where on a bonus or rights issue the*

entitlement of a shareholder would include a fraction of a share (if strict proportions were followed), and the shareholder receives in lieu of that fraction of a share, a compensatory cash amount usually from the sale of the entitlement on the market the cash sum should be deducted from the base cost of the "new holding" rather than being treated as a part disposal of the shares."

• **Revenue/Chief Inspector's CGT Manual :**

— In Paragraph 19.4.7.3 of the capital gains tax manual, the Revenue Commissioners point out that the transfer of an entitlement to a rights issue of shares (at a time when the shares have not yet been issued but when the entitlement to subscribe for them has accrued to the shareholder) is strictly speaking a part disposal by the shareholder of his shares, although the part disposal must be computed as being for a consideration which gives rise to neither a gain nor a loss. The Revenue Commissioners note that where the value of the "rights" is small, spouses both of whom are resident may deal with the matter without attributing any consideration to the rights transferred (ie effectively ignoring the transfer). Some doubt must exist as to whether the practice indicated is indeed concessional as opposed to the correct treatment. Section 584 does provide that on a rights issue, the shares being issued are to be regarded as the same asset as the original holding of shares with which they constitute a "new holding". But an unexercised provisional "right" is not included in the definition of "share" in Section 5(1) - it is specifically excluded. Arguably therefore the right, at a time when it is not exercised, does not fall within Section 584 and is in itself an independent asset. As the point is not likely to be of significance in the context of an intra spouse transaction, it is probably not worth exploring the point further.

42.4	**Exchange of Shares in same company ('Paper for Paper')**
s586	Relief is provided where shares in a company are disposed of by way of exchange for other shares in the same company; for example, where the shareholder surrenders his existing shares in exchange for other new shares in the same company. In such a case, nothing passes but the shares.

In such a case there is deemed to be no disposal and no acquisition. The new shares take the original cost and acquisition date of the old shares.

Example 223

Jimmy bought 500 £1 ordinary shares in SALT LAKE LTD on 1 January 1997 at par. In March, 1988 the company became insolvent and reorganisation took place. In exchange for his existing shares Jimmy received 1,000 non-voting preference shares; he sold the preference shares on 31 January 1999 for £3,250.

CGT is payable as follows:

		£
Sale price of pref. shares		3,250
Cost of old ord. shares...	£500	
£500 indexed at 1.033		516
GAIN		2,734

This straightforward relief where a person exchanges one lot of paper for another is sometimes more complex in real life. It is not uncommon for the consideration for the disposal of shares to consist in part of shares and debentures up front, together with further consideration payable at a later date if certain targets are achieved (an earn out). Such an arrangement raises questions as to whether the right to the additional deferred contingent consideration (the earn out amount) to be regarded as itself consisting of shares or debentures (where that is the form in which it is payable should it arise), or whether the right is to be treated as additional consideration in itself. If it is in itself additional consideration (a chose in action) then it would not consist of shares, but be a mere right to receive shares in certain circumstances. This problem was considered in the UK case of Marren v Ingles. This is discussed in Paragraph 4.4.6.

- *Revenue Commissioners published precedent :*

– In their published precedents the Revenue Commissioners have stated *"Where part of the consideration for a takeover consists of shares or securities to be issued at a future date if a contingency is satisfied, the earn out element will be treated as a security and relief under Section 586 may be due. This will apply only in so far as the earn out element does not or could not take the form of cash."*

It seems fairly clear from the context in which the precedent has been published (reference to s586) that the Revenue Commissioners do not regard debentures as being the equivalent of cash, notwithstanding that debentures may be readily turned into cash in some circumstances.

The Revenue Commissioners have a separate published precedent in relation to an earn out consisting of cash - see paragraph 5.2.11.

42.5   **Introduction of Further Consideration**

s584(4)   In a reorganisation, a shareholder, in exchange for his new shareholding, may be required to surrender his existing shares, and, in addition, contribute further consideration. Such a transaction is deemed not to be a disposal of his original shareholding. On the eventual disposal of his new shares, he will have two items of expenditure to deduct from the sale price, that is:

- the base cost (and not the market value at date of exchange) of the original shares which were surrendered in exchange for the new shares:

and

- the new consideration given at the time of the reorganisation.

For indexation purposes, (and for determining the period of ownership), the cost will retain its original base date, but the new consideration will acquire its own base date, i.e. the date the new consideration was given. In effect, the new consideration is treated as 'enhancement expenditure' for indexation purposes.

For this purpose, the term *"new consideration"* does not include:

- any surrender, cancellation or other alteration of the original shares or of the right attached thereto, or

- any consideration consisting of any application in paying up the shares or debentures or any part of them

  - of any asset of the company or

  - of any dividend or other distribution declared out of those assets but not made (but an exception is made for scrip issues taxed on the shareholder under s.56 FA 1974 - see below).

Example 224 - *Payment of New Consideration*

Johnny Mack acquired 500 ordinary shares in LEASTOWN ANIMAL PRODUCTS LIMITED on 1 January 1972; market value of the shares at 6/4/74 was £750. On a reorganisation of the company in February, 1993, Johnny was offered 1,000 new "A" ordinary shares of £1 in exchange for his existing shares and for a payment of £500 in cash. Having little choice in the matter, Johnny accepted and paid over his £500 on 15 February, and at the same time surrendered his existing shares. He disposed of his "A" shares on 1 March 1993 for £5,650.

His liability to CGT is calculated as follows (ignoring the annual exemption):

	£
Consideration Received	5,650
Cost - Original shares - MV 6/4/1974	
- indexed (£750 x 5.656)	4,242
Expenditure 15/2/83 (no indexation - sold within 12 months)	500
	4,742
Gain	908

s816   Where an issue of shares is taxable as income in the hands of the shareholder under s816 (known as a scrip dividend or shares in lieu) the cash which that shareholder could have received in lieu of the shares is treated as consideration given for those shares. Broadly speaking, s816 gives rise to an income tax charge where the share issue (by an unquoted company pre 3rd December 1997 and by any company after that date) results from the exercise of an option to receive either a cash sum or additional shares; the shareholder is deemed to be in receipt of income equal to the cash amount he could have received as an alternative to the shares.

42.6   **Shares Plus Other Consideration**

s584(5)   If in exchange for giving up his shares, a shareholder receives other consideration in addition to new shares in the same company, the relief applies to the transaction in the following manner :

* the other consideration received is deemed to be consideration for a part disposal of the original shareholding

    and

* the new shares acquire the same acquisition date as the old shares and also the same base cost (but with an adjustment to eliminate the part of the cost attributable to the part disposal).

This part disposal arises where the shareholder receives or becomes entitled to receive any consideration other than the new holding (of shares or securities) for the disposal of an interest in the original shares and in particular:

* where he is to be treated as having disposed of an interest in the original shares in consideration of a capital distribution received in respect of those shares (see paragraph 40.3)

    and

* where he receives (or is deemed to receive) consideration from other shareholders in respect of his surrender of rights derived from the original shares.

Example 225

Jim acquired 4,000 £1 ordinary shares in HAYSTACKS LTD at par on 1 January 1986. On a reconstruction on 31 December 1990 he received in exchange for his shares, 2,000 non-voting preference shares and £3,900 in cash. The market value of the preference shares at the date of issue was £2,500. In March 1999 he sold the preference shares for £2,700. His liability to CGT is calculated as follows:

Part disposal in December 1990	*£*
Consideration received in cash	*3,900*
Attributable cost	

$$\text{Cost of ordinary shares } £4,000 \times \frac{3,900}{3,900 + 2,500} = 2,438$$

£2,438 indexed at 1.188	2,896
Gain - 1990/91	1,004

Disposal in March 1999

Consideration received	2,700
Attributable cost £1,562 (i.e.. £4,000 - £2,438) indexed @ 1.414 =	2,208
GAIN - 1998/99	492

42.7   Apportionment

s584(6)

The effect of the relief which applies to a share exchange, or other transactions coming within the relief is to attribute the total cost (and acquisition date) of the old shares to the new holding (in total). Where the new holding consists of more than one class of shares or debentures in the company, an apportionment of the total cost over the various parts of the new holding may be necessary. An apportionment would, of course, only arise on a subsequent disposal of part of the new holding.

Where no part of the new holding is quoted, the apportionment of the total cost of the old holding must be done in proportion to the respective market values of the various parts of the new holding at the date of the first (and each subsequent) disposal out of that new holding.

Example 226

Joe purchased 1,000 £1 ordinary shares in CALENDARS LTD on 30 June 1988 at par. On 1 January 1990 he received 500 "A" ordinary shares and 500 preference shares in exchange for his original holding. He sold the preference shares for £750 in March 1994 and the market value of the "A" ordinary shares on that date was £1,250. None of the shares are quoted.

The gain is calculated as follows:

	£
Consideration for disposal	750

$$\text{Cost as indexed} = £1,000 \times \frac{£750}{(£750 + £1,250)*}$$

Indexed @ 1.167	438
Gain	312

* MV of ord. (£1,250) plus MV of pref. (£750).

As can be seen from this example, although the preference shares appeared to have a base cost of £1 each on the reorganisation, in consequence of the ordinary

> *shares growing more rapidly value , the preference shares are stripped of part of their real base cost (which, in effect, is transferred to the ordinary shares under the apportionment rules).*

This treatment, which calculates base cost not at the date of acquisition, but as each disposal subsequently takes place, can be a severe trap where shares and debentures are received in exchange for shares. A delay in cashing in the debentures may lead to their base cost falling below their nominal value, as values subsequently change. A gain could thus arise on the eventual encashment of debentures, even if at the date of acquisition, they appeared to have an adequate base cost.

s584(7)
A different rule applies where the new holding received in the reconstruction includes **quoted** shares or securities.

In such a case the cost of the old holding is apportioned between the various classes of shares or debentures in the new holding by reference to their respective market value on the day on which the quoted shares were first quoted. The unquoted and quoted parts of the new holding (if any) must be valued on that day, for the purposes of this apportionment.

This rule only applies where the new holding consists of more than one class of shares or debentures, and one or more of those classes had a quoted market value on a recognised stock exchange (the quotation must have been not later than three months from the date the reconstruction took effect, or such longer period allowed by the Revenue Commissioners).

43   COMPANY AMALGAMATIONS (by exchange of shares)

43.1   Overview

The relief dealt with in paragraph 42 deals with transactions within a single company. The same rules apply (with any necessary adaptations) where a company ('the acquiring company') issues shares or debentures to a person for his shares in or debentures of another company ('the subject company').

Broadly speaking, the relieving provisions will apply in this case only if:

- the acquiring company has, or in consequence of the exchange will have, control of the subject company.

  or

- the exchange is the result of a general offer made by the acquiring company to the members of the subject company. The offer must be made on conditions which if satisfied would give the acquiring company control of the subject company. (For example, the offer might be conditional upon the acquiring company obtaining 51% of the shares in the subject company).

Where the offer was made on the basis that it was conditional on the acquiring company obtaining control of the target, the conditions required for amalgamation are satisfied even if the original condition is subsequently waived and the offer becomes an unconditional offer.

Example 227

Killer Whales Plc have offered to the shareholders of Penguin Limited two shares in Killer Whales Plc for each share held in Penguin Limited. The offer is expressed to be conditional on it being accepted by holders of in excess of 50% of the shares in Penguin Limited.

The holders of 30% of the shares in Penguin Limited indicate their acceptance of the conditional offer. At that point Killer Whales Plc announce that their offer is unconditional, ie that they are prepared to acquire shares whether or not they achieve control. No further shareholders take up their offer and the transaction is concluded by Killer Whales Plc acquiring the 30% of the shares in Penguin Limited. Notwithstanding that Killer Whales Plc did not achieve control of Penguin Limited, the transaction is nonetheless entitled to be treated as an amalgamation of companies. The shareholders in Penguin Limited will not be treated as disposing of their shares.

Example 228

Some time after the events described in **Example** 227 *above Killer Whales Plc made a further offer of two of its shares for each share in Penguin Limited. The offer was not expressed to be conditional on sufficient acceptances being received to provide control to Killer Whales Plc. Twelve percent of the shareholders accepted the new offer, giving Killer Whales Plc 42% of Penguin Limited.*

This transaction, since it neither provided control nor was initially conditional on control being obtained, is not treated as an amalgamation, and the holders of the 12% of Penguin Limited who accepted the offer are treated as disposing of their shares.

Later in the same year Killer Whales Plc improved their offer to five of Killer Whales Plc shares for each two shares in Penguin Limited. The offer was not expressed to be conditional on the acquisition of control of Penguin Limited. Fifteen percent of the shares in Penguin Limited were successfully acquired as a result of this new offer. In consequence the total shareholding of Killer Whales Plc in Penguin Limited moved up to 57%. Notwithstanding that the 15% shares acquired on this occasion would not, taken in isolation, provide a holder with control of the company, and notwithstanding that the offer was not conditional on obtaining control when originally made, this is treated as an amalgamation because when the 15% acquired is added to the shareholding already possessed by Killer Whales Plc the combined shareholding is now sufficient to give them control.

Example 229

On 30 April, 1984 Jim acquired 5,000 £1 ordinary shares in PENGUINS LTD for £7,500. In June 1988, KILLER WHALES LTD made a successful takeover bid and for his shares in PENGUINS LTD Jim acquired £5,000 in cash and 10,000 £1 A ordinary shares in KILLER WHALES LTD. At the date of issue to Jim 10,000 "A" ordinary shares had a market value of £15,000. Jim disposed of these shares in March 1999 for £50,000.

The gains on Jim's disposal are calculated as follows:

1988/89 part disposal	£
Consideration received	*5,000*
Attributable Cost - 1984/85	

$$£7{,}500 \ x \ \frac{5{,}000}{15{,}000 + 5{,}000} = 1{,}875$$

	£
£1,875 indexed at 1.171	*2,196*
GAIN - 1988/89	*2,804*

1998/99 disposal	£
Consideration received	*50,000*
Attributable cost -	
1984/85 balance = £5,625	
(7,500-1,875)	
£5,625 indexed @1.502	*8,449*
GAIN - 1998/99	*41,551*

Note: *The shares acquired in KILLER WHALES LTD take the same base date (in 1984/85) and same cost (part) as the original shares in PENGUINS LTD.*

The use of similar UK *"share for share"* provisions to avoid tax is well illustrated in the case of Furniss v Dawson, although anti-avoidance legislation against this type of scheme has since been introduced in both Ireland and in the UK.

The taxpayers held shares in two family companies - "the family shares". They had negotiated the sale of the shares to a third party but before entering into a binding agreement, they took steps to avoid tax on the sale.

The taxpayers exchanged the family shares for shares in a newly formed Isle of Man company, Greenjacket. That company sold the family shares to the third party at the agreed price.

The taxpayers contended that the exchange did not constitute a disposal of the family shares as it was made in the course of a "reorganisation". They also contended that no gain arose to Greenjacket on the disposal of the family shares; this was on the grounds that Greenjacket had acquired the shares at market value, the consideration for the acquisition being an issue of shares in Greenjacket.

The Revenue contended:

- that the transactions having been carried out purely for tax purposes, Greenjacket should be regarded as the alter ego of the taxpayers:

- that any representation that Greenjacket acted independently was sham: that the company should therefore be ignored and the position determined as if Greenjacket did not exist:

- that Greenjacket should be regarded as acting as nominee or bare trustee of the taxpayers in the acquisition of the family shares; the result being that Greenjacket did not acquire "control" of the family companies:

- that there were understandings between the taxpayers and Greenjacket the effect of which was such that Greenjacket's apparent beneficial ownership of the shares was no more than bare legal ownership, so that Greenjacket never acquired control of the family companies:

- that following the decisions in W. T. Ramsay Ltd v IRC and Eilbeck v Rawling, the shares should be regard as having been disposed of by the taxpayers to the third party and the intermediate disposal to Greenjacket treated as a fiscal nullity.

Vinelott J. dismissed these contentions in finding for the taxpayers. He held that the exchange of shares and the sale of family shares by Greenjacket were genuine transactions which had enduring legal consequences; the court could not ignore these enduring legal consequences and either disregard the exchange or treat the sale agreement as if it had been entered into by Greenjacket as nominee or agent for the taxpayers. He distinguished the case from WT Ramsay Ltd v IRC, Eilbeck v Rawling, and IRC v Burmah Oil Co Ltd.

The decision of Vinelott J was upheld by the Court of Appeal.

The development of the "new approach" adopted in the Ramsay case was thought to have culminated with Furniss v Dawson. Both the Chancery Division and the Court of Appeal had given judgement in favour of the taxpayer, and as they seemed to take account of the Ramsay principle, it appeared that the judgements would be upheld by the House of Lords. It was quite a surprise when the House of Lords, not only overruled the lower Courts and gave judgement in favour of the Revenue, but extended the "new approach" even further.

Details of the Irish position are set out in paragraph 69

44   RECONSTRUCTIONS AND AMALGAMATIONS

44.1   Overview

s586; s587   The relief described in paragraph 42 also applies to certain
arrangements entered into for the purposes of or in connection with
a scheme of reconstruction or amalgamation. A transaction will
qualify for relief where under any such arrangement between the
company and the persons holding shares in or debentures of the
company, another company issues shares or debentures to those
persons in respect of and in proportion to their original holding of
shares or debentures. The original shares or debentures must be
either retained by the shareholders or cancelled.

Where the transaction qualifies, the shareholders concerned will be
treated as exchanging their original shares or debentures for those
held by them after the carrying out of the arrangement without a
disposal for CGT purposes.

A form of clawback of the relief can arise as explained in paragraph
46.

"Scheme of reconstruction or amalgamation" means a scheme for the
reconstruction of any company or companies (see paragraph 44.3) or
the amalgamation of any two or more companies (see paragraph
44.2).

- **Revenue/Chief Inspector's CGT manual :**

- The Revenue Commissioners in their capital gains tax manual at
  Paragraph 19.4.11.2 provide the following description of a
  reconstruction and an amalgamation: *"A reconstruction takes place
  where an undertaking carried on by a company is in substance preserved
  and transferred to another company consisting substantially of the same
  shareholders. An amalgamation is the blending of two or more existing
  undertakings into one undertaking, the shareholders of each blending
  company becoming substantially the shareholders in the company which
  carries on the blended undertaking."*

s587(3)   References to shares or debentures being retained include their being
retained with altered rights or in altered form whether as a result of
reduction, consolidation, division or otherwise.

The relief applies in relation to a company which has no share capital
as if references to shares or debentures of a company included
references to any interests in the company possessed by members of
the company.

A typical example of a company not having a share capital is a
company limited by guarantee. Such companies are usually, but not
necessarily, formed for charitable purposes. Where a company does
not have share capital, it nonetheless has members. Such members

will usually have rights conferred upon them by the Memorandum and Articles of Association. Whatever those rights may be, they are treated as being the same as "shares" for the purposes of the reliefs described in paragraph 44.2 (amalgamations), 44.3 (reconstructions) and 44.4 (share for undertaking). The fact that the company does not have a share capital in no way prevents it from engaging in share for share exchanges or share for undertaking exchanges!

The "share for share" two company transaction attracts relief as described in paragraph 43. That relief is set out in TCA97 s586.

s586
s587
S586(1) states that s586 is "subject to s587". TCA97 s587 provides the relief for a "share for undertaking" three party swap, normally described as a reconstruction or amalgamation. It is not clear why s586 is stated to be "subject to" s587.

S587 itself merely applies s586 to a share for undertaking transaction. The two sections are not capable of having application to the same transaction, since s587 will apply only if the shares in question are either retained by the original shareholder, or cancelled, where s586 requires that the shares be exchanged by their original owner for shares in another company.

A *"demerger"* is not included in the terms "reconstructions and amalgamations". A reconstruction involves the placing of a new corporate envelope around an existing undertaking, while remaining in the same ultimate ownership. An amalgamation involves the marriage of two undertakings. In contrast a demerger involves a divorce of undertakings into separate ownerships.

Example 230

Discord Holdings Limited is a long established family company. The original founder is dead and the shares are now held by his two sons and two daughters in equal shares. After a period of disagreement on company policy it is agreed to divide the businesses carried on by Discord Holdings Limited in four approximately equal segments, and to transfer the four segments each to a newly formed separate company, the shares in which are issued to the shareholders in Discord Holdings Limited, all of the shares in each one of the new companies going entirely to one of the family shareholders. The result is that instead of the four siblings jointly owning a company carrying on a number of businesses, each child now owns the entire of a company carrying on a single business.

Although there has been a transfer of undertakings from one corporate body into new corporate "envelopes" and although the same cast of characters comprise the shareholders in the new entities, the ownership of the various undertakings has not remained the same - any one undertaking when examined singly, is now owned by only one child, and not by the four children together. What has occurred is a demerger and not an amalgamation or reconstruction. Relief is not available in strict law.

However, the Revenue Commissioners may allow concessional treatment in a situation where a family company broken up into a number of separate units and split between the family members - see paragraph 44.8.

44.2   Amalgamations

The reorganisation provisions of the CGT Acts refers twice to amalgamations.

s586

- It does so as described in paragraph 43 above in the context of a share for share exchange, as a result of which one company comes to control another company.

s584

- In s584 the reference to amalgamations is to a transaction where one company issues shares or debentures to the shareholders of another company, in return for the transfer to it of the undertaking of the second company.

In other words the reference in s586 is to a share for share exchange, whereas the reference in s584 is to a share for undertaking exchange whereby two or more undertakings are brought together in the ownership of one company.

In the UK case of IRC -v- Ufitec Group Ltd it was held that in addition to involving a share for undertaking exchange as the result of which a number of undertakings are held in the ownership of one company, there must in a reorganisation be substantial identity of ownership of the trades so brought together, taking the position before the transfer as compared with the position after the transfer.

44.3   Reconstructions

A reconstruction has many features in common with an amalgamation. Like an amalgamation, it involves an exchange of shares and debentures for an undertaking. It also requires a substantial identity of ownership of the trade before and after the exchange. However it differs from the amalgamation in that it does not involve the bringing together into the ownership of one company of more than one undertaking.

Example 231

Company A is a company without assets, which has been newly created for the purpose of taking over the undertaking of company B. It issues shares to the shareholders of company B in return for which company B transfers its undertaking to company A. As company A did not have any existing undertaking nor was it simultaneously acquiring any other undertaking from any other company, this is a reconstruction and not an amalgamation.

If company A were also issuing shares and debentures to the shareholders of company C, in return for the transfer to it of the undertaking of company C, the overall transaction would constitute an amalgamation.

A transaction involving a reconstruction or an amalgamation, involving as it does the disposal by a company of its undertaking in return for no consideration payable to the company, or with the consideration being given directly to its shareholders, may raise issues of company law and issues relating to income tax or corporation tax on income and stamp duty which are outside the scope of this book.

44.4   **Undertaking**

The references above to the transfer of an undertaking would include transfer of part of an undertaking. *"Undertaking"* has a wide meaning and can cover much more than a trade. In particular it can cover an investment business including the holding of tenanted properties, and the holding of shares in a group of companies.

Not every transfer of assets from one company to another will constitute the transfer of the undertaking or part of the undertaking of one company to another .

The question of whether the transfer of assets constituted the transfer of undertaking was considered in the UK case, Baytrust Holding Limited -v- IRC, and also in the UK cases of McGregor -v- Adcock and Mannion -v- Johnston. In McGregor -v- Adcock the court rejected the notion that the sale of five acres out of a farm of thirty five acres constituted the sale of part of the business carried on.

Generally speaking, an undertaking involves some element of activity as opposed to the mere ownership of assets. A transfer of an undertaking, or part of an undertaking, ought to be reflected in a change in the level of activity of the purchaser and seller, after the transaction.

44.5   **Reorganisation : T. S. B.s and Building Societies**

The Finance Act 1990 introduced special provisions (now TCA97 s703) relating to the conversion of a building society or a trustee savings bank into a company.

A building society is an industrial and provident society. A trustee savings bank is usually a trust. The process of converting either into a company created under the Companies Acts involves the creation of a new legal entity, rather than the continuation in existence of the previous legal entities in an altered form. In the ordinary way therefore, there would be disposals of assets by the old entities, and acquisitions of assets by the new entities; and ownership rights in the old entities would be disposed of on being extinguished; and ownership rights in the new entities would be acquired upon creation.

s703

Since a building society is a company within the meaning of the Capital Gains Tax Acts (i.e. a body corporate other than a European Economic Interest Grouping) it might be thought that its conversion to a company would fall to be dealt with under the company amalgamation provisions of the second schedule (share for undertaking). Likewise it might be thought that the conversion of a trustee savings bank into a company would attract the provisions of the second schedule relating to the incorporation of an unincorporated business. Such however is not the case because the s703 has special provisions which, although not explicitly referring to the provisions of the second schedule of the Act, effectively appear to overrule their application. s703, which provides a comprehensive code for the CGT treatment of the conversions, is described in paragraph 44.5.1.

The cases of Foster v. Williams and Horan v. Williams, heard before the U.K. special commissioners in 1997, suggest one reason why, in the absence in the 1990 legislation, the reorganisation provisions might not apply in some circumstances to all aspects of the conversion of a Building Society. The two cases in question were concerned with the conversion of the Cheltenham and Gloucester Building Society into the form of a Plc. All account holders in the Building Society, both those who held share accounts, and those who held ordinary accounts, received payments by reason of being account holders, arising out of the conversion process. The special commissioners held that since the payments were made to account holders without regard to whether or not they were equity holders in the Building Society (i.e. holders of share accounts) it could not be said that the payments were compensation for the loss of equity status in the old Building Society. Rather the special commissioners analysed the process as one in which all account holders made a total disposal of their accounts (and all the rights attaching to those accounts) in the Building Society, in return for new accounts (of equal amounts) and the sums received, in the new Plc. The conversion process in that case did not involve the issue of shares to the account holders. The United Kingdom does not appear to have had the equivelent of our 1990 legislation.

44.5.1   Conversion of building society:

s703
Sch16

The society is not treated as disposing of assets owned by it at the conversion. The successor company is treated as having acquired them in the same manner and for the same consideration and at the same time as the society.

- The successor company is treated as having done everything which was done by the society. Accordingly it is entitled to any allowable losses of the society which had not been relieved at the conversion.

- A member of the society to whom the successor company issues shares is treated as giving consideration for them only of such new consideration as he provides the company.

- Where the successor company shares are passed to the society's members through a trust set up for that purpose and without new consideration being provided, the interposition of the trust is effectively ignored for CGT purposes. The member is treated as having received the share from the company for a nil consideration.

44.5.2   **Conversion of a trustee savings bank:**

- Assets are transferred by the bank to a successor company on a no gain no loss basis, so far as concerns the disposal only.

s704   The successor company is deemed to have acquired the
Sch17   transferred assets in the same manner and at the same time and for the same consideration as the bank did.

- Any allowable losses of the bank not relieved at the date of transfer are available to the successor company.

- The bank and the successor company are treated as being the same person for the purposes of roll over relief.

- An amalgamation of two trustee savings banks under Part IV of the Trustee Savings Banks Act 1989 is treated for CGT purposes as if the two banks were one person.

The rules relating to the conversion of a bank or of a society apply to conversions on or after 6 April 1990.

44.6   **Reorganisation of co-operative society**

s701   As a result of the process whereby large agri-food undertakings were transferred from co-operative societies (co-ops) to quoted companies, many coops became the owners of shares in quoted companies. The Finance Act 1993 introduced a relief which enabled co-ops to transfer the company shares to their members and to correspondingly reduce their own capital. The relief enables this reorganisation to take place without the co-op being treated as making a distribution, and on a no gain, no loss basis for the co-op, while the member is treated as not having disposed of his co-op shares which are cancelled, and to have the same base cost for the company shares as he had for the cancelled co-op shares.

The relief applies in the following circumstances:

s701(1)   − The co-op must be a society registered under the Industrial & Provident Societies Acts 1893 to 1978 and be an agricultural or fishery society as defined in s.18 FA 1978.

s701(2)(b)   — The transfer of shares must be on or after 6 April 1993.

s432   — The co-op must have control of the company whose shares are to
                      be transferred. "Control" has the meaning given in s432 i.e.
                      possession of or power to acquire, whether alone or with
                      associates, more than half of the share capital; dividends; or assets
                      on a winding up.

                    — The co-op must receive no consideration for the shares apart from
                      a reduction of its own capital.

                    — Each member of the co-op must receive a fraction of the shares in
                      the company proportionate to his share holding in the co-op.

s701(2)(b)   — A certain proportion of the shareholding in the co-op held by each
                      member must be cancelled without consideration apart from the
                      company shares transferred, the cancelled shares being identified
                      on a FIFO basis in respect of each member. The number of co-op
                      shares to be cancelled in respect of each member is that fraction of
                      his holding which is proportionate to the fraction of the value of
                      the co-ops assets represented by the value of the company shares.

                    This requirement is expressed in terms of the value of the co-op's
                    total assets and not of its net assets. It may give rise to anomalous
                    results, depending on the extent of borrowings and liabilities in
                    the co-op when the transfer of shares occurs.

s701(5)   — The transfer must be for commercial reasons and not part of an
                      arrangement to avoid corporation tax or C.G.T.

                    There are no particular requirements relating to the company whose
                    shares are transferred. It is not necessary that it be quoted or a
                    trading company.

Example 232

> Milk Co-operative Society owns 60% of the share capital of Food PLC. The
> Balance Sheet of the co-op shows an investment in Food PLC shares valued at
> £100,000; other assets of £20,000; and liabilities of £40,000. The £80,000 of net
> assets is financed by share capital of £10,000 and reserves of £70,000. Sean Bull
> owns 100 of the 10,000 shares, 50 of which he acquired in 1975 and 50 in 1994.
> The co-op transfers all of the Food PLC shares to its members.
>
> To avail of the relief, Milk Co-Op must cancel 10/12ths of its capital of £10,000
> i.e. £8,333. Sean Bull has the 50 shares acquired in 1975, and 33 out of the 50
> shares in 1994, cancelled. However he is not treated as having made any
> disposal, and the base cost of the cancelled shares now attaches to his Food PLC
> shares, which he is deemed to have acquired partly in 1975, and partly in 1994.
>
> The co-op is treated as disposing of the Food PLC shares on a no gain no loss
> basis, notwithstanding the different basis (just explained) on which they are
> treated as acquired by the members.

44.7   **Demutualisation of assurance company**

A mutual assurance company can be broadly described as one which does not operate to earn profits for its shareholders, but which operates so that any profits, over and above that required for the financing of its business, is returned to its policy holders. In effect, it is the policy holders to whom the benefits of the profitability of a mutual assurance company accrues, and not shareholders. Such a mutual assurance company may convert itself into a straightforward company, operating for the benefit of its shareholders, and not solely for the benefit of its policy holders. The process of conversion usually involves the existing policy holders receiving shares in the company.

The FA97 provides (in relation to demutualisation on or after 21 April 1997) rules relating to the CGT position of policy holders who receive shares in this fashion, and also of the CGT position of any trustees to whom such shares are initially issued, for allocation to policy holders.

The broad scheme of the provisions is to ensure that the policy holder is not treated as receiving a capital sum in respect of his rights in the assurance company, or in respect of his policy, but rather that he is treated as receiving the shares either for a zero base cost, or, where he pays additional new consideration for the shares, for the amount of that new consideration.

To give effect to this the legislation provides that;

• The right conferred on policy holders to receive shares is to be treated as if it were an option. The consequence of this is that once the shares are received, the acquisition of the right to receive merges with the receipt of the share, and does not become a separate event for capital gains tax purposes (see paragraph 39). However if the policy holder sold his right to receive shares before he received the shares, he would be disposing of an asset (i.e. of an option) and would be chargeable to tax accordingly. Since his base cost in the deemed option is treated by the legislation as being zero, the fact that an option is a wasting asset has no practical implications in that situation, where the option is disposed of to a third party.

• Where the policy holder receives shares on foot of the right to receive, or otherwise in connection with the demutualisation arrangement, his base cost in the shares is restricted to any new consideration given by him.

• The right to receive shares, or to subscribe on preferential terms for shares in connection with the demutualisation is regarded as a right having no value at the time it was granted. Accordingly its receipt does not constitute a capital sum derived from any existing asset of the policy holder.

- Where shares are initially transferred to trustees for transmission to policy holders, the trustees are treated as obtaining the shares for no consideration (which overrides any provisions substituting open market value or any other base cost). When they transmit them to the policy holders they are deemed to do so on a no gain no loss basis, which, since they have been deemed to acquire them for zero consideration, would imply that they are deemed to dispose of them for zero consideration.

s593   S593 confers an exemption on the holder of a life assurance policy in relation to the disposal of his rights under the policy, where the policy is issued by a company within the charge to Irish corporation tax in respect of income in its life assurance fund. Were it not for the 1997 provisions, it is arguable that the "free shares" received by a policy holder on the demutualisation of a company would, in relation to an Irish company, represent a tax free receipt, and would confer on the policy holder a base cost in the new shares equal to open market value. The 1997 legislation therefore seems to leave such a policy holder worse off. However it probably benefits the holders of policies issued by life assurance companies not within the charge to corporation tax in that they avoid a charge to tax on the occasion of the receipt of the shares.

It may however be that the process of demutualisation would involve the policyholder receiving shares in the new company, not in respect of his policy but in respect of some equity ownership rights in the society which can be regarded as distinct from his policy. That is a matter of speculation outside the remit of this book. If such were the case (and it appears to be the view of the Inland Revenue in the UK that it is) the transaction would not otherwise have been free of tax.

The treatment of life assurance generally is described in paragraph 36.

44.8   **De-Mergers and Partitions of Family Companies**

It frequently happens, that where a family trading company or group has passed into the second or third generation of ownership, the individual family shareholders may find that they would prefer to go their own way, each taking part of the trading operations under their own total control. Capital gains tax is an obstacle to such a demerger or partition of the family interests in that, if carried out in a straightforward manner, it would usually involve a double charge to capital gains tax. Usually it will involve a disposal by one or more companies of their assets, on the occasion of those assets being passed to one of the shareholders, and either an income tax charge or a capital gains tax charge on the individual shareholder on the grounds that he received a distribution from the company.

Example 233

> John, Joe and Mary are siblings. Each own one-third of the shares in Family
> Holdings Limited. Family Holdings Limited owns a shop, a pub, and an
> undertaking business, all of approximately equal value. John, Joe and Mary
> have not seen eye to eye regarding the running of the businesses. Friction is
> leading to ill-will in the family. The solution identified is to give one of the
> businesses to each of the shareholders, and allow all three to go their own way
> with no further business connections between them.
>
> The straightforward manner of achieving this result would be to liquidate the
> company and distribute one business to each shareholder, in specie. Such a
> transaction would have the result of causing the company to be treated as
> disposing of each of the three businesses and related assets, potentially giving
> rise to capital gains tax in the company. Furthermore, each of the three
> shareholders would be treated as disposing of their shares for a consideration
> equal to the value of the businesses which they receive. Once again capital gains
> tax could arise. If there was any inequality in the value of the businesses taken
> by each of the three, there would also be gift tax issues and possibly issues under
> s543 (exercising control so as to pass value out of shares).

There are of course other less straightforward methods by which the
transaction might be carried through which might provide some
prospect of reducing the potential tax liabilities on the transaction.
Fortunately however it may not be necessary to resort to artificial tax
planning.

- **Revenue Commissioners published precedent :**

— The Revenue Commissioners, in their published precedents have
stated *"Where a family trading company (or group of companies) is
broken up into several individual trading companies, such an event will
not be regarded as a disposal for CGT purposes provided that the value of
each individual's holding in the company or group remains strictly
unaltered and also provided certain other conditions are met. Prior
approval and formal undertakings will be required. Requests for this
treatment should be addressed to the Technical Services (CGT) Area at
the Office of the Chief Inspector of Taxes."*

Since the precedent was published in the context of *"Partition of
family trading companies"* it must be assumed that the reference
to the value of each individual's holding being unaffected does not
imply the continued existence of the company or group whose
partition was sought, but rather that no "value shifting" should
have occurred as between the shareholders in the process of
partitioning or de-merging the group/company. The precedent
does not spell out what further conditions or undertakings apply.

De-mergers can be achieved otherwise than by way of a liquidation.
A method frequently adopted in the UK is for a company to declare
a dividend to be satisfied by the distribution in specie to the
shareholders of shares in subsidiaries of that company. The UK has
specific legislation relating to such an approach to de-mergers, of

which Ireland does not have the equivalent. A similar approach in Ireland would lead to a charge to income tax under Schedule F, unless the Revenue Commissioners made a concession available.

45   REORGANISATIONS, ETC - ANTI-AVOIDANCE

45.1   Reorganisation of Share Capital

FA82 s63   FA82 s63 was concerned with closing a loophole in the original legislation, which enabled the relieving provisions relating to reorganisations to be used for tax-avoidance purposes. To appreciate the effect of the anti-avoidance legislation, it is necessary to understand the effect of a share for share exchange on the value of the shares disposed of in the hands of the acquiring company.

"63-(1) Neither paragraph 4 nor paragraph 5 of Schedule 2 to the CGTA 1975, (now s586 and s587)shall apply to the issue, on or after 24 June 1982, by a company of shares in the company

(a)   by way of such an exchange as is referred to in the said paragraph 4, or

(b)   under such a scheme or reconstruction or amalgamation as is referred to in the said paragraph 5,

unless it is shown that the exchange, reconstruction or amalgamation is effected for bona fide commercial reasons and does not form part of any arrangement or scheme of which the main purpose, or one of the main purposes, is avoidance of liability to tax.

(2) In subsection (1) 'shares' has the same meaning as in s.62".

These provisions now appear as s586(3) and s587(4).

Example 234

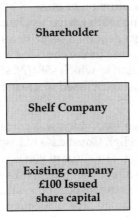

An individual owns all the shares in an existing company. The shares cost £100 in 1975. Since then, the company has prospered and in 1982 is worth £1m. The shareholder receives a cash offer for the shares, and wishes to sell. A CGT liability of (approx.) £400,000 will arise on the sale in the absence of avoidance measures.

To reduce the CGT liability, he transfers his shares in the existing company, to a new 'shelf' company in exchange for shares in that company. Under the relieving provisions of Schedule 2, no gain was chargeable on the swap of his shares for the shares in the new company.

The new 'shelf' company now owns the shares in the existing company. It acquired the shares in 1982 in return for the issue of its own shares. The new company is regarded as acquiring the shares at market value in 1982 (i.e. £1m).

This allowed the tax free disposal of the shares to the purchaser. It did not provide a tax free access to the cash in the "shelf company". That was the subject of separate planning.

Examples of this type of scheme can be seen in the cases of Floor v Davis, and Furniss v Dawson.

s625

This method of avoidance worked in the case where the shares were owned by an individual. Anti-avoidance provisions already exist to prevent this type of arrangement in the case of a company - TCA97 s625 - see paragraph 46.

S586(3) provides, in effect, that the relieving provisions which enable the shareholder to transfer his shares in exchange for others without incurring a CGT liability will not apply unless it is shown that the exchange is effected for bona fide commercial reasons, and does not form part of any arrangement or scheme of which the main purpose, or one of the main purposes, is avoidance of liability to taxation. The amendment takes effect in relation to the issue of shares by a company on or after 24 June 1982. The new provision covers all share exchanges (within s586) and all schemes of reconstruction or amalgamation (within s587).

Similar legislation is included in s.57 of the UK CGTA 1979. That legislation includes provision for prior clearance with the Board of Inland Revenue on the question of whether the transactions are being effected for bona fide commercial reasons. No such provision for clearance was included in s.63 FA 1982 [see s586(3) and s587(4)].

45.2   Debenture not a debt on a security

s541(7)

The Finance Act 1996 introduced provisions [now s541(7)] effective as regards disposals of a debenture on or after 28 March 1996, which provide that any debenture, no matter what its characteristics may be, is to be regarded as being a debt on a security for the purposes of capital gains tax if it was acquired in the course of a reconstruction, reorganisation, or amalgamation to which s584(2), s586(2), s587(2), s631, s632, or s637 apply. This is discussed in greater detail in paragraph 38.

The apparent gap in the legislation, which was corrected by s541(7) was the subject matter of the High Court case of Inspector of Taxes v Thomas Keleghan (High Court, 11 February 2000). In short, Mr Keleghan had received a debenture (not a debt on a security, and not one to which s541(7) applied as the disposal predated 28 March 1996) in a paper for paper exchange. He subsequently disposed of the debt. The High Court held that he was not liable to capital gains tax on the disposal.

46   DISPOSAL AFTER RECONSTRUCTION, ETC.

46.1   **Broad Outline**

s625   These provisions are designed to prevent avoidance of tax through the use of the reliefs provided in relation to the disposal of shares in a reconstruction or amalgamation. The anti-avoidance provisions apply where:

- a company ("the Subsidiary") ceases to be a member of a group of companies and,

- on an earlier occasion, shares in the subsidiary were disposed of by another company ("the chargeable company") which was then a member of the Group.

- in the course of an amalgamation or reconstruction in the Group.

Note: For these purposes, the term "disposal" has a special meaning as generally there is no disposal for CGT purposes where shares are transferred in the course of a reconstruction or amalgamation (see paragraph 46.8 below).

As noted above, the provisions of s625 apply "where a company ceases to be a member of a group of companies...." Those words are open to the construction that the section applies where a company ceases entirely to be in a group relationship with any other company. Alternatively it could refer to a situation where a company ceases to have a group relationship with a group headed by a specific principal company, notwithstanding that it may either remain in a group relationship with other companies, or enter into a new group relationship with other companies. However, the entire context of s625 and in particular the phrase "another company....which was then a member of that group" suggests that what is involved is a reference to a company ceasing to be in a group relationship with a specific principal company of a group, i.e. leaving a specific group, rather than ceasing to have a group relationship generally.

A company may leave a group for many reasons other than being sold by a group member to an outsider. The definition of what constitutes a group for CGT purposes, or for the purposes of corporation tax on company's capital gains, is described in paragraph 75.4. A wide variety of circumstances, including changes in shareholdings within the group, or the introduction of certain loan capital, can result in a group ceasing to exist. Such an event could trigger the application of this section.

46.2   **Application of Provisions**

Where the provisions apply, the chargeable company will be treated for all purposes of the CGT Acts as if it had sold and immediately reacquired the shares in the subsidiary immediately before the "earlier occasion". The earlier occasion is of course the time when the shares in the subsidiary were disposed of in the reconstruction or amalgamation.

The deemed date of disposal is not the date upon which the company leaves the group, but rather is immediately prior to the amalgamation or reconstruction in question. Thus the deemed disposal date could be several years prior to date on which the company leaves the group. However as noted in paragraph 46.3 , there is a ten year time limit for the application of the section. Where that the deemed disposal is in a prior year, the tax rules and tax rates which would apply to the deemed disposal may be different to those which apply in the year in which it leaves the group.

s547

The anti-avoidance legislation introduced in the FA82 in respect of reconstructions and amalgamations considerably reduces the importance of these provisions (see paragraph 41).

Example 235

Position 1

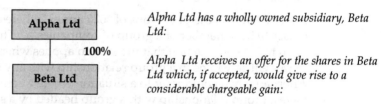

Alpha Ltd has a wholly owned subsidiary, Beta Ltd:

Alpha Ltd receives an offer for the shares in Beta Ltd which, if accepted, would give rise to a considerable chargeable gain:

Alpha Ltd disposed of the shares in Beta Ltd as follows :

Position 2

Alpha Ltd arranges for the formation of a third company, Gamma Ltd; the initial nominal share capital held by third party (see position 2 above).

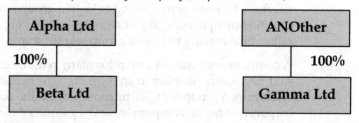

Position 3

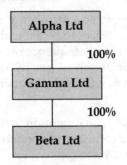

Gamma Ltd issues shares to Alpha Ltd in exchange for all the shares in Beta Ltd - the resulting structure is set out in position 3:

Gamma Ltd disposes of the shares Beta Ltd to the outside party for the agreed consideration - the resulting structure is set out in the chart of position 4

Position 4

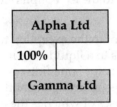 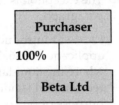

Leaving aside the argument regarding the form and substance of the transaction, (and the question as to whether Beta Ltd ever really becomes the beneficial owner of the shares in Gamma Ltd), the general tax effects would be as follows:

- *Under the reconstruction and amalgamation provision (see paragraph 42) Alpha Ltd is deemed to have made no disposal of the shares in Beta Ltd; and the shares in Gamma Ltd take the place of the Beta shares.*

- *Gamma Ltd acquires the shares in Beta Ltd at market value.*

- *Gamma Ltd disposes of the shares in Beta Ltd to the outside party without giving rise to a significant chargeable gain, assuming market value approximates the sale price.*

Under the anti-avoidance provisions outlined above, the actual tax effect is as follows:

- *Beta Ltd has left the Group which existed under position 3. Alpha Ltd is therefore deemed to have sold and immediately reacquired the shares in Beta Ltd at market value prior to the transfer of the shares to Gamma Ltd.*

- *The gain arising on the deemed disposal is taxable on Alpha Ltd.*

46.3　　　Time Limits

The legislation applies only if the "disposal" in the course of the reconstruction or amalgamation took place;

- on or after 27 November 1975 and

- within the period of ten years ending with the date on which the subsidiary ceases to be a member of the Group.

46.4   Liquidation

References to a company ceasing to be a member of a group do not apply to cases where a company ceases to be a member of a group by being wound-up or dissolved or in consequence of another member of the group being wound-up or dissolved (see the discussion of the application of this rule in Burman v Hedges & Butler in paragraph 81.4)

As noted in paragraph 81.3 there is an exception to the clawback of group relief on the occasion of a company ceasing to be a member of a group, while owning an asset transferred to it under group relief. That exception is where it leaves the group by reason of being dissolved, or by reason of another group member being dissolved. The exception is therefore similar to the exception referred to in this paragraph.

s623   FA96 s51 introduced a requirement to the exception to the application of s623, that references to a liquidation in s623 apply only where the liquidation in question is for bona fide commercial reasons and is not part of a scheme or arrangement the main purpose or one of the main purposes of which is the avoidance of tax. No similar anti-avoidance provision has been introduced in relation to the exception discussed in this paragraph.

46.5   Charge on Principal Company

s625   If before the subsidiary ceases to be a member of the group;

• the chargeable company ceases to exist or,

• a resolution has been passed or an order made for the winding-up of the company, or

• any other act has been done for the like purpose,

any CT which would have been payable by the chargeable company will be assessed and charged on the principal company in the group.

It should be noted that the charge to tax on the company which disposed of the shares in the course of an amalgamation or reconstruction may arise to it at a time when it is no longer a member of the group of which it was a member of when the transfer in question took place. The company could now be owned by shareholders who have no connection with the original group. This is a potential exposure to tax which anybody buying a company out of a group should be alert to. The fact that it has left the group does not mean that the charge will arise instead to the principal company of the group, as it would have done if the company which made the original transfer had, instead of leaving the group by way of sale, had left the group a reason of a liquidation.

If the original transferor company still exists, it is it and not the principal company which will bear the charge to tax.

s623

This clawback of relief is to be contrasted with the clawback of "group relief" under s623 (see paragraph 75). S623 imposes a clawback of group relief where a company leaves a group while owing an asset transferred to it intra group. However where the company which transferred the asset to it leaves the group simultaneously, and where the transferor and transferee company, though leaving the group together, themselves form a group, the clawback does not occur. Thus if a whole subgroup leaves a larger group, the clawback will not apply to assets which have been transferred between members of the subgroup but will apply to assets obtained by the subgroup from other members of the larger group whom they are leaving behind. In contrast, the clawback under s625 applies even where the reorganisation or reconstruction took place entirely within a subgroup, and all of the companies involved in that reconstruction or reorganisation leave the main group simultaneously, and while forming a group in their own right.

Example 236

Holding Company has two wholly owned subsidiaries, Company A and Company B. Company A itself has a wholly owned subsidiary, Company C. Company B has a wholly owned subsidiary, Company D. Company A transfers a property to Company C. Company B transfers all of the shares in Company D to a newly formed company, Company E, in return for all of the shares in Company E. Holding Company sells the shares in Company A and Company B to an unconnected person.

The transfer between Company A and Company C is an intra group transfer, under s617, and is carried out on a no gain no loss basis. When Company A leaves the Holding Company group, s623 does not operate the clawback of the group relief, because Company A and Company C leave the group simultaneously, and while forming a subgroup of their own.

The transfer of shares in Company D by Company B is not treated as a disposal by Company B on the occasion of the share swap, by reason of s584. However, when Company B, together with Company D and Company E leave the Holding Company group, s625 claws back the reconstruction and amalgamation relief by treating Company B as having disposed of the shares in Company D on the occasion of the previous share swap. It does this notwithstanding that all of the companies concerned leave the Holding Company group simultaneously, and while forming a subgroup of their own. The contrast in treatment between the lack of clawback of group relief, and the clawback of reconstruction and amalgamation relief, in economically similar circumstances, seems harsh.

46.6   **Tax Unpaid**

If any CT assessed on a company under these provisions is not paid within six months of the due date, it may be collected from :

- the company which was the principal company on the due date or the company which was the principal company on the "earlier occasion"

or

- any company taking an investment in the subsidiary as part of the reconstruction or amalgamation in the Group.

The tax may be assessed on any of these companies within two years of the due date (subject to paragraph 91.5).

A company which has to pay under this provision is entitled to recover it from the company which was liable in the first instance.

46.7   Overall Time Limit for Assessment

Notwithstanding any other limitation, an assessment to CT under these provisions may be made at any time within ten years from the time the subsidiary ceased to be a member of the group.

46.8   Disposal in the Course of Reconstruction or Amalgamation

For the purpose of these provisions, there is a disposal in the course of a reconstruction or amalgamation in a group of companies if:

- the relief applying to company amalgamations by exchange of shares applies to the disposal

and

- the companies are members of the same group

or

become members of the same group as a result of the reconstruction or amalgamation.

47   CONVERSION OF SECURITIES

47.1   Outline - conversion of securities

s585   The relieving provisions which apply in relation to reconstructions and amalgamations also apply in relation to the 'conversion of securities'.

Conversion of securities includes:

- a conversion of securities of a company into shares in the company.

- a conversion as an alternative to the redemption of the securities for cash.

• an exchange of securities required under any law

"Security includes any loan stock or similar security whether of any government or of any public authority of any company, and whether secured or unsecured but excluding securities falling within s.19 (Government and Semi-State securities)".

The term 'security' is also considered in paragraph 38 in the context of the phrase 'debt on a security'.

Example 237

On 1 January 1992 Philip acquires debentures in DEVELOPMENT LTD for £5,000. These were convertible in three years to ordinary shares at the option of the shareholder. On 1 January 1999, Philip exercised his option and received 5,000 £1 ordinary shares in return for his debentures.

In these circumstances under the general CGT rules Philip would be deemed to have disposed of his debentures on 1 January 1992 for a consideration equal to the value of the 5,000 ordinary shares. Under the relieving provisions, there is deemed to be no disposal; on a subsequent disposal of the ordinary shares, his base cost will be £5,000 and his acquisition date is 1 January 1992.

48   SHARES-IDENTIFICATION

48.1   Outline

When a share is sold, it is necessary to identify the share so that the cost can be ascertained, and the acquisition date determined for the purpose of indexation.

48.2   General Rule

s580

To remove any doubt, s580 sets out specific rules for identifying shares of the same class in the same company when some of them are disposed of. These rules apply irrespective of which shares have actually been sold or otherwise disposed of.

The principal rule is-first in-first out (F.I.F.O)

Shares are treated as being of the same "class" only if they would be treated as such if they were dealt with on a stock exchange.

• **Revenue/Chief Inspector's CGT Manual :**

− The Revenue Commissioners capital gains tax manual, at paragraph 19.4.1 notes that *bearer shares* are never of the same class as registered shares, even if their rights are otherwise identical. It also points out that shares held in the form of letters of allotment, which are not yet registered, cannot be of the same class as registered shares. However what appears to be concessional treatment is noted in Paragraph 19.4.7.8 where partly paid up shares (the balance of whose purchase money is payable within 6 months of issue) obtained in a reorganisation may be treated as being of the same class as shares in respect of which they were obtained (where they would be treated as being of the same class but for their being only partly paid up). The same concessional treatment applies to bonus or rights issue shares held in letter of allotment form, ie they may be treated as of the same class as the shares in respect of which they were obtained, provided that, were they registered, they would be so regarded anyway. It is further stated that the concessional treatment outlined above can be applied not only to bonus issue and rights issue shares, but also to purchases in the open market of additional "rights" of such shares of or additional partly paid shares. The treatment of bonus issue and rights issue shares from the viewpoint of identification of shares, is further discussed in paragraph 48.6.

Example 238

Joe had the following transactions in shares of Greenfields Ltd :

	Shares
First Purchase 1/1/1982	200
Second Purchase 31/3/1993	300
	500
First Sale 31/12/1994	(400)
balance	100
Third Purchase 30/6/1996	250
balance	350
Second Sale 31/12/1998	(150)
	200

FIRST SALE-400 SHARES IN 1994:

On this sale there is a disposal of the entire first purchase of 200 shares and there is a part disposal of the second purchase of 300 shares.

SECOND SALE-150 SHARES IN 1998:

On this sale there is a disposal of the remaining part of the second purchase of 300 shares and a part disposal of the third purchase of 250 shares.

This general rule is subject to an important exception relating to shares disposed of within 4 weeks of the acquisition of other shares of the same class. This exception is further described in 65.3 below. A further exception relating to shares qualifying for the income tax BES relief is dealt with in paragraph 9.14.2.

These share identification rules apply to identify the shares disposed of, regardless of which share the taxpayer actually transfers.

Example 239

In the previous example, the shares acquired by Joe had the following share register numbers:

Acquired on 1 January 1982	10,300 - 10,499
Acquired on 31 March 1993	20,201 - 20,500

On the occasion of the first sale on 31 December 1994 Joe handed over to the purchaser share certificates numbered 20,201 - 20,500 inclusive, and 10,400 - 10,499 inclusive.

*Notwithstanding this selection by Joe of the shares he was parting with, for CGT purposes Joe is treated as disposing of the shares indicated in **Example 229**. Joe cannot determine which shares he is to be treated as disposing of by selecting the individual shares. The identification of the shares is decided by the arbitrary rules of the legislation.*

- **Revenue/Chief Inspector's CGT Manual :**

— The Revenue Commissioners, in their capital gains tax manual at paragraph 19.3.3.2 state that in applying share identification rules where a person holds some shares in his own name, and other shares through a bare nominee, all of the shares are to be taken into account, as if they were all in the name of the beneficial owner.

48.3   Disposal within 4 Weeks of Acquisition

48.3.1   General Outline – "Bed and Breakfast"

s581   The situation that this provision is trying to deal with is best explained by an example.

Example 240

Willie bought 100,000 ordinary shares in WILLIAM LTD, when the shares were quoted at £2 each. The value has now dropped to 50p each. He hopes that the value will rise again and he will recover his investment. He wants to hold on to the shares, but he can't get relief in the meantime for the decrease in value. The loss has not been realised nor has the value become negligible. He decides, therefore, under an arrangement with his stockbroker to sell the shares, and buy them back again a few days later at the same price. He has now, in effect, realised the loss, although he still holds the shares.

In the absence of anti-avoidance provisions relief would be available for this "artificially" created loss. The legislation provides that the loss on a sale of shares, where an equivalent number of the same shares has been "reacquired" within 4 weeks of the disposal (before or after) can only be set against a subsequent gain arising on the disposal of the shares "reacquired".

s581   S581 contains provisions which

- ensure that the artificially created loss described above cannot be availed of (see paragraph 48.3.3) and also

- include a rule which has general application whether or not losses are involved, and whether or not tax planning is involved.

That rule applies on a disposal of shares of a particular class, which shares will be deemed to be the same shares as any shares of the same class acquired by the taxpayer in the 4 week period prior to the disposal.

48.3.2   Share identification rule

For the above rule to apply, the disposal and acquisition must be made by the taxpayer in the same capacity - in other words, a disposal of shares held by him beneficially would not be identified with shares which he acquired as the trustee of a trust in the preceding 4 week period.

s581(1), (2)   This rule identifies shares disposed of with shares acquired in the 4 weeks preceding the disposal. It does not identify such shares with shares acquired in a period following the disposal. Therefore this rule has no application to the facts set out in *example 236* above. The facts set out in *example 236* are affected by other elements of s581.

The rule that shares disposed of are to be primarily identified with shares of the same class acquired in the preceding 4 week period is applied to a married couple (i.e. a man and his wife living with him) as a unit. In other words, a disposal by either the husband or the wife can be identified with shares acquired in the preceding 4 week period by the other spouse.

S581 states that this extension of the rule is to apply *"with any necessary modifications"*. Since a husband and a wife are separate taxpayers for the purposes of capital gains tax, it is not clear that any modification, no matter how drastic, could render this aspect of s581 effective. It amounts to a requirement that a person be treated as disposing of an asset not owned by him, and never acquired by him, but which is in fact owned and acquired by another person. The only conceivable *"modification"* which could render such a rule effective would be to deem the acquisition by one spouse to be an acquisition by the other spouse, and the ownership of the shares acquired to be ownership by the other spouse. Such a *"modification"* would surely require express *"deeming"* provisions in the Taxes Acts, and there are no such provisions. Furthermore, the reference to *"modifications"* is a reference to modifications to the application of s581, and not to modifications to the actual facts to which they are being applied. It is not clear how s581(4), dealing with a man and his wife living together, can have application.

S581 does not make explicit reference to how it would apply to a situation where an individual disposes of shares which he owns absolutely, but has in the previous 4 week period acquired a joint interest in shares of the same class. An example would be where one spouse disposes of shares of a particular class, having in the previous 4 week period acquired shares of that class jointly with the other spouse. Even s581(4), assuming it is at all capable of application, would not seem to deal with such a situation.

There is some ambiguity in s581 in relation to the use of the phrase "four weeks". The capital gains tax acts do not provide any definition of this phrase. The Interpretation Act states that a week is a period from midnight on a Saturday to midnight on the following Saturday. It also states that a period of time expressed to end on a particular date is deemed to include that date. Is a reference to the previous four weeks a reference to the 28 days ending on and including the date specified (the date of disposal); or is it a reference to a period of 28 days ending at midnight on the Saturday prior to the date of disposal? Common sense suggests that it is the 28 day period ending with the date of disposal. However the failure to use a relatively unambiguous term such as 28 days, and the use instead of a phrase whose defined meaning is somewhat ambiguous such as four weeks must leave some residual ambiguity. The equivalent phrase in UK legislation is "30 days".

48.3.3   Losses restriction rule

Where shares are reacquired by the same person (in the same capacity) within four weeks of such a disposal, the shares reacquired are identified with the shares sold.

s581(3)   Where a loss accrues to a person on the disposal of shares, and he reacquires a share of the same class and in the same company within 4 weeks of the disposal, the loss will only be allowed as a deduction from any gain arising on the disposal of the shares which were reacquired. The loss cannot be set against other gains.

Where only part of the shares are reacquired or otherwise replaced by shares of the same class in the same company, the loss is only restricted to the extent that such shares are reacquired.

48.3.4   Married couples

s581(4)   In the case of married persons, one spouse cannot avoid the provisions by selling, and having the other spouse reacquire the shares. However, reference should be made to the comments above on s581(4) in paragraph 48.3.2.

Example 241

> *Bill bought 1,000 shares in a quoted company in January 1974 for £5,000. MV at 5/4/74 was £6,000. In June 1998 the shares were worth only £2,000. He sold the shares in June 1998 for £2,000 and purchased a further 1,000 shares in the same company the following day for £2,100.*

	£
Sale proceeds	2,000
Cost MV 1974 £6,000 @ 6.215 =	37,290
Loss using indexation	(35,290)
Reduce to actual loss (under normal rules)	3,000

This £3,000 loss can only be used against a gain arising on the subsequent disposal of the 1,000 shares acquired in 1998 for £2,100.

If he had only acquired 500 shares in June 1998, he would be allowed half of the loss (i.e. £3,000) and the balance could only be used against a gain arising on the subsequent disposal of the 500 shares acquired.

s581(4)   Provisions are included to prevent a taxpayer from getting around the anti-avoidance provisions, by buying the new shares prior to the sale of the existing shares, or by arranging for the shares to be reacquired by his spouse living with him (see paragraph 33.2 and paragraph 48.3.2).

48.4   **Shares Acquired - 6/4/'74 to 5/4/'78**

The rule under the 1975 Act regarding shares of the same class in the same company which were acquired on or after 6 April 1974, was that all such shares in that company were regarded as one single asset i.e. a 'pool' which increased or diminished with acquisitions and disposals out of that 'pool'.

When more shares of the same class were purchased, the number of shares in the pool increased as did the total cost of the pool. When shares were sold out of that pool the number of shares in the pool reduced, and the total cost of the remaining shares was reduced by the allocation to the shares being sold of a proportionate part of the total pool cost (i.e. proportionate to the number of shares being sold).

Where no disposals have been made out of the pool prior to 6 April 1978, no problem arises in applying the first in - first out rule which applies to disposals of such shares on or after 6 April 1978.

Where, however, disposals were made prior to 6 April 1978, under the pooling rule, difficulties arise in applying the first in - first out basis to subsequent disposals out of balance of that pool, because it is not possible to identify the balance of the pool held at 6 April 1978 as representing any individual share or group of shares.

The 1978 Act sets out rules for dividing the balance of the pool held at 6 April 1978 into identifiable units, for determining the acquisition date and cost of each constituent unit.

Once this has been done, the first in - first out rule can be applied on a subsequent disposal of the shares.

The 1978 Act rules are as follows:

- It is necessary to work forward from 6 April 1974. Each separate block of such shares purchased since then is treated as a separate unit, carrying a period of ownership from its date of purchase and carrying its own separate cost.

- Any disposal prior to 6/4/78 out of the total pool (under the 1975 Act rules) is treated under the 1978 Act rules as if that disposal proportionately reduced the number of shares in each separate block of such shares held at the date of the disposal, with a corresponding reduction in the cost of the remaining part of that block of shares. The position is best illustrated by an example.

Example 242

John purchased 200 ordinary shares in CRAZY RULES LTD on 1 May 1974 for £300. In December of 1974 he bought another 400 ordinary shares in that company for £700. In June 1975, he bought another 100 ordinary shares in the company for £250.

In July 1977, he sold 300 of the shares for £900. The balance of 400 shares were held by him at 6 April 1978.

For the purpose of identifying the acquisition date and cost of the balance of pool of 400 shares held at 6 April 1978, the rules set out above are applied as follows:

Cost	No.	Date
£300	200	May 1974
£700	400	Dec 1974
£250	100	June 1975
£1,250	700	

On the sale of the 300 shares in July 1977 under the pre 1978 pooling rule, the cost allowable in arriving at the gain (or loss) on the disposal would be:

300/700 x £1,250 = £536

Under the 1978 Rule, 3/7 of the May 1974 shares are deemed to have been sold, and the cost of the remaining shares (i.e. 114 shares) is reduced by 3/7 of the cost of those shares (i.e. reduced to £171). Similarly, the number of the shares purchased in December 1974 and June 1975 and the cost of those shares will be reduced by 3/7. The balance of the pool (i.e. 400 shares) held at 6 April 1978, and the balance of the pool cost (i.e. £1,250 less £536 = £714) is identified as follows:

	Balance of Shares	Attributable Cost
Purchased May 1974	114	£171
Purchased Dec 1974	229	£400
Purchased June 1975	57	£143
Balance total	400	£714

On a subsequent disposal of shares of this class the normal first in -first out rule will apply.

Example 243

William owned 450 shares in WILLIE LTD at 6 April 1978. He sold the shares
On 1 March 1998. The following information sets out details of the make up of
the pool of 450 shares which were sold.

Date	Shares purchased	Purchase price	Shares sold	Sale price
1/1/75	200	£400	-	-
1/7/75	100	£300	-	-
1/1/76	-	-	150	£450
1/7/76	350	£1,200	-	-
1/1/77	-	-	50	£250
1/3/98	-	-	450	£8,000
TOTAL	650	£1,900	650	£8,700

In calculating CGT payable on the gain arising on that disposal the constituent
parts of the block of 450 shares held at 6 April 1978 must be identified in
accordance with the 1978 Act rules in order to arrive at the allowable cost.

CALCULATIONS

(a) SALE ON 1/1/1976 -

Number of shares held 300 :

Number of shares sold 150 :

Date acquired	Shares No.	Shares Cost	Fraction sold	shares sold	shares remaining	Unsold cost
1/1/75	200	£400	150/300	100	100	£200
1/7/75	100	£300	150/300	50	50	£150

(b) SALE ON 1/1/1977

Number of shares held 500 : Number of shares sold 50 :

Date acquired	Shares No.	Shares Cost	Fraction sold	shares sold	shares remaining	Unsold cost (90%)
1/1/75	100	£200	50/500	10	90	£180
1/7/75	50	£150	50/500	5	45	£135
1/7/76	350	£1,200	50/500	35	315	£1,080

The sale proceeds of the 450 shares (i.e. £4,000) is split between the three
remaining (balance) "units" set out above, and the gain (or loss) on the disposal
in 1998 is calculated on a normal basis on the disposal of each separate unit.

JAN 1975 shares:

Sale proceeds (proportionate)	$\frac{90}{450}$ x £8,000	£1,600
Cost......£180 indexed x 6.112	=	£1,100
Loss		£500

JULY 1975 SHARES:

Sale proceeds (proportionate)	$\frac{45}{450}$ x £8,000	£800
Cost...£135 indexed x 4.936	=	£ 666
Loss		£134

JULY 1976 SHARES:

Sale proceeds (proportionate)	$\frac{315}{450}$ x £4,000	£5,600
Cost...£1,080 indexed x 4.253	=	£4,593
Loss		£1,007

48.5   **Shares Held at 6 April 1974**

Such shares, even under the 1975 Act rules were always dealt with on a first in-first out basis and all the 1978 Act does is to continue to apply that rule.

48.6   **Shares obtained in a reorganisation (or amalgamation)**

s584   Where the provisions of TCA97 s584, relating to reorganisation and reduction of share capital, and the amalgamation of companies, (see paragraphs 42 to 45 inclusive) apply the rules for identification of shares take account of the provisions of s584 and may deem shares to have been acquired on dates other than those on which they were, in fact, acquired.

The general rule applied by s584 is that new shares acquired in a transaction to which s584 has application (reorganisations, reductions, amalgamations etc.) do not represent the acquisition of a new asset, but are to be treated as being the same asset as the original shares held prior to the reorganisation etc. and acquired at the same time as those original shares.

Example 244

> *The facts are the same as in **Example 238** above, except that on 31 July 1996 the company made a bonus issue of shares, issuing one new share for each two shares then held by the shareholders.*

*Joe, whose shareholdings are described in **Example 238** had 350 shares immediately prior to the bonus issue, and received a bonus issue of 175 shares. He then proceeded to dispose of 150 shares (as before) on 31 December 1994.*

*In reality Joe acquired 175 new shares on 31 July 1996. However the application of s584 to the transaction meant that for the purposes of capital gains tax, Joe is treated as having acquired no shares at all on 31 July 1996. Instead, the 175 bonus shares are treated as having acquisition dates corresponding to the acquisition dates of the 350 "original" shares. As explained in **Example 238** - 100 of the original shares was deemed to be acquired on 31 March 1993, and 250 of them were treated as acquired on 30 June 1996. After the bonus issue of shares, Joe is treated as having acquired 150 shares on 31 March 1993 (1 extra share for every two shares acquired on that occasion) and to have acquired 375 shares on 30 June 1996 (again, an additional one share for every two shares actually acquired on that occasion).*

Example 245

On 31 December 1995 Joe purchases 1,000 £1 ordinary shares in Make Market PLC. On 31 January 1996 he purchases 500 £1 preference shares in the company. On 30 June 1996 the company makes a rights offer of preference shares to its members, permitting each holder of an ordinary share to subscribe for one preference share. Joe takes up this offer. Accordingly he acquires 1,000 preference shares.

On 31 October 1996 Joe sold 750 preference shares.

At first glance it might seem that the FIFO rules would apply as between the two dates upon which Joe (factually) acquired preference shares, in January and in July 1996. It must be borne in mind however that a rights issue is generally a reorganisation of share capital and accordingly, where s584 applies to it, as it generally will, it is not the occasion of the acquisition of shares, for the purposes of the capital gains tax legislation. In reality Joe sells 750 preference shares. For capital gains tax purposes however he has ever only acquired 500 such shares, and that in January 1996. How then are the share identification rules to be applied? Joe has factually disposed of shares that the capital gains tax legislation deems him then never to have acquired.

The actual CGT treatment on a disposal of any of the rights issue preference shares is not in doubt - it is a part disposal of the ordinary shares in respect of which the right to subscribe was obtained. But how do we identify an actual sale of preference shares with those preference shares which Joe is deemed never to have acquired but which factually he does hold and which factually he may dispose of? The CGT legislation does not provide a clear answer to this question but in the opinion of the authors the share identification rules must be applied at least initially having regard to what in fact is occurring i.e. that preference shares are being disposed of. Of the 1,500 preference shares held prior to the disposal, 500 were acquired in January 1996, and 1,000 are treated as if they were the same asset as shares acquired in December 1995 notwithstanding that they were actually acquired in August 1996. In the opinion of the authors, the shares disposed of should therefore be treated as coming firstly from the shares which have a deemed acquisition date in December 1995, and only then from the shares whose actual acquisition date is January 1996.

Once the shares which were disposed of are identified in that fashion, the computation will then proceed in accordance with s584, and will treat the transaction, insofar as it relates to the preference shares with a deemed acquisition date in December 1995 as being a part disposal of the ordinary shares acquired on that occasion, and in respect of which enhancement expenditure was incurred on the occasion of the rights issue in August 1996.

The interpretation above appears to be confirmed by the judgment in the case of Inspector of Taxes v Thomas Keleghan. That case concerned the taxation of a disposal of loan notes obtained in a share for loan note exchange. In the judgment it is stated *"There could be no question that the provisions of a schedule of a Capital Gains Tax Act could change the nature of the loan notes in this case so that they in fact remain shares in the company, with the same rights attached to them as were attached to the original shares. Were it otherwise, the holder of the notes would be entitled to notice of and to attend general meetings of the company and to participate in dividends of the company. This is of course absurd. Therefore there must be some limit to the fiction. The next step is to consider whether the fiction applies to all of the provisions of the Capital Gains Tax legislation. This again cannot be so as the fiction could not be intended to apply, for example, to the calculation of shareholdings for the purposes of s598 (retirement relief). One is therefore driven to the inevitable conclusion that the fiction only apply to the limited objects of the schedule, namely to the calculation of the amount of tax payable. This is confirmed by the wording of s545(2) which provides that the amount of the gains accruing on the disposal of assets shall be computed subject to the provisions of, inter alia, Schedule 2 CGTA 1975 (now sections 583, 584, 585, 586, 587, 588, 600, and 733 TCA 97). This is the whole purpose of the schedule and there is no logical reason why the provisions of that schedule should apply to matters other than the computation of the gain. Accordingly, when considering whether there has been a chargeable gain on the disposal of the loan notes, they must be treated as loan notes and not as the original shares in the company other than for the purpose of computing the actual amount of tax payable."*

It is true that that passage does not address the question of share identification, but it does lend support to the views expressed above.

In paragraph 48.2 reference is made to Revenue Commissioners concessional treatment of bonus issue and rights issue shares, as regards the matter of when they constitute the same class of shares as other shares.

48.7   **BES shares**

Special rules apply to identify shares disposed of where all or part of a holding was acquired under the "Business Expansion Scheme" These rules are dealt with in paragraph 9.14.

49   ACQUISITION BY A COMPANY OF ITS OWN SHARES

49.1   **Background**

Prior to 1 July 1991, there were two main constraints on a company redeeming, reducing, or purchasing its own shares:

— company law,

   and

— tax law.

In the past, company law allowed a company to issue and redeem certain preference shares. It also allowed a company to reduce its share capital, and to liquidate - which, in effect got rid of all shares.

The redemption of issued redeemable preference shares caused no particular difficulty. However, the reduction of the share capital by a limited company required Court approval and consideration of creditors rights, etc. Liquidation could be expensive, and had implications far beyond getting rid of the share capital - for example, it meant the disposal of the assets by the company, and that in itself could lead to chargeable gains.

Many companies used in tax planning were unlimited companies, as company law (and also the law dealing with capital duty) was much more flexible in the case of an unlimited company.

s130   Tax law made no distinction in a CGT context between a limited or unlimited company. The broad affect of the tax law, was to treat all or part (depending on circumstances) of the amount received by the shareholder in respect of his shares (other than in a liquidation) as an income dividend - i.e. a distribution. In broad tax terms, any profit over and above the amount subscribed for the shares (including any premium on redemption) was treated as a distribution under s130 and charged to income tax under Schedule F.

Extensive anti avoidance provisions were included in s130 and the immediately following sections to ensure that any method used to extract cash from an Irish resident company (other than liquidation) would meet with an assessment to income tax.

CA90 Pt XI   The Companies Act 1990 substantially liberalised the company law relating to companies, and in particular made it possible for a company to re-issue redeemable shares, and to purchase its own shares. It is also now possible for a subsidiary to hold shares in its own parent company. These are only some of the many changes made by the Companies Act 1990.

s173 to s176 Following from the changes in company law, the tax law was also changed to deal with the new situation - as there was little point in changing company law if the tax deterrent remained. Unfortunately, the changes in the tax legislation are very limited when compared to the changes in company law. The tax changes were introduced in the FA91. The legislation is contained in TCA97 s173 to s186, and takes affect as and from the operative date of the Companies Act 1990.

The Companies Act 1990 (Commencement) (No 2) Order 1 July 1991 gives a commencing date to those Companies Act provisions with effect from 1st July 1991.

New rules for quoted groups were introduced by FA97 (now in s175).

s176 In broad terms what the FA91 tax law (TCA97 s173 to s186) does, is to treat payments by a company in respect of the redemption, repayment or purchase of its own shares (or shares in its holding company) as being of a capital nature, rather than income (as heretofore). The provisions only extend to shares in an unquoted trading company (or a holding company of a trading group) and are subject to many conditions. There are many circumstances where such payments are outside the scope of the FA 1991 provisions, and remain to be treated as "income" transactions. In such circumstances, the payments are deemed to be distributions by the company, and taxed as income under schedule F.

s175 The FA97 provisions relating to quoted companies (s175) and their subsidiaries, in contrast, apply almost no conditions and would give capital gains treatment to redemptions and buybacks in almost every case.

49.2   Overview

FA97 s39(b) The statutory provisions which provide a special regime for the buyback of shares by a company are to be found in

s176 — s176, dealing with unquoted companies, and

s175 — s175, dealing with quoted companies and their 51% subsidiaries.

The two sets of provisions are mutually exclusive. They also are significantly different. s176 relating to unquoted companies and groups contains detailed preconditions and requirements for the transaction to be treated as not involving a distribution. In contrast, s175 relating to quoted companies is brief, and almost entirely without preconditions or requirements. It is important to bear in mind this distinction in reading the remainder of this part of the book dealing with the acquisition by a company of its own shares, as the commentary relates almost entirely to s176 dealing with unquoted companies, and has no relevance to the treatment of quoted companies and their 51% subsidiaries.

49.2.1   Quoted buybacks

S175 applies to payments made on or after the 26th day of May 1997, by a quoted company, or a 51% subsidiary of a quoted company. Where a payment is made on the redemption, repayment or purchase of its own shares by such a company, no part of that payment is treated as a distribution for the purposes of the Taxes Acts. That is so regardless of the purposes of the company in entering into the transaction, or the status of the shareholders whose shares are purchased, redeemed etc. and indeed regardless of any of the circumstances surrounding the payment, provided only that it is made by a quoted company, or a 51% subsidiary of a quoted company, "on redemption, repayment or purchase of its own shares".

s175

It is understood that prior to 27 May 1997 the Revenue Commissioners in practice did not treat the purchase by a quoted company of its shares on the stock exchange as involving a distribution, insofar as the vendor of the shares was concerned. In other words, a person who sold the shares on the stock exchange (who would not normally therefore know the identity of the purchaser) was treated as remaining within the capital gains tax code (if that was for him the relevant code) even if the purchaser turned out to be the quoted company itself. In consequence where this "concessional" treatment applied the vendor was not treated as receiving a distribution, nor was he allowed a tax credit. The purchasing company however prior to 27 May 1997 was treated as having made a distribution, with consequences for advance corporation tax etc.

Any such treatment of the vendor (insofar as it was applied) was concessional. The effect of the FA97 (now s175) is to treat both the vendor of shares, and the purchasing company, as if no distribution occurred. S175 also goes further than the previous concessional treatment in that it relates to purchases whether or not they occur on the stock exchange, and also the purchase (etc.) of its own shares by a 51% subsidiary of a quoted company.

The treatment provided for in s175 is obligatory, and not optional. Even where it might suit a shareholder to have a transaction treated as involving a distribution, rather than being entirely within the Capital Gains Tax code, that treatment is not available where a quoted company, or a 51% subsidiary of such, buys back its shares. This would have implications for bodies exempt from income tax such as pension funds etc.

The definition of "quoted" in given in paragraph 49.4.2 below.

Both s176 and s175 exclude the treatment of a buyback as involving a distribution, only insofar as Ch2 of Part 6, TCA97 would apply to treat the transaction as involving a distribution. They do not exclude the possibility of some other section of the Taxes Acts treating the transaction as involving a distribution. TCA97 s817 (discussed in paragraph 41.7) is concerned with arrangements to avoid liability to tax under Schedule F, and would not seem to be excluded by the provisions of s175 or s176 (see also comments on this issue in paragraph 49.3.1).

49.2.2   **Unquoted buybacks**

S176 applies to a payment made on or after 1 July 1991 by a company on the

- **redemption,**

- **repayment, or**

- **purchase**

of its own shares.

The company must be either :

- **an unquoted trading company, or**

- **an unquoted holding company of a trading group.**

In very broad terms, s176 relief is only allowed where the transaction is carried out for the purpose of either:

- *benefiting the trade,* or

- enabling the vendor to *pay inheritance tax* following an inheritance of those shares.

s176   Where the person is relying on the 'trade benefit' purpose, additional conditions must also be complied with regarding:

—the *residence of the vendor* of the shares,

—the substantial *reduction of the vendor's interest* in the company following the transaction,

—the *exclusion of connected persons,*

—miscellaneous anti-avoidance provisions to ensure the relief is not abused.

S176 does not apply to quoted shares, nor does it apply to shares in an investment company. For most persons s176 treatment will be a relief, but there are some circumstances in which it will not give any relief, and the taxpayer would have been better off if it were treated as an income transaction. However, in this paragraph for the sake of simplicity, the new treatment of such transactions is referred to as a relief.

For the remainder of this paragraph, the term 'vendor' is used to describe the person whose shares are being acquired by the company, whether by redemption, purchase, or otherwise. References to a person's entitlement to, or ownership of shares and profits, refers to a beneficial entitlement or ownership (except in the case of trustees and personal representatives).

This paragraph deals with the CGT consequences of a company acquiring its own shares, or shares in its parent company, and the related problems where one or more of the companies is a member of a group. This should not be taken to mean that all the transactions referred to are in fact permitted by company law. That law also contains many conditions, and limitations.

A number of the words and phrases used for the purpose of these provisions have a special meaning. The relevant definitions are set out below in paragraph 49.4.

49.3   **Unquoted shares**

49.3.1   **Broad Outline**

In broad terms, the provisions of s130 treat most payments made by a company in respect of shares to a shareholder as a distribution chargeable to income tax under Schedule F. s130 is a very wide-ranging section, and the reference to it in this text is merely a very broad view to establish the background to the CGT provisions.

s130

"(2) In relation to any company "distribution" means -

    (a)   *any dividend paid by the company, including a capital dividend;*

    (b)   *any other distribution out of the assets of the company (whether in cash or otherwise) in respect of shares in the company............."*

This part of s130 is normally regarded as treating a redemption by a company of its own share capital as a distribution for income tax purposes (although exemption from income tax is given to the extent the payment by the company is merely repaying the amount initially subscribed for the shares). However, it may not have been sufficient to deal with a payment made by a company in respect of shares in its parent company.

s135

The meaning of "in respect of shares in the company" is extended by s135.

"(a) In this chapter and s137 "in respect of shares in the company" .. .. in relation to a company which is a member of a 90% group

mean respectively in respect of shares in that company or any other company in the group...and ."

(b)   *.... in relation to a company which is a member of a 90% group , distribution includes anything distributed out of the assets of the company (whether in cash or otherwise) in respect of shares or securities of another company in the group."*

The extension of the meaning by s135 to include other group companies, is normally regarded as dealing with the situation of where a company acquires shares in its parent company.

Where the acquisition of the shares comes within the scope of the s176 provisions, any payment for the shares received by the vendor is treated as not being income for income tax purposes.

If the payment is not 'income', it will be treated as a 'capital distribution' for CGT purposes (s583 - see paragraph 40.3).

The combination of these two rules, has the affect of changing the nature of the payment from being income, to being capital. In most circumstances, this will benefit both the vendor and the company. The vendor is charged to CGT on the 'deemed' disposal profit (after deducting the indexed cost) instead of paying income tax (and also perhaps PRSI and levies in the case of an individual) on the 'profit' included in the receipt increased by the amount of the tax credit. It is even more beneficial where the shares have been acquired at market value (for CGT purposes) shortly before the disposal - e.g. on a death, or from a connected person, where no chargeable gain would arise.

The only exceptions are:

* If the shares are part of the stock of a share 'dealing' business, the transaction will be treated as income, as s176 only takes the transaction outside the distribution rules. In such a case, the receipt will remain 'income' and s176 will have no affect.

s.61(1)

* the payment is still regarded as a distribution for the purposes of the close company surcharge on investment and service companies (s176).

s176

It is not a 'relief' which has to be claimed - it is the automatic result of being within the scope of the FA91 provisions.

Example 246

Brown Holdings Ltd. issued 100,000 £1 ordinary shares in 1990, for £2 each. Of the £2 subscribed for each share, £1 represented a premium on issue. In 1995 Joe Brown inherited 1,000 of the £1 ordinary shares from his father. At the date of the inheritance they had a value of £5 each. In 1997, following two years of disagreements with the other shareholders, the company agreed to buy back from Joe the 1,000 shares which he held for an amount of £8 per share.

If the transaction is not regarded as being within the scope of the s176 as described below (and this is not a matter which is dependent on a claim being made, or which may be elected out of, or into) Joe would be treated as being in receipt of a distribution from the company in the amount of £6,000. This is calculated by deducting from the amount paid to him by the company for the shares (£8,000) the amount which was originally subscribed to the company in respect of the shares (a total of £2,000, being £2 per share). Since the company is an Irish resident company, that distribution would be treated as income liable to income tax under Schedule F. Accordingly it would fall to be disregarded in the computation relating to Joe's disposal of the shares. That computation would be as follows:

	£
Total sum received in respect of the shares	*8,000*
Disregard amount included in income tax computation	*(6,000)*
Net consideration for capital gains tax purposes	*2,000*
Base cost in respect of the shares	*5,000*
Loss	*(3,000)*

Indexation has been ignored since it would only serve to increase the loss, and indexation cannot increase an allowable loss.

If it is considered that the transaction fell within the provisions of s176 as described below, the computation prepared would be as follows:

	£
Consideration for disposal of shares	*8,000*
(No part falls to be treated as income, and accordingly no part is disregarded)	
Base cost	*(5,000)*
Indexation	*(230)*
Taxable gain	*2,770*

s817

TCA97 s817 is an anti-avoidance section aimed at preventing a shareholder in a close company from avoiding or reducing a charge to income tax under Schedule F by converting into a capital receipt of the shareholder an amount that would otherwise be available for distribution by the close company to the shareholder by way of dividend. Where the section has application, it can treat the proceeds of the disposal of shares in the close company as being a distribution made by the close company to the shareholder. In consequence, the sum would be in whole or in part chargeable to income tax under Schedule F and accordingly disregard it in a capital gains tax computation.

It is unlikely that s817 would have application to a transaction which falls within s175 or s176 since s817 does not apply to a disposal of shares where the shareholder, following on the disposal, has significantly reduced his interest in the company in question. The requirements of the buyback legislation in relation to the reduction of the shareholders interest to 75% or less, should ensure that s817 has not application to a transaction within that legislation. It was also unlikely that a transaction carried out for the benefit of the trade of a company could also be part of an arrangement or scheme to avoid income tax.

49.3.2   Treasury shares : unquoted (s184)

s184

CA90 s209

The concept of 'treasury shares' was introduced in the Companies Act 1990. The meaning of 'treasury shares' for tax purposes, take the meaning assigned to them from s.209 of the Companies Act 1990. In broad terms, they are shares which have been issued by the company, and subsequently reacquired (redemption, purchase, etc.) by that company. They are shares which have not been cancelled.

There are many restrictions in company law attached to such shares, in the area of voting rights, dividends, re-issue price, etc. There is also a restriction on the number of such shares which can be held by a company at any time.

For all purposes of the Tax Acts, and the Capital Gains Tax Acts:

(a)   any shares which are

     — held as treasury shares, **and**

     — not cancelled by the company,

     are deemed to be cancelled immediately upon their acquisition by the company.

(b)   no chargeable gain or allowable loss arises on the actual or deemed cancellation of those shares.

(c)   the re-issue of treasury shares by the company is deemed to be a new issue of shares. Accordingly it is not a disposal by the company for CGT purposes.

49.3.3   Main Conditions for relief : Unquoted

49.3.3.1   Purpose of the transaction

There are two alternative conditions relating to the purpose behind the transaction, compliance with either of which will (subject to other conditions) bring the transaction within the scope of CGT, and allow the shareholder to ignore the income tax distribution rules which would otherwise apply. The two purposes recognised by the legislation as bringing the transaction within the scope of the "new" treatment, in broad terms are:

s176

- **the transaction benefits the trade, or**

- **the proceeds of disposal are used to pay inheritance tax due in respect of those shares.**

In both cases, the company must be an unquoted trading company (or qualifying holding company). Where the vendor is relying on the 'trade benefit' purpose, there are many other additional conditions which must also be complied with. In a case where the vendor is claiming relief on the grounds that the sale proceeds are used to pay the inheritance tax due on the shares, the other conditions may be ignored.

49.3.3.2   **Trade Benefit (unquoted)**

The redemption, repayment, or purchase must be made wholly or mainly for the purpose of benefiting a trade carried on by the company (or any of its 51% subsidiaries).

Further conditions must also be met (where applicable) regarding :

— the residence of the vendor of the shares (s177) - see paragraph 49.3.4.

— the period of ownership of those shares by the vendor (s177) - see paragraph 49.3.5.

— the reduction of the vendor's interest in the company (s178) - see paragraph 49.3.6, and

— groups of companies (s179) - see paragraph 49.3.7.

Those further conditions are dealt with below.

There is no guidance in the legislation as to the exact meaning of 'benefiting' a trade. The UK Revenue have issues a statement of practice on the equivalent UK provision, and regard the following as 'benefiting' the trade:

• the removal of an outside investor who has provided equity finance to the company but now wishes to withdraw,

• the removal of a dissident shareholder (who is adversely affecting the trade)

• the removal of a controlling shareholder who is retiring to make way for new management,

• the buyout of shareholders who acquired their shares by gift or inheritance, but do not wish to retain the shares.

In addition, the acquisition of the shares by the company must not form part of a scheme or arrangement the main purpose (or one of the main purposes) of which is to enable the owner of the shares to participate in the profits of the company (or any of its 51% subsidiaries) without receiving a dividend.

- **Revenue Commissioners - tax briefing :**

— In issue 25 of "Tax Briefing" published by the Office of the Chief Inspector of Taxes in February 1997, the Revenue Commissioners published an article on *"trade benefit tests"*. In that article they stated that the test would not be met where *"the sole or main purpose of the buyback is to benefit the shareholder or to benefit a business purpose of the company other than a trade e.g. an investment activity"*. The briefing indicated that the Revenue Commissioners will normally regard a buyback of benefit in the trade in certain situations including:

  - Disagreements between shareholders over the management of the company where the disagreement is having or is expected to have an adverse effect on the company's trade and where the effect of the transaction is to remove the dissenting shareholder.

  - The purpose is to ensure that an unwilling shareholder who wishes to end their association with the company does not sell the shares to someone who might not be acceptable to the other shareholders.

Specific examples of this latter purpose were given and include:

  - An outside shareholder who had provided equity finance and now wished to withdraw that finance.

  - A controlling shareholder retiring as a director and wishing to make way for new management.

  - Personal representatives of a deceased shareholder wishing to realise the value of the shares.

  - A legatee of a deceased shareholder where they do not wish to hold shares in the company.

The article indicated that generally the examples outlined above would all involve the shareholder selling the entire of his shareholding in the company and making a complete break with the company. There might be exceptions to this need for a complete disposal e.g. a small shareholding might be retained for sentimental reasons or a controlling shareholder in a family company, on the sale of his shares so as to pass control to his children, might remain as a director for a specified period purely because an immediate departure from the company at that time would have a negative impact on the company's business.

The article indicated that the Revenue would give an advance opinion as to whether a proposed transaction would meet the requirements. Applications should be made to the Office of the Chief Inspector of Taxes.

49.3.3.3   **Proceeds used to pay inheritance tax (unquoted)**

The vendor must use the payment to discharge either:

- his liability to inheritance tax in respect of an inheritance of the company's shares. The payment must be applied within 4 months of the 'valuation date' (for CAT purposes - see s.21 CAT Act 1976) in discharging the liability,

  or

- a debt incurred by him in discharging his inheritance tax liability on an inheritance of the shares. The debt must be discharged within one week of the day on which the payment is made.

This provision applies subject to the condition that he could not have discharged that inheritance tax liability (or debt) by other means, without undue hardship (there is no guidance in the Act as to what constitutes 'undue hardship').

The requirement to apply the payment in discharging the CAT is treated as being met, where he uses 'substantially' the whole of the payment (apart from any part used to pay any CGT liability resulting from the transaction) to discharge the CAT liability. There is no guidance given in the legislation, as to what is meant by 'substantially' - but presumably is would be taken as excluding only an insignificant amount (see paragraph 30.4)

The same relief outlined above applies to the acquisition of shares by a subsidiary in its parent company, provided the acquisition of the shares would have been within the scope of these provisions if the shares had been acquired by the parent company itself.

49.3.4   **Residence of Shareholder (unquoted)**

This condition applies where the vendor is relying on the "trade benefit" purpose to give him the relief.

s177   The vendor must be resident and ordinarily resident in Ireland for the chargeable period (i.e. accounting period for a company, otherwise, the year of assessment) in which the company acquires the shares back from him. If the shares are held through a nominee, that nominee must also comply with the residence and ordinary residence condition.

For this purpose, the residence and ordinary residence of trustees and personal representatives is to be determined under the normal CGT rules - see paragraph 65.3 (trustees) and paragraph 66.2 (personal representatives).

In the case of a company, the reference to "ordinary residence" is ignored.

49.3.5   **Period of ownership of shares (unquoted)**

This condition applies where the vendor is relying on the 'trade benefit' purpose to give him the relief.

s177   The shares must be owned by the vendor for a period of 5 years up to the date they are acquired by the company.

Where the shares were transferred to the vendor by a person who was then his spouse living with him, the period of ownership by that person is counted as a period during which the shares were owned by the vendor. The only exception to this is an occasion on which the CGT Act recognises the possibility of marriage breakdown. The period of ownership of the other person does not transfer to the vendor, if, at the time of acquisition by the company, that other person is not living with the vendor, and is alive.

If the vendor became entitled to the shares under the will (or on the intestacy) of a previous owner, or is the personal representative of a previous owner:

- the period of ownership of the vendor is to include the period of ownership of that previous owner, and

- the period of ownership for the purposes of this relief is reduced from 5 years to 3 years.

In determining the period of ownership where shares of the same class in the same company were acquired by the vendor at different times,

- a 'first in - first out' rule is to be applied, and

- any previous disposal of shares of that class is to be assumed as a disposal of shares acquired later, rather than shares acquired earlier.

Where there is a reorganisation of share capital of a company (as defined for CGT purposes) the CGT Acts set out specific rules for determining the status of the new holding of shares following that reorganisation (see paragraph 42). In most cases, the new holding takes on the same cost and acquisition date as the old holding owned prior to the reorganisation. This, for example, would apply in the case of a bonus issue, an exchange of shares on a reorganisation or amalgamation, and a rights issue. The same rules apply to determine the period of ownership for the purposes of this relief, with one exception. Where further consideration is given (other than, or in addition to the original holding) the CGT rules on reorganisations will not apply. An example of this would be a rights issue. In such a case, the new shares are deemed to be acquired when they are actually acquired, and the normal CGT rules which would apply are ignored.

The following comments by the Revenue Commissioners have been published in Irish Tax Review.

TALC minutes 14 December 1998

Question : D1. Share buyback and separated spouses

In many separation and divorce cases, shares will be transferred in a private company from one spouse to another as part of the settlement. Immediately following the transfer, the spouse who has recently acquired the shares may have the shares bought back by the company, given that the spouse will probably be a minority shareholder and obviously, there will have been discord between the shareholders. While section 1030 TCA 1997 facilitates the transfer of shares from one spouse to another in these circumstances, the share buyback provisions, in particular section 177(7) TCA 1997denies the requisite period of ownership for the new spouse to qualify for buyback treatment (assuming all other conditions have been met). Is it possible that a concession could operate in this area particularly where separation/divorce proceedings are concerned.

Response

The Chief Inspector of Taxes requested a formal submission on this point. They agreed to raise the matter with Policy and Legislation Branch.

49.3.6   Reduction of vendor's interest in the company (unquoted)

This condition must be met where the vendor is relying on the 'trade benefit' purpose, in claiming relief.

s178

As a general rule, the Share Buyback legislation does not permit these rules to be used to extract small amounts of cash from a company. It provides that if the vendor owns shares in the company, and has any interest in the profits of the company after the acquisition of his shares by the company, the transaction must result in the vendor disposing of a substantial interest in both the shares and profits of the company. In effect, this means a minimum disposal of a figure in excess of 25% of his interest prior to the acquisition by the company.

As regards his shareholding, s178 provides:

'....*if the total nominal value of the shares owned by the vendor immediately after the purchase, expressed as a fraction of the issued share capital of the company at that time, does not exceed 75 per cent of the corresponding fraction immediately before the purchase*'.

Example 247

Andrew owns 3,000 shares of the total issued share capital of 30,000 shares in Redemption Ltd. He has owned the shares for the past 8 years, and has always been resident and ordinarily resident in Ireland.

In November 1993, the Redemption Ltd purchased 750 of his shares for cash.

The fraction of the total share capital he owned prior to the purchase is $\frac{3}{30}$, i.e. 10%

The fraction of the total share capital he owned after the purchase is $\frac{2250}{29250}$, i.e. 7.69%

75% of the corresponding fraction immediately before the purchase, is 7.5%

In this case he has not reduced his holding sufficiently to qualify under s178, even though he has disposed of 25% of his holding.

It should be noted that shares in Redemption Ltd acquired by the company itself, are deemed to be 'cancelled' (whether or not they are actually cancelled) as soon as they are acquired by the company (s184) - see paragraph 49.3 above. This reduces the total issued share capital, as well as the holding of the vendor. This affects the 'arithmetic' involved in the calculations. The result is that more than 25% has to go if a person is to qualify under this rule.

A similar rule applies where the vendor has 'associates' who have retained shares in the company after the acquisition by the company - in that the above rule applies as if the vendor owned the total shareholding of himself and his associates.

In addition to the test regarding the substantial reduction of his shareholding, a similar provision applies to his interest in the distributable profits of the company if he has any interest after the acquisition of his shares by the company. Once again, the substantial reduction is measured by a figure in excess of 25% - i.e. he is not regarded as substantially reducing his interest as a shareholder where:

- *'the vendor would, if the company distributed all its profits available for the distribution immediately after the purchase, be entitled to a share of those profits, and*

- *that share, expressed as a fraction of the total of those profits, exceeds 75 per cent of the corresponding fraction immediately before the purchase.'*

As in the case of the shareholdings mentioned above, the same provisions apply to any profit entitlement owned by his associates. The combined profit entitlement of the shareholder and his associates is taken into account.

The question of what profits are available for distribution are to be determined under company law - Part IV, Companies (Amendment) Act 1983, with the following amendments:

In determining the profit distribution for this purpose, the profits available for distribution (before and after the acquisition of its own shares by the company) are deemed to be increased by:

- in the case of every company - £100, and

- in the case of a company where any person is entitled to periodic fixed rate distributions, by a further amount equal to the sum required to make the distribution.

For the purpose of measuring the profit entitlement under the above rule, a person entitled to periodic distributions calculated by reference to fixed rates or amounts is deemed to be entitled to the maximum amount to which he is entitled for a year.

A company acquiring its own shares, will (in most circumstances) do so out of distributable profits. It is possible for the acquisition to totally use up the available profits. In any case where there is an acquisition of its own shares by the company, and the amount payable by the company exceeds the distributable profits immediately before the acquisition by the company of its own shares, the profits are deemed to be increased by that excess.

s179 Similar rules apply where the acquiring company is a member of a group. The 'arithmetic' is more difficult, but the fundamental principles are the same, with the addition of special arithmetic rules to determine the distributions of other members of the group (s179). A company which ceased to be a 51% subsidiary of another company prior to the acquisition of the shares, is treated as continuing to be a 51% subsidiary, if any arrangements existed under which it could again become a 51% subsidiary.

Where the whole (or a significant part) of the trade of an unquoted company ('the successor company') was previously carried on by either:

- the company making the purchase of the shares, or

- a company which is a member of a group which includes the purchasing company

the 'successor' company and its parent company (i.e. any company of which it is a 51% subsidiary) are deemed to be members of the same group - unless the 'successor' company carried on that business more than 3 years before the acquisition of the shares.

This condition (the reduction of the vendors interest in the company) is relaxed in certain circumstances - i.e..

- where the condition is not met by the vendor, but

- he agreed to the transaction in order that an associate of his could meet the requirement of that condition

- which could not be satisfied in any other way.

then, provided that result is actually produced by the transaction, the condition is deemed to be met - but only as respects so much of the share disposal as was necessary to produce that result.

The meaning of the term 'associate' is dealt with in paragraph 49.4.9.

49.3.7   Connected persons

This condition must be met where the vendor is relying on the 'trade benefit' purpose, in claiming relief.

s180   The vendor and the company acquiring the shares must not be connected immediately after the acquisition of the shares by that company. In addition, the vendor must not be connected with any other company which is a member of the same group as that company.

For this purpose, 'group' means

- a company which has one or more 51% subsidiaries, and

- which is not itself a 51% subsidiary of any other company,

- together with all its 51% subsidiaries.

As with the condition relating to the reduction of the vendors interest in the company, the requirement that he is not to be connected with the company is also relaxed in the same circumstances, i.e.

—the condition is not met by the vendor, but

—he agreed to the transaction in order that an associate of his could meet the requirement of that condition - which could not be satisfied in any other way.

Then provided that result is actually produced by the transaction, the condition is deemed to be met - but only as respects so much of the share disposal as was necessary to produce that result.

49.3.8   Scheme or arrangement

This condition must be met where the vendor is relying on the 'trade benefit' purpose, in claiming relief.

s180   The purchase must not be part of a scheme or arrangement which is designed or likely to result in the vendor (or his associates) having interests in any company, which if they existed immediately after the acquisition of the shares by the company, would have resulted in his failure to meet the substantial reduction in profits/shareholding test. This includes the additional rules for determining the reduction in the interest in a company where the acquiring company is a member of a group.

49.3.9 **Company acquiring shares from a dealer in shares**

s174

Where shares in a company are acquired (whether by purchase, redemption, or repayment) from a person who is a dealer in shares, the relief does not apply. The payment is treated as an income receipt to be taken into the computation of trading income in the hands of the dealer. It is not treated as a distribution in the hands of a dealer.

However, this exception to the general rule does not apply to the redemption:

- of certain fixed rate preference shares (as defined in s174), and

- of other preference shares, on binding terms settled before 18th April 1991 and issued before that date,

provided, in either case, the shares were issued to and continuously held by the person from whom they were redeemed.

49.3.10 **Returns**

s182

If a company makes a payment to which s176 applies, it must make a return in a prescribed form, to the appropriate Inspector of Taxes.

The return must be made with 9 months from the end of the accounting period in which the payment is made. If the Inspector requires the return at any time after the payment is made, he may request it (in writing), and it must be submitted, but he must allow at least 30 days notice.

49.3.11 **Information**

s183

If a company treats a payment as coming within the provisions of this relief, any person connected with the company who is aware of any such scheme or arrangement referred to in s180 - see end of paragraph 49.3.8 above - must give the relevant details to the Inspector within 60 days of his becoming aware of it.

Where the Inspector has reason to believe that such a scheme or arrangement exists, he may require the company, or any person connected with that company, or the recipient of the payment, to provide him with the relevant information within 60 days.

49.4 **Definitions - Share Buyback.**

49.4.1 **Overview**

A considerable number of words and phrases have a special meaning for the purposes of this relief, and are set out below.

49.4.2   **Quoted s173**

s173   A company is not a quoted company if:

— the company itself is not quoted, and

— the company is not a 51% subsidiary of a quoted company.

In this context, 'quoted' means where any class of the company's shares are listed in the official list of a stock exchange, or dealt in on an unlisted securities market.

This definition applies to both s176 on unquoted companies and s175 for quoted groups.

49.4.3   **Trading - s173**

s173   For this purpose, 'trade' does not include a trade of dealing in:

— shares

— securities

— land

— futures

— traded options

A trading company is one whose business consists wholly or mainly of the carrying on of a trade, or trades. Wholly or mainly is not defined, but is normally taken to mean that more than 50% of its turnover is derived from qualifying activities - i.e. trading, excluding share dealing, etc.

49.4.4   **Group - s173**

s173   This is defined to mean a company which has one or more 51% subsidiaries, together with those subsidiaries.

This applies to both quoted and unquoted companies.

49.4.5   **Trading group - s173**

s173   This means a group, the business of whose members (taken together) consists wholly or mainly of the carrying on of a trade (or trades).

49.4.6   **Shares - s173**

s173   - includes stock.

49.4.7   **Treasury shares - s184**

s184   - see paragraph 49.3.2.

49.4.8   **Material interest - s185(3)**

s185   The term 'material interest' in relation to a persons interest in property held on trusts, or comprised in the estate of a deceased person, means an interest which exceeds 5% of the value of all property in the settlement or estate, excluding any property in which he is not, and cannot become entitled.

49.4.9   **Associated persons - s185**

s185   Whether a person is an associate of another (in relation to a company) is to be determined under the following rules:

- *Husband and wife* (living together) are associates of one another.

- *Parents and their minor children* (under 18 years) are associates of one another,

- *Control of company:* A person who has control of a company and that company are associates of one another.

   Where a person who has control of one company has control of another company, both companies are associates of one another.

   Where one person is accustomed to act on the directions of another (in relation to the affairs of a company) both persons are associates of one another in relation to that company.

- *Estate of deceased person :*   where shares in a company are comprised in the estate of a deceased person, the personal representatives, and any person who is or may become beneficially entitled to a 'material' interest in the shares are associates of one another (in relation to that company).

- *Trustees :* Where shares of a company are held by trustees (other than bare trustees), in relation to that company the trustees are associates of the following persons (and those other persons are also associates of the trustees):

   − *the settlor* - i.e. any person who (directly or indirectly) provided property to the trustees, or who has made a reciprocal arrangement for another to do so,

   − *his/her spouse* (if living together) and minor children of the person providing the property to the trustees (see preceding line)

   − *certain beneficiaries*: i.e. any person who is or may become beneficially entitled to a material interest in the shares.

   This provision regarding trustees as associates of other persons does not apply:

   − where the shares are held by the trustees exclusively for the benefit of an exempt approved superannuation scheme, or

−where the shares are held on trusts exclusively for the benefit of employees, or employees and directors of the company (whose shares are held by the trustees), or of companies in a group to which that company belongs, or their dependents provided the trusts are not wholly or mainly for the benefit of directors or their relatives.

49.4.10   Control - s173

s11
s173

For the purpose of this relief, the short broader version of the meaning of 'control' in s11 is used, rather than the more complex version for close company purposes contained in s432 of that Act.

In broad terms it merely requires that to control a company, a person must be able to ensure that its affairs are conducted in accordance with his wishes - whether as a result of his shareholding, powers conferred by the Articles of the company, or any other means. It is a very broad nonspecific definition.

....'control' in relation to a company, means the power of a person to secure, by means of the holding of shares or the possession of voting power in or in relation to that or any other company, or by virtue of any powers conferred by the articles of association or other document regulating that, or any other company, that the affairs of the first-mentioned company are conducted in accordance with the wishes of that person...'

49.4.11   Connected persons - s186

s186

The question of whether a person is connected with a company for the purposes of this relief, is to be determined under the following rules notwithstanding the existing provisions of s10:

In determining whether a person is connected with the company :

- a person is treated as entitled to acquire anything which he is or will be entitled to acquire at a future date.

- a person is assumed to have the rights or powers of his associates as well as his own.

49.4.12   30% of shares or votes :

'A person shall.... *be connected with a company if he directly or indirectly possesses or is entitled to acquire more than 30 per cent of:*

(i)   the issued share capital of the company, or

(ii)   the loan capital and issued share capital of the company, or

(iii) the voting power in the company'.

49.4.13   **30% assets on winding up :**

A person is connected with the company if he directly or indirectly possesses or is entitled to acquire such rights as would on a winding up of the company entitle him to more than 30% of the assets available for distribution to equity holders.

49.4.14   **Control of company:**

A person is connected with a company if he has control of it.

49.4.15   **Loan Capital:**

A reference to loan capital, is a reference to any debt incurred by the company:

– for any money borrowed or capital assets acquired by the company,

– for any right to receive income created in favour of the company,

– for consideration, the value of which to the company was, at the time when the debt was incurred, substantially less than the amount of the debt, including any premium thereon.

Loans in the normal course of a money lending or banking business are excluded from being treated as 'loan capital' - provided the lender takes no part in the management or conduct of the company's business.

50   EMPLOYEE SHARES

50.1   **Broad Outline**

There are five principal tax favoured (or at least regulated!) methods by which an employee may obtain shares in his employer company or an associate. These are:

s128   • **A share option scheme for employees:**
Currently this is governed for income tax purposes by TCA97 s128 (see paragraph 39.11).

s479   • **A subscription by an employee for new shares in his employer company :**
An income tax relief is provided for this purpose in s479 (see paragraph 9.11).

s510   • **An approved profit sharing scheme :**
Relief is provided by s510 in respect of shares issued under such schemes (see 50.2 below).

s519   • **Employee share ownership trust:**
A corporation tax deduction is available to a company in respect

of payments made by it to an employee share ownership trust (see paragraph 50.3 below).

FA99 s68

• **Save As You Earn** - see paragraph 50.4 below.

The two share schemes first referred to above are primarily the subject matter of income tax reliefs and reference should be made to the companion volume, Income Tax, published by the Institute of Taxation in Ireland, for a discussion of the income tax aspects of those schemes.

50.1.1 Finance Act 1998 - antiavoidance

S122A

FA98 s15

TCA 97 s122A, inserted by the FA98, potentially has application in any situation in which an employee, or a person connected with the employee, acquires shares in the company in pursuance of a right or opportunity available by reason of the employee's employment. The section has application no matter when the shares were acquired, including at any time prior to the date when the section was first published in draft (4 March 1998). Therefore it potentially has application to shares acquired under any of the four schemes described above. Potentially it may also apply to shares acquired by an employee by reason of an opportunity arising to him out of his employment, even if his acquisition of the shares did not fall within any of the four schemes above, e.g. because his acquisition had predated the introduction of any of those schemes, and indeed even if it had predated the introduction of the Capital Gains Tax Act in 1975.

So badly drafted is this section, and so anomalous would be the consequences of applying the section as drafted to all situations to which it could apply, that it must be doubted that the section will be applied by the Revenue Commissioners, as drafted and enacted. Nonetheless it is necessary in this book to consider how the section, which is essentially an income tax section, may impact on the CGT treatment of the disposal of shares obtained by reason of an employment. The section has not been considered in detail as it is not a section directly concerned with CGT. Further details may be found in the companion volume, Income Tax, by McAteer and Reddin, published by the Institute of Taxation in Ireland.

The section operates by treating a person who acquires shares (in the circumstances described above) for an immediate payment of less than the market value, as thereby receiving a preferential loan from their employer (i.e. a loan which TCA97 s122 applies).

Where further payments are made in respect of the shares so acquired, the loan is correspondingly reduced. It is also reduced by any amount in respect of the share acquisition which is charged to income tax on the employee.

At the date the shares are disposed of :

- so that neither the employee nor any connected person has any beneficial interest in the shares thereafter, or

- the obligation to make further payments in respect of partly paid up shares ceases to be an obligation of the employee or any person connected with them, or

- The death of the employee if he still holds the shares,

the balance then remaining of the notional loan is charged on the employee to income tax under schedule D (foreign employments) or schedule E (Irish employments). The section makes no reference as to how it would interact with CGT rules.

s122A

The sum which is charged to income tax by s122A does not include the proceeds of sale (be they factual or deemed for the purposes of CGT) of the shares disposed of. The charge to tax is only on a notional amount in no way related to the proceeds of sale. Accordingly, the income tax charge does not cause any part of the proceeds of sale (actual or deemed under the CGT Acts) to be left out of account in computing a capital gains tax liability on the disposal of the shares.

The charge to income tax under s122A does not result in the person disposing of the shares being treated as having given any additional consideration for the acquisition of the shares, or as having incurred any enhancement expenditure upon them. Neither is the charge to tax an incidental cost of disposal or of acquisition as defined. Accordingly, the employee is not entitled to any additional deduction in computing capital gains tax on the disposal of the shares.

In summary, where s122A imposes an income tax charge, that fact has no impact on the computation of capital gains tax, and a double charge to tax may result from the disposal of the shares.

S122A could not have application to shares obtained in accordance with s479 (subscription by an employee for new shares in his employer company) as that section has application only where the shares issued are fully paid up and where they are subscribed for at market value at the time of subscription. It is believed to be the opinion of the Revenue Commissioners that it does not apply to shares obtained from an Approved Profit Sharing Scheme, although the wording of the legislation leaves that open to doubt.

S122A would seem capable of application to shares obtained from an employee share ownership trust, and under an approved share option scheme.

50.2   **Approved profit sharing scheme (CGT aspects)**

s510   The legislation in the s510 relating to approved profit sharing schemes envisages:

- a company making payment to trustees of certain sums of money

- the trustees applying those moneys to acquire shares in the company, either by subscription, or by purchase from existing shareholders

- The allocation by the trustees of those shares to employees in the company in accordance with the scheme rules which have been approved by the Revenue Commissioners.

s510   Generally, the trust deed for an approved profit sharing scheme will provide that once shares are allocated to an employee, they are the absolute property of the employee. In such a case the allocation is obviously the occasion of the acquisition of the shares by the employee. However, even where the trust deed may place restrictions on the employees freedom to deal with the shares, s510 provides that every participant in an approved profit sharing scheme is to be treated for the purposes of capital gains tax as being absolutely entitled to his shares as against the trustees. He is therefore treated as the absolute owner of the shares for capital gains tax purposes, even if he is not actually such as a matter of trust law. In consequence, the trust in an approved profit sharing scheme is not a settlement within the meaning of s574 (see paragraph 65.4). Rather the trustees are treated as nominees for the employee (see paragraph 64.1).

Where the trustees employ the funds provided to them by the company to either subscribe for shares in the company, or to purchase those from existing shareholders, they are acquiring an asset for the purposes of capital gains tax. In the ordinary way, their appropriation of those shares to an employee (who is thereupon treated by s510 as the absolute owner of those shares) would be the occasion of a disposal of those shares by the trustee, which could potentially give rise to a chargeable gain or allowable loss. However s510 provides that where the shares are appropriated to employees in accordance with the scheme within 18 months of having been acquired by the trustees, any gain accruing to the trustees on the appropriation of the shares is not a chargeable gain (it would follow of course that any loss arising to them in such circumstances would not be an allowable loss).

The FIFO rule is followed in order to identify (as between shares of the same class) :

— shares acquired by the trustees with

— shares appropriated by them to employees

for the sole purpose of determining whether shares are appropriated to an employee within 18 months of acquisition by the trustee. However the other share identification rule which applies generally, under which shares disposed of are identified primarily with shares of the same class acquired within a four week period, does not apply for this particular purpose (see paragraph 48.3).

Example 248

The trustees of Parian Ware Ltd. approved profit sharing scheme were allocated £100,000 by the company on 31 December 1996 in accordance with the scheme rules. On 5 January 1997 the trustees applied £100,000 in subscribing for new ordinary shares in the company. On 31 December 1997, the trustees received a further £75,000 from the company, and on 2 January 1998 used the moneys to purchase ordinary shares from one of the existing shareholders in the company. On 20 January 1998 the trustees appropriated 75,000 £1 ordinary shares amongst several employees. On 1 December 1999 the trustees appropriated the balance of shares held by them amongst employees.

The shares appropriated by the trustees on 20 January 1998 are, for the purpose of determining whether or not any gain arising to the trustees on their disposal is a chargeable gain, treated as being an appropriation of part of the shares acquired by the trustees on 5 January 1997 (thus applying the first in first out basis). The "four week rule" explained in paragraph 48.3 does not apply for that limited purpose. Since these shares were appropriated to employees within 18 months of being acquired, no chargeable gain or allowable loss can arise on their disposal by the trustees.

The shares appropriated in December 1999 would likewise be apportioned on a FIFO basis, with 25,000 of them being treated as being from the shares acquired by the trustees in January 1997. That is more than 18 months prior to the appropriation to employees and accordingly a chargeable gain or allowable loss may have arisen to the trustees on this appropriation. The balance of the shares are treated as being out of the January 1988 acquisition by the trustees, and since they were appropriated within 18 months no chargeable gain or allowable loss arises.

s581 It should be noted that while the "four week rule" does not apply for the purpose of determining whether or not shares appropriated to employees were from shares acquired by the trustees within the previous 18 month period (or outside that period) once it is determined that a chargeable gain or allowable loss may have arisen by reason of the gap between acquisition and appropriation being in excess of 18 months, it would appear that for the purpose of determining base cost, and computing the chargeable gain or allowable loss, the four week rule would have application! This may seem rather anomalous but does appear to be the clear result of s510.

Though the employee is not charged to income tax on shares being appropriated by him by the trustees, he is chargeable to income tax in respect of the initial value of the shares on any disposal of the shares by the trustees within three years of their acquisition. Thereafter, no income tax charge arises on a disposal.

Under ordinary capital gains tax rules consideration which is chargeable to income tax in the hands of the taxpayer is left out of account in computing the consideration for the disposal of an asset for capital gains tax purposes (See paragraph 8.2). As stated above, an income tax charge may arise on the taxpayer where the shares appropriated to him are disposed of by the trustee (as his actual nominee, or deemed nominee) within 3 years of their acquisition (5 years before FA97). This is subject to some exceptions.

s509   S509 specifically excludes this rule from application on such an occasion. In other words the full consideration arising from the disposal of the shares, notwithstanding that all or part of it may have been chargeable to income tax in the hands of the taxpayer, is taken into account as consideration for the disposal of the shares in computing the chargeable gain or allowable loss arising for capital gains tax purposes. The rationale for this treatment can be easily guessed at - the income tax charge is a clawback of an income tax relief under which the acquisition of the shares at no cost to the employee was not treated as a perquisite of his employment.

The employee's base cost for any shares appropriated to him by trustees under an approved profit sharing scheme was the open market value of the shares at the date of appropriation. The APSS legislation does not make specific provision for the employee's base cost but the shares are acquired by him otherwise than by way of a bargain made at arm's length, and also arguably by reason of his employment, and both their circumstances which, under s547 cause the acquisition to be deemed to be for open market value. Since there is a corresponding disposal by the trustees (notwithstanding that no chargeable gain or allowable loss will arise if it is within 18 months of their acquisition of the shares) s547(3) does not apply so as to cause the attribution of open market value by s547(1) not to apply (see paragraph 41.5).

Example 249

> Joe is allocated 1,000 £1 ordinary shares in Parian Ware Ltd. under the company's approved profit sharing scheme. The shares were acquired by the trustees for £1,000 and at the time of their appropriation to Joe, were worth £1,200. Two years and nine months after their appropriation, Joe has an urgent need for money and directs the trustees to dispose of the shares, which they do for the sum of £2,000.

s511   > Joe is chargeable to income tax on the sum of £1,200. This arises under s511. The income tax aspects are not considered further in this example or book. Joe is also liable for capital gains tax since the trustee's disposal of the shares is treated as being a disposal by Joe, acting through a nominee. Notwithstanding that part of the consideration for the disposal of the shares has been charged to income tax and would therefore normally be left out of account for capital gains tax *purposes, because a disposal arises in the context of an approved profit sharing scheme, the full consideration is taken into account for capital gains tax purposes. Joe's base cost is the open market value of the shares at the time he acquired them (£1,200) and not the cost to the trustees (£1,000). Because the trustees appropriated the shares to Joe within 18 months of having acquired them from the company, the trustees are not treated as having a chargeable gain on the occasion of their appropriation of the shares to Joe, notwithstanding that the shares had increased in value since their acquisition by the trustees.*

Where the value of shares appropriated by trustees to an employee in any one year exceeds a certain limit (currently £10,000) an income tax charge will arise on the employee either on the occasion of the disposal of those shares by the trustees (as nominee for the trustee) or on the 3rd anniversary (5th anniversary pre FA 1997) whichever first occurs. As in the example given above, notwithstanding that the consideration for the disposal by the trustees is chargeable to tax in the hands of the employee, no part of that consideration is excluded from being taken into account in a capital gains tax computation also. A capital gains tax computation of course would arise only in the event of an actual disposal by the trustees or by the employee, and it does not arise (as does the income tax charge) on the 3rd anniversary (5th anniversary pre FA 1997) of the acquisition of the surplus shares, where that occurs prior to any disposal.

It is important to remember that because the employee is deemed by s510 to be absolutely entitled as against the trustees to any scheme shares appropriated to him, a transfer of such shares by the trustees to the employee is not the occasion of a disposal by the trustees, or acquisition by the employee. It is only the initial appropriation by the trustee to the employee that is the occasion of a disposal by the trustee to the employee. Subsequent actions by the trustee occur as mere nominee for the employee.

50.3   Employee share ownership trusts

s519

The 1997 Finance Act provided a tax code for employee share ownership trusts now TCA97 s519. An employee share ownership trust is a discretionary trust created by a company for the benefit of its employees. In order that s519 should apply to it, it is necessary that it should meet detailed conditions.

s519 is primarily concerned with granting the company which transfers money to such a trust, a corporation tax deduction for those transfers. The legislation has little or no direct reference to tax on capital gains, nor does it directly provide for any tax reliefs for employees in relation to benefits resulting to them. The legislation is therefore primarily corporation tax legislation and it is not proposed to describe it here in detail - reference may be made to the companion volume published by the Institute of Taxation in Ireland, Corporation Tax.

s574   An employee share ownership trust is probably a settlement within
the meaning of s574. Although, from an overall viewpoint, the trust
might be seen as merely part of the remuneration arrangements of
the employees, and consequently involving no element of bounty,
the trust is discretionary in nature. That discretionary aspect is
probably sufficient to introduce the necessary element of bounty into
the situation. Certainly, the trustees are not nominees and, regardless
of s574, would be taxable persons in their own right in any event.

An employee share ownership trust operates typically by an
employer company transferring money to the trustees of the trust;
the trustees then acquiring shares in the employer company and
holding those shares; and the disposal of those shares by the trustees
either by direct appointment to the employees (unlikely for income
tax reasons) or by sale to an approved profit sharing scheme.

The only specific provision relating to the taxation of capital gains in
s519 in relation to employee share ownership trusts is that a transfer
by the trustees of the trust of shares to the trustees of approved profit
sharing scheme is not to be treated as giving rise to a chargeable
gain. Any other disposals e.g. an appropriation of shares absolutely
to an employee, or a sale of shares to any person other than the
trustees of an approved profit sharing scheme, is a disposal
potentially giving rise to a chargeable gain which is not exempt
under the 1997 legislation (s519).

The trustees of an employee share ownership trust may acquire
shares in any fashion. They may subscribe for shares. They may
purchase shares from existing shareholders. Generally their base cost
in the shares they acquire will be equal to the consideration which
they give for those shares. However open market value might be
substituted if the transaction is otherwise than by way of a bargain
made at arm's length. The rules relating to the acquisition cost of
shares acquired by way of subscription are dealt with in paragraph
41, and are capable of application to an employee share ownership
trust which subscribes for shares.

It is likely that an employee share ownership trust will hold shares
for a lengthy period. Accordingly, there is a strong incentive on the
trustees to dispose of shares only to an approved profit sharing
scheme. This is the only method of disposal carrying an exemption
from capital gains tax, and is the only method by which shares are
likely to be transferred to employees without an income tax liability
arising on the employee. The income tax exemption is of course
limited to £10,000 p.a. per employee.

The limit of £10,000 per annum per person on payments from an
ESOT is lifted in some circumstances. Subject to conditions, an
employee may receive up to £30,000 in one year on a once off basis
provided the shares in question were used by the ESOT as security
for borrowings for a minimum period of five years. This latter

period of security may be reduced by order by the Minister for Finance.

50.4   Save As You Earn

s519A;
s519B;
s519C

FA99 introduced a Save As You Earn scheme, copied from a similar scheme in the UK. It is to be found in s519A to s519C, and in Sch12A and Sch12B. Section 128 charges an employee to tax when he exercises (or otherwise turns to profit) share options obtained by reason of his employment. The same treatment obviously applies to a director. The essence of the Save As You Earn scheme is to eliminate that charge to income tax entirely from the transaction. The employee therefore finds that he does not suffer tax in relation to obtaining a share option, or the exercise of the share option, and will incur a liability to tax only on the occasion of disposing of the shares. That liability is to CGT.

This preferential treatment of share options is linked to an approved savings scheme. The return on this approved savings scheme is tax free. It is intended that the proceeds of the approved saving scheme would be used to finance the acquisition of shares which are the subject matter of an option.

A Save As You Earn scheme is primarily an income tax matter. For that reason it is not discussed in detail in this book. Reference should be made to "Income Tax" by McAteer & Reddin published by the Institute of Taxation in Ireland.

As noted above, where the conditions of the Save As You Earn scheme have been met, the employee will first encounter a charge to tax in relation to shares on the occasion of disposing of the shares.

FA 2000, s51

Prior to the FA 2000, the Save as you Earn legislation made no specific provision for the base cost of the employee in the shares which he obtained under the scheme. FA2000 s51 inserted a new subsection 3A into s159A. This subsection provides that where a trust or company is used for the purpose of acquiring and holding scheme shares, and passing them on to employees in due course, the trust or company in question is exempt from capital gains tax on the shares, and the base cost of the employee in the shares is the consideration given by him for their acquisition.

The topic of the base cost of an employee in respect of shares obtained on foot of an employee share option is discussed in paragraph 39.11, and will not be repeated here.

51   STRIPPING VALUE FROM ASSETS

51.1   Outline Summary of provisions

There are many ways of reducing the value of an asset prior to its disposal, leaving a smaller gain (or perhaps a loss) resulting for CGT purposes from the disposal. Some methods of achieving this result would not normally in themselves involve a disposal.

Most arrangements made to achieve such a result, involve the taking of *value* by various means out of the asset, leaving the actual asset in the same ownership, but with a substantially reduced value. The result (in the absence of specific provisions to deal with the matter) would normally be that although the greater part of the value may have been stripped from the asset, there has in fact been no disposal of any asset. The following sections of this paragraph deal with

- a number of arrangements used to try and achieve such a result, and
- the statutory provisions which attempt to ensure that any resulting advantage is not effective for CGT purposes.

The main arrangements, and corresponding statutory provisions are:

- Transfer of value derived from assets ("value shifting"). This is dealt with in paragraph 51.2

- Transferring assets from a company at an undervalue. This is dealt with in paragraph 51.3

- Asset stripping. This is dealt with in paragraph 51.4.

- Dividend stripping. This is dealt with in paragraph 51.5

- Pre-Disposal dividends. This is dealt with in paragraph 51.6

51.2   Transfer of Value Derived from Assets

51.2.1   Shares in Companies

s543   A person having control of a company will be deemed to have made a disposal (or part disposal) of his shares if he exercises his control so that value passes out of shares owned by him into other shares in the company. In such a case the transaction is treated as not at arm's length and market value must be substituted for the actual consideration (if any) passing. Market value is the actual consideration (if any) passing plus any further consideration which could have been obtained for the transfer if it was a bargain made at arm's length.

Example 250

Donal and Tim are shareholders in CHAIN SAW LTD. Donal owns 70% of the shares and Tim owns 30%. Tim is to marry Donal's daughter and Donal wishes to give Tim a gift of his share of the company. Rather than make a direct gift of the shares he arranges for a resolution to be passed in March 1996 to the effect that Tim's shares acquire all the voting power and rights to dividends. Assume the market value of the transfer of control and dividend rights is £50,000, and that Donal acquired his shares in June, 1990 for £20,000. The market value of Donal's shares after the transfer of rights is £5,000. Donal's chargeable gain is calculated as follows:

	£
Deemed Consideration for part disposal	50,000
Cost £20,000 x $\dfrac{50,000}{55,000}$ = £18,182	
Indexed @ 1.130	20,489
Chargeable Gain	29,511

The legislation, which is contained in s543 is as follows:

"(1) Without prejudice to the generality of the provisions of the Capital Gains Tax Act as to the transactions which are disposals of assets, any transaction which under this section is to be treated as a disposal of an asset

  (a) shall be so treated (with a corresponding acquisition of an interest in the asset) notwithstanding that there is no consideration and

  (b) so far as, on the assumption that the parties to the transaction were at arm's length, the party making the disposal could have obtained consideration, or additional consideration, for the disposal, the transaction shall be treated as not being at arm's length and the consideration so obtainable, added to the consideration actually passing, shall be treated as the market value of what is acquired.

(2) (a) Where a person having control of a company exercises that control so that value passes out of shares in the company owned by such person or a person with whom such person is connected, or out of rights over the company exercisable by such persons or by a person with whom such person is connected, and passes into other shares in or rights over the company, that exercise of such person's control shall be a disposal of the shares or rights out of which the value passes by the person by whom they were owned or exercisable.

  (b) Reference in paragraph (a) to a person include references to 2 or more persons connected with one another".

Subsections (3) and (4) of s543, dealing with value shifting in the case of certain land transactions, and the abrogation or extinction of certain rights, are dealt with in paragraphs 51.2.2.5 and 51.2.2.6 below.

It should be noted, that because of the amendments introduced in the 1978 Act, particularly those relating to the 'identification' of shares, differences exist in this area between Irish and UK law. The antiavoidance provisions, however, are the same. The concept of value shifting is well illustrated in the UK case of Floor v Davis. The position in that case was as follows (prior to the value shift):

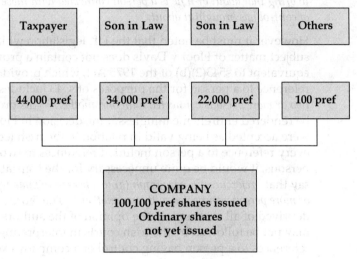

The preference shares carried a right to six sevenths of all declared dividends, and one seventh of all surplus asset on a winding up. The ordinary shares (not yet issued) carried a right to one seventh of all dividends, and six sevenths of the surplus assets on a winding up. All shares carried equal voting rights. It was resolved that a rights issue of ordinary shares be offered to all the preference shareholders. Only the 'others' accepted the offer, and were allotted 50 ordinary shares at par. At a subsequent meeting it was resolved to wind up the company. The taxpayer, and one son-in-law were not present at the meeting, nor was any vote cast on behalf of either of them. As a result of the winding up six sevenths of the surplus assets of the company passed to the others.

The main point at issue in the case was whether the words "*a person having control*" includes a situation where control belongs to more than one person. It was held by a majority (Lords Wilberforce and Keith dissenting) that the section could be so interpreted. Viscount Dilhorne, in the course of his judgement, said "*I can see no reason for not treating the passing of value out of shares owned by two or more persons as a result of the exercise by them of control and out of shares owned by persons connected with them in precisely the same way. I can see no indication that Parliament intended to secure that what would be a disposal if the control was exercised by the exercise of control by one person*" *would not be a disposal if the control was exercised by two or more and in the absence of any clear indication of such an intention (s543) must in my opinion be construed in the light of (The Interpretation Act 1937) and (s432). It is said that a minority shareholder owning say 10% of the shares would be liable to be taxed if one or more others have shares which, with his add up to a controlling situation. I do not agree that this is so. Such a minority shareholder will only have value passing out of his shares treated as a disposal if he is joined with other shareholders in the exercise of control to bring that about or if he is a person connected with those whose exercise of control has brought it about."*

s543

However it must be noted that the UK legislation which is the subject matter of Floor v Davis does not contain a provision equivalent to s543(2)(b) of the 1975 Act, which provides that a reference to a person for the purposes of s543 includes *"references to two or more persons connected with one another."* This provision would be rendered entirely meaningless if the decision in Floor v Davis were accepted as being valid in relation to the Irish legislation. If every reference to a person included references to two or more persons, it would be quite unnecessary for the legislation to go on to say that *"references in paragraph (a) to a person include references to two or more persons connected with one another."* The words would be deprived of all meaning. In the opinion of the authors Floor v Davis may not be followed by the Irish courts in interpreting s543 and references to a person having control of a company exercising his control are more likely to be taken to be references only to the exercise of control by one person, or by two or more persons who are connected with one another. It may not be taken to be a reference to the exercise of control by two or more persons who are not connected with one another. The point will remain in doubt until it is clarified by the Irish Courts.

A further point which was considered in this case was whether "exercise of control" required positive action by the person(s) having control. It was held that the passing of the resolution by which value passed out of the taxpayers shares was exercise of control even though he was not present at the relevant meeting. On this point, Viscount Dilhorn, in the House of Lords was in agreement with the observations of Sir John Pennycuick made during the course of his judgement in the Court of Appeal.

"I do not doubt that in the ordinary case of control by the holding of a majority of shares the expression "exercise of control" indicates the casting of the votes attached to those shares on the relevant resolutions, and that a shareholder could not be treated as exercising control when he is absent or inactive when the resolution is proposed. But the expression "exercise of control" is not a term of art denoting by its own force the casting of votes and nothing else, and there may be circumstances, in the case of control by more than one person, where those persons should be indeed treated as collectively exercising control without all of then actually casting their

votes. It seems to me that the circumstances here are of that character. The taxpayer and the sons-in-law acquired voting control of FNW as the first step in a series of operations designed to eventuate in the proceeds of their shares of IDM passing to a foreign company. This series of operations represented a scheme planned in advance by the three individuals acting in concert. The passing of the winding up resolution by FNW was an integral and essential operation in this scheme and was indisputably carried out in furtherance of a common and continuing intention on the part of the three individuals. On these facts it seems to me that the resolution should be regarded as an exercise by all three individuals of collective control. It is, I think, immaterial that two of the individuals did not exactly cast their votes in favour of the resolution".

s543(2)(a) refers to a person who *"exercises his control so that value passes out of shares in the company owned by him or a person with whom he is connected ......and passes into other shares in or rights over the company ...."*

On their own these words leave it unclear as to whether s543 could have application where a person exercises control so that value passes out of shares in a company owned by him and passes into other shares in the company owned by him. It would appear from the wording of s543 that it does not operate in such a case. It refers to a transaction *"notwithstanding that there is no consideration and so far as, on the assumption that the parties to the transaction were at arm's length, the party making the disposal could have obtained consideration.....for the disposal"*. A transaction to which there is only one party (i.e. the person who exercises control so that value passes from shares in the company owned by him into other shares in the same company also owned by him) would appear to be a transaction to which the concept of consideration has no relevance. Since one cannot enter into a legally binding transaction with oneself, it is difficult to visualise whether such a transaction would be or would not be a transaction at arm's length. Nor, in reality, can a person force themselves to pay additional consideration, or any consideration for a transaction with themselves. The whole concept seems to be a nonsense in such circumstances.

The reference in s543(1) to *"parties to the transaction"* is somewhat ambiguous. In the example of the passing by the members of the company of a resolution to amend the rights attaching to different classes of shares, so that value passes out of some shares and into other shares as a result, who are the parties to the transaction?

It is necessary to identify who the parties are, as it is on the assumption that those identified parties are at arm's length, that the consideration which could be obtained for the transaction is determined.

• Do the parties include the company itself?

- Do they include each and every shareholder in the company?

- Do they include each and every director of the company?

If it were accepted that the company were a party to such a transaction, might there be the necessary two parties present in an instance where a shareholder has exercised control so as to pass value from some shares owned by him, into other shares owned by him? But if the only assumption we are to make is that the shareholder and the company are at arm's length, we would still conclude that no consideration would be obtainable for the transaction, since it leaves the shareholder no better off, and no worse off than he was before. If in such a circumstance it were considered that s543 had application to the transaction, the only consequence would be to treat the shareholder as having disposed of the shares out of which the value passed, for a nil consideration. A computation based on that interpretation would, on the facts assumed, always yield either a no gain / no loss result, or a loss. It would never produce a chargeable gain.

It appears that the only logical conclusion is to suggest that s543 cannot apply to a shift of value between shares owned by the same person.

51.2.2   Interaction with other provisions

51.2.2.1   Reorganisations, etc.

s584

TCA97 s584(1) provides that references in the section to a reorganisation of a company's share capital include any case where there is more than one class of shares and where the rights attaching to shares of any class are altered.

S584 goes on to provide that in such a case the reorganisation will not be treated as being a disposal of shares, nor an acquisition of shares, but rather shares which are held as a result of the reorganisation are treated as the same shares as existed prior to the reorganisation and as were concerned in it. In other words, such a reorganisation does not give rise to a chargeable gain or allowable loss. It is a *"nothing"* in CGT terms. There is no reference in s584 to s543 and vice versa.

Neither is stated to be subject to the other. Which therefore takes precedence and overrules the other in terms of practical affect? As a general principle, it would seem logical that a provision which provides a relief from the charge to tax should take priority over a section which imposes a charge to tax. There would be no purpose in providing reliefs if they were overridden by charging sections.

s543

The overlap between s584 and s543 is considerable. The example of a transaction in which value is passed from some shares in a company into other shares in a company, which most readily comes to mind, is a transaction in which the rights attaching to two classes of shares are amended. Thus the type of transaction most likely to be within s543 is specifically and unconditionally treated as not being a disposal by s584. However as s584 is probably more specific as regards the type of transaction to which it applies than the general description of a transaction to which s543 applies, the rule that the specific provision takes precedence over the general provision would probably apply to reinforce the conclusion that the relief should take precedence over the charge.

51.2.2.2   Transfers between husband & wife

TCA97 s1028 provides that transfers of assets between spouses living together as husband and wife will be treated as being for a consideration such as would yield neither a gain nor a loss on the disposal. If the *"parties to the transaction"* referred to in s543(1) are spouses living together as husband and wife, does s543 or s1028 take precedence in determining consideration in the transaction?

s1028

S1028 applies where there is a disposal of an asset by one spouse, and a corresponding acquisition of the asset by the other spouse in the same transaction.

s543

S543 can deal with transactions which are not in the ordinary sense either a disposal of an asset nor an acquisition of an asset. That deficiency is made good where necessary by s543 which deems there to be a disposal, and (in s543(1)) deems there to be a corresponding acquisition of an interest in the asset which has been deemed to be disposed of. Accordingly a s543 transaction involving only spouses would seem capable of being within s1028. Once again, it is arguable that the relief is not overridden by the charge; and that the specific provision (s1028) takes precedence over the general provision (s543). It would also be nonsensical if actual disposals and acquisitions between spouses are covered by s1028, but one instance of a deemed disposal and acquisition (s543) was not.

51.2.2.3   Transfers between members of a group of companies

s617

The provisions of TCA97 s617, dealing with intra group transfers of assets, commence with the words *"notwithstanding any provision in the Capital Gains Tax Acts, fixing the amount of the consideration deemed to be received on a disposal or given on an acquisition...."*. From that, one might infer that s617 would take precedence over s543, so that a transaction to which s543 refers, where it occurs within a group would be on a *"no gain / no loss"* basis.

However s617(1) goes on to state *"where it is assumed for any purpose that a member of a group of companies has sold or acquired an asset, it shall be assumed also that it was not a sale to or acquisition from another member of the group."* Notwithstanding the reference to *"sale"* rather than the more usual word *"disposal"* this provision seems to clearly indicate that deemed disposals and deemed acquisitions by a member of a group are to be assumed not to have been disposals to, or acquisitions from, another group member.

s543   Transactions to which s543 apply will, in many instances, be deemed acquisitions, or deemed disposals, but not actual acquisitions or disposals. In some instances, where consideration is given by one party to the other for the consent of the second party to value being passed out of the shares, a second party may well have made a part disposal of the shares by deriving a capital sum from them. In such a case there would be a disposal by the second party. But there would be no actual acquisition in such a transaction by the first party. So s617 would not have application to such a transaction, since it requires that there should be both an acquisition and a disposal.

Since s543 merely deems an acquisition and a disposal, s617 would not have application to the transaction even if all the parties to the transaction were members of a group, by reason of the words in s617(1) quoted above. Therefore, it would seem to follow that "group relief" would not relieve a charge under the value shift provisions.

That conclusion would give rise to an anomalous situation in which actual acquisitions and disposals are within the relief, but a deemed acquisition and disposal is not within the relief. Because of the absurdity of that position, there must be doubt about the matter.

51.2.2.4   **The notional interest in the asset**

S543(1) deems that there is *"a corresponding acquisition of an interest in the asset"* where the section applies so as to deem a disposal of shares to have occurred by reason of a transaction. This notional interest in the shares out of which the value has passed has a base cost attributed to it i.e. the deemed consideration for the transaction. It is strange that the section should create this notional asset. A notional asset is incapable of being the subject matter of an actual transaction. You cannot sell it. You cannot gift it. You cannot derive a capital sum from it. It has no actual existence.

This is not in fact surprising, when one considers the nature of this anti-avoidance provision. If we look again at the facts set out in *example 250* and consider what has actually happened, the difficulties of applying this section can be more easily understood. In that case, Donal has not disposed of an asset. He owned shares before the transaction. After the transaction he still owns the same shares. What has happened, is that "value" has passed from his shares into the shares owned by Tim.

Equally, Tim has not acquired an asset. He owned shares before the transaction, and still owns the same shares after the transaction. What he has acquired is "value".

S543 applies normally where there is no actual asset passing between the persons concerned. What is passes is "value" which shifts (in the case set out in *example 250*) from Donal to Tim.

It appears that what s543 is trying to do, is to

- tax the "value" passing (as if it were an asset) on the person from whom the value has passed (as a part disposal of his asset) and

- allow the value passing as additional expenditure incurred to the person acquiring the value.

Unfortunately, the wording of s543 leaves the position obscure.

If we look again to *example 250*, we can see that what Tim has acquired is a notional interest in that from which Donal has passed value - i.e., Donal's shares. On a subsequent sale by Tim of his own shares, he has not sold any part of Donal's shares, and so it may be difficult to establish a valid case for a deduction for this additional cost equal to the amount of value passing from Donal's shares.

A sale of the shares in which this notional interest exists by the actual owner of the shares, is not a disposal of the notional interest in the shares. It is not an actual disposal nor is it a deemed disposal of the notional interest. It is in fact difficult to conceive of any circumstance in which this notional asset can be disposed of, so as to yield either a gain or a loss. The only occasion which the authors can think of is the occasion of the extinguishment of the company, on being struck off the company's register. At that point the shares would cease to have an existence, and the extinguishment of an asset is the occasion of a disposal of that asset. The extinguishment of all shares in the company (perhaps through liquidation and ultimate dissolution of the company) would surely result in the extinguishment of even a notional right in those shares, and accordingly lead to a disposal of that notional right. It is not clear however that there is any other circumstance in which the base cost attributed to that notional right can be crystallised into an allowable loss.

S543 can be fairly described as one of the more badly drafted sections in the capital gains tax legislation. Until it has been more comprehensively examined by the courts, the issues raised above regarding its interpretation must remain the subject of considerable doubt.

51.2.2.5   **Land**

s543(3)   Similar provisions apply in the case of land, where the owner of the property becomes the lessee (sale and leaseback) and the terms of the lease are subsequently changed resulting in value passing to the new owner. The value passing to the new owner as a result of the subsequent change in the terms of the lease is treated as a further disposal (at market value) by the old owner of the property.

Example 251

If the owner of freehold land transferred that land to his son, but retained a 100 year lease of the land at an annual rent of £5, the value of the interest in land disposed of would be negligible, and little or no CGT would result. If, then, the following year, the terms of the lease were changed, to provide for (say) a full market value rent with 2 years rent revisions, the land would then be worth its full value.

In such circumstances, the former owner of the freehold would be treated as making a further disposal (out of his retained leasehold interest) to the extent of the value transferred to the present owner of the freehold.

51.2.2.6   **Other Assets**

s543(4)   In the case of any asset, which is subject of any right or restriction, the abrogation or extinction of the right or restriction (or part of it) by the person entitled to enforce it, is treated as a disposal of the right or restriction by that person at market value.

An example of the circumstances in which such a deemed disposal would arise is set out in paragraph 16.4.3

51.2.2.7   **Persons acquiring the benefit**

Any transaction deemed to be a disposal under the above provisions, involves a corresponding acquisition by the recipient of the "benefit" involved.

However, the question of him receiving a deduction for the value of the benefit or value received, involves it being identified with a particular asset which is being disposed of. This may cause some difficulty as discussed in paragraph 51.2.2.4 above.

51.3   **Transfer of assets at undervalue**

51.3.1   **Broad Outline - s589**

s589   Where on or after 6 April 1974 a *close company:*

- transfers an asset to any person under a bargain not at arm's length

  and

- the transfer is for an amount less than the market value of the asset

the undervalue will be apportioned over all the issued shares in the company. The allowable cost of each share for the purpose of computing the gain or loss on a subsequent disposal is reduced by its apportioned part of the undervalue. This rule only apportions the

s552

undervalue to expenditure under s552 (which would not include enhancement expenditure). Where indexation applies, the cost before indexation is reduced, and the balance of the allowable cost is indexed. The term *close company* has the meaning assigned to it by

s430

s430 (see also paragraph 67.2).

s130

It is interesting to note, that although the transfer of assets at an undervalue to a shareholder in the company may be treated as a distribution for income tax purposes under s130 (to the extent of the undervalue), for CGT purposes the cost of the shares is reduced as well. No relief is available for the potential double charge which can arise in such circumstances. On the subsequent sale of the shares, two factors will determine the amount of the gain or loss for CGT purposes:

- the sale proceeds

- the cost (as reduced).

The CGT rules exclude from the "consideration for disposal" any amount taken into account as income, but as the undervalue taxed as a distribution is not part of the sale proceeds of the shares, no relief is available. The only item excluded from the cost for CGT purposes, is an amount deductible for income tax purposes. There are no circumstances in which income taxed as a distribution can be allowed as a 'deduction' for income tax purposes, and so no relief is available for CGT under this rule either.

In addition to the potential double tax charge which can arise in such circumstances, there is also the question of Capital Acquisitions Tax. This is clearly an area to be avoided, unless all the possible consequences have been well thought out.

There is an ambiguity in s589 in that it applies where a person transfers an asset to another person under a bargain not at arm's length and the consideration is of an amount of value less than the market value of the asset. s547, states that, for the purposes of the Act, the consideration arising on a disposal which is otherwise than by way of a bargain made at arm's length, is to be deemed to be the market value of the asset. It might be thought that s547 has application for the purpose of s589 (as it does for all other purposes of the CGT Acts). If it did have application, there would be no circumstance in which s589 could have application, since every transfer of an asset otherwise than by way of a bargain made at arm's length would be treated as being for a consideration equal to the market value of the asset. It must be assumed that the reference in s589 to consideration is to the actual consideration and not to the deemed consideration arising under s547 or under any other provision of the CGT Acts which replaces actual consideration with a notional consideration. Given the multiple taxation to which a transaction within s589 is exposed, as explained above one could only speculate that a court might take some notice of the ambiguity created by the interaction of s547 and of s589.

A company making the transfer at under value is of course disposing of an asset. Since the disposal is otherwise than by way of a bargain made at arm's length, s547 will treat the company as receiving a consideration from the disposal equal to the market value of the asset, and not the lesser amount which it in fact receives. The company (if within the charge to capital gains tax or corporation tax on companies capital gains) will thus suffer the same tax consequence as would have applied had it to transfer the asset for full value. This represents a further charge of tax to add to the several described above, which would result from the transaction.

s590(11)   These provisions apply not only to a close company but also to a company not resident in the State which would be a close company were it resident in the State (i.e. a company within s590(1) to (9) - see paragraph 67). However where the transfer in question is between members of a "non-resident group" s589 does not have application. Neither does it have application to an intra group transaction.

Example 252

A. Ltd. has 100 shares in issue. 75 are held by B Ltd., and 25 by John. All three persons are resident in the State. A Ltd. has a block of shares which cost it £100,000. They are now worth £200,000. It transfers three quarters of these shares to B Ltd. and one quarter to John. They are transferred at cost, and not at market value.

The transfer between A Ltd. and B Ltd. is a transfer of an asset within a capital gains group i.e. between a 75% subsidiary and its parent. Accordingly the transfer is treated for the purposes of corporation tax on capital gains as being on a no gain no loss basis, being a transfer within s617. In accordance with s130(3)(b), the fact that the asset is transferred at under market value to B Ltd. will not give rise to it being treated as a distribution (to the extent that it is under value). The application of s589 is avoided by reason of a specific exclusion in s616(6)(b). Accordingly s589 does not reduce the base cost which B Ltd. has in its shares in A Ltd., by reason of the under value transfer.

The treatment of the shares transferred to Tom is very different. Group relief is not available on this transfer and accordingly being with a connected party, and being otherwise than a bargain made at arm's length, it is treated as being for a consideration equal to market value. Accordingly a chargeable gain accrues to A Ltd. of £25,000. By reason of s130(3)(b) the undervalue transfer to Tom is treated as being a distribution in the amount of the under value element i.e. £25,000. This gives rise to an income tax liability in Tom's hands. Tom's base cost for his shares in A Ltd. is reduced under s589, most probably by the amount of £25,000 (assuming Tom's base cost to be sufficiently large to permit that).

Notwithstanding that s589 did not apply to the transfer between A Ltd. and B Ltd. at under value (by reason of the specific exclusion of its operation in s616) there is a further statutory provision which would have affect. That is s621 "depreciatory transactions in a group". That section operates in a way that is somewhat similar to s589 but not identical. An allowable loss arising on a disposal by B Ltd. of its shares in A Ltd. could be reduced by the amount at which the consideration given for the transfer of shares from A Ltd. to B Ltd. was under market value. That is not the same thing of course as a reduction in the base cost of shares which s589 can bring about.

S621 applies only to reduce the loss. s589, where it applies by reducing the base cost in shares, can also have the affect of increasing a chargeable gain. s621, where it applies, cannot increase a gain. s621 is discussed in greater detail in paragraph 51.4.

51.3.2 Apportionment

The legislation does not provide apportionment rules specifically for s589.

s544 S544(5) provides a general rule that the method of apportionment of 'consideration' or 'expenditure' shall be *"such method as appears to the inspector or on appeal the Appeal Commissioners to be just and reasonable".*

This is subject to specific rules which apply for specific purposes:-

- parts disposals, and

- assets derived from other assets

The difficulty here, is that the apportionment required by s589 is not an apportionment of expenditure, nor is it an apportionment of consideration, and so there must be a doubt as to the method of apportionment to use where s589 applies.

Where a company does not have a share capital (e.g. a company limited by guarantee) the apportionment required by s589 would appear to be impossible.

51.3.3 Exception

s616(6) These provisions do not apply to transfers of assets between members of an Irish resident group of companies (as defined for the purposes of corporation tax on chargeable gains-see paragraph 76.4).

51.4 Depreciatory Transactions in a Group

51.4.1 Broad Outline

s621 In the absence of anti-avoidance provisions it would be quite simple to create artificial CGT losses within a group.

If, for example, a parent company stripped the assets out of its subsidiary at a substantial undervalue, the shares in the subsidiary could be worthless. On a subsequent sale of those shares by the parent company, a substantial loss could arise.

Example 253

WHISKEY LTD owns all the shares in GIN LTD. It bought the shares in that company in 1986 for £100,000. The only asset of GIN LTD is a building which it bought in 1977 for £100,000. In March 1989, GIN LTD sells the property to WHISKEY LTD for £1. Under the group provisions no gain or loss arises.

In March 1993 WHISKEY LTD sells the shares in GIN LTD for £1.

WHISKEY LTD has a loss on the sale of the shares amounting to £99,999. The "asset strip" has left WHISKEY LTD with assets worth £99,999 which cost £1.

WHISKEY LTD still owns assets worth £100,000, only in a different form. Previously it owned the shares. Now it owns the assets. It has no overall loss. However, in the absence of anti-avoidance provisions the £99,999 loss would be allowable.

The anti-avoidance provisions dealing with transfers of assets at an undervalue as set out in paragraph 51.3 do not apply to transfers between members of a group. However, the "asset stripping" anti-avoidance provisions have the effect of taking the undervalue on the assets transferred into account in arriving at the allowable loss on the disposal of the shares.

51.4.2   **Scope of anti-avoidance Provisions**

The provisions apply where the value of shares in a GROUP company have been materially reduced by a 'depreciatory transaction' carried out on or after 6 April 1974.

51.4.3   **Meaning of "Depreciatory Transaction"**

A depreciatory transaction is defined as:

• any disposal of assets between members of a group other than at market value

    or

• any other transaction between members of a group provided the company whose shares are sold (causing the loss) or its 75% subsidiary was a party to the transaction.

CA63 s72   Such a transaction would include the cancellation of shares in a subsidiary under s.72 of the Companies Act 1963.

A payment taken into account in calculating a gain or loss (for the purposes of CT on chargeable gains) arising to the group member selling the shares is deemed not to be a depreciatory transaction.

51.4.4   **Effect of Provisions**

The provisions can only be used to reduce what would otherwise be an allowable loss. They cannot affect a gain arising on the disposal of the shares.

Where a depreciatory transaction has been carried out within a group, and the shares in the 'stripped' company are disposed of by a member of the group, any allowable loss accruing on the disposal..."*shall be reduced to such extent as appears to the inspector, or on appeal the Appeal Commissioners, or on a rehearing by a Judge of the Circuit Court, that Judge, to be just and reasonable having regard to the depreciatory transaction*".

If the person disposing of the shares is not a member of the group in which the depreciatory transaction occurred and who was not a member at the time of the depreciatory transaction, no account will be taken of a depreciatory transaction occurring while it was not a member of the group.

If a reduction in the allowable loss is made under these provisions, any gain on a subsequent disposal of shares in another group company which was a party to the transaction may be reduced, if it can be shown that part of the gain reflects the effect of the depreciatory transaction.

Example 254

> *Assume the facts to be as an **example 253** above except that 10% of the shares in Gin Ltd were held by Mr Guinness and a further 10% were held by Power Investments Ltd. The balance were held by Whisky Ltd. A cash take over offer is accepted by the three share holders following on the depreciatory transactions described in **example 253**.*

> *S621 will have no application to Mr Guinness since he is not a member of a group either at the time he makes the disposal or at the time of the depreciatory transactions. Being an individual, he cannot be a member of the group. Neither will s589 (discussed in paragraph 51.3.1) have application to him since the depreciatory transaction was within a group, and the application of s589 is excluded in the case of intragroup transfers by s616(6). Power Investments Ltd is a company, but is not a member of a group with Whisky Ltd or Gin Ltd as it does not meet the conditions regarding shareholdings etc. Accordingly s621 will not have application to Power Investments Ltd, nor will s589, for the reasons just explained. S621 will have application to Whisky Ltd as explained in **example 253**. S589 will not have application since the depreciatory transaction is intragroup.*

> *S621 has application only to intra group depreciatory transfers. S589, which seems to cover broadly similar territory, cannot have application to transactions to which s621 applies, because the application of s589 is excluded if the depreciatory transaction was intragroup.*

51.5   **Dividend Stripping**

51.5.1   **Broad Outline**

s622   The 'dividend stripping' provisions are similar to the 'asset
                 stripping' provisions outlined in the previous paragraphs.

Example 255

>   *GIN LTD owns all the shares in TONIC LTD, a company with no assets other
>   than cash. TONIC LTD has traded for many years, but now has ceased trading.
>   Its profits have been accumulated over the years. The shares originally cost GIN
>   LTD £80,000.*
>
>   *A dividend is paid to GIN LTD consisting of the total revenue reserves of
>   TONIC LTD. TONIC LTD is now worthless and on a sale of the shares by GIN
>   LTD a loss of £80,000 will arise.*
>
>   *The position is similar to that outlined in the previous paragraph. Any loss on
>   the disposal of shares coming within the scope of the 'dividend stripping'
>   provisions, is reduced in the same manner as outlined in paragraph 51.4.*

51.5.2   **Scope of the Provisions**

                 The provisions apply in any case where one company (the first
                 company) holds shares in another company (the second company):

         and

• the shareholding amounts to 10% or more of that class of shares in
  the second company (for this purpose the holdings of connected
  persons are taken into account)

         and

• the first company is not a dealing company

         and

• a distribution has been made to the first company in respect of
  those shares on or after 6 April 1974

         and

• the effect of the distribution has been to materially reduce the
  value of those shares.

"Distribution" has the meaning which it has for the purposes of the
corporation tax acts. It therefore extends beyond a dividend and
includes the various other asset transfers referred to in s130, and
other sections of the Corporation Tax Acts which deem transactions
to be a distribution.

As is the case with depreciatory transactions (s621) the dividend
stripping rules have application only:

— in the case of a loss arising. They have no application where a chargeable gain arises. Neither can it have the affect of turning a loss into a gain - at most it can reduce or cancel a loss.

— to a disposal by a company. It does not apply to a disposal by an individual or trustee.

s622

S622 operates by applying s621 in relation to any disposal of shares or securities to which s622 has application. This can occur even if the company disposing of the shares is not the company which held the shares when the offending dividend was paid. If the company disposing of the shares is a company to which the shares were transferred within "group relief" i.e. under s617 (see paragraph 76), then the section can have application to that company even though it did not receive the "depreciatory dividend". The wording of s622 is rather loose in that it states the section can have application to any company to which the holding was transferred within group relief, but does not explicitly state that it is referring to a transfer made within a group of which the company which received the depreciatory dividend, was a member. Presumably a court would read such a limitation into the section.

Example 256

*In **example 255** above, assume that Gin Limited transferred the shares in Tonic Limited to a wholly owned subsidiary of Gin Limited, Whiskey Limited. The shares are then disposed of by Whiskey Limited*

Notwithstanding that Whiskey Limited did not receive any dividend from Tonic Limited, it will be treated as if it had received the dividend which Gin Limited received. Under group relief Whiskey Limited would have been treated as having the same base cost in the shares as Gin Limited and, but for s622, would be treated as incurring an allowable loss on the disposal. However the affect of s622 is to reduce that loss, by adjusting it by a reasonable amount and in all probability by the sum of £80,000 in the example above.

A company might hold shares of more than one class in a second company. It is possible that it might receive a distribution in respect of one such class which would have the affect of reducing the value of shares of more than one class held by it. s622 applies in such circumstances only to restrict the loss on the disposal of shares of the class in respect of which the distribution was received. The loss arising on the disposal of shares of other classes (notwithstanding the extent to which the distribution may have contributed to losses on those shares) are not restricted by s622. As indicated in paragraph 51.2, dealing with s543, and the transfer of value between shares, it is unlikely (but by no means certain) that s543 would have application either in such circumstances.

As indicated above, s622 ensures that its application is preserved where the depreciated shares have been transferred intragroup prior to disposal outside the group. A similar provision to deal with the

circumstance in which the shares have been subject of a
reorganisation or reconstruction or amalgamation does not appear to
be made.

51.6   **Pre-disposal dividends**

Where a group holding company is considering of disposing of a
subsidiary company in the group, it has available to it a number of
options as to how it can realise the value of its shareholding in the
subsidiary.

It can sell the subsidiary outright, in which case the proceeds of sale
would be liable to corporation tax on companies' capital gains.

Alternatively, it might arrange to have the subsidiary distribute to it
all of the distributable reserves of the subsidiary by way of dividend,
and having thus reduced the value of the subsidiary, might sell the
subsidiary. The dividend received from the Irish resident subsidiary
would not be liable to corporation tax (other than surcharge on
undistributed investment income if a close company) and the
consideration for the sale of the shares in the subsidiary should be
reduced in broadly the amount of the dividend received from the
subsidiary, thus reducing the exposure to corporation tax on
companies' capital gains.

There is sometimes an obstacle to such a *pre-disposal dividend*. It
may be that the subsidiary to be disposed of does not have
distributable reserves, or sufficient distributable reserves to enable
its value to be reduced to a negligible amount by a suitably large
dividend. In the past this difficulty has sometimes been overcome by
arranging for the subsidiary (which is to be sold) to acquire a
subsidiary of its own; and to then transfer to that new subsidiary
some asset upon which a substantial profit may be crystallised. That
profit is then regarded as a realised profit and is available for
distribution to shareholders by way of dividend.

s623   FA96 s51 in an amendment now in s623(3) has countered this
approach by providing that where two companies leave a group as
associates (i.e. forming a mini group of their own) any dividend paid
by a member of that mini-group being disposed of to any member of
the vendor group of companies out of profits generated by the
transfer from one member to another of the mini-group of an asset, is
to be regarded as additional consideration for the disposal of the
shares in the mini-group. This is so whether or not the asset whose
disposal intra-group generated the profits out of which the dividend
was paid, is still retained within the mini-group of companies being
disposed of.

The provisions described above relating to pre disposal dividends
apply only to Irish resident companies. They do not have
application where an Irish resident company is disposing of the

shares in a non resident company or "non resident group of companies".

Example 257

Holdings PLC owns Property Ltd., a wholly owned subsidiary. Property Ltd. owns a building which cost it £1 million, and is now worth £10 million. Property Ltd. has no other assets or liabilities. Holdings PLC has a base cost for its shares in property Ltd. of £1 million.

If Holdings PLC disposed of its shares in Property Ltd for their value (presumably £10 million) a substantial capital gain would arise to it, which would be exposed to corporation tax on companies' capital gains. In order to avoid this, Holdings PLC arranges for Property Ltd. to create a new subsidiary of Property Ltd., Subco Ltd. Property Ltd. transfers its shares for a consideration of £10 million to Subco. It has thereby crystallised a distributable profit of £9 million. No chargeable gain arises since the transaction is intra group. Property Ltd. now pays a dividend to Holdings PLC of £9 million, having borrowed from a bank for the purpose. Holdings PLC can now sell Property Ltd. for its reduced value of £1 million, leaving it to the purchaser to arrange for the bank borrowings in Property Ltd. to be paid off.

Prior to FA 1996, Holdings PLC would have incurred no chargeable gain on the disposal of Property Ltd. since the consideration for the disposal amounted to £1 million only. s623 did not cause a gain to crystallise in Subco Ltd. on leaving the group with a property acquired intra group, since it was acquired from an associate company leaving the group at the same time (i.e. Property Ltd. which is now the principal company in relation to Subco).

The amendment in FA96 s51 (now s623(3)) would treat Holdings PLC as receiving consideration for its disposal of its shares in Property Ltd. of

- *£1 million, being the sale of proceeds of the shares and*

- *£9 million, being the amount of the dividend received pre-disposal.*

If in the example above Property Ltd. had shareholders funds consisting of their capital of £2 and revenue reserves of £1 million (accumulated rental income, after tax) before the transactions outlined above were entered into, then Property Ltd. would have been in a position to pay a dividend to Holdings PLC of £10 million, and thus reduce the value of its shares to £2. The application of s623(3) in such circumstances would be to treat Holdings PLC as receiving consideration for the disposal of the shares in Property Ltd. of:

- *sales proceeds of £2 and*

- *£9 million (pre-disposal dividend)*

In this case the pre-disposal dividend treated as part of the consideration for the disposal of the shares in Property Ltd. is not the entire dividend, but only that part of the dividend which was out of the gain realised on the transfer of an asset to Subco. That part of the dividend which was paid out of reserves accumulated from income arising from third parties, is not treated as additional consideration for the disposal of the shares, and would not be treated any differently than any other dividend received by Holdings PLC.

S623(3) is widely worded. As previously mentioned, it applies even where the asset whose transfer generated the profit out of which the dividend is paid, has been disposed of outside of the group before the dividend is paid. Thus, in the example above, it would not matter if Subco had managed to sell the building to a third party, before Holdings PLC sold the shares in Property Ltd.

There appears to be no time limits in s623(3). It does not appear to matter how much time may elapse between:

- the transfer of an asset between a company to be disposed of, and a subsidiary, thus crystallising distributable reserves and;

- the payment of a dividend by the company to be disposed of to the vendor group and;

- the date of sale of the shares of the company being disposed of.

It would seem the section can have application even where these three events are separated by many years, and even where the transfer of the asset intra group, and the payment of the dividend, were transactions not undertaken in contemplation of the sale of the shares in the company, and even where they were not undertaken for tax reasons at all.

s623   The wording of s623(3) is so wide in its plain meaning that it could have application to the sale of shares in a manufacturing company, where the manufacturing company had accumulated distributable reserves by selling its product to a sales subsidiary in the normal course of trade, and which sales subsidiary paid dividends to its parent out of those trading profits. Those profits would appear to be profits arising from the disposal of assets by one associated company to another, as referred to in s623(3). s623(3) is not expressed to be confined to profits generated by the transfer of chargeable assets only or only of assets on whose disposal a chargeable gain or allowable loss would arise. Presumably the Revenue would not seek to apply the section in such circumstances but it is not clear what discretion they have in the matter. The wide wording of s623(3) is unfortunate.

The wording of s623(3), is also ambiguous in another respect. s623(3) states that the pre-disposed dividend "shall be deemed....to be consideration....received by the member of the group or former member of the group in respect of a disposal which disposal gave rise to or was caused by the associated companies ceasing to be members of the group". There is no previous reference in s623(3) to "a member of the group or former member of the group" and accordingly it is not clear to what company reference is being made. The only previous references to companies in s623(3) is to "two or more associated companies". Arguably a sub-section which would have the effect of imposing a liability to tax, or increasing a liability to tax, should be more explicitly worded than this, if effect is to be given to it.

There is a further ambiguity in the wording. The pre-disposal dividend is deemed to be consideration received "in respect of a disposal" and two possible disposals are then mentioned i.e:-

- a disposal which gave rise to associated companies ceasing to be members of the group and

- a disposal which was caused by the associated companies ceasing to be members of the group. An example of the first type of disposal could be a sale by the parent company of a group of the shares in the associated companies.

An example of the second type of disposal could be the application of s623 to an asset held by one of the associated companies, obtained intra group while a group member. A single transaction, the sale of shares by the parent in the associated companies, could give rise to both types of disposal, giving rise to a liability to tax in two separate companies. The section does not indicate how one is to determine to which of the two disposals the additional consideration is to be attributed. Once again, it is arguable that the language used is less clear than that which is required to create, or to increase, a liability to tax.

There is one peculiar limitation to the application of s623 (3) (a) (II) i.e. that it is application only where two companies together leave a group, and together form a group immediately on leaving the first mentioned group. As mentioned in paragraph 81.3, where two companies simultaneously leaving a group do so by reason of becoming non-resident in Ireland, they cannot possibly themselves form a group, no matter what shareholding relationship exists between them. A group cannot consist of or include non-resident companies.

Example 258

> Company A has a wholly owned subsidiary, Company B which has in turn has a wholly owned subsidiary, Company C. All are Irish resident. Company B owned a shop in Cork which in 1996 it transferred to Company C, thereby realising, in accounting terms (but not for tax purposes by reason of group relief) a substantial distributable surplus. It immediately dividended that surplus to Company A. In 1997 Company B and Company C became non-resident immediately upon a sale to Mega Group Inc., a U.S.A. resident company.
>
> At the time when Company B and Company C ceased to be a member of the Company A group on disposal by Company A, Company B owned 100% of the shares in Company C. However they were not at that date associated companies, because they were not capable of being themselves a group of companies by reason of being non-resident companies.
>
> Accordingly, it would seem that the provisions of s623(3)(a)(ii) in relation to pre-disposal dividends does not have application to the dividend paid by Company B to Company A out of the surplus created by its transfer of a property to its fully owned subsidiary, Company C. That analysis is of course

dependent on the change of residence being absolutely simultaneous with the departure of Company B and C from the group.

s623   The provisions dealing with the pre-disposal dividend paid by companies ceasing to be a member of a group and funded from an intra group asset transfer are to be found in s623. That Section may also treat a company ceasing to be a member of a group as disposing of assets which are acquired within the previous ten years from another member of the group, where that other member does not also cease to be a member of the group at the same time, and where together, they do not, immediately after ceasing to be a member of the first mentioned group, themselves form a group. This is discussed in greater detail in paragraph 81.

The UK High Court case of Spectros International v Madden was concerned with the interpretation of a contract for the disposal of shares, which contract had been preceded by the payment of a very substantial dividend to the vendor. The case was not concerned with legislation similar to s623(3). Nonetheless, the case is of interest in considering the consequences of a pre-disposal dividend, if s623(3) did not have application. It is described in greater detail in paragraph 8.9.

52   **SHARE RELIEFS - SUMMARY CHART**

A chart summarising the main share reliefs is set out on the remaining pages of this Chapter.

COMPARISON OF MAIN SHARE RELIEFS		
	Retirement relief s598 and s599	**Roll-over relief s591**
• Holding Required	25% voting rights or 10% (provided 75% held by family)	not specified
• Residence of company	not specified	not specified
• Place of Incorporation	not specified	not specified

COMPARISON OF MAIN SHARE RELIEFS		
	Retirement relief s598 and s599	**Roll-over relief s591**
• Business of company	wholly or mainly trade/farming or 75% holding company of trading group	wholly or mainly trading or holding company of mainly 51% trading group or holding company
• Prior period of ownership	10 years	lesser of 3 years or from commencement of trade
• Working Director	Director 10 years - full time Director for 5 years	full or part time employee/direct or in group for 3 years
• Clawback	if lifetime disposals exceed £375,000 (other than to child of disponer) or on subsequent disposal by child within 10 years	On disposal of new shares if that disposal does not itself qualify for further relief
• Type of shares to which relief applies	no requirement	no requirement
• Individual only	yes	yes
• Value limit	£375,000 lifetime limit for third parties - none for child.	none
• Bona Fides requirement	no	yes
• Application of consideration	no requirement	in making qualifying investment
• unquoted company	no requirement	no requirement

NOTE : This chart is only a broad summary, and should not be relied on without reference to the discussion of the reliefs in the relevant paragraphs of the book. It is intended only as a general guide to the requirements of the reliefs. The reliefs are all subject to detailed conditions, and the chart only gives a broad summary of the main conditions.

53   LEASES - GENERAL INTRODUCTION

Sch14   TCA97 Sch14 sets out special rules for computing gains and losses
for CGT purposes on the disposal of leasehold interests.

Although the provisions deal mainly with leases of land, some of the
provisions also apply to leases of other assets.

Transactions in leases of land may be divided broadly into two
categories for CGT purposes:

- The creation of a leasehold interest by the grant of a lease; this is a
  part disposal of an asset and may involve a premium (part of
  which might be chargeable to income tax)

  and

- the sale or assignment of a leasehold interest;

It is important therefore to distinguish between the grant of a lease
and the sale or assignment of a lease (see paragraphs 54 and 55).

The term 'lease' in relation to land, includes an underlease, sublease,
or any tenancy or licence, and any agreement for a lease, etc. In the
case of land outside the State, it includes any corresponding interest.
Land includes any interest in land. The provisions set out in this
chapter apply equally to other assets in the same manner as they
apply in the case of land.

In relation to property other than land, the term 'lease' means any
kinds of agreement or arrangement under which payments are made
for the use of, or in respect of the property concerned.

54   GRANT OF LEASE

54.1   General outline - grant of lease

A lease of land may be granted out of a freehold property or out of
an existing lease. Where the lease is granted out of an existing lease
it is known as a sublease. In return for the grant of a lease a person
will usually receive a rent. Sometimes, in addition to the rent he will
receive a lump sum known as a premium; the premium is normally
payable at the time the lease is granted.

In the UK case of Clarke -v- United Real (Moorgate) Limited the
taxpayer company entered into an agreement with a life insurance
society under which, in consideration of the society repaying its past
and future costs associated with the development of the site, the

taxpayer granted a lease of the site to the society for a term of 99 years. The rent payable under the lease was below the market rent and it became lower the more the society had to pay to the taxpayer by way of reimbursement of its costs. It was held that the sums paid to the taxpayer company under the agreement constituted a premium.

Sch14 Para1   The term 'premium' is not defined in the Acts, but is stated to include:

"any like sum, whether payable to the intermediate or a superior lessor and for the purposes of this schedule any sum (other than a rent) paid on or in connection with the granting of a tenancy shall be presumed to have been paid by way of premium except in so far as other sufficient consideration for the payment is shown to have been given".

This must also be looked at in the context of the wide 'arm's length' rules which apply generally to all transactions. If the terms of the lease are not at arm's length, or if connected persons are involved, a premium may be deemed to have been paid (in addition to any actually paid) equal to the excess of the amount which could have been obtained on an 'arm's length' letting, over the amount, if any, actually paid.

In addition, in certain circumstances, a premium is deemed to have been paid. Details of these deemed premiums are set out in paragraph 60.

The grant of a lease is a part disposal of the asset (i.e. the leasehold interest or the freehold, out of which the lease was granted).

The rent receivable under a lease will, of course, be subject to income tax and not CGT. The income tax treatment of a premium, and following from that the CGT treatment of the premium, depends on whether the duration of the lease is for a period of 50 years or less, or exceeds 50 years.

In the following text, for the sake of simplicity, leases are referred to as

— a long lease (one which is for more than fifty years), and

— a short lease (one which is for fifty years or less).

A premium received on the grant of a long lease is not subject to income tax and the whole amount must be brought in for CGT as consideration for the part disposal. A premium received on the grant of a short lease will be partly subject to income tax (see paragraph 59 below); the balance only is brought in for CGT; and the detailed CGT rules for taxing the premium (or part of it) are dealt with below. The special rules for determining the duration of a lease are set out in paragraph 61.

s99   TCA97 s99 imposes a charge to income tax on the assignment of a lease (for a period not exceeding 50 years at date of grant), where the original grant was on terms below market value. The sum charged to tax is that part of the consideration for the assignment equal to the amount by which the premium (if any) on the grant of the lease was less than what could have been charged on an arm's length basis.

In so far as part of the consideration for the disposal of the lease was charged to income tax, the same amount will not be taken in as consideration in the capital gains tax computation on the disposal of the lease. However, there would not appear to be any right to take account of this actual or potential income tax charge the disposal of the lease, on the earlier occasion of the grant of the lease. As indicated above, the grant of a lease at under market value can give rise to a chargeable gain. The income tax consequences of the same grant, which only contingently crystallises on a subsequent sale, does not appear to be capable of interacting with the CGT computation on the occasion of the grant of the lease. The potential future income tax charge must be ignored in computing the consideration to be taken into account for CGT purposes on the grant of the lease. This is rather anomalous.

Example 259 Grant of Lease Out of Freehold

Jim purchased a freehold house in 1991. Having lived in it for seven years he granted a three year lease of the house to Joe in 1998 for a rent of £1,000 per annum and a premium of £5,000.

For CGT purposes the original asset (i.e. the freehold) has been divided into two parts, that is:

- *the three year leasehold interest which Jim granted to Joe.*

- *Jim's right to repossess the house at the end of the three years, and the right to receive the rent for the three year period.*

As Jim has retained a part of his original asset, he has made only a part disposal of the asset to Joe for a rent and a premium. The rent is subject to income tax and, therefore, is not subject to CGT; part of the premium only will be subject to income tax and the balance will be brought into the CGT computation, as consideration for the part disposal.

Example 260 Grant of Lease Out of a Leasehold

David owns a small premises used as an office. In 1992 he granted a 51 year lease of the premises to Luke in return for a rent and a premium. Luke set up his audit practice there and occupied the premises until 1998. In June 1998 he received an offer of a five year contract in England and decided to go there for five years. As he intended to come back to Ireland he wished to retain his leasehold interest in the premises. He, therefore, granted a five year sublease to Jenny in return for a rent and a premium.

In this case David has made a part disposal of the freehold premises. Luke has acquired an asset - i.e. a 51 year leasehold interest. When Luke granted a five year sublease he split his asset into two parts, that is:

- *the five year lease granted to Jenny, and*

- *his right to occupy the premises for the remaining part of his 51 year lease after the expiration of Jenny's five year lease, coupled with the right to receive the rent for the five year period.*

As Luke has retained part of his original asset (his 51 year lease) he has made a part disposal of that asset. The rent receivable by Luke from Jenny is subject to income tax and not to CGT. Only part of the premium received from Jenny is subject to income tax; the remaining part of the premium must, therefore, be brought in for CGT, as consideration for the part disposal.

55   SALE OR ASSIGNMENT OF LEASEHOLD INTEREST

55.1   Sale of leasehold interest is a disposal

Where a lease is sold or assigned no new interest is created and there is a disposal of the entire asset - i.e. the entire interest which the lessee owns in the lease. The amount received from the purchaser is simply consideration for the disposal of an asset, and the entire amount comes in for CGT - see the comment in paragraph 54.1 on the Income Tax Treatment of the disposal of a lease granted at undervalue.

Example 261

*If in **example 260**, Luke had not intended to return to Ireland he might have sold his leasehold interest instead of granting a five year sublease to Jenny. Had he done so, he would have retained no interest at all in the property. In that case, there would simply be a disposal of an asset for a capital sum.*

No part of the capital sum would be chargeable to income tax and the full amount would be brought into the CGT computation.

As there is less than 50 years of the lease remaining at the time of its disposal, it would be regarded as a wasting asset and the special rules applying to expenditure incurred on a lease which is a wasting asset would apply (see paragraph 57).

s99

TCA97 s99 imposes a charge to income tax on the assignment of a lease (for a period not exceeding 50 years at date of grant), where the original grant was on terms below market value. The sum charged to tax is that part of the consideration for the assignment equal to the amount by which the premium (if any) on the grant of the lease was less than what could have been charged on an arm's length basis.

In so far as part of the consideration for the disposal of the lease was charged to income tax, the same amount will not be taken in as consideration in the capital gains tax computation on the disposal of the lease. However, there would not appear to be any right to take account of this actual or potential income tax charge on disposal of the lease, on the earlier occasion of the grant of the lease. As indicated above, the grant of a lease at under market value can give rise to a chargeable gain. The income tax consequences of the same grant, which only contingently crystallises on a subsequent sale, does not appear to be capable of interacting with the CGT computation on the occasion of the grant of the lease. The potential future income tax charge must be ignored in computing the consideration to be taken into account for CGT purposes on the grant of the lease.

55.2   Cost of acquisition

A leasehold interest which is disposed of may have been acquired in a number of ways. Basically, it may have been acquired by being granted to the person making the disposal, or it may have been purchased by the person making the disposal. It could also of course have been inherited by him or gifted to him.

Where the acquisition was by way of original grant of the lease any **premium** payable for the grant will fall to be considered as part of the acquisition cost, subject to qualifications on the deductibility of such cost set out in paragraph 59.8 following.

s547

Where the lease is **granted by a connected party** (or in the other circumstances which would attract the application of s547 as explained in paragraph 16) the grant of the lease will be treated (both as regards the person granting it and the person receiving it) as being for a consideration equal to the open market value of the leasehold interest granted. That is effectively the same thing as saying that where s547 has application, the tenant will be deemed for CGT purposes to pay a premium at an open market rate for the lease, and the landlord granting the lease would be deemed (for CGT purposes) to have received such.

Where a leasehold interest is acquired by **gift or inheritance** it will be treated as having been acquired for a consideration equal to its open market value, in the same manner as any other asset, and as explained in paragraph 16.

Where a pre-existing lease is **purchased** from the existing leaseholder, the sum paid for it is treated as a cost of acquisition, as it would in relation to any other asset so acquired. Similarly, if acquired from a connected party, or otherwise in circumstances which attract the application of s.9, the acquisition will be treated for a consideration equal to the open market of the asset (see paragraph 16).

The UK case of Bayley v Rogers dealt with a lease which was acquired by virtue of a court order made under the UK Landlord and Tenant Act 1954. Under that Act, in certain circumstances a tenant was entitled to obtain a new lease from his landlord, on the termination of his old lease. Where the new lease was not granted by agreement between the tenant and the landlord, the tenant was entitled to apply to the courts to seek the grant of the new lease. The case dealt with an issue which was relevant to the acquisition cost of a lease granted to a tenant by reason of statutory rights under Landlord and Tenant legislation (or otherwise). It was argued (for the taxpayer) that the new lease which was obtained was derived from the old lease which had expired and that the provisions relating to assets derived from other assets (see paragraph 9.11) had application. If the argument was successful, part of the cost of the old lease would have been attributed to the new lease. The argument was, however, rejected by the Court. The Court recognised that the tenant *"would have had no locus standi to apply to the court for a new lease under the (Landlord and Tenant) Act (1954)"* had he not possessed the original and expired lease. Notwithstanding this however the original lease could not be said to have merged with the new one (it had already expired prior to the grant of the new one) nor had it been divided, nor had it changed its nature, nor had rights or interests in or over the original lease been created or extinguished, as referred to in s559 dealing with *"assets derived from other assets"*.

Where a lease is obtained by reason of a court order on foot of landlord and tenant legislation, it represents the acquisition of a new asset. The manner of its acquisition cannot be described as being *"by way of a bargain made at arm's length"* as referred to in s547(1)(a). It is not acquired by way of bargain at all, whether at arm's length or otherwise. It is acquired by way of a court order given on foot of a statute and the terms of the lease are determined by the Court, and not by way of bargaining between the landlord and the tenant. It would seem therefore that s547 would apply to the acquisition of a lease in such circumstances and would deem the lease to be acquired by the tenant at open market value. It is a question of fact, to be determined in every instance, as to whether a lease so granted has a market value at the date of its acquisition. If it did have such a value, it would represent an acquisition cost for the tenant, but it would also represent a deemed consideration for its grant, received by the landlord. It would seem particularly harsh on a landlord to not only be compelled by the Courts to grant a lease on terms over which he would have had little control, but to be also treated by the Courts as having received consideration for the grant which in fact he never received. Nonetheless, where the facts regarding valuations support it, such a situation would seem possible.

The UK case of Bayley v Rogers is also discussed in paragraph 61.

56 CHARGE TO CGT

TCA97 Sch14 Para 3 states that:

Sch14 Para 3 *"Subject to this Schedule, where the payment of a premium is required under a lease of land or otherwise under the terms subject to which a lease is granted, there is a part disposal of the freehold or other asset out of which the lease is granted".*

In general terms, therefore, where a lease is granted and the payment of a premium is required, there is a part disposal of the freehold or superior leasehold interest, as described above.

This specific charge refers only to the grant of a leasehold interest. The sale or assignment of a leasehold interest already in existence (which is simply a disposal of an asset) is adequately covered under the general charge to CGT.

In some case, payments made during the currency of a lease can be deemed to be 'premiums' for CGT purposes. These are dealt with in paragraph 60.

Where a lease is granted for a premium, the disposal involved is a part disposal of the interest in the property which the grantor possesses. The disposal is not a disposal of the lease which he has granted. The lease is created by the act of granting it. An asset must exist and be owned prior to disposal for a disposal of that asset to occur, subject to statutory exceptions such as in the case of options.

- **Revenue/Chief Inspector's CGT Manual :**

  - In the Revenue Commissioners capital gains tax manual at Paragraph 19.2.21.27 it is stated "The surrender of a lease by a lease holder before the lease expires and the grant to him of a new lease for the same or an extended term should not, in practice, be regarded as a disposal or part disposal of the old lease, unless a capital sum is received by the lessee. This practice avoids the necessity of obtaining valuations and of computing the gain (or less) at the date of change".

  - In the situation outlined in the quote above it is difficult to see that a chargeable gain would ever arise, whereas an allowable loss might arise, on the premature termination of the lease. The Revenue practice is therefore one which the taxpayer should consider carefully before adopting it.

57   **LEASE AS A WASTING ASSET**

57.1   **Wasted Expenditure - calculation**

Sch14 Para2   Normally expenditure attributable to a wasting asset is written off at a uniform rate over the period of its useful life (see paragraph 9 for the general rules on wasting assets). This general rule does not apply to a lease. Capital expenditure incurred on the acquisition of a lease is 'wasted' in accordance with a special Table in Sch14 Para2.

If the term of the lease is not an exact number of years, the percentage to be taken from the table is

— the percentage for the whole number of years, *plus*

— one twelfth of the difference between that and the next number of years for each odd month (14 days or more are counted as one month)

The provisions dealing with the wasting of expenditure on a lease of land are contained in Sch14 Para2.

The Table - "Lease as a wasting asset" is set out on the following page.

Sch14 Para2   A lease of land is not regarded as a wasting asset *until* the time when its duration does not exceed 50 years.

A lease for a term of fifty years or less (a 'short lease') is always a wasting asset. A lease for more than fifty years (a 'long lease') becomes a wasting asset when it has fifty years or less to run.

The operation of the table is best illustrated by an example which follows the "wasting" table for leases set out on the following page.

TABLE - LEASE AS A WASTING ASSET

Years	%	Years	%
50		25	81.1
(or more)	100.0	24	79.6
49	99.7	23	78.1
48	99.3	22	76.4
47	98.9	21	74.6
46	98.5	20	72.8
45	98.1	19	70.8
44	97.6	18	68.7
43	97.1	17	66.5
42	96.6	16	64.1
41	96.0	15	61.6
40	95.5	14	59.0
39	94.8	13	56.2
38	94.2	12	53.2
37	93.5	11	50.0
36	92.8	10	46.7
35	92.0	9	43.2
34	91.2	8	39.4
33	90.3	7	35.4
32	89.4	6	31.2
31	88.4	5	26.7
30	87.3	4	22.0
29	86.2	3	17.0
28	85.1	2	11.6
27	83.8	1	6.0
26	82.5	0	0.00

Example 262: (Without Enhancement Expenditure)

Jim purchased a leasehold interest for £15,000 from Barney when it had twenty years to run. After five years he sold it to Pat for £50,000.

Jim's deductible expenditure is calculated as follows:

(a) Take the percentage on the table relating to a lease with twenty years to run. In this case 72.8 per cent.

(b) Take the percentage on the table relating to a lease with fifteen years to run. In this case 61.6 per cent.

(c) Waste Jim's expenditure of £15,000 in the proportion which the reduction in percentage bears to the percentage at the beginning of his period of ownership

$$\frac{(i.e.\ 72.8 - 61.6)}{72.8}$$

The calculation then is:

	£
Cost of Lease	15000
Disallow £15,000 x $\frac{(72.8 - 61.6)}{72.8}$ =	2,308
Deductible expenditure to be indexed	12,692

There are special rules for determining the duration of a lease (see paragraph 61).

The notation used in Sch14 for the formula described above is

$$\frac{P(1) - P(3)}{P(1)} = \text{wasted part of expenditure} \quad \text{where}$$

P(1) is the percentage of the beginning of the period of ownership of the lease, and

P(3) is the percentage at the time of the disposal.

In the above example, **P(1)** is 72.8 and **P(3)** is 61.6.

The treatment of enhancement expenditure incurred on leasehold property is set out in the following example.

Example 263 (including Subsequent Enhancement Expenditure)

Let us take the facts in **example 260**, but in addition, let us assume that two years after he acquired the lease, Jim spent £2,000 on an extension to the buildings. At that time, the expenditure was reflected in the nature of the lease.

This does not affect the deductible expenditure of £12,692 already calculated.

The additional expenditure of £2,000 is treated as wasting away only from the time that expenditure is reflected in the nature of the lease.

The formula used in Sch14 is

$$Expenditure\ x\ \frac{P(2) - P(3)}{P(2)} = Wasted\ Expenditure \quad Where$$

P(2) is the percentage applicable to the duration of the lease at the time the expenditure is first reflected in the nature of the lease.

P(3) has the same meaning as in the previous example.

$$Wasted\ expenditure = \quad £2,000\ x\ \frac{68.7 - 61.6}{68.7} = £207$$

The allowable part of the enhancement cost is therefore £2,000 - £207 = £1,793.

The total allowable expenditure is therefore

(a) Part of Cost	£12,692
(b) Part of enhancement cost	£1,793

The cost (£12,692) is indexed from the date of acquisition of the lease. The enhancement expenditure (£1,793) is indexed from the date the expenditure was reflected in the nature of the lease.

If a lease of land is acquired at a time when it is subject to a sublease which is granted at a rent below market value, the head lease value would be depressed. In such circumstances, where it is estimated (at the time of acquisition of the head lease) that the value of that head lease when the sublease ceases will exceed the cost of the head lease, that cost will not be treated as wasting, until the sublease ceases.

57.2 Expenditure : Capital Allowances

s561

Where expenditure on the acquisition or enhancement of a lease of property qualifies for capital allowances, the lease (or part of it) may not be treated as a wasting asset. The exclusion from the wasting asset category provided by s561 for other assets qualifying for capital allowance is also applied to leases.

s561 is divided into two sub-paragraphs,

— one dealing with an asset used for business purposes throughout its entire period of ownership, and

— the other dealing with the position where it is partly used for other purposes.

s561(1)

Where the leased asset is used, from the beginning of the period of ownership of the lease solely for the purposes of a trade or profession by the person making the disposal, and any expenditure (cost or enhancement) could qualify for a capital allowances deduction, the asset is not a wasting asset.

s561(2)

Where throughout the entire period of ownership, the leased asset has been used partly for business purposes and partly for other purposes, or has not been used throughout the entire period of ownership for business purposes, or which has otherwise qualified in part only for capital allowances, the expenditure must be split into the business and non-business element. The apportionment is made in the basis of the ratio between the expenditure qualifying for allowances, and the non-qualifying element of the expenditure. The method of apportionment is dealt with in more detail in s560.

If, for example, a lessee took a 40 year lease of a building which did not originally qualify for capital allowances in the hands of the landlord, and that leasee can claim an allowance in respect of subsequent enhancement expenditure incurred by him, what is the status of the lease? Does it fall within s561(1) where no part of it is wasting, or within s561(2) where it must be apportioned?

It is clear that if it fell within s561(1) it would mean the wasting status of a lease could be changed at a later stage if any subsequent enhancement expenditure qualified for capital allowances (prior to the date of disposal).

It is interesting to note that s561(1) is not stated to be subject to s561(2). It may be possible to argue that the ejusdem generis rule applies to s561(2) to limit the category of assets which 'otherwise qualified in part only for capital allowances' to cases where the asset does not qualify because of non-business use, and not merely because the entire expenditure did not qualify because of some restriction in legislation prohibiting a full allowance.

The treatment of the expenditure which attracted capital allowances is described in paragraph 9.8.

57.3 **Leases owned at 6 April 1974**

Where a leasehold interest is owned at 6 April 1974, the owner is treated as disposing of it, and reacquiring it at that date (see paragraph 13).

The calculation of the amount of the expenditure to be wasted depends on the duration of the lease at the beginning of the period of ownership, and its duration at the date of disposal.

In determining the P(1) factor in the wasting formula, the question arises in the case of a lease owned at 6 April 1974, as to whether the period of ownership is to be taken from the actual acquisition date, or from 6 April 1974.

s28 The term 'period of ownership' is defined only for the purposes of s28, which deals with the rates of tax. It provides that in determining the rate of tax, the period is determined by reference to the actual date of acquisition (prior to 6 April 1974). This provision, however, does not apply for any other purpose, and the beginning of the period of ownership of the lease must be taken at its deemed acquisition date (i.e. 6 April 1974) and not the actual acquisition date, if earlier. The expression is also defined in s592 which deals with the lower (26%) rate of CGT.

58   INTERACTION OF CGT WITH INCOME TAX

58.1   Income Tax - Sch D, Case V rules

s544

As a general principle, any part of the consideration for disposal of an asset which come within the charge to Income Tax as income, does not come within the charge to CGT. Also, expenditure which would be deductible in arriving at taxable income may not be deducted in arriving at the allowable cost in computing a chargeable gain. The rules which apply this principle for CGT generally, do not always apply in relation to leases of land. The Capital Gains Tax legislation on leases substitutes special rules in the case of certain leases.

s551
Sch14 para6(5)

In calculating a gain on the grant of a lease of land, the part of the premium subject to income tax is normally excluded. Where however, the lease is created out of a short lease there is no exclusion for the part of the premium subject to income tax. The net premium chargeable to income tax may be deducted from any gain arising on the disposal; the deduction cannot operate to convert a gain into a loss or to increase any loss. This is set in more detail in paragraph 59.8.

For income tax the amount of a premium regarded as capital and excluded from the income tax charge is determined by the formula:

$$P \times \frac{N - 1}{50} \text{ Where}$$

P = Premium, and

N = The term (duration) of the lease

If a lease was granted out of a freehold for a term of 21 years for a rent and a premium of £50,000 the amount regarded as a capital receipt is:

$$£50,000 \times \frac{21 - 1}{50} = £20,000$$

The figure of £20,000 would be regarded as capital consideration received by the lessor for a part disposal of his freehold - see also paragraph 54.1.

59   TRANSACTIONS FOR CONSIDERATION

59.1   General

The transactions considered in the following paragraph are:

- Sale of a Long Lease (paragraph 59.2)

- Sale of a Short Lease (paragraph 59.3)

- Grant of a Long Lease out of a Freehold
  or Long Lease (paragraph 59.4)

- Grant of a Short Lease out of a Freehold or Long Lease (paragraph 59.5)

- Grant of a Short Lease out of a Short or
  Lease (paragraph 59.6)

59.2   Sale of a Long Lease

A capital sum received for the sale or assignment of a long lease does not come within the charge to income tax. If the lease at the time of disposal has more than fifty years to run it is not a wasting asset for CGT purposes. Therefore, no complications arise on the sale of a long lease with more than fifty years to run at the time of disposal.

Example 264

On January 1 1988, Joe was granted a 99 year lease out of freehold property at a full rent and a premium of £10,000. On 31 January 1993, he sold it to William for £25,000.

The gain is calculated as follows:

	£
Sale Price	*25,000*
Cost as indexed (10,000 x 1.146)	*11,460*
Chargeable Gain	*13,540*

The situation is slightly more complex if the lease has fifty years or less to run at the time of disposal, as it is now a wasting asset.

Example 265

On 1 January 1989 Joe was granted a 51 year lease out of freehold property at a full rent and a premium of £10,000. On 1 January, 1993 he sold it to William for £25,000.

The gain is calculated as follows: £   £
Consideration received   25,000
Expenditure   10,000

Less £10,000 x $\dfrac{(100 - 98.9)^*}{100}$ =   110

Deductible Expenditure   9,890
_____

£9,890 indexed at 1.109   10,968
Chargeable Gain   14,032

Note: The lease becomes a wasting asset when it has 50 years to run. The percentage for 50 years is 100; the percentage for 47 years is 98.9 (from the Table in paragraph 57.1).

59.3   **Sale or assignment of a Short Lease**

The sale or assignment of a short lease is a disposal of the entire asset (that is, the leasehold interest), which is a wasting asset. Consideration must be given to the following points:

• the full consideration for the sale is a capital receipt;

• any capital expenditure on acquisition must be "wasted" in arriving at expenditure deductible for CGT.

Example 266

On 1 January 1989, Robert was granted a 21 years lease out of a freehold for a rent and a premium of £50,000. On 1 January 1993, he sold the lease to Michael for £85,000.

The chargeable gain is calculated as follows: £   £
Consideration Received   85,000
Expenditure   50,000

Disallow 50,000 x $\dfrac{(74.6 - 66.5)}{74.6}$ =   5,429

Deductible Expenditure   44,571
_____

£44,571 indexed at 1.146   51,078
Chargeable Gain   33,922

The reader is also referred to paragraph 54.1 for further details of the inter-reaction of this area with the income tax rules.

59.4   **Grant of a Long Lease (out of a Freehold or Long Lease)**

In this case there is a part disposal out of the freehold (or long leasehold). There are no problems relating to the income tax or wasting asset provisions; no part of the cost is allowable for income tax, nor is the lease a wasting asset. In addition, no part of the proceeds is chargeable to income tax.

Example 267

On 30 June 1990, Peter was granted a 99 year lease out of a freehold property for an annual rent and a premium of £25,000. On 30 June 1992 he granted a 60 year sublease to Bill at an annual rent and a premium of £35,000. The market value of the 99 year lease subject to the sublease at 30 June 1992, was £5,000.

The gain is calculated as follows:	£	£
Consideration received		35,000
Cost	25,000	
Attributable to Part Disposal		
$25,000 \times \dfrac{35,000}{5,000 + 35,000} =$	21,875	
£21,875 indexed at 1.064		23,275
Chargeable Gain		11,725

59.5   **Grant of a Short Lease (out of a Freehold or Long Lease)**

In this case there is a part disposal out of the freehold or long lease as the case may be. The main points to be considered are:

Sch14 Para 6   Part of the consideration received (the premium) will be subject to income tax. Accordingly, that part must be excluded from the Capital Gains Tax computation Sch14 Para 6. However, see paragraph 54.1 where the lease is granted at an undervalue.

A special rule applies in the working of the part disposal formula. The numerator in the part disposal formula will be the capital portion of the premium, but the denominator will be the aggregate of the full premium plus the value of what remains Sch14 Para 6.

Sch14 Para 3   In applying the part disposal rules, the property which remains undisposed of will include a right to any rent or other payments (other than the premium). The value of such rights must be included in the value of the property which remains undisposed of Sch14 Para 3.

The rules are best illustrated by an example.

Example 268

Peter acquired a freehold property on 1 June 1989 for £30,000. On 1 June 1992 he granted a 31 year lease for a rent, and a premium of £40,000. Assume the market value of the property, subject to the lease, is £25,000 (including the value of the reversionary interest, and the right to receive the rent for the duration of the lease).

The gain is calculated as follows:

Consideration received Premium £40,000

$$\text{Capital element } £40,000 \times \frac{31 - 1}{50} = £24,000$$

Cost :

$$£30,000 \times \frac{£24,000}{£40,000^* + £25,000} = £11,077$$

Indexed @ 1.109 £12,284

Chargeable Gain £11,716

*Note: The denominator in the part disposal formula is normally the aggregate of the consideration received for the disposal and the market value of what remains. The 1975 Act specifically provides that the part of the consideration chargeable to income tax (in this case £16,000) must be excluded from the computation except when calculating the denominator of the part disposal formula.

59.6 Grant of a Short Lease Out of a Short Lease

Where a person has a short lease of property, and out of it he grants a sublease, he has made a part disposal of his leasehold interest.

Sch14, Paras 5, 6 and 7 set out special rules for computing the gain, or loss for CGT purposes in such a case.

59.7 Expenditure Attributable to Part Disposal

s557

The normal part disposal rules of s557 do not apply. Those rules are excluded by Sch 14 Para 5; and instead, the special rules set out in Sch 14 Para 5 apply. The part of the cost, and enhancement expenditure attributable to the part disposal, is the amount of that expenditure which is treated as wasting during the period of the sublease (calculated under the Table in Sch 14 Para 2). The amount calculated on this basis is restricted where the premium charged on the grant of the sublease could have been higher if the sublease was granted at the same rent as that payable under the head lease. A further restriction in the amount of expenditure allowable for CGT purposes occurs where the sublease refers only to part of the premises. These rules are illustrated in the following examples (in paragraph 59.8).

59.8 Consideration Chargeable

Sch14 Para 6

Sch14 Para 6 excludes the part of the consideration chargeable as income. Paragraph 5(2) however, gives a deduction from the gain for the amount chargeable as income for Schedule D, Case V purposes. The combined effect of those two provisions would, in effect, give a double deduction for the amount chargeable as income

— by excluding it from the sale proceeds taken into account for CGT, and

— allowing a deduction for it in the computation of a gain or loss for CGT purposes.

The answer to this apparently generous treatment is to be found in s544, which states that *'no deduction shall be allowable in a computation under this Act more than once from any sum, or from more than one sum'.* Clearly, only one deduction is allowable.

Sch14 Para 6(2) only applies to the computation of a gain or loss on the grant of a short lease out of a short lease. That rule being specific to those circumstances, would take priority over the general rule in Para 6(1) which would apply in other circumstances. Where a sublease is granted out of a short lease, the amount chargeable as income would not be excluded from the consideration brought into the computation. The gain or loss would be calculated on the basis of including the full consideration, and any resulting gain would be reduced by the amount chargeable as income.

Example 269

On 30 June 1989 Robert was granted a 31 year lease of a property for business use. He paid an initial premium of £20,000, and the annual rent was £10,000. On 30 June 1992, he ceased business. On that date he granted a sublease of the property for 21 years to Jim for a premium of £40,000 and annual rent of £10,000.

His gain is calculated as follows:

INCOME TAX POSITION
1989 PREMIUM PAID BY ROBERT:

The part of the 1989 premium chargeable to income tax (Sch D Case V) on the landlord is :

$$£20,000 - \left(£20,000 \times \frac{31 - 1}{50} \right) = £8,000$$

Robert is treated (for income tax purposes) as paying an additional rent of £8,000 over the period of the lease - i.e. 1/31 x £8,000 (£258) each full year.

1992 PREMIUM RECEIVED BY ROBERT

Robert is chargeable to income tax on

$£40,000 - \left(£40,000 \times \dfrac{21 - 1}{50}\right) =$	£24,000
He is entitled to deduct the deemed additional rent payable over the period of the sublease he has granted i.e. £258 x 21 =	£5,418
Amount chargeable under Sch D, Case V	£18,582

CALCULATION OF CGT PAYABLE:

Proceeds of disposal	£40,000

Note: *Instead of bringing in only the non-income part of the premium, the amount of the premium taxed as income is deducted from the gain-Sch14 Para 3.*

Cost: - premium paid -	£20,000

Sch 14, Para 5

The normal part disposal rules do not apply to calculations involved in the grant of a short lease out of a short lease. Instead the deductible expenditure is calculated by reference to the amount which would have 'wasted' during the period of the sublease:

balance forward	£40,000
i.e. £20,000 $\times \dfrac{85.1 - 35.4}{88.4}$ =	£11,224
indexed at 1.109 =	£12,447
	£27,553
Less amount chargeable to Income Tax (Schedule 3, paragraph 5(2) CGTA 1975)	£18,582
Gain	£8,971

In the calculation of the amount wasting during the sublease (above), the denominator of the fraction (88.4) is the figure from the table in paragraph 57.1 for the duration of the head lease i.e. 31 years. The numerators represent the figure for the duration of the head lease at the date the sublease is granted (85.1) and the figure for the duration of the head lease at the date the sublease expires (35.4).

If the premium received for the grant of the short sublease is less than the premium which would have been charged if the sublease was granted at the same rent as is payable under the head lease, the part of the cost of the head lease which is allowable in computing the gain (or loss) is reduced proportionally.

Example 270

If in **example 269,** *Robert had granted the sublease for a premium of £40,000 (as before) and an increased annual rent of £20,000, the deduction for the premium paid to the landlord in 1979 would be restricted. Let us assume that the value of the premium which could have been obtained if the sublease was granted at a rent of £10,000 per annum is £70,000.*

Amount wasted during period of	£11,244
Restricted to	
11,244 $\times \dfrac{40,000}{70,000}$ =	£6,425
Indexed @ 1.109	£7,125

59.9   **Restriction of Loss**

Sch14 Para 7   If a CGT arose on the grant of the sublease, the loss must be reduced
                  by the amount of additional rent deemed to be paid by Robert (in
                  example 262) for the duration of the sublease (i.e. £5,418). This rule is
                  contained in Sch14 Para 7. The deduction of the deemed rent from
                  the loss cannot reduce the loss below NIL.

60   **DEEMED PREMIUMS**

60.1   **Income Tax rules applied**

Sch14 Para 4   Apart from a premium arising on the grant of a lease, certain other
                  payments made by the lessee during the currency of the lease are
                  deemed to be premiums:

- a sum payable by the lessee under the terms of the lease in lieu of
  rent, or as a consideration for the surrender of the lease is deemed
  to be a premium paid for the period in respect of which the
  payment was made [Sch14 Para 4(1)].

- a sum payable by the lessee as consideration (other than rent) for
  the waiver or variation of any of the terms of the lease is deemed
  to be a premium paid for the period for which the variation or
  waiver is effective [Sch14 Para 4(2)].

- Where no consideration is paid for the waiver or variation of the
  terms of a lease, in certain circumstances a full market value
  premium can be deemed to have been paid. This happens where
  the transaction is not at arm's length', and in particular, where it is
  entered into gratuitously. The lessor is treated as receiving a
  premium of such an amount as would have been paid if the
  transaction was at arm's length.

Where such payments are deemed to be a premium, (in a case where
the payment is not in respect of the surrender of the lease), both the
lessor and lessee are treated as if the payment represented a
premium for the grant of a lease due at the time of grant of the
original lease. The calculations involved in the original grant of the
lease are amended accordingly, and any necessary adjustments, are
made. Where, however,the landlord is himself a lessee in respect of
the head lease out of which the sublease was granted, then if the
duration of that head lease is 50 years or less, the treatment of the
deemed premium is different. The payment is treated as a premium
for the grant of a lease for the period in respect of which the payment
was made. The provisions outlined in paragraph 59.6 (sublease out
of a short lease) apply in taxing the landlord-as if a new short lease
had been granted by him for that period.

Where the payment is in respect of the surrender of the lease, the
landlord is treated as disposing of his interest in the lease for the

consideration involved. In the case of the tenant, the expenditure is treated as enhancement expenditure.

s98   s98 may deem a premium to be paid where the lessee is obliged under the lease to carry out work on the premises. This provision does not apply where the expenditure concerned would be deductible from the rent for income tax purposes (i.e. repairs). The measure of the deemed premium, is the amount by which the work has increased the value of the landlord's interest in the premises. Such a deemed premium is taxed on the lessor in the normal manner. However, the lessor has, in effect, expended this amount on the premises, and provision is made to give him an allowance for it in computing any gain or loss on the disposal (or part disposal) of his interest in the property. He is treated as incurring enhancement expenditure on the property at the date the lease to which it relates was granted.

Sch14 Para 8 provides that:

Sch14 Para 8   *"Where under s98(2)..... income tax is chargeable on any amount, as being a premium the payment of which is deemed to required by the lease, the person so chargeable shall be treated for the purposes of the computation of any gain accruing to him on the disposal by way grant of the lease, and on any subsequent disposal of the asset out of which the lease was granted, as having incurred at the time the lease was granted expenditure of that amount (in addition to any other expenditure) attributable to the asset under s552(1)(b)".*

61   DURATION OF A LEASE

61.1   Duration of lease - special rules

Special rules are set out for determining the duration of a lease.

Sch14 Para 9   Where the lease can be terminated by the landlord under the terms of the lease on his giving notice to the tenant, the lease cannot be treated as being for a period beyond the earliest time at which the landlord could terminate it by giving the required notice to the tenant.

Where any of the terms of the lease (whether relating to forfeiture or any other matter) or any other circumstances render it unlikely that the lease will continue for its full term, the lease is treated as being for that shorter period. In particular, where the lease provides for increased rent or obligations on the part of the lessee from a given date, coupled with a right of the lessee to terminate the lease at that time, the term of the lease is treated as running to that date.

Where the lease provides for the extension of the lease by the lessee, the term of the lease is treated as running for as long as the lessee can extend-subject to any right of the landlord to terminate the lease.

The duration of the lease is to be decided by reference to facts which were known or ascertainable when the lease is granted.

In Irish Landlord and Tenant law, it is very difficulty for a landlord who has granted a lease to a tenant over a building which is used by the tenant for business purposes to ever terminate the tenant's right to occupation of the premises, for so long as the tenant meets his obligations under the lease. Even if the lease was for a fixed period of years, then, provided it exceeds a certain minimum number the tenant will be entitled under the Landlord & Tenant Act to obtain a new lease on the expiry of the old lease, whether or not the landlord wishes to grant such a lease. The tenant may, if necessary, seek the assistance of the Courts in compelling the landlord to grant the new lease.

Sch14 Para 9 Against such a background, it is tempting to assume that the duration of a lease, even under the special rules set out in paragraph 8 of schedule 3, is almost indefinite, and that a lease would be unlikely to constitute a wasting asset (i.e. one with expected useful life of less than 50 years). This is not the case. This particular issue was examined in the UK case of Bayley v Rogers, in the context of UK landlord and tenant legislation which, for the purposes of capital gains tax, is similar to the Irish legislation.

The case of Bayley v Rogers concerned a Mr. Rogers who in 1960 received a 14 year lease of a business premises. That lease would have expired in December 1974. Mr. Rogers made application to the Court under the UK Landlord & Tenant Act 1954 to receive a new lease on the expiration of his original lease. That new lease, to which he was entitled as of right, was granted in December 1974 by order of the Court. The taxpayer sold the lease in July 1976. Under the rules then applying in the UK for the computation of a gain, it was necessary to determine the period of ownership of the lease disposed of by Mr. Rogers in 1976. Mr. Rogers claimed that that period of ownership should date back to the grant to him of a lease originally, in 1960.

This was rejected by the Court. Browne Wilkinson J. explained his decision in the following terms

"S.29 (of the UK Landlord and Tenant Act 1954) in terms enables the court, on an application for a "new tenancy", to order the grant of a tenancy. The tenancy so ordered, the new tenancy, may differ substantially from the current tenancy which gave the tenant locus standi to apply. For example, if only part of the premises comprised in the original tenancy is used for business purposes, the new tenancy under the 1954 Act will be limited to a tenancy of that part of those premises; therefore the subject matter of the demise may be different. Secondly, the rent is not the rent reserved by the original tenancy, but, subject to certain modifications, is the open market rent of the premises at the date of the court order. Thirdly, under the other terms of the original tenancy already taken into account, the

court is not bound to order that the other terms of the new tenancy shall be the same as the terms of the old tenancy. Accordingly, it seems to me clear that a tenancy granted under part 2 of the Landlord and Tenant Act 1954 (UK) is, as the Act itself describes it, "a new tenancy", having possibly different terms, different subject matter and different rent. In those circumstances, it seems to me clear that the asset which the taxpayer disposed of in July 1976 was the lease that he was granted in December 1974, being a new tenancy, a new asset acquired for the first time on that occasion."

The case of Bayley v Rogers is relevant in considering the duration of a lease. It makes it clear that a new lease, granted to a tenant on foot of landlord and tenant legislation, is not a continuation of the old lease, but is a separate lease, and a separate asset in itself. Its duration, and the duration of the old lease, must be decided without regard to each other. It also makes clear that the reference in Sch14 Para 9 to the terms of a lease providing for its extension by the lessee, are not a reference to the situation where landlord and tenant legislation (as opposed to the lease itself) provides for the granting of a new lease (as opposed to the extension of an old lease).

The case of Bayley v Rogers also has relevance in relation to determining the base cost of a lease (see paragraph 55.2).

The UK case of Lewis v Walters dealt with the sale of a lease that had an expired term of 16 years. The Leasehold Reform Act 1967 gave the tenant the right to extend the lease for a further 50 years. Accordingly, the taxpayer claimed that the lease was not a wasting asset.

It was held that the legislation read in its ordinary and natural way required that the provision for the extension of the lease should be included among "the terms of the lease". The provision for extension relied on by the taxpayer was not in the terms of the lease - it was in the Leasehold Reform Act 1967:

Even if the statutory right in the 1967 Act was to be regarded as a term of the lease, it would not constitute a provision for the extension of the lease beyond a given date within the meaning of the legislation. It would be a new and separate lease (Bayley v Rogers considered).

In any event, the lease could not be extended by the taxpayer because the tenant had not, during his lifetime, given notice to the landlord of his desire to have an extended lease.

62   LEASES OF PROPERTY OTHER THAN LAND

62.1   Broad Outline - other leases

Some of the special provisions dealing with a lease of land, also apply to leases of other property. All the provisions set out in this chapter on leases apply with the exception of:

Schedule 3 paragraph 1 : the special "wasting" provisions on leases of land (see paragraph 57.1).

Schedule 3 paragraph 5 :the rules relating to the exclusion of the part of a premium taxed under Sch D, Case V (see paragraph 54 et seq.).

Schedule 3 paragraph 6 : the special rule dealing with the reduction of a loss for CGT purposes by the amount of the premium paid on acquisition of the main lease which is allowed for income tax purposes on the grant of a sublease of the property (see paragraph 59.9).

Sch14 Para 10   In the case of a lease of an asset which is movable property, it would be possible to have a lease for a period far in excess of the life of that asset. Sch14 Para 10 provides a rule for determining the duration of the lease in such circumstances:

"In the case of a lease of a wasting asset which is movable property, the lease shall be assumed to terminate not later than the end of the life of the wasting asset".

CHAPTER 8   ASSETS HELD IN A FIDUCIARY OR REPRESENTATIVE CAPACITY

63   NOMINEES/TRUSTEES/EXECUTORS

63.1   Broad Outline

A difficulty which inevitably arises when considering the application of the CGT rules to persons holding, and/or dealing with assets in a representative or fiduciary capacity, is the necessity to have a broad understanding of the general legal principles in the area of trust law.

The CGT legislation recognises many different capacities in which a person may hold or deal in assets of which he is not the beneficial owner. It practice, there are in effect three broad categories of persons who hold, and deal with assets in a fiduciary or representative capacity.

They are :

- Nominees (paragraph 63.2 and 64)

- Trustees of settled property (paragraph 63.3 and 65) and

- Personal representatives of deceased persons (paragraph 63.4 and 66).

It should be noted that the CGT legislation makes no special provision for discretionary trusts. Such trust arrangements fall within one or other of the three general categories described in this Chapter, depending on the form and nature of the trusts on which the assets are held. Discretionary trusts do, however, come in for special mention where it is necessary to give effect to specific antiavoidance provisions to measure the interest of a potential or actual recipient of trust funds (arising out of the exercise of their discretion by the trustees). Such antiavoidance provisions are dealt with mainly in paragraph 68.

Part 19 Chap3   The main rules dealing with the CGT aspects of assets held in a fiduciary or representative capacity are contained in TCA97 Part 19 Chapter 3.

63.2   Nominees and Bare Trustees.

This category would include not only nominees as such, but certain trustee situations, where the beneficiary is absolutely entitled as against the trustee.

The main effect of the legislation is to look through the nominee (or trustee in such circumstances) to the person on whose behalf the assets are being held — and to treat all disposals and acquisitions as being by that person, and not by the nominee or trustee.

The provisions of the legislation regarding the treatment of assets held in such circumstances are considered in paragraph 64.

63.3   **Settled Property/Trustees.**

Because of the complexities of trust law, the trustees of settled property are singled out for special treatment in the legislation. Nominees and bare trustees etc.,(as mentioned above) are excluded from the special rules applying to the trustees of settled property.

- trustees are treated as a single and continuing body of persons (distinct from the individual trustees);

- special rules apply in determining the residence of that deemed body;

- transfers to the trustees by the settlor are treated as being a disposal by the settlor at market value with a corresponding acquisition by the trustees at that value;

- appointments of absolute interests (but not of limited interests) in property out of the trust fund will normally be treated as disposals by the trustees at market value;

- there are special rules for dealing with the situation where

  - a beneficiary becomes absolutely entitled to the trust property and

  - where a life interest in trust property terminates on the death of the life tenant.

The treatment of the trustees of settled property is considered in paragraph 65.

63.4   **Personal Representatives**

During the administration period of the estate of a deceased person, the personal representatives are, in effect, neither nominees, nor trustees. They are deemed to acquire the assets of the deceased person at market value at the date of his death. However, the deceased person is deemed not to have made any disposal. In effect, gains accruing on the assets up to the date of death are tax-free. When assets are passed on by the personal representatives to a legatee, the legatee is treated as standing in the shoes of the personal representatives i.e. as acquiring the assets at market value at the date of death of the deceased person.

Where assets are sold by the personal representatives, whether to pay off liabilities, or otherwise comply with the terms of the will, any gains and losses will accrue to them, and will be taxed in their hands.

As in the case of trustees, personal representatives are deemed to be a single and continuing body of persons, and special rules are set out for determining their residence and domicile. The detailed provisions are set out paragraph 66.

The special rules only apply to the holding or dealing in assets by the personal representatives during the administration period of an estate. After the end of the administration period, where the personal representatives still hold assets on trust, they will hold they assets either as trustees of settled property or as nominees etc. for the beneficiaries of those trusts, and the rules applicable in such circumstances will apply.

For example, where under the will of a testator, property is left for life to one individual and passes absolutely to another on the death of the life tenant, the executors of the original will would hold the property during the administration period in their capacity as personal representatives, but when the administration period is complete, they would hold that property in their capacity as trustees of settled property (in trust for the life tenant and remainderman).

63.5   Special trusts

Special tax treatment applies in the case of certain trusts including:

- approved employee profit sharing schemes (see paragraph 50.2),
- employee share ownership trusts (see paragraph 50.3)
- trustees on demutualisation of a life assurance company (see paragraph 44.7)
- unit trusts (see paragraph 35)
- pension fund trustees (see paragraph 32.4)

63.6   Joint Tenants

Where property is held by two or more persons as joint tenants, the law presumes them each to have an equal share in the property. It is also a peculiar feature of a joint tenancy that on a person's death his interest in the property passes automatically in equal shares to the other joint tenants. The deceased person has no power to determine how that interest will pass - he cannot leave it in his Will. The interest of a joint tenant is spoken of as being one which passes *"on survivorship"*. Generally, joint tenants do have the power to sever a joint tenancy and to convert their interest into a tenancy in common. A tenancy in common has none of the features just described and is just a straight forward form of co-ownership of property.

- **Revenue/Chief Inspector's CGT Manual :**

—The capital gains tax manual states that where *joint tenants* dispose of a property, and do not share the proceeds equally, but choose to share in the proportions in which they contributed to the cost of the asset, this should be accepted by the Revenue for CGT purposes provided that all the joint tenants so agree in writing.

—In paragraph 19.3.7.5 of the CGT manual it is stated *"where the owner of property conveys it to joint tenants of whom he is one, there is a disposal of the whole property to the joint tenants collectively and, where appropriate, the general rule in s547 that the asset is deemed to be disposed of and acquired at its market value, should be applied."*

In this matter the Revenue instruction appear to be treating the property transferred into the joint tenancy as "settled property", and accordingly looking on the transaction as a disposal of the entire property by the original owner as "settlor" to the trustees of the settlement (the joint tenants) - notwithstanding that the original owner still retains an interest in the asset, and the property held by the joint tenancy may not constitute *"settled property"* for the purposes of the CGT Acts. The transfer of the property from the owner to the joint tenants (of which the original owner may be one) is within the very wide meaning of the term *"settlement"* - see paragraph 65.4). However, whether it amounts to *"settled property"* may depend on the circumstances of the transfer, and in particular whether an *"element of bounty"* is involved. This issue is discussed in detail in paragraph 65.4.

64   NOMINEES AND BARE TRUSTEES

64.1   Nominees

s567(2)   The relevant legislation is contained in TCA97 s567(2), which provides:

*'In relation to assets held by a person as **nominee** for another person, or as trustee for another person **absolutely entitled as against the trustee,** or for any person who would be so entitled but for being an infant or other person under disability (or for two or more persons who are, or would be jointly so entitled), the Capital Gains Tax Acts shall apply as if the property were vested in, and the acts of the nominee or trustee in relation to the assets were the acts of, the person or persons for whom the first mentioned person is the nominee or trustee (acquisitions from or disposals to the first mentioned person by that person or persons being disregarded accordingly)'.*

In such circumstances the beneficial owner for whom the nominee or trustee is holding the assets, is treated for CGT purposes as making the acquisitions and disposals which have in fact been made on his behalf by the nominee or trustee. Any gains or losses attach to the beneficial owner and not to the nominee or trustee. The tax liability will therefore be determined by reference to the residence and domicile of the beneficial owner; it will not in any way be affected by the residence or domicile of the nominee (or trustee) should it be different.

s1051

The tax arising on disposals by a nominee or bare trustee will normally be payable by the beneficial owner of the assets. There is an exception to this rule in the case of infant children, and persons under disability. S1051 extends the provisions of the Income Tax Acts relating to the assessment and collection of tax, to include CGT. It specifically applies the provision of s1045, s1046 and s1047 which particularly relate to such a situation.

s1045

"The trustee, guardian, or committee of any incapacitated person having the direction, control, or management of the property or concern of any such person, shall be assessable and chargeable to tax in like manner and to the like amount as that person would be assessed and charged if he or she were not an incapacitated person"

s1047

"Where a person chargeable to tax is an infant...the parent or guardian of the infant shall be liable for the tax in default of payment by the infant".

In the remainder of paragraph 64 specific aspects of the CGT treatment of nominees are considered,

- *"Absolutely entitled against the trustees"*: The meaning of this phrase is considered in paragraph 64.2

- *Bankruptcy:* The treatment of the assets of an insolvent person is considered in paragraph 64.3.

- *Liquidators:* Treatment of a liquidator of a company is considered in paragraph 64.4.

- *Court funds:* The treatment of funds held in court is dealt with in paragraph 64.5.

- *Mortgages:* The treatment of assets held as security for debts etc. is dealt with in paragraph in 64.6.

64.2   **Absolutely entitled against the trustees**

Apart from the initial set up of a trust, perhaps the single most important other event in the life of a trust is the point in time when the beneficiary becomes entitled to the trust assets. It could be that he has reached a particular age, or perhaps a life tenant has died, or some other event determined by the trusts upon which the assets are held has now occurred.

That single event (in relation to the assets to which the beneficiary then becomes entitled) triggers a number of CGT consequences, all of which in the absence of a specific exemption, could give rise to a charge to tax.

In very broad terms, when a beneficiary becomes *"absolutely entitled as against the trustees"* to all or part of assets held on trust:

- There is a deemed disposal of those assets at open market value *by the trustees,*

- The trustees are deemed to immediately reacquire the assets in a capacity as bare trustee (or nominee) for the benefiaciary who is now absolutely entitled to those assets, and any further dealings in the assets by the trustees are, in effect, deemed to be for and on behalf of the person for whom they now hold the asets as nominee.

- There is a deemed disposal of his interest in the settlement *by the beneficiary* now entitled to the assets, the consideration for that disposal being the value of the trust assets to which he becomes entitled.

There is a deemed disposal by both the trustees (of the assets held on trust) and by the beneficiary (of his interest under the trust) either or both of which can give rise to a charge to tax.

The deemed disposal by trustees and the corresponding exemption from the charge to CGT on the trustees in certain circumstances is discussed in paragraph 65.7. The separate deemed disposal of his interest under the settlement by the beneficiary and the exemption applying to a beneficiary in certain circumstances is set out in paragraph 65.12.

s567(1)   The meaning of the phrase 'absolutely entitled as against the trustee' is crucial. The only guidance given in the legislation to the meaning of that phrase is set out in s567(1).

"References in the Capital Gains Tax Acts to any asset held by a person as trustee for another person absolutely entitled as against the trustee, are references to a case where that other person has the exclusive right, or would have such a right if that other person were not an infant or other person under disability, subject only to satisfying any outstanding charge lien or right of the trustees to resort to the asset for payment of duty, taxes, costs, or other outgoings, to direct how that asset shall be dealt with".

The UK equivalent of s567(1) has been the subject of much judicial consideration in the UK courts.

Tomlinson v Glyns Executor and Trustee Co concerned a settlement for four infant children. The point at issue was whether they were absolutely entitled to the trust property as against the trustees. In the circumstances of the case, if the liability attached to the children (i.e. if the trustees were treated as mere nominees) no tax would have been payable on the gains which resulted from the sale by the trustees of some of the investments forming part of the trust assets. The settlement itself took the familiar form of the trustees holding the capital and income in trust "for such of the beneficiaries as shall attain the age of twenty one years (or marry under that age) and if more than one in equal shares absolutely". The very nature of the settlement ensured that nothing vested in the children until they reached the age of 21 years (or earlier marriage). If any of them died before 21 years, or marrying, they would have been entitled to nothing. The CGT position in such circumstances was clearly stated by Lord Denning MR in his judgement...

"I think that the right way of looking at [s567(1)] is to take the time when the capital gain was made, and to ask the question: If he was not an infant at that time, would he be absolutely entitled to call for his money so as himself to be able to give directions to the trustees, and to give a good receipt to them? In short, is infancy the only bar? In the present case none of these four children if they were not infants would be absolutely entitled at that time to call for the money or to give the trustees a proper receipt. Their interests were contingent on their living to the age of twenty-one...The section only applies where a child has...a vested and indefeasible interest in possession. None of these four children came within that category; none of them was absolutely entitled to the money".

A person ceases to be an infant at the age of 18 years (and not 21 years as was once the case).

Another case where the beneficiaries being absolutely entitled as against the trustees would have favoured the tax position, was the UK case of Cochrane v IRC . In that case the beneficiary was non-resident, and the gains would have escaped tax if he was absolutely entitled to the assets at the time of disposal. The deceased person nominated executor trustees to look after his estate on his death. Under the terms of his will, they were to pay his debts and expenses first and then to provide a legacy to his daughter. What remained, (the residue) was to go to his son absolutely. After the testator's death the executors sold some of the assets to pay the debts and expenses, and to provide the daughter's legacy. These sales resulted in gains, which were assessed to tax on the executors. The executors appealed the assessment contending that the son had been absolutely entitled to the assets (being the sole absolute residuary legatee) since the testator's death, and as he was non-resident, no liability arose.

It was held that the interest of the son extended only to what remained of the estate after paying the debts and providing for the legacy, and accordingly he was not entitled in any way to the assets sold to provide for those items, which were never part of the residue. Accordingly, s567(1) could not apply even if the executors were trustees within the meaning of that sub-section. In that case, the Lord President (Lord Emslie) said..."*what vested in the residuary legatee*

was a right to the 'residue' and no more. A bequest of residue vesting a
morte testatoris is not a bequest of the whole estate...'residue', said Lord
Watson in Duchess of Montrose v Stuart, 'is simply so much of his personal
estate as may remain after the whole of the antecedent purposes of the deed
have been effected – after debts and legacies have been paid'...it is for the
executors...and for them alone to determine what particular assets should be
realised...although executors may, if they choose, consider the views of the
residuary beneficiary before realising any part of the estate, they are in no
way bound to do so, and they are in no way bound to accept any 'directions'
from the residuary legatee in this connection".

s567

In Stephenson v Barclays Bank Trustee Co, the two grandchildren of
a deceased person became entitled to the residue of his estate, which
was charged with the payment of annuities in favour of his   ·
daughters. It was argued for the taxpayer that the rights of the
annuitants should be treated as 'duties, taxes, costs and other
outgoings'. This contention was firmly rejected by Walton J who
said "It appears to me quite clear that the subject matter to which [s567(1)]
is directed is the prevention of a situation where the taxpayer was able to
say and say truly that he was not absolutely entitled against the trustees
because the trustees had some personal right of indemnity of resorting to the
trust funds which took priority over the rights of the person otherwise
absolutely entitled. It does not appear to me to be in any way apt language
for use in the case of another beneficial interest arising under the same
instrument".

A similar point was considered in the UK case of Prest v Bettinson,
where a testatrix left the residue of her estate to trustees, on trust for
sale. They were directed by the will, after paying certain annuities to
distribute the proceeds of the sale of the assets equally between five
institutions, four of which were charitable. It was held that the gain
accrued to the personal representatives, and not to the charities
(which would have been exempt).

In the UK case of Crowe v Appleby it was held that a beneficiary
entitled to a proportionate share in a trust fund consisting entirely of
land, where the trustees had the power to postpone sale, was not
absolutely entitled as against the trustees, as he could not call for
immediate payment of his respective share, or interfere with the due
exercise of the trustees discretion to postpone sale.

The case had concerned certain properties which had been left by
will to trustees. The properties were held by seven of the testator's
children as life tenants, with the remainder interest in respect of each
such share being left to grandchildren. On the death of some of the
children who were life tenants, their grandchildren became entitled
to the remainder interest in respect of their share. Other life tenants
were still living at the time. In normal circumstances grandchildren
who would become entitled to the remainder interests would be
absolutely entitled as against the trustee. What prevented them from

being absolutely entitled against the trustee in this case was that the assets of the settlement consisted of property in which they held undivided shares. They were not in a position to direct the trustee to transfer any property, or any part of the property to them immediately. They would not have an absolute right to direct the trustee how to deal with their share of the trust fund until the property had been sold and converted to money.

s567(2)

In the UK case of Kidson v MacDonald the meaning of 'two or more persons who are or would be jointly so entitled' was considered in the context of the UK equivalent of s567(2). In that case, freehold land was conveyed to two individuals on trust for sale for themselves as tenants in common in equal shares, with a power to postpone the sale. When one of the individuals died, his personal representatives sold his half share in the property, and a capital gain arose. If the property was held to be 'nominee' property, the gain would be chargeable on the executors. If it was not within the 'nominee' category, the assets would be settled property (under the UK definition, which unlike the Irish definition, does not appear to require a trust for this purpose to have an element of bounty) - and the disposal of an interest in settled property in such circumstances would be exempt from CGT (see paragraph 65.12). Foster J, held that the word 'jointly' in the context of s567(2) had its normal wide meaning, and could not be confined to the narrow meaning associated with the term 'joint tenancy'.

"No authority was cited to me showing that in English law the word 'jointly' has a technical meaning, though of course, the words 'as joint tenants' do have a technical meaning. In my judgement, 'jointly' in its ordinary sense means 'common to two or more', and is therefore wide enough to include an equitable tenancy in common of English real property. If the word 'jointly' was confined to joint tenants and excluded tenants in common, an extraordinary position would arise where one joint tenant severed an equitable joint tenancy and thus they became tenants in common in equity. Up to the moment of severance it would not be settled property and the individuals would be chargeable, while after severance it would be settled property and the trustees would be chargeable. Such an extraordinary result should be avoided if a permissible construction is available which leads to a different result".

The decision in that case was closely followed by Foster J in the UK case of Harthan v Mason, where in the circumstances of the case, property was held by a number of individuals on trust for sale for themselves as tenants in common.

A specific example of a nominee is dealt with in Paragraph 37, dealing with the operations of special investment accounts by designated brokers.

64.3   **Assets of Insolvent Persons**

s569   Where assets are held by a trustee or assignee in bankruptcy, or
under a deed of arrangement (to which the Deeds of Arrangement
Act 1887 applies), the provisions of s569 apply for CGT purposes.

s569(2) provides that:

*"The Capital Gains Tax Acts shall apply as if the assets were vested in, and
the acts of the trustee or assignee in relation to the assets were the acts of the
bankrupt or debtor (acquisitions from or disposals to such person by the
bankrupt or debtor being disregarded accordingly), and tax in respect of any
chargeable gains which accrues to any such trustee or assignee shall be
assessable on and recoverable from such trustee or assignee".*

In the UK case of re McMeekin (a bankrupt) it was held that the
liability to pay the CGT in such circumstances, fell on the trustee or
assignee, and not on the bankrupt, or debtor.

Where a mortgage or charge exists over the property which is sold
by the official assignee, the question arises as to the priority between
preferential debts charged on the property prior to the adjudication
of the bankrupt, and the CGT liability arising on the sale of the
mortgaged asset. In re McMeekin the position was set out by Lowry
CJ...*"I now come to question (4) [the position of the CGT liability], which
raises the only issues that were seriously debated. In my view alternatives
(b) [CGT liability as preferred debt] and (c) [CGT as an unsecured debt] can
be dismissed immediately, since there is nothing in the relevant legislation
to contradict the ordinary law of bankruptcy, that the debts to be taken into
account, whether as preferred or unsecured debts of the bankrupt, are those
which existed at the date of adjudication. A liability for capital gains tax
arising from sales by the Official Assignee after adjudication cannot fall
into either of those categories. Nor does it create a debt personal to the
Official Assignee, in the sense that he could be rendered liable to discharge
it out of his own pocket without regard to the sufficiency of the bankrupt's
assets. The liability is to be treated as part of the costs of the administration
of the bankruptcy, which are to be discharged in priority to all debts..."*.

Although it is the trustee or assignee who will be assessed and who
has the liability to pay the tax, it would appear from s569(2) that the
gain must be computed as if the disposal was made by the bankrupt,
or debtor — which would have the effect of preserving the "annual
allowance" (not available to trustees); in addition the residence and
domicile position of the debtor, or bankrupt could be a crucial factor
in determining whether a liability arose.

On the death of the debtor, or bankrupt, special provisions apply. In
effect, the assignee or trustee is treated as a personal representative
of the deceased bankrupt or debtor, and the normal provisions
applying to disposals by personal representatives will apply. These
provisions are considered in paragraph 66.

64.4   Companies in Liquidation

s570

S570 provides that where a company is in liquidation, and the assets of the company are vested in a liquidator under s.230 of the Companies Act 1963, or otherwise, *"this Act shall apply as if the assets were vested in and the acts of the liquidator in relation to the assets were the acts of the company (acquisitions from or disposals to him by the company being disregarded accordingly)"*. CA63 s230 deals only with court liquidation, and does not affect a voluntary winding up. The section provides -

CA63 s230

"Where a company is being wound up the by Court, the Court may, on the application of the liquidator, by order direct that all or any part of the property of whatsoever description belonging to the company or held by trustees on its behalf shall vest in the liquidator by his official name and thereupon the property to which the order relates shall vest accordingly, and the liquidator may, after giving such indemnity, if any, as the court may direct, bring or defend in his official name any action or other legal proceeding which relates to that property or which it is necessary to bring or defend for the purpose of effectively winding up the company and recovering its property".

S570 is not confined to cases to which s.230 has application - note the words *"or otherwise"* in the legislation quoted above.

64.5   Funds in Court

s572

Such funds held by the Accountant attached to the High Court (or a deputy appointed by the Minister for Justice), are regarded as being held by him as nominee for the person entitled to or interested in the funds, or as the case may be, for the trustees of that person.

The same provisions apply in the case of the Circuit Court.

Example 271

Funds could be held by the Accountant in such circumstances, for example, where an award was made for the benefit of a minor child, or on the vesting in the Court of the assets of an insane person.

Example 272

A further example of this provision, is where a person dies without leaving a Will, and the assets are held by the High Court until it decides on who is to inherit the assets.

Problems can arise in this area, in that until the ultimate destination of the assets is decided, it cannot be known who the real owner is, and accordingly in the meantime there is no one for the Inspector to assess, and equally there is no one with an obligation to make a self-assessment return - in the event of a gain arising.

"Funds in Court" are defined in s572 as meaning: "any moneys (and investments representing such moneys) annuities, stocks, shares or other

securities standing to or to be placed to the account of the Accountant in the books of the Bank of Ireland or any company and includes boxes and other effects".

Where cash is required in the case of one fund, and where investments are required by another fund which has cash, it would not be unusual for the Accountant to give effect to the requirements of both funds, by an internal transfer within his own books. This could be given effect to by the mere transfer of investments from the fund requiring cash, into the fund which required the investments, with a corresponding transfer of the cash from that fund, into the fund which required the cash. The investments would of course be transferred at market value. In such circumstances, the Accountant has not disposed of any assets, and accordingly s572(3) makes specific provision for dealing with such transactions.

It provides -

"Where funds in court standing to an account in the books of the Accountant are invested or after investment are realised the method by which the Accountant effects the investment or the realisation of investments shall not affect the question whether there is for the purpose of this Act an acquisition or as the case may be a disposal of an asset representing the funds in Court standing to that account and in particular there shall for those purposes be an acquisition or disposal of assets notwithstanding that the investment of funds in Court standing to an account in the books of the Accountant or the realisation of funds which have been so invested is effected by setting off in the Accountant's books investments on one account against a realisation of investments in another".

64.6   **Assets Transferred As Security**

s537   The normal effect of a mortgage or charge on property, is to give the person who provided the money, the right (in certain circumstances) to sell the property in the name of the borrower/owner, and pay off the debt due. In some cases, it will also have the effect of transferring legal title to the lender, subject to the borrower's right to have title returned to him on payment of the debt due.

s537(1) provides that :-

'The conveyance or transfer by way of security of an asset or of an interest or right in or over it, or transfer of a subsisting interest or right by way of security in or over an asset (including a retransfer on redemption of the security), shall not be treated for the purposes of the Capital Gains Tax Acts as involving any acquisition or disposal of the asset'.

Where the lender has to resort to his right to sell the asset to obtain repayment of the amount due to him, he is treated as selling the asset as nominee for the borrower. The relevant legislation is in s537(2):

s537(2)

'Where a person entitled to an asset by way of security or to the benefit of a charge or encumbrance on an asset deals with the asset for the purpose of enforcing or giving effect to the security, charge or encumbrance, such persons dealings with it shall be treated for the purposes of this Act as if they were done through such person as nominee by the person entitled to it subject to the security, charge or encumbrance; and this subsection shall apply to the dealings of any person appointed to enforce or give effect to the security, charge or encumbrance as receiver and manager or judicial factor as it applies to the dealings of the person so entitled'.

In applying these provisions, note should be taken of the special provisions relating to 'bankruptcy' — see paragraph 64.3.

s571

Where a disposal takes place on or after 9 June 1983 s571 ensures that the tax is payable in priority to the entitlement of the lender. The person with possession of the sale proceeds, whether it be the lender or an agent appointed by him to enforce the security is made primarily responsible for payment of the CGT liability arising out of that disposal.

The provisions take effect *where a disposal is made on or after 9 June 1983* by

(a) A liquidator of a company or

(b) any person entitled to an asset by way of security or to the benefit of a charge or encumbrance on an asset or as the case may be any person appointed to enforce or give effect to the security charge or encumbrance.

s537(2)
s570

Where s537(2) — see above, or s570 (see paragraph 64.4) apply to a disposal by the lender, or by any person appointed to enforce or give effect to the security, charge or encumbrance, (the accountable person)

(a) the CGT chargeable in respect of the disposal is assessable on and recoverable from that accountable person and

(b) the tax is treated as a necessary disbursement out of the proceeds of the disposal, and is payable out of those proceeds, and

(c) the tax paid by that person is treated as discharging a corresponding amount of the liability to CGT of the debtor (who apart from this provision would be chargeable).

The tax chargeable on the "accountable person" is collected not by way of a CGT assessment, but by an assessment under Case IV of Sch D for the year of assessment in which the disposal takes place. The income tax assessment will be on whatever sum as is necessary so that when tax is chargeable on it at the standard rate for that year, the amount payable equals the amount of CGT due. If for example the CGT due for 1999/00 by such an accountable person amounted to £4,800, then the income tax assessment would be £20,000 at 24% (standard income tax rate for 1999/00).

Where the tax paid is excessive, relief is to be given by repayment or otherwise to the accountable person.

The CGT chargeable on the disposal is the liability which accrues to the "borrower", taking into account his normal reliefs and allowances. Where he has more than one gain in the period concerned, it is necessary to determine the part of the total tax liability which must be paid by the "accountable person". The rules dealing with the apportionment of the liability are illustrated in the following examples.

Example 273

This is an example of the apportionment where there is no restriction on the set-off of losses (e.g. where no development land gains are included):

	£
William is unmarried. During 1999/2000 the following gains arose:	
GAIN on sale of shares by William	5,000
GAIN on sale of mortgaged holiday home by bank	8,000
Total gains	13,000
William's own losses forward from 1998/99 (assumed)	8,000
	5,000
Annual Exemption	1,000
TAXABLE	4,000
CGT @20%	1,200

S571 does not increase the liability, it merely fixes responsibility for payment of the tax. Assuming the disposal by the bank was in September 1999, and none of the disposals are of development land, the liability would be apportioned as follows-

	£
Bank £800 x $\frac{1{,}600^*}{2{,}600^{**}}$	492
William: Balance (£800 - £492)	308
	800

* 20% of £8,000 = £1,600   **20% of £8,000 + 20% of £5,000 = £2,600

Example 274

This is an example of the apportionment rule in other cases, i.e. Where both development land and other assets are involved.

During 1999/2000 Bill made a gain of £25,000 on the disposal of development land for non-residential development. The gain is chargeable @ 40%. The land was sold by a bank enforcing its rights under a mortgage on the land. Bill also sold shares in an Irish trading company. The gain on disposal of the shares was £12,000 chargeable @ 20%.

Bill is married, but his spouse has no gains during 1999/2000.

His CGT losses forward (not on development land) from 1998/99 amount to £9,000.

The tax payable for 1999/2000 is calculated (and apportioned) as follows:

	£
Gain on shares	12,000
Losses forward	(9,000)
Taxable Gain (chargeable @ 20%)	3,000
Gain on land	25,000
Annual exemption	1,000
Taxable Gain (chargeable @ 40%)	23,000

The losses forward are set against the gain on the sale of shares, as the only losses which can be set against a development land gain are losses on the disposal of development land.

The annual exemption is set against the gain chargeable at the highest rate of CGT in that year - the development land. The tax payable on the disposal of the development land is £23,000 @40% = £9,200, and this tax is payable by the bank out of the sale proceeds of the land. The balance of the tax (on the shares) is payable by Bill. The £1,000 annual allowance available to his spouse is lost - it is not available for set off against a gain arising to Bill.

In the case of a company, the same principles apply to the apportionment of the liability between the company and the accountable person.

s571   The case of Bank of Ireland Finance v Revenue Commissioners, a 1989 High Court case, held that tax withheld from the consideration arising on the disposal by the Bank of Ireland Finance Limited as mortgagor of certain lands owned by a person to whom they had lent money, was not repayable by the Revenue to Bank of Ireland Finance Limited, but was offsetable against the capital gains tax liability of the owner of the land. This transaction predated s.56 Finance Act 1983 (now TCA97 s571).

65   SETTLED PROPERTY

65.1   Broad Outline

s579   The main provisions in the Capital Gains Tax Acts dealing with trustees of settled property are contained in s574 to s578. A major relief relating to a beneficiary of a trust is to be found in s613 together with a "deemed" disposal provision. Provisions relating to a trust going non-resident, and relating to non-resident trustees are set out in s759A to 579F inclusive. The following is a brief outline of the statutory provisions:

s567(1)   gives the meaning of the phrase 'absolutely entitled as against the trustee';

s574   deems trustees to be a single and continuing body of persons...and sets out rules for establishing the residence of that body,

s574(1)   deems all the trustees to be a single body of trustees where part of the trust property comprised in a settlement is vested in one trustee, and part in another;

S574(3)   Confirms that the rule deeming the trustees to be a single and continuing body of persons applies to a situation where part of the trust property comprised in the settlement is vested in one trustee, and part in another separate trustee.

s574(2)   allows the Revenue in certain circumstances to recover tax due by the trustees from the beneficiary, where he is absolutely entitled to the assets;

s575   treats the settling of assets on the trustees as a disposal of the entire property by the settlor at market value;

s576(1)   deems a disposal of assets by the trustees when a person becomes absolutely entitled as against them in relation to those assets;

s576(2)   allows the benefit of losses accruing to the trustees in relation to assets to be taken over by a beneficiary who becomes entitled as against the trustees to those assets;

s577(1)(a) gives the meaning of 'life interest' in relation to a settlement, and deals with annuities which are to be treated as 'life interests'.

s577(2)   extends the normal 'death' provisions to trustees where a person becomes entitled as against the trustees on the death of a person with a life interest in the property;

s577(3)   deems a disposal by the trustees in relation to assets where a life interest in those assets is terminated by the death of the person holding the life interest, otherwise than where an absolute interest is taken on such death by another beneficiary;

s577(4)   for the purposes of s577(3), deems a life interest in part of the income of the settled property to be a life interest in a corresponding part of that property,

and

where it is a life interest in income of part of settled property only, with no recourse to any other part of the settled property, the life interest is treated for the purposes of s577(3) as being a separate settlement;

s578   extends the provisions of s576 and s577 to an annuity which is not a life interest, where it ceases by reason of the death of the annuitant;

s579;   can attribute gains of a non-resident trust to an Irish
s579A;   resident beneficiary
& s579F

s579B - Impose a deemed disposal on trustees going non-resident
s579E   or becoming treaty protected.

s613   deems a beneficiary who becomes absolutely entitled as against a trustee to dispose of his interest under the settlement.

s613   exempts a gain on the disposal of an interest in settled property by a person who did not purchase that interest (e.g. the original beneficiary)

s613A   limits the exemption under s613 where the trust has been non-resident.

An explanatory outline of the main provisions affecting trustees was given by Buckley L. J. in the UK case of Berry v Warnett. [The equivalent Irish sections are substituted for the U.K. references actually used by Buckley L.J.]

"In the case of an ordinary voluntary settlement, where a settlor transfers property of his to trustees to be held on the trusts of the settlement, he makes a disposal to the trustees of the settled property which for the purposes of the Capital Gains Tax Acts is a disposal of the entire property, notwithstanding that the settlor may have some beneficial interest under the settlement [s575]. Since the trustees acquire the settled property otherwise than by way of bargains at arm's length,

(a)   the disposal by the settlor, and

(b)   the acquisition by the trustees

s547   are deemed to be for a consideration equal to the market value of the settled property [s547]. The price so deemed to have been paid by the trustees applies for the purposes of

(a)   calculating what capital gain or allowable loss is to be treated as having accrued to the settlor on the disposal, and

(b)   ascertaining the amount or value of the consideration which the trustees are to be treated as having given for the acquisition of the settled property for the purposes of calculating any capital gain or allowable loss which the trustees may later realise on a subsequent actual or notional disposal by them of the settled property or any part of it.

For this latter purpose the trustees of the settlement are given what can appropriately be called a quasi-corporate character by [s547], so that changes in the personal identities of the trustees shall not complicate the ascertainment of the capital gains liabilities in respect of dealings with the corpus of the trust property. If during the continuance of the trust the trustees sell a trust asset which was part of the property initially settled by the settlor, the trustees will realise a chargeable gain or allowable loss by reference to a notional cost of acquisition (or 'base value') equal to the market value of that asset at the date of the settlement, and the base value to the trustees for capital gains tax purposes of the newly acquired asset will be the price paid for it by the trustees. When anybody becomes absolutely entitled to the settled property or any part of it as against the trustees, the trustees are to be deemed to have disposed of that property [s576]. Under [s576] this deemed disposal is to be deemed to be for a consideration equal to the then market value of the property...A similar situation will arise [s577] on the termination of a life interest in possession in all or any part of the settled property. In this way, so long as the settled property remains in settlement and on the occasion of its ceasing to be settled by reason of some person becoming absolutely entitled to the property as against the trustees, the trustees are the persons chargeable to capital gains tax in respect of all disposals, whether actual or notional, of the settled property or any part of it. They are, or course, entitled under the general law to pay the tax out of the settled property, so that the burden falls on the beneficiaries in accordance with their several interests under the settlement".

The treatment of unit trusts, which are a special type of trust is described in paragraph 35.

Chapter 3 of Part 19, TCA97 is a separate code of CGT law as it applies to a settlement. The application of CGT to the life of a settlement (i.e. a trust with an element of bounty) can be broadly summarised as follows:

• The creation of a settlement involves a disposal of the settled assets by the settlor at OMV and their acquisition by the trustees at OMV.

• The trustees are thereafter the assessable persons in relation to the settled assets, and not the settlor or beneficiaries, although beneficiaries may have a secondary liability for CGT assessed on trustees or may be assessable on the gains of certain non resident trusts.

• The sale of trust assets by trustees is a disposal of those assets for CGT purposes by the trustees. All of the usual connected party rules apply.

• An appointment of assets to a beneficiary is a disposal at open market value (OMV) by the trustees and an acquisition at OMV by the beneficiary provided it is an absolute appointment which frees the assets from the trusts of the settlement.

- An appointment of an interest in assets to a beneficiary, which is not an absolute interest and leaves the assets subject to the trusts of the settlement, is not a disposal or part disposal of the asset or of the interest by the trustees. However it is the acquisition of an interest under the settlement by the beneficiary, at OMV.

- A disposal of an interest in settled property by a beneficiary who obtained it without giving consideration (which is the usual case) is exempt from CGT. This is subject to an exception if the trust is/has been non resident.

- On the death of a life tenant the trustees are deemed to dispose of the trust assets and reacquire them at OMV. No chargeable gain arises if the trust comes to an end on that death. A further exception arises where on the death the trustees then hold the assets for charitable purposes. Otherwise a chargeable gain may arise.

- A person who, as holder of a future interest, becomes entitled to an absolute interest in possession in assets, is deemed to then dispose of his interest in return for the assets. As noted above, in most cases (but not all) this disposal is exempt from CGT.

- The trustees are deemed to dispose of the assets on that occasion at OMV. This situation typically is how a settlement comes to an end.

- Retirement relief and principal private residence relief can be available to trustees in certain circumstances.

In short, there is a disposal/acquisition by the settlor/trustees at the start of a settlement, a disposal/acquisition by the trustees/beneficiary at the end of a settlement, and most appointments of limited interests during the life of a trust are not disposals by the trustees.

Example 275

John settles shares worth £500,000 on a discretionary settlement. His base cost was £100,000. The trustees (Irish resident) sold the shares for £750,000 and bought other shares with the proceeds. They then appointed a life interest in the shares to Mrs John, and a remainder interest in half of the shares to John's son, Jim, at a time when the new shares were worth £800,000. A year later Mrs John died. The shares were then worth £900,000. A month after her death, the trustees appointed the remaining half of the shares to Jim's wife, at a time when the overall shares were worth £1million. Indexation is ignored in this example in the interests of simplicity, as in the impact on the trust assets of the payment of CGT.

John is treated as realising a gain of £400,000 on his settlement of the assets. The trustees are treated as acquiring the assets of a base cost of £500,000.

The trustees realise a gain of £250,000 on the sale of the shares. Their base cost in the new shares is £750,000.

The appointments to Mrs John and Jim are not disposals by the trustees.

On the death of Mrs John, Jim becomes absolutely entitled to half the shares. There is a disposal by the trustee of the half but as Jim has become absolutely entitled on the death of a life tenant, the gain is exempt. So also is the gain Jim is deemed to realise on the disposal of his interest arising under the settlement.

The trustees are treated as disposing of and reacquiring the half of the shares which did not pass to him on the death of Mrs John, and realise a gain of £75,000 on that occasion [1/2 x (900,000 - 750,000)]

On the appointment of the remaining half of the shares to Mrs Jim, the trustees realise a gain of £50,000 [1/2 x (1,000,000 - 900,000)]

As noted in paragraph 33.7.4, where one spouse grants the other spouse a life interest in assets, that transaction does not attract the normal relief for intra spouse exemptions. It is not treated as a transfer between spouses but rather is treated as a transfer from one spouse to a trust, and is therefore a total disposal of the asset at open market value and may lead to a chargeable gain accruing. This is illustrated in the example in that paragraph.

65.2   Trustees-Single Continuing Body

s574

The trustees of settled property are deemed by s574(1) to be a *'single and continuing body of persons, (distinct from the persons who may from time to time be the trustees)'*. Where part of the property comprised in

s567(1)

a settlement is vested in one trustee (or set of trustees), and part in another, they are to be treated as together constituting (and insofar as they act separately, as acting on behalf of) a single body of trustees.

SLA82

This latter rule provided by s567(3), applies particularly where settled land, within the meaning of the Settled Land Act 1882, is vested in the tenant for life, and investments representing capital money are vested in the trustees of the settlement. In such circumstances the tenant for life will be a trustee, and his residence will be relevant in determining the residence of the body of trustees.

These rules were crucial to the decision in the UK case of Roome v Edwards (which is considered in detail in paragraph 65.10). In that case two separate sets of trustees held the main 1944 fund and a separate 1955 fund. The tax liability arose primarily because in the circumstances of the case, the two funds were held to be comprised in the same settlement. The residence of all the trustees of both funds (as a single body) was held to be in the UK, whereas, as separate trustee/bodies, one would have been non-resident.

s568

Trustees, in their representative capacity, are deemed not to be individuals, and as such are not entitled to any of the allowances or reliefs which normally only apply to individuals — for example, the £1,000 annual exemption or the remittance basis for foreign gains.

65.3   **Residence of a settlement**

65.3.1   **Main rule**

Notwithstanding its importance, there is only one short reference in
the legislation to the *"residence"* of a settlement - the*"single and
continuing body of persons"* for CGT purposes.

s574(1)(a)   *"...That body* (the trust) *shall be treated as being resident and ordinarily
resident in the State unless the general administration of the trusts is
ordinarily carried on outside the State and the trustees or a majority of them
for the time being are not resident or not ordinarily resident in the State".*

The trust is *deemed to be resident and ordinarily resident in Ireland*
for CGT purposes, *unless:*

- the general administration of the trust is ordinarily carried on
  abroad,

  and

- the trustees or a majority of them are not resident *or* not
  ordinarily resident in Ireland.

Unless it comes within the narrow exclusion, the trust is treated for
CGT purposes as being both resident *and* ordinarily resident in
Ireland for CGT purposes. No distinction is made between residence
and ordinarily residentce in the case of a settlement/trust.

The exclusion from this deemed Irish residence rule has two separate
requirements:

- relating to the place where the general administration of the trust
  is ordinarily carried on. That is normally a question of fact, to be
  ascertained in each case. However, as the phrase *"general
  administration"* is not defined, difficulties may arise. Further
  discussion of this point is set out below.

relating to the individual residence and ordinary residence of the
separate trustees who make up that deemed single body of persons.
It is possible that the overall taxation status of the body of trustees
could be affected by the residence status of a lone trustee.

The rules for determining the residence of an individual are
discussed in paragraph 99, and those relating to the ordinary
residence of an individual are dealt with in paragraph 100.

The wording of s574(1)(a) exclusion from Irish resident status would
appear to require that the residence status of the majority of the
separate trustees making up that single body be:

- not resident,

- *OR*

- not ordinarily resident.

The use of the word *"or"* would seem to indicate that either non resident or non ordinary resident status for any trustee would be sufficient to qualify that trustee to be included in the "non-resident catagory" in arriving at the non resident tax status of the overall body of trustees. However, the wording used in the legislation to deal with the residence and ordinary residence of the trustee body is not absolutely clear. Although it refers to the majority of trustees being not resident *or* not ordinarily resident it is not clear whether a majority being not resident (irrespective of their ordinary residence) is sufficient, and vice versa. What is the case where some trustees are non resident, and others, although Irish resident are not ordinarily resident in Ireland? The most obvious meaning of the words used is that where a majority of the trustees are not resident, and the general administration is carried on abroad, the trust (as a body) is not resident or ordinarily resident in Ireland. This is so notwithstanding that a majority of the trustees may still be ordinarily resident in Ireland, as individuals can retain ordinary residence for a period of 3 years after ceasing to be resident (see paragraph 100). The position is not absolutely clear.

The phrase *"the general administration"* in relation to a trust (as a body) is not defined . The Oxford dictionary equates the word "administer" with "manage". It's meaning may appear at first glance to be obvious, but on reflecting on the issues involved in "managing" a trust it becomes less clear. There are many separate issues involved, including:

- the management of the the trust assets involving investment decisions, etc. which may be managed by persons other than the trustees (e.g.- professional investment advisors)

- the actual physical holding of and location of the trust assets

- the keeping of financial records and bank accounts.

- the decisions of the trustees relating to distributing assets and income of the trust to beneficiaries.

- The decisions of the trustees may be made in different places on different matters affecting the trust.

In looking at the residence position of any settlement, the meaning of *"the general administration"* must be looked at in the context of the circumstances of that particular settlement. Perhaps some guidance may be obtained from the pre FA99 rules for determining the location of the central management and control of a company (also a body of persons) - see paragraph 101.

65.3.2   Effect of "Professional Trustees"

s574(1)(b)   In certain cases , Irish resident persons (such as banks) may act as trustees of a foreign trust which has no Irish connections except for the Irish trustees. In such a case the trustees (only in their capacity as trustees of that trust) will be deemed not to be resident if:

- the trustees are acting in the course of a business which consists of or includes the management of trusts,

    and

- the whole of the property in the trust consists of (or is derived from) property provided by a person who was not domiciled, resident, or ordinarily resident in Ireland at the time he provided the property.

The issues of residence, ordinary residence, and domicile are dealt with in Chapter 13.

If, on the basis of these rules the trustees or a majority of them are non-resident (or deemed to be non-resident) the general administration of the trust will be deemed to be carried on outside Ireland. Consequently, the trustees may not be subject to Irish CGT on gains arising on foreign assets and non-specified Irish assets.

Example 276

The Murphy Discretionary Trust is a trust established under Swiss law. All sources of the trust capital were provided by John Patrick Murphy from foreign funds when he was resident, ordinarily resident and domiciled in Liechtenstein. The trustees are two German residents, an Irish Bank, which also looks after the general administration of the trust, and an Irish resident Accountant.

Under the general rule, the trust is Irish resident, because:

- *the majority of the trustees are not resident or ordinarily resident outside Ireland*

    and

- *the general administration of the trust is not carried on outside Ireland.*

However, the exception to the general rule can have the effect of deeming the trust to be non-resident: i.e. in this case, on the assumption that the bank is looking after the general administration of the trust in the course of a business of managing trusts, the bank will be regarded as non-resident for the purpose of determining the residence of the trust.

If on this basis (deeming the bank to be non-resident) the majority of the trustees are non-resident (which they are) the general administration of the trust is deemed to be carried on abroad.

The trust is therefore non-resident for CGT purposes.

These rules will normally enable a foreign trust to maintain its non-resident status even though its funds are managed by an Irish trustee/manager.

FA93 s49 New detailed rules for determining the residence of trusts which have no connection with Ireland apart from an Irish trustee, were set out in the FA93. However, those new rules do not take affect until legislation has been enacted providing for the regulation of trustees by the Central Bank, and subject to such legislation, and on such date as the Minister for Finance by order appoints. No such legislation has been enacted. It is not proposed to make any comment on those proposed new rules in advance of the legislation referred to, and the required Ministerial order. These rules will affect largely, trustees based in the IFSC (see paragraph 65.14). It is understood that the rules were inadvertently repealed by FA97 and are expected to be re-enacted, although this has not yet been done.

Where a professionally managed trust is regarded as non resident in accordance with s574, it may nonetheless have to take account of Irish capital gains tax. S579 and s579A, which can attribute gains of non resident trustees to resident persons in certain circumstances, can have application to the trust. These sections are discussed in greater detail in paragraph 68.

• **Appeal Commissioners Ruling**

— The Appeal Commissioners have ruled that where personal representatives disposed of land forming part of the residue of an estate, the resulting capital gains tax liability accrued to them and not to the beneficiary of the estate.

65.4 **What is a Settlement?**

Before dealing with the main rules relating to the trustees of settlements, it is necessary to consider the meaning of the terms 'settled property', and 'settlement'.

s574 The main provisions relating to settled property and trustees are contained in s574 (as amended). However, a number of the definitions relating to the interpretation of that section are contained in TCA97 s5.

s5 SETTLED PROPERTY is defined in s5 to mean "*all property held in trust other than*

• "*property to which s567 applies*" i.e.- property held by a person as nominee for another person, or as trustee for another person absolutely entitled as against the trustees, or for any other person who would be so entitled but for being an infant or other person under disability (or two or more persons who are, or would be, jointly so entitled) - see paragraph 64, "*but does not include*

• *any property held by a trustee or assignee in bankruptcy or under a deed or arrangement"* - see paragraph 64.3.

Special provisions apply to assets held in the circumstances set out above, and dealings in those assets are excluded from the general treatment of settled property set out in s574. The special provisions are dealt with in paragraph 64. The terms 'settlement' and 'settlor' are given the meanings assigned to them by s10. This however is a repetition of the definition that was given to them by s.96(3)(h) ITA 1967.

'SETTLEMENT' is not defined as such in that section, but is stated to include

s10

'any disposition, trust, covenant, agreement, or arrangement, and any transfer of money or other property, or of any right to money or other property.

s5

It will be noted that the definition of *"settlement"* is a very wide definition. For example, it includes *"any transfer of money or other property"*. Notwithstanding that the courts have interpreted the definition in income tax cases where an identical definition was used as **being confined to transactions involving an element of bounty** (the UK case of IRC v Plummer - see also extract from judgement of :Lord Roskill in Chinn v Collins on next page) it is nonetheless clear that the definition is remarkably wide. The definition of *"settled property"* (set out above) is more narrow in that it is confined to property held in trust. S5 requires that *"settled property"* should be construed in accordance with the wide definition given to *"settlement"*. Nonetheless it is difficult to see how *"settled property"* can be construed to include anything which does not represent property held in trust.

An outright and unconditional gift of property, from a father to a son is a transaction which falls within the definition of *"settlement"*. But such an outright and unconditional gift does not involve any trust. The property which is the subject matter of the gift is not held by the son in trust. He is the absolute owner of it, free of all trusts. The example given would seem to be an example of a settlement in relation to which there is no *"settled property"*, and the requirement that *"settled property"* be construed in accordance with the wide definition of *"settlement"* would not seem capable of changing that.

s574

The terms of s574 themselves suggest that they are limited to a situation in which a trust exists. The section is written entirely on the basis that a person can be identified who is, in relation to settled property, a trustee. The section would seem incapable of operation where there is no trustee by reason of there being no trust. It is true that the courts will never allow a true trust to fail by reason of difficulty in identifying a trustee, but s574 does not seem capable of deeming a person to be a trustee, when he is not. Accordingly it seems to the authors that s574 dealing with settled property is confined to dealing with property which is the subject matter of a trust, and which in the context of the trust has been the subject matter of one of the types of transactions referred to in the definition of *"settlement"* involving an element of bounty.

It is possible to have (within the meaning of the CGT Acts) a trust which is not a settlement e.g. the sale for its open market value of the remainder interest in a specific property where the interest is created by the sale, and it is possible to have a settlement which is not a trust (e.g. an outright and unconditional gift). S574 is concerned with transactions which are both settlements and trusts.

A similar meaning attached to the phrase *'settlement'* has been the subject of much judicial consideration in the UK. Although the Irish and UK definitions are not identical for all CGT purposes, they are close enough to warrant consideration of some of the UK decided cases.

In Chinn v Collins, certain transactions carried out for the purposes of tax avoidance were held to be an *"arrangement"*.

In that case the taxpayer was a beneficiary of an English settlement which held a substantial number of shares. The settlor wished to have the shares appointed absolutely to the beneficiary. The appointment would, however, have given rise to a substantial capital gains tax liability.

To avoid this tax liability the following steps were taken:

Non-resident trustees were appointed and the general administration of the trust was transferred abroad. Shares were then appointed to the beneficiary contingent on his survival for three days from the date of the appointment. The taxpayer then sold his contingent interest in the shares to a non-resident company. He then entered into an agreement to purchase an equivalent number of shares (effectively the same shares) from the same company.

One of the Revenue contentions was that the scheme was an 'arrangement' and therefore a 'settlement' within the meaning of s.42(7) of the [UK] FA 1965.

It was held in the House of Lords that the scheme as a whole constituted an arrangement involving real bounty and accordingly was a settlement for CGT purposes. It followed that on the vesting of the contingent interest the taxpayer became absolutely entitled to the shares as against the trustees and accordingly attracted liability to tax in respect of the gains arising to the trustees on the transfer of the shares to the taxpayer. (See paragraph 68 dealing with the liability of Irish resident and domiciled beneficiaries having interests in non-resident trusts).

One of the main questions in considering whether the transactions constituted an *"arrangement"* [within the definition of *"settlement"* for the purposes of the CGT Acts] was whether there was an **element of bounty**.

On this point Lord Roskill stated:

"what the cases have sought to do is to distinguish those cases where the recipient has in return for the benefit which he has received accepted some obligation which he has to perform either before receiving the benefit or at some stated time thereafter and those cases where the recipient benefits without any assumption by him of any correlative obligation. In Plummer's case the transaction in question was for consideration. Under this scheme there was an appointment without consideration. (The taxpayer) was among the objects of the 1960 settlement but before the power of appointment was exercised there was no absolute certainty, however strong the probability that (the taxpayer) would receive any of the shares held by the trustees. In my judgement there was very real 'bounty' conferred when the trustees with the settlor's consent exercised the power of appointment in question in (the taxpayer's) favour. As Counsel for the Crown put it, when the power of appointment was exercised a blank was filled in the original settlement which left blank how the final distribution of the trust assets was to be made. That in my judgement was a clear act of 'bounty'".

Copeman v Coleman was decided under s.21 of the UK FA 1936, which defined settlement as including 'any disposition, trust, covenant, agreement, arrangement or transfer of assets'. Lawrence J in that case, said, *"is not the limitation to be read with those words — 'not being a bona fide commercial transaction'?*

In Bulmer v CIR , Penniquick J held that a commercial transaction without any element of bounty could not constitute a settlement. That case was heard under later legislation where the definition was the same as under the 1936 Act, but without the words 'or transfer of assets'.

This was followed by Buckley J in IRC v Plummer, where he said " *a transaction effected for full consideration in money or money's worth is not a settlement"* (within that definition). These principles were again followed by Goulding J in Berry v Warnett a case involving a CGT avoidance scheme - which is discussed in greater detail in paragraph 65.12.

The term 'SETTLOR' is stated to include (in relation to a settlement):

'Any person by whom the settlement was made or entered into directly or indirectly, and in particular (but without prejudice to the generality of the preceding words of this definition) includes any person who has provided or undertaken to provide funds directly or indirectly for the purpose of the settlement, or has made with any other person a reciprocal arrangement for that other person to make or enter into the settlement'.

65.5   **Property Settled on Trustees**

s575   S575 provides that a *"gift in settlement, whether revocable or irrevocable, shall be a disposal of the entire property thereby becoming settled property notwithstanding that the donor has some interest as a beneficiary under the settlement and notwithstanding that he is a trustee, or the sole trustee, of the settlement"*.

Where a settlor settles property on trustees, he is deemed by s575, to have made a disposal of the entire property. A gift in settlement would not be a bargain at arm's length, and accordingly the disposal proceeds in the case of the settlor, must be taken as being the market value of the assets at the time when they are settled on the trustees. Similarly, the trustees are treated as acquiring the assets at market value.

A person who owns an asset and declares trusts in relation to it, thereafter will hold it as a trustee. In such a case, although no transfer of legal title has occurred, the taxpayer has made a disposal to a trustee i.e. himself.

Example 277

John owns 5,000 shares in CRH PLC. He signs and seals a deed declaring that henceforth he holds the shares in trust for his wife for her life, and thereafter for his children in equal shares. The shares remain registered in John's name.

John has disposed of the shares to a trustee (i.e. himself). He has not disposed of them to his wife, nor to his children. The disposal by John is at open market value, as is the acquisition by the trustee i.e. by John, wearing a different hat. His wife and children have acquired interests arising under a settlement.

Example 278

John transfers 5,000 shares in CRH PLC to Bank of Ireland Nominees Limited to hold for himself for life and thereafter for his children.

John has disposed entirely of the 5,000 shares at open market value. He has not merely made a part disposal of the reversionary interest which is passed to the children. John has separately acquired an interest arising under a settlement - his life interest. The same result would arise if John had kept the shares registered in his own name and declared the trusts by a deed.

It should also be borne in mind that any loss on the disposal of assets to a connected person will not give rise to an unrestricted allowable loss for CGT purposes. As the settlor and trustees are normally regarded as 'connected' for CGT purposes, any losses accruing to the settlor on the 'gift in settlement' will not be allowed to him, except in the limited circumstances, where he has a subsequent gain on a further disposal to the trustees. The provisions dealing with the restriction on the use of losses on a disposal to a connected person are dealt with in paragraph 16.4.2.

Where the trustees acquire the assets by way of a 'gift in settlement', they are regarded as acquiring those assets at the market value on the date of acquisition.

In considering the question whether there has been a gift in settlement, it must first of all be decided whether there is a settlement. This question was considered in paragraph 65.4.

s10   The meaning of *"gift in settlement"* was considered in the UK case of Berry v Warnett. It is important to bear in mind, in considering the Berry v Warnett case, that the Irish and UK legislation relating to CGT and settlements is not identical. The Irish legislation applies the definition of *"settlement"* found in s.96(3)(h) ITA 1967 now s10 throughout the CGT legislation. That definition, as explained in paragraph 65.4, requires that there be an element of bounty in the arrangement or transaction, in order that a settlement should be constituted thereby. A similar definition was not adopted throughout the UK legislation and accordingly the UK legislation relating to settlements, although written in generally the same terms as the Irish legislation, applies inter alia to arrangements that do not include an element of bounty.

Berry v Warnett concerned a scheme designed to avoid CGT on the disposal of certain shares, which disposal was imminent. Mr. Berry transferred the shares to Jersey trustees as nominee. He then entered into a deed of settlement with those trustees whereby they paid to him a sum of money and he transferred the stocks and shares to the settlement, reserving to himself a life interest in the fund of the settlement. Subsequently he disposed of the life interest to a third party and, between the sum paid to him by the trustees, and that payable to the third party, realised the value of the portfolio of investments. The sum received from the trustees was a relatively small part of the total sums which he received.

Mr. Berry claimed that the transaction with the trustees constituted a part disposal only of the share portfolio, in respect of which he was liable to CGT; and that he was exempt from CGT on the disposal of the life interest under the UK equivalent of s613(4). That sub-section provides that no chargeable gain shall accrue on the disposal of an interest created by or arising under a settlement by the person for whose benefit the interest was created by the terms of the settlement or by any other person except one who acquired, or derives his title from one who acquired, the interest for a consideration in money or money's worth, other than consideration consisting of another interest under the settlement.

There was considerable difference of opinion among the judges who heard the case, which went all the way to the House of Lords. Those differences of opinion would in themselves reduce the influence which the judgement might have in Ireland, apart altogether from the difference in the underlying legislation.

The Revenue claimed that the transaction with the trustees constituted an entire disposal of the portfolio of shares and for a consideration which must be deemed to be open market value. They placed reliance on the UK equivalent of s575 which states that a gift in settlement shall be a disposal of the entire property thereby becoming settled property, notwithstanding that the donor has some interest as beneficiary under the settlement. Mr. Berry denied that the transaction with the trustees was *"a gift in settlement"*. He claimed that as the trustees had paid the full value of the reversionary interest in the portfolio, there was no element of gift involved. There could not therefore be a gift in settlement. Accordingly, he claimed that s575 (UK equivalent) had no application to the transaction. Opinions differed among the judges right up to and including the House of Lords, as to whether *"a gift in settlement"* referred only to something which was a gift, or whether it could refer to a transaction between a settlor and trustees which was not in the nature of a gift. The difficulties encountered by the UK judges in this matter are unlikely to arise in Ireland where the meaning of the phrase seems much more clear in the context of a settlement being an arrangement necessarily having an element of bounty. In the opinion of the authors, an Irish court is likely to agree with those of the judges in the UK who held that "a gift in settlement" could refer only to a transaction which is a gift.

The wording of the agreement between Mr. Berry and trustees influenced some of the judges in the case. They pointed out that, at the end of the two transactions under which the shares firstly were transferred to the trustees as nominees, and secondly the trustees received a reversionary interest in the shares, Mr. Berry had parted entirely with the power to sell (or retain if he so wished) the portfolio of shares in question. He did not retain a life interest in the portfolio of shares per se. What he had chosen to retain was a life interest in the trust fund and it was merely coincidental that for a short period that trust fund consisted of the portfolio of shares which he had previously owned absolutely. On general principles, and without reference to the special provisions relating to settled property, it was possible therefore to conclude that what was involved was not a part disposal but a complete disposal of the portfolio. This particular interpretation was set out in the judgement of Buckley LJ [(1980) STC p 647] *"it is contended that in these circumstances the taxpayer made a part disposal of shares and stock within [s534]. The words relied on are "there is a part disposal of an asset, where, on a person making a disposal, any description of property derived from the asset remains undisposed of." These words might well be held to fit the present case if it had taken the form of a grant by the taxpayer to the purchasers of a reversionary interest expectant on his own death specifically in the shares and stock, the taxpayer reserving to himself a life interest in them, thus constituting himself a trustee of the shares and stock. In such circumstances the only disposal would have been of the reversionary interest, and the life interest might be accurately described as having "remained undisposed of". But that was not the form of the transaction. The property disposed of was the shares and stock. The property in which the purchasers acquired a reversionary interest was not specifically the shares and stock, but a fund which, for the time being only, was represented by the shares and stock. Strictly speaking, nothing in my view, remains undisposed of. The taxpayer acquired a new asset consisting of a life interest under the settlement, not specifically in the shares and stock, but in the fund for the time being represented by the shares in the stock."*

Part 19 Chap 3   The comments of Buckley LJ above are interesting in the context of Irish legislation, where a *"settlement"* must contain an element of bounty. The hypothetical transaction which Buckley LJ described, involving a sale of a reversionary interest in stocks and shares, would not have been an arrangement involving any element of bounty and the resulting trust would not have been a settlement within the meaning of the Irish CGT rules (as set out in TCA97 Part 19 Chap 3). Accordingly, Part 19 Chap 3 would have had no application to it and the ordinary rules of the capital gains tax legislation, apart from Part 19 Chap 3, would have application to the trust, both in its creation, its continuation, and its termination. Indeed, it is arguable that the transaction which Buckley LJ suggests was what occurred in the Berry v Warnett case, involving the entire disposal of the stocks and shares in return for a payment of money, and a life interest in the fund of the trust, might be a transaction involving no element of bounty but merely a bargain at arm's length between two parties. In such a case Part 19 Chap 3 might have no application to that transaction either, although, on the interpretation placed on the transaction (which is not the only possible interpretation) it would have represented an entire disposal of the stocks and shares in the meaning of s534(a), and not a part disposal within the meaning of s534(b), for the reasons set out by Buckley LJ above.

In the Berry v Warnett case Buckley LJ held that in a situation where the life interest had been purchased at open market value (thereby creating a trust) the transfer of the asset to a trustee could not be said to be by way of a bargain with that trustee (whether at arms length or otherwise) and that that in itself would impose open market value on that transaction. To that limited extent, it may not have mattered whether or not the transaction described in Berry vs. Warnett would have been regarded as a transaction involving a settlement, for the purposes of Irish CGT on the occasion of the creation of the trust.

s613(4)   The exemption contained in s613(4) - which is subject to exceptions - relating to the disposal of an interest arising under a settlement does not extend to the disposal of an interest (such as a life interest or a remainder interest) arising under an arrangement or trust which is not a settlement by reason of not having an element of bounty in it. If indeed the arrangements entered into by Mr. Berry contained no element of bounty (on whatever interpretation is placed on them) then his disposal of his life interest would not have fallen within the exemption in s613(4).

s613A

The interest disposed of by Mr Berry in the case described above was an interest arising under a settlement which was or had been non resident. S613A (inserted by the FA99) would deny the exemption from a charge to tax in s613 on the disposal of an interest arising under a settlement, where the settlement had at any time been non resident. The law in Ireland therefore would no longer accommodate arrangements such as those entered into by Mr Berry.

65.6   Dealings in Assets by Trustees — Actual Disposals

Trustees, as a single continuing body, may dispose of assets in the same manner as any other person. When that body of persons disposes of an asset either a gain or a loss will arise for CGT purposes (in normal circumstances).

Whether such a gain is chargeable, or a loss allowable, depends on the residence or ordinary residence of that body, and whether the assets are specified Irish assets (see paragraph 3.4.2). The domicile of the body of trustees is not relevant for CGT purposes, as not being individuals (in their representative capacity) the remittance basis which applies to non-domiciled individuals in relation to certain foreign gains (see paragraph 3.3) cannot apply.

The absolute appointment of assets to a beneficiary is a disposal by the trustees at market value.

Changes in the identity of the persons acting as trustees (e.g. appointment of a new trustee or death or resignation of an old trustee) are not events for CGT purposes. They involve neither a disposal nor an acquisition of assets. Trustees are a continuing body of persons who are unaffected by changes in their identity. The only relevance of a change in the identity of trustees is that it may affect the residence of the trust (see paragraph 65.3).

65.7   Deemed Disposal by Trustees

65.7.1   General Outline

In addition to actual disposals by trustees, there are circumstances where trustees are deemed to dispose of assets. With the exception of charitable trusts, which are separately dealt with in paragraph 31 there are two specific instances in which the trustees are *deemed* to dispose of trust assets:

s567(1)

- When a person becomes absolutely entitled as against the trustees. The statutory definition of "absolutely entitled" is discussed in paragraph 64.2.

and

- When a life interest in the trust property ceases on the death of the life tenant, and the property does NOT cease to be settled property.

S576(1) provides:

'on the occasion when a person becomes absolutely entitled to any settled property as against the trustee all the assets forming part of the settled property to which that person becomes so entitled shall be deemed to have been disposed of by the trustee, and immediately reacquired by the trustee in his capacity as a trustee within s567(2), for a consideration equal to their market value'.

In effect, the trustees are treated as reacquiring the assets as nominee for the beneficial owner. Any further dealings in the assets would be treated as being made by the trustees on behalf of the beneficial owner. The treatment of nominees is set out in paragraph 64.

s5(3)

S5(3) provides that where the CGT Acts deem assets to be sold and immediately reacquired, the Acts do not imply that any incidental expenditure is incurred on sale or reacquisition. In other words, a deemed disposal does not entitle anyone to "deemed deductible incidental expenses" in the resulting computation. Since there can be no actual expenses associated with a deemed disposal, it follows that no incidental costs of disposal will be deductible in such a computation.

An asset ceases to be "settled property" when some person becomes absolutely entitled to the entire beneficial ownership, and either has, or is absolutely entitled to demand, the legal title to the asset, free of all trusts.

It should be noted, that there is also a deemed disposal by the beneficiary (of an interest in that settlement) when he becomes absolutely entitled as against the trustees to all or part of the trust assets. The charge to CGT arising on the beneficiary, and the exemption which applies in certain circumstances are discussed in paragraph 65.12.3.

Example 279

Under the terms of a settlement the trustees hold investments in trust for Stephen contingent on his living to the age of 25 years.

When he becomes 25 years of age, Stephen will be absolutely entitled to the assets as against the trustees. At that time, there is a deemed disposal by the trustees. They are also deemed to reacquire the assets at market value at that date as nominee for Stephen.

Stephen will have a deemed "cost" for CGT purposes equal to the market value of each and every separate investment comprised in the trustees investments to *which he becomes "absolutely entitled" at the date on which he becomes so entitled.*

An exception to the tax charge arising in such circumstances is provided where a beneficiary becomes absolutely entitled to settled property on the death of the person with a life interest in that property. In such circumstances, although there is a deemed disposal by the trustees, no chargeable gain arises; in addition, they are deemed to reacquire the assets at market value at the date of death of the person who held the life interest. Details of this exception to the main rule are set out in paragraph 65.7.3.

s577A

The FA98 has made it possible for *retirement relief* under s598 and s599 to be available in relation to the deemed disposal by the trustees on the occasion of a person becoming absolutely entitled as against them to the assets of the settlement. The relief is provided by a new s577A which applies to a deemed disposal (on the occasion of a person becoming absolutely entitled as against them) by trustees on or after 12 February 1998. The new section has application if the occasion of a person becoming absolutely entitled to assets as against the trustee is the occasion of "the relinquishing of a life interest (within the meaning of s577) by the person entitled to that interest" - see paragraph 30.12.

S577 (1)(a) provides the definition of "life interest" but makes no reference to any person relinquishing a life interest. Accordingly "the relinquishing of a life interest (within the meaning of s577)" must be construed as meaning the relinquishing (in the ordinary sense) of a life interest (as defined in s577). When does a person relinquish a life interest? It is clear that they do so when they renounce the interest in legal form, so as to cease to be entitled to it. In contrast, if a beneficiary disclaims a life interest before becoming entitled to it, they could not be said to be relinquishing a life interest to which they were entitled, and the section would not have application in those circumstances. Where a life tenant (i.e. a person entitled to a life interest) dies, he probably could not be said to relinquish his life interest, so much as that he is deprived of it. The act of death is not an act by which a person relinquishes anything - it is essentially a passive act. This is not particularly relevant however to s577A, since no tax would become payable by the trustees by reason of a deemed disposal on the death of a life tenant, the trust then coming to an end. As explained in paragraph 65.7.2, alternate relief is available to them in such circumstances.

s577

"Life Interest" as defined in s577 includes an interest per autre vie i.e. an interest for the period of the life of a person other than the person entitled to the interest. Such an interest would come to an end potentially on the death of a person not entitled to it, and the relief normally available to trustees where the trust comes to an end on the death of a life tenant is not then available, since the person who dies is not the life tenant. In such a situation, it is doubtful if the life tenant could be said "to relinquish" his life interest when it is taken from him by the death of a third party. "Relinquish" seems to denote some positive act, and would not seem sufficient to cover a situation where a life tenant is the passive victim of being deprived of his life interest by circumstances outside of his control. However, in absence of a definition of "relinquish" in the section, the matter cannot be beyond doubt.

65.7.2   Death of Life Tenant

s577

Where the death occurs of a person having a life interest in possession in all or part of settled property, s577 deems a disposal of the relevant part of that settled property by the trustees, but only to the extent that the property does not at that time cease to be settled property.

'*On the termination at any time on or after the 6th day of April, 1974, of a life interest in possession in all or any part of settled property, the whole or a corresponding part of each of the assets forming part of the settled property and not ceasing at that time to be settled property, shall be deemed for the purposes of this Act at that time to be disposed of and immediately reacquired by the trustees for a consideration equal to the whole or a corresponding part of the market value of the asset'.*

This subsection does not apply where any person becomes absolutely entitled to the assets on the death of the life tenant. The deemed disposal arises to the extent that the property does not cease to be settled property (see paragraph 65.7.1).

s577(5)

Example 280

William enjoyed a life interest in land and investments settled on trustees by his uncle in 1967. After William's death, his son will take a life interest in the property. William died on 10 September 1995.

As the life interest in the property terminated on William's death, the trustees are deemed to sell (and reacquire) the assets at market value at 10 September 1995. The resulting gain is chargeable to CGT – a loss would be allowable against other gains, subject to the normal rules.

It was contended by the Revenue in the UK case of Pexton v Bell, that on the death of a beneficiary with a life interest in one quarter of the total trust fund, the trustees were deemed to sell and reacquire the total trust fund at the date of death. The court held that only one quarter of the fund was deemed to be sold and reacquired in such circumstances.

The legislation itself provides that in certain circumstances, the property in which the life interest subsists may be regarded as a separate settlement for the purpose of determining which assets have been disposed of on the death of the life tenant - see paragraph 65.9.

In paragraph 31.3 a relief is described which applies where a charity becomes entitled to the assets on the death of the life tenant.

s577(5)   An exemption from the deemed disposal and reacquisition on the death of a life tenant is given in relation to certain *heritage houses*, or certain heritage objects, subject to conditions. The exemption applies to heritage houses and gardens, and art works which are exempt from capital acquisitions tax by reason of;

- a determination by the Revenue Commissioners or the Office of Public Works that they are of significant national, historic, aesthetic, or scientific interest and;

- have been open to the public for a specified period of time in each year.

CATA76 s55   Further details of the assets entitled to the exemption (CATA76 s55 and FA78 s39) can be found in the companion volume published by the Institute of Taxation, Capital Acquisitions Tax.

In order that the exemption from the deemed disposal and reacquisition should apply to these heritage assets, it is necessary that they should have been comprised in an inheritance taken on the death of the life tenant. "Inheritance" has a technical meaning in the Capital Acquisitions Tax Act and further reference should be made to the companion volume, Capital Acquisitions Tax, for further details.

This exemption applies only from 6 April 1997.

CATA76 s55   The exemption is subject to a clawback. If the CAT relief under CAT Act 76 s55 or FA78 s39 is clawed back by reason of the occurrence of events set out in those sections (principally the failure to continue to provide public access, or withdrawal of the determination that the objects are of significant interest, or the removal from the State of the heritage objects) capital gains tax that would otherwise have arisen on the trustees by reason of the deemed disposal and reacquisition is deemed to accrue to them in the year of assessment in which the capital acquisitions tax relief is withdrawn.

The withdrawal of the capital acquisitions tax relief can occur at any time over a period which can be as long as the lifetime of the person who has succeeded to the property as an inheritance. In an extreme case that could be as long as (say) 100 years. The trustees would seem to be exposed to a liability whose amount is difficult to determine (since it would depend on the rate applying at the date the gain is deemed to accrue i.e. at the time when the capital acquisitions tax relief is withdrawn) and at a time over which the trustees have no control. Viewed from that perspective, the exception is more of a burden on trustees than a true relief. Unfortunately the exception from the deemed disposal and reacquisition is not something which may be elected for, or not elected for. It is mandatory.

It is possible that the gain would be deemed to accrue at a time when the trust no longer exists, and even at a time when the trustees themselves may no longer be living. It must be doubtful whether a liability can be imposed at a time when the trust has ceased to exist, and at a time when there is no continuing body of persons who constitute the trustees of the trust. The point is uncertain.

The meaning of "life interest" and "life tenant" is considered in paragraph 65.8.

65.7.3   **Trustee relief - absolute interest passes on death of Life Tenant**

As set out above, the two occasions upon which the trustees are *deemed* to dispose of certain trust assets are:

s576
* where a person becomes absolutely entitled to trust assets
  − s576(1)

  and

s577
* on the death of a life tenant with an interest in possession in trust assets − s577(2).

Relief is provided where a person becomes absolutely entitled on the death of the life tenant to the trust assets in which the life interest subsisted.

s577(2)
S577(2)) provides:

'Where, by virtue of s576(1), the assets forming part of the settled property are deemed to be disposed of and reacquired by the trustee on the occasion when a person becomes absolutely entitled thereto as against the trustee, then, if that occasion is the termination of a life interest (within the meaning of this section) by the death of the person entitled to that interest-

(a)   no chargeable gain shall accrue on the disposal; and

(b)   the re-acquisition under that subsection shall be deemed to be for a consideration equal to the market value of the assets at the date of the death'.

The effect of this subsection, is to apply the normal 'death' provisions to treat the trustees as if they were personal representatives passing the asset to a beneficiary under the will of a deceased person where that person acquires absolute ownership of a trust asset on the death of a life tenant. Any gain accruing on the asset up to the date of death of the life tenant is not taxed, and the trustees hold the asset as if they were nominees for the person so entitled. The position of the person becoming entitled is discussed in paragraph 65.12.

Example 281

> *George enjoys a life interest in settled property. On his death, the property goes absolutely to his son Alan.*
>
> *When George dies there is a deemed disposal by the trustees but any gain arising is not chargeable, and a loss accruing on the disposal is not an allowable loss.*
>
> *The assets are deemed to be reacquired by the trustees at the date of George's death at market value, as nominee for Alan.*
>
> *Alan is deemed to dispose of his interest in the settlement in exchange for the settled property, and relief may also apply to that disposal - see paragraph 65.12.*

In the UK case of Crowe v Appleby it was held that where remaindermen become entitled to property on the death of a life tenant, but the life tenant was entitled to only a share in part of the settled property which consisted of land and buildings, the remaindermen did not become absolutely entitled as against the trustee on the death of the life tenant, but became so absolutely entitled only as and when the property was eventually sold and converted to cash. The case did not consider whether the property representing the interests of the remaindermen in that case remained an interest in settled property. If it had done so, the relief from the charge to tax arising on the death of the life tenant, described in this paragraph, would not apply.

s5(3)

s552(5)

In the ordinary way, the occasion of a person becoming absolutely entitled to settled property, as against the trustees, would be an actual disposal by the trustees of that property. However s576 deems a disposal to occur at the moment when the beneficiary becomes absolutely entitled against the trustee. This provision might seem unnecessary given that an actual disposal occurs in any event. The provision probably exists because the provisions relating to settlements are a self-contained code and many of the normal rules that apply to other situations do not apply to settlements. An example is the fact that on basic principles one would regard the appointment by trustees of a life interest in trust assets as being a part disposal of those assets. But for capital gains tax purposes the trustees are not treated as making either a disposal or part disposal on that occasion. The fact that the disposal that occurs on the occasion of a person becoming absolutely entitled as against the trustees is a deemed disposal and not an actual disposal as at least one consequence. S5(3) provides that on a deemed disposal and reacquisition, no deemed incidental expenses of disposal are to be taken into account. Any actual expenses incurred by the trustees in transferring the assets to the life tenant are not expenses of the deemed disposal (as opposed to the real disposal) and so would not seem to be deductible in the computation relating to the deemed disposal. However s552(5) provides that the incidental costs incurred by the trustees in transferring the asset to the beneficiary may be treated as deductible incidental costs by the beneficiary on any subsequent disposal by him of the asset. Thus although the trustees are denied a deduction for their own expenses, the beneficiary is granted a deduction of those expenses but on a later transaction.

Example 282

> The trustees of the Murphy Discretionary Trust own land. They appoint that land to Joe Murphy, one of the beneficiaries. They incur legal costs in connection with the transaction, amounting to £5000. The indexed base cost of the property was £200,000 and its open market value £500,000.
>
> Approximately a year after the appointment, Joe Murphy sold the property for £600,000 and incurred incidental costs of disposal of £10,000 on that occasion.

> **Trustees computation:**

Open market value - deemed consideration	500,000
Deduct:	
Indexed base cost	200,000
Incidental costs of disposal	nil
Chargeable gain	300,000

> **Joes Computation one year later:**

Consideration for disposal	600,000
Base cost (ignoring indexation for convenience)	500,000
Trustees costs of disposal deducxtible by Joe	5,000
Joe's incidental costs of disposal	10,000
Chargeable gain	85,000

- **Revenue/Chief Inspector's CGT Manual:**

— In the Chief Inspector of Taxes manuals at paragraph 19.2.10.5 it is stated in relation to acquisition and disposal costs

"The costs of legal and actuarial services including stamp duty on transfers and ancillary expenses incurred in varying or ending a settlement (see CIR v Chubbs Trustees) or upon determination of a life interest in possession. The allowable expenditure may include fees in respect of discharges, withdrawal fees and commission on transfer of assets to beneficiaries (but not insurance premiums) and where necessary, should be apportioned between chargeable and non-chargeable items by reference to value. - - if the costs of transfer etc have been borne by the person to whom the property is transferred, he may either be allowed a deduction for those costs or he may forego a claim and permit the trustees to treat these costs as an allowable deduction in computing their chargeable gain arising from the deemed disposal."

This statement would appear to imply that it is the Revenue practice to permit trustees a deduction for actual costs even in the context of a deemed disposal, contrary to the analysis set out above. It also indicates a concessional treatment in so far as the trustees expenses are paid by the beneficiary.

65.8   **Meaning of Life Interest**

s577   No definition of the phrase 'life interest' is given for the purpose of s577 and so it takes its normal meaning, subject to the specific items included in, and excluded from the normal meaning of that phrase by s577(1). The term 'life interest' is stated to include *'a right under the settlement to the income of , or the use or occupation of, settled property for the life of a person (or the lives of persons) other than the person entitled to the right'.*

Example 283

> *This partial definition would seem to include the following situations:*
>
> - *Joe is entitled to the use of a house for his life.*
>   *He thus has a life interest in the house.*
>
> - *Joe is entitled to the use of a house for the duration of the life of his wife.*
>   *This also is a life interest. It is known as an interest per autre vie (i.e. for another's life).*

The following two items are specifically excluded by s577(1) from the meaning of the phrase 'life interest' for the purpose of applying the rules set out in TCA97 Part19 Chap3.

Life Interest:

- *does not include any right which is contingent on the exercise of the discretion of the trustee or the discretion of some other person, and*

- *does not include an annuity, notwithstanding that the annuity is payable out of or charged on settled property or the income of settled property except where some or all of the settled property is appropriated by the trustees as a fund out of which the annuity is payable and there is no right of recourse to settled property not so appropriated, or to the income of settled property not so appropriated.*

An annuity is only regarded as a life interest where:

- property of the trust fund is appropriated by the trustees as a specific fund out of which the annuity is to be paid,

  and

- there is no right of recourse to other settled property (or income from other settled property).

Where a fund is set aside to pay a life annuity, and there is no recourse to other settled property, such an annuity is included within the meaning of the phrase 'life interest' for the purpose of applying the rules set out in Ch3 P19. Accordingly, on the death of the annuitant, a deemed disposal by the trustees takes place.

65.9   **Deemed Separate Settlements**

On the death of a life tenant, s577 deems a disposal of the relevant assets by the trustees [see paragraph 65.7.2].

For the purpose of applying this rule, and only for that purpose, s577 provides that in certain circumstances, the funds set aside to meet the income due in respect of a life interest or a life annuity, may be regarded as being a separate settlement.

In paragraph 65.10 the problems created by separate settlements and by resettlements are described. The deemed separate settlement under s577 is for the limited purposes of s577(3) and does not involve any of the consequences described in paragraph 65.10 of the creation of a separate settlement.

s577(4)

S577(4) provides:

(4)   *For the purposes of subsection (3)*

      (a)   *a life interest which is a right to part of the income of settled property shall be treated as a life interest in a corresponding part of the settled property, and*

      (b)   *if there is a life interest in a part of the settled property and, where that interest is a life interest in income, there is no right of recourse to, or to the income of, the remainder of the settled property, the part of the settled property in which the life interest subsists shall while it subsists be treated for the purposes of this subsection as being settled property under a separate settlement'.*

Example 284 - s574(4)(a)

Andrew and Charles are each entitled to a life interest in one half of the income of a settlement.

When one of them dies, only one half of the assets are deemed to be sold by the trustees, even though the interest of each extends to part of all of the trust assets.

Example 285 s577(4)(b)

Under a settlement made many years ago, William is entitled to a life interest in the income from land comprised in the settlement, while Robert is entitled to the income from the other trust investments.

The land, and the other investments, are treated as separate settlements for the purposes of s577(3); when Robert dies the investments are deemed to be sold and reacquired, and when William dies the land is deemed to be sold and reacquired.

The corresponding provision in the case of a life annuity, is contained in s577(1)(b):

s577

'Without prejudice to subsection (4)(b), where under paragraph (a)(iii) an annuity is to be treated as a life interest in relation to a settlement, the settled property or the part of the settled property appropriated by the trustees as a fund out of which the annuity is payable shall, while the annuity is payable, and on the occasion of the death of the annuitant, be treated for the purposes of subsection (3) as being settled property under a separate settlement'.

The circumstances in which an annuity is regarded as a life interest, are set out above.

In the UK case of Pexton v Bell (heard together with Crowe v Appleby)] the UK Court of Appeal dealt with a situation in which a life tenant had died but other persons who were also life tenants of the same settlement, still lived. The Inland Revenue claimed that the death of the life tenant who was entitled to a life interest in a quarter of the trust fund was the occasion that deemed disposal of the entire of the trust fund. The Court rejected this and ruled that it was the occasion of a disposal of only one quarter of the trust fund, in proportion to the interest held by the deceased life tenant.

- **Revenue/Chief Inspector's CGT Manual :**

- The Revenue Commissioners capital gains tax manual at Paragraph 19.3.5.10 states that notwithstanding that *"for certain purposes funds within the same trust are treated as separate settlements under Section 577(4)(b), any allowable losses arising on one fund are available for set-off against chargeable gains arising on another fund within the same trust. Provided that the trustees do not object, a separate assessment need not be made, even though the fund is treated as a separate settlement for computation purposes. If however, the trustees insist, separate assessments should be made."*

65.10   Separate Settlements

s576

Under general principles a disposal by trustees takes place only when they dispose of an asset. This would happen on the sale of an asset or on the absolute appointment of an asset in favour of a beneficiary. S576(1) however, deems a disposal of the assets by trustees on the occasion when any person becomes absolutely entitled to those assets as against the trustees.

In most circumstances it is quite clear whether a beneficiary has become so entitled as against the trustees. However, where the trustees exercise a power of appointment or advancement as a result of which the assets remain settled property, but interests which were not previously in existence have been created by the exercise of those powers, or perhaps where new interests have been created, serious difficulties can arise. The real question is whether the act of appointment or advancement by which those trustees declare that they hold trust property upon trust for the beneficiaries in fixed (or determined) interests itself results in those trustees (or any new trustees appointed in respect of the re-settled property) becoming a separate person for CGT purposes in respect of that property. If a new settlement is created by the appointment or advancement, the trustees of the new trusts will become absolutely entitled as against themselves as the trustees of the old trusts thus occasioning a deemed disposal for CGT purposes. The issues involved have been considered in a number of UK cases.

Before considering the UK cases on this point it is important to note that the relevant UK legislation considered in the cases did not contain a definition of *"settlement"*. As noted in paragraph 65.4, the Irish legislation does contain a definition of *"settlement"*. Furthermore, as previously noted, the UK definition of *"settled property"* differs from the Irish definition of *"settled property"* in that the Irish definition refers only to property the subject matter of trusts having an element of bounty, whereas the UK definition referred to property which was the subject matter of any trusts, with certain specified exceptions. The UK cases described below have not been reviewed by the Irish courts and until they do so, it remains to be seen whether they would follow them on their own merits, and whether any implications flow from the differences between the UK and the Irish relevant CGT legislation, as regards the definition of *"settlement"* and *"settled property"*. It must also be borne in mind that trust law in Ireland is not identical to trust law in Northern Ireland, Scotland or England.

What is in question here is not whether trustees may resettle property if they are given the power to do so by the trust deed or statute. That trustees may do so is well established. The question that arises is whether such resettled property is held as part of the original settlement, or as part of a new and separate settlement. If a resettlement results in a new and separate settlement, the trustees of that new settlement become absolutely entitled to the resettled assets as against the trustees of the original settlement and a CGT charge may result. That is the result even if the persons who constitute the trustees of both settlements are identical.

The first two of the CGT cases in which the point arose were Hoare Trustees v Gardner and Hart v Briscoe which were heard together in the UK Chancery division.

In those cases, Brightman J held that a deemed disposal takes place where the trustees of the settlement, pursuant to a power of advancement, either transfer assets to the trustees of another ad hoc settlement or execute a deed declaring a series of trusts of the advanced assets so as to take them out of head settlement and subject them to new trusts. The decision was made on the basis that the head settlement and the ad hoc settlement in relation to the advanced assets constituted two separate settlements for CGT purposes. It was also held that the trustees of the ad hoc settlement (whether or not they were the same as the trustees of the head settlement) had become absolutely entitled to the advanced assets as against the trustees of the head settlement for the purpose of CGT, notwithstanding the fact that they had no beneficial interest in those assets.

Those cases were followed by Roome v Edwards where it was held that the exercise of a joint special power of appointment under the Marriage Settlement coupled with an assignment of the life interest in possession so as to procure that the appointed funds should be held on trusts which were not exhausted, did not result in that fund becoming subject to the trusts of a separate settlement for CGT purposes.

In that case Lord Wilberforce said:

"There was a number of obvious indicia which may help to show whether a settlement, or a separate settlement from another settlement exists. One might expect to find separate and defined property, separate trusts, and separate trustees. One might also expect to find a separate disposition bringing the separate settlement into existence. These indicia may be helpful, but they are not decisive. For example, a single disposition, e.g. a will with a single body of trustees, may create what are clearly separate settlements, relating to different properties, in favour of different beneficiaries, and conversely separate trusts may arise in what is clearly a single settlement, e.g. when the settled property is divided into shares. There are so many possible combinations of fact that, even where these indicia or some of them are present, the answer may be doubtful, and may depend on an appreciation of them as a whole.

Since 'settlement' and 'trusts' are legal terms, which are also used by business men or laymen in a business or practical sense, I think that the question whether a particular set of facts amounts to a settlement should be approached by asking what a person, with knowledge of the legal content of the word under established doctrine and applying this knowledge in a practical and common sense manner to the facts under examination, would conclude. To take two fairly typical cases, many settlements contain powers to appoint a part or a proportion of the trust property to beneficiaries; some may also confer power to appoint separate trustees of the property so appointed, or such power may be conferred by law...It is established doctrine that the trusts declared by a document exercising a special power of appointment are to be read into the original settlement (see Muir v Muir). If such a power is exercised, whether or not separate trustees are appointed, I do not think that it would be natural for such a person as I have presupposed to say that a separate settlement had been created, still less so if it were found that provisions of the original settlement continued to apply to the appointed fund, or that the appointed fund were liable, in certain events, to fall back into the rest of the settled property. On the other hand, there may be a power to appoint and appropriate a part or portion of the trust property to beneficiaries and to settle it for their benefit. If such a power is exercised the natural conclusion might be that a separate settlement was created, all the more so if a complete new set of trusts were declared as to the appropriated property, and if it could be said that the trusts of the original settlement ceased to apply to it. There can be many variations on these cases each of which will have to be judged on its facts".

In the quotation above Lord Wilberforce said that "*settlement*" and "*trusts*" are legal terms which are also used by businessmen in a practical sense. Lord Wilberforce made these remarks in the context of UK CGT legislation, which did not contain a definition of "*settlement*" for the purpose of the provisions he was then dealing with. The position is different in Ireland where "*settlement*" is statutorily defined in the CGT legislation. It is difficult to say whether that fact would have affected Lord Wilberforce's judgement, had he given it in an Irish context.

The UK case of Muir v Muir referred to by Lord Wilberforce above was an important case in the area of trust law. In particular the principles set out in it, and referred to above by Lord Wilberforce, are relevant in determining whether a trust offends the rule against perpetuities (i.e. is capable of continuing for a period which is longer than the maximum period permitted by law). Lord Wilberforce has noted above that in accordance with Muir v Muir, special powers of appointment are treated as if they had formed part of the original trust deed being equivalent to blanks in the trust deed left by the settlor for the trustees to fill in. Lord Wilberforce appears to consider that where such an exercise of a special power of appointment applies, a new settlement would not normally be considered to be created. Lord Wilberforce goes on to identify some other circumstance relating to a power of appointment which he believes could lead to the creation of a new settlement. It is not clear why Lord Wilberforce considers that the rule in Muir v Muir would not apply to that power of appointment, and why accordingly, one would not reach the same conclusion as he reached earlier in relation to a special power of appointment which did fall within the rule in Muir v Muir.

In the UK case of Pilkington v CIR it was confirmed that trusts created by the exercise of a power of advancement or of re-settlement remained governed by the perpetuity period of the original settlement, according to the rule in Muir v Muir.

The notion that a settlement can sub-divide in such a manner that it creates from itself a new settlement, the trustees of which can become absolutely entitled against the trustees of the original settlement which created the new settlement, is a matter which has emerged in the UK courts. It is not a matter to which the capital gains tax legislation makes specific reference or for which it makes explicit provision. To date the matter has not come before the Irish courts, and until it does, there must be some question as to whether they would follow the approach adopted in the UK courts.

Roome v Edwards was a UK case concerned with a scheme which was effected for the sole purpose of taking assets out of a settlement without attracting a liability to CGT on the disposal by the trustees. Under a marriage settlement made in 1944, a trust fund was held by trustees for a wife (for her life) and thereafter on protective trusts for her husband during his life (should he survive her), and thereafter for their issue as they or the survivor should appoint. In 1955, the wife and husband executed a deed of appointment and release whereby investments (valued at £13,000) forming part of the 1944 fund were irrevocably appointed in trust for one of their daughters absolutely (contingent on her reaching the age of 25 years). The wife surrendered her life interest in the investments represented by the 1955 appointed fund. After the 1955 appointed fund was created, and although the two trustees of both 'funds' were the same, the two funds were administered separately. The 1955 fund, although created many years before the introduction of CGT, was the sole factor on which the scheme put into effect in 1972, failed.

The Scheme :

7 February 1972:

One of the two trustees of the 1944 fund was replaced by another.

28 February 1972:

An order was made under the Variation of Trusts Act 1958, approving an arrangement converting the husband's protected reversionary life interest in the main 1944 fund into an absolute reversionary life interest in that fund (which fund was then worth about £900,000).

15 March 1972:

The husband and wife executed a number of deeds, the consequence of which was to leave the position of the balance of the 1944 fund held on trust:

—for the wife for her life;

—with remainder to the husband for his life (after her death);

—with remainder to the two daughters in equal shares absolutely.

The above transactions were preliminary to the introduction of the tax planning aspects of the scheme.

20 March 1972:

The wife assigned her interest in the main 1955 fund to Royal Oak (A Cayman Islands Company) for market value, i.e. £375,000.
and

The husband assigned his interest in that fund also to Royal Oak for £25,000 (market value).

As a result of this transaction, there had been no disposal by the UK resident trustees. The two 'life interest' beneficiaries had disposed of their 'interest in settled property' for a total of £400,000, which by virtue of s.24(4)(a) was exempt from CGT (see paragraphs 32.13, and 65.12).

20 March 1972:

The two daughters assigned their interest in the 1944 fund to another Cayman Islands company, 'CRI', for £234,000 each.

The same provisions applied here to exempt the disposal by the daughters from CGT, as applied in the case of the assignments by the husband and wife.

21 March 1972:

The two trustees of the 1944 fund were replaced by two Cayman Island resident trustees.

It was thought that, the 1944 settlement being a separate settlement, with non-resident trustees, would now be outside the scope of the charge to CGT on any later disposals by the non resident trustees.

13 April 1981:

CRI assigned its reversionary interest to Royal Oak, which by virtue of the assignment became absolutely entitled as against the trustees to the entire balance of the 1944 fund.

It was held in the House of Lords that the 1944 fund, and the 1955 fund (which had two UK resident trustees) were one single settlement for CGT purposes. As the majority of the trustees were not non-resident (i.e. two UK and two Cayman Island trustees), the single body of trustees was automatically deemed to be UK resident (see paragraph 65.3). Accordingly, the deemed disposal by the trustees, on Royal Oak becoming absolutely entitled as against the trustees, was chargeable to CGT (on the UK resident trustees).

In Eilbeck v Rawling, the House of Lords also dismissed a taxpayer's contention that separate settlements existed. In that case, the taxpayer purchased the reversionary interest in a Gibraltar settlement for £543,600. At that time, the fund consisted of £600,000. There was power in Clause 5 of the settlement to appoint any part of the capital of the Trust Fund to the reversioner or to the trustees of any other settlement. In the latter case, it was necessary that the reversioner should be indefeasibly entitled to a corresponding interest under such other settlement. On the exercise of any such power, a compensating advance had to be made to the income beneficiary. Such a settlement was formed in Jersey by the taxpayer's brother and the Gibraltar Trustee advanced £315,000 to the Jersey settlement to be held as capital of that settlement. The Gibraltar Trustee also appointed £29,610 to compensate the income beneficiary.

The taxpayer sold his interest in the Gibraltar fund for £231,130. The Trust Fund at that stage consisted of £255,390. The taxpayer also sold his interest in the Jersey Fund for £312,100.

The taxpayer claimed that he had suffered a loss of £312,470 on the disposal of his interest in the Gibraltar settlement. He claimed that the gain realised on the disposal of his interest in the Jersey settlement was exempt on the grounds that it arose on the disposal of an interest under a settlement by the person for whose benefit the interest was created by the terms of the settlement (not having been acquired for a consideration in money or money's worth) — see paragraph 65.11.

It was held in the House of Lords that the taxpayer's interest in the Jersey Fund must be regarded as part of his interest in the Gibraltar Fund. Accordingly, the true price realised on the disposal of the taxpayer's interest was the aggregate of the sums realised from both funds so that his real loss was about £370.

Lord Fraser summarised the position as follows:

'The position was that, after the appointment, the appointed fund was held by the Jersey Trustee for purposes which, although in some respects different from those of the Gibraltar Settlement (the tenant for life being different and the closing date probably being different), were within the limits laid down in the Gibraltar settlement. In particular, the reversioner was the same and the closing date not later than the vesting date in the Gibraltar Settlement. If the difference had not been within the permitted limits the appointment would of course not been intra vires the Gibraltar Trustee. Accordingly, the true price realised on the disposal of Mr. Rawling's interest was in my opinion, the sum of the price of the retained fund in Gibraltar (£231,130) and of the appointed fund in Jersey (£312,100) amounting to £543,230. His loss was therefore about £370'.

The case of Eilbeck v Rawling was heard in the House of Lords in conjunction with the notorious Ramsay case. The judgement in the two cases (which were taken together in the House of Lords) involved the first statement of the so called Ramsay doctrine, (developed later as the Furniss v Dawson doctrine). This doctrine was an approach to the judicial consideration of tax avoidance cases which the Supreme Court in Ireland refused to follow, on the grounds that it involved an interference in the legislative sphere. Although the House of Lords held against the taxpayer in the Eilbeck v Rawling case on grounds which were not dependent on the so called "Ramsay" doctrine, it is doubtful if the judgement would be regarded as influential in the Irish courts, having regard to its association with the "Ramsay" doctrine and the perhaps over vigorous hostility displayed to tax avoidance, by the House of Lords in particular, and also by the other courts which heard the case.

In the later UK case of Bond v Pickford , Nourse J in his judgement, followed the guidelines set out by Lord Wilberforce in Roome v Edwards. In Bond v Pickford, the trustees of a discretionary settlement executed deeds of allocation as a result of which some of the trust assets were to be held on trusts in favour of specified beneficiaries. Although the trusts of the allocated funds were separate from the trusts of the main settlement, and were exhaustive of the beneficial interest in those funds, the trustees of the main settlement continued as trustees of the allocated funds. In addition, the administrative powers of the head settlement were applied to the allocated funds. In his judgement, Nourse J said...*"my view so far can be summarised by saying that I look at the deeds of allocation as if they were exhaustive appointments under special powers which automatically preserved the application of the administrative powers and provisions of the settlement and, of course, the enduring retention of the allocated funds by the trustees of the settlement. On that footing, echoing the words of Lord Wilberforce, I do not think that it would be natural for such a person as he presupposed to say that a separate settlement has been created".*

The judgement of Nourse J was upheld by the Court of Appeal, and the Revenue were refused leave to appeal to the House of Lords.

Similar issues arose in Swires v Renton, but that case did not throw any new light on the matters involved.

At the moment, the question of whether a new trust is created by the exercise of such powers by trustees is far from clear, and is likely to remain so until the Courts have given a more detailed consideration to this area of the law. However, it is possible to obtain assistance from the guidelines set out by Lord Wilberforce in Roome v Edwards. The following is a summary of those guidelines:

• Would "a person" with knowledge of the legal meaning of the word settlement, who considered the matter in a practical and common sense way come to the conclusion that a separate settlement had been created.

• Although they are not decisive in themselves the following factors may be helpful in deciding whether or not a separate settlement has been created:

  — the existence of separate and defined property

  — the existence of separate trusts

  — the existence of separate trustees

  — whether there is a separate disposition bringing the separate settlement into existence.

 — to what extent (if any) do the provisions of the head settlement apply to the appointed fund.

 — is the appointed fund liable at any time to fall back into the head settlement.

The question of when a new settlement is created by the actions of the trustees of an existing settlement is of interest, not only for the purposes of CGT (and other taxes such as capital acquisitions tax and stamp duty), but also in the context of the rule against perpetuities, which limits the maximum period of a trust. A transaction which offends the rule against perpetuities is void. The rule in the case of Muir v Muir, referred to by Lord Wilberforce above was developed arising out of such trust law concerns rather than in a taxation context. It is likely that Irish Courts, when they have to consider these matters, will be aware of the implications of their decisions for trust law generally and will not be over influenced by the extreme hostility to tax avoidance which has characterised many decisions of the UK House of Lords and especially in this area of tax law and trust law since the late 1970's.

The definition of "settlement" used for Irish CGT purposes can include an arrangement involving an element of bounty, and a trust. The word "arrangement" is a word of potentially very wide application. Where there are more than one body of trustees, and separate properties, there may nonetheless be only a single settlement if all of the trustees and trusts and properties are encompassed by a single arrangement which had an element of bounty. It can be a matter of considerable difficulty to determine whether actions taken by trustees (perhaps encouraged by beneficiaries, or including participation by beneficiaries), are or are not part of a single arrangement with the original creation of the trust. The subsequent actions taken by the trustees may not have been envisaged in a specific way by the settlor when he created the trust. But trustees are not capable of taking any action other than an action for which they have been granted a power by the settlor in the trust deed. The doctrine in Muir v Muir quoted above would suggest that the exercise of powers by trustees is the equivalent of the filling in of blanks on the original settlement, and can be seen as part of the original action of the settlor in creating the trust. Against that background, it may be difficult to demonstrate that a settlement, distinct from an original settlement, had been created by the trustees.

• **Revenue/Chief Inspector's CGT Manual :**

 — At paragraph 19.3.5.10 of the Revenue capital gains tax manual it is stated *"Separate settlements may exist in law even though they have been created by the same trust instrument and have at the same body of trustees, but a separate settlement can only exist where separate funds are held on separate trusts."*

- **Revenue/Chief Inspector's CGT Manual :**

— The Revenue Commissioners, in their capital gains tax manual at Paragraph 19.3.2 state that all assets held on identical trusts (with identical beneficiaries having the same relative interests in all assets) may be regarded as held in a single settlement notwithstanding that they were added to the trusts on separate occasions. However trustees are permitted to request in writing *"that additions to trust funds are to be regarded as creating a separate trust"*. In certain circumstances, provided the trustees agree a regime for taxing the trust which will operate irrevocably over the entire life of the trust, the Inspector is likely to accede to the request.

65.11 Losses Accruing to Beneficiary

s576(2)

When a person becomes absolutely entitled to any of the trust property, any allowable losses (including losses forward) accruing to the trustees in respect of that property (or property which is represented by that property) insofar as they are not used by the trustees up to that time, are treated from then on as accruing to the person who became entitled to the property.

On the deemed disposal, for example, when the beneficiary becomes entitled as against the trustees, a loss may arise. S576(2) provides:

'(2)   *On the occasion when a person becomes absolutely entitled to any settled property as against the trustee, any allowable loss which has accrued to the trustee in respect of property which is, or is represented by, the property to which that person so becomes entitled (including any allowable loss carried forward to the year of assessment in which that occasion falls), being a loss which cannot be deducted from chargeable gains accruing to the trustee in that year, but before that occasion, shall be treated as if it were an allowable loss accruing at that time to the person becoming so entitled, instead of to the trustee'.*

Example 286

The trustee of the Williams Family Trust hold a portfolio of shares on discretionary trusts. John Williams is amongst a class of beneficiaries for whom the trust was originally set up. He also holds shares which are his absolute property.

On 30 April 1999 the trustees appoint to John absolutely shares in Biotech Future PLC which have recently fallen in value on the stock exchange. An allowable loss of £10,000 arises. On 10 April 1999 the trustees had sold some CRH PLC shares on which a chargeable gain of £6,000 arose. On 30 June 1999 they realised a further gain of £20,000 on a sale of AIB PLC shares.

On 31 May 1999 John personally sold shares from his own portfolio, realising a gain of £15,000.

The trustees are entitled to offset £6,000 of the loss on Biotech Future PLC's shares against the gain accruing to them on the prior disposal of CRH shares.

However the balance of a loss of £4,000 in the Biotech shares is deemed to accrue to John (to whom those shares were appointed). The trustees cannot offset that £4,000 balance of loss against the gain on the AIB shares because that gain arose subsequent to the loss being crystallised on the Biotech shares. It does not matter that the Biotech loss and the AIB gain arose all in the same 1999/00 tax year.

John may offset £4,000 of the Biotech loss (which in fact was borne by the trustees) against his gain in the year 1999/00 of £15,000.

Even if John never disposed of any asset and so had no use for the £4,000 balance of the Biotech loss, it is deemed to be his loss and not that of the trustees who cannot obtain relief for it.

The appointment of assets which crystallise a loss for the trustees requires careful consideration and planning if the best results are to be obtained.

The same "transfer of losses" on a compulsory basis (no election is required or permitted) applies where the losses arose, not on the appointment of an asset to the beneficiary, but on earlier disposals by the trustees of assets now represented by the asset appointed by them to the beneficiary.

It is unclear in what circumstances an asset is to be treated as representing other assets. It might be confined to as restricted a circumstance as where shares have been obtained in exchange for other shares (see paragraphs 42 and 43). In the alternative, it may be that all assets held by a trustee represent the assets originally settled, and that a proportion of all trust losses unutilised by the trustees on the date of the appointment of an asset are to pass to the beneficiary. Any attempt at tracing the proceeds of sale of an asset to the acquisition later of other assets by the trustees would seem not to be intended, and would be impractical.

On balance it seems likely that the correct interpretation is that a proportion of all unutilised trust losses pass to the beneficiary. However there remains doubt in the matter.

65.12   Disposal of Interest Under a Settlement

65.12.1   Deemed disposal by beneficiary

s613(4)(b)   S613(4)(b) deems the beneficiary to dispose of his interest under the settlement when he becomes absolutely entitled as against the trustee to the settled property.

(b)   *Subject to paragraph (a), where a person who has acquired an interest in settled property, (including in particular the reversion to an annuity or life interest) becomes, as the holder of that interest, absolutely entitled as against the trustee to any settled property, the person shall be treated as disposing of the interest in consideration of obtaining that settled property (but without prejudice to any gain*

> accruing to the trustee on the disposal of that property deemed to be
> effected by the trustee under s576(1)).

The meaning of "absolutely entitled as against the trustee" is dealt
with in paragraph 64.2.

Provided he is within the exemption under s613(4)(a) - see
paragraph 65.12.2 below - the gain will not be chargeable to tax. In
any case where a gain would not be chargeable, a loss will not
qualify for relief for CGT purposes.

These provisions in no way interfere with the operation of s576(1) -
see paragraph 64.2 - which deems a disposal by the trustees when
the beneficiary becomes absolutely entitled to the assets. They
merely provide an exemption to the beneficiary.

65.12.2   Exemption for beneficiary on disposal of interest

s613(4)(a)

An exemption from CGT is also provided by s613 for gains arising
out of the deemed disposal by a beneficiary of his interest arising
under the settlement. That section (as amended by FA99 s90)
provides:-

'(a) *Subject to subsection (5) no chargeable gain shall accrue on the
disposal of an interest created by or arising under a settlement
(including, in particular, an annuity or life interest, and the reversion
to an annuity or life interest)*

   (i)   *by the person for whose benefit the interest was created by the
terms of the settlement or*

   (ii) *by any other person except one who acquired, or derives that
person's title from one who acquired, the interest for a
consideration in money or money's worth, other than
consideration consisting of another interest under the
settlement'.*

The exemption does NOT apply to a person who acquired his
interest under the settlement for 'consideration'. The only
exceptions to this exclusion, where the exemption will still apply, are

- where the consideration consisted of another interest under the
settlement, or

- where the person making the disposal is the person for whose
benefit the interest was originally created.

FA99 s90(1)(a)

In making the s613 exemption *"subject to subsection(5)"*, FA99 has
limited the use of the exemption where the trust has ever been
non-resident or treaty protected. The additional limitation is
discussed in paragraph 65.12.3.

In the UK case of Berry v Warnett , Buckley LJ said *"No chargeable gain arises on the disposal by a beneficiary of any beneficial interest created by or arising under a settlement, whether it is made for a consideration or voluntarily, but, if the disposal is for consideration in money or money's worth, the acquirer will be liable to capital gains tax on any subsequent disposal of that interest by him in just the same way as as anyone else who realises an investment which he has made...or on his becoming absolutely entitled to the property as against the trustees..."*.

Example 287

> *Joe created a discretionary settlement with his children included in the class of beneficiaries. Subsequently the trustees appointed a life interest to John, one of Joe's children. John needs capital to start up a business, and sells the life interest to an uncle for £100,000. The uncle then gifts the life interest to his daughter, Mary.*
>
> *Because John was a person for whose benefit the life interest was created under the terms of the settlement, he is not chargeable to tax on a disposal of the interest, notwithstanding that he received a sum of £100,000 for it. His uncle disposed of the interest when he gifted it to his daughter Mary, and since the transaction was between connected parties and was a gift, he is deemed to have made the disposal at open market value. Because the uncle is not the person for whose benefit the interest was originally created, and because he acquired it for a consideration in money or money' worth, he is not entitled to avail of the exemption described above on the occasion of his disposal of the interest by way of gift. Accordingly it is necessary for him to prepare a computation.*
>
> *If the trustees of the settlement had appointed the life interest to John in return for John transferring certain shares in a family company to the trust, John would nonetheless remain exempt in respect of his disposal of the life interest, because he was the person for whose benefit the interest was originally created, notwithstanding that he gave consideration for it.*

Example 288

> *Joe created a discretionary settlement for a class of beneficiaries which includes his children. The trustees granted a life interest to one of those children, John, in return for John transferring certain shares in a family company to the settlement. John gifted his life interest to his cousin Mary. Mary in turn transferred the life interest by gift to one of her children.*
>
> *As in **Example 287** John is entitled to avail of the exemption in respect of the disposal of his interest in the trust. Mary however is not entitled to avail of the exemption, notwithstanding that she did not give any consideration for the interest which was gifted to her. That is because she derives her title (i.e. the life interest) from a person who acquired it for a consideration in money's worth (i.e. John). Accordingly, on the occasion of her gift of the life interest to her child, there is a disposal for capital gains tax purposes which is not covered by the exemption.*

If in the example above, what John received and sold, and what his cousin Mary in turn gifted to her children, having received it by way of gift from John, was a remainder interest (i.e. one not yet in possession), then Mary's child would be deemed by s613(4)(b) to dispose of that remainder interest on the occasion when it fell into possession i.e. when she became absolutely against the trustees. Because the title was derived from a person who acquired it for a consideration in money's worth (i.e. John ultimately) an exemption would not be available to Mary's child on that occasion.

The exemption described above in relation to the disposal of an interest arising under a settlement is particularly important in the light of the fact that Section 613(4)(b) deems a beneficiary to dispose of his interest in a settlement on the occasion of becoming absolutely entitled to the assets in the settlement by virtue of that interest.

Example 289

> Taking the facts in **example 287 and 288** above, assume that the trustees also appoint out the remainder interest in the assets to a grandchild of Mary. On John's death the life interest held by Mary's child comes to an end, and Mary's grandchild becomes absolutely entitled as against the trustees by virtue of having the remainder interest. At that point Mary's grandchild is treated as having disposed of that remainder interest in return for the assets to which the grandchild became entitled. But for the exemption provided in Section 613(4)(a), the grandchild would become liable to capital gains tax at that point on the difference between the open market value of the remainder interest at the time it was acquired by him, and the open market value of the assets to which the grandchild became absolutely entitled at the later date on which he became entitled to them..
>
> As noted above, that exemption is not always available.

- **Revenue/Chief Inspector's CGT Manual :**

- The Revenue Commissioners, in their capital gains tax manual at paragraph 19.3.5.5 state *"Where the original life tenant of a settled property makes a payment to the original reversioner (remainderman) in consideration for which the reversioner surrenders the reversionary interest to the life tenant, the life tenant becomes absolutely entitled to the property as against the trustees who are consequently chargeable under s576(1). The property is deemed to have passed to the life tenant at market value but no allowance is due in respect of the life tenant's payment. The life tenant is not liable under s613(4)(b) because he becomes absolutely entitled to the property as the holder of both interests and not as the holder of the reversionary interest within the terms of s613(4)(b). Although as a result of the transaction the reversioner has disposed of the reversionary interest, no chargeable gain accrues. The above instructions also apply to a reversioner who, by making a payment to the life tenant, becomes absolutely entitled to the settled property."*

The ruling given above by the Revenue Commissioners avoids any argument that the life interest, on coming into the same ownership as the remainder interest, is deemed to merge with it and extinguish instantaneously, so that it is by reason solely of the remainder interest that the beneficiary becomes absolutely entitled against the trustees.

65.12.3   **Disposal of interest - non resident trustees**

65.12.3.1   **Broad Outline**

FA99 s90(1)(a) As noted above, the exemption which is available in relation to gains arising on the disposal of an interest created by or arising under a settlement applies (subject to conditions) to CGT which would otherwise be chargeable on

- a *deemed disposal* of that interest when the holder of the interest becomes absolutely entitled as against the trustees, and

- an *actual disposal* of that interest, including a sale of it to third parties, or a gift of it.

FA99 has placed restrictions on the application of that exemption to the latter circumstance where the trust has *ever* been *non-resident.*

The same restrictions apply where the trust has even been *"treaty protected"* - i.e.- where an Irish resident trust has been regarded for the purposes of any tax treaty between Ireland and another territory as being resident in that other territory.

This would normally only happen where

- the trust is resident in Ireland under Irish domestic law.

- the trust is also resident in another territory under the domestic law of that territory.

- the tax treaty between Ireland and that other territory provides a *"tie breaker"* clause in the fiscal domicile article of the treaty under which the trust is regarded as a resident of the other territory (in the circumstances of that particular trust).

This is a feature of most modern tax treaties. The UK treaty, for example provides in Article 4(3) - *"Where ....a person other than an individual is a resident of both Contracting States, then it shall be deemed to be a resident of the Contracting State in which its place of management is situated"* - see paragraph 84.2.1

Example 290

> *The Murphy Trust, formed in 1995 has four trustees ,two of which are resident in Ireland, and two of which are resident in the UK. The administration of the trust is carried on in Ireland up to and including 1998/99. In 1999/2000 one of the UK trustees retires, and is replaced by a UK corporate trustee, which also takes over the the general administration of the trust.*
>
> *If we assume that the Irish "trust residence rules" also apply in the UK, the trust would be resident in the UK, with two trustees and the general administration located there. It would also be deemed to be resident in Ireland as the majority of the trustees are not resident abroad.*

In such circumstances, the tie breaker clause in Article 4(3) of the Ireland/UK tax treaty would apply to make the trust resident in the UK for the purposes of the treaty.

In such circumstances, although the trust is resident in Ireland (and also resident in the UK) under the terms of the Ireland/UK tax treaty it is deemed to be a resident of the UK. In this text, such a trust is referred to as one which is *"treaty protected"* - and the provisions apply whether or not under the terms of the particular tax treaty, any of the gains are actually protected from a charge to Irish CGT or not.

65.12.3.2   Limitation on use of exemption

FA99 s90

FA99, with effect as and from a *disposal made on or after 11 February 1999* of an interest under a settlement , has limited the use of the s613 exemption where:

s613

- there has ever been a time when the trust has been resident or ordinarily resident outside the State, or,

- There has ever been a time when the trust has been regarded under a double tax agreement as resident outside the State, or

- the trust property is or includes property derived directly or indirectly from such a non-resident or treaty protected trust.

The limitation takes affect regardless of when the interest under the settlement was obtained by the holder.

In such circumstances the s613 exemption:

- *only applies* where the holder of the interest under the settlement becomes *absolutely entitled as against the trustee* to settled property (and is treated as making a disposal of an interest in consideration of that settled property) - see paragraph 65.12.1 above,

- *does not apply* to any other disposal of an interest under the settlement, eg., a sale or gift of the interest would not qualify for relief.

The rules relating to the residence of a trust (which differ significantly from residence rules relating to other entities) are explained in paragraph 65.3.

The limitation in the use of the exemption applies in a case where a trust is treated as resident in another State for the purposes of a double tax agreement, even if all or most of the assets of the trust are such as are not protected from a charge to capital gains tax under the treaty (e.g. Irish land, which generally speaking is not the subject matter of treaty protection). Other sections introduced by FA99, such as the exit charge on trusts on the occasion of going non resident, or becoming treaty protected, do distinguish between assets upon which the trust would thereafter remain within the charge to capital gains tax, and other assets. This distinction has not been carried over in the restriction on the relief for disposing of an interest arising under a settlement.

As explained in paragraph 65.13, there is protection against the exit charge on trusts where a trust becomes non resident or treaty protected by reason of the death of a trustee, and it resumes residence, or loses treaty protection, within six months of that death (e.g. by the appointment of a new Irish resident trustee). No such flexibility is provided in relation to the denial of the s613 exemption where the trust became at any time, no matter for how short a time, non resident or treaty protected.

Neither does the limitation on the use of the exemption take any account of the extent of assets in the trust at the time when it was non resident or treaty protected. It is not unusual for settlements to be created by the settlement of quite nominal sums on trustees e.g. £100. The trust may then exist for several years before other more substantial assets are added to the trust. That addition of assets could be, for example, under the Will of a deceased person who had created the initial trust in his lifetime. The denial of relief in relation to the disposal of an interest under a settlement (other than in the context of the charge on becoming absolutely entitled against the trustee) would apply if the initial £100 settlement was non resident, notwithstanding that it had become Irish resident before the settlement on it of the "real" assets i.e. the bulk of the assets. Such a draconian restriction of relief might possibly involve the application of the principle of proportionality, as explained in the Daly case, if the matter ever came before the Courts.

The limitations described above will obviously cause careful attention to be paid as to when assets added to a settlement lead to a new and separate settlement (distinct in every way from the previous settlement) being created. This is a complex matter and is discussed in paragraph 65.10. The far reaching nature of the restriction on the relief may also raise issues under EU law, where the period of non residence was residence in another Member State.

65.12.3.3 Exit Disposal by Beneficiary

As explained in paragraph 65.13, the trustees of a settlement can be subject to an "exit charge" on the occasion of the trust ceasing to be Irish resident (within the peculiar meaning of residence of a settlement). They may also be subject to an exit charge (as explained in paragraph 65.13) by reference to the occasion upon which, in relation to particular assets, they become treaty protected (see paragraph 65.12.3.1) while remaining Irish resident.

FA99 s90   An *"exit disposal"* is imposed on trust *beneficiaries* having an
            interest in the assets of the settlement, in circumstances related to
            each of the two occasions mentioned above. This is not with a view
            to imposing an "exit charge" on the beneficiary. Rather it is to
            provide a tax free uplift in base cost of the interest immediately
            before the trustees go non resident or become treaty protected. This
            is the last occasion on which a disposal of the interest (save on
            becoming absolutely entitled against the trustees) will be exempt
            from CGT. Therefore a deemed disposal on this occasion preserves
            the benefit of the exemption for the value of the interest at that point
            in time.

s613A   S613A (inserted by the FA99) and applying as regards disposals on
            or after 11 February 1999 of an interest created by or arising under a
            settlement introduced the "exit disposal" on the beneficiary.
            Because s613A applies where either or both of two circumstances
            may have occurred:

            • trustees going non resident or

            • trustees becoming treaty protected,

            it can only be described as somewhat complex. The rules are
s579B   summarised as follows:

            (1)   where s579B imposes an exit charge on the trustees on the
                  occasion of their ceasing (under Irish domestic law) to be
                  resident in Ireland,

            (2)   a beneficiary having an interest in the settlement at that time
                  and who disposes of it subsequently is treated as disposing of it
                  at open market value (and reacquiring it at that value) on the
                  occasion when the trust goes non resident, or if earlier, on the
                  occasion of the trust having become "treaty protected".

s579E   However this deemed disposal will not apply to an interest arising
            under a settlement which was created after s579E had applied to the
            trustees i.e. after they had become treaty protected.

65.12.3.4   Exit charge on trustees under s579B

s579B   Where trustees go non resident (but had already obtained double tax
            agreement protection by being treated under a double tax agreement
            as resident in another State) a beneficiary having an interest in the
            settlement on the occasion of the trustees going non resident under
            domestic law will be treated as having disposed of that interest, not
            on the occasion of the trustees going non resident, but rather on the
            prior occasion upon which they became treaty protected.

            It should be noted that the occasion of trustees becoming treaty
            protected is not in itself without other circumstances applying, the
            occasion of a deemed disposal by a beneficiary of his interest under

the settlement. Such a deemed disposal by the beneficiary can occur only if the trustees cease to be resident under Irish domestic law. The relevance of the trustees having had s579E (exit charge on becoming treaty protected) applied to them is that it ensures that the deemed disposal cannot apply to an interest created after the s579E charge has applies; and it can determine that the deemed disposal which does occur is deemed to occur at the time when they became treaty protected, rather than at a later time when the trustees became non resident under domestic law.

The exit "disposal" described above does not appear to be automatic. The mere fact of trustees becoming non resident, or becoming treaty protected does not seem in itself to be sufficient to trigger the disposal. This is because it is stated in FA99 that the new s613A shall have application only in relation to disposals of interests arising under a settlement, where the date of disposal is on or after 11 February 1999. The disposals referred to can hardly be the deemed disposals under s613A, since those deemed disposals only arise if s613A first has application. On the face of it therefore it appears that s613A will apply only where there is a real disposal of an interest arising under a settlement, or a disposal deemed under some other provision of the CGT Acts of such an interest on or after 11 February 1999.

Example 291

> Mike is the life tenant of the Russell settlement and Mary is the remainder person. On 31 March 1999 the sole trustee moved to Switzerland and became resident there. He thereupon became, as trustee, treated as resident in Switzerland for the purposes of the Switzerland/Ireland double tax agreement. s579E then had application to the settlement. On 30 June 1999 the administration of the trust was moved to Switzerland and the trustee then, under Irish domestic law, ceased to be resident in Ireland. S579B then had application to the settlement although that resulted in a charge to capital gains tax only in relation to certain Irish assets not protected by the treaty.

> On 31 December 1999 Mike sold his life interest to his brother, John. Unfortunately Mike died on 31 January in the year 2000 and Mary thereupon became absolutely entitled as against the trustees to all the trust assets and was thereupon deemed to dispose of her interest in the settlement (by s613).

> Mike's disposal of his interest to his brother occurred after 11 February 1999 and accordingly s613A has potential application. Mike will be treated as having disposed of his interest under the settlement, at open market value , and reacquired at that value on the date on which s579E applied i.e. on 31 March 1999 when the trustee became treaty protected. This is in addition to his actual disposal on 31 Decewmber.

> Mary is deemed by s613 to have disposed of her interest under the settlement on the occasion of becoming absolutely entitled to the assets i.e. on 31 January 2000. Once again s613A may have application. Mary also is treated as having disposed of her remainder interest (and reacquired it) at open market value on the occasion when the trustees became treaty protected i.e. 31 March 1999.

Mike has two disposals of his interest under the settlement. The first is a deemed disposal on 31 March 1999. That is deemed to take place immediately prior to the trustees becoming treaty protected, and at a time when they are still Irish resident. Accordingly no charge to tax will arise on Mike as the exemption in relation to a disposal of an interest under a settlement, in s613(4) will apply. On the occasion of a sale of his interest on 31 December 1999 the exemption in s613(4) no longer applies because the trustees are now non resident, and also because they are now treaty protected. Accordingly a charge to tax (with consideration being treated as being open market value by reason of the transaction being with a connected party) may arise.

The charge to tax on Mike on the occasion of his disposal of his interest on 31 December 1999 will be prepared on the basis that his base cost for the interest was the open market value at 31 March 1999. He will therefore be exposed to tax only on the increase in value (adjusted by inflation if the period exceeds 1 year) during the period of treaty protection of the trust.

Mary has had two disposals of her interest. One is the disposal deemed to occur by s613 on the occasion of her becoming absolutely entitled as against the trustees. The protection offered by s613(4) is available in relation to that deemed disposal whether or not the trustees are resident or non resident, or treaty protected, or not. The other is the deemed disposal on 31 March 1999, where the exemption applied because the trust had not then become non resident or treaty protected. Accordingly no charge to tax will arise on Mary.

s613A

It can be seen that s613A, although it reads as if it is a charging section in so far as it deems people to dispose of an interest under a settlement in various circumstances, is in fact a relieving section. Its purpose is to ensure that where a beneficiary loses the protection of s613(4) in relation to the disposal of an interest arising under a settlement, by reason of the trust becoming non resident or becoming treaty protected, that he will at least retain its benefits as regards the value of the interest at the date when he loses that protection.

The only circumstance in which s613A would seem to be a true charging section in the sense of being likely to give rise to a liability to capital gains tax, is where the interest in the settlement which is deemed by the section to be disposed of is an interest on whose disposal relief under s613(4) would not be available anyway. An example of such an interest is an interest which has been purchased by a person, rather than created for them under the settlement. Even in these circumstances s613A will not impose a charge to tax unless the holder of the interest disposes of that interest, or is deemed to do so by some other provision of the acts (other than s613A) on or after 11 February 1999.

Example 292

*Had Mike sold his interest to John in **example 291** above, on 31 December 1998 rather than 31 December 1999, John would not be deemed to have disposed of the interest which he purchased, on the occasion of the Trustees becoming non resident. That is because John did not, at any time after the 11 February 1999, actually dispose of his interest, nor was he deemed by any provision of the CGT*

Acts (other than s613A) to do so. In the absence of such a real or deemed disposal, s613A is not triggered.

If John had acquired the interest on the 31 December 1998 and had disposed of it to Mary on 30 June 1999, the following would have happened;

John would not have the benefit of the exemption in s613A in relation to the disposal of his (purchased) interest on 30 June 1999. That is because the relief is not available to a purchased interest.

John would be deemed to have also disposed of his interest and reacquired it at open market value on 31 March 1999 (the earlier of the dates upon which the trustees became non-resident or Treaty protected). Once again s613A relief would not be available to him on the deemed disposal. Accordingly, the deemed disposal at 31 March 1999 might give rise to a chargeable gain; but it would also provide him with a new base cost for the disposal which actually occurred on the 30 June 1999.

65.13   Exit charge on trust going non resident

65.13.1   General rule

FA99 s88(1)   S579B, introduced by FA99, imposes an *"exit charge"* on trustees of a settlement, where as a body they

- have been Irish resident or ordinarily resident, and

- cease to be resident or ordinarily resident in Ireland.

s579B   It applies when the trustees of settled property *"become at any time neither resident nor ordinarily resident in the State"*. In the case of trustees of settled property, unlike individuals, residence and ordinary residence are (by definition) co-terminous.

The trustees are *deemed* to

- dispose of *"defined assets"* (ALL settled property with certain specific exclusions) at the open market value of those assets immediately prior to becoming non-resident (thereby bringing any resulting gains within the charge to CGT - i.e. an exit charge) and,

- Immediately re-acquire those assets at their then open market value (changing the base cost and acquisition date of those assets for the purpose of computing a gain on a future disposal).

Example 293

Connolly Family Trust was established by the Will of John Connolly when he died in 1980. The trustees have been resident from that date up to 30 June 1999, at which date the ordinary administration of the trust is moved to the Isle of Man, the Irish trustees resign, and Isle of Man trustees are appointed. From 30 June 1999 the trust is no longer resident or ordinarily resident in the State. s579B will therefore treat it as disposing of its assets on 30 June at open market *value. This is a disposal immediately before ceasing to be resident, and accordingly is within the charge to Irish capital gains tax.*

s574(1)(a) As discussed in paragraph 65.3, in order that the trustees of settled property (as a continuing body of persons) can be regarded as non resident it is necessary both that

- the general administration be ordinarily carried on outside the State and

- that a majority of the trustees should either be not resident, *or* not ordinarily resident in the State.

There is an arguable ambiguity as to the point in time at which a trust (as a body) ceases to be resident in the State. Trustees are deemed to be a continuing body of persons having a continuity that is not affected by changes in the identity of the separate persons acting (at any particular point in time) as trustees of the trust.

In *example 293* above, the Connolly Trust was resident in Ireland up to 30 June 1999, because the separate trustees were themselves (as individuals) resident in the State up to that date. Thereafter, the separate persons who were the trustees changed and were different individuals to those who had been the trustees prior to the change, and those new trustees were not resident in the State. However, if the trustees are a continuing body of persons, it could be argued that the continuing body is resident in the State for the entire tax year during any part of which it is resident here by reason of

- the residence or ordinary residence status of any persons who are the trustees, or

- the place where the general administration is carried on.

If such an arguement could succeed, then the deemed disposal by the trustees of the Connolly Trust would not take place on June 30 1999 (as suggested in *example 293* above) but on 5 April 2000, being the end of the tax year in which the trust ceased to be resident. The point is arguable.

However, the drafting of the FA99 anti-avoidance legislation appears to proceed on the basis of the "date" of a specific event giving rise to a change in the residence of the trust. In this context it should be noted:

s579A(2) - s579A(2) in relation to a trust going non-resident uses the words *"for any year of assessment **during which** the trustees **at any time** are neither resident not ordinarily resident".*

s579C - s579C refers clearly to a temporary period (not exceeding 6 months when the residence of the trustees (as a body) changes by reason of the death of one of the trustees - see paragraph 65.13.2.4.

This matter does not in any way affect the tax year in which the deemed disposal is made, but could affect the date of disposal of assets, which in turn affects the value of those assets - which in the above example could be different at 30th June compared to the following 5th April.

The position of the Revenue Commissioners seems clear from the drafting of the legislation, which indicates the possibility of the trust being resident for part of a year only, and ignores the possibility of the trust being regarded as resident for an entire tax year where the circumstances which determine residence change at some time during a tax year.

This point is particularly relevant where the residence status of the trust (as a body) is affected by a trustee (or trustees) going non-resident. Where the trustees are individuals they will retain their Irish ordinary residence status for a period of 3 years after ceasing to be Irish resident. If it were the case that the trust did not cease to be resident by reason of a majority of the trustees retaining an ordinary resident status (albeit non-resident) the deemed disposal under s579B would not occur until three years after the trustees (as individuals) ceased to be Irish resident. Although the issue is not absolutely clear, on balance, the authors believe that the trust (in such circumstances) ceases to be Irish resident when the majority of the trustees became non-resident, even though they retained an ordinary resident status.

s579F

Although the residence status of the separate persons who are the trustees is relevant in determining the residence of the trust (as a body) s579F has application to a change in the residence of the trust rather than a change in the residence of the persons who are the trustees. Thus, even if all the trustees of a settlement become (in their personal capacity) non-resident, the trust itself would remain Irish resident for as long as the general administration was carried out in the State. That being the case, the fact that the trustees themselves (as individuals) became non-resident would not alone cause the trust to be deemed to dispose of its assets under s579F, or cause it to be regarded as non-resident for other CGT purposes.

Special treatment is afforded where the occasion of a trust becoming non resident is the death of one of the persons who are the trustees of the settlement. In such a case, if the trust becomes resident and ordinarily resident again within six months of the date of death, only assets actually disposed of by the trust in that non resident period are treated as being disposed of at open market value and the occasion of the trust becoming non resident.

65.13.2   **Defined Assets**

65.13.2.1   **General rule**

Where the trustees have become non-resident, they are deemed to dispose of the defined assets immediately prior to becoming non-resident.

s579B(4)   The defined assets are *"all assets constituting settled property of the settlement immediately before the relevant time"*. The relevant time, is the time when the trustees of the settlement became non-resident.

Certain assets are excluded from the category of assets which trustees are deemed to dispose of at open market value, on the occasion of the trust becoming non resident. Those excluded assets are set out in the following paragraphs.

65.13.2.2   **Irish branch trade assets**

s579B(5)   If immediately after the trustees become non-resident

- the trustees carry on a trade in Ireland through a branch or agency, and

- assets are situated in the State and either

    — used in or for the purposes of the trade, or

    — used or held for the purposes of the branch or agency,

such assets are excluded from the meaning of *"defined assets"*.

Any disposal of such assets, would be chargeable to CGT in any event under the normal rules applying to the disposal of assets of an Irish branch trade by a non-resident - see paragraph 3.6.

65.13.2.3   **Tax Treaty protected assets**

s579B(6)   Where under a tax treaty between Ireland and another territory,

- were certain assets (specified in that agreement) to be disposed of by the trustees (as a body) immediately before becoming non-resident

- the trustees would (under the terms of that tax treaty) not be liable to any Irish tax charge on gains arising from that disposal

such assets are also excluded from the meaning of *"defined assets"*.

It should be noted that the exclusion (from being "defined assets") by this provision only extends to assets where the trustees are not liable to tax on any gain arising from the disposal. This would not extend to assets where a liability to tax arose, but was relieved under the tax treaty (or otherwise) by a deduction for the foreign tax paid on the same disposal.

65.13.2.4   **Temporary change of residence due to death of trustee**

s579C   In broad terms, the "defined assets" catagory is limited by s579C where:

- a non-resident settlement becomes temporarily resident, or

- a resident settlement becomes temporarily non-resident,

- because of the death of a trustee and

- the original residence status of the trustees (as a body) is reinstated within 6 months of the death of the trustee.

S579C(4)   Where a non-resident settlement becomes temporarily resident because of the death of a trustee, the defined assets are limited to assets which

— would otherwise be defined assets, and

— were acquired during that temporary period of Irish residence.

Where a resident settlement becomes temporarily non-resident because of the death of a trustee, the defined assets are limited to assets which

— would otherwise be defined assets, and

— were disposed of by the trustees during that temporary period of non-residence.

Such disposals during the "non resident period" could of course attract the application of s579, s579A, or s579F (attribution of offshore gains to resident persons - paragraph 68). For the purposes of those sections, as well as for the purpose of imposing a charge to CGT on the date of going non resident, the trust will however be treated as having already disposed of the assets at open market value, and reacquired them at that value on the occasion of going non resident.

Example 294

The Jones trust has three trustees, two of whom are resident in the Isle of Man, and one of whom is resident in Ireland. The ordinary administration of the trust is carried on in the Isle of Man. On 30 June 1990 one of the Isle of Man trustees died. As a result, a majority of the trustees are no longer resident outside of the State and the trust is treated for Irish capital gains tax purposes as then becoming Irish resident. At the date of death of the trustee the trust held £1m worth of Allied Irish Bank shares which had a base cost of £100,000. On 1 July they acquired £100,000 worth of CRH shares. On 1 August a new Isle of Man resident trustee was appointed. The trust then ceased to be Irish resident. The

> trustees are treated as having disposed of the CRH shares acquired in July, but not the Allied Irish Bank shares which they had already held on the date on which they became Irish resident.

Example 295

> The Murphy trust was created by the Will of John Murphy in 1995. The trustees own Murphy's Butcher Shop in Dublin, and £100,000 worth of Allied Irish Bank shares.
>
> The ordinary administration of the trust is carried on in the Isle of Man where one trustee is resident. The second trustee is resident in Dublin.
>
> On 30 June 1999 the Irish trustee died. In consequence, (a majority of the trustees being non resident and the administration being carried on outside the State) the trust ceased to be resident. On 1 August 1999 the trust disposed of the Allied Irish Bank shares and on 1 September 1999 an Irish trustee was again appointed.
>
> Because the trust resumed Irish residence within six months of the date of death of the Irish trustee (which had occasioned it becoming non resident) it is not treated as having disposed of the butcher's shop. However it is treated as having disposed of the Allied Irish Bank shares on the date of death of the Irish trustee (ie on the occasion of going non resident). That is because it disposed of those shares (in fact as opposed to tax fiction) during the non resident period.
>
> Even if an Irish trustee had not been appointed in the six month period, the Murphy trust would not have been treated as disposing of and reacquiring the pub at open market value at 30 June 1999, because it is an asset situated in Ireland and used for the purpose of a trade carried on in Ireland by the trustees through a branch or agency.

65.13.2.5   Modification of Roll-over relief rules:

s579B(7)

Where the trustees have carried on a trade, and have claimed roll-over relief in respect of the disposal of an asset (by investing the sale proceeds in replacement assets - see paragraph 26) under the "roll-over" rules the gain would not accrue until the new replacement asset ceases to be used for trade purposes. The roll-over provisions defer the tax charge on the gain until a later date ascertained by reference to the use of the replacement asset

S579B(7) applies to shorten the deferral period by deeming the gain to arise when the trustees become non-resident (even if the asset continues to be used for trade purposes).

s579B(8)

The only exception to this shortening of the deferral period, is where the trade is carried on through an Irish branch or agency, and the asset concerned situated in Ireland, and is either

- used in or for the purposes of the trade, or

- used or held for the purposes of the branch or agency.

In such circumstances, the replacement asset would continue to be within the charge to CGT on its eventual disposal, as would the trustees in respect of the deferred gain.

65.13.2.6   Collection of tax from former trustee

s579D   S579D applies special provisions for the collection of tax arising by reason of s579B (exit charge when trust goes non resident). Any person who was a trustee of the settlement in the 12 month period prior to it going non resident may be liable in respect of the tax charge arising by reason of s579B, where that has not been paid within 6 months from its due date. A former trustee can avoid this liability only by demonstrating that when they ceased to be a trustee of the settlement there was no proposal that the trustees might become non resident.

The former trustee who is "stuck with the tax bill" under this provision is given a statutory right to recover the amount from the non resident trustees. In practice that is likely to be cold comfort since it is a statutory right not enforceable outside the State.

65.14   Trust becoming treaty protected

As explained above an exit charge is imposed on the occasion when trustees cease to be resident in the State. Because of the peculiar rule relating to the residence of a trust, it is possible for the trust to be resident in Ireland notwithstanding that all of the persons who are the trustees of the trust are resident outside of Ireland. This could occur where the general administration of the trust is carried on in Ireland. The situation could therefore arise that the occasion upon which a trust ceases to be resident in Ireland would be the occasion of the transfer of the general administration of the trust out of Ireland, rather than a change in residence by the individual trustees, where they are already resident outside of Ireland. On such an occasion it is possible that the trust would be regarded by another State as being resident in that other State by reason of the residence in that State of the persons who are the trustees. Treaty protection might therefore be available, which would defeat the exit charge described in paragraph 65.13 above.

s579E   The FA99 made special provisions to deal with this problem. They apply where trustees, who are resident in Ireland under the Irish domestic rules (which can mean as little as that the general administration of the trust is carried on in Ireland) become entitled to treaty protection such that they are shielded from an Irish capital gains tax charge on disposals of trust assets. The section will apply only if the occasion of their becoming entitled to treaty protection (while still resident under domestic rules) falls on or after 11 February 1999.

The provisions are similar to the exit charge imposed on a trust going non-resident, with the main exception that the charge only applies to assets on disposal of which the trustees would not be liable to Irish tax under the treaty.

The section provides that on the occasion described above (becoming entitled to treaty protection) the trustees are to be deemed to have disposed of all of their assets constituting settled property at open market value, and to immediately have reacquired them at open market value at that time. This constitutes an "exit charge". Because it is imposed immediately prior to treaty protection applying, a treaty will offer no protection against it.

The exit charge is imposed on settled assets only to the extent that a treaty protects those particular assets. Thus if assets included land in the State, Ireland's double tax agreements would not usually offer protection against CGT on a disposal of that land. In such circumstances, the occasion of the trustees becoming entitled to treaty protection in relation to other assets (eg foreign shares and securities held by them) would not cause them to be deemed to dispose of the Irish land.

s579E S579E applies only where the trustees are, and continue to be over the period in which treaty protection comes to apply to them, resident in Ireland for tax purposes. This does not mean that the persons who are the trustees must, in their individual capacity, be resident in Ireland. What is at issue is residence status as trustees of the settlement rather than in a personal capacity. As explained above, the trustees may be treated as Irish resident in their capacity as trustees even if their connection with Ireland is as slight as having a general administration of the trust carried on here and notwithstanding that no person who is a trustee is personally resident in Ireland.

The section applies only where trustees "become" entitled to treaty protection on or after 11 February 1999. Therefore it has no application to trustees who are already entitled to treaty protection on that date. On the face of it, the negotiation of a protocol to a treaty which merely extended double tax treaty protection already possessed in a general way by the trustees, to specific assets previously excluded from that protection, would not trigger the section. That is because it is necessary that they should become to be treated both as resident elsewhere under the treaty, and as not liable to capital gains tax. The mere extension of exemption from capital gains tax from some assets to all is not in itself be sufficient to trigger the section, where the trustees are already non resident.

Example 296

The trustees of the Romanof trust are resident in Ireland for capital gains tax purposes. The general administration of the trust is carried on in Ireland, and up to 31 March 1999, the sole trustee was also resident in Ireland. From that date he became a resident of Switzerland. The Swiss double tax agreement with Ireland would treat him as a Swiss resident for the purposes of the treaty (this is assumed, not an interpretation of the treaty) but Irish domestic law regards the trust as still resident in Ireland by reason of its general administration being carried on here. Therefore under Irish domestic law the trust does not cease to be resident and the exit charge under s579B does not apply.

The trust assets consist of shares in UK quoted companies and an estate in Ireland.

The trustees are now protected from Irish capital gains tax by the treaty, in respect of the UK shares but not in respect of the Irish estate. Accordingly the trustees are deemed by s579E to have disposed of the shares on 31 March 1999 at open market value, and to have reacquired them at open market value on that date. This is immediately before treaty protection applied, so a charge to capital gains tax may arise. They are not deemed to have disposed of the Irish land as the treaty does not protect them in respect of that land.

From 30 June 1999 the general administration of the trust is also moved to Switzerland. That is an occasion under domestic law of the trustees ceasing to be resident in Ireland and accordingly s579B has application to impose a further exit charge. This exit charge is in respect of all of their assets other than those in respect of which they would remain liable (on a disposal) to capital gains tax notwithstanding their non resident status. Therefore s579B would seek to treat the UK shares as being again disposed of at open market value, this time on 30 June 1999. However the Swiss double tax agreement protects the trustees from any charge to capital gains tax. S579B will not treat them as disposing of the Irish estate because (regardless of residence status) they remain within the charge to capital gains tax in respect of land in the State.

s597E S579E also regulates the application of roll over relief in a case where trustees came within treaty protection on or after 11 February 1999. Trustees may not "roll-over" into assets which are treaty protected. They are also deemed to have crystallised any old rolled over gains where the "new assets" into which they were rolled over become treaty protected on the occasion of the trust itself becoming treaty protected.

65.15   Return by trustees

A trustee, on the occasion of becoming non resident, or while remaining resident, on the occasion of becoming treaty protected, where that occasion is on or after 11 February 1999, is obliged to make a return within 3 months of the date of change of status, indicating the day on which the settlement was created, the identity of the settlors, and the identity of the trustees.

While these details might seem rather sparse, it should be borne in mind that the trustees in any event will have other obligations to make returns in relation to the period when they were resident, if they had income or gains in that period. This would particularly be the case in relation to gains arising by reason of the deemed disposal of assets on the occasion of either going non resident, or on the occasion of becoming treaty protected.

Settlors also have an obligation to make a return in relation to non resident settlements.

Any person who on or after 11 February 1999 transfers property (otherwise than by way of a transaction at arm's length) to non resident trustees (whom the transferor has reason to believe are non resident) is obliged to make a return within three months of the date of the transfer. The return must identify the settlement, describe the property transferred and the consideration for the transfer. The settlor will also be obliged to make a return on the occasion when he creates a settlement on or after 11 February 1999, and the settlement is either non resident or treaty protected on the occasion of its creation. Any domiciled and resident or ordinarily resident settlor is obliged within three months of the creation of the settlement to make a return identifying the settlement and the trustees, but not, curiously, the assets settled. Neither does the requirement specifically require a copy of the trust deed to be submitted. If the assets settled were other than case, the settlor would of course have a reporting obligation in any event, in relation to assets disposed of.

65.16 Charitable Trusts

The exemption available for disposals of assets to charities, and the exemption of the charity itself, are dealt with in paragraph 31.

65.17 Foreign Trusts

FA93 s49
s574

The FA93 granted an exemption from Irish taxes on income and on capital gains to certain foreign trusts. The exemption was introduced to encourage the management of foreign private trusts in the *IFSC*. It is principally relevant to income since the trusts to which it applies would not be within the charge to CGT in the State generally, being non-resident in accordance with the provisions of s574 relating to professional trustees (see paragraph 65.3.2). As the provisions are primarily relevant to income tax, they are not described further here.

The provisions were repealed by FA97, possible inadvertently.

Anti-avoidance provisions relating to non-resident trusts are dealt with in paragraph 68.

66   PERSONAL REPRESENTATIVES

66.1   Broad Outline

s573   The rules applicable to the personal representatives of a deceased person differ substantially from those which apply to trustees of settled property, and indeed, the rules applicable to nominees. The legislation dealing with the passing of assets on the death of a person, and the treatment of the personal representatives was substantially changed by the 1978 Act, although a number of the original 1975 Act rules remain unchanged. The amended provisions apply where assets of the deceased person are disposed of by the personal representative (or other person on whom the assets devolve) on or after 6 April 1978 and are in TCA97 s573.

Like trustees of settled property, personal representatives are deemed to be a body of persons distinct from the persons who from time to time may be the members of that body: the rules for determining the residence of that body, however, are different.

Unlike trustees, the passing of assets to the personal representatives on death does not give rise to a disposal for CGT purposes by the deceased person: in addition, no disposal takes place when those assets are passed on by the personal representatives to a legatee. Neither event gives rise to a CGT charge or loss.

During the course of administering the estate, the personal representatives may reach the point where assets of the deceased person may be held by them as trustees of a settlement (created by the will), and accordingly they will no longer hold the assets in their capacity as personal representatives, but as trustees of a settlement. From then on the rules applicable to trustees will apply to any dealings in the assets by the body of persons. In addition the residence of the body of persons may change, as the 'trustee' residence rules are different from those applying to personal representatives.

In broad terms, the provisions of s573 are as follows:

* There is deemed to be no disposal by the deceased person on the passing of assets to the personal representatives on his death (1975 Act).

* Assets passing on death are deemed to be acquired by the personal representatives (or other persons on whom the assets devolve) at market value at the date of death (1978 Act).

* Where assets are acquired on the death of a person by the personal representatives (or other person on whom they devolve) and those assets are then passed on by them to a person who takes them as legatee, no chargeable gain accrues to the personal representatives (or other person...etc): in addition, the legatee is deemed to have

acquired the assets at the same (deemed) time, and the same (deemed) cost as the personal representatives (1975 Act).

- The personal representatives have the obligation of providing the information to the inspector on behalf of the deceased person (making the returns, etc.), and assessments will be made on them in respect of gains accruing to the deceased person up to the date of death. Any tax due is payable by them out of the assets of the estate (1975 Act).

- Terminal loss relief is available to the personal representatives in respect of any losses accruing to the deceased person in the final year of assessment up to the date of death. The losses can be set back against gains of three years of assessment prior to that in which the death occurred (1975 Act).

66.2   Personal Representatives

s5

s799

The term 'personal representatives' is given the same meaning as in s799. In broad terms it means the executor or administrator of a deceased person's estate, and includes persons with similar functions under the law of a foreign country. For CGT purposes, personal representatives like trustees are treated as a single and continuing body of persons, distinct from the persons who from time to time are the personal representatives. As a single body, and in their representative capacity, they are deemed to have the same residence, ordinary residence and domicile as the deceased person had at the date of his death.

Personal representatives are not regarded as 'individuals' for the purpose of ascertaining their CGT liability (in their representative capacity), and as such they are not entitled to any of the reliefs or allowances which would only apply in the case of an individual. For example, they cannot get the £1,000 annual exemption, nor are they entitled to a remittance basis where they are regarded as non-domiciled.

66.3   Gains Arising to Deceased Person up to Date of Death

The provisions of the Income Tax Acts dealing with the assessment and collection of IT on income arising to the deceased person up to the date of death, apply equally to CGT.

s1048

Where a person dies, any assessments which could have been made on the deceased person if he was living, in respect of gains which arose to that deceased person before his death, can be made on his personal representatives. The tax assessed on the personal representatives is a debt due from and payable out of the Estate of the deceased person.

Where the Grant of Probate (or Letters of Administration) was made in the year of death, no assessment in respect of gains arising prior to death can be made on the personal representatives later than three years after the year of assessment in which the death occurred.

Where, however, the Grant of Probate (or Letters of Administration) was not made in the year of death, no assessment can be made later than two years after the year of assessment in which the grant was made.

However, as sometimes occurs, if, after the date of the original Grant of Probate the personal representatives lodge a corrective affidavit for the purposes of Estate Duty or CAT, or where the personal representatives are required under the CAT provisions to deliver an additional affidavit and do not deliver that additional affidavit in the year of assessment in which the deceased person died, then the assessment may be made at any time before the expiration of two years after the end of the year of assessment in which the corrective affidavit was lodged or the additional affidavit was delivered.

The personal representatives are required to deliver the tax return on behalf of the deceased person giving details of all the income and gains and other information required in a normal tax return, which, to the best of the knowledge and belief of the personal representatives, is correct.

The full annual allowance for the year of assessment in which the death occurs is available against gains arising to the deceased person in that year (up to the date of death).

66.4   Terminal Loss Relief

s573(3)   Terminal loss relief is available to the personal representatives of a deceased person. Allowable capital losses sustained by the deceased individual in the year of assessment in which he dies, to the extent that they cannot be used against his gains of that year, may be set back against the chargeable gains for the three years of assessment before the year of assessment in which he dies. Terminal loss relief only applies to the balance of the loss available after set-off of the loss against chargeable gains of the year of death.

It should, of course, be remembered that the passing of assets to the personal representatives on the death of the individual owner is not a disposal giving rise to either a gain or a loss. In addition, any disposals by the personal representatives cannot result in a loss qualifying for terminal loss relief, as it would not have been incurred by the deceased person. Terminal losses must be set against gains of later years first, in priority to setting them back against earlier years.

Example 297

Fred died in September 1998. In June 1995 he had a chargeable GAIN of £500. In August 1995 he incurred an allowable LOSS of £3,000. Chargeable GAINS for the previous three years were as follows:

1995/96	*£700*
1996/97	*£900*
1997/98	*£1,400*

This loss must first of all be set against the chargeable gains arising in June 1995 of £500, leaving a balance of £2,500 for terminal loss relief. This will be set against the later year first. It will wipe out the chargeable gains for 1997/98 and the gain of 1996/97. Any tax already paid on the basis of those gains will be repaid. The balance of £200 will be carried back against 1995/96, leaving £500 assessable in that year (which is, of course, covered by the annual allowance).

66.5   Assets Passing on Death

66.5.1   Assets to which the special "death" rules apply

s573 Special rules are set out in s573 for dealing with assets passing to the personal representatives or to a person as a legatee. Those rules only apply to assets of which the deceased was 'competent to dispose'. This means 'assets of the deceased, which he could, if of full age and capacity, have disposed of by will, assuming that all assets were situated in the State and that he was domiciled in the State'.

It also includes his severable share in any assets to which immediately before his death he was beneficially entitled as a joint tenant.

It was necessary to deem assets held as a joint tenant to be assets of which the deceased was competent to dispose of by will, since, so long as they were held in a joint tenancy, they were not in fact assets he could have disposed of as they passed by survivorship to the surviving joint tenant.

In determining whether or not assets are those which the deceased was competent to dispose of, the assumption is made that all of his assets are situated in the State. This assumption has the effect of applying the laws of Ireland to the question of whether or not the deceased would be competent to dispose of those assets.

Example 298

Pierre is a long term resident of Ireland but at his death owned his traditional family farm in France. Under French law Pierre is not free to dispose of the farm by Will. Instead it passes according to strict rules of succession under French law. In reality therefore the farm is not an asset of which Pierre is competent to dispose. However because, for the purpose of applying that test in s573, all of Pierre's assets are treated as if they were in Ireland, Pierre can be

> *regarded as being competent to dispose of the family farm since there are no "forced heirship" rules in Ireland.*

Assets acquired by the personal representatives of which the deceased was not 'competent to dispose' are dealt with under the normal CGT rules which would apply (ignoring the special "death" rules).

There is no charge to CGT where assets of which the deceased was 'competent to dispose' pass on his death to either:

- his personal representatives (or other person on whom they devolve)

- or any person acquiring the asset as legatee

In such a case there is deemed to be no disposal by the deceased person. The original rule was introduced in s.14(1)(b) and s.14(4) 1975 Act. It was not changed by the 1978 Act.

s741   The rules outlined above do not apply in relation to an asset which is a material interest in a non qualifying offshore fund. The meaning of "non qualifying offshore fund"(TCA 97 s744 and s743) is discussed in paragraph 35.12. Where the asset is such a material interest, s741 *deems* the deceased person to have disposed of his interest immediately prior to death. However, that *deeming* provision takes affect only for the purposes of TCA97 chap2 Part27, dealing with the taxation of offshore funds. Broadly speaking, post 1990 gains arising in relation to the material interest in question can be charged to income tax as a result of the deemed disposal. The deemed disposal however does not have affect for the purposes of CGT. For CGT purposes the interest is treated as not having being disposed of by the deceased, and as being acquired by the personal representative at open market value. In consequence, the loss for Capital Gains Tax purposes which the application under income tax charge under chapter 2 of part 27 dealing with offshore funds, normally involves (see paragraph 35) does not arise.

As noted in paragraph 35, "offshore fund" can include a non resident company in some circumstances and does not refer solely to foreign unit trusts. The deemed disposal for income tax purposes under s741 applies not only to an asset which is, at the date of death, a material interest in a non qualifying offshore fund, but applies also to any asset which has at any time been a material interest in a non qualifying offshore fund.

66.5.2   **Assets passing on or after 6 April 1978**

s573(2)   Where assets passing on the death of the deceased are disposed of by the personal representatives (or other person on whom they devolve), on or after 6 April 1978, they are deemed to have been acquired by those personal representatives, (or other person on whom they devolve) at market value at the date of death of the deceased person. It is important to note, that it is the date of disposal by the personal representatives (or other person on whom the assets devolve) that determines whether this rule applies — not the date of death. Any gain or loss accruing to the personal representatives on any subsequent disposal by them will be calculated by reference to the market value of the asset at the date of death, and the rules governing indexation and the higher rates will apply accordingly (where the disposal is chargeable to tax).

Where the asset is acquired from the personal representatives by a person as 'legatee', no chargeable gain accrues to the personal representatives on the disposal of that asset to the legatee. In addition, the legatee is deemed to have acquired the asset at the same deemed time and cost as the personal representatives.

Example 299 (Post 5 April 1978 Disposal)

John died in June 1999 and left shares which were valued at the date of death at £100,000 to his son Bill. Bill disposed of the shares in December 1999. The shares had been passed to Bill by the personal representatives in November 1999.

The personal representatives are deemed to acquire the asset for £100,000. They then are treated as disposing of the assets to Bill at the £100,000 value, irrespective of the actual value at the date at which they transferred them to Bill.

No gain can accrue to the personal representatives on this transaction. Bill is deemed to acquire the shares at the same value and same date as the personal representatives acquired them, i.e. at the date of John's death.

Bill has an asset treated as acquired by him in June 1999 for £100,000 (deemed) and on the subsequent disposal in December 1999 he only pays CGT on the increase in real value from the date of his acquisition. Indexation would apply to the £100,000 in the case of Bill, from his deemed acquisition at the date of death to the date of disposal (subject to the normal indexation rules) had he held the shares for at least 1 year.

The deceased person (John) is deemed not to have disposed of the assets. The effect of this is to exempt any gain accruing up to the date of death.

It can sometimes happen that although a legatee has been bequeathed a cash sum, the personal representative and the legatee may agree that a particular asset in the estate will be transferred to the legatee in whole or partial satisfaction of the entitlement to the cash sum. This would save the personal representative the bother of selling the asset to realise the cash needed to meet the bequest, and if the asset is particularly attractive to the legatee, it saves him the risk that it may be sold to somebody else. This sensible, and not unusual, transaction can have very different tax results depending on whether or not the Will specifically gave to the personal representatives a power to appropriate assets in specie in satisfaction of cash bequests. Where such a power exists, both the personal representative and the legatee is treated as if the asset appropriated to the legatee had been specifically bequested to the legatee by the deceased person. In other words no capital gains tax arises at all on the entire transaction, and the legatee has an open market value at the date of death as his base cost for the future.

If however the personal representative was not provided with the power to appropriate assets in specie in satisfaction of cash bequests, but has done so purely by agreement with the legatee, the practical effect is that the personal representative is treated as if he had sold the asset. He has a disposal and must compare the consideration at the date of disposal with the open market value at the date of death. This could result either in a chargeable gain, or an allowable loss. In the tax treatment of the legatee in such a situation his base cost is likely to be determined by the value which he and the personal representative have attributed to the asset in doing their deal. In other words by reference to the amount of the cash bequest discharged by the transfer of the asset. There is also a possibility that Section 541(3) might have application. This is discussed in Paragraph 38.3 "property in satisfaction of debt".

• **Revenue/Chief Inspector's CGT Manual :**

– The Revenue Commissioners in their capital gains tax manual at paragraph 19.3.9.10 state that where the personal representative and the legatee agree to the treatment, the legatee and the personal representative may both be treated as if the asset transferred was one bequeathed to the legatee. It would therefore be taken by him at open market value at the date of death (rather than the value of the consideration given at the date of appropriation); and the personal representative would not be treated as having made any disposal in transferring the asset to the legatee.

66.5.3 **Assets passing before 6 April 1978**

s573(2) It is important to note that s573(2) rules governing the deemed time and cost of acquisition apply only in relation to a disposal on or after 6/4/78 by the personal representatives, or other person on whom the assets devolved. Where the disposal by the personal representatives (or other such person) was prior to 6 April 1978, they were treated as acquiring the asset at the same time as the deceased acquired it, and for the same cost as the deceased person.

s573(5) The legislation governing the person who is only taking assets as legatee [s573(5)] was not changed by the 1978 Act — his position follows that of the personal representatives. He is (and was prior to the 1978 Act) treated as if ...'the personal representatives acquisition of the asset had been his acquisition of it'. This raises the question of whether a legatee acquiring assets from the personal representatives prior to 6 April 1978 is within the 1978 Act rules where the subsequent disposal by that legatee is after 5 April 1978. S573 gives two separate reliefs:

s573(2)

- subsection (2) gives the relief to the personal representatives, or other person on whom the assets devolve, by deeming their acquisition to be at market value at the date of death.

s573(5)

- subsection (5) gives relief for the transfer of assets from the personal representatives to a person taking as legatee. No mention is made in subsection (5) of the other person on whom the assets may devolve. This subsection, in effect, provides that on such a transfer, the legatee steps into the shoes of the personal representatives — he acquires the assets at market value at the date of death if the personal representatives acquisition is within the 1978 Act rules now in s573(2).

If a legatee can be considered to be a person on whom the assets 'devolve' in such circumstances, there is hardly any need for subsection (5) but that is unlikely.

SA63 s10

The Succession Act 1965 provides broadly speaking, that where the deceased left a will the assets 'devolve' on the personal representatives. Where he did not leave a will, the assets 'devolve' on the High Court pending the appointment of personal representatives.

It provides in s.10, that:

"The real and personal estate of a deceased person shall on his death, notwithstanding any testamentary disposition, devolve on and become vested in his personal representatives"

S13 of that Act provides:

SA63 s13

"Where a person dies intestate, or dies testate but leaving no executor surviving him, his real and personal estate, until administration is granted in respect thereof, shall vest in the President of the High Court who, for this purpose, shall be a corporation sole".

In the context of the way in which the CGT relief is structured in s573 and taking into account the provisions of the Succession Act 1965, it unlikely that a legatee in normal circumstances can be considered to be a person on whom the assets devolve.

However, it is understood, that in practice the Revenue Commissioners will apply the 1978 Act rules (s573(2)) in such circumstances.

Example 300 (Pre 6 April 1978 disposal)

John died in June 1977 and left a portfolio of shares worth £50,000 to his son Bill. John had acquired the shares in June 1975 for £35,000. Market value at June 1977 was £50,000. The executor passed the shares to Bill on 18 February 1978. Bill sold the shares on 3 March 1978.

Bill was treated as if he acquired the shares for £35,000 in June 1975.

s573(2)

As already mentioned, where Bill disposed of the shares after 5 April 1978, although it would appear that he is not a person on whom the asset devolved, the Revenue will in practice apply the 1978 Act rules (s573(2)) which would provide a base cost of £50,000. In most circumstances this will benefit the taxpayer.

SA65

The term 'legatee' is not defined, as such, but *'includes any person taking under a testamentary disposition or an intestacy or by virtue of the Succession Act, 1965, or by survivorship, whether he takes beneficially or as trustee, and a person taking under a donatio mortis causa shall be treated as a legatee and his acquisition as made at the time of the donor's death and, for the purposes of this definition and of any reference to a person acquiring an asset 'as legatee', property taken under a testamentary disposition or on an intestacy or partial intestacy or by virtue of the Succession Act, 1965, includes any asset appropriated by the personal representatives in or towards the satisfaction of a pecuniary legacy or any other interest or share in the property devolving under the disposition or intestacy or by virtue of the Succession Act, 1965'.*

A beneficiary entitled to the residue of the estate of a deceased person, which is charged with annuities or other bequests in favour of other beneficiaries, is not entitled to the entire balance of the estate 'subject to satisfaction of the rights of the other beneficiaries'. He is only entitled to what remains after satisfaction of those rights. Gains arising out of disposals by the executor (to provide funds to satisfy those rights) are chargeable on the executors. The disposals are not as bare trustee or nominee for the residuary legatee (Cochrane v IRC).

In the UK case of Passant v Jackson, the taxpayer was the residuary legatee of his mother's estate, which was valued at about £3,600. The only remaining asset of the estate was a house valued at £6,000, which the executor would have to sell to pay debts due by the estate, leaving approx. £3,600 balance for the taxpayer. The taxpayer, however, wished to get the house, and so he made an arrangement with the executor, whereby he provided the cash to pay the debts, and the executor executed an assent vesting the property in him.

Some years later he sold the property, and the question arose as to the deductible cost. The taxpayer claimed a deduction for the market value of the property at the date of his mother's death, and in addition, a deduction for the amount paid to the executor, as being an amount paid wholly and exclusively for the purpose of establishing or defending his title to the property.

The case came before Vinelott J in the Chancery Division, who in the course of his judgement said:

"The whole of the taxpayer's case turns on the assumption that the taxpayer acquired the legal or equitable title in the property on Mrs. Passant's death,

and must be treated as having acquired what was an interest in or a right to the residuary estate remaining after the payment of debts, legacies, and specific devises, and testamentary expenses. He had no interest in or title to the entire freehold property, and cannot be treated as having acquired that interest at a notional value of £6,000 as at the death of Mrs. Passant free from the liabilities to which the estate was subject".

The taxpayer's appeal failed, the decision of Vinelott J being, in effect, that he was only entitled to a deduction for the market value of what he inherited at the date of his mother's death, i.e. £3,600 in addition to the extra cost incurred in acquiring the balance of the interest in the property which he did not inherit at the date of death (represented by the amount paid by him to the executor).

The judgement of Vinelott J was upheld in the Court of Appeal.

66.6   **Personal Representatives Becoming Trustees**

In many circumstances the assets of a deceased person's estate will not pass absolutely to the immediate beneficiary under the will. A life interest in property, for example, could be passed to one person, with absolute entitlement to the asset passing to another on the death of the life tenant. In such a case, and indeed in many other circumstances, a trustee situation could arise.

Even where a trust situation is created by will, or by the law of intestacy, the normal rules applying to personal representatives should apply until either the administration period of the estate is completed, or the personal representatives have assented to hold the assets upon the trusts concerned. At that stage, the trustees take the assets (held by them up to that date as personal representatives) as legatee. No disposal arises for CGT purposes on the passing of the assets to themselves as legatee. Thereafter, they hold the assets subject to the relevant trusts, as trustees of settled property. A beneficiary taking assets from them subsequently, would not receive those assets as a legatee, but as a beneficiary under the settlement. The normal rule regarding dealings between trustees and beneficiaries under such a settlement would apply (see paragraph 65). It is important to note any change which may occur in the residence position of the trustees of the settlement, from that which applies to them in their capacity as personal representatives. The two separate residence rules are quite different.

66.7   **Family Arrangements**

s573(6)

If any of the dispositions of the property of which the deceased was competent to dispose (whether by will or under the law relating to intestacies or otherwise) are varied by a deed of family arrangement or similar instrument, the above provisions relating to property passing on death apply as if the variation was effected by the deceased. Consequently, no dispositions made by such a deed constitute a disposal for CGT purposes. The 'variation' must be effected within 2 years of death (or such longer time as is allowed by the Revenue Commissioners) to qualify for this relief.

- **Revenue/Chief Inspector's CGT Manual :**

— In their capital gains tax manual at Paragraph 19.3.9.15 the Revenue Commissioners state that *"the term "deed of family arrangement" may be regarded as covering any situation (including a gift by a legatee) as a result of which property disposed of by the deceased (whether by Will or in an intestacy) is, by some form of deed, redistributed within the family."*

— The manual goes on to indicate that where there are valid grounds (eg complicated estate or widely dispersed family) the Inspector may grant an extension of the two year period for a further period of 12 months. Any further extension must be submitted to head office for approval.

s573(6)

There seems to be no reason why trustees of a settlement created by the Will should not be a party to a deed of family arrangement (assuming the trust deed permits them to be so). S573(6) does not make specific reference to interaction with s574 to s577 inclusive, dealing with settlements but there would seem to be no reason why trustees should not avail of the relief, if they wished to dismantle a settlement within two years of death. Normally dismantling of a settlement will involve disposals of assets by the trustees, which could trigger liability to capital gains tax. If the dismantling of the trust can be brought within s573(6) such tax would be avoided. However the matter is not free from doubt.

The equivalent statutory provision was considered in the U.K. case of Marshall v Kerr.

Under the terms of her father's will, the taxpayer was given, absolutely, one half of her father's residuary personal estate. Her father was domiciled and ordinarily resident in Jersey and neither resident nor ordinarily resident in the United Kingdom.

The personal representative of the deceased was the Regent Trust Company Limited (Regent), a company incorporated in Jersey and at all relevant times resident there and in no other place.

The taxpayer and Regent executed an instrument of family arrangement, the effect of which was to settle her share in her father's residuary personal estate on the terms of a settlement, of which Regent was the sole trustee.

Capital payments were later made from the settlement to the taxpayer.

It was common ground that the payments were taxable under the provisions of the UK Finance Act 1981, if the taxpayer could be regarded as the settlor. It was held that the taxpayer was the settlor for these purposes.

In the House of Lords the case was decided by reference to basic principles of U.K. succession law, which principles are equally valid under Irish law. The judgement given held that the deceased could not have been the settlor. At the date the daughter entered into the deed of family arrangement, she had no entitlement to any of the assets of the estate, and by reason of the deed, never acquired such an interest. At that time, her rights consisted solely of the right to have the estate administered, but she had no right to any assets since the residue had not been ascertained. That right, which was all she possessed, was not an asset of which the deceased was competent to dispose of, never being possessed by her.

S573(6) applies only to assets of which the deceased was competent to dispose.

If the decision in Marshall v Kerr were correct, the implication would be that the provisions of s573(6), and the relief which it provides, would not have application to a deed of family arrangement entered into in relation to assets forming part of the residue of the estate of a deceased person, where the deed of family arrangement is entered into prior to the residue being ascertained, and retained for the benefit of the beneficiary nominated in the will. In practice that means that s573(6) would not have application to a deed of family arrangement relating to the residue of an estate if the deed were entered into prior to the administration of the estate being complete. Since it would not be unusual for a deed of family arrangement to be entered into prior to the administration of an estate being complete, and indeed since in many instances it may be most convenient that the deed be entered into while the administration is still in progress, it would be surprising if the intent of the legislation was that it should not apply in such a case.

Marshall v Kerr was a tax avoidance case. The UK House of Lords has shown considerable hostility to tax avoidance especially since the late 1970's. It is arguable that in the case of Marshall v Kerr that hostility may have unduly influenced them in their decision. The actual trust deed by which Mrs. Kerr created the settlement settled *"the one half share in the testators said residuary personal estate to which Mrs Kerr is entitled"*. It is arguable that it was the clear intent of Mrs. Kerr to settle, not a chose in action consisting of the right to have the estate administered, but rather the assets to which she would become entitled once the administration was complete. In fact these were the assets with which the trustees ended up. It remains to be seen if the Irish courts would follow the highly legalistic approach of the House of Lords in Marshall v Kerr, or take a more straightforward view of the nature of the transaction.

Until the matter is clarified in the Irish Courts, regard should be had to the decision in Marshall v Kerr in entering into any deeds of family arrangement.

66.8   **Acquisition on Death of Spouse**

s592   In order to establish the period of ownership for the purpose of determining the rate of tax where assets pass on the death of one spouse to the surviving spouse, the surviving spouse is deemed to have owned the asset since the date of its acquisition by the deceased spouse. (See also paragraph 33.7).

66.9   **Termination of Life Interest in settled property**

The special provisions relating to the termination of a life interest in settled property are dealt with in paragraph 65.7.

67 NON-RESIDENT ENTITIES

67.1 Offshore aspects

67.1.1 Broad outline

A wide range of provisions in the CGT Acts have application to non resident persons, including non-resident companies and non resident trusts. Most of these measures can be seen to be directed towards ensuring that resident persons do not avoid a charge to CGT by arranging that assets are held (and disposed of) by a non resident entity, rather than by themselves.

The provisions of the CGT Acts which affect offshore entities include the following:

- S29 (3) treats non-resident persons as liable to Irish Capital Gains Tax in relation to disposals of certain specified Irish Assets (see paragraph 3.4)

- S579 can attribute gains arising to certain non resident trustees, to resident beneficiaries of the trusts (see paragraph 68)

- S579A also attributes gains of a non-resident trust to Irish resident beneficiaries.

- S579B(together with the sections which follow - up to s579F) impose a "deemed disposal" of assets at open market value on a trust becoming non-resident - i.e.- they impose an "exit charge"

- S590 can attribute gains arising to a non resident company to resident share holders (see paragraph 67.2)

- S613 and s613A restricts the availability of the exemption normally available on the disposal of an interest under a settlement where the settlement has at any time been non-resident.

- S627 imposes a "deemed disposal" at open market value on a company going non-resident - i.e. it imposes an "exit charge"(see paragraph 74)

- S740 to s748 inclusive contain the code of taxation in relation to offshore funds which can charge gains arising on the disposals of interest in certain offshore funds to income tax rather than the CGT, and impose a 40% CGT rate on gains arising on the disposal of certain interests. (see paragraph 35)

- S594 denies to a life assurance policy/annuity contract issued by the company not within the charge of corporation tax (i.e. an offshore company) the exemption from Capital Gains Tax which is otherwise provided by s593 on a disposal of the policy (see paragraph 36)

- S546 (4) denies relief for a loss incurred at a time when a person was neither resident nor ordinarily resident in the state, unless the loss arises on the disposal of a specified Irish asset.

- S29 (4) denies a deduction for losses arising outside of Ireland and the UK, to a person entitled to be taxed under remittance basis. Such a person would typically be an individual not domiciled in Ireland. (see paragraph 20.2)

- S541 and s533 have the effect of treating any bank account in foreign currency, held by a resident or ordinarily resident person, as a chargeable asset notwithstanding that debts which are not a debt on a security, in general are not chargeable assets. (see paragraph 38)

Most of the provisions outlined above are aimed at imposing or increasing a tax liability. In contrast however, s29 (4) provides the remittance basis of taxation in relation to non Irish and non UK assets to a resident or ordinarily resident individual who is not domiciled in the state. (see paragraph 3.3).

In addition to the CGT measures relating to offshore matters outlined above, there are of course also income tax provisions in the Taxes Acts which impact on offshore structures. These are not described in this volume but reference may be made to the companion volume, Income Tax by McAteer and Redden, published by the Institute of Taxation in Ireland. Any consideration of the overall taxation position of an offshore entity, or of an Irish resident person having an interest in such an entity, may require that regard be had both to the CGT and to income tax provisions which can impact on it, and possibly also to Capital Acquisitions Tax.

67.1.2   History of Provisions

S579   The Capital Gains Tax Act 1975 contained the present s579, which can attribute gains arising to certain non resident trustees to resident beneficiaries of the trusts, and also s590, which can attribute gains arising to a non resident company to resident shareholders. However it did not contain any "exit charge" deeming either a company or a trust to dispose of their assets at open market value on the occasion of going non resident. An exit charge on a company going non resident was imposed in 1997 in s627. An exit charge on a trust going non resident was introduced in FA99 in s579B and the sections which follow.

In the original CGT Act 1975, although s579 could attribute to Irish resident beneficiaries the gains that in fact arose to a non resident trustee, and although s590 could attribute to Irish resident shareholders the gains which in fact arose to a non resident company, the two sections did not interact. Where a non resident trust owned a non resident company, it was not possible for the operation of the two sections together to result in gain of the non resident company being attributed to the non resident trustees, and then attributed to the beneficiaries in Ireland of the non resident trust. Only gains directly arising to the trust could be attributed under s579.

The original legislation had a further limitation in that the gains arising to a non resident company which were distributed within two years were not attributed to a resident shareholder. This was probably an attempt to avoid double taxation (once on the attribution of the gain, and once on the receipt of the distribution) but the exception to attribution applied whether or not the distribution was received by an Irish resident person.

Because of the features of the original legislation described above it became common practice to structure offshore investments in the form of an offshore trust owning an offshore company which in turn held assets which might be disposed of at a gain. Taxpayers also entered into arrangements whereby following on a gain arising to a non resident company, distributions were made to other non resident persons but at no real economic cost to the ultimate Irish owners of the company. Either approach ensured that Irish resident persons were not subjected to tax by reason of the gains arising to non resident persons.

S590
s579A
The FA99 plugged these "loopholes". It did so by replacing s590 with a new s590, and by supplementing the existing s579 (which continues in force unamended) with a new s579A. The combined effect of these changes reduces the attractions of the planning methods outlined above, and has serious implications for structures in existence when the new legislation was brought in.

s613A
The FA99 also imposed an exit charge on trusts on the occasion of their becoming non resident. It also withdrew the exemption which existed from the charge to capital gains tax on the disposal of an interest arising under a settlement, where the settlement has at any time been non resident (s613A).

The FA99 also changed the definition of a group for the purposes of group relief. The revised definition is relevant to the relief granted from the application of s590 (non resident companies) in relation to disposals made between members of "an offshore group".

The legislation relating to non resident entities is now quite complex. It may involve considering the interaction or action separately of the old s590 (pre 11 February 1999), the current s590 (post 11 February 1999), s579; and the new s579A.

The pre 11 February 1999 s590 did not interact with s579. In other words a non resident company gains to which the old s590 applied could not be attributed by s579 to the beneficiaries of a trust which owned the company. The new s590 does interact with s579, and with s579A. In consequence the gains of a non resident company owned by a non resident trust may be attributed through either s579, or s579A, to a resident beneficiary.

Where s579A has application to a gain, s579 cannot apply to that gain.

The exclusion of s579 where s579A applies so as to charge a person to tax on chargeable gains is a little ambiguous. The charge to tax under s579A cannot exceed the capital sum received from the trust by the person to whom the gain is attributed. It is therefore possible that a chargeable gain arising to a non resident trustee may not be fully charged to tax on resident persons. The ambiguity in the provision relates to the question of whether s579 can apply to so much of the chargeable gain as is not charged to tax under s579A, or whether the fact that any part of it has been charged to tax is sufficient to exclude the application of s579 to the chargeable gain. In the authors opinion the fact that the amount of a chargeable gain is attributed and charged to resident persons is less than the totality of the chargeable gain does not mean that the section has not applied so as to charge resident persons with the chargeable gain. It has applied within its own terms, which determine the amount of that tax charge but it nonetheless applies to the whole of the chargeable gain. On that basis, s579 is excluded no matter how small a proportion of the chargeable gain is ultimately charged to tax on a resident person by reason of s579A.

The detailed operation of the sections referred to above are described separately below. Before beginning a discussion of the detailed provisions of each section, it may be useful to look at an example which illustrates the interaction of the various sections both prior to 11 February 1999, and subsequently.

Example 301

The Morgan Trust was settled in 1990 by Tom Morgan, an Irish resident, ordinarily resident and domiciled person. The trustees of the trust have at all times been resident in the Isle of Man where the trust is administered. The trustees own an Isle of Man resident company, Morgan Offshore Limited.

On 1 January 1998 Morgan Offshore Limited disposed of quoted shares and realised a gain of £20,000. On the same day the trustees disposed of quoted shares held by them and realised a gain of £5,000.

On 31 December 1998 the trustees appointed £5,000 to an Irish resident and domiciled and beneficiary, Joe Morgan.

On 31 March 1999 Morgan Offshore Limited disposed of further assets and realised a gain of £30,000.

On 30 June 1999 the trustees appointed a further £50,000 to Joe Morgan.

On 31 December 1999 Morgan Offshore Limited was liquidated and the assets distributed in specie to the trustees. The liquidation of the company crystallised gains of £100,000 for the company on the disposal of its assets. The liquidation of the company crystallised gains by the trustees in relation to the shares in the company, of £75,000. On 30 June 2000 the trustees appointed £175,000 to Joe Morgan.

The disposal by Morgan Offshore Limited in 1998, which crystallised a gain of £20,000, would not have resulted in the attribution of those gains to any Irish resident person. There were no Irish resident participators in the company at that time. The pre 11 February 1999 s590 would not have attributed gains to the non resident trustees - it attributed gains only to resident and ordinarily resident persons and the trustees were not such. S579 applies only to gains which accrue to non resident trustees. Accordingly no attribution arises under the section.

The gains which accrued to the trustees in 1998, of £5,000, are attributed by s579 because Joe Morgan is domiciled and resident and is a beneficiary of the settlement. Accordingly s579(2)(a) has application to treat him as if the gains have accrued to him. The fact that he received an appointment of a similar amount of money from the trust in 1998 is not relevant or necessary in order that the attribution should have occurred. The gains would have been attributed to him whether or not he received any payment from the trust.

The disposal by the company on 31 March 1999 is in the tax year 1998/99. S579A is not capable of attributing a gain to a resident person in that tax year. The first tax year in which it can attribute gains to a resident person is the year 1999/2000. Since s579A does not have application, it is possible that s579 and the new s590 might apply. Since the gain accrued after 11 February 1999, it is the new version of s590 which has application. That version can attribute company gains to a non resident trustee, thus triggering s579. Therefore s579 can attribute to Joe Morgan the £30,000 of gains which accrued to the company notwithstanding that he has not received payment from the trust in respect of those gains.

On 6 April 1999, s579A is theoretically capable of having application to attribute gains to a resident person. It may do so in an amount not exceeding payments from 11 February 1999 onwards to that person from the trust. On 6 April there are no such payments. However, on 30 June 1999 the trustees paid £50,000 to Joe Morgan. In principle s579A can now have application to attribute post 11 February 1999 gains by Morgan Offshore Limited (which is controlled by the trust to which s579A has application) to beneficiaries. However at this point all post 11 February 1999 gains have been attributed. S579A would therefore not seem capable of action at this point. This is discussed further below.

On 31 December 1999 the company crystallises gains of £100,000. S579A can now have application to the extent of the payment by the trustees to Joe Morgan on 30 June 1999 of £50,000 and can attribute to him £50,000 of the company's gains. The balance of £50,000 of the company's gains cannot be attributed by it at this time. Because s579A has applied to the gain of £100,000, s579 cannot apply to it.

The gain by the trustees on 31 December 1999 of £75,000 cannot be attributed by s579A as there are no post 11 February 1999 payments to beneficiaries which have not already been taken into account in the attribution of offshore gains. However s579 is capable of application and can attribute the £75,000 of gains to Joe Morgan.

On 30 June 2000 the trustees pay Joe Morgan £175,000. S579A can now have application to attribute to Joe Morgan the balance of £50,000 of gains which arose to Morgan Offshore Limited on 31 December 1999, and which had not previously been attributed.

ANALYSIS OF "OFFSHORE" PROVISIONS				
	s579	**s579A**	**New s590**	**Old s590**
• Settlor requirement	Domiciled and res/ord res at gain or when settled	-	-	-
• Company	-	-	Close non-resident	Close non-resident
• Gains Charged	6/4/74 et seq.	11/2/99 et seq.	11/2/99 et seq.	6/4/74 to 11/2/99
• Apportioned to	Interest in trust	Beneficiaries	Members and loan creditors	Shareholders
• Payment requirement	(1) None if beneficiary (2) Otherwise in same or past year	Same or later year	None	None
• Cap	(1) None if beneficiary (2) Payments otherwise	payments	None	None
• Tax charged on	(1) Dom & Resident or Ord Res beneficiary (2) Dom & Res/Ord Res recipient of payment	Dom & Res/Ord Res beneficiary	Res/Ord Res participator	Res/Ord Res shareholder
• Basis apportioned	Just & reasonable	Proportionate to payments	Proportionate to interest as participator	Winding up rights

ANALYSIS OF "OFFSHORE" PROVISIONS				
	s579	s579A	New s590	Old s590
• Exemptions	Life Interest in pre 74 trust	-	Foreign trade assets: Irish specified assets: :Non res group	Foreign trade assets: Irish specified assets: :Non res group
• Loss relief	None	None	Against gain	Against gain

67.2

s590

Non-Resident companies

S590 can attribute the gains of a non resident company to Irish resident persons in certain circumstances. The FA99 substituted a new version of s590 for the pre existing version, but only by reference to disposals accruing from 11 February 1999 onwards. The pre existing version, which had application to disposals by the non resident company prior to 11 February 1999 is described in paragraph 67.3. The version of s590 which has application to gains arising currently (ie from 11 February 1999) is described in paragraph 67.2.1 below.

67.2.1.1

Which non resident companies?

Section 590(3) states that the section applies

"as respects chargeable gains accruing to a company -

(a) which is not resident in the State, and

(b) which would be a close company if it were resident in the State."

"Close company" is defined in s430 and s431. The definition excludes certain quoted companies from the ambit of the expression.

s430

The definition in s430 makes it clear that a non resident company cannot be a close company. That is the explanation for the reference in s590(3) above to a company *"which would be a close company if it were resident in the State."*

S430(1) provides that "close company" means a company which is under the control (a defined expression) of

- 5 or fewer participators, or

- of participators who are directors.

s433

"Participator" is defined for these purposes in s433 as *"a person having a share or interest in the capital or income of the company"*. This is the basic definition provided by s433. It then goes on to specifically include in the meaning of "participator" certain defined persons (see below) but it should not be forgotten that the basic definition of "participator" is that quoted above and that it is a definition of wide and general meaning. It is important not to assume that the definition is confined to the specific instances which the section clarifies are included.

The specific types of persons who are deemed to be participators (without prejudice to the general definition given above) include

s433
- any person who possesses share capital or voting rights in the company, or who is entitled to acquire such share capital or voting rights in the company.

    This obviously includes what in common parlance would be termed a "shareholder." If however a company did not have share capital, it is still possible that a person could be a participator in the company if the person had voting rights in the company. It is possible under Irish company law, and under the company law of many other States, to incorporate a company without share capital. It should be borne in mind that the fundamental definition of "participator" quoted further up does not require that the company should have share capital. Thus a person holding neither share capital (eg because the company's capital is not divided into shares) or voting rights in the company, could nonetheless be a participator in the company if, under the company's memorandum and articles of association (or foreign equivalent) that person was specified as being entitled to some part of the capital or of the income of the company.

    If a person had an option to subscribe for shares in a company, or an option to acquire voting rights, then, even at a time when the option was not exercised and at a time when they did not hold share capital or voting rights directly, they would be a "participator".

- Any loan creditor of the company. "Loan creditor" is not defined. It would include any person who has lent money to the company, but would not include a person to whom the company was indebted for the supply of goods or services.

S433(1) also includes in the definition of "participator" persons who are entitled to participate in distributions of the company or in premiums on redemption of loans or a person who is entitled to secure that income of the company will be applied directly or indirectly to their benefit. These latter provisions are essentially of an anti-avoidance nature and do not add much to the two basic
s432
examples of participator which are given - shareholders and loan creditors.

The relevance of whether or not a person is a participator is of course that the definition of "close company" confines it to a company under the control of 5 or fewer participators, or of participators who are directors. It is therefore necessary to consider what is the meaning of "control" in this context. That is defined by Section 432(2). The sub-section starts with a broad general definition: "*A person shall be taken to have control of a company if such person exercises, or is able to exercise or is entitled to acquire, control, whether direct or indirect, over the company's affairs.*" That definition is extremely wide and general and, of course, is circular in that it employs within it the very word it is seeking to define ie "control". That wide and general definition must be borne in mind when looking at the specific examples which the sub-section provides of persons who are to be treated as controlling a company. While any person who falls within the specific examples (described below) is a person controlling a company, it must be borne in mind that the fact that a person fails to fall within those examples does not mean that he does not control a company. A conclusion can be drawn only if one also has regard to the test outlined above, wide and vague though it may be.

The specific classes of persons treated as having control of a company are:

- those possessing or entitled to possess the greater part of the share capital or the issued share capital, or the voting power of the company. The reference here to "share capital" is a reference (in the author's opinion) to the nominal amount expressed in money terms of that share capital, as opposed to a reference to the number of shares in issue, or to the sums subscribed for such shares. The reference to "share capital" in contrast to "issued share capital" is presumably a reference to the authorised share capital of the company, a somewhat dated concept.

- A person who possesses or is entitled to acquire such part of the issued share capital as would, on a distribution of the income of the company among participators (other than loan creditors) entitle the person to receive the greater part of the amount so distributed.

  Shares may differ as between each other in the entitlement they confer on the holder to participate in distributions. A very small shareholding could entitle a person to the lion's share of distributions. Thus a person who has a very small shareholding but who would receive a disproportionally large distribution if the profits were distributed, could be treated as controlling a company. That would be so even if the person had no voting rights and no ability to compel the company to distribute its income. It should be borne in mind that a distribution to shareholders on the occasion of a winding-up of a company is a distribution of the company's capital and not of the company's income.

• A person entitled, should a company be wound-up or otherwise distribute its capital, to receive the greater part of the assets available for distribution among the participators. Oddly, there is no exclusion here for loan creditors such as there is in terms of distribution of income. It is therefore possible that a loan creditor could be treated as being in control of a company which had substantial indebtedness to that person but had little or no net assets.

A person may be treated as in control of a company under this provision even though they have no power to bring about the winding-up of a company, or a distribution of its assets.

s432

S432 goes on to provide certain anti-avoidance features, which enable a person to have attributed to him the rights and powers of companies controlled by the person or by him and his associates, or the rights and powers of his associates. It is not proposed to discuss these particular features here.

It will be apparent from the description above that a company may be treated as being controlled simultaneously by a wide variety of people. It may be controlled by its shareholders; it may be controlled by persons who have options to acquire shares by purchase or subscription; it may be controlled by its loan creditors; and all of them may be simultaneously and separately treated as controlling the company. In order to be a close company it is sufficient that from out of the various groups who may be treated as being participators controlling the company, a group as small as 5 can be identified who together can be treated as controlling the company. This is so, even if many hundreds of other people can also be treated as controlling the company.

Example: 302

Notwell Plc has issued share capital of £1m. It is divided into 6000 £1A ordinary shares each of which carries one vote, and which are entitled to participate in dividends only where the dividends paid in an accounting period exceed £500,000; and 4000£1B ordinary shares which are non-voting shares entitled to receive the first £400,000 in any dividends paid in an accounting period and to participate pari passu with the A ordinary shares thereafter. The company has incurred significant losses such that its net assets attributable to shareholders amount to only £1000. In the current period it has a profit after tax of £10,000. The company has been kept afloat by a term loan of £300,000 from its bank, and a loan of £100,000 from an individual, who possesses the right to convert it at par into C ordinary shares, a class of 1p shares carrying one vote per share, which is presently unissued.

The A ordinary shares are held equally by 20 unconnected persons. The B ordinary share are held by 4 individuals.

The company is controlled by the individual who has lent it money subject to conversion rights into shares because he is entitled to acquire the greater part of the voting rights of the company. It is also controlled by its bank, since the bank is a loan creditor (a participator) and would receive the greater part of the assets available for distribution to participators on a winding-up. It is also controlled by the holders of the B ordinary shares because if the entire of the company's recent £10,000 profit were distributed, they would receive the greater part of it (in fact the entire of it).

Although the company is fundamentally a widely held company it can nonetheless be a close company.

A frequently traded quoted company is not treated as a close company nor is a company which can only be treated as close by including among the participators for the purpose a company which is not a close company, and which itself controls the company.

The presence of a non-close company among the participators is relevant (as referred to above) only if both of the requirements referred to are met ie that the company in which the non close company holds shares cannot be treated as close without including the non close company among the participators who control it, for this purpose *and* if the non close company on its own, or together with another non-close company, can be treated as controlling the company.

Example 303

Subsidiary Limited has a share capital of 100 £1 ordinary shares, all ranking pari passu. These are held as to 50 by Quoted Company Plc and as to 50 by Joe Bloggs. Quoted Company Plc is not a close company.

Subsidiary Limited is not controlled either by Joe Bloggs or by Quoted Company Plc taken individually. However it is controlled by two participators ie the two shareholders. Prima facie it is therefore a close company. However one of those controlling shareholders which have to be taken into account in establishing control is a non-close company. That however does not mean that Subsidiary Limited is not a close company. Quoted Company Plc does not control Subsidiary Limited and although it must be taken into account in order to determine that Subsidiary Limited is controlled by five or fewer participators, that is not sufficient to exempt Subsidiary Limited from being a close company.

If the situation were that Quoted Company Plc held 51 shares, and Joe Bloggs 49 shares, then Quoted Company Plc on its own would control Subsidiary Limited. In such circumstances Subsidiary Limited would not be a close company because both requirements relating to control by a non-close company are met ie it cannot be treated as controlled by five or fewer participators without taking into account the non-close company, and the non-close company itself controls Subsidiary Limited.

In *example 302* above the Bank would almost certainly not be a close company (few banks are) but it controls Notwell Plc. However because Notwell Plc can be treated as a close company without having regard to the bank's involvement, this does not exempt Notwell Limited from being a close company.

Certain types of companies are not close companies. These include:

s698
- a registered Industrial and Provident Society within the meaning of Section 698

s702
- a Building Society within the meaning of s702

- a Semi-State company.

- an actively traded widely held quoted company subject to certain conditions.

The principal conditions which must be met in order that an actively traded widely held quoted company should not be treated as a closes company are:

- Shares carrying not less than 35% of the votes must be held by the public. Certain shares are treated as held by the public ie those held by a non-close company or by a non resident company which would not be close if resident; those held by an approved pension scheme; and any not held by a "principal member". "Principal member" is described below. Additionally shares are treated as not being held by the public if they are held by a director or an associate of a director; or by a company controlled by directors or their associates; or by an associated company of the company; or by any trust for the benefit of employees.

- The total percentage of the voting power possessed by the principal members must not exceed 85%. The principal members are the five members possessing the greatest voting power (provided they have at least 5% each).

Example 304

Quoted Company Plc has 100,000 £1 ordinary shares in issue. All carry equal voting rights, and all are quoted on the official list of a stock exchange and dealings in the shares occur regularly on the stock exchange.

The shares are held as to 20% by A, 29% by B, and 15% by C. The balance of 36% are held by a wide variety of persons, none of whom hold more than 1% or 2% each. B is not a close company and is a company resident in the State.

The voting power held by the principal members amounts to 64% and therefore does not breach the requirement that it should not exceed 85%. A, B and C are the principal members. The 64% of the shares held by them are not treated as being held by the public by reason of being comprised in a principal member's holding. This is so notwithstanding that B is a non-close company. The balance of 36% of the shares however are treated as held by the public (not being held by directors etc. as described above). Accordingly share capital carrying more than 35% of the voting power is held by the public and is quoted. Accordingly the company is not a close company.

If in the example above A had held 25% rather than 20%, the company would be a close company because the shares held by A (being held by a principal member) are not treated as held by the public. Only 31% of the shares would be treated as held by the public.

It will be seen that in general most closely held family companies will be close companies. The detailed provisions described above will mainly be of relevance either in a tax planning situation where a taxpayer is attempting to structure a company so that it is not a close company, or where a company which might appear to be widely held may in fact, under some of the technical rules described above, fall to be treated as a close company.

67.2.1.1   **Resident**

The second requirement, in order that s590 should apply to a non resident company, is that it should not be resident in the State. The test here is by reference to the normal domestic rules ie the place of central management and control, and registration in Ireland in certain cases. If a company is resident in Ireland under Ireland's domestic rules, but is regarded as a resident of another State under the terms of a double tax agreement, the section would nonetheless have application to the company. The test as regards residence for the purpose of s590 is purely the test under domestic law. The place of registration has no relevance, save in so far as an Irish registered company may, solely for that reason, be regarded as resident in certain circumstances.

There is no requirement that an Irish resident or domiciled person should have involved in the setting up of a company, in order that the section should apply to it. The section has application to all non resident closely held companies, no matter what their circumstances. The focus of the section is only reduced when it comes to examining the persons to whom the gains of the company are to be attributed. Only then is attention focused on persons with Irish connections.

The motive for the creation of the company is not relevant. The section applies equally to a non-resident trading company created without the intent to avoid tax just as readily as it applies to a non-resident investment company created to avoid tax.

Example 305

> Tom Murphy spent a large part of his life in Taiwan where he set up a company, Far Eastern Products Limited, which exports fireworks to the UK. In 1999 Tom transferred 30% of the shares in the company to his son, John, and 30% to his daughter, Mary. Thereafter John and Mary managed the company in Taiwan. Tom retired back to Ireland. Tom had an Irish domicile of origin which he never lost and he is therefore now both resident and domiciled in Ireland. Far Eastern

Products Limited is a Taiwanese registered company controlled by its board of directors in Taiwan (ie John and Mary since Tom no longer attends meetings).

Far Eastern Products Limited has been very profitable over the years and had built up surplus assets not required in its trade. These included £100,000 of Taiwanese government stocks. These were disposed of by the company on 28 February 2000, realising a gain of £50,000.

40% of this gain (proportionate to his interest in the company) is attributable to Tom. This is so notwithstanding that Far Eastern Products Limited is a bona fide trading company created, and existing, without any intent to avoid Irish tax, or indeed without any regard to the existence of Irish tax.

On 31 March 2000 Far Eastern Products Limited disposed of one of its factory buildings in Taiwan and realised a gain of £100,000. No part of this gain is attributable to Tom because it arises on the disposal of immovable tangible property used only for the purpose of a trade carried on by the company wholly outside the State. This aspect is discussed immediately below under the heading "excluded assets".

67.2.2   To whom may gains be attributed?

s590(4)   S590(4) states –

"subject to this section

— every person who at the time when the chargeable gain accrues to the company

— is resident or ordinarily resident in the State

— who if an individual is domiciled in the State

— and who is a participator in the company

— shall be treated for the purposes of the Capital Gains Tax Acts as if a part of the chargeable gain had accrued to that person."

In other words the persons chargeable in relation to the offshore gains are participators (as defined in paragraph 67.2.1) who are either resident or ordinarily resident in the State at the date when the chargeable gain accrues. The date when the chargeable gain accrues in most instances will be the date of the unconditional contract under which the asset is disposed of (See paragraph 15).

The person to whom gains are attributed can be an individual, or a company, or a trustee. If the participator is a resident or ordinarily resident individual, then he will be chargeable only if he is also domiciled in the State. Any other type of person is chargeable regardless of domicile.

Because individuals are chargeable only if domiciled, the section has no interaction with the "remittance basis" of taxation in relation to the disposal of assets located overseas. (See paragraph 3.3)

s590(12)   S590(12) provides a "look through" where a participator in the non resident company is itself a non resident close company. This look through can apply to any number of "non resident close companies" holding shares indirectly in the non resident close company which crystallises a gain. The effect of the look through is that if there is an Irish resident or ordinarily resident person (domiciled in the case of an individual) who is a participator in any of the chain of companies which is being "looked through" then the gain can be at least in part attributed to that Irish resident/ordinarily resident person.

Example 306

> *Offshore Limited is a "non resident close company" resident in the Isle of Man. It is in turn owned by Offshore Holdings Limited, also a "non resident" company resident in the Isle of Man. The shareholders of Offshore Holdings Limited are Joe Smith, an Irish resident and domiciled individual, and Smith Investments Limited, an Irish resident company owned solely by Joe Smith.*
>
> *On 17 April 1999 Offshore Limited disposed of quoted shares and realised a gain on the disposal of £100,000. As there are no participators in the company who are Irish resident or ordinarily resident, s590(4) does not have direct application to attribute gains. However sub-section 12 will attribute to the participators in Offshore Holdings Limited, the gains which would have been attributed to Offshore Holdings Limited. Therefore Joe Smith is treated as having gains accruing to him on 17 April 1999 of £50,000, and a similar attribution is made to Smith Investments Limited. Because Smith Investments Limited is a resident company, there is no further attribution to its shareholder, Joe Smith, of the gains attributed to it. That gain "stops" with Smith Holdings Limited which is chargeable to tax in respect of it.*

s590(2)

S590(2) applies a special treatment to a situation where a trust is a shareholder in an offshore company, or is otherwise a participator in the company or the means by which an other person is treated as a participator. The matter is most easily explained by reference to a straight forward situation in which a trust holds shares in the offshore company. In such a situation it is the trustees of the trust, and not the beneficiaries of the trust (even if they have an interest in the shares such as a life interest, or a remainder interest) which are treated as being the participator for the purposes of s590. Correspondingly, the beneficiaries are not treated as being participators. Furthermore, s590(13) explicitly confirms that trustees who are participators can have a part of the chargeable gains of a non resident company attributed even if the trustees are neither resident nor ordinarily resident in the State. As explained above, under s590(4) the section ordinarily will attribute the gains of an offshore company only to persons who are either resident or ordinarily resident in the State at the date the gains accrues. This treatment of trustees is therefore an exception to that general rule. A trustee who is a participator can have the gains attributed to him whether or not he is resident or ordinarily resident in the State. As explained above, the domicile position of a trustee is always irrelevant since it is only individuals (and a trustee is never treated as an individual) whose domicile status is taken into account.

Example 307

> *The facts are the same as in **example 306** above save that, instead of 50% of the shares being held by Smith Holdings Limited, that 50% is held equally by the trustees of the Joe Smith Junior Settlement (resident in Ireland) and by the trustees of the Joe Smith Senior Settlement (resident in the Isle of Man). Joe Smith is a life tenant of both settlements, and his wife is the remainder person in both settlements.*
>
> *One quarter of the gain will be attributed to the trustees of the Joe Smith Junior Settlement, the gain of Smith Offshore Limited being "seen through" the chain of companies to the participators in the top company. However they are not attributed further to Mr. & Mrs. Smith who, between them, hold the entire beneficial interest in the shares. Instead that one quarter of the gain is attributed to the trustees. The other quarter of the gain is attributed to the trustees of the Joe Smith Senior Settlement.*
>
> *Here something very peculiar happens. Under s590 it is not possible to further attribute the gains attributed to the trustees, to either of the beneficiaries in the trust. S590 (2) specifically prohibits that. But S579A (introduced by FA99 at the same time as this new version of s 590) now comes into play. That section (as is explained in detail in paragraph 68) is capable of attributing to Joe and Mrs. Smith the gains which Section 590 have attributed to the trustees of the Offshore Joe Smith Senior Settlement, where they have received benefits from the settlement.*
>
> *If they have not received benefits, then s579 may apply. That section has application only where non resident trustees accrue a gain. S590(13) specifically permits non resident trustees to have part of the offshore companies gain attributed to offshore trustees. So the condition for the triggering of s579 is met by s590(13). S579 will now apply to attribute to resident beneficiaries of the trust (see paragraph 68) the gains on which the non resident trustees would have been chargeable if resident. Here s590(4) comes into play. It attributes offshore company gains to the (hypothetically resident) trustees, so s579 can now re-attribute those gains to beneficiaries. Since s590 (13) can only attribute gains to non resident trustees, it falls out of sight once we assume (for the purposes of s579) that trustees are resident. Its sole function is to trigger s579. Once triggered, s590(4) does the rest.*

67.2.3.1   What can be attributed?

s592(5)

S592(5) states that the part of a chargeable gain which may be attributed to a resident or ordinarily resident participator *"shall be equal to the proportion of that gain that corresponds to the extent of the participator's interest as a participator in the company"*.

Where a gain has been "seen through" a chain of companies the reference here is to be interpreted as a reference to the participator's interest in the company in which he is a participator. It should be borne in mind that whereas gains of an offshore company can be attributed through a chain of offshore companies to a resident/ordinarily resident participator in any of the chain, that person is not, by reason of being a participator in one of the companies in the chain, a participator in any of the other companies in the chain.

s592(6)

S592(6) provides that where the aggregate amount falling to be apportioned to a person (and to persons connected with that person) does not exceed 1/20th of the gain, no attribution is to be made to the resident or ordinarily resident participator .

The starting point clearly is to determine what is the amount of the chargeable gain which accrued to the offshore company. Sub-section 15 provides that it is to be computed as if the company were within the charge to corporation tax on capital gains, ie as if it were a resident company. There are therefore no special features that have to be taken into account in the computation of the chargeable gain, other than the provisions relating to "offshore groups" which are explained in paragraph 67.3.11.

Once the chargeable gain has been computed the question of its apportionment now arises. That apportionment can be either

- directly to participators in the company who are resident or ordinarily resident in Ireland (and domiciled if individuals) or

- can be a attribution to non resident companies who are participators in the offshore company in which the gain accrued; or

- can be an attribution to non resident trustees who are participators in the offshore company to which the gain accrued.

The attribution to non resident companies and to non resident trusts is of course simply for the purpose of determining whether, under the "look through" provisions that apply to companies in s590, or under s579A, or s579 the gains can ultimately be attributed to an Irish resident or ordinarily resident participator in the other companies, or beneficiary of the settlement.

It is now necessary to determine how much shall be apportioned to each participator. That amount must *"correspond to the extent of the participator's interest as a participator in the company"*. Section 590(1) (b) requires that in determining the extent of a person's interest as a participator, regard should be had to all the factors by reference to which a person would fall to be treated as such a participator (see paragraph 67.2.1).

Example 308

John Brown holds 10% of the issued ordinary share capital of Offshore Company Limited. He has also advanced a loan to the company of £100,000. He possesses an option to subscribe for shares equivalent to a further 10% of the share capital.

In determining the extent of John Brown's interest in Offshore Company Limited, all three factors by reference to which he could be treated as a *participator - the shares, the loan, and the option - must be separately taken into account and evaluated.*

S590 (1) (c) provides that the extent of a participator's interest is to be measured by reference to the proportion of all of the interests of participators in the company, allocated on a just and reasonable basis. The "extent of the interests" is a reference not to an absolute amount of money, but to a proportion. This will expressed as (say) ½, or a ¼, or 1/10ᵗʰ etc. but not as (say) £1,000,000, or £50,000 etc. The proportion so identified will be the same as the proportion of the chargeable gain which will be attributed to that participator. Thus if the extent of the interest of a participator in a company were determined to be (say) 1/5ᵗʰ, that participator would have attributed to him 1/5ᵗʰ of the chargeable gain which accrued to the offshore company.

The criteria for determining the relative proportions of the interest of participators is "a just and reasonable apportionment". This is a somewhat unfortunate expression, because one man's justice is another man's injustice, and what is reasonable to one man will seem like pigheadedness to another.

s590

S590 does not explicitly state that you start by computing the value of the company, insofar as it is attributable to participators (ie the value of the share capital and of the loan capital of the company). Nonetheless, this would seem the most "just and reasonable" method to adopt. Once that total figure has been determined, it now falls to allocate it amongst the various interests in the company which are held by participators. Those interests can include the interests of shareholders, of loan creditors, of option holders etc.

The next issue that would seem to arise is how that total is to be apportioned. One approach would be to apportion it to each interest in the ratio of the open market value of that interest to the open market value of all interests. Such a straight forward approach however could create anomalies and difficulties. For example, if a solvent and profitable company had taken out a fixed term loan of £1,000,000 at a fixed interest rate of 12%, some years ago, that loan might now be worth a great deal more (to the creditor) on the open market than £1,000,000, consequent on the general fall in interest rates. Indeed it might well be worth at the current date closer to £2,000,000. The company is obliged only to repay capital of £1,000,000 and that is the only liability disclosed in the balance sheet. The answer probably is that the obligation to pay the very high interest rates will be reflected in the value of the share capital, and will have depressed the value of the share capital, and therefore that this factor does not need to be taken into account a second time in the valuation of the loan. Accordingly, the loan might be taken at its face value.

How do you determine the relative interests of a 10% shareholder and a 51% shareholder? The open market value of the two lots of shares will reflect very different discounts on account of their being less than 100% holdings. The 51% interest will attract a much lower discount (and therefore per share will have a higher value) than the 10% interest. Do you take the interests of the 51% shareholder to be 5.1 times the interest of the 10% shareholder, or do you take it in the ratio of the open market value of the two holdings (on which basis the 51% holding might be worth at least 10 times the 10% holding)? The words "just and reasonable" offer little guidance. The 10% shareholder might feel it unjust that an approach be taken that could result in having part of the capital gain attributed to him, since his shares are probably valued on a dividend yield basis, rather than an asset backing basis, whereas the 51% shareholder's shares may well be valued by reference to the value of the company's assets. However, the "just and reasonable" apportionment is not applied in the context of attributing gains, but rather in determining the relative proportions of interests. On balance, the author's view of justice and reasonableness would suggest that market value of the shares be taken as the basis, rather than nominal value. The matter is not beyond dispute.

The expression "just and reasonable" is used extensively in the Taxes Acts in determining the tax liability of taxpayers. In view of its vagueness, it seems an inappropriate expression to employ in the context of our Constitution granting to the Dail the exclusive rights to levy taxes. The levying of taxes should not be left to the view of the Revenue Commissioners, or of the Appeal Commissioners, or of the courts, as to what constitutes justice or reasonableness. It should be defined by the Dail.

Example 309

In *Offshore Company Limited*, the interests of all shareholders are worth £1,000,000 in total. 51% of the shares are held by C, 10% by D, 10% by E, 10% by F, and 9% by G. The company has additionally loan capital of £500,000 provided by H. A has an option to subscribe for up to 10% of the share capital of the company at par. B has an option to subscribe for up to 10% of the share capital of the company but at open market value at the date of subscription.

All of A, B, C, D, E, F, G and H are participators (see paragraph 67.2.2 where the definition is discussed.)

The task is to determine the relative proportions of their interests in Offshore Company Limited.

As explained above, the loan should probably be taken at its face value, without regard to the interest rate applying. If the interest rate is exceptionally low, this will have correspondingly inflated the value of the shares. If it is exceptionally high, it will have depressed the value of the shares. In determining proportionate value, it would therefore seem reasonable to leave the loan at its nominal amount.

As discussed above, it would seem appropriate that the relative proportions of the shares should be in accordance with their relative open market values. Solely for the purpose of this example (and not as an example of the valuation of shares), it is assumed that the 51% interest is worth 10 times a 10% or 9% interest in ordinary circumstances. In the present case however there exists options to subscribe for shares. If either of those options are exercised the 51% interest would no longer be a controlling interest in the company (in a commercial sense as opposed to CGT rules) but would then be only a 42.5% interest. For that reason, it is assumed that the open market value of the 51% interest held by C, would be not 10 times the equivalent of 10% interest, but only 7 times. Once again, it is emphasised that these valuation aspects are arbitrarily assumed for the purpose of the example and are not comments on share valuations per se.

The option held by A, to subscribe for up to 10% of the share capital at par is a very valuable option since there are only 1,000 shares in issue, compared to the open market value of the entire share capital of £1,000,000. It is therefore to all intents and purposes worth the equivalent of a 10% interest in the company, since the cost of taking it up is minimal. In contrast, the option held by B to subscribe for shares at open market value at the time of subscription, although it would have some value, would probably have a very minor value. The value, for the purposes of this example, is assumed to be so low that it can be disregarded on a just and reasonable basis.

The open market value of the share capital is £1,000,000, and of the loan capital is £500,000. One can therefore say that the proportion of the interests in the company held by H is 1/3rd. The balance of 2/3rds has to be allocated among the shareholders and option holder A. 2/3rds will be allocated in the ratio of 7:1:1:1:.9:1. The .9 relates to G's 9% interest. The option is taken to have the same value as a 10% holding. The 2/3rds must therefore be divided by 11.9. The resulting figure, when multiplied by 7 will give us the proportion held by C. When multiplied by 1, it gives us the proportion attributable to D, E. F and H. On multiplied by .9, it gives us the proportion held by G.

Therefore the ratios with which we emerge from this exercise are as follows -

A	0.06
B	0.00
C	0.38
D	0.06
E	0.06
F	0.06
G	0.50
H	0.33

The chargeable gain which has accrued to Offshore Company Limited is now to be apportioned to the participators in the ratios above.

As was stated further up, the attribution of the chargeable gain of an offshore company will not be made to a resident or ordinarily resident participator in that company where the amount to be attributed to that person any persons connected with him does not exceed $1/20^{th}$ of the gain accruing to the company.

In *example 307* above, G would be attributed .05 of the gain, ie. $1/20^{th}$ of the gain. Since the proportion does not exceed $1/20^{th}$, no apportionment is to be made to G, provided he is not connected with any of the other participators whom an apportionment is being made. The meaning of "connected" is explained in paragraph 16.4.4.

The fact that no attribution of gains is made to G does not increase the amounts being attributed to other participators. It simply means that the total gain arising to the onshore entity is not fully attributed, notwithstanding that all of the participators are resident or ordinarily resident (and if individuals, domiciled) in Ireland.

67.2.3.2   Excluded Assets

Certain disposals of assets are excluded from the application of the section.

- Disposals of movable or immovable tangible property (including a lease) used, and used only for the purposes of a trade carried on by the company wholly outside the State.

- Disposal of currency (including a bank account) where the moneys are in use for the purpose of a trade carried on by the company wholly outside the State.

- A disposal of Irish specified assets, such that the company is chargeable to either capital gains tax or corporation tax on companies capital gains in respect of the disposal (see paragraph 3.3)

The exclusions relating to trade assets do not extend to assets used for the purpose of a profession but that may be of little practical importance since there are few professions which may be carried on by a company. A more serious limitation is that the reference to trade assets is confined to tangible trade assets. That would not include intangible assets such as goodwill, patents, copyrights, rights under contracts. Such trade assets are within the scope of the section even though they might relate to a trade carried out by a non resident company wholly outside the State. The logic lying behind the discrimination between tangible trade assets and intangible trade assets is not apparent. Although the legislation does not require that the excluded trade assets be located outside the State, in practice they would have to be if they are being used solely for a trade carried on wholly outside the State.

67.2.4   **Offshore losses**

s590(11)

The attribution of offshore company chargeable gains to resident/ordinarily resident participators is by reference to each separate gain, as it accrues. In the ordinary manner, capital gains tax is charged on the total of chargeable gains arising in the tax year less allowable losses, and is not charged in respect of individual gains, one by one. However the method of attribution in s590 is to attribute individual gains to the participators, and not merely the amount upon which the offshore company would have been charged with tax had it been resident. For that reason loss relief is not automatically available to the participator in respect of offshore losses. Indeed, s590 (11) specifically confirms (although it was not necessary to do so that) that the attribution provisions of the Section do not apply to losses.

S579
s579A

However the same sub-section does provide a limited form of loss relief. The participator to whom a gain is attributed is entitled to have the section applied so as to apportion to participators any loss arising to the company in the same year of assessment, just as it apportions gains. A loss so apportioned to a participator may be used by that participator only to *"reduce or extinguish chargeable gains accruing by virtue of this section"*. In other words, the losses attributed in this fashion are "ring fenced" for offset against the gains so attributed in the same year. They cannot be offset against any other gains arising to the participator, eg on disposals by himself, or attributed to him by s579 or s579A.

However, the ring fencing is not specific to the company whose gains are apportioned. If a resident person is a participator in two offshore companies, one of which crystallised a chargeable gain, and another of which incurs a loss in the same year, he is entitled to have the loss apportioned, and to use his share of the loss against any gain apportioned to him in relation to the other company.

It would seem that the ring fenced offshore losses are to be used in priority to any other loss relief to which the participator may be entitled. Thus a participator who has loss relief available in relation to disposals by himself in the same or prior years is not obliged to use those losses against the offshore gain to the extent he can avail of an offshore loss arising in the same year.

Example 310

> Joe Smith disposed of quoted shares on which he has crystallised chargeable gains of £10,000 in the year ended 1999/2000. He has available to him unutilised losses arising on transactions in the year 1998/99 of £8,000. Also in 1999/2000 s590 has apportioned to him £2,000 of chargeable gains of an offshore company, Offshore Investments Limited. He is also a participator in Offshore Holdings Limited, another offshore company which in 1998/99 crystallised losses of £1,000, and in 1999/2000 crystallised further amount of losses of £1,000. Joe is the sole participator in this company.

Joe is entitled to offset the 1999/2000 loss of Offshore Holdings Limited against the portion of the gain of Offshore Investments Limited apportioned to him in the same year (£2,000) leaving a net £1,000 to be taken into account in computing his chargeable gains. He is not obliged to offset any part of his own losses forward from 1998/99 against the gain apportioned to him from Offshore Holdings Limited. He is not ever able to obtain relief for the £1,000 loss in 1998/99 in Offshore Holdings Ltd. This cannot be "carried forward" where not used in the year it arose. The chargeable gains are computed for the year 1999/2000 as follows -

	£
Gains on disposals by Joe Smith	10,000
Net offshore gain after offset of offshore loss	1,000
Total chargeable gains	11,000
Less - losses forward from 1998/99	8,000
Chargeable gains of year	3,000

67.2.5   Interaction with double tax agreements

s590   Double tax agreements are discussed in paragraph 85 and the discussion is not repeated here. The essence of s590 is to charge to Irish capital gains tax a person resident in Ireland, in respect of a gain in reality arising to a person resident abroad. In the ordinary way a double tax agreement would not prevent Irish taxation of an Irish resident person. A double tax agreement will usually only operate (as a broad statement) to prevent a non resident person being subjected to Irish tax. However the particular wording of the capital gains tax article of many treaties focuses not on the right of Ireland to tax (or not to tax) a non resident person. Instead it focuses on the right of Ireland to tax a gain arising on a disposal by a person who is non resident. Where the article of the treaty focuses on the right to tax the gain (as opposed to the right to tax a non resident person) it can have the result of denying Ireland the right to tax even a resident person in respect of a gain that in fact arose to a non resident person.

The point can be illustrated by Article 14(4) from the United Kingdom/Ireland double tax agreement which reads: *"Gains from the alienation of any property other than that referred to in paragraphs (1), (2), (3) and (4) of this article shall be taxable only in the contracting state in which the alienator is a resident"*. This wording focuses not on exempting a resident of the UK from CGT in Ireland, but rather on exempting certain gains from Irish taxation, without reference to the person who is being charged in respect of those gains. The wording would seem to protect an Irish resident from tax as much as it would protect a UK resident from tax, where the tax is in respect of a gain arising from the disposal of property where the person who made the disposal is not a resident of Ireland. Similar wording occurs in a number of other treaties.

It is accepted by the UK Inland Revenue that similar wording in treaties overrides and provides protection against the UK equivalent of s590. To date the Revenue Commissioners have not made a statement on the application of Ireland's treaties but the matter would seem clear enough ie treaty protection is available where a wording such as that quoted above applies.

Example: 311

Joe Bloggs is the sole shareholder in Bloggs Investments (UK) Limited. That company is managed and controlled in the UK by reason of its board of directors (consisting of UK based investment advisers and Joe Bloggs) meeting only in the UK. The company from time to time disposes of investments and crystallises gains.

Under s590, the gains of the non resident company are capable of being attributed to Joe Bloggs. However the paragraph from Article 14 of the UK Ireland treaty quoted above provides Joe Bloggs with protection. This is because the alienator of the investments (ie the person making the disposal) is a UK resident and accordingly the gain arising on the disposal may be taxed only in the UK. It is not possible for Ireland to tax anybody whether it be Joe Bloggs or Bloggs Investments (UK) Limited in respect of those gains.

67.3   Non resident companies - position pre 11/2/99

s590   S590 can attribute the gains of a non resident company to Irish resident persons in certain circumstances. The FA99 substituted a new version of s590 for the pre existing version, but only by reference to disposals accruing from 11 February 1999 onwards. The pre existing version, which had application to disposals by the non resident company prior to 11 February 1999 is described in this paragraph. The version of s590 which has application to gains arising currently (ie from 11 February 1999) is described in paragraph 67.2.1 above.

67.3.1   Broad Outline - pre 11/2/99 only

s590   S590 was replaced in its entirety by a new version of the section by FA99. The new (and current) version has been discussed in paragraph 67.2 above. The old pre 11/2/99 version remains relevant to some transactions and accordingly is discussed in paragraph 67.3, as it was prior to FA99 changes.

A person considering the purchase of an asset with potential for capital appreciation might seek to avoid tax on the eventual disposal of the asset by acquiring it through a non-resident company. The object of this would be to realise the gain in the company which, being non-resident, would be outside the charge to Irish CGT (except in respect of certain specified Irish assets - see paragraph 3).

However, the potential for avoidance in this way was foreseen and provisions to prevent it were included in s590. The affect of the provisions is to treat the gains of the non-resident company as if they arose to the shareholders of the company.

s590(2)

"Subject to this section, every person who, at the time when the chargeable gain accrues to the company

(a)   *is resident or ordinarily resident in the State,*

(b)   *if an individual is domiciled in the State, and*

(c)   *holds shares in the company,*

shall be treated for the purposes of this Act as if part of the chargeable gain had accrued to that person".

Where the immediate shareholder is another non-resident company it is necessary to look through that company, and so on through any number of non-resident companies.

Clearly the anti-avoidance provisions are not required where the gain would be subject to CGT in Ireland even in the hands of a non-resident (e.g. a gain on the disposal of Irish land), so there are exceptions to these provisions. The exceptions are dealt with in paragraph 67.4 below.

67.3.2   Scope of Provisions - pre 11/2/99 only

The provisions apply to chargeable gains accruing to a company,

s590(1)

• which is not resident in Ireland

   and

• which would be a close company if resident in Ireland.

s430

"Close company" has the meaning assigned to it by s430. In that section 'close company' is generally defined as one which is under the control of five or fewer participators or of participators who are directors. However, this general definition is substantially extended in s430 and other sections especially by the wide meaning given to the terms "participator" and "control". The effect is to bring within the definition the majority of private companies and even some quoted companies. "Close company" is discussed in paragraph 67.2.1.

67.3.3   Affect of Provisions - pre 11/2/99 only

s590(2)

Any person who holds shares in such a company (as is described in paragraph 67.3.2) at the time when the gain arises will be treated as if a part of the gain had arisen to him, if at that time

—he is resident or ordinarily resident in Ireland

and

— If an individual, is also domiciled in Ireland.

s590(8)   If one of the shareholders is itself another non-resident company which would be a close company if resident in Ireland, the gain attributed to that other non-resident company must be re-attributed to the shareholders of that company. If any of the shareholders of that other non-resident company are themselves non-resident companies which would be close companies if Irish resident, a further re-attribution of the gains is necessary through that non-resident company to its shareholders, and so on through any number of such non-resident companies.

Notwithstanding that the gain accruing to a non-resident company may be attributed to an Irish resident shareholder, the Irish resident shareholder is not granted credit for tax paid by the non-resident company on the gain in question. The legislation makes no specific provision for such a credit. If the non-resident company were resident in a state with which Ireland has a double tax agreement, some argument might be made that that agreement would entitle the Irish resident shareholder to whom the gain is attributed, to credit for the foreign tax. However, since the foreign tax wasn't paid by the Irish resident shareholder, nor did the gain in fact accrue to him, it is doubtful if a double tax agreement would grant credit. However the foreign tax paid by the non-resident company should be taken into account as a deduction when computing the amount of the gain, since it is the gain as computed in accordance with the CGT Acts that is attributed to the Irish resident shareholder.

The unilateral tax credit introduced by the FA98 extends only to a credit against corporation tax payable by an Irish resident company on a dividend received by it from a non-resident company resident in a state with which Ireland doesn't have a double tax agreement. It is not capable in any direct way of providing a credit for the tax paid by the non-resident company, on a gain which is attributed to an Irish resident shareholder. As noted in paragraph 67.3.4, where the non-resident company distributes the capital gain by way of dividend, and the recipient is an Irish resident company holding at least 25% of the share capital of the non-resident company paying the dividend, credit for the foreign tax paid on the capital gain would be available to the Irish resident company.

s5   For the purpose of looking through a company to its shareholders, the term "company" has the meaning attributed to it by s5 - i.e. any body corporate, but does not include an European Economic Interest Group. The term "company" does not include a trustee, even if the trustee is a corporate trustee. A trustee is never attributed the characteristics of either an individual or a company for CGT purposes.

A gain of a non-resident company which is attributed under s590 to a trustee, is chargeable on the trustee if he is resident or ordinarily resident in Ireland. If the trustee is not resident (or not ordinarily resident) he is not chargeable on any gains attributed to him under s590 nor is the settlement "seen through" in the same manner as a company under s590.

s590(3)

The part of the gain treated as arising to the shareholder is a proportion of the total gain equal to the proportion of the total assets of the company which he would be entitled to receive on a liquidation of the company, i.e.

$$total\ gain\ \ x\ \ \frac{asset\ entitlement}{total\ assets}$$

Example 312

Illgotten Gains Ltd is resident outside Ireland. Its shares are held as follows:

ROBERT	20%
IRENE	35%
WILLIAM	20%
WINDFALL LTD	20%
HUGH	5%

Robert, Irene and Hugh are resident and domiciled in Ireland. William is domiciled in Ireland but resident and ordinarily resident in France. Hugh owns all the shares in Windfall Ltd which is a non-resident company. The shares in Illgotten Gains Ltd rank equally in all respects, and the company does not carry on a trade.

In 1999/00 Illgotten Gains Ltd has the following chargeable gains

	£
On Irish Land	10,000
On UK Shares	15,000
On US Property	20,000
On Irish Quoted Shares	5,000

The gains which come within the scope of the anti-avoidance legislation are:

	£
On UK Shares	15,000
On US Property	20,000
On Irish Quoted Shares	5,000
Total	40,000

Note: These are gains which would not be taxable (under the general legislation) on a person who was not resident and not ordinarily resident in Ireland (see paragraph 3.4). The gain on the disposal of the Irish land would be chargeable to Irish tax in the normal manner on the company (being a gain on a "specified asset") and is not apportioned to the shareholders under s590.

The total of £40,000 must now be apportioned between the shareholders, as follows:

		£
ROBERT	20%	8,000
IRENE	35%	14,000
WILLIAM	20%	8,000
*HUGH	20%	8,000
HUGH	5%	2,000
Total		40,000

*As WINDFALL LTD would be a close company if resident in Ireland its 20% share must be apportioned between its shareholders. As Hugh is the only shareholder the 20% share of WINDFALL LTD is added to his 5% share.

The gains chargeable to CGT in Ireland for 1999/00 are therefore:

	£
ROBERT	8,000
IRENE	14,000
WILLIAM	Nil
HUGH	10,000

As William is not resident or ordinarily resident in Ireland, he is not within the charge to CGT at all in respect of the part of the gains apportioned to him.

s590(3)
The wording of s590(3) is somewhat ambiguous. The part of the chargeable gain which is to be attributed to a resident shareholder is the same proportion of the gain as "…..*the proportion of the assets of the company to which the person would be entitled on a liquidation of the company at the time when the chargeable gain accrues to the company*". The plain meaning of the words would seem to be that one has regard to the proportion of:

- all the assets of the company such as they may be at the time of the disposal, and

- which would be available to that shareholder on a winding up at that date.

In any winding up, the assets of the company are primarily available to meet the claims of creditors. It is only the balance of those assets which remains after all liabilities have been discharged that is available to shareholders. It seems possible to argue that where a company has creditors, that it is not appropriate to apportion the gain among the shareholders in the ratio of their respective shareholdings as has been done in the examples set out above. Arguably, one should calculate what proportion of the gross assets of the company would be paid to each shareholder on a winding up (after discharging the creditors out of those gross assets) and it is only the part of the gain which is proportionate to the part of the gross assets attributable to any shareholder which can be taken into account for the purposes of s590 (i.e. the effect of this would be to attribute part of the gains to the creditors). It would be surprising if such a result were intended in drafting the section in such a manner, but it seems that it could be argued that the plain meaning of the words used should be interpreted in such a manner. Any other interpretation would make it difficult to apportion to shareholders the gains of an insolvent non-resident company.

It should be noted that what is attributed under S590 to the resident shareholder is all or part of the gain arising to the non-resident company. This is not the same thing as attributing to the resident shareholder all or part of the amount on which the non-resident company would have been chargeable to tax in respect of capital gains, had it been resident in Ireland in the same year. Had it been resident, it would have been taxed not on the amount of chargeable gains arising to it, but on that amount, as reduced by losses arising in the current year, and unrealised losses forwarded from previous years in which is was resident. The attribution under S590 is of the gross gains. The losses are separately dealt with as explained in paragraph 67.3.6. This treatment differs to that applying under S579 to the gains of a non-resident trust, where they are attributed to resident beneficiaries. This is explained in Paragraph 68.11.8.

67.3.4   Exceptions - pre 11/2/99 only

s590(4)   The provisions do not apply in certain circumstances. These are where:

— **gain distributed within 2 years** : the gain is distributed within two years from the time when it accrued to the company - either by way of dividend or by distribution of capital on a dissolution of the company to shareholders or creditors of the company.

S590 (4) (a) does not actually refer to a distribution of the gain per se. Rather it refers to *"any amount in respect of the chargeable gain which is distributed –"*. The section does not provide guidance has to how to determine whether any dividend or distribution is to be regarded as being *"in respect of the gain"*. The matter is clear enough in a dissolution, since the entire assets of the company would be distributed either to creditors or the shareholders, and the distribution to one or the other or both must at least in part be in respect of the gain. Where however the company redeems some share capital only, or pays a dividend in a period in which it has not only gains, but also income, it is not clear on what basis it is to be determined that part of the proceeds of redemption of shares, or the dividend, is to be regarded as being *"in respect of the gain"*. If a dividend were specified as being out of the gain, as opposed to out of profits or other reserves, that might help settle the matter in the case of a dividend.

The reference to payments to the creditors of the company is presumably intended to cover the situation where a company is insolvent, and all of its assets are used in payment of creditors, on a liquidation. In such a case, the payments to the creditors would be at least in part *"in respect of the gain"*, whatever it may mean. Oddly enough, the use of the assets of an insolvent company to pay of the creditors does not satisfy a requirement for this exclusion of the attribution of the gain, unless a dissolution of the company occurs and indeed, strictly speaking, unless the payment occurs in the course of the dissolution. If the assets were applied in payment of creditors (under some arrangement with the creditors) prior to a dissolution, and once the company had been reduced to the worthless shell, it was then dissolved or struck off, strictly speaking, the requirements for the exclusion from attribution would not have been met. Payments to a creditor must occur on a liquidation of the company.

The shareholders to whom the distribution in respect of the gain is made in the 2 year period following the accrual of the gain, need not necessarily be the same shareholders who owned the company at the time the gain accrued.

The time limit of 2 years within which a dividend or other distribution of capital must occur commences with the date on which the gain accrues, and not at the end of the tax year, or of the accounting period, in which it accrues. The time at which a gain accrues to a company is likely to be determined by the date of the disposal (see paragraph 15).

s590(5)

S590 (5) permits the Revenue to raise an assessment on a resident person to whom the gain has been attributed, at a time when no dividend or other distribution of capital in respect of the gain has yet occurred. If later within the 2 year period from the date the gain accrued, such a dividend or other distribution of capital is paid out, a repayment or discharge of tax will be made. In practice it is unlikely that the Revenue would get round to the raising of an assessment within the 2 year period.

- **Revenue/Chief Inspector's CGT manual :**

Paragraph 19.4.13.9 of the Revenue CGT manual states *"Gains accruing to a non resident company should, however, be assessed and charged on the shareholders without waiting for the end of the two year period, i.e. in order to see whether they are, in fact, distributed and so qualify for relief. If the gains are subsequently distributed, then assessments should be amended and any necessary discharge or repayment made."*

The FA98 introduced a unilateral credit for foreign tax. It is available both where an existing treaty would provide relief and where a double taxation agreement does not exist so as to provide credit for foreign tax. The credit may be applied only against corporation tax payable by an Irish resident company on dividends paid by a company not resident in Ireland. It will apply where the company paying the dividend is not resident in the state. That unilateral tax credit can extend not only to foreign taxes suffered by the Irish resident company on the dividend, but, where it holds at least 25% of the ordinary share capital of the non resident company, to taxes paid by the non resident company (or by its associates in certain circumstances) on the profits from which the dividend was paid. Those profits could include capital gains, and the taxes for which credit would be available could include foreign taxes akin to Irish CGT. The credit would extend to taxes paid not only in the country in which the company paying the dividend is resident, but also the taxes paid in third countries. This unilateral tax credit could be relevant if a non resident company determined to distribute its gain, in order to avoid attribution of the gain to Irish resident shareholders. The unilateral tax credit is limited to corporation tax payable in Ireland by an Irish resident company in respect of dividends received from a non resident company. It is not available to individuals, and it is not available in relation to either CGT payable on a disposal of an asset, or corporation tax on companies capital gains payable on the disposal of foreign assets.

— **gain on tangible foreign trade assets :** the gain arises on a disposal of tangible property whether movable or immovable (or a lease of such property) which was used only for the purposes of a trade carried on by the non-resident company wholly outside Ireland,

— **foreign trade currency :** the gain arises on a disposal of currency or on bank balances in foreign currency which were used for the purposes of a trade carried on by the non-resident company wholly outside Ireland, or

— **CGT on specified Irish asset :** the gain is chargeable to Irish CGT in the hands of the non-resident company, being a gain on "specified Irish assets" chargeable on non-residents (see paragraph 3.4)

— **CT on specified Irish asset :** the gain is chargeable to Irish corporation tax on the non-resident company - which may be chargeable to Irish CT in respect of certain gains of an Irish branch (see paragraph 3.6).

67.3.5   Deduction for Tax paid

s590(6)   Where all or part of the gains of a non-resident company are treated as accruing to an Irish resident shareholder, and he pays the tax under these provisions on the part of the gains attributed to him (to the extent he is not reimbursed by the company for the CGT involved) he will be allowed a deduction for that tax payment in calculating a chargeable gain arising on a disposal by him of the shares in that company.

The question of any such deduction cannot arise until there is a disposal by the shareholder of the shares in the non-resident company.

Example 313

> Trevor is Irish resident and domiciled. He is a 20% shareholder in "Jersey Investments", an unlimited company, incorporated in Jersey and resident in Guernsey. The other shareholders are all German resident. During 1999/00, Jersey Investments had a number of non-Irish gains - 20% of which were attributed to Trevor, and he paid the appropriate Irish CGT charged of £8,000. No part of the CGT paid by him has been re-imbursed by the company.
>
> On the eventual disposal of his shares in Jersey Investments, Trevor is entitled to a deduction for the amount of CGT paid (and not reimbursed by the company) - i.e. "a deduction, in the computation, under this Act, of a gain accruing on the disposal by him of the shares by reference to which the tax was paid".

As is illustrated in *example 312* above, s590 can attribute a non-resident company's gains to an Irish resident shareholder even if the company is not controlled by Irish resident shareholders. It is no defence to a charge of CGT on the resident shareholder that the shares were not acquired for tax avoidance reasons, or that the residence of the company is not a matter within his control. The absence of such a defence makes s590 a penal section. It seems contrary to the spirit at least of EU law and principles.

The application of s590 may be subject to a relevant double tax agreement - see Chapter 11.

67.3.6   **Losses - pre 11/2/99 only**

s590(7)   Capital losses arising to the non-resident company described in paragraph 67.3.2 may be attributed to the shareholders in the company.

These provisions will apply to a loss arising to the non-resident company, only if it would reduce or extinguish a gain arising under these provisions in the same year of assessment to the same shareholder.

Example 314

> Dublin Bay Ltd. is an Irish resident close company. It owns all the share capital of
>
> * Liverpool Ltd, and
> * Bristol Ltd

both of which are non-resident companies (which would be close companies if they were resident in Ireland).

During their accounting year ended 31st December 1998 the companies had the following transactions:

- *Dublin Bay Ltd disposed of Irish quoted shares, the chargeable gain on disposal of which (calculated under Irish CGT rules) amounted to £50,000.*

- *Liverpool Ltd disposed of UK quoted shares, the chargeable gain on disposal of which (calculated under Irish CGT rules) would amount to £25,000.*

- *Bristol Ltd disposed of UK quoted shares, the CGT loss on disposal of which (calculated under Irish CGT rules) would amount to £40,000.*

Assuming that the conditions for the application of s590 apply (i.e.. none of the exceptions apply) the gain of £25,000 which accrued to Liverpool Ltd would be attributed to Dublin Bay Ltd.

The loss incurred by Bristol Ltd could be claimed by Dublin Bay Ltd to the extent required to offset the attributed gain of Liverpool Ltd, in effect using £25,000 of the £40,000 loss of Bristol Ltd.

The balance of Bristol's £40,000 loss cannot be used by Dublin Bay Ltd to offset its own gain of £50,000.

s590(7)

S590 (7), which permits a loss to be attributed to the shareholder insofar as it would reduce or extinguish a chargeable gain attributed to him in the same year requires that the loss and the gain should both be incurred by the same non-resident company.

It should be noted that relief for the losses of a non-resident company are available only where they arise in the tax year in which a gain arises which is attributed to the shareholder. Losses which arose in prior years, and which have not been "relieved" by granting relief against gains attributed to the shareholders in those years, cannot be relieved in a later year in that fashion. The result of this treatment is that the tax payable by the shareholder could actually exceed the tax which would have been payable by the non-resident company, had it been resident. This should be contrasted with the treatment of losses in a non-resident trust - see Paragraph 68.11.8.

Example 315

*Taking the same facts as in **example 314** above, but suppose that Liverpool Limited had, in its accounting year ended 31 December 1998, disposed of UK quoted shares of which it had incurred a loss of £10,000. Liverpool Limited had no other disposals of assets in that year, nor had Bristol Limited any disposals of assets in that year.*

Notwithstanding that if Liverpool Limited had been resident in Ireland in both 1998 and 1999, the losses in 1998 would have been offset against the gains in 1999 so that only a net £15,000 would be liable to tax in respect of chargeable gains in 1999, 1998 losses cannot be availed by Dublin Bay Limited to offset the gains of £25,000 attributed to it from Liverpool Limited in 1996. The only losses which it may avail of are those actually arising in the same year as that on which the gains attributed to it arose.

- **Revenue/Chief Inspector's CGT Manual :**

— In the Revenue Commissioners CGT manual, paragraph 19.4.13.1 it is stated *"losses of non resident company may be set off against gains for the same year but may not be carried forward to later years for purposes of apportionment. If, however, the shareholder has losses in two or more non resident companies, the shareholder's apportioned net losses of one company may be set off against apportioned net gains of the other."*

67.3.7   Double Tax Relief

s590   S590 provides two forms of relief for tax arising by reason of the operation of the section. Firstly it provides a credit relief and, where the credit relief does not have application, it provides relief by way of deduction.

Where any amount in respect of a chargeable gain is distributed within two years from the time when the chargeable gain accrued to the company, and a tax liability arises to an Irish resident or ordinarily resident person as a result, that person may credit against that tax liability any capital gains tax paid by them by reason of the previous operation of s590. Taxes against which the capital gains tax arising by reason of s590 can be credited can be either income tax (e.g. where a dividend has been received) or capital gains tax where a capital distribution or a distribution on liquidation, has been received. Credit will apply only provided the capital gains tax paid by the Irish resident or ordinarily resident person by reason of s590 has not been reimbursed by the company.

The time limit referred to above is one of two years from the time when the chargeable gain accrued to the offshore company. That is a reference to (usually) the date of the contract giving rise to the disposal which triggered the chargeable gain. See paragraph 15 for further discussion regarding date of disposal. It is not a reference to two years from the end of an accounting period, or period of account or any similar concept, during which the disposal occurred.

It is not sufficient, in order that the credit should be available, that a company be put into liquidation within two years from the date of the gain. It is necessary that the actual distribution of capital by reason of the liquidation be made within that period also.

s590   Curiously, s590(8) is expressed in terms of capital gains tax paid by the resident person by reason of s590, and in terms of a credit against income tax or capital gains tax. It makes no reference to corporation tax in respect of companies capital gains. The resident person to whom a gain was attributed under s590, and who might as a result become liable to tax, could have been a resident company liable to corporation tax in respect of companies capital gains. It is presumed by the authors that it was the intention of the draftsman to permit a resident company which has paid tax by reason of s590 to receive relief in the same manner as a non corporate taxpayer but this would require a Revenue concession

Where the distribution within two years of the date of disposal is an income distribution, it is treated as being part of a person's income which is subject to the highest marginal rate of tax for the purpose of computing the income tax against which credit is possible.

Where relief by credit is not available as described above, a relief by way of deduction is alternately available. It is available in computing a gain accruing on the disposal by the resident person who paid the tax by reason of s590, of any asset representing that person's interest as a participator in the offshore company. The asset in question need not be one held on the date on which the offshore gain crystallised and was attributed to the resident participator. However, it must be an interest in the same offshore company as that which crystallised the gain which was attributed to the resident participator under s590. Where the resident participator is a participator, not in the company which crystallised the gain originally, but in another offshore company further up the chain of ownership from the original offshore company, the credit would be against a disposal of his interest in that company in which he was a participator, rather than in relation to the disposal of an interest (which he might not possess in any event) in the company which crystallised the gain.

Example 316

> *Joe Smith (Irish resident and domiciled) owns all the shares in IOM Holdings, which has a wholly owned subsidiary, IOM Properties. The companies are non resident. IOM Properties disposed of land in UK on 30 June 1999, realising a gain of £100,000. This gain is attributed to Joe who pays £20,000 CGT. On 31 January 2000 he received a dividend from IOM Holdings, which paid it from a dividend received from IOM Properties out of the gain. The dividend amounted to £50,000. He became liable to £23,000 income tax as a result. Joe is entitled to a credit of £20,000 against that income tax liability. He is entitled to a credit for the entire of the CGT paid notwithstanding the fact that the income tax arose on a distribution of part only of the gain which had given rise to the CGT he paid.*

67.3.8   Tax Paid by Company

s590(14)

If the tax due by a shareholder under these provisions is paid by the company realising the gain or by another company holding shares in the non-resident company (which if it were resident in Ireland would be a close company) that payment is not regarded as being a sum received by the shareholders for income tax or CGT purposes.

67.3.9   Self Assessment

s590

The application of s590 is not dependant on the exercise of discretion by the Revenue Commissioners. Where the conditions for its application are met, its application would appear to be mandatory and automatic. It is not clear however that the resident person to whom gains are attributed has a reporting obligation. The affect of s590 is to treat the resident person "as if a part of the chargeable gain had accrued to that person". That would seem to fall short of stating that he could be treated as if he had disposed of assets. If he had disposed of assets, he would be obliged to disclose that fact in his annual return of income. The return of income form does not appear to require disclosure of the fact that gains are attributed to him notwithstanding that he has not disposed of assets, and is not deemed to have disposed of assets. It would seem however that a taxpayer to whom gains are attributed under this section would need to take those gains into account in computing his preliminary tax payment.

- **Revenue/Chief Inspector's CGT manual :**

- The Revenue Commissioners, in their capital gains tax manual at paragraph 19.4.13.9 advise an Inspector that an assessment should be raised in relation to gains of a non-resident company attributed to a resident shareholder without waiting for the end of the two year period during which, if the company makes a distribution of the gain, no attribution would be made to the Irish resident shareholder. The Inspector is advised that the assessment can be later amended should a distribution be made by the company in the two year time period. The advice contained in the Inspector's manual seems to come close to urging the Inspector to raise an assessment at a time when he cannot know whether or not the section under which he is raising the assessment had application! This could be interpreted as a rather cavalier attitude to the obligations of an Inspector.

67.3.10   **Offshore funds**

In certain circumstances s590 may attribute offshore gains of an offshore fund to the Irish resident shareholders of an offshore company holding an interest in the fund. This is dealt with in paragraph 35.12.

67.3.11   **Non-Resident "Groups" - limited relief for s590**

s590(11)   For the purposes of applying s590, some of the group provisions apply to non-resident companies which are in a group relationship. In deciding whether the non-resident companies are in a group relationship, the normal rules apply, with, of course, the exclusion of the requirement that the companies be resident in Ireland. Subject to this a "non-resident group" of companies :-

- in the case of a group, none of the members of which is resident in the State means that group, and

- in the case of a group, two or more members of which are not resident in the State

means the members which are not resident in the State.

The following are the group relief provisions which are applied:

—paragraph 76 (Transfers of assets between group members)

—paragraph 77 (Disposal or acquisition outside group)

—paragraph 80 (Trading stock)

—paragraph 81 (Company leaving group)

—paragraph 79 (Group Roll-over Relief)

—paragraph 46 (Disposal after reconstruction or amalgamation)

It is important not to be misled by this into believing that non-resident companies can be an effective part of, or can themselves form a capital gains group in the normal sense. This is not the case.

The reference in s590(11) to a non-resident group introduces a concept which has a very specific and limited relevance in capital gains tax legislation. It is there to provide a limited form of relief solely in the context of the attribution to resident persons of the gains of certain non-resident companies. Such an attribution can occur under s590 as explained in paragraph 67.1.

s590(16)   The concept of a "non-resident group" introduced by s590(16) is used to ensure that transactions between companies, which would not give rise to a tax charge in respect of capital gains where the companies are resident in Ireland, would not result in a chargeable gain being attributed to a resident person where the same transaction occurs between non-resident companies.

S590(4), s590(16)   Although s590(16) provides relief from the operation of s590(4) in some cases, it does not provide it in all cases. The transfer of an asset between a non-resident company, and a resident company would give rise to a gain capable of being attributed (where the conditions are met) to a resident person under s590(4) notwithstanding that a similar disposal to another non-resident company forming a non-resident group with the transferor, would not have given rise to such an attribution. This would seem to be anomalous.

Example 317

> Dublin Holdings Ltd. (a close company) is an Irish resident holding company. It has a resident 75% subsidiary, Grafton Ltd., and a non-resident 75% subsidiary, Jersey Ltd. Jersey Ltd. in turn has a non-resident 75% subsidiary, Sark Ltd.
>
> In the accounting period ended 31 December 1998 the following transactions took place between these companies:

1. Sark Ltd. sold UK quoted shares with a base cost of £100,000, to Jersey Ltd. for that amount of consideration, notwithstanding that their open market value was then £150,000.

2. Sark Ltd. sold other UK quoted shares to Dublin Holdings Ltd. Their base cost was £50,000 and the consideration paid was £100,000. However the open market value at the date of disposal was only £80,000.

3. Grafton Ltd. sold a retail property (base cost £500,000, market value £1 million) to its parent, Dublin Holdings Ltd., for £1 million.

4. Sark Ltd. disposed of UK quoted shares to an unconnected 3rd party for a consideration of £250,000. Their base cost was £100,000.

The following Irish tax consequences follow from those transactions:

Since Sark Ltd. is not Irish resident, and since the assets disposed of by Sark to Jersey were not specified Irish assets, land etc.(see paragraph 3.4.1) Sark is not within the charge to either capital gains tax or corporation tax on capital gains in respect of this disposal. If the conditions for avoiding a charge under s590(2) are not met the gain which has arisen to Sark will be deemed to have arisen to Jersey, and will in turn be deemed to have arisen to Dublin Holdings Ltd. Since Sark and Jersey are connected parties, the actual consideration passing would be disregarded in calculating the gain, and the open market value would be substituted. On that basis, a gain of £50,000 would arise. However s590(11) treats Sark and Jersey as being members of a non-resident group and, solely for the purpose of the application of s590, applies the intra group provisions explained in paragraph 75 relating to the transfer of assets between group members. Accordingly Sark is treated as having disposed of the shares to Jersey for a consideration equal to their base cost, being £100,000. No gain therefore arises and Dublin Holdings Ltd. is not exposed to a charge to corporation tax on capital gains as a result.

A disposal by Sark to Dublin Holdings Ltd. is a disposal between connected parties. Accordingly actual consideration is disregarded and open market value is substituted. The consideration is therefore deemed to be £80,000, and not the actual £100,000 contracted for. Accordingly Sark is treated as making a gain of £30,000. As Sark is not a resident company, and the assets are not specified Irish assets, Sark is not within the charge to either capital gains tax or corporation tax on capital gains in Ireland. However s590 (if the conditions for its application are met (see paragraph 43) will attribute that gain of £30,000 from Sark to its shareholder, Jersey Ltd. Since Jersey Ltd. is a non-resident company, the gain will in turn be attributed to Dublin Holdings Ltd. Dublin Holdings Ltd. will be exposed to a charge to corporation tax on capital gains on the sum of £30,000.

The disposal by Grafton Ltd. to Dublin Holdings Ltd. is a disposal between two resident companies which form a group for capital gains purposes. Accordingly the consideration passing of £1 million is disregarded and the transaction is treated as being for a sum equal to the base cost of £500,000. Accordingly no chargeable gain arises on the transaction.

The disposal by Sark Ltd. to the unconnected party of shares gives rise to a gain of £150,000. This gain is under s590 (if it applies)[see paragraph 67.2] attributed to Jersey Ltd., and since Jersey Ltd. is non-resident to Dublin Holdings Ltd. Dublin Holdings Ltd. would be chargeable to corporation tax on capital gains on the gain of £150,000.

> *Dublin Holdings Ltd. would be entitled to a deduction in respect of the corporation tax which it will pay on the gains arising to Sark on transactions 2, and 4 above but the deduction will be available to it in computing the gain or loss arising on a disposal of the shares in Jersey Ltd. (were such to occur). Although the gain on which Dublin Holdings Ltd. paid tax arose to Sark Ltd., it is on a disposal of shares in Jersey Ltd. that the deduction would be available, because it is by reason of the shareholding in Jersey Ltd. that Dublin Holdings Ltd. was liable for the corporation tax on Sark's gains.*

It should be noted that two non-resident companies, neither of which hold shares in each other, can constitute a non-resident group of companies. Where several companies would form a group (being 75% subsidiaries of a common holding company) without regard to the question of residence, the non resident members of that "group" together form a non-resident group whether or not there are direct shareholding links between them.

Example 318

> *Taking the facts of **example 317** above, assume that Dublin Holdings Ltd. directly held all of the share capital of another non-resident company, Guernsey Ltd. In such a case there would be no shareholding relationship directly between Jersey Ltd. and Guernsey Ltd., or between Sark Ltd. and Guernsey Ltd. Nonetheless, because all three of Guernsey Ltd., Jersey Ltd. and Sark Ltd. form part of what would be a group of companies if the question of residence were ignored (Dublin Holdings Ltd. being the parent of the group on that basis) they are deemed by s590(16) to constitute a non-resident group, for the purposes of relief from the provisions of s590(4).*

Where a company ceases to be a member of a non-resident group while owning as asset acquired from another member of the non-resident group in the previous 10 years, it is deemed to dispose of the asset and re-acquire it at market value. This deemed disposal is treated as occurring immediately after its acquisition, and not at the date the company ceases to be a group member. It can give rise to a gain which can be attributed to Irish residents.

Where a company leaves a group currently with an asset acquired intra group prior to 11/2/99 the deemed disposal could be subject to the *"old version"* of s590 and not the current FA99 version.

s590(16) S590(16) provides **solely for the purposes of the attribution of gains and losses under s590** a form of group relief. It does this by providing a special definition of "non resident group" and then applying s617 to s620, and s623 and s625 to that non resident group of companies, as if they constituted a resident group. The sections mentioned are the sections which grant group relief on transfers of assets within a group, and claw back on a transferee company leaving the group with an asset acquired intra group in the previous 10 years.

s1014
s5 The basic definition of a group is to be found in paragraph 75.4.3. That definition is modified for this purpose by the fact that the

restriction on the meaning of a company in s616(2) is not applied. That point should not be significant since the definition of "company" for ordinary group relief purposes is very wide indeed. In the absence of that special definition, "company" for non resident group purposes, including the definition of a non resident group is that applied by s5 -"any body corporate" other than an EEIG within the meaning of s1014.

A non resident group of companies, where the parent company of the group is itself non resident, consists of that non resident parent and its 75% subsidiaries which are non resident. Any 75% subsidiaries of that non resident parent which are resident in the State are not part of the non resident group. Therefore a transfer of assets as between a 75% subsidiary which is resident, and one which is non resident, does not fall within any form of group relief and will be a transaction between connected parties, with consideration equal to open market value.

Where the parent company of the group is Irish resident, only the 75% subsidiaries of that Irish parent which are non resident are members of the offshore group. The resident parent itself is not a member of the offshore group, notwithstanding that the group exists only by reason of it being a parent.

Example 319

> Xco, an Irish resident company owns all of the share capital in Aco (resident in Ireland), Bco (resident in the Isle of Man) and Cco (resident in the UK).
>
> Bco and Cco are in a non resident group for the purpose of s590. Transfers of assets between them will not give rise to a chargeable gain attributable under the section to resident participators. On the other hand, a transfer of assets between Aco and either Bco or Cco, would not be within the offshore group and would give rise to a chargeable gain, with the consideration being treated for these purposes as being equal to open market value.

Example 320

> Holdings Limited is an Isle of Man resident company which owns all of the share capital of Ireland Limited, a company resident in Ireland, and also all of the share capital of UK Limited, a company resident in the UK. Holdings Limited and UK Limited form an offshore group. Ireland Limited is not a member of that group.

The FA99 amended the requirements for determining whether or not a group exists. Prior to the FA99, a group was constituted merely by the holding of 75% of the ordinary share capital by one company of another. The FA99 imposed additionally a requirement regarding sharing in dividends, and sharing in assets on a winding up or otherwise. In other words it adopted the definition of "group" that had long applied for the purposes of group loss relief. That more elaborate definition of "group" applies to an offshore group. This definition is discussed in greater detail in paragraph 67.3.10.

Not only do the group relief provisions apply to the offshore group, but so also do the clawback provisions relating to group relief. Thus if a group relationship is broken, the relief originally granted may be lost. The manner in which the clawback is carried out is to deem the transferee company to have, **immediately after it acquired an asset**, to have disposed of it at open market value. The deemed acquisition does not take place at the date of the company leaving the group. Rather, when the transferee company leaves the group (having an asset obtained within the previous 10 years subject to intra group relief the company not then leaving the group as an associate of the transferee company) it is treated as having disposed of the asset on the date upon which the intra group transfer was made. That date could potentially be before 11 February 1999, the commencement date for the new s590. This is important because the new s590 and the old s590, are very different sections, in terms of their ability to effectively attribute an offshore gain to a resident taxpayer. In particular, the old s590 was ineffective for that purpose where the offshore company was owned by an offshore trust. That structure was not "seen through" by the old s590, and s579.

Where an asset had been transferred within an offshore group, disposal to a third party by the transferee company of that asset after the 11 February 1999 could give rise to a gain which would be attributable to a resident beneficiary of a non resident settlement owning the non resident company in question. But ironically the operation, after 11 February 1999 of the clawback provisions relating to the breaking of a group would have the effect, where the original transfer was before 11 February 1999, of deeming the asset to be disposed of and re acquired at open market value on the date of the intra group transfer; and any gain so thrown up would not be attributable up from the company, through the trust, to resident beneficiaries under the old s590 and s579. Thus one form of disposal may result in attribution, but another would not.

s590

There is a further ambiguity to the operation of the offshore group relief in the new s590. The new s590 is stated by s590(2) to apply "as respects chargeable gains accruing to a company on or after 11 February 1999". On the face of it therefore it is a prerequisite to its application that the offshore company should have a chargeable gain. But how does one determine whether or not a disposal by the non resident company has given rise to a gain? Arguably, since the non resident company provisions have application only once it has been determined that the section has application, the question of whether or not a disposal did give rise to a gain should be determined without regard to those non resident company provisions. Where the non resident company provisions don't apply, the "intra offshore group" transfer would have been at open market value. That could give rise to the paradox of the ultimate disposal to a third party might not yield a gain whereas if it yielded only a very small gain (ignoring the offshore group relief) and the section then had application, the provisions of the offshore group relief (by reducing the base cost of the transferee company from open market value at the date of transfer to historic cost) could produce a much larger attributable gain. Until the courts have ruled on the matter, it will not be clear whether or not the terms of s590 itself, including offshore group relief, are to be taken into account in determining whether or not a disposal gave rise to a chargeable gain after 11 February 1999, and thus to determine whether or not the section has application.

68   NON-RESIDENT TRUSTS

68.1   Broad outline

The treatment of trustees generally, and the rules for determining the residence of trustees for CGT purposes are set out in paragraph 65.

FA99 s88 Gains arising to the trustees of a non resident settlement may in certain circumstances be attributed to (i.e.- treated as arising to) persons who have an interest in the property of the trust or who have benefited from the trust.

s579A Prior to FA99, the anti avoidance rules relating to non resident trustees were contained solely in s579. That section remains in force and is discussed in paragraph 68.8. FA99 introduced an additional provisions in s579A. These additional provisions also attributes gains of a non resident settlement to beneficiaries. There now are two principal sections concerned with this same topic - s579, and s579A.

The provisions of the two sections are quite different from each other. The principal features of the two sections, and also of s590 (attribution of gains of non resident companies to resident persons) are set out in a chart in paragraph 67.1.2. The most notable difference between the two (non-resident trust) sections is that :

- s579 applies to only a limited range of trusts (ie those where the settlor was domiciled and either resident or ordinarily resident in the State) and can attribute the gains of a settlement to a beneficiary to an almost unlimited extent, and results in a CGT charge on those resident or ordinarily resident in Ireland.

- s579A has a much wider scope in that it can apply to any non resident trust, but it attributes the gains of the non-resident trust to beneficiaries in proportion to non-income benefits received by them, resulting in a CGT charge on such beneficiaries who are resident or ordinarily resident in Ireland (and if an individual, who is also domiciled in Ireland).

In considering any non resident trust, it is necessary to consider the possibility that one or the other of these sections may apply to it. Both sections cannot apply to the same gain arising to a non resident trust as s579A provides that where it applies, s579 will not apply.

68.2   **Section 579A - non resident trustees**

s579A   S579A was enacted by FA99. It has application for tax years commencing with the tax year 1999/2000. The implication of this is that it cannot attribute a gain to a resident person in a tax year earlier than 1999/2000.

In order that the section can operate so as to attribute a non resident trustees gain to a resident person, it is necessary that the resident person should take a benefit from the non resident trust. Benefits taken before the 11 February 1999 are disregarded entirely for this purpose. Insofar as a benefit taken after 11 February 1999 represents a trustee's gain which accrued prior to 11 February 1999, it also is entirely disregarded for the purposes of the section.

The section operates so as to attribute to a resident person who receives a benefit from a non resident settlement, the gains accruing to the non resident trustees in the year the benefit is taken, and in prior years. However, the attribution of gains is limited to the amount of benefits taken. Given the commencement provisions described above it follows that where the sole benefit taken by a resident person is taken prior to 6 April 1999, section 579A cannot attribute a gain to that person. That is because, if it did have application, it would attribute the gain to him in a tax year prior to 1999/2000. If however the same individual were to take a further benefit after 6 April 1999, in computing the amount of the non resident trustees gains which are attributable, gains accruing back to 11 February 1999 can be taken into account (but not those accruing prior to that date); and benefits taken back to 11 February 1999 can be taken into account in computing the cap on the amount of gains which may be attributed, but account is not taken of benefits received prior to 11 February 1999, for this purpose.

68.3   **What settlements are affected ?**

s579A(2)   The section applies to any settlement *"for any year of assessment during which the trustees are , at no time, neither resident nor ordinarily resident in the State"*...subject to the commencement rules in s579A(10).

It seems a badly worded way of referring to where the trust is **non-resident** (as the trust residence rules makes no distinction between the residence and ordinary residence of the settlement itself - see paragraph 65.3). From a literal reading it refers to resident trusts and not to non-resident trusts. It remains to be seem whether the Courts would deny the section any application by giving the words a literal meaning. In this book, the section is assumed to refer to a non-resident trust.

S579A applies to a non resident trust irrespective of the residence or domicile of the settlor. This is in contrast to s579. In principle s579A applies to every settlement in the entire world. It does not impose any tax charge on the trustees of an offshore trust, but it can impose a reporting obligation and a CGT liability on an Irish domiciled, and resident or ordinary resident beneficiary.

s579A(8)   A settlement created under a will or intestacy is to be treated as made at the date of death of the testator/intestate. The significance of this is not immediately apparent as the identity of the settlor is irrelevant to the section. Its relevance may be that, in a case where assets are not passed to the trustees of a settlement until some time has elapsed during the course of the administration of an estate (which is the common experience), the trust is none the less to be treated as having commenced at the date of death so that gains arising to the administrators of the estate, in relation to assets subsequently allocated to the trustees, are to be treated as gains arising to the trustees. This interpretation is only speculation on the part of the authors. In fact, it is doubtful if the words used are sufficient to attribute to the trustees gains which did not in fact arise to them.

As noted in paragraph 65.3.2, "professional trustees" who are Irish resident can be deemed to be non resident, and the administration can be deemed to be carried on abroad. In other words, a trust which ordinarily will be regarded as resident in the State can be treated as non resident. There appears to be no reason why s579 and s579A would not apply to such a "deemed non resident" trust just as it does to a trust which, on the basis of ordinary rules of residence of a trustee, is non resident.

68.4   Beneficiary:

"Beneficiary" is not defined for the purposes of the section. It would therefore take its normal meaning in the context of trust law. That meaning, in broad terms would refer to any person to whom the trustees are required to provide a benefit, or to whom, at their discretion, they are entitled to provide a benefit. The powers and obligations of trustees are usually contained in a trust deed. The deed will usually define the persons, or classes of persons to whom the trustees must, or to whom they may, provide benefits. Sometimes people are identified by name for this purpose. In other cases, the trust deed may merely define a class of persons, eg all of the children of a named person. In such a case the children will not have been identified individually by name, but they may be identified by reason of their relationship to the named person. The description of the class of persons who may benefit from a trust could be even more vague, eg poor of the parish of Monkstown. In such a case it may be very difficult indeed to determine who (potentially) is a beneficiary of the trust. Since however it is only beneficiaries who receive benefits from the trust that may have gains attributed to them by s579A, that is not in practice likely to be a problem to the operation of the section. Obviously anybody who receives a benefit from a trust is likely to be a beneficiary as trustees may only provide benefits to beneficiaries.

S579A

There is no explicit provision in s579A to exclude from the meaning of "beneficiary" a company. Subsection 7 does confine a charge to tax by reason of the section to beneficiaries who are domiciled in the State. However a company is capable of having a domicile and that is usually the place of registration of the company. That subsection does refer to a beneficiary in terms of "he or she". Such words might suggest that the section did not contemplate anybody who is not an individual being a beneficiary, but it would not seem sufficient grounds for confining the operation of the section to beneficiaries who are individuals. Subsection 1(a) defines "capital payments" by excluding payments chargeable to income tax on the recipient, in the case of resident beneficiaries. Again that might indicate that the section contemplates only an individual being a beneficiary. If "beneficiary" included a resident company, one would have expected the reference to income tax to be extended to include corporation tax. It would be unusual for a company to be a beneficiary of a settlement, but there is no legal impediment to a company being such a beneficiary. While the section appears to have been drafted without the possibility that the beneficiary would include a company, it seems to the authors that the section would not have application to a company which is a beneficiary. A similar ambiguity arises in the case of s579.

68.5 Capital Payments:

In order that a beneficiary can have gains attributed to him, it is necessary that he should receive a *"capital payment"* from the trust.

s579A(5)

The amount of gains attributed to any beneficiary cannot exceed the amount of *capital payments* taken by that beneficiary.

In broad terms, a *capital payment* is defined in very wide terms to include any payment or benefit other than one treated as income and is generally referred to in this book as a "benefit".

The term "payment" is widely defined and does not relate solely to payments of cash. Included in the wide definition are:

s579A(b)

- the transfer of an asset,

- the conferring of any benefit

- any occasion whereby settled property becomes property which is held by a trustee as nominee for a person who is absolutely entitled to that asset as against the trustee (see paragraph 64.2).

s579A(1)(c)   A loan to a beneficiary (or any other capital payment which is not an outright payment of money) is regarded as a capital payment to the extent of *"the value of the benefit conferred by it"*.

The expression above "conferring of any benefit", is an expression so wide as to make further exploration of the definition of payments unnecessary. Any benefit will constitute a payment. Thus if a trust permits a beneficiary to reside rent free in a property owned by the trust, that benefit of rent free occupation will constitute a payment for the purposes of the section.

However there is one limitation placed on this wide definition. Only "capital payments" are taken into account. A capital payment is defined as being one that is not chargeable to income tax on the recipient, or, where the recipient is neither resident nor ordinarily resident in the State (therefore largely excluded from Irish income tax especially in relation to foreign source payments) any payment received otherwise than as income. It also excludes any payment received by way of a bargain made at arms length.

If a person rents a property at arms length to the trustees of a settlement, the rent he receives will not constitute a capital payment for two reasons. Firstly it would be taxable on him as income if the recipient is Irish resident, or the property is Irish. Secondly, the payment would be under a transaction at arms length.

In the instance given above of a person who has the rent free occupation of an Irish property, the benefit is likely to constitute a capital payment. This is firstly because it is not by way of a transaction at arms length (self evidently). Secondly the benefit of rent free occupation is not a benefit chargeable to income tax in Ireland save in limited circumstances, such as where it is derived from an employment or office. Since in this instance it would be derived merely from a trust, but not from an employment or an office, it would not constitute income for tax purposes. This is an anomaly which could give rise to hardship. A person having rent free occupation might well have no assets with which to meet the capital gains tax bill, and the capital gains in question may not in any way accrue to his benefit. This anomaly is recognised in capital acquisitions tax where the trustees of the settlement can be compelled to pay a life tenants capital acquisitions tax liability, and may not seek to recover the payment from the life tenant. However no similar recognition of the problem has been built into s579A. Most benefits taken by a life tenant of a property are indeed income, but as illustrated, not all benefits taken by such a person are income for the purposes of s579A.

s579A(1)(d)   A beneficiary is regarded as having received a capital payment from the trustees if

- he receives it directly or indirectly from the trustees,

- it is directly or indirectly applied by the trustees in payment of any debt of the beneficiary or otherwise paid for the benefit of the beneficiary, or

- It is received by a third party at the beneficiary's direction.

It is not clear what might constitute the receipt of a capital payment "indirectly" from the trustees. Would a payment received from a company controlled by the trustees be received "indirectly" from the trustees ?

s579A(10)   Non-income benefits taken by a beneficiary before the *11 February 1999* are disregarded entirely for this purpose.

s579(10)   Insofar as a benefit taken after *11 February 1999* represents a trustee's gain which accrued prior to *11 February 1999,* it also is entirely disregarded for the purposes of the section.

68.6   Gains to be attributed:

For this purpose, the chargeable gains of the non-resident trust are measured under the normal Irish CGT rules, taking losses into account, and excluding gains on non-chargeable assets (e.g - Irish government stocks).

S579A(3)   The section requires an annual computation of all gains of the non-resident trust under Irish CGT rules - *"There shall be computed in respect of every year of assesssment for which this section applies the amount on which the trustees would have been chargeable to capital gains tax if they had been resident and ordinarily resident in the State..."*

The gains which may be attributed to beneficiaries are

- The gains in respect of which the trustees would have been chargeable to capital gains tax if they had been resident or ordinarily resident in the State in the year of assessment and

- Any gains of earlier years of assessment for which there would have been similarly chargeable, to the extent these are not otherwise attributed to beneficiaries under the section, or under Section 597F (2). The attribution under Section 579F(2) relates to migrant settlements and is described in paragraph 68.10.

Given the commencement provisions described above it follows that where the sole benefit taken by a resident person is taken *prior to 6 April 1999,* s579A cannot attribute a gain to that person. That is because, if it did have application, it would attribute the gain to him in a tax year prior to 1999/2000. If however the same individual were to take a further benefit after 6 April 1999, in computing the amount of the non resident trustees gains which are attributable, *gains accruing back to 11 February 1999* can be taken into account (but not those accruing prior to that date); and *benefits taken back to 11 February 1999* can be taken into account in computing the cap on the amount of gains which may be attributed, but account is not taken of benefits received prior to 11 February 1999, for this purpose.

Example 321

John is a beneficiary of a trust whose trustees are resident in the Isle of Man. In 1995 the trustees appointed the sum of £50,000 to John. In January 1999 they appointed £60,000 to him, and in December 1999 they appointed £100,000 to him. The non resident trustees had chargeable gains accruing to them of £100,000 in 1998, and £150,000 in June 1999.

Because John has received a benefit from the trust, trust gains may be attributed to him for capital gains tax purposes. Only the benefit taken in December 1999 is relevant for this purpose. The other benefits (being pre 11/2/1999) do not on their own cause the section to operate. Only gains arising after 11 February 1999 may be attributed, and accordingly, only the £150,000 gain which accrued in June 1999 is relevant for this purpose. All of the £150,000 gain will not be attributed to John, as the amount attributable to him on this occasion is limited to the amount of the benefits taken by him from 11 February 1999 onwards, ie to £100,000. The benefits taken prior to 11 February1999 are disregarded for this purpose.

Although s579A has not applied to the gains which arose to the trustees prior to 11 February 1999 in the circumstances outlined above, s579 may have application to those earlier gains. The operation of s579 is described in paragraph 68.8. Provided the settlor is Irish domiciled and resident or ordinarily resident either when the settlement was created, or when the gain accrued, the gains may be attributed to the Irish resident or ordinarily resident beneficiaries whether or not they have received benefits from the trust. Since John is a beneficiary of the settlement, s579 would have had application to attribute a part of the gains arising to the non resident trustees in 1998 to him. The calculation of that part is described in paragraph 68.8. However s579 does not have application to the gain arising in June 1999, because s579A has application to that gain, and, where s579A has application, s579 does not.

s579
s579A(11)

No reference is made to s579, which also may attribute the gains of a non resident trust to resident beneficiaries. It is true that s579A(11) provides that *"where this section applies so as to charge a person to tax on chargeable gains, Section 579 shall not apply in respect of those chargeable gains"*. However s579A will apply to charge a person in respect of gains only if that person has received a benefit from the settlement. S579 can apply to attribute gains to a resident person even if that resident person has not received benefits from the settlement. It is therefore possible that s579 could have application to a gain at a time when s579A could not apply, because no benefit had been provided. Despite this, s579A does not exclude such gains from attribution subsequently under s579A.

It is not clear if it is intended that the attribution under s579, where has previously occurred, is to be "undone" on the occasion when s579A has application to further re-attribute those gains. If that had been the intent, one would have expected it to be more clearly expressed, and provision to be made for repayment of tax etc. However the legislation is silent on the point. It cannot be the case that the mere possibility that s579A might apply in the future, if a benefit were provided, is sufficient to prevent s579 having application. If that were the case, s579 would never have application since s579A applies to all trusts in the world, whereas s579 applies only to those with a domiciled/resident settlor.

The section has application to all settlements throughout the world, and requires attribution of gains to all beneficiaries who have received capital payments from such settlements, but only beneficiaries to whom gains have been attributed in this fashion, who are domiciled in Ireland, will be chargeable to Irish tax on capital gains. The meaning of "domicile" is discussed in paragraph 104.

The section does not impose a CGT liability on the offshore trustees. It operates only to impose the liability on Irish domiciled and resident/ordinarily resident beneficiaries. Nonetheless the section provides that where the trustees do pay any amount of capital gains tax which would otherwise be payable by a beneficiary by reason of s579A, that payment by the offshore trustees will not be treated as being itself a capital payment to be taken into account for a further attribution of gains to the beneficiary in question. If on the other hand, a beneficiary paid the capital gains tax liability which had arisen to him by reason of the section, and the trustees compensated him by making an appointment of capital to him, that appointment would be taken into account as being a further capital payment to the beneficiary, possibly giving rise to the attribution to him of further offshore gains and therefore giving rise to further tax liabilities. It is clearly more tax efficient to allow the trustees to directly meet the Irish CGT liabilities which arise by reason of the section.

68.7 Attribution of gains:

s579A(4) Gains of a non-resident settlement are attributed to *"beneficiaries of the settlement who receive capital payments from the trustees in the year of assessment or have received such payments in any earlier year of assessment"*.

Curiously, there is no exemption from the operation of the section for charitable trusts. On the face of it, the section is capable of applying to an international charitable organisation which provides benefits to Irish persons who are in need. Such Irish beneficiaries, who may have been selected by the international charity by reason of their poverty and need, could have part of the gains in international charity attributed to them for tax purposes!

s579A(5) The "cap" on the attribution of gains to a beneficiary is set out in the limit provided by s579A(5), where it provided for the attribution of gains to be made to the beneficiaries *"in proportion to, but shall not exceed, the amounts of capital payments received by them"*. This "cap" is applied to the total amount of gains which are to be attributed. It is therefore necessary to calculate the total capital payments in the year of assessment or earlier years of assessment received by beneficiaries. That represents the limit to the amount of gains which can be attributed. That limited amount is then attributed to the beneficiaries in the proportions of the payments received by them. Logically, that should result in the payments received by each beneficiary representing a personal cap on the amount which he receives.

Example 322

In 1999/2000 John received capital payments of £100,000 from Offshore Trust. In the year 2000/2001 he received a further £100,000, and £150,000 was received by Mike in that year. In the year 2001/2002 the trustees had capital gains accruing to them of £500,000.

Of the £500,000 of capital gains which have arisen in the year 2001/2002, only £350,000 of those gains may be attributed. This represents the total of capital payments received in that or prior years (since 11 February 1999) by beneficiaries. £350,000 of gains must be attributed between John and Mike in the proportion of £200,000/£150,000, being the proportion of the payments received by them.

In the year 2002/2003 each of John and Mike receive further capital payments of £100,000 each from the trustees. In the year 2003/2004 the trustees have capital gains of £25,000 accruing to them.

In the year 2002/2003 no capital gains accrued to the trustees. Nonetheless, it is necessary to compute the amount of gains which would have accrued to them had they been resident (that would be zero) and to add to it the amount of similar gains accruing since 11 February 1999 not already attributed to beneficiaries. That amounts to £150,000. That amount may now be attributed to beneficiaries, subject to the overall limit of capital payments paid to beneficiaries. In computing that overall limit payments taken into account in prior attributions are ignored. Therefore the only payments remaining to be taken into account are the £200,000 payments in the year 2002/2003. Since that amount is greater than the amount of gains available for attribution, the entire £150,000 may be attributed to John and Mike. It is attributed to them in the proportion of the capital payments received to the extent not already attributed, ie £100,000/£100,000. Therefore each of them have attributed to them £75,000 of chargeable gains in the year 2002/2003.

In the year 2003/2004 the trustees gains of £25,000 must be taken into account. There are no prior year gains which are unattributed, so the total for attribution in the year 2003/2004 is the £25,000 only. The limit to the amount which can be attributed is the amount of capital payments since 11 February 1999 not previously attributed, and that is £50,000. Therefore the entire £25,000 may be

> attributed. That must attributed to the beneficiaries in the proportion of the
> capital payments received by them (not previously taken into account for
> attribution purposes). In this instance that is 25/25. As a result £12,500 capital
> gains is attributed to each of them in the year 2003/2004.

Where gains are attributed to a beneficiary under s579A, they are
treated as accruing to a beneficiary in the year in which they are
attributed to him. This may well be a different year to that in which
the gain accrued to the offshore trustees. That year may be an earlier
year (where the capital payments taken into account for the purpose
of attribution were received prior to the gain arising) or a later year
(where in the year in which the gain arose to the offshore trustees,
there were no capital payments in that or earlier years since 11
February 1999 to beneficiaries which had not been already taken into
account for attribution purposes). Where the capital payment which
is the basis for the attribution, is received in the same year as that on
which the capital gain arises to the offshore trustees, the gain will be
treated as arising to the beneficiary in the same year as it arose to the
offshore trustee.

Where the tax year in which the beneficiary is treated as having a
gain accruing to him is different from that in which it actually arose
to the offshore trustee (ie the year of the disposal of the asset giving
rise to the gain) reporting requirements and payment requirements
in relation to the beneficiary would be by reference to that year in
which the gain is deemed to accrue to the beneficiary. However it is
likely that the rate of capital gains tax, and many other aspects of
capital gains tax law may be determined not by the year in which the
beneficiary is treated as having the gain accrued to him, but rather
by reference to the actual date of disposal of the asset by the offshore
trustee.

Example 323

> In **example 322** above John and Mike are treated as having a chargeable gain
> accrued to them in the year 2002/03 . Nonetheless, the rate of capital gains tax
> by reference to which their tax liability on those gains would be computed would
> be the rate applicable at the date of disposal of the asset, ie a date in the year
> 2001/02 . Their entitlement to avail of loss relief on any losses which accrued to
> them on disposals of assets by themselves (as opposed to the offshore trustees)
> would be determined by reference to the tax year in which they are deemed to
> have disposed of the asset.

Such complexities are not particularly suitable to a self assessment
system of taxation.

As mentioned in paragraph 68.4, only domiciled beneficiaries are
chargeable to capital gains tax (or corporation tax on companies
capital gains) by reason of the application of s579A.

68.8   **Interaction with double tax agreements.**

In paragraph 67.2.5, it was pointed that in many instances Ireland's double tax agreements provide protection against an Irish resident being subjected to Irish CGT in respect of gains arising on disposals made by persons not resident in Ireland. The same conclusions do not necessarily arise in relation to s579 or in relation to s579A. The difficulty is that whereas s590 attributes the actual gain arising on the disposal of an asset to the resident person, both s579 and s579A attribute to a resident person, not the actual gain which arose to the non resident trustees, but rather all or part of the amount on which the trustees would have been chargeable if domiciled and either resident or ordinarily resident in the State in the year in which they made the disposal. It is therefore arguable that what s579 and s579A charge to tax is not the actual gain which arose to the non resident trustees, but rather a notional gain equal in amount to the gain which arose to the non resident trustees. The distinction might seem, and is, slight. Nonetheless, a similar distinction was relied on by the Inland Revenue in the UK case of Bricom Holdings Limited v IRC in 1997, before the Court of Appeal. In that case Bricom had challenged a charge to tax on it made under UK controlled foreign company legislation. The charge was triggered by income arising in a subsidiary of Bricom resident in another state with which the UK had a double tax agreement. Bricom argued that the double tax agreement did not permit the UK to tax the income of the non resident. The Inland Revenue argued, and the Court of Appeal agreed, that Bricom was not being taxed on that income. What it was being taxed on was on a notional amount equal to that income.

If the Bricom case were followed in Ireland (where the matter has not been considered by the Courts to date) it would seem to prevent treaty protection being available in respect of a charge to tax under s579, or in respect of a charge to tax under s579A. This would seem to apply equally where the charge to tax arises by reason of s590 attributing the gains of an offshore company to non resident trustees, and s579 or s579A then treating an Irish resident as having gains of equal amount. The final attribution in such a case would arise in respect of a notional amount, and not the original gain arising to the non resident company.

The Bricom case was decided in the UK largely on the basis of an interpretation of the UK controlled foreign company legislation, according to the usual strict interpretation of taxation legislation. It is arguable that the decision is incorrect in that it failed to apply the rather different rules of interpretation that apply in the case of double tax agreements, where a wider view must be taken of the intent of the parties to agreements. The semantic distinction on which the Court of Appeal relied in Bricom Holdings would seem alien to the notion that international treaties should be observed in a spirit of good faith. The authors are not convinced that the Bricom case would be followed in Ireland in the context of the interpretation of a treaty. However the matter is uncertain.

68.9   **Interaction with CAT**

As explained in paragraph 97.6 where CGT and CAT arise on the same event to the same person, the CGT payment may be offset against the CAT payment.

The appointment of a "capital payment" from an offshore trust to a domiciled/resident or ordinarily resident beneficiary may give rise to a capital acquisitions tax liability on the beneficiary. As indicated in the preceding parts of this section, by reason of receiving such a capital payment, the beneficiary may also become liable to capital gains tax in respect of gains accruing to the offshore trustees. It is difficult to see however that the capital gains tax liability arises "on the same event" as the capital acquisitions tax liability. The capital gains tax liability might not arise for many years after the capital payment is made and the capital acquisitions tax liability has arisen. It is dependent on the offshore trustees crystallising a post 11 February 1999 capital gain. The CGT liability appears to require two events in order that it should crystallise to the Irish domiciled beneficiary - a capital payment, and an offshore capital gain. It is not clear in the circumstances that the offset of CGT against CAT would be available.

Whereas a payment by the offshore trustees of the CGT liability of the domiciled beneficiary is not regarded as a further capital payment attracting further attribution of capital gains, such a payment might well give rise to capital acquisitions tax. The topic of capital acquisitions tax is outside the scope of this book. Readers are referred to "Capital Acquisitions Tax" by Condon and Muddiman, published by the Institute of Taxation in Ireland. Once again it would seem that such a capital acquisitions tax liability could not have a capital gains tax payment paid by the trustees offset against it. Although the capital gains tax payment may give rise to the capital acquisitions tax liability, the capital gains tax payment relates to a different event ie disposal of an asset by the offshore trustees, or a prior capital payment to the beneficiary (or perhaps both).

68.10   **Migrant Settlements**

s579F   The rules governing the residence of trustees are explained in paragraph 65.3 The residence of a trust may change over time, as the place of administration is changed, or as a trustee resigns, dies, or a new trustee is appointed.

The operation of s579A is modified where the trust to which it applies (i.e. whose trustees are currently non resident)

- had previously been resident, or

- in a tax year subsequent to that in which they realised the gain, become resident in the State.

Settlements whose residence position varies in this fashion are described in s579F as "migrant settlements".

Where a trust

- was resident in Ireland at a time when a capital payment was received by a beneficiary, and subsequently,

- in one or more years of assessment, the trust is non resident,

a capital payment made during the period when it was resident is not taken into account for the purposes of s579A in determining the extent to which capital gains accruing when the trustees are non resident can be attributed to beneficiaries. However this exclusion does not apply if the capital payment made by the trustees while Irish resident was made "in anticipation of a disposal made by the trustees in the non resident period".

Example 324

The trustees of a family trust are Irish resident in the year 1999/2000. No chargeable gains have accrued to them. A beneficiary is in financial difficulties, and since the trustees have available cash in the bank, they determine to make a capital appointment to that beneficiary (John) of £100,000. That is not sufficient to meet John's needs. To make further payments to him, the trustees would have to realise assets on which chargeable gains will crystallise. They therefore borrow £400,000 from a bank and appoint it to John. Subsequent to 5 April 2000 the trustees take up residence in the Isle of Man and on 31.12.1999 dispose of their remaining asset, crystallising a gain of £600,000 all of which arose subsequent to going non resident. They discharge their liability to the bank in respect of the £400,000 borrowed for the purpose of the appointment to John.

The £100,000 capital appointment to John out of the trustees cash resources will not be taken into account in determining the amount of the offshore gain in the year 2000/2001 that may be attributed to him. However the second capital payment, which was made in anticipation of the disposal of an asset and the crystallisation of a chargeable gain in the following tax year when they would be non resident, is taken into account. Accordingly £400,000 of the chargeable gain of £600,000. arising in the year 2000/2001, is attributed to John and is treated as having accrued to him in the year 1999/2000 (the year in which he received the capital payment). Notwithstanding that £600,000 of chargeable gains arose in the year 2000/2001, and notwithstanding that John received capital payments totalling £500,000 in a prior tax year, only £400,000 of the gain can be attributed to him under s579A. Because s579A has application to the disposal, s579 does not apply.

s579F   S579F also varies the application of s579A where a non resident trust becomes Irish resident, having had chargeable gains in its non resident periods which were not fully attributed to beneficiaries before it became resident. S579F provides that in such circumstances capital payments made to beneficiaries in periods during which the trust is Irish resident may be taken into account as if they had been capital payments made by a non resident trust to the beneficiaries. Therefore the gains of the non resident period can be attributed to beneficiaries in years in which the trust has become Irish resident.

Example 325

> *The facts are the same as in **example 324** above. In the year 2002/2003 the trustees resume Irish residence. They make a further payment of £100,000 to John. Notwithstanding that the payment is being received by John from Irish resident trustees, s579A will have application as if the trust was still non resident, and £100,000 of the chargeable gains which arose in the year 2000/2001 to the trustees can now be attributed to John.*

Strictly speaking s579F does not, where a non resident period is succeeded by a resident period, result in the application of s579A. Rather s579F(2), contains the power to attribute non resident period gains to the beneficiary. It adapts s579A(5) and s579A(7). S579A(5) provides an attribution rule, and s579A(7) limits the CGT charge to domiciled beneficiaries. Whereas s579A applies by taking into account capital payments received on a cumulative basis since 11 February 1999, save to the extent that they had been previously taken into account to attribute a gain to the beneficiary, s579F deals with the matter on a year by year basis. The non resident period gains are attributed to beneficiaries in proportion to the capital payments in a particular year of assessment in the resident period, and to an amount not exceeding those capital payments. Any non resident period gains remaining unattributed are then attributed in subsequent years of assessment, in the same manner as capital payments are made in those subsequent years of assessment. However the payments are not taken into account cumulatively for this purpose.

As in the case of s579A, s579F applies only as and from 11 February 1999. A non resident period for this purpose cannot include any year of assessment prior to 1999/2000 because it is only years of assessment to which s579A have application that can constitute non resident periods. Although s579A does take account of chargeable gains and payments from 11 February 1999 up to 5 April 1999 inclusive, it does not have application as such to any tax year prior to 1999/2000, and accordingly a non resident period cannot be earlier than 1999/2000 for the purposes of s579F.

68.11   S579 Rules

68.11.1   Broad Outline - s579

S579 has two subsection (s579 (2) and s579 (3)) each of which may cause the gains of a non resident trust to be attributed to a domiciled resident person. These two sub sections operate quite differently from each other. They each require a separate set of preconditions for their application, and the amount of the gains which may be attributed to a domiciled resident beneficiary under s579 (2) may differ from that which would be attributed under s579 (3). Comments below on the operation of attribution under s579 should be read so as to carefully distinguish between the operation of the two sub sections.

s579   S579 has application only where a chargeable gain accrues to non resident trustees. Where the section does have application, and in particular where s579 (2) has application, an assumption has to be made that the trustees are resident, in order to calculate the amount of the chargeable gain which may be attributed to beneficiaries. But the basic application of the section requires that a gain should accrue to the trustees (or be deemed to accrue to them) and unless such a gain did accrue (or was so deemed) there is no basis for proceeding to the assumption that they were resident.

The pre FA99 version of s590 (non-resident company) did not attribute gains to a shareholder who was a non-resident trustee and accordingly did not *"trigger"* s579 so as to in turn attribute the gain to a beneficiary. The FA99 version of s590 does make this attribution to a shareholder.

68.11.2   **Scope of provisions - s579**

s579(1)   The anti-avoidance provisions apply in any tax year where:

- the trustees of the settlement are neither resident nor ordinarily resident in Ireland, and

- the settlor or one of the settlors is domiciled and either

  − resident or ordinarily resident in Ireland or

  − was domiciled and either resident or ordinarily resident in Ireland when he made the settlement.

Example 326

> *Ronnie had a domicile of origin in Northern Ireland. In 1980, whilst still resident and ordinarily resident there, he settled a trust the trustees of which were resident in the Isle of Man. In 1982 Ronnie sold all his property in Northern Ireland and acquired a substantial stud farm in the Republic of Ireland, and took up residence there. By 1998 he had concluded that he had no wish to leave the Republic of Ireland and would probably live there for the remainder of his life.*

> *Prior to Ronnie becoming domiciled in the Republic of Ireland in 1998 the provisions of s579 did not have application to the Isle of Man trust because the settlor of the trust was not domiciled in the Republic of Ireland either at the time the trust was settled or in any subsequent tax year. From 1998 onwards however the provisions of s579 will have application to the Isle of Man trust in any year in which Ronnie is resident or ordinarily resident in Ireland, and for as long as he retains his domicile of choice in Ireland. This is so notwithstanding*

> that the trust was set up at a time when he had no connection with the Republic of Ireland, and possibly no intention of ever living in it.

Example 327

> John, who is domiciled, resident and ordinarily resident in the Republic of Ireland settled a trust, whose trustees were resident in Jersey, in 1980. In 1990 he gave up his home in Ireland and went to live in Tunisia, for health reasons. He has remained there ever since.
>
> S579 will have application to the trust in every tax year for so long as the trustees are not resident in Ireland, and this will continue indefinitely. Because John was domiciled and resident at the time he settled the trust, it remains within the scope of s579 even after he has ceased to be resident or ordinarily resident, and even after he ceased to be domiciled, if that occurred.

- **Revenue/Chief Inspector's CGT Manual :**

— In the Revenue Commissioners capital gains tax manual at Paragraph 19.3.5.18 it is stated that *"Time should not be spent enquiring about gains arising from foreign currency appreciation in the hands of non-resident trusts unless the amounts involved seem likely to be material."*

68.11.3   Effect of provisions - s579(2)

s579(2)   Where these provisions apply, any chargeable gains arising to the trustees may be treated as arising to a beneficiary of the trust who (having an interest in the trust property) in the year of assessment in which gain arises to the trustees is:

— domiciled in Ireland, and

— either resident or ordinarily resident in Ireland.

s579(2) provides-

"Any beneficiary under the settlement who is domiciled and either resident or ordinarily resident in the State in any year of assessment shall be treated for the purposes of this Act as if an apportioned part of the amount, if any, on which the trustees would have been chargeable to capital gains tax under Section 31, if domiciled and either resident or ordinarily resident in the State in that year of assessment, had been chargeable gains accruing to the beneficiary in that year of assessment".

The reference above to the domicile of the trustees is odd. Domicile can have no affect on the amount of capital gains in respect of which resident or ordinarily resident trustees would be liable to Capital Gains Tax. The remittance basis of taxation (see paragraph 3.3) does not apply to trustees. The reference to trustees being either resident or ordinarily resident also strikes an odd note. The rules governing the residence of a trust are such (TCA 97 s574 (1) (a)) that trustees will always be either both resident and ordinarily resident or neither resident nor ordinarily resident.

For apportionment under TCA 97 s579 (2) to occur it is therefore necessary that in the tax year:

(1)   The trustees should realise a gain to which s579A does not have application (see paragraph 68.2).

(2)   The trustees should be non resident in Ireland.

(3)   There should be one or more persons with interests in the trust assets (i.e. beneficiaries or potential beneficiaries) who are resident or ordinarily resident in Ireland.

(4)   One of the settlors (or all) should be domiciled and resident or ordinarily resident in Ireland *or* have been so domiciled and resident/ordinarily resident when he settled the trust.

All of the requirement must be met in the same tax year for the net gains of that year to be apportioned. It is not possible under s579 (2) to apportion gains of a tax year in which those conditions are not met, in a later tax year in which the conditions are met. Attributions of net gains under s597 (2) is on a tax year by tax year basis.

The split year residence relief provided by TCA 97 s822 is applicable for the purposes of income tax on employment income only. Accordingly, where a person is a beneficiary of a non resident in Ireland in a tax year, if all the conditions for attributions under s597 (2) are met in that year, he may have attributed to him gains in respect of disposals in that tax year made before he arrived in Ireland.

68.11.4   Apportionment Between Beneficiaries - s579 rules

s579(2)(b)

The gains will be apportioned between the beneficiaries under the settlement where s579(2) operates :

"...in such a manner as is just and reasonable...whether the interest be a life interest or interest in reversion so that the chargeable gain is apportioned as near as may be according to the respective value of those interests..."

Example 328

Stephen settled property on a non-resident trust in 1975, when he was resident and domiciled in Ireland. Under the terms of the settlement the income was to be divided equally between his four children until his death, when the children were to become absolutely entitled to the capital of the trust in equal shares. Chargeable gains arising to the trustees in 1998/99 amounted to £60,000.

STEPHEN'S CHILDREN are:

- PETER   who is resident and domiciled in Ireland for all years.
- MAURICE   who is resident and ordinarily resident in France for all years, but domiciled in Ireland.
- PATRICIA   who married and acquired UK domicile but is resident in Ireland for 1998/99.

- CHRIS   *who is domiciled and ordinarily resident in Ireland for all years.*

The Irish CGT position for 1998/99 is as follows:

The total gain of £60,000 is first apportioned equally between all the children (i.e. all the beneficiaries). The apportionment would be made on the basis of equal shares, as the value of their respective interests is the same.

Each child will be chargeable to Irish CGT on his or her share if that child is:

- *Resident or ordinarily resident in Ireland*

  and

- *Domiciled in Ireland*

for the year of assessment in which the gain arises to the trustees (i.e. 1998/99).

- PETER   *Chargeable on £15,000 as he is resident and domiciled in Ireland.*
- MAURICE   *Not chargeable as he is neither resident nor ordinarily resident in Ireland.*
- PATRICIA   *Not chargeable as she is not domiciled in Ireland.*
- CHRIS   *Chargeable on £15,000 as he is ordinarily resident, and domiciled in Ireland.*

In the UK case of Chinn v Collins, the taxpayer, a UK resident, was a beneficiary under a non-resident settlement. The trustees appointed trust property consisting of a large block of quoted shares in L Ltd to the taxpayer, contingent on his survival for three days.

The taxpayer sold his contingent interest under the settlement to a non -resident company (R Ltd), and then entered into an agreement to purchase from R Ltd an equivalent number of shares in L Ltd (effectively the shares held by the Trustees).

It was held that the contract between the taxpayer and R Ltd for the purchase of the shares gave the taxpayer an equitable interest in the shares. It followed that the taxpayer and not R Ltd was the beneficiary under the settlement on the vesting of the contingent interest.

Accordingly, the taxpayer was chargeable in respect of the gains arising to the trustees on the vesting of the contingent interest. In the course of his judgement, Lord Wilberforce said:

"As soon as there was an agreement for the sale of the shares by R Ltd to [the taxpayer] accompanied or followed by payment of the price, the equitable title passed at once to the purchaser, [viz the taxpayer] and all that was needed to perfect his title was notice to the trustees or nominee, which notice both had at all material times. Consequently, the trustees were bound to transfer the shares to [the taxpayer] immediately the interests vested on 1 November 1969, and [the taxpayer] was the beneficiary under the settlement as regards the shares".

The difference given to the meaning of the term "settlement" in the UK legislation and the Irish legislation is noted in Chapter 8. That difference may affect the question of whether an Irish court would follow the same approach as the UK court to the transactions in Chinn v Collins.

In that case, the Revenue also contended that it was sufficient for the purposes of the section for a beneficiary to be a beneficiary under the settlement at any time during the year of assessment in which the gain accrues to the trustees. As the case was already decided against the taxpayer on other grounds, the Lords did not venture any opinion on this point.

- **Revenue Commissioners CGT Manual :**

— At paragraph 19.3.5.23 of the Revenue Commissioners CGT manual, it is noted that in some instances the gains attributed to a life tenant could exceed the receipts he is entitled to from the trust (ie the income to which he is entitled). It is advised that such cases should be referred to head office. The point made in this paragraph highlights a possible constitutional objection to s579. A life tenant cannot directly benefit from the capital gain which accrues to the non-resident trustee. There is an inherent injustice in charging him with any part of it. The doctrine of "proportionality" as developed by the Irish courts, may have application to such a situation as that referred to.

68.11.5   Discretionary trusts - s579 rules

68.11.5.1   Broad Outline

s579

The apportionment of the gains of the non-resident settlement to the beneficiaries should cause no great difficulty where the interests of the respective beneficiaries under the settlement are easily ascertainable.

Difficulties can, however, arise in the case of a discretionary trust. In broad terms, the only right of a beneficiary under such a trust is the right to be considered as a potential recipient of benefit by the trustees. Such a beneficiary may in fact receive nothing. The fact that a discretionary beneficiary cannot call for the assets to be passed to him, does not necessarily mean that he does not have an "interest" under the settlement.

A certain amount of guidance has been given in this matter by the UK Courts, and a number of statutory rules are also provided in that area.

Many advisors may doubt that a beneficiary of a discretionary trust has an interest in the assets of the trust, in the absence of any appointment to him by the trustees. The UK courts have concluded that such an interest does exist. The Irish courts have not had to consider the matter.

68.11.5.2   Interest of discretionary beneficiary - case law

s579(2)   In the UK case of Leedale v Lewis where the UK equivalent of s579(2) was considered, it was held that a potential beneficiary under a discretionary trust has an 'interest' in the trust property. That case concerned an appeal against an assessment on the UK resident potential beneficiaries of a foreign discretionary trust, arising from a gain made by the non-resident trustees.

Lord Fraser in the course of his judgement, said *"the main question is what is the meaning of the word 'interest' in [s579(2)]. It is a word that is capable of many meanings, the appropriate meaning depending upon the context. In Attorney General v Heywood the settlor had provided that trustees had a discretion to apply the trust income for the benefit of himself and his wife and children or any one or more of them. It was held that they had reserved an 'interest' within the meaning of the Customs and Inland Revenue Act 1881. But in Gartside v IRC this House decided that a beneficiary under a discretionary trust did not have an 'interest' in the sense of s.43 of the FA 1940. Lord Reid expressed approval of the decision in Attorney General v Heywood but distinguished it because of the different context in which 'interest' was used in the 1940 Act. He said*

"If so vague a word as 'interest' is used in different Acts dealing with different problems, there is only, in my view, a slender presumption that it has the same meaning in both..."

In Gartside v IRC, Lord Wilberforce, after referring to Attorney General v Heywood and also to Attorney General v Farrell decided to treat those cases as having settled the meaning of "interest" in the different setting of the FA 1940. He said:

> *"No doubt in a certain sense a beneficiary under a discretionary trust has an 'interest'; the nature of it may, sufficiently for the purpose, be spelt out by saying that he has a right to be considered as a potential recipient of benefit by the trustees and a right to have his interest protected by a Court of Equity".*

In Leedale v Lewis, Lord Wilberforce said *"the key question is as to the meaning of the word 'interest' in [s579(2)(b)], the alternatives being whether this word refers only to such interests as can be assigned a value, or whether it is a word of more general significance capable of covering any interest, quantifiable or non-quantifiable, of a beneficiary under a trust".* Having considered the decisions in the case of Gartside v IRC, and AG v Heywood, he then went on to say that *"the word interest is one of uncertain meaning and it remains to be decided on the terms of the applicable statute which, or possibly what other, meaning the word may bear".* He then went on to make it quite clear that in his opinion an apportionment in respect of interests under a discretionary trust can, and indeed must be made.

Another point, confirmed in Leedale v Lewis, was that

—the **entire gain** must be apportioned to the potential beneficiaries of a discretionary trust, (also confirmed in the UK case of Bayley v Garrod)

—the **apportionment** should have regard to the circumstances - guided perhaps by the intentions of the settlor, as expressed in a letter of wishes to the trustees (if such exists).

If gains arising are taxable in the hands of Irish resident objects of the trust under the attribution rules, then, whether or not the tax is actually assessed, no further CGT liability can arise on subsequent payments made to the trust objects which represent those gains.

The wide scope given to s579 in the UK case of Leedale v Lewis has not been considered in the Irish courts. The Irish courts, in the Wexford Farmers case and the Daly case have identified and approved constitutional limits to the scope of Irish tax law - inter alia, the law must be fair and proportionate. The Leedale v Lewis interpretation of s579 could result in a CGT liability being imposed on a beneficiary who has received no benefit from a trust, and who may not have the financial means of discharging the liability. It remains to be seen what view the Irish courts will take on the matter.

It should be noted that the gain is apportioned in the ratio of the value of the beneficiary's interests and is not limited to the amount of such a value. If the making of any appointment from a trust within the following (say) 10 years were unlikely the present value of any beneficiary's interest may be negligible. The gain apportioned to him might significantly exceed the present value of that interest.

68.11.5.3   Interest of discretionary beneficiary - Statutory Rules

s579(3)   For the purpose of measuring an 'interest' of potential beneficiaries under a discretionary settlement, s579(3) sets out rules deeming a potential beneficiary (of a discretionary settlement) who receives payments from the trustees to have an interest in that settlement, and sets out rules for the measurement of that interest. The statutory rules apply where the beneficiary has received payments of either income or capital of the settlement

(3)   *For the purposes of this section-*

(a)   *where in any of the five years ending with that in which the chargeable gain accrues a person has received a payment or payments out of the income of the settled property made in exercise of a discretion, such person shall be regarded in relation to that chargeable gain, as having an interest in the settled*

> *property of a value equal to that of an annuity of a yearly amount equal to one-fifth of the total of the payments so received by him in the said five years, and*
>
> (b) *where a person receives at any time after the chargeable gain accrues a capital payment made out of the settled property in exercise of a discretion, being a payment which represents the chargeable gain in whole or in part, then, except so far as any part of the gain has been attributed under this section to some other person who is domiciled and resident or ordinarily resident in the State, that person shall, if domiciled and resident or ordinarily resident in the State, be treated as if the chargeable gain, or as the case may be the part of the chargeable gain represented by the capital payment, had accrued to the recipient at the time when the recipient received the capital payment'.*

s579(3) S579(3)(b) seems arbitrary and unfair in its affect. Whether a gain is to be attributed to the beneficiary to whom it is distributed is left dependent on whether the Revenue authorities have (or have not) previously applied s579 to attribute the gain to some other beneficiary. There is no provision made to allow the Revenue to re-open such a premature attribution, and re-attribute it to the actual ultimate recipient.

In the UK case of Ewart v Taylor, the taxpayer received payments from a non-resident discretionary trust during 1976/77. The payments represented gains which had arisen on disposals between 1969 and 1976. It was common ground that the gains were taxable in the hands of the discretionary objects during the years in which they arose under the principle established in Leedale v Lewis. However, the Revenue, following their then existing practice had not sought to assess the discretionary objects in respect of those gains.

It was contended on behalf of the Revenue that the payments made during 1976/77 were taxable because the gains they represented had not been assessed under the attribution rules. It was held that the gains had to be regarded as having been attributed to the taxpayer in the years in which they arose: liability to tax arose in respect of those years and could not arise again on payments representing the gains made in a later year. The fact that the taxpayer had not been assessed on gains attributable in the earlier years could not affect the position.

In the opinion of the authors, s579(3) sits uneasily with the decision in Leedale v Lewis, which would suggest that gains would be attributed to discretionary beneficiaries annually (presumably under self-assessment !) in that it seems to provide for the possibility that a gain was not attributed in the year in which it arose. In Leedale v Lewis that was rationalised as a provision to deal with the possibility that there were no domiciled and resident beneficiaries in that year.

68.11.5.4   **Statutory rules not a separate taxing code - discretionary trusts**

s579(3)   It is not clear whether s579(3) where it is applied in the case of a
beneficiary is an exhaustive measurement of the value of the interest
of that beneficiary in the settlement. If it is, it could result in a lower
value being placed on his interest than may be indicated by the
overall circumstances of the settlement.

In Leedale v Lewis, it was argued that the special provisions in the
UK equivalent of s579(3) provided a separate code for taxing
discretionary beneficiaries, so that such a beneficiary could not be
held to have an interest in the trust property unless he had received
a payment coming within these provisions. This argument,
however, was unanimously rejected in the House of Lords. In the
course of his judgement, Lord Fraser of Tullybelton said *"subsection 3
of [s579] is in my view only subsidiary to subsection (2). Paragraph (a) of
subsection (3) is concerned with the problem of converting a discretionary
payment of income into an annuity to which an approximate value can be
attached for the purposes of subsection (2). That appears to me to be all the
draftsman had in mind as the function of a valuation under subsection
(3)(a), as is shown by the lack of detailed guidance as to the assumptions to
be made about the annuity. Nothing is said about its duration; is it to be
assumed to be for the lifetime of the annuitant or for the "possibly shorter"
period that the discretion lasts? Is it to have any other conditions? Without
more detailed guidance on the nature of the annuity it cannot be valued
accurately although it may be given some approximate value which is
adequate for the purposes of subsection (2).*

*Paragraph (b) subsection (3) is intended to secure that tax would be
collected from a resident beneficiary to whom a discretionary payment is
made out of the settled property, if it is a payment which represents
previously untaxed chargeable gains".*

In the same case Lord Wilberforce said *"that subsection (3) represents
an exclusive code is in my opinion not supported by the form of the section.
On the contrary, the structure of it suggests that subsection (2) is the main
and general charging provision, subsection (3) being auxiliary and confined
to particular cases".*

Where a person is deemed to have an interest by reason of receiving
a capital payment in the 5 year period after a gain arose to the
trustees, it is his residence and domicile status in the year in which
the gain arose, and not his status in the year in which he received the
payments, that is relevent to his liability to CGT in respect of the
trustee's gain. All reporting and payment requirements also seem to
relate to that earlier year, no matter how impractical that may seem.

68.11.6   **Pre 28 February 1974 settlements (s579)**

s579(4)   In the case of any settlement made before 28 February 1974:

— **Exemption for Income beneficiary:** the provisions of s579 will not apply to any beneficiary whose interest is solely in the income of the settled property and who cannot obtain any part of the capital by the exercise of a power of appointment, or revocation, or otherwise (with or without the consent of another person). This is so no matter how the interest was acquired.

— **Deferral of payment of tax :** where a beneficiary is charged to tax under these provisions in respect of an interest in reversion in any part of the capital of the settlement, payment of the CGT may be postponed until he becomes absolutely entitled to that part of the trust funds, or disposes of all or part of his interest in the settlement, or can by any means (including with or without the consent of another person) obtain any of the funds at an earlier date. For these purposes the adding of the property to a pre-1974 settlement is treated as a new settlement of current date.

Given that a settlement could last for approximately 100 years, and even longer in jurisdictions which do not apply the rule against perpetuities, the fact that pre 1974 settlements were exempt from the application of Section 579 in certain circumstances can be important. There may be many such settlements still in existence.

Example 329

> Susan had a domicile of origin in Ireland, but had worked in Hong Kong for many years. In 1970 Susan created a settlement with trustees resident in Jersey. She was at that time still resident solely in Hong Kong. The settlement was a discretionary trust. In 1990 Susan resigned from her position in Hong Kong and returned to spend her retirement in Ireland. From 1990/91 onwards she was resident in Ireland.
>
> The terms of the settlement permitted the trustees to appoint either a limited interest in the income of the settlement, or capital, to any of a group of beneficiaries which included Susan and her husband.
>
> In 1990 Susan asked the trustees to consider supplementing her pension by appointing a life interest in the income of the trust to her. They did so. At the same time they appointed out the remainder interest in the trust (i.e. the entitlement to the capital on the death of Susan) to Susan's son, John, who was domiciled and resident in Ireland.
>
> Because the trust was pre dated 28 February 1974 and because Susan had no power to obtain for herself the capital of the trust, no part of any gains arising to the trustees can be attributed to her under s579. The fact that the trustees would obviously give serious consideration to any request by her for capital is not a relevant point. Under the trust deed only the trustees were given the power to appoint interests in the trust assets, including capital. Susan could not obtain anything for herself, although she could request the trustees to consider her circumstances. The high probability that they would look favourably on a request does mean that one could say that Susan has the power to obtain the capital for herself. The fact that the trustees might appoint capital if requested by Susan (or might not) is a distinct situation from one where Susan can obtain for herself that capital, with the consent of the trustees. More

than the consent of the trustees is required - it is actually their decision that is required and not their consent.

The appointment of a remainder interest to John unfortunately means that he cannot benefit from the special exemption for pre 28 February 1974 settlements. John's interest in the settlement (which is not an interest in possession, but is only a future interest) is an interest in the capital of the settlement. Accordingly the gains of the trustees may be attributed to John. However John is entitled to postpone payment of the CGT on the gains attributed to him until such time as Susan dies, and he becomes entitled to the capital of the trust fund.

It should be noted that even if the trustees had appointed some capital to Susan, for example to enable her to purchase a house on her return to Ireland, that appointment would have been a decision of the trustees, and not the exercise of any power by Susan by which she would have obtained the capital for herself. Once the capital is appointed to Susan, it would cease to be part of the capital represented by the settled property. It is doubtful whether in such a case the receipt of capital by Susan would enable any part of the capital gains of the trustees of pre 28 February 1974 settlement to be attributed to her. Payment of capital to her did not give her an interest in the capital at a time when it was settled property. From the very moment in which she had an interest in it, it had ceased to be settled property. That situation can be contrasted with the position of John, in the example above, where he has an interest in the capital of the settlement which will only come into possession on the death of Susan. His interest at the present time is in capital which is presently settled property. It is that fact which brings him outside the relief for pre 1974 settlements.

There is an ambiguity in the exception made for pre 1974 settlements, in that it states that the attribution of trust gains shall not apply to a beneficiary "whose interest is solely in the income of the settled property and who cannot, by means of the exercise of any power of appointment or power of revocation or otherwise, obtain from himself or herself any part of the capital represented by settled property". Read literally that would imply that the exclusion is available only to a beneficiary who does possess an interest in the income of the settled property. As noted in Paragraph 68.5.2, the U.K. courts have held that their equivalent of s579 can treat a person who is merely one of a class of beneficiaries of a discretionary trust (and to whom no interest in the trust income or assets has been appointed) as a person with an interest in the settlement. Such a person certainly does not have an interest "solely in the income of the settled property". On the literal reading, a pre 1974 discretionary trust, with no interest in possession whatever, and no future interests appointed out, would seem not to fall within the exclusion of the application of s579 to such settlements. That would be an anomalous result and could hardly be the correct interpretation. It is more reasonable to suppose that the legislation applies to any person whose interest in the settled property is not greater than or wider than an interest in its income, and may in fact be very much less i.e. may be no more than the right to be considered by the trustees when making appointments.

S579(4) dealing with pre 1974 settlements only excludes the application of s579(2) to those settlements. It does not exclude the application of S579(3). S579(3)(b) is a sub-section which, independently of s579(2) can cause the gains of a non-resident trustee to be attributed to a beneficiary of a settlement. The beneficiary in question is one who:-

- is domiciled and resident or ordinarily resident in the State and

- receives a capital payment out of the settled property in exercise of a discretion

- which payment is made after a chargeable gain has accrued to the trustees

- and which payment represents the chargeable gain in whole or in part.

Such a person can have an appropriate part of the chargeable gain (the part represented by capital payment) attributed to him. Such an attribution in the case of a pre 28 February 1974 settlement is not excluded by s579(4).

Example 330

> Susan, in **example 329** above, has capital appointed to her by the trustees after her return to Ireland, to enable her to purchase a house in Ireland. To enable them to pay some of the capital to Susan, the trustees disposed of some quoted shares and realised a gain. Notwithstanding that it is a pre 1974 settlement and that the application of s579 in attributing gains under sub-section (2) is excluded by s579 (4), the gains represented by the capital payment to Susan can be attributed to her because the attribution occurs under Section 579(3)(b) and that is not excluded by s579(4).

The attribution of the gain to Susan in the example above could have been avoided if the trustees had borrowed money, and appointed that money to Susan, and then disposed of the quoted shares to enable them to repay the bank borrowings. Even if all of those events occurred in the same tax year, provided the gain was realised after the capital was appointed to Susan, the gain could not be attributed to her under s579 (3). Regard should be had to s579A however (paragraph 68.2).

S579 (4) attempts to limit the extent of the exemption which it grants by providing that if property is added to a settlement after the settlement was originally created, that added property should be regarded for the purpose of the subsection as being in a separate settlement made at the time it was added to the original settlement.

Example 331

*Susan, in **example 330** above, inherited a substantial sum of money from her sister in 1995. She decided to add it to the trust fund held by the Jersey trustees on foot of the trusts which she had created in 1970.*

The exclusion of s579 (2) in attributing gains of the trustees to Susan (by reason of s579 (4)) will not apply to gains arising from the newly added assets. These are regarded as being held upon trusts created in 1995.

Although the principle is clear, its practical application is far from clear. No rules are provided for tracing funds added to a settlement at different times, or for relating them to assets subsequently held, on whose disposal gains might arise. If trustees pursue an active investment policy, it may become practically impossible to relate their share portfolio at a current date to assets added to the settlement on a variety of prior dates. While it might seem reasonable to apportion gains in some "just and reasonable" manner, there is no statutory basis for any such apportionment. To determine whether or not a gain falls within s579 (4), and accordingly cannot be attributed to beneficiaries not having interest in the capital, under S579(2), it is necessary to be able to precisely determine whether or not the gain arose from assets added to the settlement before 28 February 1974, or from assets added after that date. It is probable that the onus of proving that s579 (2) does not apply would lie with the taxpayer who wishes to plead that fact. In that way, the ambiguity in the legislation would work to the disadvantage of the taxpayer rather than the disadvantage of the Revenue.

The discussion so far has concentrated on the operation of s579 (2). As stated in paragraph 68.1, s579(3)(b) operates independently to attribute gains of a non resident trustee to a resident domiciled beneficiary.

s579(3)(b)

S579(3)(b) will attribute the offshore gains to an offshore beneficiary if all of the following conditions are met in a tax year:

(1) The trustees as a body are non resident in Ireland.

(2) The trustees have exercised a discretion to make a payment to a beneficiary

(3) That beneficiary is domiciled and resident or ordinarily resident in the state.

(4) That payment is capital in nature and not income.

(5) The payment is made <u>after</u> a chargeable gain has accrued to the trustees.

(6) That gain has not been attributed under s579 (2) or s579 (3) (b) to some other person.

(7) The payment of capital represented the gain in whole or in part.

(8) One of the settlors was Irish domiciled and resident or ordinarily resident either when the trust was settled or when the gain accrued to the trustees.

Where all eight conditions are met, the gain referred to in 5 above (or the part represented by the payment) may be attributed to beneficiary who received the capital payments.

s579(2)   S579(2) attributed to a beneficiary a gain equal to the <u>net</u> gain arising to a trustee in a tax year. That is the amount of all the gains, less losses, arising in that year. It does not attribute gains of prior years, and does take account of current year losses.

In contrast s579(3)(b):

- can attribute gains which arose in tax years prior to the year in which a capital payment triggers its operation, as well as gains which arose in the same tax year as that in which the payment was made, but prior to the date of the payments.

- attributes gains without deduction of losses, whether of the current or prior years.

Where s579(3)(b) operates, the gain which it attributes to the beneficiary is treated as accruing at the date of the capital payment. However it would seem that the appropriate rate of Capital Gains Tax would be determined by reference to the date of disposal of the asset, which gave rise to the gain in question and not the rate of the year in which the payment was made.

Example 332

Trust Co. are Jersey resident trustees of a trust settled by an Irish domiciled and resident settlor, John, in 1970. In November 1997 they entered into an unconditional contract for the sale of shares in a private trading company and realised a gain of £100,000 and sales proceeds of £200,000. They exercised a discretionary power to pay John £200,000, being all of the capital of the trust in May 1998. John had been resident in the UK solely from 1980/81 to 1997/98. He became resident in Ireland again in 1998/99, having moved here in June 1998. The payment to John clearly represented the £100,000 gain. It was made after the gain arose. It was made to John in a tax year in which he was domiciled and resident in Ireland. It was a capital payment and made in exercise of a discretion. As a result the £100,000 gain is deemed to accrue to John in May 1998. That was before he arrived back in Ireland, but was in a tax year in which he was Irish resident, so he is liable to CGT. The rate of CGT is determined by the date of disposal of the company by the Trustee and <u>not</u> by the date of the capital payment to John. Accordingly the rate is 40% for a pre 3 December 1997 disposal and not 20% which would apply to a May 1998 disposal.

The 1997/98 gain by the Trustees could not be attributed to John under s579 (2) because John wasn't resident or ordinarily resident in Ireland in 1997/98. S579 (2) operates on a year by year basis only. S579 (3)(6) can look backwards to find an attributable gain.

Example 333

> Assume the Trustees in **example 332** also sold quoted shares in October 1997, and incurred a loss of £20,000. Assume that they had exercised discretion to pay (out of the £200,000 proceeds of the sale of the trading company) £100,000 to John and £100,000 to his UK domiciled wife who came to Ireland with John in1998 and became resident here for 1998/99. John's wife is not **both** domiciled and resident in Ireland so s579(3)(b) cannot apply to the payment to her. It can apply to the payment to John. The legislation does not indicate how a capital payment is related to a prior gain. Is Johns £100,000 representing wholly the gain or is it only a part of the gain proportionate to the share of the total payout that he received? Common sense suggests the latter and the legislation is silent. If we assume that to be the case, £50,000 of a gain will be attributed to John. No relief will be available to him for any part of the £20,000 loss.
>
> Had the attribution been under s579 (2) he would have had only £40,000 attributed to him, allowing for relief for a proportionate part of the loss. Relief for the loss would not be available under s579 (3) (b) even if the trustees had also appointed out proceeds of the sale of the quoted shares on whose disposal the loss arose.

There is an ambiguity in condition 8 noted above. S579(1) states that the section applies inter alia where the settlor is domiciled and resident in Ireland and where gains accrue to a non resident trust. For s579(3)(b) to apply additionally the trustees must make a capital payment. Is the domicile and residence status of the settlor to be tested at the time the gain accrues to the trustee or of the time they make payment?

s579(3)(b)   The words used in s579(1) and s579(3)(b) on balance suggest that it is at the date of the capital payment that the domicile and residence status of the settlor should be tested (as well as at the date he created the settlement) rather than at the date the gain arose to the trustee. However that interpretation would lead to absurd results. The residence position of the trustee falls to be determined at the same date as the domicile and residence position of the settlor. It could, where trustees were Irish resident when a gain arose, and non resident when the payment was made, lead to double taxation of the gain. The contrary interpretations, which the words will bear, affords a more sensible results and seems to be the correct position i.e. s579(3)(b) can apply provided the trustees are non resident, and the settlor is resident/domiciled when the gain arises or the settlor is resident/domiciled when he created the trust. The sub section can apply even if the trustees become resident before making the capital payment which triggers it and even if the settlor has then ceased to be both resident and domiciled in Ireland and was not both domiciled and resident when he settled the trust.

The legislation does not grant any Irish resident beneficiary to whom the gains of a non-resident trust are attributed, credit for any foreign tax paid by the non-resident trustees on the gain in question. Since the gain did not in fact accrue to them, and since the foreign tax would not in fact have been paid by them, the resident beneficiary is unlikely to obtain a credit by reason of any relevant double tax agreement. The unilateral tax credit, which applies only to corporation tax in respect of dividends received from a non-resident company, would not have relevance.

However, a deduction would be available for the foreign tax paid by the trustee since the capital gain to be attributed to the Irish resident beneficiary is a gain computed in accordance with the Capital Gains Tax Acts.

68.11.7   Payment of Tax by Trustees

s579(5)   Where in the case of any settlement the tax liability of the beneficiary under these provisions is paid by the trustees, the amount of the payment will not be regarded as a payment to the beneficiary for the purposes of assessment to income tax or CGT.

68.11.8   Losses

s579(6)   A loss accruing to the trustees cannot be attributed to a beneficiary under these provisions.

s590(7)   This is in contrast to s590(7) which permits a limited amount of relief to a resident shareholder for the losses of a non-resident company. (see paragraph 67).

s579(2)   Although a beneficiary cannot claim the benefit of losses arising to a trustee for offset against his own gains, he does however obtain indirect benefit insofar as the losses of the trustee would seem to be required to be taken into account in determining the amount of gains to be attributed to beneficiariesunder s579(2). S579 (2) (a) attributes to the beneficiaries an apportioned part of the amount on which the trustees would have been chargeable to capital gains tax under TCA97 s31, if they were domiciled and either resident or ordinarily resident in the State in that year of assessment. S31 applies a charge to tax on chargeable gains arising in the year of assessment, less losses arising in that year and less losses carried forward from prior years. A statement in s579(6) that the section does not apply in relation to a loss accruing to the trustees of the settlement, would not seem sufficient to override s31 in calculating the amount which is to be attributed to beneficiaries. The significance of s579(6) would seem confined to ensuring that no beneficiary can claim that where the losses arising to a trustee exceed the gains arising to a trustee, the losses should be attributed to the beneficiary for the purpose of being relieved against his own gains.

The comments above relate only to a charge under s579(2). Similar treatment does not apply to a charge under s579(3). A charge in that case is based on taking each chargeable gain arising to the non resident trustees separately. It does not attribute the total amount on which the trustees would be chargeable had they been resident, for a particular tax year, as s579(2) does. It is this latter treatment which enables losses in the year to be taken into account in s579(2).

s31 Notwithstanding the wording of s31, and its application to losses which arose in prior years, it would seem that no relief is available for such prior year losses because even if the trustees were resident in a tax year (which is what we are asked to assume) they would not be entitled themselves to any relief for losses which arose in a prior year in which they were not resident and in respect of which prior year we are not asked to assume they were resident.

s579 The wording in s579 in this respect differs from s590 dealing with
s590 non-resident companies. In s579 what is to be attributed to the beneficiary is the amount on which the trustees would have been charged to tax in the State i.e. the amount of their gains less their losses. In s590, what is attributed to shareholders is the chargeable gain which accrues to the non-resident company, and not necessarily the amount in respect of which the company would have been chargeable to tax had it been resident in the State. The specific relief granted in s590 to the shareholders, in respect of the losses of the company, must be understood in that context.

Where gains are attributed to a beneficiary by reason of Section 579, that beneficiary is entitled to loss relief in the normal way in relation to any losses which have accrued to him either in that tax year, or in a prior tax year (and which were not otherwise relieved).

68.11.9 Gains on Specified Assets

It is interesting to note that there is no exclusion for gains on 'specified assets' similar to that provided in the case of non-resident companies. Presumably gains on such assets (such as Irish land) would be taxable on the trustees in the normal manner, and in practice would not be attributed to the beneficiaries under these provisions.

s579 As noted in Paragraph 68.8 above, the beneficiary to whom the non-resident trustees gains are attributed is entitled to relief for losses accruing to that beneficiary in relation to disposals by the beneficiary of his own assets. There could be circumstances in which it might be in the interest of the beneficiary, and of the trustees, to insist on strict application of s579 where trustees dispose of specified assets and realise a gain, and a beneficiary has losses available for relief. In such a case it might not make sense for the trustees to accept that they are the persons liable for tax on the specified assets which are disposed of, since if they were attributed to the beneficiary, loss relief would be available.

68.11.10   **Offshore Funds**

S579 may attribute the income gains of an offshore fund in which a trust has an interest to Irish resident beneficiaries of the trust.

This is dealt with in paragraph 35.12.

68.11.11   **Self Assessment**

s579

Although s579 may attribute gains of a non resident trustee to resident persons, it does not deem the resident persons to have disposed of the assets which were in fact disposed of by the non resident trustee. Therefore, although the resident persons may have a liability to Capital Gains Tax as a result of the operation of s579, they would not appear to have an obligation to report this in any particular form to the Revenue Commissioners. The normal return of income and gains form does require disclosure of disposal of assets, but it does not require disclosure of gains attributed to a person who has not disposed of assets.

It would seem however that a taxpayer to whom gains are attributed under this section would need to take those gains into account in computing his preliminary tax payment.

69   **FORM -V- SUBSTANCE**

69.1   **Historical Position**

For some considerable time, the approach of the Irish Courts in relation to tax avoidance schemes has been based on the principles laid down in the UK case of Duke of Westminister -v- CIR.

In that case the issue was whether payments made under a series of deeds of covenant were payments for remuneration for services or were not. The Duke had sought to reduce his liability to surtax by executing the deeds in favour of a number of employees. The deeds were not substituted for wages paid to the employees but it was understood that an employee in receipt of an annuity under the deed would accept reduced wages. The sums payable under the covenant were deductible in computing the surtax liability of the Duke whereas, of course, the wages payable were not deductible.

The Revenue contended that the payments under the deeds of covenant were, in substance, wages and this view was upheld in the High Court.

In the Court of Appeal and later in the House of Lords, it was held that the annuity payments could not be regarded as wages and therefore were allowable as a deduction in calculating the surtax liability of the Duke. Lord Russell of Kilowen set out the principles to be followed.

"The result is that payments, the liability for which arises only under the deed are not and cannot be said to be payments of salary or wages within schedule E. They cannot with any regard to the true legal position be said to arise from an employment. They are, and can only be said to be, annual payments within schedule D. Tax was deductible on payment; they are income of the recipient, and are accordingly not part of the Duke's total income for the purpose of calculating his liability for surtax.

The Commissioners and Mr. Justice Finlay took the opposite view on the ground that, as they said, looking at the substance of the thing the payments were payments for wages. This simply means that the true legal position is disregarded and a different legal right and liability substituted in the place of the legal right and liability which the parties have created. I confess that I view with disfavour the doctrine that in taxation cases the subject is to be taxed if, in accordance with a Court's view of what it considers the substance of the transaction, that the Court thinks that the case falls within the contemplation or spirit of the statute. The subject is not taxable by inference or by analogy, but only by the plain words of a statute applicable to the facts and circumstances of his case. As Lord Cairns said many years ago in Partington v Attorney General:

"As I understand the principle of all fiscal legislation, it is this; if the person sought to be taxed comes within the letter of the law he must be taxed however great the hardship may appear to the judicial mind to be. On the other hand, if the Crown, seeking to recover the tax, cannot bring the subject within the letter of the law, the subject is free, however, apparently within the spirit of the law the case might otherwise appear to be".

If all that is meant by the doctrine (of substance) is that having once ascertained the legal rights of the parties you may disregard mere nomenclature and decide the question of taxability or non-taxability in accordance with the legal rights, well and good. This is what this House did in the case of Secretary of State in Council of India v Scobie; that and no more. If, on the other hand, the doctrine means that you can brush aside deeds, disregard the legal rights and liabilities arising under a contract between parties, and decide the question of taxability or nontaxability upon the footing of the rights and liabilities of the parties being different from what in law they are, then I entirely dissent from such a doctrine".

The Duke of Westminister case was considered in this jurisdiction in O'Sullivan v P Limited. In that case, Kenny J. said

"Where a transaction is contained in a document, the liability to tax arising out of the transaction depends upon the meaning and effect of the document ascertained in accordance with the principles of construction which have been laid down by the Courts. Prior to the decision in (the Duke of Westminister case) there was some judicial support for the view that in determining liability to tax, the substance of the transaction was to be looked at; this was assumed to mean that the financial result and not the legal effect of a transaction determined liability for tax purposes. This was rejected in the Duke of Westminister case".

Following the decision in O'Sullivan v P Limited, the approach of the Irish Courts may thus be expressed as follows. In determining liability to tax, the courts do not look at the economic substance or financial result of a transaction. Provided that the transactions do not constitute a sham (i.e. purport to be something other than that what they really are) the courts will look at the actual legal effect of the transactions and determine liability to tax accordingly. This is sometimes expressed as the doctrine of form over substance. However, it is important to note that by form is meant the actual legal rights and obligations resulting from a transaction and not the apparent effects of the transaction.

Following a number of decisions in the U.K. Courts culminating in the decision of the House of Lords in Furniss v Dawson, doubt arose as to whether the principles laid down in the Duke of Westminister case and approved in O'Sullivan v P Limited were still valid as a statement of the relevant law in this country. In broad terms, the decision in Furniss v Dawson was an example of the application of the so-called "doctrine of fiscal nullity". Under this approach, the liability to tax is computed by reference to the end result of a number of transactions and by ignoring any preordained transactions which have no commercial purpose apart from the avoidance of a liability to tax.

Further confusion arose following the application by the Appeal Commissioners of the doctrine of fiscal nullity to a capital gains tax avoidance scheme which involved the creation of artificial capital losses to shelter realised gains.

Eventually, that case - P.W. McGrath v J.E. McDermott (Inspector of Taxes) reached the Supreme Court which gave its decision in July 1988 unanimously in favour of the taxpayer.

69.2   **The McGrath Case**

The relevant CGT legislation referred to in this paragraph has been significantly amended by legislation subsequent to decision of the Irish Supreme Court in the McGrath case.

The description of the case given here should not be taken as a guide to the current law in this area, particularly as regards s549, and s547 or the relief for losses.

The facts of the case were as follows

(a)   On 2nd December 1981, Mr. Patrick W. McGrath (Mr McGrath) purchased from Caversham Trustees Limited (Caversham) preference shares of Stg£1 each in Parapet Holdings Limited (Parapet) at the price of Stg£110. At the time of his purchase of those preference shares, the only other issued shares of Parapet were 90 ordinary shares which were also owned by Caversham.

Parapet was a company registered in the Isle of Man but managed and controlled in Jersey. The said preference shares were duly transferred to Mr. McGrath's name and he was registered as owner thereof in the books of Parapet.

(b)   On 8th December 1981, Mr. McGrath purchased from Parapet at the price of Stg£900 the entire issued Ordinary Share Capital in Garfish Investments Limited (Garfish), namely 500 Ordinary shares of Stg£1 each. These Ordinary Shares were subject to an option in favour of the holders of the preference shares in that company (viz. Parapet) whereby the holders of the preference shares were entitled to purchase the ordinary shares at the price of Stg£2 per share. The said shares were duly transferred into Mr. McGrath's name and he was registered as owner thereof in the books of Garfish.

(c)   The asset and liability position of Garfish at the time of Mr. McGrath's purchase of the shares was as follows:

ASSETS	**£Stg**
Cash on current account	2,970
Cash on deposit account	1,110,500
Total	1,103,470

LIABILITIES	
Share Capital Account	
500 Ordinary Shares of £1	500
1,000 Preference Shares of £1 each	1,000
Share Premium account	
Premium on 498 Preference Shares @ Stg£265 per share	131,970
Premium on 500 Preference Shares @ Stg £1,940 per share	970,000
Total	1,103,470

Garfish was registered in the Isle of Man but managed and controlled in Jersey.

(d)   On 5th January 1982, Mr. McGrath sold and duly transferred the 500 Ordinary Shares in Garfish for Stg£900 to London Law Securities Trustees Limited, a Jersey company. The sum of

Stg£900 represented the market value of the shares sold by him and duly transferred.

(e)   On 22 January 1982, Mr. McGrath sold and duly transferred the Preference Shares in Parapet for Stg£110 to London Law Securities Trustees Limited, which sum represented the value of the shares sold by him.

(f)   Mr McGrath had no connection with Caversham or with London Law Securities Trustees Limited other than that arising in connection with the transactions already mentioned.

(g)   It was accepted on behalf of the appellant that the purpose of these transactions was to secure an allowable loss for capital gains tax purposes.

s432

s547

s549

It will be noted that, at the time Mr. McGrath purchased the shares in Garfish from Parapet, he owned the greater part of the share capital of Parapet and, accordingly, was connected with it within the meaning of s432 as applied to capital gains tax by s5. By virtue of the provisions of s549 and s547 (see paragraph 16) acquisitions and disposals between connected persons are treated as if they are made at open market price.   However, in accordance with s549(6) where an asset acquired from a connected person was subject to any right enforceable by that person, or by some person connected with him, then the market value of the asset was to be taken as

— The market value of the asset ignoring the right or restriction

reduced by

— The market value of the right or restriction or the amount by which the value of the asset would be increased if the right or restriction did not exist, which ever is the less.

Under s549(7)(b), the right or restriction was ignored in calculating the market value of an asset where, inter alia, the right or restriction is an option to acquire that asset.

Accordingly, for capital gains tax purposes, the price at which Mr. McGrath was deemed to have acquired from Parapet the ordinary shares in Garfish was the market value of those shares ignoring the fact that the holders of the preference shares were entitled to acquire the ordinary shares at a price of Stg£2 each. Without taking account of such restriction, the market value of the ordinary shares was considerable.

s.5

In relation to the sale of the ordinary shares in Garfish to London Law Securities Trustees Limited, the position is that Mr. McGrath was not connected with the purchaser within the meaning of TCA97 s10. Therefore, that section had no application to the disposal. Thus, taking into account the sale proceeds of Stg£900 and the deemed market value acquisition price (which ignored the restriction) Mr.

McGrath's capital gains tax computation in respect of the acquisition and disposal of the shares in Garfish produced a very considerable capital loss. Of course, in real terms, Mr. McGrath realised no loss (apart from expenses) since he purchased and sold the ordinary shares for Stg£900. The taxpayer claimed the resultant capital loss against actual capital gains under the provisions of s31(a). The Inspector refused the claim on the basis that there was no real loss. However, the Supreme Court (following the judgement of Carroll J. in the High Court) decided the case unanimously in favour of the tax payer.

Finlay C.J., stated that the market value of an asset coming within the provisions of s549(7)(b) is not its true or real value but one artificially calculated by ignoring the existance of a restriction or right as defined. The amount of the gain accruing on the disposal of such an asset is computed at a figure which is artificial and may not coincide with the real gain. There being no express provision to the contrary contained either in the Capital Gains Tax Acts, or in any other statute, the amount of the loss accruing on the disposal of an asset coming within the provisions of s549(7) is likewise to be computed at a figure which is artificial and may not coincide with the real loss. According to Finlay CJ, these consequences followed from the plain and unambiguous meaning of s549.

The Court rejected the contention on behalf of the inspector that the doctrine of fiscal nullity should be introduced into the application of s549 so that the provisions would be inoperative unless the tax payer could establish a real loss. The Chief Justice stated that the function of the Courts in interpreting a statute of the Oireachtas is strictly confined to ascertaining the true meaning of each statutory provision. It is not a function of the Courts to add to, or delete from, existing statutory provisions. Effectively, the application of the doctrine of fiscal nullity would require the Courts to do so by providing that a condition precedent to the computation of an allowable loss pursuant to the provisions of s549(7) is the proof by the taxpayer of an economic loss equal to the artificial loss computed in accordance with the subsection.

The Chief Justice also noted that successful tax avoidance schemes may result in unfair burdens being placed on other taxpayers. However, he stated that it is the role of the Revenue Commissioners, and not the Courts, to anticipate and prohibit tax avoidance schemes. In the absence of general statutory provisions against tax avoidance, there are no grounds for the Courts to depart from the plain meaning of specific provisions of taxation laws.

The only other judgement delivered in the case was that of McCarthy J. Apart from stating that the Inspector's contention would involve the court in rewriting the legislation which it cannot do, his judgement is noteable for its rebuke of the Appeal Commissioners.

Originally, the Appeal Commissioners had found in favour of the Inspector by holding that the doctrine of fiscal nullity did apply to the transactions by which the capital loss was created. According to the Appeal Commissioners, this doctrine did not involve any over-ruling of previously accepted principles but was merely a difference in approach. However, McCarthy J. said that the doctrine of fiscal nullity clearly did reverse the Duke of Westminister case and it was not open to a tribunal, such as the Appeal Commissioners, to review principles accepted by the Superior Courts.

69.3 General Anti-Avoidance Law (s811)

s811

The Minister of Finance stated in the budget speech on 25th January 1989 that, in the light of the McGrath case, the means to counteract tax avoidance schemes must be fundamentally reviewed. He stated that he had been advised by the Revenue Commissioners that the potential loss of revenue was sufficiently large to warrant action being taken in the interest of preserving equity in the tax system and ensuring that the expected yield of revenue each year is realised. Therefore, the Government had decided to introduce measures to counter avoidance of tax in the 1989 Finance Bill.

The principal measure introduced was a general anti-avoidance provision, in s.86 FA 1989, now TCA97 s811.

s811

S811 applies to CGT as well as all other taxes which are under the care and management of the Revenue Commissioners.

At the date of writing it is understood that this section has been applied in practice in a handfull of cases but has not yet been reviewed by the Irish courts.

Where the Revenue Commissioners form an opinion that a transaction is a tax avoidance transaction, s811 permits them to make all such adjustments and do all such things as are just and reasonable in order that the tax advantage resulting from the transaction may be withdrawn or cancelled.

In order that s811 may have application, there are several steps which the Revenue Commissioners must take.

1. They must *identify a transaction* to which to apply the section. "Transaction" is very widely defined for this purpose, including scheme, plan, proposal, arrangement, understanding, course of conduct. The transaction identified could be a combination of several transactions or only a part of a larger transaction. It is for the Revenue to identify the limits to the transaction which they have selected.

2.   They must *form an opinion* that the selected transaction gave
     rise to a tax advantage. A tax advantage is a reduction,
     avoidance, a deferral, a refund or increase in a refund, of tax.

3.   They must *form the opinion* that the transaction was not
     undertaken primarily for a purpose other than to obtain the tax
     advantage.

When the Revenue complete these three steps in relation to a
transaction, it is (subject to the taxpayer's right of appeal) a tax
avoidance transaction for the purposes of this section.

The Revenue are restricted in the manner in which they may form
the opinion described above, leading to the conclusion that a
transaction is a tax avoidance transaction.

They must have regard only to:

— the results of the transaction

— the use of the transaction as a means of achieving those results

— any other means by which the results or part of them could have
  been achieved.

They may not regard as a tax avoidance transaction:

— a transaction carried out with a view to profit in the course of a
  business and not undertaken primarily to give rise to a tax
  advantage.

— a transaction undertaken to obtain the benefit of any relief or
  allowance where the transaction would not result directly or
  indirectly in the misuse or abuse of a provision.

Notice to taxpayer : Where the Revenue Commissioners have taken
the steps described above, they must give notice in writing to the
taxpayer setting out:

— the transaction which in their opinion is a tax avoidance
  transaction.

— The tax advantage which they propose to withdraw.

— The tax consequences which will ensue. By this is meant the means
  by which they propose to withdraw the tax advantage. These
  include allowing or disallowing a deduction; reallocating or
  refusing a relief, allowance or exemption; reallocating income;
  re-characterisation of any payment or other amount. This list is not
  exhaustive.

— Any double tax relief to which the taxpayer would be entitled as a
  result of the steps taken by the Revenue.

Taxpayer appeal : The taxpayer may give notice in writing to the Revenue Commissioners within 30 days of receiving such a notification, of his wish to appeal to the Appeal Commissioners. The appeal is confined to four matters:

—that the transaction is not a tax avoidance transaction

—that the tax advantage calculated is incorrect

—that the tax consequences are not just or reasonable

—that the double tax relief is incorrect.

There is provision for rehearing by the Circuit Court and for appeal on questions of law to the High Court.

70   ANTI-AVOIDANCE - GUIDE TO LOCATION

70.1   Share transactions

The CGT Acts set out a considerable amount of anti-avoidance legislation in the area of share transactions affecting individuals, companies and groups of companies.

The main provisions specific to share transactions are contained in Chapter 6.

70.2   Anti-avoidance : Summary Chart

A broad summary of the main CGT anti-avoidance provisions is set out in chart form in the following pages of this Chapter.

PRINCIPAL CGT ANTI-AVOIDANCE PROVISIONS		
ANTI-AVOIDANCE PROVISION	**STATUTORY REFERENCE**	**BOOK REFERENCE**
• Deemed remittance (of amounts not actually remitted into Ireland)	s29(5)	Para 3.3.2
• Assumption of liability treated as additional consideration	s537(3)	Paras 8.7 & 9.4
• Market value substituted for actual consideration	s547	Para 16
• Cost of share subscription restricted	s547(2)	Para16.2, & 41
• Losses incurred while non-resident restricted	s546(4)	Para 20.2
• Trust Beneficiary may be liable for CGT of trustees	s574(2)	Para 91.2

PRINCIPAL CGT ANTI-AVOIDANCE PROVISIONS		
ANTI-AVOIDANCE PROVISION	STATUTORY REFERENCE	BOOK REFERENCE
• Chattels - splitting of set : anti-avoidance	s589	Para 23.3
• Life Assurance - no indexation on disposal of foreign policy	s594	Para 32.9
• Principal Private Residence - restricted for development land	s604	Para 24
• Retirement Relief - clawback on later disposal by children within 6 years	s599	Para 30.11
• Connected Person - defined	s10	Para 16.4.4
• Connected Person - OMV substituted for actual consideration between such persons.	s549(2)	Para 16
• Connected Person - restriction of relief for losses on transactions between connected persons.	s549(3)	Paras 16.4.2, 20.7 & 38.4
• Connected series of transactions - consideration for each disposal may take account of value of total (combined) disposals.	s550	Paras 16.4.6, 23.3
• Transfer at undervalue by company - may result in reduction in base cost of shares.	s589	Para 51.3
• Non resident company - gains may be attributed to resident shareholders	s590	Para 67
• Non-resident trust - gains may be attributed to resident beneficiaries	S579: s579A	Para 68
• Value shift - gain may arise on value shifted out of shares into other shares - also applied to property other than shares.	s543	Para 51.2
• Computation of gain/loss - no sum may be deducted twice	s544(4)	Paras 4.4.7, 59.8 & 41
• Identification of shares - acqusition and disposal within 4 weeks	s581	Para 48.3.1

PRINCIPAL CGT ANTI-AVOIDANCE PROVISIONS		
ANTI-AVOIDANCE PROVISION	**STATUTORY REFERENCE**	**BOOK REFERENCE**
• Lease - deemed premium in certain circumstances	Sch14 Para 4	Para 60
• Lease - provisions relating to duration of lease	Sch14 Para 4	Para 60
• Disposal of interest arising under non-resident trust	s613A	
• Purchase of capital loss company	Sch 18A	
• Shareholders - tax due by company may be recovered from shareholders	s614	Para 91.4.1
• Company leaving group - CGT charge may arise in respect of assets acquired from other group members	s620 and s624	Para 81
• Company leaving group after reconstruction or amalgamation.	s625	Paras 45 & 46
• Depreciatory transactions in a group (asset stripping) - share base cost restricted	s621	Para 51.4
• Dividend stripping	s622	Para 51.5
• Development land disposals - many reliefs denied	s442, s443	Para 6.4
• General anti-avoidance provision	s811	Para 69.3
• Schemes to avoid tax under Schedule F	s817	Para 41.7
• Off-shore funds - gains may be charged to income tax	s740 - s747	Paras 35.1 & 35.11
• Ordinary residence - defined	s820	Para 100
• "Exit charge" on company going non-resident	s627	Para 74
• Pre-disposal dividends	s623(3)	Para 51.6

CHAPTER 10   COMPANY CHARGEABLE GAINS

71   INTRODUCTION

71.1   Company chargeable gains

When CGT was first introduced in the CGTA 1975, it was charged
and assessed as a separate tax on gains arising after 5 April 1974 on
all persons, including companies. Special provisions were
introduced in the CTA 1976, to substitute for CGT a charge to
corporation tax on capital gains on certain companies. In addition
that Act introduced special provisions for dealing with mergers,
reconstructions and other transactions between members of a group
of companies, together with certain anti-avoidance provisions
relating to companies and their shareholders.

This chapter deals with the *corporation tax provisions* insofar as
they apply to *chargeable gains*.

- The scope of the charge to corporation tax is dealt with in
  paragraph 71; and the calculation of the amount chargeable to
  corporation tax is dealt with in paragraph 72.

- Paragraph 9.5 deals with the circumstances in which interest paid
  by a company is allowed as a deduction in computing a gain or
  loss on the disposal of an asset.

- Special rules apply where assets are transferred in the course of a
  reconstruction or amalgamation of companies. Those rules are set
  out in paragraph 75.

- Paragraph 91.4 deals with the circumstances in which the tax due
  in respect of gains arising to a company, can be recovered from the
  shareholders in that company.

- Under the group relief provisions assets may be transferred
  between members of a group (as defined) without giving rise to
  chargeable gains. This relief and other reliefs which apply to
  transfers of assets between companies are dealt with in paragraph
  75.

- Where an asset which has been the subject of relief is sold outside
  the group special provisions govern the calculation of the
  chargeable gain. (paragraph 77).

- If a company owning an asset which has been the subject of group
  relief leaves the group, the company is deemed to have sold and
  reacquired the asset from the other group member. These rules
  (and the exceptions) are dealt with in paragraph 81. Relief is

provided where a company leaves a group in the course of a merger (paragraph 82).

- Provisions are included to deal with groups and development land (paragraph 78); groups and trading stock (paragraph 80); groups and roll-over relief (paragraph 79); and recovery of tax from other group members (paragraph 91.5).

- Anti-avoidance provisions dealing with depreciatory transactions in a group, dividend stripping and disposals after reconstruction or amalgamation are dealt with in paragraph 51.

- A company which ceases to be resident in the State on or after 21 April 1997 is deemed on that occasion to have disposed of its assets, and to have immediately reacquired them, at open market value. This "exit charge" does not apply in certain circumstances (principally to the extent a branch operation continues immediately after going non-resident or where the company is controlled from a State with which Ireland has a full tax treaty) and may be postponed in certain other circumstances. These provisions are dealt with in paragraph 74.

71.2   **Scope of the charge - Broad Outline**

s21   Under the general charge to corporation tax (CT), companies are chargeable in respect of all income and gains wherever arising. The
s649   corporation tax charge on gains applies where the disposal was made after 5 April 1976. Gains on disposals in the 2 years ended 5th April 1976 were chargeable to CGT. However, s649 provides that gains on development land are chargeable to CGT and not to CT (since FA82).

This general rule is modified in relation to income and gains arising to non-resident companies. A non-resident company may be within the charge to either CT or CGT or both.

s25   A non-resident company will not be within the charge to CT unless it carries on a trade in Ireland through a branch or agency. If it does carry on a trade here through a branch or agency, it is chargeable to CT on the following:

- any trading income arising directly or indirectly through or from the branch or agency and any income from property or rights used by or held by or for the branch or agency.

and

- such chargeable gains as, but for the Corporation Tax Acts would be chargeable to CGT in the case of a company which is not resident in the State (see paragraph 3.4).

Such chargeable profits (i.e. income and gains) do not include gains accruing to the company on the disposal of assets which, at or before the time when the chargeable gains accrued, were not used in or for the purposes of the trade and were not used or held or acquired for the purposes of the branch or agency.   This provision which determines whether a non-resident is chargeable to CT or CGT on gains, does not affect the basic rule applying to all non-residents that a non-resident is only chargeable on gains arising on the disposal of specified assets (see paragraph 3.4).

In the light of these rules, the position regarding tax on chargeable gains of companies may be summarised as follows:

- *Resident companies* are chargeable to CT on all gains (other than on development land disposals on or after 28 January 1982) wherever arising, if the disposal takes place on or after 6 April 1976.

- *Non-resident companies* are chargeable to CT in respect of gains on specified assets (i.e. Irish land, minerals, etc. — see paragraph 3.4) and other Irish branch assets if :-

    (i)   the company carries on or carried on a trade in Ireland through a branch or agency, and

    (ii) the assets were used *'in or for the purposes of the trade'* or *'used or held or acquired for the purposes of the branch or agency'* and

    (iii) The assets are located in the State at the date of disposal.

- *Non-resident companies* are charged to CGT in respect of chargeable gains arising on specified assets where such gains are not within the charge to CT (e.g. where they are not assets of an Irish trading branch even if the non-resident company has such a branch).

- Chargeable gains arising on the disposal of *development land* on or after 28th January 1982 are chargeable to CGT and not to CT (see paragraphs 6 and 78) irrespective of the residence of the company .

It is important to note that non-resident companies, like non-resident individuals, are chargeable only in respect of gains arising on disposals of specified assets; this rule applies irrespective of whether the gains are chargeable to CT or CGT (see paragraph 3.4).

The rules for determining the residence of a company are set out in paragraph 101.

s533

As stated above, a non-resident company is liable to tax on specified Irish assets only if those assets are located in the State at the date of the disposal of the assets. This is particularly relevant in relation to assets which are or were in use for the purpose of trade carried on here through a branch, or which were used or held or acquired for those purposes. It should be borne in mind that the location of assets is not a matter solely of common sense, or even a matter to be determined solely by reference to international law on the matter. TCA97 s533 lays down rules for determining the location of assets for the purposes of capital gains tax. These are discussed in Paragraph 3.7. Those rules may not coincide with international law, or with commercial or common sense, in some instances.

Example 334

Multinational Inc. is resident in Bermuda. It carries on a manufacturing trade through a branch in Ireland. The branch owned a very valuable machine tool, and also a small aircraft. Due to a downturn in the trade a decision was made to dispose of these two assets. The machine tool was taken to the U.K. where it was shown to a potential customer who wished to test it at his own factory. That customer agreed to purchase it while it was located at their factory in the U.K. The aircraft was sold to a Belgian airline whilst still standing at Dublin airport

Multinational Inc. carried on a trade here through a branch and accordingly was chargeable to corporation tax in respect of gains on branch assets, where those branch assets are located in Ireland at the date of disposal. Although the machine tool was a branch asset, it was located in the U.K. at the date of disposal and accordingly no chargeable gain arises on its disposal. No chargeable gain arises on the disposal of the aircraft either, notwithstanding that it was branch asset used for the purpose of their trade, and parked on the tarmac at Dublin airport. S533 states that an aircraft is situated in Ireland only if the owner is resident in Ireland. Multinational Inc. was not resident in Ireland, and accordingly the aircraft cannot be regarded as located in Ireland (notwithstanding its physical position).

As indicated in Paragraph 3.7.1, the location of an asset such as goodwill can give rise to problems in the case of a non-resident company carrying on a trade in several locations, only some of which are in Ireland. Those problems have been illustrated in Paragraph 3.7.1, in relation to a trade carried on by an individual. Some other problems arise in the case of a company.

Example 335

Multinational Inc. is resident in Bermuda and has its sole manufacturing operation in Ireland. It manufactures "Super Product - The Universal Solution" which is sold almost exclusively in India. Its large popularity in India is in part due to extensive advertising in that country, and in part due to the prestige in that country of the owner of Multinational Inc., an Indian national who is in his spare time is a famous star of the Indian cinema. The fact that the product is manufactured in Ireland is not mentioned in the company's advertising and would be unknown to all but an insignificant handful of the product's many customers and admirers. Most customers wrongly assume that it is manufactured in India.

Multinational Inc. has received an offer for its trade (but not its shares as the purchaser does not wish to assume uncertain taxation liabilities associated with the company). Where is the company's goodwill located for the purposes of computing Irish capital gains tax? If it is located in Ireland at the date of the disposal, then it will be an asset located in Ireland and in use for the purpose of a trade carried on here through a branch, and accordingly will be liable to Irish capital gains tax.

Commercial common sense suggests that no part of the goodwill whatever is located at the Irish manufacturing center and that the goodwill is entirely located in India. However s533 states that the goodwill is located wherever the trade is carried on and the trade is indeed carried on at least in part in Ireland. It is also of course carried on in India where the product is sold and distributed, and even to some extent in Bermuda, where ultimate control of the company is exercised and occasional strategic decisions are made relating the company's trade.

The company carries on only a single trade. It would not seem possible therefore to say that there is a separate trade in Ireland with a distinct goodwill, and a separate trade in India having a distinct goodwill, and that the sales price for the trade goodwill must be apportioned between the two goodwills. Unfortunately, neither case law nor the statutory provision enable any clear answer to be given to this conundrum. It is an important conundrum since many multinationals operate in Ireland through branches and occasionally dispose of goodwill.

It should be noted that the problem for Multinational Inc. could of course be solved by closing down the Irish manufacturing operation. This would not change the fact that the goodwill was an asset which had been used for the purpose of a trade carried on through a branch here - closing down the trade cannot alter that fact. However it does seem to be the case in the particular instance of goodwill that once the trade ceases to be carried on here, the goodwill ceases to be regarded as located here and provided that it is not located in the State at the date of disposal, a charge to tax in respect of the capital gain on its disposal will not arise. In contrast, the plant and machinery used in the manufacturing operation, if it were sold after the Irish manufacturing operation had been closed, would still be within the charge to tax on capital gains since it had at one time been used for a trade carried on here through a branch, and it was located in the State at the date of its disposal, notwithstanding that the branch trade was no longer then carried on.

71.3   Meaning of "company"

s4(1)

For the purposes of corporation tax "company" is defined as meaning any body corporate and also a trustee savings bank within the meaning of the Trustee Savings Bank Act 1989. However certain entities are specifically excluded from being a "company" for the purpose of corporation tax. These include a health board; a vocational education committee; a committee of agriculture, and a local authority. In principle therefore those bodies remain chargeable to capital gains tax and are not within the charge to corporation tax on companies' capital gains.

The practical significance of those exclusions is reduced by the fact that all of the excepted bodies just mentioned above are exempted from capital gains tax. It does however have the consequence that none of them are capable of being a member of a group of companies for the purpose of corporation tax on companies' capital gains.

Also excluded from the definition of "company" for the purposes of corporation tax is a European Economic Interest Grouping (EEIG). These are further described in paragraph 34.13.

Although many types of State entities have been excluded from the meaning of "company" for corporation tax purposes, a minister of state (who is a corporation sole and therefore arguably a body corporate) is not excluded.

71.4   **Overseas branches - "participation exemption"**

s847   Capital gains arising to overseas branches of certain Irish resident companies may be exempt from CGT or corporation tax on companies capital gains. This relief was introduced by the FA95. Similar reliefs exist in many European countries where they are aspects of what is known as a *"participation exemption"*. The Irish relief is subject to stringent conditions which make it unlikely that it will be availed of by many companies.

s222   The relief hinges around the resident company entering into an approved investment plan involving the creation of jobs in the State, and the investment of capital in the State. In that respect the relief appears, in a broad manner, comparable to the corporation tax relief in respect of the repatriation of dividends from overseas subsidiaries, which is contained in s222.

s847   The relief is contained in s847(6) which states that ;

- Profits or gains or losses arising from the carrying on of *qualified foreign trading activities* are to be disregarded for all the purposes of the Corporation Tax Acts.

- A gain it is not to be treated as a chargeable gain if it arises on the disposal of an asset used wholly and exclusively for the purpose of *qualified foreign trading activities* unless the asset consists of

  − land in the State

  − minerals in the State

  − exploration rights in a designated area (in the State)

  − shares in a company deriving their value from the foregoing (other than quoted shares) and unquoted shares acquired in a share for share exchange to which s584 had application, in return for shares deriving their value from the foregoing and

  − goodwill of a trade carried on in the State.

The list of assets above, which are exceptions to the CGT exemption, are broadly the same list of assets to which the 15% withholding tax requirements apply in the absence of a tax clearance certificate where consideration for the disposal exceeds the stated limit (see paragraph 94). Because they include shares received in a share swop for shares deriving their value from land, minerals etc... the list is not identical to the list of specified assets in respect of which a non resident and non ordinarily resident person may be liable to Irish CGT (see paragraph 3.4.2)

Qualified foreign trading activities are defined as trading activities carried on by the company which is qualifying for the relief, through a branch or agency outside the State and in a territory which has been specified by the Minister in the certificate given by him to the company, conferring the relief upon them.

The relief is available only to a company provided it holds a certificate from the Minister for Finance giving it entitlement to the relief. The law provides for that certificate to be given by the Finance Minister only following consultation by him with the Minister for Enterprise and Employment.

In order to obtain the certificate the company must be resident in the State and must have submitted to the Minister an investment plan.

The ***investment plan*** must :

- involve the company, or an associate company, in the provision of ***substantial new employment*** in the State and trading operations in the State carried on by the company obtaining relief, or by the associate company submitting the plan, and

- involve investment in the State of ***substantial permanent capital*** for the purposes of the plan.

The question of what constitutes substantial new employment, or substantial permanent capital investment, are set out in guidelines issued in October 1995 by the Minister for Finance.

Those guidelines provide that in the context of the required investment plan:

- ***"Substantial employment"*** means that the company's (or an associated company's) trading operations in the State must create a minimum level of sustainable employment in the order of 40 new incremental jobs. The minimum level of sustainable jobs must be created at the latest by the end of a three year period commencing from the date of start-up as specified in the certificate.

- ***"Substantial permanent capital"*** means that amount of permanent capital which is considered appropriate to the trading operations carried on or to be carried on in the State, as specified in the certificate issued by the Minister.

As noted above, a company may obtain a certificate entitling it to relief in respect of its foreign gains on the basis that another company submits and carries out the approved investment plan.

That other company carrying out the investment plan must be an associate company of the company obtaining the relief. For this purpose, the two companies are associated if one is a 75% subsidiary of the other or they are both 75% subsidiaries of a third company.

s412

S412 to s418, applying profit distribution, voting, and asset tests, are employed for the purpose of determining whether or not companies are associated as described.

An Irish resident company is normally liable to corporation tax on chargeable gains arising on the disposal of assets worldwide. The effect of the relief, where it is available, is to exempt the gain arising on the disposal of assets used exclusively for the trade carried on in specified foreign branches.

In substance therefore, it appears that such a company would be liable to tax only on chargeable gains accruing on the disposal of assets located in the State, since it is likely that any assets located outside the State would be in use for the purpose of a trade carried on through a branch outside the State.

Where a company has several branches, only those branches specified in the certificate granted by the Minister, which confers the relief, are encompassed in the relief. If a company set up a branch subsequent to having received such a certificate, that most recently formed branch would not attract the relief, unless the company had the foresight to seek its inclusion in the certificate in advance.

Where a company carries on a single trade, partly in the State and partly abroad through branches, it may well have only a single goodwill in respect of the entire trade. If the company disposed of a branch and of all the assets of the branch, it would be a question of fact as to whether it was disposing of a separate asset consisting of the separate goodwill of the branch, or whether there was involved a part disposal of the goodwill of the overall trade. Since the goodwill of the overall trade is excepted from the exemption (being the goodwill of a trade carried on in the State) and since it is also not an asset used exclusively for the purpose of the branch, it would not be entitled to the exemption.

s847(8)

S847(8) empowers an Inspector to require the company to furnish him with such information as is necessary for the purpose of giving relief under the Section.

This relief has been criticised by the EU code on Tax Competition review group and may be abolished soon.

72   AMOUNT CHARGEABLE TO C.T.

72.1   Main rule - amount chargeable to CT

s78   Notwithstanding that the tax charged on most capital gains of a company is corporation tax rather than capital gains tax, the computation of the chargeable gain which is to be subject to tax generally is the same for corporation tax, as it is for capital gains tax. For the most part, the preparation of the computation of the amount chargeable can proceed without any regard being made to the fact that it is a corporation tax computation, and not a capital gains tax computation.

There are of course certain differences where corporation tax is charged on a capital gain, rather than capital gains tax.

- *Tax Rate :* A special adjustment is required to be made to the amount chargeable to take account of the fact that the rate of corporation tax differs from the standard rate of CGT. This is explained in greater detail below.

- *Group relief :* There is an important relief which enables members of a capital gains group to transfers assets between them without crystallising a capital gain or loss. There is also a consequent provision deeming a disposal to occur when a group member leaves a group, while owning an asset transferred under the group relief provisions. These provisions are explained in paragraphs 75 to 82.

- *Trading losses* arising in the same period may be offset against capital gains of the company in that period. Trading losses surrendered from other member of a loss group may be similarly offset against capital gains. Similar provisions extend to expenses of management of the company or of other companies. This is subject to restrictions in relation to losses incurred in trades where profits would qualify for the reduced rate of 10% CT. These provisions are further explained in paragraph 73.4.

- *Interest :* As explained in paragraph 9.5, a company unlike any other body, may include certain interest charges in its computation of deductible expenditure in a computation of corporation tax on capital gains.

- *Anti-avoidance :* There are certain anti-avoidance provisions, such as those relating to depreciatory transactions in a group, that are specific to corporation tax on capital gains. These are described in paragraph 51.

- *Rollover relief* is available to a company by reference not only to its own expenditure, but a.so to the expenditure of other members of a capital gains group. This is explained in paragraph 79.

- **Development land** is not within the charge to corporation tax on capital gains, but is chargeable to capital gains tax. Special provisions under the E.U. Mergers Directive enable companies to transfer development land within a capital gains group as if it were any other asset within the charge to corporation tax on capital gains. This is to explained in paragraph 75.3.2.

- **Accounting period :** Corporation tax on capital gains is charged by reference to accounting periods of a company, and not by reference to a year of assessment.

Example 336

> Tulip Ltd. makes up its accounts each year to 30 June. In the year ended 30 June 1996 it has the following transactions:
>
> - It disposed of development land on 28 March 1996, and
>
> - it disposed of shares in a subsidiary on 1 January 1996.
>
> Tulip Ltd. is chargeable to capital gains tax in respect of the disposal of development land. That disposal took place in the year of assessment ended 5 April 1996, and the company is chargeable to capital gains tax on that disposal for that year.
>
> It is however chargeable to corporation tax on companies capital gains in respect of its disposal of shares in its subsidiary and those are chargeable for the accounting period ended 30 June 1996, being the accounting period in which the disposal occurred. The consequences as regards tax returns and tax payment are described in paragraph 87.

- The tax treatment of a disposal by a company of **units in a unit trust**, or of a **life assurance policy** differs from that applying to an individual. This is explained in paragraph 35.

Although this list of exceptions is significant, it must be emphasised that fundamentally the calculation of corporation tax on a company's capital gains proceeds as if the tax being computed was capital gains tax, and the provisions of the capital gains tax legislation, and of case law applicable to that legislation apply equally to corporation tax on company's capital gains.

s78

The legislation in the FA82 dealing with the taxation of capital gains included new provisions for applying corporation tax to such gains. The then basic rate of 40% on gains (together with the higher rates of 50% and 60% that applied between 1982/83 and 1986/87) applied to companies as they applied to other persons. Provisions were therefore required to deal with the fact that company gains were effectively chargeable at different rates of tax and at a rate which differs from the standard rate of CT for 1998 was 32%. The rates of CT applying from 1998 to 2003 and later years are set out in the table at the end of this paragraph.

These provisions apply in respect of accounting periods ending after 31 December 1981.

s78   In respect of gains arising in an accounting period ending after 31st
        December 1981, a notional amount of CGT is calculated as if the
        company was within the charge to CGT but subject to the exceptions
        to CGT rules described above. The amount of the notional CGT is
        then grossed up at the rate of CT applying for the period and the
        resulting amount is included in the profits of the company (income
        plus gains) for the period. The effect is to produce a CT liability on
        the gains equal to the notional CGT calculated.

Example 337

Blackboard Limited had the following capital gains in the year ended 31
December 1982.

Gain	Rate of Tax
£1,000	60%
£500	50%
£2,800	40%

The amount to be charged to CT (at a 50% CT rate then applicable) was
calculated as follows:

£1,000	@ 60%	£600
£500	@ 50%	£250
£2,800	@ 40%	£1,120
		£1,970

$$\text{Chargeable to corporation tax } 1{,}970 \times \frac{100}{50} = £3{,}940$$

Corporation tax @ 50% on £3,940   =   £1,970

The rates of tax used above are those applying at the time of the transactions.
The consequences of a change in the rate of CT (or the rate of CGT) is described
in paragraph 72.

At present, the rate of CGT on company chargeable gains is 20%
(gains on development land being charged to CGT and not to CT).

Where a gain chargeable to CT arises to an Irish resident company,
the amount of CGT which would be payable on that gain (as if it
were chargeable to CGT) is calculated. An amount is then included
as part of the company's profits so that when it is charged to CT at
the standard CT rate (or mixture of CT rates which apply to the
accounting periood) will yield the same amount of tax.

Example 337

> *Investments Ltd, an Irish resident company has capital gains of £5,000*
> *(measured under the CGT rules) during its accounting period of 12 months*
> *ended 31st March 1998. The appropriate rate of CGT on those gains is 20%.*
>
> *The CGT which would have been payable had the gains been chargeable to CGT*
> *is £1,000. The amount to be included in the company's profits to be charged @*
> *35%* to yield the same amount of tax is:*

$$£1,000 \ x \quad \frac{100}{35} \qquad\qquad = \qquad\qquad £2,857$$

> *As a check on the result, it can be seen that £2,857 @ 35%* = £1,000.*
>
> ** the CT rate for the 9 months to 31 December 1997 was 36%, and for the 3*
> *months to 31 March 1998 was 32%. The effective rate of CT for the year ended*
> *31 March 98 therefore is 35%.*

The FA98 had the effect of changing the corporation tax rate for the
1998 financial year (i.e - y/e 31 December 1998) from 36% to 32%. It
also reduced the rate of CGT on disposals on or after the 3 December
1997 from 40% to 20%, while retaining a 40% rate in relation to
disposals of development land, and shares deriving their value
therefrom and for material interests in offshore funds. In the
example above all of the gains arose after 3 December 1997, and
accordingly the appropriate Capital Gains Tax rate is 20%. If the
company had been liable to Capital Gains Tax, the resulting charge
would be £1000. However, as the company is liable to corporation
tax, it is necessary to further adjust the chargeable gains figure of
£5000 to a figure which, at the relevant corporation tax rate, would
yield a corporation tax liability of £1000 also.

 Because the accounting period of twelve months ends 31 March
1998 includes nine months of the financial year 1997, and three
months of the financial year 1998, it spans a period to which both the
36% corporations tax rate, and the 32% corporation tax rate had
application. The effective rate of corporation tax applying to the
accounting period is computed as the average (on a time basis) of the
rates which apply. In the example, that amounts to 35%. This
average is applied to adjust the computed amount of chargeable
gains upwards for the purpose of corporation tax, notwithstanding
that the chargeable gains in question arose in the financial year in
which the corporation tax rate was 36% (i.e. 1997).

Example 338

> *The facts are as in **example 337** above save that £3000 of the chargeable gains*
> *arose in June 1997, and £2000 of the chargeable gains arose in February 1998.*
>
> *The CGT which would have been payable had the gains been chargeable to CGT*
> *is:*

£3000 x 40%	*£1200*
£2000 @ 20%	*£ 400*
Total	*£1600*
	====

The amount of chargeable gains to be included in the companies profits for the accounting period is computed in the same manner as in *example 338* above, i.e. by adjusting them by reference to an average corporation tax rate for the accounting period ended 31 March 1998 of 35% (reflecting the fact that a 36% rate applied for nine months, and the 32% rate applied for three months, of the accounting period).

£1600 x 100/35 =	*£4571*

Had any of the gains in the example been in relation to the development land, or shares deriving their value therefrom they would not have been chargeable to corporation tax and would be excluded from the adjustments carried out above.

Example 339

*The facts are as in **example 338** above except that of the £2000 gain which arose in February 1998, £1000 related to a disposal of development land.*

The CGT which would have been payable had the gains been chargeable to CGT is:

£3000 x 40%	*£1200*
£1000 (non development land) @ 20%	*£ 200*
Total	*£1400*
	====

The £1000 gain on development land is ignored for the purpose of this stage of the calculation, as it is chargeable to CGT and not to Corporation Tax.

The adjustment to produce an amount of chargeable gains chargeable to corporation tax at the average applicable rate of 35% is as before.

£1400 x 100/35 =	*£4000*

Corporation tax chargeable on companies capital gains:

£4000 @ 35%	*£1400*

Capital Gains Tax chargeable on the company in respect of disposals of development land

£1000 @ 40%	*£ 400*
Total tax chargeable	*£1800*
	====

FA99 s71 The FA99 set out a schedule of the standard rates of corporation tax which will apply to the financial year 1998 and subsequent years.

s21(1) The rates are set out on the following table:

STANDARD RATES OF CORPORATION TAX

Financial year	Tax Rate
1998	32%
1999	28%
2000	24%
2001	20%
2002	16%
2003 et seq	12.5%

A CT Rate of 25% appliesto certain income from 1/1/2000.

72.2 **Rate of C.T. on Gains – prior to FA 1982.**

s78 Examples of the application of the provisions of s78 to the circumstances that existed prior to the FA82 (when the CGT rate was lower than the standard corporation tax rate) may be found in the 7th edition of this book and are not repeated here as no longer being of current interest.

73   RELIEF FOR LOSSES

73.1 **Broad Outline**

In considering the treatment of losses in corporation tax in respect of a company's capital gains, it is necessary to look at the matter under three headings.

- *Capital losses* arising to the company whose tax is being computed.

- *Trading losses, charges, and management expenses* (if an investment company) arising to the company whose tax is being computed.

- *Losses of other companies in a group* with the company whose losses are being computed.

The relief for losses discussed in this paragraph is solely in the context of corporation tax in respect of a company's capital gains.

As explained in paragraph 6.1 a company is chargeable to capital gains tax (and not corporation tax) on disposals of development land. A non-resident company may find itself chargeable to capital gains tax on the disposal of some assets in the State (e.g. any of the specified Irish assets to the extent not held for the purpose of a

856

branch or agency - see paragraph 3.4) and be chargeable to corporation tax in respect of other gains on branch assets.

The reliefs described below are reliefs only in respect of those gains which are chargeable to corporation tax on companies capital gains. Those reliefs described below are not available against gains which are chargeable to capital gains tax. Similarly, allowable losses arising to a company on the disposal of assets which are within the charge to capital gains tax rather than to corporation tax on companies capital gains, cannot be offset against chargeable gains arising to the company on the disposal of assets which are within the charge to corporation tax on companies capital gains.

The FA99 introduced anti avoidance provisions designed to counter purchase of losses for relief against capital gains. These are described in paragraph 73.3.

73.2

Capital losses of the company

As in the case of capital gains tax, allowable losses for the purposes of corporation tax are calculated in the same manner as are chargeable gains for that purpose. The computation prepared on the occasion of a disposal of an asset will throw up either a chargeable gain, or an allowable loss as the case may be. About the only distinction between the two in terms of computation is that indexation can neither create nor augment an allowable loss, whereas it is fully taken into account in computing a chargeable gain.

Only those losses arising to a company on the disposal of assets at a time when it is within the charge to corporation tax are allowable losses for the purposes of corporation tax on capital gains.

In calculating the notional CGT payable, relevant allowable losses are deductible. Relevant allowable losses for this purpose means:

s78(4)
"Any allowable losses accruing to the company in the accounting period and any allowable losses previously accruing to the company where it has been within the charge to CT so far as they have not been allowed as a deduction from chargeable gains accruing in any previous accounting period".

Example 340

Bells Limited had the following figures in the year ended 31 March 1998.

	£
Gain (pre 3 December 1997)	*500*
Gain (pre 3 December 1997)	*2,000*
Loss	*(1,450)*

The amount to be included for CT purposes at the standard CT rate applicable is calculated as follows:

	£
Total Gains	2,500
Total Loss	(1,450)
	2,050
CGT @ 40%	820

The amount to be included as part of the profit of the company for the year ended 31st March 1998 is calculated as follows:

$$£820 \ x \ \frac{100}{35} \ £2,343$$

The amount of £2,343 is chargeable to CT @ 35% = £820.

The calculation of the 35% CT rate is explained in *example 335.*

Only losses arising on the disposal of assets within the scope of the charge to corporation tax on capital gains are allowable losses. Since the disposal of development land is within the charge to capital gains tax and not that of corporation tax, a loss arising on the disposal of development land by a company is not offsetable or relievable for corporation tax purposes. Similarly, losses accruing to a non resident company on assets outside of Ireland (or on Irish assets not held for the purpose of its branch or agency in Ireland) arise on assets not within the scope of the charge of corporation tax on a company's capital gains, and accordingly may not be offset against or relieved against chargeable gains arising to the company which are within the charge to corporation tax e.g. on assets held for the purpose of its branch or agency in the State.

Example 341

Pierre SA is a French resident company and has a branch in Ireland. It disposes of its head office in Paris at a loss, and of part of its premises in Dublin at a gain.

Pierre SA was chargeable to corporation tax on companies capital gains in respect of its Irish disposal, without relief for the loss arising to it on the disposal of its Paris headquarters, since the latter disposal is not within the charge to corporation tax (Pierre SA being a non-resident company).

Example 342

Pierre SA is a French registered company. It was purchased from its French owners by Dublin Export Holdings Ltd, and Irish resident company on 31st March 1998. The French directors were replaced by Irish directors, and thereafter Pierre SA was resident in Ireland.

On 6th January 1998, it sold its Paris Head Office premises incurring a loss calculated under Irish CGT rules of £10,000. On 1st June 1998 it sold its warehouse at Dieppe and incurred a gain calculated under Irish CGT rules of £8,000.

It is intended that the company will make up its accounts each year to 31st December, commencing with 31st December 1998.

The accounting period of the company under Irish CT rules commences when the company comes within the charge to CT on becoming Irish resident - ie. commences on 31st March 1998, and ends on 31st December 1998.

The gain of £8,000 arises within the period and is within the scope of the charge to CT on gains arising in that accounting period to 31st December 1998.

The loss of £10,000 incurred on the disposal in January 1998 is outside the scope of the charge to CT, as it arose (at that time) to a non-resident company on the disposal of a foreign asset. Accordingly no CGT set off is available for the loss.

73.3   Buying losses: Anti Avoidance

73.3.1   Broad Outline

FA99 s57

The FA99 introduced an additional schedule to the TCA97 - "Schedule 18A", which is designed to counter the buying and selling of capital losses. As explained above, conventional group relief does not exist in relation to capital losses. The capital loss of one member of a group can be availed of in a group context only by other members transferring to the loss member an asset on which it is intended to crystallise a gain. The transfer would be made under group relief (no gain/no loss basis) and the loss company then disposes of the asset to a third party, thus crystallising a gain within the company against which it may offset its losses (group relief is explained in more detail in paragraph 75).

If a company anticipated that a chargeable gain would arise on the disposal of an asset, it might consider the acquisition of another existing company which had unutilised losses in relation to past disposals or which owned assets on whose realisation substantial capital losses could be expected to arise. Once such a company had been acquired, the asset which the group wished to dispose of could then be transferred intra group to the loss company, and be disposed of to a third party by the loss company. If the company had losses forward from previous disposals, those could be offset against the gain arising on the disposal of the asset to a third party. Alternatively, if the company had been acquired while owning an asset on which large uncrystallised losses were anticipated, those losses could be crystallised by disposal of the asset to a third party in the same accounting period. Relief would then be available for those losses.

Sch 18A

TCA97 sch 18A seeks to counter such transactions.

The scheme of Sch 18A may be very broadly described as to *ring fence*

- losses arising before becoming a member of a group, and

- subsequent losses on assets held at the date the company
  became a member of a group, to the extent they relate to the
  period prior to becoming a member,

for relief only against gains arising on the disposal of assets held
when the company became a member of the group, or against assets
held for trading purposes solely, and acquired subsequent to
becoming a member of a group, from an unconnected party. More
simply, pre-entry losses are generally available only against gains on
pre-entry assets and on trade assets acquired from third parties
subsequently.

73.3.2   What is a "pre-entry" loss?

sch 18A   A "pre-entry" loss means
para1(2)

- an allowable loss that accrued to the company prior to becoming
  a member of the relevant group.

  To the extent that the company had crystallised losses not
  previously relieved against gains, at the time it entered into a
  group relationship that loss is a pre entry loss.

- A loss arising on an asset held at the date a company became a
  member of a group even though the loss is crystallised after it
  became a member.

  Such a loss is taken to be the lower of the actual loss arising, or
  the loss that would have arisen had it been disposed of at open
  market value at the date the company entered into the group
  relationship.

Example 343

*Targetco Ltd disposed of a building on 30 June 1999 and realised an allowable
loss of £50,000 on the disposal. On 30 September 1999 it was taken over by
Predator plc. On 31 December 1999 Targetco Ltd disposed of a further property
which it had owned at 30 September 1999 and crystallised an allowable loss of
£60,000. The sales consideration was £140,000, and deductible expenditure
amounted to £200,000. The open market value of the property at 30 September
1999 (the date of the take-over of Targetco Ltd) was £175,000.*

The pre entry loss of Targetco Ltd amounts to

- *£50,000 in relation to 30 June 1999 disposal and*

- *£25,000 in relation to 31 December 1999 disposal.*

*Although a loss of £60,000 accrued on the 31 December 1999 disposal in respect
of an asset held at the date it became a member of the Predator plc group, the pre*

entry portion of the loss is only that part of the loss which would have arisen had the disposal occurred at open market value on 30 September 1999 ie £25,000.

Therefore the total "pre-entry loss" of Targetco Ltd is £75,000 in respect of the two disposals.

Example 344

Assume the same facts as in **example 343** *above, but later on 31 March 2000, Predator plc transferred quoted shares to Targetco Ltd and these were immediately disposed of by Targetco Ltd crystallising a chargeable gain of £100,000. On the same date, Targetco Ltd disposed of a property which it had held at 30 September 1999, realising a chargeable gain of £30,000.*

The total losses available in Targetco (as in **example 343***) are £100,000.*

- *£75,000 of these are pre-entry losses.*

- *£25,000 of those losses are not pre entry losses.*

£30,000 of the pre-entry losses may be offset against the £30,000 gain on the property sold on 30 September 1999 since the property was a pre-entry asset.

The £25,000 of losses which were not pre entry losses may be relieved against part of the £100,000 gain on the disposal of the quoted shares (which were not a pre entry asset but were acquired intra group subsequent to joining the group). Therefore Targetco Ltd will have net chargeable gains of £75,000, all in relation to the quoted shares.

It will also have pre-entry losses carried forward of £45,000.

73.3.3   What relief is available for a pre-entry loss?

73.3.3.1   Introduction

The rules relating to the uses that may be made of a pre-entry loss vary (slightly) depending on whether the loss in question was crystallised prior to becoming a member of the relevant group, or was one which arose subsequent to becoming a member of the group, on the disposal of an asset held at the date of entry. Because the rules are broadly similar in both situations, they are discussed together below.

73.3.3.2   Entry period gain

An accounting period of a company does not necessarily end and a new one commence on the occasion on which it becomes a member of a group. It is therefore possible that an accounting period of a company could include the period in which it was not a member of a group, and a period in which it was a member of a group. Where a company which has become a member of a group, had crystallised a loss

- prior to becoming a member of the group, but

- in the accounting period in which it joined the group,

it may obtain relief for the loss against any gain crystallised in the accounting period, provided the gain was crystallised before it became a group member.

Example 345

ACo has an accounting period ending 31 December 1999. In December 1998 it crystallised an allowable loss of £100,000, for which it was unable to obtain relief at the time as it had no chargeable gains at that time. On the 31 March 1999 it disposed of an asset and crystallised a gain of £50,000. On the 30 June 1999 it was taken over by BCo and thus became a member of a group with BCo. On the 30 September 1999 it crystallised a gain of £75,000.

ACo may utilise its 1998 loss of £100,000 to relieve the gain arising on the disposal on the 31 March 1999, because that gain was crystallised prior to becoming a member of the BCo group, and in the same accounting period as that of which it became such a member.

A Co's right to use its 1998 loss against a chargeable gain which arose on 30 September 1999 would depend on further tests described below. It would not qualify on the basis of the test described above.

There is a second circumstance in which the gain arising in the period in which a company joins a group, but which arose prior to joining the group, may benefit from loss relief in relation to a pre-entry loss. That is where the pre-entry loss arises as a result of the disposal (subsequent to becoming a member of a group but in the same accounting period as that of which the company joined the group) of an asset held at the date of entering the group. In such circumstances, that part of the loss arising on the disposal of the pre-entry asset which was attributable to the pre-entry period may be offset against the gain crystallised prior to becoming a group member, but in the same accounting period as that of which the company became a group member.

Example 346

*The facts are as in **example 345** above except that the disposal on 30 September 1999 yielded a loss of £40,000, all of which was attributable to the pre-entry period, since the market value of the asset on the 30 June 1999 (the date of entry into the group) was the same as that on 30 September 1999, when the actual disposal took place. The loss arising on the 30 September 1999 may be offset against the gain which arose on 31 March 1999.*

It is explained below that in some circumstances a company is treated as owning an asset at the date of entering the group where in fact it did not own that asset and when in fact it was owned by an associated company joining the group on the same occasion. That relaxation of rules does not apply in any circumstances to permit a loss crystallised after joining a group to be offset against a gain crystallised prior to joining a group, where the gain and the loss both arose in the same accounting period.

73.3.3.3   **Pre Entry Asset**

Where a gain arises from the disposal of the asset held by the company on the occasion of becoming a group member, a pre-entry loss on a disposal before becoming a group member may be offset against it.

Similarly where a company, after becoming a group member, disposes of a pre-entry asset at a gain, and a second pre-entry asset at a loss, the portion of the loss relating to the period prior to becoming a group member may be relieved against the gain on the disposal of the other pre-entry asset. In this instance the pre-entry portion of the loss may be off-set against all of the gain arising on the other pre-entry asset, whether it arose

- before joining the group, or

- after joining the group.

The post entry portion of the loss is unrestricted in the ability to avail of loss relief subject to normal rules.

Where two companies were in a group relationship on the occasion on which they became members of another group, any of those companies is entitled (for the purpose of the test outlined above on the use of pre-entry losses) to treat assets held by that other associated company as having been held by it on the date of entry into the new group.

Example 347

> *Dublin Limited owned Kildare Limited and Wicklow Limited as wholly owned subsidiaries. On 30 June 1999 it disposed of them to Kerry Limited with whom they then formed a group.*
>
> *On 29 June 1999 Kildare Limited had disposed of a freehold property at a loss of £100,000. On the 31 July 1999 Wicklow Limited transferred quoted shares to Kildare Limited who disposed of them on the same day, crystallising a gain of £50,000.*
>
> *But for the relaxation of rules above, the pre entry loss on the disposal of the land would not be capable of being offset against the gain arising on the shares. That would be because the shares were not assets held by Kildare Limited at the date it entered the Kerry Limited group. However because at the date it entered the Kerry Limited group, the shares were held by a company which joined the group at the same time as it did, and with which immediately before joining the Kerry Limited Group, it had been a fellow group member, it is entitled to treat those shares as being assets held by itself (Kildare Limited) at the date of entry into the Kerry Limited group.*
>
> *It must be noted that if, instead of transferring the shares from Wicklow Limited to Kildare Limited, Wicklow Limited had disposed of the shares directly to a third party, very different results would follow. As noted previously, there is no group relief in the sense of an ability to surrender capital losses from one company to another. Relief for capital losses can only be obtained by*

transferring assets intra group and crystallising a gain in the same company as that which crystallised a capital loss. Accordingly, while in the example above Kildare Limited is entitled to treat itself as the owner of the shares held by Wicklow Limited for the purposes of determining if there are any restrictions on loss relief, it is nonetheless essential to loss relief that it should be the company which actually disposes of the shares. Therefore the prior intra group transfer from Wicklow Limited to Kildare Limited was necessary for this purpose.

Example 348

Dublin Limited owned Kildare Limited and Wicklow Limited as wholly owned subsidiaries at 30 June 1999. On that date it sold the two companies and they thereupon became members of a group with Kerry Limited. Kildare Limited owned freehold premises in Kildare, and Wicklow Limited owned a farm in Wicklow on 30 June 1999. On 31 July 1999 Kildare Limited sold its freehold property and realised a gain of £300,000. On 31 August 1999 Wicklow Limited transferred its farm to Kildare Limited, which then sold it to a third party on 30 September 1999, realising a loss of £100,000. The market value at 30 September 1999 was unchanged compared to 30 June 1999, so that the loss that would have been realised by a disposal at 30 June 1999 at the then open market value was no different to that actually realised in September 1999.

Notwithstanding the fact that Kildare Limited had not owned the farm of land at the date it became a member of the Kerry Limited group:

- *because the farm of land was then owned by a company with which it had been in a group immediately prior to joining the Kerry Limited group and;*

- *because the two companies joined the Kerry Limited group at the same time.*

it is entitled solely for the purpose of determining whether there is a restriction on loss relief, to treat the farm of land as having been held by it at the moment it entered the Kerry Limited group. Accordingly it is entitled to offset the loss on the farm against the gain on the freehold property.

If the facts were the same as those above, save that Kildare Limited had disposed of the freehold property on 29 June 1999 (immediately before becoming part of the Kerry Limited group) and assuming that its accounting period was the year ended 31 December 1999, it would not have been entitled to relief against the gain on 29 June 1999 on disposal of the freehold property, for the loss crystallised on 30 September 1999 on the farm which had been transferred to it in August 1999. This is because it would now be seeking relief in respect of a gain crystallised prior to becoming a member of the Kerry Group, in respect of a loss crystallised after that date. As noted above, in such a situation it is not entitled to treat itself as the owner at the date of entering the Kerry Limited group, of assets held by another company which moved with it from another group to the Kerry Limited group at the same time.

Example 349

Dublin Limited owned as wholly owned subsidiaries, Kildare Limited, and Wicklow Limited. It sold these two companies on 30 June 1999 to Kerry Limited. Kildare Limited operated a supermarket both before becoming a member of the Kerry Limited group and after. On 31 March 1999 Wicklow Limited had purchased from one of the two co-owners, a half interest of the freehold of the property from which Kildare Limited carried on its trade. On 30 September 1999 it succeeded in purchasing the balance of the freehold from the other co-owner. On the same date it transferred the entire freehold to Kildare Limited.

In any subsequent disposal of the freehold property, Kildare Limited will be treated (for the purpose of determining if there will be any restriction on the offset of pre entry losses against a gain on the disposal of the freehold) as if it had acquired that freehold otherwise than from a group member. The fact that part of the freehold was acquired prior to becoming part of the Kerry Limited group, and part was acquired after becoming a member of the Kerry Limited group, would not affect the matter in any way.

73.3.3.4 **Trading Assets**

A pre-entry loss crystallised before a company became a member of a group may be off-set against a gain on the disposal of an asset acquired after it entered the group (from a person not a member of the group) provided it was used from the date it was acquired onwards solely for the purpose of a trade by the company in question. The trade must be one carried on by the company prior to entering the group and continuously up to the date of disposal of the asset.

Some relaxation of this condition is available in a situation where two companies were themselves in a group relationship at the time they joined the new group. In such a situation, the acquisition of the trade asset (after entry into the new group) by either of the companies will be regarded as an acquisition by the other. This section does not go on to explicitly state that the use of the asset for the purpose of a trade carried on by either of the companies is to be taken to be the use for the purpose of a trade carried on by the other company, but without that assumption, the apparent concession in the legislation would be a bit meaningless.

A loss crystallised after entering the group on a pre-entry asset may be off-set against a gain on the disposal of an asset acquired after joining the group and used from the date of its acquisition solely for trade purposes. Once again, acquisition by one company can be treated as acquisition by another where two companies had a group relationship at the time they joined the new group.

73.3.3.5 **Wide Scope of Restrictions on Loss Relief**

Sch18A Sch 18A has unexpectedly wide application. It

- applies where a company is a member of a group, in relation to losses arising prior to becoming a member of that group, and

- can also apply to a company which at any time has been a group member, notwithstanding it is no longer a group member.

If a company becomes a member of a group for even one day, its pre-entry losses are "pre-entry losses" and restricted, even after it ceases to be a group member. However, Sch 18A, para 6 (described below) can vary this result where an existing group becomes a sub-group within a new group.

Even though the legislation can be seen to be drafted to counter the purchase of loss companies, its effect is not limited to that situation.

Example 348

> *Shop Co owns several shops. On the 30 June 1999 it disposed of one of the shops at a loss. It used the proceeds of sale to capitalise a newly formed subsidiary, New Co. New Co used the proceeds to buy a shop.*

> *Shop Co became a member of a group on the occasion of creating a wholly owned subsidiary. At that moment its loss on the disposal of its shop became a pre-entry loss, and thus restricted. Even if Shop Co now liquidates New Co and thereby ceases to be in a group, it will find that its loss on the sale of the shop remains a pre-entry loss and forever remains restricted as regards its use.*

73.3.3.6   Special rules - identification of assets

Because of the restrictions on the use of pre-entry losses and in particular because such losses can be used against gains arising on the disposal of pre-entry assets, the identification of assets becomes important. The question may arise, as to whether an asset disposed of by a group was or was not the same asset as that held by a loss company at the date of entry to the group.

sch 18A para 1(8)
Assets derived from assets : Sch 18A para 1(8) deals with a situation where the value of an asset is derived in whole or in part from another asset (see a discussion of this concept in another context in paragraph 9.10). The paragraph provides that in such circumstances, if one of the assets would have been a pre-entry asset, both assets may be so treated. The paragraph itself gives the example of a freehold, where a leasehold was held at the date of entering a group, and the freehold of the property was bought out subsequently by the company.

sch 18A para 1(4)
Re-purchased assets : Where an asset was held by a company at the date it became a group member, it will not in all circumstances be a pre-entry asset. An example of where this would not occur is where the company disposed of the asset after entering the group and the disposal was to a non group member. It might seem obvious that if the company has disposed of the asset, it would not thereafter be a pre-entry asset. However the company might re-purchase that asset in which case it would be holding an asset which is the same asset it had held at the time it became a member of the group (notwithstanding that it had not been in its continuous ownership thereafter). Sch 18A (4) deals with this situation and states that the asset, once disposed of outside the group is no longer a pre-entry asset.

Part disposal of asset : Where a capital sum is derived from an asset, that is a part disposal of an asset. A part disposal of an asset is a disposal of the asset. Therefore the rule described above could have harsh consequences. The legislation avoids this by providing that where a company disposes of a pre-entry asset but, despite the disposal, retains an interest in it, that disposal will not cause it to cease to be a pre-entry asset. The most obvious situation that that covers is of course the receipt of a capital sum derived from the asset but it would equally cover any form of part disposal of the asset.

Major change in trade : There is anti avoidance legislation applied where the freedom from restriction on pre entry losses is claimed by reason of the asset on which a gain is realised being a trade asset. Where

- in any period of 3 years

- a company becomes a member of any group of companies: and at any time in that period,

- a major change in the nature or conduct of the trade occurs,

the fact that the company was carrying on the trade prior to becoming a member of its current group, will be disregarded for the purpose of the relaxation of the rules described above. Effectively this means that the relief from restriction on losses in the case of a trade asset acquired from a third party after entering the group is lost.

Revival of neglegible trade : The same result follows where a company joins a group after the scale of its activities in a trade have become small or negligible, and before any considerable revival of the trade. This is not the same as saying that a small trade is disregarded. It is necessary that the trade should have **become** small or negligible. That implies that it was at one time neither small nor negligible but it has subsequently gone into a decline. If this has occurred before it joined its current group, and before the trade having significantly recovered again, the fact that the company carried on the trade prior to becoming a member of the current group is disregarded. Accordingly an asset subsequently acquired from a third party for use in that trade will not be one against which pre entry losses may be utilised, if it is disposed of at a gain.

A major change in the nature or conduct of a trade, as referred to above is defined as being a reference to a major change in the type of property dealt in, services or facilities provided, customer, markets, or in outlets of the trade.

73.3.3.7   **Group Reorganisations**

sch 18A para
1(5)   A company will not be treated as having left one group, and joined
another group, for the purpose of determining whether there are
restrictions on its utilisation of losses, where the transaction that
caused it to become another member of another group was a
disposal of shares or securities in itself, or in another company, and
that disposal was one which the CGT Acts treat as being on a "no
gain/no loss basis."

At first sight, it might be thought that this was a reference to a
situation where a company is taken over by another company, (thus
becoming a member of its group) on a share for share basis.
However a share for share swap is not a disposal on a no gain/no
loss basis, but rather is treated by the CGT Acts as not being a
disposal at all. Accordingly that would not seem to be a situation
covered by this provision.

The most commonly encountered form of disposal which is treated
by the CGT Acts as being on a no gain/no loss basis is of course an
intra group transfer. However, by definition, an intra group transfer
will not result in a company becoming a member of a new group.
Self evidently, it remains a member of the same group both before
and after the transfer of its shares intra group.

It is not easy to see what circumstances this particular provision
relates to in practice.

73.3.3.8   **Change in Identity of Group**

Broadly speaking a group consists of a principal company and its
effective 75% subsidiaries. Where the identity of the principal
company, in relation to 75% subsidiaries changes, then a new group
comes into existence. In consequence the 75% subsidiaries may be
regarded as entering into a new group relationship. This situation
can come about in a number of ways.

Example 351

> *Holdco owns 100% of OperatingCo. Predator plc purchases all the shares in
> Holdco. Whereas OperatingCo was previously in a group which was the group
> of which Holdco was the principal company, it has now entered into a group of
> which Predator plc is the principal company.*

Example 352

> *Joe Smith owns all of the shares in Retail Limited which owns all of the shares in
> Wholesale Limited. Both are trading companies. Joe decides he wants to have a
> holding company over the structure and does a share for share swap with Holdco
> as a result of which Holdco owns all of the shares in Retail Ltd. Wholesale Ltd
> was previously a member of the Retail Ltd group and now becomes a member of
> the Holdco group. Joe Smith remains the ultimate owner.*

Example 353

> *Joe Smith owned all of the shares in Holdco which owned all of the shares in Retailco which owned all of the shares in Wholesaleco. Wholesaleco is a member of the Holdco group. Holdco is liquidated and the shares in Retailco are passed to Joe Smith in specie. Wholesaleco is now a member of the Retailco group.*

Sch18A para6 Sch 18A, para 6, has provisions that deal with the situation where an existing group of companies acquire a new principal company, so as to technically become a new group. In such a situation it provides that the time at which the members of the existing group are deemed to have become "members of the relevant group" is not the time at which they became members of the existing group, but rather the time at which the new principal company became their principal company ie the time at which they became members of the new group of which the new principal company is the head.

There is an exception to the application of para 6 in this way which should be mentioned before the significance of para 6 is explained. The exception is where the new principal company (in the circumstances outlined above where an existing group acquire a new principal company) meets the following conditions:

- It was not a principal company immediately prior to becoming a principal company of the existing group and

- Immediately after it becoming the principal company of the existing group, its assets consisted entirely, or almost entirely of the shares in what was formerly the principal company of the existing group.

Additionally, for the exclusion to apply, there should be no change in the ultimate beneficial ownership of the existing group ie the shareholders of the new principal company must be the same persons as own the shares in the holding company of the existing group prior to the principal company taking it over. A precise example of that particular exclusion from the application of para 6 is to be found in *example 353* above, where Joe Smith owned an existing group, but chose to put in a new holding company over it.

The significance of Sch 18 para 6 is that it changes the time at which various companies are deemed to have become members of a relevant group. Such a change in the time at which they are deemed to have become members changes the time at which a judgment has to be made as to whether losses are pre entry losses, and as to whether assets are pre entry assets. It also changes the time at which a judgment must be made as to whether assets were owned by other companies becoming members of the group on the same occasion.

This is a two edged sword. On the one hand, you have companies which on a previous occasion became members of a group ie of the existing group referred to. On that occasion certain capital losses of those companies may have become pre entry losses and would have become ring fenced. On the same occasion certain assets of those companies would have become pre entry assets entitled to avail of relief from the pre entry losses. Capital losses arising on assets acquired after that existing group was formed are not ring fenced in that fashion. The consequence of existing group joining another group, in circumstances to which para 6 applies is that the previous ring fencing of capital losses is lifted as the date at which one makes the judgment as to whether losses were pre entry losses is now moved forward to the point where the new principal company became the principal company of the group. However, losses that had arisen from assets acquired after the existing group was created would now become pre entry losses (whereas previously they were not). Thus potentially more losses become ring fenced, but the range of assets against which previously ring fenced losses may be offset is also potentially increased. **In effect, earlier ring fences are lifted and replaced by a ring fence determined at a later point in time.** This may either have the effect of permitting previously ring fenced losses to be offset against gains on disposals of certain assets, or it may result in previously "non ring fenced" losses becoming ring fenced. Depending on the circumstances of a particular group, it may be a good thing, or a bad thing.

As explained above, there is an exclusion from the operation of para 6. That exclusion may be broadly described as where a new holding company is inserted over an existing group without a change in the ultimate beneficial ownership. Because of that exclusion, para 6 will not apply to what is probably the most frequent occasion upon which a group acquires a new principal company. It also makes it more difficult to deliberately bring about the operation of para 6 (where it would seem to be beneficial by lifting an earlier ring fence on losses and replacing it with one calculated at a later date). Although more difficult, of course it is not impossible. As explained above, the exclusion from paragraph 6 depends on the new holding company having certain characteristics.

73.4   **Trading losses and other deductions of the company**

s396   Corporation tax is charged on a company's profits, which are comprised of the company's income together with its chargeable gains (excepting those charged to capital gains tax). It is not charged separately on the income, and on the gains, but rather on the aggregate of the two. S396 provides that a company (within the charge to corporation tax) which incurs a loss in a trade in an accounting period may;

- set off the loss against profits of any description in that accounting period. This would include not only all of its income, but also a chargeable gain if the chargeable gain is chargeable to corporation tax and;

- if the company was carrying on the trade in preceding accounting periods ending in a period immediately preceding the accounting period in which the loss arose, against the profits of those accounting periods. Again, that permits offset against both income and chargeable gains of those prior periods. The immediately preceding period is a period equal in length to the accounting period in which the loss arose and immediately prior to it.

Relief is also available for the trading losses against trading income from the same trade in succeeding accounting periods. However trading losses of a company cannot be offset against chargeable gains of that company which arise in a subsequent accounting period.

Example 354

Diversified Ltd. is a resident company. In the accounting period ended 31 December 1995, it incurred a trading loss of £20,000. It had no other transactions. In the succeeding accounting period ending 31 December 1996 it incurred a trading loss of £30,000. It disposed of quoted shares on which a chargeable gain of £15,000 arose, and it disposed of development land on which a chargeable gain of £20,000 arose.

The 1995 trading loss cannot be relieved against any of the chargeable gains (whether on the shares or on the land) because it did not arise in the same period. The trading loss of £30,000 can be offset against the gain on the disposal of shares of £15,000 (to the extent of the gain). However no part of the trading loss in the accounting period ended 31 December 1996 may be offset against the loss arising on the disposal of the development land, since that latter loss is not arising on a transaction which is within the charge to corporation tax on companies capital gains. The company will be chargeable to capital gains tax (for the tax year in which the disposal occurred rather than for the accounting period in which it arose) on that gain.

s83   An investment company resident in the State is entitled to offset expenses of management against its total profits of the same accounting period and that necessarily entitles it to offset those expenses against inter alia chargeable gains in that period. Unlike trading losses, management expenses cannot be carried back for relief to a previous period but they may be carried forward to subsequent periods for offset against the profits of those succeeding accounting periods. This is unlike trading profits, which are restricted in succeeding accounting periods to being relieved against trading income as opposed to all income and chargeable gains.

s243   A company is entitled to offset any charges on income paid by the company in the accounting period (in so far as it is paid out of the company's profits brought into charge to corporation tax) against the total profits of the period as reduced by any other relief from tax other than group relief. This relief entitles a company to offset charges against inter alia capital gains within the charge to corporation tax. The relief is available only so as to offset charges paid in the accounting period against capital gains accruing in that period. Charges paid in prior periods, or subsequent periods, cannot be offset against the capital gain of a period. The right of relief is therefore more restricted than in the case of expenses of management, or trading losses. There is a restriction on the offset of charges made by a company which avails of manufacturing relief.

s420

The topic of computation of management expenses, charges, and trading losses of the company is outside the scope of this work. Further discussion of the topic is to be found in the companion volume *"Corporation Tax"* published by the Institute of Taxation in Ireland.

Certain losses - arising principally from activities which attract the 10% rate of corporation tax and from leasing cannot be set against chargeable gains.

73.5   **Group losses**

Where two companies are in a corporation tax loss group, one company may surrender to the other any trading losses, management expenses, or charges on income, arising to it in an accounting period, insofar as they exceed the company's profits for that accounting period. A group company to whom these are surrendered may offset them against its profits for that accounting period. It may therefore offset them inter alia against capital gains chargeable to corporation tax.

Similarly, any company which is a member of a consortium may surrender its surplus trading losses, management expenses, or charges on income arising in an accounting period to one or more of its consortium members. However the amount which may be surrendered to a consortium member is only that fraction of the amounts which may be surrendered, which is proportionate to the consortium member's shareholding in the company.

s456

Where

- trading losses are incurred by a company from a trade entitled to manufacturing relief, or

- charges on income are paid by such a company,

there are restrictions on its ability to surrender such losses, and on the utilisation of such surrendered losses by a claimant company.

Although losses, management expenses, and charges, may be surrendered from one group or consortium company to another in the same accounting period, this cannot be done in respect of the losses etc. of a company which arose in a prior period, or which arise in a subsequent period to that in which a capital gain arises. In other words, group relief operates to provide relief on a "same period" only basis and does not provide relief against capital gains of a claimant company for the losses etc. of other group members in prior or subsequent periods.

It seems strange that although the trading losses of one group member may be relieved against the capital gains of another group member, the capital losses of a group member may not be relieved against the capital gains of another group member. There is no "group loss relief" for capital losses.

Example 355

Distributor Ltd. is a wholly owned subsidiary of Property Ltd. The companies therefore satisfy the requirement for being in a loss group. Property Ltd. has disposed of a property (not development land) on which a capital gain of £50,000 is crystallised. It has no income or other gains or losses in the accounting period. Distributor Ltd. incurred a trading loss in its wholesale business of £20,000 in that accounting period and also disposed of quoted shares on which a loss of £10,000 arose, in that accounting period.

Distributor Ltd. may surrender its trading loss to Property Ltd. and Property Ltd. may offset that loss against its total profits (in this case represented solely by the capital gain). However Distributor Ltd. may not surrender its capital loss to Property Ltd. nor is there any way in which, given the manner in which the transactions were carried out, that Property Ltd. can obtain relief for the capital loss in Distributor Ltd.

The difficulty that a capital loss cannot be surrendered within a group is usually overcome by ensuring that where an asset is to be disposed of by a group at a gain and another group member has capital losses (whether in a previous period or in the same period) available for relief, the asset to be disposed of is first transferred intra group to the company with the available losses (prior to an unconditional contract for sale to another party being entered into) and is then disposed of by that company to the third party purchaser. In that way the gain crystallises in the company which has the losses available for relief.

Example 356

Property Ltd. and Distributor Ltd. are the companies described in the example above. The facts are the same as in the example above except that Property Ltd. did not dispose of its property directly to a third party. Instead, once a likely purchaser had been identified it transferred the property to Distributor Ltd. Since this transfer took place within a capital gains group, neither a gain nor a loss arose on the transfer. Distributor Ltd. then contracted for the sale of the property to the identified third party purchaser. In consequence Distributor Ltd. who is treated as having acquired the property at the same base cost as it had been acquired by Property Ltd., and with the benefit of the same period of ownership and indexation, crystallises the gain of £50,000. It is able to offset against that gain its trading loss of £20,000, and its capital loss of £10,000.

74   "EXIT CHARGE" ON GOING NON-RESIDENT

74.1   Overview

s627

When a company which is resident in the State becomes non-resident *on or after 21 April 1997*, the company is on that occasion deemed to have disposed of all of its assets at open market value, and to immediately have reacquired them at the same value.

- To the extent that assets are in use in what (immediately after the company becoming non-resident) is a branch operation within the State, this deemed disposal will not take place.

- Any net gain arising to a company by reason of these provisions, and arising in relation to assets not located in Ireland will be treated as not arising until a later date, provided the company and its 75% parent (which must be resident in the State) so elect, and certain conditions are met.

- This "exit charge" does not apply to a company controlled by a company resident in anmd controlled from a country with which Ireland has a tax treaty, but not controlled by Irish residents.

No similar rule deeming a disposal and reacquisition of assets applies on the occasion of a company *becoming resident* in the State. The deemed disposal on the occasion of the company ceasing to be resident in the State could crystallise gains which had accrued to it before it had become resident in the State, in a case where the company was not always so resident.

It would seem that a company would not be able to avail of the benefits of a *double tax agreement* between Ireland and the State to which the company has changed residence, so as to avoid a charge arising under this legislation, since the deemed disposal is deemed to take place immediately prior to the company changing residence. At that point, it would usually not be a resident of the other State for the purposes of the double tax agreement.

Additionally, entitlement to *rollover relief* may be affected by a company becoming non-resident after the disposal of old assets, and before the acquisition of new assets.

A company is resident in the State under Ireland's domestic tax rules if its central management and control is exercised within the State. This *definition of residence* arises from case law, and not as a result of a statutory definition. Additionally a company is resident in the State if registered here unless it falls within several exclusions described in paragraph 101.3.

A company would cease to be resident within the State if central management and control, having been exercised within the State, ceases to be exercised there, and is exercised elsewhere.

"Central management and control" normally refers to the exercise of control by the directors of the company over its affairs, although case law indicates that, depending on the facts of the case, central management and control at the highest level may in some cases be exercised otherwise than by the board of directors. An Irish registered company not managed & controlled in Ireland could cesae to be resident here if, having been treated as being resident by reason of the place of registration, circumstances (e.g. - the residence of those who ultimately control it) changed and it fell within the exclusions described in paragraph 101.3.

s627 S627 provides that where a company which is resident in the State ceases to be so resident, two consequences will follow:

- The company is deemed to dispose of all of its assets immediately prior to becoming non-resident, at open market value, and to immediately reacquire them at that value. This has the consequence of crystallising any gain or losses inherent in these assets, at a time when the company is resident within the State and within the charge to corporation tax on companies capital gains on its world wide assets.

  If the company carries on a trade in the state through a branch or agency immediately after going non-resident, assets situated in the State and used for the purposes of the trade carried on by the branch or agency, or used or held for the purposes of the branch or agency, are not subject to the deemed disposal and reacquisition.

s597 - The company is denied the benefit of rollover relief (s597) in relation to old assets disposed of prior to going non-resident where new assets have not been acquired before going non-resident. This restriction on rollover relief does not apply to assets which, immediately after the company becomes non-resident, are Irish branch assets, as described above in relation to the exception from the deemed disposal rule.

CSA68 s2 As noted above, Irish branch assets are excluded from the disposal and restriction in rollover rules. Such assets generally have to be situated in the State on the occasion of the company going non-resident. An exception to this consists of "exploration or exploitation assets or exploration or exploitation rights". These are deemed to be situated in the State for the purposes of this legislation, whether or not they are so situated at the time the company becomes non-resident. "Exploration or exploitation assets" refers to assets used or intended for use in connection with exploration or exploitation activities, carried on in the State or in an area designated by an order under s.2 of the Continental Shelf Act, 1968.

s27 The occasion of a company ceasing to be resident in the State is the ending of an accounting period of the company. As the deemed disposals referred to above are deemed to take place immediately prior to the company going non-resident, they take place in the accounting period which ends on the occasion of the company going non-resident. This will determine the deadlines for reporting requirements, and payment of tax, in relation to the deemed disposals.

Example 357

> *Holdings Ltd. prepares its accounts annually to 30 June. On 1 October 1997 it changes residence from Ireland to the Isle of Man. It is deemed to dispose of its chargeable assets on that date, crystallising a gain of £100,000.*
>
> *An accounting period ended on 1 October 1997. Preliminary tax in respect of the capital gain (and in respect of other profits for the 3 months accounting period) is due on 1 April 1998 and a CTI return is due no later than 1 July 1998.*

The charge to tax does not apply to a company which is controlled by certain foreign persons resident in a state with which Ireland has a double tax agreement. This exclusion is described in paragraph 74.3.

74.2   **Postponement of charge**

When a company which becomes non-resident is a 75% subsidiary of a resident company (which does not at the same time become non-resident) it is possible to postpone the charge on any gains arising on the deemed disposal of assets by the company going non-resident, at least in relation to assets situated abroad which are used for the purposes of a trade carried on outside the State by the company ceasing to be resident.

For tax purposes the 75% subsidiary is one not less than 75% of whose ordinary share capital is owned directly by the other resident company.

Example 358

> *Company A owns 100% of the ordinary shares of Company B, which in turn owns 100% of the ordinary shares of Company C. All three companies are resident and carry on trades in the State. Company B and Company C simultaneously become non-resident after the directors commence holding their board meetings in the United Kingdom.*
>
> *Company B is capable of availing of the postponement of recognition of a gain on its foreign trading assets (i.e. the gain arising by reason of the deemed disposal on the occasion of going non-resident). It cannot postpone the deemed disposal of its shareholding in company C as that is not a foreign trading asset. Company C is not capable of availing of the postponement because Company C, although is indirectly wholly owned by Company A, is not a company 75% of whose shares are directly held by Company A. Its shares are held directly by Company B, and Company B is ceasing to be resident at the same time. Only companies whose shares are directly held by Company A can avail of the postponement, since Company A is the only company which remains resident.*

Example 359

> Company A owns all of the shares capital of Company B, and of Company C.
>
> The share capital of Company D (a trading company) is owned 50/50 by Company B and by Company C.
>
> All companies are resident in the State until Company D goes non-resident.
>
> Company D cannot avail of the postponement of the recognition of a gain on its foreign trading assets on the occasion of going non-resident since although Company D is indirectly wholly owned by Company A, and although all of its shares are directly held by resident companies, Company B and Company C, it cannot avail of the postponement of recognition of a gain as 75% of its ordinary shares are not directly held by one resident company.

Although the singular can import the plural where the context permits, it would not seem that the reference in the legislation to shares held directly by another company which is resident in the state is capable of applying to shares held directly by two or more companies which are resident in the State. This conclusion would arise because (as explained below) the result of applying the postponement is to shift the liability (should it eventually arise) for the net gain which would crystallise on the company going non-resident, onto the resident company which holds directly 75% of its share capital. There is no provision in the section for apportioning the re-allocation of liability to more than one resident company.

In order that the postponement of the gain arising on the deemed disposal by a company on the occasion of it going non-resident should apply it is necessary that the company which goes non-resident, and the resident parent company should jointly elect, within two years of the occasion of the company going non-resident that the postponement provisions should apply. As noted before, these postponement provisions apply only to assets which are trading assets situated outside the State.

The consequence of an election to have the postponement provisions apply are that:

- Foreign trading assets of a company which goes non-resident are excluded from the deemed disposal provisions on the occasion of going non-resident and accordingly neither a chargeable gain nor an allowable loss arises to the company on that occasion in relation to those assets.

- Instead, the net gain on the foreign assets (i.e. the chargeable gains less allowable losses which would have arisen on the foreign assets had they been deemed to be disposed of on the occasion when the company went non-resident) will be deemed to accrue to the resident parent if at any time in the following 10 years:

  - the parent itself becomes non-resident or;

—it ceases to be a direct holder of 75% of the ordinary shares of the company which has gone non-resident or;

—the company which has gone non-resident disposes of any of the foreign assets in question. In this case only an appropriate proportion of the original net gain is deemed to accrue on the occasion of the disposal of the asset in question.

If none of these three events occur within 10 years of the company going non-resident, no charge in respect of chargeable gains will accrue in relation to the foreign trading assets, by reason of the company having gone non-resident.

If any of the three events occur within a 10 year period, what occurs is that the resident parent is treated as having the net gain (or an appropriate part) accrue to it at that time. It is therefore entitled to the same relief on that occasion as it would in relation to any other chargeable gain accruing to it at the time (e.g. offset of capital losses forward, or offset of non ring fenced trading losses in the same accounting period). The appropriate rate of tax will be that which applies at the time that the gain accrues to the resident parent, and not the rate which would have applied in the case of the company which went non-resident, had the gain accrued at the time it went non-resident.

The resident parent may also avail of allowable losses of the company which went non-resident, to the extent that these have not otherwise been relieved. This is available only against the gain arising to the parent company on the deemed disposal of the foreign trading assets. To obtain relief for non-resident companies allowable losses, it is necessary that the resident parent and the non-resident subsidiary should jointly elect to treat the losses in this way. The joint election must be made within two years of the event giving rise to the crystallisation of the postponed net gain.

The allowable losses of the non-resident company which may be relieved in this fashion are those which arise to it prior to it becoming non-resident, and any allowable losses which arose to it in relation to specified Irish assets (see paragraph 3.4.2) after it had become non-resident, to the extent that they have not otherwise been utilised for relief by the company. This represents a unique example of the surrender of capital losses by one company to another, and the unique form of group relief involving a resident and a non-resident company.

Example 360

Holding Company owns all of the issued share capital of Trading Company. Trading Company owns a shop in Dundalk which it rents out, and shops in which it trades in Enniskillen, in Newry and in Belfast.

It has capital losses forward from previous accounting periods of £30,000. On 30 June 1997 it goes non-resident by commencing to hold its director's meetings in Belfast.

Holding Company and Trading Company jointly elect for the benefits of the postponement provisions, and for relief to be available to Holding Company for the capital losses forward of trading company, to the extent not utilised. The latter election is not made until the occasion of the postponed charge crystallising.

Trading Company is deemed to dispose of its rental shop in Dundalk at open market value, and to immediately reacquire it at the same value on 30 June 1997. It is not deemed to dispose of its shops in Enniskillen, Newry, or Belfast on the occasion of going non-resident. The deemed disposal of the Dundalk premises crystallises a chargeable gain of £20,000 which is offset against part of the capital losses forward.

Two years later Trading Company sells its Enniskillen shop for £300,000. Its open market value at the date it went non-resident was £200,000.

The sale of the shop by Trading Company crystallises part of the postponed net gain for Holding Company. Because only one asset out of several has been disposed of, only part of the gain will crystallise. Had Trading Company disposed of its Northern Ireland shops on the occasion of going non-resident, a gain of £20,000 would have arisen on Enniskillen, a loss of £10,000 on Newry, and a gain of £30,000 would have arisen on Belfast. Accordingly the postponed net gain amounts to £40,000. The proportion of the net gain of £40,000 which must be deemed to have crystallised is the proportion which the gain at the date of going non-resident on the asset disposed of (the Enniskillen shop) bears to the aggregate of all of the postponed gains (£50,000, disregarding the allowable loss). Therefore two fifths of the postponed gain of £40,000 is deemed to crystallise i.e. £16,000. Holding Company is entitled to claim relief against this chargeable gain of £16,000 for the remaining unutilised allowable losses of Trading company i.e. in the amount of £10,000 (the original allowable losses of £30,000 having been partly utilised on the occasion of going non-resident).

If the disposal of Enniskillen had taken place more than 10 years after Trading company having gone non-resident, no part of the postponed gain would crystallise on Holding company.

Unlike in group relief for losses, no provision is made in the section for a payment by the subsidiary which goes non-resident, to the resident parent which agrees to have the potential liability transferred to it.

As noted above, one of the events crystallising the postponed gains is where the resident parent ceases to be a direct holder of 75% of the ordinary shares of the company which has gone non resident. That could occur, for example, if the resident parent transferred the shares in the non resident company to another member of its group resident in Ireland. It would then hold the shares indirectly and no longer hold them directly. Although a transfer within a CGT group does not crystallise any gain on the shares being transferred, it does crystallise the postponed gains in relation to the company whose shares are being transferred.

s623

The occasion upon which a company goes non-resident may also be the occasion upon which it ceases to be a member of a group for the purposes of tax on capital gains. Under s623, a company which leaves the group, if it had received a transfer of assets from other group members in the previous ten years, and still holds those assets at the date it leaves the group, will be deemed to have disposed of those assets immediately after their acquisition at open market value. In the case of a company which goes non-resident and by reason of going non-resident also ceases to be a member of a group, and holds assets on that occasion which it had obtained intra group on a prior occasion, it will be deemed

s627

• under s627 to dispose of its assets at open market value at the date it goes non-resident and

• under s623 to have disposed of the assets obtained in the prior 10 years intra group and still held on the date it leaves the group, at open market value immediately following the acquisition of those assets.

On going non-resident, some assets will therefore be deemed to be disposed of at open market value on two occasions i.e. once immediately after acquisition by an intra group transfer, and once on the occasion of going non-resident.

The exceptions relating to branch trading assets, and the postponement arrangements relating to foreign trading assets apply only to the deemed disposal at the date of going non-resident, under s627, and do not apply to the deemed disposal under s623.

Example 361

Holding Company owns all of the share capital of Company A, and of Company B. All are Irish resident. On 30 June 1994 Company A transferred a rental shop premises in Ireland to Company B. On 30 June 1997 Company B became non-resident. The shop had a base cost to Company A of £100,000; it was worth £200,000 on the occasion of its transfer to Company B; it was worth £250,000 at 30 June 1997.

Indexation and incidental costs are ignored in this example for the sake of simplicity.

By reason of going non-resident and thus leaving a group at 30 June 1997 Company B is deemed to have disposed of the retail premises at 30 June 1994 at open market value at that date. That deemed transfer crystallises a chargeable gain of £100,000. It is also deemed to have disposed of the retail premises at 30 June 1997, at open market value at that date. By reason of the deemed disposal at the prior date, its base cost in the premises for the purposes of the second deemed disposal is £200,000 (open market value at 30 June 1994) and not £100,000, the base cost at which it was transferred from Company A.

The £100,000 chargeable gain is deemed to arise in 1994 accounting period, and tax is calculated by reference to the rate then applying (40%). A £50,000 chargeable gain arises in the accounting period ended 30 June 1997 and is *chargeable by reference to the rate applying to that accounting period (also, as it happens, 40%).*

Had the shop been occupied by Company B for its trade, rather than held as a rental investment, the deemed disposal at 30 June 1997 would not have arisen, since the shop would constitute the assets of an Irish branch once Company B was non-resident. Nonetheless the deemed disposal by reason of s623, at 30 June 1994, would still arise.

Had the shop been occupied by Company B for its trade and been located outside the State, say in Newry, Holding Company and Company B could have elected to postpone recognition of the 30 June 1997 gain, and pass the liability to holding company should it eventually arise in the following 10 year period. But the 30 June 1994 disposal would still be deemed to have occurred.

74.3 **Exclusion for treaty States**

The deemed disposal of assets on the occasion of going non-resident does not apply to certain companies which might be broadly described as controlled by a person resident in a state with which Ireland has a double tax agreement. However not all companies controlled by persons resident in treaty states are excluded.

In order to be excluded from the deemed disposal of assets on the occasion of going non-resident, not less than 90% of the issued share capital of a company must be held by:

— a company not resident in the State and under the control of persons resident in a state with which Ireland has a double tax agreement and not under the control of Irish residents or,

— a person or persons who are directly or indirectly controlled by a company or companies which are themselves not resident in the State, and under the control of a person or persons resident in a treaty stateand not under the control of Irish residents.

Example 362

Seashells Ltd. is an Irish resident company all of whose issued share capital is owned by Pierre, an individual resident in France.

Although Seashells Ltd. is wholly owned by a resident of a treaty state, it is not excluded from the deemed disposal of assets on the occasion of it becoming non-resident. This is because the shares are held directly by an individual i.e. by somebody who is not a company.

Example 363

Seashells Ltd. is an Irish resident company all of whose share capital is owned by Pierre Holdings SA, which in turn is wholly owned by Pierre, an individual resident in France. Pierre Holdings SA is also resident in France.

Should Seashells Ltd. cease to be Irish resident, the deemed disposal of assets under s627 will not occur because at least 90% of its share capital is held by a company controlled by a person resident in a treaty state. This would also be the result if Pierre Holdings SA were resident in the Isle of Man - it is the residence *of Pierre in a treaty state, and the fact that Pierre Holdings SA is **not** resident in Ireland that is relevant.*

Example 364

Seashells Ltd. is an Irish resident company owned by Pierre Holdings Ltd. (an Irish resident company). Pierre Holdings Ltd. is in turn wholly owned by Pierre Holdings SA, a French resident company, which is wholly owned by Pierre, an individual resident in France.

Should Seashells Ltd. cease to be Irish resident it is exempt from the deemed disposal as not less than 90% of its share capital is owned by a person (Pierre Holdings Ltd.) which is in turn controlled by a company resident not resident in the state and controlled in turn by Pierre, who is resident in a treaty state.

It should be noted that the requirement being met in *example 362* is that the person holding the share capital of the Irish company should be controlled by a company or companies resident in a treaty State. It is not necessary that not less than 90% of its share capital should be held by such a treaty State resident company. Where the company going non-resident claims exemption by reason of share capital being owned by a non-resident company controlled by a person resident in a treaty state, it is necessary that not less than 90% of its share capital should be so owned. Where alternatively it claims exemption on the grounds that the person who does hold not less than 90% of its share capital is controlled by a person resident in a treaty state, the person in the treaty state need not necessarily hold 90% of the share capital in the holding company of the company which has gone non-resident. It is sufficient that it controls it.

s432

"Control" has the meaning given by s432, and can be generally taken to be possession as a greater part of the share capital, or voting powers, or entitlement to the greater part of the assets on a winding up. It also extends to a situation where a person exercises or is able to exercise, or is entitled to acquire control, either direct or indirect, over a company's affairs - see paragraph 67.2.1.

It is sufficient that the foreign shareholding company should be controlled by a treaty resident, and not controlled by an Irish resident. It does not matter that the persons controlling the foreign company (which holds shares in the Irish company) may themselves be controlled from a non treaty state; nor does it matter that the foreign company holding shares in the Irish company may be controlled not only by persons resident in a treaty state, but may also be controlled by persons who are not resident in a treaty state, provided they are not resident in Ireland. The definition of "controlled" in s432 is exceedingly wide.

Example 365

Seashells Limited is owned by Seashells BV, a Netherlands company which in turn is owned by Seashell Holdings BV another Netherlands resident company. Seashell Holdings BV is owned by trustees resident in the Isle of Man. Seashells

Limited beats the excluded company test because its shareholder is controlled by a person resident in a treaty state (Seashell Holdings BV). The fact that it is also controlled by an Isle of Man resident trustee is irrelevant.

It is sufficient that the foreign shareholding company should be controlled by a treaty resident, and not controlled by an Irish resident. It does not matter that the persons controlling the foreign company (which holds shares in the Irish company) may themselves be controlled from a non treaty state; nor does it matter that the foreign company holding shares in the Irish company may be controlled not only by persons resident in a treaty state, but may also be controlled by persons who are not resident in a treaty state, provided they are not resident in Ireland. The definition of "controlled" in s432 is exceedingly wide.

Example 366

Seashells Limited is owned by Seashells BV, a Netherlands company which in turn is owned by Seashell Holdings BV another Netherlands resident company. Seashell Holdings BV is owned by trustees resident in the Isle of Man. Seashells Limited beats the excluded company test because its shareholder is controlled by a person resident in a treaty state (Seashell Holdings BV). The fact that it is also controlled by an Isle of Man resident trustee is irrelevant.

The test relating to ownership of share capital is by reference to all of the issued share capital.

Example 367

Seashells Ltd. has 100 £1 ordinary shares in issue, all held by Pierre, an individual resident in France. Pierre Holdings SA, a French resident company wholly owned by Pierre, holds 1,000 £1 preference shares in Seashells Ltd. They are non-voting shares, redeemable at par, and not carrying any right to a dividend.

Notwithstanding that the ordinary shares held by Pierre hold the entire value of the company, and represent the real worth of the company, at least 90% of the issued share capital is held by a company not resident in the treaty state and controlled by a resident of a treaty state and accordingly Seashells Ltd. is exempt from a deemed disposal of its assets on the occasion of it ceasing to be Irish resident.

74.4   ## Collection of tax

Tax on capital gains can arise either to a company which goes non-resident, in respect of the deemed disposal on that occasion of its assets, or on the parent of such a company, in relation to a postponed gain which subsequently crystallises in the 10 year period following the company going non-resident. Those tax liabilities may be collected by the Revenue Commissioners from any person who is a member of the same group as the company liable to the tax, or a controlling director of the company liable to the tax or of a company which controlled that company.

A person can be treated as a group member or controlling director for this purpose if they have been a group member or controlling director during the period of 12 months ending with the time when the gain accrues. As noted in paragraph 74, the gain may accrue either upon the occasion of a company going non-resident, or on a later occasion where an election has been made for postponement of the net gain in relation to foreign trading assets.

The legislation leaves it unclear as to whether it is only group members and controlling directors who have been such throughout the period of 12 months ending with the date the tax accrues, who may be made liable for the tax, or whether it is any company which was a group member at any time in the 12 month period or any person who was, at any time in the 12 month period a controlling director, who may be made liable. The better interpretation seems to be that it extends to any person who was a controlling director, or any company who is a group member, at any time in the 12 months prior to the gain accruing. The ambiguity is important because, if the interpretation suggested is correct, it has serious implications for any sale of a company.

Example 368

Holding Company sells Subsidiary Company to an unconnected individual. Some months later, that individual causes Subsidiary Company to become non resident. Because the company does not have a resident parent, Subsidiary Company cannot elect to postpone any part of the gain even if it had foreign trading assets.

If the Revenue Commissioners are unable to enforce collection of the tax arising on the deemed disposal of assets on the occasion of going non-resident, against Subsidiary Company, they may look to Holding Company, or to any controlling director of Holding Company to collect the tax.

The legislation does grant to the group member or controlling director as the case may be, from whom the tax is collected, a right to recover that tax from the non-resident company or any Irish resident parent (in relation to postponed tax). However that right of recovery may be of theoretical value only in the instance where a subsidiary has been sold by a group. Generally, such a right would not be enforced by foreign courts, since it would be seen as the indirect enforcement of Irish tax liabilities.

The only tax which may be recovered in this fashion by the Revenue Commissioners is the tax on the capital gains arising from the deemed disposal of assets on the occasion of a company going non-resident, or arising from the crystallisation of a postponed gain arising on that occasion. Other tax liabilities of the company which has gone non-resident cannot be recovered from group members or controlling directors under these provisions. Thus unpaid tax on capital gains which had accrued on disposal of assets at a time when a company is resident, cannot be recovered under these provisions from group members or a controlling director, subsequent to the company going non-resident.

The group members or controlling directors from whom the Revenue may seek to collect the tax are not treated as having the gains accruing personally to them. Nor are they made the chargeable persons in relation to the tax. They are simply persons from whom the Revenue may seek payment of a tax which is properly owing by another person. In view of the fact that the right of recovery against the company which is gone non-resident may well be of little practical value, a legislative provision which enables the Revenue to collect one taxpayer's tax liabilities from another person who may no longer have control over that taxpayer may be of doubtful constitutional validity.

s432

A *controlling director* is one who has control of a company within the meaning of s432.

"Control" is defined in that section in quite a wide way and includes possessing:-

- the greater part of the share capital or voting power of a company;

- share capital which will entitle the person to the greater part of distributions;

- rights which would entitled them to the greater part of the surplus assets of the company on a winding up.

This basic definition is widened by treating a person as being entitled to acquire anything which they are entitled to acquire at a future date. Thus if a person has an option to acquires shares, they must for these purposes to treated as the owner of the shares.

The definition is also widened by attributing to a person the rights and powers of any company which he, or he and his associates have control of and also the rights and powers of any associate of his. Thus if Joe Bloggs owns 51% of the voting shares of Holding Company, which in turn owns all of the shares in Subsidiary Company, Joe Bloggs will be treated as controlling Subsidiary Company. If he is also a director of Subsidiary Company, he would be treated for the purposes of the tax recovery legislation as being a controlling director of Subsidiary Company. However if he is not a director of Subsidiary Company, the mere fact that he is treated as controlling it will not be sufficient to expose him to liability in respect of Subsidiary Company's tax liabilities. But "director" is widely defined.

"Associate" means any relative or partner, or any trustee of a settlement in relation to which the individual or any relative of his was a settlor and, if the individual has an interest in shares which are the subject of a trust, or part of the estate of a deceased person, any other person with an interest in the shares. "Relative" means husband, wife, ancestor, lineal descendant, brother or sister.

s116
s433

"Director" is given quite a wide meaning. It includes the meaning in s116(1) and also in s433.

- It includes a member of a board of directors, where the company is managed by the board.

- Where the company is managed by a single director or similar person, that person is a director.

- Where the company is managed by the shareholders, any member is to be treated as a director.

- Any person in accordance with whose directions or instructions the directors of a company are accustomed to act is also treated as a director. However a person is not to be treated as a person in accordance with whose instructions the directors customarily act merely because they act on advice given by him in a professional capacity.

- Any person who, by any means, direct or indirect, and on his own or with one or more associates, is able to control 20% or more of the ordinary share capital of a company, and who engages in the management of the company's trade or business, or of the company, is also treated as a director.

Given the very wide scope given to the meaning of "director", it would seem impossible for any person who is de facto performing the duties of a director, and exercising the rights of a director, to avoid liability merely by avoiding formal membership of the board of directors. In particular, a 20% plus shareholder in a group, or a shareholder whose family together control 20% or more of the shares in a group would find it difficult to prove that he is not a director of every company in the group unless he can demonstrate that he has no involvement whatever in the management of the company or of its trade. Presumably safety could be obtained only by emigrating to Australia!

The definition of "controlling director" is so wide that it is evident that in any situation in which the Revenue Commissioners attempted to apply the section, there will most likely be a large range of persons to whom they might apply for payment of the tax arising by reason of a company becoming non-resident. The section provides no basis for determining which person shall be called upon to pay the tax, nor does it provide a basis for apportioning the tax over several persons. Indeed the section explicitly provides that a notice requiring payment of the tax relates to the entire of the unpaid amount of the tax and therefore apportionment over several persons is impossible. It would therefore seem necessary for the Revenue Commissioners to select, at their absolute discretion, one person from among the potentially many to whom the section could apply, and seek to recover the tax from that person.

Given the possibility, or indeed the probability, that the right of
recovery of tax by a person who has been called upon to pay it,
could prove impossible to exercise against the non-resident company
(which could after all be a foreign registered company also), there
must be doubts as to whether the courts would enforce the
provisions of this section. In the UK Vestey case, the UK House of
Lords found so repugnant the notion that the Inland Revenue in the
UK should be able to apportion at their absolute discretion the
income of a non-resident person over a selected group of resident
persons, that they reversed their prior decision on the interpretation
of the UK equivalent of s806 (transfer of assets abroad). The
constitutional restrictions on taxing powers in the UK are
significantly more lax than they are in Ireland.

In order to seek to collect the tax owing by the non-resident
company from a group member or a controlling director, the tax
must have been outstanding for at least 6 months, and a notice must
be served on the person from whom it is sought to collect the tax
within 3 years of the specified return date for the chargeable period
to which the tax liability relates. In practice that means within 3
years and nine months of the company going non-resident.

The tax which the Revenue Commissioners may seek to collect from
third parties under this section is that tax which would not otherwise
have been payable but for the company going non-resident. The
section does not indicate how this tax is to be computed. Where the
company which went non-resident had chargeable gains which
accrued to it in the accounting period at the end of which it went
non-resident, and also had deemed chargeable gains arising to it on
going non-resident, and had available to it against the totality of its
chargeable gains relief for losses (either capital losses in the same or
prior accounting period, or trading losses in the same period) it
would not be a straight forward matter to calculate what part of the
company's corporation tax in relation to chargeable gains arises by
reason of the deemed disposal of its assets on the occasion of it going
non-resident. It is likely that all reliefs for losses which arose
otherwise than by reason of the deemed disposals on going
non-resident, would be offset against the actual chargeable gains at
the period firstly. Any losses arising out of the deemed disposals
would, for this purpose of determining the tax recoverable from a
third party, be treated as offsettable primarily against the gains
arising on the same deemed disposal. However, that is mere
speculation as the legislation is silent on the matter.

Example 369

> Subsidiary company, which had made up accounts to 31 December 1996, went
> non-resident on 30 June 1997. In that 6 month accounting period allowable
> capital losses of £100,000 accrued to it on disposals. So also did chargeable gains
> of £200,000. At the beginning of the accounting period it had allowable losses

coming forward of £50,000. It incurred a trading loss (non-manufacturing) in the period of £20,000. By reason of the deemed disposal of assets on the occasion of it going non-resident, it realised chargeable gains of £750,000 and allowable losses of £200,000.

Subsidiary Company's computation for the accounting period ended 30 June 1997 would be as follows:

	£
Chargeable gains on actual disposals	200,000
Chargeable gains on deemed disposals	750,000
Allowable losses on actual disposals	(100,000)
Allowable losses on deemed disposals	(200,000)
Net chargeable gains for period	650,000
Less relief for losses forward and trading loss	70,000
Profit for period	580,000
Tax at 40% (ignoring the adjustment for the computation of corporation tax at 36% for simplicity purposes)	232,000

The amount of this liability which may be recovered from one of the group members or controlling directors would be computed as follows:

	£
Profits for accounting period as computed above	580,000
Less chargeable gains on deemed disposals	(750,000)
Add allowable losses on deemed disposal	(200,000)
Adjusted profits	30,000
Tax at 40% (for simplicity ignoring the adjustment to recompute at 36%)	12,000
Tax as calculated above	232,000
Additional tax arising on occasion of going non-resident	220,000
This reconciles as being 40% of the net gain arising on going non-resident i.e	550,000

s623 As stated above, it is only the tax liability on the deemed disposal of assets on the occasion of going non-resident which is recoverable from third parties. Certain other corporation tax liabilities may arise solely by reason of going non-resident. For example, the occasion of going non-resident may be the occasion of a company ceasing to be a member of a group. If it then possessed assets transferred to it intra group in the previous ten years, it is treated under s623, (see paragraph 81) as having disposed of those assets immediately after their acquisition. That deemed disposal could give rise to either gains or allowable losses.

It should be noted that :

- the **deemed disposals** on the occasion of **going non-resident** (arising under s627) occur at the date of going non-resident,

- the *deemed disposals* on the occasion of *leaving a group* (under s623) are deemed to occur immediately after the assets have been transferred intra group, and not at the date of leaving the group, notwithstanding that it is the occasion of leaving the group which triggers the deemed disposal.

"S623 deemed gains" are not recoverable under s627. s623 itself permits certain third parties (principally the former or current holding company of the company which has left a group) to be assessed.

s627   In *Example 359* in paragraph 74.2, the interaction of s623, and s627 in relation to going non-resident, is illustrated. Only the tax on the chargeable gain of £50,000 in that example is recoverable under s627 from controlling directors and group members. The chargeable gain of £100,000 (arising by reason of s623) may be recoverable from certain third parties under s623 - principally the group holding company, but is not recoverable from controlling directors or other group members other than the holding company.

75   RELIEFS - TRANSFERS BETWEEN COMPANIES

75.1   Summary of reliefs:

There are 3 principal reliefs which enable an asset to be transferred between companies without giving rise to a potential charge to tax on a chargeable gain. These are:

- *s615 reconstructions* - see paragraph 75.2,

- transfers within the scope of the *EU mergers directive* - see paragraph 75.3, and

- *group relief* - see paragraph 75.4

The provisions of these reliefs are summarised on the chart below. However, the chart, being only a summary, should be read in the context of the detailed treatment of each relief in the appropriate paragraphs noted above.

RELIEFS FOR TRANSFERS OF ASSETS				
	s615	s617	s631	s632
• Between companies only	yes	yes	yes	yes
• Occasion of transfer	Reconstruction of 2 or more companies /transfer of business/part	None specified	Transfer of trade	no requirement

RELIEFS FOR TRANSFERS OF ASSETS

	s615	s617	s631	s632
• Liabilities transferred as consideration	yes	yes	arguably yes	yes
• Consideration to be received by	not by transferor company other than liabilities taken over	not specified	transferor	not specified
• Clawback of relief	no	If transferee leaves group or becomes non-resident within 6 years	if securities (consideration) disposed of within 6 years	no
• Assets	any	any within charge to CT	any - but must be used for trade in State immediately after transfer	any assets
• Election	none	none	elect out of	none
• Place of incorporation	not specified	not specified	not specified	not specified
• Residence	Both must be resident	Both must be resident but 75% parent can be EU resident	not specified(but must be within charge to CT/CGT on transferred assets)	not specified
• Transferee	other party to reconstruction or amalgamation	Resident company in 75% group	must be within CT/CGT charge re. transferred assets	same as s.631
• Relationship between transferror and transferee	none specified	both resident members of a 75% group	none specified	Transferee must hold 100% of capital securities of transferor
• CT or CGT	CT only (but extends to CGT on development land)	CT only (but extends to CGT on development land)	Both CGT and CT	Both CGT and CT
• Development land	yes	yes	yes	yes

RELIEFS FOR TRANSFERS OF ASSETS				
	s615	s617	s631	s632
• Trading stock	excluded	included but deemed disposed of and reacquired	included	included but deemed disposed of and reacquired.

N.B. - see also s634 - Credit for deferred foreign tax.

Withholding tax requirements may apply even though a relief applies to avoid a gain - see paragraph 94.9

75.2 Transfer of Business on Reconstruction, etc.

75.2.1 Broad Outline

s615

Relief from tax is given where one Irish resident company disposes of a business (or part of it) to another Irish resident company, and the selling company receives no consideration for the disposal other than the acquiring company taking over the liabilities of the business.

The relief which is described in this paragraph is one of three distinct reliefs which enable assets to be transferred from one company to another company without crystallising a capital gain, or a capital loss on the occasion of the transfer.

The best known of these reliefs is of course "group relief". That relief is described in paragraph 75.4. As explained there, the relief is available only where strict conditions relating to shareholding relationships between the two companies are in place.

In contrast, the relief under s615, which is discussed below is available even where the two companies do not have a formal relationship prior to the transaction.

A further form of relief is described in paragraph 75.3 and it is that which is provided through the implementation in Ireland of the European Union Mergers' Directive. It has the particular advantage that unlike group relief, and unlike s615 relief, it is capable of extending to a transfer involving a company which is not resident in Ireland.

75.2.2 Conditions - s615 relief.

1. Both companies must be Irish resident at the time of the transfer.

2. The transfer must take place in the course of the reconstruction of any company or companies, or the amalgamation of any two or more companies.

s615

"Scheme of reconstruction or amalgamation" means a scheme for the reconstruction of any company or companies, or the amalgamation of any two or more companies (see paragraphs 42 to 44).

3. The company disposing of the business must receive no part of the consideration for the disposal other than having its business liabilities taken over by the acquiring company. However, other persons, e.g. the transferor company's shareholders may recieve consideration.

4. The relief does not apply to an asset which:

  • is trading stock of the company making the disposal or

  • will be trading stock of the company acquiring the business.

"Trading stock" means property of any description, whether real (e.g. land) or personal (e.g. intangible assets such as an option) which is either :

— property such as is sold in the ordinary course of the trade in relation to which the expression is used or would be so sold if it were mature or if its manufacture, preparation, or construction were complete, or

— materials such as are used in the manufacture, preparation, or construction of property such as is sold in the ordinary course of the said trade.

It is to be noted that the relief applies on the transfer of a *business* or part of a business. A business is not itself an asset in the ordinary sense of the word but will usually encompass a number of assets. Thus in a business which consists of a shop, the "business" will probably comprise goodwill, premises, fixtures and fittings, and trading stock as well as possibly debtors and cash in hand. It is of course on the disposal of these individual assets (insofar as they are chargeable assets which not all of those listed are) that a chargeable gain would arise and not on the transfer of a business per se. Where the transfer of a business involves the transfer of chargeable assets comprised in the business, then the relief will apply in relation to gains which would otherwise have arisen on the transfer of those assets.

The relief does not apply to the transfer of every asset between two companies. It will apply to the transfer of an asset only if the transfer of the asset is comprised in the transfer of a business or part of a business between the two companies.

Example 370

> *Farm Losses Ltd. is a company which carries on a trade of farming. It has incurred losses and enters into a scheme of reconstruction involving the transfer of its business to New Farms Ltd., in return for shares issued by that company to the shareholders in Farm Losses Ltd. Farm Losses Ltd.'s assets consist of 200 acres of land; farm machinery; and trading stock. Prior to the transfer to New Farms Ltd., Farm Losses Ltd. sold 50 acres of its land to Forestry Ltd., to provide funds with which to pay off its creditors.*

> *Farm Losses Ltd. is treated as transferring its 150 acres (balance of land remaining after the sale to Forestry Ltd)) to New Farms Ltd. on a no gain / no loss basis. No chargeable gain arises on the transfer of trading stock so relief is not necessary, and is excluded by the rules of s615 in any event. The farm machinery (although tangible wasting assets) are chargeable assets by reason of being used for a trade or profession and s615 will apply to treat them as being disposed of on a no gain / no loss basis.*

> *However in relation to the sale of the land to Forestry Ltd., Farm Losses Ltd. cannot avail of s615 relief because the sale of 50 acres does not take place in the context of the transfer of part of the business. It might also be objected that it does not take place in the course of the reconstruction of Farm Losses Ltd., although that point might be more arguable.*

Retirement relief in the UK differs from that in Ireland and involves the concept of the transfer of a business or part of a business. As a result there are several UK court judgements available which distinguish between what constitutes a simple disposal of an asset, as compared to the disposal of an asset in the course of the disposal of a business. The concept of the transfer of a business also arises in the context of value added tax, being a transaction not chargeable to value added tax when it is between two taxable persons. That provision likewise has given rise to litigation in the UK although much of the litigation on this score in the UK has been concerned with the question of whether or not the business is being transferred as a going concern. That later requirement does not arise in the context of s615. A number of the relevant UK cases are referred to in paragraph 75.2.4.

s615   S615 does require that the company transferring the assets in the course of a transfer of a business or part of a business should receive no other consideration for the transfer other than the taking over of all or part of the liabilities of the business. The section does not otherwise explicitly restrict the nature of the consideration which may be given e.g. to the shareholders in the transferor company. However since s615 relief applies only in the case of a scheme of reconstruction or amalgamation, there must be doubt as to whether it would apply where the consideration given to the shareholders in the transferor company was other than shares in the transferee company.

s584
s615   S615 relief is concerned solely with the position of the companies which are parties to the transfer of the business. It is not concerned

with the position of the shareholders in the transferor company. If those shareholders received consideration from the transferee company in return for the business transferred by the transferor company, that would in principle be a capital sum derived by them from their shares in the transferor company, or even conceivably a distribution from that company. Insofar as such consideration constitutes a capital sum, rather than a distribution chargeable to income tax under Sch. F, the shareholder receiving that consideration may be entitled to relief under the reorganisation provisions of s584 (see paragraphs 42 to 44 inclusive).

- **Revenue Commissioners published precedents:**

—In their published precedents the Revenue Commissioners have indicated that *"where a capital distribution is generated purely by an internal group restructuring undertaken for bona fide purposes, no charge under s583 will be imposed"*. Section 583 is the section which deems a disposal of shares where a person becomes entitled to a capital distribution in respect of those shares

FA65 s31
s400

The transfer of a business or part of a business by one company to another company may also have implications for other taxes such as corporation tax on income. That is outside the scope of this book but the reader may wish to refer to s400. There are also stamp duty and capital duty reliefs (e.g. S79, s80, and s119 Stamp Duty Consolidated Act 1999) which may be relevant.

75.2.3   **Operation of Relief**

The relief applies to a transfer by an Irish resident company of all or part of its 'business' to another Irish resident company, insofar as the transfer attracts corporation tax on chargeable gains. This automatically excluded CGT on development land, as such gains were not chargeable to corporation tax until this exclusion from s615 ceased in 1992 (see below).

Subject to the conditions set out above, the relief treats the transfer as being for such a consideration as gives no gain and no loss to the company transferring its assets. This effectively means a transfer at original cost (or 6th April 1974 value if the assets were held then), plus subsequent enhancement expenditure.

The real affect of this relief is to defer any gain arising on the transfer of the business assets, as the acquiring company is treated as if it had acquired the assets at the same date and cost (including enhancement expenditure) as the transferring company.

s633

The relief was extended by s633, as part of the general extension of the rules dealing with amalgamations and mergers in compliance with the European Union mergers directive of 23rd July 1990.

The overall affect of the amendment, is to extend this (s615) relief between Irish resident companies, to include '*development land*'. The disposing company is deemed to dispose of the development land at cost (or 6th April 1974 value if later) plus subsequent enhancement expenditure, and the acquiring company acquires that cost (including enhancement expenditure) and also the same acquisition date as the transferring company, preserving the indexation relief. The amendment dealing with development land applies to transfers made on or after 24 April 1992.

The extension of the relief under s615 to cover development land does not apply where relief under s631 is available — see paragraph 75.3.

s615

The extension of relief under s615 to cover development land applies only where the transfer is effected for bona fide commercial reasons and does not form part of any arrangement for the avoidance of a liability to income tax, corporation tax or capital gains tax. There is no similar requirement or restriction in relation to the operation of s615 relief, otherwise than in the context of development land.

75.2.4   Disposal of Business

The problem of when the disposal of an asset is part of the disposal of a business was considered in the UK case of Wase v Burke, albeit in the context of different UK legislation.

That case concerned a farmer who had decided to discontinue his dairy farming business. He sold his entire dairy herd firstly, and eleven months later sold his milk quota. The question at issue was whether the disposal of the milk quota was in the course of the disposal of a farming business or part of a farming business. The judge quoted from the case of Jarman v Rawlings.

"As regards any individual business asset it will only possible to say that the disposal was a sale of part of a business if all the other sales of other business assets were taken into consideration. (An) auction (of the totality of the asset of a business) could be regarded as a single transaction at least from the vendors point of view and it is to be reminded that it is a disposal that is the subject matter of inquiry and not the consequential acquisition by another party. In my view it is legitimate to have regard to simultaneous disposals entered into of other assets used in the business in assessing whether or not a particular disposal can be categorised as a sale of part of a business. I consider therefore that the sales of cattle between contract (for the sale of land) and completion (of the sale of land) could properly be taken into account by the (appeal) commissioners. Later sales seem to me clearly not evidence which supported the commissioners conclusion that there was here a disposal of part of a business unless there was some connection established at the date of completion of the land transaction which enabled later sales of cattle to be treated as part of the same transaction. The fact

that the cattle were no longer being used by the taxpayer for his dairy farming business would not in my view be a sufficient connection."

s615

Having regard to this quotation, and also other cases, the judge concluded that the disposal of the milk quota could not be related to the earlier disposal of cattle so as to constitute the disposal of the milk quota as being part of the disposal of a business or of part of a business. This case was concerned with UK retirement relief but turned on the interpretation of a similar expression to that which occurs in s615.

S615 refers to "transfer of a business" whereas the UK legislation mentioned above referred to a "disposal of a business". The reference in s615 would therefore seen to imply that not only should the disposals of assets in relation to which the relief is claimed be part of the disposal of a business , but that the transaction should also represent the acquisition of a business. The word "transfer" would seem to imply that what is passed across should be, both before and after the transaction, a business. In contrast, a requirement that it be the disposal of a business would not have required that what is disposed of should have been acquired by somebody else as a business. The UK "retirement relief" cases must be read (in considering s615 relief) with that reservation in mind.

75.2.5   Returns

Where relief is availed of under the 1992 amendment to s615 (in the case of development land) a return must be made to the inspector of taxes by the transferring company within 9 months after the end of that company's accounting period in which the transfer took place.

75.3   EU Mergers Directive - Transfer of Trade

75.3.1   EU Mergers Directive - outline of relief

The European "Mergers" Directive of 23 July 1990 required member states to introduce certain tax reliefs for transfers of assets. The implementation of the Mergers Directive in Ireland can be broadly summarised as:

- Introduction of a new relief in s631, described below, covering transfers of assets from a wholly owned subsidiary to its parent.

- Modifications of group relief (s617) and of s615 CTA 1976 relief to extend them to development land in certain circumstances.

- A credit against Irish tax on capital gains for notional tax arising on the same transfer in another member state of the EU, where that tax is not creditable under a double tax agreement by reason of being deferred and not immediately payable.

75.3.2   **EU mergers directive - relief**

s631   This relief was introduced in s631, in compliance with part of the
European Union 'mergers' directive of 23rd July 1990.

This directive addresses the taxation problems arising out of the lack
of a common taxation system for dealing with mergers, divisions,
transfers of assets and exchanges of shares between companies
located in two or more Member States of the European Union.

Article 1 of the directive states... *'Each Member State **shall** apply this
Directive to mergers, divisions, transfers of assets and exchanges of shares
in which companies from two or more Member States are involved.'*

In broad terms, the *mergers directive* deals with:

Mergers: - whereby one or more companies on being dissolved
without going into liquidation, transfers all its assets and liabilities
to another company in exchange for shares to the shareholders by
the transferor company (10% limit on cash paid) or to its parent
company,

Divisions: - whereby a company on being dissolved without
going into liquidation, transfers all its assets and liabilities to two
or more companies, in exchange for the pro rata issue of shares to
its shareholders by the transferor companies (10% limit on cash
paid).

Transfer of assets: - whereby a company transfers (without being
dissolved) all, or one or more branches of its activity (all assets and
liabilities) to another company in exchange of shares in the
company receiving the transfer.

Exchange of shares: - whereby a company acquires a majority of
the votes on another company in exchange for the issue to the
shareholders in the latter company, of shares in the acquiring
company (10% limit on cash payments).

The CGT issues involved in mergers, divisions and transfers of assets
(as defined for the directive) in broad terms involves the disposal of
the assets of a business (or branch), in exchange for the issue to the
shareholders in the disposing company of shares and debentures in
the acquiring company.

From the point of view of CGT, a number of the issues involved are
already dealt with in existing legislation, but mainly in the context of
a transfer of assets from one Irish resident company to another (see
paragraph 75.2) and transfers between members of an Irish resident
group (see paragraph 75.4). The issues are discussed further in those
paragraphs.

Further provisions were made in the FA92, mainly dealing with
transfers of assets (in exchange for shares) *between companies which*

are not necessarily resident in Ireland nor members of the same group.

The existing relief for company reconstruction and amalgamations, etc. (see Chapter 6) covers a considerable number of issues from the point of view of the share transfers involved.

There are, however, many areas covered by the directive, for which no general or specific relief is yet given in Irish tax law.

s634

S634 provides an overall relief for types of transactions specified in the directive, but which are not specifically covered by the FA92 amendments to the tax law.

The Revenue Commissioners *'may'* give such relief as appears to them to be *'just and reasonable'* for the purpose of giving effect to the provisions of the Directive.

Any application to the Revenue Commissioners for such relief must be made in writing, and be in such form as they may require.

Where a company transfers all or part of a trade carried on by it in Ireland to another company, which uses the assets for the purposes of a trade carried on in Ireland, and the **sole consideration** for the transfer is the issue to the transferring company, of securities in the receiving company, the relief gives a deferral of tax on any gains (it also defers potential losses) which would otherwise arise on the transfer of the assets, by (in effect) treating the transfer as being at 'cost' for CGT purposes.

In many ways it is similar to the relief for a transfer of a trade between two Irish resident companies under s615 (see paragraph 75.2) but makes no distinction between development land and other assets. In this case, although the two companies involved do not have to be resident in Ireland, the receiving company has to be within the charge to corporation tax or CGT immediately after the transfer, or would be chargeable if it then made a disposal of any of the assets transferred.

The term 'company' means 'company from a Member State' within the meaning of Article 3 of the directive.

Article 3 of the Directive (90/434/EEC) of 23 July 1990, defines the term 'company from a Member State' in the following manner:

"(a) takes one of the forms listed in the annex hereto";

The list (in broad terms) contains the forms of legal persons charged to a corporate tax throughout the European Union. In the case of Ireland, the list comprises:

— public companies limited by shares or guarantee,

— private companies limited by shares or guarantee,

     — bodies registered under the Industrial and Provident Societies Acts,

     — building societies registered under the Building Societies Acts.

It is interesting to note that **unlimited companies** are not included on the list for Ireland, although in the case of the UK, the list comprises all companies incorporated under UK law.

(b)   *according to the laws of a Member State is considered to be resident in that State for tax purposes and, under the terms of a double taxation agreement concluded with a third State, is not considered to be resident for tax purposes outside the Community;*

(c)   *moreover, is subject to one of the following taxes, without the possibility of an option or of being exempt....'*

In the case of Ireland and the UK, 'corporation tax' is listed. The equivalent taxes are listed for other countries.

The term 'securities' means both shares (including stock) and debentures.

Where a company only transfers part of its trade, that part is to be treated as a separate trade carried on by the transferring company.

Example 371

Deutsche Diversified GMBH owns two Irish subsidiaries. Hotels Ltd. operates a hotel in Bundoran. Hotels Ltd. has a base cost in all of its trading assets taken together of £100,000. Software Ltd. operates a call centre in Dublin. Deutshce Diversified GMBH receive an offer from Global Holidays Plc to acquire the hotel trade of its Irish subsidiary. The deal is done on the basis of the issue of 1,000 £1 ordinary shares in Global Holidays Plc, and debentures worth £1m, to Hotels Ltd. Global Holidays Plc is UK resident. Software Ltd. agree to sell its trade to its parent company, Deutsche Diversified GMBH, for cash.

S631 will apply to treat Hotels Ltd. as not having made any disposal of its hotel trade or assets. Its base cost for the shares and debentures which it has received will depend on whether or not it disposes of them at any time within a period of six years from the day on which the trade was transferred to Global Holidays Plc. If it disposes of the shares and debentures in that period, any chargeable gains that would have arisen on its disposal of its trade will be deducted from what would otherwise be the base cost of those shares and debentures i.e. their value at the date received. If, however, it does not dispose of the shares and debentures during that six year period, then its base cost in the shares and debentures will be their market value on the day received (or more precisely, the value of the assets which they gave in return for them, which would of course be the same thing).

Global Holidays Plc, however, are treated as receiving the trade and the assets of the trade which it has purchased only at the same base cost as Hotels Ltd. had in those assets. It therefore will have a base cost in all of the acquired assets of only £100,000 notwithstanding that it gave consideration worth approximately £1m for them. This is so whether or not Hotels Ltd. dispose of their shares and debentures in the six year period, so as to effectively have the deferral of CGT on the transfer of the trade clawed back from them.

The sale of the call centre by Software Ltd. to Deutsche Diversified GMBH would not be covered by the relief under s631 since that relief applies only where the consideration consists entirely of shares and debentures. However, s632 will provide relief because the transfer is from a subsidiary to its parent, and the assets in question were in use for the purpose of a trade carried on in the State, both immediately before and immediately after the transfer. Because Deutsche Diversified GMBH is not resident in Ireland, it does not form an effective group with Software Limited, and group relief under Section 617 is therefore not available. Nonetheless, Section 632 applies Section 617 to the transfer so as to give the same relief i.e. group relief on the transfer of the assets. Curiously, Section 623 (company leaving a group) is not applied, however. It is curious that CGT group relief is applied, but the normal clawback on a "group" being broken does not apply.

75.3.3   EU Mergers Directive - method of granting relief

s631(3)   If the transfer of the trade is within the conditions for the relief:

the **transferor company** is treated as:

• not making any disposal of the assets.

This means that no chargeable gains or losses can arise on the actual disposal.

the **receiving company** is treated, as if:

• it had acquired the assets itself, at the same date, and at the same cost as the transferring company, and

• all things done to the assets by the transferring company had been done by the receiving company — e.g. incurring enhancement expenditure.

This has the practical affect of treating the transfer as being made between the companies at 'cost', with the receiving company also acquiring the same acquisition date as the transferor company.

75.3.4   EU Mergers Directive - clawback of relief

s631(4)   If, at any time within **6 years** commencing with the date of the transfer, the transferor company disposes of the securities (received as consideration for the transfer) the cost of those securities is reduced by the deferred gain on the transfer of the assets.

In computing any chargeable gain on the disposal of those securities:

• the aggregate of the chargeable gains less allowable losses which would have been chargeable if there was no relief on the original transfer of the trade assets are apportioned to the securities as a whole, and

- the deductions normally allowed (before indexation) in computing the gain is reduced by the amount of those deferred gains.

If the securities are not all of the same type, the deferred gains are apportioned between the securities in proportion to the respective market values of those securities at the time of their acquisition by that company.

The affect of this is to give a reduced cost for setting against the sale proceeds in computing any gain or loss on the disposal of those securities. It also reduces the cost available for indexation.

The clawback of relief in the 6 year period commencing with the date of transfer can result in a form of double taxation. As noted above, the clawback occurs if the securities received as consideration are disposed of within a 6 year period. In such a case the gain which is deferred during the 6 year period is clawed back. However the branch assets received by the transferee company are treated as having been acquired by it at the same base cost as the transferor company had in those assets. If the transferee company disposes of those assets (at any time) it may suffer a charge to capital gains tax which was deferred on the occasion of their transfer from the transferor company. Although the two charges to tax arise on different companies, the net result, where both the securities issued for the branch assets, and the branch assets, are transferred, is to potentially charge the gain on the transfer of the assets to tax twice.

Example 372

Company A owns shops in several towns in Ireland. It transfers its branch in Ballina to Company B in return for shares issued to it by Company B. The base cost of the branch assets (premises, fixtures and fittings etc.) at the date of the transfer was £100,000. The open market value on that date was £200,000. 4 years later, Company A disposed of the shares for £250,000. Sometime later Company B sold the Ballina shop for £300,000.

For the purpose of simplicity indexation is ignored in this example.

Because Company A disposed of the securities within the 6 year period following the transfer of the branch, the relief granted is withdrawn. The method of withdrawal is to treat Company A as having a base cost in the securities of £100,000, rather than the £200,000 of consideration (the value of the branch) which it gave for the securities. The £100,000 is computed as being the consideration given i.e. - £200,000, less the deferred gain of £100,000. The reduced base cost of £100,000 is eligible for indexation, and the CGT rate applicable to the disposal of the securities is the rate applicable in the year in which the disposal of the securities takes place.

Company B has been treated as acquiring the branch assets at the same base cost as Company A had in those assets. That was the sum of £100,000. That is the case regardless of when Company B disposes of the branch assets. Accordingly Company B has a chargeable gain of £200,000 in respect of the disposal of the branch assets. Of that chargeable gain, £100,000 represents the gain which *accrued during the ownership of the assets by Company A, and which was relieved on the occasion of the transfer to Company B.*

The consequence of the disposal of the securities within a 6 year period by Company A, and the disposal of the branch assets by Company B (regardless of when that occurred) is that the £100,000 of gains deferred/relieved on the occasion of the transfer between Company A and Company B, is effectively taxed twice, once in the hands of Company A, and once in the hands of Company B.

S631 (mergers directive) can apply to a transaction even where other reliefs would otherwise have applied. Where other reliefs would have applied, the application of s631 may be undesirable in view of the "double clawback" potential which the section has. Both the transferor and transferee company may jointly elect that s631 should not apply. The election must be made before the due date for the making of a return of income by the transferring company (Company A in the example above) for the accounting period in which the transfer takes place.

Example 373

*Assume the facts to be the same as in **example 372 Assume however that Company A and Company B are in a group for capital gains tax purposes.***

The transfer of the branch assets from Company A to Company B would take place at the base cost to Company A under the group relief provisions of s617. The application of s631 changes nothing in that regard. However the application of s631 does have the result that if the Company disposes of the securities it received from Company B in return for the branch assets, within a 6 year period, its base cost in those securities is reduced by the amount of the deferred gain on the transfer of the assets. This occurs by reason of s631 solely and would not occur if the transfer were governed solely by s617. In such a case it would clearly be to the advantage of Company A and of Company B to elect out of the application of s631.

s631

It is not known what attitude the Revenue adopt in practice in the case of an intra group transfer which is within the terms of both s617, and of s631, and where an election out of s631 has not been made. It is unfortunate that in the drafting of s631, provision was not made to exclude the application of the section to intra group transfers since its application to such transfers provides no additional relief and involves only the potential clawback of relief. This is all the more strange since s632, which implements other aspects of the mergers directive, makes specific reference to s617 and applies only where s631 would not have application. There may be some implication that s631 would not have application where s617 would otherwise provide relief, but the implication is weak and could not be relied on.

75.3.5   EU Mergers Directive - exclusions from relief

s631(5)   This relief does not apply if immediately after the transfer:

- the assets transferred to the receiving company are not used for the purposes of a trade carried on in Ireland by the receiving company, or

- the receiving company would not be chargeable to corporation tax or CGT on any gains arising on a disposal (assuming there is a disposal) of any of the chargeable assets transferred, or

- any of the assets involved would not be chargeable to corporation tax or CGT in the hands of that receiving company by virtue of the provisions of a double tax treaty.

The relief applies automatically, and does not have to be claimed. However, if both companies involved do not wish to avail of the relief, they may jointly elect for it not to apply, by notice in writing to the Inspector. Such an election must be made on or before the normal tax return date for the transferring company for the accounting period in which the transfer takes place. The companies may prefer to rely on s615 or group relief if available, and therefore may elect not to avail of the "mergers directive" relief.

75.3.6   EU Mergers Directive - anti-avoidance

s635   This relief will not apply unless it is shown that the transfer of the trade is effected for bona fide commercial reasons and does not form part of any arrangement or scheme of which the main purpose (or one of the main purposes) is avoidance of liability to income tax, corporation tax, or CGT.

75.3.7   EU Mergers Directive - returns

s636   Where this relief has affect in relation to any transfer, the transferring company must make a return in the required form to the Inspector within 9 months of the end of the accounting period in which the transfer takes place.

- **Revenue Commissioners - tax briefing**

- In Issue 32 of Tax Briefing, June 1998 the Revenue Commissioners stated that no form has been devised for the purpose of the return required in relation to relief under sections 631 to 634 inclusive. The following details are required however:

  - Name, Country of tax residence and tax reference of the transferor company and also separately of the transferee company.

  - Brief description of the nature, location and value of the assets which are the subject of the transfer

- Identification of the section under which relief applies

- A certificate vouching the quantity and date of payment of tax incurred in another member state and indicating the equivalent amount paid in Irish pounds, or in Euros. This is where credit is being sought for a foreign tax suffered at source in respect of the same transaction, under s643

- Identity of the ultimate group company and its tax residency, whether or not the group parent was involved in the transaction.

The Revenue statement also drew attention to the fact that the 15% withholding tax under s980 may have application to the transaction, where the necessary certificate to pay gross was not issued.

75.4   **Group Relief - post FA99**

75.4.1   **Overview of Group Relief - post FA 99**

Group relief permits an asset to be transferred between members of a group without crystallising a capital gains tax charge on that transfer. The FA99 made important changes to the definition of what constitutes a group for these purposes. Prior to the FA99 a group:

- was confined to Irish resident group companies and

- required only a 75% ordinary share relationship between them. The ordinary shares in question were not necessarily shares having voting rights or much economic value.

The FA99 changed this situation by:

- permitting any EU resident company to be a member of a group (but not necessarily to participate in a transaction attracting group relief) and

- imposed additional requirements for the existence of a group relationship, in terms of percentage of entitlement to assets on a winding up, and entitlement to profits on a distribution.

The FA99 also provided transitional arrangements to deal with companies which either became, or ceased to be, members of a group by reason of the enactment of the FA99.

Notwithstanding these major changes to group relief, it remains important to understand the rules that related to group relief prior to the enactment of the FA99. Those rules will in many instances determine the base cost of assets held by companies, where they acquired them intra group under the old rules. Those rules therefore continue to have relevance to the computation of capital gains in a group situation. A full discussion of the old rules is set out below in paragraph 75.4.5.

Paragraph 75.4.3 below discusses group relief in the context of the definition of a group provided by the Finance Act 1999. In reading that discussion it is important to bear in mind that it is valid only in relation to an acquisition or a disposal which occurred:

— in so far as the inclusion of an EU resident (but not Irish resident) company as a member of a group is concerned, as respects accounting periods ending on or after 1 July 1998 (the legislation is retrospective) and

— as regards the application of asset distribution/profit distribution requirements for a group relationship, as and from 11 February 1999.

There are therefore strictly speaking three distinct phases of group relief:

- accounting periods ending before 1 July 1998: Groups did not include EU resident companies not resident in Ireland, and required only 75% of ordinary shares as a condition for group membership.

- any part of an accounting period ending on or after 1 July 1998 that did not extend beyond 11 February 1999; non Irish resident, EU resident companies could now be a member of a group, but the requirements for group membership are otherwise unchanged.

- transactions from 11 February 1999 onwards: EU resident companies not resident in Ireland may be members of a group, and the group relationship now requires assets entitlement on a winding up/entitlement to profits on a distribution rights as specified.

The discussion below does not deal with the second mentioned period above ie that period which at maximum stretches from 1 July 1997 to 11 February 1999. Rather the discussion will focus on the post 11 February 1999 period.

75.4.2   **Group relief - Companies resident in other EU Member States**

The FA99 amendment which permitted a company not resident in Ireland but resident in another EU member state to be a member of a group for group relief purposes was introduced as a result of a case, known as ICI v Colmer. This originated in the UK, but was referred to the European Court of Justice.

s411   The case of ICI v Colmer concerned the UK equivalent of s411. That relief is an application of group relief to losses. The statutory provisions are not the same provisions as apply for group relief for the purpose of companies capital gains but the provisions are, in material respects, similar to those in s616, where a group is defined for capital gains purposes. The conclusions reached in ICI v Colmer on the interpretation of s411, were they to be accepted by the Irish courts, would be equally applicable to the interpretation of s616.

In ICI v Colmer, ICI was a member of a consortium which owned a holding company. The holding company had several subsidiary trading companies, the majority of which were not resident in the UK, but four of which were. ICI claimed relief in respect of its share of the losses of the UK resident subsidiary trading companies. The Revenue refused relief on the grounds that the company in which ICI had invested was not a holding company within the meaning of the section, since the majority of its subsidiaries were not resident in the UK. The matter turned on the UK equivalent of s411(1)(c) which states inter alia *"references in this and in the following sections of this part to a company apply only to companies resident in the State"*. The UK equivalent of s411(1)(a) stated *"holding company" means a company whose business consists wholly or mainly in the holding of shares and securities of companies which are as 90% subsidiaries, and which are trading companies"*.

The Revenue suggested that the business of the holding company in this case was wholly or mainly the holding of shares and securities of non-resident companies and therefore not of "companies" within the meaning of the section.

The High Court dismissed the Revenue approach. It took the view that the reference in the UK equivalent of sub-section 1 to companies resident in the State did not constitute a definition of "company" but rather indicated to which companies the relieving aspects of the section were to apply - i.e. relief could be surrendered only from a resident company to another resident company but that the section could be interpreted without requiring that references to "company" be taken to be references only to resident companies for other purposes.

The Appeal Court came to a broadly similar conclusion although they did not fully endorse the basis on which the High Court reached the conclusion.

The House of Lords rejected the decision of both the High Court and of the Appeal Court and confirmed the traditional understanding that a group could be constituted only by a resident parent, and resident subsidiaries.

The European Court of Justice ruled

"Article 52 of the Treaty precludes legislation of a member state which, in the case of companies established in that state belonging to a consortium through which they control a holding company, by means of which they

exercise their right to freedom of establishment in order to set up subsidiaries in other member states, makes a particular form of tax relief subject to the requirement that the holding company's business consists wholly or mainly in the holding of shares in subsidiaries which are established in the member state concerned."

The ICI case concerned consortium relief. The implications from the judgment clearly involved other forms of group relief. They made it clear that group relief could not be denied merely because a group member who was not a party to a transfer of assets, or a surrender of losses, was not resident in Ireland (but was resident elsewhere in the EU).

The manner in which the FA99 sought to deal with the implications of the European Court of Justice judgment in the ICI v Colmer case has two controversial features.

- The amendment is stated to be effective only as regards accounting periods ending on or after 1 July 1998. Therefore it has effect as regards transactions occurring at earliest on 1 July 1997. It is arguable that the European Court of Justice decision did no more than to confirm that Ireland's pre FA99 definition of a group was, and had been at all times since we enacted the Capital Gains Tax, in breach of European law. That being the case, it is difficult to see on what basis a definition of a group (in the period prior to 1 July 1997) can be defended, if it has already been held that that definition was, before 1 July 1997, illegal. It is possible that companies who had lodged appeals against assessments relating to transactions prior to 1 July 1997 (if there be such, as may well be the case) may contest this before the courts, with every prospect of success.

- The amendment, while permitting a company resident in an EU member state other than Ireland, to be a member of a group, does not (in the view of the Revenue) permit that company to participate in a transaction which would benefit from group relief. That is so even if the non resident group member is within the charge to Irish corporation tax by reason of having a branch in Ireland. It is not clear that such discrimination against a branch operation (which would appear to be unnecessary for the protection of the Irish tax base since the charge to capital gains tax could easily have been extended to a non resident company on the disposal of assets transferred intra group) would seem to be in conflict with the interpretation of EU law laid down in ICI v Colmer, by the European Court of Justice.

The authors would expect that the European Court of Justice judgment in the case of ICI v Colmer will have implications for future Finance Acts, and that the FA99 is not the last word on the topic.

75.4.3   **Group relief - What constitutes a Group (post FA 99)**

75.4.3.1   **What constitutes a group - overview**

Group relief is expressed by s617 as relating to a situation "where a member of a group of companies disposes of an asset to another member of the group". The essential question in relation to the application of group relief on the transfer of an asset between two companies, is whether the transferor company is "a member of a group of companies" and the transferee company is "another member of that group".

s616

S616 states that a group shall consist of "a principal company and all its effective 75% subsidiaries". It does not state what constitutes a member of a group but it may be reasonably assumed the principal company and each of the "effective 75% subsidiaries" of that company are each of them members of the group, and that no other companies are members of the group. A principal company would be known in common parlance as "a parent company".

In order to be a principal company, or to be an effective 75% subsidiary, and therefore in order to be a member of a group, it is necessary that a company should be resident for tax purposes in a member state of the EU.

Example 374

> *Europa BV is a Netherlands resident company. It has two wholly owned Irish subsidiaries, Ireland 1 Limited and Ireland 2 Limited. All three companies are members of a group as defined in s616. However, as will be discussed later, this does not mean that all three companies are entitled to avail of group relief in relation to transactions between them. It is the view of the Irish Revenue that only Ireland 1 Limited and Ireland 2 Limited may make acquisitions and disposals as between each other, with the benefit of group relief. It is considered that a transaction involving Europa BV will not benefit from group relief, notwithstanding that it is a member of the group.*

S616 provides that, whereas a reference to a company in that section can include an EU resident (but not resident in Ireland) company, in the subsequent sections dealing with group relief (including s617(1) which is the section which actually grants the relief) a reference to a company is a reference solely to an Irish resident company. On the basis of this changing definition of "company" the interpretation of the Revenue Commissioners is that Europa BV can be a member of a group for the purpose of ensuring that its two wholly owned Irish subsidiaries are in a group relationship with each other (which prior to the FA99 extending a group to include Irish non resident but EU resident companies would not have been the case) but that when s617(1) refers to "a member of a group of companies" and to "another member of that group" the reference is solely to an Irish resident company. Thus a non Irish resident of a group is not able to acquire or dispose of an asset with another group member under group relief. This is so even if the non Irish resident company is within the charge to corporation tax by reason of trading in Ireland through a branch or agency.

s617

The interpretation suggested by the Revenue Commissioners for this legislation must be open to some doubt. S617(1), which is the legislation which actually grants group relief, does not make a single explicit reference to a company. As discussed above, what it refers to are " member of a group of companies" and "another member of the group". It is true that a member of a group must of necessity be a company and it may be argued that a reference to a member of a group is therefore an indirect reference to a company. On that basis it would accordingly be argued that in s617(1) a reference to a member of a group is necessarily a reference solely to an Irish resident member of the group. It may however be argued to the contrary, since s617(1) makes no explicit use of the word "company" but rather confines itself to the phrase "member of a group" that it is not a section which contains a reference to a company and accordingly is not a section subject to any constraints as regards application only to Irish resident group members.

As noted previously, if the Revenue interpretation is correct (and it is probably safe to assume that it is) then it may very well be that the section is in conflict with European law. If the Revenue view is not correct, then the legislation as drafted in the FA 99 would have serious deficiencies since the Finance Act very clearly limits the anti-avoidance legislation to transactions involving Irish resident companies only, and would not apply to a transaction involving a non resident group member. In many instances the non resident group member would not in any event be within the charge to tax in Ireland on the disposal by it of an asset transferred from another group member.

In order that a group should exist it is necessary that there should be at least two companies in existence, one of whom is an effective 75% subsidiary of the other. To be an effective 75% subsidiary, it is necessary that:

- the company should be a 75% subsidiary as defined in s9 and

- the parent should be entitled to not less than 75% of profits available for distribution to equity holders and

- the parent should be entitled to not less than 75% of the assets and available to distribution to equity holders on a winding up.

This fairly straight forward rule is subject to two further considerations.

Firstly, where a member of a group has itself got an effective 75% subsidiary, that subsidiary is also a member of the group.

Secondly, s413 to s419 TCA 97 are applied for the purpose of the tests outlined above. s418 provides that in determining how much of the profits, or assets, available for distribution that one company is entitled to in relation to another company, the entitlement can be traced through a chain of companies. Thus if company A is entitled to 50% of the profits of company B, and company B is entitled to 50% of the profits of company C, company A can be treated as entitled to 25% (50% x 50%) of the profits of company C.

s418

The combination of the two rules described above produces some contradictions.

Example 375

If company A owns 75% of the shares of company B, and company B owns 75% of the shares of company C, then (there being only one class of shares in existence in each company) it would follow that company A is not entitled to 75% of the profits of company C according to the tests outlined above. One might therefore conclude that company A and company C would not be in a group together. But they are, because company B is entitled to 75% of the profits of company C, and B and C form a group. But B in turn forms a group with company A and accordingly company A and company C are members of the same group.

There can be circumstances in which the rule in s418 will be important in order to create a group.

Example 376

Company A owns 100% of company B. Company B owns 50% of company C. Company A owns 25% of company C.

In accordance with the definition of "75% subsidiary" in s9, company A is entitled to trace a 75% shareholding in the share capital of company C by indirect means, ie through company B, as well as directly, through its own shareholding. By reason of s418 it is entitled to calculate an entitlement to profits, and to assets on a winding up, by taking into account its proportion of the entitlement of company B, as well as its direct entitlement through its shareholding in company C. Therefore company C is "an effective 75% subsidiary" of company A, notwithstanding that it is not such in regard to company B. All three companies are in a group.

Only EU resident companies can be members of a group. All references to "a company" in s616 (where a group is defined) are confined to an EU resident company. However, references in s9 (where a 75% subsidiary is defined) and in s418 (which provides a "look through" entitlement in calculating the percentage of profits and assets to which a company is entitled) to a company are not confined in that fashion. Therefore it is possible to trace the necessary relationships between EU resident companies through a chain of non EU resident companies.

Example 377

> *The facts are the same as in **example 376** above save that company A is resident in Ireland, company B is resident in the Isle of Man and company C is resident in the UK. Company C will be "an effective 75% subsidiary" of company A, and, since both are EU resident companies, will be in a group with company A. Company A is entitled to trace its percentage of shares held, and entitlement to share of profits and assets on a winding up indirectly through a non EU resident company (company B) notwithstanding that company B cannot be part of the group by reason of not being EU resident.*

> *The fact that company A and company C together constitute a group is of course irrelevant to group relief since group relief will apply to transactions only between Irish resident members of the group and in this case there is only one Irish resident member.*

The three tests which apply to determine whether or not a company is an effective 75% subsidiary of another company are examined separately below.

75.4.3.2   Group relief - 75% Subsidiary (post FA 99)

s9

This expression is defined in s9. A company is a 75% subsidiary of another company *"if and so long as not less than 75% of its ordinary share capital is owned directly or indirectly by that other company"*. It should be noted that "company" in this context can include companies resident outside of Ireland, and outside of the EU. Such companies cannot themselves be a member of a group, but they can be taken into account in determining whether or not a company is a 75% subsidiary of another company.

The test is applied to *"ordinary share capital"*. *"Ordinary share capital"* is defined to mean all the issued share capital of a company *"other than capital the holders whereof have a right to a dividend at a fixed rate, but have no other right to share in the profits of the company"*. Clearly the meaning of *"ordinary share capital"* for this purpose is wider than it would be in its ordinary sense. In fact, it would be unusual to come across share capital which is not ordinary share capital.

In order to be excluded from being ordinary share capital, the share must carry a right to a dividend at a fixed rate. "A right" suggests an entitlement to the dividend and not merely the possibility of receiving one at the discretion of the directors. It is also necessary that the shares should carry no "right" to share further in the profits of the company. That would not seem to refer to a share where the directors may, at their discretion, pay a further dividend to the shareholder.

In the case of Burman v Hedges & Butler Limited advantage was taken of the wide definition of "ordinary share" to construct a group relationship between two companies where there was little or no economic inter relationship. The ordinary shares creating the group relationship were relatively worthless. However that case did not examine the meaning of "ordinary share" in any detail - see paragraph 81.4.

Prior to the FA99 the only requirement that had to be met in order that a group should exist for capital gains tax purposes was that one company should be a 75% subsidiary of another company. In other words, one company had to hold 75% of the "ordinary share capital" of another company. Given the wide meaning of "ordinary share", it was possible to construct such relationships by means of shares that were essentially worthless and without economic significance. That is no longer possible. However, it remains as simple as ever to ensure that the first requirement for a group (post FA99) is met ie that one company is a 75% subsidiary of another.

It is also necessary, in order to meet the test that the ordinary shares held by one company in the other should be beneficially owned by the company holding them. The meaning of beneficial ownership of shares, in the context where the shares were the subject matter of put and call options, was considered in the UK case of Sainsbury v O'Connor. In that case it was held that the existence of put and call options over shares did not deprive the company holding the shares of beneficial ownership of the shares.

The UK case of Salt Shore Mutual Insurance Company Limited v Blair was dealt with by the Special Commissioners in the UK. It concerned the question of whether a company was in a group. This turned on whether or not the company, which was limited by guarantee, had share capital. It is possible for a company limited by guarantee to also have share capital and that principle was not an issue in the case. What was an issue was whether certain rights of the members constituted share capital. The Commissioners concluded that "issued share capital (by whatever name called)" meant such authorised share capital of a company as had been issued, whether or not it was called ordinary share capital, so long as it gave a right to a share in the profits. The Commissioner concluded that the particular facts of that case (which were so unlikely to recur elsewhere as to be not worth recounting) did not lead to the view that the sums paid to the company, and rights held as a result, constituted share capital.

The pre FA 99 definition of 75% subsidiary is set out in paragraph 75.4.5.3.

75.4.3.3   Group relief - profits test (post FA 99)

The second requirement in order that one company should be an effective 75% subsidiary of another is that the parent company should be beneficially entitled to not less than 75% of any profits available for distribution to equity holders of the subsidiary.

As noted above, it is possible that the parent company might hold 75% of the ordinary shares without in fact having any significant entitlements as a result. It would not necessarily follow that because 75% of the ordinary shares are held, that the holder of those shares is entitled to 75% of the profits available for distribution. Shares may be ordinary shares notwithstanding that they have no entitlement to a share in dividends, and there may be another class of shares with a prior right to profits.

s414　　S414 describes how the profits test is to be operated. It requires that one assumes that the total profits of the company in that accounting period were distributed to "equity holders". If the company did not have profits in the accounting period, then it is to be assumed that it had profits of £100, and that they were distributed.

The section provides that the test is to be applied according to the entitlement of the members to a distribution "in money" of the profits. The qualification that the test is by reference to a distribution in money is unlikely to be of relevance in most instances and would probably only have relevance in the unlikely event of some of the shares being entitled to receive a distribution in specie.

As noted, where the company has no profits, profits of precisely £100 are assumed. In such a case, if a class of shares were entitled to the first £1000 of dividends paid in a period (should the directors decide to pay any dividends) and 1% of the total of dividends paid in excess of that amount, such shares would be ordinary shares as defined above. Their actual entitlement to share in profits might be of little value, but against a test of a distribution of only £100 (where a company does not in fact have profits in the period) such shares would meet the 75% test. Equally of course, the existence of such shares could prevent another class of more valuable shares (the "real shares" in the company) from meeting the test.

s418　　S418 provides that a company's entitlement to profits available for distribution can be indirect, and traced through a chain of companies. Thus if company A owns 100% of company B which owns 75% of company C, if there is only one class of shares in each of the companies, company A will be treated as entitled to 75% of the profits of company C, by means of an indirect tracing through company B.

s411　　S411(1)(c) states *"References in this section and in the following sections of this chapter to a company shall apply only to a company which, by virtue of the law of a member state of the European Communities, is resident for the purposes of tax in such a member state."* Some of the sections following s411, as referred to, are applied for the purposes of the profits and assets on distribution tests for CGT group relief. Those sections include s414, and s415. S411 is not explicitly stated to apply for group relief purposes but it does apply for all corporation tax purposes and therefore on balance probably would have application in the interpretation of s414 and s415, as applied to CGT group relief. It is understood that it was not the intention of the Revenue that s411(1)(c) should apply so as to deny to a company the ability to trace entitlement to share of profits on a distribution, or assets on a winding up, through a chain of companies which included companies not resident in the EU. However there is always the risk that in a situation which might be viewed by the Revenue as "abusive" they might take another view of the matter. For that reason it may be prudent to obtain a specific clearance if the point is relevant to a transaction.

Example 378

> Holding Co. is an Irish resident company. It owns IOM Co, an Isle of Man resident company which in turn owns all of the share capital of Holland BV, a Netherlands resident company. Holland BV is a 75% subsidiary of Holding Co. In order that they should be in a group it is necessary that Holding Co should be able to demonstrate its entitlement to 75% of the profits on a distribution, and of the assets on a winding up of Holland BV. It is not entitled to any of these directly since it holds no shares in Holland BV. However it can trace its entitlement indirectly through other companies. The issue therefore is whether IOM Co is a "company" for this purpose. If the meaning of the word "company" is confined to EU resident companies, then a group does not exist. That would be the result of the application of s411(1)(c) to the interpretation of s414 and s415 for the purposes of group relief in relation to capital gains. Provided however the Revenue continue to accept that such a result is unintended, a group would exist between Holding Co and Holland BV. IOM Co would not be a member of that group notwithstanding that it is necessary to take it into account in order to establish the existence of the group.

In order that a group should exist it is necessary that a company claiming to be a parent should be able to trace its entitlement to a 75% share of the profits in a period available for distribution. If a company has two classes of shares, and the directors have discretion to pay a dividend on one class without also paying on the other, or to pay a dividend to the two classes at rates that differ as between the two classes of shares, then if the two classes are each held by different companies, neither company may be in a position to demonstrate that on a distribution of the profits it would receive 75% of those profits.

Example 379

> Holdco holds £1m £1 A Ordinary shares in Subco. Otherco has 1,000 B Ordinary shares of £1 each in Subco. The B Ordinary shares are redeemable at par at the discretion of the A Ordinary shareholders. The B Ordinary shares carry no votes. The directors have discretion to pay dividends on either class of share at whatever rate they choose.
>
> Although in every economic sense Holdco is the only real owner of Subco, and although Otherco has no significant interest whatever in Subco, it is not possible for Holdco to demonstrate that it has a group relationship with Subco since, the directors having a discretion as to how to pay dividends, it cannot be

demonstrated that if a dividend were paid, it would necessarily go as to 75% to the shares held by Holdco.

Where there are multiple classes of shares in a company, and more than one shareholder, unexpected difficulties can be encountered in establishing the existence of a group.

It should be noted that the test regarding distribution of profit relates to the distribution of the profits for a period to "the equity holders." This is not necessarily the same thing as a distribution to the shareholders.

75.4.3.4   **Group relief - "equity holders" (post FA 99)**

An equity holder is defined as any person

- who owns ordinary shares in the company or

- is a loan creditor of the company in respect of a loan which is not a normal commercial loan. A normal commercial loan is a loan which doesn't carry rights of conversion into shares or securities, or to acquire additional shares or securities; does not carry interest which varies in accordance with the results of the company's business and the value of its assets, or which exceeds a reasonable commercial return; in respect of which the loan creditor is entitled on repayment to an amount that does not exceed the original amount loaned, or to an amount which is reasonably comparable with that generally repayable on a quoted stock. However, s433(6)(b) provides that a bank is not to be deemed to be a loan creditor in respect of any loan capital issued or debt incurred by a company for money loaned by the bank to the company in the ordinary course of the banking business. This exclusion does not apply to all loans made by all financial institutions but only by such institutions as carry on a banking business. In Ireland a banking business may only be carried on by a body licensed by the Central Bank to be a bank.

s130   As can be seen, what might be called "s84 loans", or, in more modern parlance, s130 loans, are treated as equity where not granted by a bank. It therefore follows that any interest payable on those loans, (which may be treated as a distribution under s130, or might be so treated but for the numerous restrictions that now exist on s130) has to be taken into account as if it were a distribution of profits. This is so whether or not the interest in question is in fact treated as a distribution by s130. It therefore follows that the existence of profit participating loans , or other non "normal commercial loans" can have an impact on whether or not a group relationship exists.

Example 380

Holdco owns all of the share capital of Subco. Subco has obtained loans from Venture Capitalco. The interest on those loans varies with the profitability of Subco, and the loans are convertible into shares in Subco in certain circumstances. The total interest entitlement in the year ended 31 December 1999 of the Ventureco loans amounts to £100,000. The total profits available for distribution in that period (treating the interest as being part of that profit and not as an expense) is £200,000.

Holdco and Subco are not in a group because Holdco's entitlement to profits on a distribution of all of those profits to equity holders would amount to only 50% of the profits.

s414 The test is by reference to a hypothetical distribution of the total profits of the company in an accounting period. "Total profits" are not defined for the purpose leaving open the possibility that the reference is to accounting profits, or the possibility that the reference is to profits computed in accordance with the Tax Acts. The fact that the subject matter of discussion is the distribution of profit might be taken to point towards it being a reference to accounting profits (which are the only profits actually distributable). However the section does not actually refer to a distribution of the total profits, but rather to a distribution of an amount equal to the total profits. That would seem to deliberately break the link with accountancy concepts. Since interest on non commercial loans is also treated as an add-back for the purpose of computing that total profit (by implication rather than explicit statement) that also might indicate that we are dealing with tax concepts rather than accounting concepts. On balance the authors believe that total profits is a reference to the profits of the company (its chargeable gains and income) computed in accordance with the Tax Acts but adjusted to take account of interest on non-commercial loans. That latter adjustment is by no means straight forward since some of that interest will have been added back in arriving at profits in accordance with the Tax Acts, and some of it may not have been added back.

The manner in which s414 sets out the profit distribution test also enables one to disregard any Companies Act restrictions that may exist on the distribution of the actual profits of a company in a period. The test is applied by making the assumption that an amount equal to the profits (as calculated above) is in fact distributed. There is therefore no necessity to concern ones self with whether the directors, in the financial circumstances of the company, would have been entitled to declare any dividend. Total insolvency is not an obstacle to the application of the profits test. In extreme circumstances, s414 assumes that profits of £100 have been distributed even where there are no profits, and in the real world, no distribution of profits by the company could conceivably occur.

75.4.3.5   **Group relief - assets on a winding-up test (post FA 99)**

This is the third test which must be met in order that one company should be an effective 75% subsidiary of another company, for the purpose of CGT group relief. The actual test set out in s616 is that the parent should be beneficially entitled to not less than 75% of the assets of the company (the potential subsidiary) available for distribution to its equity holders on a winding-up.

It will be noted that once again the test is by reference to "equity holders". That term has been discussed above and can include certain loan creditors, and not simply shareholders.

s415   S415 provides rules for determining what the amount is that would be available to equity holders on a winding up of the company. The rule appears to produce a somewhat artificial result which could be important in some cases. In s414 the amount available for distribution to equity holders is treated as being the excess of *"the total amount of the assets of the company as shown in the balance sheet - - at the end of the relevant accounting period over the total amount of those of its liabilities as so shown which are not liabilities to equity holders as such"*.

s414   Normally the amount available to equity holders on a winding up would be determined by the value of the assets (which would be realised for the purpose of distributing the proceeds to them). In s414 however our attention is directed not to the value of assets, but to the amount at which they are stated in the balance sheet of the company at the end of the relevant accounting period. That amount might bear no relationship at all to the market value of those assets. It seems fairly clear that while one would expect market value to be the relevant concept in the context of a winding up, it is not what s414 is concerned with. S414 refers to "the total amount of the assets of the company as shown in the balance sheet". The use of "amount" rather than "value" and the reference to the balance sheet, all would seem to point away from any assumption that we take the open market value of assets and restate the balance sheet accordingly. Similarly, no provision is made for taking into account the costs of winding up a company. In some instances (e.g. where large redundancies may be anticipated, or where it may be necessary to break long term commercial contracts) these could be considerable. Rather we are directed to take into account the liabilities shown in the balance sheet at the end of the accounting period. Almost certainly, that balance sheet will have been prepared on a going concern basis and will take no account of liabilities that might arise on a winding up.

The interpretation outlined above (which the authors believe is correct) can produce anomalous results.

Example 381

> *Holdco owns 100% of the share capital of Subco. Subco's sole asset a property which it bought in 1980 for £100,000, which is now worth £5m on the open market. It has a liability in its balance sheet consisting of moneys borrowed from a finance company to acquire the property. This amounts to £50,000. It carries a commercial rate of interest but it entitles its holders to subscribe at par for up to 10% of the share capital of Subco on the repayment of the loan.*
>
> *On a commercial view of matters above, it would be apparent that Holdco is entitled to about 90% of the assets of Subco and one would expect on that basis that it would meet the criteria for a group. However, the loan (being convertible) is part of the equity and the finance company which owns it is an equity holder. As an equity holder, it would receive (using the test in s414) 50% of the assets as disclosed in the balance sheet, on a winding-up. That is because regard has been had to the amount at which those assets are stated in the balance sheet, and not to their market values. Accordingly a group relationship will not exist. Had the loan been from a bank, it would not constitute equity.*

It is of course unlikely that a company would be permitted to produce a balance sheet which fails to periodically revalue its properties. Nonetheless the use of book values rather than market values can produce anomalous situations.

75.4.4   Group relief - anti-avoidance

75.4.4.1   Antiavoidance - broad outline

S416 and s417 TCA 1997 apply, in determining whether one company is an effective 75% subsidiary of another. Their purpose appears to be to defeat any manipulation of share or loan rights which would otherwise assist in ensuring that the entitlement to profits and entitlement to assets tests are met.

The anti avoidance deals separately with two possible situations, as described below.

75.4.4.2   Antiavoidance - limited rights to profits or assets

s416

The section provides that if the entitlement to profits, or to assets on a winding up, of an equity holder is limited by reference to some specified amount or amounts, then the entitlement to profits and entitlement to assets tests described above are to be carried out as if that equity holder had waived his rights in relation to the share or security carrying these restricted rights.

Example 382

> *Investment Co Limited have lent money to Propertyco. The interest on the loan is to be 10% of the profits of Propertyco in each year. However, it is provided that the total amount of interest so payable shall not exceed £500,000 in any year.*

> *Investment Co Limited is an equity holder in Propertyco, since it has a "profit participating" loan advanced to it. However its entitlement to share in the profits as equity holder is limited by reference to an amount (£500,000). It would seem that s416 requires that the profit distribution test be applied on the assumption that Investment Co Limited had waived its entitlement to interest.*

Example 383

> *Aco holds all the £1 Ordinary shares in Subco. Bco holds the Preference shares in Subco. The Preference shares do not have a fixed entitlement to a dividend. The directors are entitled to pay a dividend on those shares at their discretion but the total amount of such a dividend in any one year may not exceed £0.5m.*
>
> *The ordinary shares and preference shares in Subco are "ordinary share capital" for the purposes of group relief. (See the definition of ordinary share capital in paragraph 76.4.3.2) Both Aco and Bco are equity holders.*
>
> *Bco's entitlement to share in profits is limited. We must assume, for the purpose of applying the entitlement to profits test, that Bco had waived their entitlement to a dividend in respect of the preference shares. The result would be to make it almost certain that Aco will be a parent of Subco.*

Like many pieces of anti avoidance, it is not always apparent what mischief was in the draftsman's mind when he drafted it. Some of the results of applying the section, as illustrated above, appear to be bizarre.

75.4.4.3   Antiavoidance - variable rights, over a period of time

s417   S417 is concerned with a situation where the entitlement of a shareholder or security holder either to a share of profits, or to assets on a winding up, vary over time. It is concerned with a situation where, although a particular class of shares might be entitled to 75% of the profits available for distribution on a particular date, (thus meeting the profit distribution test), that entitlement might have been very short-lived indeed and perhaps specially designed to meet the test on that date. It may well be that those shares might be entitled to almost none of the profits on almost any other date selected. Its concerns relating to share of assets on a winding up are along similar grounds.

s414   S414, in applying the profit distribution test, assumes a distribution in an accounting period. It does not specify at any particular time in that accounting period. S417, in dealing with rights to a distribution of profits, where the rights vary over time, focuses on variations in the rights such that the rights in one accounting period differ from those in another. Neither s416 nor s417 address the possibility that the rights to profits on a distribution of profits might vary within an accounting period. Bearing in mind that "accounting period" is an artificial tax concept, quite distinct from the more usual "period of account" by which companies tend to regulate their affairs and share rights, it is by no means impossible that a variation in share rights could occur within an accounting period. Such a variation within an accounting period is not explicitly addressed by s417. However, in so far as the rights in a succeeding accounting period differ from the rights at any time in the prior accounting period, it may indirectly address the issue.

S417 requires that the entitlement of an equity holder to profits on a distribution should be calculated firstly as described above, by reference to their entitlement to a share of a distribution in the relevant accounting period. It secondly requires that the same calculation be carried out by reference to any other accounting period (prior accounting period or later accounting period) in which the entitlement to a share of profits may be different. The test as regards profit distribution is then to be applied taking the lower of the two results.

Example 384

New Ventureco was founded in 1985. Holdco applied for £1m of shares (consisting of 1m £1 ordinary shares) and Venture Capitalco took up 500,000 A Ordinary shares of £1 each. The A Ordinary shares were entitled to all distributions of profits in the first five years of the company's existence, and the memorandum and articles of association provided that all profits in that period had to be distributed. They were then entitled to be redeemed at par in 1990. That redemption duly occurred. Holdco is now the sole shareholder in New Ventureco. New Ventureco has no "non commercial loans" and accordingly the only equity holder in it currently is Holdco. It might be thought that Holdco clearly meets the profit distribution test since it is currently entitled to all of the profits available for distribution. If however regard is had to the period between 1985 and 1990, when the A Ordinary share existed, then the Ordinary shares at that time had no entitlement to share in the distribution of profits. Accordingly, s417 requires that we take its current entitlement to profits not at what they are (100%) but at the lower level (0%) that applied up to 1990.

It would seem obvious that the application of s417 as described in this example does not meet any anti-avoidance requirement and is an absurdity.

Example 385

*The facts are as in **example 381** above save that all of the ordinary shares rank pari passu for dividends, but the memorandum and articles required that in the first 5 years all profits should be distributed. The A Ordinary shares were as in example 359 above duly redeemed in 1990.*

It remained the case that in the period 1985 to 1990 Holdco was not entitled to 75% of the profits available for distribution. However arguably s417 does not now have application because it is not by reason of the rights attaching to the ordinary shares held by Holdco that its entitlement to profits (as a percentage) was then less than it currently is. Rather it was simply by reason of a change in the total number of shares in issue, and not by reason of the rights attaching to the shares. Accordingly, s417 would not have application, and Holdco and New Ventureco would be in a group.

In example 384 above, it will be noted that regard has been had to share rights prior to the FA99 coming into operation. Notwithstanding that the profit and asset distribution tests are applied as and from 11 February 1999, there appears to be no restriction on the ability of an anti-avoidance section like s417 to have regard to matters prior to that date, albeit it can only do so in relation to transactions to which group relief is being potentially applied, which are on or after 11 February 1999.

The entitlement to assets on a winding up test is subject to the identical anti avoidance measures which operate in an identical fashion as that described above.

In order that s417 shall apply it is necessary that the variation in entitlement to profits, or assets on a winding up, over a period of time, should be the result of the rights of shares or securities being "of such a nature" that the percentage to which the person is entitled of profits or of assets differs over time. In the asset winding up test, the entitlement could vary over time merely by reason of balance sheet values varying over time. Loan equity holders might be entitled to a high percentage of the balance sheet at a time when those values reflect cost. On a subsequent revaluation reflecting growth in value of assets, the entitlement of the loan creditors might become relatively small, and the entitlement of shareholders might become relatively large.

s417

In the opinion of the authors, notwithstanding that the entitlement to assets on a winding up is determined by the rights attaching to shares and securities, the variation which would occur due to values of assets changing over time, or due to non commercial loans being taken on and redeemed over time would not arise from the nature of the rights attaching to the shares or securities and are not factors which would in themselves trigger s417. That matter is not beyond dispute since s417 is inherently ambiguous. In most instances the entitlement of shareholders or loan holders to profits or assets will depend both on the rights of the shares and securities held by them, and the value of the underlying assets, and not by reason of any one factor only. If however mere changes in balance sheet values were sufficient in themselves to trigger s417, it would introduce an arbitrary element into the interpretation of the section.

S417 goes on to provide that where arrangements exist which could have the effect of changing the entitlement of an equity holder to profits or to assets on a winding up, in a future period, then it is to be assumed in a current period that effect has been given to those arrangements. While one can understand why such a provision might have been inserted in an anti avoidance section, it is also the case that this provision is especially open to manipulation in a tax avoidance situation.

75.4.4.4   **Residence and Groups**

The position regarding residence of a company, and its impact on membership of a group may be summarised as follows:

—*Company resident outside the EU:* Such a company cannot be a member of a group. However it can be taken into account in tracing whether or not one company is entitled indirectly to ordinary shares, or profits available for distribution, or assets on a winding up.

—*EU resident but not resident in Ireland:* Such a company may be a member of a group. For practical purposes the significance of this is confined to a situation where it is the principal company in a group, and its membership is essential in order to bring other Irish resident companies into a group relationship. Such a company may also be "seen through" for the purpose of determining whether another company is entitled to ordinary shares, or income on distribution, or assets on a winding up, of a third company. It cannot be a transferor or a transferee of an asset to which transfer group relief would apply.

—*Irish resident company:* An Irish resident company may be a member of a group, can be a transferor or transferee of an asset in a transaction with another Irish resident group member, and it may avail of group relief on that transaction; and may be seen through for the purpose of determining whether another company is entitled to ordinary shares, profits on distribution, or assets on a winding up, of a third company.

The rules for determining the residence of a company are set out in paragraph 101.

75.4.4.5   **Special Transitional Arrangements (post FA99)**

The FA 99 has inserted two new sections, s623A and s625A, to deal with the fact that the introduction of the new definition of a group may have the effect that a company that was, until 11 February 1999, a member of a group, would cease on 11 February to be treated as a member of a group by reason of failing to meet the new tests for determining membership.

s623

One of the most important consequences of a company ceasing to be a member of a group is that, where it does so while owning an asset transferred to it intra group in the previous 10 years by a group member not ceasing to be a member of the group at the same time, it is deemed to dispose of the asset and reacquire it at open market value immediately following its acquisition intra group. This clawback is discussed in paragraph 81 and arises from s623.

s625A

The effect of s625A is to disregard the introduction of the new group rules solely for this purpose, and to treat the companies, solely in relation to the clawback under s623, as still being members of a group, until such time as they would have ceased to be a member of a group had the old group definitions continued to apply.

s625 S625 has similar "clawback" effects where a company ceases to be a member of a group while owning shares in a subsidiary, which shares were acquired in the course of a reorganisation of the group in a previous 10 years. It too will, on the occasion of the company ceasing to be a member of the group, deem the shares to have been disposed of and reacquired immediately after the reorganisation. S625A in effect ensures that a company leaving a group solely by reason of the introduction of the new definition of group membership, will be treated as still in that group until it would have left the group if the old rule had continued to apply.

Example 386

> *Holdco owned 1,000 A Ordinary shares in Subco. These shares were entitled to no votes, no dividends, and redemption at par on a winding up. B Ordinary shares were held by Realco and consisted of 10 £1 shares.*
>
> *On 1 January 1995 Subco acquired property from Holdco. Group relief would have applied to the transfer because the two companies would be treated (under s616 prior to 11 February 1999) as being in a group. That property is still held by Subco.*
>
> *On 11 February 1999 Subco and Holdco would no longer be in a group because, although Subco remains a 75% subsidiary of Holdco, it is not an effective 75% subsidiary by reason of being unable to meet the distribution of profits, and assets on a winding up tests. Notwithstanding that it has now ceased to be a member of a group with Holdco, s623 has no immediate application by reason of s623A.*
>
> *On 1 January 2000 the shares held by Holdco are redeemed at par. The effect of this transaction is that, had the old group rules which existed prior to 11 February 1999 continued, Subco would cease to be a member of the Holdco group. Accordingly Subco is now treated as having disposed of, and reacquired, at open market value the property on 1 January 1995, ie immediately after it was acquired by it in reality.*
>
> *Had Holdco retained its shares until 2005, a redemption after 10 years had elapsed from the acquisition of the property by Subco would no longer lead to the clawback described.*

75.4.5   What Constitutes a Group? (Pre FA99)

s616 The definition of a Group in the context of CGT pre FA 99 was quite different from that used for the purposes of Group relief for trade losses.

- A principal company and all its 75% subsidiaries formed a Group

- Where a principal company is a member of a Group as being a 75% subsidiary, that Group comprised all its 75% subsidiaries.

75.4.5.1   Definitions (pre FA99)

Company

s616(2)   For the purpose of the relief "company" is defined as:

- a company within the meaning of the Companies Act 1963.

- a company which is constituted under any other Act or charter or letters patent, or (although resident in Ireland) is formed under the law of a country or territory outside Ireland.

s698   - a registered industrial and provident society within the meaning of s698.

- a Building Society incorporated under or by virtue of the Building Societies Act 1989.

Except in the context of the limited relief applying in respect of the attribution of gains of non-resident groups to Irish resident beneficiaries, a non-resident company cannot be a member of a Group. This is discussed further in paragraph 67.3.11.

75.4.5.2   Principal Company

s616(1)   This means a company of which another company is a 75% subsidiary.

75.4.5.3   75% Subsidiary (pre FA 99)

s9   The meaning of a 75% subsidisary has been substantially changed by FA 99. The current (post FA 99) definition is discussed in paragraph 76.4.3.2.

A company is a 75% subsidiary of another if and so long as not less than 75% of its ordinary share capital (see paragraph 76.5) is owned directly or indirectly by that other company.

Example 387   75% Subsidiaries

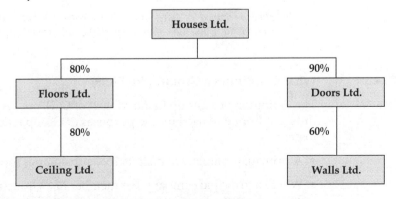

- *Doors Ltd is a 75% subsidiary of Houses Ltd.*

- *Walls Ltd is owned only as to 54% indirectly by Houses Ltd and is therefore not a 75% subsidiary.*

- *Floors Ltd is owned 80% by Houses Ltd and is therefore a 75% of that company. Ceilings is a 75% subsidiary of Floors Ltd which is therefore a principal company in its own right.*

- *Houses Ltd is a principal company as it has 75% subsidiaries. Its group comprises:-*

- *Its own subsidiaries, Floors Ltd and Doors Ltd.*

- *Ceilings Ltd which is included by virtue of the fact that it is a 75% subsidiary of Floors Ltd.*

75.4.5.4   Non-resident structures (pre FA 99)

s590(11)   Generally, a non-resident company cannot be a member of a group for the purposes of group relief pre FA 99. An exception to this rule is made in the context of the limited relief applying in respect of groups of non-resident companies for the purposes of s590.

However, in considering whether a group exists for general purposes it is necessary to examine some of the effects of non-resident companies.

Example 388

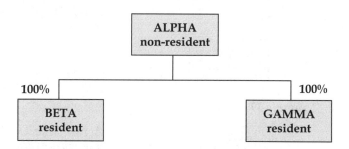

Although Beta and Gamma are Irish resident companies with a 100% relationship, there is no group relationship in this structure as there is no principal company. Alpha, the parent company, is non-resident and therefore cannot be a principal company.

Example 384

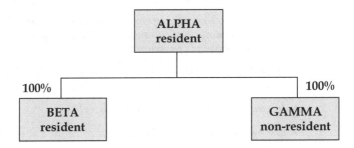

Alpha and Beta constitute a group; Gamma is not a member of the group being non-resident.

Example 389

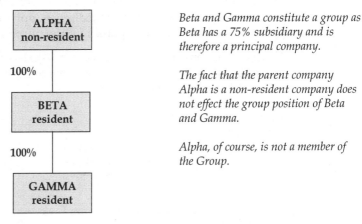

Beta and Gamma constitute a group as Beta has a 75% subsidiary and is therefore a principal company.

The fact that the parent company Alpha is a non-resident company does not effect the group position of Beta and Gamma.

Alpha, of course, is not a member of the Group.

Example 390

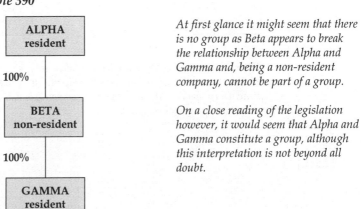

At first glance it might seem that there is no group as Beta appears to break the relationship between Alpha and Gamma and, being a non-resident company, cannot be part of a group.

On a close reading of the legislation however, it would seem that Alpha and Gamma constitute a group, although this interpretation is not beyond all doubt.

This interpretation is based on the following reasoning:

• References to a company for the purposes of the various sections of TCA97 s411 et seq dealing with group relief (on chargeable gains) apply only to a resident company. There is an exception to this rule for the purposes of the limited relief supplied to non-resident groups.

- By reason of this limitation, it is clear that a non-resident company cannot be a member of a group for ordinary relief purposes.

s411

- The question of whether a principal company has a 75% subsidiary is decided not under the provisions of s411 et seq but under s9. It is therefore possible to conclude that, in determining whether a principal company has a 75% subsidiary, shares held through non-resident companies should be taken into account.

s9

- The alternative argument is that s9 must be read in the context of the general provisions of s411 et seq so that the 'company' in s9 means resident company. It is felt that this argument has serious flaws. Also, in this context it is important to note that for group relief applicable to losses etc., the structure of the legislation is different. For the purposes of that relief, also, references to a company apply to a resident company only; but further, in determining the questions of principal company and 75% subsidiary, it is specifically stated that a company will be treated as not being the owner of any share capital which is owned directly or indirectly by a company not resident in the state.

Doubt has been cast on the analysis given above of the application of group relief by two cases, neither of them Irish.

- **Revenue Commissioners published precedent :**

— In their published precedents the Revenue Commissioners have stated *"Under s617 certain assets can be transferred within a capital gains tax group without a chargeable gain arising. Instead, the transferee company takes the asset at the same time and cost at which it was originally acquired by the transferor company. The definition of a capital gains tax group in s616 confines this relief to such group companies where both companies are resident in the State. In practice Revenue will allow similar relief in circumstances involving transfers within a non-resident CGT group where assets are transferred as part of a transfer of trade carried on in the State where profits of the trade, including chargeable gains, are chargeable to corporation tax. The assets must be in use for the purposes of the trade and there must be no discontinuance of the trade, ie the transferee will continue to carry on the trade. The transfer must also be for bona fide commercial reasons and not to avoid tax. To avail of this treatment a formal submission must be made to the Technical Services (CGT) Area of the Office of the Chief Inspector of Taxes. This will involve formal undertakings from the transferee and the group parent in relation to the asset transferred."*

It is to be noted that the concession as published relates only to a transfer of an asset in the course of the transfer of a trade or part of a trade. The concession does not go much beyond the relief provided by s631 (see paragraph 75.3) except that it is not confined to companies resident in the EU.

75.4.5.5   Ordinary Share Capital

This means all issued capital other than that where the holders have a right to a dividend at a fixed rate but no other right to share in the profits of the Company. For example, participating preference shares would be regarded as "ordinary share capital".

s616(1)

In applying the definition of 75% subsidiary, any share capital of a registered industrial and provident society will be treated as share capital.

The importance of the wide meaning attached to the term 'Ordinary Shares' was well illustrated in the UK case of Burman v Hedges and Butler Ltd discussed in paragraph 81.4.

75.4.5.6   Company Incorporated Outside Ireland

s616(1)

The terms 'Group' and 'Subsidiary' will be construed with any necessary modifications where applied to a company incorporated under the law of a country outside Ireland.

75.5   Transfers Between Group Member Companies (pre and post FA 99)

75.5.1   Transfers between group companies - outline

s617
s648

Broadly speaking, the effect of the group relief is to ensure that no chargeable gain arises on a transfer of assets between group members. Where an asset is transferred from one group member to another it is deemed to be transferred at a price which ensures that no gain and no loss arises to the company making the disposal.

The relieving provisions did not apply to transfers of development land on or after 28 January 1982 and before 24th April 1992.

s619

s589

For the purposes of the indexation provisions all members of the group are regarded as one person so that the group member acquiring the asset takes over the same base acquisition date as the member from which the asset was acquired. Accordingly, when arriving at the deemed transfer price which would give rise to no gain/no loss for the company making the disposal, indexation is not applied. The anti-avoidance provisions contained in s589 (transfer of assets at undervalue) do NOT apply to a transfer to which these provisions apply (see paragraph 51.3).

Example 391

> HEN LTD acquired an asset in 1971 for £40,000. (MV 6 April 1974 £110,000). In 1976 it had enhancement expenditure of £30,000 on the asset and then sold it to CHICKEN LTD in December 1982 for £30,000 which was its OMV then.
>
> If the two companies were not within the same group, HEN LTD would calculate its gain by deducting from the sale price, the market value at 6 April 1974 and the enhancement expenditure, both figures uplifted by indexation.
>
> However, if they are both members of the same group for CGT purposes, the asset is deemed to be transferred at a figure which give HEN LTD no gain/no loss, i.e. £140,000.

Notwithstanding that a transfer may, by reason of s617, not give rise to a gain or a loss when made between group members, a withholding tax obligation may still exist in the absence of a clearance certificate. This is discussed in paragraph 94.9.

Notwithstanding that a transfer may be within a group and accordingly will not give rise to a gain or loss, it may, if it is a transfer of shares in a company which became subject to an exit charge on going non resident, and postponed that exit charge, be the occasion of crystallising the charge. This is discussed in paragraph 74.2.

75.5.2   Group transfers - indexation

Where a company in a Capital Gains group (see paragraph 75.4) disposes of an asset acquired from another member of the group, indexation is applied as if all members of the group were one person.

Example 392

> James Limited acquired an asset in June 1974 for £20,000. The asset was transferred to Flynn Limited, another company in the CGT group, in 1980 for £75,000. Flynn Limited sold the asset in March 1998 for £175,000.
>
> The amount to be included in the profits of Flynn Limited is calculated as follows:

	£
Consideration received by Flynn Limited	175,000
Cost to James Limited (indexed) £20,000 x 6.112	122,240
Gain	57,760
Notional CGT £82,900 at 20%	16,580

> Chargeable to Corporation tax :

$$£16,580 \ x \ \frac{100}{35} \ = \ £47,371$$

> The CT payable on the gain is £47,371 @ 35% = £16,580

NOTE - the calculation of the 35% CT rate is explained in example 276.

It is important to note that these rules do not apply to gains arising to companies in respect of disposals of development land on or after 28 January 1982. Such gains are chargeable to CGT in the hands of companies and not to CT.

75.6   **State Bodies**

s616(5)   The Group relief provisions apply to bodies established by or under any enactment;

* for the carrying on of any industry or part of an industry, or

* for the carrying on of any undertaking under national ownership or control

as if they were companies as defined and as if such bodies charged with related functions and subsidiaries of any of them formed a Group; and as if two or more such bodies charged at different times with the same or related functions were members of a Group.

These rules have effect subject to any enactment by virtue of which property, rights, liabilities or activities of one such body are to be treated for corporation tax as those of another.

The bodies referred to above are deemed by s616(5) to be companies (within the defined meaning of that expression as set out in paragraph 75.4.3.1). In theory therefore such a body would be able to avail of group relief even if it were not resident in the State. In practice it is unlikely that such a body would be non resident.

The courts have not yet had to consider whether a minister of state together with companies owned by him in that capacity are capable of constituting a group for the purposes of tax on capital gains. A minister is a corporation sole and therefore arguably capable of forming part of a group for corporation tax purposes and indeed, being the principal company of such a group. A minister may well be "a company which is constituted under any other Act", as referred to in the definition of company above.

It may be necessary in each instance to consider whether the Minister is the beneficial owner of the shares in the semi state company, or whether he holds the shares as nominee for the State. In some instances the creation of companies has been governed by specific statutory provisions (other than, or in addition to, the Companies Acts) and such provisions state that the Minister must account to the Central Fund for any dividends received, and for the proceeds of sale of shares. This might indicate that in such cases he is not the beneficial owner of the shares but holds them in some form of trust. The matter is ambiguous.

75.7   **Offshore Group Relief**

As explained in paragraph 75.7 a transfer of an asset between two companies which are in a group relationship does not give rise to a chargeable gain, but is treated as being on a no gain no loss basis. It would seem unfair if a transfer between two companies which, but for the fact that they were non resident, would be treated as being in group relationship would give rise to a tax charge on a resident participator. After all, the tax charge on the resident participator is essentially to provide a "level playing field" between investors in resident companies, and in non resident companies. This is discussed in paragraph 67.3.10.

76   GROUPS, TAKEOVERS, & REORGANISATIONS

76.1   **Group Effects of Takeover**

s616(3)   A Group of companies remains the same Group so long as the same company remains the principal company of the Group. If at any time the principal company becomes a 75% subsidiary of another company, the original Group continues but with the takeover company (or its principal company) being the new principal company.

Example 393   Group Effects of Takeover

Chart A - Before Takeover

X and Y constitute a Group and A, B and C constitute a Group.

Y acquires all the share capital in A.

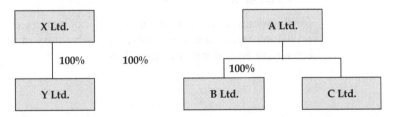

Chart B - After Takeover

After the takeover, there is a new group of 5 companies X, Y, A, B and C.

X as the principal company of that group.

A B and C are deemed not to have left the original A B C Group.

In effect, for this purpose, the old group and the new group are treated as the same - as if all companies were part of the same group.

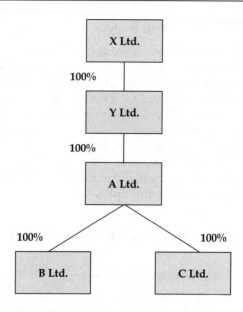

76.2   **Winding up of Group Company**

s616(4)   In deciding whether a Group exists or what companies are members of a group, special rules apply in relation to a company being wound up.

For these purposes:

• the passing of a resolution, or

• the making of an order, or

• any other act

for the winding up of a company shall not be regarded as the occasion of that company or any 75% subsidiary of that company ceasing to be a member of the Group.

Example 394 - General Example of Group Structure

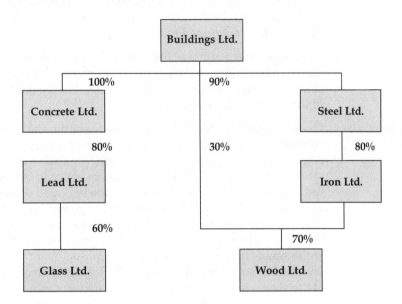

- *Concrete is a 75% subsidiary of Buildings*

- *Lead is indirectly a 75% subsidiary of Buildings*

- *Steel is a 75% subsidiary of Buildings*

- *Iron is not a 75% subsidiary of Buildings. However, Steel is a principal company (having a 75% subsidiary) and is a member of a Group with Buildings being itself a 75% subsidiary of that Company. Therefore, Iron is also a member of the Group of which Buildings is the Principal Company, (see paragraph 76).*

- *Glass is not a 75% subsidiary of any company in the Group and is therefore not a Group member.*

- *Wood is a 75% subsidiary of Buildings; 50.4% held indirectly through Steel and Iron and 30% held directly.*

76.3   **Group relief and Reorganisations**

The UK case of Westcott -v- Woolcombers Limited considered the provisions relating to transfers between group companies and the legislation on company amalgamations by an exchange of shares dealt with in paragraph 44.

In that case, a parent company transferred the shares in three companies ("the three companies") on 23rd March 1966 to its subsidiary company (Topmakers) in consideration of the issue of further shares by Topmakers to the parent. Originally, the parent company had acquired the shares in the three companies for £1,270,380. In December 1971, Topmakers sold the shares in the three companies to a fellow subsidiary (Woolcombers) for £601,235. On 7th January 1972, the three companies were put into voluntary liquidation and the value of the distributions received by Woolcombers amounted to £601,235.

The net point at issue was the allowable cost to Woolcombers of the shares in the three companies for the purpose of computing the chargeable gain or allowable loss in respect of the deemed disposal of the shares in the three companies.

s586
s617
Under the provisions of s586, the transfer of the shares in the three companies to Topmakers in consideration of the share issue constituted a reorganisation. As a result, the parent company's shares in the three companies were deemed not to be disposed of but were treated as the same asset as the newly issued shares in Topmakers.   Accordingly, as regards the parent, the newly issued shares in Topmakers took the same base cost as the shares in the three companies. What was unclear was the base cost to Topmakers of the shares in the three companies acquired by it from the parent. Did the UK legislation (in Ireland s617) apply to treat the acquisition of the shares in the three companies as an intra group transfer or was the base cost their actual value at the date of transfer? The doubt arose because the reorganisation provisions make the assumption that there is no disposal but there has to be a disposal in order for the group relief provisions to apply.

The UK Court of Appeal held that group relief provisions applied for the purposes of determining the base cost to Topmakers. The result was that Topmakers was treated as acquiring the shares in the three companies for £1,270,380. Consequently, this amount also became the base cost for Woolcombers in respect of its intra-group acquisition of the shares in the three companies from Topmakers so that a substantial capital loss accrued to Woolcombers on the liquidation of the three companies. Effectively, the loss was allowed twice, i.e. to Woolcombers Limited and also to the parent company since its base cost in respect of the newly issued shares in Topmakers was also fixed at £1,270,380. Of course, in different circumstances, the figures could produce a gain which would also would be taxed twice and this demonstrates the importance of the case.

It should be noted that the U.K. Revenue introduced amending legislation in the U.K. FA88, the effect of which is to prevent any potential double taxation or double allowance for losses.

However in the UK case of NAP Holdings v Whittles the Court of Appeal dealt with a similar set of facts. The court reached the opposite conclusion to that which was reached in the Woolcombers case. The court did not hold that Woolcombers had been wrongly decided, but rather it concluded that, because the law was consolidated in the UK subsequent to the transactions with which Woolcombers was concerned, and prior to the transactions with which NAP Holdings was concerned, the Court was entitled to look at the matter afresh in the light of the consolidated legislation. In so doing, it reached the conclusion that as a share for share exchange was to be treated as not involving a disposal of the shares which were swapped, the provisions relating to intra group transactions (which apply only where there is a disposal and an acquisition) did not apply. Accordingly they held that where a company issues shares to another group member in return for other shares transferred to it by that group member, and the share exchange provisions of the Capital Gains Tax Acts have application, the company which issued the shares is deemed to acquire at open market value the shares which it receives in exchange.

The House of Lords later reversed the decision of the Court of Appeal in the NAP Holdings case. In affect, they endorsed the Woolcombers decision.

The issue has not come before the Irish courts. It is not clear which of the two cases, the Woolcombers case or the UK Court of Appeal decision in the NAP Holdings case, would have the greatest influence with the Irish courts. The NAP Holdings case more closely accords with the view of the legislation which was traditionally held, up to the Woolcombers case. Arguably it involves fewer anomalies. On a purely technical basis the Irish legislation, in the shape of the Capital Gains Tax Acts and the Companies Capital Gains Provisions of the Corporation Tax Acts, more closely accord as a single system of legislation with the consolidated legislation being considered in the NAP Holdings case. The matter however cannot be said to be free from doubt.

On the other hand the decision by the House of Lords in the NAP Holdings case accorded closely with the perceived scheme of the provisions relating to groups of companies, that transfers within a group should not have CGT consequences and that the only acquisition should be an acquisition by a member of the group from outsiders, and the only disposal should be a disposal by the group to an outsider.

In view of the confusion in the area it is to be hoped that the matter may be clarified by a suitable amendment to what can be only described as confusing legislative provisions.

It is reported in the January 1993 edition of Irish Tax Review in the Institute Matters article (item 15) that the view of the Revenue Commissioners "was that they would not seek to double tax a gain on the basis of the Woolcombers case in the normal course of events. Obviously if a taxpayer were seeking to claim a double capital loss the claim would be contested."

NAP and Woolcombers are discussed in the March 1998 issue of Irish Tax Review in an article by Aoife Goodman BL.

Example 395

> *Company A owns a subsidiary, Company B and a second subsidiary, Company C. The base cost of Company A in the shares in Company C is £100 and at the date of the transaction to be considered they are worth £400. Company A transfers the shares of Company C to Company B in return for shares issued by Company B to Company A.*
>
> *According to the House of Lords in the NAP Holdings case Company A is to be treated as making no disposal of shares in Company C and no acquisition of shares in Company B, but the shares which it acquires in Company B are to be treated as the same shares as the shares it had held in Company C. Therefore it is to be treated as if it had a base cost for those shares of £100.*

s625

> *This analysis is further complicated by the fact that s625 (discussed in greater detail in paragraph 70) provides that were Company B to dispose of Company C out of the group, Company A is to be treated as having disposed of and reacquired at open market value the shares in Company B immediately prior to the share for share swap. The consequence of this retroactive adjustment of the transactions would of course be to give Company C a base cost in the shares in Company B equal to the open market value of those shares at the date of the share for share swap; to give Company A a similar open market value base cost for the shares received from Company C; and to expose Company A to a potential charge to tax on the deemed disposal at the market value of the shares in Company B immediately prior to the share for share swap. If the House of Lords decision in NAP Holdings is followed in Ireland, the result would be that, taking into account the operation of s625 in addition to the provisions being considered here, there should be no exposure to either a potential double charge to CGT on unwinding the whole structure, nor the possibility for getting multiple allowable losses. That aspect of the matter may well commend the House of Lords decision in the NAP Holdings case in the Irish courts.*
>
> *On the other hand, Company B is to be treated as having acquired the shares in Company C on an intra-group transaction and therefore as having the same base cost for them as Company A had i.e. £100.*

s547

> *However regard would have to be had for the provisions of s547(2) and (3), which can restrict the consideration deemed to be given on a subscription for shares in a connected party in certain circumstances. (See paragraph 41.5).*

76.4   Part disposals within a group

As a broad rule, transfers within a group to which s617 apply take place on a "no gain / no loss" basis.

The consideration which actually passes in the transaction is disregarded for this purpose and is replaced by a deemed consideration equal to the base cost of the transferor company.

s617

Part disposals are discussed in paragraph 11. In order to determine the deductible base cost or expenditure for the purpose of a part disposal computation, it is necessary to apply a formula which includes the consideration passing in the transaction. In the case of an intra group transfer, as noted above, there are two figures available for consideration - the actual consideration, and the deemed consideration under s617.

The consideration taken into account for the purpose of the part disposal computation, in the case of an intra group transfer to which s617 applies, is the actual consideration passing (or open market value where the transaction is between connected parties as it always will be in an intra group transfer), and not the deemed consideration which applies for the purposes of s617. Thus the consideration for the purpose of s617 is a notional consideration designed to give a "no gain / no loss" situation; but the consideration taken into account in the part disposal computation for the purpose of determining the amount of deductible expenditure (and hence for determining the consideration for the purposes of s617 itself) is the open market value of the asset.

Example 396

Company A and Company B are members of a capital gains tax group. Company A transfers a half ownership of a property to Company B for the sum of £100,000. At the date of the transfer, in 1996, the property was worth £300,000. Company A's base cost in the property in 1996 is £50,000.

The part disposal computation is applied as follows:

$$£50,000 \ x \ \ \frac{150,000}{150,000 = 150,000} \ \ = \ £25,000$$

The deemed consideration under s617 will be £25,000.

76.5   Exceptions to General Rule

The relief from CT on chargeable gains mentioned in paragraph 75.5 does not apply, where the disposal concerned is:

1.   *a disposal of a DEBT from a member of the group, where the disposal is effected by satisfying the debt or part of it [s617(2)].*

Example 397

SOOT LTD owes a debt of £50,000 to a non-group company. BLACK LTD, which is the parent of SOOT LTD, buys the debt from the non-group member for £45,000, and subsequently collects the £50,000 debt from SOOT LTD.

BLACK LTD has a chargeable gain of £5,000 – no relief is available under the group provisions. Black Ltd is not the original creditor, so in its hands the debt is a chargeable asset.

2.   *a disposal of REDEEMABLE SHARES in a company on the occasion of their redemption.*

Example 398

> *BLACK LTD owns 20,000 £1 redeemable preference shares in SOOT LTD (its wholly owned subsidiary) which were issued in 1975 at £1 per share. In March 1993 SOOT LTD is wound-up and the shares are redeemed at £1.50 per share by the liquidator.*

s617

> *Any chargeable gain arising to BLACK LTD on the redemption of the shares is chargeable to corporation tax. No relief is available under the capital gains tax group provisions.*

3.   *a disposal which is a CAPITAL DISTRIBUTION (see paragraph 40.3) for CGT purposes.*

Example 399

> *BLACK LTD owns all the shares in SOOT LTD. SOOT LTD is liquidated and the proceeds are distributed by the liquidator to BLACK LTD.*

> *BLACK LTD is chargeable to CT on any gains arising-no relief is available under the CGT group provisions.*

The facts in *example 396* are broadly similar to those in the UK case of Innocent v Whaddon Estates Ltd. In that case the judge held that the distribution of assets from a subsidiary to the parent company by the liquidator of the subsidiary involved three transactions for capital gains tax purposes:

- A disposal by the liquidator (treated as a disposal by the subsidiary) of the assets being distributed.

- The acquisition of the same assets by the parent company.

- A deemed part disposal or disposal by the parent of its shares in the subsidiary, by reason of the receipt of a capital distribution from the subsidiary in respect of those shares

The judge pointed our that the words in the UK equivalent of s617(2) which exclude the intra group relief provisions of s.130(1) from application to anything *"which under Section 583, is to be treated as a disposal of an interest in shares in a company in consideration for a capital distribution....from that company...."* had the affect only of excluding the third mentioned transaction above from the benefit of the intra group transfer rules. The first two transactions involved, the disposal by the subsidiary, and the acquisition by the parent, of the assets transferred by the subsidiary to its parent, fell within the group transfer provisions, but the deemed part disposal, or disposal, by the parent of its shares in the subsidiary by reason of the receipt of the capital distribution, did not fall within the intra group transfer provisions.

The relief under s617 for intra group transfers applies "where a member of a group of companies disposes of an asset to another member of the group". It is therefore somewhat surprising that the Act should explicitly exclude the disposal of a debt on the occasion of its satisfaction by another group member, and the redemption of redeemable shares. Neither transaction would ordinarily involve a disposal by one company to another company of the debt, or the shares, as the case may be. Rather they involve the extinguishment of the debt, and of the shares, without any transfer of ownership in them occurring. On the ordinary words of s617, it does not seem likely that either transaction would have fallen within the scope of the relief, and it is not therefore clear why it was considered necessary to exclude them.

This point highlights a limit to group relief. Transactions between group members can result in a disposal by one group member of an asset, without it constituting a disposal of the asset to the other group member. An example would be where one group member is in receipt of a capital sum from another group member, which capital sum is derived from an asset. In such a case the company receiving a capital sum is deemed to dispose of the asset from which it was derived; but it neither transfers that asset to the other group member, nor is it deemed to transfer it. In such a case a chargeable gain would arise, notwithstanding that the transaction was entirely intra group.

s617(3) There is one transaction involving a capital sum derived from an asset which the act specifically provides shall be treated as a disposal of an asset by one party to another, although it does not in fact involve such a disposal. It is the case where a company receives compensation for damage or injury to an asset, or for its destruction, or for the depreciation in value of an asset. In such a case the company is treated under s535 as disposing of an asset. s617(3) provides that the disposal is to be treated as being to the person who provides the consideration or compensation, where that person is another group member.

Example 400

Company A and Company B are in a group. Company A borrows a forklift truck from Company B. While it is borrowed, it is destroyed by a container falling on it. The forklift truck was not insured while out on loan to Company A. Company A pays £10,000 compensation to Company B for the destruction of the forklift truck.

Company B is treated as receiving a capital sum derived from an asset (i.e. the forklift truck). Although it did not dispose of the forklift truck to Company B, it is treated by s617(3) as making a disposal to Company B insofar as the receipt of the compensation is concerned. Accordingly the transaction is covered by group relief. The actual compensation of £10,000 is therefore disregarded, and is replaced by Company B's base cost on the forklift truck i.e. on a no gain / no loss basis.

The topic of part disposals is discussed in greater detail in paragraph 11. Compensation is discussed in paragraph 4.5.

76.6   **Extension of relief**

s632   The relief set out above in paragraph 75.5 (s617) is extended by s632, which provides that the same relief is to apply (in very limited circumstances) to a transfer from a subsidiary company to its parent company, even though one or both of the companies are non-resident.

This additional relief was part of the overall amendments brought into the law to comply with the European Union 'mergers' directive of 23rd July 1990.

The additional relief is one way only. The transfer must be from a wholly owned subsidiary company to its parent. It does not apply on a transfer from the parent company to its subsidiary.

The conditions for additional relief are very restricted, and all of the following conditions must be met:

- it must be a transfer by its wholly owned subsidiary of chargeable assets to a company which owns all the shares, stock and debentures in the transferring company,

s631   - the disposal must not be part of a transfer for which relief is available under s631 (relief for transfers of a trade — see paragraph 76.3),

- immediately after the disposal of the assets, the receiving company must commence to use the assets for the purposes of a trade carried on in Ireland by that company,

- the receiving company would be chargeable to corporation tax or CGT on any gains arising on an immediate disposal (assuming there is a disposal) of any of the chargeable assets transferred,

- all of the chargeable assets involved would be chargeable to corporation tax or CGT in the hands of that receiving company irrespective of the terms of any double tax treaty.

- The transfer must be for bona fide commercial purposes and must not be part of a scheme for the avoidance of income tax, corporation tax or capital gains tax.

s632   S632 operates, not by granting relief itself, but by deeming both the transferor and transferee company to be resident in the State for the purposes of s617. If the only obstacle to the application of group relief (s617) is that one or both of the companies is not resident in the State, then s632 corrects this deficiency and enables the relief to apply. If however there are other obstacles, then s632 will not enable s617 to apply.

s623   There is one peculiar feature to group relief, where it is applied by reason of s632 (i.e. where s632 has deemed one or other or both companies to be resident, when they are not resident). s632 does not treat the transferor and transferee company as being in a group for the purposes of the clawback of group relief under s623. It makes good the requirement regarding residency for the purposes of granting the relief under s617, but does not apply the same assumption to the clawback of relief under s623. A transferee company which receives group relief by reason of s632 is thus in a better position than a transferee company which receives group relief solely by reason of s617, and without s632 having applied to it.

Example 401

> Company A is an Irish resident company with two subsidiaries, Company B and Company C. Company B is also Irish resident but Company C is resident solely in the UK. Company A transfers a branch in the State to Company B and a branch in the State to Company C. The transfers occur in 1996. At all times Company A also has other subsidiaries resident in the State.

> In 1997 Company A sells the shares in Company B and in Company C. The sale is the occasion of Company B leaving a group of which it was a member on the occasion of the transfer to it of a branch. Since the transfer occurred within the 10 year period prior to leaving the group, Company B is treated (by s623) as disposing of the branch assets and immediately re-acquiring them at open market value, immediately after their original acquisition. The gain which would have been charged on Company A on the occasion of their transfer to Company B, but for the operation of group relief, is now charged on Company B.

> In contrast, notwithstanding that Company C was treated as being in a group with Company A on the occasion of the transfer to it of a branch in the State, so that Company A was not chargeable on the gain which arose on that occasion, Company C is not treated by s623 as leaving a group on the occasion of the sale by Company A of the shares in Company C. This is because Company C and Company A were not, as a matter of fact, members of a group on the occasion of that earlier transfer, and s632, which deems them to be a member of a group on the occasion of the transfer, operates only for the purposes of s617 (the grant of the relief) and not for the purposes of s623 (clawback of the relief). Company C is of course still within the charge to corporation tax on company's chargeable gains in respect of the branch assets, for so long as those assets are located in the State. It would therefore be chargeable to corporation tax on company's capital gains on an actual disposal to a third party of those assets.

s631
s632
S632 does not apply to any transaction to which s631 has application. S631 therefore takes precedence in its application. As noted above, it is possible to elect out of s631. However such an election only has the effect of ensuring that sub-sections 2, 3 and 4 of s631 do not apply to the transaction. These are the subsections which grant the relief under s631, and provide for its clawback. The election does not cause s.631(2) not to apply and that is the subsection which states whether or not s631 has application to a transaction. There is therefore an ambiguity as to whether an election out of s631 would permit s632 to have application since arguably, notwithstanding the election, s631 still applies to the transaction although it does not grant it relief. It would seem imprudent to elect out of s631 relief, in the hope that

s632 would grant group relief, without specific prior clearance from the Revenue that this would be so.

An example of a transaction to which s631 does not have application but to which s632 might apply would be a transfer from a subsidiary to its parent of an asset used by it for the purpose of a trade in the State, in return for cash. s631 has application only where the consideration granted consists of shares or debentures.

77   TRANSACTIONS OUTSIDE A GROUP

77.1   Transactions with non-group persons

s619   Where a group member disposes of an asset which was acquired from another group member any restriction of the loss by reference to capital allowances granted in respect of the asset must take into account allowances granted to the group company from which the asset was acquired in addition to any allowances granted to the company now disposing of the asset. This rule extends to any number of group companies through which the asset passed.

All group members are treated as the same person for the purpose of calculating the gain or loss when the asset is finally disposed of outside the group. The member disposing of the asset outside the group is deemed to be the one which initially acquired the asset when it first came into the group. Accordingly, the market value at 6 April 1974 (where applicable) and the indexation rules are preserved within a group.

Example 402

> *Michaels Ltd owns all the issued share capital in Jones Ltd and 65% of the share capital in Flood Ltd.*
>
> *In June 1976 Michaels Ltd bought a property for £50,000. In December 1977 the property was sold to Jones Ltd for £60,000. Jones Ltd extended the property in March 1978 at a cost of £25,000. Flood Ltd purchased the property from Jones Ltd for £384,000 in March 1988.*
>
> *The corporation tax position for the year ended 31st December 1988 is as follows (assuming it is not development land): In December 1977 Jones Ltd is deemed to have acquired the property for £50,000 i.e. an amount which results in no gain and no loss for Michaels Ltd. The sale of the property to Flood Ltd is a sale outside the group accordingly, a taxable gain arises to Jones Ltd calculated as follows:*

Jones Ltd-taxable gain	£
Sale proceeds	384,000
Cost (to group) indexed	
£50,000 indexed @ 4.253 = £212,650	
Enhancement expenditure	
£25,000 indexed @ 3.646 = £ 91,150	303,800
Gain	80,200

Notional CGT= 80,200 @ 20% =		16,040

$$\text{Chargeable to CT} = £16,040 \times \frac{100}{32} \quad = \quad 50,125$$

Example 403

HEAD LTD owns all the shares in NOSE LTD and MOUTH LTD. In 1940 NOSE LTD acquired an asset for £10,000. In 1977 it sold the asset to MOUTH LTD for £50,000. In March 1982 MOUTH LTD sold the asset to HEAD LTD for £100,000. HEAD LTD sold the asset to a non-group member on 2 April 1982 for £110,000.

No chargeable gain arises to NOSE LTD or MOUTH LTD under the group provisions. In calculating the gain of HEAD LTD it is treated as acquiring the asset in 1940 for £10,000; its gain will be calculated by deducting from the sale proceeds of £110,000 the 'indexed' market value at 6/4/74. (Subject to the usual computation rules).

Example 404

BLACK LTD acquired a building in 1972 for £40,000. The MV at 6 April 1974 was £50,000. On 31 March 1982 BLACK LTD sold the building to its wholly owned subsidiary, SOOT LTD for £100,000. SOOT LTD sold the building outside the group on 2 April 1998 for £350,000.

Chargeable gains are calculated as follows:

BLACK's Disposal	£
Cost (MV 6/4/74)	50,000
Deemed Sale Price	50,000
Gain/Loss	Nil

SOOT'S Disposal	£
Sale Price	350,000
Cost as indexed* £50,000 x 6.215	310,750
Chargeable Gain	39,250

Notional CGT - £39,250 @ 20% =	7,850

Chargeable to CT : £7,870 x 100/32 =	24,581

78   GROUPS AND DEVELOPMENT LAND

78.1   Broad Outline — pre-24th April 1992

s649   A gain on the disposal of development land on or after 28 January 1982 is chargeable to CGT, and not to CT. As the relief available for transfers of assets between members of a group only applies for the purposes of CT on chargeable gains, it cannot apply to gains on development land chargeable to CGT. This exclusion from group relief was changed from 24th April 1992 by FA92 s68.

79.2   Disposal of Development Land

Where such land was acquired from another group member prior to 28 January 1982, it would have been treated for the purposes of CT on gains as being acquired at the initial cost to the group. On the disposal of that land on or after 28 January 1982 and prior to 24 April 1992, any gain or loss will be computed on that basis.

Example 405

> Oak Ltd and Beech Ltd are members of a group for the purposes of CT on gains. On 30 June 1980 Oak Ltd acquired land at a cost of £100,000. The current use value of the land at that time was £20,000. On 31 December 1981 the land was transferred to Beech Ltd for £400,000. Beech Ltd sold the land on 31 March 1983 for £500,000.
>
> For the purposes of CT on gains, Oak Ltd would have been treated as transferring the land to Beech Ltd for the cost of £100,000. On the disposal in March 1983 Beech Ltd is treated as acquiring the land in June 1980 for £100,000.

	£	£
Sale Proceeds		500,000
Cost		100,000
Indexation:		
C U V 1980	20,000	
Indexed @ 1.439	28,780	
Uplift	8,780	108,780
Gain		391,220
CGT payable @ 50%*		195,610

> If the land had be transferred to Beech Ltd in February 1983, the position would have been different. The disposal by Oak Ltd would have been chargeable to CGT, and the normal CT group provisions would not apply.

Sale by Oak Ltd — February 1983	£
Sale Proceeds	400,000
Indexed cost (as above)	108,780
Gain (chargeable to CGT 50%*)	291,220

On the subsequent disposal by Beech Ltd in March 1983 its gain would be calculated as follows:

	£
Sale Proceeds	*500,000*
Cost	*400,000*
	100,000
CGT payable 60% *	*60,000*

* CGT rate applicable 1982/83.

If the asset had been held by Beech Ltd for more than 1 year, indexation would apply, but only to the extent of the uplift in the current use value between February 1983 (date of acquisition by Beech Ltd) and the date of disposal.

Even under the normal group provisions, there are circumstances in which the group member acquiring the asset is treated as acquiring it at a date subsequent to the date of its initial acquisition by the group. This would happen in the following circumstances:

- Where a group member leaves the group with an asset which it acquired from another group member, it is treated as selling the asset and reacquiring it at market value at the date the asset was acquired from the other group member (see paragraph 81).

  In such circumstances, the company selling the land on or after 28 January 1982 is treated as acquiring it at the date it is deemed to reacquire the asset under those provisions, and for a cost (and current use value) at that date. The date and cost of the initial group acquisition would not be applied in such circumstances.

- Where a group member transfers a Capital Asset which is acquired as trading stock by the group member acquiring it, the transferring member would be treated as disposing of the asset at no gain, and no loss. The group member acquiring the asset as trading stock, is treated as selling and reacquiring the asset at market value at the date of its appropriation as trading stock (see paragraph 80).

It is difficult however to visualise any circumstances in which the subsequent sale of that trading stock could give rise to a chargeable gain.

78.3   Position — on or after 24th April 1992

s649

As with other reliefs involving transfers of assets between companies, the position was amended as part of the overall compliance with the EEC 'mergers' directive of 23rd June 1990.

The amendment was introduced in FA92 s68, and took affect on and from 24th April 1992.

Assets other than development land pass from one group member to another under s617, without triggering off a chargeable gain.

The same relief is now extended to transfers of development land between members of an Irish resident group. Development land was excluded from the normal 'group relief' for transfers between group members, as that relief only applied for the purposes of corporation tax on chargeable gains. Gains on development land were not chargeable to corporation tax — they were chargeable to CGT.

The relief is now extended to include gains chargeable to CGT within the scope of the same relief (which, in effect, means that development land is now included).

The normal relief for transfers between members of a group is given by s617.

s649 S649 provides that ... *'sections s617, s621, s622,s623, s624, s625 and s626 of the CTA 97, shall apply, with any necessary modifications, in relation to capital gains tax to which a company is chargeable on chargeable gains accruing to it on a relevant disposal as they apply in relation to corporation tax on chargeable gains and references in those sections to corporation tax shall be construed as including references to capital gains tax.'* Where a company claims relief under this amendment, a return must be made in the required form to the Inspector within 9 months of the end of the transferring company's accounting period in which the disposal took place.

s617 s617 (group relief) can apply on a transfer of certain assets from a wholly owned Irish resident subsidiary to its non-resident parent, in certain circumstances, where s632 applies. This includes transfers of development land.

s631 A relief is also available under s631, in relation to a transfer of development land between companies, where the conditions relating to the relief are met. This is discussed in greater detail in paragraph 75.3.

79   GROUP ROLL OVER RELIEF

79.1   Broad Outline - Group roll-over

s620 The roll-over relief provisions are dealt with in detail in paragraph
s597 26. In applying the relief in the case of a CGT group (defined in paragraph 75.4.3) you treat the trades of all members of the group as one single trade. This means that a chargeable gain accruing to one member of the group can be rolled-over, if it and/or other group members invest the required amount in new qualifying assets within the period allowed.

Example 406

A, B and C are trading companies in an Irish resident group. A sells a factory building for £500,000, giving rise to a gain of £50,000. A acquires no new assets. B purchases a factory premises for £400,000. C acquires new plant and machinery for £200,000. The assets were acquired by B and C within 2 years of the disposal of the factory by A.

For the purposes of roll-over relief, the individual trades of A, B and C are treated as one single trade. As the qualifying assets acquired within the time limit by B and C exceed the sale proceeds of the factory by A, the gain is deemed not to arise until the new qualifying assets cease to be used for the purposes of the single group trade.

s620

S620, which applies rollover relief in a group context, does no more than deem (for the purposes only of rollover relief) all of the trades carried on by the members of a group of companies to be a single trade. It does not deem all of the members of the group to be a single person. Some ambiguity arises in applying the section where Company A and Company B are in a group; Company A disposes of qualifying assets; and Company B reinvests a similar sum of money in qualifying assets for the purpose of its trade. The effect of s620 is to regard the assets disposed of, and the assets reinvested in, as all being assets in use for the purpose of the same trade. However s620 does not deem Company A, which made the disposal, to make the reinvestment which is actually made by Company B. In such a situation it is not clear that the requirements for relief have been met. It is understood that this ambiguity does not give rise to problems in practice.

S620 will not apply to treat all of the trades carried on by members of a group as a single trade for rollover relief purposes in two situations. They are:

- Where the assets which were disposed of are disposed of to another group member or:

- Where the new assets acquired on the rollover are acquired from another group member.

It seems unlikely that the first grounds for exclusion noted above, a disposal of the old assets to another group member, could be relevant. Any such disposal should be on a no gain/no loss basis and accordingly should not give rise to the need for rollover relief.

Example 407

Company A and Company B are in a group and each of them carry on a trade. Company A sold its premises which it had in use for the purpose of its trade. It used the proceeds to purchase the premises owned by Company B. It occupied part of that premises for its own trade, and left Company B in occupation of the other part.

Rollover relief will not be available in relation to the part of the premises which remains occupied by Company B as the trade of Company B will not be treated as the trade of Company A. This is by reason of the premises having been acquired by one group member from another. However it would seem that rollover relief would be available in relation to the part of the premises which is put into use for the purpose of the trade of Company A. In that instance relief is available without regard to s620, and without the necessity of deeming all of the trades carried on by group members to be a single trade. Company A has acquired a new asset for use in its own trade and therefore made a legitimate reinvestment in new assets.

The exclusion from relief of reinvestment in assets acquired from other group members applies only where it is necessary to invoke the provisions of s620 group relief, but do not apply to the basic relief under s597, where the company making the disposal also makes the reinvestment for the purpose of its own trade.

See paragraph 81 for clawback on a company leaving a group, and paragraph 74 for details of the "exit charge" on the company going non-resident.

There is one circumstance in which all of the trades carried on by a group is not treated as a single trade for rollover relief purposes. That is where a transaction involves a company acquiring the new assets from another group company; or disposing of the old assets to another group company.

Example 408

A & B are trading companies in an Irish resident group. A sells a factory building for £500,000, giving rise to a gain of £50,000. A uses the proceeds of £500,000 to purchase a premises from B, which it then puts into use in its trade.

A is entitled to rollover relief on its expenditure on the premises purchased from fellow group member B. In this context the trade of A and the trade of B are not treated as a single trade and therefore it is possible to say that the premises is put into use for the purposes of the trade of A. It would not be possible to say that if the premises were already in use for such a common group trade.

In this example, B has made a disposal. If the asset were an asset in relation to which it was entitled to rollover relief, it could not claim that relief by reference to A's expenditure on acquiring the asset because in this transaction the trade of A and B is not treated as a single trade, and accordingly it cannot be said that the building has been put into use for the purpose of that single trade.

The deeming language used in s620, to provide a form of group relief to rollover relief is not completely satisfactory. It deems a single trade to exist in the group companies. This in itself may not be enough, strictly speaking, to provide rollover relief on a group wide basis. The section does not deem expenditure by one group company to be expenditure by another group company. Thus if Company A disposes of a trading asset, and Company B incurs expenditure on a qualifying asset, and A & B are in a group, the legislation will deem B to have incurred the expenditure for the purpose of the common trade carried on by A & B; but it does not deem A to have incurred the expenditure. Is A therefore entitled nonetheless to rollover relief?

The point is not clear and advance clearance from the Revenue may be prudent if it is relevant.

80   APPLICATION - GROUP RELIEF TO TRADING STOCK

80.1   Acquisition as Trading Stock

The general CGT rules which apply to transfers of assets to and from trading stock (other than in a group situation) are discussed in paragraph 18.

s618   Where the asset being disposed of is a chargeable asset of the group member disposing of it, and it is acquired as trading stock of the group member acquiring it, the group member acquiring it is treated as if it did not acquire it as trading stock. The normal rule for transfers within a group will therefore apply to the disposal and acquisition.

The acquiring member is then treated as if it had appropriated the asset as trading stock immediately after its acquisition i.e. as if it had sold and reacquired the asset at its market value at the date of acquisition.

Example 409

LEG LTD is the Irish resident parent company of a CGT Group. One of its 75% subsidiaries, FOOT LTD is a trading company. FOOT LTD acquired a chargeable asset for £40,000 from LEG LTD on 31 March 1988 to use as trading stock of its trade. LEG LTD originally acquired the asset in June 1975 for £20,000. Market value at the date of disposal to FOOT LTD was £100,000. FOOT LTD subsequently disposed of the asset in the course of its trade for £110,000.

LEG LTD is treated under the group provisions as disposing of the asset at cost i.e. £20,000 and FOOT LTD is treated as acquiring the asset for £20.000.

This gives LEG LTD the benefit of the group transfer provisions. FOOT LTD has acquired an asset for £20,000, and immediately after is deemed to sell it, and reacquire it for trade purposes at its market value at the date of acquisition from LEG LTD (i.e. £100,000). FOOT LTD has therefore, a chargeable gain calculated as follows:

	£	£
Deemed sale proceeds		100,000
Deemed cost	20,000	
Indexed x 4.936		98,720
Chargeable gain		1,280

- **Revenue Commissioners - tax briefing**

— The Revenue Commissioners in Issue 35 of Tax Briefing, March 1999, stated *"The reference in s596(1) TCA 1997 to "the trade" is a reference to the trade into which an asset has been appropriated so that the fact that an asset was held as a capital asset in another trade carried on by the same person does not affect the application of the section. Accordingly the section does apply where an asset already held as a capital asset in one trade is appropriated to a new trade".*

80.2   **Meaning of trading stock**

"Trading stock" does not have its ordinary meaning when used in s596 (appropriations to and from stock and trade) nor when used in s618 (transfers within a group of trading stock).

s5   TCA97 s5 provides that *"trading stock"* has the meaning which it has in s89. There it is defined as:

s89   *"Property of any description, whether real or personal, which is either*

(a)   *property such as is sold in the ordinary course of the trade in relation to which the expression is used or would be so sold if it were mature or it its manufacture, preparation, or construction were complete, or*

(b)   *materials such as are used in the manufacture, preparation, or construction of property such as is sold in the ordinary course of the said trade...."*

s89   That definition is extended by s89(1)(b) to include *"any services, article or material which would if the trade were a profession, be treated as work in progress thereof for the purposes of this section...."*

The expression used above - *"such as is sold in the ordinary course of the trade"* is somewhat ambiguous. It does indicate that in principle, a company might acquire some item for resale, and yet that item might not be *"trading stock"* if its sale would not be in the ordinary course of the trade, but would be outside that ordinary course. It is difficult to consider an example of such, but were a company obliged to accept certain goods in discharge of a trade debt, which goods were of a type it did not normally deal in, the sale of those goods might be outside the ordinary course of the trade albeit a sale in the course of the trade. In such a case those goods would not be trading stock, although held for the purpose of sale.

In the UK case of Reed v Nova Securities Ltd. which is discussed in greater detail in paragraph 80.3, Lord Templeman said at page 130;

"The members of the Court of Appeal were, however, unanimously of the view that property could only be acquired "as trading stock" if it was acquired for the purpose of being used in the course of a trade. I agree. If a company is to acquire an asset as trading stock, the asset must not only be of a kind which is sold in the ordinary course of the company's trade but

must also be acquired for the purposes of that trade with a view to resale at a profit. A company which acquired an asset for purposes other than trading would not, in my opinion, acquire the asset as trading stock even though the company habitually traded in similar assets".

In that passage, Lord Templeman states that in order to be trading stock, an asset must be acquired *"with a view to a resale at a profit".* That requirement is not found in the statutory definition in s89 and no authority is stated by Lord Templeman in the Nova Securities case for that statement. In the authors' view it is wrong. *"Loss leaders"* are a common feature of a trade. A company may purchase certain lines of stock with a view to their resale at a loss, and do so for sound commercial reasons and in particular because it will maximise the overall profit of the company from its trading activities, usually by attracting in additional customers. If Lord Templeman were correct, items purchased for resale at a loss in this fashion would not be trading stock. That could of course be the case if the legislation so stated, but the legislation does not appear to have stated that.

In the Nova Securities case, Lord Templeman also rejected the shares in that case as being trading stock on the grounds that they were completely incapable of being resold, at any price. While that may seem a reasonable view to take, if trading stock had its ordinary meaning (being usually property held for resale) it does not appear to be an explicit requirement of the statutory definition. It is also a requirement which could give rise to difficulties in relation to stock which, by reason of some defect or failure to meet some regulatory requirement, cannot legally be resold, notwithstanding that it is property such as is sold in the ordinary course of the trade and was acquired as such, as referred to in the statutory definition.

80.3   Trading stock : Optional treatment

Instead of being taxed on the gain, the taxpayer has the option of adjusting the value of the asset to be taken in as stock in trade. The value taken in for trading purposes may be reduced by the capital gain or increased by the capital loss incurred on the deemed disposal arising out of the appropriation of the asset to stock in trade. Where the trade is carried on in partnership then all parties must agree to exercise the option. In relation to appropriations of assets to trading stock on or after 30 May 1990, this option may not be exercised in relation to the appropriation of an asset on whose deemed disposal an allowable loss would arise but for the option.

Example 410

*In **example 409** the exercise of the option to adjust the value would give the following result, assuming the asset was eventually sold for £110,000.*

	£	£
Sale Proceeds		110,000
*Cost (deemed)**	100,000	
Less Gain not charged	1,280	98,720
Trading Profit		12,280

*MV on appropriation as stock in trade.

If we assume that the market value of the asset on transfer from Leg Ltd was £10,000 and the asset was eventually sold for £110,000, the position prior to 30 May 1990 would be as follows (assuming the option to adjust the value was exercised).

Capital Loss—Foot Ltd	£	£
Deemed Sale Proceeds		10,000
Deemed Cost 20,000 indexed @ 4.936		98,720
Loss		88,720
Restricted to Actual Loss		10,000

Trading Position—Foot Ltd		
Sale Price		110,000
Deemed Cost	10,000	
Add Capital Loss	10,000	20,000
Trading Profit		99,000

The effect of this optional treatment has been well illustrated in two UK cases, which however would no longer be valid in Ireland since 30 May 1990, since the optional treatment described above does not apply to losses since that date.

In the UK case of Reed v Nova Securities Ltd the taxpayer company which had traded in shares and securities for a number of years was acquired by another company, Littlewoods. On August 17 1973 Littlewoods disposed of shares and debts to the taxpayer company for £30,000 which represented their market value.

The shares and debts were not held by Littlewoods as trading stock. They had been acquired by that company for a total consideration of £3,936,765.

The taxpayer company claimed that the assets had been acquired as trading stock and that a loss arose in the sum of £3,906,765 i.e.

	£
Cost to Littlewoods	3,936,765
Less MV on transfer	30,000
Loss on appropriation as stock-in-trade	3,906,765

The taxpayer company elected to have the 'cost' of the assets for trading purposes increased by this amount, giving rise to a trading loss of £3,905,915. Group relief was claimed by three members of the Littlewoods Group in respect of this loss. (The £850 difference in the figures is accounted for by other transactions in that period).

The Inland Revenue resisted the contention that a trading loss had been incurred. They argued that the assets, because of their nature, did not become trading stock in the taxpayers hands. They contended also that the acquisition of the assets from Littlewoods was partly a tax-avoidance scheme and, following the UK decision in W. T. Ramsay Ltd v IRC, should be ignored for tax purposes.

In the High Court Walton J. rejected both these arguments in finding for the taxpayer.

The Revenue appeal against this decision was rejected in the Court of Appeal, Lawton L. J. dissenting. It was held that on the facts before them the Commissioners had not erred in law in concluding that the assets had been acquired as trading stock. Considerable importance was attached to the fact that it had not been demonstrated, and could not be inferred from the facts, that the sole or main purpose of the transaction was to secure a fiscal advantage. This distinguished the case from Coates v Arndale Properties Ltd where the Court of Appeal held in favour of the Inland Revenue, reversing the decision of the Court below.

However, in the House of Lords, it was held that for the assets to be regarded as trading stock,they must not only be of a kind normally dealt with in the ordinary course of the company's trade, but also acquired by the company with a view to resale at a profit.

Because the shares were demonstrably worthless, it was impossible that they could be sold at a profit and accordingly Lord Templeman held that they were not capable of being trading stock. The debts however were held to be trading stock since they had a value and could conceivably have realised a profit on disposal or satisfaction, and were of a type of property dealt in by the company in the course of its trade.

It is noted in paragraph 80.2 that Lord Templeman's statement that only property acquired by a company with a view to resale at a profit could be trading stock, appears to be without statutory basis. It would also appear to conflict with common sense and commercial practice. It was specifically on this point i.e. a complete inability to dispose of the shares at a profit, that the judgement in the Nova Securities case on that point turned. For that reason the case may not be regarded by Irish courts as an influential precedent nor, in the authors' opinion, is it likely to be followed by the Irish courts.

It was argued by the taxpayer that the shares in question were required as a *"job lot"* along with the debts, and were acquired in order that the company might be able to acquire the debts. Accordingly, the taxpayer argued, that the shares were trading stock notwithstanding that they were worthless. This argument was rejected by Lord Templeman who said *"the shares were not commercially saleable at any price"*. This is not the same thing as saying that they could not be resold at a profit. If indeed the shares were totally incapable of being resold, there could be strong grounds for holding that they were not trading stock, albeit their acquisition might be an expense of the trade. A complete inability to sell the shares is a separate matter from the question of whether, if they were resaleable, that resale would be at a profit or a loss.

In the UK case of Coates v Arndale Properties Ltd, the taxpayer company was a dealing company. It was a member of a Group with a development company (SPI) and an investment company (APT).

On 30 March 1973 Arndale Properties Ltd acquired a leasehold property for £3,090,000 from SPI and on the same day assigned it to APT for its then market value of £3,100,000.

By that time SPI's expenditure in connection with the property amounted to £5,313,822.

Arndale Properties Ltd had previously acted as a property dealing company within the Group, trading in properties in the course of transactions with other members of the Group.

The taxpayer company duly made its election which gave rise to a trading loss of £2,213,822, calculated as follows:

Capital Loss (on appropriation of asset as trade stock)	£
Deemed Sale Proceeds (MV) on appropriation to stock in trade	3,090,000
Deemed Cost (cost to SPI)	5,313,822
Capital Loss	2,223,822
Trading Loss (on sale to APT)	
Sale Price	3,100,000

Cost (mv on appropriation)	3,090,000
Add capital loss (election)	2,223,822
	5,313,822
Trading Loss	2,213,822

The Inland Revenue resisted the loss claim on the grounds that the taxpayer company did not acquire the property as trading stock but purely to establish a loss for fiscal purposes.

Goulding J following the principle in the UK case of Griffiths v JP Harrison (Watford) Ltd, held that the general commissioners did not err on a point of law in finding that the property had been acquired by the taxpayer company as trading stock.

The Revenue appealed the decision. Unlike the case of Nova Securities, it was admitted that Arndale had not acquired the property for a commercial purpose, but had done so merely to obtain a fiscal advantage. In those circumstances, the Court of Appeal held that the only true and reasonable conclusion on the facts, was that the property was not acquired as trading stock. Accordingly, the decision of the Commissioners was erroneous in law, and the appeal by the Revenue allowed-Griffiths v JP Harrison (Watford) Ltd distinguished.

80.4   Disposal of Trading Stock

s618   Where trading stock of one member of a group is acquired by another member of that group otherwise than as trading stock, the position is the same as for any person appropriating an asset from trading stock. The basic rules are set out in s596 (see paragraph 18).

s596   S618 treats the member disposing of the asset as appropriating the asset out of trading stock prior to the disposal. S596 then treats the asset as being reacquired for CGT purposes (by the disposing company) at the value for Income Tax (or Corporation Tax) at which it is appropriated out of stock.

The member disposing of the asset then has an asset which is no longer trading stock, and the normal rules govern the transfer to the other group member.

Example 411

Harcourt Ltd acquired an asset for £20,000 in May 1995 as trading stock. In June 1997 it transferred the asset to another member of the group, Grafton Ltd, at cost, when its full value was £30,000. Grafton Ltd did not trade, and held the asset as an investment. Grafton Ltd sold the asset in December 1997 for £40,000 on receiving an unexpected good offer.

Harcourt Ltd is treated as appropriating the asset from trade stock in June 1997, and reacquiring the asset (not as trade stock) at the value at which the asset is taken out for "income" purposes. In most circumstances, the asset will be treated as appropriated from stock at cost (see note in paragraph 18). The asset which is transferred to Grafton Ltd is treated for CGT purposes as one which has been acquired by the group in June 1997, and the gain on the disposal by Grafton Ltd will be computed accordingly:

i.e. sale proceeds	£40,000
Cost	£30,000
Gain	£10,000

81   COMPANY LEAVING GROUP – GENERAL RULE

81.1   Company leaving group - outline

s623

In the case of most relieving provisions, there will normally be anti-avoidance provisions to prevent abuse of the relief and the CGT group relief provisions are no exception.

Provisions are made to effectively charge the tax foregone on a transfer within a group if the group company which acquires the asset leaves the group with that asset. The gain accrues to the company leaving the group, but in some case, the parent of the group, or the group company from which the asset was acquired can also be held responsible for the tax involved (see paragraph 91.5).

81.2   Company leaving group - main rule

s623

Where a company ceases to be a member of a group, any asset which it acquired from other group members while it was a member of the group is deemed to be sold, and immediately re-acquired by the company leaving the group at market value, at the date of acquisition from the other group company.

This has the effect of realising the gain which was deferred on the original inter-company transfer within the group, and making it chargeable on the company leaving the group. It is a chargeable gain arising on the date of acquisition of the asset by that company and not the date the company leaves the group.

Only assets acquired intra group within ten years of the date of leaving the group are deemed disposed of in this fashion.

Example 412

The following is an Irish resident group of 4 companies:

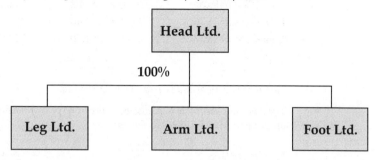

HEAD LTD owns all shares in the subsidiaries. In May 1995, an asset was bought by LEG LTD for £20,000. In May 1997, it was transferred to FOOT LTD at its market value at that time (£40,000). In March, 1998, the shares in FOOT LTD were sold to a non-group company.

Under the group provisions, LEG LTD is treated as transferring the asset to FOOT LTD at no gain no loss

i.e. Cost £20,000

As soon as Foot Ltd leaves the group it is deemed to have sold the asset in May 1997 for its market value at that date, i.e. £40,000. The gain therefore accrues to Foot Ltd in May 1997, and the normal provisions for charging a gain accruing in May 1997 on an asset acquired in May 1995 at a cost of £20,000 will apply.

Example 413

Chairs Ltd owned 90% of the ordinary shares in Desks Ltd, and 85% of the ordinary shares in Tables Ltd.

In June 1975, Tables Ltd bought a property for £40,000. Having spent £20,000 on improvements in May 1976, it sold the property to Chairs Ltd for £30,000 in March 1977.

Chairs Ltd spent a further £15,000 in improving the property in June 1977, and sold it to Desks Ltd for £60,000 in December 1979. The market value of the property at that time was £129,000.

No gain or loss arises out of the disposal of the property between the group members concerned. Desks Ltd is treated as acquiring the asset in June 1975 for £40,000, and is regarded as incurring all the subsequent enhancement expenditure on it.

Chairs Ltd sold half of the ordinary shares it held in Desks Ltd in January 1980. In March 1983, Desks Ltd sold the property to an unconnected person for £280,000.

The tax position is as follows, assuming the property could not be regarded as development land. As a result of leaving the group in January 1980, Desks Ltd is deemed to have sold and reacquired the property at market value in December 1979. The gain is calculated as follows:

				£	£
Deemed sale proceeds					129,000
Cost 1975: indexed	40,000	x 1.62	65,000		
Enhancement 1976:	20,000	x 1.40	28,000		
Enhancement 1977:	15,000	x 1.20	18,000		111,000
Gain					18,000

Tax on this gain would be payable by Desks Ltd.

The amount chargeable to corporation tax in respect of the disposal of the property in March 1983 is as follows:

Sale Proceeds			£280,000
Deemed Cost	£129,000		
Indexed @ 1.662		£214,398	
Enhancement cost	£3,000		
Indexed @ 1.662		£4.986	£219,384
Gain			£60,616
Notional CGT @ 40%			£24,246

Chargeable to CT	£24,246	x	100**	£48,492
			50	

** *50% CT Rate then applicable.*

The legislation provides for any adjustment necessary to assess and collect the tax (i.e. additional assessments, etc.) to be within the time limit allowed for assessing and collecting the tax up to a period of 10 years after the date the company ceased to be a member of the group.

Paragraph 75.4.3 describes the rules to determine whether or not a company is a member of a group, following the FA 99. The rules are complex. As described in that paragraph, the pre-conditions for the existence of a group may fail to be present for any of a large variety of reasons. Many commercial transactions which might not be expected to impact on the existence of a group, can result in a group not existing, or indeed in a group actually existing. These are described in that paragraph and will not be repeated here. What is important to bear in mind is that a company may now leave a group by reason of the failure of some of the technical requirements for group membership even though the event causing the failure may be otherwise an insignificant event without much commercial impact, and might indeed be one of which the group is quite unaware. An event as straightforward as a severe reduction in profits in an accounting period (causing the alternative test of profits equal to £100 being applied) can, depending on the structure of share capital and of loans, result in a group ceasing to exist. The fact that the group relationship may be restored shortly thereafter (on a recovery of profits) is not relevant to the fact that a company may have ceased to be a member of a group.

81.3   **Company leaving group - exceptions to main rule**

These provisions do not apply where :

(1)   the asset had been owned by that company for more than 10 years at the time when it left the group.

Prior to the 1997 consolidation of the CGT legislation, the predecessor to TCA 97 s623 (CTA 76, s135) contained an exclusion from the application of the section in respect of assets acquired by a company intra group prior to 6 April 1974.

s623   This provision is not repeated in the consolidated legislation since, in relation to the company currently seeking to be a member of a group, it would have no relevance, since the asset would necessarily have been obtained intra group more than ten years previously. The provision would have had relevance only in relation to a company ceasing to be a member of a group at times prior to 6 April 1984.

(2)   a company leaves a group while owning an asset acquired by it intra group, where the company leaves the group by reason of being dissolved, or by reason of another group member being dissolved.

This fact has been used in tax planning, most notably in the Burman v Hedges and Butler Ltd. case in the UK (see paragraph 81.4) and no doubt in many other less well publicised instances since then. s623(1)(d) (inserted by FA96) has countered this planning approach by providing that the exception to the application of s623(2) by reference to a liquidation, will apply only where the liquidation in question is for bona fide commercial reasons and is not part of a scheme or arrangement the main purpose or one of the main purposes of which is the avoidance of tax.

A company is not regarded as leaving the group if it ceases to be a member by being wound up or dissolved or because some other member of the group is wound up or dissolved.

(3)   Where two or more companies leave the group at the same time the asset acquired from one another will not be regarded as sold and reacquired as a result of those companies leaving the group provided they are a group in their own right. An

example of this would be where a company with a 75% subsidiary leaves the main group. As they are a self-contained group, assets acquired from one another are ignored in applying the normal provisions set out above.

(4)   Where a company leaves a group solely by reason of the new FA99 definition of a group - see paragraph 75.4.4.5.

Example 414

Company A has a wholly owned subsidiary, Company B which in turn has a wholly owned subsidiary, Company C. All are Irish resident. Company B in 1996 transfers a shop in Dublin to Company A and a shop in Cork to Company C. In 1997 Company A sells the shares in Company B to an unconnected third party.

Both Company B and Company C have left the "Company A group". Company C possesses an asset transferred to it when it was a member of that group. However the company which made the transfer to it, Company B, has also simultaneously left the Company A group, and Company C and Company B together continue to form a group. Accordingly s623 will not have application to the transfer from B to C, and will not cause a clawback of group relief in respect of that transfer.

Company A has also ceased to be a member of the "Company A group" by reason of the fact that it is no longer in a group relationship with any subsidiary. It possesses an asset which was transferred to it intra group while it was a member of the "Company A group". s623 will apply to deem Company A as having disposed of the Dublin Shop immediately following its transfer to it, and thereby acquired it at open market value. Had Company A ensured that it had a further subsidiary within the charge to corporation tax and resident in Ireland, at the time when it disposed of the shares in Company B, it would have remained the principal company of the "Company A group" and the s623 clawback would not have occurred. This is so even if the subsidiary in question was specially created for the purpose immediately prior to disposing of the shares in Company B, and even if it has no more activity than maintaining £100 on deposit in a bank. It need not have existed at the time of the transfer of the Dublin shop from Company B to Company A.

If in the example above the occasion of Company B and Company C ceasing to be a member of the Company A group of companies was that they ceased to be resident in Ireland, a different situation would necessarily arise. Company B would continue to be the 100% owner of Company C, but, as non-resident companies, they would not be capable of forming a group for this purpose. Accordingly Company C would be treated as disposing of the shop in Cork immediately after the shop had been transferred to it by Company B, in 1996. In this example the asset which is the subject matter of the deemed disposal was land in the state, so Company C is within the charge to tax on Capital Gains on a deemed disposal of that asset (it being one of the specified assets). The charge would be to corporation tax on companies capital gains both because the deemed disposal is deemed to take place at a time when it was a resident company, and because at the time that the deeming provision is triggered, it is in any event an asset in use for the purpose of a trade carried on by a branch in the state. The same conclusion, that Company C would be liable to corporation tax on companies capital gains in relation to a 1996 disposal, would have followed even if the shop had been located in Belfast. The deemed disposal is deemed to occur at a time when Company C is Irish resident.

s627

If a purchaser of Company B, in the example above, had maintained the Irish residence of Company B and of Company C for a short time after he had purchased them, on their subsequently going non-resident (by a transfer of Board meetings to the home country of the purchaser of Company B) would a charge under s623 arise? That question has become less relevant since s627 was enacted by the FA97, and deemed companies ceasing to be resident in the state to dispose of their assets immediately prior to so ceasing to be resident. However s627 does not have universal application (there are many exceptions to its application) and it deems the disposal to occur on a different date to the date on which s 623 may deem a disposal to occur. The question therefore remains relevant in many instances.

S616
s623

B and C form a group, and form the group at all times during which B held the shares in C. At the time of the transfer of assets from B to C, B and C formed a group. However, s616 (1) (b) provides that where that the principal company of a group is itself a 75% subsidiary of another company, then that other company is the principal company of a group encompassing all of the companies involved. Accordingly B and C were the members of a group of which A was the principal company, notwithstanding that at the same time B and C were the members of another group of which B was the principal company. When A disposed of the shares in B (in the example above) B and C ceased to be a member of a group (i.e. that of which A was the principal company) and that was a group of which they had been a member at the time that B made the transfer of the shop in Cork to C. S623 (2) applies s623 where a Company ceases to be "a member of a group of companies" and therefore applies it where it ceases to be a member of any group of companies, notwithstanding that it may remain a member of another group of companies. However s623 (3)(a)(i) disapplies s623(2) where the company leaving the group remains in a group with the company from which it obtained the asset. So s623 would not have deemed Company C to have disposed of the Cork shop immediately after its acquisition, on the occasion of the sale by Company A of Company B. However once Company B and Company C cease to be Irish resident Company C again leaves a group - the Company B group - and s623 (2) would then have application. So, potentially, would s627 albeit it would deem the disposal at the date of going non resident whereas s623 (2) deems a disposal immediately after the intra group acquisition.

The circumstances of the company and a wholly owned subsidiary simultaneously ceasing to be a member of a group by reason of going non-resident was considered in the U.K. case of Lion v. Inspector of Taxes, before the U.K. Special Commissioners in 1997.

In the case of Dunlop International v Pardoes, the UK High Court had to consider the positions of two companies which left a group by becoming non-resident. They remained related by a shareholding and one had an asset obtained intra group from the other in the previous 10 years.

Lightman J said at P473:

"Reading the definition of 'associated companies' in s278 (4) (a) into s278 (2), the subsection reads:

'Where two or more companies who by themselves would form a group of companies cease to be members of the group at the same time...'

The question arises as to what is the relevant time at which 'they would form a group of companies' and in what eventuality. The language is capable of supporting both suggested constructions. I prefer, however, the construction adopted by the Revenue for two reasons. (1) The language of the section requires focus to be made on the moment when the companies cease to be members. That is the moment when the charge created by s278 (3) arises, and that is surely the moment when the conditions in the relieving provision have to be satisfied. It is at that time that the companies leaving the group must be associated, i.e. by themselves 'would', outside the group they are leaving, form a group of companies. The word is 'would': there are not the words 'do or would'. The word 'would' affords some indication that the draftsman had in mind that the group that 'would be formed' will be different from the group that is ceasing to exist. (2) The purpose behind s278 (2) accords with this construction. The purpose must plainly be that the benefit of deferral of the tax charge conferred by s273 could safely and sensibly be continued in respect of an acquisition by one group company from another, notwithstanding their cesser of membership of that group, if at the same time they would form in whole or in part a new group. As the commissioners put it in paragraph 23 of their decision -

'...if an asset is transferred between a sub-group within a principal group, the deferral can continue if that sub-group is sold out of the principal group. If it is appropriate to defer the tax implication of gain or loss arising on the transfer of assets within a group, then it seems equally appropriate to allow that deferral to continue for so long as the asset remains within its own sub-group.'

This, however, requires that on the cesser of membership of the previous group one of the companies shall be the 75% subsidiary of the other and both shall continue resident in the United Kingdom."

This judgement was confirmed by the UK Court of Appeal.

The statutory references quoted are to equivalent UK legislation.

81.4   **Burman v Hedges & Butler (UK case) - pre FA 99**

Hedges and Butler Ltd owned 'Bushmills', and agreed to sell the shares in Bushmills for £4m to 'Seagrams'. The case concerned a scheme implemented to avoid a chargeable gain on the disposal of the shares in Bushmills to Seagrams. The basic scheme was as follows:

- Shares in a new company (Vostaka) were issued to both Hedges and Butler and Seagrams. Hedges and Butler was issued 76 participating preference shares of £1 each, and Seagrams was issued 24 £1 ordinary shares.

- The preference shares ranked equally with the ordinary shares for division of profits, but carried no voting rights, and were entitled only to a return of £1 per share on a winding-up, i.e. they were 'ordinary share capital'.

- Another company (Zagal) was formed and its total £100 share capital issued to (and beneficially owned) by Vostaka.

This left the companies in the following position:

"Group CHART"

Hedges & Butler		Seagrams
76 pref shares		24 ord shares
100%	100%	
	Vostaka	
	100%	
Bushmills	Zagal	

On account of the wide meaning of the term 'Ordinary Shares' all of the above companies with the sole exception of Seagrams, were in a group for the purpose of corporation tax on chargeable gains.

- Seagrams loaned £4m to Zagal.

- Zagal used the funds to buy the shares in Bushmills from Hedges and Butler.

The result of this was that:

- Hedges and Butler received £4m.

- Zagal now owned Bushmills.

- No chargeable gain arose on the disposal of the shares in Bushmills between two members of the same group (see paragraph 80).

The final part of the scheme, which in effect gave Bushmills to Seagrams was:

- Vostaka was wound up.

- In the liquidation, £76 (par value of the preference shares) was returned to Hedges and Butler.

- Seagrams took the remaining assets, i.e. the shares in Zagal, which in turn owned Bushmills.

Seagrams was not chargeable on any gain arising out of the distribution in the liquidation, as the shares in Zagal were worthless. That company had an asset worth £4m (Bushmills), but it also had a debt due to Seagrams of £4m.

The anti-avoidance provisions which would normally seek to withdraw the relief given on the transfer of Bushmills from Hedges and Butler to Zagal, do not operate in the case of a company leaving the group by reason of itself or its parent company being wound up (see paragraph 81.3).

The Revenue assessed Hedges and Butler on the gain arising ignoring the group relationship and challenged the scheme contending that Zagal was acting merely as a nominee for Seagrams. This argument, however, was rejected by the Special Commissioners. On appeal to the Chancery Division, the Revenue contended that as the liquidation of Vostaka was contemplated from the start, Hedges and Butler could not be regarded as the beneficial owner of the 76 preference shares: alternatively that Zagal acted as a nominee or agent for Seagrams.

Rejecting the contentions of the Revenue, Walton J held:

- As Hedges and Butler could have disposed of the 76 preference shares, and had the right to receive payment in a winding up it could not be said that it was not the beneficial owner of those shares:

- The question of whether a subsidiary was agent or nominee of the parent was one of fact to be determined by a consideration of the whole of the facts of the case. On the facts, the only true and reasonable conclusion was that Zagal was not acting as agent or nominee of Seagrams in the acquisition of the shares in Bushmills.

On the first point, Walton J, in the course of his judgement said:

"But what is the test of beneficial ownership? In the case I have just cited [Wood Preservation Ltd v Prior] it was held that the vendors under a conditional contract were in the position of persons who had a tree which they must not cut down, could not sell, and of which they could enjoy none of the fruits. That being the case, so far as I can see, there was nothing to prevent the taxpayer company parting with all their shares in Vostaka had they been so minded. Of course, they would have been foolish to do so, standing the present system of taxation. But let us assume that had it altered immediately after 13 October and before the 17th, and that it had become financially highly advantageous for them to have sold them. What was there to stop them? So far as the fruit of the tree is concerned, it appears to me that the receipt of what was distributed in the winding-up is a most important part of the fruit of the tree. Putting the matter more concisely, it appears to me that prospective length of continuation of ownership is immaterial when considering the question, "Is X at a particular moment in time the beneficial owner of shares in company Z"?

With regard to the question of a subsidiary being a nominee or agent for its parent company, he said:

"It is of course of the essence of any subsidiary company that, broadly speaking, it should conform to the wishes of its parent company. The parent company, of necessity, appoints its directors, directly or at a remove; the parent company is often its main, and frequently its sole source of finance; its directors are often directors of the parent company, who thus carry the policy of the holding company directly into the board room of the subsidiary. All these factors may, and indeed sometimes do, lead to the board of the subsidiary company pursuing policies which commend themselves to the parent company but which, viewed objectively, ought not to commend themselves to an independent board of directors. None of these factors, however, whether separately or in conjunction, lead to the conclusion that, in thus obeying, or indeed possibly being made to obey, the whims and caprices of the board of the parent company, the subsidiary company is in any manner acting otherwise than on its own behalf: it is not thereby acting as an agent or nominee for its parent company."

In considering this type of arrangement today regard should be had to the general anti-avoidance provisions of s811 (see paragraph 70). It has also been suggested that the arrangements may not produce the anticipated result for reasons not argued in the case described above.

s623(1)

S623(1)(d) has since 1996 amended the legislation to restrict the relief in relation to a company leaving a group on a liquidation, to a situation where the liquidation was for bona fide commercial reasons and not for tax avoidance reasons.

The definition of a group was amended by FA99 so currently, the arrangements described above would no longer constitute a group.

81.5   **Roll-over relief : Co. leaving group.**

Where under the group "roll-over relief" provisions (see paragraph 79) a gain arising on the disposal of an asset is rolled-over by a group company against new assets acquired by another group member, the tax deferral ceases when the member owning the "new" assets leaves the group.

81.6   **Assets Derived from Other Assets**

An asset acquired by the company leaving the group is deemed to be the same as an asset owned at a later time by that company (or its 75% subsidiary or parent company) if that other asset is derived in whole or in part from the first asset. This particularly applies where the original asset was a leasehold interest and the freehold was subsequently acquired, and the asset now held is the freehold.

81.7   **Company going non-resident**

s627   A company may cease to be a member of a group by reason of the company becoming non-resident i.e. ceasing to be Irish resident. The occasion of a company ceasing to be resident in the State may cause it to be deemed to dispose of its assets at that date under the provisions of s627, and may also be the occasion of a company leaving a group owning assets obtained intra group, in relation to which deemed disposals under s623 may arise. The interaction of these two sets of deemed disposals is discussed in paragraph 74.

81.8   **Pre-disposal dividends**

s623   In paragraph 81.3 it was noted that the application of s623 is modified, where two companies cease to be a member of a group but themselves form a group immediately afterwards. S623 will not apply so as to treat them as disposing of an asset held by them as a result of a transfer between them, on the occasion of them ceasing to be a member of the main group.

The FA 96 introduced an anti avoidance measure which also applies to companies in those circumstances i.e. where two companies leave a group and themselves form a group in their own right, and they have transferred assets between them while a member of the main group. The anti-avoidance provisions apply to a dividend paid by any of the companies leaving the group to any member of their former group out of the surplus created by the intra group asset transfer. This is discussed in detail in paragraph 51.6.

82　　COMPANY LEAVING GROUP in course of MERGER

82.1　　Company leaving group in merger - outline

s624　　The charge arising when a company leaves a group (see paragraph 81) does not apply when a company leaves the group as part of a "merger". The phrase "merger" is defined and the relief is subject to certain conditions. It must be shown that the "merger" was carried out for bona fide commercial reasons, and that the avoidance of tax was not the main, or one of the main reasons for the merger.

82.2　　Meaning of "merger"

The phrase "merger" is defined as being an arrangement whereby:

- the acquiring non-group company (or companies) acquires an interest in all or part of the business of the group company

and

- one or more members of the group acquires an interest in the business of the acquiring non-group company (or companies)

... provided the relevant conditions (mentioned below) are fulfilled.

For this purpose, a member of a group is treated as carrying on, as one business, the activities of that group.

82.3　　Merger - conditions

- At least 25% of the "interest" acquired by both the remaining group company (or companies) AND the acquiring non-group company (or companies) must be in the form of ordinary share capital.

- The balance of the "interest" acquired by the remaining group members must be in the form of share capital (of any kind) or debentures.

- The value of the interests received by the remaining group members must be substantially the same as the value received by the acquiring non-group company.

The consideration received by the remaining members of the group (apart from a part which is small by comparison with the total) must be applied in acquiring an interest in the business (shares or debentures) of the acquiring company (or companies).

82.4　　Non-Resident Companies

These provisions apply to non-resident companies in the same manner as they apply to Irish resident companies for the purposes of the exception to the charge under s590 - see paragraph 67.

83   DTR - BROAD OUTLINE OF RELIEF

83.1   Outline - DTR

s828(1), (2), (3)

s826

The authority in law under which the Government enters into arrangements for the relief of double taxation is contained principally in s826. S828 applies those sections for CGT as they apply for income tax and Corporation Tax.

A disposal or deemed disposal which may give rise to capital gains tax in Ireland, or corporation tax on companies capital gains, may also potentially give rise to taxation in some other jurisdiction. Such a situation is referred to as double taxation. Relief from that double taxation may be available in the following manner:

- A double tax agreement between Ireland and the other taxing jurisdiction may either exempt the transaction from taxation in either Ireland or the other state; reduce the rate of taxation which either Ireland or the other state may apply to the transaction; or provide that either Ireland or the other jurisdiction, as the case may be, shall provide a credit against the tax which it charged in respect of the tax paid on the transaction in the other state.

s449

- Where the foreign tax is a withholding tax, which is unusual, a unilateral tax credit may be available in Ireland under s449. This however is limited to certain companies qualifying for the reduced rate of 10% corporation tax .

FA98 s60

- An Irish resident company (only) in receipt of a dividend (only) from certain non-resident companies is entitled to credit for foreign withholding tax on that dividend, and tax on the underlying profits in some cases, under a unilateral tax credit arrangement provided for in FA98 s60 and TCA97 Sch24 Para 9A.

- Credit may be available under the EU "Mergers Directive" - see paragraphs 75.3.2 and 83.3.7.

- Where none of the reliefs described above are available, the foreign tax paid would represent deductible expenditure, being a cost of disposing of the asset.

A double tax agreement is an international treaty entered into between Ireland and another taxing jurisdiction. The purpose of a double tax agreement is to provide relief from taxation. *A double tax agreement cannot impose a charge to taxation.* Where a treaty allows for one or both States to tax a particular transaction, that statement is not intended to represent a charge to tax on that transaction. The statement does no more than make it clear that the treaty does not prevent the States from taxing the transaction should their domestic law apply a charge of tax on the transaction. A charge to taxation in Ireland arises only under the domestic law of Ireland and cannot arise under a double tax agreement entered into by Ireland.

In considering the relevance of any particular double taxation agreement entered into by Ireland, it is necessary to pay particular attention to two points:

The taxes covered by the agreement : Double taxation agreements usually apply only to specified taxes. These rarely extend to all of the taxes which Ireland or any other state imposes. Thus some taxes will be covered and others will not. The reliefs which are provided extend only to the taxes stipulated in the agreement. Many of Ireland's double tax agreements, particularly those entered into prior to 1975, do not extend to capital gains tax or to corporation tax upon companies capital gains. Foreign "federal" States often have local taxes which are not covered by an international agreement.

The persons who may avail of the treaty : Although double taxation agreements are usually entered into between sovereign States they do not necessarily, or usually, extend relief to all citizens or subjects of the States in question. The persons who may avail of a treaty are defined in the treaty. The usual term used in a treaty to described those who may avail of its reliefs is "resident of a contracting State". This expression is then defined in precise terms, which vary from treaty to treaty. Some treaty benefits are available to persons who are not a resident of either State or may have klittle connection with either.

O.E.C.D. Model Treaty : Double Tax Agreements are usually (but not always) modeled on the OECD Model Treaty. This model treaty is the subject of a commentary by the OECD on its meaning and application.

Typically a treaty is structured as follows:

- Sections defining the *taxes covered* by the treaty and the persons who may avail of the treaty reliefs.

- Sections dealing with *specific types of income and gains*. These sections usually state whether either or both states may, or may not levy tax on a specific type of income or gain, and may restrict the rates of tax which may be applied.

- A section dealing with *relief from double taxation*. This section usually provides that one State shall grant a credit against the tax levied by it for the tax charged by the other. In some cases it may be where an exemption from tax in one of the States is provided.

- A section stating *when the treaty comes into operation*. This usually is stated to be a date in the year following the year in which the treaty is finally ratified by both states. The treaty usually does not make it clear when that year might be, so that it is sometimes necessary to clarify the point with the Revenue.

Double Tax Agreements are sometimes varied or supplemented by a later agreement between the states, without being completely replaced. Such supplementary agreements are called *protocols.* The treaty with Austria provides an example of such a protocol. The treaty, which dates from 1967 did not extend to CGT until it was supplemented in 1987 by a Protocol, which dealt inter alia with CGT.

The provisions of Ireland's treaties which relate to CGT follow a common pattern, although there are minor variations between treaties.

The general rule laid down in Ireland's treaties is that capital gains may be taxed only in the State of which the alienator is a resident. This general rule is then set aside in the case of capital gains arising on the disposal of specified assets.

Typically gains on disposal of interests in land or mining or exploration rights may be taxed not only in the State of which the alienator is a resident (the general rule) but also in the State in which the assets are situated, if different. Gains on the disposal of partnership interests or shares in unquoted companies the greater part of whose assets are land or mineral rights usually may be taxed where the land or mineral rights are situated, as well as the State of which the alienator is a resident.

A similar treatment is usually applied to gains arising from the assets of a permanent establishment i.e. they may be taxed in both States.

In contrast, capital gains from ships and aircraft operated in international traffic usually may be taxed only where the enterprise realising the gain is managed and controlled.

As mentioned, there are variations between treaties. The treaties with Denmark and Finland deal separately with capital gains on the disposal of containers, reflecting the significance of shipping to both countries.

The treaty with Australia deals with all the specific assets described above, but does not mention how any other assets are to be dealt with, which is a very curious omission. If there is no general restriction placed on the right of both States to tax the same asset, why provide for such a possibility in the case of land?

The treaty with Spain grants to the state in which a company is resident the right to tax a gain on the disposal of its shares by a resident of the other State, if he had held directly or indirectly at least a 25% interest in the company during the 12 months prior to the disposal. This provision is unique amongst Ireland's treaties. Generally they permit a State in which the person disposing of shares is not a resident to tax a gain on the shares only where the company's assets consist mainly of land in that other State. Some treaties extend a similar taxation right in respect of disposal of interests in a partnership whose assets consist mainly of land (e.g. Russia, Sweden, Spain) but others, (e.g. Portugal) do not.

83.2   **TCA97 s826**

s826   S826 applies for the purposes of CGT with the modification that references to capital gains are substituted for references to income, and references to CGT are substituted for references to income tax.

Sch24   Under s826 therefore, the Government may make an order declaring that arrangements entered into with a foreign government for the relief of double taxation in respect of CGT will have the force of law. Where an order is proposed to be made, a draft thereof must be laid before Dail Eireann and the order may not be made until a resolution approving the draft has been passed by the Dail. Any such order may be revoked by a subsequent order. Where the arrangements for relief provide for a credit for foreign tax paid against Irish tax, the provisions of Schedule 24 (provisions as to relief by way of credit for foreign tax) apply for the purposes of calculating the relief (see paragraph 83.3).

Under s826 the Revenue Commissioners may make regulations generally for carrying out the provisions of that section, or any arrangements having the force of law under that section.

s826; s827   S826 is applied to corporation tax by s826 and s827.

83.3   **Credit relief - schedule 24**

Where arrangements have been entered into for double taxation relief, and these provide for credit to be allowed against Irish tax for foreign tax paid, Sch 24 will apply for the purposes of implementing the relief.

The main provisions of Sch 24 which apply are as follows:

83.3.1   **Manner of granting Credit**

Where credit is to be allowed against Irish CGT, the amount of the Irish tax payable will be reduced by the amount of the credit.

83.3.2   **Requirement as to residence**

Credit will not be allowed against capital gains tax for any year of assessment unless the person chargeable is resident in Ireland for that year of assessment.

83.3.3   **Limit on credit to be allowed**

A limit is placed on the amount of foreign tax to be allowed as a credit against Irish tax payable. The credit cannot exceed the effective overall rate of Irish tax on the gains on which the foreign tax has been paid. The rate is calculated by dividing the total Irish CGT payable for the year by the total CG of the year (as computed **under Irish law).**

83.3.4   **Calculation of Irish Tax where credit is allowed for foreign tax**

(i)   Where tax is charged on the remittance basis, the charge is made on the aggregate of the remittance and any tax credit available.

(ii)   No deduction is allowed in computing chargeable gains for the foreign tax paid.

(iii)   Except where the remittance basis applies, any part of the foreign tax paid which cannot be allowed as a credit will be allowed as a deduction in computing chargeable gains.

83.3.5   **Claim for credit relief**

Any claim for allowance by way of credit for foreign tax must be made in writing to the Inspector Taxes not later than six years from the end of the relevant year of assessment.

83.3.6   **Net basis of calculation**

FA95 s60   s.60 FA95 (now in Sch24) clarified that double taxation relief is to be computed on the so-called "net "basis rather than the "gross" basis. This distinction is relevant mainly to taxes on income, and should not have any affect on tax payable in respect of chargeable gains.

83.3.7   **Credit under mergers directive**

Under the provisions of s634 which implement the Mergers Directive of the EU, it may be possible to obtain credit in Ireland for tax which would have arisen in another member state of the EU on a transfer of assets, but for the fact that either the directive, or the domestic law of the other EU member state deferred recognition of the gain and accordingly it did not result in an immediate charge of tax.

s634

Relief under s826 is available only in respect of taxes which have become payable. s634 can grant credit for foreign taxes at a time when they have not yet become payable, and even if it is not certain that they even will become payable.

Credit under the Mergers Directive will arise where:

— A resident company transfers a foreign branch to a non-resident company.

— A transfer can include part only of the trade carried on through the branch.

— The transfer must include all of the assets used for the trade, or part of the trade, being transferred, other than cash.

— The consideration must include securities issued to the Irish resident company by the non-resident company. "Securities" includes shares and debentures. The consideration does not have to consist solely of securities, but must include some such securities. It would seem that the consideration could consist almost entirely of cash, provided some part of the consideration, no matter how small, consists of securities.

— The transfer must be treated by the other EU member state (in which the branch is located) as being on a "no gain/no loss basis" or on a basis which defers recognition of the gain until the assets are disposed of by the transferee company.

Where the conditions outlined above are met, and the other member state provides a certificate concerning the tax treatment described above, and stating the amount of tax deferred (offsetting any losses arising on the transfer of some assets against gains arising on other assets in the transfer), then credit must be granted in Ireland for the deferred tax.

It should be noted that the deferred tax referred to may never become payable. If the transfer is treated in the other member state as being on a "no gain/no loss" basis, tax would only become payable on a subsequent disposal of those assets for a consideration at least equal to the value which would otherwise have applied at the date of the first transfer. If the assets in fact fall in value subsequent to the transfer, their later disposal to a third party may not result in any tax becoming payable. This does not affect the entitlement to credit for the "deferred" tax on the occasion of the first mentioned transfer from the Irish resident company to the non-resident company.

The entitlement to a credit for the "deferred" tax arises whether or not the transferor and transferee companies are connected.

Example 415

Company A is an Irish resident company which has a branch in Belgium. It decides to amalgamate its branch with a business carried on by a Belgian company. For this purpose a new company is formed, which will be held 50/50 by the Irish resident company and the Belgian company. The new company is Newco. Newco issues 100 Bel Fr. 1 shares to the Irish company, and to the Belgian company as part consideration for the assets transferred to it, and provides the balance of the consideration (as agreed between the parties) in cash.

The transaction is not one to which s617 applies since the Irish resident company is not in a 75% group with Newco. Accordingly s632 (see paragraph 75.3) which could treat Newco as Irish resident for the purpose of the group relief, is not effective. s631 does not apply because the consideration does not consist entirely of securities issued by Newco (see paragraph 75.3).

*For the purpose of this example it is **assumed** that the transfer is treated in Belgium as being on a no gain/no loss basis (this may not be the case). The Irish resident company will be chargeable to Irish corporation tax on companies chargeable gains in respect of any gain arising on a disposal of branch assets. However it will be entitled to claim a credit against the corporation tax resulting for the amount of Belgian tax that would have arisen had Belgium not treated the transaction as being on a "no gain/no loss" basis.*

83.3.8   Unilateral Tax Credit

FA98 s60

FA98 s60 introduced a unilateral tax credit. This is an entitlement to credit for foreign taxes even in the absence of a double tax agreement. However it is confined to the situation where an Irish resident company is chargeable to tax in Ireland in respect of the receipt of a dividend paid by a company not resident in Ireland. It therefore has no direct relevance to CGT.

Sch24 Para9A, Para 9B

Where the Irish resident company holds at least 25% of the share capital of the foreign resident company which pays a dividend, it is entitled to a credit not only for taxes on the dividend, but also for taxes paid by the non resident company (and its associated companies, where it obtained profits from those associated companies). The taxes paid by the non resident companies (known as underlying tax) can include taxes paid by those companies which is akin to Irish CGT. If therefore an Irish resident company obtains a dividend from a 25% or greater held foreign resident company, and the dividend is paid out of Capital Gains which have borne tax abroad, a credit will be available for the tax paid by the foreign company on those Capital Gains.

84   **IRELAND / UK TAX TREATY**

In the remainder of this chapter

- the UK treaty is examined in detail so far as it affects capital gains.

- The provisions of other treaties which extend to capital gains tax are then examined in a manner which highlights the respects by which they differ from the UK treaty.

84.1   **Broad Outline**

The Ireland/UK tax treaty was the first to become law since the introduction of CGT in Ireland. It follows the OECD model treaty in relation to CGT as well as the other taxes.

84.2   **Terminology**

Before dealing with the detailed provisions it is necessary to consider some of the special terms used in this treaty, and tax treaties generally.

84.2.1   **'Resident Of'**

It is important to distinguish between the terms 'RESIDENT IN' and 'RESIDENT OF'. The first is a term used in general tax law (in some countries) to describe the status of a person in relation to that country for the purposes of the general charge to tax there. Very broadly speaking, and subject to the many exceptions, a person is taxable in a country if he is resident in that country. Different countries have their own tests for deciding whether a person is resident there for tax purposes.

The term *'resident of'* is used in tax treaties. Broadly speaking, a person chargeable to tax in both countries who is a 'resident of' one of them would be entitled under the treaty to claim exemption in the other (each treaty usually includes exceptions to this rule). Where exemption is not available because of the exceptions mentioned, relief will normally be available under the treaty by way of credit.

The term is defined in each treaty. For example, in the Ireland/Netherlands treaty 'resident of Ireland' means:

"(1) *any company whose business is managed and controlled in Ireland;...*

(2) *any other person who is resident in Ireland for the purposes of Irish tax and not resident in the Netherlands for the purposes of Netherlands tax".*

Most of Ireland's treaties define the term in the same manner. It should be noted that, in that case, a person resident in both countries for tax purposes would not usually be a 'resident of' either.

In the Irish/UK treaty, however, a much more comprehensive definition of the term 'resident of' is included. Under this definition it is much easier than normal to qualify as a 'resident of' either Ireland or the UK. Article 1 states that "This convention shall apply to persons who are resident of one or both of the contracting States". If a person does not qualify as a resident of one or both of the countries, no relief is available under the tax treaty even by way of tax credit.

The full definition of 'resident of' for the purposes of the Ireland/UK treaty is a follows:

ARTICLE 4

Fiscal Domicile

(1) *For the purposes of this Convention, the term "resident of a Contracting State" means, subject to the provisions of paragraphs (2) and (3) of this Article, any person who, under the law of that State, is liable to taxation therein by reason of his domicile, residence, place of management or any other criterion of a similar nature; the term does not include any individual who is liable to tax in that Contracting State only if he derives income from sources therein. The terms 'resident of Ireland' and 'resident of the UK' shall be construed accordingly.*

(2) *Where by reason of the provisions of paragraph (1) of this Article an individual is a resident of both Contracting States, then his status shall be determined in accordance with the following rules:*

   (a) *he shall be deemed to be a resident of the Contracting State in which he has a permanent home available to him. If he has a permanent home available to him in both Contracting States, he shall be deemed to be a resident of the Contracting State with which his personal and economic relations are closer (centre of vital interests);*

   (b) *if the Contracting State in which he has his centre of vital interests cannot be determined or if he has not a permanent home available to him in either Contracting State, he shall be deemed to be a resident of the Contracting State in which he has an habitual abode;*

   (c) *if he has an habitual abode in both Contracting States or in neither of them, he shall be deemed to be a resident of the Contracting State of which he is a national;*

   (d) *if he is a national of both Contracting States or of neither of them, the competent authorities of the Contracting States shall settle the question by mutual agreement.*

(3) *Where by reason of the provisions of paragraph (1) of this Article a person other than an individual is a resident of both Contracting*

States, then it shall be deemed to be a resident of the Contracting State in which its place of effective management is situated.

84.2.2   **Enterprise of a Contracting State**

An 'enterprise of Contracting State' is one which is carried on by a 'resident of' that State.

84.2.3   **Permanent Establishment**

The definition is as follows:

ARTICLE 5

Permanent Establishment

(1) *For the purposes of this Convention, the term "permanent establishment" means a fixed place of business in which the business of the enterprise is wholly or partly carried on.*

(2) *The term "permanent establishment" shall include especially:*

   (a) *a place of management;*

   (b) *a branch;*

   (c) *an office;*

   (d) *a factory;*

   (e) *a workshop;*

   (f) *a mine, oil well, quarry or other place of extraction of natural resources;*

   (g) *an installation or structure used for the exploration of natural resources.*

(3) *The term "permanent establishment" shall not be deemed to include:*

   (a) *the use of facilities solely for the purposes of storage, display or delivery of goods or merchandise belonging to the enterprise;*

   (b) *the maintenance of a stock of goods or merchandise belonging to the enterprise solely for the purpose of storage display or delivery;*

   (c) *the maintenance of a stock of goods or merchandise belonging to the enterprise solely for the purpose of processing by another enterprise;*

   (d) *the maintenance of a fixed place of business solely for the purpose of purchasing goods or merchandise, or for collecting information, for the enterprise;*

   (e) *the maintenance of a fixed place of business solely for the purpose of advertising, for the supply of information, for scientific*

> *research or for similar activities which have a preparatory or auxiliary character, for the enterprise.*

(4) *A person acting in a Contracting State on behalf of an enterprise of the other Contracting State – other than an agent of independent status to whom the provisions of paragraph (6) of this Article apply – shall be deemed to be a permanent establishment in the first-mentioned State if he has, and habitually exercises in that State, an authority to conclude contracts in the name of the enterprise, unless his activities are limited to the purchase of goods or merchandise for the enterprise.*

(5) *A person carrying on activities in connection with the exploration or exploitation of the sea bed and subsoil and their natural resources situated in a Contracting State shall be deemed to be carrying on a trade through a permanent establishment in that Contracting State.*

(6) *An enterprise of a Contracting State shall not be deemed to have a permanent establishment in the other Contracting State merely because it carries on business in that other State through a broker, general commission agent or any other agent of an independent status, where such persons are acting in the ordinary course of their business.*

(7) *The fact that a company which is a resident of a Contracting State controls or is controlled by a company which is a resident of the other Contracting State, or which carries on business in that other State (whether through a permanent establishment or otherwise), shall not of itself constitute either company a permanent establishment of the other.*

84.3   Scheme of Relief — General

It is important to remember that the provisions of tax treaties are relieving provisions and do not impose a charge to tax. Therefore, it is stated that a gain "may be taxed" in a particular contracting State, the gain is taxable there only if the domestic legislation imposes a charge to tax on such gains. A tax treaty does not impose a charge to tax where domestic tax law has not done so.

The scheme of relief in the Ireland/UK treaty is set out in the following sub-paragraphs.

84.4   Assets Generally

Article 14 of the treaty with the UK sets out specific rules concerning which of the two States, or whether both States might, tax gains arising on the disposal of specific types of assets. The rules relating to those assets specifically dealt with in the article are described below.

The article provides, in Clause 5, a general rule for assets of a type not specifically referred to in the article i.e. for assets generally. It provides that capital gains from assets not specifically dealt with in the article should be taxed only where the "alienator" is a resident. "Alienator" is not specifically defined but in the context clearly means the person owning the asset and making the disposal. There is however an important exception to this rule. The clause goes on to state that where an individual is subject to tax in the state in which he is a resident only by reference to amounts received in that state (i.e. *under the remittance basis*) the restriction of the right to tax the gain to the state of which he is a resident will not apply to so much of the gains as is not received in that state.

Example 416

Pierre is domiciled in France but resident in Ireland. He owns a painting which is hanging in his brother's house in London. He sends it to an auction in London and disposes of it for £10,000. The capital gain arising is £2,000. Pierre lodges the proceeds of sale to his bank account in France, and transfers £1,000 from that account into his account in Dublin.

The £1,000 transferred by Pierre is treated in Ireland as a remittance of part of the gain on the disposal, and to that extent the gain is charged to tax in Ireland. The balance of £1,000 of the gain, which is retained in France and not remitted into Ireland, is not taxed in Ireland.

Under Article 14(5) of the UK Treaty, the UK is permitted to charge tax on the £1,000 of the gain which escaped Irish tax, but is not permitted to charge tax on the £1,000 of the gain taxed in Ireland. Ireland, as the country of residence of the alienator, was alone entitled to tax that gain. Of course UK domestic law would not actually impose a charge to CGT on Pierre in the circumstances outlined above. However the treaty would permit the UK to do so, if it chose to amend its domestic law.

84.5   Ships and Aircraft

A special provision applies to disposals of ships and aircraft operated in international traffic and movable property pertaining to the operation of such ships and aircraft. It is provided that gains arising from such disposals are taxable only in the country of which the person making the disposal is a resident.

84.6   Shares

Clause 2 of Article 14 deals with shares. It provides that a capital gain from the alienation (disposal) of shares deriving their value or the greater part of their value, directly or indirectly from immovable property may be taxed in the state in which the immovable property is situated. However this rule does not apply to shares quoted on the stock exchange.

The clause makes no reference to the state in which the person making the disposal is resident, where that is not the state in which the land is located from the which the shares derive their value. Because the clause places no restriction on the right of the country of residence to tax the gain, its affect is to leave that country with an unrestricted right to tax the gain.

Example 417

John, who is resident in Ireland and not resident in the UK, owns all of the share capital in Land Holdings Ltd. It is an unquoted company and its only asset is a building in London. John disposes of the shares.

Article 14(2) of the UK treaty permits the UK to tax John in respect of the disposal. It does not of course impose such a charge to tax - that is a matter for UK domestic law. All the article is doing is to make it clear that there is no restriction on the UK's right to tax the gain. Ireland also may tax the gain (as indeed it does under its domestic law).

The article does not state how it is to be determined as to whether shares derive the greater part of their value directly or indirectly from immovable property. It is notoriously difficult to determine from what shares derive their value. The comparable article in other treaties often use an alternative phrase which is much easier to understand - shares in a company the greater part of whose assets consist of immovable property.

The treatment outlined above does not apply to shares quoted on a stock exchange (no matter where that stock exchange might be). Because such quoted shares have been specifically mentioned however, they do not fall into the general rule for assets not specifically dealt with, which is described above. The true affect therefore of the reference to quoted shares in Article 14(2) is to provide that the UK cannot tax a gain on the disposal of quoted shares deriving their value from immovable property in the UK, when disposed of by a resident of Ireland.

Example 418

John disposes of his shares in British Land PLC, which is a quoted company deriving its value from land in the UK. John is resident in Ireland and not resident in the UK.

Article 14(2) would not permit the UK to tax John on a gain arising on the disposal of the British Land PLC shares. In fact the UK domestic law does not seek to impose such a charge. The Article does not restrict the right of Ireland (as a country of residence) to tax the gain.

84.7   **Property of Permanent Establishment**

The treaty permits a resident of one country, in certain circumstances, to be chargeable in respect of gains arising on disposals of movable property situated in the other. The charge to tax is allowed to arise where the property situated in that country:

(a)   is part of the business property of a permanent establishment situated there

or

(b)   is property pertaining to a fixed base available to the person making the disposal for the purpose of performing professional services.

Example 419

George is resident in the UK and is a "resident of " the UK for the purposes of the treaty provisions. For some years he carried on a trade in Ireland through a branch. On 30 June 1994 he sold the business in Ireland and gains arose on the disposal of the business premises and the goodwill of the Irish branch.

George's position regarding Irish capital gains is as follows:

s.4

- *GAIN ON DISPOSAL OF IRISH BUSINESS PREMISES*

    The treaty provides that gains arising on disposals of immovable property may be taxed in the country in which the property is located. Therefore, this gain may be taxed in Ireland although George is resident in and is a resident of the UK but only if a charge arises under Irish domestic law. In this case a charge under Irish Law does arise as gains on disposals of Irish land by non-residents are taxable in Ireland (1975 Act s.4).

    As he is resident in the UK, George will also be subject to UK tax on the gain. Irish tax payable will be available as a credit in arriving at any UK tax payable (under the treaty credit provisions).

- *GAIN ON DISPOSAL OF GOODWILL*

    Goodwill is regarded as movable property. Generally under the terms of the treaty, gains arising on disposals of movable property are taxable in the country of which the person making the disposal is a resident. However, George falls into one of the exceptions outlined above as the goodwill forms part of the business property of George's permanent establishment in Ireland. Accordingly, the gain on the goodwill is subject to Irish tax but only if a charge arises under Irish domestic law. In fact, a charge does arise in Ireland as non-residents are subject to Irish tax in respect of gains arising on assets situated in Ireland and used for the purposes of a trade carried on here through a branch (1975 Act s.4).

    Again, Irish tax paid will be allowed as a credit against George's UK liability.

84.8   **Immovable Property**

Capital gains from the disposal of immovable property may be taxed in the country in which the property is situated. Unquoted shares deriving their value (or the greater part of their value) from immovable property (directly or indirectly) may be taxed in the country in which the property is situated.

Example 420

Bill is a "resident of" the UK and disposes of land situated in Ireland. Under general tax law Bill is resident in the UK for tax purposes.

Any gain arising may be taxed in Ireland as the property is situated there. The fact that it may be taxed in Ireland does not exclude it from any charge to UK tax which may arise. Accordingly, as Bill is resident in the UK he is also subject to UK tax on the gain. Of course, under the credit relief provisions, credit will be available against UK tax for Irish CGT paid.

Example 421

Tony is resident in Ireland for tax purposes and is a "resident of Ireland" for the purposes of the treaty. He disposes of land situated in the UK.

Tony is chargeable to Irish CGT on any gains arising as he is resident in Ireland for tax purposes. Under the terms of the treaty, the gain "may be taxed" in the UK. However, UK domestic law does not impose a charge to tax in respect of gains arising to a non-resident on the disposal of UK land. (In this case the law in the UK is different from that in Ireland). Accordingly, no UK tax arises on the gain.

The term immovable property would include items such as land and buildings. The treaty does not provide an exhaustive definition but states that:

- the term is to be defined in accordance with the law of the country in which the property is situated, and

- the term is to include:

    (i)   property accessory to immovable property

    (ii) livestock and equipment used in agriculture and forestry

    (iii) rights to which the provisions of general law respecting landed property apply

    (iv) usufruct of immovable property and rights to variable or fixed payments as consideration for the working of, or the right to work mineral deposits

The term does not include ships, boats and aircraft.

84.9   **Credit Relief**

Where, under the terms of the treaty, gains are chargeable in both countries (e.g. resident of UK disposing of land in Ireland) relief is granted by way of tax credit.

Tax on gains arising from sources in the UK is allowed as a credit against Irish tax paid in respect of those gains. The exact manner in which credit is actually granted in Ireland is governed by the rules relating to credit relief outlined in paragraph 83.3.

Tax on gains arising from sources in Ireland is allowed as a credit against UK tax paid in respect of those gains. Again, the credit granted in the UK will be calculated by reference to the detailed UK rules governing credit relief.

85   OTHER TAX TREATIES

85.1   Ireland/Australia

The definition of *"Resident of -"* is the same as in the UK treaty except that a person who would otherwise be a resident of Australia is to be regarded as such only if he is taxable in Australia on income from sources in Ireland or, if that income is exempt from Australian tax, it is so exempt solely because it is subject to Irish tax.

The Australian treaty is unusual in that it does not appear to include any explicate rule to deal with taxation of gains arising from *assets not explicitly referred to* in the provisions relating to capital gains. In the absence of any provision in the treaty to deal with this matter there would seem to be no restriction on the right of either or both states to tax gains on assets not explicitly referred to.

The provision relating to *Ships or Aircraft* operated in international traffic are generally similar to that in the UK treaty. It does explicitly require that the ship/aircraft should be so operated while owned by the enterprise gaining the benefit of the relief. This is not explicitly stated in the UK treaty although it might be inferred in it.

The provision relating to *shares* states that shares in the company whose assets consist principally of land or exploration rights situated in one of the contracting states, may be taxed in the state in which the land or exploration rights are situated. There is a similar provision in relation to an interest in a partnership or trust the greater part of whose value is derived directly or indirectly from land or exploration rights.

The reference to shares does not exclude quoted shares.

Gains from the disposal of *land* or exploration rights may be taxed where that land or those rights is situated.

The arrangements for *credit for taxes* and capital gains are similar to those in the UK treaty.

85.2   Ireland/Austria

The meaning of *"Resident of"* is the same as in the UK treaty.

The provision relating to *assets not specifically referred to* in the provisions relating to capital gains is the same as in the UK treaty.

The provision relating to *Ships and Aircraft* operated in international traffic states that gains on such disposals may be taxed only in the contracting state in which the place of effective management of the enterprise which owns them is situated. This wording is slightly different from the UK treaty.

The provision relating to *shares* is the same as in the UK treaty.

The provisions relating to *permanent establishment assets* are the same as in the UK treaty.

Capital gains arising from the disposal of *land* may be taxed in the state in which the land is situated.

The arrangements for *credit for taxes* and capital gains are similar to those in the UK treaty.

85.3   Ireland/Czech Republic

The definition of *"resident of"* is the same as in the UK treaty.

The rule relating to gains arising on *assets not specifically referred to* in the treaty is the same as in the UK treaty except that it does not contain the proviso relating to gains which are taxable only on a remittance basis.

The treatment of *ships and aircraft* in international traffic is the same as in the UK treaty. It extends also to movable property relating to the operation of such ships and aircraft.

The rule relating to *shares* is generally the same as that in the UK treaty. However it applies to quoted shares as well as unquoted. Shares in a company whose assets consist principally of land or mineral rights in either of the states can be subjected to taxation in that state.

The rule relating to the *property of a permanent establishment,* or fixed base for the provision of personal services, is the same as that in the UK treaty.

Gains from the disposal of *land or mineral rights* may be taxed in the state in which they are situated.

The provisions relating to *credit for taxes paid* in another state are the same as in the UK treaty.

85.4   Ireland/Denmark

The definition of *"Resident of"* with respect to an individual is the same as in the UK treaty. The tie-breaker clause for a company resident in both states or neither is the same as that described for the Finland treaty below.

The rule relating to gains from the disposal of *assets not specifically referred to* in the provisions relating to capital gains are the same as in the UK. However, when an individual has been a resident of a contracting state for the period of five years or more prior to the disposal that contracting state may tax him in respective of capital gains on shares accruing up to the date at which he becomes a resident of the other contracting state.

The provisions relating to gains from *Ships and Aircraft* operated in international traffic differ from those in the UK treaty. The Danish treaty provides such gains will be taxable only in the contracting state in which the place of effective management of the enterprise is situated. The clause does not explain what enterprise it is referring to but it must be presumed that it is the enterprise which operates the ships or aircraft. The clause goes on to provide that the benefits of that provision apply to Scandinavian Airlines Systems (SAS) but only proportional to such gains of SAS as correspond to the participation in the consortium held by the Danish partner of SAS (DDL).

Gains from the *disposal of containers* (including trailers, barges and related equipment for the transport of containers) used for the transport of goods and merchandise are taxable only in the contracting state in which the place of effective management of the enterprise operating them is situated except where the containers are used for transport solely between places which are within the other contracting state.

The provisions relating to gains on the disposal of *shares* extend also to interests in a partnership and are expressed in terms of a company or partnership the assets of which consist principally of land situated in a contracting state or of shares in a company the assets of which consist principally of such land. The clause provides that the gains on such shares or interests in a partnership may be taxed in the State in which the land is situated provided that, under the laws of that State, such gains are subject to the same taxation rules as gains from the disposal of land. The provision is an unusual provision not found in other treaties. In principle it would deny the country in which the land is situated the right to tax such gains if it applied a different system of taxation to them than it applied to the disposal of land per se.

It is likely that the Irish rules relating to the taxation of land would be the same rules as would apply on the disposal of shares derived their value from land notwithstanding that in some detail there would be necessary differences (e.g. rules relating to the granting of leases would not apply to shares).

The rule relating to *immovable property of a permanent establishment* is the same as in the UK treaty.

Gains arising from the disposal of *land* may be taxed in the state in which the land is situated.

The Danish treaty does not make explicit provision for credit in Denmark for Irish tax on capital gains, although it does make such provision in relation to tax on income. The treaty makes the normal provision in relation to *credit in Ireland for Danish tax* on capital gains.

The treaty provides that where gains are partly relieved from tax in one state and an individual was taxed in the other state only on a *remittance basis* on those gains, then the reliefs under the treaty are to be applied only in respect of the amounts remitted.

85.5 Ireland/Estonia

The definition of *"resident of"* with respect to an individual is the same as in the UK treaty. However in the case of a person who is not an individual, the tiebreaker clause provides that the matter shall be settled by mutual agreement. Paragraph 2 of the Protocol to the treaty provides that in attempting to reach such agreement, the place of effective management, and the place of incorporation will be taken into account. In the absence of mutual agreement, the person is not entitled to benefits under the treaty!

Gains from the alienation of property not specifically referred to in the article on capital gains is taxable only in the country of residence of the alienator. However either state is entitled to levy a tax on gains on any property on a resident of the other state if he was resident in the first mentioned state in the three years prior to the disposal of the property and held the property at the time he became a resident of the other state.

Gains arising from the disposal of ships, aircraft or containers are not specifically referred to and therefore would be taxable only in the country of residence.

Gains on the disposal of shares and partnership interests and interests under a trust, where the greater part of the assets of the entity in question consist of land in the other contracting state may be taxed in the contracting state in which the land is situate. There is no specific exclusion of quoted shares.

Gains on the disposal of the movable property of a permanent establishment (including a disposal of the permanent establishment itself) may be taxed in the state in which it is situate.

Gains on the disposal of land and mineral rights may be taxed in the state in which they are situate.

The rules relating to credit for tax oblige each state to provide credit for the tax levied by the other.

85.6   **Ireland/Finland**

The definition of *"Resident of "* is the same in the Finnish treaty as in the UK treaty so far as concerns individuals. The Finnish treaty differs from the UK as regards companies. The Finnish treaty provides that a company which is resident of both contracting states or neither of them under the standard rule is to be regarded as a resident of Ireland if its place of effective management is situated in Ireland; and is to be regarded as a resident of Finland if its place of effective management is situated in Finland or if it is incorporated in Finland and its place of effective management is not situated in Ireland.

The rule relating to gains from *assets not specifically referred to* in the provisions with relation to capital gains is the same as in the UK except that the proviso relating to gains taxed only on a remittance basis does not appear.

Gains arising to an enterprise carried on by a resident of a contracting state from the disposal of *ships, aircraft or containers* (including trailers, barges and related equipment for the transport of containers) operated in international traffic, or movable property pertaining to the operation of such, are taxable only in that State. This differs from the UK treaty in containing a reference to containers. The expression "enterprise of a contracting state" is also different from the expression used in the UK treaty (resident of a contracting state) but that is not likely to result in any difference in practice.

The rule relating to *shares* is the same as in the UK treaty. It also in the Finnish treaty extends to an interest in a partnership or trust the assets of which consist principally of immovable property situated in a contracting state or of shares deriving the greater part of their value from lands situated in a contracting state. Gains from the disposal of such an interest in a partnership or trust may be taxed in the contracting state in which the land is situated.

Quoted shares are those quoted on the Irish or Helsinki Stock Exchange, or any other Stock Exchange agreed on between the Tax Authorities of the two states.

The *permanent establishment gains* clause is the same as in the UK treaty.

Gains arising from the disposal of *land* may be taxed in the state in which the land is situated.

The provisions relating to *credit in one state for tax charged by the other state* are as in the UK treaty. The Finnish treaty does not explicitly refer to a credit in Finland for Irish tax on capital gains. It may be that the provisions relating to Irish tax on income are intended to extend to capital gains.

85.7 **Ireland/Hungary**

The definition of *"resident of"* is the same as in the UK treaty.

The rule relating to gains from *property not specifically referred to* in other provisions in relation to capital gains is the same as in the UK treaty except that the proviso relating to gains taxable on a remittance basis does not apply.

The rule relating to *ships or aircraft* operated in international traffic is the same as in the UK treaty. It also extends to road transport vehicles operating in international traffic, and movable property relating to the operation of such ships, aircraft or road transport vehicles.

The rule relating to *shares* extends to quoted as well as unquoted shares, and to partnerships. Gains from the alienation of shares whose assets consist principally of rights in land or mineral rights situated in a contracting state may be taxed in that contracting state. The same rule applies to shares in a company whose assets consist principally of shares in a company such as has been just described, but the article does not go on to consider the further tier of ownership i.e. where a company's assets consist principally of shares in a company whose principal assets consist in turn of shares in another company, whose assets consist of land situated in a state.

The rule relating to movable *property of a permanent establishment* or fixed base for the rendering of independent personal services, is as in the UK treaty.

Gains on the disposal of *land or mineral rights* may be taxed in the state in which they are situated.

The provisions relating to *credit for tax is paid* in the other state are the same as in the UK treaty.

85.8 **Ireland/Israel**

The definition of *"resident of"* is broadly similar to that in the UK treaty, except that in determining residence, "centre of vital interests" receives priority over the place where a person has a permanent home available to them.

The rule relating to gains on the disposal of *assets not specifically referred to* in the provisions relating to capital gains is the same as in the UK treaty.

The provisions relating to the disposal of *ships or aircraft* operating in international traffic (and movable property connected therewith) are the same as those in the UK.

The rules relating to *shares* differ from those in the UK. Gains on the disposal of shares (quoted or unquoted) arising to a resident of one state on the disposal of shares in a company resident in the other state may be taxed in that other state only if the resident of the other state who is disposing of them had owned either directly or indirectly at any time within a two year period preceding the disposal, shares giving the right to 10% or more of the voting powers in the company. Indirect ownership extends to ownership by a related person. Gains from the disposal of shares 50% or more of whose assets consist directly or indirectly of land or mineral rights situated in a contracting state may be taxed in that state. This includes both quoted and unquoted shares. Gains from the disposal of an interest in a partnership, or trust, or estate whose property consists principally of land or mineral rights situated in a contracting state can be taxed in that state.

The rules relating to gains on movable *property of a permanent establishment* are the same as in the UK treaty.

Gains arising on the disposal of *land or mineral rights* may be taxed in the state in which they are situated.

The provisions relating to *credit for taxes paid* are similar to those in the UK treaty.

85.9   Ireland/Italy

The double tax agreement with Italy dates from 1973 and predates the introduction of capital gains tax. Capital gains tax is not specifically referred to as among the Irish taxes covered.

Article 2 (2) states that taxes on gains from the alienation of moveable or immovable property are to be regarded as taxes on income. Nonetheless, it seems unlikely that the convention could apply to capital gains tax.

85.10   Ireland/Korea

The definition of *"Resident of "* is as in UK treaty.

The rule relating to gains from the disposal of *assets not specifically referred to* in the provisions relating to capital gains is the same as that in the UK except that there is no proviso relating to gains taxed only on a remittance basis.

The rule relating to gains from the disposal of *ships or aircraft* operated in international traffic is worded differently to that of the UK although its effect is probably the same. Gains from the disposal of such ships or aircraft which form part of the assets of an enterprise carried on by a resident of one of the states, shall be taxable only in that state.

The treatment in the Korean treaty of *shares* is similar to that in the UK treaty except that the reference in the Korean treaty is to shares in a company the property of which consists directly or indirectly principally of land situated in a contracting state, rather than the UK formula which is a reference to shares deriving their value or the greater part of their value directly or indirectly from immovable property etc.

The Korean treaty, like some other recent Treaties, defines a *quoted share* as one quoted on either the Korean or Irish Stock Exchange, or any other Stock Exchange that the competent Authorities of the contracting states may mutually agree. In contrast the UK treaty does not attempt to define this expression. This could be relevant to an Irish company quoted only on NASDAQ.

The rule relating to *immovable property of a permanent establishment* is as in the UK treaty.

Gains arising from the disposal of *land* may be taxed in the state in which the land is situated.

The provisions relating to *credit for taxes paid* in another state are the same as in the UK treaty.

85.11   Ireland/Latvia

The residence rules are in line with those of the UK treaty. The tiebreaker for a person who is not an individual is "mutual agreement", and if this is not reached, no benefits are available. Paragraph 2 of the protocol to the treaty provides that the place of effective management, and the place of incorporation, will be taken into account in attempting to reach mutual agreement.

Gains from the alienation of property not specifically referred to are taxable only in the State of residence. However each State retains the right to tax a former resident for the first three years after giving up residence.

The rule relating to ships and aircraft is the same as that in the UK.

Shares deriving value from land may be taxed by the State in which the land is situated. This does not extend to interests in partnership or in trusts (unlike the Estonian treaty negotiated about the same time).

The rule relating to the movable property of a permanent establishment is the same as in the UK.

Gains arising from the disposal of land or mineral rights may be taxed in the State in which they are situate.

The provisions relating to taxes paid in another State are the same as in the UK treaty.

85.12 **Ireland/Lithuania**

The rule relating to residence is as stated in Latvia above.

The rule relating to gains on the disposal of assets not specifically referred to is that they may be taxed only in the State of residence of the alienator.

The rule relating to ships and aircraft in international traffic is the same as that in the UK.

Shares deriving their value from land may be taxed in the State in which the land is situated. The same rule applies to partnership interests and trust interests.

The rules relating to gains on a permanent establishment are the same as in the UK treaty.

Gains from the disposal of land may be taxed in the State in which the land is situated.

The provisions for credit for taxes paid in another State are the same as in the UK treaty.

85.13 **Ireland/Malaysia**

The rule relating to "resident of" is generally the same as in the UK treaty. Where a person who is not an individual is dual resident, the tiebreaker is the place of effective management. Article 24 confines the benefits of the treaty, in a remittance basis case, to so much as is actually remitted.

Gains on the disposal of assets not specifically referred to in the provisions relating to capital gains tax are taxable in the country of residence of the alienator.

Gains from the disposal of ships or aircraft operated in international traffic, and movable property relating to their operation, are taxable only in the country of residence of the alienator.

Gains from shares, or interest in a partnership whose assets consist principally of land (either directly or indirectly) may be taxed in the country in which the land is situated.

Gains from the disposal of movable property of a permanent establishment (including of the entire permanent establishment) may be taxed in the State in which it is situated.

Gains from the disposal of land may be taxed where the land is situated.

The provisions relating to credit for foreign taxes are broadly the same as in the UK treaty but do include a "tax sparing clause" in relation to certain Malaysian tax incentives which is valid up to 31 December 2009.

85.14   **Ireland/Mexico**

The rule in relation to "resident of" is the same as in the UK treaty. Where a person other than an individual is dual resident, they will be treated as resident where their place of effective management is situated.

Gains on the disposal of property not specifically mentioned in the CGT article, or surprisingly, in Article 12 relating to royalties, are taxed only in the state of residence in the alienator.

Article 12 dealing with royalties includes under that heading gains derived from the disposal of a right or property in relation to literary, artistic or scientific work including films, recordings, patents, trademarks, designs and models, plans, secret formula or process, industrial commercial or scientific equipment, and business information. Gains on the disposal of such rights or property contingent on the productivity, use or disposition of them, may be taxed in the country in which they are located in an amount not exceeding 10% of the gross royalties (so defined).

Gains from the alienation of ships and aircraft in international traffic and movable property related to such are taxable only in the country of residence of the alienator.

Gains from the disposal of shares, interests in a partnership, or interests in a trust the greater part of whose assets consist directly or indirectly of land may be taxed in the state where the land is situated.

Gains on the disposal of shares by a resident of one State can be taxed in the other State where the holding, in the 12 month period prior to the disposal, amounted to at least 25% of the company. There is an exclusion in the case of reorganisations, mergers or divisions.

The rule relating to permanent establishments is as in the UK.

Gains arising from the disposal of land may be taxed in the State in which the land is situated.

Credit is provided for foreign tax in the normal manner but subject to a limitation where income is taxed only on a remittance basis.

85.15   **Ireland/New Zealand**

The rule relating to *"Resident of "* is the same as in the UK treaty.

The rule relating to gains on the disposal of *assets not specifically referred to* in the provisions relating to capital gains is the same as that in the UK treaty with one exception. Each contracting state is permitted to tax gains from property not specifically referred to, if the alienator was a resident of that state at any time during the ten years preceding the disposal.

The provisions relating to the disposal of *Ships or Aircraft* operating in international traffic are the same as those in the UK.

The rules relating to gains from *shares* are the same as those in the UK. They additionally apply to an interest in a partnership the assets of which consist principally of land within a contracting state or shares deriving the greater part of their value from land situated in a contracting state, and permit a gain on the disposal of an interest in such a partnership to be taxed in the contracting state in which the land is situated.

The rules relating to *gains on a permanent establishment* are the same as in the UK treaty.

Gains arising from the disposal of *land* may be taxed in the state in which the land is situated.

The provisions relating to *credit for taxes paid* in another state are the same as in the UK treaty.

85.16   **Ireland/Poland**

The definition of *"resident of"* is the same as in the UK treaty.

The rule relating to gains from *assets not specifically referred to* in other provisions in relation to capital gains is the same as in the UK treaty except that the proviso in relation to gains taxable on a remittance basis does not appear.

The provision relating to *ships and aircraft* operated in international traffic are generally similar to that in the UK treaty. The provision extends to cover all transport vehicles operated in international traffic and movable property pertaining to the operations of ships, aircraft and road transport vehicles.

The provision relating to *shares* states that shares in a company whose assets consist principally of land, or mineral rights or other natural resources situated in one of the contracting states may be taxed in the state in which the land or mineral rights etc. is situated. The same rule applies to a company whose assets consist principally of shares in such a company. The article does not refer to shares in a company whose assets consist principally of shares in another company which in turn has assets consisting principally of land or mineral rights situated in one of the states. A partnership whose assets consist principally of land or mineral rights in one of the states is treated similarly to shares in a company. The reference to shares does not exclude quoted shares.

Gains from the disposal of *land or mineral rights* may be taxed where that land or right is situated.

Gains relating to the alienation of the movable *property of a permanent establishment* or fixed base for the purpose of independent personal services, or from the disposal of the entire permanent establishment or fixed base, may be taxed in the state in which the permanent establishment or fixed base is situated.

The arrangements for *credit for taxes paid* on capital gains is similar to those in the UK treaty.

85.17   **Ireland/Portugal**

The definition of *"Resident of"* is the same as in the UK treaty.

The rule relating to gains from *property not specifically referred to* in other provisions in relation to capital gains is the same as in the UK treaty except that the proviso relating to gains taxable on a remittance basis does not appear.

The provision relating to gains from *Ships or Aircraft* operated in international traffic provides that they should be taxable only in the contracting state in which the place of effective management of the enterprise is situated. This differs from the UK treaty in that the reference is to the place of effective management, rather than the state of which the alienator is a resident.

The rule relating to *shares* is generally the same as that in the UK treaty except that it applies to quoted shares as well as to unquoted and the reference is to shares in the company the assets of which consist principally of immovable property situated in a contracting state, rather than the UK reference to shares deriving the greater part of their value directly or indirectly from immovable property in a contracting state.

The rule relating to a *permanent establishment* is the same as in the UK treaty.

Gains arising from the disposal of *land* may be taxed in the state in which the land is situated.

The provisions relating to *credit for taxes paid* in another state are the same as in the UK treaty.CGT Book

85.18   **Ireland/Russia**

The definition of *"Resident of"* is as in the UK treaty except that in the tie-breaker clause for individuals, the word "Citizens" is substituted for the word "Nationals" used in the UK treaty.

The rule relating to gains from *assets not specifically referred to* in the treaty provisions on capital gains is the same as in the UK treaty except that the proviso in relation to gains taxed on a remittance basis does not appear in the Russian treaty.

The rule relating to **Ships and Aircraft** operated in international traffic differs slightly from that in the UK treaty in that the reference is to "Means of transport operated in international traffic" rather than specifically to ships or aircraft; and it provides that the gains may be taxed not only in the state of which the alienator is a resident but also in the other contracting state if the place of effective management of the operation is situated in that other state.

The rule relating to **shares** differs in detail from that of the UK treaty. The Russian treaty provides that shares in a company (including a quoted company) or an interest in a partnership, the assets of which consist as to 50% or more of immovable property situated in the other contracting state, or of shares in a company whose assets consist as to 50% or more of immovable property situated in the other contracting state, may be taxed in the other contracting state. Shares or interests in a partnership which forms part of the movable property of a permanent establishment are dealt with under the permanent establishment rule.

The rule relating to the **immovable property of a permanent establishment** is the same as that in the UK treaty.

Gains arising from the disposal of **land** may be taxed in the state in which the land is situated.

The provisions relating to **credit for taxes paid in another state** are the same as in the UK treaty.

86.19   **Ireland/Slovakia**

The definition of "resident of" is the standard definition. The tie-breaker for companies is place of effective management.

Gains from disposing of property not specifically referred to below are taxable only where the person making the disposal is a resident for the treaty purposes.

Gains from the disposal of ships or aircraft operated in international traffic, and related movable property, are taxable only in the contracting state which the place of effective management of the enterprise is situated. Note that that is not necessarily the place of residence - effective management is usually located in the same place as central management and control, but not always.

Gains from the disposal of land may be taxed both in the country of residence and in the country in which they are located. So also may gains on the disposal of shares, or an interest in a partnership or under a trust, where the greater part of the assets consist of land. "Land" for these purposes includes mineral rights etc and livestock and what is loosely described as "property accessory to immovable property".

The reference to shares deriving their value from land is not confined to unquoted shares.

The rules relating to permanent establishment property are similar to those in the UK treaty.

The provisions for credit for foreign taxes are the usual ones.

85.20   **Ireland/South Africa**

The definition of "resident of" as regards a resident of Ireland is as in the UK treaty, but as regards South Africa is an individual who is ordinarily resident in South Africa, or any other person whose place of effective management is in South Africa. The tiebreaker for non-individuals is the place of effective management..

Gains from the disposal of property not specifically referred to is taxable only in the State where the alienator is resident. However the State has the right to tax a person in the three years after he ceases to be resident, in relation to any property held when he ceased to be resident.

Gains from the disposal of ships, aircraft or containers operated in international traffic and related movable property, are taxable only in the State of residence of the alienator.

Gains on unquoted shares deriving their value from land in the State may be taxed in that State.

The rules relating to land, and permanent establishments are similar to those in the UK treaty.

Gains arising from the disposal of land may be taxed in the State in which the land is situated.

The rules relating to credit for foreign taxes are the usual provisions, with limitation where the income is taxed on a remittance basis, of the amount remitted.

85.21   **Ireland/Spain**

The definition of *"Resident of "* is the standard definition used in the UK treaty.

The rule relating to gains arising on *assets not specifically referred to* in the treaty is the same as in the UK treaty except that it does not contain the proviso relating to gains which are taxable only on a remittance basis.

The treatment of *Ships and Aircraft* in international traffic is the same as in the UK treaty.

The treatment of gains from the disposal of *shares* differs from that in the UK treaty. Gains from the alienation of shares or other rights in a company, or in a partnership, whose assets consist principally of immovable property situated in a contracting state, or of shares in a company whose assets consist principally of such immovable property, may be taxed in the contracting state in which the immovable property is situated. Gains from the alienation of other shares of a company which is the resident of a contracting state may be taxed in that contracting state where the recipient of the gain owned directly or indirectly 25% or more of the capital of that company in the twelve months preceding the disposal.

The rules relating to the *immovable property of a permanent establishment* are the same as the UK.

Gains arising from the disposal of *land* may be taxed in the state in which the land is situated.

The provisions relating to *credit for taxes paid* in another state are the same as in the UK treaty.

85.22   **Ireland/Sweden**

The definition of *"Resident of -"* is the standard definition as used in the UK treaty.

The rule regarding *gains not specifically referred to* in the treaty, is the same as that in the UK treaty with one exception. The exception is that either state may tax an individual on gains from the alienation of property not otherwise specifically dealt with in the treaty during the ten year period after the individual ceased to be a resident of the contracting state in question.

The Taxation of *Ships and Aircraft* operated in international traffic and movable property relating to that operation is the same as in the UK treaty.

The Swedish treaty provisions relating to the taxation of *shares* are the same as those in the UK treaty. However the Swedish treaty also provides that an interest in a partnership or trust the assets which consist principally of an immovable property situated in a contracting state, or shares deriving their value or the greater part of their value directly or indirectly from immovable property situated in a contracting state, may be taxed in the contracting state in which the immovable property is situated.

Gains arising from the disposal of *land* may be taxed in the state in which the land is situated.

85.23   **Ireland/Switzerland**

The definition of *"Resident of -"* is the UK definition except that any *partnership* organised under the laws of Switzerland is deemed a resident of Switzerland. There is no corresponding provision relating to a partnership organised under the laws of Ireland.

The rule regarding *gains not specifically referred to* in the treaty is the same as that in the UK treaty, except that it does not contain the proviso in the UK treaty relating to amounts not remitted into the state of which the alienator is a resident, where the resident is taxable there only on a remittance basis.

The Swiss treaty differs from the UK treaty in the treatment of gains from *Ships and Aircraft* operated in international traffic. The Swiss treaty states that such gains shall be taxed in the state in which the enterprise's effective management is situated. That is not necessarily the state of which the enterprise is a resident e.g. a Swiss partnership managed in Ireland would be a resident of Switzerland for treaty purposes but would be taxable in Ireland on gains from relevant ships and aircraft, and not in Switzerland.

The Swiss treaty differs from the UK as regards the treatment of *shares.* It does not exclude shares quoted on a stock exchange from the treatment generally applied to shares deriving their value from land.

Whereas the UK treaty refers to shares deriving value from land, the Swiss treaty refers to shares "the property of which consists principally of" land.

It does not contain the proviso to the *permanent establishment* provision of the UK treaty that gives to the state of which the alienator is a resident, sole taxing rights on shares deriving their value from land situated in that State, even if the shares are moveable property of a permanent establishment in the other state.

Except as noted above, the provisions relating to *moveable assets* of a permanent establishment are as in the UK treaty.

Gains arising from the disposal of *land* may be taxed in the state in which the land is situated.

The provisions relating to *credit for taxes paid* in another state are the same as in the UK treaty

85.24   **Ireland/USA**

A new treaty with the United States came into force for corporation tax purposes from 1 January 1998, and for income tax and capital gains tax purposes from 6 April 1998. Persons entitled to the benefit of the previous treaty were entitled to retain those benefits for a period of one year i.e. up to 31 December 1998. Where such an election is made for any purpose, the election applies for all the purposes of the treaty. Thus an election to take the benefits of the old treaty for withholding tax purposes would govern all tax purposes. The old treaty did not cover capital gains tax, and accordingly such an election would deprive a taxpayer of the benefits of the new treaty in relation to capital gains tax, for 1998.

The definition of "resident of" includes, as would be expected, any person liable to tax by reason of domicile/residence etc., as in the UK treaty. Additionally, however, a US citizen or alien lawfully admitted for permanent residence in the United States is regarded as a resident of the United States provided such person has a substantial presence, permanent home or habitual abode in the United States. The definition also includes Governments of each State, non-commercial semi-State entities, and pension funds relating to such. A US regulated investment company and a US real estate investment trust (REIT) are regarded as residents of the United States. A collective investment undertaking (within the meaning of the 1989 legislation) is regarded as a resident of Ireland.

The tie-breaker for individuals takes the following order of priority:

- availability of permanent home
- centre of personal and economic interests
- habitual abode
- a national
- mutual agreement

Unlike most treaties, it does not automatically follow that a person who is a resident of one or other of the States is entitled to the benefits of the treaty. Additionally a person must meet elaborate requirements in a "limitation of benefits" article. These requirements (in Article 23 of the treaty) are too complex to be described here. In the May 1998 issue of Irish Tax Review there is a "decision tree" (by Paul Reck, Deloite Touche) which summarises the tests imposed by Article 23.

Gains derived from land and buildings may be taxed in the State in which they are situated, and in the country of residence of the alienator. In Ireland unquoted shares deriving the greater part of their value directly or indirectly from land in Ireland receive the same treatment.

Gains from the disposal of a permanent establishment, or moveable assets of such a permanent establishment, may be taxed in both states.

Gains on the disposal of ships, aircraft, or containers operated in international traffic or personal property relating to such property are taxable only in the State of residence. All other gains are also only taxable in the State of which the alienator is a resident.

The provisions relating to credit for taxes paid are the same as in the UK treaty.

85.25   **Ireland D. T. R. agreements:**

State	*Deals with CGT*
Austria	yes
Australia	yes
Belgium	no (note 1)
Canada	no
Cyprus	no (note 1)
Czech Republic	yes
Denmark	yes
Estonia	yes
Finland	yes
France	no
Germany	no
Hungary	yes
Israel	yes
Italy	no (note 1)
Japan	no (note 1)
Korea	yes (note 1)
Latvia	yes
Lithuania	yes
Luxembourg	No
Malasia	yes
Mexico	yes
Netherlands	no (note 1)
New Zealand	yes (note 1)
Pakistan	no
Poland	yes
Portugal	yes
Russia	Yes
Slovakia	yes

State	*Deals with CGT*
Sweden	yes
Spain	yes
Switzerland	yes
UK	yes
South Africa (limited agreement)	No
USA (new treaty)	yes
Zambia	no

Note 1: The treaty has an article which refers to capital gains but does not extend to CGT.

86   **CARE & MANAGEMENT OF CGT**

86.1   **Responsibility for administration of CGT**

s849   CGT is under the care and management of the Revenue
              Commissioners.

              In exercising that care and management, the Revenue
              Commissioners have not designed a separate set of rules for CGT.
              For the main part they have adopted the income tax rules which
              apply to CGT as they apply to an assessment of income to income
              tax under Schedule D. The income tax rules governing

              — assessment,

              — appeals

              — payment

              — collection

              — other matters

              as they apply to CGT are set out in the remaining pages of this
              chapter, together with a few additional rules which apply only to
              CGT.

              Assessments to CGT will be made by Inspectors or other such
              officers as the Revenue Commissioners appoint.

              CGT (as with income tax) is a self-assessment tax with responsibility
              for making the return and paying the tax resting primarily on the
              taxpayer.

              The Revenue Commissioners, by reason of their responsibility for the
              care and management of the tax, have power to grant concessional
              treatment that is not in strict accordance with the legislation where
              circumstances suggest to them that it is proper to do so.

              Details of concessions granted are now published by the Revenue
              Commissioners under the Freedom of Information Act.

              Any known past concessional treatments referred to in this book
              should not be relied on in relation to any transaction without prior
              consultation with the Revenue Commissioners.

              The following comments by the Revenue Commissioners have been
              published in Irish Tax Review.

TALC minutes 14 December 1998

Authority of Statements of Practice and Operational Procedures

Question : A substantial amount of material has been made available by the Revenue Commissioners under differing formats such as Operational Procedures, Statements of Practice, Tax Briefing Articles and Revenue Interpretation Leaflets. Would it be possible for Revenue to provide some guidance to tax practitioners and taxpayers as to the authority of these statements? For example, can it be taken that all Inspectors of Taxes will operate on the basis of these various position statements?

Response : The Chief Inspector of Taxes advised that they would expect all Revenue officials to follow procedures set out in Statements of Practice. The status of information issued under the Freedom of Information Act was also raised, and in particular the status of Revenue precedents. CIOT advised that if a case is on all fours with the precedent, then Revenue will follow the precedent.

The UK case of Steibelt v Paling had to consider whether the exercise by the Inland Revenue of a statutory discretion could be subject to review by Appeal Commissioners. The Court concluded that while the exercise of statutory discretion by the Revenue could be the subject matter of judicial review, it could not be reviewed by Appeal Commissioners. The case concerned a discretion granted to extend the period during which expenditure had to be incurred in order to avail of roll over relief.

87   RETURNS, INFORMATION AND PAYMENT

87.1   Application of Income Tax Provisions

s913(2)

The provisions of the ITAs relating to the making of returns, etc., subject to any necessary modification, apply to CGT as they apply to Income Tax.

In addition to s913(2) applying the income tax provisions to CGT, s1052, s1053 and s1060, TCA97 includes specific CGT provisions. The CGT provisions specifically included are:

- s914 (returns by issuing houses, stockbrokers, auctioneers, etc.)
- s915 (returns by nominee shareholders)
- s916 (returns by parties to a settlement)
- s917 (returns relating to non-resident companies and trusts)
- s945 (appeals)
- s980 (withholding tax)

The provisions are also extended to require that returns include details of:

— assets acquired,

— the person from whom assets were acquired,

— the consideration for the acquisition of an asset.

87.2   Obligation to Make A Return

s951   Every person who is chargeable to capital gains tax for a year of assessment is required to make a return for that year in a form prescribed by the Revenue Commissioners. The return is usually made in the same form as that used for income tax. The obligation exists even if a return has not been requested by an inspector. Additionally any person who is requested by an inspector to make a return in respect of a year of assessment is obliged to do so.

s913   Notwithstanding that a reorganisation of shares or reduction of capital is treated for CGT purposes in certain circumstances as not involving the acquisition or disposal of assets, such transactions must be reported in a CGT return, in accordance with s913. The same requirement applies to a corporation tax return in respect of a company's capital gains.

The obligation to make a CGT return extends not only to individuals and trustees, but also to *companies*. A company may be within the charge to CGT in respect of disposals of development land or on other disposals of certain Irish assets if it is not within the charge to corporation tax.

s951   Although an inspector may exclude a person from the obligation to make a return in respect of income tax, he does not have a similar power in relation to CGT.

The precedent partner in a *partnership* is obliged to make a return in respect of the partnership.

A *spouse* may satisfy the obligation of both parties to a marriage by making a joint return.

87.3   Time Limit for Submission of Return

s950   The deadline for submission of a return is 31st January in the calendar year following the end of the relevant year of assessment. Thus the deadline for a CGT return for 1999/2000 is 31st January 2001. This deadline applies if it is later than any deadline which would otherwise arise - e.g. where an inspector has requested a return. The deadline for a CGT return by a company is as stated, and may be different to the deadline for the company's corporation tax return.

Example 419

> *Exco Ltd. is an Irish resident manufacturing company. During its financial year ended 31 December 1997, it disposed of 2 acres of land situated beside its factory. The land had outline planning permission, and was development land (see paragraph 6). It also disposed of a portfolio of quoted shares, in that period.*
>
> *Exco Ltd. is chargeable to corporation tax in respect of the gains on the shares, and must include the details of that disposal in its corporation tax return for the accounting period ended 31 December 1997. That return is due by 30 September 1998.*

s1084

> *The disposal of the development land (not part of the corporation tax profits for the period) must be included on a CGT return which is due not later than 31 January 1999.*

Where a taxpayer commenced a trade or profession in a year of assessment and neither the taxpayer or his/her spouse carried on another trade or profession in that year which had commenced prior to that year, the due date of a return *for surcharge purposes* for 1995/96 and later years is the due date of the return for the following year of assessment.

In other words, a taxpayer who starts up a new business is given a "year of grace" in terms of making his first return for that business. Although the provision in relation to this "year of grace" would appear to be principally relevant in relation to a return of income under the income tax laws, it would seem to be applied for capital gains tax purposes also where a trade commences and the gains would be included on the same return.

87.4   Fraudulent or Negligent Return

s1084

s1084 is applied for the purposes of CGT returns under self assessment. In consequence a return which is delivered fraudulently or negligently and is not corrected before the deadline for returns, is deemed not to have been delivered by the deadline. The same consequence applies where a person becomes aware of a return being incorrect and fails to correct the return without unreasonable delay.

"Fraudulently or negligently" in this context have their ordinary meaning and would not refer to an innocent error by a reasonably careful taxpayer.

87.5   Surcharge for Late Return

s1084

Where the return is made within two months of the due date, the surcharge is an amount equal to 5% of the tax, or £10,000 if lower.

Where the return is made more than 2 months late, the surcharge is 10%, or £50,000 if lower.

For 1994/95 and prior years, the surcharge applied at a flat rate of 10% of the tax, without limit or reference to the degree of lateness of delivery of the return.

This surcharge on CGT is itself a charge of CGT.

87.6   Returns of a partnership

s913
s880

A return of income of a partnership under s880 must include:

(i)   with respect to any disposal of partnership assets during a period to which the return relates, the same particulars as if the partnership were liable to tax on any chargeable gain accruing on a disposal, and

(ii)   particular of the partnership assets acquired during the period.

87.7   Reorganisations etc.

s630

Where a company transfers assets in a manner which attracts relief under s630 et seq. provisions implementing the Mergers Directive (see paragraph 75.3), it must make a return of such transfers. Similar requirements apply to transfers which are treated by reason of s586 or s587 as not constituting disposals (share for share, share for undertaking etc.).

87.8   Penalties

s1077

Where a person fails to comply with the requirements relating to returns for CGT purposes, Part 47 (Penalties, Revenue Offences, interest on overdue tax and other sanctions) of TCA97 apply to that person for the purposes of CGT as they apply for the purposes of IT.

TCA97, Part 47 imposes fines and penalties of fixed amounts (up to £1,200) in a variety of circumstances including failure to comply with demands for returns, making or assisting in making incorrect returns or declarations and similar matters.

s1076

The FA99 permits the recovery of certain of these penalties from the company secretary, where they have not been paid within three months. It also imposes a fine directly on the company secretary. Where the secretary is not an individual resident in the State a resident individual who is a director may become liable for the penalties. Also in certain circumstances a company treasurer, a company auditor, or a receiver may become liable. In the case of a non resident company, the agent, manager, factor or other representative of the company may be liable for the penalties.

87.9   **Returns by Issuing Houses, Stockbrokers, etc..**

s914   An *issuing house* or other person carrying on a business of effecting public issues of shares or securities in any company, or placings of such shares or securities, may be required to make a return of public issues or placings effected by him in the course of his business.

A *member of a stock exchange* in the State may be required to make a return giving particulars of any transactions effected by him in the course of his business in the period specified in the notice requiring the return and giving particulars of:

(i)   the parties to the transaction

(ii) the number or amount of the shares or securities dealt with in respect of transactions, and

(iii) the amounts or values of the considerations.

A person (other than a member of a stock exchange in the State) *who acts as an agent* in the State in transactions in shares or securities may be required to make a return giving particulars of any transactions effected by him in the period specified in the notice giving particulars of:

(i)   the parties to the transactions

(ii) the number or amount of the shares or securities dealt with in the respective transactions and,

(iii) the amount or value of the considerations.

87.10   **Returns by Auctioneers, etc.**

s914   An auctioneer, and any person carrying on a trade of dealing in any description of tangible movable property, or of acting as an agent or intermediary in dealings in any description of tangible movable property, may be required to make a return giving particulars of any transactions effected by or through him in which any asset which is tangible movable property is disposed of for a consideration in excess of £15,000.

In the case of transactions effected in the period from 6th April 1994 to 5th April 1995, the reporting limit was £5,000.

Prior to 6th April 1994 the reporting limit was £2,000.

87.11   **Returns by Nominee Shareholders**

s915   A person who is acting as a nominee shareholder may be required to furnish the names and addresses of the persons on whose behalf the shares are registered in his name.

87.12   **Returns by Party to a Settlement**

s916   The Revenue Commissioners may by notice in writing require any person being a party to a settlement to furnish them with such particulars relating to the settlement as they (the Commissioners) think necessary for the purposes of the CGT Acts.

87.13   **Returns Relating to Non-Resident Companies & Trusts**

s917   A person who:

- holds shares or securities in a non-resident company, or

- is beneficially interested in a non-resident trust, or

- acts as agent for or on behalf of a person who is beneficially interested in settled property of a non-resident trust,

may be required by the Revenue Commissioners to give them such particulars as are necessary to enable them to consider whether the liability falls on shareholders of the non-resident company or beneficiaries of the non-resident trust under the anti-avoidance provisions (see paragraphs 67 and 68).

s917A   S917A (inserted by the FA99) has application were on or after 11 February 1999 property is transferred to a non-resident trust. The section requires the transferor to make a return to the Revenue Commissioners identifying the settlement and the property. The return must be made within three months from the day on which the property is transferred. Only transfers which are otherwise than at arms length need be returned.

The requirement to make a return applies only where the transferor knows or has reason to believe, that the trustees are not resident in ordinarily resident in the state. It would be unusual for a transferee of property to trustees, under a transaction which is not at arms length, not to be aware of their residence status.

The settlor of a settlement created on or after 11 February 1999 is obliged to make a return, if the trustees are not resident, or are resident but treaty protected on the occasion of the creation of the settlement. The return must identify the trustees and the settlor. The return must be made within three months from the day on which the settlement is created.

s917C   S917C requires trustees, on the occasion of becoming non-resident or on the occasion of becoming treated protected (where either event occurs on or after the 11 February 1999) to make a return. The return must be made within three months of going non-resident or becoming treaty protected, as the case maybe. The return must identify the settlor and the trustees, and the date which the settlement was created.

88   PRELIMINARY TAX

88.1   Payments on account of CGT

s952   Every person on whom CGT is chargeable for a year of assessment is obliged to make a payment of Preliminary Tax in respect of that year. In principle Preliminary Tax is a separate tax to CGT. Since it becomes payable by reason of a CGT liability and is credited against that liability, it can be thought of for practical purposes as a payment on account of CGT.

s952(4)   A person who has received an assessment for a tax year before the due date for payment of Preliminary Tax is exempted from the obligation to pay Preliminary Tax. Instead they have an obligation to pay CGT at the same due date as that for Preliminary Tax, so the exemption is of little practical significance.

s952(2)   The amount of Preliminary Tax which is payable is the taxpayer's estimate of his liability for the year. The consequences of a failure to pay this amount fully, or of a shortfall between the amount estimated and paid and the final CGT liability for the year may give rise to an interest liability (see paragraph 89).

Preliminary Tax is payable whether or not it is demanded by the Revenue.

s953   The Revenue do not have the power to issue Notices of Preliminary Tax in the case of CGT as they do in the case of income tax. They do have that power in the case of corporation tax, including where it applies to a company's chargeable gains. A Notice of Preliminary Tax can give rise to an enforceable tax liability in certain circumstances.

s952(5)   A payment of Preliminary Tax (on account of CGT) is applied in reduction of the taxpayer's CGT liability for the year of assessment in respect of which it is paid and not that of the tax year in which it is paid.

s953(7)   Any excess of a payment over the liability to CGT for the same period must be repaid to the taxpayer. There is no statutory right to offset it against any other tax liability of the taxpayer for that period or any other period.

A repayment of Preliminary Tax attracts interest at the appropriate rate set by the Minister for Finance from time to time, and this interest is exempt from income tax.

s950(1);
s955(5)(a)   Preliminary Tax in respect of CGT is distinct in character from Preliminary Tax paid by or due from the same taxpayer in respect of income tax (or of corporation tax in the case of a company). Strictly speaking an overpayment of Preliminary Tax in respect of CGT may

not be offset against an underpayment of Preliminary Tax in respect of income, and vice versa.

88.2 **Due date for payment of tax**

In broad terms, there are THREE separate circumstances in which CGT can become payable:

1. *Due to a liability to pay Preliminary Tax in respect of CGT*

2. *Due to the raising of an assessment to CGT*

3. *Due to the amendment of an assessment.*

The due date for the tax is described below separately in respect of each circumstance.

s958 *Preliminary Tax* for a year of assessment is due and payable by 1 November following the end of the year of assessment. This is one year later than the due date for Preliminary Tax in respect of income tax for the same year.

FA98 s45 FA98 s45 has provided for the possibility of the Minister for Finance making an order which would change the due date for preliminary tax from 1 November in a year to 30 November in a year. At the date of writing no such order has been made. Were such an order to be made, the order would also change the due date for the making of a return in respect of capital gains from 31 January in the tax year following the year at which the disposal occurs, to 30 November in the tax year following the year at which the disposal occurs.

Raising of an assessment: Apart from Preliminary Tax which becomes due whether or not it is demanded, CGT can become payable by reason of an assessment. If the assessment is raised before the due date for Preliminary Tax for the relevant year of assessment, the tax becomes due on the Preliminary Tax due date. If the assessment is raised after that date, the tax becomes due on the later of:

• the due date for a CGT return in respect of the year of assessment in question; or

• 30 days after the raising of the assessment.

However this due date does not apply in one circumstance. If the taxpayer's payment of Preliminary Tax in respect of CGT for a year of assessment does not equal at least his CGT liability for the year as finally determined or if it is not paid by its due date, the due date for CGT arising on an assessment is the Preliminary Tax due date for the year of assessment in question.

For tax years 1997/98 and prior years, a taxpayer who paid a preliminary tax payment by its due date, of at least 90% of his CGT liability for the year as finally determined, could rely on the due date for the balance of tax being as described in the two bullet points above. For the tax year 1998/1999 and later years the position differs as between CGT and Income Tax. For income tax purposes, a timely payment of 90% of the tax due remains sufficient to ensure that, in most instances, the due date for tax will be thirty days following the raising of an assessment. For CGT, a 100% payment of the tax liability on a timely basis is required, which makes little sense, since it ensures that there will be no tax due on foot of an assessment. In practice therefore if any tax is due in respect of CGT on foot of an assessment raised, it seems that the due date for that assessment will always be the due date for preliminary tax for the same year i.e. at present 1 November in the tax year following the year in which the disposal occurred. This seems a startling conclusion to arrive at from the now very elaborate provisions of s958 (4), which provide at the due date for CGT shall be the preliminary tax payment date, unless, where a variety of conditions are met it shall be - the preliminary tax payment date!

The authors speculate that what is in mind is that in certain circumstances a CGT liability for the year of assessment may be affected by events that occur many years later (e.g., in the case of corporation tax on companies capital gains, a company leaving a group while owning an asset acquired intra group in the previous ten years). It may be that where the liability as determined prior to the occurrence of an event subsequent to the year of assessment in question affecting the total of that liability, had been 100% paid by a preliminary tax payment made on time, that the tax arising by reason of the subsequent event (e.g., a company leaving a group as mentioned) will be treated as arising in 30 days after the date of the assessment. However that is only the authors speculation.

s958   The provisions of s958(10) in relation to the collection of tax by the Collector General by direct debiting of the tax payers bank account do not apply in relation to Capital Gains Tax. S958(5(b)) and s958(10) provide a method of determining the due date for payment of income tax by reference to whether the payment equals the sum due for the pre preceeding chargeable period. No similar provision applies to CGT.

Amendment of an assessment : The due date for the CGT arising on the amendment of an assessment depends on whether the assessment was raised before or after a full and true CGT return for the period was delivered.

If the assessment was made after the return was delivered; or if it had been previously amended after the return was delivered, the due date is 30 days after the date of the amendment.

Otherwise the tax arising on the amendment is due on the same due date as applied to tax on the assessment. This due date is taken to be the date which applied prior to the amendment being made. The significance of this is that an amendment to an assessment alters the final liability for the year, and so may affect the question of whether or not the Preliminary Tax payment equalled at least 90% of the final liability. As described above, this can affect the due date for tax arising from an assessment.

s955   The reference above to a *full and true return* is a reference to a return in which the taxpayer has made a full and true disclosure of all material facts necessary for the making of an assessment. Where a taxpayer is in doubt as to the law in some matter, he will not fail to make such a full and true return by reason of any resulting error if he makes the return to the best of his knowledge and belief and draws the inspector's attention to the doubt. This is known as an *expression of doubt.*

A return which is incorrect is regarded as not delivered but only if the error was due to fraud or negligence. A return prepared conscientiously and honestly will always be regarded as delivered, but if innocent errors cause it to deprive the inspector of all the facts needed to accurately assess the CGT liability, it may be regarded as not being a full and true return. Fraudulent or careless error may lead to a surcharge. Other errors can only affect the due date for tax.

There are one or two minor exceptions to the due dates outlined above for the payment of tax arising on an assessment.

s1042   — where the tax arises by reason of an assessment raised on a non resident in accordance with s1042 (as described in paragraph 90.1) the due date is the later of 3 months after the date of disposal of the asset, or 2 months after the raising of the assessment.

s977   — where an assessment is raised to recover tax owing by a company from the shareholder, under s977 (see paragraph 91.4.2) the due date for tax on foot of such an assessment is not clear from the legislation. The rules outlined above represent rules relating to the due date for tax specified in an assessment made for a relevant chargeable period. It is not clear that an assessment under s977 made on a shareholder is such an assessment.

s978   — tax recoverable from the donee of a gift on foot of an assessment raised under s978. The same comments as in relation to an assessment to recover tax from a shareholder of a company, apply here. The due date is ambiguous.

s1006A   s1006A (inserted by the FA 2000) permits the Revenue to offset claims for repayment of tax against any outstanding tax. Thus a claim for repayment of income tax to a taxpayer could be offset against capital gains tax owing by that taxpayer. The operation of the section requires regulations not published at the date of writing. These regulations will deal with the order of priority of various liabilities under the Act against which any claim or overpayment is to be offset.

s1006B   S1006B (inserted by the FA 2000) gives power to the Revenue Commissioners to appropriate payment from a taxpayer to any taxes owning by that taxpayer. This may be done only where the Revenue Commissioners cannot determine what the taxpayer's instructions were, as to the liability against which the payment was to be offset. In other words, the taxpayer is entitled to specify which out of several tax liabilities he is paying with a payment. Where the taxpayer so specifies, the payment may be offset only against the taxes the taxpayer has indicated. But if the taxpayer sends in a payment without indicating which tax he intends to pay, then s1006B will have application. The application of the section requires regulations to be made by the Revenue Commissioners and these were not made at the date of writing.

89   INTEREST ON OVERDUE TAX

89.1   General

Interest on overdue tax is charged at the rate of 1% per month (or part of a month) occurring after 31 March 1998. Prior to that date the rate applicable was 1.25% per month (or part of a month). No interest can be charged if the tax is paid within 2 months of the due date.

89.2   Penalty Interest

Where for any accounting period, an assessment is made to recover an undercharge to CT, which is attributed to the fraud or neglect of any person, the amount of the undercharge carries interest at the rate of 2% per month (or part of a month) from the date the tax would have been payable if it was included in an assessment made 6 months after the end of the accounting period, up to the actual date of payment. This is instead of the normal charge to interest for late payment of tax.

For this purpose, "neglect" is defined as negligence or failure to give any notice, to make any return, statement or declaration, or to produce or furnish any list, document or other information required by or under the enactments relating to CT.

Where there was a reasonable excuse for not providing the required information, there is deemed to be no neglect provided the matter was rectified without unreasonable delay after the excuse ceased.

90 ASSESSMENT OF CGT

90.1 Assessments

s954

As noted in paragraph 88, Preliminary Tax in respect of CGT may become due and payable without the raising of a demand or assessment. Where an inspector is satisfied that a preliminary tax payment has discharged all of the CGT liability, he may elect not to raise an assessment. A taxpayer is entitled to receive an assessment if he demands it.

Such a situation may arise if a taxpayer believes he has overpaid preliminary tax, and seeks a refund. Until an assessment is raised, no refund is possible, nor is there access to the appeal procedures.

s954(1)

An assessment may not be raised before the earlier of:

- A return for the year of assessment being made by the taxpayer, or

- The due date for a CGT return for the year of assessment (i.e. 31st January following the end of the year of assessment)

s954(7)

These earliest times for the raising of an assessment do not apply to:

—an assessment on a non-resident in respect of certain Irish assets.

—an assessment in relation to the 15% withholding tax on certain land disposals.

—an assessment on a donee to collect CGT on a gift. This assessment must be made within two years of the gift.

s955

An assessment for a year may not be raised or amended more than 6 years after the end of the year of assessment in which a full and true return (see 88.2) is made in respect of the year.

Example 423

Joe Smith disposes of an asset on 30th June 1993. He does not make a CGT return for 1993/94 by its due date of 31st January 1995 but delivers it on 30th April 1995. An assessment cannot be raised earlier than 31st January 1995 or raised or amended later then 5th April 2002 (being 6 years after the end of the tax year in which he delivers the return).

This time limit for the amendment of an assessment is subject to so many exceptions as to be of little practical significance. The time limit is principally relevant to the raising of an assessment.

s955(2)(b)

*An assessment may be **amended** outside the 6 year time limit described above:*

- *on the determination of an appeal by reason of the liability being affected by an event which occurs after the return is delivered.*

- *to correct a calculation error*

- *to bring the assessment into line with the facts disclosed in a return*

- *to correct estimates in a return when accurate figures become available.*

s954(2)   Generally an assessment must be in accordance with the return made by the taxpayer. The inspector may make the assessment to the best of his knowledge and belief if:

   • the taxpayer has not made a return, or

   • the inspector is not satisfied with the return.

s954(5)   Where the amount of tax assessed is the same as that computed by the taxpayer in his return, or where no return has been made for the tax year, the only detail which need be stated on the assessment is the amount of CGT payable.

s956   An inspector may not make *enquiries* regarding capital gains more than 6 years after the end of the tax year in which a return for the year under enquiry was made even if it is not a full and true return (see paragraph 88.2). Since a return prepared fraudulently or negligently is deemed not to have been delivered, the time limit does not apply in such a case. Neither does it apply where the inspector believes the return to have been prepared fraudulently or negligently, even if he is mistaken in that belief, provided he has a reason for his belief.

s1042   **The Revenue may assess a person who is neither resident nor ordinarily resident otherwise than in accordance with the rules outlined above. (s954 and s1042)).**

            Although Capital Gains Tax is ordinarily chargeable in respect of the chargeable gains arising to a person in a year of assessment, as reduced by allowable losses accruing in that year, s1042, in respect of disposals made after 17th July 1982, permits the Inspector to assess a person who is neither resident nor ordinarily resident at the time when the disposal is made, in respect of a chargeable gain accruing on a disposal without waiting until the end of the year of assessment. A non resident may therefore be assessed separately in respect of each disposal occurring during a year, or in respect of any group of disposals and the assessment may be raised during the year at any time subsequent to the disposal.

            Tax so assessed and charged is payable within 3 months of the time when the disposal is made or within 2 months of the making of the assessment, whichever is later.

            Where a non resident is assessed in this fashion, he would still seem to be obliged to make a return under the self assessment system as described in paragraph 87. There does not appear to be any obligation on him to make an "interim return" in relation to separate disposals during the year.

            Where a non resident is seeking to obtain a tax clearance certificate in order to avoid the application of CGT withholding tax (see paragraph 94) the raising of an assessment under the provisions of s1042 may be resorted to in order to have the liability agreed and paid prior to the date of the payment of the consideration.

The other rules relating to the amending of an assessment, and appeals against assessments, and the making of enquiries by an Inspector of Taxes etc.., as described above, all continue to apply to an assessment raised under the provisions of s1042 on a non resident, as they do to any other assessment.

An assessment on a company in respect of corporation tax on companies capital gains must be made in respect of an accounting period rather than in respect of a year of assessment. It is not clear how an assessment can be raised on a company in respect of a gain arising when it does not have an accounting period. Some relatively inactive companies can find themselves "between accounting periods" especially after the cessation of a trade.

90.2 Other Special Assessment Rules

The rules described above relating to the time for the raising for assessments cannot apply to an assessment raised to recover tax from a shareholder in a company (see paragraph 91.4) or from the donee of a gift (see paragraph 91.3). The raising of such assessments are subject to a 2 year time limit, and not to the time limits described above in relation to assessments generally. The rules described above relating to the amendment of assessments would also not seem to apply to such assessments.

90.3 Statement of Affairs

s909

An Inspector dissatisfied with a tax return may require the taxpayer to deliver a statement of assets. The FA92 extended this to Capital Gains Tax and extended the provisions.

The extended provisions apply where for the purposes of income tax or capital gains tax a person is required to deliver a tax return to an Inspector of Taxes or to the Inspector of Returns. The Inspector may require the taxpayer by notice in writing to submit a statement of affairs. The requirement will extend to a spouse where there is joint assessment.

Following receipt of the Statement of Affairs, the Inspector may also by notice, require delivery of evidence in support of this Statement of Affairs.

The Statement of Affairs must include:

- a statement of all the assets wherever situated to which the taxpayer is beneficially entitled and all the liabilities to which he is liable;

- any assets to which a minor child is beneficially entitled would also be included in the Statement of Affairs, where;

- the assets were disposed of by the individual (whether to the minor child or not) prior to their acquisition by the child, or

- the consideration for the acquisition of the assets by the child was provided directly or indirectly by the taxpayer.

- similar information with regard to a spouse jointly assessed.

The legislation also extends to persons required to file a return in a representative capacity or as a trustee of a trust.

The Statement of Affairs must include in relation to each asset:

— a full description,

— its location on the relevant date,

— the cost of acquisition to the person beneficially entitled thereto,

— the date of acquisition and if acquired otherwise than through a bargain at arm's length, the name and address of the person from whom it was acquired and the consideration, if any, given to that person in respect of its acquisition.

A Statement of Affairs must be signed by the person by whom it is delivered and must include a declaration by that person that it is, to the best of his knowledge, correct and complete.

The Revenue Commissioners may require that the declaration be made on oath.

91   COLLECTION OF TAX FROM OTHERS

91.1   Broad overview

There are a number of circumstances set out in the Capital Gains Tax Acts where the tax can be assessed on and collected from a person other than the person who made the disposal of the asset.

91.2.1   Collection of Tax from beneficiary of trust

s574

If CGT is assessed on trustees, and the tax is not paid within six months of the due date, the tax can be assessed on and collected from any person ..."*who as against the trustees is absolutely entitled to*"...the asset on the disposal of which the tax liability arose. Such a person can only be held responsible for the tax (or the part of it) proportionate to the amount of that asset (or the proceeds of the sale of it, etc.) which has actually been transferred to him.

This rule is provided by s574(2), which states:-

'where any amount of capital gains tax assessed on the trustees, or any one trustee, of a settlement in respect of a chargeable gain accruing to the trustee is not paid within six months from the date when it becomes payable by the trustees or trustee, and before or after the expiration of that period of six months the asset in respect of which the chargeable gain accrued, or any part of the proceeds of sale of that asset, is transferred by the trustees to a person who as against the trustees is absolutely entitled to it, that person may at any time within two years from the time when that amount of tax became payable be assessed and charged (in the name of the trustees) to an amount of capital gains tax not exceeding the amount of capital gains tax chargeable on an amount equal to the amount of the chargeable gain and, where part only of the asset or of the proceeds was transferred, not exceeding a proportionate part of that amount'.

It would be noted from the above that the right to proceed against a beneficiary is not unlimited. The beneficiary can be pursued only where

- he has had transferred to him absolutely by the trustees the asset in respect of which the gain accrued or

- he has had transferred absolutely to him the proceeds of sale of the asset upon which the gain accrued.

An obvious example of the first circumstance described above is where the trustees of a discretionary settlement appoint an asset absolutely to a beneficiary. Such an appointment represents a disposal by the trustees of the asset. The very transfer to the beneficiary may generate a gain. Any tax on that gain can be recovered from the donee in the circumstances outlined above. That however is not the only circumstance where the absolute transfer of an asset may bring with it secondary liability in respect of the gains of the trustees. If the trustees had derived a capital sum from an asset in the past and now transfer that asset absolutely to a beneficiary, the beneficiary is exposed to the CGT on the previous part disposal by the trustees (the receipt of a capital sum) as well as the final disposal of the asset by the trustees (the appointment to the beneficiary).

In the second instance above where the beneficiary may have a secondary liability, it is only where the proceeds of sale are absolutely appointed to him. The word "sale" is often given a narrow technical meaning as being the disposal of an asset for money. The appointment to a person of a capital sum derived from the asset would not be the proceeds of sale and the appointment of such a sum would not seem to carry with it any secondary liability under this provision. Thus if the proceeds of liquidation of a company were appointed to a beneficiary, rather than the shares in the company itself, or the sales proceeds of the shares, secondary liability would not appear to be created for the beneficiary.

It should be noted however that s978 (discussed in paragraph 91.3) is capable of having application to a beneficiary of a settlement. The definition of "gift" for the purpose of s978 would seem wide enough to encompass the appointment to a beneficiary of assets from a settlement. The comments above need to be read in that light.

91.2.2 Collection of Tax from Former Trustees

s579D

S579D applies special provisions for the collection of tax arising by reason of s579B (exit charge when trust goes non resident). Any person who was a trustee of the settlement in the 12 month period prior to it going non resident may be liable in respect of the tax charge arising by reason of section 579B, where that has not been paid within six months from its due date. A former trustee can avoid this liability only by demonstrating that when he ceased to be a trustee of the settlement there was no proposal that the trustee might become non - resident. The former trustee from whom tax is collected under s579D is given a statutory right to recover the amount from the non-resident trustee. In practice, unless the non - resident trustee has Irish assets, that statutory right is unenforceable.

91.3 Gifts-recovery of tax from donee

s978

Where a capital gain arises on a gift and the tax is not paid within 12 months from the due date the donee may be assessed and charged to tax in the name of the donor.

The donee (subject to any terms or conditions of the gift) will be entitled to recover the tax from the donor as a simple contract debt in any court of competent jurisdiction.

Under this head, references to a donor, in the case of an individual who has died, includes references to his personal representatives.

References to a gift include references to any transaction which was not by way of bargain made at arm's length, or so far as money or money's worth passes under the transaction without full consideration in money or money's worth.

91.4 Recovery of Tax from Shareholders

91.4.1 Broad Outline

s614

In certain circumstances, the Revenue can recover the CT due on chargeable gains made by a company, from the shareholders in that company. Where this happens, the shareholder is given the right to recover the tax concerned from the company.

91.4.2   **Circumstances of Charge on Shareholders**

s977   Where an Irish resident company makes a 'capital distribution' on or
after 6th April 1976, to any connected person out of the proceeds of
disposal of a chargeable asset, or where the disposal of the asset is
made by way of a capital distribution to that connected person, the
tax due from the company in respect of that disposal can be assessed
on and collected from that connected person.

This only applies where an assessment has been raised and the
company has not paid the tax concerned within six months of the
due date. The assessment can be made on the connected person (in
the name of the company) at any time within 2 years of the due date.

The term *capital distribution* is dealt with in paragraph 40.3. For
the purposes of this provision, a capital distribution does not include
one which represents a reduction of capital. This phrase is not
defined, and presumably has its normal meaning.

s10   The definition of 'connected persons' is contained in s10 (see
paragraph 16.4.4).

91.4.3   **Limit on Amount Recoverable**

The amount recoverable from the connected person cannot exceed
the lower of:

— the value of the capital distribution received (or receivable) by him

   or

— a proportion of the tax due by the company in respect of the gain,
equal to the proportion of the total capital distribution out of the
proceeds (or representing the asset) received by him.

Example 424

> *William owns 40% of the shares in an Irish resident company (WILLIE LTD).*
> *The other shares are owned by 2 other persons. The company disposed of its*
> *only asset in March 1993. The amount of the gain included in the profits*
> *chargeable to CT is £30,000. The tax due (40% rate) would amount to £12,000.*
> *In May 1994, the company is put into liquidation, and the liquidator makes a*
> *capital distribution to the shareholders, of which William's share (40%)*
> *amounts to £5,000. The company does not pay the tax due within 6 months of*
> *the due date.*
>
> *The amount of tax recoverable from William cannot exceed the lower of the two*
> *following figures:*
>
> * *£5,000 (the amount received by him)*
>
> * *£4,800 (40% of tax due — same proportion as his share of the distribution*
>   *made by the company)*

The tax due by William on the capital distribution received by him is not in any way affected by the above provisions. He calculates his gain on that distribution in the normal manner.

Any tax paid by William in respect of the company's liability may be recovered by him from the company.

91.5   Recovery of Tax from Group Members

91.5.1   Broad Outline

s626

If a chargeable gain accrues to a company at a time when it is a member of a capital gains group, the CT payable on that gain, if it is not paid within six months, can be assessed and charged (in the name of the company with the gain) on the principal company of that CGT group. It can also be assessed and charged on any other group member from which the asset giving rise to the gain was acquired. This applies even if the company from which the asset was acquired is no longer a member of the group, provided it was a member at any time in the two years prior to the disposal giving rise to the gain.

s623(5)

As explained in paragraph 81, the occasion of a company leaving a group while owning an asset obtained intra group within the previous 10 years can be the occasion of the company being deemed to dispose of that asset at open market value. Where the tax resulting from that deemed disposal is not paid within 6 months from the date when it becomes payable, the tax may be assessed and charged on:

- A principal company of the group from which a subsidiary's departure triggered the gain. Tax may be assessed on the company which was the principal company when the subsidiary left the group, or on a company which is the principal company of the group upon the date on which the tax becomes due.

- A company owning, on the date the tax becomes due, the asset whose deemed disposal gives rise to the charge.

It will be noted that the persons whom the Revenue Commissioners are authorised to assess and charge may be persons who had no connection whatever with the subsidiary which is primarily liable for the tax. The principal company which may be assessed could be a company which was not a member of the group at any time during which the subsidiary was a member of the group - it could have become a principal company of the group subsequent to the departure from the group of the subsidiary. The company holding the asset at the date the tax falls due could be an unconnected third party who purchased the asset at arm's length. The selection of the person to be assessed with the tax lies in the discretion of the Revenue Commissioners. Such wide ranging discretion would appear to be unconstitutional.

1022

91.5.2   Time Limit

s623,
s626

Such an assessment, to be valid, must be made within two years of the date on which the tax becomes payable.

91.5.3   Recovery from Others

Any other group member which pays the tax due under the above provisions, has the right to recover that tax from the group member who realised the gain, or from the group principal company.

91.5.4   Company ceasing to be resident

s628

Where a company ceases to be resident in the State it is deemed on that occasion to dispose of its assets at open market value. Where the tax on that deemed disposal is not paid within 6 months of it becoming due and payable, it may be recovered by the Revenue Commissioners from other group members, or from controlling directors (which is very widely defined). This recovery mechanism is discussed in greater detail in para 74.4.

91.6   Reconstructions

s625

A reconstruction or amalgamation to which s586 or s587 applies can expose the principal company of a group for the tax of another group member. This is described in paragraph 44.1..

91.6.1   Agents, etc. of non-resident

The position of an Irish agent, factor, receiver, or manager of a non-resident is discussed in paragraph 94.12.

91.7   Liquidators

The present position of liquidators and mortgage holders is described in paragraph 97.5, and also in paragraphs 64.4 and 64.6.

92   APPEALS

92.1   Appeal - Time Limit

s945

An appeal against a CGT assessment must be made with 30 days after the date of the notice of assessment and must be made in writing.

s29(8)

S29(8) makes provision for an appeal against the determination by the Revenue Commissioners as to a taxpayer's domicile or ordinary residence. The time limit for such an appeal is two months from the date of notice of the Revenue Commissioners' decision. The appeal procedures are otherwise as described here in relation to an assessment. Hence the identity of the settlor is irrelevant to the section. Its relevance may be that, in a case where assets are not passed to the trustees of a settlement until some time has elapsed during the course of the administration of an estate (which is the common experience), the trust is nonetheless to be treated as having commenced at the date of death so that gains arising to the administrators of the estate in relation to assets subsequently allocated to the trustees are to be treated as gains arising to the trustees. This interpretation is only speculation on the part of the authors. In fact, it is doubtful if the words used are sufficient to attribute to the trustees gains which did not in fact arise to them.

Although a gain or a loss may arise on a disposal, an appeal is possible against only against an assessment in respect of the taxable gains for a period. That figure will be the amount of gains arising in the period, as reduced by relief for losses of that period and of prior periods if not already relieved. If disposals in an assessable period all give rise to losses, and no gains arise in that period, it is not possible, in the event of a failure to agree the amount of those losses with the Inspector at the time, to take the matter to appeal at that time. The taxpayer must wait until he has occasion to claim relief for the losses against a subsequent gain, before the question of the availability, computation or allowability of the losses can be brought before the Appeal Commissioners by way of an appeal against an assessment in respect of taxable gains.

Example 425

John inherited a farm of land from his father on 30 June 1997. At that time John was advised by a valuer that the farm was worth £200,000. On 30 November 1998 John signed an unconditional contract for the sale of the farm for £160,000, to an unconnected party. John had no other disposals of assets in the year ended 5 April 1998. In the following year John disposed of quoted shares on which he made a taxable gain of £10,000.

John disclosed his disposal of the farm in his return of income and gains (form 11) for the year ended 4 April 1998. He attached a computation in relation to the disposal, showing an allowable loss of £40,000 (ignoring acquisition and disposal costs for the sake of simplicity).

The Inspector of Taxes indicated that he did not accept the value attributed by John to the land at the date of acquisition, and that he did not consider that an allowable loss had arisen. Notwithstanding this, John is not able to take the matter of the computation of the loss to appeal until such time as the Inspector raises an assessment in relation to the taxable gains for the year ended 5 April 1999, which is the year in which John can first claim relief for the losses.

The inability to take the computation of losses to appeal until there is a taxable gain against which they can be relieved imposes requirements on the taxpayer to ensure that he retains adequate records to prove his loss, and indeed that he actually remembers that he had the loss! Especially where valuation issues are concerned, it can be unsatisfactory that these cannot be resolved until possibly many years after the event at a time when records and memories may no longer be adequate.

92.2   Appeals – Manner of Making

s955   Where a taxpayer believes that an assessment has been raised or amended out of time, or enquiries are being pursued by an inspector beyond the time limits described above, he may appeal the matter to the appeal commissioners, subject to further appeal from their decision to the courts.

s957   No appeal may be made

- against an assessed amount which is strictly in accordance with the return made or had previously been agreed by the taxpayer with the inspector

- until a CGT return has been delivered for the period *and* any tax computed in accordance with it that return has been paid.

The constitutionality of these restrictions on the right of appeal have not been tested in the courts. Some opinions have been expressed that they may be open to challenge.

s957   A notice of appeal must specify:

- each amount or matter in the assessment which is in dispute

- state in detail the grounds of appeal as respect each such amount or matter.

To date the courts have not clarified the meaning of 'in detail' in relation to grounds of appeal. A similar requirement exists in Australia. There a court upheld an assessment to Income Tax on a volunteer fireman in respect of travel expenses paid to him. He had claimed they were wholly, necessarily and exclusively incurred in the performance of his duties. This was rejected and the judge confirmed the assessment although he was of the opinion that no employment existed (the fireman being a volunteer) in relation to which a liability could arise. This ground of appeal had not been specified by the fireman and so was ignored by the court.

A taxpayer may pursue only those grounds of appeal specified in detail in the notice of appeal, unless the Appeal Commissioners or Courts hold that there is a further ground which he could not reasonably have specified at the time. This latter case might arise where an assessment contains no details as to how the assessment was computed

An amendment to an assessment may be appealed in the same manner.

The provisions restricting a taxpayer in the conduct of his appeal to the grounds of appeal specified in a notice of appeal may not fit in well with the legislation relating to appeals. The legislation relating to appeals requires the Appeal Commissioner to form an opinion on the accuracy of the assessment raised by the inspector, having regard to such information as the Appeal Commissioner considers necessary for the purpose, and to such representations as the taxpayer makes to him. It is not clear that the Appeal Commissioner can be restricted in the matters which he takes into account (or in the enquiries which he may make) in arriving at a conclusion relating to the accuracy of the assessment, by reason of any deficiency in the appeal notice.

92.3   **Application of Income Tax Provisions**

The following provisions of the Income Tax Acts apply, with any necessary modifications, to an appeal against a CGT assessment as they would apply to an IT assessment.

The provisions relating to:

- the appointment of times and places for the hearing of appeals;

- the giving of notice to each person who has given notice of appeal of the time and place appointed for the hearing of his appeal;

- the determination of an appeal by agreement between the appellant or his agent and an inspector of taxes or such other officer;

- the determination of an appeal by the appellant giving notice of his intention not to proceed with the appeal;

- the hearing, determination or dismissal of an appeal by the Appeal Commissioners including the hearing, determination or dismissal of an appeal by one Appeal Commissioner;

- the assessment having the same force and effect as if it were an assessment in respect of which no notice of appeal had been given where the person who has given notice of appeal does not attend before the Appeal Commissioners at the time and place appointed;

- the extension of the time for giving notice of appeal, and the re-admission of appeals by the Appeal Commissioners and the provisions which apply where court proceedings have been taken;

- the rehearing of an appeal by a judge of the Circuit Court and the statement of a case for the opinion of the High Court on a point of law;

- the payment of tax in accordance with the determination of the Appeal Commissioners notwithstanding that an appeal is required to be reheard by a judge of the Circuit Court or that a case of the opinion of the High Court on a point of law has been required to be stated or is pending;

- the procedures for appeal

with any necessary modification, apply to an appeal under any of the provisions of the CGT legislation which provides for an appeal to the Appeal Commissioners as if the appeal were an appeal against an assessment to income tax.

FA98 s134 FA98 s134 has made provisions for the publication (in anonomysed form) of the decisions of the appeal commissioners. The appeal commissioners would be entitled to publish past decisions as well as decisions given after the passing of the FA 1998. Those CGT decisions published at 31 March 2000 are reflected in the text.

92.4 Regulations Relating to Appeals

s950 The Revenue Commissioners may make regulations with respect to appeals. Each regulation must be laid before the Dail, and will have effect unless a resolution annulling the regulation is passed in the Dail within the next 21 sitting days. The broad areas where the regulations may be made are as follows:

- in relation to the conduct of appeals against the assessments and decisions on claims under the CGTs

- entitling persons to appear on appeals in addition to those who would already be entitled

- regulating the time within which appeals or claims may be brought or made

- providing for matters to be determined by a tribunal where two or more persons are affected by the market value of an asset on a particular date or an apportionment, or any other matter

- enabling an Inspector of Taxes or other officer of the Revenue Commissioners to disclose certain information relating to the valuation of assets to a person entitled to appear on such an appeal.

When an inspector of taxes is of the opinion that a person who has sent to him a notice of appeal was not entitled to make that appeal the inspector may reject the appeal notice. However he must specify in writing to the taxpayer the grounds for that rejection. The taxpayer is then entitled to appeal to the Appeal Commissioners against the decision of the inspector of taxes to disallow his original notice of appeal.

s957 An example of an appeal which an inspector might reject is one which is made out of time. Other instances in which the inspector might feel that a right of appeal does not exist is where the appeal is against an amount which is assessed in accordance with the return made; or where the chargeable person had defaulted in the making of a return (s957).

93   MARRIED PERSONS

93.1   Income Tax rules applied

s1029   A return of chargeable gains accruing to a married woman in a year of assessment during which she is married and living with her husband may be required either from her or (if she has not claimed separate assessment) from her husband.

s1022   S1022 (assessment of, and collection from married couples) applies with any necessary modifications in relation to CGT as it applies to income tax.

s1019; s1021   The general changes made in the area of returns, assessments and repayments for income tax in FA93, apply equally to CGT. A married woman can now make the joint return in the name of herself and her husband, whereas previously the joint return had to be made by her husband.

A more detailed discussion of the position of married persons regarding the assessment and collection of tax due on gains arising to either spouse is set out in paragraph 33.

94   WITHHOLDING TAX

94.1   General Rules : withholding tax

s980   On the sale of certain assets the person by or through whom payment is made is obliged to withhold an amount of CGT from the sale proceeds and pay it over to the Revenue. The requirement to deduct tax from the sale proceeds only applies to certain assets specified in the legislation, and where the consideration for the disposal exceeds :

FA98 s74
- £ 50,000 - Pre 24 May 1989

- £100,000 - 24 May 1989 to 27 March 1998

- £150,000 post 27 March 1998.

FA2000 s87
- £300,000 post 23 March 2000

The provision is basically designed to collect tax in the case of a non-resident where later collection may be impossible. The rules, however, apply to all disposals whether by an Irish resident or by a non-resident.

The basic charge to the withholding tax applies on *payment of the consideration for acquiring an asset* to which Paragraph 11, Schedule 4 applies. This is extended to capital sums derived from assets as explained in paragraph 94.4.

The rate of withholding tax is 15%, and is chargeable on the full consideration (irrespective of the gain or loss arising on the disposal).

Tax does not have to be withheld by the purchaser of an asset (or a person paying over a capital sum in certain circumstances) where the vendor, or person receiving the capital, is able to produce a *clearance certificate* from the Inspector of Taxes authorising the payments to be made gross. An Irish resident taxpayer making a disposal is entitled to such a clearance certificate as of right, provided he applies for it in time.

A non-resident person will receive such a certificate only where he has satisfied the inspector that he has no liability, or satisfies him as to the amount of the liability and that tax will be paid by him. In practice it is rare for a non-resident person to receive a clearance certificate, because the time constraints in commercial transactions usually make it difficult for the non-resident to agree his liability with the inspector, and to discharge his tax, prior to the date upon which the withholding might arise.

As a general rule, the Revenue Commissioners will not issue a clearance certificate after the date upon which the withholding of tax should have been deducted (in the absence of a clearance certificate).

The due date for accounting for the 15% withheld in relation to the acquisition/disposal of an asset (as noted in paragraph 94.8.3) is 7 days from the time at which the asset is acquired. It is not usual for a person to acquire an asset in advance of paying over the consideration for the asset but this can happen. In some instances the payment of consideration may be deferred, or it may be payable by instalments. The application of the provisions relating to the due date for accounting for the 15% withholding tax in such a situation is ambiguous.

Example 426

> John sells land worth £400,000 on terms that he is to be paid £250,000 on the conveyance of the land to the purchaser, and the balance of £150,000 one year thereafter. The balance of the money is to be secured on the land until it is paid. John is a non-resident and fails to apply for or obtain a tax clearance certificate in relation to the transaction.
>
> The transaction raises two questions:
>
> • Is the transaction to be regarded as one in which the land is disposed of for a consideration of £250,000 plus a debt of £150,000, giving rise to an obligation to withhold £60,000 on the occasion when the £250,000 deposit is paid over, and to account for it to the Revenue Commissioners within 7 days of that date?
>
> • Is it a transaction in which the consideration consists of a sum of £400,000 payable in two instalments, with no obligation to withhold arising until the payment of the second instalment (being the point at which the consideration

paid over exceeds £300,000). In such a case what is the due date for accounting to the Revenue for the tax so withheld? It could hardly be 7 days after the acquisition of the land, since that would be almost a year prior to the withholding arising.

If John, in *example 413* above, had sold the land for a deposit of £10,000 and the balance of £390,000 left outstanding and charged on the land for a period of a year, the problem would become even more difficult. The money passing at the date on which the purchaser acquires the asset is too little to enable a withholding in respect of the full consideration to be made at that time. Has John disposed of the asset for a consideration from which a deduction cannot be made (largely a debt) and must he therefore account to the Revenue Commissioners for the 15% of the total consideration, if necessary out of his own resources and subject to recovery from the purchaser ?

Unfortunately the legislation is ambiguously worded. A definitive answer to the difficulties which arise is not possible and taxpayers encountering these difficulties, or anticipating them, would be advised to discuss the problem with the Revenue Commissioners in advance.

94.2   **Assets subject to withholding tax**

s980(2)   The assets to which the withholding tax applies are:

(a)   Irish land and buildings;

(b)   Minerals in Ireland or any rights, interests or other assets in relation to mining or minerals or the searching for minerals;

(c)   Exploration or exploitation rights within the limits of the the Irish Continental Shelf;

(d)   Unquoted shares in a company deriving their value or the greater part of their value directly or indirectly from (a) to (c) above;

(e)   Unquoted shares, acquired under the relieving provisions of s584 (see Chapter 6) in exchange for shares specified in (d) above.

(f)   The goodwill of a trade carried on in Ireland.

FA 2000 s87   These are the only assets subject to the withholding tax, and even then, it only applies where the consideration for the disposal exceeds £300,000 (current limit - see paragraph 94.1).

FA95 s76   Part (e) above was inserted into s980 by the FA95, and has effect in relation to a payment of money or money's worth made on or after 2nd June 1995.

What this additional sub-paragraph seems to be concerned with, is that on a reorganisation of share capital where (in broad terms) existing shares are exchanged for new shares or debentures in the company, the owner of the old existing shares:

- would be deemed not to have made any disposal of his existing shares, and

- the new shares would be treated as being the old shares from the point of view of cost and acquisition date [ie. *the original shares (taken as a single asset) and the new holding (taken as a single asset) shall be treated as the same asset acquired as the original shares were acquired*].

On a later disposal of the new shares or debentures by a non-resident, if those new shares did not derive value from Irish land (or other specified assets) the withholding tax would not have applied. Equally, on disposal of the shares through liquidation, or on a redemption of debentures where the company making the payment does not acquire any asset, the withholding tax provisions would not apply, and it may be difficult for the Irish Revenue to recover any tax on the disposal at a later stage.

The actual words of s980(2)(e) are: "*shares other than shares quoted on a stock exchange, to which s584 applies, whether by virtue of that section or any other section, so that, as respects a person disposing of those shares, they are treated as the same shares **as shares specified in paragraph (d)**, acquired as the shares so specified were acquired*".

This FA95 addition of the additional paragraph (e) to the list of specified assets for withholding tax closes that loophole, and puts the new holding, whether it be of shares or debentures, in the same category as the old shares.

The withholding tax always applied solely to assets within the scope of the charge to CGT - see paragraph 3 (Chapter 1) for details of the territorial scope of the tax. The extension of the withholding tax to the shares listed in the new paragraph (dd) is strange, as the legislation does not actually extend the CGT charging section to such shares or debentures (which may not derive value from the specified assets) in the ownership of a non-resident. It now appears that a withholding tax applies to assets which in the hands of a non-resident may not be within the charge to CGT. This may cause some difficulty in the operation of the new provisions.

The question of unquoted shares deriving value from such assets is also dealt with in paragraph 2 (Chapter 1).

The extension of the withholding tax requirements to shares not deriving their value from land (which the person disposing of them had acquired in a share for share swap) makes it important for a purchaser of Irish shares for a consideration in excess of £300,000 to always make inquiries as to the manner in which the purchaser acquired those shares. There is no clearance procedure provided for to enable a purchaser to confirm with the Revenue whether or not shares not deriving their value from land were the subject of reorganisation relief (share for share swap) on their acquisition by the vendor. Neither would a purchaser usually be aware, or be entitled as of right to discover, whether the "old shares" which were swapped for the "new shares" derived their value from land or other specified assets.

94.3   Disposal of asset in parts

s980

Aggregation is not applied to the withholding tax provisions. The specific disposal is either for a consideration of £300,000 or more, or it is not within the scope of the provisions.   The taxpayer is not concerned with yesterday's disposal, or what will happen tomorrow. He is concerned only with a single disposal.

There are, of course, provisions to ensure that where a single asset is disposed of in parts, in certain circumstances those parts will be aggregated and treated as a single disposal.

Where an asset owned at one time by one person is disposed of by him in parts

— to the same person, or

— to persons acting in concert, or

— to connected persons,

whether or not on the same or different occasions, the several disposals are all treated as one single disposal for the purpose of determining whether the withholding tax applies, and if so, the amount of withholding tax.

Where the disposal of a single asset is made in parts, but is not made to the same person, or connected persons, etc., it would appear that each separate disposal would stand alone in applying these provisions.

94.4   Capital Sum derived from asset

s535

A *capital sum derived from an asset* is deemed to be a disposal of that asset. The area of capital sums, and the identification of which asset (if any) the capital sum is derived from is complex. The area is dealt with in paragraph 4.4.4 (Chapter 1).

FA95 s76

The FA95 inserted a new paragraph (10A) into para 11 of Sch 4, which brings certain capital sums within the scope of the withholding tax.

s980(11)(a)   *"Subject to Paragraph (b) where there is a disposal of assets by virtue of a capital sum being derived from those assets, the person paying the capital sum shall, notwithstanding that no asset is acquired by that person, be treated for the purposes of ...(the withholding tax provisions)... as acquiring the assets disposed of for a consideration equal to the capital sum, whether that sum is paid in money or money's worth, and .."*.. all the withholding tax provisions are to apply (subject to any necessary modifications) to that transaction.

The requirements of s980 relate to withholding 15% from the consideration apply only when a person acquires an asset. When a person derives a capital sum from an asset, he is deemed by the Act to dispose of the asset. However, that transaction would not ordinarily result in the person who pays the capital sum acquiring any asset. It is in this context that the FA95 provision, which deems, for the purposes of the 15% withholding tax legislation, that the person who pays a capital sum acquires an asset, is significant. It ensures that the requirements to impose a 15% withholding tax liability (potentially) are in place.

FA96 s59   FA96 s59 excluded from the category of payments in relation to which the withholding tax might have to be accounted for, payments made under an insurance policy in relation to damage to an asset. But for that amendment, compensation paid by an insurance company to a householder whose house was destroyed by fire would, if the sum exceeded £300,000 and a clearance certificate was not produced, have required the insurance company to withhold 15%. This is no longer necessary.

Example 427

> *An example where the extended provisions of the FA95 might apply would be a case where a local authority pays a capital sum to a farmer in respect of the diminished value of land retained by the farmer but adjacent to a new road scheme being developed by the council.*

A further example of a capital sum derived from an asset to which withholding tax would have application is the grant of a lease at a premium, where the whole of the premium was not taken into account for income tax purposes, as generally it will not be. A premium on a lease may require either withholding tax or a clearance certificate.

"Capital sum" has been defined for the purpose of these provisions as including money's worth. The provision would seem to have application even in a situation where a liquidator of a company deriving its value from Irish land, transfers property in specie to a shareholder in the course of the liquidation, in satisfaction of his rights as shareholder. Such a transaction involves a disposal by the liquidator of land, and a disposal (or part disposal) by the shareholder of shares. The land received by the shareholder would seem to be a capital sum derived from his shares, and the liquidator would seem to be a person who has *paid* such a capital sum to him. Where the shareholder does not produce a tax clearance certificate, it would seem that the liquidator would be obliged to account to the Revenue Commissioners for 15% of the value of the land.

s583

Some doubt exists in this area because a disposal of shares by reason of a distribution by the liquidator is a disposal by reason of the receipt of a capital distribution (s583) rather than by reason of the receipt of a capital sum derived from an asset (s535) as referred to in the FA95 extension of the withholding tax obligations.

94.5   Rate of Withholding Tax

s980

The rate of withholding tax is 15%.

94.6   Amount on which withholding Tax is chargeable

94.6.1   Broad Outline

The withholding tax is chargeable on the full proceeds of disposal.

It should be noted that where the consideration exceeds £300,000 even by £1, the entire sales proceeds are subject to the withholding tax. It is not only the excess over £300,000 which is subject to the withholding tax.

94.6.2   VAT on sale proceeds:

The full disposal proceeds include any amount of VAT chargeable on the transaction.

Some contracts for the sale of land state an agreed amount of consideration but provide in the detailed conditions in relation to the sale, that should VAT be chargeable on the transaction the consideration may be increased by a corresponding amount. There has been some controversy in the past as to whether the obligation to withhold or account for tax is computed by reference to the basic agreed consideration, or to consideration as adjusted for VAT, where VAT arises.

Where VAT does arise on a transaction in such circumstances it is clear that account has to be taken of the price as adjusted for the VAT both in determining whether the consideration passing does not exceed £300,000 and in calculating the amount which must be withheld or accounted for.

Example 428

John who is a non-resident, sold a building for £296,000. He was entitled to, and did, charge the purchaser VAT on the sale in the amount of £42,285. He did not have a clearance certificate at the closing of the sale.

> *The total consideration to be taken into account is £338,285 (i.e. VAT inclusive). The purchaser must withhold £37210.*

94.7   Notional sale proceeds

In certain circumstances in the computation of capital gains tax the actual consideration arising on the disposal of an asset is disregarded, and a notional consideration equal to its open market value is taken into account instead. An example would be a transaction between connected parties. In transactions between companies in a group, the actual consideration may be disregarded, and would be replaced by the transferor's base cost in the asset. In such cases the withholding tax obligations apply to the actual agreed consideration, and not to the notional consideration which may be substituted for them in the computation of the transferor's tax

s980   liability. This is because s980 imposes withholding tax *"upon payment of the consideration"* in an amount of *"15% of the said payment"*.

The only payment involved in the transactions is the actual payment. The notional consideration is not the subject matter of a payment nor does the legislation ever deem a payment of the notional consideration to be made. For the same reason, although a gift would be deemed to be both a disposal by the donor, and an acquisition by the donee, at open market value, a withholding tax obligation does not arise on a gift because no *payment of consideration* is involved.

Example 429

> *John sells shares deriving their value from land to his son, Joe, for the sum of £150,000, at a time when their open market value is £400,000.*

> *If John does not produce a tax clearance certificate, Joe will be obliged to withhold 15% of £150,000, upon making the payment. However for the purposes of computing John's CGT liability on the disposal, the consideration will be taken to be £400,000, and that also would be Joe's base cost of the shares.*

94.8   Non-money Consideration

94.8.1   Broad Outline

s917   Where an asset (subject to these withholding tax provisions) is acquired after 2nd June 1995 and the consideration given for the disposal is in such a form that tax cannot be withheld, special provisions apply.

It should be noted that these provisions, which place onerous responsibilities on the person acquiring the asset, were substantially amended in relation to acquisitions of assets after 2nd June 1995 [the date of passing of the FA95]. The previous provisions had affect in relation to assets acquired in similar circumstances in the period between 17th July 1982 and 2nd June 1995. In a case involving acquisitions in that earlier period, the reader is referred to the 6th edition of this book (FA94 edition).

These provisions only apply where the Inspector has not issued a clearance certificate exempting the person paying the consideration from the withholding tax provisions. Details of the circumstances in which an exemption certificate will be issued are set out in paragraph 94.9 below.

In broad terms, the FA95 provisions place two separate obligations on the person acquiring the asset:

- **an obligation to make a return of information** to the Revenue regarding the transaction, and

- **an obligation to actually pay the withholding tax** at 15% of the estimated value of the asset acquired.

94.8.2   **Return of information:**

The person acquiring the asset must notify the Revenue Commissioners in writing, giving details of the following:

—the asset acquired;

—the consideration for acquiring the asset,;

—market value of that consideration (estimated where necessary to the best of that person's knowledge and belief)), and

—name and address of the person making the disposal.

This information must be given to the Revenue Commissioners within *seven days* of the date on which the acquisition is made.

94.8.3   **Payment of withholding tax**

s980   In addition, the person acquiring the asset, must pay to the Collector General an amount of CGT equal to 15% of the estimated market value of that asset which he has acquired. This provision only applies to the acquisition of an asset within the scope of the charge to the withholding tax on or after 2nd June 1995.

Where the person acquiring the asset is required to account for withholding tax under the above provisions,

- it is payable by that person in addition to any CGT payable by him by virtue of any other provisions of the CGT legislation, and

- is due within *seven days* of the time at which he acquires the asset, and

- is payable without the making of an assessment.

However, the tax can be assessed on the person acquiring the asset if any part of the tax remains unpaid on the due date.

Where the person acquiring the asset pays the tax due under the above provisions, he is given a right (under s980) to recover that amount from the person from whom he acquired the asset *"as a simple contract debt in any court of competent jurisdiction."*

Where a clearance certificate, exempting the transaction from withholding tax (see paragraph 94.9) is issued to the person acquiring the asset, that person:

— *"shall not be entitled thereafter to so recover the said sum, and*

— *shall be repaid the said amount of tax".*

This provision is somewhat confusing, in that it can only apply to a clearance certificate issued after the transaction has occurred . If a clearance certificate is issued prior to the date of the transaction, the transaction is exempt from the withholding tax, and none of the above provisions have any relevance. However, where the clearance certificate is not available at the time of the transaction, but is produced later, all this provisions does is to stop proceedings for recovery of the tax from the person from whom the asset was acquired, and substitute a refund (presumably from the Revenue - although that is not stated in the legislation).

Any doubts raised by the above comments should not be relied on as justification for failing to withhold tax.

Where an Irish resident purchaser has not had a clearance certificate produced to him relating to a transaction to which withholding tax legislation has application, he would be wise to protect himself by applying the withholding tax.

94.9   Exemption from withholding tax

The person who is chargeable to CGT on the disposal of the asset may apply to the Inspector for a certificate exempting the transaction from the withholding tax provisions.

Provided the Inspector is satisfied that the person applying for the exemption is in fact the person who is making the disposal, and that:

- he is resident in the State (NOTE :prior to 6th April 1995 the requirement was for him to be ordinarily resident).

  or

- no amount of CGT is payable in respect of the disposal

  or

- the CGT chargeable for the year of assessment for which he is chargeable in respect of this disposal, and the tax chargeable on any gains accruing in any earlier years of assessment on a previous disposal of the asset, has been paid,

s980

the inspector is required to issue a certificate to the person making the disposal, and a copy of that certificate to the person who is acquiring the asset. Provided all the conditions for the issue of the clearance certificate are met, the actual issue of the certificate is mandatory on the Inspector. He has no choice in the matter. In the case of The State (FIC Ltd) v E O'Ceallaigh (Inspector of Taxes) the High Court held that the Inspector was not entitled to engage in a wide ranging investigation of a taxpayers affairs or title or the transaction before issue of a certificate under s980.

The certificate has the effect of exempting the transactions specified in that certificate from the withholding tax provisions.

In the case of a disposal by an Irish resident, the application for an exemption from withholding tax is made to the Inspector of Taxes who normally deals with that person's income and gains. The normal grounds on which an exemption is applied for is that the person making the disposal is 'resident in Ireland'.

To claim exemption on other grounds (i.e. no gain arises, etc..) may take a considerable period of time to process (to prove the facts to the satisfaction of the Inspector) and may cause unnecessary delays. However, a non-resident seeking to obtain a clearance certificate, has no choice but to rely on these other grounds.

s617

The obligation to operate withholding tax in the absence of a clearance certificate applies whether or not a gain would result on the disposal. For example, an intra group transfer to which s617 would have application so as to treat the disposal as being on a no gain/no loss basis, would still require a clearance certificate if a withholding tax is not to be applied. Obviously in such a case, if a withholding tax were applied, the company making the disposal would be entitled to a refund of the tax. Nonetheless, if the withholding tax were not applied, the purchasing company would be exposed to interest and possibly penalties because of its failure to withhold and account for the tax.

In the case of Pine Valley Developments Ltd, Healy Holdings Ltd, and Daniel Healy v Minister for the Environment & the Attorney General the Revenue Commissioners sought to have 15% withheld from an award of damages arising out of a planning appeal application. The High Court refused to order such a withholding on the grounds that the payment was to be made to a person who was ordinarily resident in the State.

That person had not been issued with a CGT tax clearance certificate for reasons not stated. The Judge said *"In all these circumstances it seems to me that the Inspector of Taxes ought to have issued to the plaintiff a tax clearance certificate. In accordance with equitable principles I will*

1038

treat that as done which ought to have been done" and ordered that tax should not be withheld from the payment.

FA83 s56

In the case of Bank of Ireland Finance Ltd. v Revenue Commissioners, Justice Carroll ruled that Bank of Ireland Finance Ltd. were not entitled to repayment of £15,000 withheld by a purchaser of land being sold by the bank as mortgagor. The bank did not own the land, but had an equitable mortgage over it in respect of sums lent to the owner. It was as mortgage holder that the bank were selling the land. They had not obtained a clearance certificate and the purchaser withheld 15%. The bank claimed that they were entitled to the entire proceeds of sale, and were not liable to any capital gains tax on the disposal, since it was not their asset that was being disposed of. The judge ruled that the 15% withheld was properly offsetable against any capital gains tax liability of the owner of the land, and was not refundable to the bank. This case related to a transaction entered into prior to 9 June 1983, when the law was amended by FA83 s56 to provide that capital gains tax is payable in priority to the entitlement of any lender secured on the property.

- **Revenue Commissioners published precedent :**

— In a published Revenue precedent it is stated that *"A Local Authority completing a compulsory purchase of land is not obliged to operate tax clearance, since the Local Authority is not entering into a contract with the land-owner. It is exercising its powers under a statutory scheme for land acquisition. This applies whether the price paid for the land has been agreed between the Local Authority and the land-owner, or has been fixed by arbitration. Where the local authority enters into a contract with a land-owner for purchase of land it would be obliged to operate tax clearance, even though it could compulsorily acquire the land."*

The Revenue precedent quoted it not easy to relate to the legislation which is not expressed in terms of "a sale" or in terms of the existence of a contract. Rather it is expressed in terms of "payment of the consideration for acquiring an asset to which this section applies." The Local Authority certainly acquires an asset, and the moneys which it gives over to the person from whom the asset is compulsorily acquired is seen to be "consideration" notwithstanding the absence of a freely entered into bargain.

- **Revenue Commissioners - tax briefing :**

— Issue 35 of Tax Briefing, March 1999 contains an article by the Revenue Commissioners on the operation of clearance certificates. The article emphasises that an application for a clearance certificate should be addressed to the local tax office, and not to the Revenue Commissioners at Dublin Castle. It also states *"Applications should be posted so that they are received in the tax office at least 5 working days in advance of the closing date. (This may mean actual posting of the application 6 to 7 days in advance of the closing date)."*

It also states that if the closing date on a contract has elapsed at the time of making the application, confirmation will be required that the consideration has not passed and a revised closing date must be specified. The implication of this statement is that "retrospective clearance certificates" will not be issued ie a clearance certificate will be issued only at a time before the necessity for withholding has arisen, by reason of the payment of the consideration.

The article goes on to state that the application must be signed by the person chargeable (ie the vendor) and cannot be signed by an agent on his behalf. In the case of a company it should be signed by the secretary of the company. In the case of a corporation or other body of persons the application should be made by the treasurer, auditor or receiver. For trusts or unadministered estates the application should be made by the trustees or the personal representative. Where there are multiple vendors, a single application should be made but it should be signed by all of the vendors. However in the case of a joint disposal by husband and wife, an application signed by one spouse only will be accepted.

94.10   **Returns and Assessment**

The person liable to withhold CGT on payment of the sale proceeds must "forthwith" deliver an account of the proceeds and withholding tax to the Revenue Commissioners. The Inspector will then raise an assessment to charge the tax. The CGT is due for payment the day following the date of the assessment.

Where the Inspector is not satisfied with the returns he may estimate the amount he feels is due, and assess the person accordingly. The normal appeal procedures apply.

94.11   **Adjustment of Liability**

Where CGT has been assessed and paid under the provisions outlined above, the person making the disposal is entitled to relief if the CGT withheld from the proceeds exceeds his actual liability on the disposal of the asset concerned. Any adjustment will be dealt with by way of repayment when the actual liability is agreed. The repayment does not attract interest.

94.12   **Irish Agent of non-resident**

s1034   Even where an Inspector issues a certificate authorising payment of the proceeds in full, any Irish resident by or through whom the payment is made should be aware of the provisions of s1034, which applies equally to IT and CGT.

"A person not resident in the State, whether a citizen or Ireland or not, shall be assessable and chargeable in the name of any trustee, guardian, or committee of such person, or of any factor, agent, receiver, branch or manager, whether such factor, agent, receiver, branch or manager has the receipt of the profits or gains or not, in like manner, and to the like amount as such non-resident person would be assessed and charged if he were resident in the State and in the actual receipt of such profits or gains".

95   LIABILITY OF TRUSTEES, ETC.

95.1   Trustees of settlement

s568

CGT chargeable on gains accruing to trustees of a settlement, or CGT due from the personal representatives of a deceased person may be assessed and charged on any one or more of those trustees or personal representatives.

A trustee or personal representative is not treated as an individual for CGT purposes. Among other things this means that they are not entitled to the £1,000 annual exemption.

96   VALUATION OF ASSETS : POWER TO INSPECT

96.1   Power to inspect assets

s911

An Inspector or other authorised officer may inspect any property for the purpose of ascertaining its market value and the person having the custody or possession of the property must permit them to do so at any reasonable time.

Penalties are provided for any person who "obstructs, molests, or hinders" the Inspector or officer.

97   PAYMENT OF CAPITAL GAINS TAX

97.1   Broad Outline - payment of CGT

The manner for determining the due date for payment of CGT is described (for most circumstances) in paragraph 88.

97.2   Unremittable Gains

s1005

Where a gain arises on the disposal of a foreign asset, and the taxpayer can PROVE to the satisfaction of the Revenue Commissioners that the gain cannot be remitted into Ireland because of legislation in the foreign country, or because of action taken by the government of that country, the Revenue may take the amount of those unremittable gains out of the assessment.

In effect, he is only assessed on the part of the gain (if any) remitted into Ireland.

This lasts for as long as the Revenue are satisfied that the gain is unremittable for the reasons set out above. If it subsequently becomes remittable, the gain is assessed, and the tax collected.

There is a right of appeal against a decision by the Revenue Commissioners not to "defer" assessing the unremittable gain, or any part of it.

The wording of the UK equivalent provision is different to s1005 but the relief is given on similar grounds. In the UK case of Van-Arkadie v Plunket, the taxpayer who was assessed on his proportionate share of gains accruing to a non-resident company (see paragraph 43) claimed to have the charge deferred as the remittance of the gain was prohibited by the law of the country in which the gain arose. The company (in which the taxpayer was a minority shareholder) was not resident in the UK, and was incorporated in Rhodesia (now Zimbabwe). The then Government prohibited the payment out of the country of dividends and distributions of assets to UK resident shareholders. The company, however, never declared dividends nor distributed assets in the period concerned. It was decided that the relief did not apply.

In the course of his judgement, Vinelott J said

"[s1005]...is concerned only with the case where a chargeable gains accruing on an actual or deemed disposal is represented by something, money, or money's worth, which comes into the hands of the taxpayer. It is only in respect of that money or money's worth that it can be sensibly asked whether the taxpayer was unable to transfer it to the United Kingdom, and whether the inability was due to the laws of the territory where the gain accrued...It is said that it is unfair that [s1005] should not apply in circumstances where the reason for not distributing the gain which accrued to a non-resident company might have been the circumstance that if it had been distributed it would in turn have been blocked in the jurisdiction where the company was incorporated. It is quite clearly not possible to assume that the reason for non-distribution would always or even mainly be the knowledge by the shareholders that gains distributed by the company would be blocked. In the present case I know nothing of the circumstances of the company or of the other shareholders; all I know is that the taxpayer is only a minority shareholder".

It is clear that Vinelott J. was not satisfied, on the available evidence, that the company would have distributed the gain even if such a distribution was not blocked by the Rhodesian Government.

However, even if he had been so satisfied, it would appear from his judgement that it would not have affected the decision.

97.3   Payment by Installments

s981   Where the sale proceeds are payable by instalments after the date of disposal, and over a period exceeding eighteen months, the gain is calculated in the normal manner as if the sale proceeds were payable at the date of disposal. If any part of the proceeds subsequently prove to be irrecoverable, an adjustment will be made to the amount of tax payable.

If the Revenue are satisfied that it would cause undue hardship to collect all the tax on the due date, they may allow the tax to be paid by instalments over a period not exceeding 5 years, and not going beyond the date of receipt of the final instalment.

97.4   Preferential Payment

s982   "The priority attaching to assessed taxes under s.4 of the Preferential Payment in Bankruptcy (Ireland) Act 1889, and Sections 78 and 285 of the Companies Act 1963, shall apply to capital gains tax".

97.5   Liquidators and Mortgagors, etc..

s571   Where a disposal takes place on or after 9 June 1983 s571 ensures that the tax is payable in priority to the entitlement of any lender who may be entitled to the property (under a mortgage, etc.). The person with possession of the sale proceeds, whether it be the lender or an agent appointed by him to enforce the security is made primarily responsible for payment of the CGT liability arising out of that disposal.

The details of the provisions are set out in paragraphs 64.4 and 64.6.

The case of Bank of Ireland Finance v Revenue Commissioners, a 1989 High Court case, held that tax withheld from the consideration arising on the disposal by the Bank of Ireland Finance Limited as mortgagor of certain lands owned by a person to whom they had lent money, was not repayable by the Revenue to Bank of Ireland Finance Limited, but was offsetable against the capital gains tax liability of the owner of the land. This transaction predated s.56 FA83.

97.6   Credit against CAT

FA85 s63   Where a person makes a gift of an asset to another, or transfers an asset at an undervalue, the transaction may come within the scope of two separate taxes.

• Capital Acquisitions Tax (on the recipient), and

- Capital Gains Tax (on the person making the disposal)

The combined effect of both taxes could take a substantial part of the value of the gift.

Prior to 30th January 1985, the value of the gift for CAT purposes was reduced by the CGT payable, and the recipient charged to CAT on the reduced value.

FA85 s63

S.63 FA85 introduced a relief whereby credit against the CAT itself is given for the CGT paid.

Where CAT is payable on the happening of an event (on or after 30th January 1985), and that event is a disposal of an asset for CGT purposes, then in calculating the amount of CAT payable, credit is allowed for the amount of CGT payable. The amount of the credit is to be the lesser of the capital gains tax and capital acquisitions tax attributable to the relevant asset. As credit is given against the tax payable, no deduction is given for the CGT in arriving at the value of the benefit received for CAT purposes.

Example 430

John is about to get married. To "set him up" and help him obtain a home, his father decides to make him a gift. The father sells CRH plc shares for £250,000. He gifts the £250,000 to John.

The sale of the shares generated a taxable gain of £30,000. The gift of £250,000 generated capital acquisitions tax of (assumed £25,000). It is not possible to offset the CGT on the sale of the shares against the CAT on the gift of the sales proceeds, because the sale of the shares and gift of the proceeds were two separate events. The two charges to tax did not arise on the same event.

Had John's father gifted him the shares in CRH plc, and had John then sold the shares, the commercial result would be the same i.e. John would have received a gift worth £250,000 from his father. However, in this case the same amount of CGT and CAT would arise but they would arise on the same event, i.e. on the occasion of the gift of shares from the father to John. Accordingly, CGT would be offsetable against the CAT leaving no net CAT payable.

A difficulty can arise where a transfer attracts tax reliefs in the case of either CGT or CAT, and these are subsequently clawed back. The circumstances in which this is most likely to arise is described in the example below:

Example 431

*John, in **Example 430** above, also receives a gift from his father of shares in the family trading company, in order to mark his marriage. The gift qualifies both for retirement relief in the case of capital gains tax, and business property relief in the case of capital acquisitions tax. These two reliefs are mandatory and automatic and are not reliefs which may be elected into, or out of, as of right.*

Three years later John got wanderlust and decided to move to Australia. He sold back to his father the shares in the family trading company. Because he has disposed of the shares within the "claw-back period" in relation to both the CGT

> and CAT reliefs, the claw-back provisions of those reliefs now operate. An assessment will be raised on John in relation to the capital gains which would have arisen on the occasion of his father's transfer of shares to him, but for the relief. He will also become liable to capital acquisitions tax. However his liability in relation to the capital acquisitions tax arises by treating the original gift to him as not having been entitled to business property relief, and the raising of a CAT assessment upon him in relation to the gift three years previously.

> The question therefore arises whether the CAT (now treated as arising on the gift from the father) and the CGT (becoming due by reason of the disposal of the shares but calculated by reference to the CGT that would otherwise have arisen on the gift) arise on the same event. If they arise on the same event, they may be offset. But if they do not arise on the same event they may not be offset.

> There is a real ambiguity here. Is the event upon which the two tax charges arise the sale by John of the shares three years after they were gifted to him? Or is it the sale which triggers the CGT but the original gift which gave rise to the CAT albeit affected by the later sale?

In the opinion of the authors the offset should be possible on the basis that the relief should not be affected by what are essentially assessment mechanisms. It is not the original gift which has within it the ability to give rise to these tax charges. It is the subsequent sale that triggers legislative provisions that give rise to the tax charge. Both tax charges are to some degree computed by reference to the prior gift (the CGT is computed as to its amount and relevant tax rate by reference to the prior gift, and the CAT is computed and assessed by reference to the prior gift). But neither charge to tax could have arisen other than by reason of the sale and immediately before the sale the gift had not managed to give rise to either charge. That is not beyond doubt and any person intending to rely on the offset in such circumstances should seek explicit Revenue clearance.

The due date for CGT is usually later than the due date for CAT. CGT is offsetable against CAT and not vice versa i.e. it is the CGT which must be paid, and it is the payment of CAT which is relieved. In practice the Revenue Commissioners will usually agree that CAT need not be paid, where CGT (once it has been paid) will be offsetable against the CAT. However this should be verified on each occasion.

97.7   Repayments of CGT

If a person has made a payment of capital gains tax or of preliminary tax on account of capital gains tax or has suffered a withholding tax, and the payment or withholding tax exceeds his liability to capital gains tax for the relevant period of assessment, he is entitled to a repayment of the excess.

s591(14)   Where the repayment is a repayment of preliminary tax, the repayment carries interest in most instances. There are however some specific prohibitions on payment of interest on repayments of tax even where it is preliminary tax e.g. s591(14) dealing with roll-over relief on shares.

A repayment of withholding tax does not attract interest on the basis of any statutory provision.

Repayment of tax arising out of an order of a Court would entitle the taxpayer to interest on bases which lie outside the capital gains tax legislation.

98   BROAD OUTLINE

Disposals of certain Irish assets (the specified assets) are within the charge to Irish CGT irrespective of the residence or ordinary residence of the person making the disposal. In respect of disposals of other assets, the gain is chargeable only if the person making the disposal is resident or ordinarily resident in Ireland. Where an individual is chargeable to CGT (by reason of residence or ordinary residence) the charge will, in certain circumstances, be limited where that individual is not domiciled in Ireland.

This topic is discussed in detail in paragraph 3.

The terms resident, ordinarily resident and domicile are, therefore, of fundamental importance for CGT purposes.

s819 - s824   Until the FA94 introduced a statutory definition (now s819 to s824) (see paragraph 100), the only statutory guidance on the general meaning of the terms "resident" and "ordinarily resident" for CGT purposes was contained in s.2 of the 1975 Act (now s5).

s2   S2 stated that "resident and ordinarily resident have the same meanings as in the Income Tax Acts". In addition, s.15 of the 1975 Act (now s574(1)) includes special provisions dealing with the residence of trustees of settled property (see paragraph 65.3) and personal representatives of deceased persons (see paragraph 66).

Neither the CGT Acts nor the IT Acts include any guidance as to the meaning of domicile which therefore has the meaning assigned to it in general law, as explained in paragraph 104.

99   RESIDENT INDIVIDUAL (POST FA 94)

99.1   Residence - broad Outline

s819   Prior to the FA94, there was no comprehensive statutory definition to enable an individual to determine whether he was resident in Ireland (see paragraph 102). A comprehensive definition was provided by FA94 s150, now s819.

The changes to the meaning of "resident" and of "ordinarily resident" in the FA94 are of major significance to CGT. In particular the new definition leaves an individual ordinarily resident (and therefore subject to CGT) for the first three tax years of his non-residence. That period of extended liability can be three years and 11 months long. The change has made it difficult to avoid a CGT liability by ceasing to be resident for a period. It also has significance (perhaps unintentionally) for non-domiciled individuals who spend sufficient time in Ireland to acquire ordinary residence, and then return to their home abroad. Such individuals remain liable to Irish CGT for at least 3 years, subject to any double tax agreement that may be applicable. This is significant especially as regards their UK source gains which are not taxable on the remittance basis.

99.2   Residence - statutory rules

s819   FA94 Part VII introduced a statutory definition of "resident" and of "ordinarily resident" in relation to an individual. These definitions or tests replace the rules which previously existed and which are described below. An individual is resident in the State in any year of assessment in which he:

- Spends a total of 183 days or more in the State or;

- Spends more thant 30 days in the State in that year, and in that year and the previous year together spent 280 days or more in the State or;

- Elects to be resident, being in the State with the intention of being resident the following year and in circumstances which make that likely.

For the purposes of the tests described above a person is regarded as present in the State on a day in which he is *present at midnight*.

s822   The "split year" residence treatment which may apply in the case of employment does not apply for CGT purposes.

100   ORDINARILY RESIDENT (POST FINANCE ACT 1994)

100.1   Ordinary Residence - statutory rules

An individual is ordinarily resident in the State in any tax year in which he has been resident in the State in the three previous tax years. Once he becomes ordinarily resident, he remains so until a tax year in which he has been non-resident in each of the three previous tax years.

s820   A new arrival does not become ordinarily resident until his fourth consecutive tax year of residence. A departing person who was ordinarily resident retains that status for the first three tax years of his non-residence.

Example 432

> *Joe Smith arrives in Ireland on 30 June 1994 and remains until 30 June 1999.*
>
> *Joe is resident in 1994/95 to 1999/2000 inclusive. He becomes ordinarily resident in 1997/98 and does not cease to be ordinarily resident until 2002/03.*

The new rules both as regards residence and ordinary residence apply generally from 6 April 1994. They did not apply until 6 April 1995 to individuals who:

- were resident in 1991/92 but not in 1992/93 or 1993/94

- were resident in 1992/93 but not in 1993/94

- were resident in 1993/94 but would not under the old rules be resident in 1994/95

- left the State in 1992/93 or 1993/94 and then ceased to be ordinarily resident under the old rules, and did not recommence ordinary residence before 1994/95, under the old rules.

See paragraph 104.5 regarding a special appeal procedure on rulings regarding ordinary residence.

101   RESIDENT — COMPANY

101.1   Broad Outline - Company residence

Prior to the FA 99 the residence of a company was determined, for Irish taxation purposes, solely by reference to its place of central management and control.

This test remains a basis upon which a company may be regarded as being resident in Ireland. However, with effect from the **11 February 1999** a company which is **registered in Ireland** may, in certain circumstances, be regarded as resident in Ireland for tax purposes even if its central management and control is not exercised in Ireland.

The concept of central management and control is discussed below.

101.2   Central Management and control :

A Company is resident in a place where the central management and control exists. The place of incorporation of a Company is not necessarily the place of residence of a Company, although it may be a factor to be taken into account if the location of the management and control is uncertain.

In DeBeers Consolidated Mines Limited v Howe, Lord Loreburn said

"...the Company resides for purposes of income tax where its real business is carried on...I regard that as a true rule and the real business is carried on where the central management and the control actually abides".

Control in this context is that normally exercised by the directors and *not* shareholder control.

The location of the residence of a Company is a question of fact. Normally, the Company would be resident where the Directors' meetings are held. This test, of course, of not conclusive because it must be established that the central management and control of the Company is exercised by the Directors at those meetings.

In deciding the location of the management and control, it may be necessary to take into account factors such as the place where the Company's business is carried on, and whether and to what extent control has been delegated by the directors.

101.3   Irish registered company

FA99 s82   The Finance Act 1999, with effect from 1 October 1999, will treat certain Irish registered companies which are not managed and controlled in Ireland, as being resident in Ireland for tax purposes. Such companies were popularly known (prior to the Finance Act 1999) as Irish registered non resident companies or IRNRs. Not all IRNRs have been rendered Irish resident by the Finance Act 1999. The exceptions from Irish registration causing a company to be treated as resident in Ireland for the purposes of the Income Tax Acts and Capital Gains Acts are -

- Any company regarded for the purposes of a double tax agreement as resident in territory other than Ireland, and as not being resident in Ireland.

   Generally double tax agreements will provide a special rule to determine where a company is to be regarded as resident for the purpose of the treaty. This topic is discussed further in paragraph 84.2.1.

- Any company meeting both a trading test, and control test, is exempt.

The trading test for this purpose is that the company should either

   − carry on a trade in the State or

   − be related to a company which carries on a trade in the State.

A company is related to another company if it is a 50% subsidiary or holding company of that company, or if they are 50% fellow subsidiaries of another company. For the purpose of determining whether the companies are related, the definition of a group (see paragraph 75.4) is applied with 50% being substituted for 75% in each place where the reference occurs. In other words, there is a requirement for holding at least 50% of the ordinary share capital; entitlement to at least 50% of profits available for distribution; and entitlement to at least 50% of the assets available on a winding up. However companies resident no matter where can be taken into account for the purpose of determining group relationships as it is not confined to companies resident in EU member States or treaty states.

The control test requires that the company be under the control, whether direct or indirectly of a person resident in an EU member State or a treaty State, and that person should be not under the control, whether directly or indirectly, of any person who is not a resident of an EU member State or treaty state. The latter requirement (not under the control etc) relates not to the company but to the EU treaty State resident who controls it.

s432

"Control" for these purposes is broadly the definition in s432 as discussed in paragraph 16.4.5. The definition in s432 is modified appropriately to take account of the fact that the topic under discussion is control by EU treaty State residents, and not control by five or fewer participators (which is the topic in s432).

It should be noted that for the purposes of the control test, Ireland is a member State of the EU. Accordingly control by Irish persons will meet the test.

The trading test can be met by a trade no matter how large or small that trade may be. The trade does not have to be carried on solely in Ireland - if it is carried on in Ireland it could part only of a much larger trade, carried on in Ireland through a branch.

Where a company meets the trade requirement described above, it may also be excluded from residence if it, or a company to which it is related, has the principal class of its shares substantially and regularly traded on a recognised stock exchange in the EU or in a treaty State.

The new test applies to all companies incorporated on or after 11 February 1999, with effect from the date of incorporation. It applies to companies incorporated prior to 11 February 1999 with effect from 1 October 1999.

102   RESIDENT : INDIVIDUAL (PRE FA 94)

102.1   Broad Outline - Old Residence rules

The term *resident* has the same meaning for CGT as it has in the income tax Acts.

ITA67 s199,
ITA67 s206

The provisions in the Income Tax Acts which dealt with the general meaning of the term "resident" were (prior to FA 1994) contained in s.199 and s.206 ITA 1967. The provisions did not define the term resident but only stated certain circumstances in which a person would or would not be held to be resident.

S.199 deals with persons who have been ordinarily resident in Ireland, and who may have left for occasional residence abroad. S.206 deals with persons who are in Ireland for temporary purposes only.

These sections read as follows:

SECTION 199 ITA 1967

"Every person whose ordinary residence has been in the State shall be assessed and charged to tax, notwithstanding that at the time the assessment or charge is made he may have left the State, if he has so left for the purpose only of occasional residence outside the State, and shall be charged as a person actually residing in the State upon the whole amount of his profits or gains, whether they arise from property in the State or elsewhere, or from an allowance, annuity or stipend (save as herein excepted) or from any trade, profession or employment in the State or elsewhere".

SECTION 206 ITA 1967

"A person shall not be charged to tax under Sch D as a person residing in the State, in respect of profits or gains received in respect of possessions or securities outside the State, who is in the State for some temporary purpose only, and not with any view or intent of establishing his residence therein, and who has not actually resided in the State at one time or several times for a period equal in the whole to six months in any year of assessment, but if any such person resides in the State for the aforesaid period, he shall be so chargeable for that year".

102.2

Tests - pre 6 April 1994:

Arising out of sections 199 and 206, and related Court decisions, a number of generally accepted tests have arisen which are applied by the Revenue Commissioners in deciding the residence of an individual for tax years prior to 6 April 1994. These are as follows:

- If he did not maintain a place of abode in Ireland for his use and his visits were not habitual, but occasional only, an individual would not be regarded as resident in Ireland, unless he had been in Ireland in the tax year for a period or periods which in aggregate amount to or exceed six months in a tax year.

- If the individual maintained a place of abode in Ireland available for his use, he would be held to be resident for any tax year in which he made a visit to Ireland irrespective of the length of his

FA87 s4

stay, unless he was an Irish domiciled person working full-time abroad.

- Even if he did not maintain a place of abode in Ireland available for his use and did not spend periods in Ireland in the tax year equal to or greater than six months, an individual would be regarded as becoming resident if he visited Ireland year after year (so that his visits become in effect part of his habit of life) and those visits were for substantial periods of time. Three months would normally be regarded as a substantial period of time and visits would normally be regarded as becoming habitual after four years. Where however, it was indicated from the start that there would be regular visits for substantial periods, the individual could be regarded as resident from the first year.

- In addition to the above tests, an individual would, of course, become resident in Ireland for any tax year in which he came here to take up permanent residence.

While these tests were useful in considering the residence of an individual, it should be borne in mind that the question of residence in any particular case can only be determined by reference to the facts of that case. Also, subject to the specific sections mentioned the term 'resident' has its ordinary meaning at times prior to 6 April 1994.

In the course of his judgement in the UK case IRC v Lysaght , Lord Buckmaster stated that the question is one of fact. It is worth quoting at some length his comments on this concept.

"the distinction between questions of fact and questions of law is difficult to define, but according to the Respondent whether a man is resident or ordinarily resident here must always be a question of law dependent upon the legal construction to be placed upon the provisions of an Act of Parliament. I find myself unable to accept this view. It may be true that the word 'resides' or 'residence' in other Acts may have special meanings, but in the IT Act, it is, I think, used in its common sense and it is essentially a question of fact whether a man does or does not comply with its meaning. It is, or course, true that if the circumstances found by the Commissioners in the Special Case are incapable of constituting residence, their conclusion cannot be protected by saying that it is a conclusion of fact, since there are no materials upon which that conclusion could depend. But if the incidents relating to visits in this country are of such a nature that they might constitute residence, and their prolonged or repeated repetition would certainly produce that result, then the matter must be a matter of degree; and the determination of whether or not the degree extends so far as to make a man resident or ordinarily resident here is for the Commissioners and it is not for the Courts to say whether they would have reached the same conclusion".

That the word "resident" has it ordinary meaning was also illustrated by Viscount Cave LC in the UK case of Levene v IRC when he said:-

"My Lords, the word 'resides' is a familiar English word and is defined in the Oxford English Dictionary as meaning "to dwell permanently or for a considerable time, to have ones usual or settled abode, to live in or at a particular place. No doubt, this definition must for present purposes be taken subject to any modification which may result form the terms of the ITA and Schedules; but, subject to that observation, it may be accepted as an accurate indication of the meaning of the word 'reside'".

The position may be considered in further detail under five main headings. Four of the headings are the four basic tests outlined above and the fifth is the proposition in S199 which deals with persons who have been ordinarily resident in Ireland and who may have left for occasional residence abroad. The headings therefore are as follows:

- PHYSICAL PRESENCE in Ireland (not habitual and no place of abode).

- Maintenance of a PLACE OF ABODE in Ireland available for use.

- HABITUAL VISITS to Ireland for SUBSTANTIAL PERIODS.

- Person Coming to Ireland for PERMANENT RESIDENCE.

- Person WHO HAS BEEN ORDINARILY RESIDENT in Ireland taking up Residence Abroad (s.196 ITA 1967).

102.3   Physical Presence in Ireland (not habitual and no place of abode)

Arising out of s.206, an individual who is in Ireland for some temporary purpose only and not with a view to establishing his residence here was treated as resident for tax purposes only if he spent at least six months in aggregate in Ireland in the relevant year of assessment.

ITA67 s206

In the UK case of Wilkie v CIR it was held that the term "six months" means six calendar months and it was confirmed also that for this purpose, periods spent here which are less than one day are to be calculated in hours. Generally, six months is regarded as 183 days whether or not the year in question is a leap year. Also, in general practice the day of arrival is counted, but the day of departure is not.

Where a person was held to be resident in a particular tax year, by reason of physical presence here, he was treated as resident for the full tax year and not just for the period or periods of his stay. However, it is understood that certain concessions applied in this area.

102.4   **Maintenance of a Place of Abode (in Ireland Available for Use)**

If an individual maintained a place of abode in Ireland available for his use and visited the country at any time during the tax year, he would be treated as resident here for that year of assessment. In the UK case of Loewenstein v de Salis, a Belgian visited the UK each year, but never stayed for more than six months. While in the UK, he used a hunting box owned by a UK Company, in which he held the majority of the shares. He was held to be resident in the UK.

The UK case of Cooper v Cadwalader concerned an American who was ordinarily resident in New York. He rented a house and shooting rights in Scotland where he spent about two months in each relevant year. He was held to be resident in the UK.

An American who lived for twenty years in a yacht moored in English territorial waters was held to be resident in the UK (Brown v Burt).

In the UK case of re Young, a master mariner who had a house in Scotland for his wife and family was held to be resident in the UK in the tax year in which he only spent 88 days in the country. This case was followed in the UK case of Rogers v CIR where a mariner had a home in the UK, but was abroad for the full tax year.

FA87 s4   By virtue of FA87 s4, the question whether an Irish domiciled individual was resident in Ireland was to be determined without reference to any place of abode maintained in the State for his use if he was engaged full time in a trade, profession, office or employment and no part of the trade or profession was carried on in the State or all the duties of the office or employment (apart from incidental duties) were performed outside the State.

Although contained in a chapter of the FA87 dealing with income tax, it is understood to be the view of the Revenue Commissioners that FA87 s4, has general application - i.e. including for capital gains tax purposes.

102.5   **Habitual Visits to Ireland (for Substantial Periods)**

This heading concerns a person who has not been resident or ordinarily resident in Ireland, but who made visits to Ireland regularly for substantial periods.

In the UK case of Levene v CIR the taxpayer who was a British subject, had given up a house in London and was living mainly abroad. However, in each relevant tax year he spent between four and five months in the UK. He was held to be resident and ordinarily resident in the UK for the relevant years.

A taxpayer who had gone to live with his family in Ireland and who had no definite place of abode in the UK came to the UK every month for business purposes. On each visit he stayed about a week and normally resided at an hotel. He was held to be resident and ordinarily resident in the UK (IRC v Lysaght).

102.6   Coming for Permanent Residence

Any person coming to Ireland to take up permanent residence here is clearly not coming for 'temporary purposes only' and was regarded as resident in Ireland. In practice, the Revenue Authorities by concession allowed a period of 10 days grace either side of 5 April in applying this rule. If, for example, an individual arrived in Ireland to take up permanent residence here on 28 March 1991, he would (in practice) not be regarded as resident for 1990/91.

102.7   Irish resident - leaving

ITA67 s199   Under s.199 ITA 1967, a person who has been ordinarily resident in Ireland will continue to be chargeable to tax notwithstanding that he may have left Ireland for the purpose of occasional residence abroad.

In the UK case of Levene v CIR - see paragraph 103.5 - the taxpayer was held to have gone abroad for the purpose of occasional residence only and was therefore held to be resident in the UK for the years in question.

However, in the UK case of IRC v Coombe, a British subject who had been ordinarily resident in the UK left for the United States to take up a three year apprenticeship. During that period, he had no place of abode in the UK but paid occasional visits for the purpose of his employment, staying at hotels. It was held that his period abroad was not for 'occasional residence only' and he was therefore held not to be resident in the UK.

103   ORDINARILY RESIDENT (Pre FA94)

Like the term 'resident' the term 'ordinarily resident' was not statutorily defined until the FA94. Accordingly, it was difficult to distinguish between the different meanings of the two terms.

In Levene v IRC Viscount Cave LC said:

"the expression 'ordinary residence'...connotes residence in a place with some degree of continuity and apart from temporary absences. So understood, the expression differs little from the residence used in the Acts; and I find it difficult to imagine a case in which a man were not resident here is yet ordinarily resident here".

In the Lysaght case two of the Lords gave an outline of the term:

"ordinary residence means in my opinion no more than the residence is not casual and uncertain, but that the person held to reside does so in the ordinary course of his life"(Lord Buckmaster).

"I think the converse to ordinary is extraordinary, and that part of the regular order of a man's life adopted voluntarily and for settled purposes is not extraordinary"(Viscount Summer).

104   DOMICILE

104.1   Broad Outline

Domicile has no special meaning for tax purposes. It takes its meaning from general law. The concept of domicile is a complex subject, the full details of which are not required for the purposes of dealing with CGT. It is proposed therefore to outline only the main principles involved.

Domicile is a connection which a person has with a territorial system of law and not necessarily with a specific country. A person, for example, can be domiciled in New York, or perhaps California, but not in the USA. Similarly, a person can be domiciled in Scotland, or in England or Northern Ireland, but not in the UK.

The concept of domicile under Irish law is the same as that in England and other countries which operate a common law system, (subject to certain local modifications for specific purposes).

104.2   Domicile of Origin

Every person must have a domicile and accordingly, the law attributes to a child at birth the domicile of his father if the child is legitimate and of the mother if he is illegitimate. A foundling is domiciled in the jurisdiction where he is found. The domicile attributed to a child at birth is know as the domicile of origin.

The domicile of origin can be abandoned and a new domicile acquired — a domicile of choice. However, there is always a presumption in favour of the existing domicile, and the burden of proof always lies with the person alleging a change of domicile. If the evidence is conflicting or not decisive, the Courts will normally decide in favour of the existing domicile. There is seldom any doubt about the domicile of origin and the main difficulty is normally encountered when dealing with the question of whether or not a person has acquired a domicile of choice.

Generally, a person cannot have two domiciles. However, in certain circumstances the general concept may be modified by local law for a specific purpose. In such a case, a person will be deemed to be domiciled in a particular jurisdiction for that specific purpose, although, for other purposes under general law, he may actually be domiciled elsewhere. This point is illustrated by the special rules on domicile contained in the UK legislation on Inheritance Tax. A further example can be found in the Matrimonial Causes Act 1959 (Australia), which applies an Australian domicile rather than a State domicile for the purposes of divorce proceedings etc.

The 1997 High Court case of Claire Proes v Revenue Commissioners confirmed that an individual who had replaced an Irish domicile of origin with an English domicile of choice did not cause their Irish domicile of origin to revive merely by reason of subsequently residing in Ireland for several years for temporary reasons. The individual maintained connections with England and intended to return to England when circumstances permitted and did not intend to live in Ireland indefinitely. The case also emphasises that domicile is very dependent on the facts of every case.

104.3   Domicile of Choice

To acquire a domicile of choice, a person must establish physical presence in the new country and an intention to remain there indefinitely. A declaration of intent to acquire a new domicile is not sufficient. Residence in a new country for a long period does not establish a new domicile if there is no intention to remain there indefinitely.

The new residence must be freely chosen and not prescribed or dictated by any external necessity such as the duties of office, the demands of creditors, or the relief from illness; and it must be residence fixed not for a limited period or a particular purpose, but general and indefinite in its future contemplation. Residence originally temporary, or intended for a limited period may afterwards become general and unlimited, and in such a case as soon as the change of purpose or animus manendi, can be inferred, the fact of domicile is established.

If a domicile of choice is abandoned, the domicile of origin revives unless and until a new domicile of choice is established.

104.4   Domicile of Dependence

A minor child has the domicile of his father, or, in certain circumstances, of his guardian.

The Domicile and Matrimonial Proceedings Act 1973 provides for the domicile of a married woman to be determined in the same manner as any other individual: she no longer takes the domicile of her husband when she marries as was the position prior to that Act.

104.5　　　**Appeal procedures regarding domicile.**

S29(8) and (9) provide an appeal procedure in relation to disputes on domicile. The appeal procedure provided is identical to that in relation to an appeal against an assessment (involving potentially Appeal Commissioners, Circuit Court and the Superior Courts). The one important difference is that the period for giving notice of intention to appeal is two months from the date on which notice is given to the taxpayer of a decision by the Revenue Commissioners regarding their domicile status. The normal time limit (section 945) for appeals against assessments is only 30 days.

The same special appeals procedure applies to rulings regarding ordinary residence.

TABLE OF CASES

GENERAL NOTE

In considering any aspect of statute law it is necessary to review the cases which have come before the courts for assistance in interpreting that law. Although the Irish law relating to capital gains tax has been on the statute books since 1975, no substantial body of law has yet been built up through decisions in the Irish courts.

However, the law in the UK relating to capital gains tax has been in operation since 1965 and a substantial number of cases have been decided in the UK courts. The statute law in both countries is similar in many respects.

It is, therefore, possible to look to some of the UK court decisions for assistance in interpreting the Irish law although care must be taken to ensure that the legislation relating to the point at issue is the same in both countries. In a number of cases, the law is different, and others were decided purely on the facts of the particular case and have no general application.

In considering the UK case law it is necessary to bear in mind that the Irish courts are not bound by decisions of the UK courts, and in some cases have taken a different view. Nevertheless, the UK decisions carry considerable weight in relation to the interpretation of equivalent Irish legislation. The reader is also referred to paragraph 1.2 which deals in more detail with this matter.

A list of the court decisions referred to is set out below.

Cases referred to	*Para*

A

Aberdeen Construction Group v IRC (1978) STC 127	7.1, 8.2, 8.9, 9.1.4, 9.10, 38.2, 40.2.
American & Foreign Insurance Association v Davis 32 TC 1	34.12
Anderton v Lambe (1981) STC 43	26.1.1
Aspden v Hindersley (1982) STC 206	15.1
Atkinson v Dancer (1988) STC 758	30.1
Attorney General v Farrell (1931) 1 KB 81	68.11.5.2
Attorney General v Heywood (1887) 19 QBD 326	68.11.5.2

B

Bank of Ireland Finance v Revenue Commissioners (1989) Vol IV ITR p217	64.6, 94.9, 97.5
Bayley v Rogers (1980) STC 544	9.10, 55.2, 61.1

Bayley v Garrod (1983) STC 287   68.11.5.2
Batey v Wakefield (1981) STC 521   24.3
Baytrust Holdings v IRC [1971] 1 WLR 1333, Ch D   44.4
Belville Holdings Ltd (HC)   18.2
Bentley v Pike (1981) STC 360   9.1.2.2
Berry v Warnett (1978) STC 504   65.1, 65.4, 65.12.2
Beveridge v Ellam (1996) STC 77   4.5.1
Birch v Delaney 2 STC 127   6.9
Bond v Pickford (1982) STC 403 (1983) STC 517   65.10
Booth v Buckwell (1980) STC 578   8.2, 8.9
British Colombia Fir & Cedar Lumber Co. 48 TLR 284   4.5
Bricom Holdingsa Ltd v IRC (1977) STC 1179   68.9
British Transport Commission v Gourley(1956) AC 185   4.6
Bromarin AG & Another v IMD Investments (1988) STC 244   20.10
Brown v Burt 5 TC 667   102.4
Bulmer v CIR 44 TC 1   65.4
Burmah Steamship Co v IRC 16 TC 67   4.5.1
Burman v Hedges & Butler (1979) STC 136   46.4, 75.4.3.2, 75.4.5.5,
        81.3, 81.4
Burman v Westminster Press Limited (1987) STC 669   22.2
Butler v Evans (1980) STC 613   3.7.2.2

C
Campbell Connolly & Co Ltd v Barnett (1994) STC 50   26.5
Carlisle and Silloth Golf Club v Smith 6 TC 198   34.12
Carter v Sharon 20 TC 229   3.3.4
Chaloner v Pallipar Investments (1996) STC 234   4.4.4
Chaney v Watkis (1986) STC 89   9.1.4
Chinn v Collins (1981) STC 1   65.4, 68.11.4
CIR v Chubbs Trustees 47 TC 353   9.2.1, 65.7.3, 65.9
Clarke v Mayo (1994) STC 57   26.5
Clarke v United Real (Moorgate) Ltd (1988) STC 273   54
Cleveleys Investment Trust v IRC (1975) STC 457   38.2
Coates v Arndale Properties Ltd. (1984) STC 637   80.3
Cochrane v IRC (1975) STC 335   64.2, 66.5
Cooper v Cadwalder 5 TC 101   102
Copeman v Coleman 22TC 594   65.4
Coren v Keighley 48 TC 370   8.8.1
Couch v Catons Administrators (1996) STC 201   9.2
Craddock v Zevo Finance Co Ltd 27 TC 267   8.2
Crowe v Appleby (1976) STC 301   64.2, 65.7, 65.9
Currie v Misa (1875) LR 10 Ex 153   8.2

D

Davenport v Chilver (1983) STC 426   3.5.3, 4.2.4, 4.2.6, 4.2.7, 4.4.5,
   4.4.6

Davenport v Hasslacher (1977) STC 254   30.4

Davis v Henderson SC (1995) 308   4.4.5, 27.3

Davis v Powell (1977) STC 32   4.2.6, 4.4.5

De Beers Consolidated Mines Ltd. v Howe 5TC 198   101

Deeny v Gooda Walker (1996) STC 299   4.5.1, 4.6

Dilleen, Ed J v T A Kearns (HC 1993)   39.1, 39.3.1, 39.3.2

Dodd v Mudd (1987) STC 141   26.1.1

Drummond v Austin Brown (1984) STC 321   4.2.6, 4.4.5, 4.4.6

Duchess of Montrose v Stuart 15R (HL) 19   64.2

Duke of Westminster v CIR 19 TC 490   1.2, 69.1

Dunlop International v Pardoes (1988) STC 459   81.3

Dunstan v Young Austen and Young Limited (1989) STC 69   42.2.2.2

E

Eastham v Leigh London and Provincial Properties Ltd
   46 TC 687   15.2

Eglen v Butler (1988) STC 872   24.11

Eilbeck v Rawling (1981) STC 174   43.1, 65.10

Electricity Commission (Balman's Electric Light Company
   purchase) Act 1950 (1957) SR(NSW) 100   29.3

Emmerson v Computer Time International Ltd. (1977) STC 170   9.1.5

Ensign Shipping Co v IRC 12 TC 1169   4.5

Ewart v Taylor (1983) STC 721   68.11.5.3

F

Fielder v Vedlynn (1992) STC 553   8.3

Fleming v Bank of New Zealand (1990) AC 577   8.3

Floor v Davis (1979) STC 379   51.2.1

Foster v Williams (1977) STC SCD 112   44.5

Fox v Stirk & Bristol Electrical Regional Officer (1970)
   2QB463CA   24.2

Frampton v IRC (1985) STC 186   34.12

Furniss v Dawson (1982) STC 267 (1983) STC 549
   (1984) STC 153   43.1, 65.10, 69.2

G

Garner v Pounds Ship Owners & Ship Brokers (1997) STC 551   7.1,
   8.8.1, 8.3, 8.10, 9.13, 39.2

Gartside v IRC (1968) 1 AllER 121   68.11.5.2

Glenboig Union Fireclay Co v IRC 12 TC 427   4.5.1

Golding v Kaufman (1985) STC 152   39.3.2
Goodwin v Curtis (1996) STC 1146   24.2, 24.10
Gordon v IRC (1991) STC 174   29.3
Griffin v Craig-Harvey (1994) STC 54   24.7
Griffiths v JP Harrison 40 TC 281   80.3
Gubay v Kington (1984) STC 99   33.2

H
Harmel v Wright (1974) STC 88   3.3.2
Harrison v Nairn Willamson (1978) STC 67   16.2, 41
Hart v Briscoe (1978) STC 89   65.10
Harthan v Mason (1980) STC 94   64.2
Helen Slater Charitable Trust v IRC (1980) STC 150   31.4
Herron, Peter C & Others v Minister for Communications(1985)
    Vol III, ITR, p298   4.6
Hinchcliffe v Crabtree 47 TC 419   17.4
Hoare Trustees v Gardner (1978) STC 89   65.10
Honour v Norris (1992) STC 304   24.3
Horan v Williams (1977) STC 112   44.5

I
ICI v Colmer (1993) STC 710   75.4.2
Income Tax Commissioners for London v Gibbs 24 TC 221   34.12
Innocent v Whaddon Estates (1982) STC 115   76.5
Inspector of Taxes v Thomas Keleghan   8.4, 38.2, 45.2, 48.6
IRC v Brackett   3.6.1
IRC v Burmah Oil Company Ltd (1982) STC 30   42.3, 48.1
IRC v Coombe 17 TC 405   102
IRC v Lysaght 13 TC 486   102, 103
IRC v Plummer (1979) STC 793   65.4, 65.5
IRC v Helen Slater Securities Ltd (1980) STC 150   31.4
IRC v Ufitec Group Ltd (1977) STC 363   44.2

J
Jarman v Rawlings (1994) STC 1005   30.1, 75.2.4
Johnson v Edwards (1981) STC 660   15.1
Jones v Wilcock SC (1996) 389   24.10

K
Kearns, Ed gentlemen v Thomas Dileen HC 1993   39.1, 39.3.1, 39.3.2
Kidson v McDonald (1974) STC 54, 49 TC 503   64.2
Kirby v Thorn (1986) STC 200, (1987) STC 621   4.2.3, 4.2.4, 4.4.2

Kneen v Martin 19 TC 33   3.3.2

L

Lang v Rice (1984) STC 172   4.5.1
Larner v Warrington (1985) STC 442   20.5
Leahy v AG for New South Wales (1959) AC 457   34.12
Leedale v Lewis (1982) STC 835   68.11.5.2, 68.11.5.4, 68.11.5.4
Levene v IRC 13 TC 486   102, 103
Lewis v Lady Rook (1992) STC 171   24.3
Lewis v Walters (1992) STC 97   10.6, 61.1
Lion v Insp. of Taxes (1977) STC SCD 133   81.3
Loewenstein v De Salis 10 TC 424   102.4
Loffland Bros. North Sea Inc v Goodbrand (1997) STC 102   8.8, 8.10,
    9.1.2.2
London & Thames Haven Oil Wharves v Attwooll 43 TC 491   4.5
Lyon v Pettigrew (1985) STC 369   15.1, 15.2

M

McGrath, PW v JE McDermott IRLM, Vol. 8, No. 11 1.2, 16.4.3, 39.1.2,
    39.3.2, 69.2
McGregor v Adcock (1977) STC 206   30.1, 44.4
McMahon (Inspector of Taxes) v Albert Noel Murphy
    ITR, Vol. IV, p 125   6.2, 17.1
McMeekin re (1974) STC 429, 48 TC 725   64.3
Makins v Elson (1977) STC 46   24.2
Mannion v Johnston (1988) STC 758   44.4
Mara v Hummingbird SC (1977) 103   6.9
Markey v Sanders (1987) STC 256   24.3
Marren v Ingles (1979) STC 637 4.2.7, 4.4.4, 4.4.6, 5.2.11, 8.2, 8.8, 9.1.2,
    38.2
Marshall v Kerr (1991) STC 686   66.7
Marson v Marriage (1980) STC 177   4.4.6, 8.8, 38.2
Meuthen-Campbell v Walters (1979) QB 525   24.3
Milton v Chilvers (1995) STC 57   26.5
Mooney, JJ v Noel McSweeney ITR, 1996, p51   38.2
Moore v Thompson (1986) STC 170   24.2
Morgan v Gibson (1989) STC 568   6.2
Muir v Muir (1943) AC 468   65.10
Murphy, S v Dataproducts (Dublin) Ltd (1988) 1RIO
    Vol IV, p12   3.6.3

N

N Ltd v Insp of Taxes (unreported)   18.1

National Provincial Bank Ltd v Hastings Carmart Ltd
    1965 AC 1247   4.2.3
Nap Holdings v Whittle (1993) STC 592   76.3

O
O'Brien v Bensons Hosiery (Holdings) Ltd. (1979) STC 735 4.2.5, 4.2.8
O'Ceallaigh, E v Financial Indemnity Co Ltd.(HC 1983)   94.9
O'Coindealbhain, E P (Insp of Taxes) v KN Price (1988)
    Vol IV, p1   26.4
Oram v Johnson (1980) STC 222   9.1.3.1
Osborne Steel Barrell Co Ltd v IRC 24 TC 293   8.2
O'Sullivan, JM v Julia O'Connor 2 ITC 352   3.3.2
O'Sullivan v P Ltd 3 ITC 355   69.1

P
Palmer v Maloney (1998) STC 425   30.4
Partington v Attorney General (1869) LR   1.2
Passant v Jackson (1985) STC 133   66.5
Patuck v Lloyd 26 TC 284   3.3.2
Pennine Raceways v Kirklees M C (1989) STC135   4.4.4, 4.4.5,4.6
Pexton v Bell (1976) STC 301   65.7.2, 65.9
Pilkington v CIR 40 TC 416   65.10
Pinewood Developments Ltd, Healy Homes Ltd & Daniel Healy v
    Minister for the Environment and Ireland HC 1983,
    No 1715   4.4.6, 94.9
Prest v Bettinson (1980) STC 607   31.4., 64.2
Proes, Clare v Recvenue Commissioners (unreported)   104

R
R v British Colombia Fir and Cedar Lumber Co 48 TLR 284   4.5
R v IRC ex Parte Commerabank AG (1993) STC 605   83
Rajas Commercial College v Singh & Co (1976) STC 282   4.5.1
WT Ramsay Ltd v IRC (1981) STC 174   38.2, 43.1, 80.3
Randell v Plumb (1975) STC 191, 50 TC 392   8.8, 9.9, 39.10
Rank Xerox v Lane (1979) STC 740   32.11
Reed v Nova Securities Ltd. (1985) STC 124   80.2, 80.3
Revenue v ORMG, SC 1983   6.4, 34.12
Richart v J Lyons & Company Ltd. (1989) STC 8   26.4
Rogers v CIR ITC 225   102.4
Roome v Edwards (1981) STC 96   65.2, 65.10

S

Sainsbury v OConnor (1991) STC 318	39.1, 39.10, 75.4.3.2
Salt Shore Mutual Insurance Co v Blair	75.4.3.2
Sansom v Peay (1976) STC 494	24.9
Scottish Provident Institution v Allen, 4 TC 419	3.3.2, 3.3.3
Sharkey v Wernher (36 TC 275)	18.2
Spectros International v Madden (1997) STC 114	8.3, 8.9, 51.6
Stanton v Drayton Commercial Inv Co Ltd (1982) STC 585	8.2, 9.1.2, 41, 49
Steele v European Vinyls Holdings BV (1996) STC 785	16.4.4
Stephenson v Barclays Bank Trust Co Ltd (1975) STC 151, 50 TC 374	64.2
Steibelt v Paling (1999) STC 594	26.5, 26.6.4
Sterne v The Queen (1896) 1 QB 211	3.7.2.1
Stoke on Trent City Council v Wood Mitchell & Co Ltd (1979) STC 197	4.6
Strange v Oppenshaw (1982) STC 416	4.4.3, 39.2, 39.10
Swaine v VE 3 ITC 389	6.9
Swires v Renton (1991) STC 490	65.10

T

Tarmac Roadstone Holdings Ltd v Williams SC (1996) 409	38.2
Taylor Clark International v Lewis (1997) STC 499	38.2
Temperley v Visabell (1974) STC 64, 49 TC 129	26.1.1
Thompson v Moyse (1960) 3 ALL ER	3.3.2
Thompson v Salah 47 TC 559	9.4
Tomlinson v Glyns Executor & Trust Co 45 TC 600	64.2
Turner v Follet (1973) STC 148, 48 TC 614	4.4.2

V

Van-Arkadie v Plunket (1983) STC 54	97.2
Vartry v Lynes (1976) STC 508	24.2
Vestey v IRC (1980) STC 10	74.4

W

Wase v Burke (1996) STC 18	75.2.4
Watkins v Kidson (1979) STC 464	6.2
Watton v Tippett (1996) STC 101	4.2.11, 11.2, 26.1.1
Welbeck Securities Limited v Powlson (1987) STC 468	39.3.2
Westcott v Woolcombers Limited (1987) STC 600	76.3
West Suffolk County Council v W Rought Ltd 1957 AC 403	4.6
Whimster v IRC 12 TC 813	2
Whittles v Uniholdings (1995) STC 185	9.1.2, 38.2

Wilkie v CIR 32 TC 495   102.3
Williams v Bullivant (1983) STC 107   20.5
Williams v Merrylees (1987) STC 445   24.3
Wood Preservation v Prior 45 TC 112   81.4

Y
Young v Phillips (1984) STC 520   3.7.2.1, 4.2.9
Young, Re. I TC 57   102.4

Z
Zim Properties Ltd. v Proctor (1985) STC 90   4.2.6, 4.2.7, 4.2.8,
                                                4.4.4, 4.4.5, 4.4.6, 6.2

TABLE OF STATUTES

PREFERENTIAL PAYMENT IN BANKRUPTCY (IRELAND) ACT 1889

Section	Paragraph
s.4	97.4

PARTNERSHIP ACT 1890

Section	Paragraph
s20	34.2
s39	34.2

SETTLED LAND ACT 1892

Section	Paragraph
	65.2

VOCATIONAL EDUCATION ACT, 1930.

Section	Paragraph
	32.7

AGRICULTURE ACT, 1931

Section	Paragraph
	32.7

FINANCE ACT 1931

Section	Paragraph
S28	31.1

INTERPRETATION ACT 1937

Section	Paragraph
s.11	3.4.2, 34.1, 34.12

CONSTITUTION OF IRELAND (1937)

Section	Paragraph
15.2.1	1.2
41.3.2	33.8.1

LOCAL GOVERNMENT ACT 1941

Section	Paragraph
s.2	32.7

HARBOURS ACT 1946

Section	Paragraph
Sch 1	32.1

ADOPTION ACTS 1952 (to 1991)

Section	Paragraph
	16.4.4

EXCHANGE CONTROL ACT 1954

Section	Paragraph
	17.3

STATE PROPERTY ACT 1954

Section	Paragraph
s31	16.2, 20.5

FINANCE (MISCELLANEOUS PROVISIONS) ACT 1956

Section	Paragraph
s.22	32.8

GREYHOUND INDUSTRY ACT 1958

Section	Paragraph
s2	26.11

COMPANIES ACT 1963

Section	Paragraph
s.72	42.2.1, 51.4.3
s.78	98.4
s.230	64.4
s.285	98.4

LOCAL GOVERNMENT (PLANNING & DEVELOPMENT) ACT 1963

Section	Paragraph
s.2	6.2
s.3	6.2
s.4	6.2
s.29	6.4

SUCCESSION ACT 1965

Section	Paragraph
s.10	66.5
s.13	66.5

DIPLOMATIC RELATIONS & IMMUNITIES ACT 1967

Article	Paragraph
34	32.12
49	32.12

CONTINENTAL SHELF ACT 1968

Section	Paragraph
s1	3.4.2, 3.7
s2	74.1

VAT ACT 1972

Section	Paragraph
13.3	9.12

VAT REGULATIONS 1972

Section	Paragraph
	9.12

EUROPEAN COMMUNITIES (RETIREMENT OF FARMERS) REGULATIONS 1974

Section	Paragraph
	32.5

CAPITAL ACQUISITIONS TAX ACT, 1976

Section	Paragraph
s.55	65.7.2
s.158	49.4.10
Sch2 Para9	30.4

AGE OF MAJORITY ACT 1985

Section	Paragraph
s2	33.9
s39	34.2

STATUS OF CHILDREN ACT 1987

Section	Paragraph
	30.11

STATUTORY INSTRUMENT 78 OF 1989

Section	Paragraph
	35.1, 35.6

TRUSTEE SAVINGS BANK ACT 1989

Section	Paragraph
	73.2

COMPANIES ACT 1990

Section	Paragraph
Part IX	49.1, 49.3
s209	49.3.2

FINANCE ACT 1991

Section	Paragraph
s42	30.1

FINANCE ACT 1992

Section	Paragraph
s36	35.9, 39.3.2
s62	41.5

IRISH HORSERACING INDUSTRY ACT 1994

Section	Paragraph
s2	6.4

LOCAL GOVERNMENT PLANNING & DEVELOPMENT ACT 1994

Section	Paragraph
	6.2

FAMILY LAW ACT 1995

Section	Paragraph
s52	33.8.3.2

FAMILY LAW (DIVORCE) ACT 1996

Section	Paragraph
s10	33.8.2.1
Part III	33.8.2.3

HARBOURS ACT 1996

Section	Paragraph
s.96	26
s.97	26

DUBLIN DOCKLANDS DEVELOPMENT AUTHORITY ACT 1997

Section	Paragraph
s28(1)	26.11

TAXES CONSOLIDATION ACT 1997

Section	Paragraph
s2	34.12
s3	27.3
s4	3.4.2, 71.3, 84.7
s5	3.6.1, 3.7.2, 34.12, 34.13, 35.16, 40.2, 65.4, 65.7, 66.2, 67.3.3, 67.3.11, 69.2, 80.2
s6	33.9
s7	33.9
s8	33.9
s9	26.12.3, 75.4.3.2, 75.4.5.3, 75.4.5.5, 75.5.6.4
s10	16.4.4, 33.8.4, 33.9, 34.1, 65.4, 65.5, 91.4.2
s11	49.4.10
s13	3.4.2
s15	65.9
s20	4.4.7
s21	71.2, 72.1
s25	71.2
s27	74.1
s28	2.1, 3.1, 4.1, 4.2.1, 5.1, 7.1, 57.3
s29	3.1, 3.2, 3.3.1, 3.3.2, 3.3.5, 3.4.2, 3.4.3, 3.5.1, 3.5.3, 3.6.2, 3.6.3, 3.7.2, 20.2 , 64, 92.1, 104.4
s30	34.1, 34.8
s31	20.3, 68.11

s44	8.3
s55	32.3, 40.2
s61	49.3.1
s71	3.3.2
s72	3.3.2, 3.3.5
s73	6.4
s76	4.4.7
s78	4.4.7, 20.10, 72.1, 72.2, 73.2
s79	9.1.2.2, 38.9
s80	38.8
s83	73.4.5
s89	80.2
s98	60.1
s99	8.4, 54.1, 55.1
s100	8.4
s116	74.4
s122A	41.5, 50.1.1
s128	39.11, 50.1
s128A	39.11.2
s129	4.4.7, 40.3
s130	40.3, 49.1, 49.3, 51.3.1, 75.4.3.4
s135	49.3.1
s173	49.1, 49.4
s174	49.1, 49.3.9
s175	49.1, 49.2
s176	49.1, 49.2, 49.3
s177	49.3.4, 49.3.5
s178	49.3.6
s179	49.3.6
s180	49.3.7, 49.3.8
s182	49.3.10
s183	49.3.11
s184	49.3.2, 49.4
s185	49.4
s186	49.4.11
s191	32.8
s222	71.4
s226	32.6
s232	27.5
s235	6.4
s243	73.4
s280	9.8
s289	9.8
s295	9.8
s312	9.8
s396	73.4
s400	75.2.2
s411	75.4.3, 75.4.5.4

s412	71.4, 75.4.2
s413	75.4.3
s414	75.4.3.3, 75.4.3.4, 75.4.4.3, 75.4.4.4
s415	75.4.3.2, 75.4.3.5
s416	75.4.3.2, 75.4.4.2
s417	75.4.3.2, 75.4.4.3
s418	75.4.3.2
s419	75.4.3.2
s420	73.4
s430	51.3.1, 67.2.1, 67.3.2
s431	41.6
s432	16.4.5, 44.6, 67.2.1, 69.2, 74.3, 74.4, 101.3
s433	67.2.1, 74.4
s449	83.1
s451	35.13
s456	73.5
s479	9.13.1, 9.15, 50.1, 68.8
s481	9.13.1, 9.13.4.1, 9.13.4.2, 9.13.4.3
s486B	9.14
s498	9.13.2.3, 9.13.2.4, 9.13.2.5
s506	9.13.2.1, 9.13.2.2, 9.13.2.6, 9.15
s509	50.2
s510	50.1, 50.2
s511	50.2
s519	50.1, 50.3
s519A	50.4
s519B	50.4
s519C	50.4
s532	4.2.1, 4.2.4, 4.4.4, 38.1
s533	3.7.1, 71.2
s534	4.2.4, 4.4.1, 4.4.3, 24.3, 65.5
s535	3.5.3, 4.4.1, 4.4.4, 4.4.7, 4.5.3, 39.3.2, 40.3, 44.7, 94.11
s536	28
s537	4.4.1, 8.7, 9.4, 64.6
s538	4.3, 4.4.2, 20.4, 20.5, 39.3.2
s539	15.1
s540	4.4.2, 39
s541	38, 45.2
s541A	4.3, 38.2, 38.6
s542	15.1, 15.2
s543	51.2.1, 51.2.2
s544	4.4.7, 9.1.1, 12.1, 51.3.2, 58.1
s546	3.4.3, 20.1, 20.2, 20.3
s547	3.5.4, 4.2.5, 6.2, 8.1, 8.2, 8.9, 9.5, 11.3, 16.1, 16.2, 16.3, 37.2, 39.11, 41, 46, 55.2, 65.1, 69.2, 76.3
s548	17.1, 17.2, 17.4, 17.5, 17.6
s549	9.1.2.2, 9.1.4, 16.2, 16.3, 16.4, 20.7, 33.8.4, 34.6, 37.2, 41.1, 69.2

s550	16.4.6
s551	4.4.7, 8.4, 8.5, 8.6, 58.1
s552	8.2, 9.1.1, 9.1.2, 9.1.4, 9.2, 9.5, 9.7, 9.11, 51.3.1
s553	9.5
s554	9.1.1
s555	9.8, 20.6
s556	13, 14.1, 14.3, 14.4
s557	11.1, 11.2, 59.7
s559	9.10, 10.6, 39.2
s560	10.1, 10.2, 10.4, 10.6, 22.1, 57.2
s561	10.3, 10.4, 57.2
s562	3.4.2, 3.5.1, 9.9
s563	8.3, 8.8.1, 8.9, 8.10
s564	32.10
s565	9.6
s567	4.4.1, 64.1, 64.2, 65.1, 65.2, 65.7
s568	3.3.1, 19.1, 65.2, 95.1
s569	4.4.1, 64.3
s570	64.4, 64.6
s571	64.6, 97.5
s572	37.2, 64.5
s573	4.4.1, 8.1, 33.7.3, 66.1, 66.4, 66.5, 66.6
s574	50.3, 65, 91.2
s575	65
s576	65
s577	65.1, 65.7, 65.8, 65.9
s577A	30.1, 30.12, 65.7
s578	65.1
s579	35.11.6, 65.1, 67.1.2, 67.2.4, 68.11
s579A	5.1, 65.1, 65.13, 67.2.4, 68.2 to 68.7
s579B	3.6, 65.1, 65.12, 65.13, 67.1.2
s579C	65.1, 65.13
s579D	65.1, 65.13, 91.2.2
s579E	65.1, 65.14
s579F	65.1, 65.13, 68.10
s580	9.13.4.3, 9.15, 48.2
s581	9.13.4.3, 48, 50.2
s582	41.5
s583	4.4.7, 40.3, 40.4, 41.4, 94.11
s584	5.2.10, 5.2.12, 35.14, 38.10, 41.4, 42, 44.2, 48.6, 51.2.2, 75.2.2
s585	38.1, 38.2, 47.1
s586	16.2, 30.7, 38.10, 41.4, 44.1, 44.2, 45.1, 76.3
s587	16.2, 38.10, 41,44, 45.1
s589	51.3.1, 7.5.1
s590	5.1, 35.11.6, 51.3.1, 67.1, 67.2, 67.3, 68.11.7, 75.4.5.4, 82.4
s591	26.12.1, 26.12.3

s592	3.5.1, 5.2.1, 5.2.3, 5.2.4, 5.2.5, 5.2.6, 5.2.7, 5.2.8, 5.2.9, 5.2.10, 33.7.3, 66.8, 67.2.3
s593	32.9, 44.7
s594	3.9, 32.9, 36.3
s595	36.2
s596	18.1, 80.4
s597	6.4, 26, 74.1, 79
s598	30, 65.7.1
s599	30, 65.7.1
s600	29, 30.7
s601	19.1, 19.3, 19.4, 19.5, 37.2
s602	21.3, 23, 32.1
s603	1.2, 21.2, 22, 23
s604	24, 27.3
s605	27.1, 27.2, 27.4
s606	32.14.2
s607	32.1.1, 32.2, 35.7, 37.2
s608	32.4.1
s609	31.4
s610	32.7
s611	31.1, 31.3
s613	32, 65
s613A	65
s614	91.4.1
s615	75.2
s616	51.3.3, 75, 76, 81.3
s617	51.2.2, 75, 76, 78, 94
s618	80
s619	75.5.1, 77
s620	79
s621	20.9, 51.4.1
s622	20.9, 51.5.1
s623	40.1, 46, 51.6, 74.1, 74.2, 75.4.4.5, 76.6, 81, 91.5.1
s623A	75.4.4.5
s624	82
s625	45.1, 46.1, 46.5, 76.4.4.5, 77.3, 92.6
s625A	75.4.4.5
s626	91.5.1
s627	23.14, 74.1, 74.2, 84.3, 81.7
s628	91.5.4
s630	87.7
s631	75.3, 76.6, 78
s632	76.6
s633	75.2.3
s634	75.3.2, 83.3.7
s635	75.3.6
s636	75.3.7
s640	6.9

s641	6.9
s643	8.4, 26.12.2
s648	3.1, 6.2, 75.5
s649	6.7, 20.8, 71.2, 78
s649A	6.6
s650	6.6
s651	6.3
s652	6.4, 26.11, 27.5
s653	6.5
s654	27.5
s655	27.3
s698	67.2.1, 76.4.5.1
s701	44.6
s702	67.2.1
s703	44.5
s704	44.5.2
s707	4.4.7
s711	36.5.1
s719	36.5.1
s720	36.5.1
s722	36.5.1
s723	36.6
s731	35.2, 35.15
s733	35.14
s734	35.2, 35.12
s737	35.2, 35.10
s738	35.2, 35.7
s739	35.7
s740	35.2
s741	66.5
s743	35.11.2
s744	35.11.4
s745	35.11.1
s746	35.11.6
s747	35.11.2, 35.11.3, 42.1
s751A	42.1
s751B	32.1.2
s757	8.4
s784A	32.4.2
s797	4.4.7
s799	66.2
s806	75.4
s811	39.3.2, 69.3
s812	32.3
s815	32.1.1
s816	42.2, 42.6
s817	41.6, 49.3.1
s819	98, 99

s820	100.1
s821	98
s824	98
s826	83.2
s827	83.2
s828	9.3, 83.1
s838	37.2
s847	71.4
s849	86.1
s880	87.6
s909	90.3
s911	96.1
s913	87.1, 87.2, 87.6
s914	87.9, 87.10
s915	87.11
s916	87.12
s917	87.13, 94.7.4, 94.8
s917A	87.13
s917B	87.13
s917C	87.13
s931	33.3
s945	92.1
s950	87.3, 88.1, 92.4
s951	87.2
s952	88.1
s953	88.1
s954	90.1
s955	88.1, 88.2, 90.1, 92.2
s956	39.10, 90.1
s957	92.2, 92.4
s958	88.2
s977	88.2, 91.4.2
s978	88.2, 91.3
s980	94
s981	8.8.1, 97.3, 97.4
s982	97.4
s1003	32.14.3
s1005	97.2
s1006A	89.2
s1006B	89.2
s1014	34.13, 67.3.11
s1015	33.2
s1019	93.1
s1021	93.1
s1022	93.1
s1023	33.8.4
s1026	33.8.4
s1028	5.2.8, 9.1, 19.2, 33, 37.2, 51.2.2.2

s1029	93.1
s1030	33.8.3
s1031	33.8.2
s1034	94.12
s1039	3.6.1
s1042	88.2, 90.1
s1045	64.1
s1047	64.1
s1048	66.3
s1051	64.1
s1076	87.8
s1077	87.8
s1084	30.11, 87.3, 87.4, 87.5
Sch14 Para1	54
Sch14 Para2	10.1, 53, 54, 56, 57.1
Sch14 Para3	56, 57, 59
Sch14 Para4	60.1
Sch14 Para5	59.8
Sch14 Para6	58.1, 59.5, 59.8
Sch14 Para7	59.9
Sch14 Para8	60.1
Sch14 Para9	61.1
Sch14 Para10	62.1
Sch15 Para1	32.7
Sch16	44.5.1
Sch17	44.5.2
Sch18A	73
Sch24	83.2, 83.3.8
Sch20	35.12.5
Sch24	9.3
Sch26	26.1.1

FINANCE ACT 1998

Section	Paragraph
s15	50.1.1
s42	35.13
s45	88.2
s65	5.1
s66	35.12.1
s67	4.4.2, 20.5
s68	20.5
s69	30.12
s70	5.2
s71	26.1.1
s72	30.4
s73	26.11
s74	94.1
s75	33.6

s134	92.3
Sch2	4.2.1, 9.1.2.2, 38.2, 38.6

FINANCE (NO 2) ACT 1998

Section	Paragraph
s3	5.1, 6.1.2, 6.1.3

FINANCE ACT 1999

Section	Paragraph
s56	see TCA97 s.616, s623A, s625A & s626A
s57	73.3.1
s58	see TCA97 s746
s59	32.12, 42.1
s65	37.2
s68	50.1.1
s69	50.3
s71	72.1
s78	72.4, 76.4
s82	101.3
s87	35.7, 35.8
s88	- See TCA97 s579A-s579F
s89	67.2
s90	65.12.2, 65.12.3
s91	6.1.2.1
s92	See s917
s93	32.1

FINANCE ACT 2000

Section	Paragraph
s23	32.4.2
s27	39.11.2
s51	50.4
s53	36.5.2
s58	36.4
s62	36.6
s86	6.1.2.1
s87	94.1, 94.2
s88	33.8.3.2, 33.8.5

INDEX

A

Abandonment of option...39.3

Accountant
    deduction for costs of...9.2

Acquisition
    arms length rules...16
    no corresponding disposal...16.2
    cost - in case of share issues...41.5
    cost - in case of leases...55.2

Administration
    appeals...92
    assessment - see assessment
    care & management of CGT...86
    collection - see collection
    date payable...88, 97
    deduction of tax at source...94
    income tax provisions...87.1
    interest on overdue tax...89
    information and returns - see returns & information
    penalties...87.8
    power to inspect property...96
    preliminary tax...88
    returns...87.2 et seq.

Advertising
    deduction for cost of,...9.2

Aer Lingus, Aer Linte, Aer Rianta (securities issued by)...32.1

Agent
    deduction for costs of...9.2
    acting for non-resident...94.12

Agency or Branch (Irish)...3.6

Agricultural Credit Corporation (securities issued by)...32.1

Aircraft
    location of...3.7.1
    DTR provisions (ships /aircraft)...83 et seq.

Alienation of capital...3.3.4

Amalgamation or Reconstruction...43, 44

Annual allowance/exemption for individuals
    affect of special investment accounts (no allowance)...37.2
    different rates of tax...19.5
    general rule...19.1
    married persons... 19.2, 33.6
    not available to trustees, personal representatives, etc...65.2, 66.2

not available in year retirement relief claimed...19.4
year of death...19.3
Annual payment
    meaning of...32.11
Annuities
    capitalised value as consideration...8.6
    exemption... 32.11, 36.2
    terminating on death of life interest...65.7.2
    foreign...36.3
    regarded as life interest...65.8
Annullment of marriage...33.8.6
An Post (securities issued by)...32.1
Anti-avoidance provisions
    acquisition cost of shares...41.3, 41.4
    assets acquired without a disposal...16.2
    bed and breakfast...48.3
    company transferring assets at undervalue...51.3
    depreciatory transactions in a group...51.4
    disposal of assets in series of transactions...16.4.6, 94.3
    disposal of shares in subsidiary...51.4
    dividend stripping...51.5
    extraction of profits...41.7
    form v substance...69
    general anti-avoidance legislation...69.3
    liquidation of companies...64.4
    non-resident companies...67
    non-resident trusts...68
    pre-disposal dividends...51.6
    "Ramsay" doctrine...69
    recovery of tax from other group members...91.5, 91.6
    remittances...3.3
    reorganisations and amalgamations...42, 43, 44, 45, 46
    reverse Nairn Williamson arrangements...16.2, 41.3
    roll over relief, assets acquired to dispose of at a gain...26.10
    share transactions...41.4
    transfer of value derived from assets (value shifting)...51.2
Appeals...17.6, 92
Apportionment of consideration...8.9
Approved profit sharing scheme...50.2
Arms Length Rules...16
Art
    exemption for works of art...32.14
Assessments
    generally...90
    insolvent persons...64.3
    married persons...33.3, 33.4

non-resident...90.1
options...39.10
other group companies...91.5
Trustees and personal representatives...95
withholding tax...94.9
Asset stripping and dividend stripping...51
Assets
acquired from trust...9.11
acquired under contract...15.1
business assets replaced...26, 27
capital sums derived from...4.4.4, 4.4.6, 4.4.7
chargeable...4.2
compensation proceeds reinvested...25, 28
compensation, whether chargeable to CGT...4.2.6
created on disposal...4.2.4
derived from other assets...9.10, 10.6, 39.3.1, 81.6
disposal of...4
held in fiduciary or representative capacity...63 to 66
insolvent persons, of...64.3
insurance proceeds reinvested...25, 28
land & buildings...4.2.11
letters of allotment...4.2.9
limitations on transfer...4.2.5
location of...3.7
lost or destroyed...4.4, 4.5, 20.4
meaning of...4.2
negligible value...20.5
owned at 6.4.74...13
ownership prior to disposal necessary...4.2.4
part disposals...4.4.1, 4.4.3, 11
partnership...34
power to inspect...96
pre entry assets....73.3.3.3
restored or replaced...25, 26, 27, 28
right to receive (is an asset)....4.2.7
right to sue (is an asset)...4.2.8
right or restriction over assets...16.4.3
seized...4.2.6, 25, 27
time of disposal...15
transfer as security...64.6
transfer, limits on...4.2.5
transfer at undervalue by company...51.3
valuation...17, 96
wasting...10, 57
Associations...34

Auctioneers
    deduction for costs of...9.2
    returns by...87.10
Authorised Unit Trusts
    General...35
    in IFSC...35.8.5, 35.13
Authorised Investment Company
    General...35.8
    in IFSC...35.12
Avoidance Schemes - see anti-avoidance...

B
Bank
    bank balance in foreign currency...38.7
Bankruptcy...64.3
Bare Trustees...63.2, 64.1
Basic rate of tax...5.1
Basis of charge to CGT...2
"Bed and Breakfast"...48.3.1
Betting winnings...32.8
Bord Failte...32.7
Bord na Mona (securities issued by)...32.1
Bord Gais Eireann (securities issued by)...32.1
Bord Telecom Eireann (securities issued by)...32.1
Branch or Agency
    branch assets, non-resident company exit charge...74.1
    Irish assets of...3.6
    Irish Branch...3.4, 3.6
    foreign branch relief...71.4
Building society
    reorganisations...44.5
Buildings - see Land and Buildings
Business
    assets replaced...25, 26, 27
    chattels...21, 22.2
    business use of principal private residence...24.5
    compensation for re-invested...25, 28
    disposal on retirement...30
    relief for investment in corporate trades...9.13
    transfer to company...29
    transfer to company - interaction with retirement relief...30.13
    transfer on reconstruction or amalgamation...75.2
Business Expansion Scheme
    general...9.13
    share indentification... 9.13.2.4, 48.7

special investment schemes (life assurance)...35.10

special investment accounts (brokers)...37.2

Buyback of own shares by company...49

C

Calculation of gain (see also consideration, deductible expenditure)

asset transferred as security...8.7

capital allowances...8.5, 9.8, 10.3, 57.2

consideration...8

capitalised rent or income...8.6

contingent liability...9.9

discounted or contingent proceeds...8.8

deductible expenditure...9

disposal proceeds...8

Euro, change to...38.2

foreign currency...38.2, 38.6

incidental costs...9.2

indexation...14

main rules...7

part disposals...11

receipts taxed as income...8.4

wasting assets...10

Calls on shares...41.6

Capital Allowances...8.5, 9.8, 10.3, 20.6, 57.2

Capital acquisitions tax...97.6

Capital Distributions...40.3

Capitalised value of rent or income...8.6

Capital sum derived from assets

charge to tax, and meaning of...4.4.4

compensation, whether income or capital receipt...4.5.1

date of disposal...15.1

derived from what asset ?...4.4.6

insurance...4.4.4

meaning of capital sum...4.4.7

not derived from asset...4.4.5

relief for reinvestment of proceeds...25, 28

right to receive...4.2.7

right to sue...4.2.8

withholding tax...94

Caravan

use as principal private residence...24.2

Care & Management...86

Case law, significance of UK decisions...1.2

Central Bank of Ireland...32.7

Charge or mortgage on property...9.4, 64.6, 97.5

Charge to tax... 2

Charity
    general exemption...31.1, 31.4
    disposal to...31
    trusts...31.3, 65.16

Chattels
    broad overview...21, 22, 23
    business chattels...22, 23
    location...3.7
    losses on chattels...23.4
    Marginal relief...23.2
    non wasting chattels...23
    part disposal...23.5
    sets of chattels...23.3
    wasting...22
    worth £2,000 or less...21, 23

Child
    meaning of...16.4.4, 30.11, 33.9
    transfer of family business assets to , retirement relief...30

CIU's and Unit trusts...35

Co-Habiting couples...33.8, 33.10

Collection of tax
    "exit charge" - company going non-resident...74.4, 91.5.4
    general...97
    installments...97.3
    recovery from agent...91.6.1
    recovery from donee...91.3
    recovery from liquidator...97.5
    recovery from mortgage holder...91.7
    recovery from other group members...46.5, 46.6, 91.5, 91.6
    recovery from shareholders...91.4
    recovery from trust beneficiary...91.2
    withholding tax at source...94

Collective Investment Undertakings
    charge to CGT pre Finance Act 1989...35.13
    charge to CGT 1989 - 1993...35.6
    charge to CGT post Finance Act 1993...35.7
    Double tax agreements...35.13
    IFSC...35.12
    offshore funds...35.11
    overview of CGT treatment...35.1
    overview in chart form...35.2
    reduced rate of CGT to 1989/90...35.4, 35.5
    reorganisations...35.14
    residence...35.8
    special investment schemes...35.10
    unit linked undertakings...35.9

Committee of Agriculture...32.7

Commodity futures
    annual allowance/exemption does not apply...23.6
Companies - see also groups of companies
    acquisition of own shares...49
    amalgamation...43, 44
    authorised investment company...35.7
    basis of charge...71 et seq.
    buyback of own shares...49
    capital distribution...40.3
    changes in CT rate...72.1
    connected persons...4.2, 16.4.4, 41.2
    corporation tax on gains...71
    development land...78
    distributions...16.2, 35.7, 40.3
    extraction of profits (anti-avoidance)...51
    exit charge on company going non-resident...74
    fixed capital PLC...35
    family company (retirement relief)...30.4
    going non-resident, exit charge...74
    group relief...75.4 et seq.
    liquidation...64.4, 75.9, 97.5
    losses of company...73.2
    meaning of "company...71.3, 75.4.5.1
    meaning of control...16.4.5
    mergers directive (EU)...75.3
    non-resident...74, 75.4.5.4, 75.7
    overseas branches...71.4
    reconstructions and amalgamations...42 et seq., 75.2
    recovery of tax from directors...74.4
    recovery of tax from shareholders...91.4
    recovery of tax from other group members...91.5
    reorganisation of share capital...42
    residence of company...101
    strike off - company...20.5
    SICAV and SICAF...35
    transfer of assets between companies, relief for...75
    transfer of assets at undervalue...51
    transfer of business to...29
    transfer of trade - EU mergers directive...75.3
    transfer of business on reconstruction...75.2
    variable capital investment company...35
Compensation for damages
    charge to tax...4.2.6
    deduction of tax from payment (Gourley's case)...4.6
    exempt... 4.5.2, 32.8
    income or capital receipt...4.5.1
    insurance...4.5.3
    proceeds reinvested (relief)...25, 28

right to sue is asset...4.2.8
statutory...4.2.6, 4.4.5
Compulsory Purchase Orders
   date of disposal...15.1
   development land...6
   farm land & road widening...6.4
   relief where proceeds reinvested...25, 27
Computation of gain - see also Calculation of gain...7
Conditional contract
   time of disposal...15.2
   meaning of...15.2
   options...39
Connected Persons
   acquisition cost of shares...41.2
   arms length rules...16.2, 16.4
   definition...16.4.4
   form over substance...69
   losses...16.4.2, 20.7, 38.4
   special investment accounts (brokers)...37.2
   transfer subject to right or restriction...16.4.3
Consideration
   amount of consideration...8.2
   apportionment between assets...8.9
   arms length rules...16
   cannot be valued...16.2
   capital allowances...8.5
   capitalised value of annuity...8.6
   connected persons...16.3, 41.2
   contingent, unascertainable...4.2.7, 4.4.6, 8.8
   distributions...40.3
   deemed disposal at market value...16.2, 41.2
   deemed acquisition at market value...16.1, 41.2
   deduction of tax from...94
   discounted or contingent...8.8
   exclusion by reference to income tax...8.4, 8.5
   general rules for computing...8
   leasehold interests...53 to 62
   meaning of consideration...8.2
   non-money consideration, withholding tax...94.7
   part disposals...11
   payable by instalments...97.3
   special investment accounts (brokers)...37.2
   VAT...9.13
Consular & Diplomatic officials...32.12
Continental shelf...3.4.2
Contingent liabilities...9.9
Contingent proceeds...4.2.7, 4.4.6, 8.8

Contract
    time of disposal under...15.1
    conditional contract...15.2
Contingency
    contingent liabilities...9.9
    contingent proceeds...4.2.7, 4.4.6, 8.8
    "earnouts"...8.8.2
Control
    meaning of...16.4.5
Conversion of securities...47
Co-operative society - reorganisation...44.6
Corporation tax on chargeable gains...71
Court, funds in...64.5
Covenants, payments under...32.11
Copyright, location of...3.7
Coras Iompair Eireann, securities of...32.1
Credit relief...83, 84
Credit against capital acquisitions tax...97.6
Currency (general)...4.2.1, 9.1.6, 38.2, 38.6, 38.7, 38.8, 38.9
Currency (change to Euro)...4.2.1, 38.2, 38.6

D
Damages
    buildings - may be separated from land...4.2.11
    compensation - exemption...32.8
    deduction of tax on payment (Gourley's case)...4.6
    right to sue is an asset...4.2.8
    statutory compensation...4.2.6, 4.4.5
    whether chargeable to CGT...4.2.6
    whether income or capital...4.5.1
Date payable...88, 97
Death
    annual allowance/exemption - year of death...19.3
    assets passing on death... 66.5
    assets passing to trustee...66.6
    acquisition on death of spouse...66.8
    death of spouse, period of ownership for retirement relief...30.7
    family arrangements...66.7
    gains up to date of death...66.3
    general...66.1
    of life tenant...65.7.2
    personal representatives... 66.2, 66.6
    post 5/4/78 position...66.5.2
    pre 5/4/78 position...66.5.3
    special investment accounts (brokers)...37.2

spouse...66.8

terminal loss...66.4

Debenture

debenture not a debt on a security, antiavoidance re. exchanges...45.2

Debts

acquired from trustee...38.5

acquisition of property in satisfaction of debt...38.3

are an asset...4.2.1, 4.2.7

bank balances in foreign currency...38.7

debenture swaps...38.10

general...38.1

group relief exception...76.5

location of...3.7.1

loss on debt acquired from connected person...38.4

on a security...38.2, 45.2

right to recover a sum is an asset...4.2.7

Deduction of tax at source...94

Deductible Expenditure

allowable for income tax...9.1,

assets acquired from trust...9.11

assets derived from other assets...9.10

BES shares...9.13.2

capital allowances...9.8

contingent liabilities...9.9

cost of acquisition...9.1

enhancement expenditure...9.1

expenditure on asset...9.1.3

foreign currency...9.1.2.2

foreign tax...9.3

general rule...9.1

grants...9.6

incidental costs...9.2

indexation...14

insurance...9.7

interest...9.5

leases...57, 58

notional costs...9.1

options...39.3.1

own labour...9.1.2.1

part disposals...11

qualifying for capital allowances...9.8, 10.3, 57.2

share issues, cost of acquisition...41

share schemes...9.13

trustees costs of transferring assets to beneficiary...9.11

VAT...9.12

wasting expenditure...10

Deemed consideration
    bargain not at arns length...16
    connected persons (transaction with)...16
    earnouts...8.8.2
Deemed disposal
    "exit charge" on company going non-resident...74
    on company leaving group...81
Deferred annuities and life assurance...32.9, 36.2
Deferred payment of purchase price...8.8
Demutualisation of life assurance company...44.7
Dependent relative - principal private residence relief...24.11
Deposit, forfeited...39.8
Depreciatory transaction...51
Derived
    asset from which capital sum is derived...4.4.6
    shares deriving value...3.5
Designated variable capital company...35
Destruction or loss of asset
    buildings may be separated from land...4.2.11
    charge to tax...4.4.2
    compensation - capital or revenue...4.5.1
    losses...20.4
    relief for reinvestment of compensation proceeds...28
Development Land (see also, land)
    companies...6.7
    CPO relief (restrictions)...6.4, 27.5
    Dublin Docks Development Authority, disposal to...26.11
    general...6.1
    group relief...75
    income tax charge...6.9
    indexation...6.3
    losses...6.5, 20.8
    meaning of...6.2
    merger relief...75.3.2
    principal private residence...24.12
    reorganisation relief...75.2
    residential development, disposal for...6.1
    roll-over relief (restrictions)...6.4, 26.11
    roll-over on disposal by Greyhound tracks, etc..26.11
    small gains exception...6.6
Director, collection of company tax from...74.4
Diplomatic & Consular officials...32.12
Discounted proceeds...8.8
Discretionary trusts - see trusts

Disposal
    after reconstruction...46
    arms length provisions...16.3
    as security...64.6
    by contract...15
    capital sum derived from asset...4.4.4
    compulsory purchase orders...6.4, 25, 27
    deemed, at market value...16.3
    general rule...4.1
    hire purchase...15.1
    interest in settled property...65.12
    in series of transactions...16.4.6, 23.3
    loss or destruction of asset...4.4, 20.4, 28
    meaning of...4.4
    non chargeable assets...4.2
    of encumbered property...64.6
    of interest under settlement...65.12
    of trading stock...18, 80.4
    on retirement...30
    options...39
    part disposals...4.4.3, 11
    pre-disposal dividend...51.6
    proceeds, relief for reinvestment...25 to 28
    receipt of capital sum...4.4.4
    reinvestment of disposal proceeds, relief...25 to 28
    seizure...4.2.6, 27
    time of disposal...15
    to charities...31
    to connected person...16
    to spouse (general rule)...33.7
    to spouse (following separation)...33.8.3.2
    to spouse (following divorce)...33.8.2.2
    to the State...31
    trading stock, to or from...18, 80
    within four weeks of acquisition...48.3
Distribution
    arms length rules...16.2
    by unit trust, fund, collective investment undertaking, UCITS...35.7
    capital distribution...40.3, 75.4
    from special investment scheme (life assurance)...35.10
Dividend, pre-disposal...51.6
Dividend stripping...51.5, 51.6
Divorce (see also Husband & Wife)
    transfers of assets between former spouses, relief for...33.8
    former spouses not connected persons...33.10
Domicile...3.1, 3.2, 3.3, 104

Donee, recovery of tax from...91.2.1

Double taxation relief
    collective investment undertakings...35.13
    credit under EU "mergers directive"...83.3.7
    exit charge - company going non-resident...74
    foreign tax relief...9.3
    general note...83.1, 83.2, 83.3
    other than UK...85
    UK agreement...84
    Unilateral relief...83.3.8

Double Taxation agreements
    Australia...85.1
    Austria...85.2
    Czech Republic...85.3
    Denmark...85.4
    Estonia...85.5
    Finland...85.6
    Hungary...85.7
    Israel...85.8
    Italy...85.9
    Korea...85.10
    Latvia...85.11
    Lithuania ...85.12
    Malasia... 85.13
    Mexico...85.14
    New Zealand...85.15
    Poland...85.16
    Portugal...85.17
    Russia...85.18
    Slovakia...85.19
    South Africa ...85.20
    Spain...85.21
    Sweden...85.22
    Switzerland...85.23
    USA...85.24
    U.K....84

Due date for payment...88

E
"Earnouts"...8.8.2

Electricity Supply Board - securities issues by...32.1

Employment
    approved profit sharing scheme...50.2
    arms length rules, assets acquired in connection with...16.2
    contract of employment is asset...4.2.5
    employee shares...50
    employee share purchase scheme...9.15

employee share ownership trusts...50.3

grants...32.6

principal private residence and employments...24.4.2

retirement relief...30

share options...39.11

Encumbered property...9.4, 64.6, 91.7

Enhancement expenditure...9.1

Environment damage to - roll-over relief on development land...26.11

Euro, substitution of Irish Punt for...4.3, 38.6

Euro, currency of Ireland...4.3, 38.2

European Economic Interest Grouping (EEIG)...34.13

European Union

Grants paid by...9.6

non-discrimination - definition of groups...75.4.2

Farmers retirement scheme...32.5

Mergers Directive...75.3

Securities of...32.1

Exchange Control - affect on open market value...17.3

Exchange of shares...43

Exchange gains of trade...38.9

Exemptions and Reliefs

annuities and covenants...32.11, 36.2

annual allowance...19.1

charities...31

death...66

debts...38

disposal of interest under settlement...65.12

disposal of business assets (roll-over)...25, 26

divorced spouses, transfers between...33.8.2

government securities...32.1

married spouses , transfers between.....33.7

scheme for retirement of farmers...32.5

separated spouses, transfers between...33.8.3

superannuation schemes...32.4

woodlands...32.10

Exempt persons (and bodies)...32.7

Exempt unit holders, trust for...35

Exit charge on company going non-resident...74

Expenditure, deductible - see Deductible expenditure

Exploration or Exploitation rights

charge to tax...3.4.2

location of...3.7

withholding tax...94

F

Farmers, scheme for retirement...32.5

Family arrangements...66.7

Family company
    retirement relief...30.5
    liquidation & retirement relief...30.6
    sale of shares & retirement relief...30.9

Farming

Conacre letting (affect on retirement relief)...30.4
    CPO relief for development land...27.5
      Milk Quota...26.1.1
    retirement relief...30
    EU scheme for retirement of farmers...32.5

Films, relief for investment in...9.13.4

Fixed Capital PLC...35

Foreign Branch - see branch assets

Foreign currency
    bank balances...38.6, 38.7
    calculation of deductible expenditure and sale proceeds...9.1.6
    exchange gains, trade...38.9
    loans in foreign currency...38.8

Foreign tax (see also double taxation agreements)
    credit relief...83
    deduction for...9.3
    unilateral relief...83.3.8

Foreign trusts...65.17

Forfeited deposits...39

Form v Substance...69

Forestry exemption...32.10

Fraudulent or negligent returns...87.4

Friendly Societies...32.7

Funds (investment)...35

Funds in Court...64.5

Futures
    contracts...32.2
    exemptions...32.2
    held by superannuation scheme...32.4

G

Gambling, exemption...32.8

General anti-avoidance provisions...1.2, 69

General outline of CGT...1

Gifts
    art (works of)...32.14

deemed disposal...4.4, 16.1
open market value rules...16
prior to 20/12/74...16.3
recovery of tax from donee...91.2

Gift Tax - see capital acquisitions tax

Going concern
meaning, re. transfer of business to company...29.3

Goodwill
as a specified asset...3.4.2
attached to buildings...3.7.2.2
CPO relief...27
holding company may possess...4.2.4
location of...3.7
roll-over relief...26.1
retirement relief...30
withholding tax...94

Gourley's case (adjustment of amount of damages for tax)...4.6

Government and other securities
general exemption...32.1
held by special investment schemes (life assurance)...35.10
installment savings scheme...32.8
UCITS, Funds, Unit Trusts, and Collective Investment
Undertakings...35.8

Grants
assets held at 6/4/74...14.2
affect on indexation...14.4
employment grants...32.6
general treatment...9.6

Groups of Companies
affect of take-over...76.1
assets derived from other assets...81.6
capital distributions - exception to relief...40.3
company leaving group...81
company, meaning of for group relief...75.4.5.1
company leaving group, as a result of liquidation...81.3
debts - exception to relief...76.5
depreciatory transactions...51
development land...78
disposal after reconstruction or amalgamation...46
disposal or acquisition outside group...77
dividend stripping...51.5
foreign registered company...75.4.5.6
group relief...75.4
inter-company transfer of assets...75.4
interaction of reliefs for reconstructions and group relief...76.3
liquidation, leaving group as a result of...76.2
losses...20.10, 73.2

mergers directive (EU)...75.3
non-resident group & companies...75.4.5.4, 75.7
part disposals - in groups...76.4
recovery of tax from other group members...91.5
residence, and groups...75.4.4.4
roll-over relief in a group...79
sale of shares in subsidiary...51
semi-State companies, and Ministers...75.6
share redemption - exception to relief...76.5
takeover, effect on group relief...76.1
trading stock...80
transfer of value from shares...51.2
what is a group...75.4.3
winding up of group company...76.2

H

Hansard record of UK Parliamentary debates...1.2

Harbour Authority - securities of...32.1

Health Board...32.7

Hepatitis compensation...32.8

Hire Purchase...15.1

Holding company
    reduced rate of CGT...5.2
    retirement relief...30.4

Housing Finance Agency...32.1

Husband and Wife
    acquisition on death of spouse...66.8
    annual allowance...19.2, 33.6
    assessment...33.3
    connected persons, general application...16.4
    connected persons, position following divorce...33.10
    disposal to spouse, relief...33.7
    disposal to spouse following separation, relief...33.8.3
    disposal to former spouse following divorce, relief...33.8.2
    general...33.1
    losses...33.5
    married woman living with husband...33.2
    principal private residence...24.8
    returns...87
    separate assessment...33.4
    separation, divorce...33.8, 33.10
    special investment accounts...37.2
    transfer of value from shares...51.2
    transfers between, and period of ownership for retirement relief...30.7

I

Identification of shares...9.13, 48

IFSC
    authorised investment company...35.8
    UCITS, funds, and collective investment undertakings...35.12

Incidental costs of acquisition and disposal...9.2

Incorporation...29

Income - capital value of, as consideration...8.6

Income or capital
    capital value of right to income...8.6
    compensation for loss of profits...4.5
    compensation payments...4.2.6, 4.4.5, 4.5
    disposal of part of business...4.5
    receipts in computation...8.4

Income tax
    application of appeals provisions...92.3
    application of income tax administration provisions...88.1
    development land taxation...6
    expenditure allowable for...9.13
    interaction with CGT, leases...58
    receipts taxed as income...8.4
    relief for investment in shares...9.13.1, 9.15

Indexation
    assets owned at 6/4/74...13
    collective investment undertakings, ...35.7
    development land...6.3
    exceptions...14.3
    enhancement expenditure...14.2
    events prior to 6 April 1974...12, 14.3
    general overview...14.1
    grant aided expenditure...14.4
    funds and UCITS...35.7
    multipliers...14.1
    qualifying taxpayers...14.1
    qualifying expenditure...14.1
    restrictions...6.3, 14.3, 14.4
    special investment schemes (brokers)...37.2
    unit trusts...35.8
    wasting assets...10.5

Informally separated spouses...33.8.4

Industrial Credit Company - securities of...32.1

Information and returns - see returns and information

Inheritance Tax - see capital acquisitions tax

Injury...32.8

In-laws - connected persons...16.4.4

Insolvent persons...64.3, 91.7, 97.6

Instalments, payment by...97.3

Inspection, Power of...96

Insurance (see also - life assurance)
    capital sum derived from assets...4.4.4
    compensation proceeds for assets lost or destroyed...4.5.3
    demutualisation of assurance company...44.7
    premium paid...9.7
    reinvestment of compensation proceeds (relief)...28
    withholding tax...94

Interest charged to capital...9.5

Interest deductible...9.5

Interest on overdue tax...89

Irish assets
    charge to tax on non-resident...3.4
    deduction of tax at source...94
    Irish currency, channge to Euro...4.3, 38.2, 38.6
    Irish registered company...101.3

Irish Telecommunications Investments - securities...32.1

Irish Thoroughbred Marketing Ltd...32.7

Issuing houses and stockbrokers
    returns...87.9
    special investment schemes (life assurance)...35.10
    special investment accounts (brokers)...37.2

J
Jointly, meaning of...64.1

L
Land and Buildings - see also development land
    buildings may be seperated from land...4.2.11
    compulsory purchase order, relief...27
    deduction of tax at source...94
    development land generally - see development land...6
    development land and groups...78
    disposal on retirement...30
    foreign branch relief exception...71.4
    goodwill & buildings...3.7.2.2
    income tax charge re. dealing in land, etc...6.9
    in Ireland: charge on non-residents...3.4
    leasehold interests...53 to 62
    location of rights over...3.7
    principal private residence...24
    roll-over relief...26
    shares deriving value from...3.5
    transfer of value derived from...51.2.2.5

with development value...6, 78
withholding tax...94.2

Land Bonds...32.1

Leasehold interests in land
    charge to CGT...56
    consideration chargeable...59.8
    cost of acquisitions...55.2
    deemed premiums...60
    duration of a lease...61
    expenditure attributable to part disposal...59.7
    expenditure qualifying for capital allowances...57.2
    general note on leases...54
    grant of a lease, general note...54.1
    grant of a long lease out of a freehold or long lease...59.4
    grant of a short lease out of a freehold or long lease...59.5
    grant of a short lease out of a short lease...59.6
    interaction of CGT with income tax (premiums)...58
    lease as a wasting asset...57
    merger with superior interest...10.6
    options, re lease...39.9
    owned at 6th April 1974...57.3
    premiums, meaning of...54.1
    property other than land...62
    restriction of expenditure on wasting assets...10.4
    restriction of loss on grant of sub-lease...59.9
    sale of a leasehold interest, general note...55
    sale of a long lease...59.2
    sale of a short lease...59.3
    statutory compensation on termination of lease...4.4.6
    transfer of value...51.2
    wasting asset...57

Leases - other than land...62

Legal costs
    deduction for...9.2
    cost of establishing or defending title...9.1.5
    costs of variation of settlement...9.2.1

Legatees...66

Letters of allotment - as an asset...4.2.9, 3.7.2.1

Liability - capital sum derived from...4.4.5

Life assurance
    companies...36.5
    demutualisation of assurance company...44.7
    exemption...36.2
    foreign life assurance companies...36.3
    overview...36.1
    special investment policies...35.10, 36.6

time of disposal...15.1
unit linked collective investment undertakings...35.9
Life assurance and deferred annuities...32.9
Life interest in settled property...65.8, 65.9
Liquidation of companies...64.4, 97.5
general...64.4
leaving group as a result of liquidation...81.3
payment of tax...97.5
retirement relief...30.6
winding up of group company...81
Loan
foreign currency loan...38.8
assets transferred as security for...64.6
Local Authorities
certification re roll-over relief on development land...6.4, 26.11
CPO relief...6.4, 27
securities of...32.1
exemption...32.7
Location of assets...3.7
Losses
accruing to beneficiary of trust...65.11
anti-avoidance - re. shares in group of companies...20.9
asset stripping and dividend stripping...51
asset with negligible value...20.5
buying capital losses...73.3
bed & breakfast...48.3
capital allowances...9.9, 20.6, 57.2
chattels...23.4
company losses...73.2
connected persons...16.4.2
debt acquired from connected person...38.4
depreciatory transactions...51
development land...6.5
general...20.1
groups...20.10
in year of death...66.4
leases...59.9
loss buying...73.3
married persons...33.5
non allowable losses...20.2
non-resident companies...67.2.4, 67.3.6
non-resident trusts...68.3
pre-entry losses...73.3
restriction, grant of sub-lease...59.9
special investment accounts...37.2
terminal loss relief...66.4
trading stock - restrictions on losses on transfer

to & from stock...18.1, 80
use of losses...20.3
Loss or destruction of asset...20.4
Lottery prize exemption...32.8

M
Market value...17
Married persons - see Husband and Wife
Merged assets
assets derived from other assets...9.10
wasting assets & indexation...10.5
Mergers
company leaving group in course of merger...82
Merger Directive of EU...75.3
transfer of business on reconstruction or amalgamation...75.2
transfer from subsidiary to parent EU mergers directive relief...75.3
transfer of trade...75.2
Mineral rights
charge to tax on non-residents...3.4.2
foreign branch relief exclusion...71.4
location of...3.7
shares deriving value from...3.5
withholding tax...94.2
Milk Quota...26.1.1
Minister...75.6
Ministerial Order under State Property Act s31...20.5
Minor, meaning of...33.9
Miscellaneous reliefs and exemptions...32
Mortgage on property...9.4 16.4.3, 97.5

N
Nationalisation...4.2.6
National Gallery...32.14
National Lottery prize exemption...32.8
National Treasury Managment Agency...32.7
Negligible value - loss claim...20.5
Nominees...63.2, 64.1
Nominee shareholders, returns...87.11
Non-resident
agent acting for...94.12
assessment...90.1
charge to tax...3.4
companies...81.7

exit charge on going non-resident...74
groups...75.4
Irish branch or agency...3.6
losses...20.2, 67.3.6, 68.11
trusts...68

Non-resident companies
anti-avoidance provisions...67
group relief... 75.4
losses...67.2.4, 67.3.6

Non-resident trusts
apportionment between beneficiaries...68.7, 68.1.4
discretionary trusts...68.11.5.2, 68.11.5.4
gain on specified Irish assets...68.6, 68.11.9
general provisions (anti-avoidance)...68.1, 68.2
losses...68.11.8
offshore funds...67.3.9, 68.11.10
pre 23/2/74 settlements...68.11.6
returns...87.13
payment of tax by trustees...68.11.7

Notional sale proceeds...3.3.3

Nullity, decree of...33.8.6

O

Offshore funds...35.1, 35.12, 67.3.9, 68.11.10

Offshore Group relief...75.7

Open market value
appeals against valuation...17.6
applies to connected persons...16.4.1
exchange control restrictions...17.3
general rule...17.1
quoted shares...17.4
unit trusts...17.5

Options (and forfeited deposits)
as an asset...4.2.1
abandonment of option...4.4.2, 39.3
assessment and returns...39.10
deferred payment...39.11.2
employee shares options...39.11
exercise of option...39.2
forfeited deposits...39.8
general rules...39.1, 39.2
meaning of option...39.1
options re leases and non-sale transactions...39.9
put and call option...39.7
quoted options and traded options...39.5
trade assets...39.4
traded option held by superannuation scheme...32.4

transfer of option...39.6
wasting asset...39.6
Ordinary residence
effect of...2
meaning of...100
Overdue tax interest on...97
Overseas branch Relief...71.4
Owner occupier -see principal private residence

P
Part disposals
apportionment of expenditure...11
chattels...23.5
capital sum derived from asset...4.4.4
definition...4.4.3
generally...11
in a group...76.4
leasehold interests...59.7
Partnership
connected persons...16.4.4
general rule...34.1
returns...34, 87.6
residence of...34.11
UK statement of practice...34.3
Patents, location of...3.7
Payment by instalments...97.3
Payment of tax...88.1, 94.8.3, 97
Penalties...87.8
Penalty interest...89.2
Pension - see superannuation scheme
Period of ownership - buy-back of shares...49.3.5
Period of ownership - principal private residence...24
Permanent establishment...83, 84.2.3
Personal injury...32.8
Personal representatives of deceased persons (See - death)...66
Persons chargeable...3
Planning permission - compensation...4.4.5
Plant and Machinery - see also capital allowances
as a wasting asset...10.4
CPO...27
replacement of...26
Power to inspect property...96
Preferential payment in bankruptcy...97.4

Preliminary tax
  obligation to pay...88

Premium on lease...53 to 62

Principal private residence
  absence for period...24.4.2
  change in use or structure...24.6
  condition of employment...24.4.2
  development land...24.12
  dependent relative occupying...24.11
  foreign employment...24.4.2
  foreign residence...24.13
  general rules, exemption...24
  last 12 months of ownership...24.4.2
  married persons...24.8
  more than one residence...24.77
  part used for trade purposes...24.7
  profit motive...24.10
  separate building...24.3
  settled property...24.9

Prizes exemption...32.8

Prize Bonds...32.8

Profit sharing scheme (employee)...50.2

Purchase by company of own shares...49

Q

Quoted shares, valuation of...17.4

R

Rates of tax
  annual allowance - use of, with different tax rates...19.5
  CT rate re company chargeable gains...72
  reduced rate (pre 2/12/97)....5.2
  reduced rate - unit trusts...35.4, 35.5
  special investment schemes...35.10
  standard rate - 20%...5.1
  unit trusts, funds, UCITS, Collective investment
  undertaking...35.9
  withholding tax...94

Receipts taxed as income...4.5

Receiver...64.4

Reconstructions - see also amalgamations, mergers, etc
  disposal after amalgamation or reconstruction...46

Recovery of tax
  exit charge on company going non-resident...74, 91.5.4
  from beneficiary of trust...91.2
  from donee or gift...91.3

from mortgage holder...91.7

from other members of group...91.5

from liquidator...91.7

from shareholders...91.4

Reinvestment of disposal proceeds, relief for...25, 26, 27, 28

Relief for investment of insurance/compensation proceeds...25, 28

Relief for replacement of business assets - roll-over relief...25, 26

Remittance basis

liability of non-domiciled person...3.3

meaning of remittance...3.3.2

remittances - notional proceeds ?...3.3.3

alienation of capital...3.3.4

anti-avoidance...3.3.5

Rent

capitalised value as consideration...8.6

payment of arrears by liquidator...9.1.3

Reorganisation and collective investment undertaking...35.14

Reorganisation of share capital

BES and reorganisations...9.13.2

building society...44.5.1

collective investment undertakings...35.14

demutualisation of assurance company...44.7

general...42

group relief - interaction...76.3

reduced tax rate...5.2

returns...87.7

share identification...48

trustee savings bank...44.5.2

Research and development...9.13.3

Residence

affect of...3.2, 3.3

company residence...101

companies & groups...75.4.4.4, 75.5.4.4

"exit charge" on company going non-resident...74

individuals...99, 102

meaning of...98 et seq.

of company...101

ordinary residence...100, 103

partners...34.11

principal private residence, relief for...24

trustees...65.3

unit trusts...35.8

Restoration or replacement of assets...25, 26, 27, 28

Retirement relief

amount of relief...30.3

annual allowance (cannot be claimed)...19.4

calculation of limit to relief...30.8

chargeable business assets...30.4

conditions for relief...30.2

disposal to child of owner...30.11

family company...30.5

general...30.1

holding company...30.9

interaction with relief for transfer of business to company...30.7, 30.13

interaction with roll-over relief...30.13

liquidation of family company...30.6

marginal relief...30.10

no annual allowance...19.4

period of ownership...30.7

qualifying assets...30.4

sale of shares in family company...30.9

trustees, application to...30.12

Returns and information...49.3.10, 75.3.7, 87.2 et seq. 97.8.2, 94.10

Rights - human rights as an asset ?...4.2.3

Rights issues (shares)...42.3

Roads

road widening - CPO relief for development land...27.5

Roll-over relief

application to non-trade activities...26.7

assets used partly for non-trade purposes...26.4

cessation of trade - commencement of new trade...26.6.4

company going non-resident - deferrment of "exit charge"...74.2

compulsory Purchase Order...6.4, 15.1, 27

damage to environment - development land...26.11

delay in reinvestment...26.5

development land...6.4, 26.11

general...26.1

groups...79, 81.5

interaction with retirement relief...30.13

profit motive...26.10

qualifying assets...26.1

reinvestment of proceeds...26.2, 26.3

shares, disposal by entrepreneur...26.12

sporting bodies, assets of...26.9

time limit...26.5

two or more trades...26.6

RTE - securities of...32.1

S

Sale of property, deduction cf tax...94

Savings certificates...32.8

Scope of the charge to tax - see territorial scope

Securities - see shares and securities

Security
  acquisition or disposal of asset subject to security...8.7, 9.4, 16.4.3
  conversion of...47
  asset transferred as...64.6
  debt on a security...38.2
  strips of securities...32.3

Semi-state company stocks...32.1

Separate assessment...33.4

Separated spouses connected persons...33.10

Set of assets...16.4.6, 23.3

Settled property - see trustees

Settlement, meaning of (see also trusts, trustees)...65.4

Settlement, returns...87.12

Settlor, liability of (on settling assets on trustees)...64, 65

Shannon - collective investment undertakings, and funds...35.12

Shares and Securities
  acquisition by company of its own shares or securities...49
  anti-avoidance...41.4, 45
  base cost...41
  bed & breakfast...48.3
  BES shares - identification...48.7
  bonus issue...42.2.3
  business expansion scheme...9.13.2
  buy back by company of its own shares...49
  calls on shares...41.6
  capital distributions...40.3
  company amalgamations...43
  conversion of securities...47
  co-operative society reorganisation...44.6
  cost of acquisition...41
  deductible expenditure...9.13, 41
  deriving value from land, minerals, or trade...3.5
  employee shares...50
  employee share purchase scheme...9.15, 50
  exchange of shares...42.4
  exempt securities...32.1
  extraction of profits...41.7
  film companies, relief for investment in shares...9.13.4
  general overview...40.1
  government stocks...32.1
  harbour authority stocks...32.1
  identification...9.13, 9.14.2.4, 48
  income tax relief...9.13
  issued by Aer Lingus, Aer Linte, Aer Rianta...32.1
  issued by An Post...32.1

issued by Agricultural Credit Corporation...32.1
issued by Bord na Mona ...32.1
issued by Bord Gais Eireann...32.1
issued by Bord Telecom Eireann ...32.1
issued by Coras Iompair Eireann, ...32.1
issued by Electricity Supply Board...32.1
issued by European Union...32.1
issued by Harbour Authority...32.1
issued by Industrial Credit Company...32.1
issued by Irish Telecommunications Investments...32.1
issued by RTE...32.1
issue of shares - acquisition cost...41
letters of allotment, as an asset...3.7.1, 4.2.9
life assurance companies - demutualisiation...44.7
location of...3.7
local authority stocks...32.1
meaning of shares...40.2
mergers...43
open market value...17.2, 17.4, 41.2
ordinary shares, meaning of for group relief...75.4.3
pooling...48.4
profit extraction...51
purchased and sold within 4 weeks...48.3
recovery of CGT from shareholders...91.4
redeemable preference shares - group relief exclusion...75..4.3
reduced rate of CGT ...5.2
reduction of capital...42
relief for investment in...9.13, 9.15
reorganisations and BES...9.13.2
reorganisation and reduction of share capital...42
reorganisation within a group of companies...76.2
research & development relief, CGT aspects...9.13.3
retirement relief...30
reverse Nairn Williamson scheme...41.3
rights issues...40.4, 42.3
rollover relief...26.11
sale of, in family company (retirement relief)...30.9
sale of rights...40.4
semi-State company securities...32.1
share redemption exception to group relief...76.3
share schemes attracting income tax relief...9.13.1
share transactions - general note...40
share issues - cost of acquisition...41
strips of securities...32.3
transfer of assets at undervalue by a company...51.3
transfer of value derived from...51
treasury shares...49.4.7

valuation of...3.5.4, 17.2, 17.4
withholding tax...94

Ships
location of...3.7

SICAVand SICAF
generally...35
in IFSC...35.12
reorganisations...35.14

Special investment accounts...37

Special investment schemes...35.11

Special investment policies...36.6

Specified Irish assets...3.4.2

Sport
sporting body - roll-over relief on development land...6.4, 26.11

Spouse - see also husband & wife
connected persons, definition...16.4.4

State
bodies...75.6
disposal to...31
semi-state company stocks...32.1
State Properety Act, waiver by Minister..20.5.

Statement of affairs, obligation to provide...90.3

Statutory compensation...4.2.6

Stock - see trading stock

Stock exchange - see shares & securities

Stockbrokers
returns...87.9
special investment accounts...37.2

Strike off of company...20.5

Strips of securities...32.3

Substance v Form...69

Superannuation schemes...32.4

Surcharge for late return...87.5

Sweepstake winnings...32.8

T

Takeover, effect on group...76

Tangible movable property - see Chattels

Taxi - "cosy" driver - affect on retirement relief...30.6

Taxi plate - Revenue precedent...26.1.1

Terminal loss relief...66.4

Termination of life interest...65.7.2, 66.9

Territorial scope of the charge to CGT
branch assets...3.6

broad outline...3.1
location of branch assets...3.6.2
meaning of branch...3.6.1
non-residents...3.4
residence and domicile, affect of...3.2
resident & non-domiciled...3.3
remittances, meaning of...3.3.2
remittances & notional proceeds...3.3.3
remittances & alienation of capital...3.3.4
remittance anti-avoidance...3.3.5
specified Irish assets...3.4.2
shares deriving value from land, minerals, etc...3.5

Time limits
compulsory purchase orders - relief...27.4
payment...96
principal private residence election...24.7
reinvestment of compensation/insurance proceeds...26.5
returns...87.3
roll-over relief...26.5

Time of disposal...15

Tote Ireland Ltd...32.7

Tourism bodies - exemption...32.7

Trade - see also trading stock
assets used for purpose of Irish branch, charge on
non-residents...3.4
carried on by non-resident company...3.4
freedom to trade not an asset...4.2.3
principal private residence, used for trade...24.5
retirement relief...30
trading stock and group relief...80
transfer of business on reconstruction or amalgamation...46
transfer of business to a company...29

Trademarks, location of...3.7

Trading Stock
disposals to or from...18, 80
groups of companies...80
meaning of...80.2

Trade Unions - exemption...32.7

Transfer
at undervalue...16, 51.3
between companies...76
between group members (to & from trading stock)...18, 80
between spouses (general rule)...33.7
between spouses following separation...33.8.3
between spouses following divorce...33.8.2
of assets to trust...65.5
of business on retirement...30

of business to company...29
of business on reconstruction or amalgamation...44.3
of trade...44
of value derived from assets...51
on death... 66
to trustee of will trust...66.6
Trustee Savings Bank
    reorganisation...44.5.2
Trustees
    absolute interest passing on death...65.7.3
    absolutely entitled as against trustee...64.2
    appointment of property to beneficiary...65.7
    assessment of...95
    assessment on beneficiary of trust gains...91.3
    assets of insolvent persons...64.3
    bare trustees...63.2, 64.1
    becoming treaty propected...65.13.2.3
    beneficiary becoming entitled...65.7
    broad outline (CGT and Trustees)...65.1
    charitable...65.16
    charity, transfer to or by trustees...31.3, 65.16
    companies in liquidation...64.4
    connected persons...16.4
    cost of transferring assets...9.11
    cost of variation of settlement...9.2.1
    dealing in assets...65.6
    death of life tenant...65.7.2
    debts...38.5
    deemed disposals...65.7
    discretionary trusts...68.11.5
    disposal of interest in settled property...32.13, 65.12
    employee share ownership trusts...50.3
    entitled as against trustees...65.2
    exit charge on going non resident...65.13
    exit charge on disposal by beneficiary...65.12.3.3
    foreign trusts...65.15
    funds in court...64.5
    life interests...65.8, 65.9
    limited interest passing on death...65.7.2
    losses accruing to beneficiary...65.11
    nominees...63.2, 64.1
    non-resident...35.11, 65.3, 87.13
    passing of losses to beneficiary...65.11
    principal private residence...24.9
    property settled on trust...65.5
    recovery of tax from beneficiary... 91.3
    residence of...65.3
    retirement relief, application to...30.12

returns...87.13
security (assets transferred as)...64.6
settled property - broad outline...65.1
separate settlements...65.9, 65.10
single continuing body...65.2
unit trusts, CIU's etc...35
what is a settlement...65.4

Trusts
death of life tenant...65.7.2
debts acquired from trustee...38.5
CIU's & Unit trusts...35
discretionary trusts...68.101.5disposal of interest arising under
settlement...32.13, 65.12
foreign trusts...65.17
general outline...65.1
losses accruing to beneficiary...65.11
personal representatives becoming trustee...66.6
retirement relief, application to...30.12
separate settlements...65.9, 65.10
settlement, meaning of...65.4
settlor, meaning of...65.4
unit trusts, CIU's etc...35

Trustee Savings Bank...44.5.2

U

UCITS...35

Unincorporated associations...34.12

Unit Trusts - see also collective investment undertakings
charge to CGT...35
FA 2000 tax regime...35.8
general rule and overview...35.1, 35.2
in IFSC...35.8.3, 35.13
reduced rate of CGT...35.5
residence...35.9
unauthorised unit trusts...35.16
valuation...17.5

Unremittable Gains...97.2

Undertaking, meaning of...44.4

Unilateral credit relief for foreign tax...83.3.8

USA, DTR agreement...85.24

V

Value
acquisition cost of shares...41
appeals...17.6
arms length rules...16

negligible value - losses...20.5
open market value...17
shares...3.5.4, 17.4
shares deriving value from land, minerals or trade...3.5
transfer of assets at under value...51
transfer of value out of shares...51
transfer of value out of land...51

Value added tax...9.12, 94.6.2

Valuation
appeals...17.6
consideration...8.2, 9.1.5
fees, deduction for...9.2
general rules...17
market value rules...16, 17
power to inspect assets...96
shares...3.5.4, 17

Valuer, deduction for costs of...9.2

Variable Capital Investment Company...35

Vocational Educational Committee...32.7

W
Wasting assets
assets qualifying for capital allowances...10.3
chattels...21 to 23
compensation proceeds...28.2
general...10.1
indexation...10.5
lease as wasting asset...57
merged assets...10.6
method of restricting expenditure...10.4
options...39.1, 39.6
restriction of deductible expenditure...10.2

Wife - see Husband and Wife

Withholding tax...94

Woodlands
exemption...32.10
CPO relief and development land...27.5

• Publishing Programme

The Institute of Taxation in Ireland is committed to the publication of taxation titles which provide a valuable up-to-date reference source for tax consultants and students. Books are written by eminent tax consultants who are specialists in their particular area of taxation. Many of the publications are the sole comprehensive publication on the relevant tax in Ireland. These publications are available at discount prices to Institute members and subscribers.

The Institute publishes twenty four taxation titles:

Direct Tax Acts

Law of Capital Acquisitions Tax

Law of Value Added Tax

Stamp Acts

Taxation Summary, Republic of Ireland

Income Tax

The Taxation of Capital Gains

Corporation Tax

The Law of Stamp Duties

Valuation of Shares in Private Companies

Capital Acquisitions Tax

Value Added Tax

VAT on Property

Finak

PRSI & Levy Contributions

Tax Implications of Marital Breakdown

Double Taxation Agreements

Case Law for the Tax Practitioner

Pensions: Revenue Law & Practice

Trust & Succession Law: A Guide for Tax Practitioners

Taxes Consolidation Act, 1997: The Busy Practitioner's Guide

Seminar & Conference Papers

Capital Allowances

Taxation of Property Transactions